EYEWITNESS *TRAVEL GUIDES*

EUROPE

EYEWITNESS TRAVEL GUIDES

EUROPE

DK

LONDON, NEW YORK,
MELBOURNE, MUNICH AND DELHI
www.dk.com

PROJECT EDITORS Ferdie McDonald, Claire Marsden
ART EDITOR Paul Jackson
EDITORS Sam Atkinson, Simon Hall, Andrew Szudek
DESIGNERS Anthony Limerick, Sue Metcalfe-Megginson,
Rebecca Milner
PICTURE RESEARCHERS Katherine Mesquita, Alex Pepper, Lily Sellar
MAP CO-ORDINATOR Casper Morris
DTP DESIGNER Maite Lantaron

MAPS
Ben Bowles, Rob Clynes, James Macdonald
(Colourmap Scanning Ltd)

PHOTOGRAPHERS
Max Alexander, Demetrio Carrasco, Kim Sayer, Linda Whitwam

Reproduced by Colourscan, Singapore
Printed and bound by South China Printing Co., Ltd, China

First published in Great Britain in 2001
by Dorling Kindersley Limited
80 Strand, London WC2R 0RL

Reprinted with revisions 2002, 2003, 2004

Copyright © 2001, 2004 Dorling Kindersley Limited, London
A Penguin Company

A CIP CATALOGUE RECORD IS AVAILABLE FROM THE BRITISH LIBRARY.

ISBN 0 7513 4832 5

FLOORS ARE REFERRED TO THROUGHOUT IN ACCORDANCE WITH EUROPEAN
USAGE; IE THE "FIRST FLOOR" IS THE FLOOR ABOVE GROUND LEVEL.

**The information in this
Dorling Kindersley Travel Guide is checked regularly.**
Every effort has been made to ensure that this book is as up-to-date
as possible at the time of going to press. Some details, however,
such as telephone numbers, opening hours, prices, gallery hanging
arrangements and travel information are liable to change. The
publishers cannot accept responsibility for any consequences arising
from the use of this book, nor for any material on third party
websites, and cannot guarantee that any website address in this
book will be a suitable source of travel information. We value the
views and suggestions of our readers very highly. Please write to:
Publisher, DK Eyewitness Travel Guides,
Dorling Kindersley, 80 Strand, London WC2R 0RL, Great Britain.

◁ **The Hôtel de Ville, Brussels' magnificent town hall** *(see pp224–5)*

**Enjoying the evening sunshine in
a café overlooking a Greek harbor**

CONTENTS

**Punting on the Cam beside Queens'
College, Cambridge** *(see p73)*

Field of sunflowers, a common crop in central and southern France

Leaning Tower of Pisa rising behind the Baptistry *(see p411)*

The spectacular hilltop Monestir de Montserrat in Catalonia *(see pp316–17)*

HOW TO USE THIS GUIDE

THIS DORLING KINDERSLEY travel guide helps you to get the most from your visit to Europe. *Visiting Europe* maps the continent, and gives tips on practical considerations and travel. *Europe at a Glance* gives an overview of some of the main attractions and a brief history. The book is divided into seven sections, each covering a group of two, three, or four countries. The chapter on each country starts with a historical portrait and a map of the country. The main sightseeing section then follows, with maps of the major cities. For each country there is a section of practical and travel information, followed by listings of recommended hotels and restaurants.

EUROPE MAP

The colored areas shown on the map on the inside front cover indicate the 19 country chapters in this guide.

1 At a Glance
The map here highlights the most interesting cities, towns, and regions in the countries covered in the section (in this example Italy and Greece).

Each country chapter has color-coded thumb tabs.

2 Introduction to a Country
This section gives the reader an insight into the country's geography, historical background, politics, and the character of the people. A chart lists the key dates and events in the country's history.

3 Country Map
For easy reference, sights in each country are numbered and plotted on a map. The black bullet numbers (eg. ❸ *) also indicate the order in which the sights are covered in the chapter.*

Sights at a Glance lists the numbered sights in alphabetical order.

For the larger countries there is an index of the practical and listings pages at the end of the chapter.

4 City Map
This plots individual sights within the most important cities. The sights within a city such as Rome are indicated with clear bullet numbers (eg. ③), in contrast to the black bullets used on the country maps.

Visitors' Checklist gives all the practical information needed to plan your visit.

Sights at a Glance lists the numbered sights within the city.

5 Major Sights
Historic buildings are dissected to reveal their interiors, while museums and galleries have color-coded floor plans to help you find the most important exhibits.

Stars indicate the features that no visitor should miss.

6 Detailed Information
Cities, towns and other sights are described individually. Their entries appear in the same order as the numbering on the country map at the beginning of the section.

Each entry begins with essential practical information, including the address and telephone number of the local tourist information office. Opening times are given for major sights and museums.

7 Practical Information
This section covers subjects such as visas, security, travel, shopping, and entertainment. The larger countries are covered in greater detail.

Directory boxes give contact information for the services and venues mentioned in the text.

Climate charts *(see p13)* are provided for each country.

VISITING
EUROPE

Putting Europe on the Map

THE CONTINENT OF EUROPE stretches as far east as Russia's Ural Mountains, a total surface area of 10.4 million sq km (4 million sq miles). However, the 20 countries covered in this guide occupy a much smaller area, being concentrated in the northwestern and central parts of the continent and along the Mediterranean coast in the south. These countries are shown on this map in dark green. They include the nations that make up the European Union, the political association of Western European states based in Brussels *(see p228)*. The map also shows the principal international airports and the major road links. Europe's rail network is shown on the map on the inside back cover.

Satellite Photograph of Europe
This image shows the range of landscapes on the European continent, from the frozen coast of northern Scandinavia, through fertile plains on either side of the Alps and Pyrenees, to the balmy regions of the Mediterranean.

0 kilometers 250

0 miles   250

KEY

- ✈ International airport
- — Major road
- — Minor road
- --- Ferry route
- ▪▪▪ International boundary

ATLANTIC OCEAN

NORTH SEA

Faroe Islands

Shetland Islands

Bergen

Stavanger

Kristians

Orkney Islands

Inverness

Aberdeen

Glasgow   Edinburgh

NORTHERN IRELAND   Belfast

Newcastle

Galway

DUBLIN

GREAT

IRELAND

BRITAIN

Cork

Birmingham

Cardiff

Harwich

LONDON

AMSTERDAM

Southampton

Dover

NETHERLANDS

Calais

BRUSSELS Dussel

Le Havre

BELGIUM

St-Malo

Luxembourg

Rennes

PARIS

Metz

Nantes

Tours

Dijon

FRANCE

BERN

SWI

Lyon Geneva

Bay of Biscay

Bordeaux

Mil

Turin

A Coruña

Gen

Bilbao

Toulouse

Nic

Marseille

Oporto

SPAIN

Zaragoza

Co

Ajacci

PORTUGAL

MADRID

Barcelona

LISBON

Valencia

Palma

Menorca

Sar

Ibiza

Mallorca

Faro

Seville

Granada

Alicante

Cáglia

Gibraltar

Málaga

MEDITERRANEAN

Tangier

Algiers

Melilla

MOROCCO

ALGERIA

DISTANCE CHART

Distance by road in kilometers
Distance by road in miles

ATHENS								
2564 1593	BERLIN							
3023 1878	**782** 486	BRUSSELS						
3227 2005	**1057** 657	**327** 203	LONDON					
3883 2413	**2342** 1455	**1568** 974	**1732** 1076	MADRID				
2967 1844	**1076** 669	**302** 188	**415** 258	**1267** 787	PARIS			
1902 1182	**1520** 945	**1501** 933	**1802** 1120	**2093** 1301	**1460** 907	ROME		
3650 2268	**1035** 643	**1594** 991	**1820** 1131	**3222** 2002	**1861** 1156	**2622** 1629	STOCKHOLM	
2188 1360	**589** 366	**1335** 830	**1838** 1142	**2932** 1822	**1623** 1009	**1834** 1140	**1601** 995	WARSAW

PRACTICAL INFORMATION

Millions of visitors travel to Europe for reasons many Europeans take for granted – the rich diversity of history, architecture, art, and landscape. In Western Europe tourist facilities are generally of a high standard, while in the former Communist countries of Eastern Europe their scope and quality have improved significantly over the past

The European Union Flag

decade. As a result, the whole of Europe is more accessible. This section gives information on practical matters such as passport formalities and how to get around. Many countries are members of the European Union, with certain laws in common, but there are also notable differences. In each country chapter a *Practical Information* section gives specific details for visitors.

WHEN TO GO

The best time to visit Europe depends on your itinerary, but most people prefer the summer months, between May and September. Due to the diverse geography of Europe, the weather has wide variations. Summers in northwestern Europe can be cool and rainy, while in the east they can be unbearably hot. The Mediterranean, with its hot, dry summers and relatively mild winters, has the balmiest climate, but crowds are a major drawback, particularly in July and August, making May and June better times to visit. August is the busiest month because this is when most French, Italian, and Spanish citizens take their vacations.

The climate of parts of Scandinavia is extreme: in winter in the north the sun rises only for a few hours and the roads can be blocked by snow, while summertime attracts many visitors, drawn by the prospect of enjoying the "midnight sun".

The mountainous areas of Europe have unique climates. The Pyrenees, Alps, and Apennines all have short summers and long winters with heavy snowfall. Consequently, these regions offer wonderful opportunities for skiing.

EUROPEAN TIME ZONES

The 20 countries covered in this guide fall across three time zones. Great Britain, Ireland, and Portugal are on GMT (Greenwich Mean Time), while the other European countries are one hour ahead

(+1), except for Greece, which is two hours ahead (+2). So, for example, London, Dublin, and Lisbon are five hours ahead of New York, while Paris and Budapest are six hours ahead, and Athens is seven hours ahead.

In Europe the clocks go forward by one hour in March (Daylight Saving), and go back in the fall, usually in October.

PASSPORTS AND VISAS

Most western European countries belong to the European Union. Based in Brussels, this European authority has the power to pass certain laws affecting all member states. There are 15 member states so far and 10 more countries are joining the Union in 2004.

In 1999, the following EU members agreed to eliminate passport controls between them: Germany, France, Spain, Portugal, Belgium, Luxembourg, the Netherlands, Italy, and Austria. In theory it is sufficient to carry an identity card when traveling between these countries, but it is worth carrying your passport just in case. The other EU countries (Britain, Denmark, Finland, Greece, Ireland, and Sweden) have yet to sign up to this agreement, and so passports are needed by everyone entering or leaving.

If you are arriving in Europe from a non-EU country, a passport is required. However, since 1999 visitors from the United States, Canada, Japan, New Zealand, Norway, and Switzerland no longer require visas for short visits to those

countries in the agreement (Germany, France, Spain, Portugal, Belgium, Luxembourg, the Netherlands, Italy, and Austria). Instead, you should receive an official entry stamp on your passport when entering the country (or from a police station within 72 hours). For longer stays, a visa may be required. Check this with the embassy of the country you plan to visit.

Some countries require a visa regardless of your length of stay; refer to the individual *Practical Information* sections in each chapter for full details.

STUDENT CARDS

As well as various bus and rail tickets that offer discounts on European travel *(see p18)*, students with a recognized student card may be eligible for a wider range of discounts. The best card is the International Student Identity Card (ISIC), which gives discounts on all kinds of goods and transport, as well as cheap admission to many museums, galleries, and other sights. Most students can obtain this card from their educational establishment at home but it can also be obtained abroad from an ISIC issuing office or from branches of STA Travel *(see p17)*. For US students, this card also includes some medical cover.

CUSTOMS AND DUTY-FREE

Since 1999 duty-free goods are no longer available for purchase when traveling between EU countries; these goods can only be bought on entry to or exit from the European Union as a whole. The allowances are as follows: tobacco (200 cigarettes, 50 cigars, or 250g of loose tobacco); alcohol (1 liter of strong spirits, 2 liters of alcohol under 22 percent proof, and 2 liters of wine); coffee (500g), and perfume (60ml).

When entering a country you will be asked to declare certain items from abroad and pay duty on any amount that exceeds that country's allowance; the nature of these goods will vary from country to country. This process applies on returning to your home country with goods acquired in Europe.

VALUE ADDED TAX

IN THE EU, ALL GOODS and services (except certain items such as food and children's clothes) are subject to a Value Added Tax, known as VAT, which is included in most prices. If you are not a European Union citizen, you may get a refund of this tax, but it can be a lengthy process.

The easiest way to do this is to shop where you see the "Euro Free Tax" sign, although the stores that offer this service may be expensive or sell only luxury goods. After showing your passport to the shop assistant and completing a form, the VAT will be deducted from your bill.

In certain countries you need to keep your receipts and VAT forms and present them at the Tax Refund desk with your unopened purchases when you leave the country. These forms are processed and a refund will eventually be sent to your home address.

PERSONAL SECURITY

EUROPE IS ONE of the safest places to travel, but you should always take certain safety measures. If you are traveling alone and especially at night, it is best to avoid deserted and poorly lit buildings, and places such as back streets and parking lots. If you should be a victim of an attack or robbery, report it

immediately to the local police. Pickpockets are common throughout Europe, but certain crimes are worse in certain countries – specific information is given in the *Practical Information* section of each country chapter.

By far the safest way of carrying money is in the form of traveler's checks (*see p14*), which allow you to keep your hard cash to a minimum. Never leave your belongings unattended, and make sure they are adequately insured before you leave home. Keep your valuables well concealed, especially in crowds. It is advisable to wear minimal jewelry when going out; leave it in your hotel safe instead.

INSURANCE AND MEDICAL TREATMENT

TRAVEL INSURANCE is essential to cover any loss or damage to your possessions and for unexpected medical and dental treatment. Many major credit cards (including American Express) offer some insurance if you purchase your flights or vacation package with them, so check this before buying a separate policy. If possible, buy one which pays for medical treatment on the spot, rather than a policy

which reimburses you later. Most general insurance policies do not cover potentially dangerous activities such as climbing, skiing, and scuba diving – these cost extra. If you plan to do any of these, check that you will be covered.

CONVERSION CHART

Officially the metric system is used throughout Europe, but Imperial measures are commonly used in Britain. British pints and gallons are 20 percent larger than US measures.

Imperial to Metric
1 inch = 2.54 centimeters
1 foot = 30 centimeters
1 mile = 1.6 kilometers
1 ounce = 28 grams
1 pound = 454 grams
1 US pint = 0.47 liter
1 UK pint = 0.55 liter
1 US gallon = 3.8 liters
1 UK gallon = 4.6 liters

Metric to Imperial
1 millimeter = 0.04 inch
1 centimeter = 0.4 inch
1 meter = 3 feet 3 inches
1 kilometer = 0.6 mile
1 gram = 0.035 ounce
1 kilogram = 2.2 pounds
1 liter = 2.1 US pints
1 liter = 1.76 UK pints

THE CLIMATE OF EUROPE

As a continent that ranges south from the Arctic Circle to just north of the tropics, Europe experiences a diversity of climates, yet because it is influenced by the warm Gulf Stream its climate is overall much more temperate than other areas at the same latitudes. The *Practical Information* section for each country contains a panel like the one below giving details of average temperatures, rainfall, and sunshine for each season of the year.

ROME			
°C/F	29/84	22/72	
	18/64 19/66	13/55 12/54	
	9/48		4/40
0°C 32°F			
☀	6 hrs	10 hrs	7 hrs	5 hrs
☂	51 mm	21 mm	95 mm	87 mm
month	Apr	Jul	Oct	Jan

Average daily maximum temperature

Average daily minimum temperature

Average daily hours of sunshine

Average monthly rainfall

Communications and Money

IN THE 21ST CENTURY communications are developing quickly so that few places in Europe remain completely out of touch. With the advent of cell phones, e-mail access on computers, and internet cafés, ways to communicate are now more numerous, easy, and relatively cheap. Many hotels and restaurants readily accept most credit cards, so cash is normally only needed for smaller transactions or in remote spots. The introduction of a common currency (the euro) in 12 countries should also make life much easier for the traveler on a European tour.

TELEPHONES

THESE DAYS, when more and more people have a cell or mobile phone, the need for a public telephone may be less urgent. However, be aware that not all cell phones work everywhere. If you want to use your cell phone abroad you need to arrange this with your service provider. Also, most US cell phones do not work in Europe and vice versa – but you can now buy phones that work in both continents.

Most European countries have excellent public telephones in towns and cities. In the more isolated regions, it is less likely that you will come across a telephone kiosk where you can make international calls.

MAIL SERVICES

MAIL SERVICES are generally fast and efficient, with letters and cards typically taking five days to reach North America, or a week to get to Australasia. The mail service does vary across the continent, however, and in some areas, such as Eastern Europe and in remote parts of Greece the service may be much slower.

If your trip involves moving through countries and you are not staying at a hotel, you can still receive mail by using the Poste Restante system. This usually can be set up at main post offices in large towns. Just ask for mail to be sent to you care of Poste Restante. When you collect your mail, you need to take confirmation of your identity, such as an identity card or passport. Mail from overseas is usually kept for one month.

INTERNET CAFÉS

THE HUGE INCREASE in home computers with Internet access means that many people now use the Internet for e-mail communications. Now there are also public Internet access points, usually called internet cafés, in the majority of cities all over the world. These are ideal for sending home messages to your friends and family. You just pay a fee for a fixed amount of time on the Internet, which varies according to local use and rates. Many of these places also offer the facilities to make telephone calls, print, scan, upload, and download information, for extra payments. They are also often cafés in the usual sense.

CHANGING MONEY

AS EUROPE comprises so many different nations, each with their own currency, you can find that you spend a fair amount of time looking for an exchange bureau. This situation has improved now that the euro has become the official legal currency in the 12 participating countries. It was introduced on January 1, 2002, and during a short transition period both euros and local currencies were used simultaneously. All the old currencies have now been phased out leaving the euro as the sole currency.

Currency exchanges (bureaux de change) can be found in most towns – particularly within banks or post offices. Banks usually tend to offer the best rates. Most airports, central train stations, large hotels, and border posts also have currency exchanges.

For safety, most visitors use traveler's checks when abroad because, unlike cash, they can be replaced by the bank if they are lost or stolen. However, this is fast becoming an unnecessary precaution. If you have a plastic card with a pin number for your bank account or credit card, and as long as you belong to a global network such as Plus/Visa, or Cirrus/Mastercard, ATM machines can provide instant access to your funds. Just be aware that credit cards begin charging interest instantly if you take out cash. You can find ATM machines in banks, shopping malls, and stations.

INTERNATIONAL DIALING CODES

The list below gives the international dialing codes for the countries covered in this guide. When calling from the US and Canada prefix all numbers by "011';'; from Australia by "0011;" from New Zealand by "00." When calling from within Europe, use the "00" prefix. If you are unsure, call international directory inquiries.

• Austria	43	• Luxembourg	352
• Belgium	32	• Netherlands	31
• Czech Republic	420	• Norway	47
• Denmark	45	• Poland	48
• Finland	358	• Portugal	351
• France	33	• Spain	34
• Germany	49	• Switzerland	41
• Greece	30	• Sweden	46
• Hungary	36	• United Kingdom	44
• Ireland (Republic)	353	(Great Britain and	
• Italy	39	Northern Ireland)	

THE EURO

ON JANUARY 1, 2002 the Euro (the common currency of the European Union) was introduced into general circulation. Twelve countries have replaced their traditional currencies with the Euro:

Austria, Belgium, Finland, France, Germany, Greece, Ireland, Italy, Luxembourg, Netherlands, Portugal and Spain chose to join the new currency; the UK, Denmark and Sweden stayed out, with an option to review their decision, and have retained

their existing currencies and exchange rates. Each country using the Euro produces their own coins, which have one common European side, but these, like the notes which are all uniform in design, can be used anywhere inside participating member states.

Bank Notes

Euro bank notes have seven denominations. The 5-euro note (grey in color) is the smallest, followed by the 10-euro note (pink), 20-euro note (blue), 50-euro note (orange), 100-euro note (green), 200-euro note (yellow); and 500-euro note (purple). All notes show the stars of the European Union.

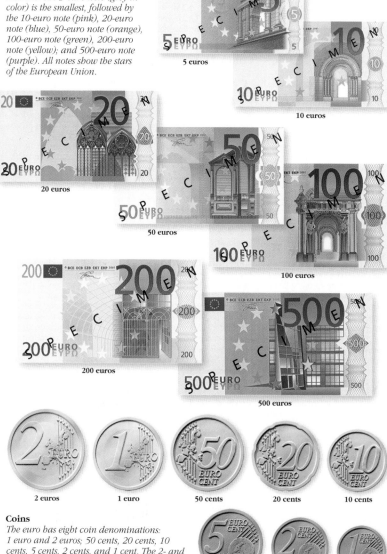

5 euros

10 euros

20 euros

50 euros

100 euros

200 euros

500 euros

2 euros

1 euro

50 cents

20 cents

10 cents

Coins

The euro has eight coin denominations: 1 euro and 2 euros; 50 cents, 20 cents, 10 cents, 5 cents, 2 cents, and 1 cent. The 2- and 1-euro coins are both silver and gold in color. The 50-, 20-, and 10-cent coins are gold. The 5-, 2-, and 1-cent coins are bronze.

5 cents

2 cents

1 cent

Europe by Air

WITH ITS NETWORK of international flights, Europe is one of the most accessible parts of the world to reach by air. Compared with North America and Australasia, European flights are a relatively cheap, quick and convenient way to get to and around Europe. In an industry previously dominated by state-run carriers and major private airlines, the recent rise of budget airlines offering "no-frills" flights has opened up many new destinations and made air travel more affordable.

FLYING TO EUROPE

IF YOU ARE TRAVELING from a major international airport, you will usually be able to find a direct flight to many European cities. Main destinations include London, Paris, Amsterdam, Rome, Milan, and Frankfurt. Most of the major North American airlines such as Delta, Air Canada, American, and Continental have frequent flights to all parts of Europe, as does Qantas from Australia. For more details on flights to specific destinations, see the *Travel Information* sections for individual countries.

Although most major airports are based on the outskirts of European capitals and other big cities, all can be reached by efficient train, bus, taxi, and sometimes subway services. Many of the smaller airlines use less convenient airports, with a longer transfer time but this is reflected in their cheaper fares.

EUROPEAN NATIONAL AIRLINES

MOST EUROPEAN countries have a national carrier which serves international destinations, and these usually offer frequent flights per day to their home countries at convenient times.

Scheduled flights on national airlines usually provide more legroom (essential on long flights) and a better quality of in-flight service than charter airlines, with complimentary items such as headphones and drinks. Fares can be more expensive but it is worth shopping around for the best deals. The largest national carriers include **British Airways**, **Air France**,

Iberia (Spain), **KLM** (the Netherlands), **Lufthansa** (Germany), **Alitalia** (Italy), and **SAS** (Scandinavia).

FLIGHT TIMES

AS A ROUGH GUIDE, flights from New York to London take about 6 hours 30 minutes, to Paris and Frankfurt 7 hours 30 minutes, and to Rome 8 hours 30 minutes. Flights from Sydney to London take around 23 hours via Bangkok, to Paris 23 hours via Singapore, to Frankfurt 22 hours via Singapore, and to Rome 25 hours via Bangkok. Flights from Auckland to London take about 24 hours, and to Frankfurt 23 hours.

KEEPING COSTS DOWN

AS A RULE, European air fares are cheaper between November and March (with the exception of Christmas and Easter weeks), while the high season is from June to mid-September. A "shoulder season" of moderate prices exists between these months. Try, if you can, to travel mid-week, because tickets are cheaper and airports are less busy.

Whatever season you travel, there are ways of saving money on air fares. A good way to start is to contact a travel agent that specializes in budget travel, such as **STA Travel** in the US. If you are young (under 25), a student, or a senior citizen, you will usually find special reduced-fare air tickets. Otherwise, you save money when you book in advance. If you can book 14 to 21 days ahead, APEX (Advanced Purchase Excursion) or Super APEX

tickets are available direct from the airlines and are much cheaper. With these there is a minimum stay requirement of 7 days but they can still be good value. It is cheaper still to buy air tickets through a travel agent. Be aware, however, that the cheaper the ticket, the more inflexible it usually is. You may not be able to alter, transfer, or cancel your flight, or if you do there may be stiff penalties, so check the conditions beforehand.

It is always cheaper to book a return (round-trip) ticket with fixed dates rather than an "open" return. You can also get an "open jaw" return, which allows you to enter via one city and exit via another (not necessarily in the same country). This is useful if you are doing a grand tour, but "open jaw" tickets are often more expensive than regular returns. Companies such as **Trailfinders** in the UK, and **STA Travel** in the US, offer their own versions of these.

Depending on how far you have to travel, round-the-world (RTW) tickets can also work out cheaper than the standard long-haul returns. These enable you to fly around the world on specified routes, as long as you don't backtrack on yourself.

Look out for good deals from established travel agents and package operators that are advertised in newspapers and travel magazines. Airlines will quote you the regular price for a ticket, but they can often reduce this if they have unsold seats. Consolidators, or "bucket shops", buy unsold tickets in bulk (often for off-season travel) and sell them at cheaper rates.

Standby tickets are also economical, but you have to be flexible about your date and time of departure; be aware that you sometimes have to wait (possibly for days) for a cancellation.

CHARTER FLIGHTS

IT IS ALWAYS worth investigating charter flight fares. There are quite a few companies that book whole planes or blocks of seats in advance, then resell the tickets at more competitive rates. The main drawback with these tickets is that they are usually non-refundable. They also tend to land at remote airports and at wildly unsocial hours. The level of in-flight service and comfort is usually lower, too.

PACKAGE DEALS

ONE OF THE EASIEST ways to arrange your visit to Europe is to book a package vacation. These are offered by all the major airlines, as well as various reputable independent companies, such as **Central Holidays** and **American Express**. They normally include flights, transfers, and accommodations, and sometimes side trips and food, and the cost is sometimes far less than if you were to buy these separately. While an excellent way of reducing the strain of organizing your vacation, the downside with a package tour is that it usually involves traveling in large numbers on specific flights to a hotel which, because the price has been pared to the bone, may not offer a high standard of food or facilities. On the other hand, there are specialist package tour operators that do offer top quality hotels and use scheduled flights.

FLY-DRIVE

MANY AIRLINES, as well as numerous travel companies, offer fly-drive packages, which combine air fares and car rental. These deals are often worth considering, as they give you flexibility and offer a saving over arranging the two parts separately.

INTERNET BOOKING

THE INTERNET is becoming a popular way of booking tickets. Two of the best sites for this are **Expedia** and **Opodo**. Expedia has a system called a "Fare Tracker" whereby you fill in a form online and they e-mail you information when tickets become available. The US company **Europebyair** also provides excellent deals on flights to Europe. It offers a FlightPass for non-European citizens, valid for 62 European cities and one-way flights between these destinations for a very reasonable price.

FLIGHTS WITHIN EUROPE

THERE IS an extensive flight network serving most major cities, making it quick and easy to fly within Europe. If you are traveling some distance, and especially between Great Britain and other parts of Europe, flying

can be the least expensive way to go. Indeed, if you want to get to destinations such as Portugal or Greece quickly, flying is almost the only option. However, between major cities, such as Berlin and Paris, you could go by train, which is almost as quick and cheap, and saves the trouble of getting to an airport *(see p18)*.

It is best to avoid flying between major cities on Friday evenings and early Monday mornings because these flights can be crowded with European commuters.

As with transatlantic flights, you can get cheaper tickets by booking early. The best cities for finding good deals from "bucket shops" are London, Athens, and Amsterdam.

LOW-COST AIRLINES

RECENT YEARS have seen the emergence of so-called "no frills" airlines in Europe, such as **Ryanair**, **easyJet**, **Air Berlin** and **Eurowings**, which offer very competitive prices. A return flight from London to Berlin, for example, can cost as little as £50 ($70). To keep prices down, there is usually less legroom, on-board catering is minimal or costs extra, and outlying airports may be used, but unless you must have these benefits, the price justifies the inconvenience.

DIRECTORY

EUROPEAN NATIONAL AIRLINES

Alitalia
📞 800-223 5730 (US).
📞 02-9244 2400 (Aus).
🖳 www.alitalia.com

Air France
📞 800-237 2747 (US).
📞 02-9244 2100 (Aus).
🖳 www.airfrance.com

British Airways
📞 800-AIRWAYS (US).
📞 1-300 767 177 (Aus).
🖳 www.britishairways.com

Iberia
📞 800-722 4642 (US).
🖳 www.iberia.com

KLM
📞 800-447 4747 (US).
📞 1-300 303 747 (Aus).
🖳 www.klm.nl

Lufthansa
📞 800-645 3880 (US).
📞 1-300 655 727 (Aus).
🖳 www.lufthansa.com

SAS
📞 800-221 2350 (US).
📞 300 727 707 (Aus).
🖳 www.sas.se

TRAVEL AGENTS

STA Travel
10 Downing St, New York,
NY 10014, US.
📞 800-777-0112.
🖳 www.statravel.com

Trailfinders
215 Kensington High St,
London W8, UK.
📞 020-7937 5400
(for transatlantic travel).
📞 020-7937 1234
(for European travel).
🖳 www.trailfinders.com

PACKAGE DEALS

American Express
📞 800-346 3607.
🖳 www.americanexpress.com/travel

Central Holidays
📞 800-935 5000.
🖳 www.centralholidays.com

INTERNET BOOKING

Europebyair
🖳 www.eurair.com

Expedia
🖳 www.expedia.com

Opodo
🖳 www.opodo.com

LOW-COST AIRLINES

Air Berlin
🖳 www.airberlin.com

easyJet
🖳 www.easyjet.com

Eurowings
🖳 www.eurowings.com

Ryanair
🖳 www.ryanair.com

Europe by Train

Trains are generally a popular, reliable, and comfortable means of travel, which also gives visitors the chance to enjoy the passing countryside. With the Channel Tunnel in operation between Britain and France, it is now possible to travel all the way from Scotland to mainland Greece by rail, and the number of passes and discounts on offer ensure that costs need not be high.

Types of Train

All kinds of train serve the rail network in Europe, from the slow local lines of remote regions, to diesel-powered intercity expresses. For the latter, such as the French TGV (*Train à Grande Vitesse*), the Spanish AVE (*Alta Velocidad Española*), and the German ICE (InterCity Express), you usually need to reserve a seat, and they are more expensive.

A pan-European rail system is still a dream of the European Union, but there has been some progress. The French operate TGV trains to Zürich, Bern, Turin, and Milan, where they link up with Italy's Pendolino trains; Brussels is connected to Paris, Amsterdam, Cologne, and Geneva by the high-speed Thalys network, while Germany's ICE system also runs to Bern, Switzerland.

Overnight trains are popular, offering couchettes, or bunks (usually four or six per compartment), or the more desirable sleepers (usually two or three beds per compartment). The price of a sleeper tends to be higher (three times the couchette price), but it is worth it if comfort is important.

Rail Passes for Non-Europeans

The cheapest way of seeing Europe by rail is to buy one of the many passes available. For non-Europeans the most popular of these is the Eurailpass from **Eurail**, or if you are under 26, the Eurail Youthpass. It is best to buy these tickets in the US or Australia before traveling because they can be 10 percent cheaper than if you wait and buy them in Europe. You can also buy these on the Internet through Eurail

and **Rail Europe**. These passes do not include the supplements payable on many of the faster trains: the EC (EuroCity), IC (InterCity), and EN (EuroNight) trains. You must pay these before boarding – if you don't and are caught by a conductor you will then have to pay the supplement plus a fine.

The Eurailpass offers unlimited travel in 17 European countries. These include Austria, Belgium, Denmark, Finland, France, Germany, Greece, Hungary, Ireland, Italy, Luxembourg, the Netherlands, Norway, Portugal, Spain, Sweden, and Switzerland. It is available as a consecutive-day pass if you want to make frequent short hops by train, or as a flexipass if you are on a trip with extended stop-overs. It is also valid for some ferries.

Other variations on the Eurailpass include the Saver Flexipass, which gives at least a 15 percent reduction per person when two or more people are traveling together. The Youth Flexipass is an option for those under 26 years of age, and applies whether you are traveling in a group or alone.

For further information on national train services and passes in individual countries see the *Travel Information* section for each country.

Passes for Europeans

For europeans the best pass is the Inter-Rail, which is also available from Rail Europe or from main train operators in individual countries. The Inter-Rail pass divides 28 countries in Europe into eight zones and is for anyone under 26 years old who has been resident in a European country for at

least six months. For those over 26 years, there is the Inter-Rail 26-Plus. What you pay depends on the number of zones you want to travel in and the length of your stay.

Eurostar/Eurotunnel

Connecting london's Waterloo Station to Lille and the Gare du Nord in Paris the **Eurostar** foot passenger train service provides the fastest link between the two capitals. It also operates to Brussels' Gare du Midi. These journeys only take three hours.

The **Eurotunnel** company operates a service between Folkestone in Great Britain and Calais in France that has drive-in compartments for vehicles. For a day trip it costs a set price per car with passengers (the more passengers, the cheaper the cost per person). Daytime journeys are more expensive than those departing after 10 o'clock at night.

Europe by Road and Ferry

WHILE MANY PREFER the ease of traveling by train when they want to get somewhere fast, traveling by car gives you the chance to stop at will and explore many areas of Europe on the way. Car ferries and the Channel Tunnel have extended Europe's boundaries into the Scottish Hebrides and down to the Aegean.

DRIVING PERMITS

MANY NON-EUROPEAN licenses can be used in Europe, but an international driving permit is worth having, if only to make life easier when renting or leasing a vehicle (you have to be at least 21 years of age when renting). Be aware that it is mandatory to have an international permit in parts of Eastern Europe. The permit lasts for one year.

DRIVING IN EUROPE

IN GREAT BRITAIN, Northern Ireland, the Republic of Ireland, Cyprus, Malta, and Gibraltar people drive on the left-hand side of the road. The rest of Europe drives on the right. Remember that in most of Europe distances are measured in kilometers (1 km equals 0.6 miles). The exceptions are Great Britain and Ireland, which work in both metric and Imperial measurements. Most highways have a speed limit of around 100–135 km/h (60–80 mph). The fastest roads are in Germany where the speed limit is 210 km/h (130 mph) on the *Autobahnen*. Roads are very congested during August, the vacation month, especially during the first and last weekends and on routes to the coast.

The cost of driving in Europe varies from country to country. Italian *autostrade*, French *autoroutes*, and Spanish *autopistas* are regularly punctuated by toll booths, while a one-time fee must be paid on entering Switzerland and Austria. However, all roads are free in the Netherlands, Great Britain, and Germany, although tolls are charged on certain bridges.

Fuel prices vary enormously across Europe. Gibraltar, Andorra, and Luxembourg are by far the cheapest, while France, Italy, and the Netherlands are the most expensive, with Spain, Great Britain, and Switzerland somewhere in between. The difference in price can be up to 30 percent. Unleaded gas is used almost exclusively in Scandinavia and Western Europe, but it is rarely available in the east.

CAR RENTAL

CAR RENTAL is a competitive business in Europe, so prices are generally quite affordable. The biggest car rental companies in Europe are Europcar, Avis, Hertz, Sixt, and Budget, all of which offer an excellent level of service. Local contact details are given in the *Travel Information* section for each country. There are also US companies that specialize in European car rentals. These include firms such as **Europcar**, **Kemwel**, **Europe by Car**, and **Auto Europe**.

TRAVELING BY BUS

DOMESTIC BUS SERVICES provide an alternative to the rail network throughout Europe, and while these are cheaper, they are also generally much slower and offer less in terms of comfort and amenities. The exceptions are Portugal, Greece, and parts of Spain, where buses have superseded trains, and Hungary, which has a bus system that is as good as the rail network. In most European countries, buses are best used as extensions of the railway, affording access to villages and remoter regions. Advance bookings for these are rarely needed.

International buses are also a second-best to express trains, but the tour options are worth considering. One example, **Eurolines,** offers passes that allow you to visit 31 European capitals over a 15-, 30- or 60-day period.

TRAVELING BY FERRY

ONCE IN EUROPE you may need to go by boat to get to the more outlying areas. Many of the islands of Greece and Scotland, for example, are only accessible by sea. Or, if you start your trip to Europe by flying into Great Britain, it is possible to continue by ferry, catamaran, or hydrofoil to Ireland, France, Belgium, the Netherlands, and Spain. Companies to contact are **P&O**, **Hoverspeed/Seacat**, and **P&O Stena Line**.

It can also be easier and cheaper to travel by sea than by air from Spain to the Balearic Islands, from Italy to Sardinia and Sicily, and to Greece from Italy. For further details, see the *Travel Information* section of the individual countries.

DIRECTORY

CAR RENTAL

Auto Europe
☏ 888-223 5555 (US).
🅦 www.autoeurope.com

Europcar
☏ 877-940 6900 (US).
🅦 www.europcar.com

Europe by Car
☏ 800-223 1516 (US).
🅦 www.europebycar.com

Kemwel
☏ 877-820 0668 (US).
🅦 www.kemwel.com

TRAVELING BY BUS

Eurolines
☏ 0870-514 3219 (UK).
🅦 www.eurolines.co.uk

FERRY SERVICES

Hoverspeed/Seacat
☏ 0870-524 0241 (UK).

P&O
☏ 0870-242 4999 (UK).

P&O Stena Line
☏ 0870-600 0600 (UK).

EUROPE AT
A GLANCE

The Landscapes of Europe

A WIDE RANGE OF CLIMATIC and geological conditions has forged an impressive variety of landscapes in Europe. Although the appearance of much of the land has changed dramatically since mankind began to cultivate it around 7,000 years ago, there are still many remote and wild regions, such as the spectacular peaks of the Alps and the Pyrenees. As well as being simply beautiful in their own right, Europe's diverse landscapes offer endless opportunities for outdoor activities.

Norway
Indenting the country's west coast, the wild and rugged Norwegian fjords are a truly spectacular sight, offering some of the most breathtaking scenery in Scandinavia.

Great Britain
Dartmoor in southwest England is a wilderness of great natural beauty. The windswept open moorland at the area's bleak and isolated heart has inspired many romantic tales.

ATLANTIC OCEAN

NORTH SEA

IRELAND

GREAT BRITAIN

NETHERL

BELGIUM
LUXEMBO

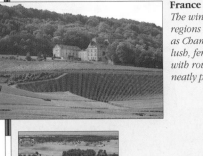

France
The wine-producing regions of France, such as Champagne, boast lush, fertile vegetation, with row upon row of neatly planted vines.

Bay of Biscay

FRANCE

PORTUGAL

SPAIN

MEDITERRANEAN S

Portugal
The interior of southern Portugal is largely characterized by parched plains, dotted with cork oaks and olive trees, and vast dusty wheat fields stretching uninterrupted to the horizon.

0 km   250

0 miles   250

◁ **The many islands of Stockholm, capital of Sweden**

Hungary

North of the Hungarian capital, the Danube flows through a verdant landscape of vineyards, orchards, and thickly wooded hills. Known as the Danube Bend, this is one of the river's most beautiful stretches.

Switzerland

Switzerland's landscape is dominated by the Alps, Europe's highest mountain range. Dramatic, snow-covered peaks, stunning vistas, and a range of first-class winter sports facilities draw millions of visitors to this part of Europe every year.

Greece

The Greek mainland and islands have some of Europe's finest coastal scenery. There are thousands of beaches, ranging from small rocky coves backed by pine-clad cliffs to broad swathes of golden sand.

Great Museums and Galleries

THE MUSEUMS AND GALLERIES of Europe include national collections, the former collections of Europe's royal and noble families, and a whole host of smaller local institutions. The museums highlighted here are those with the largest and richest collections, which ought to be included in the itinerary of every visitor to Europe. Between them they contain many of the world's best-known and best-loved artistic treasures. These range from archaeological finds from the early civilizations of the Middle East, through pieces from Egyptian, Greek, and Roman times, to masterpieces of the Renaissance and other great periods of European art.

Rijksmuseum, Amsterdam
The Rijksmuseum (see pp256–ᵢ is known for its Rembrandts and other great Dutch paintinɡ of the 17th century. Frans Haᵢ Wedding Portrait is a joyful celebration of Dutch life.

British Museum, London
A vast collection of antiquities and other artifacts from all over the world is is housed inside Britain's national museum (see pp52–3). There is a fascinating display of mummies and other exhibits from Ancient Egypt.

Louvre, Paris
The celebrated home of the Mona Lisa *and the* Venus de Milo, *the Louvre also houses Jean Watteau's melancholy study* Gilles *or* Pierrot *(c.1717), one of many French works on display (see pp158–60).*

Prado, Madrid
The former royal collection in Madrid (see pp288–90) contains the finest assembly of Spanish paintings in the world. Of many highly individual works, Goya's Saturn Devouring One of his Sons *is one of the most powerful.*

ATLANTIC
OCEAN

NORTℏ
SEA

IRELAND

GREAT
BRITAIN

NET⏌

BEI
LUXℰ

Bay
of
Biscay

FRANCE

PORTUGAL

SPAIN

MEDITERRANℰ

0 km	250
0 miles	250

Pergamon Museum, Berlin
This fabulous collection of antiquities includes the famous blue-tiled Ishtar Gate from Babylon, dating from the 6th century BC (see p532).

Kunsthistorisches Museum, Vienna
Based on the imperial collections of the Habsburgs, the museum (see p596) houses archaeology, paintings, and sculpture, such as this woodcarving of the Madonna (c.1495) by Tilman Riemenschneider.

Baltic Sea

POLAND

NORWAY

SWEDEN

FINLAND

ERMANY

CZECH REPUBLIC

AUSTRIA HUNGARY

ITALY

GREECE

Uffizi, Florence
The Uffizi (see pp422–4) was built originally as the "offices" of the Medici rulers of Florence. Transformed into a gallery in 1581, the building now displays such masterpieces as The Annunciation *by da Vinci.*

Vatican Museums, Rome
Classical and Early Christian statues excavated in Rome over the centuries include this charming Good Shepherd *(4th century AD). The vast papal museum (see pp396–8) also holds great paintings by Michelangelo and Raphael commissioned during the Renaissance.*

The History of Europe

IN THIS TIMELINE of European history, important political and social events appear on the upper half of the page, while the lower half charts contemporary developments in art and architecture. In the art and architecture section the emphasis is on structures and works of art that both illustrate major historical trends and can still be seen today. They are described in more detail in the main sightseeing section of the book.

451–429 BC The great general Perikles presides as uncrowned king of Athens. He establishes democracy in the city and commissions great buildings such as the Parthenon (see pp478–80). However, he also involves Athens in Peloponnesian Wars (431–404), in which Sparta and its allies defeat Athens

FROM PREHISTORY TO THE EARLY MIDDLE AGES

From prehistoric times Europe saw a succession of civilizations that flourished then collapsed. Much of our knowledge of the period comes only from archaeological remains, although the Mycenaeans did leave written inscriptions. Later periods are chronicled in Greek and Roman histories. However, many of these were written long after the events they describe and tend to be a blend of legend and fact.

c.1500 BC Mycenaean culture dominates mainland Greece This gold death mask from Mycenae, known as the "Mask of Agamemnon," is on display at the National Museum of Archaeology in Athens (see p476)

750–600 BC Greek colonists spread to Sicily, southern Italy, Marseille, and Spain

c.800 BC Rise of Etruscans in Italy

509 BC Romans expel Etruscan kings and found republic

c.2300 BC Start of Bronze Age in Europe

2000–1100 BC Series of Minoan civilizations in Crete

c.1000 BC Iron-working reaches central Europe from the Near East

PREHISTORY				CLASSICAL
2500 BC	2000 BC	1500 BC	1000 BC	500 BC
MINOAN AND MYCENAEAN				GREEK AND ETRUSCAN

c.1200 BC Collapse of Mycenaean culture

447 BC Work begins on the Parthenon, the great temple dedicated to Athena on the Acropolis in Athens (see pp478–80)

6th century BC Etruscan sarcophagi topped with lifelike terra-cotta sculptures of the deceased (see p405)

c.1450 BC Mycenaeans (see p491) take over palace of Knossos. Palaces in mainland Greece start to exhibit pillared, frescoed halls, ideas borrowed from the Minoans

4th century BC Magnificent Greek theater built at Epidaurus (see p491)

c.1700 BC First Minoan palace at Knossos on Crete destroyed. A new palace was immediately built to replace it. This colorful scene is one of many fine Minoan frescoes in the Irákleio Archaeological Museum in Crete (see p500)

6th century BC Greek vases of the red-figure type start to appear. The figures are left in the color of the clay, silhouetted against a black glaze. They often show scenes of myth and legend, such as the Trojan War

ART AND ARCHITECTURE

Artistic styles in prehistoric Minoan and Mycenaean cultures were strongly influenced by Egyptian and Middle Eastern models. However, during the Hellenistic period the trend was reversed. Following Alexander the Great's conquests, Greek styles of sculpture, temple architecture, and ceramics were exported to Egypt and as far east as Afghanistan. The Romans were great admirers of the Greeks and the growth of the Roman Empire helped spread the Greek aesthetic throughout western Europe.

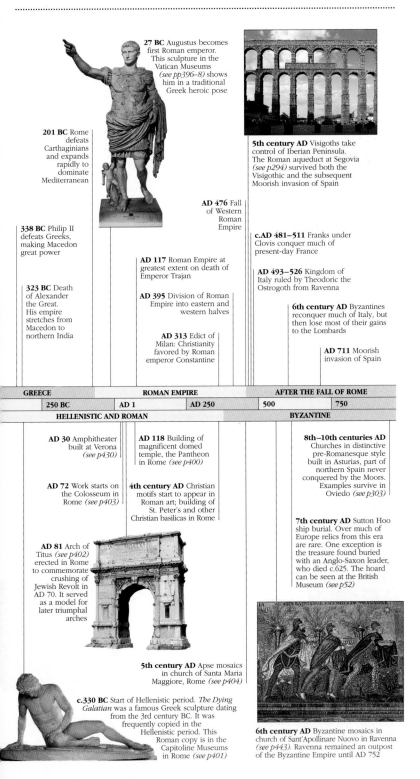

27 BC Augustus becomes first Roman emperor. This sculpture in the Vatican Museums *(see pp396–8)* shows him in a traditional Greek heroic pose

201 BC Rome defeats Carthaginians and expands rapidly to dominate Mediterranean

338 BC Philip II defeats Greeks, making Macedon great power

323 BC Death of Alexander the Great. His empire stretches from Macedon to northern India

5th century AD Visigoths take control of Iberian Peninsula. The Roman aqueduct at Segovia *(see p294)* survived both the Visigothic and the subsequent Moorish invasion of Spain

AD 476 Fall of Western Roman Empire

c.AD 481–511 Franks under Clovis conquer much of present-day France

AD 117 Roman Empire at greatest extent on death of Emperor Trajan

AD 493–526 Kingdom of Italy ruled by Theodoric the Ostrogoth from Ravenna

AD 395 Division of Roman Empire into eastern and western halves

6th century AD Byzantines reconquer much of Italy, but then lose most of their gains to the Lombards

AD 313 Edict of Milan: Christianity favored by Roman emperor Constantine

AD 711 Moorish invasion of Spain

GREECE	ROMAN EMPIRE	AFTER THE FALL OF ROME

250 BC	AD 1	AD 250	500	750

HELLENISTIC AND ROMAN	BYZANTINE

AD 30 Amphitheater built at Verona *(see p430)*

AD 118 Building of magnificent domed temple, the Pantheon in Rome *(see p400)*

8th–10th centuries AD Churches in distinctive pre-Romanesque style built in Asturias, part of northern Spain never conquered by the Moors. Examples survive in Oviedo *(see p303)*

AD 72 Work starts on the Colosseum in Rome *(see p403)*

4th century AD Christian motifs start to appear in Roman art; building of St. Peter's and other Christian basilicas in Rome

7th century AD Sutton Hoo ship burial. Over much of Europe relics from this era are rare. One exception is the treasure found buried with an Anglo-Saxon leader, who died c.625. The hoard can be seen at the British Museum *(see p52)*

AD 81 Arch of Titus *(see p402)* erected in Rome to commemorate crushing of Jewish Revolt in AD 70. It served as a model for later triumphal arches

5th century AD Apse mosaics in church of Santa Maria Maggiore, Rome *(see p404)*

c.330 BC Start of Hellenistic period. *The Dying Galatian* was a famous Greek sculpture dating from the 3rd century BC. It was frequently copied in the Hellenistic period. This Roman copy is in the Capitoline Museums in Rome *(see p401)*

6th century AD Byzantine mosaics in church of Sant'Apollinare Nuovo in Ravenna *(see p443)*. Ravenna remained an outpost of the Byzantine Empire until AD 752

From the Middle Ages to the 18th Century

During this period many of the states of present-day Europe gradually took shape, with powerful centralized kingdoms, notably Spain, Portugal, France, and England, emerging from the medieval feudal system. The Middle Ages were marked by wars between kings and nobles and even between popes and emperors. The Catholic church owned extensive lands and was a powerful political force. However, its influence over much of northern Europe was lost in the Reformation of the 16th century with the emergence of Protestantism.

1096–9 First Crusade; knights of northern Europe capture Jerusalem

1066 Norman conquest of England

9th century Vikings terrorize Europe, gaining control of much of England, Scotland, Ireland, and northern France. The Isle of Lewis chessmen (11th century) give a striking picture of the members of a Viking court. Carved of walrus ivory, they can be seen in the British Museum (see pp52–3)

896 Magyars reach eastern Europe, laying foundation of present-day Hungary

1054 East-West Schism: Roman Church splits definitively with Eastern Orthodox Church

800 The Frankish king, Charlemagne, is crowned Holy Roman Emperor

955 Saxon king Otto defeats Magyars

12th and 13th centuries Emperors and popes fight for control of Germany and Italy. Frederick I Barbarossa, Holy Roman Emperor, quarreled frequently with the pope but set off on the Third Crusade, only to drown in 1190 before he reached the Holy Land

12th and 13th centuries Gradual reconquest of Spain and Portugal from the Moors

12th century Venice grows rich supplying the crusades and trading with the east

EARLY MIDDLE AGES				**MIDDLE AGES**	
800	**900**	**1000**	**1100**	**1200**	
BYZANTINE AND ROMANESQUE					**GOTHIC**

c.800 *Book of Kells*, the greatest of the Irish illuminated copies of the Bible (see p125)

1064 Work begins on Pisa's Duomo (see p411), a magnificent example of Italian Romanesque

1071 Completion of St. Mark's, Venice's great Byzantine basilica (see pp434–5)

10th century Beginnings of Romanesque architecture, characterized by rounded Roman arches, delicate arcades, and tall bell towers

9th and 10th centuries Irish High Crosses (see p125)

11th century Christianity reaches Norway – building of striking wooden "stave" churches (see p656)

c.785 Start of building of the Mezquita in Córdoba, capital of the Moorish Caliphate in Spain (see pp326–7). The *mihrab* (prayer niche) is framed by a beautiful horseshoe arch. Spanish buildings retained Moorish features like this even after the completion of the reconquest of Spain in 1492

late 11th century Building of Durham Cathedral (see p77), England's finest Norman (Romanesque) church

c.1194 Chartres Cathedral, France (see pp180–81) rebuilt in new Gothic style. Pointed arches and ribbed vaulting create possibility of soaring height in church design

Art and Architecture

The Middle Ages in Europe produced remarkable ecclesiastical architecture: first in the Romanesque style, then the even more spectacular Gothic. The Renaissance turned its back on the Gothic with the rediscovery of Classical principles, while Renaissance art was based on scientific understanding of perspective and anatomy, and also on the idealism of Classical sculpture.

c.1267–1336 Life of Giotto, who introduces a new realism to Italian painting. *St. Francis appears to the Monks at Arles* is one of a series of magnificent frescoes he painted for the Basilica di San Francesco in Assisi (see pp406–7)

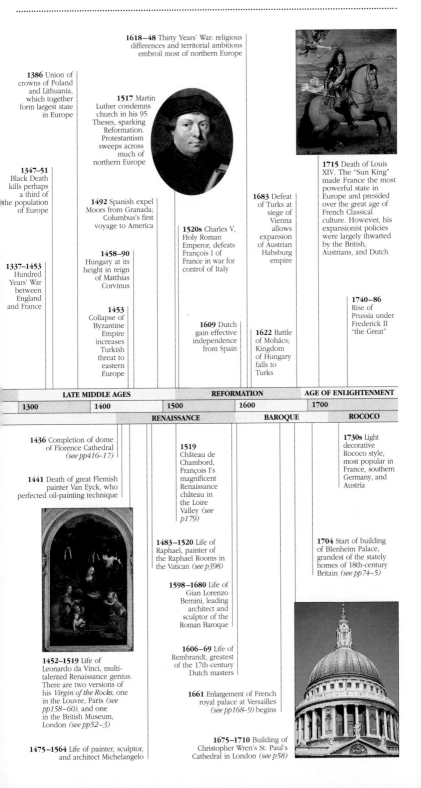

1618–48 Thirty Years' War: religious differences and territorial ambitions embroil most of northern Europe

1386 Union of crowns of Poland and Lithuania, which together form largest state in Europe

1517 Martin Luther condemns church in his 95 Theses, sparking Reformation. Protestantism sweeps across much of northern Europe

1715 Death of Louis XIV. The "Sun King" made France the most powerful state in Europe and presided over the great age of French Classical culture. However, his expansionist policies were largely thwarted by the British, Austrians, and Dutch

1347–51 Black Death kills perhaps a third of the population of Europe

1492 Spanish expel Moors from Granada; Columbus's first voyage to America

1683 Defeat of Turks at siege of Vienna allows expansion of Austrian Habsburg empire

1520s Charles V, Holy Roman Emperor, defeats François I of France in war for control of Italy

1337–1453 Hundred Years' War between England and France

1458–90 Hungary at its height in reign of Matthias Corvinus

1740–86 Rise of Prussia under Frederick II "the Great"

1453 Collapse of Byzantine Empire increases Turkish threat to eastern Europe

1609 Dutch gain effective independence from Spain

1622 Battle of Mohács; Kingdom of Hungary falls to Turks

LATE MIDDLE AGES	REFORMATION	AGE OF ENLIGHTENMENT
1300 1400	1500 1600	1700
RENAISSANCE	BAROQUE	ROCOCO

1436 Completion of dome of Florence Cathedral (see pp416–17)

1441 Death of great Flemish painter Van Eyck, who perfected oil-painting technique

1519 Château de Chambord, François I's magnificent Renaissance château in the Loire Valley (see p179)

1730s Light decorative Rococo style, most popular in France, southern Germany, and Austria

1483–1520 Life of Raphael, painter of the Raphael Rooms in the Vatican (see p398)

1704 Start of building of Blenheim Palace, grandest of the stately homes of 18th-century Britain (see pp74–5)

1598–1680 Life of Gian Lorenzo Bernini, leading architect and sculptor of the Roman Baroque

1606–69 Life of Rembrandt, greatest of the 17th-century Dutch masters

1452–1519 Life of Leonardo da Vinci, multi-talented Renaissance genius. There are two versions of his *Virgin of the Rocks*, one in the Louvre, Paris (see pp158–60), and one in the British Museum, London (see pp52–3)

1661 Enlargement of French royal palace at Versailles (see pp168–9) begins

1675–1710 Building of Christopher Wren's St. Paul's Cathedral in London (see p58)

1475–1564 Life of painter, sculptor, and architect Michelangelo

THE FRENCH REVOLUTION TO THE PRESENT

The French Revolution established a supposedly democratic republic, but the need for a central authority allowed the brilliant general Napoleon to take power and proclaim himself Emperor. The Old Regime died hard and after Napoleon's defeat, many of the old rulers of Europe were restored to their thrones. In time, however, birthright and tradition had to give way to technological progress, the growth of capitalism, the rising power of the bourgeoisie, and the spread of workers' movements. Greater democracy gave the vote to more and more of the population, but wherever democracy broke down, there was the danger it would be replaced by a totalitarian regime, such as the Nazis in Germany and the Communist regimes of the old Soviet Bloc.

1830–40 George Stephenson's *Rocket* becomes the prototype for steam locomotives. Following the success of the Liverpool–Manchester line, opened in 1930, the spread of railroads speeds the Industrial Revolution in Britain

1805 Napoleon defeats Austrians at Austerlitz; by 1807 he controls most of western and central Europe

1812 Defeats in Peninsular War and Russia weaken French hold on Europe

1804 Napoleon crowns himself Emperor of the French

1831 Creation of Kingdom of Belgium

1789 French Revolution leads to execution by guillotine of Louis XVI and reign of terror in 1793. In 1794 more moderate elements take over

1815 Napoleon defeated at Waterloo; Congress of Vienna more or less restores status quo in Europe

1838–1901 Reign of Queen Victoria: apogee of British Empire

1848 Year of revolutions throughout Europe

1852 Napoleon III becomes Emperor of France

1860 Unification of most of Italy

1870 Franco-Prussian War; German victory allows Bismarck to achieve unification of Germany

AGE OF ENLIGHTENMENT		INDUSTRIAL REVOLUTION			AG
1775	1800	1825	1850	1875	
NEOCLASSICAL	EMPIRE	REGENCY	REALISM		IMPRESSIONIS

1785 *The Oath of the Horatii* by Jacques Louis David, French Neoclassical painter. This incident from early Roman history extols the republican spirit that would inspire the French Revolution. The painting hangs in the Louvre, Paris *(see pp158–60)*

c.1814 Goya's powerful paintings recording French atrocities in the Peninsular War, *May 2, 1808* and *May 3, 1808*. They hang in the Prado, Madrid *(see pp288–90)*

1841–1919 Life of Pierre Auguste Renoir, one of the greatest of the artists associated with the Impressionist movement

c.1800 Empire style in fashion and furnishings. Many aspects of design in Europe influenced by Napoleon's Egyptian expedition

1852–70 Second Empire style; rebuilding of Paris by Haussmann *(see p164)*

1874 Claude Monet uses the word "Impression" in title of a painting, giving rise to the term Impressionism

1883 Gaudí begins work on la Sagrada Família cathedral in Barcelona *(see pp312–13)*

1890 Suicide of Dutch painter Van Gogh, unrecognized in his lifetime, now the most sought-after of Post-Impressionist painters *(see p259)*

ART AND ARCHITECTURE

Revivalist styles dominated 19th-century architecture, with imitations of Classical, Gothic, and Renaissance buildings. In contrast, painting evolved radically following the example of the French Impressionists. In the 20th century new building materials – steel, concrete, and glass – were the inspiration of Modernism. Modern art meanwhile experimented with every conceivable form of expression from Surrealism to Conceptual Art.

1857–65 The Ringstrasse built in Vienna, an example of grand 19th-century city planning. This photograph (c.1880) shows horse-drawn trams passing in front of the Staatsoper *(see p595)*

1914 Outbreak of World War I. Millions die as trench warfare along Western Front reaches stalemate

1944 Normandy Landings. Allied forces create second front, which leads to eventual defeat of Germany in 1945

1949 Berlin Air Lift stops Russian blockade of West Berlin

1989 Collapse of Communism in Eastern Europe. Poland, Hungary, Czechoslovakia, and other countries oust Communist rulers. Reopening of Berlin Wall leads to reunification of Germany in 1990

1939 Outbreak of World War II. Germany overruns Poland, then, in 1940, France

1956 Hungarian uprising against Communist rule crushed by Russian tanks

1918 Defeat of Germany, following American entry into war in 1917

1957 Treaty of Rome: European Economic Community marks beginning of European Union

1995 Membership of European Union reaches 15, with entry of Sweden, Finland, and Austria

1901 First award of Nobel prizes in Sweden and Norway

1936–9 Spanish Civil War

1933 Hitler comes to power in Germany

1968 Student protests in France and many other parts of Europe

1919 Treaty of Versailles (1919) creates new states, including Poland, Czechoslovakia, Hungary, and Finland

1973 Carnation Revolution in Portugal

2002 Introduction of common currency, the euro, in 12 countries of the European Union

F IMPERIALISM			THE EUROPEAN UNION	
1900	1925	1950	1975	2000
ART NOUVEAU	ART DECO AND MODERNISM		POST-MODERNISM	

1999 Sir Norman Foster's striking additions to the old Reichstag building in Berlin *(see p530)*

1907 First exhibition of Cubist works by Picasso and others

1919 Foundation of Bauhaus in Weimar *(see p543)*, which exerts worldwide influence on architecture

1937 *Guernica* painted by Pablo Picasso in reaction to bombing of Basque civilians in Spanish Civil War. The painting is currently on show at the Centro de Arte Reina Sofía, Madrid *(see p291)*

1997 Astonishing sculptural forms used by American architect Frank Gehry for new Guggenheim Museum in Bilbao *(see p304)*

1920s and 1930s The term Art Deco is given to design and architecture using modern materials and clean, geometrical shapes

1992 Barcelona Olympics. The city's glorious 20th-century buildings by Gaudí and others are restored and the old port is transformed *(see pp306–15)*

1890s Era of Art Nouveau. The posters of Czech-born Alfons Mucha typify the style, also known as Jugendstil or Secession. Many artists break away from the official academy of their country, notably in Vienna and Berlin

1977 Opening of the Centre Pompidou in Paris *(see p153)*. The design by Renzo Piano, Richard Rogers, and Gianfranco Franchini places service ducts and escalators on the outside of the building

THE
BRITISH ISLES

The British Isles at a Glance

THE ISLANDS of Great Britain and Ireland lie to the northwest of continental Europe and have remained relatively isolated throughout their history. Great Britain consists of three countries, England, Scotland, and Wales, each with a distinctive way of life and traditions. These three, together with Northern Ireland, form the United Kingdom. In the south of Ireland, the Republic of Ireland is a separate country. London, one of Europe's liveliest cities, offers the greatest range of cultural attractions. The islands have a rich variety of land-scapes, from rolling green hills to windswept moors and craggy mountains in the Scottish Highlands.

The Highlands *(see p87) is an area prized for its beauty and diversity of wildlife. This region of mountains and glens is home to many animal species rarely found living wild elsewhere in the British Isles.*

Dublin *(see pp112–21), Ireland's capital, has a lively atmosphere. Many of its finest public buildings, such as the Custom House, date from the 18th century.*

IRELAND
(See pp108–39)

Killarney *(see p127) is a typical friendly Irish town in County Kerry. The surrounding area is renowned for its spectacular scenery, with three huge lakes, waterfalls, and some of the country's highest mountains.*

Inverness

Fort William

Glasgow

Belfast

Galway

DUBLIN

Caernarfon

Killarney   • Cork

Plym

◁ **A tranquil corner of England's Lake District**

Edinburgh (see pp82–6) *is the administrative and cultural capital of Scotland. Its castle, which dates back to the 12th century, gives spectacular views of the entire city.*

LOCATOR MAP

Aberdeen •

• EDINBURGH

• Carlisle

• York

• Manchester
• Liverpool

GREAT BRITAIN
(See pp32–107)

• Birmingham

• Cambridge

Oxford **•**

ff
• Bristol
Bath

• LONDON

• Brighton

Exeter

0 km   75

0 miles   75

York (see pp78–9) *is a city of historical treasures, with many relics from the Roman and Viking ages. Its magnificent minster has the largest collection of medieval stained glass in Britain, and the city walls are well preserved.*

London (see pp42–63) *was founded by the Romans in the 1st century AD. The oldest part of the capital is the City, where Sir Christopher Wren's masterpiece, St. Paul's Cathedral, stands.*

Bath (see pp70–71) *is named after the Roman baths that stand at the heart of the old town, next to the splendid medieval abbey. The city is full of elegant Georgian terraces, built in local honey-colored limestone.*

GREAT BRITAIN

S EPARATED FROM THE REST OF EUROPE *by the English Channel, Britain has been assiduous in preserving its traditions. However, the island can offer the visitor much more than stately castles and pretty villages. A diversity of landscape, culture, literature, art, and architecture, as well as a unique heritage, results in a nation balancing the needs of the present with those of the past.*

Britain's character has been shaped by its geographical position as an island. Never successfully invaded since 1066, its people have developed their own distinctive traditions, and although today a member of the European Union, Britain continues to delight in its nonconformity. Britain's heritage can be seen in its ancient castles, cathedrals, and stately homes with their gardens and parklands. It is also evident in the many age-old customs played out across the nation throughout the year.

For a small island, Great Britain encompasses a surprising variety in its regions, whose inhabitants maintain distinct identities. Scotland and Wales are separate countries from England with their own legislative assemblies. They also have their own surviving Gaelic languages and unique traditions.

The landscape is varied, too, from the mountains of Wales, Scotland, and the north, through the flat expanses of the Midlands and eastern England, to the soft, rolling hills of the south and west. The long, broad beaches of East Anglia contrast with the rocky inlets along much of the west coast.

Despite the spread of towns and cities over the last two centuries, rural Britain still flourishes. The countryside is dotted with farms and charming villages, with picturesque cottages and lovingly tended gardens. The most prosperous and densely populated part of the nation is the Southeast, close to London, where modern office buildings bear witness to the growth of service and high-tech industries.

HISTORY

Britain began to assume a cohesive character as early as the 7th century AD, as Anglo-Saxon tribes migrating from the continent absorbed existing Celtic and Roman influences and finally achieved supremacy in England.

Punting on the River Cherwell, Oxford

◁ **St. Martin-in-the-Fields church and the fountains of London's Trafalgar Square**

However, they suffered repeated Viking incursions and were overcome by the Normans at the Battle of Hastings in 1066, when William the Conqueror founded the royal lineage which still rules the country today. The disparate cultures of the Normans and Anglo-Saxons combined to form the English nation, a process nurtured by Britain's position as an island. Scotland's four divided kingdoms had also unified under one monarch by this time, with the crowning of Duncan I in 1034.

The next 400 years saw English kings extend their domain at home as well as abroad. Wales was conquered in 1282, and by 1296 control was also gained over Scotland. The Scots rose up again, however, winning back their independence under Robert the Bruce in 1314. The Tudor monarchs consolidated England's strength and laid the foundations for Britain's future

Queen Elizabeth I
(reigned 1558–1603)

commercial success. Henry VIII recognized the importance of sea power and, under his daughter, Elizabeth I, English sailors ranged far across the world. The total defeat of the Spanish Armada in 1588 confirmed Britain's position as a major maritime power.

The Stuart period saw the English and Scottish crowns unite, but internal struggles eventually led to the Civil War in 1642. By the time of the Act of Union with Scotland in 1707, however, the whole island was united and the foundations for representative government had been laid. The combination of internal security and maritime strength allowed Britain to seek wealth overseas. By the end of the Napoleonic Wars in 1815, Britain was the world's leading trading nation. The opportunities offered by industrialization were seized, and by the reign of Queen Victoria (1837–1901), a colossal empire had been established across the globe. Challenged by Europe and the rise of the US, and drained by its role in two world wars, Britain's influence waned after 1945. By the 1970s almost all its former colonies had become independent Commonwealth nations.

KEY DATES IN BRITISH HISTORY

AD 43–410 Roman occupation of Britain

440–50 Start of Angle, Saxon, and Jute invasions

1034 Duncan I becomes first king of all Scotland

1066 William the Conqueror defeats King Harold and becomes the first Norman king of England

1256 First Parliament to include ordinary citizens

1533–4 Henry VIII forms Church of England

1535 Act of Union with Wales

1558–1603 Reign of Elizabeth I

1603 Union of English and Scottish crowns; James VI of Scotland becomes James I of England

1642 Civil War breaks out

1649 Charles I executed. Commonwealth declared by Parliament

1707 Act of Union with Scotland

1721 Robert Walpole becomes Britain's first Prime Minister

1837–1901 Reign of Queen Victoria. Industrial Revolution leads to growth of British Empire

1924 First Labour government

1948 National Health Service introduced

1973 Britain joins European Community

1999 Formation of Scottish Parliament and Welsh Assembly

SOCIETY AND POLITICS

British cities are melting-pots for people not just from different parts of the country but also from overseas. Irish immigration has long ensured a flow of labor into the country, and since the 1950s hundreds of thousands have

The colorful costumes of Notting Hill Carnival, an annual multicultural celebration held in London

The Eden Project, Cornwall, an entertaining educational center devoted to mankind's relationship with plants

come from former colonies in Africa, Asia, and the Caribbean, many of which are members of the Commonwealth. Nearly five percent of Britain's 58 million inhabitants are from non-white ethnic groups – and about half of these were born in Britain. The result is a multicultural society that can boast a wide range of music, art, food, and religions.

Britain's class structure is based on a subtle mixture of heredity and wealth. Even though many of the great inherited fortunes no longer exist, some old landed families still live on their estates, and many now open them to the public. The monarchy's position highlights the dilemma of a people seeking to preserve its most potent symbol of national unity in an age suspicious of inherited privilege. Without real political power, although still head of the Church of England, the Queen and her family are subject to increasing public scrutiny.

Democracy has deep foundations in Britain. With the exception of the 17th-century Civil War, power has passed gradually from the Crown to the people's elected representatives. During the 20th century, the Labour (left wing) and Conservative (right wing) parties have, during their periods in office, favored a mix of public and private ownership for industry and ample funding for the state health and welfare systems.

A cricketing pub sign showing the 18th-century version of the game

CULTURE AND THE ARTS

Britain has a famous theatrical tradition stretching back to the 16th century and William Shakespeare. His plays have been performed on stage almost continuously since they were written, and the works of 17th- and 18th-century writers are also frequently revived. Modern British playwrights, such as Tom Stoppard, draw on this long tradition with their vivid language and by using comedy to illustrate serious themes.

In the visual arts, Britain has a strong tradition in portraiture, caricature, landscape, and watercolor. In modern times David Hockney and Francis Bacon, and sculptors Henry Moore and Barbara Hepworth have enjoyed worldwide recognition. Britain has also become famous for its innovative fashion designers, such as Vivienne Westwood and Alexander McQueen.

The indigenous film industry produces occasional international hits such as *Four Weddings and a Funeral* and *The Full Monty*. British television is famous for the high quality of its news, current affairs, and nature programs, as well as for its drama.

The British are great sports fans. Soccer, rugby, cricket, and golf are popular both to watch and to take part in. An instantly recognizable English image is that of the cricket match on a village green. The British also make use of their national parks as enthusiastic walkers and hikers.

Exploring Great Britain

BRITAIN'S MAIN ATTRACTION is its capital, London, but there are many other noteworthy towns to explore throughout the country. Highlights include the university cities of Cambridge and Oxford, the historic centers of York and Bath, and Edinburgh, the capital of Scotland. In the sparsely populated regions of Northern England, Wales, and Scotland, the land itself becomes the center of attention – the Lake District, Snowdonia, and the Isle of Skye are all areas of outstanding natural beauty.

SIGHTS AT A GLANCE

Brighton's Palace Pier viewed from the promenade

KEY

✈	Airport
⛴	Ferry port
—	Highway
—	Major road
—	Railroad
····	Channel Tunnel
▬▬▬	International border
– –	Administrative border

DISTANCE CHART

LONDON							**Distance in kilometers**	
179 111	**BIRMINGHAM**						Distance in miles	
241 150	**164** 102	**CARDIFF**						
599 372	**466** 290	**600** 373	**EDINBURGH**					
626 389	**470** 292	**602** 374	**72** 45	**GLASGOW**				
851 529	**853** 448	**853** 530	**254** 158	**269** 167	**INVERNESS**			
296 184	**130** 81	**278** 173	**343** 213	**344** 214	**597** 371	**MANCHESTER**		
341 212	**332** 206	**261** 152	**784** 427	**785** 426	**1038** 545	**451** 250	**PLYMOUTH**	
333 207	**208** 129	**381** 237	**301** 187	**344** 214	**550** 342	**106** 66	**532** 331	**YORK**

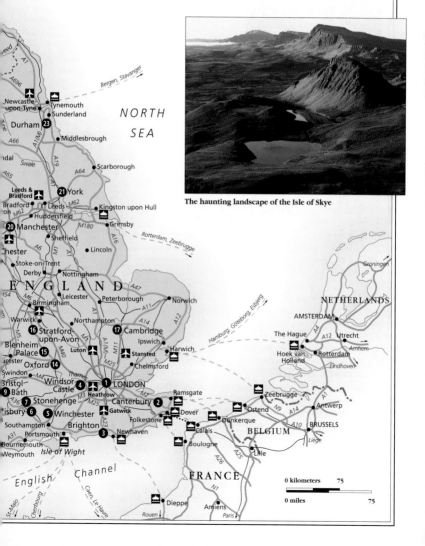

The haunting landscape of the Isle of Skye

Bergen, Stavanger

Newcastle-upon-Tyne
Tynemouth
Sunderland
Durham **23**
Middlesbrough

NORTH SEA

Scarborough

Leeds & Bradford
Bradford
Leeds **21** York
Huddersfield
20 Manchester
Sheffield
Kingston upon Hull
Grimsby

Rotterdam, Zeebrugge

Chester
Stoke-on-Trent
Derby Nottingham
Lincoln

E N G L A N D

Leicester Peterborough Norwich

NETHERLANDS

Birmingham
Warwick
16 Stratford-upon-Avon
Blenheim Palace **15**
Oxford **14**
Northampton
17 Cambridge
Ipswich
Luton Stansted Harwich
Chelmsford

AMSTERDAM

The Hague Utrecht
Hoek van Holland Rotterdam
Arnhem
Eindhoven

Hamburg, Göteborg, Esbjerg

Groningen

Swindon
Bristol
Bath **9**
Stonehenge **7**
Salisbury **6**
Windsor Castle **4**
Heathrow
1 LONDON
Canterbury **2**
Ramsgate
Dover
Folkestone
Winchester **5**
Gatwick
Brighton **3**
Newhaven
Southampton
Portsmouth
Bournemouth
Weymouth
Isle of Wight

Calais
Dunkerque
Ostend
Zeebrugge
Antwerp
BRUSSELS
Lille
BELGIUM
Liège

English Channel

FRANCE

Caen, Le Havre

Dieppe
Amiens
Rouen
Paris

St-Malo
Cherbourg

| 0 kilometers | 75 |
| 0 miles | 75 |

St. Andrews

Aberdeen **28**

Orkney Isles
Shetland Isles

London ❶

THE LARGEST CITY IN EUROPE, London is home to about seven million people. Founded by the Romans in the first century AD as an administrative center and trading port, the capital is the principal residence of British monarchs, as well as the center of government and business, and is rich in historic buildings. In addition to its many museums and galleries, London is an exciting city, with a vast array of entertainments. Developments completed in the year 2000, such as the Tate Modern art gallery and London Eye ferris wheel (the highest in the world), have added to the city's range of attractions.

Millennium Foot Bridge leading to the Tate Modern on Bankside

Summer relaxation along the banks of the Thames at Richmond

SIGHTS AT A GLANCE

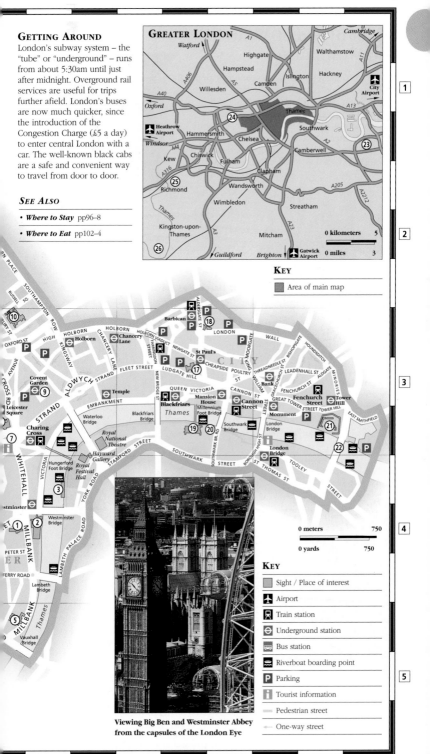

GETTING AROUND

London's subway system – the "tube" or "underground" – runs from about 5:30am until just after midnight. Overground rail services are useful for trips further afield. London's buses are now much quicker, since the introduction of the Congestion Charge (£5 a day) to enter central London with a car. The well-known black cabs are a safe and convenient way to travel from door to door.

SEE ALSO

GREATER LONDON

Watford
Highgate
Walthamstow
Hampstead
Islington
Hackney
Camden
City Airport
Willesden
Thames
Oxford
Southwark
Heathrow Airport
Hammersmith
Chelsea
Camberwell
Kew
Chiswick
Fulham
Clapham
Richmond
Wandsworth
Streatham
Wimbledon
Kingston-upon-Thames
Mitcham
Guildford
Brighton
Gatwick Airport

A1 A11 Cambridge
A406 A5
A40 A13
M4 A2 A23
A316 A205 A212
A3

0 kilometers 5
0 miles 3

KEY

Area of main map

BARBICAN
ALDERSGATE ST
LONDON WALL
HOLBORN
HOLBORN VIADUCT
St Paul's
CHEAPSIDE
POULTRY
THREADNEEDLE ST
LEADENHALL ST
Bank
FENCHURCH ST
CANNON ST
Mansion House
Cannon Street
Monument
Fenchurch Street
Tower Hill
EAST SMITHFIELD
London Bridge
TOOLEY STREET
BOROUGH HIGH ST
THOMAS ST
SOUTHWARK STREET
Southwark Bridge
London Bridge

OXFORD ST
HIGH
HOLBORN
CHANCERY LANE
Chancery Lane
KINGSWAY
AVENUE
Covent Garden
Leicester Square
STRAND
ALDWYCH
Temple
FLEET STREET
LUDGATE HILL
NEW BRIDGE ST
QUEEN VICTORIA
Blackfriars
Blackfriars Bridge
Thames
Millennium Foot Bridge
Charing Cross
EMBANKMENT
Waterloo Bridge
Royal National Theatre
Hayward Gallery
Hungerford Foot Bridge
Royal Festival Hall
YORK ROAD
STAMFORD STREET
WHITEHALL
VICTORIA
Westminster
Westminster Bridge
LAMBETH PALACE ROAD
Lambeth Bridge
PETER ST
MILLBANK
FERRY ROAD
MILLBANK
Vauxhall Bridge
Thames

0 meters 750
0 yards 750

KEY

| | Sight / Place of interest |
| Airport |
| Train station |
| Underground station |
| Bus station |
| Riverboat boarding point |
| Parking |
| Tourist information |
| Pedestrian street |
| One-way street |

Viewing Big Ben and Westminster Abbey from the capsules of the London Eye

D   E   F

Street-by-Street: Whitehall and Westminster

WESTMINSTER HAS BEEN at the center of political and religious power in England since the 11th century, when King Canute built a palace here and Edward the Confessor founded Westminster Abbey. Whitehall is synonymous with the ministries concentrated around it. On weekdays the streets are crowded with civil servants, replaced at weekends by a steady flow of tourists.

Downing Street
No. 10 has been the prime minister's official residence since 1732, when Sir Robert Walpole was given the house by George II.

The Cabinet War Rooms, now open to the public, were Winston Churchill's World War II headquarters.

St. Margaret's Church is a favorite venue for political and society weddings.

★ **Westminster Abbey**
The abbey (see pp46–7) is London's oldest and most important church. The north façade is a Victorian addition.

Central Hall was built in 1911 as a Methodist meeting hall. In 1946 it hosted the first General Assembly of the United Nations.

Dean's Yard
This secluded grassy square is surrounded by picturesque buildings from different periods, many used by Westminster School.

Statue of Richard the Lion-Heart (1860)

The Burghers of Calais is a cast of Auguste Rodin's 1886 original sculpture in France.

KING CHARLES STREET

STOREY'S GATE

GREAT GEORGE STREET

BROAD SANCTUARY

PARLIAMENT SQUARE

ST MARGARET STREET

GREAT COLLEGE STREET

ABINGDON STREET

**Entrance to
Horse Guards**

**Trafalgar
Square**

WHITEHALL

The Cenotaph
(1920) is a war
memorial by Sir
Edwin Lutyens.

RICHMOND TERRACE

VICTORIA EMBANKMENT

**Westminster
Pier** is the
main starting
point for
river trips.

**Westminster
station**

STREET

**★ Houses of
Parliament**
The seat of
government is
dominated by the
clock tower, holding
the 14-ton bell Big
Ben, hung in 1858.
Its deep chimes are
broadcast daily on
BBC radio.

Banqueting House
*Inigo Jones designed this
elegant Palladian building
in 1622. It is famous for
this ceiling painted by
Rubens for Charles I.*

The Norman Shaw Buidings
were the site of the original
Scotland Yard, headquarters of
the Metropolitan Police.

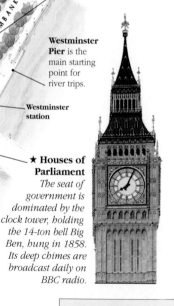

KEY

– – – Suggested route

0 meters   100

0 yards   100

STAR SIGHTS

★ Westminster Abbey

**★ Houses of
Parliament**

Westminster
Abbey ①

See pp46–7.

Houses of
Parliament ②

SW1. ☎ 020-7219 3000.
⊖ *Westminster.* 🚌 *3, 11, 12, 24, 29,
53, 70, 77, 77a.* 📷 *call (08700) 906
3773 for summer visiting times.*
Ⓦ www.parliament.uk

S INCE THE 16TH CENTURY this
site has been the seat of the
two Houses of Parliament:
the House of Commons,
made up of elected Members
of Parliament (MPs) and the
upper house, the House of
Lords. The latter, formerly
filled with hereditary peers,
bishops, and life peers, was
reformed in 2000.

The present Neo-Gothic
building by Sir Charles Barry
replaced the original palace,
which was destroyed by fire
in 1834. Westminster Hall
survived the fire, and still has
a magnificent 14th-century
hammerbeam roof.

To hear debates in either of
the houses from the visitors'
galleries, you can stand in
line on the day. Debates start
at 2:30pm. However, to attend
the popular Prime Minister's
Question Time, you have to
apply for tickets to your local
MP or to your embassy.

London Eye ③

South Bank SE1. ☎ 0870-5000 600.
⊖ *Waterloo, Westminster.* 🚌 *26,
76, 77, 211, 341, 381.* ◯ *daily.*
● *Dec 25, Jan 6–26.* 📷 🗐 ⚌
Ⓦ www.londoneye.co.uk

R EACHING TO A height of
135 m (443 ft) above the
Thames River, this is the
highest Ferris wheel in the
world, and was installed to
mark the Millennium. Its
passenger capsules offer a
gentle, 30-minute ride as the
wheel makes a full turn, with
breathtaking views over the
city and for up to 42 km (26
miles) around. "Flights" are
on the hour or half-hour and
need to be booked as the
wheel is very popular with
both Londoners and tourists.

Westminster Abbey ①

W ESTMINSTER ABBEY has been the burial place of
Britain's monarchs since the 11th century and the
setting for many coronations and royal weddings. It
is one of the most beautiful buildings in London, with
an exceptionally diverse array of architectural styles,
ranging from the austere French Gothic of the nave to
the astonishing complexity of Henry VII's chapel. Half
national church, half national museum, the abbey is
crammed with an extraordinary collection of tombs
and monuments honoring some of Britain's greatest
public figures, from politicians to poets.

North Entrance
*The mock-medieval stonework,
like this carving
of a dragon, is
Victorian.*

Statesmen's Aisle
contains monuments
to some of the
country's greatest
political leaders.

The Cloisters, built
mainly in the 13th and
14th centuries, link the
Abbey church with the
other buildings.

★ **Nave**
*Built under the direction
of master mason Henry
Yevele, the nave reaches to
a height of 31 m (102 ft),
and is the highest in
England. The ratio of
height to width is 3:1.*

CORONATION

The coronation ceremony
is over 1,000 years old
and since 1066, with the
crowning of William the
Conqueror on Christmas
Day, the abbey has been
its sumptuous setting. The
coronation of Queen
Elizabeth II in 1953 was
the first to be televised.

Flying Buttresses
*The massive flying buttresses
help transfer the great weight
of the 31-m (102-ft) high nave.*

STAR FEATURES

★ **Nave**

★ **Henry VII Chapel**

★ **Chapter House**

★ Henry VII Chapel
The chapel, built in 1503–19, has superb late Perpendicular vaultings and choir stalls dating from 1512.

WILLIAM SHAKESPEARE 1564–1616
BURIED AT STRATFORD-ON-AVON

Poets' Corner
Among the great poets honored here are Shakespeare (above), Chaucer, and T.S. Eliot.

The Sanctuary, built by Henry III, has been the scene of 38 coronations.

VISITORS' CHECKLIST

Broad Sanctuary SW1.
📞 020-7222 5152. 🚇 St. James's Park, Westminster.
🚌 3, 11, 12, 24, 29, 53, 70, 77, 77a, 88, 109, 159, 170.
🚤 Westminster Pier.
Cloisters ⬜ 8am–6pm daily.
Royal Chapels, Poets' Corner, Choir, Statesmen's Aisle & Nave ⬜ 9:30am–3:45pm Mon–Fri, 9:30am–1:45pm Sat.
Museum ⬜ 10:30am–4pm daily. 🎟 for Royal Chapels, Poets' Corner, Chapter House, Museum, Statesmen's Aisle, Nave. 🎥 ♿ limited. ✝
Evensong: 5pm Mon–Fri, 3pm Sat & Sun.
🌐 www.westminster-abbey.org.uk

★ Chapter House
This beautiful octagonal room, remarkable for its 13th-century tiled floor, is lit by six huge stained-glass windows showing scenes from the abbey's history.

The museum has many of the abbey's treasures, including wood, plaster, and wax effigies of monarchs.

The Pyx Chamber is where the coinage was tested in medieval times.

HISTORICAL PLAN OF THE ABBEY

The first abbey church was established as early as the 10th century, but the present French-influenced Gothic structure was begun in 1245 at the behest of Henry III. Because of its unique role as the coronation church, the abbey escaped Henry VIII's dissolution of Britain's monastic buildings (1536–9) during the Protestant Reformation.

KEY

▨	Built before 1400
▨	Built in 1503–19
▨	Completed by 1745
☐	Completed after 1850

St. Edward's Chapel
The Coronation Chair is housed here, along with the tombs of many medieval monarchs.

The Victoria Monument, Buckingham Palace

Buckingham Palace ④

SW1. [📞] 020-7766 7300.
[Ⓔ] St. James's Park, Victoria, Green Park. [🚌] 7, 11, 16, 24, 25, 211, 239.
State Rooms [○] Aug 1–Sep 28: daily. [🎫] [📷] [♿] phone first.
Queen's Gallery [📷] **Changing of the Guard** 11:30am daily or alternate days (subject to change). [📞] 020-7766 7300. [W] www.royal.gov.uk

THE QUEEN's official London home is a very popular attraction. Conversion of the 18th-century Buckingham House was begun for George IV in 1826, but the first monarch to occupy the palace was Queen Victoria, in 1837. When the monarch is in residence the Royal Standard flag is flown.

The palace tour takes visitors up the grand staircase and through the splendor of the state rooms. The royal family's private apartments are not open to the public.

In the Music Room royal babies are christened, and state guests presented. The Queen carries out many formal ceremonies in the richly gilded Throne Room, and the Ballroom is used for state banquets and investitures.

Valuable works of art, such as *The Music Lesson* (c.1660) by Dutch master Jan Vermeer, are on display in the Picture Gallery. A selection of works from the monarch's art collection, one of the finest and most valuable in the world, is displayed in the **Queen's Gallery**, a small building located to one side of the palace. The famous Changing of the Guard takes place on the palace forecourt. Crowds gather to watch the colorful half-hour parade of guards, dressed in red jackets and tall, furry hats called bearskins, exchanging the palace keys.

State coaches and other official vehicles may be viewed at the Royal Mews nearby. The star exhibit is the gold state coach built for George III in 1761, with fine panels by Giovanni Cipriani.

Overlooking the forecourt, the East Wing façade of the palace was redesigned by Aston Webb in 1913. He also created the spacious, tree-lined avenue known as the Mall, which leads from the palace to Trafalgar Square. Used for royal processions on special occasions, the Mall is closed to traffic on Sundays. The national flags of foreign heads of state fly from its flagpoles during official visits.

The avenue follows the edge of St. James's Park, a reserve for wildfowl, and popular picnic spot in the heart of the city. Originally a marsh, the park was drained by Henry VIII and incorporated into his hunting grounds. Later, Charles II redesigned it as a fashionable promenade, with an aviary along its southern edge (from which Birdcage Walk takes its name). In summer, concerts are held on the park bandstand.

Tate Britain ⑤

Millbank SW1. [📞] 020-7887 8000.
[Ⓔ] Pimlico. [🚌] 3, 77a, 88, 507, C10.
[🚐] between Tate Britain and Tate Modern. [○] daily. [●] Dec 24–26. [🎫] for major exhibitions. [♿] [📷]
[W] www.tate.org.uk

FOUNDED IN 1897, the Tate Gallery, now called Tate Britain, focuses primarily on British art. Many of the modern works formerly kept here have been moved to the Tate Modern *(see p59)*, housed in a stunningly transformed power station at Bankside, further down the Thames river.

Recently expanded, Tate Britain shows the world's largest display of British art, ranging from Tudor times to the present day, in line with the original intention of the gallery's sponsor, sugar magnate Sir Henry Tate.

One of the most exquisite early works is a portrait of a bejeweled Elizabeth I (c.1575), by Nicholas Hilliard. The influence of the 17th-century Flemish artist Sir Anthony van Dyck on English painters can be seen in William Dobson's *Endymion Porter* (1642–5) and the works of Thomas Gainsborough (1727–88).

Some fine examples of William Hogarth's sharply satirical pictures, which remain popular today, are usually on display. The famed horse paintings of George Stubbs include *Mares and Foals in a Landscape* (1760).

The portico of the Tate Britain building, dating from 1897

The Trafalgar Square façade of the National Gallery

Tate Britain holds a large number of paintings by the visionary poet and artist William Blake (1757–1827). His work was imbued with a mystical intensity, a typical example being *Satan Smiting Job with Sore Boils* (c.1826). England's great 19th-century landscape artists, Constable and Turner, are also well represented. John Constable's famous *Flatford Mill*, painted in 1816–17, is one of his many depictions of the Essex countryside. The Clore Gallery, open since 1987, houses the works of J.M.W. Turner (1775–1851), who left his paintings to the nation on condition that they were kept together. His watercolor *A City on a River at Sunset* (1832) is a highlight.

The Tate also holds many works by the 19th-century Pre-Raphaelites, including J.E. Millais' *Ophelia* (1851–2), as well as the works of several modern and contemporary artists, such as Henry Moore, Francis Bacon, Wyndham Lewis, and David Hockney.

National Gallery ⑥

Trafalgar Sq WC2. 020-7747 2885. Charing Cross, Leicester Sq, Piccadilly Circus. 3, 6, 9, 11 & many others. daily. Jan 1, Dec 24–26. via Sainsbury Wing entrance. www.nationalgallery.org.uk

LONDON'S LEADING art museum, the National Gallery has over 2,200 paintings, most on permanent display. The collection was started in 1824 when George IV persuaded a reluctant government to purchase 38 major paintings. These became the core of a national collection of European art that now ranges from Giotto in the 13th century to the 19th-century Impressionists. The gallery's particular strengths are in Dutch, Italian Renaissance, and 17th-century Spanish painting.

The gallery's paintings are hung in chronological order. In 1991 the modern Sainsbury Wing was added to the main Neoclassical building (1834–8) to house the impressive Early Renaissance collection (1260–1510). *The Leonardo Cartoon* (c.1500), a chalk drawing by Leonardo da Vinci of the Virgin and Child, St. Anne, and John the Baptist, is one of the highlights. Other important Italian painters represented include Masaccio, Piero della Francesca, and Botticelli. Perhaps the most famous of the Northern European works is *The Arnolfini Marriage* by Jan van Eyck (1434).

Most of the gallery's other exhibits are housed on the first floor of the main building. Among the 16th-century paintings, *The Adoration of the Kings* (1564) by Flemish artist Pieter Brueghel the Elder is notable. *Christ Mocked* (1490–1500) by Hieronymus Bosch is included in the Netherlandish and German section. The superb Dutch collection gives two entire rooms to Rembrandt. Annibale Carracci and Caravaggio are strongly represented among Italian painters. Spanish artist Diego Velázquez's only surviving female nude, the *Rokeby Venus* (1647–51), is one of the most popular and well-known of the 17th-century works of art. The great age of 19th-century landscape painting is perhaps best represented by Constable's *The Hay Wain* (1821), a masterpiece of changing light and shadow.

In the Impressionist section, Renoir's *Boating on the Seine* (1879–80) demonstrates the free, flickering touch used by the movement's artists to capture the fleeting moment. Other 19th-century highlights include Van Gogh's *Sunflowers*, Monet's *Waterlilies*, Rousseau's *Tropical Storm with Tiger*, and Seurat's *Bathers at Asnières*.

Lesser paintings of all periods are displayed on the lower floor of the main building. The better of the gallery's two restaurants is located in the Sainsbury Wing.

Bathers at Asnières (1884) by Georges Seurat, in the National Gallery

The West End

THE WEST END is the city's social and cultural center, right next to the London home of the royal family. Stretching from the edge of Hyde Park to Covent Garden, the district bustles all day and late into the night. Whether you are looking for art, history, street- or café-life, it is the most rewarding area in which to begin an exploration of the city. Monuments, shops, cinemas, and restaurants radiate out from Trafalgar Square, and the entertainment scene is at its liveliest in the busy streets around Chinatown, Soho, and Leicester Square. From the garish lights of boisterous Piccadilly Circus to genteel St. James's Square, the West End embraces all aspects of London life, and caters to every budget.

Trafalgar Square by night with Nelson's Column in the foreground

Trafalgar Square ⑦

WC2. 🚇 Charing Cross. 🚌 3, 6, 9, 11, 12, 13, 15, 23, 24, 29, 53, 77a, 88, 91, 139, 159, 176, 453.

LONDON'S MAIN VENUE for rallies and outdoor public meetings, Trafalgar Square was conceived by John Nash and mostly constructed during the 1830s. The 50-m (165-ft) tall column commemorates Admiral Lord Nelson, Britain's most famous sea lord, and dates from 1842. Edwin Landseer's four lions were added 25 years later. Today the square is very popular with tourists.

Admiralty Arch, designed in 1911, separates courtly London from the hurly-burly of Trafalgar Square. The central gate is opened only for royal processions. The restored buildings on the square's south side were built in 1880 as the Grand Hotel. The north side is now taken up by the National Gallery and its Sainsbury Wing (see p49). In the northeast corner stands **St. Martin-in-the-Fields**. This 18th-century church by James Gibbs became a model for the Colonial style of church-building in the US.

Adjoining the National Gallery, the **National Portrait Gallery** depicts Britain's history through portraits, photographs, and sculptures. Subjects range from Elizabeth I to photographs of politicians, actors, and rock stars.

Further north, Leicester Square is at the heart of the West End entertainment district with the city's leading cinemas and lively nightclubs, while London's Chinatown attracts a steady throng of diners and shoppers. Bordering it, Shaftesbury Avenue is the main artery of London's theaterland.

🏛 **National Portrait Gallery**
2 St Martin's Place WC2. 📞 020-7306 0055. 🕙 daily. ⬤ Jan 1, Good Fri, Dec 24–26. 👟 🎧 audio guide. 🖥 www.npg.org.uk

Piccadilly ⑧

W1. 🚇 Piccadilly Circus, Green Park. 🚌 9, 14, 19, 22, 38.

THE THOROUGHFARE called Piccadilly links Hyde Park Corner with Piccadilly Circus, but the name also refers to the surrounding area. Today Piccadilly has two contrasting faces: a bustling commercial district full of shopping arcades, eateries, and cinemas; and St. James's, to the south, which still focuses on a wealthy, glamorous clientele.

Piccadilly Circus, with its dazzling neon lights, is a focal point of the West End. It began as an early 19th-century crossroads between Piccadilly and John Nash's Regent Street. Briefly an elegant space, edged by curving stucco façades, by 1910 the first electric advertisements had been installed.

Crowds congregate beneath the delicately poised figure of Eros, the Greek god of love. Erected in 1892 as a memorial to the Earl of Shaftesbury, a Victorian philanthropist, the statue was originally intended to represent an angel of mercy.

Among the many notable sights along Piccadilly, the **Royal Academy**, founded in 1768, houses a permanent art collection, including a Michelangelo relief of the *Madonna and Child* (1505). Its annual summer exhibition is renowned for clever juxtaposition of new and established works.

The tranquil **St. James's Church** was designed by Sir Christopher Wren in 1684,

Alfred Gilbert's 1892 statue of Eros in Piccadilly Circus

A street performer in front of crowds at Covent Garden's Piazza

and the recently restored 18th-century **Spencer House** contains fine period furniture and paintings. This Palladian palace was built for an ancestor of Princess Diana.

Shopping in and around Piccadilly is very expensive, especially in Bond Street, where many famous designer labels have stores, and in the Burlington Arcade, which is patrolled by beadles. On Piccadilly itself, Fortnum and Mason, founded in 1707, is one of London's most prestigious food stores, while the grand Ritz hotel is a popular afternoon tea venue for the suitably dressed. Jermyn Street is renowned for high quality men's clothing.

South of Piccadilly is St. James's Square, laid out in the 1670s and dominated by a statue of William III. It has long been the most fashionable address in London. Pall Mall, named after the 17th-century game of *palle-maille* (a cross between croquet and golf) once played here, is lined with gentlemen's clubs, which admit only members and their guests. It leads to the 16th-century **St. James's Palace**, built for Henry VIII and briefly a royal residence. The palace is still the official headquarters of the Court of St. James, to which ambassadors are accredited. Opposite is the **Queen's Chapel**, the first Classical church in England.

🏛 Royal Academy
Burlington House, Piccadilly W1.
📞 020-7300 8000. ⬛ *daily.* ⬤ *Dec 24–25.* 🎫 *reserve in advance.*
⬛ 🌐 www.royalacademy.org.uk

🏛 Spencer House
27 St. James's Pl SW1. 📞 020-7499 8620. ⬛ *daily.* ⬤ *Jan & Aug.* 📷 *compulsory.* ⬛

Covent Garden ⑨

WC2. ⬤ *Covent Garden.* 🚌 *1, 6, 9, 11, 13, 15, 23, 59, 68, 77a, 91, 168, 171, 176.* ⬛ *daily.*

OPEN-AIR CAFES, street entertainers, stylish shops, and markets make Covent Garden a magnet for visitors. The name derives from a medieval convent garden which supplied Westminster Abbey with produce.

At its center is the Piazza, designed by 17th-century architect Inigo Jones as an elegant residential square, after an example from the Tuscan town of Livorno. For a time, houses around the Piazza were highly sought-after, but decline accelerated when a fruit and vegetable market developed. In 1973 the market moved to a new site and Covent Garden was revamped. Today only **St. Paul's Church** remains of Inigo Jones's buildings. Samuel Pepys saw a Punch and Judy show under the portico in 1662, and street entertainment has been a tradition here ever since.

The **Royal Opera House**, designed in 1858 by E.M. Barry, but totally renovated in 1997–9, is home to the Royal Opera and Royal Ballet Companies. Many of the world's greatest performers have appeared on its stage.

Covent Garden has many theatrical associations. The site of the **Theatre Royal**, completed in 1812, has been occupied by a theater since 1663. **St. Martin's Theatre** is home to the world's longest running play, *The Mousetrap*.

Other attractions include the **London Transport Museum** and an area of "alternative" shops around Neal Street and Neal's Yard. The **Lamb and Flag** (1623) in Rose Street is one of London's oldest pubs.

🏛 London Transport Museum
Covent Garden WC2. 📞 020-7379 6344. ⬛ *daily.* ⬤ *Dec 24–26.* 🎫 *by appt.* ⬛
🌐 www.ltmuseum.co.uk

Statue of a resting ballerina, facing the Royal Opera House

British Museum ⑩

THE OLDEST PUBLIC MUSEUM in the world, the British Museum was established in 1753 to house the collections of the physician Sir Hans Sloane (1660–1753). Sloane's artifacts have been added to by gifts and purchases from all over the world, and the museum now contains innumerable items stretching from the present day to prehistory. Robert Smirke designed the main part of the building (1823–50), but the architectural highlight is the modern Great Court, with the world-famous Reading Room at its center. The 94 galleries, which cover 2.5 miles (4 km) of floorspace, cover civilizations from ancient Assyria to modern Japan.

PREHISTORIC AND ROMAN BRITAIN

RELICS OF PREHISTORIC Britain are on display in six separate galleries. The most impressive items include the Mold gold cape made from a sheet of decorated gold; an antlered headdress worn by hunter-gatherers some 9,000 years ago; and "Lindow Man," a 1st-century AD sacrificial victim who lay preserved in a bog until 1984. Some superb Celtic metalwork is also on show, alongside the silver Mildenhall Treasure and other notable Roman pieces. The Hinton St. Mary mosaic (4th century AD) features a roundel containing the earliest known British depiction of Christ.

MEDIEVAL, RENAISSANCE, AND MODERN OBJECTS

THE SPECTACULAR Sutton Hoo ship treasure, the burial hoard of a 7th-century Anglo-Saxon king, is on display in Room 41. This superb find, made in 1939, revolutionized scholars' understanding of Anglo-Saxon life and ritual. The artifacts uncovered include a helmet and shield, Celtic hanging bowls, the remains of a lyre, and gold and garnet jewelry.

Adjacent galleries contain a collection of clocks, watches, and scientific instruments. Some exquisite timepieces are on view, including a 400-year-old clock from Prague, designed as a model galleon; in its day it pitched, played

Reconstruction of the ceremonial helmet found at Sutton Hoo

music, and even fired a cannon. Also nearby are the famous 12th-century Lewis chessmen, and a gallery housing Baron Ferdinand Rothschild's (1839–98) remarkably varied treasures. The most spectacular of these is a gold enameled reliquary of the Holy Thorn (Christ's Crown of Thorns), dating from the 15th century.

The museum's modern collection includes Wedgwood pottery, illustrated books, glassware, and a series of Russian revolutionary plates.

WESTERN ASIA

NUMEROUS GALLERIES at the museum are devoted to the Western Asian collections, covering 7,000 years of history. The most famous items are the 7th-century BC Assyrian reliefs from King Ashurbanipal's palace at Nineveh, but of equal interest are two large human-headed bulls from 7th-century BC Khorsabad, and an inscribed Black Obelisk of Assyrian King Shalmaneser III. Rooms 51–59 on the upper floor contain pieces from ancient Sumeria, part of the Oxus Treasure (which lay buried for over 2,000 years), and the museum's collection of clay cuneiform tablets. The earliest of these are inscribed with the oldest known pictographs (c.3300 BC).

ANCIENT EGYPT

EGYPTIAN SCULPTURES can be found in Room 4 on the main floor. These include a fine red granite head of a king, thought to be Amenophis III, and a colossal statue of king Ramses II. Also on show is the Rosetta Stone, which was used by Jean-François Champollion (1790–1832) as a primer for deciphering Egyptian hieroglyphs. An extraordinary array of mummies, jewelry, and Coptic art can also be found in rooms 61–66 upstairs, including a famous bronze cat with a gold nose-ring. The various instruments used by embalmers to preserve bodies before entombment are all displayed.

Ancient Egyptian tomb painting, *The Festival of Sekhtet* (1410 BC)

The Portland Vase, depicting the betrothal of Peleus and Thetis

GREECE AND ROME

THE GREEK and Roman collections include the museum's most famous treasure, the Elgin Marbles. These 5th-century BC reliefs from the Parthenon once comprised a marble frieze which decorated Athena's temple at the Acropolis in Athens. Much of it was ruined in battle in 1687, and most of what survived was removed between 1801 and 1804 by the British diplomat Lord Elgin, and sold to the British nation. Other highlights include the Nereid Monument, and sculptures and friezes from the Mausoleum at Halicarnassus. The beautiful 1st-century BC cameo-glass Portland Vase is located in the Roman Empire section.

ORIENTAL ART

FINE PORCELAIN and ancient Shang bronzes (c.1500–1050 BC) are highlights of the museum's Chinese collection. Particularly impressive are the ceremonial ancient Chinese bronze vessels, with their enigmatic animal-head shapes. The fine Chinese ceramics range from delicate tea bowls to a model pond almost a thousand years old. Adjacent to these is one of the finest collections of Asian religious sculpture outside India. These include an assortment of sculpted reliefs which

The Young Prince with his Parents (c.1600), an Indian miniature

once covered the walls of the Buddhist temple at Amarati, and which recount stories from the life of the Buddha. A Korean section contains some gigantic works of Buddhist art.

Islamic art, including a stunning jade terrapin found in a water tank, can be found in Room 34. Rooms 92–4 house the Japanese galleries, with a Classical teahouse in Room 92 and many delightful *netsuke* (small ivory carvings) gracing the lobby.

AFRICA

AN INTERESTING collection of African sculptures, textiles, and graphic art can be found in Room 25, located in the basement. Famous bronzes from the Kingdom of Benin stand alongside modern African prints, paintings, and drawings, plus an array of colorful fabrics.

THE GREAT COURT AND THE OLD READING ROOM

Surrounding the Reading Room of the former British Library, the £100-million Great Court opened to coincide with the new millennium. Designed by Sir Norman Foster, the Court is covered by a wide-span, lightweight roof, creating London's first ever indoor public square. The Reading Room itself has been restored to its original design, so visitors can sample the atmosphere which Karl Marx, Mahatma Gandhi, and George Bernard Shaw found so agreeable. From the outside, however, it is scarcely recognizable; it is housed in a multi-level construction which partly supports the roof, and which also contains a Center for Education, temporary exhibition galleries, bookshops, cafés, and restaurants. Part of the Reading Room also serves as a study suite where those wishing to learn more about the Museum's collections have access to information.

The Great Court and Reading Room of the British Museum

Madame Tussaud's and the London Planetarium ⑪

Marylebone Rd NW1. 📞 0870-400 3000. 🚇 Baker St. 🕐 daily. ⬤ Dec 25. 📷 ♿ 🌐 www.madame-tussauds.com & www.london-planetarium.com

Wooden rowboats available to rent on Regent's Park boating lake

M ADAME TUSSAUD began her wax-modeling career making death masks of victims of the French Revolution. In 1835, after moving to England, she set up an exhibition of her work in Baker Street, near the museum's present site.

Traditional techniques are still used to create the figures of royalty, politicians, actors, pop stars, and sporting heroes. In the renowned Chamber of Horrors some of the original French Revolution death masks are displayed, and vivid scenes of murders are recreated. Visitors travel in stylized taxi-cabs in the final section "witnessing" momentous events in the city's history, from the Great Fire of 1666 to the Swinging Sixties.

Situated next door is the London Planetarium, where a spectacular star show explores some of the mysteries of the planets and the solar system.

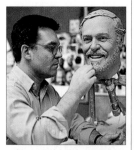

Making a model of singer Luciano Pavarotti at Madame Tussaud's

Regent's Park ⑫

NW1. 📞 020-7486 7905. 🚇 Regent's Park, Great Portland St, Camden Town. 🕐 daily. ♿ London Zoo 📞 020-7722 3333. 🕐 daily. ⬤ Dec 25. 📷

T HIS AREA OF land was enclosed as a park in 1812. John Nash designed the scheme and originally envisaged a kind of garden suburb, dotted with 56 villas in a variety of Classical styles. Eight villas were eventually built inside the park (three survive round the edge of the Inner Circle).

The boating lake boasts many varieties of water birds. In summer Queen Mary's Gardens are full of flowers and Shakespeare productions are staged at the Open Air Theater nearby. Musical performances are also held at the bandstand on the weekend. Broad Walk provides a picturesque stroll north from Park Square towards Primrose Hill.

London Zoo, with its vast animal enclosures, borders the park, and is also an important center of wildlife research and conservation work.

Hyde Park ⑬

W2. 📞 020-7298 2100. 🚇 Hyde Park Corner, Knightsbridge, Lancaster Gate, Marble Arch. 🕐 dawn–midnight daily. ♿

T HE ANCIENT MANOR of Hyde was part of the lands of Westminster Abbey seized by Henry VIII at the Dissolution of the Monasteries in 1536. James I opened the park to the public in the early 17th century, and it was soon one of the city's most fashionable public spaces. Unfortunately it also became popular with duelists and highwaymen, prompting William III to have 300 lights hung along Rotten Row, the first street in England to be lit at night. Today Rotten Row is used for horseback riding.

In 1730 the Westbourne River was dammed by Queen Caroline to create an artificial lake – the Serpentine. Today cafés, restaurants, and the Serpentine Gallery, which has exhibitions of modern art, dot the fringes of the lake, which is a popular venue for boating and swimming.

At the southeast corner of Hyde Park stands Apsley House, the grand former home of the Duke of Wellington. Now a museum of memorabilia to the great politician and soldier, the lavish interiors designed by Robert Adam are also worth seeing.

Statue of Peter Pan in Kensington Gardens

A law passed in 1872 made it legal to assemble an audience and address it on whatever topic you chose. Since then, Speaker's Corner, at the northeast corner of the park, has been the established venue for budding orators. Crowds gather on Sundays to listen to lively speeches.

Adjoining Hyde Park are Kensington Gardens, the former grounds of Kensington Palace, which were opened to the public in 1841. A royal residence for centuries, the palace was Princess Diana's home until her untimely death.

Attractions in the gardens include the bronze statue of J. M. Barrie's fictional Peter Pan (1912), by George Frampton, and the Round Pond where model boats are sailed. The dignified Orangery (1704) is now an upscale café.

Street-by-Street: South Kensington

THE NUMEROUS MUSEUMS and colleges created in the wake of the Great Exhibition of 1851 *(see pp56–7)* continue to give this neighbourhood its dignified character. Visited as much by Londoners as tourists, the museum area is liveliest on Sundays and on summer evenings during the Royal Albert Hall's famous season of classical "Prom" concerts *(see p126).*

The Royal Albert Hall
Opened in 1870 and modeled on a Roman amphitheater, this magnificent concert hall hosts a range of events.

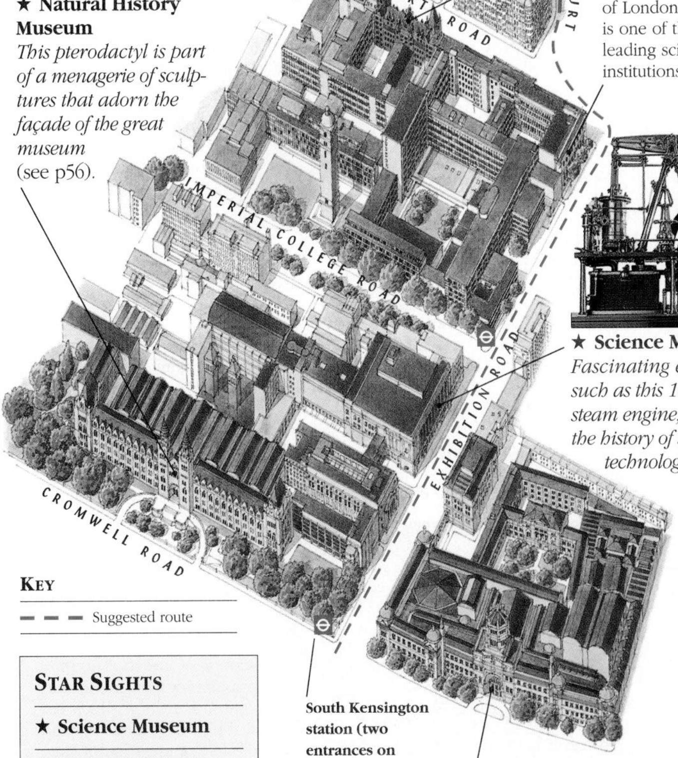

The Memorial to the Great Exhibition is surmounted by a bronze statue of its instigator, Prince Albert.

to Kensington Gardens

The Royal College of Music, founded in 1882, exhibits historic musical instruments from around the world.

★ **Natural History Museum**
This pterodactyl is part of a menagerie of sculptures that adorn the façade of the great museum (see p56).

Imperial College, part of London University, is one of the country's leading scientific institutions.

★ **Science Museum**
Fascinating exhibits, such as this 18th-century steam engine, celebrate the history of science and technology (see p56).

KEY

— — Suggested route

STAR SIGHTS

★ Science Museum

★ Natural History Museum

★ Victoria and Albert Museum

South Kensington station (two entrances on Exhibition Road)

| 0 meters | 100 |
| 0 yards | 100 |

★ **Victoria and Albert Museum**
The museum has a fine collection of decorative arts from around the world (see p57).

Children exploring the "Pattern Pod" at the Science Museum

Science Museum ⑭

Exhibition Rd SW7. ⊖ South Kensington. ▥ 9, 10, 14, 52, C1. ☎ 0870-870 4868. ◯ daily. ● Dec 24–26. ▨ for special exhibitions only. ▣ ♿ ⬡ www.sciencemuseum.org.uk

Cᴇɴᴛᴜʀɪᴇs ᴏꜰ scientific and technological development are illustrated and explained at the Science Museum – from Ancient Greek and Roman medicine to space exploration and nuclear fission.

The massive and impressive collection, exhibited on five floors, includes steam engines, spacecraft, and early mechanical computers. The museum aims to bring entertainment to the process of learning, with numerous interactive displays for children and staff on hand to provide explanations. Of equal importance is the social context of science: how inventions have transformed day-to-day life, and the process of discovery itself.

The best of the displays are "Flight," which gives visitors the opportunity to experiment with aeronautical concepts, and "Launch Pad," designed to give 7- to 13-year-olds a knowledge of basic scientific principles. A plasma ball is one of many hands-on exhibits. "The Exploration of Space" exhibits the scarred Apollo 10 spacecraft which carried three astronauts to the moon and back in May 1969. There is also a video of the Apollo 11 moon landing a few weeks later.

More down-to-earth, but just as absorbing, is "Food for Thought," which reveals the impact of science and technology on every aspect of diet, explored through demonstrations and historic reconstructions, such as an 18th-century kitchen.

Other popular sections include "Optics," which has holograms, lasers, and color-mixing experiments, and "Power and Land Transport," which displays working steam engines, vintage trains, cars, and motorbikes.

The Wellcome Wing is devoted to contemporary science and technology. "Antenna" is a constantly updated exhibition devoted to the latest scientific breakthroughs. "Pattern Pod" introduces younger children to the patterns of science in a fun and colorful way. "Digitopolis" explores our relationship with digital technology, including virtual reality. "In Future" is a multi-user game in which partici-pants decide how current scientific research could affect the future. Our understanding of human identity is the subject of "Who Am I?", where visitors can learn about genetics and current biomedical discoveries. The wing also contains an IMAX® cinema, a spacecraft simulator, and a café.

Natural History Museum ⑮

Cromwell Rd SW7. ⊖ South Kensington. ▥ 14, 49, 70, 74, 345, C1. ☎ 020-7942 5000. ◯ daily. ● Dec 24–26. ▣ ♿ ⬡ www.nhm.ac.uk

Tʜɪs ᴠᴀsᴛ cathedral-like building, designed by Alfred Waterhouse, is the most architecturally flamboyant of the South Kensington museums. Its richly sculpted stonework conceals an iron and steel frame. This building technique was revolutionary when the museum first opened in 1881. The imaginative displays tackle fundamental issues such as the ecology and evolution of the planet, the origin of species, and the development of human beings – all explained through a dynamic combination of the latest technology, interactive displays, and traditional exhibits.

Triceratops skull, Natural History Museum

The museum is divided into the Life and Earth Galleries. In the former, the Ecology exhibition begins its exploration of the complex web of the natural world, and man's role in it, through a convincing replica of a moonlit rainforest buzzing with the sounds of insects. The most popular exhibits are in the Dinosaur section which has real dinosaur skeletons and life-like animatronics. "Creepy Crawlies," with specimens from the insect and spider world, and the Mammals exhibition, enable visitors to see endangered and danger-ous creatures close-up. The

The colorful "Antenna" section in the Science Museum Wellcome Wing

extinct dodo is among the many species displayed in the Bird Gallery.

The Earth Galleries explore the history of Earth and its wealth of natural resources, and offer the opportunity to experience the rumblings of an earthquake. The Darwin Center gives the chance to go behind the scenes to observe zoological specimens and to find out more about the museum's scientific research.

Victoria and Albert Museum ⑯

Cromwell Rd SW7. ● *South Kensington.* ▭ *14, 74, C1.* ☎ *020-7942 2000.* ○ *daily.* ● *Dec 24–26.* ⊠ *for special exhibitions.* 🎫 ⚙
Ⓦ *www.vam.ac.uk*

Façade of the Victoria and Albert Museum

Oᴿɪɢɪɴᴀʟʟʏ ꜰᴏᴜɴᴅᴇᴅ in 1852 as a Museum of Manufactures – to inspire students of design – the V&A, as it is popularly known, has 11 km (7 miles) of galleries on four floors. The museum was renamed by Queen Victoria in 1899, in memory of her late husband, and contains one of the world's richest collections of fine and applied arts.

Since 1909 the museum has been housed in a building designed by Sir Aston Webb. The galleries are currently undergoing a major rehanging, which has started with the creation of the luxurious British Galleries on levels 2 and 4. Here design and decorative arts from 1500 to 1900 are displayed to great effect.

Donatello's marble relief of *The Ascension* is included in the sculpture collection along with sculptures from India and the Middle and Far East. Craftsmanship in porcelain, glass, and pottery is displayed across 21 galleries, with rare pieces by Picasso and Bernard Leach, intricate Near Eastern tiles, and a wide selection of Chinese pieces.

The most celebrated item in the vast array of furniture is

18th-century wooden doll, Victoria and Albert Museum

the *Great Bed of Ware*, made around 1590. The Victorian designers who decorated the plush Morris, Gamble, and Poynter Rooms recreated historic styles with newer industrial materials. The fully furnished interiors offer a vivid picture of social life through their displays of furniture and other domestic objects.

Among exhibits in the 20th-Century Gallery is Daniel Weil's painting *Radio in a Bag* (1983). The V&A has a wide collection of musical instruments and metalwork, including a 16th-century salt cellar, the *Burghley Nef*. The Whiteley Silver galleries also explore the history and techniques of silvermaking. The *Eltenberg Reliquary*, made in Cologne in the late 12th century, takes pride of place in the Medieval Treasury situated on level 1.

Among the textiles, weapons, jewelry, metalwork, glass, and paintings of the Nehru Gallery of Indian Art is the automated *Tippoo's Tiger* (c.1790), which mauls a European soldier when activated. Eight galleries, devoted to the arts of the Far East, display rare jade and ceramics, a giant Buddha's head from AD 700–900, and a Ming canopied bed. Among exhibits in the T. T. Tsui Gallery of Chinese Art is a watercolor on silk from the Qing Dynasty (1644–1912). The Toshiba Gallery focuses on Japanese art, including Samurai armor and woodblock prints. The world-renowned Dress Collection is displayed on level 1. It is devoted to fashionable clothing from the mid-1500s to the present day. The figures here are fully dressed, complete with contemporary accessories.

The museum also houses valuable illustrated documents in the National Art Library and the national collection of photographs with images from 1856 to the present.

The City and Southwark

DOMINATED BY gleaming office blocks, befitting its status as London's financial and business center, the City is also the oldest part of the capital. The Great Fire of 1666 obliterated many of its buildings, and much of the reconstruction was undertaken by Sir Christopher Wren. St. Paul's Cathedral is the most magnificent of his surviving works. Humming with activity in business hours, the City empties at night. Southwark, on the south bank of the Thames, was a refuge for prostitutes and gamblers in the Middle Ages. Theaters, including the Globe, where many of Shakespeare's plays were performed, and other places of entertainment were built along the waterfront in the second half of the 16th century.

Spacious interior of St. Paul's Cathedral in the City

St. Paul's Cathedral ⑰

Ludgate Hill EC4. 🍴 020-7246 8348.
😑 St. Paul's, Mansion House. 🚌 4, 11, 15, 17 & others. 🕐 9:30am– 3:45pm Mon–Sat; for services only Sun, Dec 25 & Good Fri. 🎦 📷
🖊 www.stpauls.co.uk

REBUILT ON THE SITE of a medieval cathedral after the Great Fire of 1666, this magnificent Baroque building, designed by Sir Christopher Wren, was completed in 1710.
St. Paul's has been the setting for great ceremonial events, including the funeral of Sir Winston Churchill in 1965 and the wedding of Prince Charles and Lady Diana in 1981.
At 110 m (360 ft) high, the dome is the second largest in the world, after that of St. Peter's in Rome. Supported by a brick cone, the lantern weighs a massive 850 tonnes. The dome's gallery affords a splendid view over London.
Modifications to Wren's original plan include the

towers of the west front, the double colonnade of the west portico, and the balustrade – added against his wishes in 1718. Pediment carvings on the west portico show the Conversion of St. Paul.
Wren created a cool and majestic interior. The nave, transepts, and choir are arranged in the traditional shape of a cross. Its climax is in the great open space of the crossing, below the main dome, which is decorated with monochrome frescoes by Sir James Thornhill, a leading architectural painter of the time. From the south aisle, 259 steps ascend to the

Whispering Gallery, so-called because of the unusual acoustics. The north aisle is vaulted with small domes like those of the nave ceiling.
Much of the fine wrought ironwork was created by Jean Tijou, a Huguenot refugee. The intricate carvings of cherubs, fruits, and garlands on the choir stalls are the work of Grinling Gibbons.
Memorials to famous figures, such as Lawrence of Arabia and Lord Nelson, can be seen in the crypt. The inscription on Wren's tomb is fitting: "Reader, if you seek his memorial look all around you."

Museum of London ⑱

London Wall EC2. 🍴 020-7600 3699. 😑 Barbican, St. Paul's.
🕐 Mon–Sat & public hols, Sun pm.
🔴 Jan 1, Dec 24–26. 🛗
🖊 www.museumoflondon.org.uk

THIS MUSEUM traces life in London from prehistoric times to the 20th century.
Objects from Roman London include a brightly colored 2nd-century fresco, while from the Tudor city an example of an early English delft plate, made in 1602 at Aldgate, bears an inscription praising Elizabeth I.
The 17th-century section contains the shirt Charles I wore on the scaffold, and an audio-visual display recreating the Great Fire of 1666. A dress in Spitalfields silk, dating from 1753, is among the many fine costumes on show.
One of the most popular exhibits is the lavishly gilded Lord Mayor's State Coach, built in 1757 and still used for the Lord Mayor's Show held in November of each year.
The Victorian Walk takes visitors back to the time of Charles Dickens, recreating the atmosphere of 19th-century London. The current layout is liable to change due to ongoing renovations.

Roman wall painting in the Museum of London

Sculpture from inaugural exhibition in the vast Turbine Hall, Tate Modern

Tate Modern ⑲

Bankside SE1. 📞 020-7887 8000.
🚇 Southwark, Blackfriars, Waterloo.
🚌 45, 63, 100, 381, 344, RV1.
🕐 daily. ⬤ Dec 24–26. 🎫 special
exhibitions. ♿ 🅦 www.tate.org.uk

O NE OF THE WORLD'S most
important collections of
20th-century art now has a
worthy home in this imposing,
former power station with its
vast, cathedral-like spaces.

Originally designed by
Sir Giles Gilbert Scott, the
architect of London's red
telephone kiosks, the huge
Bankside building had been
disused since 1981, when it
was acquired by the Tate
Gallery. Swiss architects were
responsible for the building's
redesign, which allows the
works of art to be displayed
in a dynamic style suited to
their innovative spirit. The
gallery opened in 2000.

Unusually, the permanent
collection is exhibited in four
themed groups: landscape,
still life, the nude, and history.
The paintings and sculptures
embrace Surrealism, Abstract
Expressionism, Pop Art,
Minimal and Conceptual Art.

Major works include
Picasso's *The Three Dancers*,
Dalí's *The Metamorphosis of
Narcissus*, and Andy Warhol's
Marilyn Diptych. There are
also regular temporary
exhibitions of works by lesser-
known artists, and by more
controversial newcomers. At
the top of the building are
two new floors, enclosed in
glass. One is a restaurant with
superb views. Natural light
from these floors filters down
to the upper galleries.

Shakespeare's Globe ⑳

New Globe Walk SE1. 📞 020-7902
1500. 🚇 London Bridge, Mansion
House. 🕐 daily. ⬤ Dec 25–26.
Performances mid-May–Sep.
🎫 🅦 every 30 mins.
🅦 www.shakespeares-globe.org

A DETAILED REPRODUCTION of
an Elizabethan theater has
been built on the riverside
close to the site of the original
Globe, Shakespeare's
"wooden O" where many of
his plays were first performed.
Open to the elements, the
theater operates only in the
summer. Seeing a play here
can be a lively experience,
with "groundlings" (those
with cheap standing-room
tickets) in front of the stage
encouraged to cheer or jeer.
An informative tour of the
theater is offered by "resting"
Globe actors, and visitors can
enjoy being center stage
among them. Beneath the
theater is the Underglobe,
where every aspect of
Shakespeare's work is vividly
brought to life through the
use of modern technology
and traditional crafts.

Tower of London ㉑

See pp60–61.

Tower Bridge ㉒

SE1. 📞 020-7940 3985. 🚇 Tower
Hill, London Bridge. **The Tower
Bridge Exhibition** 🕐 daily.
⬤ Dec 24–26. 🎫 ♿
🅦 www.towerbridge.org.uk

T HIS FLAMBOYANT piece of
Victorian engineering,
completed in 1894, soon
became a symbol of London.
Its two Gothic towers contain
the mechanism for raising the
roadway to permit large ships
to pass through. The towers
are made of a supporting
steel framework clad in stone.
When raised, the roadway
creates a space 40 m (135 ft)
high and 60 m (200 ft) wide.
In its heyday it was raised
and lowered five times a day.

The bridge now houses **The
Tower Bridge Exhibition**,
with displays which bring its
history to life. There are fine
river views from the walkways
between the towers, and the
steam engine room which was
in use until 1976 can be visited.

**Tower Bridge, a symbol of
Victorian London**

Tower of London ㉑

Tower of London raven

S OON AFTER HE BECAME KING in 1066, William the Conqueror built a fortress here to guard the entrance to London from the Thames Estuary. In 1097 the White Tower, which today occupies the center of the complex, was completed in stone; other fine buildings have been added over the centuries. The Tower has served as a royal residence, armory, treasury, and most famously as a prison for enemies of the Crown. Many were tortured and among those who met their death here were the "Princes in the Tower," the sons and heirs of Edward IV. Today the Tower is a popular attraction, housing the Crown Jewels and other fine exhibits. Thirty seven Yeoman Warders, known as "Beefeaters," guard the complex and live here. Its most celebrated residents are seven ravens. Legend claims that the kingdom will fall if they desert the Tower.

Beauchamp Tower
Many high-ranking prisoners were held here, often with their own servants. The tower was built by Edward I around 1281.

Tower Green was the execution site for aristocratic prisoners, away from crowds on Tower Hill, where many had to submit to public execution. Seven people died here, including two of Henry VIII's six wives, Anne Boleyn and Catherine Howard.

Two 13th-century curtain walls protect the tower.

Queen's House
This Tudor building is the sovereign's official residence at the Tower.

Main entrance from Tower Hill

THE CROWN JEWELS

The world's best-known collection of precious objects, now displayed in a splendid exhibition room, includes the gorgeous regalia of crowns, scepters, orbs, and swords used at coronations and other state occasions. Most date from 1661, when Charles II commissioned replacements for regalia destroyed by Parliament after the execution of Charles I. Only a few older pieces survived, hidden by royalist clergymen until the Restoration. These included Edward the Confessor's sapphire ring, now incorporated into the Imperial State Crown. The crown was made for Queen Victoria in 1837 and has been used at the coronation of every monarch since.

The Sovereign's Ring (1831)

The Sovereign's Orb (1661), a hollow gold sphere encrusted with jewels

★ Jewel House

Among the magnificent Crown Jewels is the Scepter with the Cross (1660), which contains the world's largest diamond.

VISITORS' CHECKLIST

Tower Hill EC3. **(** 0870-756 6060. **⊖** *Tower Hill; Docklands Light Railway to Tower Gateway.* **🚌** *15, X15, 25, 42, 78, 100, D1, D9, D11.* **🚢** *from Westminster to Tower Pier.* **◻** *Mar–Oct: 9am–6pm Mon–Sat, 10am–6pm Sun; Nov–Feb: 9am–5pm Tue–Sat, 10am–5pm Sun, Mon (last adm: 1 hour before closing).* **◻** *Jan 1, Dec 24–26.* **🐾** **♿** *limited, except Jewel House.* ***Ceremony of the Keys:*** *9:30pm daily.* **W** *www.hrp.org.uk*

★ White Tower

When the tower was finished in 1097, it was London's tallest building at 27 m (90 ft) high.

★ Chapel of St. John

This austere yet beautiful Romanesque chapel is a particularly fine example of Norman architecture.

Traitors' Gate

The infamous entrance was used for prisoners brought from trial in Westminster Hall.

Bloody Tower

Edward IV's two sons were put here by their uncle, Richard of Gloucester (subsequently Richard III), after their father died in 1483. The princes, depicted here by John Millais (1829–96), disappeared mysteriously and Richard was crowned later that year. In 1674 the skeletons of two children were found nearby.

STAR SIGHTS

★ Jewel House
★ White Tower
★ Chapel of St. John

London: Farther Afield

O VER THE CENTURIES, London has steadily expanded to embrace the scores of villages that surrounded it. Although now linked in an almost unbroken urban sprawl, many of these areas have managed to retain a strong individual character. Portobello Road has hosted a market since 1837, while Notting Hill, once farmland, is now covered with townhouses. Greenwich and Richmond recall the days when the Thames was an important artery for transport and commerce. The riverside around Richmond and Kew to the southwest of London was a favorite site for the great country retreats of the aristocracy. Perhaps the grandest riverside residence of all is the royal palace of Hampton Court, set in elaborate, luxuriant gardens.

View from the hill at Greenwich of the 17th-century Queen's House

Greenwich ㉓

SE10. 🚊 *Greenwich, Maze Hill, & Docklands Light Railway to Cutty Sark, Greenwich.* 🚢 *from Westminster.*

B EST KNOWN as the place from which the world's time is measured, Greenwich also marks the historic eastern approach to London by land and water. The area is steeped in maritime and royal history.

The meridian line that divides the earth's eastern and western hemispheres passes through the **Royal Observatory Greenwich** (now housing a museum) and millions of visitors have been photographed standing with one foot on either side of it. Designed by Christopher Wren, the building is topped by a ball on a rod, dropped at 1pm every day since 1833 so that ships' chronometers could be set by it.

Because of its historic links with time, Greenwich was chosen as the site for Britain's year 2000 exhibition – the **Millennium Dome**.

The exquisite **Queen's House,** designed by Inigo Jones, has been restored to how it looked in the late 17th century. Highlights are the unusually-shaped main hall and the intriguing spiral "tulip staircase".

The adjoining **National Maritime Museum** has exhibits ranging from primitive canoes, through Elizabethan galleons, to modern ships. Nearby, the **Old Royal Naval College** was designed by Christopher Wren in two halves so the Queen's House could retain its river view. The chapel and the Painted Hall are open to the public.

Other sights worth visiting include the **Cutty Sark**, a 19th-century clipper ship, and the **Gipsy Moth**, in which Francis

Clock tower of the Old Royal Observatory, Greenwich

Chichester sailed single-handedly round the world.

🏛 Royal Observatory Greenwich
Greenwich Park SE10. 📞 *020-8858 4422.* ⏱ *daily.* ⬤ *Dec 24–26, Jan 1.* ♿ *limited.* 🌐 *www.rog.nmm.ac.uk*
🏛 Queen's House and National Maritime Museum
Romney Rd SE10. 📞 *020-8858 4422.* ⏱ *daily.* ⬤ *Dec 24–26.* ♿ *limited.* 🌐 *www.nmm.ac.uk*

A colorful antique shop on London's Portobello Road

Notting Hill and Portobello Road ㉔

W11. 🚇 *Notting Hill Gate, Ladbroke Grove.* 🏠 *Fri & Sat.*

N OTTING HILL and Portobello Road have been a focus for the Caribbean community since the peak years of immigration in the 1950s and '60s. Today this is a trendy residential district, whose vibrant cosmopolitan spirit is captured in the 1999 film starring Julia Roberts and Hugh Grant.

The West Indian flavor is best experienced during Europe's largest street carnival. First held in 1966, it takes over the entire area on the August bank holiday weekend. For three days costumed parades flood through the crowded streets.

Portobello Road market has a bustling atmosphere with hundreds of stands and shops selling a variety of collectables. The southern end consists almost exclusively of stands selling antiques, jewelry, and souvenirs popular with tourists.

Richmond and Kew ㉕

SW15. ⊖ Kew Gardens, Richmond.
🚋 to Kew Bridge, Richmond.

THE ATTRACTIVE VILLAGE of
Richmond took its name
from a palace built in 1500 by
Henry VII (formerly the Earl
of Richmond), the remains of
which can be seen off the
green. The vast **Richmond
Park** was once Charles I's
royal hunting ground. In
summer, boats sail from central
London to Richmond and Kew.
   The nobility continued to
favor Richmond after royalty
had left, and some of their
mansions have survived. The
Palladian villa, **Marble Hill
House**, was completed in 1729
for the mistress of George II.
   On the opposite side of the
Thames, **Ham House**, built in
1610, had its heyday later that
century when the aristocratic
Lauderdale family moved in.
Syon House has been
inhabited by the Dukes and
Earls of Northumberland for
over 400 years. Attractions
include lavish Neoclassical
interiors, remodelled by Robert
Adam in the 1760s, landscaped
parkland by Capability Brown,
and a spectacular conservatory.
   On the riverbank to the
south, **Kew Gardens**, the most
complete botanic gardens in
the world, is flawlessly
maintained, with examples of
nearly every plant that can be
grown in Britain. Highlights
are the Palm House, with
thousands of exotic tropical
blooms, and the delicate plants
of the Temperate House. The
Gardens became a UNESCO
World Heritage Site in 2003.
Near the river, **Kew Bridge
Steam Museum** is housed in
an old water pumping station.

An aerial view of the impressive Hampton Court Palace

⚜ Syon House
London Rd, Brentford. 📞 020-8560
0881. **House** ⭘ mid-Apr–Oct: Wed,
Thu, Sun. **Gardens** ⭘ daily.
⬤ Dec 25–26. 🅰

❀ Kew Gardens
Kew. 📞 020-8332 5655. ⊖ Kew
Gardens. 🚌 65, 237, 267, 391, 419.
⭘ daily. ⬤ Dec 25, Jan 1. 🅰

Deer grazing in Richmond Park,
former royal hunting ground

Hampton Court ㉖

East Molesey, Surrey. 📞 0870-752
7777. 🚉 🚋 Hampton Court.
🚌 111, 216, 267, 411. ⭘ daily.
⬤ Dec 24–26. 🅰 🅰 ♿

CARDINAL WOLSEY, chief
minister to Henry VIII,
began building Hampton Court
as his country residence in
1514. A few years later, in the
hope of retaining royal favor,
he gave it to the king. The
palace was extended first by
Henry, and again at the end of
the 17th century by William III
and Mary II, with the help of
Christopher Wren.
   From the outside the palace
is a harmonious blend of
Tudor and English Baroque.
A remarkable feature is the
Astronomical Clock, created
for Henry VIII in 1540.
   Inside, Wren's Classical
royal rooms, such as the
King's Apartments, contrast
with Tudor architecture, such
as the Great Hall. The stained-
glass window here shows
Henry VIII flanked by the
coats of arms of his six wives.
Superb woodwork in the
Chapel Royal, including the
massive reredos by Grinling
Gibbons, dates from a major
refurbishment by Queen
Anne (c.1711). In the Queen's
Gallery, where entertainments
were often staged, the marble
chimneypiece is by John Nost.
Many of the state apartments
are decorated with furniture,
paintings, and tapestries from
the Royal Collection. The
King's Staircase has wall
paintings by Antonio Verrio.
Nine canvases depicting the
Triumph of Julius Caesar
(1490) are housed in the
Mantegna Gallery.
   The restored Baroque privy
garden, originally created for
William and Mary, features
radiating avenues of majestic
limes and formal flowerbeds.
The Fountain Garden still has
a few yews planted during
their reign. Other attractions
are the maze and the Great
Vine, planted in 1768.

The distinctive Palm House at London's famous Kew Gardens

Canterbury ❷

Kent. 🏘 50,000. 🚊 🚌
ℹ️ The Buttermarket, Sun Street
(01227-378 100). 🏛 Wed & Fri.

CANTERBURY WAS an important Roman town even before St. Augustine arrived in 597, sent by the pope to convert the Anglo-Saxons to Christianity. The town rose in importance, soon becoming the center of Christianity in England.

Under the Normans, the city maintained its position as the country's leading archbishopric. A new cathedral was built on the ruins of the Anglo-Saxon cathedral in 1070. It was enlarged and rebuilt many times; as a result it embraces examples of all styles of medieval architecture.

The most poignant moment in the cathedral's history came in 1170 when Thomas à Becket, the Archbishop of Canterbury and enemy of King Henry II, was murdered here. **Trinity Chapel** was built to house Becket's remains.

Until the Dissolution the cathedral was one of the chief places of pilgrimage in all Christendom. The *Canterbury Tales* by Geoffrey Chaucer (c.1345–1400), one of the greatest works of early English literature, tells of a group of pilgrims traveling from London to Becket's shrine in 1387.

Adjacent to the ruins of **St. Augustine's Abbey** is **St. Martin's Church**, one of the oldest in England.

The domes and minarets of the Royal Pavilion, Brighton

Beneath Canterbury's streets lies the **Roman Museum**, the highlight of which are the foundations of a Roman house.

⛪ Cathedral
Christ Church Gate. 📞 01227-762 862. 🕐 daily. 🔴 during services and concerts, Dec 25. 💷 ♿ 📷
🌐 www.canterbury-cathedral.org

Brighton ❸

East Sussex. 🏘 250,000. 🚊 🚌
ℹ️ 10 Bartholomew Sq (0906-711 2255). 🏛 Mon–Sat. 🎭 International Arts Festival (May).

AS THE NEAREST south coast resort to London, Brighton is perennially popular.

The spirit of the Prince Regent (later George IV) lives on in the magnificence of the **Royal Pavilion**, originally a farmhouse where the prince resided with the Catholic widow Mrs. Fitzherbert after

their secret marriage. As his parties became more lavish, George needed a suitably extravagant setting. In 1815 he employed architect John Nash to transform the house into the fantastic Oriental palace that we see today. Completed in 1822, the exterior remains largely unaltered.

Traditional seaside fun is centered around Brighton's pebble beach. The **Palace Pier**, a late-Victorian pleasure ground, is now filled with amusement arcades. Also worth visiting is the maze of shops and winding alleys from the original village of Bright-helmstone, called **The Lanes**.

🏛 Royal Pavilion
Old Steine. 📞 01273-290 900.
🕐 daily. 🔴 Dec 25, 26. 💷 📷 ♿
🌐 www.royalpavilion.org.uk

Windsor Castle ❹

See pp66–7.

Winchester ❺

Hampshire. 🏘 35,000. 🚊 🚌
ℹ️ Guildhall, The Broadway (01962-840 500). 🏛 Wed–Sat.

THE CAPITAL of the ancient kingdom of Wessex, the city of Winchester was also the headquarters of England's Anglo-Saxon kings.

William the Conqueror built one of his first English castles here. The only surviving part is the **Great Hall**, erected in 1235 to replace the original. It is now home to the legendary Round Table of King Arthur,

Canterbury Cathedral dominating the skyline

said to have been built by the wizard Merlin but actually made in the 13th century.

The **Westgate Museum** is one of two surviving 12th-century gatehouses in the city wall. The room (once a prison) above the gate has a glorious 16th-century painted ceiling.

Winchester has been an ecclesiastical center for many centuries. Its fine **cathedral** was begun in 1079. Originally a Benedictine monastery, it has preserved much of its Norman architecture despite numerous modifications. The writer Jane Austin is buried here. Built around 1110, **Wolvesey Castle**, once home of the bishops of Winchester, now lies in ruins.

🏰 Great Hall

Castle Ave. 📞 01962-846 476. ⬤ daily. ● Dec 25, 26. ♿

The 13th-century Round Table in the Great Hall, Winchester

Salisbury ❻

Wiltshire. 👥 40,000. 🚇 🚌 🛈 Fish Row (01722-334 956). ⬤ Tue & Sat. 🎪 Salisbury Festival (May).

SALISBURY WAS founded in 1220, when the Norman hilltop settlement of Old Sarum was abandoned in favor of a site amid lush water meadows, where the Nadder, Bourne, Avon, Ebble, and Wylye meet.

A **cathedral** was built here in the early 13th century. It is a fine example of the Early English style of Gothic architecture, typified by tall, pointed lancet windows. The magnificent landmark spire is the tallest in England.

The spacious and tranquil **Close**, with its schools, alms-houses, and clergy housing,

The awe-inspiring megaliths of Stonehenge, Salisbury Plain

makes a fine setting for Salisbury's cathedral. In the medieval King's House, the **Salisbury and South Wiltshire Museum** has displays on early man, Stonehenge, and Old Sarum.

Beyond the walls of the Cathedral Close, Salisbury developed its chessboard layout, with areas devoted to different trades, perpetuated in street names such as Fish Row and Butcher Row.

Leaving the close, you reach the busy High Street leading to the 13th-century **Church of St. Thomas**, which has a lovely carved timber roof (1450). Nearby on Silver Street, **Poultry Cross** was built in the 15th century as a covered poultry market. In the bustling **Market Place** many of the brick and tile-hung Georgian façades conceal medieval houses.

🏛 Cathedral

The Close. 📞 01722-555 120. ⬤ daily. 🎟 donation. ♿

🏛 Salisbury and South Wiltshire Museum

The Close. 📞 01722-332 151. ⬤ Mon-Sat (Aug: Sun pm). ● Dec 24-26. 🎟 ♿ limited.

Stonehenge ❼

Off A303, Wiltshire. 📞 01980-624 715. 🚌 3 from Salisbury. ⬤ daily. ● Jan 1, Dec 24-26. 🎟 🎫 ♿

BUILT IN SEVERAL STAGES from about 3000 BC onward, Stonehenge is Europe's most famous prehistoric monument. We can only guess at the rituals that took place here, but the alignment of the stones leaves little doubt that the circle reflects the changing trajectory of the sun through the sky and the passing of the seasons.

Stonehenge's monumental scale is all the more impressive given that the only available tools were made of stone, wood, and bone. To quarry, transport, and erect the huge stones, its builders must have had the command of immense resources and pools of labor.

Stonehenge was completed in about 1250 BC; despite popular belief, it was not built by the Druids, who flourished in Britain 1,000 years later.

A collection of ceremonial bronze weapons, jewelry, and other finds excavated at Stonehenge can be seen in the museum in Salisbury.

Sculpture by Elisabeth Frink (1930–93) in Cathedral Close, Salisbury

Windsor Castle ❹

T HE OLDEST CONTINUOUSLY inhabited royal residence in Britain, the castle, originally made of wood, was built by William the Conqueror in 1070 to guard the western approaches to London. He chose the site because it was on high ground and just a day's journey from his base in the Tower of London. Successive monarchs have made alterations that render it a remarkable monument to royalty's changing tastes. King George V's affection for it was shown when he chose Windsor for his family surname in 1917. The castle is an official residence of the present queen, who often stays here at weekends.

Albert Memorial Chapel
First built in 1240, it was rebuilt in 1485 and finally converted into a memorial for Prince Albert in 1863.

King Henry VIII Gate

Castle Hill and main entrance

★ St. George's Chapel
The architectural highlight of the castle, this chapel was built between 1475 and 1528 and is an outstanding Late Gothic work. Ten monarchs are buried here.

The Round Tower
was first built in wood by William the Conqueror. In 1170 it was rebuilt in stone by Henry II. It now houses the Royal Archives and Photographic Collection, but is not open to the public.

Statue of Charles II

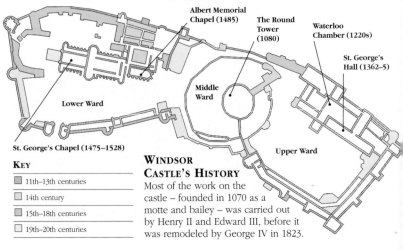

Albert Memorial Chapel (1485)

The Round Tower (1080)

Waterloo Chamber (1220s)

St. George's Hall (1362–5)

Middle Ward

Lower Ward

St. George's Chapel (1475–1528)

Upper Ward

KEY

☐	11th–13th centuries
☐	14th century
☐	15th–18th centuries
☐	19th–20th centuries

WINDSOR CASTLE'S HISTORY
Most of the work on the castle – founded in 1070 as a motte and bailey – was carried out by Henry II and Edward III, before it was remodeled by George IV in 1823.

Drawing Gallery
This chalk etching of Christ by Michelangelo is part of the Resurrection Series. *It belongs to the Royal Collection, a small selection of which is shown here at any one time.*

VISITORS' CHECKLIST

Castle Hill. **C** *0207-321 2233.*
O *9:45am–5:15pm (Nov–Feb: 4:15pm) daily (last adm: 1 hr before closing).* **O** *Good Fri, Dec 25–26.* **St. George's Chapel** *5:15pm Mon–Sat; Sun (for worshippers only).*

The Audience Chamber is where the Queen greets her guests.

The Queen's Ballroom

Queen Mary's Dolls' House was designed by Sir Edwin Lutyens in 1924. Every item was built on a 1:12 ratio. The wine cellar contains genuine vintage wine.

Waterloo Chamber
The walls of this banqueting hall, first built in the 13th century, are lined with portraits of the leaders who played a part in the defeat of Napoleon.

Brunswick Tower

The East Terrace Garden was created by Sir Jeffry Wyatville for King George IV in the 1820s.

★ State Apartments
These rooms hold many treasures, including this late 18th-century state bed in the King's State Bedchamber, used for the visit in 1855 of Napoleon III.

STAR FEATURES

★ St. George's Chapel

★ State Apartments

The Fire of 1992
A devastating blaze began during maintenance work on the State Apartments. St. George's Hall was destroyed but has been rebuilt.

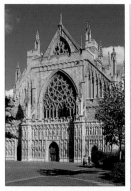

West front of the Cathedral Church of St. Peter in Exeter, Devon

Devon and Cornwall ❽

🚉 🚌 *Truro (Cornwall), Exeter (Devon).* ℹ️ *Boscawen Street, Truro (01872-274 555); Paris Street, Exeter (01392-265700).*

MILES OF STUNNING coastline dominate this magical corner of Britain. Busy seaside resorts alternate with secluded coves and fishing villages rich in maritime history. Inland, lush pastures contrast with stark and treeless moorland.

Britain's most westerly point, **Land's End**, is noted for its remote and wild landscape. Nearby, the former Benedictine monastery of **St. Michael's Mount** rises dramatically from the waters of Mount Bay off Cornwall's southern coast. On the north coast, **St. Ives**, with its crescent of golden sands, is internationally renowned for its two art museums, the Barbara Hepworth Museum and the Tate Gallery St. Ives.

The **Eden Project** in St. Austell was built in 1998–2000 in an old Cornish china clay pit. The aim of this vast educational and research center is to teach visitors about the vital relationship between plants, people, and resources in an informative and fun way. Two bulbous "greenhouses," huge segmented geodesic domes known as biomes, dominate the site, which holds some 4,500 species of plants.

The administrative capital of Cornwall is **Truro**, a city of gracious Georgian buildings and cobbled streets. Here, the Royal Cornwall Museum has displays on mining, smuggling, and Methodism.

Devon's capital is **Exeter**, a lively city with fine Roman and medieval relics. The mainly 14th-century Cathedral Church of St. Peter is one of the most superbly ornamented cathedrals in Britain.

Devon's most popular recreation area is **Dartmoor National Park**. At its heart is a bleak and windswept landscape, dotted with tors – outcrops of granite rock – and grazed by herds of wild ponies.

🏛️ **Eden Project**
St. Austell. 📞 *01726-811 911.* 🚉 *St. Austell, then local bus.* 🕐 *daily.* ⬤ *Dec 24–25.* ♿
ⓦ *www.edenproject.com*

🏛️ **Dartmoor National Park**
Devon. 🚉 🚌 *to Exeter, Plymouth, Totnes then local bus.* ℹ️ *Visitor Centre, Princetown (01822-890414).*

Bath ❾

See pp70–71.

A wild Dartmoor pony, a familiar sight in Devon's national park

Bristol ❿

Avon. 🏛️ *400,000.* 🚆 🚉 🚌 ℹ️ *The Annex, Wildscreen Walk, Harbourside.* 🏢 *daily.* 🎭 *Harbor Festival (Jul–Aug), International Balloon Fiesta (Aug).*

THE CITY OF BRISTOL, at the mouth of the Avon, was once the main British port for transatlantic trade, pioneering the era of the ocean-going steam liner. The city grew rich on the transportation of wine, tobacco, and, in the 17th century, slaves.

There is a covered market in the city center, part of which occupies the **Corn Exchange**, built by John Wood the Elder in 1743. **St. John's Gate** has colorful statues of Bristol's mythical founders, King Brennus and King Benilus.

Bristol's **cathedral** took an unusually long time to build. The choir was begun in 1298, the transepts and tower were finished in 1515, but the nave took another 350 years to build.

Designed by Isambard Kingdom Brunel, the **SS Great Britain** was the world's first large iron passenger ship. Launched in 1843, it traveled 32 times round the world. The ship now stands in the dock where it was originally built, undergoing restoration.

The **Bristol Industrial Museum's** diverse collection of vehicles and models illustrates the astonishing range of products made in Bristol over the last 300 years.

The **Arnolfini Gallery** is a showcase for contemporary art, dance, drama, and film. It is on the harborside, which is lined with cafés, bars, and galleries.

Cornwall's wild and rugged southern coastline

Wales

WALES IS A COUNTRY of outstanding natural beauty, with varied landscapes. Visitors come to climb dramatic mountain peaks, walk in the forests, fish in the broad rivers, and enjoy the miles of untainted coastline. The country's many seaside towns have long been popular with British vacationers. As well as outdoor pursuits, there is the vibrancy of Welsh culture, with its strong Celtic roots, to be experienced. The Welsh have their own language, which has survived despite the pervasive use of the English tongue.

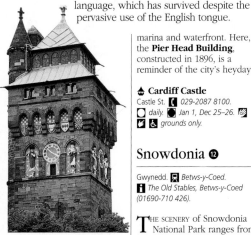

Cardiff Castle's clock tower, a 19th-century addition by Burges

Cardiff ⓫

Glamorgan. 🚶 285,000. ✈ 🚃 🚍
ℹ 16 Wood St (029-2022 7281).
🎷 Cardiff Festival (Jul/Aug).

CARDIFF WAS first occupied by the Romans, who built a fort here in AD 75. In the 1830s the town began to develop as a port, and by 1913 it was the world's leading coal exporter. Confirmed as the Welsh capital in 1955, it is now devoted to commerce and administration.

Cardiff Castle began as a Roman fort. It was renovated in the 19th century by William Burges, who created an ornate mansion rich in medieval images and romantic detail.

Cardiff's civic center is set around Alexandra Gardens. The Neoclassical **City Hall** (1905) is dominated by its huge dome and clock tower. The **Crown Building** now houses the Welsh Office, responsible for Welsh government affairs.

To the south of the center, the docklands are being transformed by the creation of a marina and waterfront. Here, the **Pier Head Building**, constructed in 1896, is a reminder of the city's heyday.

♠ Cardiff Castle
Castle St. **ℹ** 029-2087 8100.
◯ daily. ● Jan 1, Dec 25–26. 📷 ♿ grounds only.

Snowdonia ⓬

Gwynedd. 🚉 Betws-y-Coed.
ℹ The Old Stables, Betws-y-Coed (01690-710 426).

THE SCENERY of Snowdonia National Park ranges from rugged mountain country to moors and beaches. The area is well known as a destination for hikers, and villages such as **Betws-y-Coed** and **Llanberis** are busy hill-walking centers.

The main focus of this vast area is **Snowdon**, which at 1,085 m (3,560 ft) is the highest peak in Wales. Hikers wishing to explore Snowdonia's peaks should be wary of sudden weather changes. In summer, less intrepid visitors can take the Snowdon Mountain Railway from Llanberis to Snowdon's summit.

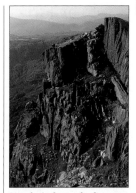

Snowdonia, famous for dangerous peaks and popular with climbers

Caernarfon ⓭

Gwynedd. 🚶 10,000. 🚌 **ℹ** Castle St (01286-672 232). 🏪 Sat.

ONE OF THE MOST famous castles in Wales looms over this busy town, created after Edward I's defeat of the last native Welsh prince, Llywelyn ap Gruffydd, in 1283. The town walls merge with modern streets that spread beyond the medieval center and open into a market square.

Caernarfon Castle was built as a seat of government for North Wales. It contains several interesting displays, including the **Royal Welsh Fusiliers Museum** and an exhibition tracing the history of the Princes of Wales.

On the hill above the town are the ruins of **Segontium**, a Roman fort built around AD 78.

♠ Caernarfon Castle
Y Maes. **ℹ** 01286-677 617.
◯ daily. ● Jan 1, Dec 24–26. 📷 📷

Caernarfon Castle, one of the forbidding fortresses built by Edward I

Street-by-Street: Bath ❾

BATH OWES ITS MAGNIFICENT Georgian townscape to the bubbling pool of water at the heart of the Roman baths. The Romans transformed Bath into England's first spa resort and it regained fame as a spa town in the 18th century. At this time the two brilliant John Woods (Elder and Younger) designed the city's fine Palladian-style buildings. Today, the traffic-free heart of this lively town is full of street musicians, museums, and enticing shops.

The Circus
This is a daring departure from the typical Georgian square, by John Woo the Elder (1705–54

No. 1 Royal Crescent is a museum which provides a glimpse of 18th-century aristocratic life.

No. 17 is where the 18th-century painter Thomas Gainsborough lived.

Assembly Rooms and Museum of Costume

★ Royal Crescent
Hailed as the most majestic street in Britain, this graceful arc of 30 houses (1767–74) is the masterpiece of John Wood the Younger. West of Royal Crescent, Royal Victoria Park (1830) is the city's largest open space.

Jane Austen (1775–1817), the writer, stayed at No. 13 Queen Square on one of many visits to Bath in her youth.

Milsom Street and New Bond Street contain some of Bath's most elegant shops.

Theatre Royal (1805)

KEY

– – – Suggested route

0 meters   100

0 yards   100

THE KING'S SPRING

STAR SIGHTS

★ **Royal Crescent**

★ **Roman Baths**

★ **Bath Abbey**

Pump Rooms
These tearooms once formed the social hub of the 18th-century spa community. They contain this decorative drinking fountain.

VISITORS' CHECKLIST

Avon. 🏠 *85,000.* ✈ *Bristol International Airport, 32 km (20 miles) W.* 🚉 *Dorchester St.* 🚌 *Manvers St.* 🛈 *Abbey Chambers, Abbey Church Yard (0870-444 6442).* 🗓 *daily.* 🎭 *International Festival (May–Jun).* **Roman Baths Museum** 🕐 *daily.* 🔴 *Dec 25–26.* 🚫 ♿ *limited.*

Pulteney Bridge
This charming bridge (1769–74), designed by Robert Adam, is lined with shops and links the center with the magnificent Great Pulteney Street.

The Building of Bath Museum shows how, in the 18th century, the city was transformed from a medieval wool town into one of Europe's most elegant spas.

★ Roman Baths
Built in the 1st century, this bathing complex is one of Britain's greatest memorials to the Roman era.

★ Bath Abbey
The splendid abbey stands at the heart of the old city in the Abbey Church Yard, a paved piazza enlivened by buskers. Its unique façade features stone angels climbing Jacob's Ladder to heaven.

Great Pulteney Street

Parade Gardens
Courting couples came to this pretty riverside park for secret liaisons in the 18th century.

Sally Lunn's House (1482) is one of Bath's oldest houses.

Train station

The massive dining hall at Christ Church College, Oxford University

Oxford ⑭

Oxfordshire. 145,000. 🚉 ✈
ℹ️ 15–16 Broad St (01865-726 871).
🛒 Wed, Thu. 🎪 St. Giles Fair (Sep).

O XFORD HAS long been a
strategic point on the
western routes into London –
its name describes its position
as a convenient spot for crossing the river (a ford for oxen).

English students expelled
from Paris founded the
university in 1167. The
development of England's
first university created the
spectacular skyline of tall
towers and "dreaming spires."

Many of the 36 colleges that
make up **Oxford University**
were founded between the
13th and 16th centuries and
cluster around the city center.
The colleges were designed
along the lines of monastic
buildings but were surrounded
by beautiful gardens.

Christ Church, the largest
of the Oxford colleges, dates
from 1525 when Cardinal
Wolsey founded it as an
ecclesiastical college. It has
produced 16 British prime
ministers in the last 200 years.
Other colleges worth visiting
are **All Souls**, **Magdalen**,
Merton, **Lincoln**, and
Corpus Christi.

The university's library,
the **Bodleian**, was
founded in 1320. One
of its most famous
rooms is the
Divinity School
(1488), which has
a beautiful Gothic
vaulted ceiling.
The Baroque
rotunda named the
Radcliffe Camera
(1748) is a
reading room.

Oxford is more
than just a uni-
versity town and
there is a wealth of interesting
sights aside from the colleges.

One of the best British
museums outside London, the
Ashmolean Museum was
opened in 1683. Its exceptional
art collection includes works
by Bellini, Raphael, Turner,
Rembrandt, Michelangelo,
Picasso, and a large group
of Pre-Raphaelites. There are
also fine Greek and Roman

Radcliffe Camera,
Bodleian Library, Oxford

carvings, a collection of
stringed musical instruments,
and the Alfred Jewel which is
more than 1,000 years old.

Carfax Tower is all that
remains of the 14th-century
Church of St. Martin, demolished in 1896. Watch the
clock strike the quarter hours,
and climb to the top for a
panoramic view of the city.

The **Martyrs' Memorial**
commemorates the three
Protestants burned at the
stake on Broad Street –
Bishops Latimer and Ridley
in 1555, and Archbishop
Cranmer in 1556 –
during the reign of
Catholic Queen
Mary.

**St. Mary the
Virgin Church** is
the official church
of the university,
and is said to be
the most visited
parish church
in England.

Two of Oxford's
most interesting
museums adjoin
each other. The
**University Museum of
Natural History** contains
relics of dinosaurs as well as
a stuffed dodo. The **Pitt Rivers
Museum** has one of the
world's most extensive ethnographic collections – including
masks and tribal totems from
Africa and the Far East – and
archaeological displays.

Completed in 1669, the
Sheldonian Theatre was the
first building designed by
Christopher Wren, the famous
architect, and was built as a
place to hold university degree
ceremonies. The beautiful
ceiling depicts the triumph of
religion, art, and science over
envy, hatred, and malice.

🏛 **Ashmolean Museum**
Beaumont St. 📞 01865-278 000. 🕐
Tue–Sat, Sun pm & public hols. 🔴 Jan
1, Good Fri, Dec 25–28. 📷 Sat. 🚻

🏛 **University Museum and
Pitt Rivers Museum**
Parks Rd. 📞 01865-272 950/270 927.
🕐 University: daily; Pitt Rivers: pm daily.
🔴 Easter, Dec 24–26. 🚻 limited.

Blenheim Palace ⑮

See pp74–5.

The Great Quadrangle of All Souls College, Oxford University

Stratford-upon-Avon ⑯

Warwickshire. 🏘 22,000. 🚆 🚌 🛈
Bridge Foot (01789-293 127). 🅿 Fri.
🎭 Shakespeare's Birthday (Apr 23).

SITUATED ON THE west bank of the River Avon, Stratford-upon-Avon attracts more tourists than anywhere else in Britain outside London. Eager hordes flock to see buildings connected with William Shakespeare, born here in 1564. The town is also the provincial home of the Royal Shakespeare Company, whose performances are staged at the **Royal Shakespeare Theatre**.

The High Street turns into Chapel Street, the site of **New Place**. Shakespeare died here in 1616, and it is now a herb and knot garden. The playwright is buried at **Holy Trinity Church**. Bought for the nation in 1847, when it was a public house, **Shakespeare's Birthplace** was restored to Elizabethan style.

Shakespeare monument at Holy Trinity Church, Stratford

Another native of Stratford, John Harvard, emigrated to America and in 1638 left his estate to a new college, later renamed Harvard University. **Harvard House** displays family mementos.

No tour of Stratford would be complete without a visit to **Anne Hathaway's Cottage**. Before her marriage to Shakespeare Anne lived 1 mile (1.5 km) from the town. Despite fire damage, the cottage is still impressive, with some original 16th-century furniture.

Cambridge ⑰

Cambridgeshire. 🏘 120,000. 🚆 🚌
🛈 Wheeler St (01223-322 640).
🅿 daily. 🎭 Folk Festival (July).

CAMBRIDGE HAS BEEN an important town since Roman times, being located at the first navigable point on the River Cam. When, in 1209, a group of religious scholars broke away from Oxford University after academic and religious disputes, they came here. Student life dominates the city, but it is also a thriving market center serving a rich agricultural region.

Cambridge University has 31 colleges, the oldest being **Peterhouse** (1284) and the newest **Robinson** (1979). Many of the older colleges have peaceful gardens backing onto the River Cam, which are known as the "Backs." An enjoyable way to view these is to rent a punt (a long narrow boat propelled by using a pole) from one of the boat-yards along the river – with a "chauffeur" if required. The layout of the older colleges, as at Oxford, derives from their early connections with religious institutions, although few escaped heavy-handed alterations in the Victorian era.

Henry VI founded **King's College** in 1441. Work on the chapel – one of the most important examples of late medieval English architecture – began five years later, and took 90 years to complete. Henry himself decided that the building should dominate the city and gave specific instructions about its dimensions. He also stipulated that a choir of six lay clerks and 16 boy choristers – educated at the College school – should sing daily at services.

The awe-inspiring choir of King's College Chapel, Cambridge

This still happens in term time but today the choir also gives concerts all over the world.

St. John's College, whose alumni include the Romantic poet William Wordsworth, spans the Cam and boasts one of the town's most beautiful bridges. Known as the Bridge of Sighs, it is based on its Venetian namesake.

One of Britain's oldest public museums, the **Fitzwilliam Museum** has works of exceptional quality and rarity, especially antiquities, ceramics, paintings, and manuscripts. These include paintings by Titian and the 17th-century Dutch masters, an impressive collection of works by the French Impressionists, and most of the important British artists of the past 300 years.

🏛 **Fitzwilliam Museum**
Trumpington St. 📞 01223-332 900.
⭕ Tue–Sun & public hols. ⬤ until after Easter 2004 for renovation; Jan 1, Good Fri, May Day, Dec 24–31. 🎟 donation. 📷 Sun pm. ♿ limited.

Bridge of Sighs, St. John's College, Cambridge University

Blenheim Palace ⑮

A FTER JOHN CHURCHILL, the 1st Duke of Marlborough, defeated the French at the Battle of Blenheim in 1704, Queen Anne gave him the manor of Woodstock and had this palatial house built for him in gratitude. Designed by Nicholas Hawksmoor and Sir John Vanbrugh, it is one of the country's most outstanding examples of English Baroque. The magnificent palace grounds, at the center of which is a huge lake, owe their present appearance to the great 18th-century landscape designer, Lancelot (Capability) Brown. Blenheim Palace was the birthplace, in 1874, of the wartime British prime minister, Winston Churchill. Today the palace is the home of the 11th Duke of Marlborough, John George.

★ Long Library
This 55-m (183-ft) long room was designed by Vanbrugh as a picture gallery. The stucco work on the ceiling is by Isaac Mansfield (1725).

The Grand Bridge
was built in 1708. It has a 31-m (101-ft) main span and contains rooms within its structure.

The Chapel holds a marble monument to the 1st Duke of Marlborough, sculpted in 1733.

★ Water Terrace Gardens
These splendid gardens were laid out in the 1920s by French architect Achille Duchêne in 17th-century style, with detailed patterned beds and fountains.

STAR SIGHTS

★ Long Library

★ Saloon

★ Water Terrace Gardens

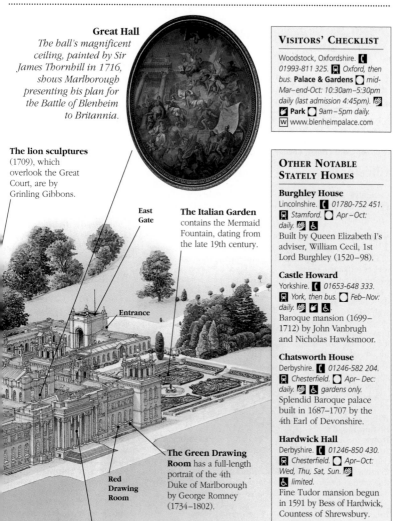

Great Hall
The hall's magnificent ceiling, painted by Sir James Thornhill in 1716, shows Marlborough presenting his plan for the Battle of Blenheim to Britannia.

The lion sculptures
(1709), which overlook the Great Court, are by Grinling Gibbons.

East Gate

The Italian Garden
contains the Mermaid Fountain, dating from the late 19th century.

Entrance

The Green Drawing Room has a full-length portrait of the 4th Duke of Marlborough by George Romney (1734–1802).

Red Drawing Room

OTHER NOTABLE STATELY HOMES

Burghley House
Lincolnshire. 📞 01780-752 451. 🚉 Stamford. ⭕ Apr–Oct: daily. 💰 ♿
Built by Queen Elizabeth I's adviser, William Cecil, 1st Lord Burghley (1520–98).

Castle Howard
Yorkshire. 📞 01653-648 333. 🚉 York, then bus. ⭕ Feb–Nov: daily. 💰 📷 ♿
Baroque mansion (1699–1712) by John Vanbrugh and Nicholas Hawksmoor.

Chatsworth House
Derbyshire. 📞 01246-582 204. 🚉 Chesterfield. ⭕ Apr–Dec: daily. 💰 ♿ gardens only.
Splendid Baroque palace built in 1687–1707 by the 4th Earl of Devonshire.

Hardwick Hall
Derbyshire. 📞 01246-850 430. 🚉 Chesterfield. ⭕ Apr–Oct: Wed, Thu, Sat, Sun. 💰 ♿ limited.
Fine Tudor mansion begun in 1591 by Bess of Hardwick, Countess of Shrewsbury.

★ Saloon
The murals and painted ceiling of the state dining room are by French artist Louis Laguerre (1663–1721). The room is used once a year on Christmas Day.

EIGHTEENTH-CENTURY GARDENS

Styles of gardening in Britain expanded alongside architecture and other fashions. The 18th century brought a taste for large-scale "natural" landscapes, characterized by woods, lakes, and a seeming lack of boundaries. The pioneer of this new style was the famous landscape designer Lancelot (Capability) Brown (1715–83). His nickname came from his habit of telling clients that their land had "great capabilities." In 1764 he relandscaped the grounds of Blenheim Palace, creating the magnificent, huge lake. Today his reputation is controversial, because in creating his idyllic landscapes he swept away many of the beautiful formal gardens previously in vogue.

Capability Brown (1715–83)

Detail of a carving on the façade of Bishop Lloyd's House, Chester

Chester ⑱

Cheshire. 🏛 125,000. 🚆 🚌
ℹ️ Town Hall, Northgate St (01244-402 111). 🛒 Mon–Sat.

FIRST SETTLED BY the Romans in AD 79, the main streets of Chester are now lined with timber buildings, many dating from the 13th and 14th centuries. These are the **Chester Rows**, which, with their two tiers of stores and continuous upper gallery, anticipate today's multistory shops by several centuries. Their oriel windows and decorative timber-work are mostly 19th century. The façade of the 16th-century **Bishop Lloyd's House** in Watergate Street is the most richly carved in Chester. The Rows are at their most attractive where Eastgate Street meets Bridge Street.

A town crier calls the hour and announces news from the Cross – a reconstruction of a 15th-century stone crucifix. South of here, the **Grosvenor Museum** explains Chester's history. To the north is the **cathedral**. The choir stalls have splendid misericords and delicate spirelets on the canopies. The cathedral is surrounded on two sides by high city walls, originally Roman but rebuilt at intervals. Also worth seeing is the **Roman amphitheater** just outside town, built in AD 100.

🏛 **Grosvenor Museum**
Grosvenor St. 📞 01244-402 008.
⏰ Mon–Sat, Sun pm. ● Jan 1, Good Fri, Dec 24–26. ♿ limited.

Liverpool ⑲

Liverpool. 🏛 450,000. ✈ 11 km
(7 miles) SE. 🚆 🚌 ℹ️ Queens
Sq (09066-806 886). 🛒 Sun.

DURING THE 17th and 18th centuries, Liverpool's westerly seaboard gave it a leading role in the Caribbean slave trade. After the city's first ocean steamer set sail from here in 1840, would-be emigrants to the New World poured into the city, including a large number of Irish refugees from the potato famine.

Liverpool's waterfront is overlooked by the well-known **Royal Liver Building**. The 19th-century warehouses around Albert Dock have been re-developed as museums, galleries, restaurants, and shops. Among these, the **Maritime Museum** and the **Tate Gallery Liverpool**, which houses one of the best collections of contemporary art in England outside of London, are well worth visiting. Liverpool is famous as the home town of the phenom-enally successful Beatles. The **Beatles Story** is a walk-through exhibition which charts their meteoric rise to fame in the 1960s.

Clock tower of the Royal Liver Building, Liverpool

One of the most prestigious art galleries in the city is **The Walker**. Paintings range from early Italian and Flemish works to 20th-century art.

Liverpool's Gothic-style **Anglican Cathedral**, com-pleted in 1978 by Sir Giles Gilbert Scott, is the world's largest. The Roman Catholic **Metropolitan Cathedral of Christ the King** (1962–7) is a striking circular building sur-mounted by a stylized crown of thorns 88 m (290 ft) high.

🏛 **Tate Gallery Liverpool**
Albert Dock. 📞 0151-709 3223.
⏰ Tue–Sun. ● Dec 24–26 & 31, Jan 1, Good Friday. ♿
🏛 **The Walker**
William Brown St. 📞 0151-478 4199. ⏰ Mon–Sat, Sun pm. ● Jan 1, Dec 23–26. 📷 🎫 by appt. ♿

Manchester ⑳

Manchester. 🏛 2.5 million. ✈ 18 km
(11 miles) S. 🚆 🚌 ℹ️ Lloyd St
(0161-234 3157). 🛒 daily.

MANCHESTER is famous as a pioneer of the industrial age, with its cotton spinning machines and early railways.

Among the city's many fine 19th-century buildings are the Neo-Gothic **cathedral**, the **Royal Exchange**, now a theater and restaurant, and the **Free Trade Hall**, once the home of Manchester's famous Hallé Orchestra. The **Manchester Ship Canal**, which opened in 1894, is a magnificent feat of engineering.

The **Museum of Science and Industry in Manchester** captures the city's spirit of industrial might with a display of working steam engines and

Modern city blocks on the banks of the Manchester Ship Canal

Lush, green fields below the Skiddaw fells in the Lake District

an exhibition on the Liverpool and Manchester Railway. Another museum of note is the **Whitworth Art Gallery**, with its splendid collection of contemporary art, textiles, and prints. The Turner watercolors are a highlight. Housed in a 19th-century porticoed building, the **City Art Galleries** contain an excellent selection of British art, as well as early Italian, Flemish, and French paintings.

🏛 **Whitworth Art Gallery**
University of Manchester, Oxford Rd. 【 0161-275 7450. ◯ Mon–Sat & Sun pm. ◯ Dec 24–Jan 2, Good Fri. ♿

The Lakeland poet William Wordsworth

York ㉑

See pp78–9.

Lake District ㉒

Cumbria. 🚇 Kendal; Windermere. 🚌 Kendal; Keswick; Windermere. 🛈 Town Hall, Highgate, Kendal (01539-725 758); Moot Hall, Market Sq, Keswick (01768-772 645).

THE LAKE DISTRICT boasts some of the country's most spectacular scenery, with high peaks, lonely fells, and beautiful lakes. The area constitutes Britain's largest national park and offers a range of outdoor activities, from hill walking to boating.

Kendal is the southern gateway to the Lake District. Of interest here is the Museum of Lakeland Life and Industry, housed in the stable block of the 18th-century Abbot Hall. The nearest lake to Kendal is Windermere, over 16 km (10 miles) long. A year-round car ferry connects the lake's east and west shores, and summer steamers link the main towns on the north-south axis.

Among these, one of the most popular is **Bowness**, where the Windermere Steamboat Museum has a collection of superbly restored watercraft.

Ambleside, another attractive lakeside town, is a good base for walkers and climbers. Nearby is Hill Top, the 17th-century farmhouse where the author Beatrix Potter wrote many of her famous children's stories.

The Lake District's most famous son, the Romantic poet William Wordsworth (1770–1850), lived for a while at **Grasmere**, on the shores of the lake of the same name, north of Ambleside. His home, Dove Cottage, contains a museum dedicated to his life.

To the west of Windermere lie Coniston Water and picturesque **Duddon Valley**, popular walking country.

In the northern part of the Lake District **Keswick**, with its lake, Derwent Water, has been a busy vacation destination since Victorian days. The Keswick Museum and Art Gallery holds original manuscripts of Lakeland writers such as Robert Southey (1774–1843) and Wordsworth. To the east of the town lies the ancient stone circle of Castlerigg. North of Keswick is Skiddaw, England's fourth highest peak and a straightforward climb for anyone reasonably fit.

Durham ㉓

County Durham. 🚇 🚌 🛈 Millenium Place (0191-384 3720). 🅟 Sat.

DURHAM WAS BUILT on a rocky peninsula in 995. The site was chosen as the last resting place for the remains of St. Cuthbert. The relics of the Venerable Bede were brought here 27 years later, adding to the town's attraction to pilgrims.

Durham's **cathedral**, built between 1093 and 1274, is a striking Norman structure. The vast dimensions of the 900-year-old columns, piers, and vaults, and the lozenge, chevron, and dogtooth patterns carved into them, are its main innovative features. The exotic Galilee Chapel, begun in 1170, was inspired by the mosque at Córdoba, Spain (see pp326–7).

The Norman **castle**, begun in 1072, served as an Episcopal Palace until 1832, when Bishop William van Mildert gave it away to found Britain's third university here. In the castle grounds, Tunstal's Chapel was built around 1542 and has some particularly fine woodwork, including a unicorn misericord. The castle keep, sited on a mound, is now part of the university.

⛪ **Durham Castle**
【 0191-334 3800. ◯ univ hols: daily; term: Mon, Wed, Sat (pm), Sun. 📷

Moorish-style arches in the 12th-century Galilee Chapel, Durham Cathedral

Street-by-Street: York ㉑

THE CITY OF YORK has retained so much of its
medieval structure that walking into its center is
like entering a living museum. Many of the ancient
timbered houses, which overhang narrow, winding
streets such as the Shambles, are protected by a
conservation order. Cars are banned from the
center, so there are always student bikes
bouncing over cobbled streets. The chief glory
of York is its cathedral, the Minster. The city
also has 18 medieval churches, 5 km
(3 miles) of medieval city walls, and many
elegant Jacobean and Georgian buildings.

York's medieval city walls
still encircle the old city. It is
possible to walk round them,
although there are large gaps.
The gates are known as "bars."

At Monk Bar the
gatehouse retains
a working portcullis.

★ York Minster
*The 15th-century choir
screen is lined with
statues of the kings
of England from
William I to Henry VI.*

Thirsk

St. Mary's Abbey

**The Yorkshire
Museum** contains
a fine collection of
fossils, discovered
at Whitby in the
19th century.

Lendal Bridge

Train station,
bus station,
National Rail-
way Museum,
and Leeds

**Ye Old Starre
Inne** is one of
the oldest
pubs in York.

In Coffee Yard,
look out for the
carved figure of
a red devil, relic
of a medieval
print shop.

Guildhall
*This two-headed
medieval roof boss
is on the 15th-
century Guildhall,
situated beside the
River Ouse and
restored after bomb
damage during
World War II.*

St. Olave's Church
*The 11th-century church, next to the gate-
house of St. Mary's Abbey, was founded by
the Earl of Northumbria in memory of
St. Olaf, King of Norway. To the left is the
Chapel of St. Mary on the Walls.*

★ Jorvik
The many artifacts on show here illustrate the time when York was a strategic Viking town.

Whip-Ma-Whop-Ma-Gate
is York's tiniest street. The name means "neither one thing nor the other street."

Merchant Adventurers' Hall

★ York Castle Museum
Converted from two 18th-century prisons, the museum features reconstructions of old York and the cell of the notorious highwayman Dick Turpin (1706–39).

Coppergate
is where the Town Crier shouts the daily news at 11am.

St. Mary's Church

Clifford's Tower (c.1250)

→ **Hull**

0 meters 100
0 yards 100

KEY

– – – Suggested route

STAR SIGHTS

★ **York Minster**

★ **Jorvik**

★ **York Castle Museum**

Exploring York

To the Romans the city of York was Eboracum, to the Saxons it was Eoforwic, and to the Vikings Jorvik. Danish street names are a reminder that from 867 York was a major Viking settlement. **Jorvik**, the Viking museum, is built underground on an archaeological site excavated at Coppergate. The very latest technology brings the sights and smells of 10th-century York dramatically to life.

Between 1100 and 1500 York was England's second city. **York Minster**, the largest Gothic church in northern Europe, was begun in 1220. It has a remarkable collection of medieval stained glass. The vast Great East Window (1405–8) depicts the Creation. In 1984 a disastrous fire in the south transept destroyed the roof and shattered its magnificent rose window. This has since been restored.

Much of York's wealth in the late Middle Ages came from the cloth trade. The **Merchant Adventurers' Hall**, the headquarters of a powerful guild of traders, is a beautifully preserved timber-framed building that dates from the mid-14th century.

In the 19th century York's position on the route to Scotland made it a major rail center. Train enthusiasts should head for the **National Railway Museum**, the largest of its kind in the world, where the rolling stock on show includes Queen Victoria's royal carriage.

🏛 **National Railway Museum**
Leeman Rd. 📞 *01904-621261.*
☐ *daily.* ● *Dec 24–26.* ♿

The square central tower of York Minster rising above the city

Scotland

S COTLAND'S LANDSCAPE IS BREATHTAKING, with sparkling
lochs, awesome mountains, and windswept isles.
The ruggedness of its climate and natural environment
has helped to forge a tough, self-reliant nation, whose
history has been characterized by resistance to English
domination. Castles, many in ruins, are found all over
the country – a legacy of its turbulent past. Culturally,
Edinburgh has always been the country's chief attraction,
but the rival city of Glasgow, despite the collapse of its
traditional heavy industries, has much to offer too.

The imposing City Chambers in George Square, Glasgow

Edinburgh ㉔

See pp82–6.

Glasgow ㉕

🏛 *735,000.* ✈ 🚆 🚌 🛈 *11 George Square (0141-204 4400).* 🎫 *Sat, Sun.* 🎷 *Jazz Festival (Jul).*

G LASGOW'S ERA OF great
prosperity was the
industrial 19th century. Coal
seams in Lanarkshire fueled
the city's cotton mills and
ironworks, belying its Celtic
name, *Glas cu*, meaning "dear
green place." Relics of this
manufacturing past contrast

starkly with the glossy image
of modern Glasgow, renowned
for its galleries and museums.
The deprived East End stands
side by side with the restored
18th-century Merchant City
and Victorian George Square.

Glasgow's **cathedral** was
one of the few to escape
destruction during the Scottish
Reformation and is a rare
example of an almost complete
13th-century church. The
crypt contains the tomb of
St. Mungo. In the cathedral
precinct, the **St. Mungo
Museum of Religious Life
and Art** is the first
of its kind in the
world, illustrating
religious themes
with a superb
range of artifacts.

It is in the more
affluent West End,
to where merchants
retreated from
industrial Clydeside,
that Glasgow's most
important galleries and
museums can be found. The
**Kelvingrove Art Gallery
and Museum** is home to a
splendid collection of art,
with works by Botticelli,
Giorgione, Rembrandt, Degas,
Millet, and Monet, while the
Scottish Gallery contains the
famous *Massacre of Glencoe*
by James Hamilton (1853–94).

Stained glass by Charles Rennie Mackintosh

From June 2003 for two years
most of the collection will be
moved to the McLennan
Galleries on Sauchiehall Street
while the gallery is renovated.

The **Hunterian Art Gallery**
houses Scotland's largest print
collection and paintings by
major European artists from the
16th century to the present. A
display of works by Glasgow's
most celebrated designer,
Charles Rennie Mackintosh
(1868–1928), is supplemented
by a reconstruction of No. 6
Florentine Terrace, where he
lived from 1906 to 1914.

South of the river, the Pollok
Country Park is the site of the
Burrell Collection, star of
Glasgow's renaissance. Highlights include magnificent
examples of 15th-century
stained glass and tapestries, a
bronze bull's head (7th century
BC) from Turkey, Matthijs
Maris' *The Sisters* (1875), and
a self-portrait by Rembrandt
(1632). On the same site,
Pollok House is an attractive
Georgian building. It holds
one of Britain's best collections
of 16th- to 19th-
century Spanish
paintings.

Other sights
worth visiting are
the **Tenement
House**, a modest
apartment in
a tenement block
preserved from
Edwardian times,
and **Provand's
Lordship** (1471), the city's
oldest surviving house. The
House for an Art Lover is a
showcase for the work of
Charles Rennie Mackintosh.
For a social history of the city
from the 12th to the 20th
century, visit the **People's
Palace**, a cultural museum
located in the city's East End.

🏛 **Kelvingrove Art
Gallery and Museum**
Argyle St, Kelvingrove. 🕿 *0141-287 2699.* ⭘ *daily.* ⬤ *from May 2003 for 2 years.* 🎫 🔲

🏛 **Hunterian Art Gallery**
82 Hillhead St. 🕿 *0141-330 5431.* ⭘ *Mon–Sat.* ⬤ *Dec 24–Jan 5 & public hols.* 🔲 *restricted.*

🏛 **Burrell Collection**
Pollok Country Park. 🕿 *0141-287 2550.* ⭘ *daily.* ⬤ *Jan 1–2, Dec 24–25.* 🎫 🔲

The Burrell Collection in Pollok Country Park on Glasgow's outskirts

The 15th-century Stirling Castle, atop its rocky crag

Stirling 26

🏠 28,000. 🚉 🚌 🛈 41 Dunbarton Rd (01786-475 019).

LOCATED BETWEEN the Ochil Hills and the Campsie Fells, Stirling grew up around its castle, historically one of Scotland's most important fortresses. **Stirling Castle** is one of the finest examples of Renaissance architecture in the country. Dating from the 15th century, it was last defended, against the Jacobites, in 1746, and stands within sight of no fewer than seven battlefields. One of these – Bannockburn – was where Robert the Bruce defeated the English in 1314.

Stirling's Old Town is still protected by the original 16th-century walls, built to keep out Henry VIII. Two buildings stand out among a number of historic monuments in the town: the medieval **Church of the Holy Rude** and **Mar's Wark**, with its ornate façade.

♣ Stirling Castle
Castle Wynd. 📞 01786-450 000. 🕐 daily. ● Jan 1–2, Dec 25–26. 📷 🎥 🚻 limited.

St. Andrews 27

Fife. 🏠 14,000. 🚉 Leuchars. 🚌 🛈 70 Market St (01334-472 021).

SCOTLAND'S OLDEST university town and one-time ecclesiastical capital, St. Andrews is now a shrine for golfers from all over the world. Its main streets and cobbled alleys, lined with grand university buildings and medieval churches, converge on the ruined 12th-century **cathedral**. Once the largest in Scotland, it was later pillaged for stones to build the town. **St. Andrew's Castle** was built for the bishops of the town in 1200.

The Royal and Ancient Golf Club, founded in 1754, has a magnificent links course and is the ruling arbiter of the game. The city has other golf courses, open to the public for a modest fee, and is home to the **British Golf Museum**.

🏛 British Golf Museum
Bruce Embankment. 📞 01334-460 046. 🕐 Easter–mid-Oct: daily; mid-Oct–Easter: Thu–Mon. 📷 🚻

An old railway poster illustrating the lure of St. Andrews for golfing enthusiasts

Aberdeen 28

🏠 220,000. ✈ 13 km (8 miles) NW. 🚉 🚌 🛈 Union St (01224-288 828). 🛒 Thu, Fri, Sat.

EUROPE'S offshore oil capital, Aberdeen is also one of Britain's most important fishing ports, and hosts Scotland's largest fish market.

Among its fine buildings is the 16th-century home of a former provost (mayor) of the city. Period rooms inside **Provost Skene's House** span 200 years of design and include the 17th-century Great Hall, a Regency Room, and a Georgian Dining Room. The Painted Gallery holds one of Scotland's most important cycles of religious art, dating from the 17th century.

Founded in 1495, **King's College** was the city's first university. The chapel has stained-glass windows by Douglas Strachan.

St. Andrew's Cathedral is the Mother Church of the Episcopal Communion in the United States. Coats of arms on the ceiling depict the American states.

Housed in a historic building overlooking the harbor, **Aberdeen Maritime Museum** traces the city's long seafaring tradition.

🕎 Provost Skene's House
Guestrow. 📞 01224-641 806. 🕐 Mon–Sat. ● Dec 25–31, Jan 1–2.

GOLF

Scotland's national game was pioneered on the sandy links around St. Andrews. The earliest record dates from 1457, when golf was banned by James II on the grounds that it was interfering with his subjects' archery practice. Mary, Queen of Scots enjoyed the game and was berated in 1568 for playing straight after the murder of her husband Darnley. Scotland has several other world-class golf courses, including Royal Troon, Gleneagles, and Carnoustie.

Victorian engraving of Mary, Queen of Scots at St. Andrews

Edinburgh ❷

IT WAS NOT UNTIL the reign of James IV (1488–1513) that Edinburgh gained the status of Scotland's capital. Overcrowding made the Old Town a difficult place to live, and led to the construction of a Georgian New Town in the late 1700s. Today, Edinburgh is second only to London as a financial center in the British Isles, and houses the new Scottish parliament building, situated next to the old Palace of Holyroodhouse. Edinburgh hosts a celebrated annual International Festival every August. One of the world's premier arts jamborees, it features drama, dance, opera, music, and ballet. The more eclectic "Fringe" developed in parallel with the official event, but has now exceeded it in terms of size. It is estimated that the population of the city doubles from 400,000 to 800,000 every August.

View of Princes Street from the top of Calton Hill

GETTING AROUND

Central Edinburgh is compact, so walking or cycling is an excellent way to explore the city. Other options include a comprehensive bus service and a multitude of black taxis. Avoid exploring the center by car, because the streets tend to be congested with traffic, and parking may be difficult. Car use has been actively discouraged in recent years.

SEE ALSO

- **Where to Stay** p101
- **Where to Eat** p107

SIGHTS AT A GLANCE

Calton Hill ⑧
Edinburgh Castle ①
Greyfriars Kirk ⑤
Palace of Holyroodhouse ⑨
National Gallery of Scotland ④
New Town ②
Royal Mile ③
Royal Museum and
    Museum of Scotland ⑥
Scottish National Portrait
    Gallery ⑦

An audience of thousands at the Military Tattoo in Edinburgh
Castle, held during August each year

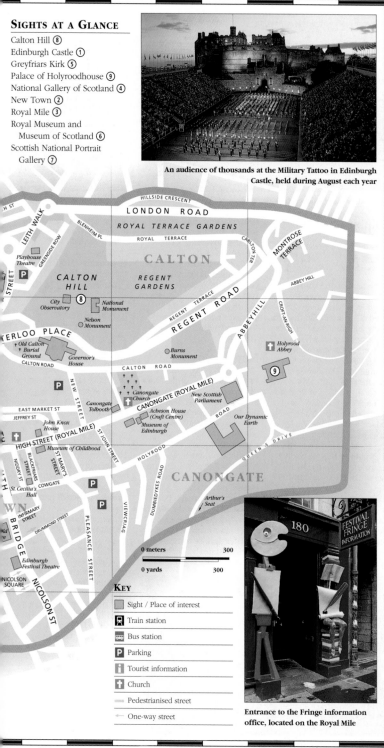

0 meters 300

0 yards 300

KEY

◼ Sight / Place of interest

🚉 Train station

🚌 Bus station

Ⓟ Parking

ℹ Tourist information

✝ Church

— Pedestrianised street

← One-way street

Entrance to the Fringe information
office, located on the Royal Mile

The battlements of Edinburgh Castle rising above Princes Street Gardens

Edinburgh Castle ①

Castle Hill. 📞 *0131-225 9846.* ⬤ *daily.* ⬤ *Dec 25–26.* 🏷 📷 ♿ Ⓦ www.historic-scotland.gov.uk

STANDING ON the basalt core of an extinct volcano, the castle is an assemblage of buildings dating from the 12th to the 20th centuries, reflecting its changing role as fortress, palace, military garrison, and state prison. The castle was a favorite royal residence until the Union of 1603, after which monarchs resided in England.

The Scottish regalia are displayed in the 15th-century **Palace** where Mary, Queen of Scots gave birth to James VI. The castle also holds the Stone of Destiny, a relic of ancient Scottish kings seized by the English, and returned in 1996. The castle's oldest existing building is the 12th-century **St. Margaret's Chapel**. A stained-glass window depicts the queen of Malcolm III, after whom it is named.

Other important buildings include the 15th-century **Great Hall**, meeting place of the Scottish parliament until 1639, and the **Governor's House** (1742), which has Flemish-style crow-stepped gables. A 15th-century Burgundian siege gun, known as Mons Meg, is kept in the castle vaults, where French graffiti recall the prisoners held here during the 18th- and 19th-century wars.

New Town ②

THE FIRST PHASE of the "New Town," to the north of Princes Street, was built in the 18th century to relieve the congested and unsanitary conditions of the old town. **Charlotte Square**, with its lavish town houses, was the climax of this phase. On the north side, the **Georgian House**, owned by the National Trust of Scotland, has been furnished to show the lifestyle of its 18th-century residents.

The most magnificent of the later developments is the **Moray Estate**, by James Gillespie Graham, where a linked series of large houses forms a crescent, an oval, and a twelve-sided circus.

🏛 **Georgian House**
7 Charlotte Sq. 📞 *0131-226 3318.* ⬤ *Mar–Dec: daily.* 🏷 ♿ *limited.*

Royal Mile ③

COMPOSED OF four ancient streets which formed the main thoroughfare of medieval Edinburgh, the Royal Mile linked the castle to Holyrood Palace. A walk starting from the castle takes you past many of the city's oldest buildings and a number of interesting museums.

The lower floors of **Outlook Tower** date from the early 17th century and were once the home of the Laird of Cockpen. Its 19th-century **Camera Obscura** remains a popular attraction. A little further on, **Gladstone's Land** is a 17th-century merchant's house which has been carefully restored and richly furnished. Another fine mansion, built in 1622, has been converted into a **Writers' Museum**, housing memorabilia of Robert Burns, Sir Walter Scott, and Robert Louis Stevenson.

St. Giles Cathedral, properly known as the High Kirk of Edinburgh, was the base from which Protestant minister John Knox led the Scottish Reformation. His house, also on the Royal Mile, is open to the public. The cathedral's Thistle Chapel has impressive rib-vaulting and carved heraldic canopies. It honors the knights of the Most Ancient and Most

Charlotte Square in the New Town

Noble Order of the Thistle. Just past St. Giles, the Italianate **Parliament House**, built in the 1630s, has housed the Scottish Courts since the 1707 Act of Union with England and Wales.

Farther east, opposite **John Knox's House** (1450), there is a good **Museum of Childhood**, while **Canongate Tolbooth** (1591) tells the social history of Edinburgh – from plagues to punk rock.

Thistle Chapel, St. Giles Cathedral, Royal Mile

Gladstone's Land

477B Lawnmarket. (0131-226 5856. 🟊 Apr–Oct: Mon–Sat, Sun pm. 🖾

National Gallery of Scotland ④

The Mound. (0131-556 8921. 🟊 daily. 🖾 by appt. 🖾 W www.natgalscot.ac.uk

ONE OF SCOTLAND'S finest art galleries, the National Gallery of Scotland has an impressive collection of British and European paintings. Designed by William Henry Playfair, it was opened in 1859. Many of the works of art are still exhibited as they were in the 19th century. Serried ranks of paintings hang on deep red walls behind a profusion of statues and period furniture.

Some of the highlights among the Scottish works are the society portraits by Allan Ramsay and Henry Raeburn, including the latter's *Reverend Robert Walker Skating on Duddingston Loch* (c.1800), an image reproduced annually on thousands of Christmas cards.

German works include Gerard David's almost comic-strip treatment of the *Three Legends of St. Nicholas*, dating from the early 16th century. Italian paintings include a fine *Madonna* by Raphael, as well as works by Titian and Tintoretto. From Spain there is a delightful genre painting of *An Old Woman Cooking Eggs* by Velázquez (c.1620).

An entire room is devoted to *The Seven Sacraments* by Nicholas Poussin, dating from around 1640. Dutch and Flemish painters represented include Rembrandt, Van Dyck, and Rubens, while among the British offerings are important works by Reynolds and Gainsborough.

Greyfriars Kirk ⑤

Greyfriars Place. (0131-226 5429. 🟊 Apr–Oct: Mon–Sat; Nov–Mar: Thu pm. 🖾 🖾

GREYFRIARS KIRK played a key role in Scotland's history. In 1638 the National Covenant was signed here, marking the Protestant stand against Charles I's imposition of an episcopal church. Throughout the wars of the 17th century, the kirkyard was used as a mass grave for executed Covenanters. The Martyrs' Monument is a sobering reminder of the many Scots who lost their lives. Greyfriars is also known for its association with a faithful dog, Bobby, who lived beside his master's grave from 1858 to 1872. Greyfriars Bobby's statue stands outside Greyfriars Kirk.

Greyfriars Bobby

Royal Museum and Museum of Scotland ⑥

Chambers St. (0131-225 7534. 🟊 Mon–Sat, Sun pm. 🖾 🖾 W www.nms.ac.uk

A GREAT VICTORIAN glass palace, completed in 1888, houses the **Royal Museum of Scotland**. It started life as an industrial museum, but acquired an eclectic array of exhibits, ranging from stuffed animals to ethnographic artifacts.

In 1993 work began on a site next door, to display Scotland's impressive array of antiquities. The resulting **Museum of Scotland**, opened in 1998, tells the story of the country, starting with its geology and natural history, through to later industrial developments. Among its many stunning exhibits is St. Fillan's Crozier, said to have been carried at the head of the Scottish army at Bannockburn in 1314.

An Old Woman Cooking Eggs by Velázquez, National Gallery of Scotland

The view from Duncan's Monument at the top of Calton Hill, Edinburgh

Scottish National Portrait Gallery ⑦

1 Queen St. ☏ 0131-556 8921.
◯ daily. ✔ by appt. ♿
🖳 www.natgalscot.ac.uk

AN INFORMATIVE exhibition on the royal house of Stuart is just one of the attractions at the Scottish National Portrait Gallery. The displays detail the history of 12 generations of Stuarts, from the time of Robert the Bruce to Queen Anne. Memorabilia include Mary, Queen of Scots' jewelry and a silver traveling canteen left by Bonnie Prince Charlie at the Battle of Culloden. The upper gallery has portraits of famous Scots, including one of the country's best-loved poet Robert Burns (1759–96) by Alexander Nasmyth. Others portrayed include Flora MacDonald, who helped Bonnie Prince Charlie escape after his defeat by the English in 1745, philosopher David Hume (1711–76), novelist Sir Walter Scott (1771–1832), and Ramsay MacDonald, who became Britain's first Labour prime minister in 1924.

Calton Hill ⑧

City center east, via Waterloo Pl.

CALTON HILL, at the east end of Princes Street, is a large open space dotted with Neoclassical monuments. It has one of Edinburgh's more memorable if baffling landmarks – a half-finished "Parthenon". Conceived as the National Monument to the dead of the Napoleonic Wars, building began in 1822 but funds ran out and it was never finished. Nearby, the **Nelson Monument**, commemorates the British victory at Trafalgar, providing a fine vantage point over the city and its environs. The Classical theme continues with Duncan's Monument and the old **City Observatory**, designed by William Playfair in 1818 and based on Athens' Tower of the Winds. Tours and free lectures are arranged here by the Astronomical Society of Edinburgh.

Palace of Holyroodhouse ⑨

East end of the Royal Mile. ☏ 0131-556 1096. ◯ daily. ● check for seasonal closures. 🎟 ♿ limited.

QUEEN ELIZABETH II's official Scottish residence, the palace was built by James IV in the grounds of an abbey in 1498. It was later the home of James V and his wife, Mary of Guise, and was remodeled in the 1670s for Charles II. The Royal Apartments (including the Throne Room and Royal Dining Room) are used for investitures and for banquets whenever the Queen visits. A chamber in the so-called James V tower is believed to have been the scene of David Rizzio's murder in 1566. He was the Italian secretary of Mary, Queen of Scots. She witnessed the grisly act, which was authorized by her jealous husband, Lord Darnley. Bonnie Prince Charlie, last of the Stuart pretenders to the English throne, also held court at Holyrood Palace, in 1745.

The adjacent Holyrood Park, a former royal hunting ground, is home to three lochs, a large number of wildfowl, and the Salisbury Crags. Its high point is the hill known as Arthur's Seat, an extinct volcano and well-known Edinburgh landmark. The name is probably a corruption of Archer's Seat.

The grand 17th-century façade of Holyrood Palace

The Highlands

Stock images of scottishness – clans and tartans, whisky and porridge, bagpipes and heather – originate in the Highlands. Gaelic-speaking Celts arrived from Ireland before the 7th century, establishing small fishing and cattle-raising communities. Nowadays the region has oil and tourist industries. Inverness, the Highland capital, makes a good starting point for exploring Loch Ness and the Cairngorms. The Isle of Skye has some of Britain's most dramatic scenery.

Sea lochs on the Isle of Skye, dominated by the Cuillin peaks

Snow-covered peaks of the Cairngorms, viewed from Aviemore

Cairngorms ㉙

🚉 🚌 *Aviemore.* 🛈 *Grampian Rd, Aviemore (0845-225 5121).*

Rising to a height of 1,309 m (4,296 ft), the Cairngorm mountains form the highest landmass in Britain.
Cairn Gorm itself is the site of one of Britain's first ski centers. Transportation to the 28 ski runs is provided daily from **Aviemore**. The chairlift that climbs Cairn Gorm affords superb views over the Spey Valley. **Rothiemurchus Estate** has a visitor center offering guided walks.
The **Cairngorm Reindeer Center** organizes walks in the hills among Britain's only herd of reindeer, and ospreys can be observed at the **Loch Garten Nature Reserve**.
Drivers can see bison, bears, wolves, and wild boar in the **Kincraig Highland Wildlife Park**.

Inverness ㉚

🚶 *60,000.* 🚉 🚌 🛈 *Castle Wynd (0845-225 5121).* 🌐 *www.host.co.uk*

Inverness is the center of communication, commerce, and administration for the Highlands. Dominating the high ground above the town is **Inverness Castle**, a Victorian building of red sandstone. Below the castle, the **Inverness Museum and Art Gallery** provides a good introduction to the region's history. Its exhibits include a fine collection of Inverness silver. The **Scottish Kiltmaker Visitor Centre** offers an insight into the history, culture, and tradition of the kilt.
In summer **Jacobite Cruises** (call 01463-233 999 for information) runs regular boat trips along the Caledonian Canal and on the famous **Loch Ness**, southwest of Inverness. The Loch is 39 km (24 miles) long and up to 305 m (1,000 ft) deep. On the western shore, the ruins of the 16th-century **Urquhart Castle** can be seen. The **Official Loch Ness Exhibition Centre** provides information about the Loch and its mythical monster.

🏛 **Museum and Art Gallery**
1 Castle Wynd. 📞 *01463-237 114.* ⏰ *Mon–Sat.* ⬤ *Jan 1–2, Dec 25–26.* ♿

Isle of Skye ㉛

🚶 *10,000.* ⛴ *from Mallaig or Glenelg.* 🚌 🛈 *Bayfield House, Portree (0845-225 5121).*

Skye, the largest of the Inner Hebrides, can be reached by the bridge linking Kyle of Lochalsh and Kyleakin. The coast is shaped by a series of dramatic sea lochs, while the landscape, from Quiraing, a plateau of volcanic towers and spikes in the north, to the Cuillins, one of Britain's most spectacular mountain ranges, is majestic. Bonnie Prince Charlie (1720–88) escaped here from the mainland disguised as a maidservant following the defeat of his army at Culloden.
Skye's main settlement is **Portree**, with its colorful harbor. **Dunvegan Castle** on the island's northwest coast has been the seat of the Clan MacLeod chiefs for over seven centuries. South of here, the **Talisker distillery** produces one of the best Highland malts.

The ruins of Urquhart Castle on the western shore of Loch Ness

Practical Information

COLORFUL PAGEANTRY, ANCIENT HISTORY, and a varied countryside attract millions of tourists to Britain each year. Facilities for visitors have improved considerably in recent years, with major urban centers offering a good variety of restaurants and hotels. The affluent southern region is more expensive than the rest of Britain. Telephone and postal systems are efficient, and violent crime is uncommon.

WHEN TO VISIT

BRITAIN'S TEMPERATE maritime climate does not produce extremes of heat or cold, but weather patterns shift constantly, and the climate can differ widely in places only a short distance apart. The southeast is generally drier than elsewhere. Be sure to pack a mix of warm and light clothing and an umbrella. Walkers can be surprised by bad weather.

Britain's towns and cities are all-year destinations, but many attractions open only between Easter and October. Some hotels are crammed at Christmas and New Year. The main family holiday months, July and August, and public holidays, are always busy. Spring and fall offer a good compromise: fewer crowds and relatively fine weather.

TOURIST INFORMATION

THE **British Tourist Authority (BTA)** has offices in a number of major cities worldwide. In Britain, tourist information is available in many towns and public places, including airports, main train and bus stations, and at some sites of historical interest. These bureaux offer general tourist advice and will also reserve accommodations.

Both the regional and national tourist boards have comprehensive lists of local attractions and registered accommodations. The monthly magazine of the **BTA**, *In Britain*, available in tourist offices, contains articles about worthwhile places to visit and also includes an events diary. A charge may be made for more detailed maps and books.

For route planning, road atlases and local maps and guidebooks are available in most bookstores.

OPENING HOURS

MANY BUSINESSES and shops are closed on Sundays, though trading is now legal. Museums and galleries are generally open from 10am to 5 or 6pm, with many opening later in the day on Sundays. Those outside the capital are normally closed for one day or one afternoon a week. On public holidays, known as bank holidays in Britain, banks, offices, most shops, and some restaurants will be closed.

VISA REQUIREMENTS AND CUSTOMS

A VALID PASSPORT is needed to enter Britain. Visitors from the European Union (EU), the United States, Canada, New Zealand, and Australia do not require a visa to enter the country. Anyone who arrives in Britain from a member country of the EU can pass through a special channel at customs, but random checks are still made to detect any prohibited goods.

When entering from outside the EU go through the green customs channel if you have nothing to declare, and the red channel if you have goods which exceed allowances.

PERSONAL SECURITY

BRITAIN IS NOT a dangerous place for visitors, and it is most unlikely that your stay will be blighted by crime. Due to past terrorist attacks, there are occasional security alerts, notably on the underground, but these are mainly false alarms, often due to people accidentally leaving a bag or parcel lying around.

POLICE

THE SIGHT of a traditional British "bobby" patrolling the streets in a tall hat is now less common than the police patrol car with flashing lights and sirens. However, policemen on foot can still be found, and are courteous and helpful. If you have anything stolen, you should report the theft at the nearest police station.

THE CLIMATE OF GREAT BRITAIN

The moderate British climate rarely sees winter nights colder than -15° C (5° F), even in the far north, or summer days warmer than 30° C (86° F) in the south. Despite the country's reputation, annual rainfall is quite low – less than 100 cm (40 in) – and heavy rain is rare. The Atlantic coast, warmed by the Gulf Stream, gives the west a warmer, wetter climate than the east.

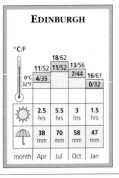

LONDON

°C/F			
		22/72	
	13/55	14/58	16/60
0°C 32°F	7/44		10/50
			7/45
			3/38
☀	5 hrs	6 hrs	3.5 hrs	1.5 hrs
☂	39 mm	45 mm	50 mm	44 mm
month	Apr	Jul	Oct	Jan

EDINBURGH

°C/F			
		18/62	
	11/52	11/52	13/56
0°C 32°F	4/39		7/44	16/61
			0/32
☀	2.5 hrs	5.5 hrs	3 hrs	1.5 hrs
☂	38 mm	70 mm	58 mm	47 mm
month	Apr	Jul	Oct	Jan

EMERGENCY SERVICES

IN AN EMERGENCY, dial 999 to reach police, fire, and ambulance services, which are on call 24-hours a day. Calls are free from any public or private phone. In coastal areas this number also applies for calls to the voluntary coastguard rescue service. You can also turn up at a hospital emergency room at any time. Emergency medical treatment in a British National Health Service (NHS) emergency room is free, but any kind of additional medical care could prove to be very expensive.

HEALTH ISSUES

YOU CAN BUY a wide range of medicines from pharmacies, which in Britain are known as chemists. Boots is the best-known chain store. If you are likely to need prescription drugs, either bring your own or get your doctor to write out the generic name of the drug (as opposed to the brand name). Some pharmacies are open until midnight, and doctors' offices (known as surgeries) are normally open morning and early evening.

FACILITIES FOR THE DISABLED

THE FACILITIES on offer for disabled visitors to Britain are steadily improving: new buildings offer elevators and ramps for wheelchair access, and adapted toilets. Many banks, theaters, and museums provide aids for the visually or hearing impaired. Given advance notice, rail, ferry, and bus personnel will help disabled passengers. The Disabled Person's Railcard provides discounted rail fares. Hertz offers hand-controlled vehicles for rental at no extra cost. For more general information about services contact **RADAR, Holiday Care Service**, or **Mobility International**.

BANKING AND CURRENCY

BRITAIN'S CURRENCY is the pound sterling (£), which is divided into 100 pence (p). Scottish banknotes are also legal tender in England and Wales, but you may find that not all stores will take them.

Banking hours vary, but the minimum opening times are 9:30am to 3:30pm, Monday to Friday. Most banks cash traveler's checks, and have

cash machines (ATMs) that accept most cards. You can also change money at private bureaux de change, which are located in major tourist areas and operate longer hours than banks. Exchange rates and commission charges can vary considerably.

Although credit cards are widely accepted in Britain, smaller stores, guesthouses, and cafés may not have the facilities for card transactions.

COMMUNICATIONS

PUBLIC TELEPHONE booths are available throughout Britain and may be card- or coin-operated. In major towns and public places, some booths are equipped with facilities to accept credit cards and offer internet access. It is less costly to telephone in the evenings and at weekends.

Post offices are usually open from 9am to 5:30pm Monday to Friday, and until 12:30pm on Saturday. Sub-post offices are located in local stores. Stamps can be purchased from any outlet which displays the sign "Stamps sold here." Mail boxes come in several shapes, but are always painted red.

Travel Information

Since it is an international gateway for air and sea traffic, traveling to Britain poses few problems. By air, visitors have a large choice of carriers serving Europe, Australasia, and North America. Bus travel is an inexpensive form of transportation from Europe, while traveling by train has been transformed by the advent of the Channel Tunnel. Traveling within Britain itself is fairly easy. There is an extensive road network reaching all parts of the country. The national rail network is improving and services to the smaller towns are good. Bus travel is the least expensive option; it serves most areas but can be slow.

FLYING TO GREAT BRITAIN

Britain has about 130 airports but only a handful of these are equipped for long-distance travel. The largest is London's Heathrow, one of Europe's central routing points for international travel. It is served by most of the world's leading airlines, with direct flights from nearly all the major cities. Other international airports include London Gatwick, London Stansted, Manchester, Birmingham, Newcastle, Glasgow, and Edinburgh.

British Airways has flights to destinations across the world. Other British airlines include **Virgin Atlantic**, with routes to the US and Far East, and **bmi british midland international**, which flies to the US and Western Europe. Ryanair and easyJet provide low-cost flights to Europe.

American airlines offering services to Britain include **American Airlines, Delta Air Lines,** and United, while from Canada, the main carrier is **Air Canada**. From Australasia, **Qantas** and **Air New Zealand** vie for passengers with many Far Eastern rivals.

CHARTERS AND PACKAGE DEALS

Charter flights offer relatively inexpensive seats, but have less flexible departure times than standard scheduled flights. Packages are also worth considering, as airlines and tour operators can put together a great range of flexible deals to suit your needs. These can include car rental or rail travel.

DOMESTIC FLIGHTS

Britain's size means that internal air travel only makes sense over long distances, such as from London to Scotland, or to one of the many offshore islands.

The **British Airways** shuttle flights between London and cities such as Glasgow, Edinburgh, and Manchester are extremely popular with business travelers. At peak times of the day, flights leave every hour, while at other times there is usually a flight every two hours.

TRAVELING IN LONDON

In London, daily, weekly, and monthly tickets called Travelcards are valid on all public transportation. However, if you are only using buses, it is better to buy a daily or weekly bus pass. Both types of pass are available at most newsagents and train or underground stations.

Fares in London are based on six train zones and two bus zones; there is a standard charge for travel within each zone and between zones, regardless of the distance traveled. The area covered by each zone varies slightly between buses and trains.

London also has express train services to Britain's two busiest airports, Heathrow and Gatwick, which leave from Paddington and Victoria stations respectively at regular intervals. The journey time is 15 minutes to Heathrow, and 30 minutes to Gatwick.

When traveling by bus, you pay the driver as you enter, or the conductor (if there is one) during your journey. The sightseeing buses that drive past many of London's historic sights are often run by private companies and will not accept bus passes or Travelcards.

All-night bus services are available in London from about 11pm until early morning. You can use Travelcards and bus passes on these. Night buses carry the letter N before the route number, and most pass through Trafalgar Square.

Taxis are available at every major train station, as well as at ranks near hotels and all over central London. All licensed cabs must carry a "For Hire" sign, which is lit up whenever they are free. The famous black cabs are the safest taxis to use in London since all the drivers are licensed and they also know where they are going. Most cab drivers expect a tip.

Sometimes, the best way to see London is on foot, but however you choose to get around, try to avoid the rush hours from 8 to 9:30am, and 4:30 to 6:30pm.

LONDON UNDERGROUND

The underground in London, known as the tube, is one of the largest systems of its kind in the world. London tube trains run every day, except December 25, from about 5:30am until after midnight. Fewer trains run on Sundays. The 12 tube lines are color-coded and maps are available at every station, while maps of the central section are displayed on each train. If you are making multiple journeys by tube, it is best to buy a daily or weekly Travelcard *(see above)*.

RAIL TRAVEL

Britain has a privatized rail network that covers the whole of the country. It consists of several regional services, such as Great North Eastern Railways and Great Western Trains. **Virgin Trains**, which runs many cross-country routes, operates two other networks – West Coast Trains and Cross Country Trains. The system is generally quite reliable.

The main stations in London all serve different areas of the country; Euston serves the Midlands and northwest, King's Cross serves the northeast and Scotland, Liverpool Street serves East Anglia, Waterloo and Paddington serve the West Country and Wales, and Victoria and Charing Cross serve the South Coast.

First-class tickets for most journeys are available, and roundtrip fares are less costly than two one-way tickets. There are four discount fare types for adults: Apex and Superapex tickets must be booked at least a week or 14 days in advance; Savers and Supersavers cannot be used during peak hours.

If you plan to do much traveling by train around Britain, buy a rail pass. These can be bought from BR agents abroad, such as **Rail Europe** and **CIE Tours International**. The All Line Rail Rover allows unlimited travel within Great Britain. Passes are available for families and young persons.

LONG-DISTANCE BUSES

IN BRITAIN, long-distance express buses and ones used for sightseeing excursions are usually referred to as coaches. Coach services are generally less expensive than rail travel. Journey times, however, are longer and much less predictable on crowded roads. Tickets can be purchased at major international airports, **Victoria Coach Station** – the main terminal for journeys into and out of London – and most large travel agents. The largest British coach operator is **National Express**. Another major operator is **Scottish Citylink**, with services between London, the North, and Scotland.

TRAVELING BY ROAD

THE MOST STARTLING difference for most foreign motorists in Britain is that one drives on the left, with corresponding adjustments at traffic circles and junctions. Distances are measured in miles. Traffic density in towns and at busy holiday times can cause long delays. Parking is a particular problem in towns and cities.

Renting a car in Britain can be expensive. One of the most competitive national companies is **Autos Abroad**, but small local firms may undercut even these rates. International car rental companies such as **Avis**, **Budget**, and **Hertz** also operate in Britain. You need a valid driver's license and a passport when you rent. Most companies will not rent to novice drivers, and set age limits (usually 21–70).

FERRY SERVICES

ABOUT 20 car and passenger services travel regularly across the Channel and the North and Irish seas, the major ones including **P&O** and **Stena Line**. Fares vary greatly according to the season, time of travel, and duration of stay.

Seacat (catamaran) services between Dover and Calais and between Folkestone and Boulogne are run by **Hoverspeed**. A larger Super Seacat operates outside the winter months between Newhaven and Dieppe.

CHANNEL TUNNEL

THE CHANNEL TUNNEL offers a nonstop rail link between Britain and Europe. **Eurostar** services (for foot passengers) run from Waterloo International station in London to Lille and Paris in France, and Brussels in Belgium. Traveling from London direct to Paris or Brussels takes about 3 hours.

The **Eurotunnel** service (commonly known as the Shuttle) transports vehicles between Folkestone and Calais in about half an hour.

DIRECTORY

AIRLINES

Air Canada
℡ 0870-524 7226 (UK).
℡ 888-247 2262 (US and Canada).

Air New Zealand
℡ 0800-028 4149 (UK).
℡ 0800-737 000 (NZ).

American Airlines
℡ 0845-789 789 (UK).
℡ 800-433 7300 (US).

bmi british midland international
℡ 0870-607 055 (UK).

British Airways
℡ 0845-773 3377 (UK).
℡ 800-403 0882 (US).

Delta Air Lines
℡ 0800-414 767 (UK).
℡ 800-241 4141 (US).

Qantas
℡ 020-8846 0321 (UK).
℡ 13 13 13 (Australia).

Virgin Atlantic
℡ 01293-747 747 (UK).
℡ 800-862 8621(US).

RAIL TRAVEL

CIE Tours International
℡ 800-243 8687 (US).

National Rail Inquiries
℡ 0845-748 49 50.

Rail Europe
℡ 0870-584 8848.
W www.raileurope.co.uk

Virgin Trains
℡ 0870-789 1234.

BUS COMPANIES

National Express
℡ 0870-580 8080.
W www.gobycoach.com

Scottish Citylink
℡ 0870-550 5050.

CAR RENTAL

Autos Abroad
℡ 020-7287 6000.

Avis
℡ 0870-590 0500.
W www.avis.co.uk

Budget
℡ 0800-181 181.
W www.budget.com

Hertz
℡ 0870-840 0084.
W www.hertz.com

FERRY SERVICES

Hoverspeed
℡ 0870-5240 241.

P&O
℡ 0870-600 0600.

Stena Line
℡ 0870-570 7070.
W www.stenaline.co.uk

CHANNEL TUNNEL SERVICES

Eurostar
℡ 0870-518 6186.
W www.eurostar.com
(for foot passengers).

Eurotunnel
℡ 0870-535 3353
(for cars & buses).

Shopping

WHILE THE WEST END of London is undeniably Britain's most exciting place to shop, many regional centers offer nearly as wide a range of goods. Moreover, regional shopping can be less stressful, less expensive, and remarkably varied, with craft studios, farm shops, street markets, and factory showrooms adding to the enjoyment of bargain-hunting. Britain is famous for its country clothing: wool, tartan, waxed cotton, and tweed are all popular, along with classic prints such as Liberty or Laura Ashley. Other particularly British goods include antiques, floral soaps and scents, porcelain, glass, and local crafts.

OPENING HOURS

IN GENERAL, you can assume most stores in Britain will open during the week from 9am or 10am until 5pm or 6pm. Hours on Saturdays may be shorter. Few town-center stores open on Sundays, unless it is near Christmas. Some stores open late for one evening a week – usually Thursday – while in villages the shops may close at lunchtime for an hour, or for one afternoon each week. Market days vary from town to town; some markets are held on Sundays.

OUT-OF-TOWN SHOPPING CENTERS

THESE LARGE COMPLEXES, similar to American malls, are rapidly increasing around Britain. The advantages of car access and easy, cheap parking are undeniable, and most centers are accessible by public transportation. The centers usually feature clusters of popular upscale stores, with many services offered, such as toilets, cafés, nurseries, restaurants, and movies.

DEPARTMENT STORES

CERTAIN big department stores are only found in London, but others have provincial branches. **John Lewis**, for example, has shops in 22 locations. It sells a huge range of fabrics, clothing, and household items, combining quality service with good value. **Marks & Spencer**, with 303 branches throughout Britain, is even more of a

household name, famed for its good-value clothing and prepared food. The sizes of all chain stores, and the range of stock they carry, will differ from region to region.

The most famous of London's many department stores is **Harrods**, with 300 departments, 4,000 employees, and a spectacular Edwardian food hall. Nearby, **Harvey Nichols** stocks designer clothing and boasts the city's most stylish food hall. Gourmets should make a pilgrimage to **Fortnum and Mason**, which has stocked high-quality food for nearly 300 years. **Selfridges** sells virtually everything, from fine cashmeres to household gadgets. **Liberty**, the West End's last privately owned department store, still sells the hand-blocked silks and Oriental goods for which it was famous when it first opened in 1875.

CLOTHING STORES

ONCE AGAIN, London has the widest range, from *haute couture* to cheap and cheerful ready-made items. Shopping for clothing in the regions, however, can often be less tiring. Many towns popular with tourists – Oxford, Bath, and York for instance – have independently-owned clothing stores where you receive more personal service. Or you could try one of the chain stores found throughout the country for stylish, reasonably priced clothes, as well as younger and less expensive fashions.

Traditional British clothing – waxed Barbour jackets and Burberry trench coats – are

found in outlets such as **The Scotch House**, **Burberry**, and **Gieves and Hawkes**, while **Laura Ashley** is renowned for its floral print dresses. For kilts and tartans, the best place is **Hector Russell**, found in both Edinburgh and Glasgow.

London is the place for designer fashions, however, as many designers have specialized outlets here. **Vivienne Westwood**, doyenne of the punkish avant-garde, uses London as her British base.

MARKETS

LARGE TOWNS and cities usually have a central covered market that operates most weekdays, selling everything from fresh produce to pots and pans. Many towns hold weekly markets in the main square.

The fashionable markets of London are **Covent Garden**, **Portobello Road**, and **Camden Lock**, where you can find an assortment of second-hand clothes, handmade crafts, and antiques. **Brick Lane** is an authentic East End market.

FOOD AND DRINK

SUPERMARKETS are a good way to shop for food. The range and quality of items in stock is usually excellent. Several large chains compete for market share and as a result, prices are generally lower than smaller shops. However, the smaller town-center stores such as local bakeries, greengrocers, or markets, may give you a more interesting choice of fresh regional produce, and more personal service.

Alcoholic beverages are available in a huge variety of shops around Britain, many of them wine merchants, such as the chain store **Oddbins**. For whisky, Scotland is the place to go; **Cadenheads** and **The Whisky Shop** both have a wide variety of rare scotches.

BOOKS AND MAGAZINES

THE CAPITAL IS the hub of Britain's book trade, as many of the country's leading publishers are located within central London. Charing Cross

Road is the focal point for those searching for new, antiquarian, and secondhand volumes, and it is the home of **Foyle's**, with its massive but notoriously badly organized stock. Large branches of such chains as **Waterstone's** and **Borders** (which also sells magazines) are here, although they can also be found in most cities and major towns.

GIFTS AND SOUVENIRS

MOST REPUTABLE large stores can arrange to ship expensive items back home for you. If you want to buy things that you can carry in a suitcase, the choice is wide. You can purchase attractive, well-made, portable craft items all over the country, especially in those areas that are popular with tourists. For slightly more unusual presents, have a look in museum shops and at the range of items available in National Trust and English Heritage properties.

Some chain stores are very convenient places to pick up attractive gifts and souvenirs. **The Body Shop** sells natural cosmetics and toiletries in recyclable plastic packaging, while **Past Times** sells modern reproductions of ancient British jewelry designs, including Celtic, Roman, and Tudor pieces. For designer gifts, try the **Conran Shop** in London, which sells stylish accessories for the home.

ART AND ANTIQUES

BRITAIN'S LONG HISTORY means there are many interesting artifacts to be found. Many towns, such as Brighton, have dozens of antique shops. You might also like to visit a jumble or flea market in the hope of picking up a bargain.

The largest collection of original photographs for sale in the country is at the **Photographers' Gallery** in London. For paintings, **Maas Gallery** in London's Mayfair district excels in Victorian masters. In Scotland, **The Scottish Gallery** has everything from jewelry to pieces by well-known Scottish artists, while **Heritage House** is a treasure trove of antiques.

DIRECTORY

DEPARTMENT STORES

Fortnum and Mason
181 Piccadilly, London W1.
020-7734 8040.

Harrods
87–135 Brompton Rd, London SW1.
020-7730 1234.

Harvey Nichols
109–125 Knightsbridge, London SW1.
020-7235 5000.

John Lewis
69 St. James Centre, Edinburgh EH1.
0131-556 9121.
One of many branches.

Liberty
210–220 Regent St, London W1.
020-7734 1234.

Marks & Spencer
173 & 458 Oxford St, London W1.
020-7935 7954.
Two of many branches.

Selfridges
400 Oxford St, London W1.
0870-377 377.

CLOTHING STORES

Burberry
165 Regent Street, London W1.
020-7930 3343.

2 Brompton Rd, London SW1.
020-7581 2151.

Gieves & Hawkes
1 Savile Row, London W1.
020-7434 2001.

Hector Russell
110 Buchanan St, Glasgow G1.
0141-221 0217.

Laura Ashley
256–258 Regent St, London W1.
020-7437 9760.
One of many branches.

Vivienne Westwood
6 Davies St, London W1.
020-7629 3757.

MARKETS

Brick Lane
Brick Lane, London E1.
dawn–1pm Sun.

Camden Lock
Chalk Farm Rd, London NW1.
9:30am–5:30pm Mon–Fri, 10am–6pm Sat–Sun.

Covent Garden
The Piazza, London WC2.
9am–5pm daily.

Portobello Road
Portobello Rd, London W10.
7am–5:30pm Sat.

FOOD AND DRINK

Cadenheads
172 Canongate, Edinburgh EH8.
0131-556 5864.

Oddbins
64 Cannon St, London EC4.
020-7332 0606.
One of many branches.

The Whisky Shop
Unit 12 Princes Square, 48 Buchanan St, Glasgow G1.
0141-226 8446.

BOOKS AND MAGAZINES

Borders
120 Charing Cross Rd, London WC2.
020-7379 8877.
One of many branches.

Foyle's
113–119 Charing Cross Rd, London WC2.
020-7437 5660.

Waterstone's
128 Princes St, Edinburgh.
0131-226 2666.
One of many branches.

GIFTS AND SOUVENIRS

The Body Shop
32–34 Great Marlborough St, London W1.
020-7437 5137.
One of many branches.

Conran Shop
Michelin House, 81 Fulham Rd, London SW3.
020-7589 7401.

Past Times
155 Regent Street, London W1.
020-7734 3728.
One of many branches.

ART AND ANTIQUES

Heritage House
3b Yorkhill Quay Estate, Glasgow G3.
0141-334 4924.

Maas Gallery
15a Clifford St, London W1.
020-7734 2302.

Photographers' Gallery
5 & 8 Great Newport St, London WC2.
020-7831 1772.

The Scottish Gallery
16 Dundas St, Edinburgh.
0131-558 1200.

Entertainment

Lsporting events. Britain, with an array of world-class cultural and sporting events. Around the country, theaters, opera houses, concert halls, and other venues host a wide range of performing and dramatic arts programs. The summer months also see numerous open-air arts festivals. Ticket prices are often less expensive outside the capital. Britain offers hundreds of special interest holidays for those wanting to acquire a new skill or learn a new sport. Walking, sailing, skiing, pony-trekking, and golfing holidays are popular. Soccer, rugby, and cricket are favorite sports.

ENTERTAINMENT LISTINGS

For information about what's on in London, check the *Evening Standard* or the listings magazine *Time Out* (published every Wednesday). All the quality broadsheet newspapers have detailed arts reviews and listings of cultural events in London and throughout the country. Local newspapers, libraries, and tourist offices can supply details of regional events.

TICKETS

Ticket availability varies from show to show. You may be able to buy a ticket at the door, especially for a mid-week matinee, but for the more popular West End shows seats may have to be reserved weeks or even months in advance through agencies – ubiquitous in central London – or by telephone or in person at theater box offices. Half-price tickets for some same-day shows can be obtained from Leicester Square. Beware of counterfeit tickets offered by touts.

THEATER

Britain has an enduring theatrical tradition dating back to Shakespeare. London is the place to enjoy theater at its most varied and glamorous. The West End alone has more than 50 theaters. The **Barbican** and the **Royal National Theatre** stage a mixture of classics and challenging new productions. The major commercial theaters, showing more popular plays and musicals, are located along Shaftesbury Avenue and the Haymarket, and around Covent Garden and Charing Cross Road.

Outside the capital, at Stratford-upon-Avon, the **Royal Shakespeare Theatre** presents a year-round program of the great bard's works. Bristol's **Theatre Royal** is the oldest working theater in Britain. Good productions are staged at the Manchester **Royal Exchange**, and the **Traverse** in Edinburgh.

Open-air theater is a feature of city life in the summer with street entertainers at London's Covent Garden and other urban centers. London's Globe theater (*see pp58–59*) stages performances of Shakespeare's plays, and open-air theaters at Regent's Park and Holland Park also have a summer program.

Perhaps the liveliest theatrical festival in Britain is the two-week **Edinburgh Festival** held in late summer. Many seaside resorts also have a summer theater season.

MUSIC

A diverse musical repertoire can be found in a variety of venues across Great Britain. London, in particular, is one of the world's great centers for music, and home to several world-class orchestras and chamber groups. As well as classical concerts, there are dozens of rock, reggae, soul, folk, country, jazz, and Latin concerts taking place on every day of the week. There are also numerous nightclubs that play everything from 70s disco to the very latest house-music beats.

Major pop-concert venues in the capital include **Wembley Arena** and **Carling Apollo**. The **Royal Albert Hall** hosts a range of concerts, including the popular classical Proms. The **Wigmore Hall**, the **Barbican Concert Hall**, and the **Royal Festival Hall** are also notable classical venues. The **Royal Opera House** is a world-class venue, and home to the Royal Opera. English National Opera performs at the **London Coliseum**. Classical open-air concerts are also held at Marble Hill House and **Kenwood House** during the summer.

A wide range of musical events is staged in towns and cities across Great Britain. Liverpool and Manchester have excellent orchestras and are also centers for modern music, while **Glyndebourne** hosts an annual opera festival. Wales has a very strong choral tradition, while northern England is renowned for booming brass bands. Scotland, of course, is famous for its bagpipers.

DANCE

Classical ballet is performed at the **Royal Opera House**, home of the Royal Ballet, and the **London Coliseum** where the English National Ballet usually performs. The **Place Theatre**, **Sadler's Wells**, and the **Institute for Contemporary Art** (**ICA**) are major venues for contemporary dance.

Birmingham is home to the Birmingham Royal Ballet and is the best place to see performances outside London. Traditional English Morris dancing or the Scottish Highland fling and Celtic dancing (*ceilidhs*) can be enjoyed at local festivals.

CINEMA

The latest movies can be seen in any large town. Premieres with international film stars are usually held at London's Leicester Square cinemas. The capital now has a 3D cinema, the **BFI London IMAX**. Young children may see films graded U (universal) or PG (parental guidance). Cinema prices vary widely; some are less expensive at off-peak times, such as Mondays or afternoons. For first nights of new releases it is advisable to book in advance.

SPECIAL INTEREST VACATIONS

HUNDREDS OF options are available from any kind of sport, to arts and crafts, such as painting, calligraphy, and jewelry-making, and a wide range of educational courses to suit all levels.

Reservations can be made with organizers or through a travel agent. The English and Scottish Tourist Boards have pamphlets on some of these activities.

OUTDOOR ACTIVITIES

BRITAIN HAS an extensive network of long-distance footpaths and shorter trail routes for walkers, together with designated cycle routes and bridle paths.

There are 2,000 golf courses in Britain and many clubs welcome visiting players (bring confirmation of your handicap). Green fees vary widely. Tennis courts can be found in every town and many hotels.

Sailing is popular in the Lake District, and the south coast resorts have plenty of pleasure craft. Boating on the Thames and on Britain's network of canals is a common summer pursuit. Surfers and windsurfers head for the West Country and South Wales.

The best game fishing (trout and salmon) is in the West Country, Wales, and Scotland. Soccer, rugby, cricket, and horse-racing are all popular sports in Britain. Details of matches and meetings can be found in national newspapers. During the last week of June and the first week of July, the Wimbledon tournament attracts many visitors to the **All England Lawn Tennis and Croquet Club**.

Among adventure sport options are rock-climbing and mountaineering, aeronautical sports and gliding. Skiing and other winter sports are possible in Scotland. Ice-skating rinks are located in major cities and horse-riding centers are found throughout the country, with pony-trekking in tourist areas.

DIRECTORY

THEATER

Barbican
Silk St, London EC2.
020-7638 8891.

Bristol Old Vic
King St
Bristol BS1.
0117-987 7877.

Edinburgh Festival
The Hub, Castlehill,
Edinburgh EH1.
0131-473 2001.

Royal Exchange
St. Anne's Square,
Manchester M2.
0161-833 9833.

Royal National Theatre
South Bank Centre,
London SE1.
020-7452 3000.

Royal Shakespeare Theatre
Stratford-upon-Avon CV37.
01789-403 403

Traverse
Cambridge St,
Edinburgh EH1.
0131-228 1404.

MUSIC

Glyndebourne
Lewes, East Sussex BN8.
01273-813 813.

Kenwood House
Hampstead Lane,
London NW3.
020-8348 1286.

Carling Apollo
Queen Caroline St,
London W6.
0870-606 3400.

London Coliseum
St. Martin's Lane,
London WC2.
020-7836 0111.

Philharmonic Hall
Hope St, Liverpool L1 9BP.
0151-709 3789.

Royal Albert Hall
Kensington Gore,
London SW7.
020-7589 3203.

Royal Festival Hall
South Bank Centre,
London SE1.
020-7960 4242.

Royal Opera House
Floral St, London WC2.
020-7304 4000.

Symphony Hall
International Convention
Centre, Broad St,
Birmingham B1 2EA.
0121-644 5003.

Wembley Arena
Empire Way, Wembley,
Middlesex HA9.
0870 739 0739.

Wigmore Hall
36 Wigmore St,
London W1.
020-7935 2141.

DANCE

ICA
Nash House, Carlton
House Terrace, The Mall,
London SW1.
020-7930 3647.

Place Theatre
17 Duke's Road,
London WC1.
020-7387 0161.

Sadler's Wells
Rosebery Ave, London EC1.
020-7863 8000.

CINEMA

BFI London IMAX
Waterloo Rd, London SE1.
020-7902 1234.

OUTDOOR ACTIVITIES

All England Lawn Tennis and Croquet Club
Church Road, Wimbledon,
London SW19.
020-8944 1066.

Association of Pleasure Craft Operators
Parkland House,
Audley Ave, Newport,
Shropshire TF10.
01952-813 572.

British Activity Holiday Association
22 Green Lane, Hersham,
Surrey, KT12.
01932-252 994.

British Mountaineering Council
177–179 Burton Rd,
Manchester M20.
0870 010 4878.

British Waterways
Willow Grange, Church Rd,
Watford, WD1.
01923-201 120.

English Golf Union
National Golf Centre,
The Broadway,
Woodhall Spa, Lincs LN10.
01526-354 500.

Outward Bound
Watermillock,
Nr Penrith,
Cumbria CA11.
08705-134 227.

Ski Club of Great Britain
57–63 Church Road,
London SW19.
0845-458 0780.

Where to Stay in Great Britain

T HE RANGE OF ACCOMMODATIONS available in Britain is extensive, and whatever your budget you should find something to suit you. London, unsurprisingly, is much more expensive than the rest of the country, but even here there are numerous affordable yet comfortable hotels. Out in the country, B&Bs (offering bed and breakfast) and guest houses are often economical places to stay.

	NUMBER OF ROOMS	RESTAURANT	PRIVATE PARKING	GARDEN OR TERRACE
LONDON				
WESTMINSTER: *Goring* ①①①① 15 Beeston Place, Grosvenor Gardens, SW1 0JW. **Map** C4. ☏ 020-7396 9000. FAX 020-7834 4393. W www.goringhotel.co.uk A grand Edwardian building is the setting for this family-run hotel. Traditional immaculate standards are maintained, and the restaurant is superb. ■ TV ▨	74	▪	●	▪
WESTMINSTER: *Jolly St. Ermin's* W www.jollyhotels.it ①①①① 2 Caxton Street, SW1H 0QW. **Map** C4. ☏ 020-7222 7888. FAX 020-7222 6914. A late-Victorian hotel close enough to Westminster to have once had its own tunnel link to the House of Commons. The public rooms are very imposing, but the bedrooms are more modest in style. ■ TV ▨	290	▪	●	
WESTMINSTER: *Royal Horseguards* W www.thistlehotels.com ①①①① 2 Whitehall Court, SW1A 2EJ. **Map** D4. ☏ 0870 333 9122. FAX 0870 333 9222. Overlooking the river, this grand 19th-century hotel has comfortable public rooms, including the smart and formal Granby's Restaurant. The style of the bedrooms varies from Classical opulence to contemporary smartness. ■ TV ▨	280	▪		
WEST END: *Hazlitt's* W www.hazlittshotel.com ①①①① 6 Frith Street, W1D 3JA. **Map** C3. ☏ 020-7434 1771. FAX 020-7439 1524. Set in three 18th-century houses, this hotel's interior is furnished with Victorian antiques, with "mod cons" unobtrusively incorporated. ■ ▨ TV	23			
WEST END: *22 Jermyn St* W www.22jermyn.com ①①①① 22 Jermyn Street, SW1Y 6HL. **Map** C3. ☏ 020-7734 2353. FAX 020-7734 0750. A warren of luxurious suites and studios catering for the business visitor. The rooms are lavishly decorated and beautifully maintained. ■ ♿ ▨ TV	18			
WEST END: *Ritz* ①①①① 150 Piccadilly, W1J 9BR. **Map** C3. ☏ 020-7493 8181. FAX 020-7493 2687. W www.theritzlondon.com This grand old late 19th-century hotel still draws the crowds. The marbled rooms are undeniably grand – especially the restaurant. ■ TV ▨	133	▪		▪
WEST END: *Savoy* W www.savoygroup.com ①①①① Strand, WC2R 0BP. **Map** D3. ☏ 020-7836 4343. FAX 020-7240 6040. A flamboyant Art Deco hotel with glorious waterfront views, combining period character with modern comforts. ■ ≋ ♿ ▨ TV	260	▪	●	
WEST END: *Waldorf* W www.lemeridien-waldorf.com ①①①① Aldwych, WC2B 4DD. **Map** D3. ☏ 020-7836 2400. FAX 020-7836 7244. Still smart, this superior hotel is no longer quite the exclusive haunt of its heyday. All rooms have recently been refurbished. ■ TV ♿ ▨	303	▪	●	
REGENT'S PARK: *La Place* W www.hotellaplace.com ①① 17 Nottingham Place, W1V 5LG. **Map** B2. ☏ 020-7486 2323. FAX 020-7486 4335. A well-appointed, pleasant town house, producing simple meals in its basement restaurant. Bedrooms are well furnished. ■ TV ▨	20	▪		
REGENT'S PARK: *Melia White House* W www.solmelia.com ①①① Albany Street, NW1 3UP. **Map** C2. ☏ 020-7387 1200. FAX 020-7387 6788. Large and impressive, this complex of suites and apartments provides high standards of accommodation. There is a smart, classy restaurant, a comfortable cocktail lounge, and a popular bistro. ■ TV ♿ ▨	582	▪	◆	▪
REGENT'S PARK: *The Landmark* ①①①① 222 Marylebone Road, NW1 6JQ. **Map** B3. ☏ 020-7631 8000. FAX 020-7631 8080. W www.landmarklondon.co.uk Palatially restored, Marylebone's railroad hotel now boasts an eye-popping atrium of soaring palm trees. ■ TV ♿ ▨ ≋	299	▪	●	

Map references refer to map of London on pp42–3

<table>
<tr><td>

Price categories are for a standard double room per night, inclusive of breakfast, service charges, and any additional taxes such as VAT:

£ under £100
££ £100–£150
£££ £150–£200
££££ over £200

</td><td>

RESTAURANT
Hotel restaurant or dining room usually open to non-residents unless otherwise stated.

PRIVATE PARKING
Parking provided by the hotel in either a private car park or a private garage very close by.

CREDIT CARDS
Major credit cards are accepted in those hotels where the credit card symbol is shown.

</td></tr>
</table>

		NUMBER OF ROOMS	RESTAURANT	PRIVATE PARKING	GARDEN OR TERRACE
REGENT'S PARK: *Langham Hilton* W www.hilton.com ££££ 1c Portland Place, W1B 1JA. **Map** C2. 020-7636 1000. FAX 020-7323 2340. The Langham offers a lavish, Hilton-style recreation of its former Victorian splendor, in addition to contemporary "mod cons." Rooms are sumptuous, as is the famous ballroom.		429	■		
HYDE PARK: *Knightsbridge Green* ££ 159 Knightsbridge, SW1X 7PD. **Map** B4. 020-7584 6274. FAX 020-7225 1635. W www.thekghotel.co.uk A long-established, upscale B&B, which is popular with women travelers. Tea and coffee are available all day in the Club Room. ● *Dec 24–26.*		28			
HYDE PARK: *Beaufort* £££ 33 Beaufort Gardens, SW3 1PP. **Map** B4. 020-7584 5252. FAX 020-7589 2834. W www.thebeaufort.co.uk Sheer elegance partially excuses the high tariffs of this classy little place near Harrods. Personal service and pampering are what you pay for.		28			
HYDE PARK: *Basil Street* W www.thebasil.com ££££ 8 Basil Street, SW3 1AH. **Map** B4. 020-7581 3311. FAX 020-7581 3693. An old-fashioned hotel with an unpretentious Edwardian air and enduring popularity. Its brasserie-wine bar is superb, and excellent value for the area. Many of the regular "Basilites" are women.		80	■		
HYDE PARK: *Berkeley* W www.savoy-group.co.uk ££££ Wilton Place, SW1X 7RL. **Map** B4. 020-7235 6000. FAX 020-7235 4330. The discreet entrance to this august hotel leads to a dignified marble hallway with Lutyens paneling. Bedrooms display unusual individuality.		200	■	●	
HYDE PARK: *Dorchester* W www.dorchesterhotel.com ££££ 53 Park Lane, W1A 2HJ. **Map** B3. 020-7629 8888. FAX 020-7409 0114. Conspicuous, flamboyant grandeur dominates this old hotel. Eating places include the famous Grill Room and the exotically themed Oriental restaurant. The voluptuous bedrooms are triple-glazed on the Park Lane side.		250	■	●	
HYDE PARK: *Mandarin Oriental* ££££ 66 Knightsbridge, SW1X 7LA. **Map** B4. 020-7235 2000. FAX 020-7235 4552. W www.mandarinoriental.com This landmark hotel overlooking Hyde Park offers superb rooms and facilities, and an oriental health spa.		220	■	●	
SOUTH KENSINGTON: *Aster House* W www.asterhouse.com ££ 3 Sumner Place, SW7 3EE. **Map** B4. 020-7581 5888. FAX 020-7584 4925. Several houses in this elegant terrace are discreet, upmarket hotels, but few have such reasonable tariffs. Bedrooms are all non-smoking.		14			■
SOUTH KENSINGTON: *Five Sumner Place* ££ 5 Sumner Place, SW7 3EE. **Map** B4. 020-7584 7586. FAX 020-7823 9962. W www.sumnerplace.com This Victorian terraced town house is elegant and stylish, and provides a welcome quiet haven from the bustle and noise of central London.		15			■
SOUTH KENSINGTON: *Blakes* ££££ 33 Roland Gardens, SW7 3PF. **Map** A5. 020-7370 6701. FAX 020-7373 0442. W www.blakeshotel.co.uk The green façade distinguishes Blakes instantly, and a glimpse at the exotic interior declares this is no ordinary hotel. Every bedroom is unique.		46	■		■
SOUTH KENSINGTON: *Cadogan* ££££ 75 Sloane Street, SW1X 9SG. **Map** B4. 020-7235 7141. FAX 020-7245 0994. These premises evoke the grandeur and formality of yesteryear. Now solidly respectable; mobiles and laptops are banned in public areas.		65	■	●	■

For key to symbols see back flap

Price categories are for a standard double room per night, inclusive of breakfast, service charges, and any additional taxes such as VAT: **£** under £100 **££** £100–£150 **£££** £150–£200 **££££** over £200	**RESTAURANT** Hotel restaurant or dining room usually open to non-residents unless otherwise stated. **PRIVATE PARKING** Parking provided by the hotel in either a private car park or a private garage very close by. **CREDIT CARDS** Major credit cards are accepted in those hotels where the credit card symbol is shown.	NUMBER OF ROOMS	RESTAURANT	PRIVATE PARKING	GARDEN OR TERRACE

	Rooms	Restaurant	Private Parking	Garden or Terrace
SOUTH KENSINGTON: *Gore* W www.gorehotel.co.uk **££££** 189 Queen's Gate, SW7 5EX. **Map** A4. **(** 020-7584 6601. **FAX** 020-7589 8127. This idiosyncratic Victorian hotel is located above a pair of chic restaurants. Bedrooms vary from tiny singles to Tudor fantasies with their own minstrels' galleries.	53	■		
THE CITY AND SOUTHWARK: *Tower Thistle* W www.thistlehotels.com **£££** St. Katherine's Way, E1W 1LD. **Map** F3. **(** 020-7481 2575. **FAX** 020-7488 4106. A 1970s concrete ziggurat just below Tower Bridge, opposite Butler's Wharf. The rooms are small, but have excellent views of the river.	801	■	●	
NOTTING HILL: *Abbey Court* W www.abbeycourt.co.uk **££** 20 Pembridge Gardens, W2 4DU. **(** 020-7221 7518. **FAX** 020-7792 0858. This lavishly decorated town house provides luxury B&B service. Bedrooms vary, but all are decorated with handsome Victorian antiques. There are a good number of single rooms for the solo traveler.	22			■
NOTTING HILL: *Pembridge Court* W www.pemet.co.uk **£££** 34 Pembridge Gardens, W2 4DX. **(** 020-7229 9977. **FAX** 020-7727 4982. This elegant town house is comfortable and civilized, with displays of costume accessories – gloves, fans, and purses – in the rooms.	20			
NOTTING HILL: *Portobello* W www.portobello-hotel.co.uk **£££** 22 Stanley Gardens, W11 2NG. **(** 020-7727 2777. **FAX** 020-7792 9641. An eccentric establishment with dark and sophisticated decor in a mix of Victorian and Edwardian styles. Rooms range from tiny to lavish.	24	■		

SOUTHERN ENGLAND

	Rooms	Restaurant	Private Parking	Garden or Terrace
BRIGHTON: *Dove* **£** 18 Regency Square, Brighton BN1 2FG. **(** 01273-779 222. **FAX** 01273-746 912. Only a few minutes' walk to the sea, this family-run hotel in a Regency house has pristine modern bedrooms. Service is efficient and friendly.	9			
BRIGHTON: *Topps* **£** 17 Regency Square, Brighton BN1 2FG. **(** 01273-729 334. **FAX** 01273-203 679. This smart hotel is a set in pair of beautifully furnished Regency town houses. Most bedrooms have gas-coal fires and large bathrooms.	15			
BROXTED: *Whitehall, Church End* **££** Broxted, nr Stansted Airport, Essex CM6 2BZ. **(** 01279-850 603. **FAX** 01279-850 385. W www.whitehallhotel.co.uk Useful for the airport, this Elizabethan manor house has large bedrooms and an excellent restaurant. ● *Dec 25–30.*	26	■	●	■
CANTERBURY: *Thanington* W www.thanington-hotel.co.uk **£** 140 Wincheap, Canterbury, Kent CT1 3RY. **(** 01227-453 227. **FAX** 01227-453 225. Only minutes from the town center, this smart Georgian house offering B&B is immaculately kept throughout. ● *Dec 25.*	15		●	■
WINCHESTER: *Wykeham Arms* **£** 75 Kingsgate Street, Winchester, Hampshire SO23 9PE. **(** 01962-853 834. **FAX** 01962-854 411. One of the oldest pubs in town, the Wykeham Arms retains all of its original charm. The bars are lit by low lights and log fires. ● *Dec 25.*	13	■	●	■

THE WEST COUNTRY AND WALES

	Rooms	Restaurant	Private Parking	Garden or Terrace
BATH: *Sydney Gardens* W www.sydneygardens.co.uk **£** Sydney Road, Bath, Avon BA2 6NT. **(** 01225-464 818. **FAX** 01225-484 347. An Italianate Victorian villa just outside Bath offering B&B. A delight to stay in, with high standards of comfort and service.	6		●	■

Map references refer to map of London on pp42–3

BATH: *Queensberry* W www.bathqueensberry.com £££ 29
Russell Street, Bath, Avon BA1 2QF. (01225-447928. FAX 01225-446 065.
Three 18th-century terraced houses form a smart hotel in the heart of Bath.
The fine bedrooms are decorated with style. ● Dec 24–29.

BEDDGELERT: *Sygun Fawr Country House* £ 9
Beddgelert, Gwynedd LL55 4NE. (& FAX 01766-890 258. W www.sygunfawr.co.uk
An old hotel which retains its original beams, very well placed for climbing
and walking in Snowdonia. Bedrooms are bright and pretty. ● Jan.

BRANSCOMBE: *Bulstone Hotel* W www.childfriendlyhotels.com £ 11
Higher Bulstone, Branscombe, Sidmouth, Devon EX12 3BL. (0129-768 0000.
The Bulstone offers excellent facilities for families – suites with parents' and
children's rooms, a parents' kitchen, a playroom, and an outdoor play area.

BRISTOL: *Berkely Square Hotel* £££ 42
15 Berkely Square, Cliffton, Bristol BS8 1HB.
(0117-925 4000. FAX 0117-925 2970. W www.cliftonhotels.com
A smart and comfortable town house, with a stylish cocktail bar and a
restaurant in the basement. The hotel is cheaper at weekends.

CARDIFF: *St. David's Spa* W www.thestdavidshotel.com £££ 132
Havannah Street, Cardiff CF10 5SD. (029-2045 4045. FAX 029-2031 3075.
An extremely modern waterfront development which attracts mostly
businessmen. A maritime feel both inside and out is completed by
the massive metallic "fin" which juts out of the roof.

PORTHKERRY: *Egerton Grey Country House* W www.egertongrey.co.uk ££ 10
Porthkerry, nr Cardiff CF6 9BZ. (01446-711 666. FAX 01446-711 690.
A part-Victorian, part-Edwardian house close to Cardiff airport, though its size
and location make it seem a million miles away. The decor combines both
comfort and sophistication. Excellent food is served in the restaurant.

PORTMEIRION: *Portmeirion* W www.portmeirion-village.com ££ 40
Portmeirion, Gwynedd LL48 6ET. (01766-770 228. FAX 01766-771 331.
It is a unique experience to stay in this bizzare Mediterranean-style
village, created by Welsh architect Sir Clough Williams-Ellis. The hotel
itself is no disappointment, with many exotic interiors.

ST. IVES: *Garrack* W www.garrack.com ££ 18
Burthallan Lane, St. Ives, Cornwall TR26 3AA. (01736-796 199. FAX 01736-798 955.
A family-run hotel above St. Ives, within easy reach of the town
center. The standard of decor in the bedrooms varies.

SEION LLANDDEINIOLEN: *Tyn Rhos Country House* £ 14
Seion Llanddeiniolen, Caernarfon, Gwynedd LL55 3LE.
(01248-670 489. FAX 01248-670 079. W www.tynrhos.co.uk
A stylishly decorated hotel with a civilized air and very hospitable
staff. Good food is served in the restaurant. ● Dec 23–30.

VERYAN: *Nare Hotel* W www.narehotel.co.uk ££££ 40
Carne Beach, Veryan, Truro, Cornwall TR2 5PF. (01872-501 111. FAX 01872-501 856.
A modern hotel, with a Victorian-style interior. Most rooms have exceptional
views looking straight out to sea. There is also a gym.

CENTRAL ENGLAND

BIRMINGHAM: *Marriot Hotel* W www.marriot.com ££ 104
12 Hagley Road, Five Ways, Birmingham B16 8SJ. (0121-452 1144. FAX 0121-456 3442.
An elegant, Edwardian-style hotel, complete with a leisure club, spa, an
excellent cocktail bar, and a restaurant.

CAMBRIDGE: *Sorrento Hotel* W www.sorrentohotel.com £ 30
196 Cherry Hinton Road, Cambridge, Cambridgeshire CB1 7AN.
(01223-243 533. FAX 01223-213 463.
An attractive family-run hotel, boasting an excellent Italian restaurant.

CAMBRIDGE: *Lensfield Hotel* ££ 36
53 Lensfield Road, Cambridge, Cambridgeshire CB2 1EN.
(01223-355 017. FAX 01223-312 022. W www.lensfieldhotel.co.uk
The Lensfield is conveniently located within walking distance of the city center.
The restaurant serves English, French, and Greek cuisine. ● Dec 20–Jan 5.

		NUMBER OF ROOMS	RESTAURANT	PRIVATE PARKING	GARDEN OR TERRACE
Price categories are for a standard double room per night, inclusive of breakfast, service charges, and any additional taxes such as VAT: **£** under £100 **££** £100–£150 **£££** £150–£200 **££££** over £200	**RESTAURANT** Hotel restaurant or dining room usually open to non-residents unless otherwise stated. **PRIVATE PARKING** Parking provided by the hotel in either a private car park or a private garage very close by. **CREDIT CARDS** Major credit card are accepted in those hotels where the credit card symbol is shown.				
OXFORD: *Cotswold House* W www.cotswoldhouse.co.uk **£** 363 Banbury Road, Oxford OX2 7PL. **(** 01865-310 558. FAX 01865-310 558. A small, friendly guesthouse two miles from the city center, located on a main residential road. 🔲 TV 🔲		8		●	
OXFORD: *Old Parsonage* W www.oxfordcity.co.uk/hotels **£££** 1 Banbury Road, Oxford OX2 6NN. **(** 01865-310 210. FAX 01865-311 262. This very comfortable hotel has a relaxed atmosphere and is an excellent base for sightseeing in Oxford and the outlying countryside. ● *Dec 23–28.* 🔲 TV 🔲		30	■		■
STRATFORD-UPON-AVON: *Caterham House* **£** 58–59 Rother Street, Stratford-upon-Avon, Warwickshire CV37 6LT. **(** 01789-267 309. FAX 01789-414 836. A centrally placed B&B in two adjoining Georgian houses. Very attractive inside and out, the hotel is comfortable, stylish, and well-run. ● *Dec 24–25.* 🔲 TV 🔲		10		●	■
WILMCOTE: *Pear Tree Cottage* **£** 7 Church Road, Wilmcote, Stratford-upon-Avon, Warwickshire CV37 9UX. **(** 01789-205 889. FAX 01789-262 862. W www.peartreecot.co.uk This charming part-Elizabethan cottage is a B&B, but has a kitchen for the use of guests. Rooms are furnished with antiques. ● *Dec 24–Jan 10.* 🔲 TV 🔲 🔲		5		●	■

NORTHERN ENGLAND

		NUMBER OF ROOMS	RESTAURANT	PRIVATE PARKING	GARDEN OR TERRACE
CHESTER: *Chester Grosvenor* @ reservations@chestergrosvenor.co.uk **££££** Eastgate, Chester CH1 1LT. **(** 01244-324 024. FAX 01244-313 246. Situated close to the Chester Rows in the center of town, the Grosvenor has individually designed bedrooms, conference rooms and a business center. There is a choice of a Michelin-starred restaurant or a brasserie. 🔲 TV 🔲 🔲		85	■	●	
DURHAM: *Georgian Town House* W www.thegeorgiantownhouse.co.uk **£** 10 Crossgate, Durham DH1 4PS. **(** & FAX 0191-386 8070. A lovely Georgian house in the heart of the city, decorated with imagination and flair. Bedrooms are bright and breakfasts are good. ● *Christmas & New Year.* 🔲 TV		8			
LAKE DISTRICT: *Roundthorn Country House* W www.roundthorn.co.uk **£** Beacon Edge, Penrith, Cumbria CA11 8SJ. **(** 01768-863 952. FAX 01768-864 100. An elegant Georgian house set in landscaped gardens on the edge of the Beacon, with panoramic views of the surrounding area. Light snacks are served on request in the evenings. 🔲 TV 🔲		10		●	■
LAKE DISTRICT: *Thistle Grasmere* @ grasmere@thistle.co.uk **££** Keswick Road, Grasmere, Cumbria LA22 9PR. **(** 0870 333 9135. FAX 0870 333 9235. A lovely Edwardian building with tastefully modernized facilities. The lake shore setting is fabulous. There is a bar. 🔲 TV 🔲		72	■	●	■
LAKE DISTRICT: *Holbeck Ghyll* **£££** Holbeck Lane, Windermere, Cumbria LA23 1LU. **(** 01539-432 375. FAX 01539-434 743. W www.holbeckghyll.com Located in a superb position with views over the lake to the mountains, this imposing Victorian house offers very attentive and courteous service. 🔲 TV 🔲		21	■	●	■
LEEDS: *42 The Calls* W www.42thecalls.co.uk **£££** 42 The Calls, Leeds LS2 7EW. **(** 01132-440099. FAX 01132-344 100. Chic and stylish, this city hotel has a quiet, informal atmosphere. The rooms are well equipped and there is a Michelin-starred restaurant. ● *Dec 25 & 26.* 🔲 TV 🔲 🔲		41	■		
MANCHESTER: *The Midland Crowne Plaza* @ www.crowneplaza.com **££** Peter Street, Manchester M60 2DS. **(** 0161-236 3333. FAX 0161-932 4100. Located in the heart of the city, this venerable hotel dates back to Victorian times. Facilities include a gym and a swimming pool. 🔲 TV 🔲 🔲		303	■		■

YORK: *Holmwood House* W www.holmwoodhousehotel.co.uk £ | 14
114 Holgate Road, York YO24 4BB. 01904-626 183. FAX 01904-670 899.
This exceptional B&B, about 15 minutes' walk from the center of the city,
is a very comfortable place to stay. The breakfasts are delicious. 🖥 TV 🌐

YORK: *Middlethorpe Hall* W www.middlethorpe.com £££ | 30
Bishopthorpe Road, York YO23 1GB. 01904-641 241. FAX 01904-620 176.
A superbly restored and beautifully furnished manor just outside York, with
top-class standards and service. Facilities include a spa and sauna. 🖥 TV 🌐

SCOTLAND

ABERDEEN: *Maryculter House Hotel* @ sales@maryculterhousehotel.co.uk £ | 23
South Deeside Road, Maryculter, Aberdeen AB12 5GB. 01224-732 124. FAX 01224-733 510.
A historic hotel set in quiet, rural surroundings on the banks of the River Dee,
with riverside walks close by. 🖥 TV 🌐 limited. 🌐

EDINBURGH: *Duthus Lodge* W www.edinburghguesthouse.com £ | 7
5 West Coates, Edinburgh EH12 5JG. 0131-337 6876. FAX 0131-313 2264.
A splendid family-run Victorian establishment offering excellent
service in tastefully decorated and comfortable surroundings. 🖥 TV 🌐

EDINBURGH: *Apex Hotel* @ mail@apexhotels.co.uk ££ | 175
31–35 Grassmarket, Edinburgh EH1 2HS. 0131-300 3456. FAX 0131-220 5345.
A comfortable modern building in the historic Grassmarket, surrounded by
shops and eating places. Some bedrooms overlook the castle. 🖥 TV 🌐

EDINBURGH: *Melvin House Hotel* W www.melvinhouse.co.uk ££ | 22
3 Rothesay Terrace, Edinburgh EH3 7RY. & FAX 0131-225 5084.
FAX 0131-226 5085. @ reservations@melvinhouse.demon.co.uk
Situated within easy walking distance of Princes Street, this fine example of
Victorian architecture has a galleried library and elegant public rooms. 🖥 TV 🌐

EDINBURGH: *Channings* W www.channings.co.uk £££ | 46
15 South Learmonth Gardens, Edinburgh EH4 1EZ. 0131-315 2226. FAX 0131-332 9631.
Close to the city center, this hotel consists of five converted Edwardian houses.
Smart and well kept, Channings still preserves a friendly atmosphere. 🖥 TV 🌐

EDINBURGH: *Caledonian* W www.hilton.co.uk ££££ | 251
4 Princes Street, Edinburgh EH1 2AB. 0131-222 8888. FAX 0131-222 8889.
This hotel is an institution in Edinburgh. Centrally located, it is a popular
place for people to meet. The hotel restaurant is excellent. 🖥 TV 🌐

GLASGOW: *Babbity Bowster* W www.babbitybowster.com £ | 6
16–18 Blackfriars Street, Glasgow G1 1PE. 0141-552 5055. FAX 0141-552 7774.
An unusual hotel with immense character. Behind the finely
restored Adam façade are a few simple, neat bedrooms. 🖥 🌐

GLASGOW: *Malmaison* @ glasgow@malmaison.com ££ | 72
278 West George Street, Glasgow G2 4LL. 0141-572 1000. FAX 0141-572 1002.
Beautifully decorated rooms, all with satellite TV and CD players, provide
a stylish stay. The brasserie serves Mediterranean cuisine. 🖥 TV 🌐

GLASGOW: *One Devonshire Gardens* W www.onedevonshiregardens.com ££££ | 38
1 Devonshire Gardens, Glasgow G12 0UX. 0141-339 2001. FAX 0141-337 1663.
The ultimate smart town-hotel with lavish furnishings and stylish decor.
Service is first-class and there is the Michelin-starred Amaryllis restaurant. 🖥 TV 🌐

INVERNESS: *Dunain Park* W www.dunainparkhotel.co.uk £££ | 13
Inverness, Highland IV3 8JN. 01463-230 512. FAX 01463-224 532.
Surrounded by a large garden, this is a convenient and peaceful base
for exploring the area. The staff are very hospitable. 🖥 TV 🌐

ISLE OF SKYE: *Dunorin House Hotel* W www.dunorin.com £ | 10
Dunvegan, Isle of Skye, Highland IV55 8GZ. & FAX 01470-521 488.
Enjoying outstanding views of the Cuillin mountains, this family-run hotel
has a relaxing atmosphere and an excellent menu. ● Nov–Mar. 🖥 TV 🌐

ISLE OF SKYE: *Viewfield House* W www.viewfieldhouse.com £ | 12
Portree, Isle of Skye, Highland IV51 9EU. 01478-612 217. FAX 01478-613 517.
Guests are made very welcome in this rambling 200-year-old family house, with a
splendid Victorian interior and good dinner menu. ● mid-Oct–mid-Apr. 🖥 🌐 TV 🌐

Where to Eat in Great Britain

T HE BRITISH RESTAURANT SCENE has moved far from its once dismal
reputation. This is partly due to an influx of foreign chefs and
cooking styles; you can now sample a wide range of international
cuisine throughout Britain. Home-grown restaurateurs have risen
to the challenge of redeeming British food too, and the indigenous
cooking has improved out of all recognition since the early 1990s.

	GOOD WINE LIST	FIXED-PRICE MENU	VEGETARIAN DISHES	OUTDOOR TABLES

LONDON

WEST END: *Food for Thought* £
31 Neal Street, WC2. **Map** D3. (020-7836 0239.
A daily changing menu at this vegetarian restaurant features various quiches
and stir-fried vegetables, and there are always some dishes which cater for
vegans. If you bring your own wine, there is no corkage charge.

			●	

WEST END: *Harbour City* ££
46 Gerrard Street, W1. **Map** C3. (020-7439 7120.
An astonishing range of *dim sum* is served at lunchtimes by urbane staff. The
restaurant is very popular with the local Cantonese population. ● *Dec 24–26.* ✂ ✉

	●	■	●	

WEST END: *Melati* ££
21 Great Windmill Street, W1. **Map** C3. (020-7437 2745.
Service is swift at this authentic Indonesian restaurant spread over three
bustling floors. Try the excellent Singapore *laksa* (rice noodles with seafood
in coconut milk). Book ahead, or be prepared to queue. ● *Dec 25–26.* ✉

		■	●	

WEST END: *Mildred's* ££
45 Lexington Street, W1. **Map** D3. (020-7494 1634.
Excellent international vegetarian food is the specialty here, with dishes
such as white bean falafel in chili sauce, or tahini tortilla wraps. ✂

			●	■

WEST END: *Bertorelli's* £££
44a Floral Street, WC2. **Map** D3. (020-7836 3969.
This slick Italian operation close to the Opera House in Covent Garden is used
by pre-theater diners. Upstairs is a grand restaurant, while downstairs a simpler
café specializes in reliable pasta and pizza dishes. ● *Sun.* ⅙ ✉

	●	■	●	

WEST END: *The Gay Hussar* £££
2 Greek Street, W1. **Map** C3. (020-7437 0973.
One of London's few Hungarian eateries, with a wood-paneled and
velvet-upholstered interior. Specialties include chilled wild-cherry soup,
stuffed cabbage, pressed boar's head, and rich goulash with egg dumplings.
● *Sun, public hols.* ✉

		■	●	

WEST END: *Criterion Brasserie* ££££
Piccadilly Circus, W1. **Map** C3. (020-7930 0488.
The spectacular ceiling mosaics give the decor a Byzantine feel and
make this one of the most striking restaurant interiors in London.
The menu is modern European and very varied. ● *Sun lunch, public hols.* ✂ ✉

	●	■	●	

WEST END: *Mezzo* ££££
100 Wardour Street, W1. **Map** C3. (020-7314 4000.
Mezzo consists of two restaurants, a café, bakery, patisserie, and three bars.
Mezzonine offers good-value Asian and Mediterranean dishes, Mezzo more
sophisticated, classic dishes. ● *Sun, Dec 24–25, Jan 1.* ⅙ ✉

	●	■	●	

WEST END: *Quaglino's* £££££
16 Bury Street, SW1. **Map** C3. (020-7930 6767.
Modern British brasserie reflecting its 1930s origins, with interior design by Sir
Terence Conran, serving classic dishes such as calves liver and bacon. ✉

	●		●	

WEST END: *Green's Restaurant and Oyster Bar* £££££
36 Duke Street, St James's, SW1. **Map** C3. (020-7930 4566.
Amid classic "gentleman's club" decor, with banquettes and booths, fish and
oysters from County Cork are a particular feature. ● *Sun: May 1–Aug 31.* ✉

	●		●	

REGENT'S PARK: *Lemonia* ££
89 Regent's Park Road, NW1. **Map** B1. (020-7586 7454.
Traditional and modern Greek dishes are served in a brasserie-style
setting filled with plants. There is also a conservatory. ● *Dec 25–26.* ✉

			●	■

Map references refer to map of London on pp42–3

	GOOD WINE LIST	FIXED-PRICE MENU	VEGETARIAN DISHES	OUTDOOR TABLES

Price categories are for a three-course meal for one, half a bottle of house wine, and all unavoidable extra charges such as cover, service, and VAT:

£ under £15
££ £15–£25
£££ £25–£35
££££ £35–£50
£££££ over £50.

FIXED-PRICE MENU
A good value fixed-price meal, at lunch, dinner, or both, usually of three courses.

VEGETARIAN DISHES
Vegetarian specialties served, sometimes for both starters and main courses.

CREDIT CARDS
Major credit cards are accepted in those restaurants where the credit card symbol is shown.

HYDE PARK: *Hard Rock Café*   £££
150 Old Park Lane, W1. **Map** C4. [020-7629 0382.
Teenagers and would-be youths queue for this joint to eat good char-grilled burgers to the compelling beat of rock music. ● *Dec 25.* 🔁 🍽

HYDE PARK: *The Fifth Floor*   ££££
Harvey Nichols, 109–125 Knightsbridge, SW1. **Map** B4. [020-7235 5250.
A stylish store restaurant popular with shoppers, business diners, and lunching ladies. Modern British food is combined with Mediterranean and Asian influences. ● *dinner Sun; Dec 25–6.* ♿ 🍽

HYDE PARK: *Deca*   £££££
23 Conduit Street, W15. **Map** C3. [020-7493 7070.
An elegant setting for superstar chef, Nico Ladenis, to exercise his classical French gastronomic artistry. The wine list is superb. ● *public hols.* 🍽

HYDE PARK: *Le Gavroche*   £££££
43 Upper Brook Street, W1. **Map** B3. [020-7408 0881.
Le Gavroche is the high temple of haute cuisine – formal, clubby, and expensive. Eating here is a sophisticated, memorable experience. The food is flawless and the service first-class. ● *lunch, Sat, Sun, public hols; Dec 23–Jan 3.* 🍽

SOUTH KENSINGTON: *Cactus Blue*   ££
86 Fulham Road, SW3. **Map** A5. [020-7823 7858.
An innovative Southwest American menu is served amid Native American Indian art. A wide range of tequilas is available to sip and savor. ♿ 🍽

SOUTH KENSINGTON: *Salloos*   ££££
62–64 Kinnerton Street, SW1. **Map** B4. [020-7235 4444.
This upscale Pakistani restaurant offers a serene dining room, carefully prepared lamb dishes, and faultless service. ● *Sun, public hols.* 🍽

SOUTH KENSINGTON: *Le Suquet*   ££££
104 Draycott Avenue, SW3. **Map** B4. [020-7581 1785.
A lively but relaxed French seafood restaurant. Highlights include foil-wrapped sea bream, scallops in garlic, and the seafood platter. ● *Christmas week.* 🍽

SOUTH KENSINGTON: *Bibendum*   £££££
Michelin House, 81 Fulham Road, SW3. **Map** B4. [020-7581 5187.
A modern-international menu is served in the Bibendum's retro-chic interior. Risottos are especially recommended. The wine list can be pricey. ♿ 🍽

THE CITY AND SOUTHWARK: *The Place Below*   £
St. Mary-Le-Bow Church, Cheapside, EC2. **Map** E3. [020-7329 0789.
Lunchtime crowds pack the 11th-century crypt of this church for soups, salads, and hot vegetarian dishes, such as spinach and potato curry with dhal. ● *evenings, Sat, Sun, public hols.* 🔁 🍽

THE CITY AND SOUTHWARK: *Baltic*   £££
74 Blackfriars Road, SE1. **Map** E4. [020-7928 1111.
The Baltic serves East-European dishes spanning seafood, classic Georgian, Polish, Russian, and Hungarian cuisines. ♿ 🍽

THE CITY AND SOUTHWARK: *Oxo Tower*   ££££
Oxo Tower Wharf, Barge House Street, SE1. **Map** D3. [020-7803 3888.
This renovated version of the old Oxo stock cube company building now holds a brasserie, restaurant, and bar. Serving Asian-influenced food, the Tower offers superb views and a large terrace for summer dining. ♿ 🍽

NOTTING HILL: *Mandola*   ££
139–143 Westborne Grove, W11. [020-7229 4734.
Sudanese cuisine is served in a "traditional Khartoum" setting. Bring your own wine; there is a minimal corkage charge. ● *Mon lunch, Dec 25–26, Jan 1.* 🍽

<table>
<tr><td>

Price categories are for a three-course meal for one, half a bottle of house wine, and all unavoidable extra charges such as cover, service, and VAT:

£ under £15
££ £15–£25
£££ £25–£35
££££ £35–£50
£££££ over £50.

</td><td>

FIXED-PRICE MENU
A good value fixed-price meal, at lunch, dinner, or both, usually of three courses.

VEGETARIAN DISHES
Vegetarian specialties served, sometimes for both starters and main courses.

CREDIT CARDS
Major credit cards are accepted in those restaurants where the credit card symbol is shown.

</td></tr>
</table>

	GOOD WINE LIST	FIXED-PRICE MENU	VEGETARIAN DISHES	OUTDOOR TABLES
NOTTING HILL: *Kensington Place* **££££** 205 Kensington Church Street, W8. ☏ 020-7727 3184. A minimalist venue attracting a dedicated crowd and serving modern international cuisine with exciting reinterpretations. ● *Dec 25, Jan 1.* 🚻 🛇	●	■	●	
GREENWICH: *Spread Eagle* **£££** 1–2 Stockwell Street, Greenwich, SE10. ☏ 020-8853 2333. One of the few reliable restaurants in Greenwich. Set meals of hearty, straight-forward food are served in this dark and rather quaint 17th-century coaching inn. Try the excellent lamb with tomatoes and black olives. ● *lunch Mon–Sat.* 🛇 🛇	●	■	●	●
RICHMOND: *Nightingales* **£££** Petersham Hotel, Nightingale Lane, Richmond-upon-Thames. ☏ 020-8940 7471. A picturesque Thames view adds to the pleasure of the mostly traditional English cooking at this Victorian hotel. ● *dinner Sun & public hols.* 🛇 🛇	●	■	●	●
<div align="center">**SOUTHERN ENGLAND**</div>				
BRIGHTON: *Food for Friends* **£** 17–18 Prince Albert Street, Brighton. ☏ 01273-202 310. This vegetarian wholefood café in the Lanes offers friendly service, generous helpings, and imaginative cooking. The pine interior is decorated with pot plants. ● *Dec 25–26.* 🚭 🛇 🛇			●	
BRIGHTON: *Black Chapati* **£££** 12 Circus Parade, New England Road, Brighton. ☏ 01273-699 011. Adventurous and eclectic "Indian" cooking fizzes with original ideas in a stark café setting just outside the town center. The service is efficient, and the atmosphere friendly and welcoming. ● *Sun, Mon.* 🛇 🛇			●	
BRIGHTON: *Terre à Terre* **£££** 71 East Street, Brighton. ☏ 01273-729 051. Close to the pavilion, pier, and the Lanes, this vegetarian restaurant has an imaginative international menu. ● *lunch Mon.* 🚭 🛇 🛇			●	
CANTERBURY: *Marlowe's* **££** 55 St. Peter's Street, Canterbury, Kent. ☏ 01227-462 194. Friendly staff and a good atmosphere make Marlowe's a popular place to eat. The extensive menu includes a wide choice of Mexican specialties and vegetarian fare, as well as the traditional fish and chips. 🛇 🛇			●	
SALISBURY: *Harpers* **££** 6–7 Ox Row, Market Place, Salisbury, Wiltshire. ☏ 01722-333 118. A light, friendly first-floor restaurant offers unpretentious roasts and casseroles. Worth a visit for the views over historic Salisbury. ● *Sun evening.* 🚭 🛇	●	■	●	
<div align="center">**THE WEST COUNTRY AND WALES**</div>				
BATH: *The Bath Priory* **£££££** Weston Road, Bath. ☏ 01225-331 922. This palatial but relaxing country-house hotel in lovely gardens offers French and English cooking in a variety of themed rooms. 🚭 🛇 🛇	●	■	●	●
BRISTOL: *Lords* **££££** 43 Corn Street, Bristol. ☏ 0117-926 2658. French and Mediterranean influences combine in the delicious creations on offer in the basement of a bank building. The fish dishes are good, as is the choice of desserts. ● *Sun, lunch Sat; Dec 25–Jan 2, Easter week, last 2 weeks Aug.* 🛇	●	■	●	
BRISTOL: *Riverstation* **££££** The Grove, Bristol. ☏ 0117-914 4434. The old river police station is now this design-award winning restaurant. It serves freshly prepared European cuisine. ● *Dec 24–28.* 🚭 🛇 *limited.* 🛇	●	■	●	■

CARDIFF: *La Brasserie/Champers/Le Monde* £££
60 St. Mary Street, Cardiff. 029-2023 4134.
A bustling complex of French brasserie (fish and grills), tapas bar, and pub-like fish restaurant, all of which have a friendly atmosphere and good wines. ● Sun.

CARDIFF: *Woods Brasserie* £££
Pilotage Building, Stuart Street, Cardiff. 029-2049 2400.
A listed building with a view over Cardiff Bay. The food is modern British in style, with fish a specialty. ● Mon, dinner Sun; Dec 25–26 & 31, Jan 1.

DARTMOUTH: *Carved Angel* ££££
2 South Embankment, Dartmouth, Devon. 01803-832 465.
The menu here features local salmon and shellfish, but changes in winter to make use of local game, such as wild duck. The restaurant also sells its own brand of cooking oils, jams, and relishes. ● Mon, dinner Sun; Dec 24–26.

EXETER: *Thai Orchid* £££
5 Cathedral Yard, Exeter, Devon. 01392-214 215.
Authentic Thai cuisine is expertly served within a 15th-century building. Fresh orchids on every table. ● Sun, Dec 25–26, Jan 1.

LLANBERIS: *Y Bistro* £££
43–45 High Street, Llanberis, Gwynedd. 01286-871 278.
Hungry walkers flock to this restaurant at the foot of the Snowdon railroad. The menu has a good range of hearty main courses. ● Sun, lunch daily.

PENZANCE: *Harris's* £££
46 New Street, Penzance, Cornwall. 01736-364 408.
Game (when in season) and locally farmed meat are a match for the superb fish dishes that make this place a treat for diners. The lunch menu is good value. ● lunch Sun (dinner Sun in winter), Mon in winter.

ST. IVES: *Russets* ££££
18a Fore Street, St. Ives, Cornwall. 01736-794 700.
This seafood restaurant in St. Ives' main thoroughfare is casual, laid-back, and yet surprisingly lively. Local artists' work hangs from the walls. ● Jan.

DARTMOOR: *22 Mill Street* ££££
22 Mill Street, Chagford, Devon. 01647-432 244.
Modern European cuisine is served in this light and airy restaurant. Dishes include crab lasagne and roasted sea bass. ● lunch Wed–Sat; mid-Jan, first week Jun.

CENTRAL ENGLAND

BIRMINGHAM: *Chung Ying Garden* ££
17 Thorp Street, Birmingham. 0121-666 6622.
A flamboyant Cantonese food palace which offers a giant range of specialties, including light *dim sum* for the peckish.

CAMBRIDGE: *Restaurant Twenty-two* £££
22 Chesterton Road, Cambridge, Cambridgeshire. 01223-351 880.
Courteous service complements pleasingly inventive food in this restaurant's Victorian setting. Variety is one of the Twenty-two's key strengths, as the three-course menus change every month. ● Sun, Mon, lunch daily.

CAMBRIDGE: *Midsummer House* £££££
Midsummer Common, Cambridge, Cambridgeshire. 01223-369 299.
An intimate restaurant serving fixed-price menus of great complexity. Puddings are luscious and elaborate. ● Sun, Mon. limited.

OXFORD: *Al-Shami* ££
25 Walton Crescent, Oxford. 01865-310 066.
This bustling Lebanese restaurant serves *tabouleh, ful medames* (spiced fava beans with egg), and other favorites, with authentic desserts to follow.

OXFORD: *Cherwell Boathouse* £££
Bardwell Road, Oxford. 01865-552 746.
Located in a romantic punting spot on the River Cherwell, the Boathouse serves Mediterranean food with a twist. ● dinner Sun.

STRATFORD-UPON-AVON: *Opposition* ££
13 Sheep Street, Stratford-upon-Avon, Warwickshire. 01789-269 980.
A bustling bistro with live music offering simple pre-theater suppers. The daily specials are chalked on large blackboards. ● Sun.

For key to symbols see back flap

<table>
<tr><td colspan="2">

Price categories are for a three-course meal for one, half a bottle of house wine, and all unavoidable extra charges such as cover, service, and VAT:

£ under £15
££ £15–£25
£££ £25–£35
££££ £35–£50
£££££ over £50.

</td><td colspan="2">

FIXED-PRICE MENU
A good value fixed-price meal, at lunch, dinner, or both, usually of three courses.

VEGETARIAN DISHES
Vegetarian specialties served, sometimes for both starters and main courses.

CREDIT CARDS
Major credit cards are accepted in those restaurants where the credit card symbol is shown.

</td></tr>
</table>

	GOOD WINE LIST	FIXED-PRICE MENU	VEGETARIAN DISHES	OUTDOOR TABLES
STRATFORD-UPON-AVON: *Russons* £££ 8 Church Street, Stratford-upon-Avon, Warwickshire. 📞 01789-268 822. This rustic 16th-century buildng fits the Shakespearian location. A varied menu offers lunches, pre-theater dinners, and inexpensive meals. ● Sun, Mon.			●	
NORTHERN ENGLAND				
CHESTER: *Francs* ££ 14 Cuppin Street, Chester, Cheshire. 📞 01244-317 952. An ever-popular brasserie where French rock beats out over tasty *plats du jour*. Sundays are family days when under-10s eat for three pounds.		■	●	
DURHAM: *Bistro 21* £££ Aykley Heads House, Aykley Heads, Durham. 📞 0191-384 4354. The eclectic modern cooking here has enough variety to satisfy almost any taste. The atmosphere is relaxed and informal. ● Sun, public hols; Dec 25.	●	■	●	■
LAKE DISTRICT: *Moon* ££ 129 Highgate, Kendal, Cumbria. 📞 01539-729 254. A creative bistro with many vegetarian specialties. The style is pleasantly informal, but ingredients are always up to the mark. ● Mon, lunch daily.			●	
LAKE DISTRICT: *Quince and Medlar* ££ 13 Castlegate, Cockermouth, Cumbria. 📞 01900-823 579. Adventurous vegetarian cooking is served in a modest house near the castle. The menu is award-winning. ● Sun, Mon, lunch daily.			●	
LAKE DISTRICT: *Sheila's Cottage* ££ The Slack, Ambleside, Cumbria. 📞 01539-433 079. Tasty baking takes place in this converted stable-block cottage. A range of tea breads and cakes supplements savory dishes such as Cumbrian sugar-baked ham. ● Tue, dinner Wed; Nov–Easter; Dec 25–Jan 12.			●	
LAKE DISTRICT: *Miller Howe* ££££ Rayrigg Road, Windermere, Cumbria. 📞 01539-442 536. The main reasons for visiting this restaurant are the elaborate and theatrical dishes. Miller Howe is located in a beautiful hotel. ● lunch daily; Jan 6–25.	●	■	●	■
LEEDS: *Brasserie Forty-four* ££££ 44 The Calls, Leeds. 📞 0113 234 3232. This waterfront warehouse complex combines bright, sophisticated cooking and a lively atmosphere with stylish accommodation. ● lunch Sat, Sun.		■	●	
LIVERPOOL: *60 Hope Street* ££££ 60 Hope Street, Liverpool. 📞 0151-707 6060. FAX 0151-707 6016. Spread over three floors of a Georgian building, the modern interior is relaxed and vibrant, with quality service and superb food. ● Sun & public hols.	●	■	●	
MANCHESTER: *Siam Orchid* ££ 54 Portland Street, Manchester. 📞 0161-236 1388. Manchester's best Thai restaurant has a great range of dishes, including many vegetarian choices. There are also influences from other parts of Southeast Asia. Beware the fiery sauces; quell them with Singha beer. ● lunch Sat, lunch Sun.		■	●	
MANCHESTER: *Moss Nook* ££££ B5166 nr airport, Greater Manchester. 📞 0161-437 4778. Moss Nook offers a superb presentation of gastronomic medleys. Try the *menu surprise*, a selection of seven dishes chosen by the chef. ● Sun, Mon, lunch Sat.	●	■	●	
YORK: *Little Betty's* ££ 46 Stonegate, York. 📞 01904-622 865. A wide range of Yorkshire and Swiss specialties, home-made cakes, and light lunches are served in this medieval building. ● dinner daily.			●	

YORK: *Melton's* £££
7 Scarcroft Road, York. 01904-634341.
This small restaurant in a Victorian terrace is good value and welcoming, serving varied Anglo-French food. *dinner Sun, lunch Mon.* limited.

SCOTLAND

ABERDEEN: *The Silver Darling* £££
Pocra Quay, Footdee, North Pier, Aberdeen. 01224-576 229.
Located on the north side of Aberdeen harbor, this restaurant offers superb seafood, which varies with the daily catch. *Sun, lunch Sat; Dec 24–Jan 6.*

AVIEMORE: *Corrour House Hotel* £££
Inverdruie, nr Aviemore, Inverness. 01479-810 220.
A family-run Victorian hotel with superb views of the Cairngorm Mountains. Traditional Scottish fare is served in a pretty setting. *mid-Nov–Dec.*

EDINBURGH: *Susie's Diner* £
53 West Nicolson Street, Edinburgh. 0131-667 8729.
A friendly wholefood vegetarian café centrally located near Edinburgh University. The good-quality ingredients are impeccably flavored.

EDINBURGH: *Daniel's* ££
88 Commercial Street, Leith, Edinburgh. 0131-553 5933.
One of the best of the new conservatory restaurants, situated opposite the Scottish Office. Serves hearty Alsace cuisine. *Jan 1, Dec 25.*

EDINBURGH: *Atrium and Blue Bar Café* £££
10 Cambridge Street, Edinburgh. 0131-228 8882.
An ultra-stylish interior by the Traverse Theatre complements the light, simple, but exciting cooking here. This is the cutting edge of modern British cookery; Mediterranean influences dominate. *Sun.* limited.

EDINBURGH: *Martin's* £££
70 Rose Street North Lane, Edinburgh. 0131-225 3106.
An excellent city-center restaurant offering a range of imaginative, contemporary Scottish cuisine. The superb Celtic cheeseboard is highly recommended. *Sun, Mon, lunch Sat; Dec 24–Jan 20.*

GLASGOW: *Willow Tea Room* £
217 Sauchiehall Street, Glasgow. 0141-332 0521.
Tucked away above a jeweler's shop, this reconstructed Mackintosh tearoom has a good range of light lunches and afternoon teas. *evenings, Jan 1–2, Dec 25–6.*

GLASGOW: *Camerons, Glasgow Hilton* ££££
1 William Street, Glasgow. 0141-204 5511.
This is theme-park Scotland, but both food and service are beyond reproach at this business hotel and restaurant. *Sun, lunch Sat.*

GLASGOW: *Ubiquitous Chip* ££££
12 Ashton Lane, Glasgow. 0141-334 5007.
The light-hearted individuality suggested by the name reveals itself most in the upstairs bistro. The food is good, with hugely varied treatments of Scottish fare.

INVERNESS: *Adam's Dining Room* ££££
Culloden House Hotel, off A96 at Culloden, Inverness. 01463-790 461.
The food is country-house style at this historic hotel, with sauces, jellies, sorbets, mousses, and fresh meat, game, and fish dishes.

ISLE OF SKYE: *The Three Chimneys* ££££
Colbost, nr Dunvegan, Isle of Skye. 01470-511 258. FAX 01470-511 358.
Once a stone-built crofter's cottage, this award-winning restaurant offers seafood and game lovingly prepared with fresh local ingredients. Accommodations are also available. *last three weeks in Jan.*

ST. ANDREWS: *The Peat Inn* ££££
On B940 nr St. Andrews, Fife. 01334-840 206.
Highly accomplished modern cooking with regional produce makes this one of the best hotel-restaurants in Britain. *Sun, Mon.*

STIRLING: *The River House Restaurant* ££
Castle Business Park, Craigforth, Stirling. 01786-465 577.
This restaurant extends out over a lake to offer an interesting venue. The modern ambience has food to match. *Dec 25–26, Jan 1.*

For key to symbols see back flap

IRELAND

IT IS EASY TO SEE IRELAND *as a lush, green island dotted with quaint, thatched cottages and friendly pubs filled with music, wit, and poetry. Despite the contrasting reality of rapid economic growth and fundamental political change, the tourist industry helps sustain this image of rural bliss, and the genuine good humor of the people invariably makes Ireland a most welcoming place to visit.*

History and religion have created two communities in Ireland, with the Protestant majority in the North determined to remain part of the United Kingdom. Bombings and shootings in Northern Ireland have tarnished the world's view of the country, but the Good Friday Agreement of 1998 has brought new hopes for peace.

Despite the Troubles, the Irish retain a positive attitude that is both easy-going and forward-looking. Both parts of the island have young, highly educated populations. The Republic of Ireland, formerly among the poorer countries of the European Union, has become one of its success stories. EU subsidies have improved the transport infrastructure and many multinationals, especially computing, chemical, and telecommunications companies, have established subsidiaries in Ireland. Since 1990, the economy has seen annual economic growth of between 7 and 11 percent. Young people are not only staying in Ireland, but actually returning from abroad. Despite this high-tech revolution, agriculture remains a mainstay of the economy, with dairy cattle feeding on rich meadowlands and sheep grazing on the poorer upland pastures. The traditional Irish talent for breeding and training racehorses is undiminished. Tourism thrives with more than 5.5 million visitors to the Republic each year and Dublin is one of Europe's hotspots for a weekend break.

HISTORY

In the past Ireland's isolation cut it off from many of the major events of European history. Roman legions never invaded and the country's early history is shrouded in myths of warring gods and heroic High Kings.

Dingle, a lively, friendly fishing harbor in southwest Ireland

◁ **The ruined Rock of Cashel, once a fortress of the kings of Munster, then seat of a medieval bishopric**

O'Connell Street in Dublin just after the Easter Rising of 1916

The bellicose Celtic tribes were quick to embrace Christianity in the 5th century AD. Until the Viking invasions of the 9th century, Ireland enjoyed an era of relative peace. Huge monasteries were founded, where scholarship and the arts flourished. The Vikings never succeeded in gaining control of the island, but in 1169 the English arrived with greater ambitions. Many Irish chiefs submitted to Henry II of England, and his Anglo-Norman knights carved out large fiefdoms for themselves.

Direct English control was usually limited to the "Pale", the well-defended area around Dublin. Matters changed when in 1532 Henry VIII broke with the Catholic church. Ireland became a battleground between Irish Catholics and English armies dispatched to crush resistance. Irish lands were confiscated and granted to Protestants from England and Scotland. England's conquest was completed with William of Orange's victory over James II in 1690. During the English Ascendancy, repressive Penal Laws denied Irish Catholics the most basic freedoms, but opposition to English rule was never totally quashed.

The Famine of 1845–8 was the bleakest period of Irish history. Over two million either died or were forced to emigrate. A campaign for Home Rule gathered strength, but it took the war of 1919–21 to force the issue. The Treaty of 1921 divided the island in two. The South became the Irish Free State, gaining full independence in 1937. The Catholic minority in Northern Ireland suffered under Protestant rule and in the late 1960s began to stage civil rights protests. The situation quickly got out of hand. The British sent in troops and acts of terrorism and sectarian violence took the place of reasoned dialogue.

KEY DATES IN IRISH HISTORY

8th century BC Humans first inhabit Ireland

600 BC Arrival of Celts from Europe and Britain

AD 432 St. Patrick brings Christianity to Ireland

795 First Viking invasion

999 Viking king of Dublin defeated by Irish High King, Brian Boru

1169 Anglo-Norman invasion; Henry II of England proclaims himself overlord of Ireland

1541 Henry VIII declared King of Ireland

1690 William of Orange defeats James II at Battle of the Boyne

1695 Penal Laws restrict civil rights of Catholics

1801 Act of Union with Britain

1828 Catholic Emancipation Act

1845–8 Potato Famine leaves one million people dead and prompts massive emigration

1921 Anglo-Irish treaty divides Ireland into the Irish Free State and Northern Ireland

1937 The Irish Free State becomes entirely independent of Britain and is renamed Éire

1969 British troops sent to Northern Ireland

1998 Good Friday Agreement sets out framework for self-government in Northern Ireland

LANGUAGE AND CULTURE

Ireland was a Gaelic-speaking nation until the 16th century, when English rule sent the language into decline. The Republic today is officially bilingual and 35 percent of adults claim to know some Gaelic. Many speak it fluently, but perhaps only 3 percent use it regularly. Some degree of knowledge is needed for university entrance and careers in the public sector. Irish culture, on the other hand, is in no danger of being eroded. The people have a genuine love of legends, literature, and songs, and festivals play an important part in community life. Traditional and modern music flourishes, whether at well-attended concerts or impromptu sessions in the local pub.

Traditional Irish dance

Exploring Ireland

Dublin is Ireland's chief attraction, a small friendly capital with most of its sights and lively nightlife concentrated in the center. Elsewhere the pace of life is slow and the country's great appeal is in its landscape: from the lush green pastures, bogs, and lakes of the center of the island to dramatic mountains and bleak, rocky headlands in the southwest. Touring by car is the most convenient way to explore Ireland. In Northern Ireland roads are generally good; in the Republic they can be agreeably empty, but vary enormously in quality.

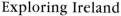

Jaunting car for hire in Killarney

SIGHTS AT A GLANCE

Aran Islands **15**
Belfast **16**
Bunratty Castle **12**
Cashel **7**
Castletown House **2**
Connemara **14**
Cork **8**
Dingle **11**
DUBLIN pp112–121 **1**
Galway **13**

Giant's Causeway **17**
Glendalough **4**
Kilkenny **5**
Killarney **10**
Kinsale **9**
Newgrange **3**
Old Bushmills Distillery **18**
Ulster-American Folk Park **19**
Waterford **6**

KEY

✈ Airport
⚓ Ferry port
— Highway
— Major road
— Railroad
▪▪▪ International border

0 km _____ 35

0 miles _____ 35

Dublin ●

ALTHOUGH IT IS a fairly small city, Ireland's capital is famous for its many pubs, and its rich cultural heritage attracts millions of visitors each year. The Liffey river runs through the middle of the city, and is the original source of its prosperity. The first harbor in Dublin was established in the early 9th century, when Vikings founded one of their largest settlements outside Scandinavia on the site of the present city. Since then, it has suffered wars and conflict over many centuries. In the 20th century Dublin established its own identity and today it is a thriving, modern city, rich in history and proud of its past. Dublin and its surrounding county have a population of just over one million.

SIGHTS AT A GLANCE

Christ Church Cathedral ⑨
Dublin Castle ⑦
Dublinia ⑩
Grafton Street ⑤
The Liffey ⑪
Merrion Square ②
National Gallery ③
National Museum ④
O'Connell Street ⑫
Parnell Square ⑬
St. Patrick's Cathedral ⑧
Temple Bar ⑥
Trinity College ①

Greater Dublin
(see inset map)
Guinness Store House ⑭
Phoenix Park ⑮

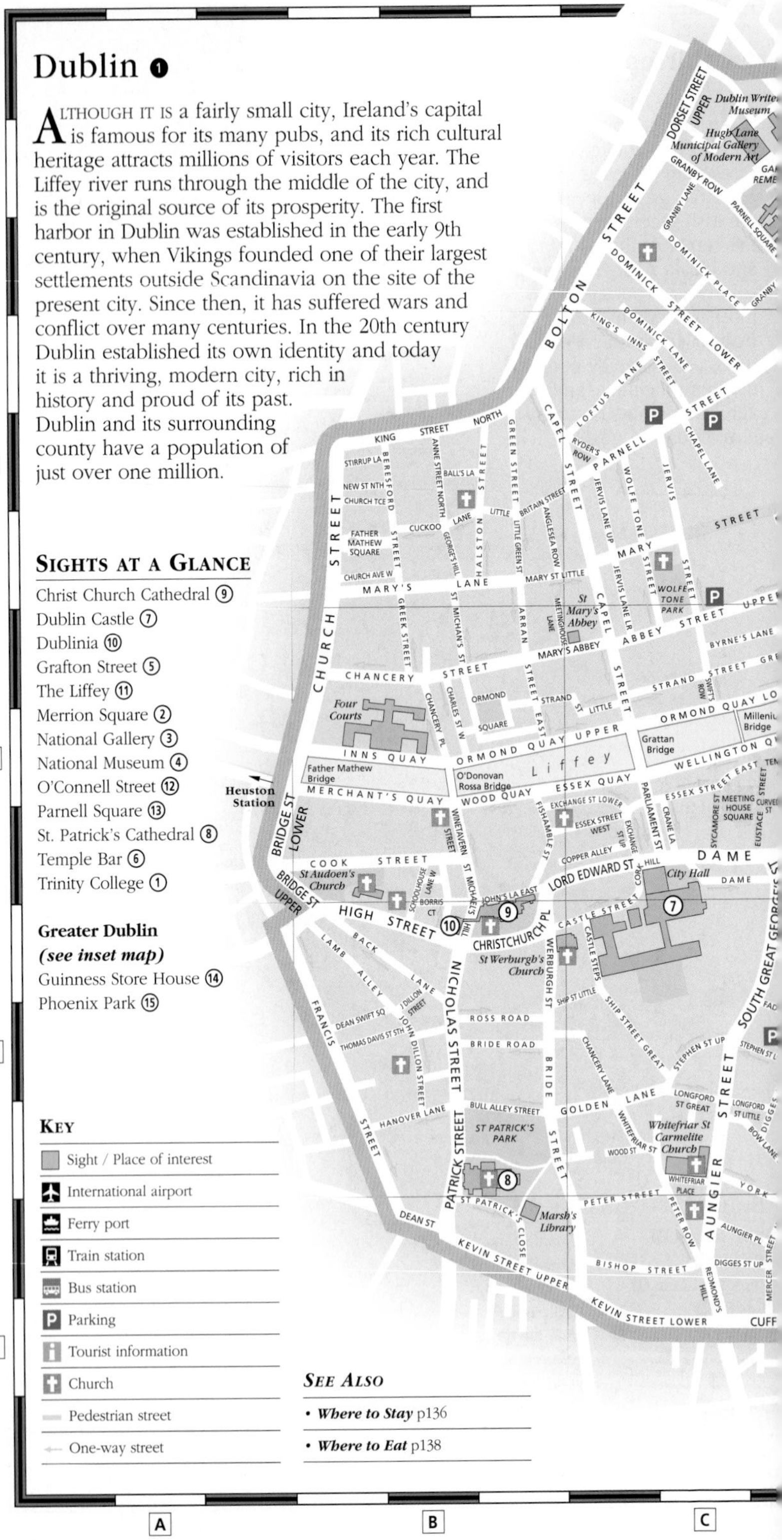

KEY

▨	Sight / Place of interest
✈	International airport
⛴	Ferry port
🚆	Train station
🚌	Bus station
P	Parking
ℹ	Tourist information
✝	Church
—	Pedestrian street
←	One-way street

SEE ALSO

• *Where to Stay* p136

• *Where to Eat* p138

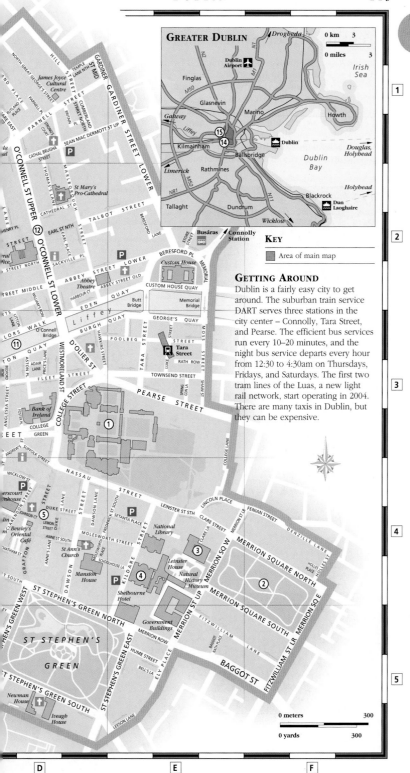

GREATER DUBLIN

Drogheda

0 km 3

0 miles 3

Dublin Airport

Finglas

Galway

Glasnevin

Marino

Howth

Irish Sea

Liffey

Kilmainham

Dublin

Ballsbridge

Dublin Bay

Douglas, Holyhead

Limerick

Rathmines

Holyhead

Tallaght

Dundrum

Blackrock

Dun Laoghaire

Wicklow

KEY

Area of main map

GETTING AROUND

Dublin is a fairly easy city to get around. The suburban train service DART serves three stations in the city center – Connolly, Tara Street, and Pearse. The efficient bus services run every 10–20 minutes, and the night bus service departs every hour from 12:30 to 4:30am on Thursdays, Fridays, and Saturdays. The first two tram lines of the Luas, a new light rail network, start operating in 2004. There are many taxis in Dublin, but they can be expensive.

0 meters 300

0 yards 300

Street-by-Street: Southeast Dublin

T HE AREA AROUND COLLEGE GREEN, dominated by the
façades of the Bank of Ireland and Trinity College,
is very much the heart of Dublin. The alleys and malls
cutting across busy pedestrianized Grafton Street boast
many of Dublin's better stores, hotels, and restaurants.
Just off Kildare Street are the Irish Parliament, the
National Library, and the National Museum. To escape
the city bustle many head for sanctuary in St. Stephen's
Green, which is overlooked by fine Georgian buildings.

Dublin ←
Castle

The Bank of Ireland
is a grand Georgian
edifice, originally built
as the Irish Parliament.

Statue of Molly
Malone (1988)

Grafton Street
Bewley's Oriental Café is the social hub of
this busy pedestrian street, alive with
talented street performers (see p117).

St. Ann's Church
This striking façade
of the 18th-century
church was
added in 1868.
The interior
features lovely
stained-glass
windows.

The Mansion House
has been the offical
residence of Dublin's
Lord Mayor since 1715.

Fusiliers' Arch (1907)

St. Stephen's Green
This relaxing city park is surrounded by
many fine buildings. In summer, lunchtime
concerts attract tourists and workers alike.

/ O'Connell
/ Bridge

★ **Trinity College**
*The focal point of
Parliament Square,
the largest of Trinity's
spacious quadrangles,
is the elegant Italianate
bell tower known as the
"Campanile". Designed
by Sir Charles Lanyon,
it was erected in 1853*
(see p116).

NASSAU STREET

FREDRICK STREET

LESWORTH STREET

KILDARE STREET

National Library
*Saintly cherubs appear on the frieze
around the library's magnificent
old reading room, once a hangout
of novelist James Joyce.*

Leinster House
was taken over
as the seat
of the Irish
Parliament
in 1922.

★ **National Museum**
*The collection of Irish
antiquities includes this
mysterious bronze object
from the 2nd century AD,
known as the Petrie
Crown* (see p117).

The Shelbourne Hotel
*Built in 1867, the hotel dominates
the north side of St. Stephen's
Green. It is popular with tourists
and locals for afternoon tea.*

STAR SIGHTS
★ Trinity College
★ National Museum

0 meters   50

0 yards   50

KEY

– – – Suggested route

**View down the central aisle of
Trinity College's Old Library**

Trinity College ①

College Green. **01-608 2308.**
DART to Tara Street. **10, 14, 15,
45, 46, 48 & many others. Old Library
and Treasury** ☐ *daily (Oct–May:
pm only Sun).* ● *10 days at Christmas.*
W www.tcd.ie/library

Trinity was founded in 1592
by Elizabeth I on the site
of an Augustinian monastery
as a bastion of Protestantism.
It was not until the 1970s that
Catholics started entering the
university. Its cobbled quads
and lawns still have a monastic
feel, providing a pleasant
haven in the heart of the city.
In front of the main entrance
on College Green are statues
of two of Trinity's most famous
18th-century students, playwright Oliver Goldsmith and

political writer Edmund Burke.
Literary alumni of more recent
times include the playwrights
Oscar Wilde (1854–1900) and
Samuel Beckett (1906–89).

The oldest surviving part of
the college is the red-brick
building (the Rubrics) on the
east side of Library Square,
built around 1700. The Old
Library itself dates from 1732.
Its spectacular Long Room
measures 64 m (210 ft) from
end to end. It houses 200,000
antiquarian texts,
marble busts of
scholars and the
oldest harp in
Ireland. Below
the Library is the
Treasury, where
the college's
most precious
volumes – the
beautifully
illuminated
manuscripts
produced in
Ireland from the
7th to the 9th
century – are
kept. The most
famous, the *Book of Kells (see
p125)*, may have been created
by monks from Iona, who fled
to Kells in 806 after a Viking
raid. The scribes embellished
the text with intricate patterns
as well as human figures and
animals. Almost as fine is the
Book of Durrow, which dates
from the late 7th century.

**Portrait of St Matthew
from the Book of Kells**

Merrion Square ②

DART to Pearse. *5, 7A, 8, 10,
45 & many others.*

Merrion square is one of
Dublin's largest and
grandest Georgian squares.
Covering about 5 ha (12 acres),
the square was laid out by
John Ensor around 1762.

On the west side are the
impressive façades of the
Natural History Museum, the
National Gallery
and the front
garden of
Leinster House,
seat of the Dáil
and the Seanad
(the two houses
of the Irish
Parliament). The
other three sides
of the square are
lined with lovely
Georgian town
houses. Many
have brightly
painted doors
and original
features such as
wrought-iron balconies,
ornate doorknockers and fan-
lights. The oldest and finest
houses are on the north side.

Many of the houses – now
predominantly used as office
space – have plaques detailing
famous former occupants,
such as Catholic emancipation
leader Daniel O'Connell, who

Façade of Trinity College, Dublin, the Republic's most prestigious university

Georgian town houses overlooking Merrion Square gardens

lived at No. 58, and poet W.B. Yeats (No. 82). Oscar Wilde spent his childhood at No. 1.

The attractive central park has colorful flower and shrub beds. In the 1840s it served a grim function as a soup kitchen, feeding the hungry during the Great Famine.

National Gallery ③

Merrion Square West. **☎** 01-661 5133.
☒ DART to Pearse. **🚌** 5, 7, 13, 44, 47, 48 & 48A. **◯** daily (pm only Sun).
◯ Good Fri & Dec 24–26. **✦ ⬤ ⬤**
⬤ ⬤ 🍴 ⬤ www.nationalgallery.ie

THIS PURPOSE-BUILT GALLERY was opened to the public in 1864. More than 600 works are on display and, although there is a strong emphasis on Irish landscapes and portraits, all major schools of European painting are represented. The ground-floor rooms show Irish and British art, including a whole section dedicated to the works of Jack B. Yeats (1871–1957). There are also paintings by his father and sisters.

Over the years the gallery has benefited from many generous bequests. Playwright George Bernard Shaw left a third of his estate to it. The Shaw Fund Gallery is an elegant hall, lined with full-length portraits, dating from the 17th century onward, and lit by magnificent Waterford Crystal chandeliers.

On the first floor works are hung in broadly chronological order according to nation. The Italian, French, Flemish and Dutch collections

account for most of the space. Caravaggio's *The Taking of Christ*, a major attraction, hung unrecognized for years in the Dublin Jesuit House of Study, until rediscovered in 1990.

National Museum ④

Kildare St. **☎** 01-677 7444. **☒** DART to Pearse. **🚌** 10, 11, 13 and many others. **◯** Tue–Sat & 2–5pm Sun.
◯ Good Fri & Dec 25. **✦ ⬤ ⬤ ⬤**
ground floor only. **🅦** www.museum.ie

THE NATIONAL MUSEUM of Ireland was built in the 1880s to the design of Sir Thomas Deane. Its splendid domed rotunda features marble pillars and a zodiac mosaic floor. The ground floor holds *Ór – Ireland's Gold*, a collection of Bronze Age finds, including many beautiful pieces of jewelry. Objects from the later Iron Age Celtic period are on display in the Treasury. There are also many well-known treasures from the era of Irish Christianity (*see pp124–5*).

The Road to Independence exhibition covers events between 1900 and 1921. The objects associated with the 1916 Easter Rising include the Republican flag that flew

***The Taking of Christ* by Caravaggio (1602), one of the highlights of the National Gallery**

briefly over Dublin's General Post Office in O'Connell Street (*see p120*).

The first floor houses Viking artifacts and the Ancient Egypt gallery. The Viking exhibition features coins, pottery, and swords excavated in the 1970s from the Viking settlement, discovered beside the Liffey at Wood Quay near Christ Church Cathedral (*see p119*).

The Museum has another branch at Benburb Street, west of the city center. Housed in the vast Collins Barracks, established in 1700 by William III, this annex is a more modern museum, and is gradually being extended to fill all four barrack blocks. The principal exhibits are the museum's collections of furniture, silver, and scientific instruments.

7th-century plaque depicting the Crucifixion, National Museum

Grafton Street ⑤

🚌 14, 15, 46 & many others.

THE SPINE OF DUBLIN'S most stylish shopping district runs south from College Green to the glass St. Stephen's Green Shopping Centre. This busy pedestrianized strip, with its energetic buskers and talented street theater artists, boasts one of Dublin's best department stores, Brown Thomas, and the popular lunch and coffee venue, Bewley's Oriental Café.

At the junction with Nassau Street is a statue by Jean Rynhart of *Molly Malone* (1988), the celebrated "cockles and mussels" street trader of the well-known Irish folk song.

Shoppers in Temple Bar

Temple Bar ⑥

🚌 11, 16A, 16B, 19A. ⛪ St. Andrews church (01-605 7700). **Project** 39 East Essex Street. 📞 01-881 9613. ⏱ 11am–7pm Mon–Sat; shows nightly. 🖥 ♿

THE AREA OF cobbled streets between Dame Street and the Liffey are named after Sir William Temple who acquired the land in the early 1600s. The term "bar" meant a riverside path. In the 1800s it was home to small businesses, but over the years went into decline. In the early 1960s the land was bought up with plans for redevelopment. Artists and retailers took short-term leases but stayed on when the plans were scrapped and Temple Bar prospered. Today it is an exciting place, with restaurants, bars, clubs, shops, and galleries. Organizations based here include the **Irish Film Centre**, which has two screens, as well as a bookshop and café, **Project**, a contemporary arts center for theater, dance, music, film, and visual art, and the **Gallery of Photography**, the only Irish art gallery devoted solely to photographs.

St. Patrick's Cathedral ⑧

St. Patrick's Close. 📞 01-475 4817. 🚌 49A, 49B, 54A, 65A, 65B, 123. ⏱ daily. 🖼 ♿

IRELAND'S LARGEST CHURCH was founded beside a sacred well where St. Patrick is said to have baptized converts around AD 450. It was originally just a wooden chapel, but in 1192 Archbishop John Comyn commissioned a magnificent new stone structure.

Jonathan Swift, Dean of St. Patrick's from 1713

The cathedral is 91 m (300 ft) long; at the western end is a 43-m (141-ft) tower, restored by Archbishop Minot in 1370 and now known as Minot's Tower. Much of the present building dates back to work completed between 1254 and 1270. Thanks to the generosity of Sir Benjamin

Dublin Castle ⑦

FOR SEVEN CENTURIES Dublin Castle was a symbol of English rule, ever since the Anglo-Normans built a fortress here in the 13th century. Nothing remains of the original structure except the much-modified Record Tower. After a fire in 1684, the Surveyor-General, Sir William Robinson, laid down the plans for the Upper and Lower Castle Yards in their present form. On the first floor of the south side of the Upper Yard are the luxurious State Apartments, formerly home to the British-appointed Viceroys of Ireland. They are still used for state occasions.

Picture Gallery

Entrance to State Apartments

Bermingham Tower has been adapted to house the magnificent Chester Beatty Library and Gallery of Oriental Art.

Octagonal Tower (c. 1812)

Record Tower

St. Patrick's Hall
This grand hall is hung with banners of the defunct Knights of St. Patrick. The 18th-century ceiling paintings are allegories of the relationship between Britain and Ireland.

The Throne Room dates from 1740. The throne itself is said to have been presented to William of Orange after his victory at the Battle of the Boyne (see p110).

Guinness, the cathedral underwent extensive restoration during the 1860s.

The interior is dotted with memorials. The most elaborate is the one erected in 1632 by Richard Boyle, Earl of Cork, in memory of his second wife Katherine. It is decorated with painted carvings of members of the Boyle family. Others remembered in the church include the harpist Turlough O'Carolan (1670–1738) and Douglas Hyde (1860–1949), Ireland's first President.

Many visitors come to see the memorials associated with Jonathan Swift (1667–1745), Dean of St. Patrick's and a scathing satirist, best known as the author of *Gulliver's Travels*. In the north transept is "Swift's Corner," which has various memorabilia such as an altar table and a bookcase holding his death mask. On the southwest side of the nave, two brass plates mark his grave and that of his beloved "Stella", Ester Johnson.

Christ Church Cathedral ⑨

Christchurch Place. **℡** *01-677 8099.* 🚌 *49A, 49B, 50, 54A, 65A, 65B, 66, 77, 123.* ☐ *daily.* 🚻 *limited.*

THE CATHEDRAL was commissioned in 1172 by Richard de Clare, known as Strongbow, the Anglo-Norman conqueror of Dublin, and by Archbishop Laurence O'Toole. It replaced an earlier wooden church built by the Vikings. At the Reformation, the cathedral passed to the Protestant Church of Ireland. By the middle of the 19th century it was in very bad repair, but was completely remodeled by architect George Street in the 1870s. Even so, the north wall, the one closest to the river, still leans out alarmingly as a result of subsidence. As part of the remodeling, the Old

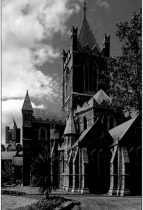

Christ Church Cathedral viewed from the east, with the Old Synod Hall behind

Synod Hall was built and linked to the cathedral by an attractive covered bridge.

In the dark, dusty crypt are fragments of monuments and stonework removed from the cathedral during its restoration. There are also the mummified bodies of a cat and a rat found in an organ pipe in the 1860s.

The nave has some fine early Gothic arches. At the west end is a memorial known as the Strongbow Monument. The large effigy in chain armor is probably not Strongbow, but the curious half-figure beside it may be part of his original tomb. The Chapel of St. Laud houses a casket containing the heart of St. Laurence O'Toole.

Dublinia ⑩

St. Michael's Hill. **℡** *01-679 4611.* 🚌 *49A, 49B, 54A, 123.* ☐ *daily.* ● *Dec 24–26 & bank hols.* 🚻 🚻 **w** www.dublinia.ie

HOUSED IN the Neo-Gothic Synod Hall, which is linked by a bridge to Christ Church Cathedral, the Dublinia covers the period of Dublin's history from the arrival of the Anglo-Normans in 1170 to the closure of the monasteries in the 1540s. An audiotape-guided tour takes visitors through lifesize reconstructions of the medieval city. Up until 1983, the Synod Hall was home to the ruling body of the Church of Ireland.

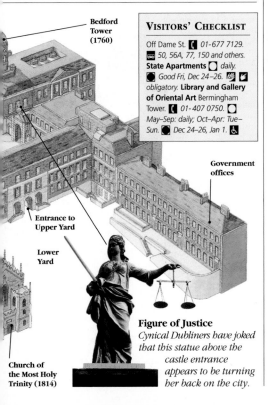

Bedford Tower (1760)

Entrance to Upper Yard

Lower Yard

Church of the Most Holy Trinity (1814)

Government offices

VISITORS' CHECKLIST

Off Dame St. **℡** *01-677 7129.* 🚌 *50, 56A, 77, 150 and others.* **State Apartments** ☐ *daily.* ● *Good Fri, Dec 24–26.* 🚻 🚻 *obligatory.* **Library and Gallery of Oriental Art** Bermingham Tower. **℡** *01-407 0750.* ☐ *May–Sep: daily; Oct–Apr: Tue–Sun.* ● *Dec 24–26, Jan 1.* 🚻

Figure of Justice
Cynical Dubliners have joked that this statue above the castle entrance appears to be turning her back on the city.

James Gandon's Four Courts overlooking the River Liffey

The Liffey ⑪

🚌 25, 25A, 51, 66, 66A, 67, 67A, 68, 69 and many others.

THOUGH MODEST in size compared with the rivers of other capital cities, the Liffey features strongly in Dubliners' everyday lives and holds a special place in their affections. The handiest pedestrian link between Temple Bar *(see p118)* and the north of the city is **Ha'penny Bridge**. This attractive, cast-iron bridge, originally called Wellington Bridge, was opened in 1816. Its official name now is the Liffey Bridge. Its better-known nickname comes from the toll of a halfpenny levied on it up until 1919.

The two most impressive buildings on the Liffey are the **Custom House** and the **Four Courts**, both designed by

Carved head representing the River Liffey on the Custom House

James Gandon at the end of the 18th century. In 1921, supporters of Sinn Fein celebrated their election victory by setting light to the Custom House, seen as a symbol of British imperialism. The building was not fully restored until 1991, when it reopened as government offices. A series of 14 magnificent heads by Edward Smyth, personifying Ireland's rivers and the Atlantic Ocean, form the keystones of arches and entrances.

The Four Courts suffered a similar fate during the Irish Civil War of 1921–2, when it was bombarded by government troops after being seized by anti-Treaty rebels. Here too, the buildings were restored to their original design. A copper-covered lantern dome rises above a Corinthian portico crowned with the figures of Moses, Justice and Mercy.

O'Connell Street ⑫

🚌 3, 10, 11, 13, 16A, 22A, 22B, 120 and many others.

DUBLIN'S MAIN thoroughfare, formerly called Sackville Street, was renamed in 1922 after Daniel O'Connell, who was known as the "Liberator"

The monument to Daniel O'Connell

for his tireless campaigns for Catholic rights in the 19th century. The street was laid out in the 18th century as an elegant residential parade, but the construction of Carlisle (now O'Connell) Bridge in 1790 turned it into the city's principal north-south route. As a result, little remains of its intended grandeur.

A few venerable buildings survive, including the **General Post Office**. Built in 1818, the GPO became a symbol of the 1916 Easter Rising. Members of the Irish Volunteers and Irish Citizen Army seized the building on Easter Monday, and Patrick Pearse read out the Proclamation of the Irish Republic from its steps. The rebels remained inside for a week, but shelling from the British eventually forced them out. During the following weeks, 14 of the leaders were caught and shot. Inside the building is a sculpture of the mythical Irish hero Cuchulainn, dedicated to those who died.

A walk up the central mall is the most enjoyable way to inspect the series of sculptures lining the route. At the south end stands a massive memorial to Daniel O'Connell, unveiled in 1882. In the middle is the Monument of Light, an elegant stainless steel spire erected in 2003. At the north end is the obelisk-shaped monument to Charles Stewart Parnell (1846–91).

Parnell Square ⑬

🚌 3, 10, 11A, 13, 16A, 16B, 19A, 22A, 22B. **Dublin Writers Museum** 18 Parnell Sq North. 📞 01-872 2077. ⬜ daily. ⬤ 25 & 26 Dec. 📷 **Hugh Lane Municipal Gallery** Charlemont House. 📞 01-874 1903. ⬜ Tue–Sun. ⬤ Dec 24–25 & public hols. 📷

THE SQUARE at the top of O'Connell Street looks sadly neglected. Even so, it contains a number of noteworthy sights, including the **Rotunda Hospital**, Europe's first purpose-built maternity hospital, founded in 1745. Its chapel has some fine Rococo stuccowork. The former grand supper room of the hospital is now the **Gate Theatre**, famous for producing new plays.

On the north side of the square, two grand 18th-century townhouses have been converted into museums: the **Dublin Writers Museum**, devoted to Irish literature, and the **Hugh Lane Municipal Gallery of Modern Art**. The latter houses the Impressionist paintings bequeathed to Dublin Corporation by Sir Hugh Lane, who died on the torpedoed liner *Lusitania* in 1915. The square also contains a **Garden of Remembrance** opened in 1966 on the 50th anniversary of the Easter Rising.

Arthur Guinness

Guinness Store House ⑭

St. James's Gate, Dublin 8. 📞 01-408 4800. 🚌 51B, 78A, 123. ⬜ daily. ⬤ Good Fri, Dec 24–26, Jan 1. 📷 ♿ 🅿 🍴 📷
Ⓦ www.guinnessstorehouse.com

GUINNESS is a black beer, known as "stout," renowned for its distinctive malty flavor and smooth creamy head. The Guinness brewery site at St James's Gate is the largest brewery in Europe and exports beers to more than 120 countries.

The World of Guinness exhibition is housed in a 19th-century warehouse, used for hop storage until the 1950s. It chronicles 200 years of brewing at St James's Gate. The tour starts in a Victorian kieve (or mash filter), and goes on to examine all other stages of the brewing process. Displays show how production methods have changed over the years since 1759, when Arthur Guinness took over the backstreet brewery. Guinness started brewing ale, but was aware of a black beer called "porter," popular in London's markets. He developed a new recipe for porter (the word "stout" was not used until the 1920s). So successful was the switch that he made his first export shipment in 1769.

The tour ends with an audiovisual show, followed by a visit to the sampling bar where you can enjoy a couple of glasses of draft Guinness.

The Phoenix Column

Phoenix Park ⑮

Park Gate, Conyngham Rd, Dublin 8. 🚌 10, 25, 26, 37, 38, 39. ⬜ daily. **Visitor Center** 📞 01-677 0095. ⬜ mid-Mar–Oct: daily; Nov–mid-Mar: Sat & Sun. 📷 ♿ limited. **Zoo** 📞 01-677 1425. ⬜ daily. 📷 🅿 📷 🍴 ♿

JUST TO THE WEST of the city center, ringed by an 11-km (7-mile) wall, is Europe's largest enclosed city park. The name "Phoenix" is said to be a corruption of the Gaelic *Fionn Uisce*, or "clear water," referring to a spring near the **Phoenix Column**, crowned by a statue of the mythical bird. The park originated in 1662, when the Duke of Ormonde turned the land into a deer park. It was opened to the public in 1745.

Near Park Gate is the lakeside **People's Garden**. A little further on are the **Zoological Gardens**, which are renowned for the breeding of lions, including the one that introduces MGM movies.

The park has two very conspicuous monuments. The **Wellington Testimonial** is a 63-m (204-ft) obelisk, begun in 1817 and completed in 1861. Its bronze bas-reliefs were made from captured French cannons. The 27-m (90-ft) steel **Papal Cross** marks the spot where the pope said Mass in front of one million people in 1979. Buildings within the park include two 18th-century houses: **Áras an Uachtaráin**, the Irish President's official residence, for which 525 tickets are issued every Saturday for a free guided tour, and **Deerfield**, home of the US ambassador. **Ashtown Castle** is a restored 17th-century tower house, now home to the **Phoenix Park Visitor Centre**.

The Gallery of Writers at the Dublin Writers Museum, Parnell Square

Southeast Ireland

E NJOYING THE WARMEST climate in Ireland, the Southeast has always presented an attractive prospect for invaders and settlers. Its highlights include the Neolithic tombs in the Valley of the Boyne, early Christian monastic sites, and towns such as Waterford that grew from Viking settlements. It is also the setting for many great 18th-century houses built by the ruling English aristocracy. The wildest landscapes of the region are to be found in the forested hills and desolate moorland of the Wicklow Mountains south of Dublin.

Elegant stuccoed hall and staircase in Castletown House

Castletown House **❷**

Celbridge, Co. Kildare. **📞** 01-628 8252. **🚌** 67, 67A from Dublin. **🕐** Easter–Sep: daily (pm only Sat, Sun & public hols); Oct: Mon–Fri & Sun; Nov: Sun pm only. **🎫 🎥** obligatory. **📷 ♿**

B UILT IN 1722–32 for William Conolly, Speaker of the Irish Parliament, Castletown was Ireland's first grand Palladian-style country house. Most of the interiors were commissioned by Lady Louisa Lennox, wife of Conolly's great-nephew, Tom, who lived here in the late 18th century. It was she who added the magnificent long gallery at the top of the house, with its Pompeiian-style friezes, cobalt-blue walls and niches framing Classical statuary. From the long gallery

visitors can admire the curious obelisk-topped memorial to Speaker Conolly erected by his widow in 1740.

A portrait of Lady Louisa is incorporated in the superb Rococo stuccowork by the Francini brothers in the staircase hall. Another personal reminder of Lady Louisa is the print room, the last surviving, intact example of its kind. In the 18th century, ladies pasted prints directly on to the wall and framed them with elaborate festoons. Castletown remained in the family until 1965.

Newgrange **❸**

8 km (5 miles) E of Slane, Co. Meath. **🚉** to Drogheda. **🚌** to visitor centre via Drogheda. **Brú na Bóinne Interpretive Centre** **📞** 041-988 0300. **🕐** daily. **●** Dec 24–27. **🎫** obligatory. **🚫** in tomb. **📷 🎥 ♿**

T HE ORIGINS of Newgrange, one of the most important passage graves in Europe, are steeped in mystery. Built around 3200 BC, the grave was rediscovered in 1699. When it was excavated in the 1960s, archaeologists realized that at dawn on the winter

solstice (December 21) a beam of sunlight shines through the roof box, a rectangular opening above the entrance to the tomb and a feature unique to Newgrange. The light travels along the 19-m (62-ft) passage and hits the central recess in the burial chamber. It is thus the world's oldest solar observatory.

Between 1962 and 1975 the grave and the mound, or cairn, covering it were restored. The retaining wall at the front of the cairn was rebuilt using white quartz and granite stones found scattered around the site. It is estimated that the original tomb, created by people who had neither the wheel nor metal tools, may have taken up to 70 years to build. About 200,000 tons of loose stones were transported to build the cairn. Larger slabs were used to make the circle around the cairn and the retaining kerb. Many of the kerbstones and the slabs lining the passage and chamber are decorated with zigzags, spirals, and other geometric motifs.

Each of the three recesses in the central chamber contained a chiseled "basin stone" that held funerary offerings and the bones of the dead. The chamber's corbeled ceiling has proved completely water-proof for 5,000 years.

Newgrange is very popular, especially in summer, so visits are by tour only and you have to wait your turn at the **Brú na Bóinne Interpretive Centre**. This has displays on the area's Stone Age heritage. The tour includes the nearby tomb at Knowth. The last one starts at 3:15pm in winter and at 5:15pm in midsummer.

Aerial view of Newgrange, showing the cairn and circle of standing stones

Round tower at Glendalough

Glendalough ④

Co. Wicklow. 🚌 *St. Kevin's Bus from Dublin.* **Ruins** ⭕ *daily.* 🅿️ *in summer.* **Visitors' Center** 📞 *0404-45352.* ⭕ *daily.* ⬤ *Dec 24–27.* 📷 ♿ *limited.*

THE STEEP, WOODED slopes of Glendalough, the "valley of the two lakes," harbor one of Ireland's most atmospheric ruined monasteries. Founded by St. Kevin in the 6th century, it functioned as a monastic center until the Dissolution of the Monasteries in 1539.

Most of the buildings date from the 8th to 12th centuries. The reconstruction *(see pp124–5)* shows how the monastery may have looked in its heyday. The main ruins lie near the smaller Lower Lake. You enter the monastery through the double stone arch of the gatehouse, from where a short walk leads to a graveyard with a restored round tower in one corner. Other ruins include the roofless cathedral, the tiny Priest's House and the 12th-century St. Kevin's Cross. Below, nestled in the lush valley, stands a small oratory. It is popularly known as St. Kevin's Kitchen, because its belfry resembles a chimney.

A path along the south bank of the river leads to the Upper Lake and some of the earliest buildings associated with St. Kevin. Here, the scenery is wilder and you are better able to enjoy the tranquillity of Glendalough.

Kilkenny ⑤

Co. Kilkenny. 🚶 *20,000.* 🚉 🚌 ℹ️ *Shee Almshouse, Rose Inn St (056-775 1500).* 🎭 *Kilkenny Arts Week (Aug).*

IN A LOVELY SETTING beside the River Nore, Kilkenny is Ireland's most attractive inland city. Many of its houses feature the local black limestone, known as Kilkenny marble. The city is proud of its heritage and hosts a major arts festival. It is also a brewery city, filled with atmospheric old pubs.

Built in the 1190s, **Kilkenny Castle** was the seat of the Anglo-Norman Butler family from the late 14th century up until 1967. With its drum towers and solid walls, the castle retains its medieval form, but has undergone many alterations. The Long Gallery, rebuilt in the 1820s to house the Butler art collection, has a striking hammer-beam and glass roof. The painted ceiling has a strong Pre-Raphaelite feel, with motifs inspired by the Book of Kells *(see p125)*.

The area known, in the days of segregation, as Englishtown boasts the city's grandest buildings, such as Rothe House, a fine Tudor merchant's house, built around two courtyards. The area of narrow alleyways or "slips" is part of Kilkenny's medieval heritage.

The Irishtown district is dominated by **St. Canice's Cathedral** and a round tower that you can climb for a good view of the city. The Gothic cathedral dates from the 13th century. It has a finely sculpted west door and an array of 16th-century tombs with beautiful effigies of the Butler family in the south transept.

🗝️ **Kilkenny Castle**
The Parade. 📞 *056-772 1450.* ⭕ *daily.* ⬤ *Good Fri, 10 days at Christmas.* 📷 📹 *obligatory.* 🖥️ ♿ *limited.*

Waterford ⑥

Co. Waterford. 🚶 *44,000.* 🚉 🚌 🚉 ℹ️ *The Granary, Merchant's Quay (051-875 823).* ⬤ *Fri.* 🎭 *International Festival of Light Opera (Sep).*

IRELAND'S OLDEST city, Waterford was founded by the Vikings in 914, and later extended by the Anglo-Normans. Its commanding position on the Suir estuary made it southeast Ireland's main port. The 18th century saw the establishment of local industries, including the world-famous glassworks.

The remains of the city walls define the area fortified by the Normans. The largest surviving structure is **Reginald's Tower**, overlooking the river. Although the city retains its medieval layout, most of the finest buildings are Georgian, including **Christchurch Cathedral**, designed in the 1770s by local architect John Roberts. In the summer, from June to August, you can admire the waterfront by taking a pleasure cruise on the river.

Waterford Crystal decanter

The **Waterford Crystal Factory** lies 2.5 km (1.5 miles) south of the center. The original factory was founded in 1783, but closed in 1851. A new factory opened in 1947.

🏛️ **Waterford Crystal Factory**
Kilbarry. 📞 *051-332 500.* ⭕ *Mar–Oct: 8:30am–6pm daily; Nov–Feb: 9am–5pm Mon–Fri.* 📷 📹 ♿ 🌐 *www.waterfordvisitorcentre.com*

Tomb of 2nd Marquess of Ormonde in St. Canice's Cathedral, Kilkenny

Early Celtic Christianity

IRELAND BECAME CHRISTIAN in the 5th century, following the missions of St. Patrick and others. The situation was soon reversed, with many Irish missionaries, such as St. Columba and St. Columbanus, sailing to Great Britain, France, and beyond. The Irish church developed more or less free from the control of Rome, but nevertheless had strong links with the east. As in Egypt, the Christian faith inspired a proliferation of hermitages and remote monasteries. Decorative motifs in illuminated manuscripts reflect Egyptian Christian imagery, and materials used in making the inks came from the Middle East. The advent of the Vikings in the 9th century forced the monasteries to take defensive measures, but they continued to flourish despite frequent raids.

Conical roof

Lookout window

Wooden floor

Movable ladder

Round towers, first built in the 10th century, were bell towers and refuges from Viking raids. The entrance could be 4 m (13 ft) above ground and was reached by a ladder.

CELTIC MONASTERY
This reconstruction shows Glendalough in about 1100. Monasteries were probably the largest centers of population in Ireland before the Vikings started to found towns.

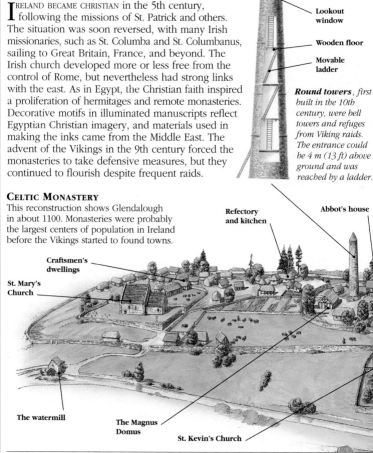

Refectory and kitchen

Abbot's house

Craftsmen's dwellings

St. Mary's Church

The watermill

The Magnus Domus

St. Kevin's Church

IRELAND'S HIGH CROSSES
High Crosses are found in parts of Britain as well as Ireland, yet in their profusion and craftsmanship, Irish crosses are exceptional. The ringed cross has become a symbol of Irish Christianity and is still imitated today. The medieval High Crosses were carved between the 8th and 12th centuries. Early ones, such as the 8th-century cross at Ahenny, bore spirals and interlacing patterns, but in the 9th and 10th centuries a new style emerged with sculpted scenes from the bible, "sermons in stone," aimed at educating a largely illiterate population.

Muiredach's Cross at Monasterboice is the finest surviving example of a cross carved with biblical scenes. This panel shows the Fall of Man: Eve offering Adam the apple in the Garden of Eden and Cain slaying Abel.

Ornamental High Cross at Ahenny

Cross of the Scriptures, Clonmacnoise

THE BOOK OF KELLS

The most richly decorated of all the Irish illuminated manuscripts dating from the 8th–10th centuries, the Book of Kells contains the four gospels in Latin, copied onto leaves of high-quality vellum. It is remarkable both for the beauty of the script and for the inspired fantasy of the illumination. There is no record of its existence before the early 11th century, but it was probably created in about 800. It would have taken many years of work by the scriptorium of a monastery. It may have been brought to Kells by monks from Iona who fled to Ireland after a Viking raid in 806. The manuscript was moved to Trinity College *(see p116)* in the 17th century for safe-keeping.

Page of the Genealogy of Christ from the Book of Kells

WHERE TO SEE EARLY CHRISTIAN SITES IN IRELAND

Important early Christian sites besides Glendalough include Clonmacnoise, the Rock of Cashel *(see p126)*, Clonfert, Kells, and Devenish Island. Though most of the monastic buildings are ruins, they have usually continued to be used as cemeteries right up to modern times. Monasteries were built on the Aran Islands *(see p129)* and even on the remote rocky Skellig Michael off the Dingle Peninsula. Round towers and High Crosses are preserved all over Ireland, often standing beside churches of much more recent construction.

Clonmacnoise was founded in the 6th century. The monastery was noted for its piety and scholarship. Now it is an atmospheric collection of ruins in a remote spot on the Shannon. This carved Romanesque doorway is part of the Nun's Church.

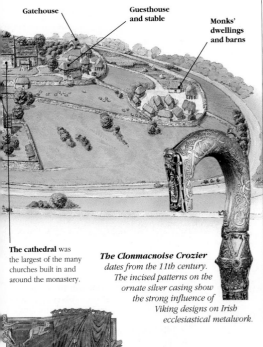

Gatehouse

Guesthouse and stable

Monks' dwellings and barns

The cathedral was the largest of the many churches built in and around the monastery.

The Clonmacnoise Crozier dates from the 11th century. The incised patterns on the ornate silver casing show the strong influence of Viking designs on Irish ecclesiastical metalwork.

The Voyage of St. Brendan is a fantastic legend of early medieval Irish Christianity. The 6th-century saint and his followers set sail into the Atlantic in a small boat, sighting volcanic islands, ice floes, whales, and even, some say, America.

Devenish Island has a fine restored round tower and enjoys a peaceful setting on Lower Lough Erne. Lake islands were popular as monastic sites.

Southwest Ireland

MAGNIFICENT SCENERY has attracted visitors to this region since Victorian times. Killarney and its romantic lakes are a powerful magnet for tourists, as is the attractive coastline of Cork and Kerry, where rocky headlands jut out into the Atlantic and colorful fishing villages nestle in the bays. Yet much of the southwest remains unspoiled, with a friendly atmosphere and authentic culture still alive in Irish-speaking pockets.

The Rock of Cashel

Cashel ⓦ

Co. Tipperary. 🏠 2,500. 🚌 ℹ️
Heritage Centre, Main St (062- 62511).
Rock 🎫 062-61437. ⭕ *daily.*
⬤ *Dec 25–26.* 📷 🎥 ♿ *limited.*

THE TOWN'S great attraction is the magnificent medieval Rock of Cashel. Many people stay overnight to enjoy eerie floodlit views of the rocky stronghold rising dramatically out of the Tipperary plain. The Rock was a symbol of royal and ecclesiastical power for more than a thousand years. From the 5th century AD it was the seat of the Kings of Munster, rulers of southwest Ireland. In 1101, they handed

Cashel over to the Church, and it flourished as a religious center until a siege by a Cromwellian army in 1647 ended in the massacre of its 3,000 occupants.

A good proportion of the medieval complex still stands, though the main building, the Gothic cathedral, is roofless. The earlier Cormac's Chapel is an outstanding example of Romanesque architecture. Other prominent features of the Rock are a restored round tower and the weatherbeaten St. Patrick's Cross. The carved figure on the east face of the cross is said to be St. Patrick.

Cork ⓧ

Co. Cork. 🏠 136,000. ✈️ 🚌
ℹ️ *Tourist House, Grand Parade (0214-273 251).* 🎷 *Jazz Festival (Oct); Film Festival (Oct).*

CORK CITY derives its name from the marshy banks of the River Lee – its Irish name Corcaigh means marsh – where St. Finbarr founded a monastery around AD 650. The center of Cork today occupies an island between two arms of the river. Its waterways,

bridges, and narrow alleys, combined with the Georgian architecture of the old Quays, give Cork a continental feel. In the 18th century many of today's streets were waterways lined with warehouses and merchants' residences.

Noted for its chic bars, ethnic restaurants, bookshops, and boutiques, Paul Street is the hub of the liveliest district in town. The nearby **Crawford Art Gallery** has some fine Irish works of art.

A prominent landmark is the steeple of **St. Anne Shandon** on a hill in the north of the city. It is topped by a weather vane in the shape of a salmon. Visitors can climb up and ring the famous Shandon bells.

🏛️ **Crawford Art Gallery**
Emmet Place. 🎫 *0214-273 377.*
⭕ *9am–5pm Mon–Sat.* ⬤ *public hols.* 🍴 🛍️ 📷 ♿

The battlemented keep and other ruined towers of Blarney Castle

ENVIRONS: Beautiful countryside surrounds Cork, especially along the valley of the Lee river. Popular outings include a tour of the whiskey-making **Old Midleton Distillery**, and a trip to **Blarney Castle** and the legendary stone that bestows magical eloquence on all who kiss it. There are also plenty of opportunities for outdoor activities such as walking, riding, and fishing.

🏛️ **Old Midleton Distillery**
Midleton, Co. Cork. 🎫 *0214-613 594.* ⭕ *daily.* ⬤ *Dec 24–27, Dec 31-2 Jan.* 📷 🎥 📷 ♿
♣ **Blarney Castle**
Blarney, Co. Cork. 🎫 *0214-385252.*
⭕ *daily.* ⬤ *Dec 24–25.* 📷 ♿

South channel of the Lee river flowing through the city of Cork

Newman's Mall in the quaint village of Kinsale

Kinsale 9

Co. Cork. 🏠 3,500. 🚌 ℹ️ *Pier Road (0214-772 234).* 🚣 *Regatta (Aug); Festival of Fine Food (Oct).*

FOR MANY VISITORS to Ireland, Kinsale heads the list of places to see. One of the prettiest small towns in Ireland, it has had a long and checkered history. The defeat of the Irish forces and their Spanish allies at the Battle of Kinsale in 1601 signalled the end of the old Gaelic order.

An important naval base in the 17th and 18th centuries, Kinsale today is a popular yachting center. It is also famous for the quality of its cuisine – the town's annual Festival of Fine Food attracts food lovers from far and wide.

Charles Fort, one of the finest remaining examples of a star-shaped bastion fort in Europe, was built by the English in the 1670s to protect Kinsale against foreign naval forces. It can be reached by taking the signposted coastal walk from the quayside.

⚓ **Charles Fort**
3 km (2 miles) E of Kinsale. 📞 *0214-772 263.* ⬜ *Mar–Oct: daily; Nov–Feb: Sat & Sun.* 🈯

Killarney 10

Co. Kerry. 🏠 11,000. 🚉 🚌 ℹ️ *Beech Road (064-31633).*

KILLARNEY is often derided as "a tourist town" but this does not detract from its cheerful atmosphere. The infectious Kerry humor is personified by the wise-cracking "jarveys," whose families have run jaunting cars (pony and trap

rides) here for generations. The town does get very crowded in the summer but this is inevitable, given the lure of the **Lakes of Killarney**. The three lakes and many of the heather-covered hills surrounding them lie within **Killarney National Park**. Although the landscape is dotted with ruined castles and abbeys, the lakes are the focus of attention: the moody watery scenery is subject to subtle shifts of light and color. Well-known beauty spots include the Meeting of the Waters, the Ladies' View, so called because it delighted Queen Victoria's ladies-in-waiting in 1861, and the Gap of Dunloe, a dramatic mountain pass. The largest of the lakes, Lough Leane, is dotted with uninhabited islands. Boat trips across the lake run from Ross Castle on the shore nearest Killarney.

Overlooking the lakes is **Muckross House**, an imposing mansion built in 1843 in Elizabethan style, set in beautiful landscaped gardens. It houses a museum of Kerry Life, with displays on the history of southwest Ireland, and a craft center.

The town is also the starting point for the popular **Ring of Kerry** tour around the Iveragh Peninsula. Allow a day's drive to enjoy its captivating mountain and coastal scenery.

🏠 **Muckross House**
4 km (2.5 miles) S of Killarney. 📞 *064-31440.* ⬜ *daily.* ⬛ *Christmas week.* 🈯🅿️🛍️🚻♿

Dingle 11

Co. Kerry. 🏠 2,000. 🚌 ℹ️ *Mar–Oct: Main St (06691-51188).* 🏷️ *Fri.*

THIS ONCE REMOTE Irish-speaking town is today a thriving fishing port and popular tourist center. Brightly painted – often fairly hippy – craft shops and cafés abound. Along the quayside are lively bars offering music and seafood. The harbor is home to Dingle's biggest star, Fungie the dolphin, who has been a permanent resident since 1983 and can be visited by boat or on swimming trips.

Gallarus Oratory, a tiny dry-stone Early Christian church

ENVIRONS: Dingle makes a good base for exploring the scattered archaeological remains of the Dingle Peninsula. The most fascinating site is the **Gallarus Oratory**, northwest of Dingle. This miniature dry-stone church, shaped like an upturned boat, was built between the 6th and 9th centuries. West of Dingle, along the coast road, are the Iron Age fort of Dunbeg and some Early Christian beehive huts.

The Upper Lake, smallest and most remote of the Lakes of Killarney

Bunratty Castle ⑫

THIS FORMIDABLE 15TH-CENTURY CASTLE is one of Ireland's major tourist attractions. Its most important residents were the O'Briens, Earls of Thomond, who lived here from around 1500 until the 1640s. The interior has been restored to look as it did under the so-called "Great Earl," who died in 1624. The adjacent Folk Park and the mock medieval banquets held in the castle attract busloads of visitors, but despite its commercialization, Bunratty is well worth a visit. The Folk Park recreates rural life at the end of the 19th century, with a whole village, complete with stores, a school, and dwellings ranging from a laborer's cottage to an elegant Georgian house.

VISITORS' CHECKLIST

Bunratty, Co. Clare. ☎ 061-361 020. ▭ from Limerick, Ennis & Shannon Airport. **Bunratty Castle** ◯ 9:30am–5:30pm daily (Jun–Oct: 9am). **Folk Park** ◯ 9:30am–5:30pm (Jun–Aug: 9am–6pm) daily. ● Good Fri, Dec 24–26. ▨ ⅱ ⅃ to Folk Park. ⎁ www.shannonheritage.com

Great Hall
The castle's grandest room served as banqueting hall and audience chamber. Among the furnishings bought by the owner, Lord Gort, when he set about restoring the castle in the 1950s was this Tudor standard.

South Solar
This richly paneled "solar," or upper chamber, was a guest apartment.

Anteroom

The North Solar
was the Great Earl's private apartment.

The Murder Hole was designed for pouring boiling water or pitch onto the heads of attackers.

Entrance

The Earl's Robing Room
also served as a private audience chamber.

North Front
The entrance, raised well above ground level to deter invaders, is typical of castles of the period.

Main Guard
This was where the castle's soldiers ate, slept, and listened to music from the Minstrels' Gallery.

The imposing Kylemore Abbey on the shores of Kylemore Lough, Connemara

Galway ⑬

Co. Galway. 🏛 56,000. 🚉 🚌
ℹ The Fairgreen, Foster St (091-537
700). 🛥 Sat. 🎭 Arts Festival (mid-
Jul); Galway Races (late Jul/Aug);
Oyster Festival (late Sep).

GALWAY IS THE CENTER for the
Irish-speaking regions in
the West of Ireland and a lively
university city. In the 15th and
16th centuries it was a prosperous trading port, controlled
by 14 merchant families, or
"tribes." Its allegiance to the
English Crown cost the city
dear when, in 1652, it was
sacked by Cromwell's forces.
In the 18th century Galway
fell into decline, but in recent
years, its fortunes have revived
through high-tech industries.

The city stands on the banks
of the Corrib river. Many of
the best stores, pubs, theaters,
and historic sights are packed
into the narrow lanes of the
"Latin Quarter" around Quay

Colourful shopfronts lining Quay Street
in Galway's "Latin Quarter"

Street. Nearby is the Collegiate
Church of St. Nicholas, the
city's finest medieval building.
To the south stands the 16th-
century Spanish Arch, where
ships from Spain unloaded
their cargoes. Across the
Corrib, facing the arch, is the
Claddagh. The only remnants
of this once close-knit, Gaelic-
speaking community are its
friendly pubs and Claddagh
rings – betrothal rings that are
traditionally handed down
from mother to daughter.

Connemara ⑭

Co. Galway. 🚌 to Clifden or
Letterfrack. ℹ Mar–Oct: Galway
Road, Clifden (095-21163). **National
Park Visitors' Center** 📞 095-41
054. ◻ Mar–Oct: daily. 🎦 ◻ ♿

THIS WILD REGION to the west
of Galway encompasses
bogs, mountains, and rugged
Atlantic coastline. The small
market town of Clifden is
a convenient and popular
base for exploring.
Starting from Clifden, the
Sky Road is an 11-km
(7-mile) circular route
with spectacular ocean
views. South of Clifden,
the coast road to Round-
stone skirts a massive bog,
impromptu landing site
of the first transatlantic
flight made by Alcock
and Brown in 1919.
**Connemara National
Park** near Letterfrack
includes some spectacular
scenery, dominated by the
mountains known as the
Twelve Bens. Here visitors
have a chance to spot
red deer and the famous
Connemara ponies.

Nearby **Kylemore Abbey** is a
19th-century romantic, battlemented fantasy. It became
an abbey when Benedictine
nuns, fleeing from Belgium
during World War I, sought
refuge here. The building is
now a select girls' boarding
school, but its gardens, with
restaurant, shop, and
spectacular lakeside setting
make it a popular destination.

Aran Islands ⑮

Co. Galway. 🏛 900. ✈ from Inverin
(091-593 034). 🛥 from Rossaveal
(091-561 767); from Doolin (Easter–
Oct: 065-707 4455). ℹ Kilronan,
Inishmore (099-61263). **Heritage
Center** ◻ daily. 🛍 🎦 ♿

INISHMORE, INISHMAAN, and
Inisheer, the three Aran
Islands, are formed from a
limestone ridge. The largest,
Inishmore, is 13 km (8 miles)
long and 3 km (2 miles) wide.
The attractions of the islands
include the austere landscape
crisscrossed with dry-stone
walls, stunning coastal views,
and prehistoric stone forts.
The islands are a bastion of
traditional Irish culture with
most of the islanders engaged
in fishing, farming, or tourism.
Ferries sail at least once a day
in winter and several times
daily in summer. Cars cannot
be taken to the islands.

At Kilronan on Inishmore,
jaunting cars (ponies and traps)
and minibuses wait by the pier
to give tours; bicycles can also
be hired. Nearby, the **Aran
Heritage Center** is dedicated
to the disappearing Aran way
of life. The islands are famous
for their distinctive knitwear
and traditional costumes.

Northern Ireland

THE PROVINCE OF NORTHERN IRELAND was created after the partition of the island in 1921. Its six counties (plus Donegal, Monaghan, and Cavan, which became part of the Republic) were part of Ulster, one of Ireland's four traditional kingdoms. Though densely populated and industrialized around Belfast, away from the capital the region is primarily agricultural. It also has areas of outstanding natural beauty, notably the rugged Antrim coastline around the Giant's Causeway.

Mosaic of St. Patrick's journey to Ireland in St. Anne's Cathedral

Belfast ⓰

Co. Antrim. 🏘 500,000. ✈ 🚉 🚌
🛈 47 Donegall Place (028-9024 6609). 🎪 Royal Ulster Agricultural Show & Lord Mayor's Show (May); Belfast Festival at Queen's (Nov).

BELFAST WAS THE ONLY CITY in Ireland to experience the full force of the Industrial Revolution. Its shipbuilding, linen, rope-making, and tobacco industries caused the population to rise to almost 400,000 by the end of World War I. The wealth it enjoyed is still evident in its imposing banks, and other public buildings. The Troubles and the decline of traditional industries have since damaged economic life, but Belfast remains a handsome city and most visitors are agreeably surprised by the genuine friendliness of the people.

Most of Belfast's main streets (and bus routes) radiate out from the hub of Donegall Square. In its center stands the vast Portland stone bulk of the 1906 **City Hall** with its huge central copper dome. Statues around the building include Queen Victoria at the front and, on the east side, Sir Edward Harland, founder of the Harland and Wolff shipyard, which built the *Titanic*. A memorial to those who died when the ship sank in 1912 stands close by.

Sights in and around the square include the **Linen Hall Library**, the late-Victorian **Grand Opera House** in Great Victoria Street, and Belfast's most famous pub, the **Crown Liquor Saloon**, which dates back to the 1880s.

The Neo-Romanesque **St. Anne's** in Donegall Street is the Protestant cathedral, consecrated in 1904. The interior is remarkable for the vast mosaics added by the two Misses Martin in the 1920s. Lord Carson (1854–1935), implacable opponent of Home Rule, is buried in the south aisle.

Away from the center, Belfast has pleasant suburbs unaffected by the civil strife of recent times. The area around **Queen's University** to the south of the city has two major attractions in the **Ulster Museum** and the **Botanic Gardens**. The museum covers

Detail of Titanic Memorial outside Belfast City Hall

all aspects of Ulster, from archaeology to technology. Treasures include jewelry from the *Girona*, a Spanish Armada ship that sank off the Giant's Causeway in 1588.

🏛 **Ulster Museum**
Botanic Gardens. 📞 028-9038 3000.
🕐 daily (Sat & Sun: pm only). 🎫 🔲
📷 ♿ 🌐 www.ulstermuseum.org.uk

Giant's Causeway ⓱

Co. Antrim. 🚉 to Portrush. 🚌 from Portrush, Bushmills, or Coleraine.
Visitors' Center (028-2073 1855). 🕐 daily. 🔲 🎫 on request. ♿ limited.

THE SHEER STRANGENESS of the Giant's Causeway and the bizarre regularity of its basalt columns has made it the subject of numerous legends. The most popular tells how the giant, Finn MacCool, laid the causeway to provide a path across the sea to his lady love, who lived on the island of Staffa in Scotland, where similar rock formations are found. The more prosaic geological explanation is that 61 million years ago, in a series of massive volcanic eruptions, molten lava poured from narrow fissures in the ground, filling in the valleys and burning the vegetation

The ornate Victorian interior of the Crown Liquor Saloon

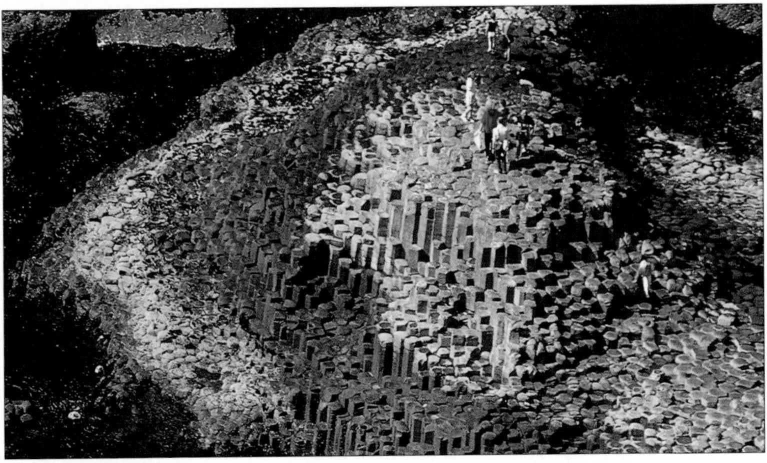

The extraordinarily regular columns of the Giant's Causeway exposed at low tide

that grew here. The basalt lava cooled rapidly. In the process it shrank and cracked evenly into polygonal-shaped blocks. Towards the end of the Ice Age, erosion by sea ice exposed the rocks and shaped the Causeway. Most of the columns are hexagonal, but some have four, five, eight, or even ten sides. They are generally about 30 cm (12 in) across. There are in fact three causeways, the Grand, Middle, and Little. Distinctive features have been given poetic names, such as the "Honeycomb" and the "Wishing Chair."

Tourists are ferried by the busload from the visitors' center to the shore. Nothing, however, can destroy the magic of the place, and it is easy to escape the crowds by taking one of the coastal paths.

Old Bushmills Distillery ⓲

Bushmills, Co. Antrim. 028-2073 1521. from Giant's Causeway & Coleraine. Apr–Sep: daily; Oct–Mar: pm Sat & Sun. 2 weeks at Christmas. obligatory. limited.

Bushmills has an attractive square and an excellent river for salmon and trout fishing, but its main claim to fame is whiskey. The Old Bushmills plant prides itself on being the oldest distillery in the world, its "Grant to Distil" dating from 1608.

In 1974 Bushmills joined the Irish Distillers Group based at the Midleton plant near Cork *(see p126)*, but its brands have retained their distinctive character. "Old Bushmills" is unusual in that it is made from a blend of single malt and a single grain. The tour of the distillery, which features audio-visual displays, ends with a sampling session in the "1608 Bar," which is housed in the former malt kilns.

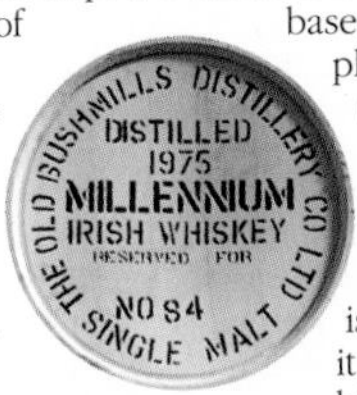

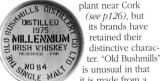

Whiskey barrel at Old Bushmills

Ulster-American Folk Park ⓳

Co. Tyrone. 028-8224 3292. from Omagh. Easter–Sep: daily; Oct–Easter: Mon–Fri.

One of the best open-air museums of its kind, the Folk Park grew up around the restored boyhood home of Judge Thomas Mellon (founder of the Pittsburgh banking dynasty). The park's permanent exhibition, called "Emigrants," examines why two million people left Ulster for America during the 18th and 19th centuries. It also shows what became of them, following stories of both fortune and failure.

The park has more than 30 historic buildings, some of them original, some replicas. There are settler homesteads (including that of John Joseph Hughes, the first Catholic Archbishop of New York), churches, a schoolhouse, and a forge, some with craft displays, all with costumed interpretative guides. There's also an Ulster streetscape, a reconstructed emigrant ship, and a Pennsylvania farmstead, complete with log barn, corn crib, and smokehouse. The six-roomed farmhouse is based on one built by Thomas Mellon and his father in the early years of their new life in America.

A fully stocked library and database allow the descendants of emigrants to trace their family roots. Popular American festivals, such as Halloween and Independence Day, are celebrated at the park.

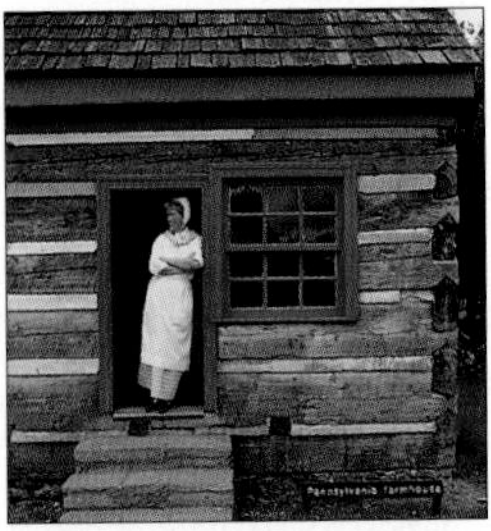

Pennsylvania log farmhouse at the Ulster-American Folk Park

Practical & Travel Information

IRELAND'S CAPITAL CITIES compare favorably to any in Europe for ease of transportation and communications, but in remoter areas the pace of life is much slower. Banks may open only two days a week and public transportation can be infrequent. The division of Ireland into the Republic and Northern Ireland, with separate currencies and communication systems, complicates matters further. Travel in Ireland is best enjoyed if you adopt the Irish approach and just take your time.

TOURIST INFORMATION

BEFORE LEAVING for Ireland you can get information from **Bord Fáilte** (Irish Tourist Board) or **Northern Ireland Tourist Board** (NITB) offices. Regional tourist offices provide more detailed information, including accommodations.

In summer, all the sights are open but crowds are naturally at their biggest. In winter many sights keep shorter hours or open only at the weekend and some close down completely.

VISA REQUIREMENTS

VISITORS FROM the EU, US, Canada, Australia, and New Zealand need a valid passport but not a visa for entry into the Republic or Northern Ireland. UK nationals do not need a passport to enter the Republic, but may find one useful as proof of identity.

SAFETY AND EMERGENCIES

IRELAND IS ONE of the safest places to travel in Europe. Petty theft, such as pick-pocketing, is seldom a problem outside certain parts of Dublin and a few other large towns. Tourist offices and hoteliers will gladly point out the areas to be avoided. In Northern Ireland, the main security risk in the recent past has been the threat of bombings, though even at the height of the Troubles this hardly ever affected tourists. Visitors may find, on the rare occasion, they are confronted by a police checkpoint. If you see a sign indicating a checkpoint ahead, slow down and use low beams. Have your passport handy as proof of identity.

Travel insurance for the UK will not cover you for the Republic, so make sure you have an adequate policy.

The police are called the Gardaí in the Republic and the Police Service of Northern Ireland (PSNI) in the north.

BANKING AND CURRENCY

THE UNIT OF CURRENCY in the Republic prior to 2002 was the punt, or Irish pound (IR£). However, on January 1, 2002, the punt was replaced by the euro *(see p15)*.

Northern Ireland uses British currency – pounds sterling (£). These currencies are not inter-changeable. Alongside the Bank of England currency in the North, four provincial banks issue their own notes, for use only in the province.

Banking hours are from 10am to 4pm, although some banks close for lunch from 12:30 to 1:30pm. In the smaller towns in the Republic, banks are often open only one or two days a week.

COMMUNICATIONS

MAIN POST OFFICES in the Republic and Northern Ireland are usually open from 9am to 5:30pm during the week and from 9am to 1pm on Saturdays. The postal service in Northern Ireland is much faster than that in the Republic, where it can take at least six days for a letter to reach the United States.

Most phones in the Republic are operated by EIRCOM, and in Northern Ireland by British Telecom. Both offer efficient, up-to-date card- and coin-operated public phones.

FLYING TO IRELAND

FLIGHTS FROM MOST large European cities arrive at Dublin Airport. The major airline operating between Britain and the Republic is **Aer Lingus**, although rival **Ryanair** has grown fast. Aer Lingus and **Continental Airlines** fly direct from the US to Shannon Airport, 16 km (10 miles) outside Limerick, as well as to Dublin Airport. Aeroflot flies from Shannon to Moscow via Amsterdam or via Dublin.

There are flights for pilgrims to Knock International Airport from Dublin, London Stansted, and Manchester Airport.

Cork airport is served by flights from London (Heathrow and Stanstead), Paris, Birmingham, Manchester, and Bristol airports amongst others.

British Airways and **bmi British Midland** fly to Belfast International Airport from London Heathrow; British Airways also flies from Manchester and Glasgow. There are two easyJet flights every day from Amsterdam to Belfast.

THE CLIMATE OF IRELAND

Rain can be the scourge of a holiday in Ireland, especially on the west coast. However, strong winds off the Atlantic mean that the weather often changes with astonishing speed. Though the rainfall is heavy, winters are mild and there is little snowfall except on the higher mountains. Dublin and the sheltered east coast have the warmest climate and least rainfall.

DUBLIN			
°C/F	19/67		
	12/53 11/51	13/56	
0°C 3/38		7/45	7/45
32°F			2/35
☀ 5 hrs	5 hrs	3 hrs	2 hrs
☂ 46 mm	52 mm	67 mm	69 mm
month Apr	Jul	Oct	Jan

ARRIVING BY SEA

FERRIES FROM PORTS in Britain and France are a popular way of getting to Ireland, especially with groups and families intending to tour the country by car. There are large seasonal variations in fares.

Irish Ferries and **Stena Line** operate regular daily crossings from Holyhead, Pembroke, and Fishguard in Wales to Dublin Port, Dun Laoghaire, and Rosslare. The fastest routes take about 1 hour 40 minutes. There are also Irish Ferries services from Holyhead to Dublin and to Rosslare from Cherbourg and Roscoff. Brittany Ferries go from Roscoff to Cork.

The fastest crossing to Belfast is the 1 hour 45 minute Stena Line service from Stranraer in Scotland. **P&O Irish Sea** cross to Larne (north of Belfast) from Cairnryan in Scotland, and **Norse Merchant** runs a regular service from Liverpool to Dublin and Belfast.

You can buy combined coach/ferry and rail/ferry tickets from coach offices or train stations all over Britain.

RAIL TRAVEL

ALTHOUGH the more rural areas in the Republic are not served by rail, **Irish Rail** (Iarnród Éireann) operates a service to most large towns. Dublin has two main train stations: Connolly serves the north and the line south along the coast to Rosslare; Heuston serves Cork and the southwest, and Galway and the west. Dublin's local rail service, the DART (Dublin Area Rapid Transit), links towns between Malahide (County Dublin) and Greystones (County Wicklow) with the center of Dublin.

There are two main routes out of Belfast: a line westward to Londonderry, and Ireland's only cross-border service, a high-speed service linking Belfast and Dublin.

BUSES AND TAXIS

THE REPUBLIC's national bus company, **Bus Éireann**, operates routes to all cities and most of the towns. **Ulsterbus** runs an excellent service in Northern Ireland, with express links between all major towns.

A "Rambler" ticket allows passengers a period of unlimited bus travel in the Republic. In the North, a "Freedom of Northern Ireland" ticket offers the same benefits.

Taxis in Ireland range from saloon cars to people carriers. Cruising taxis are rare. The most likely places to find taxis are at train and bus stations, hotels, and taxi stands.

CAR RENTAL

CAR RENTAL FIRMS do good business, so in summer it is wise to book ahead. Car rental – particularly in the Republic – can be expensive and the best rates are often obtained by reserving in advance. Broker companies, such as **Holiday Autos** in the UK, will shop around to get the best deal. If you intend to cross the border in either direction, you must inform the rental company, as there may be an additional insurance premium.

In both the Republic and in Northern Ireland, motorists drive on the left as in Great Britain (see p91).

DIRECTORY

TOURIST BOARDS

Bord Fáilte
In Ireland:
Baggot St Bridge, Dublin 2.
01-602 4000.
www.ireland.travel.ie

In the UK:
1 Regency St,
London SW1 14XT.
020-7518 0800.

In the US:
345 Park Avenue,
New York, NY 10154.
800-223 6470.

Northern Ireland Tourist Board
In Northern Ireland:
St. Anne's Court,
59 North St, Belfast BT1.
028-9023 1221.
www.ni-tourism.com

In the UK:
103 Wigmore St,
London W1U 1QS.
020-7518 0800.

In the US:
345 Park Avenue, 17th
Floor, New York, NY 10154.
212-418 0800.

EMBASSIES

Australia
Fitzwilton House,
Wilton Terrace, Dublin 2.
01-664 5300.

Canada
65–68 St. Stephen's
Green, Dublin 2.
01-417 4100.

UK
Merrion Rd, Dublin 4.
01-205 3700.

US
42 Elgin Rd, Ballsbridge,
Dublin 4.
01-668 7122.

EMERGENCY SERVICES

Police, Ambulance, and Fire services
999 (Republic and NI).

AIRLINES

Aer Lingus
01-886 8888 (Dublin).
0845-084 4444 (UK).
800-223 6537 (US).
www.aerlingus.com

bmi British Midland
01-407 3036 (Dublin).
0870-607 0555 (UK).
www.flybmi.com

Continental Airlines
01-672 7070 (Dublin).
800-321 324 (US).
www.continental.com

Ryanair
01-609 7800 (Dublin).
081-830 3030 (UK).
www.ryanair.com

FERRY COMPANIES

Irish Ferries
1890-313131 (Dublin).
0870-517 1717 (UK).

Norse Merchant
028-9077 9090 (NI).
0870-600 4321 (UK).

P&O Irish Sea
1800-409 049 (Dublin).
0870-242 4777 (UK).

Stena Line
01-204 7777 (Dublin).
08705-707 070 (UK).

RAIL TRAVEL

Irish Rail (Iarnród Éireann)
35 Abbey St Lower,
Dublin 1.
01-836 6222.

Northern Ireland Railways
East Bridge St, Belfast BT1.
028-9089 9411.

BUS COMPANIES

Bus Éireann
01-836 6111.

Ulsterbus/Translink
028-9066 6630.

CAR RENTAL

Holiday Autos
0870-400 0000 (UK).

Shopping & Entertainment

IRELAND OFFERS A WIDE RANGE of quality handmade goods, including Aran sweaters, Waterford crystal, fine Irish linen, and Donegal tweed. As with its produce, the best entertainment is local and highly individual. Ireland's cities are well served by theaters, cinemas, and concert venues, but there are many other local events including arts festivals with traditional music and dance. Not to be overlooked is the entertainment provided by a night in an Irish pub. Finally, the beautiful countryside offers the chance to unwind by walking, riding, fishing, or playing a round of golf.

WHERE TO SHOP

THE CHOICE OF PLACES to shop in Ireland ranges from tiny workshops to large factory outlets, and from chic boutiques to high-street chain stores.

In Dublin, the Temple Bar area contains a number of fashionable craft shops. One of the largest shopping centers in the city is St. Stephen's Green Shopping Centre, full of clothes and craft shops. Near Grafton Street is the Powerscourt Townhouse Shopping Centre.

CRAFTS

CRAFTS are a flourishing way of life in rural Ireland. The Crafts Council of Ireland, with branches in Kilkenny and Dublin (where it is part of **DESIGNYARD**), recommends good small-scale specialist stores. Outlets particularly worth visiting include the **Kilkenny Design Centre** and **Bricín**, which sell a wide selection of items.

Established in 19th-century Ulster, the **Belleek Pottery** produces creamy china with intricately worked decorative motifs, such as shamrocks and flowers. **Royal Tara China**, in Galway, is Ireland's leading fine bone china manufacturer, with designs inspired by Celtic themes.

Waterford Crystal is undoubtedly the most famous name in Irish glass-making but there are many other names of similar quality. **Galway Irish Crystal** is an excellent make, available as elegant ornaments and gifts. Jerpoint Abbey in County Kilkenny inspires stylish local designs by **Jerpoint Glass**.

With a tradition that dates back to Celtic times, distinctive jewelry is produced all over Ireland. The Claddagh ring of Galway is the most famous – a lovers' symbol with two hands cradling a crowned heart.

Aran sweaters are sold all over Ireland, but particularly in County Galway and on the Aran Islands. A well-known outlet for these and other knitwear products is **Blarney Woollen Mills**. Donegal tweed is a byword for quality, noted for its texture and subtle colors. It can be bought at **Magee and Co** in Donegal.

Damask linen was brought to Northern Ireland in the late 17th century by Huguenot refugees. The North is still the place for linen, with sheets and table linen on sale in Belfast at **Smyth's Irish Linen**.

Smoked salmon, farmhouse cheeses, handmade preserves, and, of course, Irish whiskey make perfect last-minute gifts.

ENTERTAINMENT LISTINGS AND TICKETS

THE TOURIST BOARD for the Republic, **Bord Fáilte**, and the **Northern Ireland Tourist Board** *(see p133)* both publish a yearly *Calendar of Events* that lists major fixtures and events around the country. The regional tourist offices also provide local information.

Tickets are often available on the night but it is safer to book in advance. Most venues will accept credit card bookings. Try the main listings magazine *In Dublin* – available from all newsagents – for information about the city's nightlife. The free *Dublin Event Guide* is available from pubs and cafés.

IN MANY IRISH CITIES, the main theaters host a wide range of concerts, events, and plays. In central Belfast, the **Grand Opera House** and **Lyric Theatre** put on an interesting program. Dublin's two most famous theaters the **Abbey** and the **Gate Theatre** are renowned for their productions of Irish and international plays, as is the **Cork Opera House**.

Keep an eye out for smaller theater groups around the country. The **Druid Theatre** in Galway puts on an original repertoire and Waterford boasts a resident drama company at the **Garter Lane Theatre**.

Other venues for classical music include Dublin's great auditorium, the **National Concert Hall**, the **Crawford Art Gallery** in Cork, and the **Ulster Hall** in Belfast.

The **Waterford Festival of Light Opera** and the **Wexford Festival of Opera** attract opera lovers from around the world. Wexford revives neglected operas while Waterford puts on more mainstream operas and musicals. Dublin's opera venue is the **Point Theatre**.

A lack of large-capacity rock venues has led to concerts in Ireland being staged at outdoor sites during the summer. Die-hard rock and jazz fans should search out the musical pubs for Irish bands.

IRISH MUSIC AND DANCE

THE IRISH PUB has helped keep traditional music alive and provided the setting for the musical revival that began in the 1960s. Nights of Irish music and song are scheduled in pubs such as An Phoenix and The Lobby in Cork, and The Laurels in Killarney. However, sessions of informal or impromptu music are commonplace. Wherever you are, the locals will advise you of the nearest musical pubs.

Popular dance spectaculars have raised the profile, if not the understanding, of real Irish country dance. Visit **Comhaltas Ceoltóirí Éireann**, in Monkstown near Dublin, or any of its branches around the country for genuine traditional music and dance nights all year.

IRISH FESTIVALS

THE IRISH are expert festival organizers, staging a week of street entertainment, theater, music, and dance to celebrate almost everything under the sun *(see Directory for listings)*.

IRISH PUBS

THE IRISH PUB is known for its convivial atmosphere and the "crack" – the Irish expression for fun. Wit is washed down with the national drinks of whiskey or Guinness.

City pubs often have grand interiors, a testament to the importance of the brewing and distilling industries in Victorian times. In the countryside, pubs provide an important focus for far-flung rural communities and some even double as shops.

Pubs vary greatly throughout the country, so be sure to try out a few wherever you visit. Dublin is famed for its literary pubs; the Dublin Literary Pub Crawl is an entertaining way to get a feel for the city's booze-fuelled literary heritage. Spontaneous music sessions are common in the many pubs of Kilkenny and County Clare. Some of the most picturesque establishments are in Cork and Kerry. Galway's tourists and student population guarantee a lively pub atmosphere.

OUTDOOR ACTIVITES

NO MATTER WHERE you are in Ireland, the countryside is never far away. Horses thrive on the green turf and racing is a national passion. A day at the track during Galway Race Week in July is a great social event. Those who want to do more than just watch should try horse riding through the unspoiled countryside.

Another way to experience the countryside is to take a river or canal cruise. **Emerald Star** has a fleet of cruisers for use on the waterways. Alternatively you may want to play golf at one of Ireland's beautiful golf courses, or try some fishing. Maps and locations for fishing are available from the **Central Fisheries Board**. The **Golfing Union of Ireland** can advise on golf courses.

Detailed information on a wide range of outdoor activities is available from the **Northern Ireland Tourist Board**, **Bord Fáilte** *(see p133)*, and local tourist offices.

DIRECTORY

CRAFTS

Belleek Pottery
Belleek, Co. Fermanagh.
(028-6865 8501.

Blarney Woollen Mills
Blarney, Co. Cork.
(021-438 5280.

Bricín
26 High Street, Killarney, Co. Kerry.
(064-34902.

DESIGNYARD
12 Essex Street East, Dublin 2.
(01-677 8453.

Galway Irish Crystal
Merlin Park, Galway.
(091-757 311.

Jerpoint Glass
Stoneyford, Co. Kilkenny.
(056-24350.

Kilkenny Design Centre
Castle Yard, Kilkenny.
(056-22118.

Magee and Co
The Diamond, Donegal.
(073-22660.

Royal Tara China
Tara Hall, Mervue, Galway.
(091-751 301.

Smyth's Irish Linen
65 Royal Ave, Belfast.
(028-9024 2232.

Waterford Crystal
Kilbarry, Waterford.
(051-373 311.

ENTERTAINMENT VENUES

Abbey Gate Theatre
Abbey St Lower, Dublin 1.
(01-878 7222.

Cork Opera House
Emmet Place, Cork.
(021-427 4308.

Crawford Art Gallery
Emmet Place, Cork.
(0214-273 377.

Druid Theatre
Chapel Lane, Galway.
(091 568 617.

Garter Lane Theatre
22A O'Connell St, Waterford.
(051-877 153.

Gate Theatre
Cavendish Row, Dublin 1.
(01-874 4045.

Grand Opera House
Great Victoria St, Belfast.
(028-9024 0411.

Lyric Theatre
55 Ridgeway St, Belfast.
(028-9038 1081.

National Concert Hall
Earlsfort Terrace, Dublin 2.
(01-475 1666.

Point Theatre
East Link Bridge, North Wall Quay, Dublin 1.
(01-836 3633.

Ulster Hall
Bedford St, Belfast.
(028-9032 3900.

MUSIC, DANCE, AND FESTIVALS

Comhaltas Ceoltóirí Éireann
32 Belgrave Sq, Monkstown, Co. Dublin.
(01-280 0295.

Dublin Theatre Festival
Assorted drama (Oct).
47 Nassau St, Dublin 2.
(01-667 8439.

Galway Arts Festival
Theater, traditional music, and dance (late Jul–Aug).
Black Box Theatre, Dyke Rd, Terryland, Galway.
(091-509 700.

Kilkenny Arts Week
Crafts, poetry, classical music, and films (Aug).
92 High St, Kilkenny.
(056-63663.

Waterford Festival of Light Opera
Light opera (late Sep–Oct).
For information contact the Theatre Royal.
(051-874 402.

Wexford Festival of Opera
Opera (Oct–Nov).
Theatre Royal, High St, Wexford.
(053-22144.

IRISH PUBS

Dublin Literary Pub Crawl
37 Exchequer St.
(01-670 5602.

OUTDOOR ACTIVITIES

Central Fisheries Board
Mobhi Boreen, Glasnevin, Dublin 9.
(01-837 9206.

Emerald Star
The Marina, Carrick-on-Shannon, Co. Leitrim.
(078-20234.

Golfing Union of Ireland
Glencar House, 81 Eglinton Rd, Dublin 4.
(01-269 4111.

Where to Stay in Ireland

THE CHOICE OF ACCOMMODATIONS in Ireland is enormous: you can stay in an elegant 18th-century country house, a luxurious (or slightly run-down) castle, a Victorian town house, an old-fashioned commercial hotel, or a cozy village inn. Whether you are staying in exclusive luxury or modest self-catering accommodations, one thing you can be certain of in Ireland is that you'll receive a warm welcome.

		NUMBER OF ROOMS	PRIVATE PARKING	RESTAURANT	PUBLIC BAR
DUBLIN					
SOUTHEAST DUBLIN: *Georgian Hotel*	€€€	75	■	●	■
18 Baggot St Lower, Dublin 2. **Map** F5. [01-661 8832. FAX 01-661 8834.					
Close to St. Stephen's Green, this small, stylish hotel has comfortable bedrooms and a good traditional restaurant in the basement *(see p138)*.					
SOUTHEAST DUBLIN: *Russell Court*	€€€	46	■	●	■
21–25 Harcourt St, Dublin 2. **Map** D5. [01-478 4066. FAX 01-478 1576.					
Jolly hotel near St. Stephen's Green with young staff and a lively atmosphere in the evenings. There's a choice of bars and a more formal restaurant.					
SOUTHEAST DUBLIN: *Buswells*	€€€€	69		●	■
25 Molesworth St, Dublin 2. **Map** E4. [01-676 4013. FAX 01-676 2090.					
A short walk from Grafton Street, this old family favorite has recently been sold and thoroughly refurbished. A friendly, comfortable place to stay.					
SOUTHEAST DUBLIN: *Davenport*	€€€€€	118	■	●	
Merrion Sq, Dublin 2. **Map** F4. [01-661 6800. FAX 01-661 5663. W www.ocallaghanhotels.ie					
With its Neoclassical façade and vast marble-floored atrium of a lobby, the Davenport has the style of a grand gentleman's club.					
SOUTHEAST DUBLIN: *Shelbourne Hotel*	€€€€€	190	■	●	■
27 St. Stephen's Green, Dublin 2. **Map** D4. [01-676 6471. FAX 01-661 6006.					
The city's most distinguished hotel. Although it has every facility for the business traveler, it manages to retain a personal atmosphere.					
SOUTHWEST DUBLIN: *Avalon House*	€	60			
55 Aungier St, Dublin 2. **Map** C4. [01-475 0001. FAX 01-475 0303. W www.avalon-house.ie					
These cheap and cheerful accommodations have over 300 beds. The hotel is centrally located, with clean bedrooms and a self-service restaurant.					
SOUTHWEST DUBLIN: *Jury's Christchurch Inn*	€€	182		●	■
Christchurch Place, Dublin 8. **Map** B4. [01-454 0000. FAX 01-454 0012.					
The hotel offers spruce modern facilities, a good bar and restaurant, and neat, well-equipped rooms at reasonable prices.					
SOUTHWEST DUBLIN: *Clarence*	€€€€€	50	■	●	■
6–8 Wellington Quay, Dublin 2. **Map** C3. [01-407 0800. FAX 01-407 0820.					
A stylish restaurant sets the standard for the rest of this trendy Temple Bar hotel, bought and refurbished by the rock band U2.					
NORTH OF THE LIFFEY: *Gresham Hotel*	€€€€€	288	■	●	■
23 O'Connell St Upper, Dublin 1. **Map** D2. [01-874 6881. FAX 01-878 7175.					
One of Dublin's oldest and best known hotels. It is a popular rendezvous spot so the public areas are always busy. The bedrooms are comfortable.					
FARTHER AFIELD: *Glenogra Guesthouse*	€€	13	■	●	
64 Merrion Rd, Ballsbridge, Dublin 4. [01-668 3661. FAX 01-668 3698. W www.glenogra.com					
Attractive, stylish guesthouse convenient for Dun Laoghaire and the centre of Dublin. Bedrooms are charming and comfortable.					
FARTHER AFIELD: *Berkeley Court Hotel*	€€€€€	188	■	●	■
Lansdowne Rd, Dublin 4. [01-660 1711. FAX 01-660 2365. W www.jurysdoyle.com					
The very smart lobby area sets the standard for this luxury hotel, which is well located for Lansdowne Road stadium.					
REST OF IRELAND					
BELFAST: *Duke's Hotel*	££	20		●	■
65 University St, Belfast BT7 1HL. [028-9023 6666. FAX 028-9023 7177.					
W www.dukes-hotel.com					
A modern hotel offering comfort, style, and international cuisine in the heart of the city. It has a good public bar.					

Map references refer to map of Dublin on pp112–13

Price categories are for a standard double room (not per person) for one night, including tax, service charges, and breakfast. Prices for Belfast are in pounds sterling.

€ under €50 (under £50)
€€ €50–125 (£50–100)
€€€ €125–200 (£100–150)
€€€€ €200–250 (£150–200)
€€€€€ over €250 (over £200)

PRIVATE PARKING
Parking provided by the hotel in either a private car park or a private garage close by.

RESTAURANT
The hotel has a restaurant for residents which also welcomes non-residents – usually only for evening meals.

PUBLIC BAR
The hotel has a bar open to non-residents and residents alike.

		NUMBER OF ROOMS	PRIVATE PARKING	RESTAURANT	PUBLIC BAR
BELFAST: *The Europa Hotel* €€€ Great Victoria St, Belfast BT2 7AP. [028-9027 1066. FAX 028-9032 7800. W www.hastingshotels.com An imposing building right by the Grand Opera House. The hotel is ideal for business people and tourists, with very good restaurants.		240		●	■
CASHEL: *Cashel Palace Hotel* €€€€€ Main St, Cashel, Co. Tipperary. [062-62707. FAX 062-61521. W www.cashel-palace.ie A beautiful Palladian house built as the archbishop's palace in the 1730s. The hotel is set in a peaceful garden, right in the center of town.		23	■	●	
CLIFDEN: *Erriseask House* €€ Ballyconneely, Connemara, Co. Galway. [095-23553. FAX 095-23639. This modern farmhouse is stylishly decorated, with light, comfortable rooms. Only a short walk from the sea, the hotel offers superb food.		12	■	●	
CORK: *Lotamore House* €€ Tivoli, Cork, Co. Cork. [0214-822 344. FAX 0214-822 219. W www.lotamorehouse.com This guesthouse in a converted Georgian manor is surrounded by lovely grounds with good views of the harbor and Blackrock Castle. Five minutes' drive from Cork city center.		20	■		
DINGLE: *Benners Hotel* €€€€ Main St, Dingle, Co. Kerry. [066-915 1638. FAX 066-915 1412. W www.bennershotel.com An efficient, American-owned hotel right in the center of town, with a choice of bars, a restaurant, and comfortable bedrooms.		52	■	●	■
GALWAY: *Ardilaun House* €€€€ Taylor's Hill, Galway, Co. Galway. [091-521 433. FAX 091-521 546. W www.ardilaunhousehotel.ie A short distance from the center, this smart hotel is popular with business people and tourists. Friendly, efficient service.		89	■	●	■
GALWAY: *Great Southern Hotel* €€€€€ Eyre Sq, Galway, Co Galway. [091-564 041. FAX 091-566 704. W www.gshotels.com The rooftop swimming pool is an unusual feature of this large, rambling Victorian hotel in the heart of the city. There are plenty of facilities.		99	■	●	■
KILKENNY: *Butler House* €€€ 16 Patrick St, Kilkenny, Co. Kilkenny. [056-65707. FAX 056-65626. W www.butler.ie The former dower house of Kilkenny Castle, right in the heart of town. The elegant 18th-century building is stylishly decorated throughout.		13	■		
KILLARNEY: *Dunloe Castle Hotel* €€€ Co. Kerry. [064-44111. FAX 064-44583. The modern buildings of this hotel are located in lovely grounds close to the ruins of a 13th-century castle. Facilities are excellent. ● *Oct–Mar.*		102	■	●	■
KINSALE: *Old Bank House* €€€ 11 Pearse St, Kinsale, Co. Cork. [0214-774 075. FAX 0214-774 296. A listed Georgian building, formerly a branch of the Munster and Leinster Bank. It has finely proportioned, comfortable rooms and excellent staff.		17			
LETTERFRACK: *Rosleague Manor House* €€€€ Connemara, Co. Galway. [095-41101. FAX 095-41168. W www.rosleague.com A substantial Georgian house, overlooking Ballinakill Bay and well placed for Connemara National Park. The Rosleague has a comfortable, relaxed atmosphere and an excellent restaurant. ● *Nov–Easter.*		20	■	●	■
WATERFORD: *Waterford Castle Hotel* €€€€€ The Island, Ballinakill, Waterford, Co. Waterford. [051-878 203. FAX 051-879 316. Guests are ferried across the river to this romantically sited, 15th-century castle. Log fires blaze in luxurious, lofty rooms.		19	■	●	■

For key to symbols see back flap

Where to Eat in Ireland

THANKS TO THE ISLAND's high-quality fish and other fresh produce, Irish cooking now ranks among the best in Europe; the town of Kinsale in County Cork has established itself as "Gourmet Capital of Ireland." If your budget is small, it is still possible to eat well. In both city and rural locations, there are small cafés, pubs, and family-style restaurants serving good-value meals.

	VEGETARIAN DISHES	OPEN LATE	FIXED-PRICE MENU	GOOD WINE LIST
DUBLIN				
SOUTHEAST DUBLIN: *Kilkenny Shop Restaurant* €€ The Kilkenny Shop, 6–10 Nassau St. **Map** E4. 01-677 7066. A busy restaurant, overlooking Trinity College playing fields, offering traditional Irish cooking (including breakfast) and an extensive cheeseboard.	●		●	
SOUTHEAST DUBLIN: *L'Ecrivain* €€€€ 109 Baggot St Lower. **Map** F5. 01-661 1919. In the heart of Georgian Dublin, French classics here have an Irish touch, such as breast of guinea fowl with a black pudding mousse.	●	■		■
SOUTHEAST DUBLIN: *The Commons* €€€€ 85–6 Newman House, St. Stephen's Green South. **Map** D5. 01-478 0530. Specially commissioned paintings by Irish artists share the honors with gourmet specialties. Aperitifs can be taken in the pretty courtyard.	●	■	●	■
SOUTHEAST DUBLIN: *The Fado* €€€€ Mansion House, Dawson Street. **Map** F5. 01-676 7200. Part of the Mansion House, the stunning Belle Epoque dining room is the setting for Irish cuisine with a French influence.	●	■		
SOUTHWEST DUBLIN: *Leo Burdock's* € 2 Werburgh St. **Map** B4. 01-454 0306. Dublin's oldest fish-and-chips takeout attracts a mix of patrons. The fish are fresh, and the chips made from top-grade Irish potatoes.		■		
SOUTHWEST DUBLIN: *Elephant and Castle* €€€€ 18 Temple Bar. **Map** D3. 01-679 3121. This boisterous American-style restaurant serves upscale cooked-to-order food, from tortillas to hamburgers. It is popular for brunch on Sunday.	●	■	●	■
NORTH OF THE LIFFEY: *Chapter One Restaurant* €€€€ Below Dublin Writers Museum, Parnell Square. **Map** C1. 01-873 2266. Portraits of Irish writers adorn the walls of this restaurant. The deep-fried Parmesan and sage gnocchi and king scallops with leeks and mussels are excellent.	●	■	●	■
NORTH OF THE LIFFEY: *Flanagan's Restaurant* €€€€ 61 O'Connell St Upper. **Map** D2. 01-873 1388. A popular family restaurant, Flanagan's is great value for money. The extensive menu ranges from burgers and salads to vegetarian and pasta dishes.	●	■		
FARTHER AFIELD: *Abbey Tavern* €€€ Abbey St, Howth. 01-839 0282. A 16th-century tavern complete with open turf fires and Irish music sessions, just off Howth harbour, and specializing in seafood. Book ahead.	●	■		■
FARTHER AFIELD: *Pier 32* €€€€ 22–23 Pembroke St Upper, Dublin 2. 01-676 1494. The regularly changing menu includes seafood and regional dishes. Try the delicious champ (mashed potatoes, spring onions, and butter).		■	●	■
REST OF IRELAND				
ARAN ISLANDS: *Dún Aonghasa & Aran Fisherman Restaurant* €€€€ Kilronan, Inishmore. 099-61104. In a building overlooking the harbor, chef Grace Flaherty uses fish fresh from Galway Bay for dishes such as seafood chowder and grilled shark.	●	■		■
BELFAST: *Cayenne* £££££ 7 Lesley House, Shaftesbury Sq. 028-9033 1532. Celebrity chefs Paul and Jeanne Rankin are the owners of this city center restaurant, which serves delicious Asian-influenced dishes.	●	■	●	■

Map references refer to map of Dublin on pp112–13.

		VEGETARIAN DISHES	OPEN LATE	FIXED-PRICE MENU	GOOD WINE LIST

Price categories are for a three-course meal for one, half a bottle of house wine, and any unavoidable charges, such as cover or service. Prices for Belfast are in pounds sterling.

€ under €15 (under £10)
€€ €15–20 (£10–15)
€€€ €20–30 (£15–25)
€€€€ over €30 (£25–50)

OPEN LATE
The restaurant remains open with a full menu available after 10pm.
FIXED-PRICE MENU
A good-value fixed-price menu on offer at lunch, dinner, or both, usually with three courses.
GOOD WINE LIST
Denotes a wide range of good wines, or a more specialized selection of wines.

BLARNEY: *Phelan's Woodview House* €€€€
Tweedmount. ☎ 0214-385 197.
This intimate restaurant often draws diners from nearby Cork. Make sure you sample chef Billy Phelan's hot seafood parcel. ● *lunch daily, Sun, Mon.* ✂ ♿ 🍷
| ● | ■ | ● | ■ |

BUNRATTY: *Mews Restaurant* €€€€
Bunratty House Mews. ☎ 061-364 082.
Downstairs in this 1846 mansion, the original kitchen, staff quarters, and wine cellars form one of the best restaurants in the country. ● *lunch daily, Jan.* ✂ 🍷
| ● | | ● | |

CASHEL: *Chez Hans* €€€€
Rockside. ☎ 062-61177.
In a former Wesleyan chapel, Hans-Peter Matthiä creates wonderfully innovative versions of traditional dishes. ● *lunch daily, late Jan, late Sep.* ✂ ♿ 🍷
| ● | | ● | ■ |

CLIFDEN: *O'Grady's Seafood Restaurant* €€€€
Market St. ☎ 095-21450.
Award-winning O'Grady's offers wonderful seafood, such as baked fillet of cod with a Calvados cream glaze, as well as superb vegetarian choices including an avocado and blue cheese mousse in puff pastry. ● *late Mar–Nov.* ✂ 🍷
| ● | | ● | ■ |

CORK: *Arbutus Lodge Hotel* €€€€
Montenotte. ☎ 0214-501 237.
The bar serves good-value lunchtime food. The more formal restaurant offers gourmet dinners mixing Irish, French, and other international cuisines. ♿ ✂ 🍷
| ● | | ● | ■ |

DINGLE: *Fenton's Bistro* €€€€
Green St. ☎ 066-915 2172.
This bright popular bistro opens for the season and uses local produce. The cooking is a fusion of traditional Irish and Mediterranean. ● *Mon, Nov–Mar.* ✂ 🍷
| ● | | ● | ■ |

GALWAY: *The Park Room* €€€€
Forster St, Eyre Sq. ☎ 091-564 924.
Inside the Park House Hotel, this restaurant offers a well-priced menu of Irish specialties such as honey-glazed rack of lamb, all prepared with local ingredients. ✂ ♿ 🍷
| ● | | | |

KILLARNEY: *Gaby's* €€€€
27 High St. ☎ 064-32519.
The best seafood restaurant in town, decorated with seafaring memorabilia. Specialties include lobster, shellfish, oysters, and Atlantic salmon. ● *Sun, lunch daily.* ✂ ♿ 🍷
| ● | | | ■ |

KILKENNY: *Langton's Restaurant and Bar* €€€€
69 John St. ☎ 056-65133.
At Langton's, fresh fish and traditional dishes are served in the bright conservatory restaurant. Stuffed mussels are among local favorites. ✂ ♿ 🍷
| ● | | ● | ■ |

KINSALE: *Man Friday* €€€€
Scilly. ☎ 0214-772 260.
This restaurant overlooking the harbor has won culinary awards galore, with specialties such as black sole with seafood stuffing. ● *lunch daily.* ✂ ♿ 🍷
| ● | | | ■ |

KINSALE: *Max's Wine Bar* €€€€
Main St. ☎ 0214-772 443.
Max's has been one of Kinsale's leading gourmet restaurants for over 20 years. The emphasis is on fresh local ingredients, meat, and fish. ● *Tue & Nov–Feb.* ✂ 🍷
| ● | ■ | ● | ■ |

WATERFORD: *O'Grady's* €€€€
Cork Rd. ☎ 051-378 851.
An innovative use of fresh local ingredients characterizes the delectable fare at this bright restaurant near the Waterford Crystal factory. ✂ 🍷
| ● | | | |

FRANCE AND THE
LOW COUNTRIES

France and the Low Countries at a Glance

FRANCE DOMINATES the northwest of continental Europe. To the northeast of France lie Belgium and the Netherlands, known as the Low Countries because they occupy flat plains and land reclaimed from the sea. South of Belgium is the tiny state of Luxembourg. France has some of Europe's greatest attractions, notably the culture and nightlife of Paris. Visitors often choose to tour just one or two of the country's regions: the mountains of the Alps or the Pyrenees, one of the historic wine-growing areas, or the warm south. Belgium and the Netherlands have many historic cities full of fine museums and art galleries. Visiting these countries can be rewarding because all the major sights lie within easy reach of each other.

Paris *(see pp150–71), France's capital, is a city of distinctive districts. Montmartre, the hilltop artists' quarter, is dominated by the Sacré Coeur.*

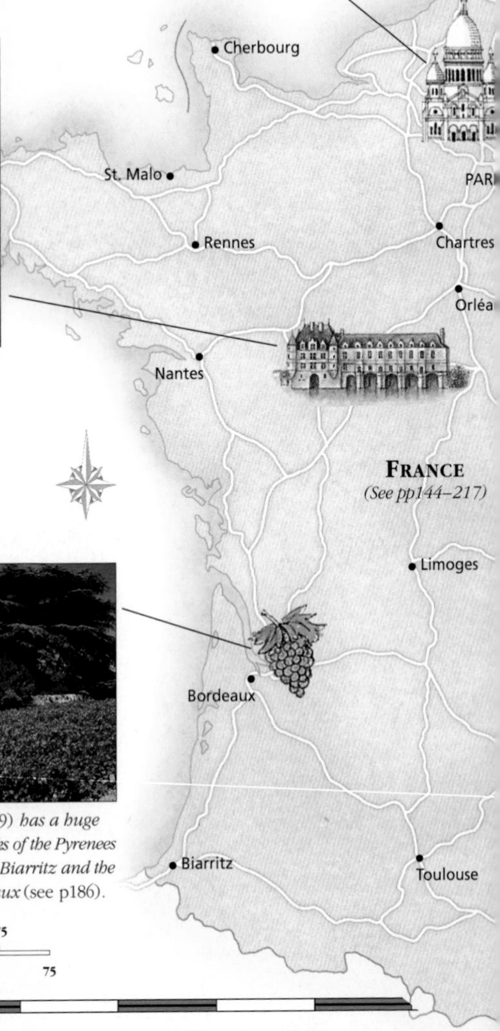

The Loire Valley *(see pp176–9) is one of France's most popular regions for touring. It is dotted with magnificent châteaux, built by kings and nobles during the Renaissance. One of the finest is Chenonceau.*

Southwest France *(see pp188–9) has a huge variety of attractions, from the peaks of the Pyrenees to Atlantic seaside resorts such as Biarritz and the world-famous vineyards of Bordeaux (see p186).*

- Cherbourg
- St. Malo
- Rennes
- Nantes
- PAR
- Chartres
- Orléa
- Limoges

FRANCE
(See pp144–217)

- Bordeaux
- Biarritz
- Toulouse

0 km   75

0 miles   75

◁ **A field of poppies in northeast France, where the battles of World War I were fought**

NETHERLANDS
(See pp244–271)

● AMSTERDAM

● BRUSSELS

BELGIUM AND LUXEMBOURG
(See pp218–243)

● LUXEMBOURG CITY

● Reims

Nancy

Strasbourg

● Troyes

● Dijon

● Besançon

nt-
d

● Lyon

● Grenoble

Cannes ●

● Marseille

LOCATOR MAP

Amsterdam (see pp248–59) *is a unique city, criss-crossed by canals, its relaxed atmosphere a refreshing change from Europe's other traffic-clogged capital cities.*

Brussels (see pp222–9), *the capital of Belgium, thrives as the headquarters of the European Union. The Grand Place, with its soaring Gothic town hall, is one of Europe's most spectacular squares.*

Dijon (see pp184–5) *flourished in the Middle Ages under the powerful dukes of Burgundy. The former palace where the dukes held court now houses the prestigious Musée des Beaux Arts, with its rich collection of art and sculpture.*

The South of France (see pp190–97) *is one of the traditional playgrounds of Europe's rich and famous, where grand hotels, luxury yachts, and pristine beaches contrast with picturesque old fishing ports.*

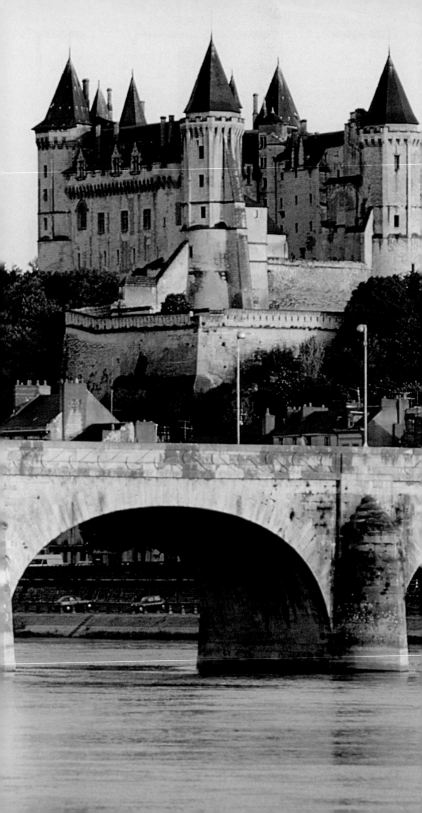

FRANCE

THE BEST ADVOCATES *for visiting France are the French themselves, convinced as they are that their way of life is best, and their country the most civilized on earth. The food and wine are justly celebrated, while French literature, art, cinema, and architecture can be both profound and provocative. France is a country that stimulates the intellect and gratifies the senses.*

France belongs to both northern and southern Europe, encompassing regions ranging from Brittany, with its Celtic maritime heritage, and Germanic Alsace-Lorraine, to the Mediterranean sunbelt and the peaks of the Alps and Pyrenees. The capital, Paris, is the country's linchpin, with its intellectual excitement, intense tempo of life, and notoriously brusque citizens.

Strangely, as life in France becomes more city-based and industrialized, so the desire grows to safeguard the old, traditional ways and to value rural life. The idea of life in the country – *douceur de vivre* (the Good Life), long tables set in the sun for the wine and anecdotes to flow – is as seductive as ever for residents and visitors alike. Nevertheless, the rural way of life has been changing. Whereas in 1945 one person in three worked in farming, today it is only one in 16. France's main exports used to be luxury goods such as perfumes, Champagne, and Cognac; today, these have been overtaken by cars, telecommunications equipment, and fighter aircraft. The French remain firmly committed to their roots, however, and often keep a place in the country for vacations or their retirement.

HISTORY

Though famous for the rootedness of its peasant population, France has also been a European melting pot, from the arrival of the Celtic Gauls in the 1st millennium BC, through to the Mediterranean immigrations of the 20th century. Roman conquest by Julius Caesar had an enduring impact but, from the 4th and 5th centuries AD, Germanic invaders destroyed much of the Roman legacy. The Franks provided political leadership in the following centuries, but when their line died out in the late 10th century, France was politically fragmented.

The traditional game of *boules* or *pétanque*, still a popular pastime – especially in the south

◁ The Château de Saumur, one of the many fairy-tale castles of the Loire Valley

The Capetian dynasty gradually pieced France together over the Middle Ages, a period of economic prosperity and cultural vitality. The Black Death and the Hundred Years' War brought setbacks, and French power was seriously threatened by the dukes of Burgundy and the English crown. In the Renaissance period, François I (reigned 1515–47) dreamt of making France a major power, but was thwarted by the Habsburg Emperor Charles V. The Reformation then plunged the country into religious conflict. However, the 17th century saw France, under Louis XIV, rise to dominate Europe militarily and intellectually.

Napoleon, the brilliant general who rose to be Emperor of France

In the Age of Enlightenment French culture and institutions were the envy of Europe. The ideas of Voltaire and Rousseau undermined the authority of the Church and the state, nowhere more than in France itself. The Revolution of 1789 ended the absolute monarchy and introduced major social and institutional reforms, many of which were endorsed by Napoleon, whose empire dominated Europe at the start of the 19th century. Yet the Revolution also inaugurated the instability that has remained a hallmark of French politics: since 1789, France has seen three forms of monarchy, two empires, and five republics.

Throughout the political turmoil of the 19th century, France remained a leading source of literary and artistic movements. In painting, the French Impressionists were the inspiration for the development of modern art and would-be painters began to flock to Paris instead of Rome. France also retained its position as the arbiter of taste in fashion, food, wine, and good manners.

Rivalry with Germany dominated French politics for most of the late 19th and early 20th centuries. The population losses in World War I were traumatic for France, while during 1940–44 the country was occupied by Germany. Yet since 1955, the two countries have proved the backbone of the developing European Union.

MODERN POLITICS

For much of the 20th century, domestic politics was marked by confrontations between Left and Right. In 1958 the problems of governing the country led to the introduction of a new constitution – the Fifth Republic – with Charles de Gaulle as president.

KEY DATES IN FRENCH HISTORY

1200–700 BC Arrival of the Celts during Bronze and Iron Ages

51 BC Romans complete conquest of Gaul

AD 481 Frankish leader Clovis becomes first Merovingian king

800 Coronation of Charlemagne, greatest of the Carolingians, as Holy Roman Emperor

1180–1223 Reign of Philip Augustus

1337–1453 Hundred Years' War with England

1562–93 Wars of Religion

1660–1715 Reign of Louis XIV

1789 French Revolution

1804 Napoleon crowned emperor

1815 Defeat of Napoleon: monarchy restored

1848 Revolution; short-lived Second Republic

1852–70 Second Empire under Napoleon III

1919 Treaty of Versailles following defeat of Germany in World War I

1940 Germans overrun France

1958 Fifth Republic with Charles de Gaulle as president

1968 May uprising of students and workers brings downfall of de Gaulle

---

The student uprising of May 1968, which challenged all the old assumptions of the French ruling elite

Relaxing in the sun at a traditional French café

Avant-garde art and literature and modern architecture enjoy strong patronage in France. Exciting architectural projects range from new buildings in Paris – the Louvre pyramid and La Grande Arche at La Défense – to the post-modern housing projects of Nîmes and Marseille in the south.

CONTEMPORARY SOCIETY

Social change has resulted from the decline in the influence of the Catholic Church. Parental authoritarianism has waned and there is a much freer ambience in schools – two trends resulting from the May 1968 uprising.

French social life, except between close friends, has always been marked by formality – handshaking, and the use of titles and the formal *vous* rather than the intimate *tu*. However, this is changing, especially among the young, who now call you by your first name, and use *tu* even in an office context. Standards of dress have become more informal too, though the French are still very concerned to dress well.

However, in 1968 protesting students and striking workers combined to paralyse the country and de Gaulle resigned the following year.

The old divide between Left and Right has given way to a more center-focused consensus fostered by François Mitterrand, Socialist President from 1981 to 1995, and forced on the Conservative Jacques Chirac, who succeeded him, by the election of Socialist Lionel Jospin as Prime Minister in 1997.

Tempting display of *charcuterie* and cheeses on a Lyon market stall

France is a country where tradition and progress are found side by side. The Euro has taken over, yet some people still calculate in old Francs, replaced back in 1960. France's agribusiness is one of the most modern in the world, but the peasant farmer is deeply revered. France has Europe's largest hypermarkets, which have been ousting local grocers. Although American in inspiration, they are French in what they sell, with wonderful displays of cheeses and a huge range of fresh vegetables, fruit, and herbs.

The Republican spirit, however, lives on in strikes and mass demonstrations. Unemployment – France's worst social problem – has led to growing racism against Arab immigrants, many of whom are from former French colonies in North Africa.

LANGUAGE AND CULTURE

Culture is taken seriously in France: writers, intellectuals, artists, and fashion designers are held in high esteem. The French remain justly proud of their cinema, and are determined to defend it against pressures from Hollywood. Other activities – from the music industry to the French language itself – are subject to the same protectionist attitudes.

The TGV, France's impressive high-speed train

Exploring France

FRANCE IS A LARGE COUNTRY and, although it has over 60 million inhabitants, is less densely populated than most of its western European neighbors. Paris belongs to northern Europe, while the south is Mediterranean in climate and lifestyle. Distances limit the amount of the country you can visit, though train services are good and there is an extensive network of highways. Popular tourist destinations include the châteaux of the Loire, the mountains of the Alps and Pyrenees, historic wine-growing regions (*see pp186–7*), and the resorts of the Côte d'Azur.

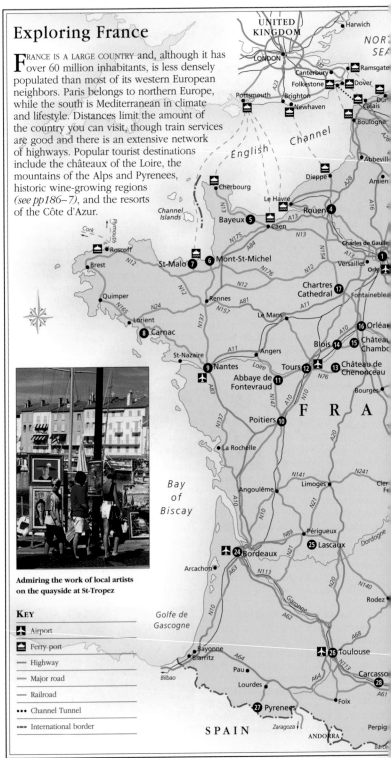

Admiring the work of local artists on the quayside at St-Tropez

KEY

✈	Airport
⛴	Ferry port
—	Highway
—	Major road
—	Railroad
•••	Channel Tunnel
---	International border

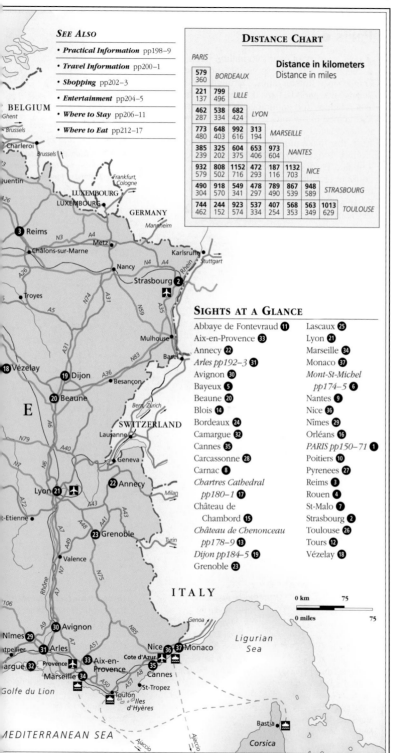

DISTANCE CHART

Distance in kilometers
Distance in miles

PARIS								
579 / 360	BORDEAUX							
221 / 137	799 / 496	LILLE						
462 / 287	538 / 334	682 / 424	LYON					
773 / 480	648 / 403	992 / 616	313 / 194	MARSEILLE				
385 / 239	325 / 202	604 / 375	653 / 406	973 / 604	NANTES			
932 / 579	808 / 502	1152 / 716	472 / 293	187 / 116	1132 / 703	NICE		
490 / 304	918 / 570	549 / 341	478 / 297	789 / 490	867 / 539	948 / 589	STRASBOURG	
744 / 462	244 / 152	923 / 574	537 / 334	407 / 254	568 / 353	563 / 349	1013 / 629	TOULOUSE

SIGHTS AT A GLANCE

Abbaye de Fontevraud ⑪
Aix-en-Provence ㉝
Annecy ㉒
Arles pp192–3 ㉛
Avignon ㉚
Bayeux ⑤
Beaune ⑳
Blois ⑭
Bordeaux ㉔
Camargue ㉜
Cannes ㉟
Carcassonne ㉘
Carnac ⑧
Chartres Cathedral pp180–1 ⑰
Château de Chambord ⑮
Château de Chenonceau pp178–9 ⑬
Dijon pp184–5 ⑲
Grenoble ㉓

Lascaux ㉕
Lyon ㉑
Marseille ㉞
Monaco ㊲
Mont-St-Michel pp174–5 ⑥
Nantes ⑨
Nice ㊱
Nîmes ㉙
Orléans ⑯
PARIS pp150–71 ①
Poitiers ⑩
Pyrenees ㉗
Reims ③
Rouen ④
St-Malo ⑦
Strasbourg ②
Toulouse ㉖
Tours ⑫
Vézelay ⑱

0 km 75
0 miles 75

Paris ❶

Paris is a city of over two million people, and has been the economic, political, and artistic hub of France since Roman times. During the medieval and Renaissance periods, Paris dominated northern Europe as a religious and cultural center. The city was rejuvenated in the mid-19th century, when its slums were replaced with the elegant avenues and boulevards that make modern Paris a delight to stroll around. Today the city strives to be at the heart of a unified Europe. Chic cafés, gourmet restaurants, and fashionable shopping are the major attractions for many visitors.

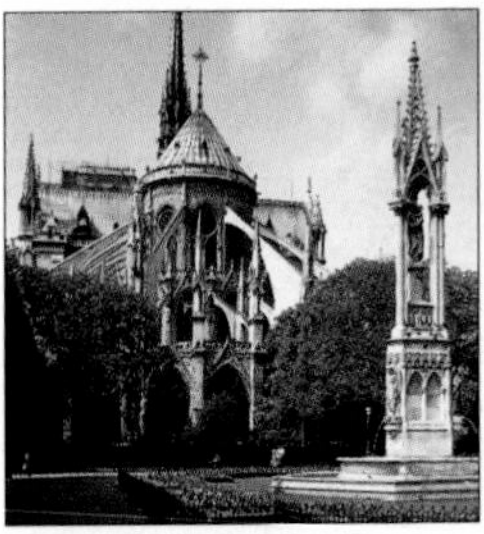

Notre-Dame viewed from the tranquil setting of Square Jean XXIII

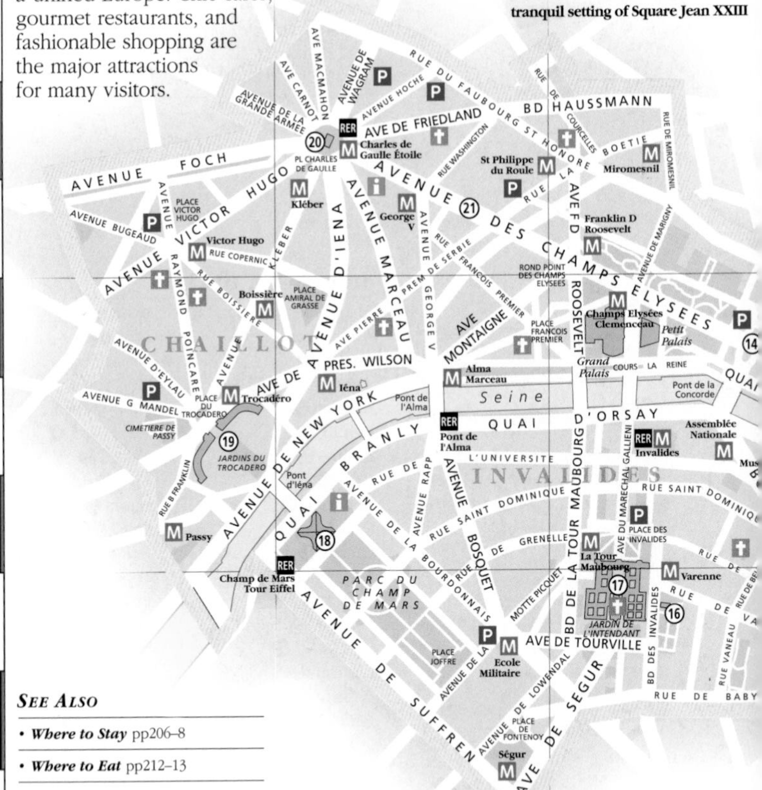

See Also

- *Where to Stay* pp206–8
- *Where to Eat* pp212–13

Sights at a Glance

Arc de Triomphe ⑳
Centre Pompidou ④
Champs-Elysées ㉑
Eiffel Tower ⑱
Ile de la Cité ①
Les Invalides ⑰
Jardin du Luxembourg ⑨
Jardin des Tuileries ⑫
Musée du Louvre pp158–60 ⑪
Musée de l'Orangerie ⑬
Musée d'Orsay ⑮
Musée Picasso ⑤
Musée Rodin ⑯
Notre-Dame pp154–5 ②
Palais de Chaillot ⑲
Panthéon ⑧
Place de la Bastille ⑦
Place de la Concorde ⑭
Place des Vosges ⑥
St-Germain-des-Prés ⑩
Sainte-Chapelle ③

Greater Paris *(see inset map)*
Basilique de St-Denis ㉘
Bois de Boulogne ㉖
Château de Fontainebleau ㉛
Château de Vaux-le-Vicomte ㉚
Château de Versailles pp168–9 ㉗
Cimetière du Père Lachaise ㉔
La Défense ㉕
Disneyland Paris ㉙
Montmartre ㉒
Parc de la Villette ㉓

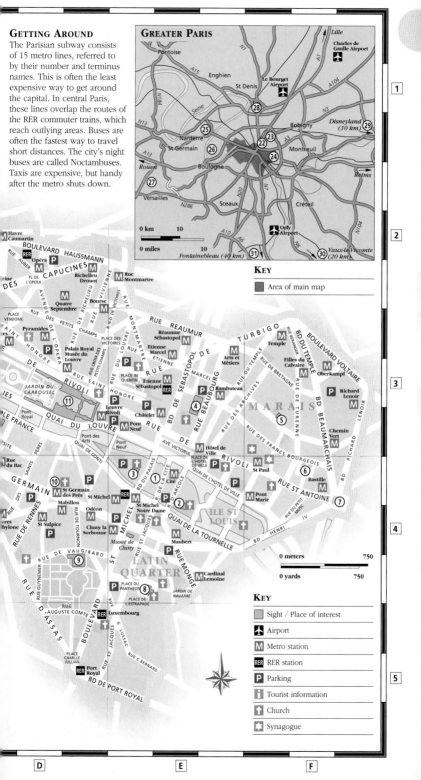

GETTING AROUND

The Parisian subway consists of 15 metro lines, referred to by their number and terminus names. This is often the least expensive way to get around the capital. In central Paris, these lines overlap the routes of the RER commuter trains, which reach outlying areas. Buses are often the fastest way to travel short distances. The city's night buses are called Noctambuses. Taxis are expensive, but handy after the metro shuts down.

GREATER PARIS

Lille

Charles de Gaulle Airport

Pontoise

Enghien

N1

A15

A1

A104

Le Bourget Airport

St Denis

Seine

28

N3

N13

Bobigny

Disneyland (10 km)

29

25

Nanterre

St Germain

22 23

A3

26

24

Montreuil

A13

Rouen

Boulogne

27

Versailles

N20

N7

N2

Reims

Sceaux

Créteil

N286

Fontainebleau (40 km)

31

A10 A6

Orly Airport

N6

N104

30

Vaux-le-Vicomte (20 km)

0 km   10

0 miles   10

KEY

Area of main map

Havre Caumartin M

BOULEVARD HAUSSMANN

RUE AUBER

RER

Opéra M

PL DE L'OPERA

CAPUCINES

Richelieu Drouot M

Rue Montmartre M

RUE DES

cine

AVENUE DE L'OPERA

Quatre Septembre M

Bourse M

RUE VIVIENNE

RUE REAUMUR

Réaumur Sébastopol M

TURBIGO

BD DU TEMPLE

Temple M

RUE BERANGER

BOULEVARD VOLTAIRE

PLACE VENDOME

Pyramides M

RUE DE RICHELIEU

RUE DES PETITS CHAMPS

PLACE DES VICTOIRES

RUE CROIX DES PETITS CHAMPS

Etienne Marcel M

RUE ETIENNE MARCEL

Arts et Métiers M

RUE DE BRETAGNE

Filles du Calvaire M

RUE DE TURENNE

Oberkampf M

SAINT HONORE

M

DE

Palais Royal Musée du Louvre M

RUE SAINT HONORE

RUE DU

PLACE M QUENTIN

Etienne Sébastopol M RER

BD DE SEBASTOPOL

RUE MONTORGUEIL

Rambuteau M

RUE DES ARCHIVES

MARAIS

Richard Lenoir P

BD BEAUMARCHAIS

BD RICHARD LENOIR

JARDIN DU CARROUSEL

11

DE RIVOLI

Louvre Rivoli M

Châtelet M

4

RUE BEAUBOURG

5

Chemin Vert M

Pont Royal

QUAI DU LOUVRE

Pont Neuf M

RUE DE

AVE VICTORIA

Hôtel de Ville M

RIVOLI

RUE DES FRANCS BOURGEOIS

Bastille M

LE FRANCE

Pont des Arts

QUAI DE CONTI

Pont Neuf

BD DU PALAIS

Cité M

PLACE DE L'HOTEL DE VILLE

QUAI DE L'HOTEL DE VILLE

St Paul M

6

RUE ST ANTOINE

7

site

Rue du Bac M

RER

St Germain des Prés M

10

St Michel M RER

RUE DE LA CITE

RUE D'ARCOLE

2

St Michel Notre Dame M

Pont Marie M

RUE DU PETIT MUSC

BD HENRI IV

GERMAIN

RUE DE RENNES

Mabillon M

Odéon M

St Sulpice M

RUE DE TOURNON

Cluny la Sorbonne M

BD ST MICHEL

RUE ST JACQUES

3

1

Musée de Cluny

QUAI DE LA TOURNELLE

ILE ST LOUIS

bylone

RUE DES SAINTS PERES

res

RUE DE VAUGIRARD

9

LATIN QUARTER

RUE MONGE

Maubert M

Cardinal Lemoine M

RUE GUYNEMER

PLACE DU PANTHEON

8

PLACE DE L'ESTRAPADE

JARDIN DE NAVARRE

RUE D'ASSAS

AUGUSTE COMTE

RUE

BOULEVARD ST JACQUES

Luxembourg RER

RUE ST JACQUES

PLACE CAMILLE JULLIAN

Port Royal RER

RUE C BERNARD

RUE DE LUSSAC

BD DE PORT ROYAL

0 meters   750

0 yards   750

KEY

Sight / Place of interest

✈ Airport

M Metro station

RER RER station

P Parking

ℹ Tourist information

✝ Church

✡ Synagogue

Western end of the Ile de la Cité, where the island is crossed by the Pont Neuf

Ile de la Cité ①

M *Pont Neuf, Cité.* **Conciergerie**
1 Quai de l'Horloge. **C** *01-53 73
78 50.* ◯ *daily.* ● *Jan 1, May 1,
Nov 1 & 11, Dec 25.* 🖼 🗹

THIS BOAT-SHAPED island on
the Seine is the nucleus of
Paris. The capital's name
derives from the Parisii, one
of the Celtic tribes who lived
here in the 3rd century BC.
The settlement was later
expanded by the Romans, the
Franks, and the Capetian kings.
Remains of the earliest
buildings can be seen in the
Crypte Archéologique,
below the square in front of
the mighty Notre-Dame
cathedral, which stands at
one end of the island. At the
other end is another Gothic
masterpiece: the Sainte-
Chapelle church, surrounded
by the huge complex of
buildings forming the **Palais
de Justice**. One of these, the
sinister-looking **Conciergerie**,
was a prison from 1391 until
1914. During the French
Revolution the prison filled to
overflowing, and Marie-
Antoinette was held in a tiny
cell here until her execution
in 1793. The Conciergerie has
a superb Gothic Hall and a
14th-century clock tower.
Crossing the western end of
the island is the oldest bridge
in Paris, the oddly named
Pont Neuf (new bridge),
which dates back to 1578.

The colorful Marché aux
Fleurs et Oiseaux takes place
daily in the Place Louis Lépine
and is the city's most famous
flower market. On Sundays
caged birds are also sold.

Notre-Dame ②

See pp154–5.

Sainte-Chapelle ③

4 Boulevard du Palais. **C** *01-53 73 78
50.* **M** *Cité.* ◯ *daily.* ● *Jan 1, May
1, Nov 1 & 11, Dec 25.* 🖼 🖵 🗹

HAILED AS ONE of the great
architectural masterpieces
of the Western world, in the
Middle Ages this church
was likened to "a
gateway to heaven."
Sainte-Chapelle was built
in 1248 to house sacred
relics, including Christ's
Crown of Thorns,
purchased from the
Byzantine emperor at
great expense by the
devout King Louis IX.
The church consists of
two chapels. The lower
chapel was used by
servants and minor
officials, while the
exquisite upper chapel,
reached by means of a
narrow, spiral staircase,
was reserved for the
royal family and courtiers.
This chapel has many

glorious stained-glass
windows, separated by
pencil-like columns soaring
15 m (50 ft) to the star-
studded roof. Over 1,100
biblical scenes from the Old
and New Testaments are
depicted, as well as the story
of how the relics were
brought to Sainte-Chapelle.
The 86 panels of the circular
Rose Window, which are best
seen at sunset, tell the story
of the Apocalypse.
Badly damaged during the
Revolution, and converted
into a flour warehouse, the
church was renovated a
century later by architect
Viollet-le-Duc. The spire,
erected in 1853, rises 75 m
(245 ft) into the air.

The Gothic Sainte-Chapelle church

Centre Pompidou ④

Centre d'Art et de Culture Georges Pompidou, Pl G Pompidou. 📞 01-44 78 12 33. Ⓜ Rambuteau, Châtelet, Hôtel de Ville. ⓇⒺⓇ Châtelet-Les-Halles. 🚌 21, 29, 38, 47 & many others. **Musée National d'Art Moderne** 🕐 11am–9pm Wed–Mon. 💲 🚫 ♿ Ⓦ www.centrepompidou.fr

WITH ITS SKELETON of struts, ducts, and elevators scaling the outside of the building, and offering fine views of the city, this famous cultural center has room for a vast exhibition area inside.

Among the artists featured in the Musée National d'Art Moderne are Matisse, Picasso, Miró, and Pollock, representing such schools as Fauvism, Cubism, and Surrealism. Star attractions are *Sorrow of the King* (1952) by Matisse, and Georges Braque's *The Duo* (1937). A library is housed on the first, second, and third floors, while temporary exhibitions are held on the first and sixth floors.

Outside, the Piazza is usually full of crowds watching the street performers. On one side of the square, the Atelier Brancusi is a reconstruction of the workshop of Romanian-born artist Constantin Brancusi (1876–1957), who left his entire *oeuvre* to the nation.

Musée Picasso ⑤

Hôtel Salé, 5 Rue de Thorigny. 📞 01-42 71 25 21. Ⓜ St-Sébastien Froissart. 🕐 Wed–Mon. ⬤ Jan 1, Dec 25. 💲 🚫 📷 ♿

THE SPANISH-BORN artist Pablo Picasso (1881–1973) spent most of his life in France. On his death, the French state inherited many of his works in lieu of death duties, opening a museum to display them in 1985. Housed in a 17th-century mansion originally built for a salt tax collector, the collection comprises over 200 paintings, 158 sculptures, 83 ceramic works, and some 3,000 sketches and engravings. The full extent of Picasso's artistic development is presented, from the somber Blue period *Self-Portrait*

Pipes and ducts on the outside of the Centre Pompidou

(1901) to Cubist collages and Neoclassical works such as *Pipes of Pan*. Highlights include *The Two Brothers* (1906) and *The Kiss* (1969).

The museum also features a sculpture garden and exhibits works from Picasso's private art collection, including paintings by Rousseau, Renoir, Cézanne, Braque, Balthus, Miró, and Matisse.

Place des Vosges ⑥

Ⓜ Bastille, St-Paul.

THIS PERFECTLY symmetrical square, laid out in 1605 by Henri IV, and known as Place Royale, was once the residence of the aristocracy. Considered among the most beautiful in the world by Parisians and visitors alike, the square is surrounded by 36 houses, nine

on each side. Built of brick and stone, with dormer windows over arcades, they have survived intact for almost 400 years. Today, the historic houses accommodate antiques shops and fashionable cafés.

The square has been the scene of many historical events over the centuries, including a three-day tournament in celebration of the marriage of Louis XIII to Anne of Austria in 1615. Among the square's famous former residents are the literary hostess, Madame de Sévigné, born here in 1626, Cardinal Richelieu, pillar of the monarchy, and Victor Hugo, who lived in one of the houses for 16 years.

Place de la Bastille ⑦

Ⓜ Bastille.

NOTHING REMAINS of the infamous prison stormed by the revolutionary mob on July 14, 1789, the event that sparked the French Revolution. A row of paving stones from No. 5 to No. 49 Boulevard Henri IV traces the line of former fortifications.

The 52-m (170-ft) hollow bronze Colonne de Juillet stands in the middle of the traffic-clogged square to honor the victims of the July Revolution of 1830. On the south side of the square (at 120 Rue de Lyon) is the 2,700-seat **Opéra Bastille**, completed in 1989, the bicentennial of the French Revolution.

Central fountain and fine Renaissance houses in the Place des Vosges

Notre-Dame ②

N O OTHER BUILDING embodies the history of Paris more than Notre-Dame. It stands majestically on the Ile de la Cité, cradle of the city. Built on the site of a Roman temple, the cathedral was commissioned by Bishop de Sully in 1159. The first stone was laid in 1163, marking the start of two centuries of toil by armies of medieval architects and craftsmen. It has been witness to great events of French history ever since, including the coronation of Napoleon Bonaparte (1804) and the state funeral of Charles de Gaulle (1970). During the Revolution, the building was desecrated and rechristened the Temple of Reason. Extensive renovations (including the addition of the spire and gargoyles) were carried out in the 19th century by architect Viollet-le-Duc.

★ West Front
Three main portals with superb statuary, a central rose window, and an openwork gallery are the outstanding features of the cathedral's façade.

The South Tower houses Emmanuel, the cathedral's most sonorous bell.

★ Galerie des Chimières
The cathedral's grotesque gargoyles (chimières) perch menacingly around ledges high on the façade.

The West Rose Window depicts the Virgin in a medallion of rich reds and blues.

STAR FEATURES

- **★ West Front and Portals**
- **★ Flying Buttresses**
- **★ Rose Windows**
- **★ Galerie des Chimières**

The Kings' Gallery features 28 kings of Judah gazing down from above the main door.

★ Portal of the Virgin
A statue of the Virgin surrounded by saints and kings decorates this massive 13th-century portal.

★ **Flying Buttresses**
*Jean Ravy's spectacular flying buttresses
at the east end of the cathedral have a
span of 15 m (50 ft).*

The Spire, designed
by Viollet-le-Duc,
soars to a height of
90 m (295 ft).

VISITORS' CHECKLIST

6 Place du Parvis-Notre-Dame.
[C] 01-42 34 56 10. [M] Cité.
[bus] 21, 38, 85, 96 to Ile de la
Cité. [○] 8am–6:45pm daily
(Treasury: 10am–6:45pm daily;
towers: 2:45pm daily.)
[†] 8am, 9am, noon, 6:15pm
Mon–Fri; 8am, 9am, noon,
6:30pm Sat; 8am, 8.45am,
10am, 11:30am, 12:30pm,
6:30pm Sun. [⌨] for Treasury
and towers. [✶]

★ **South Rose Window**
*The south façade window, with its
central depiction of Christ, is an
impressive 13 m (43 ft) in diameter.*

The Treasury
houses the
cathedral's
religious
treasures,
including
ancient
manuscripts
and reliquaries.

The transept was
completed during the
reign of Louis IX, in
the 13th century.

Statue of Virgin and Child
*Against the southeast pillar
of the crossing stands the
14th-century statue of the
Virgin and Child. It was
brought to the cathedral
from the chapel of St. Aignan
and is known as Notre-Dame
de Paris (Our Lady of Paris).*

The Cathedral from the Left Bank
*Notre-Dame's spectacular island setting
is enhanced by the trees of Square
Jean XXIII, a formal garden laid out
at the eastern end of the Ile de la Cité.*

Street-by-Street: Latin Quarter

Since the middle ages this riverside quarter has been dominated by the Sorbonne – it acquired its name from early Latin-speaking students. The area is generally associated with artists, intellectuals, and a bohemian way of life, and has a history of political unrest. In 1871 the Place St-Michel became the center of the Paris Commune, and in May 1968 it was one of the sites of the student uprisings that briefly engulfed the city.

★ **St-Séverin**
Begun in the 13th century, this beautiful church took three centuries to build and is a fine example of the Flamboyant Gothic style.

★ **Boulevard St-Michel**
The northern end of the Boul'Mich, as it is affectionately known, is a lively mélange of cafés, bookshops, and clothes stores, with nightclubs and experimental film houses nearby.

Cluny-La Sorbonne

Little Athens
takes its name from the many Greek restaurants situated in its picturesque streets.

★ **Musée National du Moyen Age**
The museum holds a fine collection of medieval art, with many beautiful tapestries. This detail is from the late 15th-century series of tapestries The Lady with the Unicorn.

| 0 meters | 100 |
| 0 yards | 100 |

La Sorbonne

Seat of the University of Paris until 1969, the Sorbonne was established in 1257 by Robert de Sorbon, confessor to Louis IX, to enable poor scholars to study theology. It achieved fame as a center of learning in the late Middle Ages. The first printing house in France was founded here in 1469. Suppressed during the Revolution for opposition to liberal, 18th-century philosophical ideas, and re-established by Napoleon in 1802, the Sorbonne split into 13 separate universities in 1969. Lectures are still held on the original site.

View of the Panthéon from the Jardin du Luxembourg

Panthéon ⑧

Place du Panthéon. 📞 01-44 32 18 00. Ⓜ Maubert-Mutualité, Cardinal-Lemoine. ⬜ daily. ⬤ Jan 1, May 1, Nov 11, Dec 25. 🎫 ✔

Famous as the last resting place of some of France's greatest citizens, this magnificent church was built between 1764 and 1790 to honor Sainte Geneviève, patron saint of Paris. During the Revolution it was turned into a pantheon, to house the tombs of the illustrious.

Based on Rome's pantheon, the temple portico has 22 Corinthian columns, while the tall dome was inspired by that of St. Paul's in London (*see p58*). Geneviève's life is celebrated in a series of 19th-century nave murals. Many French notables rest in the crypt, including Voltaire, Rousseau, and Victor Hugo. The ashes of Pierre and Marie Curie are also held here.

Jardin du Luxembourg ⑨

Ⓜ Odéon. Ⓡ Luxembourg. ⬜ daily.

This graceful and historic area offers a peaceful haven in the heart of Paris. The gardens, which cover 25 ha (60 acres), were opened to the public in the 19th century by their then owner, the Comte de Provence. They are centered around the Luxembourg Palace, which was built for Marie de Médicis, the widow of Henri IV, and is now the home of the French Senate. Dominating the gardens is an octagonal lake surrounded by formal terraces, where sunbathers gather on fine summer days.

St-Germain-des-Prés ⑩

3 Place St-Germain-des-Prés. 📞 01-43 25 41 71. Ⓜ St-Germain-des-Prés. ⬜ daily. ✔

Originating in 548 as a basilica to house holy relics, this is the oldest church in Paris. St-Germain had become a powerful Benedictine abbey by the Middle Ages, but was largely destroyed by fire in 1794. Major restoration took place in the 19th century. A single tower survives from the original three, housing one of the most ancient belfries in France. Famous tombs include that of 17th-century philosopher, René Descartes.

After World War II, the area attracted writers and artists, including one of the leading figures of the Existentialist movement, Jean-Paul Sartre, and writer Simone de Beauvoir. Bars and cafés, such as *Les Deux Magots* and the *Café de Flore*, which were their daily haunts, are now popular with tourists.

St-Julien-le-Pauvre, one of the oldest churches in Paris, dates back to the 12th century.

Maubert-Mutualité

Key

– – – Suggested route

Star Sights

★ **Musée National du Moyen Age**

★ **Boulevard St-Michel**

De Médicis fountain in the Jardin du Luxembourg

Musée du Louvre ⑪

THE MUSÉE DU LOUVRE, containing one of the world's most important art collections, has a history dating back to medieval times. First built as a fortress in 1190 by King Philippe-Auguste, it lost its dungeon and keep in the reign of François I, who commissioned a Renaissance-style building. Thereafter, four centuries of kings and emperors improved and enlarged the palace. It was first opened as a museum in 1793 under the First Republic. Major renovations were completed in 1998.

The Louvre's east façade, added in the 17th century

Pyramid entrance

The Jardin du Carrousel was once the grand approach to the Tuileries Palace, which was set ablaze in 1871 by insurgents of the Paris Commune.

BUILDING THE LOUVRE

Over many centuries the Louvre was enlarged by a succession of French rulers and latterly by the state, shown below with their dates.

MAJOR ALTERATIONS

- ☐ Reign of François I (1515–47)
- ☐ Catherine de' Médici (about 1560)
- ■ Reign of Henri IV (1589–1610)
- ■ Reign of Louis XIII (1610–43)
- ■ Reign of Louis XIV (1643–1715)
- ■ Reign of Napoleon I (1804–15)
- ■ Reign of Napoleon III (1852–70)
- ☐ François Mitterrand (1981–95)

The Carrousel du Louvre underground visitors' complex (1993), with galleries, shops, restrooms, parking, and an information desk, lies beneath the Arc de Triomphe du Carrousel.

Denon Wing

The inverted glass pyramid brings light to the subterranean complex, echoing the new main entrance to the museum in the Cour Napoléon.

★ Arc de Triomphe du Carrousel
This triumphal arch was built to celebrate Napoleon's military victories in 1806.

STAR FEATURES

★ **Perrault Colonnade**

★ **Medieval Moats**

★ **Arc de Triomphe du Carrousel**

THE GLASS PYRAMID

Plans for the modernization and expansion of the Louvre were first conceived in 1981. These included the transfer of the Ministry of Finance from the Richelieu wing to offices elsewhere and a new main entrance.

This took the form of a metal and glass pyramid designed by architect I.M. Pei. Opened in 1989, the pyramid enables the visitor to see the surrounding buildings, while allowing light down into the underground visitors' reception area.

VISITORS' CHECKLIST

Entrance through Pyramid or directly from metro. **C** 01 40 20 53 17. **M** Palais-Royal, Louvre Rivoli, Musée du Louvre. 21, 27, 39, 48, 68, 69, 72, 95. **RER** Châtelet-les-Halles. **P** Carrousel du Louvre (entrance via Ave du Général Lemmonier); Place du Louvre, Rue St-Honoré. **Museum** 9am–6pm Thu–Sun; 9am–9:45pm Mon & Wed. Jan 1, May 1, Nov 11, Dec 25. **Hall Napoléon** (including History of the Louvre, Medieval Louvre, temporary exhibitions, restaurants, bookshop.) 9am–10pm (6pm for exhibitions) Wed–Mon. same as museum. (half price after 3pm and all day Sun; free 1st Sun of month.) partial. phone 01 40 20 53 17. **W** www.louvre.fr

Cour Marly is a glass-roofed courtyard that houses the famous *Marly Horses*, sculpted by Antoine Coysevox (1706) and Guillaume Coustou (1745) for the royal château at Marly.

Richelieu Wing

The Hall Napoléon, where temporary exhibitions are held, is situated under the pyramid.

Sully Wing

Cour Carrée

★ **Perrault's Colonnade**
The east façade, with its majestic rows of columns, was built by Claude Perrault, who worked on the Louvre with Louis Le Vau in the mid-17th century.

The Salle des Caryatides is named after the four monumental statues created by Jean Goujon in 1550 to support the upper gallery. Built for Henri II, it is the oldest room in the palace.

The Cour Napoléon dates mostly from the 19th century.

Philippe-Auguste's old fortress, with its distinctive tower and keep, was transformed into a royal residence by Charles V in about 1365.

★ **Medieval Moats**
The base of the twin towers and the drawbridge support of Philippe-Auguste's fortress can be seen in the excavated area.

Exploring the Louvre's Collection

OWING TO THE VAST SIZE of the Louvre's collection, it is useful to set a few viewing priorities before starting. The collection of European paintings (1400–1848) is comprehensive, with over half the works by French artists. The extensively renovated departments of Oriental, Egyptian, Greek, Etruscan, and Roman antiquities are of world renown and feature numerous new acquisitions and rare treasures. The hugely varied display of *objets d'art* includes furniture, jewelry, scientific instruments, and armor.

The famously enigmatic *Mona Lisa* (c.1504) by Leonardo da Vinci

EUROPEAN PAINTING: 1400 TO 1848

NOTABLE FLEMISH paintings include Jan van Eyck's *Madonna of the Chancellor Rolin* (c.1435). The fine Dutch collection features *Self-portrait* and *Bathsheba* (1654), both by Rembrandt. Among important German works are a *Venus* (1529) by Lucas Cranach and a portrait of Erasmus by Hans Holbein.

Italian paintings are arranged chronologically, and include Fra Angelico's *Coronation of the Virgin* (1435) and the celebrated *Mona Lisa* (1504) by Leonardo da Vinci.

Outstanding French works are represented by Enguerrand Quarton's *Villeneuve-lès-Avignon Pietà* (1455) and the delightfully frivolous *The Bathers* (1770) by Fragonard.

Among English artists featured are Gainsborough, Reynolds, and Turner, while the Spanish collection has portraits by Goya and works by El Greco and Zurbarán.

EUROPEAN SCULPTURE: 1100 TO 1848

THE FRENCH SECTION opens with a 12th-century figure of Christ and a head of St. Peter. Several works by French sculptor Pierre Puget (1620–94) are assembled in a glass-covered courtyard. Other masterpieces of French sculpture, including Jean-Antoine Houdon's busts of Diderot and Voltaire, stand in the Cour Marly. A notable Flemish sculpture is Adrian de Vries's long-limbed *Mercury and Psyche* (1593). Michelangelo's *Slaves* and Benvenuto Cellini's *Fontainebleau Nymph* are among the many splendid Italian works.

ORIENTAL AND EGYPTIAN ANTIQUITIES

IMPORTANT works of Mesopotamian art include one of the world's oldest documents, a basalt block, bearing a proclamation of laws by Babylonian King Hammurabi, from about 1750 BC.

The warlike Assyrians are represented by delicate carvings, and a fine example of Persian art is the enameled brickwork depicting the king's archers (5th century BC).

Egyptian art on display, dating from between 2500 and 1400 BC, and mostly produced for the dead, includes lifelike funeral portraits, such as the *Squatting Scribe*, and several sculptures of married couples.

GREEK, ETRUSCAN, AND ROMAN ANTIQUITIES

THE FAMOUS Greek marble statues here, the *Winged Victory of Samothrace* and the *Venus de Milo*, both date from the Hellenistic period (late 3rd to 2nd century BC). A highlight of the Roman section is a 2nd-century AD bronze head of the Emperor Hadrian. Other fine pieces include a bust of Agrippa and a basalt head of Livia. The star of the Etruscan collection is the terra-cotta sarcophagus of a married couple. Among the vast array of earlier fragments, a geometric head from the Cyclades (2700 BC) and a swan-necked bowl hammered out of a gold sheet (2500 BC) are noteworthy.

OBJETS D'ART

MORE THAN 8,000 items feature in this collection, many of which came from the Abbey of St-Denis, where the kings of France were crowned. Treasures include a serpentine plate from the 1st century AD and a golden scepter made for King Charles V in about 1380. The French crown jewels include the splendid coronation crowns of Louis XV and Napoleon, scepters, and swords. The Regent, one of the purest diamonds in the world, worn by Louis XV at his

Venus de Milo

coronation in 1722, is also on show.

An entire room is taken up with a series of tapestries, the *Hunts of Maximilian*, executed for Emperor Charles V in 1530. The large collection of French furniture ranges from the 16th to the 19th centuries, and includes pieces by exceptional furniture-maker André Charles Boulle. He is particularly noted for his technique of inlaying copper and tortoiseshell. Among more unusual items is Marie-Antoinette's inlaid steel and bronze writing desk.

Neoclassical statues and urns in the Jardin des Tuileries

Jardin des Tuileries ⑫

Ⓜ *Tuileries, Concorde.* ⏱ *7:30am–7:30pm daily.*

THESE GARDENS once belonged to the Palais des Tuileries, a palace which was razed to the ground during the time of the Paris Commune in 1871.

The gardens were laid out in the 17th century by André Le Nôtre, royal gardener to Louis XIV. He created a Neoclassical garden with a broad central avenue, regularly spaced terraces, and topiary arranged in geometric designs. Recent restoration has created a new garden with lime and chestnut trees and striking modern sculptures. Also in the gardens, two royal tennis courts built in 1851 and known as the *Jeu de Paume* – literally "game of the palm" – now host exhibitions of contemporary art.

Musée de l'Orangerie ⑬

Jardin des Tuileries, Place de la Concorde. ☎ *01-42 97 48 16.* Ⓜ *Concorde.* ⬤ *for renovation until early 2004.*

PAINTINGS FROM Claude Monet's crowning work, his celebrated water lily series, fill the two oval ground-floor rooms of this museum. Known as the *Nymphéas*, most of the canvases were painted between 1899 and 1921 in the garden at Giverny, Normandy, where Monet lived from 1883 until his death at the age of 86.

This superb work is complemented by the Walter-Guillaume collection of artists of the Ecole de Paris, from the late Impressionist era to the inter-war period. This is a remarkable concentration of masterpieces, including a room of dramatic works by Soutine. Among a number of paintings by Cézanne are still lifes, portraits such as *Madame Cézanne*, and landscapes. The collection also features *The Red Rock*. There are 24 canvases by Renoir, one the most notable of which is *Les Fillettes au Piano*. Picasso is represented by early works such as *The Female Bathers*. Henri Rousseau has 9 paintings, including *The Wedding* and *Le Carriole du Père Junier*. Among outstanding portraits is that of *Paul Guillaume* by Modigliano. Works by Sisley, Derain, and Utrillo are also featured. All the works are bathed in the natural light that filters through the windows of the museum.

Entrance to the great collection of Impressionist and other paintings at the Musée de l'Orangerie

Place de la Concorde ⑭

Ⓜ *Concorde.*

ONE OF Europe's most magnificent and historic squares, covering over 8 ha (20 acres), the Place de la Concorde was a swamp until the mid-18th century. It became the Place Louis XV in 1763 when royal architect Jacques-Ange Gabriel was asked by the king to design a suitable setting for an equestrian statue of himself. He created an open octagon, with only the north side containing mansions.

The statue, which lasted here less than 20 years, was replaced by the guillotine (the Black Widow, as it came to be known), and the square was renamed Place de la Révolution. On January 21, 1793, Louis XVI was beheaded here, followed by over 1,300 other victims, including Marie Antoinette, Madame du Barry, Charlotte Corday (Marat's assassin), and revolutionary leaders Danton and Robespierre. The blood-soaked square was optimistically renamed Place de la Concorde after the Reign of Terror finally came to an end in 1794.

The grandeur of the square was enhanced a few decades later when the 3,200-year-old Luxor obelisk was presented to King Louis-Philippe as a gift from the viceroy of Egypt (who also donated Cleopatra's Needle in London). Two fountains and eight statues personifying French cities were also installed.

Obelisk in Place de la Concorde

Flanking the Rue Royale on the north side of the square are two of Gabriel's Neoclassical mansions, the Hôtel de la Marine and the exclusive Hôtel Crillon.

Interior of the Musée d'Orsay, showing original station architecture

Musée d'Orsay ⑮

1 Rue de Bellechasse. 【 01-40 49 48 14. Ⓜ Solférino. ℝℰℝ Musée d'Orsay. 🚌 24, 68, 69, 84 & many others. ◯ Tue–Sun. ● Jan 1, May 1, Dec 25. 📷 ⚑ ♿

ORIGINALLY BUILT as a rail terminus in the heart of Paris, Victor Laloux's superb building, completed in 1900, narrowly avoided demolition in the 1970s. In 1986 it reopened as the Musée d'Orsay, with much of the original architecture preserved. The majority of the exhibits are paintings and sculptures dating from between 1848 and 1914, but there are also displays of furniture, the decorative arts, cinema, and the newspaper industry. The social, political, and techno-logical context in which these diverse visual arts were created is explained.

Paintings from before 1870 are on the ground floor, presided over by Thomas Couture's massive *Romans in the Age of Decadence* (1847). Neoclassical masterpieces, such as Ingres' *La Source*, hang near Romantic works like Delacroix's turbulent *Tiger Hunt* (1854), and canvases by Degas and Manet, including the latter's *Le Déjeuner sur l'Herbe* and *Olympia* (1863).

The museum's central aisle overflows with sculpture, from Daumier's satirical busts of members of parliament to Carpeaux's exuberant *The Dance* (1868). Decorative arts and architecture are on the middle level, where there is

also a display of Art Nouveau, including Lalique jewelry and glassware. Impressionist works on the upper level include Renoir's *Moulin de la Galette* (1876). Matisse's *Luxe, Calme et Volupté* is among highlights of the post-1900 collection.

Musée Rodin ⑯

77 Rue de Varenne. 【 01-44 18 61 10. Ⓜ Varenne. ◯ Tue–Sun. ● Jan 1. 📷 ♿ restricted.

AUGUSTE RODIN (1840–1917), widely regarded as one of France's greatest sculptors, lived and worked here in the Hôtel Biron, an elegant 18th-century mansion, from 1908 until his death. In return for a state-owned flat and studio, Rodin left his work to the nation, and it is now exhibited here. Some of his most celebrated sculptures are on display in the attractive garden and include *The Burghers of Calais*, *The Thinker*, *The Gates of Hell*, and *Balzac*. The garden also has a stunning array of some 2,000 rose bushes.

The indoor exhibits are arranged in chronological order, spanning the whole of Rodin's career. Major works in the collection include *The Kiss* and *Eve*.

Rodin's *The Kiss* (1886) at the Musée Rodin

Les Invalides ⑰

Ⓜ La Tour-Maubourg, Varenne. ℝℰℝ Invalides. 🚌 28, 49, 63, 69 & many others. **Hôtel des Invalides** 【 01-44 42 37 70. ◯ daily. ● Jan 1, May 1, Nov 1, Dec 25. **St-Louis-des-Invalides** 【 01-44 42 37 65. ◯ daily. **Dôme Church** 【 01-44 42 37 72. ◯ daily. ● Jan 1, May 1, Jun 17, Nov 1, Dec 25. 📷 ⚑ ♿ restricted.

THIS VAST ensemble of monumental buildings is one of the most impressive architectural sights in Paris. The imposing **Hôtel des Invalides**, from which the area takes its name, was commissioned by Louis XIV in 1671 for his wounded and homeless veterans. Designed by Libéral Bruand, it was completed in 1676 by Jules Hardouin-Mansart. Nearly 6,000 soldiers once resided here; today there are fewer than 100. Behind the Hôtel's harmonious Classical façade – a masterpiece of French 17th-century architecture – are several museums.

The **Musée de l'Armée** is one of the most comprehensive museums of military history in the world, with exhibits covering all periods from the Stone Age to World War II. Among items on display are François I's ivory hunting horns and a selection of arms from China, Japan, and India. The **Musée de l'Ordre de la Libération** was set up to honor feats of heroism during World War II, while the **Musée des Plans-Reliefs** has an extensive collection of detailed models of French forts and fortified towns, considered top secret until as late as the 1950s.

St-Louis-des-Invalides, the chapel of the Hôtel des Invalides, is also known as the "soldiers' church." It was built from 1679 to 1708 by Jules Hardouin-Mansart, to Bruand's design. The stark, Classical interior is designed in the shape of a Greek cross and has a fine 17th-century organ by Alexandre Thierry.

The **Dôme Church** was begun in 1676 to complement the existing buildings of Les Invalides, and to reflect the splendor of Louis XIV's reign. Reserved for the exclusive use of the Sun King himself, the resulting masterpiece is one of the greatest examples of *grand siècle* architecture and a monument to Bourbon glory. The crypt houses the tomb of Napoleon – six coffins with an enormous red sarcophagus on a pedestal of green granite. Marshal Foch, the World War I hero, is also buried here.

Façade of the Hôtel des Invalides, showing the splendid gilded dome

Eiffel Tower ⑱

VISITORS' CHECKLIST

Champ-de-Mars. 📞 01-44 11 23 11. Ⓜ Bir Hakeim. RER Champ-de-Mars. 🚌 42, 69, 72, 82. ◯ daily. 🏛 🚹 limited. 🅿 🍴

Built for the Universal Exhibition of 1889, and to commemorate the centennial of the Revolution, the 324-m (1,063-ft) Eiffel Tower (Tour Eiffel) was meant to be a temporary addition to the Paris skyline. Designed by Gustave Eiffel, it was fiercely decried by 19th-century aesthetes. It was the world's tallest building until 1931, when New York's Empire State Building was completed. A number of crazy stunts have been attempted here. In 1912 a local tailor launched himself from the tower using a cape as wings. He plunged to his death.

Double-decker elevators take visitors to the top level, which can hold up to 400 people at a time.

The Jules Verne Restaurant is one of the best in Paris, offering excellent food and panoramic views.

The third level, 276 m (905 ft) above the ground, offers superb views. On a clear day it is possible to see for 72 km (45 miles) – as far as Chartres Cathedral (*see pp180–81*).

The second level, at 115 m (376 ft), is reached either by elevator or by 359 steps from the first level.

The Eiffel Tower at night

THE EIFFEL TOWER IN FIGURES

- There are a total of 1,665 steps from bottom to top
- The tower is held together by a total of 2.5 million rivets
- It never sways more than 7 cm (2.5 in)
- The tower weighs 10,100 tons
- 50 tons of paint are used every seven years

The first level, at 57 m (187 ft), can be reached by elevator or by 345 steps. There is a post office here.

Trocadéro fountains in front of the Palais de Chaillot

Palais de Chaillot ⑲

Place du Trocadéro 17. **Ⓜ** *Trocadéro.*
Museums ◯ *Wed–Mon.* 📷 ✓

THE PALAIS DE CHAILLOT, with its curved colonnaded wings, each culminating in a vast pavilion, was designed in Neoclassical style for the 1937 Paris Exhibition by Azéma, Louis-Hippolyte Boileau, and Jacques Carlu. It is adorned with sculptures and bas-reliefs, and the pavilion walls are inscribed in gold with words composed by the poet and essayist Paul Valéry.

The square between the two pavilions is highly decorated with bronze sculptures, ornamental pools, and shooting fountains. Steps lead down from here to the **Théâtre National de Chaillot**, famous for its avant-garde productions.

The basement of the palace houses Paris's main film institute, the **Cinémathèque Française**, founded by Henri Langlois in 1936. The institute screens a daily-changing schedule of movie classics. Frequent retrospectives offer an opportunity to catch some of the all-time screen greats.

Viollet-le-Duc's **Museé des Monuments Français** (1882), a collection of models and life-size casts of famous French buildings and monuments, has now become part of a vast new architecture complex. This enlarged Architecture Museum has extended exhibition spaces, a library, and an archive center.

The **Musée de l'Homme** in the west wing traces human evolution through a series of anthropological, archaeological, and ethnological displays. The African exhibits are particularly striking, with frescoes from the Sahara, musical instruments, sculpture, and magical figures.

Next door is the **Musée de la Marine**, devoted to French naval history. The exhibits include Napoleon's barge, models of the fleet he assembled in 1805 for a planned invasion of Britain, and displays on underwater exploration and fishing vessels.

The centerpiece of the lovely Jardins de Trocadéro is a long rectangular ornamental pool, bordered by stone and bronze-gilt statues. The gardens are richly laid out with trees, walkways, small streams, and bridges – a romantic place for a quiet evening stroll.

BARON HAUSSMANN

A lawyer by training and civil servant by profession, Georges-Eugène Haussmann (1809–91) was appointed Prefect of the Seine in 1853 by Napoleon III. For 17 years Haussmann was responsible for the urban modernization of Paris. With a team of the best architects and engineers, he demolished the chaotic, insanitary streets of the medieval city and created a well-ventilated and ordered capital in a geometrical grid. He also increased the number of street-lights and sidewalks, giving rise to the cafés that enliven modern Parisian street life. The plan involved redesigning the area at one end of the Champs-Elysées and creating a star of 12 avenues centered around the new Arc de Triomphe.

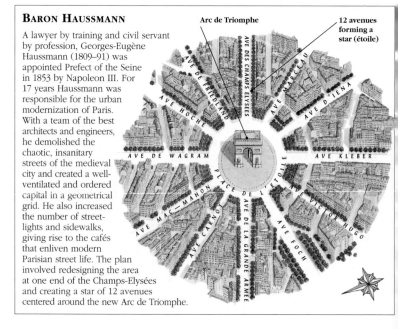

The east façade of the Arc de Triomphe

Arc de Triomphe ⑳

Place Charles de Gaulle. 📞 01-55 37 73 77. Ⓜ Charles de Gaulle–Etoile. 🚌 22, 30, 31, 73, 92. ◯ daily. ⬤ Jan 1, May 1, Jul 14, Nov 11, Dec 25. 🖼 🗹

AFTER HIS GREATEST victory, the Battle of Austerlitz in 1805, Napoleon promised his men they would "go home beneath triumphal arches." The first stone of what was to become the world's most famous triumphal arch was laid the following year. But disruptions to architect Jean Chalgrin's plans – combined with the demise of Napoleonic power – delayed completion of this monumental structure until 1836. Standing 50 m (164 ft) high, the Arc is encrusted with flamboyant reliefs, shields, and sculptures, depicting military scenes such as the Napoleonic battles of Austerlitz and Aboukir.

On Armistice Day, 1921, the body of the Unknown Soldier was placed beneath the arch to commemorate the dead of World War I. The flame of remembrance which burns above the tomb is rekindled by various veterans organizations each evening. Today, the Arc de Triomphe is the customary rallying point for many victory celebrations and parades.

The viewing platform on top of the Arc overlooks the length of the Champs-Elysées. On the other side, a fine view stretches as far as La Défense.

Champs-Elysées ㉑

Ⓜ Franklin D. Roosevelt, George V, Champs-Elysées Clemenceau. **Grand Palais** Porte A, Ave Eisenhower. 📞 01-44 13 17 30. ◯ for temporary exhibitions. 🖼 🗹 ♿ **Petit Palais** Ave Winston Churchill. 📞 01-42 65 12 73. ⬤ for renovation until 2004. 🖼 🗹 for exhibitions.

PARIS'S MOST FAMOUS and popular thoroughfare had its beginnings in about 1667, when landscape gardener André Le Nôtre extended the royal view from the Tuileries by creating a tree-lined avenue. The Champs-Elysées (Elysian Fields) has also been known as the "triumphal way" since the homecoming of Napoleon's body from St. Helena in 1840. With the addition of cafés and restaurants in the late 19th century, the Champs-Elysées became the most fashionable boulevard in Paris.

The formal gardens that line the Champs-Elysées from Place de la Concorde to the Rond-Point have changed little since they were laid out by architect Jacques Hittorff in 1838, and were used as the setting for the 1855 World's Fair. The Grand Palais and the Petit Palais were also built here for the Universal Exhibition of 1900.

The exterior of the massive **Grand Palais** combines an imposing Neoclassical façade with a riot of Art Nouveau ironwork. A splendid glass roof is decorated with colossal bronze statues of flying horses and chariots at its four corners. The Great Hall, the main area of the Palais, is currently closed for renovation, but temporary exhibitions are still being held in the Galeries Nationales du Grand Palais.

Facing the Grand Palais, the **Petit Palais** – also currently closed – houses the Musée des Beaux-Arts de la Ville de Paris. Arranged around a pretty semicircular courtyard and garden, the palace is similar in style to the Grand Palais, with Ionic columns, a grand porch, and a dome echoing that of the Invalides across the river. The exhibits are divided into medieval and Renaissance *objets d'art*, paintings, and drawings; 18th-century furniture and *objets d'art*; and works by the French artists Gustave Courbet, Jean Ingres, and Eugène Delacroix.

Musée des Beaux-Arts de la Ville de Paris, in the Petit Palais

The deceptively rustic exterior of Au Lapin Agile, one of the best known nightspots in Paris

Montmartre ㉒

M *Abbesses, Anvers, Barbès-Roche-chouart, Château-Rouge, Lamarck-Caulaincourt.* 🚌 *30, 54, 80, 85.*
Sacré-Coeur 35 Rue du Chevalier de la Barre. **[** *01-53 41 89 00.* **O** *daily.*
🎟 *for crypt and dome.* **&** *restricted.*

THE STEEP HILL of Montmartre has been associated with artists for 200 years. Théodore Géricault and Camille Corot came here at the start of the 19th century, and in the early 20th century Maurice Utrillo immortalized the streets in his works. Today, street artists of varying talents continue to exhibit their work in the Place du Tertre, and thrive on the tourist trade. Exhibitions at the **Musée de Montmartre** usually feature works of artists associated with the area, while the **Musée d'Art Naïf Max Fourny** houses almost 600 examples of naive art. The **Espace Montmartre Salvador Dalí** displays over 300 works by the Surrealist painter and sculptor.

Much of the area still preserves its rather louche, prewar atmosphere. Former literary haunt **Au Lapin Agile**, or "Agile Rabbit," is now a club. The celebrated **Moulin Rouge** nightclub is also in the vicinity.

The name Montmartre, thought to derive from martyrs tortured and killed here around AD 250, is also associated with the grandiose **Sacré-Coeur**. Dedicated to the Sacred Heart of Christ, the basilica was built as a result of a vow made at the outbreak of the Franco-Prussian War in 1870. Businessmen Alexandre

Façade of the Romano-Byzantine Sacré-Coeur

Legentil and Hubert Rohault de Fleury promised to finance its construction should France be spared from the impending Prussian onslaught. Despite the war and the Siege of Paris, invasion was averted and work began in 1876 to Paul Abadie's designs. The basilica, completed in 1914, is one of France's most important Roman Catholic shrines. It contains many treasures, including a figure of the *Virgin Mary and Child* (1896) by Brunet.

Below the forecourt, Square Willette is laid out on the side of a hill in a series of descending terraces. A funicular railway takes visitors up from the bottom of the gardens to the foot of the steps of the basilica.

Parc de la Villette ㉓

30 Ave Corentin-Cariou. **M** *Porte de la Villette.* 🚌 *75, 139, 150, 152, 250A.* **Cité des Sciences [** *01-40 05 80 00.* **O** *Tue–Sun.* 🎟 **&**

THE OLD slaughterhouses and livestock market of Paris have been transformed into this massive urban park, designed by Bernard Tschumi.

The major attraction of the site is the **Cité des Sciences et de l'Industrie**, a hugely popular science and technology museum. Architect Adrien Fainsilber has created an imaginative interplay of light, vegetation, and water in the high-tech, five-floor building, which soars to a height of 40 m (133 ft). At the museum's heart is the Explora exhibit, a fascinating guide to the worlds of science and technology. The Géode, a giant entertainment sphere, houses a huge hemispherical cinema screen. In the auditorium of the Planetarium, special effects projectors create exciting images of the stars and planets.

Also in the park, the **Grande Halle** was the old cattle hall, and has been turned into a huge exhibition space. The **Cité de la Musique** is a quirky but elegant complex that holds a music conservatory – home of the world-famous Paris *conservatoire* since 1990 – and a concert hall. Built as a venue for pop concerts, the **Zénith theater** seats over 6,000 spectators.

Cimetière du Père Lachaise ㉔

16 Rue du Repos. **M** *Père-Lachaise, A Dumas.* **C** *01-55 25 82 10.* **O** *daily.*

PARIS'S MOST prestigious cemetery is set on a wooded hill overlooking the city. The land was once owned by Père de la Chaise, Louis XIV's confessor, but it was bought by order of Napoleon in 1803 to create a completely new cemetery. This became so popular with the Parisian bourgeoisie that its boundaries were extended six times during the 19th century. Here are buried celebrities such as the writer Honoré de Balzac, the famous playwright Molière, the composer Frédéric Chopin, singer Edith Piaf, and actors Simone Signoret and Yves Montand. Famous foreigners interred in the cemetery include Oscar Wilde and the singer Jim Morrison. The Columbarium, built at the end of the 19th century, houses the ashes of American dancer

Monument to Oscar Wilde in the Père Lachaise Cemetery

Isadora Duncan, among others. The equally charismatic Sarah Bernhardt, famous for her portrayal of Racine heroines, also reposes at Père Lachaise. Striking funerary sculpture and famous graves make this a pleasant place for a leisurely, nostalgic stroll.

La Défense ㉕

RER *La Défense.* **La Grande Arche**
C *01-49 07 27 57.* **O** *daily.*

THIS SKYSCRAPER business city on the western edge of Paris is the largest office development in Europe and covers 80 ha (198 acres). It was launched in 1957 to create a new home for leading French and foreign companies. **La Grande Arche** is an enormous hollow cube, spacious enough to contain Notre-Dame cathedral. Designed by Danish architect Otto von Spreckelsen in the late 1980s, the arch houses an exhibition gallery and offers superb views over the city.

Bois de Boulogne ㉖

M *Porte Maillot, Porte Dauphine, Porte d'Auteuil, Sablons.* **O** *24 hrs daily.* **to** *specialist gardens and museum.*

LOCATED BETWEEN the river Seine and the western edges of Paris, this 865-ha (2,137-acre) park offers a vast belt of greenery for strolling, cycling, riding, boating, picnicking, or spending a day at the races. The Bois de Boulogne was once part of the immense Forêt du Rouvre. In the mid-19th century Napoleon III had the area redesigned and landscaped by Baron Haussmann along the lines of Hyde Park in London (*see p54*). A number of self-contained parks include the Pré Catelan, which has the widest beech tree in Paris, and the Bagatelle gardens, with architectural follies and an 18th-century villa famous for its rose garden. The villa was built in just 64 days as the result of a bet between the Comte d'Artois and Marie-Antoinette.

By day the Bois is busy with families, joggers, and walkers, but after dark it is notoriously seedy – and best avoided.

Kiosque de l'Empereur, on an island in the Grand Lac, Bois de Boulogne

Château de Versailles ㉗

VISITORS PASSING THROUGH the dazzling state rooms of this colossal palace, or strolling in its vast gardens, will soon understand why it was the glory of the Sun King's reign. Started by Louis XIV in 1668, the palace grew from a modest hunting lodge built for his father, Louis XIII, to become the largest palace in Europe, housing some 20,000 people. Architect Louis Le Vau built the first section, which expanded into an enlarged courtyard. From 1678, Jules Hardouin-Mansart added the north and south wings and the superb Hall of Mirrors. He also designed the chapel, completed in 1710. The interiors were largely the work of Charles Le Brun, and the great landscape gardener, André Le Nôtre, redesigned the gardens with their monumental fountains.

★ Hall of Mirrors
This magnificent room, 70 m (233 ft) long, was the settting for great state occasions. It was here that the Treaty of Versailles was ratified at the end of World War I.

Marble Courtyard
The courtyard is decorated with marble paving, urns, and busts. Above the gilded central balcony, the figures of Hercules and Mars flank the clock on the pediment.

The South Wing
originally housed the apartments of great nobles. It is now a history museum.

Ministers' Courtyard

Royal Courtyard

The ornate main gate, designed by Mansart, is crowned by the royal coat of arms.

Statue of Louis XIV

★ Chapelle Royale
Mansart's last great work, this Baroque chapel was Louis XIV's final addition to Versailles. The beautiful interior is decorated with Corinthian columns and superb Baroque murals.

STAR FEATURES

★ Chapelle Royale

★ Hall of Mirrors

The 17th-century Fountain of Neptune by Le Nôtre and Mansart

North Wing
The chapel, Opera House, and picture galleries occupy this wing, which originally housed royal apartments.

Parterres (flowerbeds)

The Opera House in the North Wing was completed for the 1770 marriage of the future Louis XVI and Marie-Antoinette.

Exploring the Palace

The main rooms of the palace are on the first floor. Around the Marble Courtyard are the private apartments of the king and queen. Visitors can see the King's Bedroom, where Louis XIV died, aged 77, in 1715. The room next door, the Cabinet du Conseil, was where the monarch would receive ministers and family members.

On the garden side, the state apartments are richly decorated with colored marbles, carvings in stone and wood, murals, and gilded furniture. Each is dedicated to an Olympian deity. Louis XIV's throne room, the Salon d'Apollon, designed by Le Brun, is dedicated to the god Apollo. A copy of the famous portrait of Louis by Hyacinthe Rigaud hangs above the fireplace. The war theme of the Salon de la Guerre is reinforced by a stucco relief of Louis XIV riding to victory. The high point of the tour is the Hall of Mirrors, with its 17 great mirrors reflecting the light from tall arched windows.

Among the other major attractions are the Chapelle Royale and the **Musée des Carrosses** (coach museum) opposite the palace.

The Gardens of Versailles

The gardens are a fitting counterpart to the colossal palace. Immediately in front of the palace is the Water Parterre, decorated with superb bronze statues. Paths lead through the formal gardens, with their regularly patterned flowerbeds and hedges, to groves, lakes, fountains, and architectural features such as the Colonnade (1685), a circle of marble arches designed by Mansart. The largest stretch of water is the Grand Canal, where Louis XIV held spectacular boating parties.

The gardens contain two smaller palaces. The **Grand Trianon**, built of stone and pink marble, was designed by Mansart in 1687 as a discreet hideaway for Louis XIV and his mistress, Madame de Maintenon. The nearby **Petit Trianon** (1762) was built for Madame de Pompadour, Louis XV's mistress. It later became a favorite retreat of Marie-Antoinette. Behind it is the Hameau, a mini-village where the queen would dress up as a shepherdess and play with a flock of groomed and perfumed lambs.

Marie-Antoinette's beloved Petit Trianon

Basilique de St-Denis ㉘

1 Place de la Légion-d'Honneu, St-Denis. **M** *St-Denis-Basilique.* **RER** *St-Denis.* **C** *01-48 09 83 54.* ○ *daily.* ● *Jan 1 , May 1, Dec 25.*

C ONSTRUCTED BETWEEN 1137 and 1281, the basilica is on the site of the tomb of St. Denis, the first bishop of Paris, who was beheaded in Montmartre in AD 250. According to legend, his decapitated figure, clutching his head, was seen here, and an abbey was erected to commemorate the martyred bishop. The basilica was the first church to be built in the Gothic style of architecture.

From as early as the 7th century St-Denis was a burial place for French rulers, and all the queens of France were crowned here. During the Revolution many tombs were desecrated and scattered, but the best were stored, and now represent a fine collection of funerary art. Memorials include those of Dagobert (died 638), François I (died 1547), Henri II (died 1559) and Catherine de' Medici (died 1589), and Louis XVI and Marie-Antoinette (died 1793).

Of the medieval effigies, the most impressive are of Charles V (1364) and a 12th-century likeness in enameled copper of Blanche de France with her dog. Their mask-like serenity contrasts with the realistic Renaissance portrayal of agony in the sculptures of the mausoleum of Louis XII and Anne de Bretagne.

Disneyland Paris ㉙

Marne-la-Vallée, Seine-et-Marne. **R** *TGV from Lille or Lyon.* **RER** *Marne-la-Vallée-Chessy.* **—** *from CDG & Orly airports.* **C** *01-64 74 40 00.* ○ *daily.*

T HE THEME PARK, which lies 32 km (20 miles) east of Paris, covers 60 ha (150 acres). It is divided into five themed areas. Although these rely heavily on Hollywood nostalgia, Disneyland Paris has tried to give the park a European touch.

"Frontierland," inspired by the Wild West of 19th-century America, can be explored on paddlewheel steamboats. A roller coaster trundles through mountain scenery.

In "Adventureland" visitors encounter characters and tales from adventure fiction, including Caribbean pirates and the Swiss Family Robinson.

Small-town America at the turn of the century is evoked in "Main Street." Authentic details include horse-drawn vehicles and a traditional barber's shop.

Young children will enjoy "Fantasyland," devoted to Disney characters and tales, where they can fly with Peter Pan or search the Alice in Wonderland maze for the Queen of Hearts' castle.

"Discoveryland" has futuristic architecture and sophisticated technology. Here, visitors can choose to be miniaturized by a hapless inventor or sent on a thrilling space trip.

Château de Vaux-le-Vicomte ㉚

Maincy, Seine-et-Marne. **R** **RER** *Melun, then taxi.* **C** *01-64 14 41 90.* ○ *late Mar–Nov 11: daily.*

L OCATED 64 km (40 miles) southeast of Paris, just north of Melun, the château enjoys a peaceful rural setting. Nicolas Fouquet, a powerful court financier to Louis XIV, challenged architect Le Vau and decorator Le Brun to create the most sumptuous palace of the day. The result was one of the greatest 17th-century French châteaux. However, it also led to his downfall. Louis was so enraged – because its luxury cast the royal palaces into the shade – that he had Fouquet arrested and confiscated all his estates.

As befits Fouquet's grand tastes, the interior is a gilded banquet of frescoes, stucco, caryatids, and giant busts. The Salon des Muses boasts Le Brun's magnificent frescoed

The tomb of Louis XII and Anne de Bretagne in the Basilique de St-Denis

Château de Vaux-le-Vicomte seen across the formal gardens designed by Le Nôtre

ceiling of dancing nymphs and poetic sphinxes. La Grande Chambre Carrée is decorated in Louis XIII style with paneled walls and an impressive triumphal frieze, evoking Rome.

Much of Vaux-le-Vicomte's fame is due to French landscape gardener André Le Nôtre (1613–1700). At Vaux he perfected the concept of the *jardin à la française*: avenues framed by statues and box hedges, water gardens with ornate pools, and geometrical parterres "embroidered" with floral motifs.

Château de Fontainebleau ③

Seine-et-Marne.  01-60 71 50 60. ☐ Wed–Mon.

FONTAINEBLEAU was a favorite royal residence from the 12th to the mid-19th century. Its charm lies in its relative informality and its spectacular setting in a forest 65 km (40 miles) south of Paris. The present château dates back to François I. Drawn to the area by the local hunting, the Renaissance king created a decorative château modeled on Florentine and Roman styles. Subsequent rulers enlarged and embellished the château, creating a cluster of buildings in various styles from different periods. During the Revolution the apartments were looted by a mob, and remained bare until the 1800s when Napoleon refurbished the whole interior.

The Cour du Cheval Blanc, once a simple enclosed courtyard, was transformed by Napoleon into the main approach to the château. At one end is the Escalier du Fer-à-Cheval (1634), an imposing horseshoe-shaped staircase.

The interior suites showcase the château's history as a royal residence. The Galerie François I has a superb collection of Renaissance art. The Salle de Bal, a Renaissance ballroom designed by Primaticcio (1552), features emblems of Henri II on the walnut coffered ceiling and reflected in the parquet floor. The apartments of Napoleon I house his grandiose throne, in the former Chambre du Roi. The complex of buildings also contains the Musée Napoléon, in which eight rooms recreate different scenes from the Emperor's life.

Nearby is the Chapelle de la Sainte Trinité, designed for Henri II in 1550. The chapel acquired its vaulted and frescoed ceiling under Henri IV, and was completed during the reign of Louis XIII.

If you have time, the gardens of the palace are also worth exploring. The Jardin Anglais is a romantic "English" garden planted with cypresses and exotic species. The Jardin de Diana features a bronze fountain of Diana the huntress.

The Salle de Bal of Henri II, Château de Fontainebleau

Northern France

NORTHERN FRANCE'S MAIN sights span thousands of years of history, from the awesome megaliths of Carnac, through the 18th-century grandeur of Nancy's town architecture, to Strasbourg's futuristic Palais de l'Europe, seat of the European Parliament. Its cities boast some of the country's greatest cathedrals, such as those of Reims and Rouen. The region's most famous religious monument is Mont-St-Michel, whose evocative silhouette has welcomed pilgrims since the 11th century.

Strasbourg's fine Gothic cathedral surrounded by historic buildings

Strasbourg ❷

Bas Rhin. 🏙 *250,000.* ✈ *15 km (8 miles) SW.* 🚃 🚌 ℹ *17 Place de la Cathédrale (03-88 52 28 22).* 🎭 *International Music Festival (Jun–Jul).* 🔲 *www.strasbourg.com*

LOCATED HALFWAY between Paris and Prague, this cosmopolitan city is often known as "the crossroads of Europe." It is also home to the European Parliament.

A boat trip along the waterways that encircle Strasbourg's Old Town takes in the **Ponts-Couverts** – bridges with medieval watchtowers – and the old tanners' district, dotted with attractive half-timbered houses.

Dating from the late 11th century, the **Cathédrale Notre-Dame** dominates the city. There are wonderful views from the top of its spire.

The grand Classical **Palais Rohan** houses three museums: the Musée des Beaux Arts, the Musée Archéologique, and the Musée des Arts Décoratifs, which has one of the finest displays of ceramics in France.

Also worth visiting is the **Musée d'Art Moderne et Contemporain**, featuring works of art dating from 1860 to the present, and the **Musée Alsacien**, which contains exhibits on local traditions, arts, and crafts.

Reims ❸

Marne. 🏙 *185,000.* 🚃 🚌 ℹ *2 Rue Guillaume de Machault (03-26 77 45 25).* 🔲 *www.tourisme.fr*

RENOWNED THROUGHOUT the world from countless champagne labels, Reims has a rich historical legacy.

The city's most famous monument is the magnificent Gothic **Cathédrale Notre-Dame**, begun in 1211. For several centuries the cathedral was the setting for the coronation of French kings. Highlights are the 13th-century Great Rose Window and the west façade, decorated with over 2,300 statues.

On the eve of a coronation, the future king spent the night in the **Palais du Tau** (1690), the archbishops' palace adjoining the cathedral. Its 15th-century banqueting hall, the Salle du Tau, with its barrel-vaulted ceiling and Arras tapestries, is a star attraction.

Among other fine historic buildings are the 17th-century **Ancien Collège des Jésuites**, with its Baroque interior, and the **Basilique St-Remi**, the oldest church in Reims.

Relics of the town's Roman past include the **Crypto-portique**, part of the former forum, and the **Porte Mars**, a triumphal Augustan arch.

The **Musée de la Reddition** occupies the building that served as Eisenhower's French headquarters during World War II. It was here, in 1945, that the general received the Germans' surrender, which ended the war.

ENVIRONS: A short drive south of Reims is **Epernay**. Here you can visit the cellars of a number of distinguished champagne "houses," including those of Moët et Chandon.

🏛 **Cathédrale Notre-Dame**
Place du Cardinal Luçon. 📞 *03-26 47 55 34.* 🕐 *daily.* 🎫 *by appt.* ♿

Rouen ❹

Seine Maritime. 🏙 *103,000.* ✈ *11 km (7 miles) SE.* 🚃 🚌 ℹ *25 Place de la Cathédrale (02-32 08 32 40).*

FORMERLY A CELTIC trading post, Roman garrison, and Viking colony, Rouen became the capital of the Norman Duchy in 911. Today it is a rich and cultured city that boasts a wealth of splendid historical monuments.

Statuary on the west façade of Reims' Cathédrale Notre-Dame

Detail from the 11th-century Bayeux Tapestry

Rouen's Gothic cathedral, the **Cathédrale Notre-Dame**, has an impressive west façade, made famous by the great Impressionist painter Claude Monet (1840–1926), who made almost 30 paintings of it. A number of these can be seen in the city's excellent **Musée des Beaux Arts**.

From the cathedral, the Rue du Gros Horloge leads west, passing under the city's Great Clock, to the Place du Vieux Marché, where Joan of Arc was burnt at the stake in 1431.

The Flamboyant Gothic **Eglise St-Maclou** and the Gothic **Eglise St-Ouen** are two of Rouen's finest churches. The Eglise St-Ouen is noted for its restored 14th-century stained-glass windows.

Also of interest is the **Musée de la Céramique**, which displays around 1,000 pieces of Rouen faïence – colorful glazed earthenware – as well as other pieces of French and foreign china.

The former family home of Gustave Flaubert (1821–80) has been converted into a museum containing memorabilia from this famous French novelist's life.

🏛 **Musée des Beaux Arts**
Square Verdrel. 📞 02-35 71 28 40.
⬜ Wed–Mon. ● public hols. 🎟 ♿

Bayeux ❺

Calvados. 🏘 15,000. 🚉 🚌 🛈
Pont-St-Jean (02-31 51 28 28).

T HE MAIN reason for making a stop at this small town in Normandy is to see the world-renowned Bayeux Tapestry. This incredible work of art and important historical document depicts William the Conqueror's invasion of England and the Battle of Hastings in the 11th century from the Norman perspective. It was probably commissioned by Bishop Odo of Bayeux, William's half-brother. The 70-m (230-ft) long embroidered hanging is displayed in a renovated seminary, the **Centre Guillaume-le-Conquérant**, which also gives a detailed audio-visual account of the events leading up to the Norman conquest.

Apart from its tapestry, a cluster of 15th–19th-century buildings and the Gothic **Cathédrale Notre-Dame** are Bayeux's principal attractions.

Bayeux was the first town in Nazi-occupied France to be liberated by the Allies following the D-Day landings in 1944. On the southwest side of the town's ring road, the **Musée Mémorial de la Bataille de Normandie** traces the events of the Battle of Normandy in World War II.

🏛 **Centre Guillaume-le-Conquérant**
Rue de Nesmond. 📞 02-31 51 25 50.
⬜ daily. ● Jan 1, Dec 25. 🎟 ♿

Mont-St-Michel ❻

See pp174–5.

St-Malo ❼

Ille-et-Vilaine. 🏘 53,000. 🚢 🚉 🚌
🛈 Esplanade St-Vincent (02-99 56 64 48).

O NCE A FORTIFIED island, St-Malo stands in a commanding position at the mouth of the river Rance. In the 16th–19th centuries the port won prosperity and power through the exploits of its seafaring population.

Intra-muros, the old walled city, is encircled by ramparts that provide fine views of St-Malo and its offshore islands. Within the city walls is a web of narrow, cobbled streets with tall 18th-century buildings housing many souvenir shops, seafood restaurants, and creperies.

St-Malo's castle, the **Château de St-Malo** dates from the 14th and 15th centuries. The great keep today houses an interesting museum charting the city's history. In the three-towered fortification known as the **Tour Solidor**, to the west of St-Malo, is a museum devoted to the ships and sailors that rounded Cape Horn.

Carnac ❽

Morbihan. 🏘 4,600. 🚌 🛈 74
Avenue des Druides (02-97 52 13 52).

T HIS POPULAR seaside town is probably most famous as one of the world's great prehistoric sites. As long ago as 4000 BC thousands of ancient granite rocks were arranged in mysterious lines and patterns in the country-side around Carnac by Megalithic tribes. Their original purpose is uncertain, though they are thought to have religious significance or to be related to an early astronomical calendar. Celts, Romans, and Christians have since adapted them to their own beliefs.

You can see some of the menhirs at the Kermario site, on the town outskirts, while in the center, the **Musée de Préhistoire** gives an insight into the area's ancient history.

Menhirs (prehistoric standing stones) in a field near Carnac

Mont-St-Michel ➏

S HROUDED BY MIST, engulfed by sea, soaring proud above glistening sands – the silhouette of Mont-St-Michel is one of the most enchanting sights in France. Now linked to the mainland by a causeway, the island of Mont-Tombe (Tomb on the Hill) stands at the mouth of the river Couesnon, crowned by a fortified abbey that almost doubles its height. Lying strategically on the frontier between Normandy and Brittany, Mont-St-Michel grew from a humble 8th-century oratory to become a Benedictine monastery that had its greatest influence in the 12th and 13th centuries. Pilgrims known as *miquelots* journeyed from afar to honor the cult of St. Michael, and the monastery was a renowned center of medieval learning. After the French Revolution the abbey became a prison. It is now a national monument that draws some 850,000 visitors a year.

★ Abbey Church
Four bays of the Roman-esque nave in the abbey church survive. Three were pulled down in 1776, creating the West Terrace.

Gautier's Leap
Situated at the top of the Inner Staircase, this terrace is named after a prisoner who leaped to his death here.

St. Aubert's Chapel,
built on an outcrop of rock, dates from the 15th-century and is dedicated to Aubert, the founder of Mont-St-Michel.

Gabriel Tower

The ramparts – a series of fortified walls with imposing towers – were built following attacks by the English during the Hundred Years' War.

Entrance

VISITING THE ABBEY

The abbey is built on three levels, which reflect the monastic hierarchy. The monks lived on the highest level *(shown here)*, in an enclosed world of church, cloister, and refectory. The abbot entertained his noble guests on the middle level. Soldiers and pilgrims further down on the social scale were received at the lowest level. Guided tours begin at the West Terrace at the church (highest) level and end on the lowest level in the almonry, where alms were distributed to the poor.

La Merveille is the name given to the buildings on the north side of the church.

Abbey Church

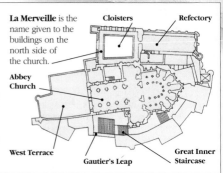

Cloisters

Refectory

West Terrace

Gautier's Leap

Great Inner Staircase

★ Cloisters
With their elegant English Purbeck marble columns, the cloisters are a beautiful example of early 13th-century Anglo-Norman style.

VISITORS' CHECKLIST

to Pontorson, then bus.
Boulevard de l'Avancée
(02-33 60 14 30). St-Michel
de Printemps (May).
Abbey 02-33 89 80 00.
May–Sep: 9am–5:30pm;
Oct–Apr: 9:30am–5pm.
Night visits during summer.
Jan 1, May 1, Nov 1 & 11,
Dec 25. 12:15pm
Tue–Sun.
www.monum.fr

★ La Merveille
The main three-story monastic complex, added to the church's north side in the early 13th century, is known as La Merveille (The Miracle). The Knights' Room, on the middle floor, has magnificent Gothic rib-vaulting and finely decorated capitals.

Eglise St-Pierre

Liberty Tower

King's Tower

The Arcade Tower
provided lodgings for the abbot's soldiers.

STAR FEATURES

★ Abbey Church

★ La Merveille

★ Cloisters

★ Grande Rue

★ Grande Rue
Now crowded with tourists and souvenir shops, the pilgrims' route, followed since the 12th century, climbs up past the Eglise St-Pierre to the abbey gates.

The Loire Valley

RENOWNED FOR ITS SUMPTUOUS CHATEAUX, the relics of royal days gone by, the glorious valley of the Loire is rich in both history and architecture. As the Loire runs through the heart of France, so the region embodies the essence of the French way of life. Its sophisticated cities, luxuriant landscape, and magnificent food and wine add up to a modern paradise. The Loire has long been described as exemplifying *la douceur de vivre*: it combines a leisurely pace of life, a mild climate, and the gentle ways of its inhabitants. The overall impression is one of an unostentatious taste for the good things in life.

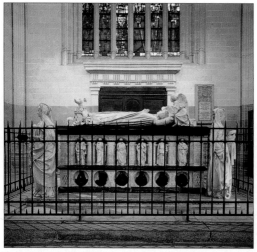

Tomb of François II in Cathédrale St-Pierre et St-Paul, Nantes

Nantes ⑨

Loire-Atlantique. 🏠 270,000. ✈ 🚊 🚃 🖪 *Place du Commerce (02-40 20 60 00).* 🖴 *Tue–Sun.*

THE ANCIENT PORT of Nantes was the ducal capital of Brittany for 600 years, but is now considered a part of the Pays de la Loire. Many of its fine 18th- and 19th-century buildings were built on profits from maritime trade. Modern-day Nantes is a lively city, with good museums, chic bars and shops, and wide open spaces.

The **Cathédrale St-Pierre et St-Paul** was begun in 1434, but not completed until 1893. It is notable for its sculpted Gothic portals and Renaissance tomb of François II (1435–88), the last duke of Brittany.

The **Château des Ducs de Bretagne** (closed for restoration until 2006) was the birthplace of Anne of Brittany, who irrevocably joined her fiercely independent duchy to France by her successive marriages to Charles VIII and Louis XII. A smaller royal lodging lies to the west of it. It was here, in Brittany's Catholic bastion, that Henri IV signed the 1598 Edict of Nantes, which granted all Protestants freedom of worship.

The **Musée des Beaux-Arts** is known for its splendid array of paintings representing key movements from the 15th to the 20th centuries.

Packed with mementos, books, and maps, the **Musée Jules Verne** is dedicated to the life and works of the famous writer (1828–1905).

🏛 **Musée des Beaux-Arts**
10 Rue Georges Clemenceau.
☎ 02-51 17 45 00. 🕐 *Wed–Mon.* 🌑 *public hols.* 🈂 🛗

Poitiers ⑩

Vienne. 🏠 84,000. ✈ 🚊 🚃 🖪 *45 Place Charles de Gaulle (05-49 41 21 24).* 🖴 *Tue–Sun.*

THREE OF THE greatest battles in French history were fought around Poitiers, the most famous in 732 when Charles Martel halted the Arab invasion. Today the town is a modern and dynamic regional capital with a rich architectural heritage in its historic center.

Behind the Renaissance façade of the **Palais de Justice** is the 12th-century great hall of the palace of Henry II and Richard the Lion-Heart. This is thought to be the scene of Joan of Arc's examination by a council of theologians in 1429.

Notre-Dame-la-Grande, whose west front is covered with superb 12th-century Poitevin sculpture, stands out among the city's churches, as does the 4th-century **Baptistère St-Jean**, one of the oldest Christian buildings in France. The latter contains Romanesque frescoes.

The **Musée Sainte-Croix** has archaeological exhibits, as well as paintings and sculpture.

ENVIRONS: Located 7 km (4.5 miles) north of Poitiers, **Futuroscope** is a theme park dedicated to state-of-the-art visual technology. The crystal-like Kinemax cinema has the largest screen in Europe.

🏛 **Futuroscope**
Jaunay-Clan. ☎ 05-49 49 30 00. 🕐 *daily.* 🌑 *Nov 3–Feb 6.* 🈂

The high-tech Kinemax cinema at Futuroscope, near Poitiers

Abbaye de Fontevraud ⓫

Maine-et-Loire. 🚌 📞 02-41 51 71 41. ⬜ daily. ⬤ Jan 1, Nov 1 & 11, Dec 25. 🅿️ 🚻 ♿

FONTEVRAUD ABBEY, founded in 1101, was the largest of its kind in France. It now hosts concerts and exhibitions.

The abbey's nuns lived around the Renaissance Grand Moûtier cloisters, and the leper colony's nurses were housed in the St-Lazare priory, now the abbey's hotel. Little remains of the monastic quarters, but the St-Benoît hospital survives. Most impressive is the octagonal kitchen in the Tour Evraud, a rare example of secular Romanesque architecture.

In the nave of the abbey church, the painted effigy of Henry Plantagenet (1133– 1189), Count of Anjou and King of England, lies by those of his wife Eleanor of Aquitaine, who died here in 1204, and their son, Richard the Lion-Heart (1157–1199).

Tours ⓬

Indre-et-Loire. 👥 140,000. ✈ 🚉 🚌 ℹ 78 Rue Bernard Palissy (02-47 70 37 37). 🛒 Tue–Sun.

THE PLEASANT cathedral city of Tours is built on the site of a Roman town, and became an important center of Christianity in the 4th century under St. Martin. In 1461 Louis XI made the city the French capital. However, during Henri IV's reign, the city lost favor with the monarchy and the capital left Tours for Paris.

The medieval old town, Le Vieux Tours, is full of narrow streets lined with beautiful half-timbered houses. St. Martin's tomb lies in the crypt of the New Basilica, built on the site of the medieval Old Basilica. Two towers, the **Tour Charlemagne** and the **Tour de l'Horloge**, survive from the earlier building.

Nearby, the vaulted cellars of the 13th-century **Eglise St-Julien** now form the **Musée des Vins de Touraine**, where

exhibits include a Renaissance winepress and displays on early viticultural history.

The foundation stone of the **Cathédrale St-Gatien** was laid in the early 13th century. Building work continued until the mid-16th century, and the cathedral provides an illustration of how the Gothic style developed over time.

The **Château Royal de Tours**, a royal residence between the 13th and 15th centuries, houses the Historial de Touraine, which illustrates the region's history in waxworks.

Château de Chenonceau ⓭

See pp178–9.

Blois ⓮

Loir-et-Cher. 👥 60,000. 🚉 🚌 ℹ Voûte du Château (02-54 90 41 41). 🛒 Tue–Thu & Sat.

A POWERFUL FEUDAL stronghold in the 12th century, Blois rose to glory under Louis XII, who established his court here in 1498. The town remained at the center of French royal and political life for much of the next century. Today, Blois is the quintessential Loire town. The partly pedestrianized old quarter is full of romantic courtyards and fine mansions.

François I's staircase, Château de Blois

Home to kings Louis XII, François I, and Henri III, no other Loire château has such a sensational history as the **Château de Blois**. It was here, in 1588, that the ambitious Duc de Guise, leader of the Catholic Holy League, was murdered on the orders of Henri III. The building itself juxtaposes four distinct architectural styles, reflecting its varied history.

Among Blois' most impressive religious monuments are the beautiful three-spired **Eglise St-Nicolas**, formerly part of a 12th-century Benedictine abbey, and the **Cathédrale St-Louis**, which dominates the eastern half of the city. The cathedral is a 17th-century reconstruction of a Gothic church that was almost destroyed in 1678.

🔱 **Château de Blois**
Place du Château. 📞 02-54 90 33 33. ⬜ daily. ⬤ Jan 1, Dec 25. 🅿️ 🚻

The historic town of Blois, viewed from across the Loire

Château de Chenonceau 🔞

Cᴴᴇɴᴏɴᴄᴇᴀᴜ, sᴛʀᴇᴛᴄʜɪɴɢ romantically across the River Cher, is considered by many to be the loveliest of the Loire châteaux. Surrounded by elegant formal gardens and wooded grounds, this pure Renaissance building began life as a modest manor and water mill. Over the centuries it was transformed by the wives and mistresses of its successive owners into a palace designed solely for pleasure. The story of these ladies is told in the château's *son et lumière* (literally "sound and light") shows, held nightly during the summer months.

Chambre de Catherine de' Medici
Henri II's wife Catherine made her own mark on Chenonceau's design, with this sumptuous bedchamber.

Formal Gardens
The current designs of the formal gardens created by Diane de Poitiers and Catherine de' Medici date from the 19th century.

Louise de Lorraine's room was painted black and decorated with monograms, tears, and knots in white after the assassination of her husband, Henri III.

The Cabinet Vert was originally covered with green velvet.

The Tour des Marques survives from the 15th-century castle of the Marques family.

Chapel
The chapel has a vaulted ceiling and sculpted pilasters. The stained glass, destroyed by a bomb in 1944, was replaced in 1953.

Grande Galerie
The elegant gallery is Florentine in style. It was created by Catherine de' Medici in 1570–76 as an addition to the bridge built for Diane de Poitiers.

The arched bridge
over the Cher was
designed by Philibert
de l'Orme in 1559 for
Diane de Poitiers. It
was built on the site
of the old water mill.

DIANE DE POITIERS

Diane de Poitiers was
Henry II's lifelong mistress,
holding court as queen of
France in all but name. Her
beauty inspired many
French artists, who often
depicted her in the role
of Diana, the Classical
goddess of the hunt.

In 1547 Henry offered the
Château de Chenonceau
to Diane, who improved
the palace by creating
stunning formal gardens
and an arched bridge
over the River Cher.

After Henry's accidental
death in 1559, Diane was
forced to leave Chenon-
ceau by his widow
Catherine de' Medici, in
exchange for the fortress-
like Château de Chaumont.
Diane retired to Anet, and
remained there until her
death in 1566.

The Château de Chambord on the banks of the Closson

Château de Chambord ⓑ

Loir-et-Cher. 🚌 to Blois, then taxi or
bus. 📞 02-54 50 40 00. 🕐 daily.
● Jan 1, May 1, Dec 25. 🎫 ✔

THE BRAINCHILD of the extravagant François I, the
château began as a hunting
lodge in the Forêt de Boulogne. In 1519 the original
building was razed and
Chambord begun, to a design
probably initiated by
Leonardo da Vinci. By 1537
the keep, with its towers and
terraces, had been completed
by 1,800 men and three master
masons. The following year,
François I began building a
private royal pavilion on the
northeast corner, with a
connecting two-story gallery.
His son, Henri II, continued
the west wing with the chapel,
and Louis XIV completed the
440-roomed edifice in 1685.

The innovative double-helix
Grand Staircase was supposedly designed by Leonardo
da Vinci. The two flights of
stairs ensure that the person
going up and the person
going down cannot meet.

Orléans ⓰

Loiret. 🏙 113,000. ✈ 🚉 🚌
🛈 6 Rue Albert 1er (02-38 24 05 05).
🎭 Fête Jeanne d'Arc (May 7–8).

ORLEANS WAS the capital of
medieval France, and it
was here that Joan of Arc
battled the English in 1429,

during the Hundred Years'
War. Later captured by the
enemy and accused of witch-
craft, she was burned at the
stake in Rouen at the age
of 19. Since her martyrdom,
Joan has become a pervasive
presence in Orléans.

A faded grandeur lingers in
Vieil Orléans, the old quarter
bounded by the imposing
Cathédrale Sainte-Croix,
the Loire, and the Place du
Martroi. The **Maison Jeanne
d'Arc** was rebuilt in 1961 on
the site where Joan lodged in
1429. Inside, audiovisual
exhibits recreate her life.

A selection of European art
of the 16th to early 20th
centuries is on display at the
Musée des Beaux-Arts.

🏛 Maison Jeanne d'Arc

3 Place du Général de Gaulle. 📞 02-
38 52 99 89. 🕐 May–Oct: Tue–Sun;
Nov–Apr: pm Tue–Sun. ● Jan 1, Apr
28–29, May 1 & 8, Nov 1, Dec 25. 🎫

The lofty interior of the
Cathédrale Sainte-Croix, Orléans

Chartres Cathedral ⑰

ACCORDING TO ART HISTORIAN Emile Male, "Chartres is the mind of the Middle Ages manifest." Begun in 1020, the Romanesque cathedral was destroyed by a devastating fire in 1194. Only the north and south towers, south steeple, west portal, and crypt remained. Inside, the sacred *Veil of the Virgin* relic was the sole treasure to survive. Peasant and lord alike labored to rebuild the church in just 25 years. Few alterations were made after 1250 and, fortunately, Chartres was left unscathed by the Wars of Religion and the French Revolution. The result is an authentic Gothic cathedral with a true "Bible in stone" reputation.

Elongated Statues
These statues on the Royal Portal represent Old Testament figures.

The taller of the two spires dates from the start of the 16th century. Flamboyant Gothic in style, it contrasts sharply with the solemnity of its Romanesque counterpart.

Gothic Nave
As wide as the Romanesque crypt below it – the largest in France – the Gothic nave reaches a lofty height of 37 m (121 ft).

★ **Stained-Glass Windows**
Donated by the guilds between 1210 and 1240, the cathedral's glorious stained glass is world-renowned.

★ **Royal Portal**
The Royal Portal (1145–55) and part of the west front survive from the original Romanesque church. The central tympanum has a carving of Christ in Majesty.

STAR FEATURES

★ **South Porch**

★ **Royal Portal**

★ **Stained-Glass Windows**

The Labyrinth
is inlaid in the nave floor. Pilgrims used to follow the tortuous route by crawling on their knees, echoing the Way of the Cross.

CHARTRES' STAINED GLASS

Over 150 stained-glass windows in the cathedral illustrate biblical stories and daily life in the 13th century (bring binoculars if you can). During both World Wars the windows were dismantled piece by piece and removed for safety. Some windows were restored and releaded in the 1970s, but much more remains to be done. Each window is divided into panels, which are usually read from left to right, bottom to top (earth to heaven). The number of figures or abstract shapes used is symbolic: three stands for the Church; squares and the number four symbolize the material world or the four elements; circles represent eternal life.

The vaulted ceiling is supported by a network of ribs.

Apsidal Chapel
This chapel houses the oldest cathedral treasure, the Veil of the Virgin *relic. Supposedly worn by the Virgin Mary, the artifact brought many pilgrims to Chartres during the Middle Ages.*

The St. Piat Chapel, built between 1324 and 1353, contains many artifacts, relics, and treasures.

South Rose Window
The cathedral has three massive rose windows. That on the south front (c.1225) illustrates the Apocalypse, *with Christ in Majesty.*

★ South Porch
Sculpture on the massive South Porch (1197–1209) reflects a selection of New Testament teaching.

Burgundy and the French Alps

Burgundy is France's richest province, historically, culturally, and gastronomically. The region's fine wines have inspired awe for centuries, and every year the historic town of Beaune hosts one of the most famous wine auctions in the world. Dijon is a splendid city, filled with the great palaces of the old Burgundian nobility. The majestic French Alps attract visitors for winter sports, and, in summer, walking and a host of water sports on the glittering mountain lakes.

Tympanum sculpture showing Christ and the apostles at Basilique Ste-Madeleine, Vézelay

Vézelay ⑱

Yonne. 🏛 600. 🚆 **Basilique Ste-Madeleine** 🚪 03-86 33 39 50. 🚉 Sermizelles, then bus. 🕙 daily. 📷

Tourists come to Vézelay to visit the picturesque **Basilique Ste-Madeleine**. In the 12th century, at the height of its glory, the abbey claimed to house the relics of Mary Magdalene, and it was a starting point for the pilgrimage to Santiago de Compostela in Spain (see p302).

The star attractions of the Romanesque church are the tympanum sculpture (1120–35) above the central doorway, the exquisitely carved capitals in the nave and narthex, and the immense Gothic choir.

Dijon ⑲

See pp184–5.

Beaune ⑳

Côte D'Or. 🏛 22,000. 🚆 🚌 🏛 Rue de l'Hôtel-Dieu (03-80 26 21 30). 📷 Charity Wine Auction (third Sun Nov).

The indisputable highlight of the old center of Beaune is the **Hôtel-Dieu**. The hospice was founded in 1443 for the town's inhabitants, many of whom were left poverty-stricken after the Hundred Years' War. Today it is considered a medieval jewel, with its superb multicolored Burgundian roof tiles. It houses many treasures, including the religious masterpiece, Rogier van der Weyden's *Last Judgement* polyptych.

The Hôtel des Ducs de Bourgogne, built in the 14th–16th centuries, houses the **Musée du Vin de Bourgogne**, with displays of traditional winemaking equipment.

Further to the north is the 12th-century Romanesque church, the **Collégiale Notre-Dame**, which has a collection of fine 15th-century tapestries.

🏛 Hôtel-Dieu
Rue de l'Hôtel-Dieu. 🚪 03-80 24 45 00. 🕙 daily. ● Dec–Mar: 11:30am–2pm daily. 📷 📷

Lyon ㉑

Rhône. 🏛 432,000. 🛬 25 km (16 miles) E. 🚆 🚌 🏛 Place Bellecour (04-72 77 69 69). 🚢 daily.

France's second city, dramatically situated on the banks of the Rhône and Saône rivers, has been a vital gateway between the north and south since ancient times.

Vieux Lyon, the oldest part of the city, is the site of the Roman settlement of Lugdunum, the commercial and military capital of Gaul founded by Julius Caesar in 44 BC. Vestiges of this prosperous city can be seen in the superb **Musée de la Civilisation Gallo-Romaine**. There are also two excavated Roman amphitheaters: the **Grand Théâtre**, built in 15 BC to seat 30,000 spectators, and the smaller **Odéon**.

Other major sights are the 19th-century mock-Byzantine **Basilique Notre-Dame de Fourvière**, and the **Cathédrale St-Jean**, begun in the 12th century. Vieux Lyon's fine Renaissance mansions are the former homes of bankers and silk merchants.

THE DUKES OF BURGUNDY

In the 14th and 15th centuries the dukes of Burgundy built up one of the most powerful states in Europe, which included Flanders and parts of Holland. From the time of Philip the Bold (1342–1404) the ducal court became a center of art, chivalry, and immense wealth. The duchy's demise came with the death of Charles the Bold in 1477.

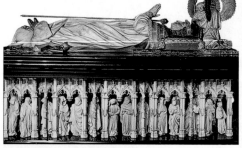

Tomb of Philip the Bold in Dijon's Musée des Beaux Arts (see p184)

Cathédrale St-Jean at the foot of the slopes of Vieux Lyon

The excellent **Musée des Beaux Arts** showcases the country's largest and most important collection of fine arts after the Louvre. The modern works, dating from after the mid-1900s, have found a new home in the **Musée d'Art Contemporain** in the north of the city. An exquisite display of silks and tapestries, some dating back to early Christian times, can be seen in the **Musée Historique des Tissus**.

fi Musée de la Civilisation Gallo-Romaine
17 Rue Cléberg. ☎ 04-72 38 81 90. ☐ Wed–Sun. ● public hols. ▨ ♿

Annecy ㉒

Haute Savoie. 👥 51,000. 🚉 🚌 ❚ 1 Rue Jean Jaurès (04-50 45 00 33). 🛒 Tue, Fri, Sat, Sun am.

ANNECY IS ONE of the most beautiful towns in the Alps, set at the northern tip of Lac d'Annecy and surrounded by snow-capped mountains.

A stroll around the town's small medieval quarter, with its canals, flower-covered bridges, and arcaded streets,

is one of the main attractions of a stay here. Look out for the formidable **Palais de l'Isle**, a 12th-century prison in the middle of the Thiou canal.

The turreted **Château d'Annecy**, perched high on a hill above the town, affords fine panoramic views.

The clear waters of the lake are perfect for swimming and water sports, while boat trips leave from the Quai Thiou.

ENVIRONS: One way to enjoy the area's spectacular scenery is to take a boat to **Talloires**, a tiny lakeside village, noted for its hotels and restaurants.

Grenoble ㉓

Isère. 👥 200,000. ✈ 🚉 🚌 ❚ 14 Rue de la République (04-76 42 41 41). 🛒 Tue–Sun.

ANCIENT CAPITAL of Dauphiné, Grenoble is a busy and thriving city, attractively located at the confluence of the Drac and Isère rivers, in the shadow of the mighty Vercors and Chartreuse massifs.

A cable car from the Quai Stéphane-Jay on the north bank of the Isère takes you up to the 16th-century **Fort de la Bastille**, where you are rewarded with magnificent views of the city and surrounding mountains. From here, paths lead down through pretty gardens to the excellent **Musée Dauphinois** at the foot of the hill. Housed in a 17th-century convent, the museum contains displays on local history, arts, and crafts.

On the other side of the river, the focus of life is the Place Grenette, a lively square lined with sidewalk cafés. Nearby, the Place St-André is the heart of the medieval city, overlooked by Grenoble's oldest buildings, including the 13th-century **Eglise St-André** and the 15th-century **Palais de Justice**.

Also worth visiting is the **Musée de Grenoble**, the city's principal art museum. With works by Chagall, Picasso, and Matisse, the modern collection is especially good.

fi Musée de Grenoble
5 Place de Lavalette. ☎ 04-76 63 44 44. ☐ Wed–Mon. ● Jan 1, May 1, Dec 25. ▨ ♿

Annecy's 12th-century Palais de l'Isle on the Thiou canal

Street by Street: Dijon ⓲

THE CENTER of Dijon is noted for its architectural splendor – a legacy from the dukes of Burgundy *(see p182)*. Wealthy parliament members also had elegant *hôtels particuliers* (private mansions) built in the 17th and 18th centuries. The capital of Burgundy, Dijon today has a rich cultural life and a renowned university. The city's great art treasures are housed in the Palais des Ducs. Dijon is also famous for its mustard and *pain d'épice* (gingerbread), a reminder of the town's position on the medieval spice route. A major rail hub during the 19th century, it now has a TGV link to Paris.

Hôtel de Vogüé
This elegant 17th-century mansion is decorated with Burgundian cabbages and fruit garlands by Hugues Sambin.

★ **Notre-Dame**
This magnificent 13th-century Gothic church is best known for its many gargoyles, the Jacquemart clock, and, on the north wall, the sculpted owl (chouette), said to bring good luck when touched.

Musée des Beaux Arts
The collection of Flemish masters here includes this 14th-century triptych by Jacques de Baerze and Melchior Broederlam.

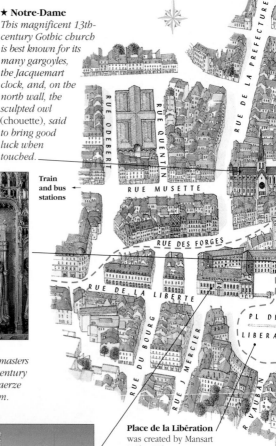

Train and bus stations

RUE ODEBERT

RUE QUENTIN

RUE DE LA PREFECTURE

RUE MUSETTE

RUE DES FORGES

RUE DE LA LIBERTE

RUE DU BOURG

RUE J. MERCIER

R. VAUBAN

PL DE LIBERA

Place de la Libération
was created by Mansart in the 17th century.

★ **Palais des Ducs**
The dukes of Burgundy held court here, but the building seen today was mainly built in the 17th century for the parliament. It now houses the Musée des Beaux Arts.

Rue Verrerie
*This cobbled street in
the old merchants'
quarter is lined
with medieval half-
timbered houses.
Some, such as Nos.
8, 10, and 12, have
fine wood carvings.*

Visitors' Checklist

Côte d'Or. ![icon] 151,000.
![icon] 5 km (3 miles) SSE. ![icon] ![icon]
Cours de la Gare. ![icon] Place Darcy
(03-80 44 11 44). ![icon] Tue, Thu–
Sat. ![icon] Festival de Musique
(Jun); Fêtes de la Vigne (Sep).
Musée des Beaux Arts ![icon] 03-
80 74 52 70. ![icon] Wed–Mon.
![icon] main public hols. ![icon] ![icon]
Musée Magnin ![icon] 03-80 67
11 10. ![icon] Tue–Sun. ![icon] some
public hols. ![icon]

★ St-Michel
*Begun in the 15th century
and completed in the 17th
century, St-Michel's façade
combines Flamboyant Gothic
with Renaissance details. On
the richly carved porch, angels
and biblical motifs mingle
with mythological themes.*

Musée Magnin
*A collection of French and
foreign 16th–19th-century
paintings is displayed
among period furniture in
this 17th-century mansion.*

The Eglise St-Etienne
dates from the 11th century
but has been rebuilt many
times. Its characteristic
lantern was added in 1686.

RUE VERRERIE
RUE PROUDHON
RUE JJ
R CHAUDRONNERIE
ROUSSEAU
RUE VANNERIE
RUE JEANNIN
RUE LAMONNOYE
PL STE CHAPELLE
R VAILLANT
PL DU THEATRE
PL ST MICHEL
RUE CHABOT CHARNY
RUE DU VIEUX COLLEGE
RUE BUFFON
RUE LEGOUZ GERLAND

Star Sights

★ Palais des Ducs

★ Notre-Dame

★ St-Michel

Key

– – – Suggested route

0 meters   100

0 yards   100

The Wines of France

WINEMAKING IN FRANCE dates back to pre-Roman times, although it was the Romans who disseminated the culture of the vine and the practise of winemaking throughout the country. The range, quality, and reputation of the fine wines of Bordeaux, Burgundy, and Champagne in particular have made them rôle models the world over. France's everyday wines can be highly enjoyable too, with plenty of good-value *vins de pays* and *vins de table* now emerging from the southern regions. Many wine producers offer tours and have their own tasting rooms, where visitors can try a selection of wines without feeling pressurized to buy.

Château Cos d'Estournel, in the Bordeaux region, produces a rich and fruity Cabernet Sauvignon. The grandeur of its exotic design is typical of château architecture.

THE WINE REGIONS OF FRANCE

Each of the 10 principal wine-producing regions has its own identity, based on grape varieties, climate and soil, and local culture. Around 40 percent of all French wines are included in the *appellation d'origine contrôlée* system, which guarantees their style and geographic origin, though not their quality.

BORDEAUX WINES

Bordeaux is the world's largest fine wine region, and, for its red wines, certainly the most familiar outside France. The great wine-producing areas lie close to the banks of the rivers Gironde, Garonne, and Dordogne. These rivers, and the river port of Bordeaux itself, have been crucial to the region's wine trade; some of the prettiest châteaux line the river banks, enabling easy transportation. Grape varieties used include Cabernet Sauvignon, Merlot, and Petit Verdot (red); Sémillon and Sauvignon Blanc (white).

Château Pitray

Château Thieuley

HOW TO READ A WINE LABEL

Even the simplest label will provide a key to the wine's flavor and quality. It will bear the name of the wine and its producer, its vintage if there is one, and whether it comes from a strictly defined area (*appellation contrôlée* or VDQS) or is a more general *vin de pays* or *vin de table*. It may also have a regional grading, as with the *crus classés* in Bordeaux. The shape and color of the bottle are also guides. Most good-quality wine is bottled in green glass, which helps to protect it from light.

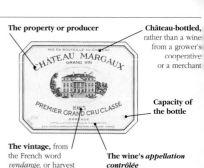

The property or producer

Château-bottled, rather than a wine from a grower's cooperative or a merchant

Capacity of the bottle

The vintage, from the French word *vendange*, or harvest

The wine's *appellation contrôlée*

Burgundy Wines

The tiny vineyards in each of Burgundy's wine-producing regions, from Chablis in the north to Beaujolais in the south, can produce wines that, at their best, are unequalled anywhere else. This is unmissable territory for the "serious" wine-lover, with its time-honored traditions and dazzling *grands crus*. Grape varieties used include Pinot Noir, Gamay, and César (red); Pinot Blanc and Chardonnay (white).

Domaine François Raveneau   **Domaine Michel Lafarge**

Champagne *is a region synonymous with the finest sparkling wines. The skill of the blenders, using reserves of older wines, creates consistency and excellence year on year. Champagne bubbles are produced by fermenting yeast inside the bottle – traditional methods are still used all over the region. In a process called* remuage, *bottles are gradually rotated in order to loosen the sediment, which is ultimately removed from the wine.*

Tours of Major Wineries

Winemakers are usually happy to welcome tourists in summer, but try not to visit at harvest time (Sep–Oct). Whatever time of year you visit, be sure to make an appointment in advance.

Bordeaux
Château Cheval Blanc
Saint Emilion. (*05-57 55 55 55.*
FAX *05-57 55 55 50.*

Château Haut-Brion
Pessac. (*05-56 00 29 30.*
FAX *05-56 98 75 14.*

Château Margaux
Margaux. (*05-57 88 83 83.*
FAX *05-57 88 31 32.*

Château Mouton-Rothschild
Pauillac. (*05-56 59 22 22.*
FAX *05-56 73 20 44.*

Burgundy
Clos de la Barre
Meursault. (*03-80 21 22 17.*
FAX *03-80 21 61 64.*

Maison Louis Latour
18 Rue des Tonneliers, Beaune.
(*03-80 24 81 00.*
FAX *03-80 22 36 21.*

Champagne
Krug
5 Rue Coquebert, Reims.
(*03-26 84 44 20.*
FAX *03-26 84 44 49.*

Moët & Chandon
20 Avenue de Champagne,
Epernay. (*03-26 51 20 00.*
FAX *03-26 51 20 21.*

Piper Heidsieck
51 Boulevard Henry Vasnier,
Reims. (*03-26 84 43 00.*
FAX *03-26 84 43 49.*

KEY

☐ Alsace and Lorraine

☐ Bordeaux

☐ Burgundy

☐ Champagne

■ Jura and Savoie

☐ Languedoc-Roussillon

☐ The Loire Valley

☐ Provence

☐ The Rhône Valley

☐ Southwest France

Chardonnay vines *in the* grand cru *vineyard of Corton-Charlemagne produce some of the greatest white Burgundies of all. The Chardonnay grape is now cultivated not only in Burgundy and Champagne, but all over the world. In the Loire valley and southern France, it is used for* vins de pays.

Southwest France

THE SOUTHWEST IS FARMING FRANCE, a green and peaceful land nurturing crops from sunflowers to walnuts. Other key country products include forest timber, Bordeaux wines, and wild mushrooms. Major modern industries, including aerospace, are focused on the two chief cities, Bordeaux and Toulouse. Visitors are mainly drawn to the wine chateaux, the ski slopes of the Pyrenees, and the prehistoric caves of the Dordogne. The major sights of this favored region include some of France's most celebrated Romanesque buildings.

Monument aux Girondins, Place des Quinconces, Bordeaux

Bordeaux ②④

Gironde. 🏛 215,000. ✈ 🚊 🚌 🛈 12 Cours du 30 Juillet (05-56 00 66 00). 🍴 daily. 🎉 Fête du Vin Nouveau (Oct).

BUILT ON a curve of the Garonne river, Bordeaux has been a major port since pre-Roman times and for centuries a focus and crossroads of European trade. The export of wine has always been the basis of the city's prosperity, and today the Bordeaux region produces over 44 million cases of wine per year.

Along the waterfront, a long sweep of Classical façades is broken by the Esplanade des Quinconces, with its statues and fountains. At one end, the Monument aux Girondins (1804–1902) commemorates the Girondists sent to the guillotine by Robespierre during the Terror (1793–5).

Buildings of architectural interest include the massive **Basilique St-Michel**, begun in 1350, which took 200 years to complete, and the 18th-century **Grand Théâtre**, a magnificent example of the French Neoclassical style. The **Musée des Beaux Arts** holds an excellent collection of paintings, ranging from the Renaissance to our time.

🏛 **Musée des Beaux Arts**
20 Cours d'Albret. 📞 05-56 10 20 56. 🕐 Wed–Mon. 🔴 public hols. 🈺 ♿

ENVIRONS: The tourist office in Bordeaux organizes tours to the various wine châteaux of the region *(see pp186–7)*, including **Latour**, **Margaux**, and **Cheval Blanc**.

Lascaux ②⑤

Montignac. 📞 05-53 51 95 03. 🕐 Feb–Mar & Nov–Dec: Tue–Sun; Apr–Oct: daily. 🔴 Jan, Dec 25. 🈺

LASCAUX is the most famous of the prehistoric sites in the Dordogne region. Four young boys and their dog came across the caves and their astounding Palaeolithic paintings in 1940, and the importance of their discovery was swiftly recognized.

Lascaux has been closed to the public since 1963 because of deterioration, but an exact copy, known as Lascaux II, has been created a few minutes' walk down the hillside, using the same materials. The replica is beautiful and should not be spurned: high-antlered elk, bison, and plump horses cover the walls, moving in herds or files, surrounded by arrows and geometric symbols thought to have had ritual significance.

Toulouse ②⑥

Haute-Garonne. 🏛 360,000. ✈ 🚊 🚌 🛈 Donjon du Capitole (05-61 11 02 22). 🍴 daily. 🎉 Piano (Sep), Jazz (Oct).

TOULOUSE, the most important town in southwest France is the country's fourth largest metropolis, and a major industrial and university city.

The area is also famous for its aerospace industry; Concorde, Airbus, and the Ariane space rocket all originated here. The **Cité de l'Espace** features a planetarium and interactive exhibits related to the exploration of space.

The church known as **Les Jacobins** was begun in 1229 and took over two centuries to finish. The Gothic masterpiece features a soaring, 22-branched palm tree vault in the apse. The belltower (1294) is much imitated in southwest France.

Palm vaulting in the apse of Les Jacobins, Toulouse

A picturesque village set in a lush valley among the foothills of the Pyrenees mountains

Toulouse became a center of Romanesque art in Europe due to its position on the route to Santiago de Compostela *(see p302)*. The largest Romanesque basilica in Europe, the **Basilique de St-Sernin**, was built in the 11th–12th centuries to accommodate pilgrims. The **Musée des Augustins** has sculptures from the period, and incorporates cloisters from a 14th-century Augustinian priory. Also featured are French, Italian, and Flemish paintings.

The 16th-century palace known as the **Hôtel d'Assézat** now houses the Fondation Bemberg, named after local art lover Georges Bemberg. His fine collection covers Renaissance art and 19th- and 20th-century French paintings.

🏛 Musée des Augustins
21 Rue de Metz. **C** *05-61 22 21 82.*
○ *Wed–Mon.* **●** *Jan 1, May 1, Dec 25.* 🎫 🚻 &

Pyrenees ㉗

✕ *Pau.* **🚃 🚍** *Bayonne & Pau.*
ℹ *Place des Basques, Bayonne (05-59 46 01 46); Place Royale, Pau (05-59 27 27 08).*

THE MOUNTAINS dominate life in the French Pyrenees. A region in many ways closer to Spain than France, over the centuries its remote terrain and

tenacious people have given heretics a hiding place and refugees an escape route.

The **Parc National des Pyrénées** extends 100 km (62 miles) along the French–Spanish frontier. It boasts some of the most splendid alpine scenery in Europe, and is rich in flora and fauna. Within the park are 350 km (217 miles) of footpaths.

The region's oldest inhabitants, the Basque people, have maintained their own language and culture. **Bayonne** on the Atlantic coast is the capital of the French Basque country, and has been an important town since Roman times. **Biarritz**, west of Bayonne, has

two casinos and three good beaches, with the best surfing in Europe. A short distance south, **St-Jean-de-Luz** is a sleepy fishing village that explodes into life in summer. A main attraction is the Eglise St-Jean Baptiste, where Louis XIV married the Infanta Maria Teresa of Spain in 1660.

A lively university town with elegant architecture, **Pau** is the most interesting large town in the central Pyrenees. It has long been a favorite resort of affluent foreigners.

Other places of interest include the many mountain ski resorts, the shrine at **Lourdes**, and the pretty hilltop town of **St-Bertrand-de-Comminges**.

THE MIRACLE OF LOURDES

In 1858, a 14-year-old girl named Bernadette Soubirous experienced 18 visions of the Virgin at the Grotte Massabielle near the town of Lourdes. Despite being told to keep away from the cave by her mother – and the local magistrate – she was guided to a spring with miraculous healing powers. The

church endorsed the miracles in the 1860s, and since then many people claim to have been cured by the holy water. A huge city of shrines, churches, and hospices has since grown up around the spring, with a dynamic tourist industry to match.

Pilgrims at an open-air mass in Lourdes

The South of France

THE SOUTH IS FRANCE'S most popular holiday region, drawing millions of visitors each year to the resorts of the Riviera and the Côte d'Azur, and to the vivid landscape and historic villages of Provence. Painters such as Cézanne, van Gogh, and Picasso, have been inspired by the luminous light and brilliant colors of the region. Agriculture is still a mainstay of the economy, but the new high-tech industries of Nice now make a significant contribution to the region's prosperity.

Château Comtal in the restored citadel of Carcassonne

Carcassonne ㉘

Aude. 🏛 45,000. 🚇 🚌 🛈 Tour Narbonnaise, La Cité (04-68 10 24 36). 🗓 Tue, Thu & Sat. 🎪 Festival de la Cité (all of Jul).

THE CITADEL of Carcassonne is a perfectly restored medieval town. It crowns a steep bank above the Aude river, a fairy-tale sight of turrets and ramparts overlooking the Basse Ville below.

The strategic position of the citadel between the Atlantic and the Mediterranean led to its original settlement, consolidated by the Romans in the 2nd century BC.

At its zenith in the 12th century the town was ruled by the Trencavels, who built the château and cathedral. The Cathars, a persecuted Christian sect, were given sanctuary here in 1209 but, after a two-week siege, the town fell to the Crusaders sent to eradicate them. The attentions of architectural historian Viollet-le-Duc led to Carcassonne's restoration in the 19th century.

Flanked by sandstone towers, the defenses of the **Porte Narbonnaise** included two portcullises, two iron doors, a moat, and a drawbridge. A fortress within a fortress, the **Château Comtal** has a surrounding moat, five towers, and defensive wooden galleries on the walls.

Within the Romanesque and Gothic **Basilique St-Nazaire** is the famous Siege Stone, inscribed with scenes said to depict the siege of 1209.

Nîmes ㉙

Gard. 🏛 137,000. ✈ 🚇 🚌 🛈 6 Rue Auguste (04-66 58 38 00). 🗓 daily.

AN IMPORTANT crossroads in the ancient world, Nîmes is well known for its bullfights and Roman antiquities. The city has had a turbulent history, and suffered particularly in the 16th-century Wars of Religion, when the Romanesque **Cathédrale Notre-Dame et St-Castor** was badly damaged. In the 17th and 18th centuries the town prospered from textile manufacturing, one of the most enduring products being denim or *serge de Nîmes*.

All roads in the city lead to the amphitheater, **Les Arènes**. Built at the end of the 1st century AD, it is still in use today as a venue for concerts, sporting events, and bullfights.

The **Maison Carrée** is an elegant Roman temple, the pride of Nîmes. Built by Augustus' son-in-law Marcus Agrippa, it is one of the best preserved in the world, with finely fluted Corinthian columns and a sculpted frieze.

Set in the Roman wall is the **Porte d'Auguste**, a gateway built for travelers on the Domitian Way, which passed through the center of Nîmes. Nearby is the **Castellum**, a tower used for storing water brought in by aqueduct. The water was distributed around the town by a canal system. A display of Roman statues, ceramics, glass, coins, and mosaics can be seen at the **Musée Archéologique**.

Five floors of Nîmes' controversial arts complex, the **Carré d'Art**, which stands opposite the Maison Carrée, lie underground. The complex incorporates a library, a roof-terrace restaurant around a huge glass atrium, and the Musée d'Art Contemporain.

🏛 Musée Archéologique
13 bis Boulevard Amiral Courbet. 📞 04-66 76 74 80. 🕐 Tue–Sun. 🔴 Jan 1, May 1, Nov 11, Dec 25. 📷

ENVIRONS: To the northeast of the city lies the **Pont du Gard**, a 2,000-year-old aqueduct. The Romans considered this to be the best testimony to the greatness of their empire, and at 49 m (160 ft) it was the highest bridge they ever built.

The Pont du Gard, outside Nîmes, a major feat of Roman engineering

Avignon ⏰

Vaucluse. 🏘 100,000. 🚉 🚍 🚌
ℹ 41 Cours Jean Jaurès (04-32 74
32 74). 🎭 Tue–Sun. 🎪 Le Festival
d'Avignon (mid-Jul–mid-Aug).

MASSIVE RAMPARTS enclose
one of the most fascin-
ating towns in southern France.
The huge **Palais des Papes** is
the dominant feature, but the
town contains other riches. To
the north of the Palais is the
13th-century **Petit Palais**, once
the Archbishop of Avignon's
residence. It has received such
notorious guests as Cesare
Borgia and Louis XIV. Now a
museum, it displays Romanesque and Gothic sculpture
and paintings of the Avignon
and Italian Schools, with works
by Botticelli and Carpaccio.
    Avignon boasts some fine
churches, such as the 12th-
century **Cathédrale de Notre-
Dame-des-Doms**, with its

**Open-air performance at
the annual Avignon Festival**

Romanesque cupola and
papal tombs, and the 14th-
century **Eglise St-Didier**.
    The **Musée Lapidaire**
contains statues, mosaics,
and carvings from pre-Roman
Provence. The **Musée Calvet**
features a superb array of
exhibits, including Roman
finds. It also gives an overview
of French art during the past
500 years, with works by
Rodin, Manet, and Dufy.

The Place de l'Horloge is the
center of Avignon's social life.
Under the town hall's Gothic
clock tower stands a merry-
go-round from 1900. Until the
19th century, brightly-patterned
calicoes called *indiennes* were
printed nearby. These inspired
today's Provençal patterns.
    From mid-July until mid-
August, the Avignon Festival
takes place at the Palais des
Papes. France's largest festival,
it includes ballet, drama, and
classical concerts. The "Off"
festival has street theater and
music from folk to jazz.
    Also worth seeing is the
Pont St-Bénézet. Built from
1171–1185, it once had 22
arches, but most were destroyed by floods in 1668. One
of the remaining arches bears
the tiny Chapelle St-Nicolas.

🏰 **Palais des Papes**
Place du Palais. 📞 04-90 27 50 74.
🕐 daily. 🎫 🎥

PALAIS DES PAPES
Pope Clement V moved the papal court to
Avignon in 1309. Here it remained until 1377,
during which time his successors transformed
the modest episcopal building into the present
magnificent palace.

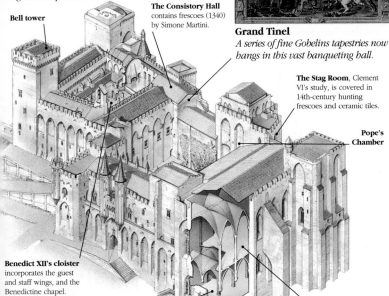

The Consistory Hall
contains frescoes (1340)
by Simone Martini.

Bell tower

Grand Tinel
*A series of fine Gobelins tapestries now
hangs in this vast banqueting hall.*

The Stag Room, Clement
VI's study, is covered in
14th-century hunting
frescoes and ceramic tiles.

**Pope's
Chamber**

Benedict XII's cloister
incorporates the guest
and staff wings, and the
Benedictine chapel.

The Great Audience Hall is
divided into two naves by
five sculpted columns.

The Great Chapel was
once covered in green
tapestries ornamented
with red roses.

Street-by-Street: Arles ③

FEW OTHER TOWNS IN PROVENCE combine all the region's charms so well as Arles. Its position on the Rhône makes it a natural gateway to the Camargue *(see p195)*. Its Roman remains, such as Constantine's baths and the amphitheater, are complemented by the ocher walls and Roman-tiled roofs of later buildings. Van Gogh spent time here in 1888–9, but Arles is no longer the industrial town he painted. Visitors are now its main business, and entertainment ranges from the Arles Festival to bullfights. A bastion of Provençal tradition and culture, its museums are among the best in the region. For enthusiasts, an inclusive ticket is available giving access to all museums. All the tourist sites in Arles are within comfortable walking distance of the central Place de la République.

The Musée Réattu houses 18th-century and modern art, including witty Picasso sketches, paintings by the local artist Jacques Réattu (1760–1833), and sculptures by Russian-born Ossip Zadkine (1890–1967).

View of Arles from the opposite bank of the Rhône

The Palais Constantine was once a grand imperial palace. Now only its vast Roman baths remain, dating from the 4th century AD.

The Museon Arlaten was founded in 1904 by the Provençal poet Frédéric Mistral with his Nobel Prize money, and is devoted to the culture and customs of his beloved Provence.

The Hôtel de Ville, the town hall, has an impressive vaulted ceiling.

★ Eglise St-Trophime
This fine Romanesque church has an ornate 12th-century portal carved with saints and apostles.

L'Espace Van Gogh is dedicated to the famous artist's life and works.

STAR SIGHTS
★ Les Arènes
★ Théâtre Antique
★ Eglise St-Trophime

Egyptian Obelisk
This ancient obelisk with fountains at its base (one of which is shown here) came from the Roman circus across the Rhône.

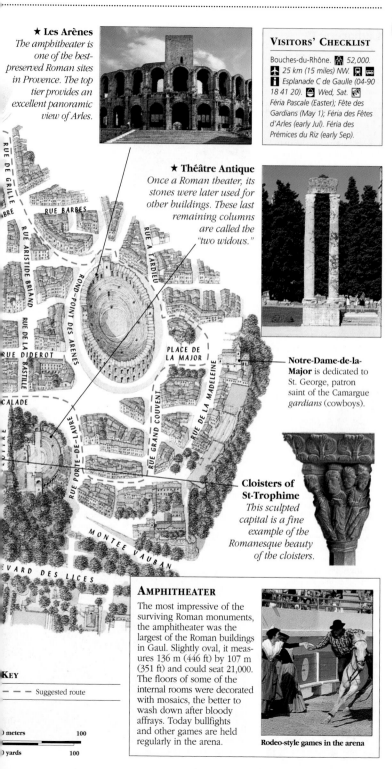

★ **Les Arènes**
The amphitheater is one of the best-preserved Roman sites in Provence. The top tier provides an excellent panoramic view of Arles.

VISITORS' CHECKLIST

Bouches-du-Rhône. ⛨ 52,000.
✈ 25 km (15 miles) NW. 🚆 🚌
🛈 Esplanade C de Gaulle (04-90
18 41 20). 🚏 Wed, Sat. 🎡
Féria Pascale (Easter); Fête des
Gardians (May 1); Féria des Fêtes
d'Arles (early Jul). Féria des
Prémices du Riz (early Sep).

★ **Théâtre Antique**
Once a Roman theater, its stones were later used for other buildings. These last remaining columns are called the "two widows."

RUE DE GRILLE
RUE BARBÈS
BRÉ
RUE ARISTIDE BRIAND
RUE DE LA BASTILLE
RUE DIDEROT
CALADE
ROND-POINT DES ARÈNES
RUE A TARDIEU
PLACE DE LA MAJOR
RUE PORTE-DE-LAURE
RUE GRAND COUVENT
RUE DE LA MADELEINE
MONTÉE VAUBAN
BOULEVARD DES LICES

Notre-Dame-de-la-Major is dedicated to St. George, patron saint of the Camargue *gardians* (cowboys).

Cloisters of St-Trophime
This sculpted capital is a fine example of the Romanesque beauty of the cloisters.

AMPHITHEATER

The most impressive of the surviving Roman monuments, the amphitheater was the largest of the Roman buildings in Gaul. Slightly oval, it measures 136 m (446 ft) by 107 m (351 ft) and could seat 21,000. The floors of some of the internal rooms were decorated with mosaics, the better to wash down after bloody affrays. Today bullfights and other games are held regularly in the arena.

Rodeo-style games in the arena

KEY

– – – Suggested route

0 meters   100
0 yards   100

Camargue 🕲

Bouches-du-Rhône. 🚗 🚌 ℹ️ *5 Ave Van Gogh, Stes-Maries-de-la-Mer (04-90 97 82 55).* 🎪 *Pèlerinage des Gitans (end May & end Oct).*

THIS FLAT, sparsely populated land is one of Europe's major wetland regions and natural history sites. Extensive areas of salt marsh, lakes, pastures, and sand dunes cover a vast 140,000 ha (346,000 acres). The native white horses and black bulls are tended by the region's cowboys, or *gardians*. Numerous seabirds and wildfowl also occupy the region.

Bullfights are advertised in **Saintes-Maries-de-la-Mer**, the region's main tourist center, which has a sandy beach offering water sports and boat trips. A few kilometers inland, the information center at **Pont-de-Gau** offers wonderful views over the flat lagoon. Photographs and documents chronicle the history of the Camargue and its diverse flora and fauna. Most of the birds that live in or migrate through the region, including the thousands of flamingoes which come here to breed, can be seen at the nearby **Parc Ornithologique du Pont-de-Gau**.

Camargue gardian

In the north of the region, a traditional Provençal *mas* or farmhouse, Mas du Pont de Rousty, has been converted to accommodate the fascinating **Musée Camarguais**. Displays here provide an introduction to the customs and traditions of the Camargue.

🦅 **Parc Ornithologique du Pont-de-Gau**
Pont-de-Gau. 📞 *04-90 97 82 62.* ⭕ *daily.* 🎫 ♿
🏛 **Musée Camarguais**
Parc Naturel Régional de Camargue, Mas du Pont de Rousty. 📞 *04-90 97 10 82.* ⭕ *Apr–Sep: daily; Oct–Mar: Wed–Mon.* ⚫ *public hols.* 🎫 ♿

Impressionist painter Cézanne's studio in Aix-en-Provence

Aix-en-Provence 🕳

Bouches-du-Rhône. 🏚 *126,000.* 🚗 🚌 ℹ️ *2 Place Général de Gaulle (04-42 16 11 61).* 🛍 *daily.*

PROVENCE'S FORMER capital is an international students' town, with a university that dates back to 1409. The city was transformed in the 17th century, when ramparts, first raised by the Romans in their town of Aquae Sextiae, were pulled down, and the mansion-lined Cours Mirabeau was built.

North of the Cours Mirabeau lies the town's old quarter. **Cathédrale St-Sauveur** creaks with history. The jewel of the church is the triptych of *The Burning Bush* (1476) by Nicolas Froment, currently undergoing restoration until 2004. The modest **Atelier Paul Cézanne**, a studio designed by Cézanne himself, is much as he left it when he died in 1906.

The main museum is the **Musée Granet**. François Granet (1775–1849) left his collection of French, Italian, and Flemish paintings to Aix. Work by Provençal artists is also shown, some by Granet.

🏛 **Musée Granet**
13 Rue Cardinale. 📞 *04-42 38 14 70.* ⭕ *Wed–Mon.* ⚫ *for renovation work until 2006.* 🎫

Marseille 🕴

Bouches-du-Rhône. 🏚 *800,000.* 🛫 *25 km NW.* 🚢 🚗 🚌 ℹ️ *4 La Canebière (04-91 13 89 00).* 🛍 *daily.*

FRANCE'S MOST important port and oldest major city is centered on the surprisingly attractive Vieux Port. On the north side are the commercial docks and the old town, rebuilt after World War II.

The old town's finest building is the **Vieille Charité**, a large, well-restored 17th-century hospice, now used as an exhibition center. The first floor has a small but rich collection of ancient Egyptian artifacts.

Marseille's finest piece of religious architecture is the **Abbaye de St-Victor**, founded in the 5th century. There are crypts containing catacombs, sarcophagi, and the cave of the martyr St. Victor.

During postwar rebuilding the Roman docks were uncovered. The **Musée des Docks Romains** mainly displays large storage urns once used for wine, grain, and oil. In the Centre Bourse shopping center is the **Musée d'Histoire de Marseille**. Reconstructions of the city at the height of the Greek period make this a good starting point for a tour.

Old harbor of Marseille, looking towards the Quai de Rive Neuve

The Food of the South of France

It's a heady experience just to stand, look, and sniff in a Provençal market. Tables sag under piles of braided pink garlic, colorful fresh peppers, tomatoes, eggplants, zucchini, and asparagus. In the fall and winter an earthy scent fills the air, with wild mushrooms, Swiss chard, walnuts, and quinces crowding the stalls. The waters of Coastal Provence provide a

Rosemary

bountiful sea harvest, including plump mussels, oysters, and *tellines* (tiny clams). The area is especially famous for its fish dishes, notably *bouillabaisse*. Lamb is the most common meat in Provence; the best comes from the Camargue, where lambs graze on herbs and salt-marsh grass. The South supplies France with the first of the season's peaches, cherries, and apricots.

Fish liquor

Red snapper

Bouillabaisse, *a fish soup originating in Marseille, is a luxury today. It consists of an assortment of local seafood including monkfish, mullet, snapper, scorpion fish, and conger eel, flavoured with tomatoes, saffron, and olive oil. Traditionally, the fish liquor is served first with croutons spread with rouille, a spicy mayonnaise. The fish is eaten afterwards.*

Croutons

Rouille (meaning "rust"), a mayonnaise with chillies and garlic

Monkfish

Conger eel

Red mullet

OLIVES AND OLIVE OIL

Most of the olive crop is crushed for oil. Ripe olives are black and the unripe ones are green; both can be preserved in brine or oil. At the end of the olive harvest *tapenade* is popular, a paste of black olives, capers, anchovies, and olive oil eaten with bread.

Fougasse *is a flattish, lattice-like bread variously studded with black olives, anchovies, onions, and spices. The sweet version is flavoured with almonds.*

Black olives

Tapenade

Olive oil

Aïoli *is a sauce made of egg yolks, garlic, and olive oil. It is served with salt cod, boiled eggs, snails, or raw vegetables.*

Ratatouille *is a stew of onions, eggplants, zucchini, tomatoes, and peppers, cooked in olive oil and garlic.*

Salade Niçoise *comes in many versions but always includes lettuce, green beans, tomatoes, black olives, eggs, and anchovies.*

The Côte d'Azur

THE CÔTE D'AZUR is, without doubt, the most celebrated seaside in Europe. Almost everybody who has been anybody for the past 100 years has succumbed to its glittering allure. Today the Côte d'Azur is busy all year round, with the beaches and nightlife still the major attractions. Between Cannes and Menton, the coast forms the glamorous French Riviera, playground of the rich and famous. The bustling city of Nice lies at the area's heart, richly deserving the title "capital of the Côte d'Azur."

BEACHES OF THE CÔTE D'AZUR

The sun-drenched coastline of the Côte d'Azur is one of the busiest in Europe. To the east lie the Riviera's big, traditional resorts, while to the west are smaller towns in coves and bays. Beaches are sandy west of Antibes, and more shingly to the east.

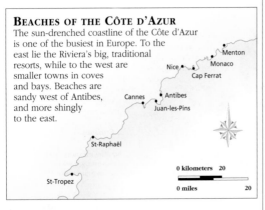

0 kilometers 20

0 miles 20

Exploring the Côte d'Azur

The Côte d'Azur is the most popular destination in France for sun-worshipers, with its seaside vacation towns and long, golden beaches. **St-Tropez** is currently the trendiest resort; Tahini-Plage is the coast's showcase for fun, sun, fashion, and glamor. By contrast, the family resort of **St-Raphaël** is peaceful, with excellent tourist facilities.

East of **Cannes**, at the western edge of the Riviera, **Juan-les-Pins** is a lively resort. Its all-night bars, nightclubs, and cafés make it popular with teenagers and young adults.

Founded by the Greeks, **Antibes** is one of the oldest towns along this stretch of coast, and home to a large museum of Picasso's work, donated by the artist himself.

Clifftop walks replace seafront promenades around the wooded peninsula of **Cap Ferrat**, where grand villas and private beaches can be glimpsed between the trees.

At the eastern edge of the Riviera, past the glitz of the casinos and hotels of **Monaco**, the beaches of **Menton** are the warmest along the coast; sunbathers enjoy a beach climate all year round.

Harborside at St-Tropez on the Côte d'Azur

Uma Thurman arriving at the Cannes Film Festival 2000

Cannes ㉟

Alpes-Maritimes. 🏠 70,000. 🚌 🚉 ☷ 🛈 Palais des Festivals, 1 La Croisette (04-93 39 24 53). ☷ daily.

THE FIRST THING that most people associate with Cannes is its many festivals, especially the International Film Festival held each May. The first Cannes Film Festival took place in 1946 and, for a while, it remained a small and exclusive affair. The mid-1950s marked the change from artistic event to media circus, but Cannes remains the international marketplace for moviemakers and distributors. The annual festival is held in the huge **Palais des Festivals**.

There is, however, more to the city than this glittering event. The Old Town is centered in the Le Suquet district, which is dominated by the church of **Notre-Dame de l'Espérance**, built in the 16th and 17th centuries in the Provençal Gothic style.

The famed **Boulevard de la Croisette** is lined with palm trees. Luxury boutiques and hotels look out over fine sandy beaches.

Nice ㊱

Alpes-Maritimes. 🏠 345,000. ✈ 🚉 🚌 🛈 5 Promenade des Anglais (04-92 14 48 00). ☷ Tue–Sun. 🎭 Carnival (Feb).

THE LARGEST resort on the Mediterranean coast, Nice has the second busiest airport in France. Its temperate winter climate and verdant subtropical vegetation have long attracted visitors, and today it is also a center for business conferences and package travelers.

There are many art museums in Nice, two of which devote themselves to the works of particular artists. The **Musée Matisse** displays drawings, paintings, bronzes, fabrics, and artifacts. The **Musée Chagall** holds the largest collection of works by Marc Chagall, with paintings, drawings, sculpture, stained glass, and mosaics.

A strikingly original complex of four marble-faced towers linked by glass passageways houses the **Musée d'Art Contemporain**. The collection is particularly strong in Neo-Realism and Pop Art. The **Musée des Beaux Arts** displays works by Dufy, Monet, Renoir, and Sisley.

A 19th-century palace, the **Palais Masséna** is filled with paintings of the Nice school, works by the Impressionists, Provençal ceramics, folk art, and a gold cloak once worn by Napoleon's beloved Josephine.

The onion domes of the **Cathédrale Orthodoxe Russe St-Nicolas**, completed in 1912, make this Nice's most distinctive landmark.

🏛 **Musée Matisse**
164 Ave des Arènes de Cimiez.
📞 04-93 81 08 08. 🔲 Wed–Mon.
⬤ some public hols. 🖼 ⬤

🏛 **Musée Chagall**
36 Ave du Docteur Ménard.
📞 04-93 53 87 20. 🔲 Wed–Mon.
⬤ Jan 1, May 1, Dec 25. 🖼 ⬤

A quiet stretch along Nice's 5 km (3 miles) of beachfront

Skyscrapers and apartment blocks of modern Monte Carlo in Monaco

Monaco ③⑦

Monaco. 🏙 30,000. ✈ (Nice). 🚉
ℹ 2a Boulevard des Moulins (092-16 61 16). ⬤ daily. 🎪 International Circus Festival (Jan–Feb).

Aʀʀɪᴠɪɴɢ ᴀᴍᴏɴɢ the towering skyscrapers of Monaco today, it is hard to envisage the turbulence of its history. At first a Greek settlement, later taken by the Romans, it was bought from the Genoese in 1297 by the Grimaldis who, in spite of bitter family feuds, still rule as the world's oldest monarchy. Monaco covers 1.9 sq km (0.74 sq miles) and, although its size has increased by one-third in the form of landfills, it still occupies an area smaller than New York's Central Park.

The best-known section of Monaco is Monte Carlo. People flock to the annual car rally held here in January, but the area owes its renown mainly to its **Grand Casino**. Source of countless legends, it was instituted by Charles III to save himself from bankruptcy in 1856. So successful was this money-making venture that, by 1870, he was able to abolish taxation for his people. Designed in 1878 and set in formal gardens, the casino gives a splendid view over Monaco. Even the most exclusive of the gaming rooms can be visited, but their tables are for the big spenders only.

Across the harbor lies Monaco-Ville, the seat of government. The interior of the 13th-century **Palais Princier**, with its priceless furniture and magnificent frescoes, is open to the public during the prince's absence.

The aquarium of the **Musée Océanographique** holds rare species of marine plants and animals. Marine explorer Jacques Cousteau established his research center here.

The lavish surroundings of the Belle Epoque Grand Casino

Practical Information

FRANCE IS JUSTIFIABLY PROUD of its many attractions, for which it has good tourist information facilities. Both in France and abroad, French Government Tourist Offices are an invaluable source of reference for practical aspects of your stay, especially for those with special needs. If you are unfortunate enough to need medical or emergency assistance, France has excellent hospitals, ambulance, fire, and police services. The country also has a modern communications network, making it easy to keep in touch by telephone, post, or e-mail.

VISA REQUIREMENTS AND CUSTOMS

CURRENTLY there are no visa requirements for EU nationals or visitors from the United States, Canada, Australia or New Zealand who plan to stay in France for under three months. Visitors from most other countries require a tourist visa. Non-EU visitors can, with some exceptions, reclaim the French sales tax (TVA) on goods if they spend over a certain amount in one shop and get a *détaxe* receipt.

TOURIST INFORMATION

ALL MAJOR CITIES and large towns have *offices de tourisme*. Small towns and even villages have *syndicats d'initiative*. Both will give you town plans, advice on accommodations, and information on regional recreational and cultural activities.

You can also get information before you leave for France from **French Government Tourist Offices**, or by contacting local tourist offices (see individual town headings in this guide) or the appropriate CRT (Comité Régional de Tourisme) – ask the FGTO for the address.

PERSONAL SECURITY

VIOLENT CRIME is rare in France – even a major city such as Paris is surprisingly safe. However, muggings and brawls do occur, so avoid isolated or poorly lit places, especially at night. Women should take extra care, especially when traveling alone. Also beware pickpockets, who are active in large cities.

POLICE

THERE ARE TWO types of police in France. The *Police Nationale* look after large towns and cities. If you need to contact them, find the *Commissariat de Police* (police headquarters). Small towns, villages, and country areas are policed by the *Gendarmerie Nationale*. If you need to report a crime in these places, go to the local *mairie* (town hall).

OPENING HOURS

GENERALLY, OPENING hours for tourist sights are from 10am–5:40pm with one late evening per week. Most close on public holidays.

National museums and sights are normally closed on Tuesdays, with a few exceptions which close on Mondays. Municipal museums normally close on Mondays. Churches are open every day but sometimes shut at lunchtime.

FACILITIES FOR THE DISABLED

FACILITIES FOR the disabled vary in France. Details of services in most towns can be obtained from the **CNRH** (Comité National pour la Réadaptation des Handicapés). The **Association des Paralysés de France** provides information on wheelchair access.

MEDICAL TREATMENT

ALL EUROPEAN UNION nationals are entitled to French social security coverage. However, treatment must be paid for at the time, and hospital rates vary widely. Reimbursements may be obtained if you have the correct documents before you travel, but the process is long and complicated.

All travelers, particularly non-EU nationals, should, therefore, consider purchasing travel insurance before they arrive. In the case of a medical emergency call **SAMU** (*Service d'Aide Médicale Urgence*). However, it is often faster to call **Sapeurs Pompiers** (the fire

---

THE CLIMATE OF FRANCE

Set on Europe's western edge, France has a varied, temperate climate. An Atlantic influence prevails in the northwest, with westerly sea winds bringing humidity and warm winters. The east experiences Continental temperature extremes with frosty, clear winters and often stormy summers. The south enjoys a Mediterranean climate, with hot, dry summers and mild winters.

PARIS

°C/F	Apr	Jul	Oct	Jan
	14/58	24/75	15/59 16/61	
	7/44		9/49	7/44
0°C 32°F				2/35
☀	6 hrs	8 hrs	4.5 hrs	2 hrs
☂	50 mm	58 mm	55 mm	55 mm

NICE

°C/F	Apr	Jul	Oct	Jan
	17/63	27/80 19/67	21/70	
	10/50		13/55	13/55
0°C 32°F				5/41
☀	7.5 hrs	11 hrs	6.5 hrs	5 hrs
☂	62 mm	16 mm	108 mm	83 mm

service), who offer a first aid and ambulance service. This is particularly true in rural areas.

Casualty departments *(service des urgences)* in public hospitals can deal with most medical problems. Your consulate should be able to provide you with details of an English-speaking doctor in the area. Pharmacists can also suggest treatments for many health problems. Look for the green cross sign outside pharmacies.

BANKING AND CURRENCY

THE FRENCH UNIT of currency is now the euro. This was introduced into general circulation in January 2002. A transition period has allowed euros and francs (the French currency prior to 2002) to be used together, although the franc should be phased out by mid-2002.

The best way to take currency is often as traveler's checks, as in the case of theft, they are replaceable. These can be obtained from **American Express**, **Thomas Cook**, or your bank.

Most credit cards are widely accepted, but, because of the high commissions charged, American Express is often not. The most commonly used credit card is Carte Bleue/Visa. Eurocard/MasterCard (Access

in UK) is also often accepted. Credit cards issued in France contain a microchip and are called "smart cards", but many machines can also read cards with magnetic strips. If you find your conventional card cannot be read in the smart card slot get the cashier to swipe the card through the magnetic reader. You may be asked to tap in your PIN code *(code confidentiel)* on a small keypad.

You can also use credit cards in most banks to withdraw cash; either from an ATM (automatic teller machine), which should have an English language option, or from a cash desk. Banks are usually open Mon–Fri, from 9am–4:30 or 5:15pm, with some also open on Saturday morning. Many close for lunch, and many, especially in the south, are closed on Monday.

COMMUNICATIONS

PAYPHONES IN FRANCE take coins or plastic telephone cards *(télécartes)*. Cards are cheaper and more convenient to use than coins. They are sold in either 50 or 120 units and can be bought at post offices, tobacconists *(tabacs)*, and newsagents. For local calls, a unit lasts up to six minutes. Many phones now

also accept credit cards (with a PIN number). Post offices have telephone booths *(cabines)* where you can telephone first and pay after the call. This is cheaper than making long-distance calls from hotels. The Minitel electronic phone directory, shopping, and information service can also be used in most post offices.

La Poste (the Post Office) used to be called the P.T.T. *(postes, télégraphes, téléphones)*, and some road signs still give directions to the P.T.T. The postal service in France is fast and reliable. However, it is not cheap, especially when sending a parcel abroad.

At La Poste, postage stamps *(timbres)* are sold singly or in *carnets* of seven or ten. They are also sold at *tabacs*. At post offices you can also use telephone directories *(annuaires)*, buy phonecards, cash or buy money orders *(mandats)*, and make international calls.

Post offices usually open from 9am–5pm Mon–Fri, often with a break for lunch, and 9am–noon on Saturdays. Mail boxes are yellow, and often have separate slots for the town you are in, the *département*, and other destinations *(autres destinations)*.

Internet cafés are slowly making an appearance, especially in major towns.

Travel Information

FRANCE HAS HIGHLY advanced transportation systems, with Paris at the hub of its air, rail, and road networks. Paris's two main airports have direct flights to North America, Africa, Japan, and the rest of Europe. The city's six major railway stations connect it to some 6,000 destinations in France, and provide links to the whole of Europe. An extensive, well-developed road network makes it easy to reach all parts of the country by car or bus. France is also well connected by sea, with frequent ferry crossings from the UK to ports on the Channel.

FLYING TO FRANCE

FRANCE IS SERVED by nearly all international airlines. Paris is the major airline destination in France, but there are a number of other international airports across the country. Some airports near the border, such as Geneva, Basle, and Luxembourg, can also be used for destinations in France.

The main French airline is **Air France**, which has services to major cities across the world. The main British airlines with regular flights to France are **British Airways** and **British Midland**. Inexpensive flights from the UK to various French destinations are available from carriers such as **easyJet** and **Ryanair**. Major airlines including **American Airlines**, **Delta**, and **United** operate flights from the United States. **Air Canada** flies from several cities in Canada, and **Qantas** provides flights from Australia and New Zealand.

AIR FARES

AIRLINE FARES are at their highest during the peak summer season in France, usually from July to September. Fierce competition between airlines, however, means there are often discounts on offer.

APEX fares are booked in advance. They cannot be changed or cancelled without penalty and there are also minimum and maximum stay requirements. Packages are also worth considering, as airlines and tour operators can put together a great range of flexible deals to suit your needs. These can include car rental and rail travel, enabling you to continue overland.

DOMESTIC FLIGHTS

THERE ARE A number of domestic airlines that fly between the cities of France, some of which only operate within one region; others also fly to French-speaking countries, with Air France offering the largest number of routes. However, unless you are eligible for discounts, you may find it cheaper and faster to travel on the high-speed trains, given the time it can take to reach the airports.

FERRY SERVICES

THERE ARE SEVERAL crossings between the UK and French ports. **P&O Stena** operates between Dover and Calais, with frequent crossings (75-90 minutes). **P&O Portsmouth** operates between Portsmouth and Le Havre (5 hrs 30 mins) or Cherbourg (5 hrs). There is also an express catamaran service from Portsmouth to Cherbourg (2 hrs 45 mins).

Brittany Ferries runs a nine-hour service from Portsmouth to St-Malo, a six-hour service from Portsmouth to Caen, and a six-hour service from Plymouth to Roscoff. **Hoverspeed** operates high-speed Seacat catamarans between Dover and Calais (45 mins) and Folkestone and Boulogne (55 mins). A larger Super Seacat operates outside the winter months between Newhaven and Dieppe (2 hrs).

CHANNEL TUNNEL

THE CHANNEL TUNNEL (Tunnel sous La Manche) was inaugurated in 1994. A car-carrying shuttle service, which is operated by **Eurotunnel**, runs between Folkestone and Calais. The passenger service, **Eurostar**, links London and Paris (2.5 hrs).

GETTING AROUND PARIS

CENTRAL PARIS is compact, and the best way to get around is often to walk. Public transportation in the city is good, however, with an efficient metro (subway) system, frequent buses, and a commuter train service (RER). These are all operated by the Paris transportation company, RATP.

There are many types of ticket available, sold at metro and RER stations, and most can be used on any RATP service, including buses. Single bus tickets can also be bought from the driver when boarding. All tickets used on buses must be stamped in the machine on board.

Single RATP tickets are valid in metro/RER zones 1 or 2, or for any bus journey. *Carnets* (books of ten single tickets), are more economical if you plan to make a number of journeys. Various passes are also available, which entitle you to unlimited travel in certain zones for a set number of days.

RAIL TRAVEL

FRANCE HAS ALWAYS been known for the punctuality of its trains. The French state railway, the **Société Nationale des Chemins de Fer (SNCF)**, provides an excellent rail network which covers nearly all of France. The fastest services are provided by the high-speed TGV *(Trains à Grande Vitesse)* trains, which link most major cities.

Overnight services are popular in France, and most long-distance trains have *couchettes* (bunks), which you must reserve for a fee. Reservations are also compulsory for all TGV services, trains on public holidays, and for a *siège inclinable* (reclinable seat). Information on the various rail services and fares is available from the **Rail Europe** office in London. In France, leaflets are available at most stations. There are a number of special tickets available, including ones for over 60s, families, and under 26s. There are also special tickets for those doing a lot of train travel.

Automatic ticket and reservation machines *(billetterie automatique)* are found at main stations. They take credit cards or coins. You can also check train times, fares, and make reservations by phoning **SNCF**. Both reservations and tickets must be validated in one of the orange *composteur* machines near the platforms before boarding the train.

TRAVELING BY ROAD

FRANCE HAS one of the densest road networks in Europe, with modern motorways which allow quick and easy access to all parts of the country. However, you can save money on tolls and explore France in a more leisurely way by using some of the other high-quality roads, such as RN *(route nationale)* and D *(départementale)* routes.

Most motorways in France have a toll system *(autoroutes à péage)*, which can be quite expensive, especially over

long distances. There are some short sections which are free, however, usually close to major centers. Tolls can be paid with either credit cards or cash. Where only small sums are involved, you throw coins into a large receptacle and the change is given automatically.

Speed limits in France are shown in km/h. The limit in all towns, unless shown otherwise, is 50 km/h (30 mph). On major roads, higher limits are usually shown. On the *autoroutes* the usual limit is 130 km/h (80 mph), but this is reduced to 110 km/h (70 mph) when it is raining. On-the-spot fines may be demanded for speeding offences, and there are severe penalties for drink-driving.

Sunday is usually a good time to travel in France, as there are very few trucks on the road. Try to avoid traveling at the French holiday rush periods known as the *grands départs*. The worst times are weekends in July, and at the beginning and end of August.

All the main international car-rental companies operate in France. It is worth ringing around before you leave for

France as there are many special offers for rentals booked and prepaid in the UK or US. Good deals are often available from **Autos Abroad**, brokers who use cars owned by other car rental companies, such as Budget and National Citer. Booking in this way may work out at half the price of the standard rental.

BUSES

LONG-DISTANCE buses generally operate only where there is not a good train service in operation (for example, between Geneva and Nice). SNCF (the state railway) operates some bus routes and issues regional TER *(Transports Express Régionaux)* timetables and tickets. **Eurolines** serves a wider range of destinations within France, as well as providing services to hundreds of major cities across Europe. They also offer excursions and arrange accommodations.

There are also many local buses, which run from the town's *Gare Routière*.

DIRECTORY

AIRLINES

Air Canada
08-20 87 08 71.
800-247 2262 (Can).
www.aircanada.ca

Air France
08-20 82 08 20.
0845-084 5111 (UK).
800-237 2747 (US).
www.airfrance.com

American Airlines
08-01 87 28 72.
800-433 7300 (US).
www.AA.com

British Airways
08-25 82 54 00.
0845-773 3377 (UK).
www.britishairways.com

British Midland
01-41 91 87 04.
0870-607 0555 (UK).
www.flybmi.com

Delta Air Lines
08-00 35 40 80.
800-241 4141 (US).
www.delta.com

easyJet
0870-600 0000 (UK).
www.easyjet.com

Qantas
08-20 82 05 00.
800-0014 0014 (Aus).
www.qantas.com

Ryanair
0871-246 0000 (UK).
www.ryanair.com

United Airlines
08-10 72 72 72.
800-241 6522 (US).
www.united.com

FERRY SERVICES

Brittany Ferries
08-25 82 88 28.
0870-536 0360 (UK).
www.brittanyferries.com

Hoverspeed
00-80 12 11 12.
0870-524 0241 (UK).
www.hoverspeed.com

P&O Portsmouth
08-25 01 30 13.
0870-242 4999 (UK).
www.poferries.com

P&O Stena Line
08-20 01 00 20.
0870-600 0600 (UK).

CHANNEL TUNNEL

Eurostar
08-92 35 35 39.
0870-518 6186 (UK).
www.eurostar.fr

Eurotunnel
03-21 00 61 00.
0870-535 3535 (UK).
www.eurotunnel.com

RAIL TRAVEL

Rail Europe
0870-530 0003 (UK).
www.raileurope.co.uk

SNCF, Paris
08-92 35 35 39.

CAR RENTAL

Autos Abroad
0870-066 7788 (UK).
www.autosabroad.net

Avis
0220-050 505 (UK).
08-20 05 05 05 (Paris).
www.avis.fr

Europcar
0870-607 5005 (UK).
08-25 86 18 61 (Paris).
www.europcar.fr

Hertz
0870-844 8844 (UK).
08-25 86 18 61 (Paris).
www.hertz.com

BUSES

Eurolines
08-92 69 52 52.
www.eurolines.co.uk

Shopping

Shopping in France is a delight. Whether you go to the hypermarkets and department stores, or seek out the many small specialist stores and markets, you will be tempted by the stylish presentation and high quality of the goods on offer. France is especially renowned for its wine, with a vast selection available, from cheap table wines to classic vintages. French food is also excellent, in particular the cheeses, cured meats, patés, cakes, and pastries. France also offers world-famous fashion, pottery and porcelain, crystal, and fine-quality antiques.

Opening Hours

Food shops open at about 7am and close around noon for lunch. After lunch most are open until 7pm or later. Bakeries often stay open until 1pm or later.

Shops that do not close at lunchtime include some supermarkets, department stores, and most hypermarkets.

General opening hours for non-food shops are around 9am–6pm Mon–Sat, often with a break for lunch. Many are closed on Monday mornings.

Food shops (and newsagents) are open on Sunday mornings. Virtually every shop in France is closed on Sunday afternoon, except for the last weeks before Christmas when hypermarkets remain open all day. Smaller shops may be closed one day of the week, usually Monday. However, those in tourist regions are often open every day in the high season.

Larger Shops

Hypermarkets (hypermarchés or grandes surfaces) can be found on the outskirts of every sizeable town: look for signs indicating centre commercial. Among the biggest are Carrefour, Casino, Auchan, and Continent. Discount petrol is often sold, and most, but not all, now have pumps which take credit cards.

Department stores (grands magasins), such as the cheap and cheerful Monoprix and Prisunic, are often found in town centers. Others, like the more upscale **Au Printemps** and **Galeries Lafayette**, can be found both in town and out-of-town centers.

Specialist Shops

One of the pleasures of shopping in France is that specialist shops for food still flourish despite the new large supermarkets. The boulangerie, for bread, is frequently combined with a pâtisserie selling cakes and pastries. The traiteur sells prepared foods. Cheese shops (fromagerie) and other shops specializing in dairy products (laiterie) may also be combined, while the boucherie (butcher's) and charcuterie (pork butcher's/delicatessen) are often separate shops. For general groceries go to an épicerie. An épicerie fine is a delicatessen.

Markets

Markets are found in towns and villages all over France. To find out where the market is, ask a passerby for le marché. Markets usually finish promptly at noon and do not reopen in the afternoon.

Look for local producers, including those with only one or two special items to sell, as their goods are often cheaper and of better quality.

By law, price tags include the origin of all produce: pays means local. Chickens from Bresse are marketed wearing a red, white, and blue badge giving the name of the producer as proof of authenticity. If you are visiting markets over several weeks, look for items just coming into season, such as fresh walnuts, the first wild asparagus, truffles, early artichokes, or wild strawberries. The special seasonal markets held throughout France are the best places to find these

items, and there are often foires artisanales held at the same time, which sell local produce, arts, and crafts.

Regional Produce

French regional specialties can be bought outside their area of origin, although it is interesting to buy them locally. Provence, in the south, prides itself on the quality of its olive oil, while the southwest is notable for its patés. Central France is famous for snails, cured meats, and Roquefort cheese. Cheese is also an important product of the temperate north, the best-known varieties being Brie and Camembert.

Popular drinks are also associated with particular regions. Pastis, made from aniseed, is popular in the south, while Calvados, made from apples, is from the north.

Location also determines quality. Lyon's culinary importance stems from the many locally produced cheeses, the proximity of Bresse for chickens, Charolais for beef, and the Alsace region for sausages.

Wine

In wine-producing areas, follow the dégustation (tasting) signs to vineyards (domaines) where you can taste the wine. You will be expected to buy at least one bottle. Wine cooperatives sell the wine of small producers. Here you can buy wine in five- and ten-liter containers (en vrac), as well as in bottles. The wine is often rated AOC, appellation d'origine contrôlée, selling at less than F10 a liter. As wine sold en vrac is "duty-free," customers receive a laissez-passer (permit) indicating their destination. Bottled wine sold by co-ops is duty-paid.

Clothing

France is famous for its fashion, and elegant clothes can be found even in quite small towns. Paris, however, is the home of haute couture. There are 23 couture houses listed with the Fédération

Française de la Couture, and most of these are concentrated on the Right Bank around Rue du Faubourg-St-Honoré and Avenue Montaigne. Famous names include **Yves Saint Laurent**, **Chanel**, **Guy Laroche**, **Christian Lacroix**, **Nina Ricci**, and **Christian Dior**. Other top designers include **Hermès**, **MaxMara**, and **Giorgio Armani**.

Men don't have the luxury of *haute couture* dressing: their choice is limited to ready-to-wear, but most of the big name womenswear designers also produce a range for men. A good example is **Gianni Versace**, with his classic Italian clothes for men. On the Right Bank, the household name designers include Giorgio Armani, the stylish **Pierre Cardin**, Yves Saint Laurent, and **Lanvin**, who is particularly popular for his beautifully made leather accessories. If time is short and you want to make all your purchases under one roof, try the *grands magasins*. These stores offer a wide choice of fashions, and prices will be more within most people's budgets. Au Printemps, for example, is huge, with separate buildings for menswear, household goods, and womens' and children's clothes. The beauty department, with its vast perfume selection, is definitely worth a visit. **Le Bon Marché**, on the Left Bank, was the first department store in Paris, and is the most chic, with an excellent food hall. Galeries Lafayette has a wide range of clothes at all price levels. **La Samaritaine** is one of the oldest shops in Paris, and full of bargains.

ART AND ANTIQUES

YOU CAN BUY fabulous art and antiques from stores, galleries, and flea-markets all over France. The best places to visit in Paris are **Le Louvre des Antiquaires**, a huge building containing around 250 antique dealers, and the famous **Marché aux Puces de St-Ouen** flea market (open Saturday to Monday). To avoid paying duty, you will need a certificate of authenticity when exporting objets d'art over 20 years old and any goods over a century old that are worth more than 150,000. Seek professional advice and declare them at customs if in doubt.

TAX-FREE SHOPPING

VISITORS RESIDENT outside the European Union can reclaim the sales tax, TVA, on French goods if they spend more than 305 in one shop, get a *détaxe* receipt, and take the goods out of the country within six months. The form should be handed in at customs when leaving the country, and the reimbursement will be sent to you.

Exceptions for *détaxe* rebates are food and drink, medicines, tobacco, cars, and motorbikes. More information is available from the **Centre des Renseignements des Douanes**, but this is usually in French.

DIRECTORY

CLOTHING

Chanel
42 Ave Montaigne,
75008 Paris.
☎ 01-47 23 74 12.

5 Bld de la Croisette,
06400 Cannes.
☎ 04-93 38 55 05.

Christian Dior
30 Ave Montaigne,
75008 Paris.
☎ 01-40 73 54 44.

38 Bld de la Croisette,
06400 Cannes.
☎ 04-92 98 98 00.

Christian Lacroix
73 Rue du Faubourg-St-Honoré, 75008 Paris.
☎ 01-42 68 79 04.

Gianni Versace
62 Rue du Faubourg-St-Honoré,
75008 Paris.
☎ 01-47 42 88 02.

Giorgio Armani
6 Place Vendôme,
75001 Paris.
☎ 01-42 61 55 09.

Guy Laroche
20 Rue Trémalle,
75008 Paris.
☎ 01-40 69 68 00.

Hermès
24 Rue du Faubourg-St-Honoré,
75008 Paris.
☎ 01-40 17 47 17.

Lanvin
32 Rue Marbeuf,
75008 Paris.
☎ 01-53 75 02 20.

15 Flg St-Honoré,
75008 Paris.
☎ 01-44 71 33 33.

MaxMara
37 Rue du Four,
75006 Paris.
☎ 01-43 29 91 10.

Nina Ricci
39 Ave Montaigne,
75008 Paris.
☎ 01-40 88 45 45.

Pierre Cardin
27 Ave Marigny,
75008 Paris.
☎ 01-42 66 68 98.

Yves Saint Laurent
19 Ave Victor Hugo,
75016 Paris.
☎ 01-45 00 64 64.

104 Rue Paradis,
13006 Marseille.
☎ 04-91 37 12 34.

DEPARTMENT STORES

Le Bon Marché
24 Rue de Sèvres,
75007 Paris.
☎ 01-44 39 80 00.

Galeries Lafayette
40 Bld Haussmann,
75009 Paris.
☎ 01-42 82 34 56.

11 Rue Ste Catherine,
33000 Bordeaux.
☎ 05-56 90 92 71.

6 Rue Maréchal Foch,
06400 Cannes.
☎ 04-97 06 25 00.

Au Printemps
64 Bld Haussman,
75009 Paris.
☎ 01-42 82 50 00.

La Samaritaine
19 Rue de la Monnaie,
75001 Paris.
☎ 01-40 41 20 20.

ART AND ANTIQUES

Le Louvre des Antiquaires
2 Place du Palais-Royal,
75001 Paris.
☎ 01-42 61 57 94.

Marché aux Puces de St-Ouen
Rue des Rosiers,
St-Ouen, 75018 Paris.

TAX-FREE SHOPPING

Centre des Renseignements des Douanes
84 Rue d'Hauteville,
75010 Paris.
☎ 08-25 30 82 63.
FAX 01-53 24 68 30.

Entertainment

THE ENTERTAINMENT CENTER of France is Paris. Whether your preference is for drama, ballet, opera, jazz, cinema, or dancing the night away, Paris has it all. Across the rest of the country the arts are also well represented, and there are a number of internationally-renowned arts festivals throughout the year. With a varied physical, as well as cultural, landscape, there are also many possibilities for outdoor sports and activities, including golf, tennis, walking, and skiing. Specialist holidays cater to those interested in French language, food, and wine.

ENTERTAINMENT LISTINGS

TWO OF THE best listings magazines in Paris are *Pariscope* and *L'Officiel des Spectacles*. Published every Wednesday, you can pick them up at any newsstand. Local newspapers and *offices de tourisme* are the best places to find entertainment listings for the regions.

BOOKING TICKETS

DEPENDING ON THE event, tickets can often be bought at the door, but for popular events it is wiser to purchase tickets in advance, at the box office or at **FNAC** chains. Theater box offices open daily from about 11am–7pm. Most accept credit card bookings by telephone. In Paris, the **Kiosque Théâtre** sells left-over tickets for up to half the price the day of performance.

THEATER

FROM THE GRANDEUR of the **Comédie Française** to slapstick farce and avant-garde drama, theater is flourishing in Paris. Founded in 1680 by royal decree, the Comédie Française is the bastion of French theater, aiming to keep classical drama in the public eye. In an underground auditorium in the Art Deco Palais de Chaillot, the **Théâtre National de Chaillot** stages lively productions of main-stream European classics. The **Théâtre National de la Colline** specializes in contemporary drama. Among the most important of the independents is the **Comédie des Champs-Elysées**, while

for over 100 years the **Palais Royal** has been the temple of risqué farce.

Excellent theaters and pro-ductions are also to be found in major cities across France, and there are big theater festivals held in Nancy (June) and Avignon (July; *see p191*).

MUSIC

THE MUSIC SCENE in Paris has never been so busy, especially with the emergence of many internationally successful contemporary French groups. There are numerous first-class venues in the city, with excellent jazz, opera, contemporary, and classical music concerts.

Opened in 1989, the ultra-modern 2,700-seat **Opéra de Paris Bastille** stages classic and modern operas. Produc-tions from outside France are staged at the **Opéra Comique**.

The **Salle Pleyel** is Paris's principal concert hall and home of the Orchestre de Paris. Paris's newest venue is the **Cité de la Musique** in the Parc de la Villette.

Top international and pop acts are usually to be found at huge arenas such as the **Palais Omnisports de Paris-Bercy** or the **Zénith**. A more intimate atmosphere is found at the legendary **Olympia**.

Paris is, perhaps, most renowned for its jazz, and the best talent in the world can be heard here on any evening, especially throughout October during the jazz festival. All the great jazz musicians have performed at **New Morning**, which also hosts African, Brazilian, and other sounds. For Dixieland go to **Le Petit Journal St-Michel**.

Jazz is also popular across France, and big international jazz festivals are held right through the year, in Cannes (February; *see p196*), Antibes and Juan-le-Pins (July), and Le Mans (April). Opera and classical music are also widely performed, notably at the Aix festival during July *(see p195)*.

CLUBS AND CABARET

MUSIC IN PARIS nightclubs tends to follow the trends set in the US and Britain, although home-grown groups, especially those playing garage, are popular and influential both here and abroad.

Balajo, once frequented by Edith Piaf, and the ultra-hip **Folies Pigalle**, once a strip joint, are particularly up-to-the-minute with their music. **La Locomotive** attracts a mixed crowd to its three-level mainstream house nights. For a more Latin touch, try **La Java**. The dance floor of this club, where Edith Piaf once performed, now sways to Cuban and Brazilian sounds.

When it comes to picking a cabaret, the rule of thumb is simple: the better-known places are best. The **Folies-Bergères** is the oldest music hall in Paris and probably the most famous in the world. It is rivaled by the **Moulin Rouge**, birthplace of the cancan.

CINEMA

PARIS IS THE WORLD'S capital of film appreciation. There are now more than 300 screens within the city limits, distributed among 100 cinemas. Most are concentrated in cinema belts, which enjoy the added appeal of nearby restaurants and shops. The Champs-Elysées has the densest cinema strip in town, where you can see the latest Hollywood smash or French *auteur* triumph, as well as some classic re-issues.

The cinemas on the Grands Boulevards include two notable architectural land-marks: the 2,800-seat **Le Grand Rex**, with its Baroque decor, and the **Max Linder Panorama**, which was refurbished in the 1980s.

The largest screen in France is the new **Gaumont** flagship in the Place d'Italie district. On the Left Bank, the area around Odéon-St-Germain-des-Prés has taken over from the Latin Quarter as the city's heartland for art and repertory cinemas.

OUTDOOR ACTIVITIES

A COUNTRY AS richly diverse in culture and geography as France offers an amazing variety of sport and leisure activities. Information on current leisure and sporting activities in a particular region is available from the tourist offices listed for each town in this guide.

Golf is popular in France, especially along the north and south coasts and in Aquitaine. You will need to take your handicap certificate with you if you want to play. Tennis is also a favorite sport, and there are courts to rent in almost every town.

More than 30,000 km (19,000 miles) of *Grandes Randonneés* (long distance tracks) and shorter *Petites Randonneés* cover France. The routes are clearly way-marked, and vary in difficulty, including long pilgrim routes, alpine crossings, and tracks through national parks. Some routes are open to mountain bikes and horses.

The mountains provide for excellent skiing and mountain-eering. The Atlantic coast around Biarritz offers some of the best surfing and wind-surfing in Europe. Sailing and waterskiing are popular all round France, and swimming facilities are generally good, although beaches in the south can be crowded in August.

SPECIALIST VACATIONS

F RENCH GOVERNMENT Tourist Offices *(see p199)* have extensive information on travel companies offering special interest vacations. Send off

for *The Traveller in France Reference Guide*. Vacations are based on subjects such as the French language, wine appreciation, and cooking, as well as craft activities and organized nature trips.

SPECTATOR SPORT

T HE MAIN SPORTING action in France revolves largely around soccer, rugby, tennis, and horse racing. There are various stadia and circuits all over the country; the best are near major cities, particularly Paris. Here, the **Stade de France** and the **Palais Omnisports de Paris-Bercy** host all the major events. **Parc des Princes** is home to the top Paris soccer team Paris St-Germain.

Cycling is also a very popular sport in France, and there is racing action across the country. The most famous event is the annual Tour de France held during July.

Where to Stay in France

FRENCH HOTELS ARE GRADED by a system that awards from nought to four stars. They range from historic châteaux with magnificent furnishings and food to informal family-run hotels. In high season some will offer only full *pension* (all meals) or *demi-pension* (breakfast and dinner). A popular option for a self-catering vacation is a *gîte*, a rural home often in a converted farmhouse.

	NUMBER OF ROOMS	PRIVATE PARKING	RESTAURANT	GARDEN OR TERRACE
PARIS				
ILE ST-LOUIS: *Hôtel du Jeu de Paume* @ info@jeudepaumehotel.com €€€ 54 Rue St-Louis-en-l'Ile, 75004. **Map** E4. **(** 01-43 26 14 18. **FAX** 01-40 46 02 76. A welcoming, exemplary family hotel. Features include a glass-walled lift, wooden beams, old terra-cotta paving, and a sauna. ▤ TV ▧	30			▪
MARAIS: *Hôtel de la Place des Vosges* @ hotel.place.des.vosges@gofornet.com €€€ 12 Rue de Birague, 75004. **Map** F4. **(** 01-42 72 60 46. **FAX** 01-42 72 02 64. A charming old building close to one of the prettiest squares in Paris. The largest rooms, on the top floor, have good views. ▤ TV ▧	16			
MARAIS: *Hôtel de la Bretonnerie* W www.delabretonnerie.com €€€€ 22 Rue Ste-Croix de la Bretonnerie, 75004. **Map** E4. **(** 01-48 87 77 63. **FAX** 01-42 77 26 78. Situated on a charming street, this is one of the most comfortable hotels in the Marais. Spacious bedrooms with antique furniture. ▤ TV ▧	29			
BEAUBOURG: *Hôtel Beaubourg* W www.hotelbeaubourg.com €€€ 11 Rue Simon Lefranc, 75004. **Map** E3. **(** 01-42 74 34 24. **FAX** 01-42 78 68 11. An extremely comfortable and well-equipped hotel, tastefully restored and decorated, with a pretty courtyard garden. ▤ TV ▧	28			▪
BEAUBOURG: *Hôtel Britannique* W www.hotel-britannique.fr €€€€ 20 Avenue Victoria, 75001. **Map** E4. **(** 01-42 33 74 59. **FAX** 01-42 33 82 65. A reasonably priced, friendly, family-run hotel in a renovated 19th-century building. ▤ TV ▧	39			
LATIN QUARTER: *Esmeralda* €€€ 4 Rue St-Julien-le Pauvre, 75005. **Map** E4. **(** 01-43 54 19 20. **FAX** 01-40 51 00 68. The decor reflects contrasting ages and styles behind old stone walls and under beamed ceilings. The best rooms overlook Notre-Dame. ▤	19			
LATIN QUARTER: *Hôtel des Grandes Ecoles* W www.hotel-grandes-ecoles.com €€€ 75 Rue du Cardinal Lemoine, 75005. **Map** E4. **(** 01-43 26 79 23. **FAX** 01-43 25 28 15. A charming cluster of three small houses enclose a well-maintained garden. The rooms are delightfully decorated, and all were updated in 2001. ▤ ▧	51	▪		▪
LATIN QUARTER: *Hôtel des Grands Hommes* €€€€ 17 Place du Panthéon, 75005. **Map** E5. **(** 01-46 34 19 60. **FAX** 01-43 26 67 32. W www.hoteldesgrandeshommes.com Sorbonne teachers frequent this quiet family hotel close to the Jardin du Luxembourg. The attic rooms have views of the Panthéon. ▤ TV ▤ ▧	31			
LUXEMBOURG QUARTER: *Récamier* €€ 3 bis Place St-Sulpice, 75006. **Map** D4. **(** 01-43 26 04 89. **FAX** 01-46 33 27 73. A family hotel with no television sets or restaurant. Try to get a room which looks onto both the courtyard and the square. ▤ ▧	30			
LUXEMBOURG QUARTER: *Hôtel de l'Abbaye* W www.hotel-abbaye.com €€€€ 10 Rue Cassette, 75006. **Map** D4. **(** 01-45 44 38 11. **FAX** 01-45 48 07 86. Once an abbey, this elegant hotel still basks in a tranquil atmosphere. There is a pretty courtyard. ▤ TV ▤ ▧	44		●	▪
ST-GERMAIN-DES-PRÉS: *Artus Hotel* W www.artushotel.com €€€ 34 Rue du Buci, 75006. **Map** D4. **(** 01-43 29 07 20. **FAX** 01-43 29 67 44. A trendy hotel with minimalist decor, which attracts a young crowd. Several suites have balconies and big whirlpool baths. ▤ TV ▧	27			
ST-GERMAIN-DES-PRÉS: *Hôtel de Fleurie* W www.hotel-de-fleurie.fr €€€ 32 Rue Grégoire de Tours, 75006. **Map** D4. **(** 01-53 73 00 00. **FAX** 01-53 73 70 20. A welcoming, family-run hotel with a delightful facade, light interiors, and comfort throughout. ▤ TV ▤ ▧	29			

Map references refer to map of Paris on pp150–51

				NUMBER OF ROOMS	PRIVATE PARKING	RESTAURANT	GARDEN OR TERRACE

Price categories for a standard double room (not per person) for one night, including tax and service charges, but not including breakfast.

€ under €60
€€ €60–90
€€€ €90–150
€€€€ €150–260
€€€€€ over €260

PRIVATE PARKING
Parking is provided by the hotel in either a private car park or a private garage close by. You may have to pay for this facility.

RESTAURANT
Hotel restaurants are for guests but can usually be used by non-residents.

CREDIT CARDS
Major credit cards are accepted in those restaurants where the credit card symbol is shown.

Hotel	Price	Rooms	Private Parking	Restaurant	Garden or Terrace
ST-GERMAIN-DES-PRÉS: *Hôtel d'Orsay* W www.hotel-esprit-de-france.com 91 Rue de Lille, 75007. **Map** C3. 01-47 05 85 54. FAX 01-45 55 51 16. Under new management, the entire hotel has been renovated. It is close to the Musée d'Orsay and has a splendid rooftop view.	€€€	41			■
TUILERIES: *Hôtel Brighton* W www.hotel-esprit-de-france.com 218 Rue de Rivoli, 75001. **Map** D3. 01-47 03 61 61. FAX 01-42 60 41 78. The bedrooms have high moulded ceilings and large windows looking either onto the courtyard or the Jardin des Tuileries.	€€€	65			
TUILERIES: *Hôtel de Crillon* W www.crillon.com 10 Place de la Concorde, 75008. **Map** C3. 01-44 71 15 00. FAX 01-44 71 15 02. Occupying an unrivaled position in the heart of the city, this hotel offers luxurious yet restrained elegance. Magnificent terrace.	€€€€€	147		●	■
TUILERIES: *Ritz* W www.ritzparis.com 15 Place Vendôme, 75001. **Map** D3. 01-43 16 30 30. FAX 01-43 16 36 68. After a century, this hotel still lives up to its discreet, high reputation. Original Louis XVI furniture, fireplaces, and chandeliers.	€€€€€	175	■	●	■
INVALIDES: *Hôtel le Pavillon* @ patrickpavillon@aol.com 54 Rue Saint Dominique, 75007. **Map** C3. 01-45 51 42 87. FAX 01-45 51 32 79. A small, quiet family-run hotel. Although the rooms are somewhat small, they are pleasantly decorated. During summer months, breakfast is served in the courtyard.	€€	18			■
INVALIDES: *Hôtel de Suède St-Germain* W www.hoteldesuede.com 31 Rue Vaneau, 75007. **Map** C4. 01-47 05 00 08. FAX 01-47 05 69 27. This elegant, late 18th-century style hotel overlooks the park of the Hôtel Matignon, home of the prime minister.	€€€	39			■
INVALIDES: *Hôtel Bourgogne & Montana* @ info@bourgogne-montana.com 3 Rue de Bourgogne, 75007. **Map** C3. 01-45 51 20 22. FAX 01-45 56 11 98. A relaxing, intimate hotel with an air of sobriety. Features include a mahogany bar, old lift, and circular hall with pink marble columns.	€€€€	32			■
EIFFEL TOWER: *Grand Hôtel Lévêque* @ info@hotelleveque.com 29 Rue Cler, 75007. **Map** B4. 01-47 05 49 15. FAX 01-45 50 49 36. Very reasonable hotel with a superb location and friendly owners. Rooms vary in price and size, but all are bright and airy.	€€	50			
CHAILLOT: *Raphaël* W www.raphael-hotel.com 17 Avenue Kléber, 75106. **Map** B2. 01-53 64 32 00. FAX 01-53 64 32 01. Many films are shot in the Neo-Gothic bar of this timeless hotel where stars shelter from the paparazzi. A Turner hangs in the hall.	€€€€€	90		●	■
CHAMPS-ELYSÉES: *Résidence Lord Byron* W www.escapade-paris.com 5 Rue Chateaubriand, 75008. **Map** B2. 01-43 59 89 98. FAX 01-42 89 46 04. This small, discreet hotel has a courtyard garden for summer breakfasts. The bedrooms are relatively quiet but not large.	€€€€	31			■
CHAMPS-ELYSÉES: *Bristol* W www.hotel-bristol.com 112 Rue du Faubourg St-Honoré, 75008. **Map** 3 A4. 01-53 43 43 00. FAX 01-53 43 43 01. This is one of the city's finest hotels. The large rooms are sumptuously decorated with carefully selected antiques and have magnificent bathrooms.	€€€€€	174	■	●	■
CHAMPS-ELYSÉES: *Four Seasons George V* W www.fourseasons.com 31 Avenue George V, 75008. **Map** 2 E5. 01-49 52 70 00. FAX 01-49 52 71 10. A legendary hotel dotted with secret salons, old furniture, and paintings, with an excellent restaurant.	€€€€€	245	■	●	■

Price categories for a standard double room (not per person) for one night, including tax and service charges, but not including breakfast.

€ under €60
€€ €60–90
€€€ €90–150
€€€€ €150–260
€€€€€ over €260

PRIVATE PARKING
Parking is provided by the hotel in either a private car park or a private garage close by. You may have to pay for this facility.

RESTAURANT
Hotel restaurants are for guests but can usually be used by non-residents.

CREDIT CARDS
Major credit cards are accepted in those restaurants where the credit card symbol is shown.

	Price	NUMBER OF ROOMS	PRIVATE PARKING	RESTAURANT	GARDEN OR TERRACE
MONTMARTRE: *Timbôtel* W www.timhotel.com 11 Rue Ravignan, 75018. 01-42 55 74 79. FAX 01-42 55 71 01. This is one of Montmartre's most delightful hotels. It borders a quiet, charming square and there are good views from the top floors.	€€€	60			
MONTMARTRE: *Terrass* W www.terrass-hotel.com 12 Rue Joseph-de-Maistre, 75018. 01-46 06 72 85. FAX 01-42 52 29 11. There are panoramic views over the rooftops of Paris from the upper floors. A few bedrooms retain their original Art Deco woodwork.	€€€€	100		●	
VERSAILLES: *Hôtel de Clagny* 6 Impasse de Clagny, 78000. 01-39 50 18 09. FAX 01-39 50 85 17. Conveniently close to the station and in a quiet location. The rooms are simply furnished and unremarkable but the welcome is genuine.	€	22			
VERSAILLES: *Trianon Palace* W www.westin.com 1 Bd de la Reine, 78000. 01-30 84 50 00. FAX 01-30 84 50 01. Undoubtedly the most splendid hotel in the region, deserving the accolade "palace", blending in with the Classical lines of the Versailles park. The gourmet restaurant is the jewel in the crown.	€€€€€	192	■	●	■
FONTAINEBLEAU: *Grand Hôtel de l'Aigle Noir* W www.hotelaiglenoir.com 27 Place Napoléon Bonaparte, 77300. 01-60 74 60 00. FAX 01-60 74 60 01. This prestigious mansion overlooks the Château de Fontainebleau and its vast park. Gourmet cuisine and impeccable service.	€€€€	53	■	●	

NORTHERN FRANCE

	Price	NUMBER OF ROOMS	PRIVATE PARKING	RESTAURANT	GARDEN OR TERRACE
CARNAC: *Lann Roz* @ hotel.lann-roz@dub-internet.fr 36 Avenue de la Poste, 56340. 02-97 52 10 48. FAX 02-97 52 24 36. A friendly hotel with a pretty garden ten minutes' walk from the beach. The restaurant has a fine wine list.	€€	13	■	●	
REIMS: *Hôtel Crystal* W www.hotel-crystal.fr 86 Place Drouet d'Erlon, 51100. 03-26 88 44 44. FAX 03-26 47 49 28. This old-fashioned hotel borders the liveliest square in Reims, yet is surprisingly quiet. In summer breakfast is served on the terrace.	€	31			■
REIMS: *Boyer les Crayères* W www.gerardboyer.com 64 Bd Henri Vasnier, 51100. 03-26 82 80 80. FAX 03-26 82 65 52. This is a renowned hotel on the gastronomic and champagne-tasting trail. Discreetly sumptuous, it occupies a Belle Epoque mansion, set in attractive grounds on the outskirts of Reims.	€€€€€	19	■	●	■
ROUEN: *Hôtel de Bordeaux* @ interhotel.rouen@wanadoo.fr 9 Place de la République, 76000. 02-35 71 93 58. FAX 02-35 71 92 15. A functional, friendly, and well-run hotel overlooking the Seine on one side and the cathedral towers on the other. English spoken.	€	48			
ROUEN: *Hôtel Notre Dame* W www.hotelnotredame.com 4 Rue de la Savonnerie, 76000. 02-35 71 87 73. FAX 02-35 89 31 52. The staff are friendly and helpful, the rooms are spacious and recently renovated, some of them with views of the river and cathedral.	€	30			
ST-MALO: *Hôtel Elizabeth* W www.st-malo-elizabeth.com 2 Rue des Cordiers, 35400. 02-99 56 24 98. FAX 02-99 56 39 24. Situated within the ramparts of the old town, the building has a 16th-century façade. English satellite TV is available.	€€€	17	■		
STRASBOURG: *Au Cerf d'Or* 6 Place de l'Hôpital, 67000. 03-88 36 20 05. FAX 03-88 36 68 67. The main hotel has more charming rooms, but the annex offers a small pool and sauna. Nearby are several waterfront restaurants.	€€	43		●	■

STRASBOURG: *Régent Petite France* W www.regent-hotels.com €€€€€ | 72
5 Rue des Moulins, 67000. 03-88 76 43 43. FAX 03-88 76 43 76.
The city's most prestigious and ideally located deluxe hotel. Set in
a converted watermill, it overlooks the Petite France district. TV 📺 🍴

THE LOIRE VALLEYEY

CHAMBORD: *Hôtel Saint-Michel* €€ | 38
41250 Chambord. 02-54 20 31 31. FAX 02-54 20 36 40.
Book ahead at this old-fashioned hotel and ask for a room with a view
of the château. The restaurant is stuffy but the cuisine good. TV 🍴

CHARTRES: *Le Grand Monarque* @ info@bw-grand-monarque.com €€€ | 55
22 Place des Epars, 28005. 02-37 21 00 72. FAX 02-37 36 34 18.
This converted 16th-century staging post, with massively thick walls, is part of
of the Best Western chain and has a recommended gourmet restaurant. TV 🍴

CHENONCEAUX: *Hostel du Roy* W www.hotelduroy.com € | 32
9 Rue du Dr Bretonneau, 37150. 02-47 23 90 17. FAX 02-47 23 89 91.
A sprawling hotel-restaurant with simple but appealing bedrooms and
a dining room hung with hunting trophies. Local wines served. TV 🍴

FONTEVRAUD-L'ABBAYE: *Hôtellerie Prieuré St-Lazare* €€ | 52
49590 Fontevraud-L'Abbaye. 02-41 51 73 16. FAX 02-41 51 75 50.
W www.hotelfp-fontevraud
This atmospheric hotel is housed in the former St-Lazare priory, within the
famous abbey complex, and has a good gourmet restaurant. TV 🍴

NANTES: *Hôtel la Perouse* W www.hotel-laperouse.fr €€ | 47
3 Allée Duquesne, 44000. 02-40 89 75 00. FAX 02-40 89 76 00.
This chic hotel which opened in 1993 offers crisp, contemporary design
and efficient service. It is reasonably quiet for a city hotel. TV 📺 🍴

POITIERS: *Château Clos de la Ribaudière* W www.ribaudiere.com €€ | 41
Chasseneuil-du-Poitou, 86360. 05-49 52 86 66. FAX 05-49 52 86 32.
A restored 19th-century house in a riverside park 10km from Poitiers – a
haven of peace and comfort away from the busy city. TV 🍴

TOURS: *Hôtel Balzac* € | 18
47 Rue de la Scellerie, 37000. 02-47 05 40 87. FAX 02-47 05 67 93.
Cozy and welcoming, this old-fashioned hotel is situated between the
theater and the cathedral. Drinks are served in the courtyard. TV 🍴

TOURS: *Hôtel de l'Univers* W www.hotel-univers-loirevalley.com €€€€ | 85
5 Boulevard Heurteloup, 37000. 02-47 05 37 12. FAX 02-47 61 51 80.
Statesmen, including Winston Churchill, and royals have stayed at this
luxurious Belle Epoque hotel. Some rooms have antique furniture. TV 📺 🍴

BBURGUNDY AND THE FRENCH ALPS

ANNECY: *Hôtel de l'Abbaye* W www.hotelabbaye-annecy.com €€€ | 18
15 Chemin de l'Abbaye, 74940. 04-50 23 61 08. FAX 04-50 27 77 65.
A charming hotel-restaurant occupying a former 15th-century
Dominican friary surrounded by gardens. TV 🍴

BEAUNE: *Hôtel le Parc* @ hotel.le.parc@wanadoo.fr €€ | 25
13 Rue du Golf, Levernois, 21200. 03-80 24 63 00. FAX 03-80 24 21 19.
A quiet, quaint country hotel on the outskirts of Beaune, set in a beautiful
park. A good base for visiting the nearby vineyards. TV 🍴

BEAUNE: *Hôtel du Cep* W www.hotel-cep-beaune.com €€€€ | 57
27 Rue Maufoux, 21200. 03-80 22 35 48. FAX 03-80 22 76 80.
An elegant hotel in the old town, renovated in Renaissance style. Each
bedroom is named after a wine of the Côte d'Or vineyards. TV 📺 🍴

DIJON: *Hostellerie le Sauvage* € | 22
64 Rue Monge, 21000. 03-80 41 31 21. FAX 03-80 42 06 07.
This city hotel is conveniently located for the main sights and the historic
center. TV 🍴

GEVREY-CHAMBERTIN: *Hôtel des Grands Crus* W www.hoteldesgrandscrus.com €€ | 24
Route des Grands Crus, 21220. 03-80 34 34 15. FAX 03-80 51 89 07.
A light and airy, old-style hotel with wonderful views over the vineyards.
It has no restaurant but there are several good ones in the village. 🍴

For key to symbols see back flap

<table>
<tr><td colspan="2">

Price categories for a standard double room (not per person) for one night, including tax and service charges, but not including breakfast.

€ under €60
€€ €60–90
€€€ €90–150
€€€€ €150–260
€€€€€ over €260

</td></tr>
</table>

PRIVATE PARKING
Parking is provided by the hotel in either a private car park or a private garage close by. You may have to pay for this facility.

RESTAURANT
Hotel restaurants are for guests but can usually be used by non-residents.

CREDIT CARDS
Major credit cards are accepted in those restaurants where the credit card symbol is shown.

		NUMBER OF ROOMS	PRIVATE PARKING	RESTAURANT	GARDEN OR TERRACE
GRENOBLE: *Parc Hôtel* W www.park-hotel-grenoble.fr 10 Place Paul-Mistral, 38027. 04-76 85 81 23. FAX 04-76 46 49 88. Grenoble's leading modern hotel offers comfortably furnished rooms with many amenities. The staff are friendly and helpful. TV ▤ ▨	€€€€	52	▦	●	
LYON: *Hôtel Carlton* W www.libertel-hotels.com 4 Rue Jussieu, 69002. 04-78 42 56 51. FAX 04-78 42 10 71. In the heart of the Presqu'île near the Rhône, this pleasantly renovated hotel still retains traces of its elegant Belle Epoque days. TV ▤ ▨	€€€€	83			
LYON: *Cour des Loges* W www.courdesloges.com 6 Rue du Boeuf, 69005. 04-72 77 44 44. FAX 04-72 40 93 61. A luxury hotel occupying four renovated Renaissance mansions in the heart of Vieux Lyon. Bedrooms are modern in style. TV ▤ ▨	€€€€€	62	▦	●	▦
VÉZELAY: *L'Espérance* W www.marc.meneau.esperance.com St-Père-sous-Vézelay, 89450. 03-86 33 39 10. FAX 03-86 33 26 15. Some of the rooms overlook the garden; others are in a renovated mill. Above all, guests come for the famous restaurant. TV ▤ ▨	€€€€	34	▦	●	▦
SOUTHWEST FRANCE					
BIARRITZ: *Hôtel Windsor* W www.hotelwindsorbiarritz.com Grande Plage, 64200. 05-59 24 08 52. FAX 05-59 24 98 90. Standing above the famous Grande Plage, and with recently decorated family rooms, this is a great spot for a lively holiday. TV ▨	€€	48	▦	●	
BORDEAUX: *Grand Hôtel Français* W www.grand-hotel-francais.com 12 Rue du Temple, 33000. 05-56 48 10 35. FAX 05-56 81 76 18. A good-value hotel in the center of town with attractively decorated, comfortable, and quiet rooms. TV ▤ ▨	€€	35		●	
MARGAUX: *Relais de Margaux* W www.relais-margaux.com Chemin de l'Ile Vincent, 33460. 05-57 88 38 30. FAX 05-57 88 31 73. The high price at this luxurious hotel is money well spent. Peaceful setting, handsome grounds, pool, tennis, and exquisite food. TV ▤ ▨	€€€€	64	▦	●	▦
PAU: *Grand Hôtel du Commerce* @ hotel.commerce-pau@wanadoo.fr 9 Rue Maréchal-Joffre, 64000. 05-59 27 24 40. FAX 05-59 83 81 74. Conveniently located near the royal château, this popular, traditional hotel has comfortable rooms and a reasonable restaurant. TV ▨	€	51		●	▦
ST-JEAN-DE-LUZ: *Le Parc Victoria* W www.parcvictoria.com 5 Rue Cépé, 64500. 05-59 26 78 78. FAX 05-59 26 78 08. A glorious garden and swimming pool set off this Victorian mansion, furnished in the style of the 1930s, near the beach. TV ▤ ▨	€€€€€	18	▦	●	▦
TOULOUSE: *Hôtel Albert 1er* W www.hotel-albert1.com 8 Rue Rivals, 31000. 05-61 21 17 91. FAX 05-61 21 09 64. A good value hotel, centrally situated with cheerful rooms and modern bathrooms. Small lounge and breakfast room, but no restaurant. TV ▨	€	50	▦		
TOULOUSE: *Hôtel Jean-Mermoz* W www.hotel-mermoz.com 50 Rue Matabiau, 31000. 05-61 63 04 04. FAX 05-61 63 15 64. Modern hotel in the center of town which is comfortable, friendly, and surprisingly quiet. Pleasant garden and restaurant. TV ▤ ▨	€€	52	▦		▦
THE SOUTH OF FRANCE					
AIGUES-MORTES: *Hôtel Saint-Louis* W www.lesaintlouis.fr 10 Rue de l'Amiral-Courbet, 30220. 04-66 53 72 68. FAX 04-66 53 75 92. Charming hotel, tucked within the stout stone walls of the city built by the saint-king Louis IX. A good base for exploring the Camargue. TV ▨	€€	22	▦	●	

AIX-EN-PROVENCE: *Hôtel des Augustins* €€€ 29
3 Rue de la Masse, 13100. (*04-42 27 28 59.* FAX *04-42 26 74 87.*
A converted 12th-century monastery with spacious rooms in traditional
Provençal style. A haven of peace in the heart of Aix. 🔧 TV 📋 🅿️

ANTIBES: *Mas Djoliba* W www.hotel-djoliba.com €€€ 13
29 Avenue de Provence, 06600. (*04-93 34 02 48.* FAX *04-93 34 05 81.*
A traditional Provençal hotel a short walk from the center and beach.
Set in a pretty garden, with comfortable rooms in a rustic style. 🔧 TV 🏊 🅿️

ARLES: *Hôtel d'Arlatan* W www.hotel-arlatan.com €€€€ 47
26 Rue du Sauvage, 13631. (*04-90 93 56 66.* FAX *04-90 49 68 45.*
Situated in the heart of Arles, this hotel dates from the 16th century.
Stone walls and a cavernous fireplace decorate the salon. 🔧 TV 📋 🏊 🅿️

AVIGNON: *Hôtel d'Europe* W www.hotel-d-europe.fr €€€€ 44
12 Place Crillon, 84000. (*04-90 14 76 76.* FAX *04-90 14 76 71.*
Avignon's most refined hotel has vast, elegant bedrooms and a salon
bedecked with tapestries above a marble floor. Superb restaurant. 🔧 TV 📋 🅿️

AVIGNON: *Hôtel de la Mirande* W www.la-mirande.fr €€€€€ 20
4 Place de la Mirande, 84000. (*04-90 85 93 93.* FAX *04-90 86 26 85.*
An exquisite establishment with richly decorated rooms in Provençal
style and fine antiques. There is a relaxing inner courtyard. 🔧 TV 📋 🅿️

CANNES: *Hôtel Molière* W www.hotel-moliere.com €€€ 24
5–7 Rue Molière, 06400. (*04-93 38 16 16.* FAX *04-93 68 29 57.*
This 19th-century town house, just five minutes' walk from the sea, has
bright, comfortable rooms and terraces overlooking the floral garden. 🔧 TV 📋 🅿️

CANNES: *Carlton Inter-Continental* W www.cannes.interconti.com €€€€€ 326
58 Bd de la Croisette, 06400. (*04-93 06 40 06.* FAX *04-93 06 40 25.*
Home to stars during the film festival and business people the rest of the
year. A private beach allows you to book in straight from your yacht. 🔧 TV 📋 🅿️

CARCASSONNE: *Hôtel le Donjon* W www.bestwestern-donjon.com €€€ 62
Les Ramparts, 2 Rue du Comte-Roger, 11000. (*04-68 11 23 00.* FAX *04-68 25 06 60.*
Right in the heart of the medieval city, this superb 14th-century building is
full of modern comforts, with 20 more rooms in an annex nearby. 🔧 TV 📋 🅿️

MONTE CARLO: *L'Hermitage* W www.montecarlo.com €€€€€ 229
Square Beaumarchais, 98000. (*00 377-92 16 40 00.* FAX *00 377-92 16 38 52.*
The vast cream Belle Epoque palace is known for its glass-domed Winter
Garden foyer, sumptuous pink-and-gold restaurant, and marble terrace. 🔧 TV 📋 🏊 🅿️

NICE: *Hôtel Windsor* W www.hotelwindsornice.com €€ 57
11 Rue Dalpozzo, 06000. (*04-93 88 59 35.* FAX *04-93 88 94 57.*
A friendly, family-run hotel with a palmed garden. Simple bedrooms
with modern murals, some with French windows, and balconies. 🔧 TV 📋 🏊 🅿️

NICE: *Le Négresco* W www.hotel-negresco-nice.com €€€€€ 140
37 Promenade des Anglais, 06000. (*04-93 16 64 00.* FAX *04-93 88 35 68.*
The most famous hotel on the Riviera, recently renovated to even
more lofty heights of Belle Epoque grandeur. 🔧 TV 📋 🅿️

NÎMES: *Hôtel Kyriad* W www.hotel-kyriad.com €€ 28
10 Rue Roussy, 30000. (*04-66 76 16 20.* FAX *04-66 67 65 99.*
A peaceful location and well-equipped bathrooms and bedrooms
make this modernized hotel good value. 🔧 TV 📋 🅿️

NÎMES: *Imperator Concorde* W www.hotel-imperator.com €€€ 62
Quai de la Fontaine, 30900. (*04-66 21 90 30.* FAX *04-66 67 70 25.*
Nîmes' grandest hotel stands close to 17th-century gardens and
fountains, and some remarkable Roman architecture. 🔧 TV 📋 🅿️

ST-JEAN-CAP-FERRAT: *Clair Logis* W www.hotel-clair-logis.fr €€ 18
12 Avenue Centrale, 06230. (*04-93 76 51-81.* FAX *04-93 76 51 82.*
This seductively old-fashioned villa with its large, mature garden is
very good value. The larger rooms are in the main building. 🔧 TV 🅿️

ST-TROPEZ: *Lou Cagnard* € 19
Avenue P Roussel, 83990. (*04-94 97 04 24.* FAX *04-94 97 09 44.*
A very popular, good-value hotel in the newest part of town, a short walk
from the port. Cheerful bedrooms and pleasant courtyard. 🔧 TV 🅿️

For key to symbols see back flap

Where to Eat in France

THE VARIETY OF places to eat in France is enormous. Throughout the day, the ubiquitous café is ideal for a coffee and a snack, while, for something more substantial, bistros and brasseries offer full menus. Restaurants are usually only open in the evening, but encompass the whole gamut of French cooking, from simple and inexpensive country fare to the very finest *haute cuisine*.

	FIXED-PRICE MENU	GOOD WINE LIST	OUTDOOR TABLES

PARIS

ILE DE LA CITÉ: *Le Vieux Bistrot*   €€€€

14 Rue du Cloître-Notre-Dame, 75004. **Map** E4. 01-43 54 18 95.
An authentic, honest bistro, frequented by many Parisian restaurateurs and
entertainment stars. The food here is unpretentious and very good. *Dec 24–25.*

		●	■

THE MARAIS: *Baracane*   €€

38 Rue des Tournelles, 75004. **Map** F4. 01-42 71 43 33.
In spite of its touristy location this tiny restaurant, serving cuisine from the southwest
such as *cassoulet* and duck, has good quality food at reasonable prices. *lunch Sat, Sun.*

■		

THE MARAIS: *Au Bourguignon du Marais*   €€€

52 Rue François Miron, 75004. **Map** E4. 01-48 87 15 40.
Sip a superior wine with your meal here at little more than shop prices, in the informal
bistro atmosphere. Classic French home cooking and excellent cheeses. *Sat pm–Sun.*

	●	

BEAUBOURG: *Benoît*   €€€€€

20 Rue St Martin, 75004. **Map** E3. 01-42 72 25 76.
This is the Rolls-Royce of Paris bistros. The excellent traditional cuisine includes
assorted cold salads, house *foie gras*, and *boeuf à la mode*.

■	●	

LES HALLES: *Au Pied de Cochon*   €€€

6 Rue Coquillière, 75001. **Map** D3. 01-40 13 77 00.
This famous institution in the heart of Les Halles is open every day, all day and
all night, serving copious amounts of grilled pigs' trotters and shellfish. Hearty
cuisine and atmosphere, but be prepared to queue after 10pm.

		■

LATIN QUARTER: *Loubnane*   €€

29 Rue Galande, 75005. **Map** E4. 01-43 26 70 60.
This Lebanese restaurant serves generous *mezes* under the watchful eye of a patron
whose main aim in life is the happiness of his customers. *Mon.*

■		■

LATIN QUARTER: *La Tour d'Argent*   €€€€€

15–17 Quai de la Tournelle, 75005. **Map** E4. 01-43 54 23 31.
Established in 1582, La Tour d'Argent consistently maintains top-class status. The wine
cellar must be one of the best in the world. A necktie is essential. *Mon, Tue am.*

■	●	

LUXEMBOURG QUARTER: *Polidor*   €

41 Rue Monsieur-le-Prince, 75006. **Map** D4. 01-43 26 95 34.
Artists, poets, and writers have been attracted to this homely bistro for decades;
James Joyce was once a regular customer. Traditional French bistro menu.

■		

LUXEMBOURG QUARTER: *Au Petit Marguéry*   €€€

9 Bld de Port-Royal, 75013. **Map** E5. 01-43 31 58 59.
Cold lobster *consommé* with caviar, mushroom salad with *foie gras*, and cod
cooked with spices are some of the unusual dishes served here. *Sun, Mon.*

■		

ST-GERMAIN-DES-PRÉS: *Le Petit St-Benoît*   €€

4 Rue St-Benoît, 75006. **Map** D4. 01-42 60 27 92.
This is the place for anyone who is on a budget or who wants to mix with
the locals. The food is simple and tasty, and good value. *Sun.*

TUILERIES QUARTER: *Le Grand Véfour*   €€€€€

17 Rue de Beaujolais, 75001. **Map** D3. 01-42 96 56 27.
An 18th-century three-star Michelin restaurant, considered to be one of the most attractive
in Paris and *the* place for special occasions. A necktie is essential. *Fri pm, Aug.*

■	●	

OPÉRA QUARTER: *Chartier*   €

7 Rue du Faubourg Montmartre, 75009. **Map** E2. 01-47 70 86 29.
This cavernous restaurant packs in the crowds with its quick service and basic
French food at budget prices. Popular with local *habitués*, the place
bustles with an infectious bonhomie.

■		

Map references refer to map of Paris on pp164–5

Price categories are for a three-course meal for one, including half a bottle of house wine, tax, and service: € under €25 €€ €25–40 €€€ €40–55 €€€€ €55–75 €€€€€ over €75	**FIXED-PRICE MENU** A good-value fixed-price menu on offer at lunch, dinner, or both, often with three or more courses. **CREDIT CARDS** The credit card symbol indicates that major credit cards are accepted (MasterCard, Visa). Other cards, including American Express and Diners Club, may also be taken.	FIXED-PRICE MENU	GOOD WINE LIST	OUTDOOR TABLES

OPERA QUARTER: *A G Le Poète* €€ 27 Rue Pasquier, 75008. **Map** C2. 01-47 42 00 64. Soft lighting and red velvet decor provide a romantic setting for inspired cooking, with dishes such as red mullet and baby scallops with wild nettles. ● *Sun; 3 weeks Aug.*	■		
INVALIDES QUARTER: *Thoumieux* €€€ 79 Rue St-Dominique, 75007. **Map** C3. 01-47 05 49 75. A good, efficiently run restaurant where the ingredients are fresh, and virtually everything is made on the premises. The *cassoulet* is a house specialty. ● *Dec 24–25.*	■		
EIFFEL TOWER QUARTER: *La Serre* €€ 29 Rue de l'Exposition, 75007. **Map** B4. 01-45 55 20 96. A small, cozy neighborhood restaurant of a type that is becoming increasingly rare in Paris. Rustic specialties include *pot au feu* and *cassoulet.* ● *Sun, Mon.*	■		
CHAILLOT QUARTER: *La Butte Chaillot* €€€ 110 bis Ave Kleber, 75116. **Map** B2. 01-47 27 88 88. Sophisticated cuisine and modern decor attract a very stylish crowd.	■		
CHAILLOT QUARTER: *Alain Ducasse* €€€€€ 25 Ave Montaigne, 75008. **Map** B3. 01-53 67 65 00. Among the *trompe l'oeil* and sculptures, M. Ducasse creates the great classic dishes, worthy of its three Michelin stars. A necktie is essential. ● *Sun, Sat, lunch Mon–Wed; Jul 15–Aug 15.*		●	
CHAMPS-ELYSÉES: *La Fermette Marbeuf 1900* €€€ 5 Rue Marbeuf, 75008. **Map** B3. 01-53 23 08 00. Come here to dine amid the stunning Belle Epoque decor. La Fermette serves commendable brasserie-style food, with a set menu and good wine.	■	●	■
CHAMPS-ELYSÉES: *Au Petit Colombier* €€€€ 42 Rue des Acacias, 75017. **Map** A2. 01-43 80 28 54. The slightly rustic ambience of this comfortable restaurant complements the traditional cuisine. An excellent place for a relaxing evening. ● *mid-Jul–mid-Aug.*	■	●	
MONTPARNASSE: *La Cagouille* €€€ 10–12 Place Constantin Brancusi, 75014. **Map** D5. 01-43 22 09 01. This is considered one of the best fish restaurants in Paris. The shellfish platter is recommended. Also look out for the seasonal items on the menu.	■	●	■
MONTPARNASSE: *La Coupole* €€€ 102 Bld du Montparnasse, 75014. **Map** D5. 01-43 20 14 20. This is a lively and boisterous place all through the day and night. It has been popular with artists and thinkers since 1927. Serves vegetarian dishes.	■		
MONTMARTRE: *Le Maquis* €€ 69 Rue Caulaincourt, 75018. 01-42 59 76 07. A pleasant bistro where you can enjoy a simple but delicious meal on the tree-shaded terrace. The menu is very good value.	■		■
MONTMARTRE: *Beauvilliers* €€€€ 52 Rue Lamarck, 75018. 01-42 54 54 42. Stepping into this restaurant, you are imbued with a sense of *joie de vivre.* Chef Edouard Carlier's cuisine is always exciting. A necktie is essential. ● *Sun.*	■	●	■
VERSAILLES: *Les Trois Marches* €€€€€ Trianon Palace Hotel, 1 Bld de la Reine. 01-39 50 13 21. The restaurant is part of the sumptuous palace overlooking the formal gardens. The *haute cuisine* matches the splendor of the place. ● *Sun, Mon; Aug.*	■	●	■
FONTAINEBLEAU: *Le Caveau des Ducs* €€€ 24 Rue de Ferrare. 01-64 22 05 05. Offers standard, but reasonably well-priced classic French cuisine in intimate, rustic surroundings near the fabulous Château de Fontainebleau.	■	●	■

For key to symbols see back flap

Price categories are for a three-course meal for one, including half a bottle of house wine, tax, and service:

€ under €25
€€ €25–40
€€€ €40–55
€€€€ €55–75
€€€€€ over €75

FIXED-PRICE MENU
A good-value fixed-price menu on offer at lunch, dinner, or both, often with three or more courses.

CREDIT CARDS
The credit card symbol indicates that major credit cards are accepted (MasterCard, Visa). Other cards, including American Express and Diners Club, may also be taken.

	FIXED-PRICE MENU	GOOD WINE LIST	OUTDOOR TABLES

NORTHERN FRANCE

BAYEUX: *Le Lion d'Or* €€€
71 Rue St-Jean. 02-31 92 06 90.
This 17th-century inn serves delicious food. Try the unusual *foie gras* of duck with honey, or the mouth-watering forest mushroom tart. ● *lunch Mon–Sat, 20 Dec–20 Jan.*
| | ■ | ● | |

MONT-ST-MICHEL: *Hôtel Saint-Pierre* €
Grande-Rue. 02-33 60 14 03.
Lamb grazed on the salt marshes – *agneau pré-salé* – features on the menu of this restaurant, housed in a 15th-century building. Crab and salmon are other favorites.
| | ■ | | ■ |

MONT-ST-MICHEL: *La Mère Poulard* €€€€€
Grande-Rue. 02-33 89 68 68.
Visitors from all over Europe come here to sample the famous *omelette Mère Poulard,* cooked in a long-handled pan over a wood fire.
| | ■ | ● | |

NANTES: *La Taverne de Maître Kanter* €
1 Place Royale. 02-40 48 55 28.
Part of a reliable chain, this Alsatian tavern excels with its offerings of *choucroute* (sauerkraut) and cold meats. Try the good beers, too.
| | ■ | | ■ |

REIMS: *Le Vigneon* €€
Place Paul Jamot. 03-26 79 86 86.
With its use of local produce and cooking techniques, this is a restaurant for those with an interest in the champagne region. Its popularity makes booking essential.
| | ■ | ● | |

REIMS: *Les Crayères* €€€€€
64 Bld Vasnier. 03-26 82 80 80.
Set in ample grounds, this celebrated restaurant runs tours of its wine cellar. Specialties include smoked salmon and cream of caviar. ● *Mon, lunch Tue; Dec 26–Jan 15.*
| | ■ | ● | |

ROUEN: *La Marmite* €€
3 Rue Florence 02-35 71 75 55.
This attractive restaurant is housed in an 18th-century building. Often stays open late, providing romantic candle-lit atmosphere. ● *dinner Sun, Mon; first 2 weeks Aug.*
| | ■ | ● | |

ROUEN: *Restaurant Grill* €€€€
9 Quai de la Bourse. 02-35 71 16 14.
Unusual house specialties include crayfish salad with chutney, and *pigeon à la rouennaise.* Vegetarian dishes can be ordered. ● *dinner Sun, Mon; first 3 weeks Aug.*
| | ■ | ● | |

ST-MALO: *Le Bémétin* €€
Les Roches Scultés-Rothéneuf. 02-99 56 97 64.
A pleasant restaurant overlooking the sea, with efficient and friendly service.
| | ■ | | ■ |

STRASBOURG: *Zum Strissel* €€
5 Place de la Grande Boucherie. 03-88 32 14 73.
An old-fashioned wine cellar in a 14th-century building near the cathedral. Serves meat stews, onion tart, and pitchers of Alsatian wines. ● *Sun, Mon; 10 days Feb, Jul.*
| | ■ | ● | ■ |

STRASBOURG: *Au Crocodile* €€€€€
10 Rue de l'Outre. 03-88 32 13 02.
This is probably Strasbourg's most exclusive restaurant. Recommended dishes include baked perch and crayfish tails with lentils. ● *Sun (Jun–Apr), Mon; 3 weeks Jul, Dec 25–Jan 2.*
| | ■ | ● | |

THE LOIRE VALLEY

BLOIS: *Le Duc de Guise* €
15 Place Louis XII. 02-54 78 22 39.
A boisterous family-orientated Italian restaurant by the château. The pizzas are cooked in traditional fashion, in wood-fired ovens. ● *Mon, Sun.*
| | ■ | | ■ |

BLOIS: *L'Grangeuedu Chateau* €€€
1 Avenue Jean Laigret. 02-54 78 036.
Situated in the winter garden of a 15th-century castle, this restaurant offers a
sophisticated French menu. Aug–Sep: lunch Mon; Oct–May: dinner Wed–Sun.

CHARTRES: *Le Buisson Ardent* €
10 Rue au Lait. 02-37 34 04 66.
With a splendid view of the cathedral, this restaurant is in the oldest part
of Chartres. Offers fish specialties such as pike-perch filet. dinner Sun, Wed.

FONTEVRAUD-L'ABBAYE: *La Licorne* €€€
Allée Sainte-Cathérine. 02-41 51 72 49.
The elegant setting and pretty courtyard, plus the oysters and asparagus, make
this a popular place to dine. Reservations are recommended in summer.
dinner Sun, Mon, dinner Wed (Sept–Apr); Dec 15–Jan 15.

NANTES: *La Cigale* €€
4 Place Graslin. 02-51 84 94 94.
The interior of this Belle Epoque brasserie is decorated with tiles and gilding;
the quality and choice of cuisine here are also exceptional.

ORLÉANS: *La Chancellerie* €€
27 Place du Martroi. 02-38 53 57 54.
This brasserie is located on the main square and is always busy. Staple brasserie
fare is enlivened by the wines. There is also a separate restaurant. Sun pm.

ORLÉANS: *Les Antiquaires* €€€
2 Rue au Lin. 02-38 53 52 35.
A popular place with locals for its inventive cuisine. In season, Sologne game is
served, including the house specialty, young partridge casserole. Sun, dinner Mon.

POITIERS: *Maxime* €€
4 Rue St-Nicolas. 05-49 41 09 55.
A chic restaurant for sophisticated palates. Dishes include tender game, duck, truffles,
and ravioli of cooked oysters. dinner Sun, Sat (Nov–Feb); Jul 14–Aug 21.

TOURS: *L'Atelier Gourmand* €
37 Rue Etienne-Marcel. 02-47 38 59 87.
The chef here extends a warm welcome, producing specialties that include goat's
cheese and sweet pepper flan, and spare ribs of pork. lunch Sat–Mon, mid-Dec–5 Jan.

TOURS: *Jean Bardet* €€€€€
57 Rue Groison. 02-47 41 41 11.
The gastronomic temple of the Loire, with two Michelin stars and a dazzling
wine list. Diners can revel in all kinds of lobster, scallop, and salmon dishes.

BURGUNDY AND THE FRENCH ALPS

BEAUNE: *La Bouzerotte* €€
Bouze lès Beaune. 03-80 26 01 37.
In winter, a roaring fire makes this the coziest place in Burgundy. In summer, enjoy
dinner on the terrace. The hearty regional dishes are all cooked to order.
Mon, Tue; Feb 10–Mar 1; 1 week Sep; Dec 24–Jan 1.

BEAUNE: *Jean Crotet* €€€€€
Route de Combertault, Levernois. 03-80 24 73 58.
"Serious" cuisine is served up in this beautiful old mansion. The Bresse chicken
and Bourgogne snails are cooked to perfection. Tue–Wed.

DIJON: *Le Bistrot des Halles* €
10 Rue Bannelier. 03-80 49 94 15.
At lunchtime this bistro is packed. Next to the market, it attracts local
people, who come here to enjoy the pâté and *boeuf bourguignon*. Sun–Mon.

DIJON: *Jean-Pierre Billoux* €€€€
13 Place de la Libération. 03-80 38 05 05.
Run by the most renowned chef in Dijon, Jean-Pierre's cooking effectively combines
traditional country ingredients with novel modern flavors. dinner Sun, Mon; 1 week Aug.

GRENOBLE: *Amerindia* €€
4 Place des Gordes. 04-76 51 58 39.
A bright and cheerful restaurant based on a South American theme, with a good
choice of vegetarian options on the menu. Sun, lunch Mon (Oct–Apr); last week Dec.

		FIXED-PRICE MENU	**GOOD WINE LIST**	**OUTDOOR TABLES**

Price categories are for a three-course meal for one, including half a bottle of house wine, tax, and service:

€ under €25
€€ €25–40
€€€ €40–55
€€€€ €55–75
€€€€€ over €75

FIXED-PRICE MENU
A good-value fixed-price menu on offer at lunch, dinner, or both, often with three or more courses.

CREDIT CARDS
The credit card symbol indicates that major credit cards are accepted (MasterCard, Visa). Other cards, including American Express and Diners Club, may also be taken.

GRENOBLE: *Le Berlioz* €€ 4 Rue de Strasbourg. ▐ 04-76 56 22 39. Housed in an 18th-century mansion, this delightful restaurant features a different seasonal menu with regional specialties each month. ● *Sun; Aug.* ⚑			■	
LYON: *Le Mercière* €€ 56 Rue Mercière. ▐ 04- 78 37 67 35. A busy, top-value restaurant where booking is essential. The fixed-price menu provides very substantial dishes, and the *à la carte* is a rare treat. ⚑		■	●	■
LYON: *Léon de Lyon* €€€€€ 1 Rue Pléney. ▐ 04-72 10 11 12. The expert chef and owner serves local food with a modern twist in a two-story building set on the Presqu'île in the heart of the city. The seasonal menu changes constantly through the year. ● *Sun, Mon, lunch Sat (Apr–Sep); first 3 weeks Aug.* ⚑		■	●	

SOUTHWEST FRANCE

BAYONNE: *Le Cheval Blanc* €€€ 68 Rue Bourgneuf. ▐ 05-59 59 01 33. Creative traditional cooking. Try the roasted hake with onions and sweet peppers, and the chocolate Amandine with wild cherries for dessert. ● *dinner Sun, Mon, Feb school hols.* ⚑			●	
BIARRITZ: *Plaisir des Mets* €€€ 5 Rue Centre. ▐ 05-59 24 34 66. Enjoy the fish dishes and seafood in a Belle Epoque brasserie. The local wines are of a high caliber. ● *Sep–Jun: dinner Tue, Wed; last 2 weeks Jun, last 2 weeks Nov.* ⚑		■		
BIARRITZ: *Les Platanes* €€€€€ 32 Ave Beausoleil. ▐ 05-59 23 13 68. Top-flight cooking, using only fresh produce, in a friendly setting. The dining room will only seat 25 so it is advisable to book well ahead. ● *Mon, Tue.* ⚑		■		
BORDEAUX: *Chez Philippe* €€€ 1 Place du Parlement. ▐ 05-56 81 83 15. A casual, lively spot specializing in fresh fish and shellfish, with the deserved reputation of being the best fish restaurant in Bordeaux. ● *Sun, Mon; first 3 weeks Aug.* ⚑		■		■
BORDEAUX: *La Tupiña* €€€€€ 6 Rue Porte de la Monnaie. ▐ 05-56 91 56 37. This restaurant prides itself on its traditional, seasonal specialties of southwest France. Meat, poultry, and game dishes are cooked over an open fire in a friendly atmosphere. ⚑		■	●	■
BORDEAUX: *Le Chapon Fin* €€€€€ 5 Rue de Montesquieu. ▐ 05-56 79 10 10. Crayfish ravioli, young pigeon, and local oysters are some of the treats in store at this luxurious Belle Epoque restaurant where Edward VII once dined. ● *Sun–Mon, Aug.* ⚑		■	●	
PAU: *Chez Pierre* €€€ 16 Rue Louis-Barthou. ▐ 05-59 27 76 86. A fine chef, an elegant setting in a 19th-century town house, and a series of creative dishes have ensured the reputation of this restaurant. ● *Sun, lunch Mon, lunch Sat; first week Jan, first 2 weeks Aug.* ⚑		■		
PAU: *La Gousse d'Ail* €€€ 12 Rue du Hédas. ▐ 05-59 27 31 55. A pleasant, brick and stucco restaurant with beams and a big fireplace. Its excellent value makes it stand out in an area full of bistros. ● *lunch Tue–Wed & Sat.* ⚑		■		■
TOULOUSE: *La Côte de Bœuf* €€€ 12 Rue des Gestes. ▐ 05-61 21 19 61. Small, efficient, and supremely friendly restaurant offering huge steaks and known for its generous portions. ● *lunch, Sun; 3 weeks Aug.* ⚑		■		■

TOULOUSE: *Les Jardins de l'Opéra* €€€€
1 Place du Capitole. [05-61 23 07 76.
Without question one of the best places to eat in Toulouse. Situated in a pretty
courtyard, it produces great local cuisine. ● Sun–Mon, 1 week Jan, Aug.

THE SOUTH OF FRANCE

AIX-EN-PROVENCE: *Le Bistro Latin* €€
18 Rue de la Couronne. [04-42 38 22 88.
Excellent meals at good prices, and imaginative local specialties such as roast sole
with fennel cream. ● Sun, lunch Mon, last week Aug.

AIX-EN-PROVENCE: *L'Aix Quis* €€€
22 Rue Victor Leydet. [04-42 27 76 16.
Stylish fish and meat dishes are the heart of this restaurant's menu, which is fast
becoming the culinary centre of Aix. Delicious six-course menu. ● Sun–Mon.

ARLES: *L'Escaladou* €€
23 Rue de la Porte de Laure. [04-90 96 70 43.
This pretty Provençal restaurant is close to the bullring in the center of town.
Choose the good local fish, served with piles of fresh vegetables.

ARLES: *L'Olivier* €€€
1 bis, Rue Réattu. [04-90 49 64 88.
Fine Provençal food is served, with only the freshest ingredients used for dishes like
honey-coated roast pigeon. ● Sun, lunch Mon (Oct–May: dinner Mon), Nov, 2 weeks Jan.

AVIGNON: *La Fourchette* €
17 Rue Racine. [04-90 85 20 93.
A relaxed alternative to Avignon's smarter restaurants. Prices are reasonable with a
good range of mouthwatering desserts. ● Sat, Sun; 2 week Feb, 2 week Aug, first week Sept.

AVIGNON: *Hiély-Lucullus* €€€
5 Rue de la République. [04-90 86 17 07.
Avignon gastronomes have been flocking here for 60 years. Try specialties such as
foie gras and *meringue glacée*. ● Tue, Wed; last 2 weeks Aug, last 2 weeks Jun.

CANNES: *Royal Gray* €€€€
38 Rue des Serbes. [04-92 99 79 60.
It is difficult to eat more lavishly than at the Royal Gray, long the doyen of
Cannes' restaurants. & ● Sun–Mon; mid-Jul–Aug: Sat.

CARCASSONNE: *Brasserie le Donjon* €
4 Rue Porte d'Aude. [04-68 25 95 72.
An elegant, refreshingly modern brasserie in an otherwise medieval town.
Menu includes regional specialties of *foie gras* and *cassoulet*. ● dinner Sun (Nov–Mar).

MARSEILLE: *Dar Djerba* €€
15 Cours Julien. [04-91 48 55 36.
An intimate North African restaurant serving delicious couscous. ● lunch Mon; 2 weeks Aug.

MARSEILLE: *Miramar* €€€€
12 Quai du Port. [04-91 91 10 40.
Fish and seafood are the specialties, with the *bouillabaisse* one of the most authentic
found anywhere in France – but at a price. ● Sun, Mon; 3 weeks Aug, 2 weeks Jan. &

MONACO: *Le Périgourdin* €€
5 Rue des Oliviers. [00377-93 30 06 02.
Two minutes' walk from the casino, this friendly restaurant offers all the riches of
Périgord cuisine – such as *foie gras* – at bargain prices. ● lunch Sat, Sun; last 2 weeks Aug.

NICE: *Nissa Socca* €
5 Rue Sainte-Réparate. [04-93 80 18 35.
Features vast plates of *socca* (chickpea bread), with pasta and carafes of red wine.
Crowded, it usually takes over the street in summer. ● Sun, lunch Mon; 2 weeks Jun. &

NICE: *Le Chantecler* €€€€€
Le Négresco Hotel, 37 Promenade des Anglais. [04-93 16 64 00.
Long the bastion of gastronomy in Nice, the restaurant retains immaculate
standards of food and service. Seafood and fish feature strongly. ● mid-Nov–mid-Dec. &

NÎMES: *Nicolas* €
1 Rue Poise. [04-66 67 50 47.
Regional fare at good prices in a friendly atmosphere. ● lunch Sat & Sun, Mon.

BELGIUM AND LUXEMBOURG

FAMED FOR ITS MAGNIFICENT FLEMISH ART *and Gothic architecture, Belgium, like neighboring Luxembourg, is a melting pot of various influences including Dutch, French, and German. The histories of the two countries have long been interlinked, but culturally and linguistically they are distinct. Luxembourg, a major financial center, is one of the smallest states in Europe.*

In recent times, both Belgium and Luxembourg have largely avoided the limelight, but it was here, in the Middle Ages, that the first great towns of Northern Europe were born, and where the first experiments with oil paintings were made. Today, Brussels, as the center of government for the European Union, is theoretically the capital of Europe, but its reputation remains overshadowed by those of the larger European capitals.

Perhaps more than any other country in Europe, Belgium is most aptly defined by contrasts. The division between the Flemish inhabitants of the north and the French-speaking Walloons in the south is mirrored by a geographical divide; the estuarial plains of Brabant and Flanders give way to the rolling hill-country of the Ardennes, which stretches south and east through the castle-dotted woods of Luxembourg.

HISTORY

At the start of the 12th century, commerce became the guiding force in Europe, and the centers of trade quickly grew into powerful cities. Rivers and canals were keys to the growth of the area's towns; Brussels, Ghent, Ypres, Antwerp, and Bruges became the focus of a cloth trade between Belgium, France, Germany, Italy, and England.

In 1369 Philip, Duke of Burgundy, married the daughter of the Count of Flanders, and a few years later the Low Countries and eastern France came under the couple's Burgundian rule. A century later, the death of Mary of Burgundy left her husband, the Habsburg Emperor Maximilian, ruler of Belgium. In 1488 Brussels and the rest of Flanders rebelled against this new power, but the Austrians prevailed, largely because of a plague which decimated the population in 1490.

European Parliament building rising above the trees of Parc Léopold, Brussels

◁ **Detail of the façade of the Hôtel de Ville in the Grand Place, Brussels**

By 1555 the Low Countries had passed into the hands of the Spanish Habsburgs, whose Catholic repression of the Protestants sparked the Dutch Revolt. In the course of the wars that led to Dutch independence (1568–1648), the predominantly Catholic southern part of the Low Countries remained under Spanish rule. In 1700 the Spanish Habsburg dynasty died out, and England, Austria, and other powers united to oppose French designs on the region in the War of the Spanish Succession. When the war came to an end in 1713, the Treaty of Utrecht transferred Belgium and Luxembourg to the Austrian Habsburgs.

King Leopold I, the first king of the Belgians, crowned in 1830

Belgium was again ruled by foreign powers between 1794 and 1830. First, by the French Republicans, and then,

after Napoleon's defeat, by the Dutch. William I of Orange was appointed King of the Netherlands at the Congress of Vienna in 1815, and his autocratic style, together with a series of anti-Catholic measures, bred considerable discontent, especially among the French-speaking Walloons. An uprising in 1830 ousted the Dutch and made Leopold I king of a newly independent Belgium. Nine years later Luxembourg, a Grand-Duchy since 1815, also gained independence.

Both countries' economies flourished throughout the 19th century, but all was eclipsed with the start of World War I. In 1940 the Germans invaded again, this time under Hitler's command.

Belgium's history in the latter half of the 20th century was dominated by the ongoing language debate between the Flemings and the Walloons. The constitution was redrawn, creating a federal state with three separate regions: Flanders, Wallonia, and Brussels.

KEY DATES IN THE HISTORY OF BELGIUM AND LUXEMBOURG

56 BC Julius Caesar conquers the Low Countries

963 AD Count Siegfried establishes Luxembourg

1229 Brussels granted its first charter

1430 Under Burgundian rule, Brussels becomes the major administrative center of the region

1482 The region falls under Austrian sovereignty

1519 Charles V, ruler of Burgundy, becomes Holy Roman Emperor.

1555–1794 Spanish and Austrian rule

1794 French Republican armies take over

1815 Belgium and Luxembourg pass to William I of Orange, King of the Netherlands

1830 Belgium gains independence

1839 Luxembourg gains independence

1914 Both countries invaded by Germany

1940 Nazi troops occupy both countries

1958 EEC headquarters set up in Brussels

1962 Act of Parliament divides Belgium into Dutch- and French-speaking regions

1967 NATO headquarters move to Brussels

1988 Flemish and Walloon regions of Belgium granted fiscal autonomy

LANGUAGE AND CULTURE

In the north of Belgium, the Flemish have their roots in the Netherlands and Germany, while the Walloons of the south are related to the French. French

A glass of Chimay, a popular Belgian beer

is one of the official languages of Luxembourg, and German is widely spoken, but the indigenous language is Letzeburgesch, a dialect of German which is spoken by all. Artistically, Belgium is best known for its 17th-century painters (including Rubens, van Dyck, and Jordaans), and more recently for its Art Nouveau style of architecture. Today it is one of the world's most popular producers of chocolate and beer.

Exploring Belgium and Luxembourg

BRUSSELS IS NOT ONLY the capital of Belgium but also of Europe, as the center of government for the European Union. The city lies in the center of the country on the flat, fertile Brabant plain. Today, its excellent communications make it an ideal place from which to explore the historic towns of Antwerp, Ghent, and Bruges. Toll-free motorways compare favorably with any in France, train travel is swift and competitively priced, and there are good bus services in the areas not covered by trains. Transport in Luxembourg is equally good, with the hub of communications in Luxembourg City itself.

The medieval market square, seen from the Belfort tower, Bruges

SIGHTS AT A GLANCE

Antwerp ❷
Bruges pp232–4 ❸
BRUSSELS pp222–9 ❶

Ghent ❹
Luxembourg ❻
Waterloo ❺

Picturesque Château de Vianden, Luxembourg

KEY

✈ Airport
⛴ Ferry port
— Highway
— Major road
— Railroad
▪▪▪ International border

Brussels ●

WITH ALMOST ONE MILLION inhabitants, Brussels is the capital not only of Belgium, but also of Europe, as the center of the European Union. The city is divided into two main areas. Historically the poorer area, where workers and immigrants lived, the Lower Town is centered around the splendid 17th-century Grand Place. The Upper Town, traditional home of the aristocracy, is an elegant area that encircles the city's green oasis, the Parc de Bruxelles. Some of the most striking buildings in this part of the city are the shiny postmodern structures of European institutions.

SEE ALSO

- *Where to Stay* p240
- *Where to Eat* p242

Tintin statue at the Centre
Belge de la Bande Dessinée

SIGHTS AT A GLANCE

Cathédrale Sts-Michel et
Gudule ⑤
Centre Belge de la
Bande Dessinée ④
Grand Place ①
Manneken Pis ③
Musée du Costume et
de la Dentelle ②
Musées Royaux des
Beaux-Arts ⑥
Palais Royal ⑦
Parc du Cinquantenaire ⑩
Parliament Quarter ⑨
Place du Grand Sablon ⑧

Greater Brussels
(see inset map)
Bruparck ⑫
Musée Horta ⑪

GETTING AROUND

Brussels' Lower Town is well served by trams. However, many streets are pedestrianized, and usually the quickest way of getting around is on foot. In the Upper Town, the best option is to take one of the buses that run through the district. Brussels' metro stations are well placed for the main sights of interest, and the system offers a fast and efficient way of reaching the suburbs.

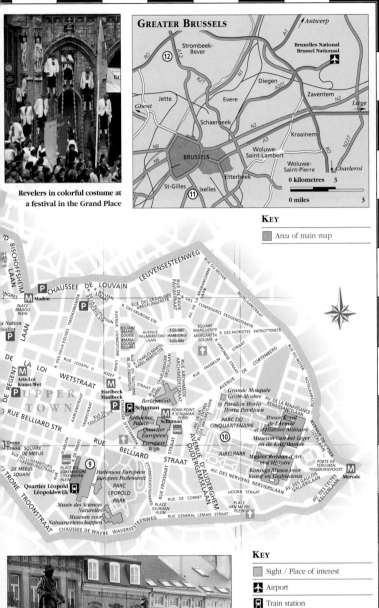

Revelers in colorful costume at
a festival in the Grand Place

GREATER BRUSSELS

Antwerp

Strombeek-Bever

⑫

Bruxelles National
Brussel Nationaal

Diegen

Ghent

Jette

Evere

Zaventem

Liege

Schaerbeek

Kraainem

Woluwe-Saint-Lambert

BRUSSELS

Woluwe-Saint-Pierre

Charleroi

Etterbeek

St-Gilles

⑪

Ixelles

0 kilometres 3

0 miles 3

KEY

Area of main map

BISCHOFFSHEIM LAAN

CHAUSSEE DE LOUVAIN

LEUVENSESTEENWEG

RUE DU NOYER

RUE DE FAVE PAVIASTRAAT

RUE DES BRABANÇONNE

Madou

PLACE MADOU PLEIN

CONGRES

R. DES GRAVELINES GREVELINGENSTR

R. DES EBURONS STR

AV. DES CONFEDERES EEDGENOTENSTR

Nation Naties

LAAN

SQUARE MARIE-LOUISE LOUIZA SQUARE

AVENUE PALMERSTON LAAN

SQUARE AMBIORIX SQUARE

SQUARE MARGUERITE MARGARETA SQUARE

RUE DES PATRIOTES PATRIOTTENSTR

DE REGENT

R. DES DEUX EGLISES TWEEKERKEN

AVENUE LIVINGSTONE LAAN

CHARLES MARTEL KAREL MARTELSTR

RUE DU CARDINAL RUE FRANKLIN

DE CORTENBERG

RUE DU NOYER NOTELAARSTR

LA LOI WETSTRAAT

RUE JOSEPH II

RUE ARCHIMEDE ARCHIMEDESTRAAT

AV. DE LA RENAISSANCE RENAISSANCELAAN

Arts-Loi Kunst-Wet

AARLENSTRAAT

THYRESTRAAT

RUE DE TOULOUSE STR

Maelbeek Maalbeek

CHAUSSEE D'ETTERBEEK

Schuman

ROND POINT R SCHUMAN PLEIN

Grande Mosquée Grote Moskee

Pavillon Horta Horta Paviljoen

Musée Royal de l'Armée et d'Histoire Militaire

Museum van het Leger en de Krijgskunde

UPPER TOWN

RUE BELLIARD STR

Residence Palace

Schuman

Quartier Européen Europese Wijk

AVENUE D'AUDERGHEM AUDERGEMSELAAN

PARC DU CINQUANTENAIRE

⑩

AVENUE DE LA RENAISSANCE

AVENUE DE LASER

Trone Troon

SQUARE DE MEEÛS

RUE DU LUXEMBOURG LUXEMBURGSTRAAT

PLACE DU LUXEMBOURG LUXEMBURG PLEIN

RUE BELLIARD

ETTERBEEKSESTEENWEG

RUE FROISSART

JUBELPARK

Musées Royaux d'Art et d'Histoire

Konings Musea voor Kunst en Geshiedenis

PORTE DE TERVUREN TERVUURSEPOORT

Merode

DE MEEÛS SQUARE

⑨

Parlement Européen Europees Parlement

PARC LEOPOLD PARK

RUE DE CORNET

AV. DES NERVIENS NERVIERSLAAN

AV. DES GAULOIS GALLIERSLAAN

AV. DE CELTES KELTENLAAN

Quartier Léopold Léopoldswijk

Musée des Sciences Naturelles

Museum voor Natuurwetenschappen

RUE GENERAL LEMAN STRAAT

HOORN STRAAT

PLACE VAN MEYEL PLEIN

TROONSTRAAT

CHAUSSEE DE WAVRE WAVERSESTEENWEG

RUE JOURDAN PLEIN

KEY

	Sight / Place of interest
✈	Airport
🚉	Train station
Ⓜ	Metro station
🚊	Main tram stop
🚌	Main bus stop
P	Parking
ℹ	Tourist information
✝	Church
—	Pedestrian street

Bronze statues in the Place du Petit Sablon in the Upper Town

D E F

Grand Place, Brussels' historic main square

Grand Place ①

Ⓜ *Bourse, Gare Centrale.* 🚌 *29, 34, 47, 48 & many others.* 🚊 *3, 52, 55, 56, 81.* **Musée de la Ville** *Maison du Roi.* 📞 *02-279 4350.* ◯ *Tue–Fri, am Sat & Sun.* ● *Jan 1, May 1, Nov 1 & 11, Dec 25.* 🖼 📷 *by prior arrangement.* ♿ *limited.*

THE GEOGRAPHICAL, historical, and commercial heart of the city, the Grand Place is the first port of call for most visitors to Brussels. A market was held on this site as early as the 11th century. During the first half of the 15th century, Brussels' town hall, the Hôtel de Ville, was built, and city traders began to add individual guildhalls in a medley of styles. In 1695, however, two days of cannon fire by the French destroyed all but the town hall and two façades. Trade guilds were urged to rebuild their halls to

La Maison du Roi, built on the site of old bread, meat, and cloth halls

designs approved by the town council, resulting in the splendid Baroque ensemble that can be seen today.

Occupying the entire south-west side of the square, the Gothic **Hôtel de Ville** *(see p225)* is the architectural masterpiece of the Grand Place. Opposite it stands **La Maison du Roi** (1536). Despite its name, no king ever lived here; the building was used as a temporary jail and a tax office. Redesigned in Gothic style in the late 19th century, it is now home to the Musée de la Ville, which contains 16th-century paintings and tapestries, and a collection of around 650 costumes created for the Manneken Pis.

On the square's eastern flank, the vast Neoclassical edifice known as **La Maison des Ducs de Brabant** was designed by Guillaume de Bruyn and consists of six former guildhalls. Facing it are **Le Renard**, built in the 1690s for the guild of haberdashers, and **Le Cornet** (1697), the boatmen's guildhall, whose gable resembles a 17th-century frigate's bow. **Le Roi d'Espagne**, also known as La Maison des Boulangers, was built in the late 17th century by the wealthy bakers' guild. The gilt bust over the entrance represents St. Aubert, patron saint of bakers. Today, the building houses one of the Grand Place's best-loved bars, whose first floor offers fine views of the bustling square.

Musée du Costume et de la Dentelle ②

Rue de Violette 6. 📞 *02-213 4450.* Ⓜ *Gare Centrale.* 🚌 *34, 48, 95, 96.* ◯ *Mon– Fri 1:30–5pm, Sat & Sun 2–4:30pm.* ● *Wed.* 🖼 📷 *on request.* ♿

HOUSED IN two 18th-century gabled houses, this museum is dedicated to one of Brussels' most successful exports, Belgian lace, which has been made here since the 12th century. The ground floor has a display of costumes showing how lace has adorned fashions of every era. Upstairs is a fine collection of antique lace from France, Flanders, and Italy.

Manneken Pis ③

Rues de l'Etuve & du Chêne. Ⓜ *Gare Centrale.* 🚌 *34, 48, 95, 96.* 🚊 *3, 52, 55, 56, 81.*

THE TINY STATUE of a young boy relieving himself is Brussels' most unusual sight. The original bronze statue by Jérôme Duquesnoy the Elder was first placed on the site in 1619. After it was stolen and damaged by a former convict in 1817, a replica was made and returned to its revered site. The inspiration for the statue is unknown, but the mystery only lends itself to rumor and fable and increases the little boy's charm. One **Manneken** theory claims that in **Pis statue** the 12th century the son of a duke was caught urinating against a tree in the midst of a battle, and was thus commemorated in bronze as a symbol of the country's military courage. When, in 1698, a city governor provided a set of clothes with which to dress the statue, he began a tradition that is still observed today. Visiting heads of state donate miniature versions of their national costume for the boy, and now a collection of 650 outfits, including an Elvis suit, can be seen in the Musée de la Ville.

Hôtel de Ville

THE IDEA OF ERECTING A TOWN HALL to reflect Brussels'
growth as a major European trading center had
been under consideration since the end of the 13th
century, but it was not until 1401 that the first foundation stone was laid. Completed in 1459, the Hôtel de
Ville emerged as the finest civic building in the country,
a stature it still enjoys. Jacques van Thienen was
commissioned to design the left wing, where he used
ornate columns, sculptures, turrets, and arcades. Jan
van Ruysbroeck's elegant spire helped seal the
building's reputation. Tours are available of the interior,
which contains 15th-century tapestries and works of art.

VISITORS' CHECKLIST

Grand Place. 📞 02-279 4365.
Ⓜ Bourse, Gare Centrale.
🚌 many routes. 🚊 3, 52, 55,
56, 81. 🕐 (for guided tours)
3:15pm Tue & Wed, 10:45am,
12.15pm Sun (Apr–Sep). ⬤
public hols & election days. 📷

★ Maximilian Room
*This lavish hall, used today
by the city council, takes its
name from the portrait of
Maximilian I of Austria over
the fireplace. It contains
18th-century tapestries
depicting the history of
6th-century King Clovis.*

★ Council Chamber
*This room was where
the ruling council of
Brabant used to meet.
Ancient tapestries and
gilt mirrors line the
walls above an
inlaid floor.*

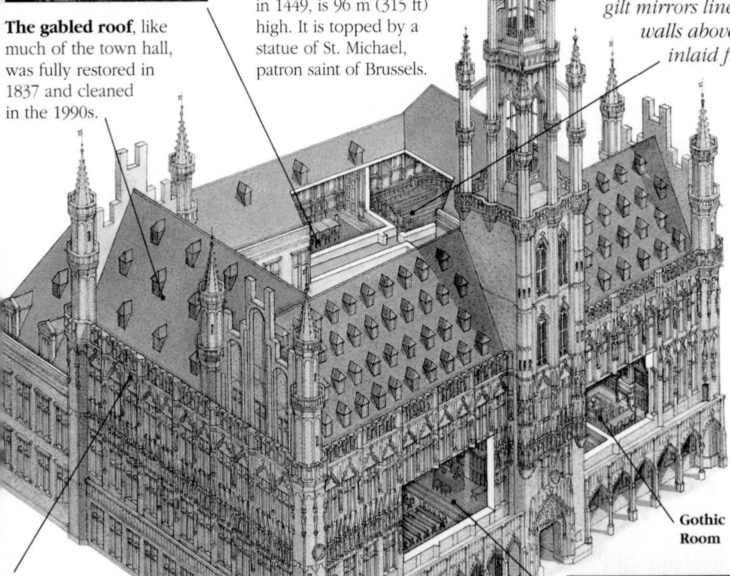

The tower, begun
in 1449, is 96 m (315 ft)
high. It is topped by a
statue of St. Michael,
patron saint of Brussels.

The gabled roof, like
much of the town hall,
was fully restored in
1837 and cleaned
in the 1990s.

**137 stone
statues** adorn
the façades.

Gothic
Room

STAR FEATURES

★ Council Chamber

★ Maximilian Room

Wedding Room
*A Neo-Gothic style dominates
this civil marriage office. Its
ornate carved timbers include
mahogany inlaid with ebony.*

Art Nouveau entrance hall of the Centre Belge de la Bande Dessinée

Centre Belge de la Bande Dessinée ④

20 Rue des Sables. 02-219 1980.
38, 58, 61. 56, 81, 90.
Ⓜ Botanique, Rogier, Centrale.
10am–6pm Tue–Sun. Jan 1,
Dec 25.

THIS UNIQUE museum pays
tribute to the Belgian
passion for comic strips, or
bandes dessinées, and to world-
famous comic strip artists
from Belgium and abroad.

One of the exhibitions
shows the great comic strip
heroes, from Hergé's Tintin –
who made his debut in 1929
– to the Smurfs and the
Flemish comic strip characters
Suske and Wiske. Other
displays explain the stages of
putting together a comic strip.
There is also a series of life-
size cartoon sets, of special
appeal to children. The
museum holds 6,000 original
plates, and a valuable archive
of photographs and artifacts.

The collection is housed in
a beautiful building, built in
1903–6 to the design of the
Belgian Art Nouveau architect
Victor Horta *(see p229)*.

Cathédrale Sts-Michel et Gudule ⑤

Parvis Ste-Gudule. 02-217 8345.
29, 60, 63, 65, 66, 71. 92,
93, 94. Ⓜ Centrale. daily. to
crypt and treasury. call in advance.

BELGIUM'S FINEST surviving
example of Brabant
Gothic architecture, the
Cathédrale Sts-Michel et

Gudule is the national church
of Belgium. There has been a
church on this site since at
least the 11th century. Work
began on the Gothic cathedral
in 1225 under Henry I, Duke
of Brabant, and continued
over a period of 300 years.

The cathedral interior is
relatively bare, due to
Protestant ransacking in 1579
and thefts during the French
Revolution. Over the west
door, however, is a magnificent
16th-century stained-glass
window of the Last Judgment.
Another splendid feature is
the flamboyantly carved
Baroque pulpit in the central
aisle, the work of an Antwerp-
born sculptor, Hendrik Frans
Verbruggen. In the crypt you
can see the remains of the
original Romanesque church,
which dates back to 1047.

Musées royaux des Beaux-Arts ⑥

Rue de la Régence 3. 02-508
3211. 25, 27, 38, 60, 71, 95, 96.
92, 93, 94. Ⓜ Parc, Centrale.
10am–5pm Tue–Sun. public
hols. call in advance.
www.fine-arts-museum.be

SIX CENTURIES of art, both
Belgian and international,
are displayed in the two
museums that make up the

The Assumption of the Virgin (c.1615) by Rubens at the Musées royaux des Beaux Arts

The white limestone façade of the Cathédrale Sts-Michel et Gudule

Musées Royaux des Beaux-
Arts, the Musée d'Art Ancien
(15th–18th centuries) and the
Musée d'Art Moderne (19th
century–present day). Both
museums have colored
"routes," which guide the
visitor through galleries
representing the different
schools and periods of art.

The Musée d'Art Ancien
holds one of the world's finest
collections of works by the
Flemish Primitive School. A
work of particular note is *The
Annunciation* (c.1415–25) by
the Master of Flémalle. The
trademarks of the Flemish
Primitives are a lifelike vitality
and a clarity of light. The
greatest exponent of the style
was Rogier van
der Weyden
(c.1400–64), the
official city painter
to Brussels, who has
several splendid
works on display
at the museum.

Peter Brueghel the
Elder (c.1525–69),
one of the most
outstanding Flemish
artists, settled in
Brussels in 1563. His
earthy scenes of
peasant life remain
his best known
works, and are
represented here by
paintings such as
The Bird Trap (1565).

Another highlight
of the Musée d'Art
Ancien is the world-
famous collection of
works by Peter Paul

Rubens (1577–1640). *The Assumption of the Virgin* stands out among his religious canvases. Other notable paintings include van Dyck's *Portrait of Porzia Imperial with her daughter Maria Francesca* (1620s) and *Three Children with Goatcart* by Frans Hals (c.1582–1666).

Opened in 1984, the Musée d'Art Moderne is situated in a unique setting: eight levels of the building are underground. Works in the 19th-century section vary greatly in style and subject matter, from Neoclassicism, exemplified by David, to Realism, Impressionism, and Symbolism.

The Fauvist painter Rik Wouters' *Woman in a Blue Dress in front of a Mirror* (1914) is one of many works by leading Belgian artists of the 20th century. Foreign artists include Matisse, Paul Klee, and Chagall. The biggest attraction of this part of the museum, however, is the collection of paintings by the Belgian Surrealists, including René Magritte (1898–1967). Surrealism had its roots back in the 16th century, with the phantasmagoria of Bosch and Peter Brueghel the Elder. One of Magritte's most famous works, on show here, is *The Domain of Arnheim* (1962) – an eerie composition showing an eagle-mountain rearing over a small bird's nest.

Palais Royal ⑦

Place des Palais. **[** 02-551 2020.
[21, 27, 38, 60, 71, 95, 96.
[92, 93, 94. **M** Trône, Parc.
○ 10:30am– 4:30pm Tue–Sun.
● mid-Sep–mid-Jul. **[** **[**

THE OFFICIAL home of the Belgian monarchy, this is one of the finest 19th-century buildings in the Upper Town. Construction began in the 1820s on the site of the old Coudenberg Palace. Work continued under Léopold II (reigned 1865– 1909), when much of the exterior was completed. The most lavish state reception rooms include the Throne Room, with 28 wall-mounted chandeliers, and the Hall of Mirrors. The latter,

The recently restored, 19th-century Palais Royal

similar to the Hall of Mirrors at Versailles *(see pp168–9),* is where ceremonial occasions are held, and guests presented to the king and queen.

Place du Grand Sablon ⑧

[27, 48, 95, 96. **[** 91, 92, 93, 94.
M Centrale, Louise.

LOCATED ON THE slope of the escarpment that divides Brussels in two, the Place du Grand Sablon is like a stepping stone between the upper and lower towns. The name "sablon" derives from the French "sable" (sand), and the square is so called because this old route down to the city center once passed through sandy marshes.

Terrace café in the upscale Place du Grand Sablon

Today this is an area of upscale antiques dealers, fashionable restaurants, and trendy bars, where you can stay drinking until the early hours of the morning.

At the far end of the square stands the lovely church of **Notre-Dame du Sablon**, built in the Brabant Gothic style, and boasting some glorious stained-glass windows. On the opposite side of the road to the church is the **Place du Petit Sablon**. In contrast to the busy café scene of the larger square, these pretty formal gardens are a peaceful

Notre-Dame du Sablon window

spot to stop for a rest. Sit and admire the 48 bronze statues by Art Nouveau artist Paul Hankar, each representing a different medieval guild of the city. At the back of the gardens is a fountain, built to commemorate Counts Egmont and Hoorn, the martyrs who led a Dutch uprising against the tyrannical rule of the Spanish under Philip II. On either side of the fountain are 12 further statues of prominent 15th- and 16th-century figures, including Gerhard Mercator, the Flemish geographer and mapmaker.

The triumphal central archway and surrounding colonnades of the Parc du Cinquantenaire

Parliament Quarter ⑨

🚌 21, 27, 34, 38, 54, 60, 80, 95, 96.
Ⓜ Maelbeek, Trône, Schuman.

THE VAST, MODERN steel and glass complex, located just behind the Quartier Léopold train station, is one of three homes of the European Parliament (the other two are Strasbourg and Luxembourg). This gleaming building has its critics: the huge structure housing the hemicycle that seats the 600-plus MEPs has been dubbed "Les Caprices des Dieux" ("Whims of the Gods"), which refers both to the shape of the building, similar to a French cheese of the same name, and to its lofty aspirations. Many people also regret that to make way for the building, a large part of the once-lively Quartier Léopold has been lost. Though there are still plenty of bars and restaurants here, a lot of the charm has gone.

Postmodern building known as "Les Caprices des Dieux" in Brussels' Parliament Quarter

Parc du Cinquantenaire ⑩

Avenue de Tervuren. 🚌 27, 28, 36, 67.
🚊 81, 82. Ⓜ Schuman, Mérode.
Musées Royaux d'Art et d'Histoire
📞 02-741 7211. ⏰ Tue–Sun.
⬤ public hols. 🎟 **Musée Royal de l'Armée et d'Histoire Militaire**
📞 02-737 7811. ⏰ Tue–Sun.
⬤ Jan 1, Dec 25. 🎟 **Autoworld**
📞 02-736 4165. ⏰ 10am–6pm daily (5pm in winter). ⬤ Jan 1, Dec 25.

THE FINEST of Léopold II's grand projects, the Parc and Palais du Cinquantenaire were built for the Golden Jubilee celebrations of Belgian independence in 1880. The park was laid out on unused marshland. The palace, at its entrance, was to comprise a triumphal arch, based on the Arc de Triomphe in Paris (see p165),

---

BRUSSELS AND THE EUROPEAN UNION

In 1958, following the signing of the Treaty of Rome in the previous year, the European Economic Community (EEC), now the European Union (EU), was born, and Brussels became its headquarters. Today, the city remains home to most of the EU's institutions. The European Commission, the EU body that formulates policies, is currently based in various buildings as its intended home, the Berlaymont building, is being restored. The city is also one of the seats of the European Parliament, which currently has around 700 members, known as MEPs (Members of the European Parliament). The most powerful institution is the Council of Ministers, composed of representatives of each member state. Each nation has a certain number of votes, according to its size. The Council must approve all legislation for the EU, often a difficult task to accomplish given that most Europe-wide legislation will not be to the liking of every state.

The signing of the Treaty of Rome, 1957

and two large exhibition areas. By the time of the 1880 Art and Industry Exposition, however, only the two side exhibition areas had been completed. Further funds were found, and work continued for 50 years. The arch was completed in 1905. Until 1935, the large halls on either side of the central archway were used to hold trade fairs, before being converted into museums.

Also known as the Musée du Cinquantenaire, the excellent **Musées Royaux d'Art et d'Histoire** contain a vast array of exhibits. Sections on ancient civilizations cover Egypt, Greece, Persia, and the Near East. Other displays feature Byzantium and Islam, China and the Indian subcontinent, and the Pre-Columbian civilizations of the Americas. Decorative arts from all ages include glassware, silverware, porcelain, lace, and tapestries. There are also religious sculptures and stained glass.

The **Musée Royal de l'Armée et d'Histoire Militaire** deals with all aspects of Belgium's military history. There are new sections on both World Wars, as well as a separate hall containing historic aircraft.

Housed in the south wing of the Cinquantenaire Palace, **Autoworld** has one of the best collections of auto-mobiles in the world.

Part formal gardens, part tree-lined walks, the Cinquantenaire park is popular with Brussels' Eurocrats and families at lunchtimes and weekends.

Musée Horta ⑪

Rue Américaine 23–25. ☎ 02-543 0490. 🚌 54. 🚊 81, 82, 91, 92. Ⓜ Albert, Louise. ◯ 2–5:30pm Tue–Sun. ◉ public hols.

ARCHITECT Victor Horta (1861–1947) is considered by many to be the father of Art Nouveau, and his impact on Brussels architecture is unrivaled by any other designer of his time. A museum dedicated to his

Elegant Art Nouveau staircase at the Musée Horta

unique style is today housed in his restored family home, to the southwest of the city. Horta himself designed the house, between 1898 and 1901. The airy interior of the building displays trademarks of the architect's style – iron, glass, and curves – in every detail, while retaining a functional approach. Most impressive are the dining room, with its ornate ceiling featuring scrolled metalwork, and the central staircase. Decorated with curved wrought iron, the stairs are enhanced further by mirrors and glass, bringing natural light into the house.

Bruparck ⑫

Boulevard du Centenaire. ☎ 02-474 8377. 🚌 84, 89. 🚊 23, 81. Ⓜ Heysel. **Mini-Europe** ☎ 02-478 0550. ◯ daily. 🅿 **Océade** ☎ 02-478 4944. ◯ daily. 🅿 **Kinepolis** ☎ 02-474 2600. ◯ for performances only. **Atomium** ☎ 02-475 4777. ◯ daily. 🅿 🍴 🖥 🛈

LOCATED ON the outskirts of the city, this theme park is popular with families. The most visited attraction is **Mini-Europe**, which has over 300 miniature reconstructions (built at a scale of 1:25) of Europe's major sights, from Athens' Acropolis to London's Houses of Parliament.

For film fans, **Kinepolis** has 29 cinemas, including an IMAX cinema with a semi-circular 600-sq m (6,456-sq ft) screen.

If warmth and relaxation are what you are looking for, **Océade** is a tropically heated water park that features giant slides, wave machines, and even artificial sandy beaches.

Towering over Bruparck is Brussels' most distinctive landmark, the **Atomium**. Designed by André Waterkeyn for the 1958 World's Fair, represents an atom of iron magnified 165 billion times, the structure has a viewing platform at the top.

The Atomium, rising 100 m (325 ft) over the Bruparck

Bronze statue of Silvius Brabo in Antwerp's Grote Markt

Antwerp ❷

🏃 500,000. ✈ 🚇 🚌 🛈 15 Grote Markt (03-232 0103).
🌐 www.visitantwerpen.be

IN THE MIDDLE AGES Antwerp was a thriving hub of the European cloth trade, and the principal port of the Duchy of Brabant. Today, it is the main city of Flemish-speaking Belgium, and the center of the international diamond trade.

At the heart of the city's old medieval district is the Grote Markt. The Brabo Fountain, at its center, has a statue of the soldier Silvius Brabo, said to be the nephew of Julius Caesar. The square is overlooked by the ornately gabled **Stadhuis** (Town Hall), built in 1564, and the Gothic **Onze Lieve Vrouwe Kathedraal** (Cathedral of Our Lady), which dates back to 1352.

Among the paintings inside the cathedral are two triptychs by Antwerp's most famous son, Peter Paul Rubens (1577–1640).

The narrow, winding streets of the old town are lined with fine medieval guildhalls, such as the **Vleeshuis**, or Meat Hall, once occupied by the Butchers' Guild. Dating from the early 16th century, it is built in alternate stripes of stone and brick, giving it a streaky bacon-like appearance.

When Rubens died in 1640, he was buried in the family's chapel at the lovely sandstone **Sint Jacobskerk** (1491–1656), also located in the old town.

One of the most prestigious of Antwerp's many museums is the **Koninklijk Museum voor Schone Kunsten**, which houses an impressive collection of ancient and modern art. Works from the 17th century include masterpieces by the "Antwerp Trio" of van Dyck (1599–1641), Jordaens (1593–1678), and Rubens. More modern exhibits include works by the Surrealist René Magritte (1898–1967) and Rik Wouters (1882–1916).

Other museums catering to special interests are the **Diamond Museum**, recently updated and now housed in a large building near to the central station, and the **Museum Plantin-Moretus**, which is devoted to the early years of printing and celebrates the achievements of Antwerp's most successful printer, Christopher Plantin.

Rubenshuis was Rubens' home and studio for the last 30 years of his life. A tour takes you round his living quarters, equiped with period furniture, as well as his studio and the *kunst-kamer*, or art gallery, where he exhibited both his own and other artists' work, and entertained friends and wealthy patrons.

🏛 **Koninklijk Museum voor Schone Kunsten**
Leopold de Waelplaats 1–9. 📞 03-238 7809. 🚋 8. ◯ 10am–5pm Tue–Sun. ● public hols. 🎫 ♿

🏛 **Rubenshuis**
Wapper 9–11. 📞 03-201 1555. 🚌 1, 23, 290. 🚋 4, 8. ◯ 8:30am–4:30pm Tue–Sun. ● public hols. 🎫

Bruges ❸

See pp232–4.

Stone gatehouse of Ghent's medieval Het Gravensteen

Ghent ❹

🏃 228,000. 🚇 🚌 🚋
🛈 Botermarkt 17A, (09-266 5232).
🌐 www.gent.be

THE HEART of Ghent's historic center was built in the 13th and 14th centuries when the city prospered as a result of the cloth trade. The closure of vital canal links in 1648, however, led to a decline in the town's fortunes. In the 18th and 19th centuries Ghent flourished again as a major industrial center.

Dominating the old medieval quarter is the imposing **Het Gravensteen**, or Castle of the Counts. Parts of the castle, once the seat of the Counts of

Jacob Jordaens' joyous *As the Old Sang, the Young Play Pipes* (1638) in the Koninklijk Museum voor Schone Kunsten, Antwerp

The Pacification Hall in Ghent's Stadhuis, with its impressive tiled floor

Flanders, date back to the 12th century, although most parts, including the gate-house, were built later.

Many of Ghent's finest historic buildings are found on Graslei, a picturesque street that borders the river Leie. The street is lined with well-preserved guildhalls dating from the Middle Ages.

The magnificent **St Baafskathedraal** has features representing every phase of the Gothic style. In a small side chapel is one of Europe's most remarkable paintings, Jan van Eyck's *Adoration of the Mystic Lamb* (1432). Opposite the cathedral stands the huge 14th-century **Belfort** (belfry). From the top of the tower you can enjoy splendid views of the city. From here it is a short walk to the **Stadhuis** (Town Hall), whose Pacification Hall was the site of the signing of the Pacification of Ghent (a declaration of the Low Countries' repudiation of Spanish rule) in 1576.

Ghent's largest collection of fine art, covering all periods up to the 20th century, is in the **Museum voor Schone Kunsten**, some 20 minutes' walk southeast of the center. There are works by Rubens and his contemporaries Jacob Jordaens and Anthony van Dyck. Occupying an elegant 18th-century townhouse, the **Museum voor Sierkunst** is a decorative arts museum, with lavishly furnished 17th-, 18th-, and 19th-century period rooms. An extension covers modern design, from Art Nouveau to contemporary works.

♠ Het Gravensteen
Sint-Veerleplein. **[** 09-225 9306.
○ 9am–5:15pm daily. 🖼

🏛 Museum voor Schone Kunsten
Citadelpark. **[** 09-222 1703.
○ Tue–Sun & late 2003–2006 for renovation. 🖼

Waterloo **❺**

🏘 30,000. 🚊 🚌 **ℹ** Chaussée de Bruxelles 218 (02-354 9910).
W www.waterloo.be

THIS SMALL TOWN is most famous for its association with the Battle of Waterloo, which saw Napoleon and his French army defeated by the Duke of Wellington's troops on June 18, 1815. The best place to start a visit here is the **Musée Wellington**, which occupies the inn where Wellington stayed the night before the battle. Its narrow rooms are packed with curios alongside plans and models of the battlefield.

The **Musée de Cires** (Wax-work Museum) has models of soldiers dressed in period uniforms, while the **Eglise St-Joseph** contains dozens of memorial plaques to the British soldiers who died at Waterloo.

For an excellent view over the battlefield, head for the **Butte de Lion**, a 45-m (148-ft) high earthen mound, 3 km (2 miles) south of the town. Next to it is a gallery where Louis Demoulin's fascinating circular painting *Panorama de la Bataille* is displayed.

🏛 Musée Wellington
Chaussée de Bruxelles 147. **[** 02-354 7806. **○** 9:30am–6:30pm daily. 🖼

The Butte de Lion viewed from the battlefield of Waterloo

THE BATTLEFIELDS OF BELGIUM

Belgium's strategic position between France and Germany has long made it the battleground or "cockpit" of Europe. Napoleon's defeat at Waterloo was just one of many major conflicts resolved on Belgian soil. In the early 18th century French expansion under Louis XIV was thwarted here, and more recently Belgium witnessed some of the bloodiest trench warfare of World War I, including the introduction of poison gas at Ypres (Ieper). Today there are several vast graveyards, where the tens of thousands of soldiers who died on the Western Front lie buried.

Aftermath of Passchendaele (Third Battle of Ypres), 1917

Street-by-Street: Bruges ❸

Traditional organ grinder

W ITH GOOD REASON, Bruges is one of the most popular tourist destinations in Belgium. The city owes its preeminent position to the beauty of its historic center, whose winding lanes and picturesque canals are lined with splendid medieval buildings. These are mostly the legacy of the town's heyday as a center of the international cloth trade, which flourished for 200 years from the 13th century. During this golden age, Bruges' merchants lavished their fortunes on fine mansions, churches, and a set of civic buildings of such extravagance that they were the wonder of northern Europe. Today, the streets are well maintained: there are no billboards or high-rises, and traffic is heavily regulated.

View of the River Dijver
A charming introduction to Bruges is provided by the boat trips along the city's canals.

Bus and train stations

Onze Lieve Vrouwekerk
Dating from 1220, the Church of Our Lady employs many styles of architecture and contains a Madonna and Child by Michelangelo.

Hans Memling Museum and St. Janshospitaal
This 12th-century hospital continued to operate until 1976. It contains a well-preserved 15th-century dispensary.

| 0 meters | 10 |
| 0 yards | 100 |

★ **The Markt**
Medieval gabled houses line this 13th-century market square at the heart of Bruges, which still holds a market each Saturday.

VISITORS' CHECKLIST

🏠 117,000. 🚉 Stationsplein.
🚌 Stationsplein, Markt.
ℹ️ Burg 11 (050-44 8686).
W www.brugge.be

Oude Griffie, or Old Recorder's House

Blind Donkey Alley
This tiny alley leads from the Burg to the 18th-century Vismarkt (Fish Market).

BURG

WOLLESTRAAT

ROZENHOEDKAAI

Heilig Bloed Basiliek
(see p234)

DIJVER

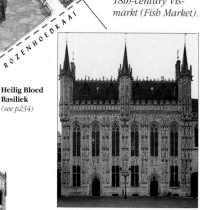

★ **Stadhuis**
One of the oldest and finest town halls in Belgium, this was built between 1376 and 1420. Inside, the beautifully restored Gothic hall is noted for its 1385 vaulted ceiling.

Groeninge Museum
(see p234)

The Arentshuis Museum
has a display of antique lace, and paintings by Frank Brangwyn (1867–1956).

Gruuthuse Museum
(see p234)

The Belfort
Built in the 13th century, the Belfort, or Belfry, is a stunning octagonal tower where the city's medieval charter of rights is held.

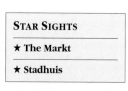

KEY

– – – Suggested route

STAR SIGHTS

★ **The Markt**

★ **Stadhuis**

🏛 Groeninge Museum

Dijver 12. ☏ 050-44 8711.
🕙 9:30am–5pm Tue–Sun. ● Jan 1,
Dec 25. 📷

Bruges' premier fine art
museum holds a superb
collection of early Flemish
and Dutch masters. Artists
featured include Rogier van
der Weyden (c.1400–1464),
Jan van Eyck (d.1441), and
Hans Memling (c.1430–94).
Van Eyck's *Virgin and Child
with Canon* (1436), a richly
detailed painting noted for
its realism, and Memling's
Moreel triptych (1484) are
among the museum's most
outstanding exhibits. Painted
in the early 16th century, the
Last Judgment triptych is one
of a number of works at the
museum by Hieronymus
Bosch (c.1450–1516). Peter
Brueghel the Younger (1564–
1638) is also well represented.
Later Belgian works include
paintings by Surrealists Paul
Delvaux (1897–1994) and
René Magritte (1898–1967).

**Panel of Hans Memling's *Moreel*
triptych in the Groeninge Museum**

today contain a collection
of fine and applied arts. The
exhibits range from wood
carvings, tapestries, porcelain,
and ceramics, to medical
instruments and weaponry.
The authentic kitchen and
beautiful oak-paneled chapel
(1472) transport visitors
back to medieval times.

🔓 Heilig Bloed Basiliek

Burg 10. ☏ 050-33 6792. 🕙 daily.
Museum ● Mon, Wed pm (in winter).

The Basilica of the Holy Blood
is Bruges' holiest church,
holding one of the most sacred
relics in Europe. In the upper
chapel, rebuilt after it was
destroyed by the French in
the 1790s, is a 17th-century
tabernacle, which houses a
phial said to contain a few
drops of blood and water
washed from the body of
Christ by Joseph of Arimathea.

**Fifteenth-century oak-paneled
chapel in the Gruuthuse Museum**

🏛 Gruuthuse Museum

Dijver 17. ☏ 050-44 8762.
🕙 9:30am–5pm Tue–Sun. ● Jan 1,
Dec 25. 📷

The Gruuthuse Museum
occupies a large medieval
mansion close to the Dijver
Canal. In the 15th century it
was inhabited by a merchant
(the Lord of the Gruuthuse),
who had the exclusive right
to levy a tax on "gruit," an
imported mixture of herbs
added to barley during the
beer-brewing process. The
mansion's labyrinthine rooms,
with their ancient chimney-
pieces and wooden beams,
have survived intact, and

🏨 Begijnhof

Wijngaardplein 1. ☏ 050-33 0011.
🕙 daily.

Béguines were members of a
lay sisterhood founded in
1245, who did not take vows,
but led a devout life. The
begijnhof, or *béguinage*, is
the walled complex in a town
that housed the Béguines. In
Bruges this is an area of quiet
tree-lined canals edged by
white, gabled houses. Visitors
can enjoy a stroll here and
visit the simple church, built
in 1602. One of the houses,
now occupied by Benedictine
nuns, is open to the public.

🏛 Brugse Brouwerij-Mouterijmuseum

Verbrand Nieuwland 10. ☏ 050-33
0699. 🕙 10:30am–5:30pm daily.
● Mon, Tue. 📷

Before World War I there
were 31 breweries operating
in Bruges. On display at this
museum, northeast of the
Markt, are documents and
artifacts that tell the story of
beer and brewing in the city.
Next door, De Gouden Boom
is a working brewery, founded
in 1584. It produces the spicy
wheat beer (known as *bière
blanche*), Brugs Tarwebier.

🏛 Museum voor Volkskunde

Rolweg 40. ☏ 050-33 0044.
🕙 9:30am–5pm Tue–Sun.

This excellent folk museum
occupies an attractive terrace
of brick almshouses in the
northeast of the town. Each of
the houses is dedicated to a
different aspect of traditional
Flemish life. Several crafts are
represented, and visitors are
shown a series of typical
historical domestic interiors.

Pretty 17th-century almshouses, home to the Museum voor Volkskunde

Luxembourg

ONE OF EUROPE'S SMALLEST sovereign states, the Grand Duchy of Luxembourg is often overlooked by travelers in Europe. The capital, Luxembourg City, is well known as a world center of international finance, but behind the modern face of the city lies a rich history stretching back over 1,000 years. The northern half of the country boasts some spectacular scenery, especially the Ardennes, a region of dense forests, deep valleys, and hilltop castles. Historic towns such as Vianden and Echternach are good bases for exploring the countryside and offer plenty of opportunities for outdoor activities.

View of Luxembourg City with its aqueduct and hilltop historic center

Luxembourg City

82,000. 6 km (4 miles) E. Place d'Armes (22 28 09). www.luxembourg-city.lu/touristinfo

LUXEMBOURG CITY enjoys a dramatic location, set atop hills and cliffs rising above the Alzette and Pétrusse valleys. The town grew up around a castle, built on a rocky promontory known as the Rocher du Bock in AD 963. The castle was destroyed in the late 19th century by the city's inhabitants, but some of the fortifications have been preserved, most famously the Bock and Pétrusse **Casemates**. These huge networks of under-ground defensive galleries, which date back to the 17th century, not only provided shelter for thousands of soldiers, but also housed workshops, kitchens, bakeries, and slaughterhouses. The **Crypte Archéologique du Bock**, currently closed for renovation, has displays on the history of the city's fortifications.

Luxembourg City's **Palais Grand Ducal** has been the official royal residence since 1890. The oldest parts of the building, which used to be the town hall, date from the latter half of the 16th century. Nearby, the **Cathédrale Notre-Dame** was begun in 1613. Inside is a fine Baroque organ gallery by Daniel Muller.

Two museums worth visiting are the **Musée National d'Art et d'Histoire**, which has a good archaeological section and a collection of ancient and modern sculpture and paintings, and the **Musée de l'Histoire de la Ville de Luxembourg**, which focuses on the city's historical past.

♣ Casemates
Bock Casemates Montée de Clausen. ☐ Mar–Oct: 10am–5pm.
Pétrusse Casemates Place de la Constitution. ☐ Easter, Whitsun, & Jul–Sep: 11am–4pm.

⌂ Musée National d'Art et d'Histoire
Place Marché aux Poissons.
47 93 301. ☐ 10am–5pm Tue–Sun.

Vianden

1,600. 1a Rue du Vieux Marché (83 42 57). **Château de Vianden** 84 92 91. ☐ Apr–Sep: 10am–6pm; Oct, Mar: 10am–5pm; Nov–Feb: 10am–4pm. ● Sat in winter.

SURROUNDED BY medieval ramparts, Vianden, in the Luxembourg Ardennes, is a popular tourist destination. The main attraction is the 11th-century **Château de Vianden**. Its rooms feature a range of architectural styles, from the Romanesque to the Renaissance. A cable car takes visitors to the top of a nearby hill, giving superb views of the castle.

Echternach

4,000. Porte St-Willibrord (72 02 30). **Abbey Basilica** ☐ daily. **Abbey Museum** ☐ Apr–Oct: 10am–noon, 2–5pm daily. www.mullerthal.lu

LOCATED IN Petite Suisse (Little Switzerland), a picturesque region of wooded hills northeast of the capital, Echternach is dotted with fine medieval buildings, including the 15th-century turreted **Town Hall**. The star sight, however, is the **Benedictine abbey**, founded by St. Willibrord in the 7th century. The crypt of the abbey basilica (c.900) contains some glorious frescoes. There are excellent walks and cycle routes in the surrounding countryside.

Medieval Town Hall in the Place du Marché, Echternach

Practical & Travel Information

VISITORS TO BELGIUM AND LUXEMBOURG can expect high levels of service and comfort in all aspects of their stay. Public transportation is clean and efficient, and there are abundant tourist information facilities, in addition to all the other modern conveniences one expects of a highly developed country. Brussels and Luxembourg City are among the safest capital cities in Europe and, due to their small size, can be easily explored on foot.

TOURIST INFORMATION

IN BELGIUM, the **Tourist and Information Office of Brussels** publishes maps and guides, and also offers a Brussels Card. This "tourist passport" includes a three-day pass to all public transport in the Brussels region, combined with unlimited access to 30 museums.

Luxembourg's **National Tourist Office** is located in the train station in the capital. It sells the Luxembourg Card, which gives unlimited travel on public transport nationwide, as well as admission to over 30 sites of interest, and reductions on many others. The card, which is valid for one, two, or three days between Easter and October, can also be bought at hotels, campsites, youth hostels, and train and bus stations.

Local tourist information offices can be found in most towns and villages throughout Belgium and Luxembourg.

OPENING HOURS

MOST SHOPS and businesses in Belgium and Luxembourg are open from 10am until 5 or 6pm Monday to Saturday, with some local shops closing for an hour at lunch. Some stores open at noon on Mondays. In the major cities and towns many shops are open on Sundays and until later in the evening.

In both countries most museums are closed on Mondays. Outside the high season (April to September), be prepared to find many sights of interest closed.

VISA REQUIREMENTS

CITIZENS OF the EU, US, Australia, New Zealand, and Canada do not require a visa to enter either Belgium or Luxembourg, but must present a valid passport and hold proof of onward passage. Bear in mind that in Belgium it is a legal requirement to carry ID on one's person at all times.

SAFETY AND EMERGENCIES

BELGIUM AND Luxembourg are safe countries, with street crime against visitors a relatively rare occurrence. However, in Brussels it is inadvisable to wander alone at night in the poorer areas to the west and north of the city center, and in the city's parks, especially at Botanique.

In case of emergencies, the numbers to call are listed in the Directory opposite.

LANGUAGE

THE TWO PRINCIPAL languages of Belgium are Dutch, spoken in Flanders, and French, the language of the Wallonians. There is also a German-speaking enclave in the far east of the country. In the capital both languages are used on all street signs and in place names.

Luxembourg has three official languages: French, German, and Letzeburgesch, or Luxembourgeois. In both Belgium and Luxembourg, especially in the capital cities, many people speak English.

BANKING AND CURRENCY

BOTH BELGIUM and Luxembourg have replaced their traditional currencies, the Belgian franc and the Luxembourg franc, with the Euro. On January 1, 2002, Euro notes and coins came into general circulation and these can be used anywhere inside the participating member states (*see p15*).

Banking hours are from 9am to 4pm in Belgium and 9am to 4.30pm in Luxembourg. In both countries most of the banks close for an hour at lunch-time, and some of the city branches open on Saturday mornings.

COMMUNICATIONS

BELGIAN POST offices are open from 9am to 5pm Monday to Friday. In Luxembourg the hours are 9am to noon and 1.30pm to 5pm Monday to Friday. Some larger branches open on Saturday mornings.

Many public payphones in Belgium and Luxembourg accept only phonecards, available at newsagents and post offices. In Brussels you can use cash in the phone booths in metro stations. There are no local area codes in Luxembourg.

THE CLIMATE OF BELGIUM AND LUXEMBOURG

Belgium and Luxembourg have a temperate climate, characterized by constant low rainfall throughout the year. Winters are usually chilly and damp, and rain may turn to snow or sleet. Summers are warmer and much brighter, but the evenings can still be cool. Spring is the driest season.

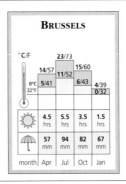

BRUSSELS

°C/F			
	23/73		
	14/57	15/60	
0°C 5/41	11/52	6/43	4/39
32°F			0/32

☀	4.5 hrs	5.5 hrs	3.5 hrs	1.5 hrs
☂	57 mm	94 mm	82 mm	67 mm
month	Apr	Jul	Oct	Jan

ARRIVING BY AIR

Belgium's PRINCIPAL airport is Brussels National Airport, known locally as Zaventem. Flights into Luxembourg arrive at Findel Airport, 6 km (4 miles) east of Luxembourg City.

Airlines flying to Belgium and Luxembourg include **SN Brussels Airlines** (Belgium) and **Luxair** (Luxembourg), British Airways, American Airlines, KLM, and Lufthansa. Brussels is also served by Air Canada and Delta Air Lines. Most flights from Canada and the US go via another European city. Virgin Express and Ryanair have low-cost flights between Brussels and various European cities.

ARRIVING BY SEA

Belgium CAN BE easily reached by ferry from Britain several times daily. **Norfolkline** has a number of crossings a day between Dover and Dunkirk. **P&O Ferries** also operates regular crossings from Dover to Calais (France) and from Hull to Zeebrugge.

RAIL TRAVEL

Belgium IS AT the heart of Europe's high-speed train networks. **Eurostar** services between Brussels' Gare du Midi and London's Waterloo station take just under three hours. The **Thalys** network links Brussels with Amsterdam, Paris, Cologne, and Geneva.

Within Belgium train services are operated by **Belgian National Railways** (Société Nationale de Chemins de Fer Belges/Belgische Spoorwegen). The network is modern and efficient, and usually the best way to travel between major cities and towns. Luxembourg's rail system is run by **Chemins de Fer Luxembourgeois (CFL)**. In both countries a variety of rail passes is available. The Benelux Tourrail pass allows unlimited travel on any five days within a month's period in Belgium, Luxembourg, and the Netherlands.

TRAVELING BY BUS

In BELGIUM THE TWO main long-distance bus operators are **De Lijn**, which covers routes in Flanders, and **TEC**, which provides services in Wallonia. Bus terminuses are usually close to train stations.

Luxembourg benefits from an extensive bus network, which compensates for the more limited rail system. One-day passes are available, and can be used on both long-distance and inner-city buses from the time of purchase until 8am the next day. Benelux Tourrail passes are valid on buses operated by Chemins de Fer Luxembourgeois.

TRAVELING BY CAR

Drivers FROM the UK can reach mainland Europe by the car train service offered by Eurotunnel. Within Belgium and Luxembourg the freeways and main roads are well-maintained and fast. Variations between the French and Flemish spellings of town names can be confusing for visitor drivers in Belgium; it is advisable to find out both names of your destination before beginning your journey. All the major car rental firms are represented in Belgium and Luxembourg, but renting a vehicle is fairly expensive.

DIRECTORY

TOURIST OFFICES

Belgium
Tourist and Information Office of Brussels, Grand Place 1, 1000 Brussels.
☎ 02-513 8940.
w www.
belgium-tourism.net

Luxembourg
National Tourist Office, Gare Centrale, Luxembourg City.
☎ 42 82 82 20.

UK
Belgian Tourist Office, 225 March Wall, London E14 9FJ
☎ 0906 550 8919.
☎ 0800 954 5245.

Luxembourg Tourist Office, 122–124 Regent Street, London W1B 5SA.
☎ 020-7434 2800.
w www.luxembourg.co.uk

US
Belgian Tourist Office, 780 3rd Ave, Suite 1501, New York, NY 10017–7076.
☎ 212-758 8130.

Luxembourg Tourist Office, 17 Beekman Place, New York, NY 10022.
☎ 212-935 8888.

EMBASSIES

UK (Belgium)
Rue Arlon 85, B-1040 Brussels.
☎ 02-287 6211.

UK (Luxembourg)
14 Blvd Roosevelt, L-2450 Luxembourg City.
☎ 22 98 64.

US (Belgium)
Blvd du Régent 27, B-1000 Brussels.
☎ 02-508 2111.

US (Luxembourg)
22 Blvd Emmanuel Servais, L-2535 Luxembourg City.
☎ 46 01 23.

EMERGENCY NUMBERS

Belgium
Police ☎ 101.
Ambulance and fire services ☎ 100.

Luxembourg
Police ☎ 113.
All other services ☎ 112.

AIRLINES

SN Brussels Airlines
☎ 07-035 1111 (Belgium).
☎ 0207-559 9787 (UK).
☎ 800-955 2000 (US).
w www.flysn.com

Luxair
☎ 4798 4242 (Luxembourg).
w www.luxair.lu

FERRY COMPANIES

Norfolkline
☎ 0870-870 1020 (UK).

P&O Ferries
☎ 0870-600 0600 (UK).

RAIL TRAVEL

Belgian National Railways
☎ 02-528 2828.

Chemins de Fer Luxembourgeois
☎ 49 90 49 90.

Eurostar
☎ 0870-518 6186 (UK).
☎ 02-528 2828 (Belgium).

Thalys
☎ 07-066 7788 (Belgium).

BUSES

De Lijn
☎ 01-544 0711.

TEC
☎ 01-023 5353.

Shopping & Entertainment

BELGIUM IS AN IDEAL PLACE to shop for luxury goods, from fine chocolates and cutting-edge fashion to mounted diamonds. As a virtually duty-free zone, Luxembourg attracts tourists in search of cheap cigarettes and alcohol. For relatively small cities, Brussels and Luxembourg City offer a wide range of cultural events. Those who prefer outdoor activities will find plenty to entertain them. The flat Flanders region in Belgium is ideal cycling country, while the hilly Ardennes and the Petite Suisse area of Luxembourg are popular with hikers.

WHERE TO SHOP

FOR LUXURY ITEMS and gifts, one of Brussels' best shopping arcades is the **Galéries Saint-Hubert**. It houses several jewelry stores, the Belgian leather bag maker Delvaux, fine chocolate shops, and smart boutiques, including women's fashion designer Kaat Tilley. The **Galéries d'Ixelles** is full of tiny ethnic shops and cafés, while the quaint **Galérie Bortier** is the place to shop for antiquarian books and maps.

Top fashion designers are well represented in Brussels. Their outlets can be found on Avenue Louise and Boulevard de Waterloo. For the original creations of the Antwerp Six and of new wave designers, try Rue Antoine Dansaert.

Less expensive, mainstream stores, including Belgium's only department store Inno, are located in the Rue Neuve. Inno is not spectacular by British or American standards.

The principal shopping areas in Luxembourg City are the Grand Rue and its side streets, and the Auchan shopping center which is found on Kirchberg.

WHAT TO BUY

BELGIAN CHOCOLATE is considered by many to be the finest in the world. Among the internationally renowned *"grandes maisons de chocolat"* with stores in Brussels are **Godiva** and **Wittamer**. The sweet-toothed will also be tempted by the edible chocolate sculptures produced by **Pierre Marcolini** and by the wares of fine biscuit specialist **Dandoy**.

Another famous Belgian export is lace, though a fall in the number of people entering the trade in recent years has resulted in a shortage of authentic, handmade goods. Before purchasing an item, make sure it has not been manufactured in the Far East. Places to shop for authentic Belgian lace include **Maison F. Rubbrecht** in Brussels and the **Gruuthuse Lace Shop** in Bruges. The latter is especially good for antique pieces.

Specialty Belgian beers can be bought at Brussels' **Beer Mania**, while **Little Nemo** and **La Bande des Six Nez** specialize in comic-strip memorabilia. If you plan to invest in diamonds, or simply wish to gaze and admire, **Diamondland** in Antwerp is a good place to start.

Among the best buys in Luxembourg are fuel, tobacco, and alcohol, due to the low rate of duty imposed on such goods. One of the country's most famous manufacturing names is **Villeroy & Boch**, makers of fine porcelain and tableware. Their flagship store is in the Rue du Fossé in the capital. There is also a factory outlet northwest of the city center where you can buy seconds at 20 percent discount.

MARKETS

FROM 9AM ON Saturdays and Sundays, Brussels' Place du Grand Sablon is the site of a fine antiques market. Also worth visiting is the huge, vibrant market around the Gare du Midi (Sundays, 6am to 1pm), with its mix of North African and home-grown delicacies, including oils, spices, and exotic herbs.

BOOKSTORES

IN BRUSSELS, **Waterstone's** sells English-language magazines and books. For international newspapers, go to the **Librairie de Rome**.

English-language books and newspapers can be bought in Luxembourg City at the **Magasin Anglais**.

ENTERTAINMENT LISTINGS

THE PRINCIPAL source of entertainment information in Belgium is *The Bulletin*, published weekly in English, and available from news-stands throughout the country. The magazine's listings section, *What's On*, is distributed free to hotels in the capital.

Details of events in Luxembourg are published in the "Culture" section of *L'Agenda du Luxembourg*, available from the National Tourist Office.

OPERA, CLASSICAL MUSIC, AND DANCE

BRUSSELS' OPERA HOUSE, **La Monnaie**, is among Europe's finest venues for opera. The season runs from September to June, and most productions are sold out many months in advance.

Designed by Victor Horta in 1928, the **Palais des Beaux-Arts** is home to the Belgian National Orchestra and boasts the city's largest auditorium for classical music. The main concert season lasts from September to June.

Regular performances of contemporary dance by several leading Belgian companies take place at the Art Deco **Kaaitheater** and the **Halles de Schaerbeek**.

Luxembourg's Printemps Musical is a festival of classical music concerts and ballet that takes place in the capital throughout April and May. Principal venues include the **Conservatoire de Musique de la Ville de Luxembourg** and the **Théâtre Municipal**. The City Tourist Information Office on the Place d'Armes is able to provide more information and assist with ticket reservations.

JAZZ, ROCK, AND BLUES

ONE OF THE BEST places to catch good jazz acts in Brussels is **Sounds**, a large venue featuring some of Belgium's top artists. The club also has Blues nights. On Saturday and Sunday afternoons, it is worth stopping at **L'Archiduc**, a refurbished Art Deco bar in the center of town, where you can listen to jazz in a relaxed atmosphere. **Ancienne Belgique** hosts up-and-coming guitar bands, folk, Latin, and techno acts.

CINEMA

AT BRUSSELS' Bruparck (*see p229*), the 29-screen Kinepolis cinema complex shows Hollywood block-busters and major British and French releases. Real movie fans should not miss a visit to the Musée du Cinéma in the Palais des Beaux-Arts complex. The museum shows classic films, from Chaplin to Taran-tino, with nightly programs of silent movies sometimes with a live piano accompaniment.

OUTDOOR ACTIVITIES

BELGIUM AND Luxembourg have extensive networks of cycle tracks, and you can rent bicycles easily from a number of outlets, including many train stations. For route details the best source of information is the local tourist information office. The US-based **CBT Tours** organizes cycle tours in Belgium.

Tourist offices throughout Belgium and Luxembourg also offer walking guides and maps. To arrange hiking tours in the popular Ardennes area, contact Belgium-based **TQ3**.

In Luxembourg, the lake at Echternach offers plenty of opportunities for swimming, sailing, and windsurfing, while the rivers of the Ardennes region are fine territory for canoeing and kayaking. To obtain further information on the latter, contact the **Fédération Luxembourge-oise de Canoë-Kayak**. For information on the whole range of sporting activities available contact the **City Tourist Office**.

Where to Stay: Belgium & Luxembourg

IN BOTH BELGIUM AND LUXEMBOURG, hotels at the top end of the market offer exceptional standards of comfort and convenience to their largely corporate clients, and their prices reflect this. However, some offer substantial discounts at weekends and during the summer months, and there are also plenty of mid-range family-run and chain establishments for those on a more modest budget.

Brussels

Hotel	Number of Rooms	Private Parking	Restaurant	Weekend Discounts
Lower Town: *Windsor* €€ Place Rouppe 13, 1000. **Map** B3. Tel *02-511 2014.* Fax *02-514 0942.* A cheerful, clean hotel, located about 15 minutes' walk from the city center. The hotel is proof positive that staying in Brussels need not be expensive.	35			■
Lower Town: *Arenberg NH* €€€ Rue d'Assaut 15, 1000. **Map** C3. Tel *02-501 1616.* Fax *02-501 1818.* @ nh-hotels@nh-hotels.be The decor of some of the rooms in this charming hotel, located on a quiet street, is loosely inspired by Belgium's classic cartoon heroes.	155	■	●	■
Lower Town: *Aris* €€€ Rue du Marché-aux-Herbes 78–80, 1000. **Map** C3. Tel *02-514 4300.* Fax *02-514 0119.* W www.arishotel.be This comfortable and efficient hotel, located right next to the Grand Place, is ideal for families, as it offers duplex rooms for four people at very reasonable rates. Breakfast is included in the price.	55			■
Lower Town: *Art Hotel Siru* €€€ Place Rogier 1, 1210. **Map** C2. Tel *02-203 3580.* Fax *02-203 3303.* @ art.hotel.siru@skynet. be W www.comforthotelssiru.com The Siru was refurbished in the late 1980s. Over 100 Belgian artists contributed to the decoration of the hotel's splendid private and public rooms.	101		●	
Lower Town: *Crowne Plaza* €€€ Rue Gineste 3, 1210. **Map** C2. Tel *02-203 6200.* Fax *02-203 4011.* W www.crowneplaza.com Revamped in 1998, this hotel combines period elegance with all the convenience of modern facilities.	356		●	■
Lower Town: *Amigo* €€€€€ Rue de l'Amigo 1–3, 1000. **Map** B3. Tel *02-547 4747.* Fax *02-513 5277.* W www.hotelamigo.com A six-story hotel, with luxuriously decorated rooms, superb facilities, and friendly service. The price includes breakfast.	174	■	●	■
Upper Town: *Argus* €€ Rue Capitaine Crespel 6, 1050. **Map** C4. Tel *02-514 0770.* Fax *02-514 1222.* W www.hotel-argus.be The rooms at this quiet hotel are clean and comfortable. Prices drop considerably at weekends and throughout July and August.	41	■		■
Upper Town: *Sabina* €€ Rue du Nord 78, 1000. **Map** D2. Tel *02-218 2637.* Fax *02-219 3239.* W www.hotelsabina.be A friendly, well-kept hotel, occupying an elegant 19th-century building. Inside, wood panelling and fireplaces add to the cozy atmosphere.	24	■		■
Upper Town: *Hilton* €€€€ Boulevard de Waterloo 38, 1000. **Map** C4. Tel *02-504 1111.* Fax *02-504 2111.* W www.hilton.com The Hilton offers large, comfortable rooms, Michelin-star restaurant, and a range of services, including a fitness center.	434	■	●	■
Upper Town: *Le Sablon* €€€€ Rue de la Paille 2–8, 1000. **Map** C4. Tel *02-513 6040.* Fax *02-511 8141.* W www.hotellesablon.be Behind the late 19th-century façade is a light, contemporary interior. The hotel has its own sauna.	32			■
Upper Town: *Astoria* €€€€€ Rue Royale 103, 1000. **Map** C3. Tel *02-227 0505.* Fax *02-217 1150.* W www.sofitel.com This opulent Belle Epoque hotel recalls Brussels' glory days of the early 20th century. Rooms are double-glazed to keep out traffic noise.	118	■	●	■

Map references refer to map of Brussels on pp222–3

Average prices for a double room, including service. € under €60 €€ €60–110 €€€ €110–175 €€€€ €175–250 €€€€€ over €250	**PRIVATE PARKING** Parking provided in a private car park or private garage. Some hotels charge for use of private parking facilities. **RESTAURANT** Hotel has a dining room or restaurant serving lunch and/or dinner for guests. **WEEKEND DISCOUNTS** Substantial reductions in the room rate at weekends.	NUMBER OF ROOMS	PRIVATE PARKING	RESTAURANT	WEEKEND DISCOUNTS

REST OF BELGIUM

ANTWERP: *Firean* €€€ Karel Oomsstraat 6, 2018 Antwerp. (03-237 0260. FAX 03-238 1168. W www.firean.com A small, family-run hotel with a warm atmosphere. Although it is not centrally located, trams run from outside the hotel to the city center. 🚗 TV 🗄 🌿	15	■	●	
ANTWERP: *Hilton* €€€€€ Groenplaats, 2000 Antwerp. (03-204 1212. FAX 03-204 1213. W www.antwerp.hilton.com Situated in the heart of the old town, the Hilton has large, well-equipped rooms. Facilities include two restaurants, a sauna, and a solarium. 🚗 TV 🗄 ♿ 🌿	211		●	■
BRUGES: *de Pauw* €€ Sint-Gilliskerkhof 8, 8000 Bruges. (050-33 7118. FAX 050-34 5140. W www.hoteldepauw.be The de Pauw is a family-run hotel, offering great value for money and warm, friendly service. All the rooms have their own bathroom and a TV. 🌿	8	■		
BRUGES: *'t Bourgoensch Hof* €€€ Wollestraat 39, 8000 Bruges. (050-33 1645. FAX 050-34 6378. W www.bourgoensch-hof.be The rooms at this cozy hotel are decorated in Flemish style, and some have views of the canal. There is a very good restaurant. 🚗 TV 🌿	22	■	●	
BRUGES: *Hotel de Tuilerieen* €€€€€ Dijver 7, 8000 Bruges. (050-34 3691. FAX 050-34 0400. W www.hoteltuilerieen.com This canalside hotel occupies a beautiful 15th-century mansion, close to some of the city's best museums. Room rates vary considerably. 🚗 TV 🗄 ♨ ♿ 🌿	45	■		
GHENT: *Erasmus* €€ Poel 25, 9000 Ghent. (09-224 2195. FAX 09-233 4241. @ hotel.erasmus@proximedia.be An immaculate family-run hotel with a lovely wood-beamed lounge and rooms with stone fireplaces. There is also a small private garden. 🚗 TV 🌿	11			
GHENT: *Gravensteen* €€€ Jan Breydelstraat 35, 9000 Ghent. (09-225 1150. FAX 09-225 1850. W www.gravensteen.be Housed in a 19th-century mansion, the Gravensteen has been refurbished in the Second Empire style. 🚗 TV 🌿	49	■		■

LUXEMBOURG

ECHTERNACH: *Saint Hubert* €€ 21 Rue de la Gare, L-6440 Echternach. (72 03 06. FAX 72 87 72. W www.hotelst-hubert.lu The Saint Hubert is in a pedestrian zone in the town center. Rooms are simple but comfortable, and the restaurant serves tasty French fare. 🚗 TV 🌿	18	■	●	
LUXEMBOURG CITY: *Parc Belle-Vue* €€ 5 Avenue Marie-Thérèse, L-2132. (45 61 41 1. FAX 45 61 41 222. @ bellevue@hpb.lu This family-run hotel has splendid views of the Pétrusse Valley and city fortifications. Suites are available and there is a lovely garden. 🚗 TV 🌿	58	■		■
LUXEMBOURG CITY: *Grand Hôtel Cravat* €€€€ 29 Boulevard Roosevelt, L-2450. (22 19 75. FAX 22 67 11. @ contact@hotelcravat.lu All the rooms at the Grand Hôtel Cravat are beautifully furnished and equipped with a full range of modern conveniences. 🚗 TV 🌿	60		●	■
LUXEMBOURG CITY: *Le Royal* €€€€€ 12 Boulevard Royal, L-2449. (241 61 61. FAX 22 59 48. W www.hotelroyal.lu Choose from a range of rooms and suites at this luxurious hotel. The superb facilities include an indoor pool, a sauna, and a health center. 🚗 TV 🗄 ♿ 🌿	210	■	●	■
VIANDEN: *Heintz* € 55 Grand Rue, L-9410 Vianden. (83 41 55. FAX 83 45 59. W www.hotel-heintz.lu Housed in a former monastery, the Heintz combines antique furnishings with modern comforts. ● *Easter, mid-Nov–Apr.* 🚗 TV 🌿	26	■	●	■

Where to Eat: Belgium & Luxembourg

B ELGIANS LOVE FOOD, and the quality of their cooking reflects this. The top gastronomic restaurants are concentrated in Brussels, where it is said that it is impossible to eat badly, but everywhere you can find unpretentious establishments offering generous servings of local specialities. Luxembourg has its fair share of haute-cuisine restaurants, many of which offer a good-value set meal at lunchtime.

	FIXED-PRICE MENU	OUTDOOR TABLES	VEGETARIAN DISHES

BRUSSELS

	FIXED-PRICE MENU	OUTDOOR TABLES	VEGETARIAN DISHES
LOWER TOWN: *Brasserie Horta* € Rue des Sables 20. **Map** C2. **[** 02-217 7271. The restaurant at the Centre Belge de la Bande Dessinée *(see p226)* serves cheap, hearty portions of old Belgian favorites, such as spicy Marolles-style meatballs, beef stewed in beer, and homemade *frites*. **●** evenings. **[&] [✉]**	■	●	■
LOWER TOWN: *Chez Léon* € Rue des Bouchers 18. **Map** C3. **[** 02-513 0426. **[W]** www.chezleon.be A casual eatery near the Grand Place, offering a wide range of *moules-frites* (mussels and fries) dishes at great prices. Children under 12 eat free. **[✉]**	■	●	■
LOWER TOWN: *Chez Patrick* €€ Rue des Chapeliers 6. **Map** C3. **[** 02-511 9815. Favorites at this family-run eatery are *choucroute* (cabbage and sausage hotpot) or chicken *waterzooi* (boiled chicken in a creamy sauce). **●** Sun & Mon. **[&] [✉]**		●	
LOWER TOWN: *La Roue d'Or* €€€ Rue des Chapeliers 26. **Map** C3. **[** 02-514 2554. The menu at this upscale Art Nouveau brasserie blends Belgian and French cuisine. Try pig's trotter vinaigrette or snails in garlic butter. **●** mid-Jul–mid-Aug. **[✉]**	■		
LOWER TOWN: *La Truite d'Argent* €€€ Quai au Bois à Brûler 23. **Map** B2. **[** 02-219 9546. The fresh, inventive cuisine at this intimate fish restaurant includes millefeuille of salmon and five different preparations of lobster. **●** lunch Sat, Sun. **[✉]**	■	●	
LOWER TOWN: *L'Ogenblik* €€€€ Galerie des Princes 1. **Map** C3. **[** 02-511 6151. **[W]** www.ogenblik.resto.be This French restaurant serves creative dishes, including sea bass with eggplant caviar and calf sweetbreads with cheese-topped zucchini. Draws a local crowd. **●** Sun. **[✉]**			■
LOWER TOWN: *Comme Chez Soi* €€€€€ Place Rouppe 23. **Map** B3. **[** 02-512 2921. **[W]** www.commechezsoi.be Unquestionably Brussels' best restaurant, achieving three Michelin stars. The game, *foie gras*, and caviar are superlative, as is the Art Nouveau decor. Tables must be reserved weeks in advance. **●** Sun & Mon. **[✉]**	■		
UPPER TOWN: *Entrée des Artistes* €€ Place du Grand Sablon 42. **Map** C4. **[** 02-502 3161. This unassumingly trendy brasserie has a French menu, featuring dishes such as toast with mushrooms, salmon steaks, and lobster. **[✉]**	■	●	■
UPPER TOWN: *Au Vieux Saint-Martin* €€€ Place du Grand Sablon 38. **Map** C3. **[** 02-512 6476. A professional establishment on the elegant Sablon, with crisp modern decor, and swift, courteous waiters. The menu features regional specialities. **[✉]**		●	
UPPER TOWN: *La Porte des Indes* €€€ Avenue Louise 455. **Map** C4. **[** 02-647 8651. An upscale Indian restaurant serving traditional cuisine from around the sub-continent. The "Brass Plate" menu allows you to try several dishes. **●** lunch, Sun. **[✉]**	■		■
GREATER BRUSSELS: *Le Sésame* € Rue Defacqz 7. **[** 02-647 5181. An excellent restaurant, specializing in refined Algerian cooking at reasonable prices. Informal but attentive service. **[&] [✉]**			■
GREATER BRUSSELS: *Shanti* €€ Avenue A. Buyl 68. **[** 02-649 4096. This popular vegetarian restaurant in the Ixelles district offers a relaxed setting, with classical music at lunchtime and jazz in the evening. **●** Sun & Mon. **[✉]**	■		■

Map references refer to map of Brussels on pp222–3

Price categories for a three-course meal for one, including cover charge, service, and half a bottle of wine or other drinks:

€ under €25
€€ €25–40
€€€ €40–50
€€€€ €50–60
€€€€€ over €60

FIXED-PRICE MENU
A good-value fixed-price menu on offer at lunch, dinner, or both, usually with three courses.

VEGETARIAN DISHES
Restaurant serves a selection of dishes suitable for vegetarian diners.

	FIXED-PRICE MENU	OUTDOOR TABLES	VEGETARIAN DISHES

REST OF BELGIUM

		FIXED-PRICE MENU	OUTDOOR TABLES	VEGETARIAN DISHES
ANTWERP: *'t Zolderke* Hoofdkerkstraat 7, Antwerp. 03-233 8427. The menu at this light and airy French restaurant features old classics such as steak in peppercorn or bearnaise sauce with fries. ● *lunch weekdays.* 🌿	€€	■		■
ANTWERP: *De Matelote* Haarstraat 9, Antwerp. 03-231 3207. Located in the old town, De Matelote is reputed to be Antwerp's best fish restaurant, with a varied menu. Reservations essential. ● *Sun, Mon.* 🌿	€€€€€	■		
BRUGES: *Den Dyver* Dijver 5, Bruges. 050-33 60 69. This excellent restaurant, located close to the Markt, specializes in Flemish dishes cooked in beer. ● *Wed, lunch Thu.* 🌿	€€€	■	●	■
BRUGES: *de Karmeliet* Langestraat 19, Bruges. 050-33 8259. Impeccable service, lavish surroundings, and exquisite Belgian/French cuisine have earned de Karmeliet three Michelin stars. ● *dinner Sun, lunch Mon; Jun–Sep: Sun, Mon; Jan, last 2 weeks Aug* 🌿	€€€€	■	●	■
BRUGES: *'t Bourgoensche Cruyce* Wollestraat 41, Bruges. 050-33 79 26. If you want a romantic meal, the canalside 't Bourgoensche Cruyce is the place to go. The perfect setting is matched by superior cuisine. The seafood dishes are especially recommended. ● *Tues, Wed; 1st week Jul.* 🌿	€€€€	■		■
GHENT: *Pakhuis* Schuurkensstraat 4, Ghent. 09-223 5555. This popular brasserie occupies a huge converted warehouse. Its special attractions are the oyster bar and the fresh shellfish served daily. ● *Sun.* 🌿	€€	■		■
GHENT: *'t Buikske Vol* Kraanlei 17, Ghent. 09-225 1880. The trendy Patershol district is home to scores of upscale restaurants, and 't Buikske Vol rates as one of the best. The beautifully prepared dishes range from river fish *waterzooi* to sweetbreads with rabbit. ● *Sun, Wed, lunch Sat.* 🌿	€€€	■		
WATERLOO: *A Côté de* Chaussée de Bruxelles 119, 1410 Waterloo. 02-351 0652. A relaxed, informal establishment that specializes in meat fondues. The restaurant attracts a young crowd. ● *lunch Mon–Sat.* 🌿	€€		●	

LUXEMBOURG

		FIXED-PRICE MENU	OUTDOOR TABLES	VEGETARIAN DISHES
LUXEMBOURG CITY: *Il Riccio* 6 Rue Beaumont. 22 40 82. This relaxed Tuscan restaurant is popular with tourists and locals alike. The tasty dishes are served by friendly staff. ● *Sun, dinner Mon, public hols.* 🌿	€€			■
LUXEMBOURG CITY: *Mousel's Cantine* 46 Montée de Clausen. 47 01 98. Located next to the Mousel brewery, this welcoming eatery serves generous portions of traditional, hearty fare – braised ham, sausages, broad beans and fried potatoes. Wash your meal down with a mug of local beer. 🌿	€€	■	●	
LUXEMBOURG CITY: *Clairefontaine* 9 Place de Clairefontaine. 46 22 11. A Michelin-star French restaurant, frequented by executives and politicians. The menu includes king prawns with cauliflower and herb salad, fish and game dishes. Jacket and tie required. ● *Sun, lunch Sat; 3 weeks in Aug; 2nd or 3rd week in Feb.* 🅿 🌿	€€€€€	■	●	■

For key to symbols see back flap

THE NETHERLANDS

S ITUATED AT THE MOUTH OF THE RIVER RHINE, *the Netherlands is a man-made country that owes its life to the sea: much of the land once lay under water, and a maritime trading tradition was the principal source of the nation's wealth, most notably in the 17th century. The Netherlands is also one of the world's most liberal countries, with a long history of cultural and racial tolerance.*

The shape of the Netherlands (or Holland, as it is also known) has changed dramatically over the last 2,000 years. Medieval maps show nearly half of the country under water, but since then large areas have been reclaimed from the sea; the current shoreline is maintained by a drainage system of windmills, dykes, and canals.

With some 16 million people in just 41,547 sq km (16,041 sq miles) of land, it is the third most densely populated country in Europe (after Monaco and Malta), but this is barely perceptible to the visitor. Only when arriving by plane do you see how much of the area is still covered with water, and how little precious land remains. The orderly Dutch cities and towns never seem overcrowded, but homes are often small, with steep, narrow staircases and modest gardens. Given the fragility of their environment, it is understandable that the Dutch are so good at preserving it.

The three biggest cities – Amsterdam, the capital, Rotterdam, the industrial hub, and the Hague, the seat of government – are all in the west of the country, part of the urban conglomeration known as the Randstad.

HISTORY

Between the 4th and 8th centuries AD, after the collapse of the Roman Empire, the area corresponding to present-day Holland was conquered by the Franks. As with all the Low Countries, it was later ruled by the House of Burgundy, before passing into the hands of the Habsburgs. When the Habsburg Empire was divided in 1555, the region came under the control of the Spanish branch of the family, which caused the Dutch Revolt of 1568, led by William I of Orange. The Dutch Republic was finally established in 1579, with the Treaty of Utrecht, but it took until 1648 for the Spanish officially to recognize its sovereignty.

Skating on a frozen Dutch river, flanked by drainage windmills

◁ **Boats anchored at the canalside in Amsterdam**

The battle for independence and the need for wealth to fight the Spanish armies stimulated trading success overseas. The Dutch colonized much of Indonesia and established a profitable empire based on spice. The Dutch East India Company thrived, and in the New World Holland briefly ruled over large parts of Brazil. Tulip bulbs were imported from Turkey and cultivated behind the dunes, thus beginning a lucrative flower industry that still flourishes today. However, war with England radically trimmed Dutch sea-power by the end of the 17th century, and from then on the country's fortunes waned. In 1795 French troops ousted William V of Orange, and in 1813, with the retreat of Napoleon, the Netherlands united with Belgium, its neighbor, an arrangement which lasted for 17 years.

William I of Orange (1533–84), leader of the Dutch Revolt

The Netherlands remained neutral in both World Wars, and although it escaped occupation in 1914, the Nazi invasion of 1940 left lasting scars on the nation. In the 1960s the country became a haven for the hippy counter-culture, an influence which is still visible today.

LANGUAGE AND CULTURE

Dutch, or Netherlandic, is a Germanic language which derives from the speech of the Western Franks. A number of dialects are spoken, and in Friesland the dialect (Fries) shows Celtic influences. Nevertheless as in so many European countries, the dialects are disappearing due to the popularity of national television stations on which a standardized version of Dutch is usually spoken.

Culturally, Holland has a huge amount to offer. Its rich history is reflected in countless old buildings and its large number of fine museum collections. The compact size of the city centers makes it easy to stroll along a canal, admiring gabled houses, and step into a museum for an hour or two, before ending the day at a nearby café or pub. The Dutch also have much to boast in the realm of the performing arts, so visitors should find time to enjoy one of the world-famous orchestras or modern dance companies, or attend an organ concert in an old church, or simply spend an evening in one of Amsterdam's jazz clubs.

A fiercely independent people, the Dutch have long been champions of freedom, and have a traditional tolerance of minorities. Jews have been welcome for centuries, and although Catholicism was banned after independence, the authorities turned a blind eye to its practice. Today that tolerance is extended to asylum seekers, gays and lesbians, and people of different backgrounds. A respect for the right to live one's own life underlies the liberal laws on prostitution and drugs.

KEY DATES IN DUTCH HISTORY

300–700 Region ruled by the Franks

1419 Philip the Good of Burgundy begins to unify the Low Countries

1482 The Netherlands pass by marriage to the Austrian Habsburgs

1555 Philip II of Spain inherits the Netherlands

1568 The Dutch Revolt ends Spanish rule

1579 The northern districts unite, forming the Republic of the United Netherlands

1602 The Dutch East India Company founded

1634 Tulip mania begins

1606–69 Life of Rembrandt

1648 Spain recognizes Dutch independence

1794–1813 The Napoleonic era brings the Netherlands under French control

1914–18 Holland is neutral during World War I

1940–45 The country is occupied by Germany throughout most of World War II

1949 The Dutch East Indies gain independence, becoming Indonesia

1957 The Netherlands signs the Treaty of Rome, and joins European Community

1981 Amsterdam is recognized as the cultural capital of the Netherlands

Exploring the Netherlands

ALTHOUGH THE NETHERLANDS' seat of government is at The Hague, Amsterdam is the nominal capital, and it is here that the main cultural attractions can be found. The folkloric villages of Marken and Volendam are only a short drive away, as are the towns of Alkmaar, famous for its traditional cheese market, Haarlem, with its nearby bulbfields, and Utrecht, with its medieval churches. The port of Rotterdam, the pottery center of Delft, and the university town of Leiden lie to the south and west.

THE NETHERLANDS

See main map

Groningen

NETHERLANDS

AMSTERDAM

Enschede

The Hague

Rotterdam

GERMANY

Eindhoven

Antwerp

Cologne

BELGIUM

0 km   90

0 miles   90

SIGHTS AT A GLANCE

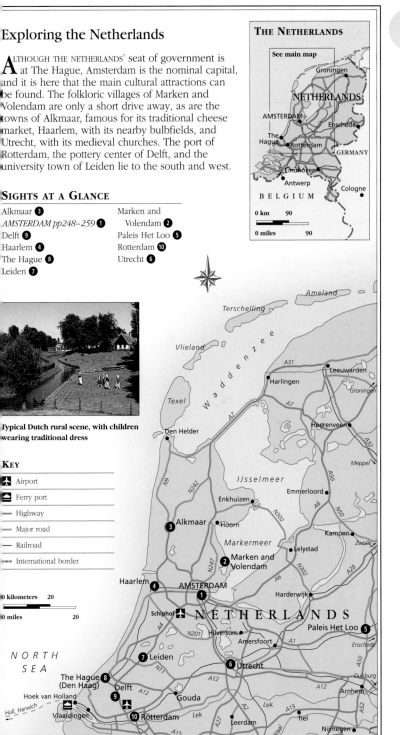

Typical Dutch rural scene, with children wearing traditional dress

KEY

✈ Airport

⛴ Ferry port

— Highway

— Major road

— Railroad

⋯ International border

0 kilometers   20

0 miles   20

Amsterdam ❶

A MSTERDAM WAS FOUNDED around 1200 as a small fishing village on marshland at the mouth of the Amstel river. The young township grew to become the chief trading city of northern Europe, and, in the 17th century, the center of a massive empire. With a population of almost 800,000, today Amsterdam is a place where beauty and serenity coexist happily with a slightly seamy side. From the seedy nightspots of the Red Light District, to the grace and elegance of the city's 17th-century canal houses and the rich cultural heritage of its museums, Amsterdam boasts a variety of attractions.

SIGHTS AT A GLANCE

Amsterdams Historisch
  Museum ⑨
Anne Frankhuis ⑩
Begijnhof ⑨
Golden Bend ⑫
Joods Historisch Museum ⑤
Jordaan ⑪
Koninklijk Paleis ⑦
Museum Amstelkring ②
Museum Het Rembrandthuis ④
Nederlands
Scheepvaartmuseum ⑭
Nemo ⑬
Nieuwe Kerk ⑥
Oude Kerk ①
Plantage ⑮
Red Light District ③
Rijksmuseum pp256–7 ⑯
Stedelijk Museum ⑱
Van Gogh Museum ⑰

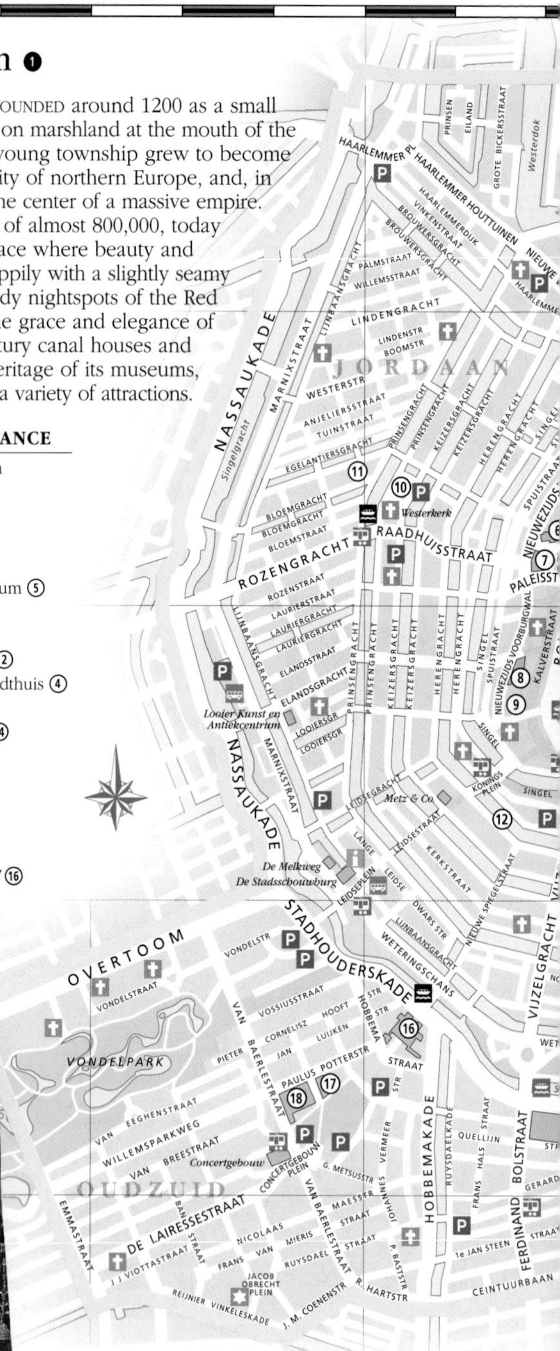

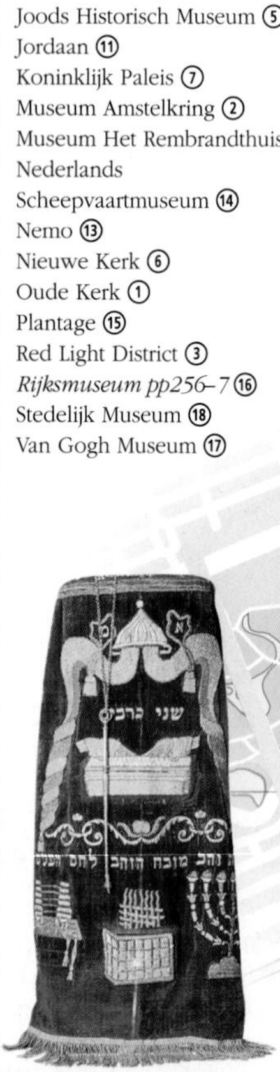

18th-century Torah mantle,
Joods Historisch Museum

SEE ALSO

• *Where to Stay* pp268–9

• *Where to Eat* pp270–71

GETTING AROUND

The most useful tram routes for tourists are lines 1, 2, 4, 5, 7, 9, 14 and 16, which go south from Centraal Station and branch out to all the main sights. Lines 13, 14, and 17 lead west to Jordaan. Buses 22 and 32 serve Nemo and the Scheepvaartmuseum, which you cannot reach by tram. A canalbus service runs from the Singelgracht to Centraal Station, stopping at the city's major landmarks.

17th-century clandestine Catholic church, at the Museum Amstelkring

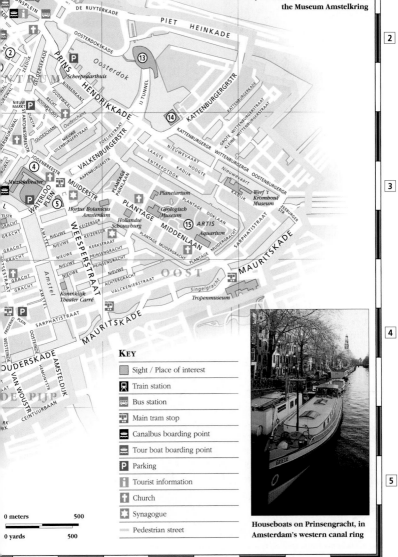

KEY

■	Sight / Place of interest
▤	Train station
▥	Bus station
▦	Main tram stop
▧	Canalbus boarding point
▨	Tour boat boarding point
P	Parking
i	Tourist information
✝	Church
✡	Synagogue
---	Pedestrian street

0 meters 500

0 yards 500

Houseboats on Prinsengracht, in Amsterdam's western canal ring

The Oude Kerk, a calm and peaceful haven at the heart of the Red Light District

Oude Kerk ①

Oudekerksplein 23. 📞 020-625 8284. 🚊 4, 9, 14, 16, 24, 25. ⬤ daily (Sun: pm only). ⬤ Jan 1, Dec 25. ✝ 11am Sun. 📷 ♿ Ⓦ www.oudekerk.nl

Tᴴᴇ ᴏʀɪɢɪɴs ᴏғ the Oude Kerk (Old Church) go back to the early 13th century, when a wooden church was built on a burial ground on a sand bank. The present Gothic structure is 14th century, and has grown from a single-aisled church into a basilica. As it expanded, the building became a gathering place for traders and a refuge for the poor. Though many of its paintings and statues were destroyed following the Alteration in 1578, the delicate 15th-century vault paintings on the gilded ceiling escaped damage. In 1755 the paintings were hidden with layers of blue paint and were not revealed until 200 years later in 1955. The Oude Kerk's beautiful stained-glass windows were also undamaged in the ransackings of the late 16th century. The Lady Chapel, which dates from 1552, contains some of the best stained glass. The magnificent oak-encased Great Organ, the work of Jan Westerman, was added to the church in 1724.

Museum Amstelkring ②

Oudezijds Voorburgwal 40. 📞 020-624 6604. 🚊 4, 9, 16, 24, 25. ⬤ daily (Sun and public hols: pm only). ⬤ Jan 1, Apr 30. 📷 📷 Ⓦ www.museumamstelkring.nl

Tᴜᴄᴋᴇᴅ ᴀᴡᴀʏ on the edge of the Red Light District is a restored 17th-century canal house, with two smaller houses to the rear. The combined upper floors conceal a Catholic church,

The opulent 17th-century parlour at the Museum Amstelkring

known as Ons' Lieve Heer op Solder (Our Dear Lord in the Attic). After the Alteration, when Amsterdam officially became Protestant, many such clandestine churches sprang up around the city. Built in 1663, the one here served the Catholic community until 1887, when the nearby St. Nicolaaskerk was completed. Above the mock marble altar is Jacob de Wit's glorious painting *The Baptism of Christ* (1716). The tiny box bedroom where the resident priest slept is hidden off a bend in the stairs.

The lower floors of the building became a museum in 1888, and today contain elegantly refurbished rooms, as well as a fine collection of church silver, religious arti-facts, and paintings. Restored to its former opulence, the parlour is a splendid example of a living room in the Dutch Classical style of the 17th century.

Red Light District ③

🚊 4, 9, 14, 16, 24, 25.

Pʀᴏsᴛɪᴛᴜᴛɪᴏɴ ɪɴ Amsterdam dates back to the city's emergence as a port in the 13th century. By 1478 it had become so widespread that attempts were made to contain it. Prostitutes straying outside their designated area were marched back to the sound of pipe and drum. A century later the Calvinists tried to outlaw the practice,

The Death of the Virgin Mary by Dirk Crabeth, one of three restored stained-glass windows in the Oude Kerk's Lady Chapel

but their attempts were half-hearted, and by the mid-17th century prostitution was openly tolerated. In 1850 Amsterdam had a population of 200,000 and a total of 200 brothels, most of which catered for rich clients.

Today, Amsterdam's Red Light District, known locally as de Walletjes (the little walls), is centered around the Oude Kerk. The area is criss-crossed by a network of tiny lanes lined with garish sex shops and seedy clubs. At night the little alleys assume a somewhat sinister aspect, and it is not wise to wander around alone, but by day hordes of visitors generate a festive atmosphere, and among the sleaze there are interesting restaurants, bars, and cafés, and beautiful canalside houses to be discovered.

Museum Het Rembrandthuis ④

Jodenbreestraat 4. ☎ 020-520 0400.
Ⓜ Nieuwmarkt. 🚊 9, 14. ◯ daily
(Sun and public hols: pm only).
◯ Jan 1. 🎦 🎫
W www.rembrandthuis.nl

BORN IN LEYDEN, Rembrandt (1606–69) worked and taught in this house from 1639 until 1660. He lived in the ground-floor rooms with his wife, Saskia, who died here in 1642, leaving the artist with a baby son, Titus. Many of the artist's most famous paintings were created in the first-floor studio, which, along with the other rooms in the house, has been restored and refurbished to show exactly how it looked in the 17th century. On display is an excellent selection of Rembrandt's etchings and drawings, including various self-portraits showing the artist in different moods and guises. There are also landscapes, nude studies, and religious pieces, as well as temporary exhibitions of other artists' works.

Interior of the Grote Synagoge, part of the Joods Historisch Museum

Joods Historisch Museum ⑤

Jonas Daniel Meijerplein 2–4. ☎ 020-626 9945. Ⓜ Waterlooplein. 🚊 9, 14. 🚌 Muziektheater. ◯ daily.
◯ Yom Kippur. 🎦 🎫 on request.
♿ W www.jhm.nl

THIS COMPLEX of four synagogues was built in the 17th and 18th centuries by the Ashkenazi Jews, who arrived in Amsterdam from eastern Europe in the 1630s.

The house where Rembrandt lived and worked in the mid-17th century

At first restricted to working in certain trades, the Ashkenazi Jews were granted full civil equality in 1796. Their synagogues were central to Jewish life in Amsterdam until the devastation caused by the Nazi occupation of World War II, which left them empty. The buildings were restored in the 1980s and connected by internal walk-ways. In 1987 they opened as a museum dedicated to Jewish culture and the history of Judaism in the Netherlands.

The impressive Grote Synagoge, with its bright and airy interior, was designed by Elias Bouman and first opened in 1671. Next door is the Nieuwe Synagoge (New Synagogue), built in 1752. It is dominated by the wooden Holy Ark (1791), which came from a synagogue in Enkhuizen in northern Holland.

Religious art and artifacts on display include Hanukah lamps, Torah mantles, and scroll finials. The Haggadah Manuscript (1734) is an illuminated manuscript with the order of service for the Passover celebrations.

18th-century Torah scroll finial

Nieuwe Kerk ⑥

Dam. 📞 020-638 6909. 🚋 1, 2, 4, 5 & many others. ⭕ during exhibitions only. 📷 ♿

DATING FROM the late 14th century, Amsterdam's second parish church was built as the population outgrew the Oude Kerk *(see p250)*. During its turbulent history, the Nieuwe Kerk (New Church) has been destroyed by fire, rebuilt, and then stripped of its treasures after the Alteration of 1578, when the Calvinists took civil power. It reached its present size in the 1650s.

Albert Vinckenbrinck's flamboyant carved pulpit (1664) is the focal point of the church interior, reflecting the Protestant belief that the sermon is central to worship. Other notable features include Jacob van Campen's ornate Great Organ (1645) and, in the apse, the tomb of the famous 17th-century commander-in-chief of the Dutch Navy, Admiral de Ruyter (1607–76), by Rombout Verhulst.

Rombout Verhulst's memorial to Michael de Ruyter in the apse of the Nieuwe Kerk

Koninklijk Paleis ⑦

Dam. 📞 020-624 8698. 🚋 1, 2, 4, 5 & many others. ⭕ phone for details or consult website. ● public hols and when Queen in residence. 📷 🎫 Sep 20–Jun 30: Fri only. ♿ 🌐 www.kon-paleisamsterdam.nl

THE KONINKLIJK PALEIS, still used occasionally by the Dutch royal family for official functions, was built as the Stadhuis (Town Hall). Work began on this vast sandstone edifice in 1648, after the end of the 80 Years' War with Spain. It dominated its surroundings, and more than 13,600 piles were driven into the ground for the foundations.

The splendid Classical façade of the 17th-century Koninklijk Paleis

The Classically inspired design by Jacob van Campen (1595–1657) reflects the city's mood of confidence after the Dutch victory. Civic pride is also shown in the allegorical sculptures by Artus Quellin (1609–68), which decorate the pediments, and in François Hemony's statues and carillon.

Inside, the full magnificence of the architecture is best appreciated in the huge Burgerzaal (Citizens' Hall). Based on the assembly halls of ancient Rome, this 30-m (98-ft) high room runs the length of the building, and boasts a superb marble floor inlaid with maps of the eastern and western hemispheres, as well as epic sculptures by Quellin. Most of the furniture on display, including the chairs, clocks, and chandeliers, dates from 1808, when Louis Bonaparte took over the building as his royal palace.

Amsterdams Historisch Museum ⑧

Kalverstraat 92, Nieuwezijds Voorburgwal 357, St. Luciensteeg 27. 📞 020-523 1822. 🌐 www.ahm.nl 🚋 1, 2, 4, 5, 9 & many others. ⭕ daily. ● Jan 1, Apr 30, Dec 25. 📷 🎫 ♿

THE CONVENT of St. Lucien was turned into a civic orphanage in the latter half of the 16th century. The original red-brick convent was enlarged over the years, and in 1975 it opened as the city's historical museum.

The permanent exhibitions are housed around the inner courtyard of the complex. Clear signposting allows the visitor either to concentrate on a specific period – *The Young City, The Mighty City,* or *The Modern City* – or to take a grand tour through the entire history of Amsterdam.

The museum's largest section, *The Mighty City,* focuses on trade, commerce, and culture during the period of Amsterdam's Golden Age. Items on display range from a globe belonging to the famous cartographer Willem Blaeu to a late 18th-century model of an East Indiaman.

Amsterdam's wealth from trade attracted great artists, who chronicled the era in extraordinary detail. There are views of the city and the port, and portraits of prominent and ordinary citizens. Some works, such as Jacob de Wit's *Maid of Amsterdam* (1741), celebrate the glory of the city in heroic, allegorical style. Others give a realistic picture of the life of the paupers and orphans. The paintings of anatomy lessons include one by Rembrandt, *The Anatomy Lesson of Dr. Jan Deijman* (1656). This shows the dissection of "Black Jan," a convicted criminal who had been hanged.

In the Civic Guards' Gallery hangs a series of group portraits of the various militia companies charged with defending law and order in the city in the 16th and 17th centuries. Paintings by Rembrandt and Cornelis Anthonisz stand out among lesser-known works.

One of the museum's most extraordinary exhibits is the 17th-century 5.30-m (17-ft) statue of Goliath that stands in the restaurant.

Statue of Goliath (c.1650) in the Amsterdams Historisch Museum

Begijnhof ⑨

Spui. 🚊 *1, 2, 4, 5 & many others.*

T HE BEGIJNHOF was built in 1346 as a sanctuary for the Béguines, a lay Catholic sisterhood who lived like nuns, although they took no monastic vows. In return for lodgings within the complex,

these worthy women undertook to educate the poor and look after the sick. Although none of the earliest dwellings survives, the rows of beautiful houses that overlook the Begijnhof's well-kept green include Amsterdam's oldest surviving house, Het Houten Huis, at No. 34. Dating from around 1420, it is one of only two wooden-fronted houses in the city, since timber buildings were banned in 1521 after a series of catastrophic fires. On a wall directly behind No. 34 is a collection of fascinating stone plaques, illustrating biblical themes.

The southern side of the square is dominated by the Engelse Kerk (English Church), which dates from the 15th century and retains its original medieval tower. The church was confiscated after the Alteration and rented to a group of English and Scottish Presbyterians in 1607. Directly opposite is the Begijnhof Chapel (Nos. 29–30), a well-preserved clandestine church, where the Béguines worshipped in secret until religious tolerance was restored in 1795. It once housed relics of the 1345 Miracle of Amsterdam. Four stained-glass windows and a collection of paintings depict scenes of the Miracle.

Anne Frankhuis ⑩

Prinsengracht 263. 📞 020-556 7100. 🚊 *13, 14, 17, 20.* 🚋 *Prinsengracht.* 🕐 *daily (Jan 1 & Dec 25: pm only).* ● *Yom Kippur.* 📷 🅦 *www.annefrank.nl*

F OR TWO YEARS during World War II, the Frank and Van Daan families, both Jewish, hid here until their betrayal to the Nazis. The 13-year-old Anne began her famous diary in July 1942. First published in 1947 as *Het Achterhuis (The Annex)*, and since translated into dozens of languages, the journal gives a moving account of growing up under persecution, and of life in confinement. Anne made her last entry in August 1944, three days before her family was arrested.

Visitors to the Anne Frankhuis climb to the second floor where an introductory video is shown. You then enter the annex where the families hid via the revolving bookcase that concealed its entrance. The rooms are now empty, except for the posters in Anne's room and Otto Frank's model of the annex as it was during the occupation. The house also has exhibitions on World War II and anti-Semitism. Try to arrive early – with 500,000 visitors a year, the museum gets very crowded.

Family photograph of Anne Frank (1929–45)

Attractive gabled houses and central green of Amsterdam's Begijnhof, which is still occupied by single women

The Westerkerk, designed by Hendrick de Keyser, overlooking Prinsengracht in Jordaan

Jordaan ⑪

🚊 13, 14, 17.

THE JORDAAN grew up at the same time that Amsterdam's Grachtengordel (Canal Ring) was being developed in the first half of the 17th century. The marshy area to the west of the more fashionable canals was set aside as an area for workers whose industries were banned from the town center. Its network of narrow streets and waterways followed the course of old paths and drainage ditches. Immigrants fleeing religious persecution also settled here. It is thought that Huguenot refugees called the district *jardin* (garden), later corrupted to "Jordaan."

Flowing through the heart of the district are the tranquil tree-lined canals known as the Egelantiersgracht and the Bloemgracht. The canalside residences of the Egelantiersgracht were originally settled by artisans, while the Bloemgracht was a center for dye and paint manufacture. One of the most charming spots along the Egelantiersgracht is **St. Andrieshofje** at Nos. 107–114. This *bofje*

(almshouse) was built in 1617 and the passage that leads to its court-yard is decorated with splendid blue and white tiles.

The 85-m (272-ft) high tower of the **Westerkerk** soars above Jordaan's streets, and gives panoramic views of the city. Begun in 1620, the church has the largest nave of any Dutch Protestant church.

Historically a poor area, recently Jordaan has taken on a bohemian air. Among the old workers' houses are quirky shops selling anything from designer clothes to old sinks, and lively brown cafés and bars, which spill onto the sidewalks in summer.

Golden Bend ⑫

🚊 1, 2, 4, 5, 9, 14 & many others.
Kattenkabinet ☎ 020-626 5378.
🕐 9am–2pm Tue –Fri; pm Sat & Sun.
⬤ public hols.

THE MOST impressive canal-side architecture in the city can be seen along the section of the Herengracht between Leidestraat and

Vijzelstraat. This stretch of canal is known as the Golden Bend because of the great wealth of the shipbuilders, merchants, and politicians who began building houses here in the 1660s. Most of the opulent mansions have been turned into offices or banks, but their elegance gives an insight into the lifestyle of the earliest residents.

Two of the finest and best-preserved buildings are No. 412, designed by Philips Vingboons in 1664, and No. 475, with its two sculpted female figures over the front door. Built in 1730, the latter is an example of the Louis XIV style, which became popular in the 18th century. The **Kattenkabinet** (Cat Museum), at No. 497, is one of the few houses on the Golden Bend accessible to the public. It is well worth visiting for its rather unusual collection of feline artifacts. Also on view here are some splendid paintings by Jacob de Wit (1695–1754) and an attractive formal garden.

Ornate capital from the façade of a building on the Golden Bend

THE GRACHTENGORDEL

Faced with a rapidly growing population, at the beginning of the 17th century Amsterdam's town planner, Hendrick Staets, formed an ambitious project to quadruple the size of the city. In 1614, work began

on cutting three new residential canals, collectively known as the Grachtengordel (Canal Ring), to encircle the existing city. Built for the wealthiest citizens, the grand houses along the Keizers-gracht (Emperor's Canal), Herengracht (Gentleman's Canal), and Prinsengracht (Prince's Canal) represent Amsterdam's finest archi-tecture, and are a testimony to the city's Golden Age.

Seeing the world through a soap bubble at Nemo

Nemo ⑬

Oosterdok 2. █ 020-531 3233.
▣ 22. ☐ 10am–5pm Tue–Sun. ▨
& �bW www.e-nemo.nl

Iᴺ JUNE 1997 Holland's
national science center
moved to this curved building
that protrudes 30 m (98 ft)
over the water. Divided into
five themed zones (Inter-
activity, Technology, Energy,
Science, and Humanity),
which are updated every
three years, the center
presents technological
innovations in a way that
allows visitors' creativity full
expression. You can interact
with virtual reality, operate
the latest industrial equipment
under expert supervision,
harness science to produce
a work of art, participate in
countless games, experiments,
demonstrations, and work-
shops, and take in a variety
of lectures and films.

Nederlands Scheep-vaartmuseum ⑭

Kattenburgerplein 1. █ 020-23
2222. ▣ 22, 32. ▣ Oosterdok,
Kattenburgergracht. ☐ Tue–Sun
(mid-Jun–mid-Sep: daily). ● Jan 1,
Apr 30, Dec 25. ▨ &
ⓦ www.scheepvaartmuseum.nl

Oɴᴄᴇ ᴛʜᴇ ᴀʀsᴇɴᴀʟ of the
Dutch Navy, this vast
Classical sandstone edifice
was built in 1656. It is
supported by 18,000 piles
driven into the bed of the
Oosterdok. The Navy stayed
in residence here until 1973,
when the building was
converted into the National
Maritime Museum, holding
the largest collection of boats
in the world. Displays of real
ships, models, and maps give
a chronological survey of the
country's seafaring tradition.

One of the museum's finest
original exhibits is a 17-m
(54-ft) long gilded barge, made
in 1818 for King William I.
The vessel was last used in
1962 for Queen Juliana's
25th wedding anniversary
celebrations. Another major
attraction is a full-size model
of a Dutch East Indiaman, the
Amsterdam. During the 16th
century the Dutch East India
Company used such vessels to
sail as far as China, Japan, and
Indonesia in the development
of the spice trade. Moored in
a dock behind the museum
building, the Amsterdam is
today "crewed" by actors,
who re-enact life aboard one
of these vast wooden ships.

Seals basking in a pool at the Artis zoological complex in Plantage

Plantage ⑮

▣ 6, 9, 14. **Artis** Plantage Kerklaan
40. █ 020-523 3400. ☐ daily. ▨
☑ & **Hortus Botanicus
Amsterdam** Plantage Middenlaan 2.
█ 020-625 8411. ☐ daily. ● Jan 1,
Dec 25. ▨ ☑ & **Hollandse
Schouwburg** Plantage Middenlaan
24. █ 020-626 9945. ☐ daily.
● Yom Kippur. &

Pʟᴀɴᴛᴀɢᴇ ɪs a part of the city
that is often overlooked by
tourists. Its name dates from
the time when it was an area
of green parkland beyond the
city wall, where 17th-century
Amsterdammers spent their
leisure time. Though much of
the greenery has gone, there
is still a lot to see and do here.

The area is dominated by
Artis, a zoological complex
founded in 1838, which has
more than 5,000 animal
species. There are also three
greenhouses, a planetarium,
a geological museum, an
excellent aquarium, and a
modest zoological museum.

Nearby, the **Hortus
Botanicus Amsterdam**
began as a small apothecaries'
herb garden in 1682 and now
contains one of the world's
largest botanical collections.

Plantage has a strong Jewish
tradition, and many monu-
ments commemorate Jewish
history in Amsterdam. Formerly
a theater, the **Hollandse
Schouwburg** is now a somber
memorial to the 104,000 Dutch
Jewish victims of World War II.
More than 60,000 Jews were
held here before being deported to concentration camps.

William I's royal barge on display at the Nederlands Scheepvaartmuseum

Rijksmuseum ⑯

T HE RIJKSMUSEUM is a familiar Amsterdam landmark and possesses an unrivaled collection of Dutch art, begun in the early 19th century. The huge museum opened in 1885 to bitter criticism from Amsterdam's Protestant community for its Neo-Gothic style. The main building will undergo extensive renovation until 2008, during which time the most famous treasures will be on view in the south wing (Philips Wing).

Second floor

Winter Landscape with Skaters (1618)
Mute painter Hendrick Avercamp specialized in intricate icy winter scenes.

The Gothic façade
of Cuypers' building is red brick with elaborate decoration, including colored tiles.

★ **The Kitchen Maid** (1658)
The light falling through the window and the stillness of this domestic scene are typical of Jan Vermeer's style.

KEY TO FLOORPLAN

- ☐ Dutch history
- ☐ Dutch painting
- ☐ European painting
- ☐ Sculpture and decorative art
- ☐ Prints and drawings
- ☐ Asiatic art
- ☐ Temporary exhibitions
- ☐ Non-exhibition space

Entrance

STAR PAINTINGS

★ **The Night Watch by Rembrandt**

★ **St. Elizabeth's Day Flood**

★ **The Kitchen Maid by Vermeer**

★ **St. Elizabeth's Day Flood** (1500)
An unknown artist painted this altarpiece, which shows a disastrous flood in 1421. The dykes protecting Dordrecht were breached, and 22 villages were swept away by the flood water.

Entrance

Study collections

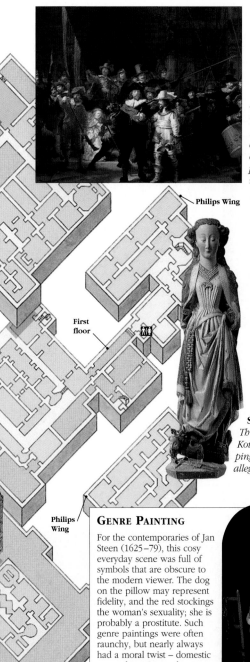

VISITORS' CHECKLIST

Stadhouderskade 42. **C** *020-674 7047.* **2, 5, 6, 7, 10, 20.**
Stadhouderskade. **10am–5pm daily.** *Jan 1.*
W www.rijksmuseum.nl

★ **The Night Watch** *(1642)*
The showpiece of Dutch 17th-century art, this vast canvas by Rembrandt was commissioned as a group portrait of an Amsterdam militia company.

Philips Wing

GALLERY GUIDE

There are entrances on either side of the driveway under the building – the left leads into the Dutch history section, the right to prints and drawings, sculpture and applied art, and then continues on up the stairs. On the first floor is a huge ante-chamber, with a shop and information desk. The entrance on the left begins with early Dutch painting, leading to the acclaimed 17th-century collection. Some disruption can be expected until 2008 due to major renovation work.

First floor

St. Catherine *(c.1465)*
This sculpture by the Master of Koudewater shows the saint stamping on Emperor Maxentius, who allegedly killed her with his sword.

Philips Wing

GENRE PAINTING

For the contemporaries of Jan Steen (1625–79), this cosy everyday scene was full of symbols that are obscure to the modern viewer. The dog on the pillow may represent fidelity, and the red stockings the woman's sexuality; she is probably a prostitute. Such genre paintings were often raunchy, but nearly always had a moral twist – domestic scenes by artists such as ter Borch and Honthorst were symbolic of brothels, while other works illustrated proverbs. Symbols like candles or skulls indicated mortality.

Jan Steen's symbolic *Woman at her Toilet*, painted in about 1660

Ground Floor

Exploring the Rijksmuseum

T HE RIJKSMUSEUM is almost too vast to be seen in a
single visit. If you have only one chance to go, you
should start with the incomparable 17th-century Dutch
paintings, taking in Rembrandt, Frans Hals, Vermeer,
and many other Old Masters. However, the collection
of Asiatic artifacts and the sculpture and applied arts
departments are equally wonderful, while the Dutch
history section also provides a rewarding experience.

**The heavily ornamented Neo-Gothic
façade of the Rijksmuseum**

EARLY PAINTING AND
FOREIGN SCHOOLS

A LONGSIDE Flemish and
Italian art are religious
works by Netherlandish
painters, such as *The Seven
Works of Charity* (1504) by
the Master of Alkmaar, Jan
van Scorel's *Mary Magdalene*
(1528), and Lucas van Leyden's
triptych, *Adoration of the
Golden Calf* (1530).

DUTCH PAINTING OF
THE GOLDEN AGE

T HE 17TH CENTURY was a
golden age for Dutch art.
By this time, religious themes
had been replaced by secular
subjects, such as realistic
portraiture, landscapes, still
lifes, seascapes, domestic
interiors, and animal portraits.

The most famous artist of
this era is Rembrandt, whose
works here include *Portrait of
Titus in a Monk's Habit* (1660),
Self-Portrait as the Apostle Paul
(1661), and *The Jewish Bride*
(1663), as well as the brilliant
The Night Watch (see p257).

Also not to be missed
are Jan Vermeer's
(1632–75) serenely
light-filled interiors,
such as *The Kitchen
Maid (see p257)* and
*The Woman Reading a
Letter* (1662). Of several
portraits by Frans Hals
(1580–1666) the
best-known are *The
Wedding Portrait* and
The Merry Drinker
(1630). *The Windmill
at Wijk* by Jacob van
Ruisdael (1628–82) is a
great landscape by an
artist at the height of
his career. Other artists
whose works contribute
to this unforgettable
collection include Pieter
Saenredam (1597–1665), Jan
van de Capelle (c.1624–79),
and Jan Steen *(see p257)*.

LATER DUTCH PAINTING

P ORTRAITURE and still lifes
continued to dominate
18th-century Dutch painting.
The evocative *Still Life with
Flowers and Fruit* by Jan van
Huysum (1682–1749) stands
out among works on display

here. Other 18th-century
artists represented are Adriaan
van der Werff (1659–1722) and
Cornelis Troost (1696–1750).

The 19th-century collection
features works by the Hague
School, a group of Dutch
artists who came together
around 1870 in Den Haag.
Their landscape work captures
the atmospheric quality of
subdued Dutch sunlight.
Look out for Anton Mauve's
Morning Ride on the Beach
(1876) and the beautiful
Polder landscape, *View near
the Geestbrug*, by Hendrik
Weissenbruch (1824–1903).

SCULPTURE AND
APPLIED ARTS

E XHIBITS IN THIS section span
several centuries, ranging
from religious medieval
sculpture to Art Nouveau
glass. Highlights that capture
the wealth of the Golden Age
include an exquisite display
of glassware, Delftware, and
diamond-encrusted jewelry.

ASIATIC ART

R EWARDS OF THE Dutch
imperial trading past are
on show in this section. Some
of the earliest artifacts are the
most unusual: tiny bronze
Tang-dynasty figurines from
7th-century China, and granite
rock carvings from Java (c.8th
century). Later exhibits include
Chinese parchment paintings,
inlaid Korean boxes, and
decorative Vietnamese dishes.

The Jewish Bride by Dutch Master, Rembrandt (1606–69)

The Bedroom at Arles, painted during van Gogh's stay in France

Van Gogh Museum ⑰

Paulus Potterstraat 7.
📞 020-570 5200. 🚃 2, 3, 5, 12, 16.
🕐 daily. ⬤ Jan 1. ♿ 👍
🖥 www.vangoghmuseum.nl

VINCENT VAN GOGH (1853–90), born in Zundert, began painting in 1880. He worked in the Netherlands for five years, before moving to Paris, and then settling at Arles *(see pp192–3)* in the south of France in February 1888. There he painted over 200 canvases in 15 months. During his time in France, however, van Gogh suffered recurrent nervous crises, hallucinations, and depression. After a fierce argument with his contemporary, French artist Gauguin, he cut off part of his own ear and his mental instability forced him into an asylum. Van Gogh's final years were characterized by tremendous bursts of activity. During the last 70 days of his life he painted 70 canvases. In July 1890 he finally shot himself and died two days later. At the time of his death he was on the verge of being acclaimed.

Van Gogh's younger brother Theo, an art dealer, amassed a collection of 200 of his paintings and 500 drawings.

Vincent van Gogh in 1871

These, together with around 850 letters written by the artist to Theo, form the core of the museum's outstanding collection. Famous works on display include *The Potato Eaters* (1885), from the artist's Dutch period, *The Bedroom at Arles* (1888), painted to celebrate his achievement of domestic stability in the Yellow House in Arles, and *Vase with Sunflowers* (1889). One of van Gogh's last paintings is the dramatic *Wheatfield and Crows* (1890). The menacing crows and violence of the sky show the depth of the artist's mental anguish in the last few weeks before his death. Also on show are selected works by van Gogh's friends and contemporaries, as well as temporary exhibitions.

Stedelijk Museum ⑱

Paulus Potterstraat 13. 📞 020-573 2911. 🚃 2, 3, 5, 12, 16. 🕐 daily, but with some disruption to exhibits due to renovation work until 2006. ⬤ Jan 1. ♿ 👍 🖥 www.stedelijk.nl

THE STEDELIJK MUSEUM was designed to hold a personal collection bequeathed to the city in 1890 by art connoisseur Sophia de Bruyn. It is housed in a late 19th-century Neoclassical building, adorned

with statues of famous artists and architects. In 1938, the museum became the national museum of modern art, showing works by well-known names such as Picasso, Matisse, Chagall, and Monet. Constantly changing exhibitions reflect the latest developments not only in painting and sculpture, but also in printing, drawing, photography, video, and industrial design.

Among the museum's best collections are works by the Dutch painter Mondriaan (1872–1944). One of the founding members of De Stijl (The Style) – an artistic movement which espoused clarity and simplicity – Mondriaan went on to produce many abstract geometrical compositions, such as *Composition in Red, Black, Blue, Yellow, and Grey*.

Another highlight of the museum is the Cobra collection, with a number of works by Karel Appel (born 1921), including his colorful *Man and Animals* (1949).

Other artists represented in the Stedelijk's exhibitions include the American photographer Man Ray (1890–1977), the Russian Kazimir Malevich (1878–1935), founder of the abstract movement Suprematism, and the Swiss sculptor and experimental artist, Jean Tinguely (1925–91), who created humorous sculptures from junk and recycled metal.

Statue of 16th-century artist Pieter Aertsen on the Stedelijk's façade

A typical 17th-century gabled timber house in Marken

Marken and Volendam **2**

Marken 2,000. **Volendam** 18,000.
Zeestraat 37 (0299-363747). Sat.

LOCATED ON the shores of the Marker Meer, and less than an hour's drive from Amsterdam, Marken and Volendam are extremely popular with tourists, who are drawn to these picturesque towns by their old-world character. In spite of the crowds, it is worth spending a few hours exploring their narrow streets and canals, lined, as they are, with attractive 17th-century gabled timber houses. You may even spot the local inhabitants wearing traditional dress.

Places to look out for in particular include the **Marker Museum** in Marken, an old fisherman's dwelling that now houses a heritage center, and

Volendam's **Spaander Hotel** situated at No. 15 Haven. The walls of the hotel's café are covered with numerous works by late 19th-century artists who came here to paint views of the pretty town.

Alkmaar **3**

94,000. Waaggebouw, Waagplein 2–3 (072-5114 284). cheese market: Apr–Aug: Fri 10am–12:30pm.

ALKMAAR IS one of the few Dutch towns to maintain its traditional cheese market, which has been held here since medieval times. Every Friday morning in summer local producers lay out Gouda and Edam cheeses in the Waagplein, and from here porters sporting colorful straw hats take them off on sledges for weighing at the **Waaggebouw** (Weigh House). This imposing building, altered in 1582 from a 14th-century chapel, also houses the **Hollandse Kaasmuseum**, where local cheese-making techniques are explained.

Alkmaar's massive Gothic church, the **Grote Kerk**, was completed in 1520 and contains the tomb of Floris V, Count of Holland. The nave is dominated by the 17th-century organ, built by Jacob van Campen and painted by Cesar van Everdingen.

🏛 **Hollandse Kaasmuseum**
Waaggebouw, Waagplein 2.
072-5114 284. Apr–Oct: Mon–Sat.

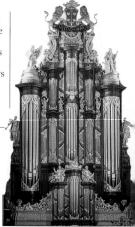

The soaring pipes of the famous organ in Haarlem's Grote Kerk

Haarlem **4**

153,000. Stationsplein 1 (0900-616 1600). Mon. Haarlem Jazz Festival (mid-Aug).

HAARLEM IS the center of the Dutch printing, pharmaceutical, and bulb-growing industries. Most of the city's main attractions are within easy walking distance of the Grote Markt, a lively square overlooked by the Gothic **Grote Kerk**. Also known as Sint Bavo's, this huge church was built between 1400 and 1550. Its highly decorative organ (1735) has been played by both Handel and Mozart. Also on the Grote Markt, the **Stadhuis** (Town Hall) dates from 1250 and displays a mixture of architectural styles. The oldest part of the building is the beamed medieval banqueting hall of the counts of Holland.

The **Amsterdamse Poort**, the medieval gateway that once formed part of the city's defenses, was built in 1355.

Haarlem is well known for its *hofjes* (almshouses), which began to appear in the 16th century. Established in 1610, **St. Elisabeth's Gasthuis** now houses a historical museum. The **Frans Hals Museum** occupies the almshouse where the famous artist (1580–1666) supposedly lived out his last years. In addition to a superb collection of paintings by Hals himself, there is a selection of

Porters carrying cheeses on sledges at Alkmaar's traditional market

Dutch paintings and applied art dating from the 16th and 17th centuries.

🏛 Frans Hals Museum

Groot Heiligland 62. 📞 023-5115 775. ⬜ Tue–Sat, pm Sun. ⬤ Jan 1, Dec 25. 📷 🎫 ♿

Paleis Het Loo ❺

Koninklijk Park 1, Apeldoorn. 📞 055-577 2400. 🚉 to Apeldoorn, then bus. ⬜ Tue–Sun. ⬤ Jan 1. 📷 🎫 ♿

STADHOLDER William III built Het Loo in 1686 as a royal hunting lodge. Generations of the House of Orange used the lodge as a summer palace, which came to be regarded as the "Versailles of the Netherlands." The building's Classical façade belies the opulence of the interior. Among the most lavish apartments are the Royal Bedroom of William III (1713), with its wall coverings and draperies of rich orange damask and blue silk, and the Old Dining Room (1686). In the latter half of the 20th century, old prints, records, and plans were used to carefully recreate Het Loo's beautiful formal gardens.

The sumptuously decorated Royal Bedroom of Stadholder William III

Utrecht ❻

🏙 234,000. 🚉 🚌 🛈 Vinkenburg-straat 19 (0900-128 873 248).

UTRECHT WAS founded by the Romans in AD 47 to protect a strategic river crossing on the Rhine. The

BULBFIELDS OF THE NETHERLANDS

Bulb species cultivated in the Netherlands include lilies, gladioli, daffodils, hyacinths, irises, crocuses, and dahlias. The most famous bulb of all, however, is the tulip. Originally

from Turkey, it was first grown in Dutch soil by Carolus Clusius in 1593. Occupying a 30-km (19-mile) strip between Haarlem and Leiden, the Bloembollen-streek is the most important bulb-growing area in the country. From late January the polders bloom with a succession of brightly colored bulbs, building to a climax in mid-April when the tulips flower. If you do not have a car, there are plenty of organized tours that visit the bulbfields, or you can rent a bicycle from Haarlem train station.

A blanket of color formed by tulips in the Bloembollenstreek

town was one of the first places in the Netherlands to embrace Christianity, and in the Middle Ages it grew into an important religious center. The city retains many of its medieval churches and monasteries. The **Domkerk**, Utrecht's cathedral, was begun in 1245. Today, only the north and south transepts, two chapels, and the choir remain, along with the 15th-century cloisters and a chapterhouse. The **Domtoren**, which has always stood apart from the cathedral, is one of the tallest towers in the Netherlands, at 112 m (367 ft). Completed in 1382, on the site of the small 8th-century church of St. Willibrord, it affords magnificent views of the city.

Among Utrecht's many museums are the **Museum Catharijneconvent**, which deals with the troubled history of religion in the Netherlands and owns an award-winning collection of medieval art, and the **Nederlands Spoorweg-museum**, a superb railway museum, housed in the former 19th-century Maliebaan station. At the heart of the collection at the **Centraal Museum** is a series of portraits by artist Jan van Scorel (1495–1562). The museum also owns Gerrit

Rietveld's Schröderhuis, which was designed in 1947 and is considered the apogee of De Stijl (see p259) architecture. The house is open to the public at No. 50 Prins Hendriklaan.

🏛 Museum Catharijneconvent

Lange Nieuwstraat 38. 📞 030-2313 835. ⬜ Tue–Sun. ⬤ Jan 1, Apr 30. 📷 ♿

🏛 Centraal Museum

Nicolaaskerkhof 10. 📞 030-2362 362. ⬜ Tue–Sun. ⬤ Jan 1, Apr 30, Dec 25. 📷

Utrecht's massive Gothic Domtoren, which dominates the city

Leiden ❼

🏚 115,000. 🚊 🚌 🛈 Stationsweg 2d (0900-222 2333). 🏪 Wed, Sat.

L EIDEN IS a prosperous town that dates back to Roman times. Its famous university is the oldest in the Netherlands, founded in 1575 by William of Orange. Created in 1587, the university's botanical garden, the **Hortus Botanicus der Rijksuniversiteit Leiden**, is still open to the public.

One of Leiden's biggest attractions is the **Rijksmuseum van Oudheden** (National Museum of Antiquities). Established in 1818, the museum houses an outstanding collection of Egyptian artifacts, including the 1st-century AD Temple of Taffeh. There are also displays of textiles, musical instruments, Etruscan bronzework, and fragments of Roman mosaics and frescoes.

The magnificent Gothic **Pieterskerk** was built in the 15th century. Its interior is rather austere, but there is a splendid organ (1642), enclosed in gilded woodwork.

Dating back to 1640, the old Lakenhal (Cloth Hall) now houses the **Stedelijk Museum**, with exhibitions of art and furniture from the 16th century onward. The pride of the collection is Lucas van Leyden's Renaissance triptych, *The Last Judgment* (1526–7). Leiden also has an excellent ethnological museum, the **Rijksmuseum voor Volkenkunde**, which reopened in April 2001 after undergoing an extensive restoration program.

Hortus Botanicus, the tranquil botanical gardens of Leiden University

🏛 **Rijksmuseum van Oudheden**
Rapenburg 28. 📞 071-5163 163.
🕐 Tue–Sun. 🌑 Jan 1, Oct 3, Dec 25.
🎫 ♿

🏛 **Rijksmuseum voor Volkenkunde**
Steenstraat 1. 📞 071-5168 800.
🕐 Tue–Sun. 🌑 Jan 1, Oct 3, Dec 25. 🎫 ♿

The Hague ❽

🏚 446,000. 🚊 🚌 🛈 Koningin Julianaplein 30 (0900-340 3505).
🏪 Mon, Wed, Fri, Sat.

T HE POLITICAL CAPITAL of the Netherlands, The Hague (Den Haag or 's-Gravenhage) is home to prestigious institutions, such as the Dutch parliament and the International Court of Justice.

When The Hague became the seat of government in 1586, it was a small town built around the castle of the counts of Holland. That same castle, much rebuilt, stands at the heart of the city, and forms part of the Binnenhof, where today's parliament sits.

The fairy-tale, double-turreted Gothic **Ridderzaal** (Hall of the Knights), the 13th-century dining hall of Count Floris V, is open to the public when parliament is not in session.

An outstanding collection of works by Dutch Masters Rembrandt, Jan Vermeer, and Jan Steen is assembled in the Royal Picture Gallery at the **Mauritshuis**. More Dutch Golden Age paintings are on view at the **Museum Bredius** and the **Galerij Prins Willem V**.

The **Haags Gemeentemuseum** has an applied arts section that includes the world's largest collection of paintings by De Stijl (see p259) artist Piet Mondrian.

Formerly called Het Oude Hof (the Old Court), the **Paleis Noordeinde** is a splendid 17th-century palace built in the Classical style. It is used as a temporary residence by Queen Beatrix.

🏛 **Ridderzaal**
Binnenhof 8a. 📞 070-364 6144.
🕐 Mon–Sat (call in advance).
🌑 public hols. 🎫 📷 obligatory.

🏛 **Mauritshuis**
Korte Vijverberg 8. 📞 070-302 3456. 🕐 Tue–Sun. 🌑 Jan 1, Dec 25. 🎫 📷 ♿

🏛 **Galerij Prins Willem V**
Buitenhof 35. 📞 070-302 3456.
🕐 Tue–Sun. 🌑 Jan 1, Dec 25. 🎫

ENVIRONS: Only a 15-minute tram ride from the center of Den Haag, **Scheveningen** has clean, sandy beaches and several good seafood restaurants. The resort also has a Sea Life Center and a small marine biology center, the Zee Museum.

The Binnenhof, home of the Dutch parliament, in The Hague

Delft ⑨

🏛 95,000. 🚊 🚌 ℹ Hippolytus-
buurt 4 (015-215 4051). 🚢 Thu, Sat.

THE CHARMING town of Delft
is most famous for its
blue-and-white pottery,
known as Delftware, which
was introduced to the
Netherlands by immigrant
Italian potters in the 16th
century. **De Porceleyne Fles**
is one of two Delftware
potteries still in operation,
and is open for guided tours.

Delft is also the resting
place of William of Orange
(1533–84), who commanded
the Dutch Revolt against
Spanish rule from his
headquarters in the town.
His richly-decorated tomb
lies in the **Nieuwe Kerk**,
built between 1383 and 1510,
but subsequently restored
following damage
caused by fire and
explosion. The
former convent
that William used
as his military
headquarters, and
where he was
assassinated by
order of Philip II
of Spain, is now
home to the
**Stedelijk
Museum Het
Prinsenhof**. The museum
contains a rare collection of
antique Delftware, as well as
tapestries, silverware, medieval
sculpture, and portraits of the
Dutch royal family.

Hand-painted
17th-century
Delft tiles

Other sites of interest are
the **Volkenkundig Museum
Nusantara**, an ethnological
museum, whose exhibits
were brought back from
Indonesia by traders working
for the Dutch East India
Company, and the **Oude
Kerk**, which dates from the
13th century. The church
holds the tomb of one of the
town's most famous sons, the
artist Jan Vermeer (1632–75).

🏛 **Nieuwe Kerk**
Markt. 📞 015-2123 025.
🕐 Mon–Sat. 📷

🏛 **Stedelijk Museum
Het Prinsenhof**
St. Agathaplein 1. 📞 015-2602 358.
🕐 Tue–Sat, Sun pm. 🔴 Jan 1,
Dec 25. 📷

**Delft's Nieuwe Kerk, with its
soaring 100-m (328-ft) high tower**

Rotterdam ⑩

🏛 602,000. ✈ 6 km (4 miles) NW.
🚊 🚌 ℹ Coolsingel 67 (010-414
0000). 🚢 Tue, Fri, Sat.

ROTTERDAM occupies a
strategic position where
the Rhine meets the North
Sea. Barges from the city
transport goods deep into
the continent, and ocean-
going ships carry European
exports around the world.

Following damage during
World War II, the Oudehaven,
Rotterdam's old harbor area,
has been rebuilt in daring
and avant-garde styles. The
pyramid-shaped **Gemeente
Bibliotheek** (Public Library)
is similar to the Pompidou
Center in Paris (see p153),
while Piet Blom's **Kijk-Kubus**
(Cube Houses) of 1982 are
extraordinary apartments set
on a series of concrete stilts
and tilted at angles.

The excellent **Museum
Boijmans-van Beuningen**
holds Netherlandish and
Dutch art, from the medieval
paintings of Jan van Eyck to
modern works using laser
technology. Among its
most famous exhibits are a
number of paintings by Peter
Brueghel and Rembrandt.

Other museums of note are
the **Historisch Museum
Rotterdam**, the city's main
historical museum, the
Wereldmuseum Rotterdam,
with its superb ethnological
collection, and the **Maritiem
Museum Rotterdam**, whose
highlight is an iron-clad warship, De Buffel, built in 1868.

For a spectacular view of
the city, take the elevator up
the 185-m (600-ft) high **Euro-
mast**. Built in 1960, it is the
tallest construction in the
country, and has a restaurant
and an exhibition area.

🏛 **Museum Boijmans-van
Beuningen**
Museumpark 18–20. 📞 010-441
9400. 🕐 Tue–Sun. 🔴 Jan 1,
Apr 30, Dec 25. 📷 ♿

🏛 **Historisch Museum
Rotterdam**
Korte Hoogstraat 31. 📞 010-217
6767. 🕐 Tue–Sun. 🔴 Jan 1,
Apr 30, Dec 25. 📷 ♿

🏛 **Wereldmuseum
Rotterdam**
Willemskade 25. 📞 010-270 7172.
🕐 Tue–Sun. 📷 ♿

**Peter Brueghel the Elder's _The Tower of Babel_ (c.1553) in the Museum
Boijmans-van Beuningen in Rotterdam**

Practical & Travel Information

THE NETHERLANDS IS A STRAIGHTFORWARD country to travel in, and visitors should find its citizens, who are often multilingual, helpful and friendly. One of the joys of a visit to Amsterdam is the relatively car-free environment. Trams, bicycles, and pedestrians are given a higher priority in the center than motor vehicles. Outside the capital, the Dutch public transportation network is one of the most highly developed in Europe.

TOURIST INFORMATION

THE NBT (**Netherlands Board of Tourism**) has offices in many cities worldwide. Within the Netherlands, the state-run tourist information organization is the Vereniging Voor Vreemdelingenverkeer, known as the **VVV**. They have around 450 offices throughout the country. Courteous and friendly staff provide information on sights, transportation, and events, and will also change money and reserve hotel rooms.

The Museum Card (*Museumjaarkaart*), available from branches of the VVV, is valid for a year, and allows admission to over 400 museums and galleries throughout the country.

VISA REQUIREMENTS AND CUSTOMS

CITIZENS OF THE EU, Australia, New Zealand, the US, and Canada need only a valid passport to enter the Netherlands. Those visitors coming from non-EU states can reclaim VAT on certain goods. Call the freephone customs information line (0800-0143) for further details.

SAFETY AND EMERGENCIES

AFTER A RECENT cleanup by the authorities, Amsterdam is much safer than many North American and European cities. Drugs-related crime is still a problem, but tourists should not be affected by this, as long as they act sensibly, and avoid certain areas after dark, in particular the Zeedijk district.

In case of emergencies, the appropriate number to call is listed in the directory opposite.

HEALTH ISSUES

MINOR HEALTH problems can be dealt with by a chemist (*drogist*), who stocks non-prescription drugs. If you need prescription medicines, go to a pharmacy (*apotheek*), open from 8:30am to 5:30pm Monday to Friday.

Attracted by the canals, mosquitoes can be an irritant in Amsterdam, so bring plenty of repellent sprays and antihistamine creams with you.

MUSEUM OPENING TIMES

MANY STATE-RUN museums are closed on Mondays, and open from 10am to 5pm, Tuesday to Saturday, and from 1 to 5pm on Sunday. Most museums adopt Sunday hours for national holidays, apart from New Year's Day, when they are always closed.

BANKING AND CURRENCY

ON JANUARY 1, 2002, the Dutch unit of currency, the guilder, was replaced by the euro (*see p15*).

Banks open from 9 or 10am to 4 or 5pm, Monday to Friday. Some city branches close at 7pm on Thursdays and open on Saturday mornings. Banks are usually the best place to change money, but official bureaux de change, the GWK (*grenswissel-kantoor-bureaus*), also have reasonable exchange rates. Credit cards are not as widely accepted in the Netherlands as in other European countries.

COMMUNICATIONS

PUBLIC TELEPHONES are identifiable by the green and white logo of the PTT, the Dutch state-run telecoms company. Few phone booths still take coins. You can buy phonecards at post offices, newsstands, and train stations.

Most post offices are open Monday to Friday from 9am to 5pm. Apart from offering the normal postal services, they also change currency and traveler's checks, and have telephone and fax services. Stamps can be bought at tobacconists or souvenir stores, as well as at post offices.

FLYING TO THE NETHERLANDS

CARRIERS OPERATING non-stop flights from the US to the Netherlands include charter operator **Martinair**, **Delta Air Lines**, **United Airlines**, and **Northwest Airlines/KLM**. Seven airlines fly direct from the UK to the Netherlands, among them **British Airways** and lowcost airlines including **Ryanair** and **easyJet**. The least expensive way to get from Amsterdam's Schiphol Airport to the city center is by the airport rail service. Trains

THE CLIMATE OF THE NETHERLANDS

The Netherlands has a temperate climate. Winters are frequently freezing, and spring and autumn can be chilly. July and August are the warmest months, but North Sea winds often make it seem cooler. You should expect rainfall all year round, but spring is generally the driest season. The heaviest rainfall occurs in the autumn, especially in November.

AMSTERDAM

°C/F	Apr	Jul	Oct	Jan
high	13/55	22/72	14/58	5/51
low	4/39	12/54	7/45	1/34
sun	5 hrs	6.5 hrs	3 hrs	1.5 hrs
rain	35 mm	57 mm	70 mm	56 mm
month	Apr	Jul	Oct	Jan

leave for Centraal Station seven times each hour between 5:40am and 1am, after which they run hourly. The journey takes 20 minutes. Schiphol Airport station is also connected to other cities in the Netherlands.

ARRIVING BY SEA

FERRY COMPANIES offering car and passenger services from the UK to the Netherlands include **P&O North Sea Ferries**, with daily sailings from Hull to Rotterdam, and **Stena Line**, which operates services between Harwich and the Hook of Holland. P&O operates regular crossings from Hull to Zeebrugge in Belgium.

RAIL TRAVEL

INTERNATIONAL RAIL routes provide a fast and efficient link between Amsterdam and many other European cities. From Centraal Station high-speed **Thalys** trains run to Brussels in 2 hours 30 minutes, and to Paris in just over 4 hours. In both Paris and Brussels, passengers can change to the Eurostar for an onward connection to London.

The Dutch rail system, operated by Nederlandse Spoorwegen, is one of the most modern and efficient in Europe, with an extensive route network. The **OVR** (Openbaar Vervoer Reisinformatie) has information on rail trips for tourists, plus details of special fares. It does not, however, issue tickets, which you buy at the ticket office. If you need to arrange rail travel abroad, visit the offices of **Nederlandse Spoorwegen Internationaal**, located in Amsterdam's Centraal Station.

TRAVELING BY BUS

LONG-DISTANCE BUS travel is an inexpensive, if tiring, way to reach the Netherlands. **Eurolines** and **Hoverspeed City Sprint** have at least two daily services from the UK to Amsterdam, crossing the English Channel by ferry and hovercraft respectively.

Buses in the Netherlands are reliable and efficient. The *strippenkaart* (ticket strip), available in multiples of 15, allows you to travel on buses all over the Netherlands, as well as on trams and the metro in city centers. The city is divided into zones, and each unit, or strip, covers one zone, even when changing between bus, tram, and metro. You can buy a *strippenkaart* at VVV offices, newsstands, or train and bus stations.

TRAVELING BY CAR

AN EVER-EXPANDING highway system makes it easy to travel to the Netherlands from anywhere in Europe. Major roads in the Netherlands (marked N) are generally well-maintained, but Dutch highways (labeled A) have narrow lanes, traffic lights, and sometimes no hard shoulder. When driving in towns, especially in Amsterdam, be careful of cyclists and trams.

Most of the principal international car rental firms have offices in Amsterdam and at Schiphol Airport, but local Dutch companies are significantly less expensive.

Shopping & Entertainment

THE NETHERLANDS IS JUSTLY famous for its cheeses, beers, and flowers, available at specialist stores and super-markets across the country. Amsterdam is a cosmopolitan city, so it is also easy to find a selection of foreign and ethnic goods, from Indonesian beads to French designer wear. The famous brown cafés and coffee shops are an important part of Dutch social life, and visitors to the Netherlands should not miss the chance to try one.

OPENING HOURS

STORES IN the Netherlands are usually open from 9 or 10am to 6pm Tuesday to Saturday, and from 1 to 6pm on Monday. In the larger cities, many shops stay open until 9pm on Thursdays.

WHERE TO SHOP

MOST OF AMSTERDAM'S large department and clothing stores are located in the Nieuwe Zijde, especially along Kalverstraat. The city's best-known department stores are **De Bijenkorf**, often described as the Dutch Harrods, **Metz & Co**, and **Maison de Bonneterie**. Less expensive ones include Vroom & Dreesman and Hema. For luxury fashion, the classy PC Hooftstraat and Van Baerlestraat are lined with chic designer boutiques, such as MEXX and The People of the Labyrinths.

The streets crossing Amster-dam's Canal Ring, such as Herenstraat and Hartenstraat, contain many specialist stores, selling everything from ethnic fabrics to handmade dolls.

WHAT TO BUY

ONE FAMOUS Dutch export is Delftware, the blue-and-white pottery from Delft (*see p263*). Only two factories still make it, though imitation pieces are found in tourist stores all over the country. A certification stamp indicates that an article is genuine. In Amsterdam, the **Galleria d'Arte Rinascimento** and **Holland Gallery de Munt** stock authentic Delftware.

The Dutch are keen beer drinkers. As well as brand names like Heineken, Grolsch, and Amstel, there are many

local specialties, such as Zatte, a rare, bottle-fermented beer, and Wieckse Witte, a white beer. Specialist store **De Bierkoning** offers the widest choice and best advice.

You can usually buy a good selection of Dutch cheeses at supermarkets, including any branch of **Albert Heijn**, street markets, or specialist food stores. Instead of buying the ubiquitous Edam, try one of the many varieties of Gouda. Mature Gouda has a rich, salty taste and crumbly texture, while young Gouda is fresh and curdy.

Other items for which the Netherlands is famous are flowers, which you can buy at Amsterdam's **Maison Rivièra**, among many other places, and diamonds. For the latter, visit the diamond-cutting center **Stoeltie Diamonds**.

MARKETS

THE DUTCH love street trading and almost every town has at least one open-air market. In Amsterdam, the best-known are the Albert Cuypmarkt in Albert Cuyp-straat, with an assortment of Dutch and ethnic food, cheap clothes, and flowers, and the Waterlooplein flea market, in Oude Zijde. The Looier Kunst en Antiekcentrum, at No. 109 Elandsgracht, is a covered market boasting the largest collection of art and antiques in the Netherlands.

ENTERTAINMENT LISTINGS AND TICKETS

THE MONTHLY magazine, *Day by Day*, is available from VVV offices (*see pp264–5*) for a small fee; free issues can be found in some hotels and restaurants. The free monthly *Uitkrant* also has

entertainment listings for the capital, and is easy to follow for non-Dutch speakers.

The main reservations office for entertainment and cultural activities in Amsterdam is the **AUB** (Amsterdam Uitburo). The VVV and Dutch Tourist Information Office will also book tickets for some venues.

ENTERTAINMENT VENUES

AMONG AMSTERDAM'S many theater venues are the **Theater Bellevue**, the **Stads-schouwburg**, and the **Felix Meritis**. For experimental theater, head for **De Brakke Grond** and other venues located along the street known as the Nes. The **Koninklijk Theater Carré** hosts long-running international musicals.

Dance is an important aspect of cultural life in the Netherlands. The Dutch National Ballet is housed in Amsterdam's large-capacity **Muziektheater**, while experimental dance can be enjoyed at **De Meervaart** and the Stadsschouwburg. The Muziektheater is also home to the Dutch National Opera.

The focus for Amsterdam's classical music scene is the **Concertgebouw**, home to the celebrated Royal Concertgebouw Orchestra.

The Netherlands has a huge number of jazz venues. In Amsterdam the internationally renowned **Bimhuis**, the **De IJsbremer**, and the **Alto Jazz Café** are worth visiting. The North Sea Jazz Festival, held in Den Haag in July, attracts some of the biggest names in the industry, while Rotterdam's **Dizzy** is another top venue.

For most Amsterdammers, rock and pop are synonymous with two venues, **Paradiso** and **De Melkweg**, both of which offer a highly varied program. Big-name bands also play at Rotterdam's Ahoy and Utrecht's Vredenburg stadiums.

BROWN CAFÉS AND COFFEE SHOPS

THE TRADITIONAL Dutch "local pub," the brown café, is characterized by dark wooden furnishings, low ceilings, dim lights, and a fog of tobacco smoke. It is a warm and friendly place, and often a social focus for the local neighborhood. There are hundreds in Amsterdam, but one of the best is the tiny and characterful **'t Doktertje**.

For many visitors, a stay in the Netherlands is incomplete without a trip to a smoking coffee shop. At this type of establishment cannabis is openly sold and smoked. Though technically illegal, the sale of soft drugs is tolerated by the Dutch authorities if it remains discreet. **Siberië** is one of the smaller, more relaxed places in Amsterdam, while **The Bulldog** is more commercial and tourist-filled.

CANAL TOURS

THERE ARE MANY operators in Amsterdam offering canal tours. In addition to the daytime sightseeing trips, there are night cruises, which often feature cheese-and-wine refreshments, a stop at a pub, or a romantic candlelit dinner. **Lovers** cruises are the most reasonably-priced, while **P. Kooij** are more upscale.

CYCLING

IT IS CLAIMED that there are more bicycles in the Netherlands than inhabitants. The endlessly flat landscape and thousands of miles of well-maintained cycle tracks make cycling an extremely popular activity, even within cities. **Yellow Bike** organizes excursions in and around Amsterdam between April and October, while the US-based **Euro-Bike and Walking Tours** arranges week-long tours around the whole country. **Cycletours Holland** has a number of "bike-and-boat" itineraries covering the main regions of interest. For those who wish to do things independently, bicycles can be rented easily from many outlets across the country, and at over 100 train stations. The VVV are able to supply detailed route maps.

DIRECTORY

DEPARTMENT STORES

De Bijenkorf
Dam 1, Amsterdam.
(020-552 1700.
Wagenstraat 32, Den Haag.
(070-426 2700.

Maison de Bonneterie
Rokin 140–142,
Amsterdam.
(020-531 3400.

Metz & Co
Leidsestraat 34–36,
Amsterdam.
(020-520 7020.

SPECIALIST ITEMS

Albert Heijn
Jodenbreestraat 21,
Amsterdam.
(020-624 1249.

De Bierkoning
Paleisstraat 125,
Amsterdam.
(020-625 2336.

Galleria d'Arte Rinascimento
Prinsengracht 170,
Amsterdam.
(020-622 7509.

Holland Gallery de Munt
Muntplein 12,
Amsterdam.
(020-623 2271.

Maison Rivièra
Herenstraat 2–6,
Amsterdam.
(020-622 7675.

Stoeltie Diamonds
Wagenstraat 13–17,
Amsterdam.
(020-623 7601.

ENTERTAINMENT TICKETS

AUB
Leidseplein 26, Amsterdam.
(0900-0191.

ENTERTAINMENT VENUES

Alto Jazz Café
Korte Leidsedwarsstraat
115, Amsterdam.
(020-626 3249.

Bimhuis
Oudeschans 73–77,
Amsterdam.
(020-623 1361.

De Brakke Grond
Vlaams Cultureel Centrum,
Nes 45, Amsterdam.
(020-626 6866.

Concertgebouw
Concertgebouwplein 2–6,
Amsterdam.
(020-573 0573.

Dizzy
's-Gravendijkwal 127,
Rotterdam.
(010-477 3014.

Felix Meritis
Keizersgracht 324,
Amsterdam.
(020-623 2321.

De IJsbremer
Weesperzijde 23,
Amsterdam.
(020-668 1805.

Koninklijk Theater Carré
Amstel 115–125,
Amsterdam.
(0900-252 5255.

De Meervaart
Meer en Vaart 300,
Amsterdam.
(020-410 7700.

De Melkweg
Lijnbaansgracht 234a,
Amsterdam.
(020-531 8181.

Het Muziektheater
Amstel 3, Amsterdam.
(020-625 5455.

Paradiso
Weteringschans 6–8,
Amsterdam.
(020-626 4521.

Stadsschouwburg
Leidseplein 26,
Amsterdam.
(020-624 2311.

Theater Bellevue
Leidsekade 90,
Amsterdam.
(020-530 5301.

BROWN CAFÉS & COFFEE SHOPS

't Doktertje
Rozenboomsteeg 4,
Amsterdam.
(020-626 4427.

Siberië
Brouwersgracht 11,
Amsterdam.
(020-623 5909.

The Bulldog
Leidseplein 13–17,
Amsterdam.
(020-627 1908.

CANAL TOURS

Lovers
Opposite Prins Hendrikkade
26, Amsterdam.
(020-530 1090.

P. Kooij
Opposite Rokin 125,
Amsterdam.
(020-623 3810.

CYCLING

Cycletours Holland
Buiksloterweg 7a,
Amsterdam.
(020-627 4098.

Euro-Bike and Walking Tours
PO Box 990, Dekalb,
IL 60115, USA.
(1-800-321 6060.

Yellow Bike
Nieuwezijds Kolk 29,
Amsterdam.
(020-620 6940.

Where to Stay in the Netherlands

Accommodations in Amsterdam range from luxurious five-star hotels to cheap hostels for those on a budget. In between are scores of B&Bs (bed and breakfasts), many in pretty canal houses, whose interiors are often maintained in period style. Elsewhere in the Netherlands, standards of accommodation are generally high, with prices comparable to those of other western European countries.

	NUMBER OF ROOMS	PRIVATE PARKING	RESTAURANT

AMSTERDAM

CENTRAL CANAL RING: *Hotel Maas* €€€
Leidsekade 91, 1017 PN. **Map** B3. (020-623 3868. FAX 020-622 2613. @ info@hotelmaas.nl
The Maas enjoys a quiet location, but is close to the city's main entertainment venues. Children are welcome, with babysitting services available. 🖥 TV 📧 🖾
| 28 | | |

CENTRAL CANAL RING: *Ambassade* €€€€
Herengracht 341, 1016 AZ. **Map** C3. (020-555 0222. FAX 020-555 0277.
@ info@ambassade-hotel.nl
Amsterdam's most luxurious canalside B&B is stylish, comfortable, and professionally run, with beautifully furnished lounges and bedrooms. The 24-hour room service provides simple meals and drinks. 🖥 TV 🖾
| 59 | | |

EASTERN CANAL RING: *Prinsenhof* €€
Prinsengracht 810, 1017 JL. **Map** D4. (020-623 1772. FAX 020-638 3368.
@ info@hotelprinsenhof.com
A simple but well-kept B&B with canal views. The rooms are tastefully decorated, but only three have a private bathroom. There are steep staircases. 🖾
| 11 | | |

MUSEUM QUARTER: *Jan Luyken* €€€€
Jan Luijkenstraat 58, 1071 CS. **Map** B4. (020-573 0730. FAX 020-676 3841.
@ jan-luyken@bilderberg.nl
Close to the city's top museums, this hotel occupies an elegant 19th-century building and has good facilities. Family rooms are available. 🖥 TV 🖾
| 62 | | |

NIEUWE ZIJDE: *Rho* €€€
Nes 5–23, 1012 KC. **Map** C3. (020-620 7371. FAX 020-620 7826. @ info@rhohotel.com
The Rho has clean, modern bedrooms. A good range of amenities, including a bar, make it great value for money. 🖥 TV 🖔 🖾
| 160 | ● | |

NIEUWE ZIJDE: *Estheréa* €€€€
Singel 305, 1012 WJ. **Map** C3. (020-624 5146. FAX 020-623 9001. @ estherea@xs4all.nl
This attractive, long-established hotel is popular with groups. Rooms at the front have canal views, but the rear bedrooms are bigger. 🖥 TV 🖾
| 75 | | |

NIEUWE ZIJDE: *NH Barbizon Palace* €€€€€
Prins Hendrikkade 59–72, 1012 AD. **Map** D2. (020-556 4564.
FAX 020-624 3353. @ nhbarbizon-palace@nh-hotels.nl
Elegant decor and first-class facilities, including business services and a superb restaurant *(see p270)*, guarantee a perfect stay at this hotel. 🖥 TV 🖔 🖾
| 275 | ● | ■ |

NIEUWE ZIJDE: *Sofitel* €€€€€
Nieuwezijds Voorburgwal 67, 1012 RE. **Map** C2. (020-627 5900.
FAX 020-623 8932. @ H1159@accor-hotels.com
A good-quality chain hotel, but somewhat noisy due to its location on a busy street. You can expect the full range of modern conveniences. 🖥 TV 📧 🖔 🖾
| 148 | | ● |

OUDE ZIJDE: *The Grand Sofitel Demeure* €€€€€
Oudezijds Voorburgwal 197, 1012 EX. **Map** C3/D2. (020-555 3111.
FAX 020-555 3222. W www.thegrand.nl
Housed in a 17th-century building, this magnificent hotel has luxurious, well-equipped rooms, a swimming pool, and a fitness center. 🖥 TV 📧 🖾
| 182 | ● | ■ |

PLANTAGE: *Intercontinental Amstel Amsterdam* €€€€€
Prof. Tulpplein 1, 1018 GX. **Map** D4. (020-622 6060. FAX 020-622 5808. @ amstel@interconti.com
This stunning hotel is undisputedly Amsterdam's best. Luxuries include a Turkish bath and a limousine service to Schiphol airport. 🖥 TV 📧 🖔 🖾
| 79 | ● | ■ |

WESTERN CANAL RING: *Canal House* €€€
Keizersgracht 148, 1015 CX. **Map** C2. (020-622 5182. FAX 020-624 1317. @ info@canalhouse.nl
Antique furnishings adorn some of the individually decorated rooms at this small, quiet hotel. To preserve the ambience, children are not welcome. 🖥 🖾
| 26 | | |

Map references refer to map of Amsterdam on pp248–9

	NUMBER OF ROOMS	PRIVATE PARKING	RESTAURANT

Price categories are for a standard double room per night, including breakfast, tax, and service:

€ up to €55
€€ €55–115
€€€ €115–180
€€€€ €180–270
€€€€€ over €270

PRIVATE PARKING
Parking provided in a private car park or private garage. Some hotels charge for use of private parking facilities.

RESTAURANT
Hotel has a restaurant or dining room, serving lunch and/or dinner for guests.

CREDIT CARDS
Major credit cards are accepted in those hotels where the credit card symbol is shown.

FARTHER AFIELD: *Van Ostade Bicycle Hotel* €€ | 16 | ● |
Van Ostadestraat 123, 1072 SV. **Map** C5. (020-679 3452. **FAX** 020-671 5213.
W www.bicyclehotel.com
This friendly B&B in the untouristy De Pijp area has spartan but clean rooms (six with a private bathroom). Staff are helpful and you can rent bicycles on the spot.

FARTHER AFIELD: *Toro* €€€€ | 22 |
Koningslaan 64, 1075 AG. **Map** A4. (020-673 7223. **FAX** 020-675 0031. @ toro@ams.nl
The charming Toro has the air of a small, country house. It enjoys a peaceful location next to a park, a short tram ride from the city center. 🛏 TV ◉

REST OF THE NETHERLANDS

APELDOORN: *Bilderberg Hotel de Keizerskroon* €€€ | 94 | ● | ▦ |
Koningstraat 7, 7315 HR Apeldoorn. (055-521 1744. **FAX** 055-521 4737.
@ keizerskroon@bilderberg.nl W www.keizerskroon.nl
In a spectacular woodland setting, conveniently located for the Paleis Het Loo, this superior hotel offers a range of modern luxuries. 🛏 TV ◉

DELFT: *Museumhotel* €€€ | 51 |
Oude Delft 189, 2611 HD Delft. (015-214 0930. **FAX** 015-215 3079. W www.museumhotel.nl
An elegant, canalside hotel with modern bedrooms. Its name refers to the Delftware in every room, specially commissioned for the hotel. 🛏 TV ◉

THE HAGUE (DEN HAAG): *Golden Tulip Hotel Corona* €€€ | 36 | ● | ▦ |
Buitenhof 39–42, 2513 AH Den Haag. (070-363 7930. **FAX** 070-361 5785. W www.corona.nl
At this smart, city-center hotel you can choose between the standard Art Deco rooms and lavish Louis XVI-style suites. 🛏 TV ◉

THE HAGUE (DEN HAAG): *Hotel des Indes* €€€€€ | 76 | ● | ▦ |
Lange Voorhout 54–56, 2514 EG Den Haag. (070-361 2345. **FAX** 070-361 2350.
W www.desindes.com
Established in 1881, this stately hotel is close to the city's main shops, theaters, and museums. It offers modern comfort and first-class facilities. 🛏 TV ◉

HAARLEM: *Golden Tulip Lion d'Or* €€€ | 34 | | ▦ |
Kruisweg 34–36, 2011 LC Haarlem. (023-532 1750. **FAX** 023-532 9543. W www.goldentulip.nl
This fine early 19th-century establishment is located near the Market Square. The large, well-equipped rooms are tastefully furnished. 🛏 TV 🍽 ◉

LEIDEN: *De Doelen* €€ | 16 |
Rapenburg 2, 2311 EV Leiden. (071-512 0527. **FAX** 071-512 8453. W www.dedoelen.com
Housed in a 17th-century patrician's house and located near the town center, this small hotel has comfortable, spacious rooms, some retaining original period features. 🛏 TV ◉

ROTTERDAM: *Best Western Savoy Hotel* €€€€ | 94 |
Hoogstraat 81, 3011 PJ Rotterdam. (010-413 9280. **FAX** 010-404 5712.
W www.edenhotelgroup.com
The Savoy is located near the Oudehaven, Rotterdam's old harbor area. All the rooms are well-equipped, and the hotel's amenities include conference suites, a bar and a restaurant, and 24-hour room service. 🛏 TV ◉

UTRECHT: *Maliehotel* €€€ | 45 |
Maliestraat 2, 3581 SL Utrecht. (030-231 6424. **FAX** 030-234 0661. W www.maliehotel.nl
Occupying a 19th-century house in a quiet street, about 15 minutes' walk from the town center, this hotel offers simple, but well-kept accommodations. There is a garden and à terrace. 🛏 TV ◉

VOLENDAM: *Spaander* €€ | 80 | ● |
Haven 15–19, 1131 EP Volendam. (0299-363595. **FAX** 0299-369615. @ info@spaander.com
The Spaander's lively hotel, café, and restaurant are packed with paintings and ornaments in the Dutch equivalent of High Victorian style. 🛏 TV ♿ ◉

Where to Eat in the Netherlands

ALTHOUGH THE NETHERLANDS does not boast the gastronomic reputation of France or Italy, the chance of finding good food at a reasonable price is high. As well as Dutch restaurants, there are plenty of other establishments serving culinary delights from around the world. Amsterdam, in particular, is full of ethnic restaurants, and the city offers some of the best Indonesian cuisine in Europe.

	OUTDOOR TABLES	VEGETARIAN DISHES	GOOD WINE LIST

AMSTERDAM

CENTRAL CANAL RING: *Swaagat* € ● ▣
Lange Leidsedwarsstraat 76. **Map** C3. ☎ 020-638 4702.
A good-value Indian restaurant. There are no beef or pork dishes, making it especially popular with Indian diners, and vegetarians are well catered for. The set menus are delicious. ♿ ☙

CENTRAL CANAL RING: *Dynasty* €€€ ● ▣ ●
Reguliersdwarsstraat 30. **Map** C3. ☎ 020-626 8400.
Dynasty offers upscale Southeast Asian cuisine in a well-designed interior. There is a good choice of first-class wines to complement the herbs and spices in the food. In summer ask for a table on the attractive open-air terrace. ● *Tue.* ☙

CENTRAL CANAL RING: *Het Tuynhuys* €€€ ● ●
Reguliersdwarsstraat 28. **Map** C3. ☎ 020-627 6603.
The menu at this excellent restaurant, which occupies an old coach house, combines French and Mediterranean influences. ● *lunch Sat & Sun.* ♿ ☙

EASTERN CANAL RING: *Tempo Doeloe* €€ ▣
Utrechtstraat 75. **Map** D4. ☎ 020-625 6718.
The chef here serves up authentic Indonesian cuisine at this highly recommended restaurant. Friendly, hospitable staff are always at hand to help you choose between the many dishes. ● *lunch daily, Sun.* ☙

EASTERN CANAL RING: *Van Vlaanderen* €€€ ●
Weteringschans 175. **Map** D4. ☎ 020-622 8292.
Oysters with watercress and sorrel and Bresse pigeon with escalope of duck liver are just two of the interesting choices at this modern French restaurant which has recently received a Michelin star. ● *Sun, Mon.* ☙

MUSEUM QUARTER: *Cadans* €€€ ▣ ●
Roelof Hartstraat 6–8. **Map** C5. ☎ 020-676 5201.
French and Mediterranean cuisines along with top-quality ingredients are blended to perfection to produce an exciting menu. This philosophy is reflected in the restaurant's striking interior. ● *Sun.* ☙

NIEUWE ZIJDE: *Krua Thai* € ● ▣
Spuistraat 90a. **Map** C2. ☎ 020-620 0623.
Thai hospitality and enthusiasm add greatly to the enjoyment of this small, casual restaurant's range of fragrant specialties. ● *Mon, lunch daily.* ☙

NIEUWE ZIJDE: *Lucius* €€ ●
Spuistraat 247. **Map** C2. ☎ 020-624 1831.
Lucius is one of only a few specialist seafood restaurants in Amsterdam, offering a wide selection of dishes. There is a good wine list. ● *lunch daily.* ♿ ☙

NIEUWE ZIJDE: *Vasso* €€€€ ● ▣ ●
Rozenboomsteeg 10–14. **Map** C3. ☎ 020-626 0158.
This rustic, Italian restaurant has daily specials, a regional set menu, and a seasonal menu. Advance reservations are essential. ● *lunch daily.* ☙

NIEUWE ZIJDE: *Vermeer/NH Barbizon Palace* €€€€ ▣ ●
Prins Hendrikkade 59–72. **Map** D2. ☎ 020-556 4885.
Now with two Michelin stars, the Vermeer will appeal to anyone interested in modern French-based cooking. Try the cheek of veal and morilles and coquilles St-Jacques. ● *Sun, lunch Sat.* ♿ ☙

OUDE ZIJDE: *Café Roux/Grand Amsterdam* €€€€ ● ▣ ●
Oudezijds Voorburgwal 197. **Map** C3/D2. ☎ 020-555 3560.
Visit Café Roux for a unique opportunity to sample dishes made famous by Albert Roux at a very reasonable price. The restaurant offers a wonderful mix of French, modern British, and even Moroccan dishes. ☙

Map references refer to map of Amsterdam on pp248–9

				OUTDOOR TABLES	VEGETARIAN DISHES	GOOD WINE LIST

Price categories are for a three-course meal for one, excluding wine, plus all unavoidable extra charges, such as cover, service, and tax:
€ under €23
€€ €23–27
€€€ €27–35
€€€€ over €35

OUTDOOR TABLES
Tables for eating outdoors, often with a good view.

VEGETARIAN DISHES
A restaurant that serves dishes which are suitable for vegetarian diners.

GOOD WINE LIST
The restaurant offers a wide range of quality wines.

CREDIT CARDS
Major credit cards are accepted in those restaurants where the credit card symbol is shown.

		OUTDOOR TABLES	VEGETARIAN DISHES	GOOD WINE LIST
PLANTAGE: *La Rive* Prof. Tulpplein 1. **Map** D4. 020-622 6060. An elegant riverside dining room is the setting for this two Michelin-starred restaurant, serving French and Mediterranean cuisine. ● *Sun, lunch Sat.* 🔥 🗩	€€€€		▦	●
WESTERN CANAL RING: *De Groene Lanteerne* Haarlemmerstraat 43. **Map** C3. 020-624 1952. Traditional French dishes are served in this romantic restaurant, which is furnished in the Old-Dutch style. Owner Roberto Plueg was once a wine merchant, which explains the astounding selection of wines on offer. ● *Sun, lunch daily.* 🗩	€€€€		▦	●
REST OF THE NETHERLANDS				
ALKMAAR: *Bios Food & Wines* Gedempte Nieuwesloot 54a, Alkmaar. 072-512 4422. This restaurant enjoys a unique setting in a former cinema auditorium. Diners sit at tables on the balconies. The cuisine is French-Mediterranean. ● *Mon.* 🗩	€€€	●	▦	●
DELFT: *L'Escalier* Oude Delft 125, Delft. 015-212 4621. Good food in a traditional Dutch atmosphere for a reasonable price. The service is friendly and helpful. Vegetarian meals must be booked. ● *Sun.* 🔥 🗩	€€€	●	▦	
HAARLEM: *De Karmeliet* Spekstraat 6. 023-531 4426. Located just off the Grote Markt, this informal restaurant specialises in French and Spanish cuisine. The *tapas* selection is definitely worth sampling. 🗩	€€	●	▦	
THE HAGUE (DEN HAAG): *Le Bistroquet* Lange Voorhout 98, Den Haag. 070-360 1170. Le Bistroquet is a favorite haunt of The Hague's politicians. Mediterranean cooking is accompanied by first-class wines. ● *Sun, lunch Sat.* 🔥 🗩	€€€€	●	▦	●
THE HAGUE (DEN HAAG): *The Raffles* Javastraat 63, Den Haag. 070-345 8587. The menu at this attractively decorated restaurant has a wonderful selection of Indonesian dishes and a good variety of wines. ● *Sun.* 🔥 🗩	€€€€		▦	●
LEIDEN: *Het Prentenkabinet* Kloksteeg 25, Leiden. 071-512 6666. Reasonable prices, good service, and the superb creations of chef Martin van der Ham have ensured a loyal following at Het Prentenkabinet. The menu comprises classical Mediterranean dishes. 🔥 🗩	€€€	●	▦	
ROTTERDAM: *Parkheuvel* Heuvellaan 21, Rotterdam. 010-436 0766. With three Michelin stars, this is one of the best restaurants in Zuid-Holland. The service is informal but spot on. ● *Sun, lunch Sat.* 🔥 🗩	€€€€	●	▦	●
SCHEVENINGEN: *Seinpost* Zeekant 60, Scheveningen. 070-355 5250. At Seinpost you can enjoy delicious, well-prepared fish dishes and admire the sea view at the same time. Exemplary service. ● *Sun.* 🔥 🗩	€€€€		▦	●
UTRECHT: *Algarve* Biltstraat 98, Utrecht. 030-271 8408. Located just outside the city center, this authentically decorated restaurant specializes in traditional Portuguese fish and meat dishes. ● *Mon, Tue.* 🔥 🗩	€€€		▦	
UTRECHT: *Tussen Hemel en Aarde* Oudegracht 99, Utrecht. 030-231 1864. This atmospheric restaurant (the name means "Between Heaven and Earth") is housed in an old castle in the heart of the town. Excellent food. ● *Sun.* 🔥 🗩	€€€	●	▦	●

THE IBERIAN PENINSULA

The Iberian Peninsula at a Glance

A WONDERFUL, WARM CLIMATE and superb beaches have made the Iberian Peninsula a popular package-tour destination, drawing millions of visitors to well-known areas such as the Algarve in Portugal, and the Costa del Sol in Spain. But there are also tranquil fishing villages, first-class museums and galleries, and a wealth of splendid architecture, from the grand monuments left by the region's Moorish rulers to ultramodern, 20th-century designs. The Catholic faith has deep roots in Portugal and Spain. As well as spectacular cathedrals, there are many colorful religious festivals that take place all year round, making a visit all the more enjoyable.

0 km   75

0 miles   75

Sa
Oviedo
Lugo
Santiago de Compostela
León
Valladolid
Oporto
Salamanca

PORTUGAL
(See pp352–381)

Toledo (see pp296–8) *has one of the largest cathedrals in Christendom, a massive Gothic structure that soars above the rooftops of the perfectly preserved medieval town.*

T

Lisbon (see pp356–65) *rises above the estuary of the Tagus on a series of a hills. The oldest part of the city is crowned by the restored battlements of the Castelo de São Jorge.*

LISBON

Ciu

Córdob

Seville

Seville (see pp328–31) *is regarded as the soul of Andalusia. The city's famous bullring is arguably the finest in the whole of Spain and a perfect venue for a first experience of the* corrida, *or bullfight.*

Málaga

◁ **The rocky coast of Galicia, northwestern Spain**

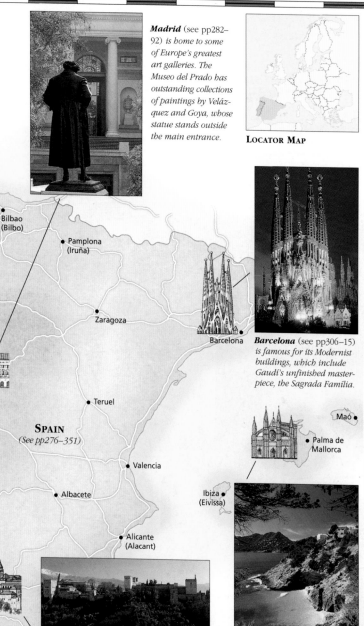

Madrid (see pp282–92) is home to some of Europe's greatest art galleries. The Museo del Prado has outstanding collections of paintings by Velázquez and Goya, whose statue stands outside the main entrance.

LOCATOR MAP

Bilbao
(Bilbo)

Pamplona
(Iruña)

Zaragoza

Barcelona

Barcelona (see pp306–15) is famous for its Modernist buildings, which include Gaudí's unfinished masterpiece, the Sagrada Família.

Teruel

SPAIN
(See pp276–351)

Valencia

Maó

Palma de
Mallorca

Albacete

Ibiza
(Eivissa)

Alicante
(Alacant)

Granada (see pp320 and 322–3), in the foothills of the snowcapped Sierra Nevada, is unmissable for its Moorish heritage. Its greatest monument is the stunning Alhambra palace.

The Balearic Islands (see p319) are often associated with mass tourism, but away from the busy resorts, there are hundreds of unspoiled coastal villages and beautiful coves to be discovered.

SPAIN

T HE FAMILIAR IMAGES OF SPAIN – *flamenco dancing, bullfighting, tapas bars, and solemn Easter processions – do no more than hint at the diversity of this country. Spain has four official languages, two major cities of almost equal importance, and a greater range of landscapes than any other European country. These contrasts make Spain an endlessly fascinating place to visit.*

Separated from the rest of Europe by the Pyrenees, Spain reaches south to the coast of North Africa, and has both Atlantic and Mediterranean coastlines. The country's climate and scenery vary dramatically, from the snow-capped peaks of the Pyrenees, through the green meadows of Galicia and the orange groves of Valencia, to the dry, barren regions in the south.

Madrid, Spain's capital, lies geographically in the center of the country. The *madrileños* – as the city's inhabitants are known – have an individualistic spirit and a sardonic sense of humor that set them apart from other Spaniards. Madrid may be the nominal capital, but it is rivaled in commerce, sport, and the arts by Barcelona, the main city of Catalonia.

In the last 50 years Spain has undergone more social change than anywhere else in western Europe. In the first half of the 20th century, it was largely a poor, rural country. Gradually people flooded into the cities, leaving the rural areas depopulated. The 1960s saw the beginning of spectacular economic growth, partly due to a burgeoning tourist industry. Since then Spain has become a major player in European and world affairs.

HISTORY

From the 11th century BC the coastal regions of the Iberian Peninsula were colonized by sophisticated eastern Mediterranean civilizations, starting with the Phoenicians, then the Greeks and the Carthaginians. Celts mixed with native Iberian tribes, forming the Celtiberians. The Romans arrived in 218 BC to take possession of the peninsula's huge mineral wealth. The fall of the Roman Empire in the 5th century AD left Spain in the hands of the Visigoths, invaders from the north. Their poor political organization,

The colorful art of bullfighting, still a strong tradition all over Spain

◁ View from a typical hilltop Castilian town across the vast plains of central Spain

The Moor Boabdil surrendering Granada to the Catholic Monarchs

however, meant they were easily conquered by the Moors, who arrived from North Africa around 711.

Within a few years the Moors controlled almost the entire peninsula. Europe's only major Muslim territory, the civilization of Al Andalus excelled in mathematics, geography, astronomy, and poetry, and by the 9th century Córdoba was Europe's leading city.

In the 11th century, northern Christian kingdoms initiated a military reconquest of Al Andalus. The marriage, in 1469, of Fernando of Aragón and Isabel of

Castile – the so-called Catholic Monarchs – led to Spanish unity. They took Granada, the last Moorish stronghold, in 1492. In the same year Columbus discovered the Americas, and the conquistadors began plundering the civilizations of the New World.

The 17th century was a golden age for Spain – a time of outstanding artistic and literary output. This brilliance occurred, however, against a backdrop of economic deterioration and ruinous wars with France and the Low Countries. Spain's misfortunes continued in the 19th century, with an invasion by Napoleon's troops, leading to the War of Independence (Peninsular War). In the course of this century, Spain also lost all her South and Central American colonies. The late 19th century was a time of national decline, with anarchism developing as a response to rampant political corruption. Political instability led to

General Franco, Nationalist leader in the Spanish Civil War

dictatorship in the 1920s and, a decade later, the Spanish Civil War. The victor, the Nationalist General Franco, ruled by repression until his death in 1975. Since then Spain has been a democratic state.

KEY DATES IN SPANISH HISTORY

1100 BC Arrival of Phoenicians, first in a wave of settlers from across the Mediterranean

218–202 BC Romans oust Carthaginians from southeastern Spain

5th century AD Fall of the Roman Empire; Visigoths take control of Spain

711 Moors invade Spain and defeat Visigoths

756 Independent emirate established at Córdoba; Moorish civilization flourishes

11th century Christian kingdoms begin reconquest of Moorish territories

1492 Catholic Monarchs capture Granada, last Moorish stronghold. Columbus reaches America

1561 Madrid becomes capital of Spain

17th century Spain's Golden Age; a period of great artistic and literary achievements

1808–14 Spanish War of Independence

1898 Spain loses her last American colony, Cuba

1936–9 Spanish Civil War; Nationalist General Franco emerges victor

1975 Death of Franco; restoration of Bourbon monarchy as Juan Carlos I is proclaimed king

1986 Spain joins the EC (now EU)

1992 Barcelona hosts the Olympic Games

DEVELOPMENT AND DIPLOMACY

After the death of the dictator General Franco in 1975, Spain became a constitutional monarchy under King Juan Carlos I. The post-Franco era, up until the mid-1990s, was dominated by the Socialist Prime Minister Felipe González, whose party, PSOE, was responsible for major improvements in roads, education, and health services. Spain's entry to the European Community in 1986 triggered a spectacular increase in the country's prosperity. Its international reputation was given a further boost in 1992 when Barcelona hosted the Olympic Games and Seville was the site of Expo '92.

With the establishment of democracy, the 17 autonomous regions of Spain have acquired considerable powers. A significant number of Basques favor independence for the Basque Country. The Basque terrorist group ETA, whose campaign of violence continues today, is one of the major problems facing the present government, headed by José María Aznar of the Partido Popular.

RELIGION, LANGUAGE, AND CULTURE

Following the Christian Reconquest in the Middle Ages, a succession of rulers tried to impose a common culture, but today Spain remains a culturally diverse nation. Several regions have maintained a strong sense of their own identities. Catalonia, the Basque Country, Valencia, the Balearic Islands, and Galicia have their own languages, which are in everyday use, and, in some cases, have supplanted Castilian as the first language of the region.

During the Middle Ages Spain gained a reputation for religious intolerance. The Inquisition, established by the Catholic Monarchs, saw thousands of non-Catholics tortured, executed, or expelled from the country. Today, Spain enjoys complete religious freedom. Nevertheless, Catholicism is still a powerful influence in society. Saints' days and other important events in the Christian calendar are marked by many traditional ceremonies, enthusiastically maintained in towns and villages throughout modern Spain.

Religious procession in a Seville street during *Semana Santa* (Holy Week)

THE SPANISH WAY OF LIFE

The Spanish are known for their natural sociability and zest for living. They commonly put as much energy into enjoying life as they do into their work. The stereotypical "mañana" ("leave it until tomorrow") is a myth, but many people fit their work around the demands of their social life, rather than be ruled by the clock. The day is long in Spain, and the Spanish have a word, *madrugada*, for the time between midnight and dawn, when city streets are often still full of revelers enjoying themselves. Eating out is an important social activity, with friends and family often meeting up in a pavement café or restaurant for a chat and a meal.

Underpinning Spanish society is the extended family. In the past, a lack of efficient public services has forced the Spanish to rely on close relatives, rather than institutions, to find work or seek assistance in a crisis. It is not uncommon for three generations to live under one roof, and even life-long city dwellers refer fondly to their *pueblo* – the town or village where their family comes from, and which they return to as often as they can.

Spaniards socializing over drinks and a meal at a sidewalk café

Exploring Spain

Although many visitors to Spain come for the
beaches alone, increasingly tourists are drawn
by the country's rich cultural heritage. The most
popular destinations are Madrid and Barcelona,
which boast world-class museums and a wealth
of medieval and modern architecture. For those
with time to travel further afield, Seville, Granada,
and Córdoba in the far south are the best places
to see relics of Spain's Moorish past. Spain is
Europe's third largest country, so getting around
can be time-consuming. However, there is a
reliable network of trains, as well as
good highways and bus services.

**Ciutadella harbor, on the island of
Menorca, at twilight**

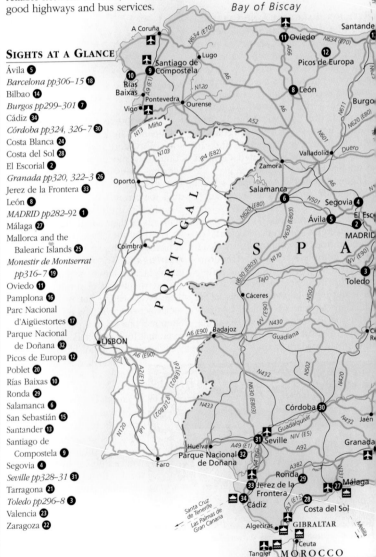

DISTANCE CHART

Distance in kilometers
Distance in miles

MADRID								
621 388	BARCELONA							
397 248	**620** 388	BILBAO						
400 250	**908** 568	**795** 497	CÓRDOBA					
544 340	**997** 623	**939** 587	**187** 117	MALAGA				
623 389	**1129** 706	**707** 442	**977** 611	**1153** 721	PONTEVEDRA			
538 336	**1046** 654	**933** 583	**138** 86	**219** 137	**922** 576	SEVILLE		
352 220	**349** 218	**633** 396	**545** 405	**648** 341	**975** 609	**697** 436	VALENCIA	
325 203	**296** 185	**324** 203	**725** 453	**869** 543	**833** 521	**863** 539	**326** 204	ZARAGOZA

KEY

✈ Airport
⛴ Ferry port
— Highway
— Major road
— Railroad
--- International border

0 km   80

0 miles   80

The Giralda in Seville, a legacy of Spain's Moorish rulers

Madrid ❶

19th-century *taberna* (taverna),
one of the few left in Madrid today

S PAIN'S CAPITAL, a city of over three million people,
is situated close to the geographical center of
the country, at the hub of both road and rail
networks. The origins of the city date back to AD
852, when the Moors built a fortress near the
Manzanares river and a small community grew up
around it. It was not until 1561, however, that the
city became the capital of a newly formed nation-
state. In the following centuries, under the Habsburgs
and then the Bourbons, the city acquired some of its
most notable landmarks, including the splendid
Plaza Mayor and the Palacio Real. At the same time,
the blossoming city attracted some of Spain's most
outstanding artists, such as court painters Velázquez
and Goya, whose works can be admired in the
world-famous Museo del Prado.

KEY

⬜	Sight / Place of interest
✈	Airport
🚉	Train station
Ⓜ	Metro station
🚌	Main bus station
Ⓟ	Parking
ℹ	Tourist information
✝	Church
—	Pedestrian street

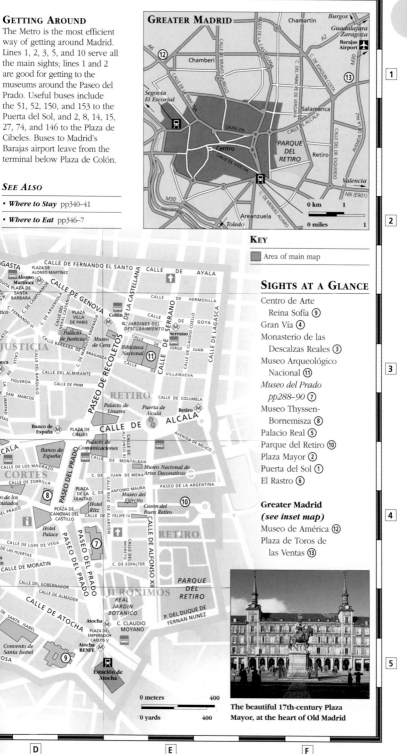

GETTING AROUND

The Metro is the most efficient way of getting around Madrid. Lines 1, 2, 3, 5, and 10 serve all the main sights; lines 1 and 2 are good for getting to the museums around the Paseo del Prado. Useful buses include the 51, 52, 150, and 153 to the Puerta del Sol, and 2, 8, 14, 15, 27, 74, and 146 to the Plaza de Cibeles. Buses to Madrid's Barajas airport leave from the terminal below Plaza de Colón.

SEE ALSO

- **Where to Stay** pp340–41

- **Where to Eat** pp346–7

GREATER MADRID

KEY

Area of main map

SIGHTS AT A GLANCE

Centro de Arte
  Reina Sofía (9)
Gran Vía (4)
Monasterio de las
  Descalzas Reales (3)
Museo Arqueológico
  Nacional (11)
Museo del Prado
  pp288–90 (7)
Museo Thyssen-
  Bornemisza (8)
Palacio Real (5)
Parque del Retiro (10)
Plaza Mayor (2)
Puerta del Sol (1)
El Rastro (6)

**Greater Madrid
(see inset map)**
Museo de América (12)
Plaza de Toros de
  las Ventas (13)

The beautiful 17th-century Plaza Mayor, at the heart of Old Madrid

Old Madrid

WHEN FELIPE II CHOSE MADRID as his capital in 1561, it was a small Castilian town of little importance. In the following years, it was to grow into the nerve center of a mighty empire. During the reign of the Habsburg dynasty, many royal monasteries, churches, and private palaces were built. In the 17th century the Plaza Mayor was added, and the Puerta del Sol became the spiritual and geographical heart not only of Madrid but of all Spain. Old Madrid's splendid Bourbon palace, the Palacio Real, was built under Felipe V in the first half of the 18th century.

Bear and strawberry tree, the symbol of Madrid, Puerta del Sol

Puerta del Sol ①

Ⓜ Sol.

WITH ITS MANY shops and cafés, the Puerta del Sol ("Gateway of the Sun") is one of Madrid's liveliest areas. The square marks the site of the original eastern entrance to the city, once occupied by a gatehouse and a castle. In the late 19th century the area was the center of café society.

An imposing statue of Carlos III (reigned 1759–88) stands at the center of the square. On its southern edge is the austere, red-brick Casa de Correos, dating from the 1760s. Originally the city's post office, it later became the headquarters of the Ministry of the Interior. During the Franco regime, the police cells below the building were the site of human rights abuses. Outside the building, a symbol on the ground marks Kilometer Zero, considered the center of Spain's road network.

On the opposite side of the square is a bronze statue of the symbol of Madrid – a bear reaching for the fruit of a *madroño* (strawberry tree).

The Puerta del Sol has witnessed many important historical events. On May 2, 1808 the uprising against the occupying French forces began in the square, and in 1912 the liberal prime minister José Canalejas was assassinated here.

Plaza Mayor ②

Ⓜ Sol.

FOR HUNDREDS of years this beautiful 17th-century square was a center of activity, with bullfights, executions, pageants, and trials by the Inquisition taking place here.

The first great public event was the beatification of the city's patron, St. Isidore, in 1621. Perhaps the greatest occasion, however, was the arrival from Italy of Carlos III (Carlos VII of Naples) in 1760. He became king of Spain after his half-brother, Fernando VI, died without an heir.

Façade of the Casa de la Panadería on the Plaza Mayor

Designed by architect Juan Gómez de Mora, the square was started in 1617 and built in just two years. At its center is an equestrian statue of Felipe III, who ordered the square's construction.

The elegant arcades that line the Plaza Mayor are today filled with cafés and craft shops. One of the more interesting buildings is the Casa de la Panadería, whose façade is decorated with splendid allegorical paintings.

On Sundays the square is the venue for a collectors' market, with stalls selling coins, stamps, books, and other items.

Decorated chapel, Monasterio de las Descalzas Reales

Monasterio de las Descalzas Reales ③

Plaza de las Descalzas 3. **C** 91-454 88 00. **W** www.patrimonionacional.es **Ⓜ** Sol, Callao. **◯** 10:30am–12:45pm, 4–5:45pm Tue–Thu & Sat, 10:30am–12:45pm Fri, 11am–1:45pm Sun & public hols. **●** Jan 1 & 6, Apr 16–19, May 1 & 15, Sep 9, Dec 24–25, 31. **◙** (except Wed for EU residents).

THIS RELIGIOUS building is one of the rare surviving examples of 16th-century architecture in Madrid. Around 1560, Felipe II's sister, Doña Juana, decided to convert the medieval palace which stood on this site into a convent.

Doña Juana's rank accounts for the massive store of art amassed by the Descalzas Reales (Royal Barefoot Sisters), which includes a fresco of

The vast Palacio Real, Madrid's 18th-century Bourbon palace

Felipe IV's family and, above the main staircase, a ceiling by Claudio Coello. The Sala de Tapices contains stunning tapestries, while paintings on display include works by Brueghel the Elder, Titian, Zurbarán, Murillo, and Ribera.

Gran Vía ④

M *Plaza de España, Santo Domingo, Callao, Gran Vía.*

A MAIN TRAFFIC ARTERY of the modern city, the Gran Vía was inaugurated in 1910.

Lined with cinemas, tourist shops, hotels, and restaurants, this grand avenue also has many buildings of architectural interest. At the Alcalá end of the street, the French-inspired Edificio Metrópolis and the Edificio la Estrella (No. 10) are both worth seeing. The latter is a good example of the eclectic mix of Neoclassical design and ornamental detail

One of the many 1930s Art Deco buildings lining the Gran Vía

that was fashionable when the street was first developed. Look out for some interesting carved stone decoration, such as the striking gargoyle-like caryatids at No. 12.

Further along the Gran Vía, around the Plaza del Callao, are a number of Art Deco buildings, including the well-known Capitol cinema and bingo hall, built in the 1930s.

Palacio Real ⑤

Calle de Bailén. **C** *91-454 88 00.* **W** *patrimonionacional.es* **M** *Ópera, Plaza de España.* **🚌** *3, 25, 33, 39, 148.* **🕐** *Apr–Sep: 9am–6pm Mon–Sat, 9am–3pm Sun & hols; Oct–Mar: 9:30am–5pm Mon–Sat, 9am–2pm Sun & hols.* **●** *for official functions.* **🎫** *(except Wed for EU residents).* **📷 ♿**

M ADRID'S VAST and lavish Palacio Real (Royal Palace) was commissioned by Felipe V after the royal fortress that had occupied the site for centuries was ravaged by fire in 1734. The palace was the home of Spanish royalty until the abdication of Alfonso XIII in 1931. Today it is used by the present king for state occasions only.

The exuberant decor of the interior reflects the tastes of the Bourbon kings, Carlos III and Carlos IV. The walls and ceiling of the Porcelain Room, commissioned by the former, are covered in green and white royal porcelain, which is embossed with cherubs and wreaths. Named after its Neapolitan designer, the Gasparini Room is equally

lavishly decorated. In the adjacent antechamber hangs a portrait of Carlos IV by Goya. Other star attractions within the palace are the Dining Room, with its fine ceiling paintings and superb Flemish tapestries, and the 18th-century Throne Room.

Shoppers browsing around the Rastro flea market

El Rastro ⑥

Calle de la Ribera de Curtidores. **M** *La Latina, Embajadores.* **🕐** *10am–2pm Sun & public hols.*

M ADRID'S FAMOUS flea market was established in the Middle Ages. Its heyday came in the 19th century, but today there are still plenty of locals, as well as tourists, who come to the Calle de la Ribera de Curtidores to browse around the many stalls selling a huge range of wares – from new furniture to second-hand clothes. The market's other main street is the Calle de Embajadores, which runs down past the dusty Baroque façade of the Iglesia de San Cayetano.

Street-by-Street: Paseo del Prado

Banco de España sculpture

I**N THE LATE** 18TH CENTURY, before the museums and lavish hotels of Bourbon Madrid took shape, the Paseo del Prado was laid out and soon became a fashionable spot for strolling. Today the Paseo's main attraction lies in its museums and art galleries. Most notable are the Museo del Prado (just south of the Plaza Cánovas del Castillo) and the Museo Thyssen-Bornemisza, both displaying world-famous collections of paintings. Among the monuments built under Carlos III are the Puerta de Alcalá, the Fuente de Neptuno, and the Fuente de Cibeles, which stand in the middle of busy roundabouts.

Paseo del Prado
Based on the Piazza Navona in Rome, the Paseo was built by Ca III as a center for the arts and sciences in Madrid.

Banco de España
Spain's central reserve bank is housed in this massive building with three façades at the Plaza de Cibeles.

Banco de España

CALLE DE ALCALÁ

CALLE DEL MARQUES

CALLE DE LOS MADRAZO

DE CUBAS

BARQUILLO

ZORRILLA

★ Museo Thyssen-Bornemisza
Petrus Christus's Our Lady of the Dry Tree *(c.1450) is one of many early Flemish works in this excellent art collection* (see p291).

Tourist information ↓

The Congreso de los Diputados, home of the Spanish parliament, witnessed the country's transition from dictatorship to democracy.

The Plaza Cánovas del Castillo is dominated by a sculpted fountain of the god Neptune in his chariot.

Hotel Palace

PLAZA CÁNOVAS CASTILLO

Mus del Pra

| 0 meters | 100 |
| 0 yards | 100 |

STAR SIGHTS

★ **Museo Thyssen-Bornemisza**

★ **Puerta de Alcalá**

★ **Plaza de Cibeles**

Palacio de Linares
This grandly decorated late 19th-century palace now houses the Casa de América, an organization that promotes Latin American culture.

Palacio de Comunicaciones

★ **Puerta de Alcalá**
Sculpted from granite, this former gateway into the city is especially beautiful when floodlit at night.

PLAZA DE LA

CALLE DE ALCALÁ

INDEPENDENCIA

CALLE DE ALFONSO XI

CALLE DE MONTALBAN

CALLE DE ALFONSO XII

CALLE JUAN DE MENA

★ **Plaza de Cibeles**
A fountain with a statue of the Roman goddess Cybele stands in this square.

DE LA LEALTAD

CALLE ANTONIO MAURA

→ **Parque del Retiro**

The Museo Nacional de Artes Decorativas was founded in 1912 as a showcase for Spanish ceramics and interior design.

RUIZ DE ALARCON

ALLE FELIPE IV

The Monumento del Dos de Mayo commemorates the War of Independence against the French.

The Hotel Ritz, with its *belle-époque* interior, is one of the most elegant hotels in the whole of Spain.

KEY

– – – Suggested route

Museo del Ejército
This huge collection of military memorabilia (see p291) is housed in part of the former Retiro Palace.

Museo del Prado ⑦

THE PRADO MUSEUM houses the world's greatest assembly of Spanish paintings from the 12th to the 19th centuries, including major works by Velázquez and Goya. It also houses impressive foreign collections, particularly of Italian and Flemish works. The Neoclassical building was designed in 1785 by Juan de Villanueva on the orders of Carlos III. It opened as a museum in 1819 to display the royal collection of fine and decorative arts. The Casón del Buen Retiro, the Prado's annex, has recently been renovated and contains 19th- and 20th-century paintings.

★ Velázquez Collection
The Triumph of Bacchus (1629), Velázquez's first portrayal of a mythological subject, shows the god of wine (Bacchus) with a group of drunkards.

The Three Graces
(c.1635)
This was one of the last paintings by the Flemish master Rubens, and was part of his personal collection. The three women dancing in a ring – the Graces – are the daughters of Zeus, and represent Love, Joy, and Revelry.

The Garden of Delights *(c.1505)*
Hieronymus Bosch, known as El Bosco in Spanish, was one of Felipe II's favorite artists, and is especially well represented in the Prado. This enigmatic painting is part of a triptych depicting paradise and hell.

Main entrance

STAR EXHIBITS

★ **Velázquez Collection**

★ **Goya Collection**

The museum's façade,
dating from the 18th century, illustrates the Neoclassical move towards dignity away from the excesses of Baroque architecture.

The second floor, recently opened to the public, contains collections of works by Goya and the 18th-century European School.

VISITORS' CHECKLIST

Paseo del Prado. **91-330 28 00.** Atocha, Banco de España. 6, 10, 14, 19, 27, 34, 37, 45. 9am–7pm Tue–Sun. Jan 1, Good Fri, May 1, Dec 25. (free Sun). **Casón del Buen Retiro:** Calle de Alfonso XII 28. **91-330 28 00.** 9am–7pm Tue–Sun. Jan 1, Good Fri, May 1, Dec 25. www.museoprado.mcu.es

First floor

Stairs to lower floor,

★ Goya Collection
In The Clothed Maja *and* The Naked Maja *(both c.1800), Goya tackled the taboo subject of nudity, for which he was later accused of obscenity.*

The Martyrdom of St. Philip *(c.1639)*
The Valencian José de Ribera moved to Naples as a young man. He was influenced by Caravaggio's use of light and shadow, known as chiaroscuro, as seen in this work.

Ground floor

KEY TO FLOORPLAN

- Spanish painting
- Flemish and Dutch painting
- Italian painting
- French painting
- German and British painting
- Sculpture
- Temporary exhibitions
- Non-exhibition space

GALLERY GUIDE

The best way to enter the Prado is through the new, modern reception center situated between the main building and the church behind. The works are arranged in schools, with the oldest works displayed on the lowest floors. The magnificent Velázquez collection is located on the first floor, along with other 17th-century Spanish works.

Exploring the Prado's Collection

THE IMPORTANCE OF THE PRADO is founded on its royal collections. The wealth of foreign art, including many of Europe's finest works, reflects the historical power of the Spanish crown. The Low Countries and parts of Italy were under Spanish rule for hundreds of years. The 18th century was an era of French influence, following the Bourbon accession to the Spanish throne. The Prado is worthy of repeated visits, but if you go only once, see the Spanish works of the 17th century.

SPANISH PAINTING

RIGHT UP TO THE 19th century, Spanish painting focused on religious and royal themes. There are a few examples of Spain's early medieval art in the Prado, such as the anonymous mural paintings from the Holy Cross hermitage in Maderuelo. Spanish Gothic art can be seen in the works of Bartolomé Bermejo and Fernando Gallego.

Renaissance features began to emerge in the paintings of Pedro de Berruguete and Fernando Yáñez de la Almedina, whose work shows the influence of Leonardo da Vinci. Among examples of 16th-century Mannerism are paintings by Pedro Machuca and Luis de Morales "the Divine". One of the great masters of this period was the Cretan-born artist El Greco, who made his home in Toledo. The distortion of the human figure, typical of the Mannerist style, is carried to extreme in his painting *The Adoration of the Shepherds* (1612–14).

The Golden Age of the 17th century produced such great artists as José de Ribera and Francisco de Zurbarán. Works by both are on display in the Prado. This period, however, is best represented by the work of Diego Velázquez, Spain's leading court painter. Examples of his royal portraits and religious and mythological paintings are displayed, including his masterpiece *Las Meninas* (1656), a portrait of the Infanta Margarita surrounded by her courtiers.

Another great Spanish painter, Francisco de Goya, revived Spanish art in the 18th century. His later work embraces the horrors of war, as seen in *The 3rd of May* (1814), and culminated in a somber series known as *The Black Paintings*.

FLEMISH AND DUTCH PAINTING

EXCEPTIONAL FLEMISH works of art include Rogier van der Weyden's masterpiece, *The Deposition* (c.1430), and some of Hieronymus Bosch's major paintings, such as the *Temptation of St. Anthony* (c.1500) and *The Haywain* (c.1485–90). Among the 16th-century paintings is the superb *Triumph of Death* (1562) by Brueghel the Elder. There are nearly 100 canvases by the 17th-century Flemish painter Peter Paul Rubens, of which the greatest is *The Adoration of the Magi*. The two most notable Dutch paintings on display are both by Rembrandt: *Artemisia* (c.1500) and a fine self-portrait.

The Adoration of the Shepherds (1612–14) by El Greco

ITALIAN PAINTING

THE MOST REMARKABLE Italian paintings are Botticelli's dramatic wooden panels that depict *The Story of Nastagio degli Onesti*, Raphael's *Christ Falls on the Way to Calvary* (1516), and *Christ Washing the Disciples' Feet* (c.1547) by Tintoretto. Venetian masters Titian – Charles V's court painter – and Veronese are equally well represented. Also on display are works by Giordano, Fra Angelico, Caravaggio, and Tiepolo, master of Italian Rococo.

Fra Angelico's The Annunciation (c.1430), from the Early Renaissance

FRENCH AND GERMAN PAINTING

MARRIAGES BETWEEN French and Spanish royalty in the 17th century brought French art to Spain. This section contains a selection of works by Poussin, Jean Ranc, Claude Lorrain, and Antoine Watteau.

German art is represented by Albrecht Dürer's lively *Self-Portrait* (1498), as well as by the works of Lucas Cranach and the late 18th-century court painter Anton Raffael Mengs.

CASÓN DEL BUEN RETIRO

RECENTLY RENOVATED and extended, the Casón del Buen Retiro houses mainly late 19th- and early 20th-century works, Neoclassical and Romantic art, and paintings on historical themes. There are some splendid works by Mariano Fortuny and the Impressionist Joaquín Sorolla.

spacious interior of the Museo Thyssen-Bornemisza

Museo Thyssen-Bornemisza ⑧

Paseo del Prado 8. 91-369 01 51.
www.museothyssen.org M Banco
de España, Sevilla. 1, 2, 5, 9, 14,
15, 20. 10am–7pm Tue–Sun.

THIS MAGNIFICENT museum houses a collection of art assembled by Baron Heinrich Thyssen-Bornemisza and his son, Hans Heinrich. From its beginnings in the 1920s, the collection was intended to illustrate the history of Western art, from the 14th to the 20th century. Among the museum's exhibits are masterpieces by Titian, Goya, and Van Gogh.

The remarkable series of Dutch and Flemish works is a strong point of the collection. Highlights include Jan van Eyck's *The Annunciation* (c.1435–41), Petrus Christus's *Our Lady of the Dry Tree* (c.1450), and among the later works *The Toilet of Venus* (c.1629) by Peter Paul Rubens.

On the ground floor is modern and contemporary art, among which are Picasso's *Harlequin with a Mirror* (1923) and Edward Hopper's *Hotel Room* (1931).

A new extension, due to open by 2004, will house the Carmen Thyssen-Bornemisza collection, including many Impressionist works.

Centro de Arte Reina Sofía ⑨

Calle Santa Isabel 52. 91-467
50 62. www.museoreinasofia.mcu.es
M Atocha. 6, 14, 18, 19, 27, 45,
55, 68. 10am–9pm (2:30pm Sun)
Wed–Mon. main public hols.
(free Sat pm & Sun).

HOUSED IN AN 18th-century former general hospital, this superb museum traces art through the 20th-century, with major works by such influential artists as Picasso, Salvador Dalí, Joan Miró, and Eduardo Chillida. There is also space dedicated to some of the most

important movements of the post-World War II era, such as Abstract, Pop, and Minimal Art.

The highlight of the collection is, without doubt, Picasso's *Guernica* (1937). This Civil War protest painting was inspired by the mass air attack in 1937 on the Basque village of Gernika by German pilots flying for the Nationalist air force. The painting was returned to Spain from a New York gallery after democracy was restored in Spain in 1981.

Parque del Retiro ⑩

91-409 23 36. M Retiro, Ibiza,
Atocha. daily.

THE RETIRO PARK formed part of Felipe IV's royal palace complex. All that remains of the palace is the Casón del Buen Retiro (now part of the Prado museum) and the Museo del Ejército, Madrid's Army Museum. In 2005 the latter is due to move to the Alcázar in Toledo *(see p298)*.

First fully opened to the public in 1869, the Retiro remains a popular place for relaxing in Madrid. The park has a pleasure lake, where rowing boats can be hired. On one side of the lake, in front of a half-moon colonnade, stands an equestrian statue of Alfonso XII.

To the south of the lake are two attractive palaces. The Neoclassical Palacio de Velázquez and the Palacio de Cristal (Crystal Palace) were built by Velázquez Bosco in 1887 as exhibition venues.

Colonnade and statue of Alfonso XII (1901) overlooking the Parque del Retiro's boating lake

Roman floor mosaic in the Museo Arqueológico Nacional

Museo Arqueológico Nacional ⑪

Calle de Serrano 13. [91-577 79 12. W www.man.es M Serrano, Retiro. 🚌 1, 9, 19, 51, 74. ⏰ 9:30am–8:30pm (6:30pm Jul & Aug) Tue – Sat, 9:30am–2:30pm Sun. ● main public hols. 🎫 (free Sat pm & Sun). ☑ ⛪

Founded by Isabel II in 1867, Madrid's National Archaeological Museum has hundreds of fascinating exhibits, ranging from the prehistoric era to the 19th century.

One of the highlights of the prehistoric section is the exhibition on the ancient civilization of El Argar (1800–1100 BC) – an advanced agrarian society that flourished in southeast Spain. There is also a display of jewelry uncovered at the Roman settlement of Numantia, near Soria.

The museum's ground floor is largely devoted to the period between Roman and Mudéjar Spain, and contains some impressive Roman mosaics.

Outstanding pieces from the Visigothic period include a collection of 7th-century gold votive crowns from Toledo province, known as the Treasure of Guarrazar.

Also on show are examples of Andalusian pottery from the Islamic era and various Romanesque exhibits, among them an ivory crucifix carved in 1063 for King Fernando I and his wife, Doña Sancha.

Steps outside the museum's entrance lead underground to an exact replica of the Altamira caves in Cantabria – complete with their paintings of the Paleolithic era. These famous caves contain some of the world's finest prehistoric art. The earliest engravings and drawings date back to around 18,000 BC. The boldly colored bison paintings date from around 13,000 BC.

Museo de América ⑫

Avenida de los Reyes Católicos 6. [91-549 26 41. M Moncloa. ⏰ 9:30am–3pm Tue – Sat, 10am–3pm Sun. ● some public hols. 🎫 (free on Sun). ⛪ W www.mcu.es/nmuseos/america

This fine museum houses a collection of artifacts relating to Spain's colonization of the Americas. Many of the exhibits, which date back to prehistoric times, were brought to Europe by the early explorers of the New World.

The collection is arranged thematically, with individual rooms on, for example, society, religion, and communication. One of the highlights of the museum is the rare Mayan *Códice Tro-cortesiano* (AD 1250–1500) from Mexico – a hieroglyphic parchment illustrated with scenes of everyday life. Also worth seeing are the Treasure of the Quimbayas, pre-Columbian gold and silver items dating from AD 500–1000, and the display of contemporary folk art from some of Spain's former American colonies.

Plaza de Toros de las Ventas ⑬

Calle de Alcalá 237. [91-356 22 00. M Ventas. ⏰ for bullfights and concerts only. **Museo Taurino** [91-72 18 57. ⏰ 9:30am–2:30pm Mon–Fri, 10am–1pm Sun. ⛪

Las Ventas is undoubtedly one of the most beautiful bullrings in Spain. Built in 1929 in Neo-Mudéjar style, it replaced the city's original bullring which stood near the Puerta de Alcalá. Outside the bullring are monuments to two renowned Spanish bullfighters: Antonio Bienvenida and José Cubero.

Adjoining the bullring, the **Museo Taurino** contains bullfighting memorabilia, such as portraits and sculptures of famous matadors. There is also a display of the tools of the bullfighter's trade, including capes and *banderillas* – sharp darts used to wound the bull *(see opposite)*.

Plaza de Toros de Las Ventas, Madrid's magnificent bullring

The Art of Bullfighting

BULLFIGHTING IS A sacrificial ritual in which men (and a few women) pit themselves against an animal bred for the ring. In this "authentic religious drama," as the poet Federico García Lorca described it, the spectator experiences the same intensity of fear and exaltation as the matador. There are three stages, or *tercios*, in the *corrida* (bullfight). The first two, which involve a team of men both on horseback and

Poster for a bullfight

on foot, are aimed at progressively weakening the bull. In the third, the matador moves in for the kill. Despite opposition on the grounds of cruelty, bullfighting is still very popular. For many Spaniards, the *toreo*, the art of bullfighting, is a noble part of their heritage. However, fights today are often debased by practises designed to disadvantage the bull, in particular shaving its horns to make them blunt.

The toro bravo (fighting bull), *bred for courage and aggression, enjoys a full life prior to its time in the ring. Bulls must be at least four years old before they can fight.*

Manolete *is regarded by most followers of bullfighting as one of Spain's greatest matadors ever. He was finally gored to death by the bull Islero at Linares, Jaén, in 1947.*

The matador wears a *traje de luces* (suit of lights), a colorful silk outfit embroidered with gold sequins.

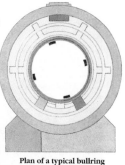

Banderillas, barbed darts, are thrust into the bull's back muscles to weaken them.

Joselito *was a leading matador, famous for his purist style. He displayed superb skill with the capote (red cape) and the muleta (matador's stick). Following a short retirement, he has returned to the ruedos (bullring).*

THE BULLRING

The audience at a bullfight is seated in the *tendidos* (stalls) or in the *palcos* (balcony), where the *presidencia* (president's box) is situated. Opposite are the *puerta de cuadrillas*, through which the matador and team arrive, and the *arrastre de toros* (exit for bulls). Before entering the ring, the matadors wait in a *callejón* (corridor) behind *barreras* and *burladeros* (barriers). Horses are kept in the *patio de caballos* and the bulls in the *corrales*.

Plan of a typical bullring

KEY

- ☐ Tendidos
- ☐ Palcos
- ☐ Presidencia
- ☐ Puerta de cuadrillas
- ☐ Arrastre de toros
- ☐ Callejón
- ☐ Barreras
- ☐ Burladeros
- ☐ Patio de caballos
- ☐ Corrales

Central Spain

MUCH OF SPAIN'S VAST CENTRAL PLATEAU, the *meseta*, is covered with wheat fields or dry, dusty plains, but there are many attractive places to explore. Spain's largest region, Castilla y León, has a rich history. It boasts some of the country's most splendid architecture, from Segovia's famous Roman aqueduct, to the Gothic cathedrals of Burgos and Léon and the Renaissance grandeur of Salamanca's monuments. Ávila's medieval city walls are a legacy of the long struggles between the Christians and the Moors. Dotted with windmills and medieval castles, Castilla-La Mancha is home to the historic town of Toledo, another popular destination.

The Library at El Escorial, with its 16th-century frescoed ceiling

El Escorial ❷

El Escorial. 📞 91-890 59 04. 🚇 from Atocha or Chamartín, Madrid. 🚌 661, 664 from Moncloa, Madrid. ◯ Tue–Sun. ● public hols. 🎫 (except Wed for EU residents). 🖼

FELIPE II's imposing palace of San Lorenzo de El Escorial was built in 1563–84 in honor of St. Lawrence. The austere, unornamented building set a new architectural style – known as "Herreriano" after the palace's architect, Juan de Herrera. Its interior was conceived as a mausoleum and contemplative retreat rather than a splendid residence.

Among the most impressive parts of the palace is the **Library**, with a collection of over 40,000 books and manuscripts. Its ceiling is decorated with 16th-century frescoes by Tibaldi. The **Royal Pantheon**, a huge mausoleum made in marble, contains the funerary urns of Spanish monarchs.

Some of the most important works of the royal Habsburg collections, including Flemish, Italian, and Spanish paintings, are housed in the **Museum of Art**, located on the first floor. Other fine works of art can be found in the chapter houses, with their fresco-adorned ceilings, and in the basilica.

In contrast to the artistic wealth of other parts of the palace, the royal apartments are remarkably humble.

Toledo ❸

See pp296–8

Segovia ❹

Segovia. 🏠 54,000. 🚊 🚌 🚍 ℹ Plaza Mayor 10 (921-46 03 34).

SEGOVIA IS ONE of the most spectacularly sited cities in Spain. The old town is set high on a rocky spur, surrounded by the Eresma and Clamores rivers. With its cathedral, aqueduct, and castle dominating the skyline, the view of the town from the valley below at sunset is magical.

Perched on a rocky outcrop at the city's western end is the **Alcázar**, an archetypal fairytale castle with gabled roofs, turrets, and crenellation. Begun in the 12th century, the castle assumed its present form between 1410 and 1455, though it had to be largely rebuilt following a fire in 1862. The castle contains a museum of weaponry and several sumptuous apartments.

Dating from 1525, Segovia's **cathedral** was the last great Gothic church to be built in Spain. It replaced the old cathedral, destroyed in 1520 when the Castilian towns revolted against King Carlos I. Other churches in the old town include the Romanesque **San Juan de los Caballeros**, which has an outstanding sculpted portico, **San Esteban**, and **San Martín**. Segovia's Roman **aqueduct** was built in the 1st century AD and remained in use until the late 19th century.

♠ Alcázar
Plaza de la Reina Victoria Eugenia. 📞 921-46 07 59. ◯ daily. ● Jan 1 & 6, Dec 25. 🎫 (free Tue). 🖼 🚻

ENVIRONS: The vast palace of **Riofrío**, 11 km (7 miles) southwest of the city center, was built as a hunting lodge on the orders of Felipe V's widow Isabel Farnese, in 1752. Today it houses a hunting museum.

Segovia's distinctive Alcázar, perched high above the city

Section of Ávila's 11th-century city walls

Ávila ❺

Ávila. 🏛 50,000. 🚊 🚌 ℹ *Plaza de la Catedral 4 (920-21 13 87).*

THE PERFECTLY PRESERVED medieval walls that encircle this historic city were built in the 11th century by Christian forces as a defense against the Moors. Of the nine gateways in the walls, the most impressive is the **Puerta de San Vicente**. Ávila's **cathedral**, whose unusual exterior is carved with beasts and scaly wild men, also forms part of the walls.

Ávila is the birthplace of St. Teresa (1515–82), one of the Catholic Church's greatest mystics and reformers. The **Convento de Santa Teresa** occupies the site of the home of this saint, who also lived for many years in the **Monasterio de la Encarnación**.

Among the city's finest churches are the 12th-century **Iglesia de San Vicente** and the Romanesque-Gothic **Iglesia de San Pedro**.

Beyond the town center, the beautiful **Real Monasterio de Santo Tomás** contains the tomb of Tomás de Torquemada (1420–98), the notorious head of the Spanish Inquisition.

Salamanca ❻

Salamanca. 🏛 160,000. ✈ 15 km (9 miles) E. 🚊 🚌 ℹ *Plaza Mayor 14 (923-21 83 42).*

HOME TO ONE of the oldest universities in Europe, Salamanca is also Spain's best showcase of Renaissance and Plateresque architecture.

The city's famous **university** was founded by Alfonso IX of León in 1218. The 16th-century façade of the main building on the Patio de las Escuelas is a splendid example of the Plateresque style. This form of early Spanish Renaissance architecture is so called because of its fine detail, which resembles ornate silverwork – *platero* in Spanish means silversmith.

The 16th-century, mainly Gothic **new cathedral** and the 12th- to 13th-century, Romanesque **old cathedral** stand side by side. A highlight of the old cathedral is the richly colored altarpiece (1445) by Nicolás Florentino.

The main ... was buil... 18th cen... for its sup... of the Spa... Among the... lining the s... Baroque tow... and the Royal Pavilion, from where the royal family used to watch events in the square.

Other fine monuments located in the heart of the city include the 16th-century **Iglesia-Convento de San Esteban**, with its lovely ornamented façade, and the **Convento de las Dueñas**, which preserves Moorish and Renaissance features.

The **Museo Art Nouveau y Art Deco** holds an important collection of 19th- and 20th-century paintings, jewelry, ceramics, and stained glass.

On the city outskirts, the 1st-century AD Roman bridge, the **Puente Romano**, offers a good view over the entire city.

🏛 **Universidad**
Patio de las Escuelas 1. 📞 923-29 44 00. 🕐 *daily.* ● *Dec 25.* 💷 (except Mon am).
🏛 **Museo Art Nouveau y Art Deco**
Calle Gibraltar 14. 📞 923-12 14 25. 🕐 *Tue–Sun.* 💷 except Thu am.

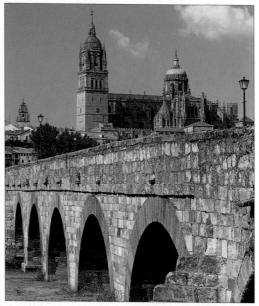

View of Salamanca's twin cathedrals from the Puente Romano

Street-by-Street: Toledo ❸

PICTURESQUELY SITED on a hill above the River Tagus is the historic center of Toledo. Behind the old walls lies much evidence of the city's rich history. The Romans built a fortress on the site of the present-day Alcázar. In the 6th century AD the Visigoths made Toledo their capital, and left behind many churches. After it was captured from the Moors by Alfonso VI in 1085, the city became the capital of the Christian kingdom of Castile. During the Middle Ages, Toledo was a melting pot of Christian, Muslim, and Jewish cultures, and it was during this period that the city's most outstanding monument – its cathedral – was built. In the 16th century the painter El Greco came to live in Toledo, and today the city is home to many of his works.

Puerta de Valmardón

Iglesia de San Román
This church contains a museum relating the city's past under the Visigoths.

0 meters   100
0 yards   100

★ Iglesia de Santo Tomé
This church, with a beautiful Mudéjar tower, houses El Greco's masterpiece, The Burial of the Count of Orgaz.

Sinagoga del Tránsito and Casa-Museo de El Greco

CALLE DE SAN ROMÁN

CÁRDENAL LORENZANA

CALLE DE ALFONSO X

CALLE DE ALFONSO XII

CALLE DE LA TRINIDAD

Archbishop's Palace

Taller del Moro
Once used as a workshop by craftsmen building the cathedral, this Mudéjar palace now houses a museum of Mudéjar ceramics and tiles.

STAR SIGHTS

★ Iglesia de Santo Tomé

★ Museo de Santa Cruz

★ Cathedral

e Puerta del
has a double
orish arch and
two towers.

Ermita del Cristo de la Luz

This small mosque, the city's only remaining Muslim building, dates from around AD 1000.

Tourist information, bus and train stations

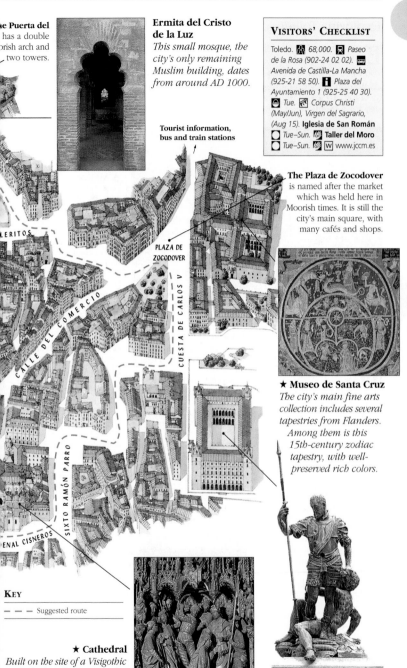

The Plaza de Zocodover
is named after the market which was held here in Moorish times. It is still the city's main square, with many cafés and shops.

PLAZA DE ZOCODOVER

CUESTA DE CARLOS V

CALLE DEL COMERCIO

SIXTO RAMÓN PARRO

ENAL CISNEROS

ERITOS

★ Museo de Santa Cruz
The city's main fine arts collection includes several tapestries from Flanders. Among them is this 15th-century zodiac tapestry, with well-preserved rich colors.

KEY

– – – Suggested route

★ Cathedral
Built on the site of a Visigothic cathedral and a mosque, this impressive structure is one of the largest cathedrals in Christendom (see p298). The beautiful Gothic high altar reredos (1504) is the work of several artists.

Alcázar
In the central patio of the fortress is a replica of the statue Carlos V y el Furor. The original is housed in Madrid's Museo del Prado.

Exploring Toledo

EASILY REACHED FROM MADRID by rail, bus or car, Toledo is best explored on foot. To visit all the main sights you need at least two days, but it is possible to walk around the medieval and Jewish quarters in a long morning. To avoid the heavy crowds, go midweek and stay for a night, when the city is at its most atmospheric.

Toledo cathedral rising above the rooftops of the medieval quarter

⛪ Cathedral

Calle Arco Palacio 2. **⚡** 925-22 22 41.
Choir, Treasury, Chapterhouse, and Sacristy ◯ Mon–Sat, pm Sun. 🈯 🈂 🅱

The splendor of Toledo's cathedral reflects its history as the spiritual heart of the Spanish church and the seat of the Primate of all Spain. The present cathedral stands on the site of a 7th-century church. Work began in 1226, but the last vaults were not completed until 1493. This long period of construction explains the cathedral's mixture of styles: the exterior is pure French Gothic, while inside, Spanish decorative styles, such as Mudéjar – a hybrid Christian-Islamic style – and Plateresque, are used.

Among the cathedral's most outstanding features are the polychrome reredos of the high altar (1504), and the choir. In the treasury is a 16th-century Gothic silver monstrance, over 3 m (10 ft) high. The monstrance is carried through the streets of Toledo during the Corpus Christi celebrations. Standing out from the mainly Gothic interior, the Transparente is a stunning Baroque altarpiece of marble, jasper, and bronze, sculpted by Narciso Tomé.

🏛 Museo de Santa Cruz

Calle Cervantes 3. **⚡** 925-22 10 36.
◯ daily (except Sun pm). 🈯 (free Sat pm & Sun).

Recently refurbished, this museum of fine arts has a superb collection of medieval and Renaissance tapestries, paintings, and sculptures. There are also works by the Cretan artist El Greco, as well as examples of two typical Toledan crafts: armor and damascened swords, the latter made by inlaying blackened steel with gold wire. The museum is housed in a fine Renaissance building.

The Assumption (1613) by El Greco, in the Museo de Santa Cruz

⛪ Iglesia de Santo Tomé

Plaza del Conde 4. **⚡** 925-25 60 98.
◯ daily. 🈯 except Wed pm for EU residents.

Visitors come to this church mainly to admire El Greco's masterpiece, *The Burial of the Count of Orgaz*. The church is thought to date back to the 12th century, and its tower is one of the best examples of Mudéjar architecture in the city.

♣ Alcázar

Cuesta de Carlos V. **⚡** 925-22 30 38. ● for renovation until 2006.

Charles V's fortified palace stands on the site of former Roman, Visigothic, and Muslim fortresses. In 1936 it was almost completely destroyed during a 70-day siege by the Republicans. The restored building houses an army museum and a library, which holds a valuable collection of books and manuscripts dating back to the 11th century.

⛪ Sinagoga del Tránsito

Calle Samuel Leví. **⚡** 925-22 36 65.
◯ Tue–Sun. 🈯 (free Sat pm & Sun).

A wonderfully elaborate Mudéjar interior is hidden behind the humble façade of this 14th-century former synagogue. Next to the synagogue is an interesting museum dedicated to the Sephardic (Spanish Jewish) culture.

🏛 Casa-Museo de El Greco

Calle Samuel Leví. **⚡** 925-22 40 46.
◯ Tue–Sun. 🈯 (free Sat pm & Sun).

It is uncertain whether El Greco actually lived in or simply near to this house, now a museum containing a collection of his works. Canvases on display include the superb series *Christ and the Apostles*. Below the museum, on the ground floor, is a chapel with a fine Mudéjar ceiling and works of art by painters of the Toledan School, such as Luis Tristán, a student of El Greco.

🏰 Puerta Antigua de Bisagra

When Alfonso VI of Castile conquered Toledo in 1085, he entered it through this gateway – the only one in the city to have kept its original 10th-century military architecture. The towers are topped by a 12th-century Arab gatehouse.

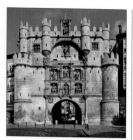

The Arco de Santa María in Burgos, adorned with statues and turrets

Burgos ❼

Burgos. 🏛 *166,000.* 🚃 🚌 ❶ *Plaza de Alonso Martínez 7 (947-20 31 25).*

FOUNDED IN 884, Burgos was the capital of the united kingdoms of Castile and León from 1073 until 1492. A few hundred years later, Franco chose Burgos as his headquarters during the Civil War.

Approaching the city via the bridge called the Puente de Santa María, you enter the old town through the grand **Arco de Santa María**. The other main route into Burgos is the Puente de San Pablo, where a statue commemorates local hero El Cid (1043–99). Born Rodrigo Díaz de Vivar, this great warrior fought for both the Moors and the Christians in the Reconquest, and for his heroism was named El Cid, from the Arabic *Sidi* (Lord). He is immortalized in the anonymous poem, *El Cantar del Mío Cid* (1180).

Not far from the statue of El Cid stands the **Casa del Cordón**, a 15th-century former palace (now a bank). It was here that the Catholic

Monarchs welcomed Columbus on his return, in 1497, from the second of his famous voyages to the Americas.

Burgos's **cathedral** *(see pp300–301)* is the city's most prominent landmark. Nearby, the **Iglesia de San Nicolás** boasts a fine 16th-century altarpiece, while the **Iglesia de San Lorenzo** has a splendid Baroque ceiling.

The **Museo de Burgos** contains archaeological and fine art collections.

West of the city is the 12th-century **Real Monasterio de Huelgas**, a former convent that houses a textile museum.

🏛 Museo de Burgos
Calle Calera 25.
🎫 947-26 58 75.
⏱ *Tue–Sun.* 🏷
(except Sat & Sun). ♿
❶ Real Monasterio de Huelgas
Calle de los Compases.
🎫 947-20 16 30.
⏱ *10am–1:15pm & 3:45–5:45pm Tue–Sat, 10:30am–2:15pm Sun & public hols.* ● *Jan 1 & 6, Apr 18, May 1, Jun 20 & 30, Dec 8, 24, 25, 31.* 🎫 ♿ 🏷 *(except Wed for EU residents).*

León ❽

León. 🏛 *131,000.* 🚃 🚌 ❶ *Plaza de la Regla 4 (987-23 70 82).*

FOUNDED AS a camp for the Romans' Seventh Legion, León became the capital of the kingdom of León in the

Middle Ages. As such, it played a central role in the early years of the Reconquest.

The city's Gothic **cathedral**, on Plaza de la Regla, dates from the mid-13th century. As well as some glorious stained glass, it has a splendid west front, decorated with a series of 13th-century carvings.

The **Colegiata de San Isidoro** is built into the Roman walls encircling the city. Here, the Romanesque **Panteón Real** (Royal Pantheon) is decorated with carved capitals and 12th-century frescoes.

León's old quarter is a maze of narrow alleyways, lined with bars, cafés, churches, and old mansions.

The **Hostal de San Marcos** was founded in the 12th century as a monastery for pilgrims on route to Santiago *(see p302).* A gem of Spanish Renaissance architecture, the present building was begun in 1513 for the Knights of Santiago. Today it houses a luxurious hotel and the **Museo de León**.

Statue of El Cid, Burgos's most famous son

🏛 Museo de León
Plaza de San Marcos. 🎫 *987-24 50 61.* ⏱ *Tue–Sun.* ● *main public hols.* 🏷 *(except Sat & Sun).*

ENVIRONS: 30 km (19 miles) east of León, the 10th-century **Iglesia de San Miguel de Escalada** is one of the finest surviving churches built by the Mozarabs – Christians influenced by the Moors.

Detail from a 13th-century carving decorating the west front of León's cathedral

Burgos Cathedral

S PAIN'S THIRD-LARGEST CATHEDRAL was founded in 1221 by Bishop Mauricio under Fernando III. The groundplan – a Latin cross – measures 84 m (276 ft) by 59 m (194 ft). Its construction was carried out in several stages over three centuries, and involved artists and architects from across Europe. The style is almost entirely Gothic, and shows influences from Germany, France, and the Low Countries. In the Middle Ages the cathedral was an important stopping point for pilgrims on the road to Santiago *(see p302)*. Burgos's most celebrated son, the medieval hero of the Reconquest, El Cid, is buried in the cathedral, alongside his wife, Jimena.

Christ at the Column, by Diego de Siloé

West Front
The lacy, steel-grey spires soar above a sculpted balustrade depicting Castile's early kings.

Lantern

Tomb of El Cid

★ Golden Staircase
This elegant Renaissance staircase (1523) by Diego de Siloé links the nave with a tall door (kept locked) at street level.

STAR FEATURES

★ Golden Staircase

★ Constable's Chapel

★ Crossing

Capilla de Santa Ana
The altarpiece (1490) in this chapel is by the sculptor Gil de Siloé. The central panel shows the Virgin with St. Joachim.

Capilla de Santa Tecla

Puerta de Santa María (main entrance)

The Capilla de la Presentación (1519–24) is a funerary chapel with a star-shaped, traceried vault.

Retrochoir
Several of the reliefs around the chancel were carved by Philippe de Bigarny. This expressive scene, which was completed in 1499, depicts the road to Calvary.

VISITORS' CHECKLIST

Plaza de San Fernando. 947-20 47 12. 9:30am–1pm 4–7pm Mon–Sat, 9:30–11:45am 4–7pm Sun & public hols. 9am, 10am, 7:30pm daily; 11am Mon–Sat; noon, 1pm, 2pm Sun.

Capilla de San Juan Bautista and museum

★ Constable's Chapel
The tomb of the High Constable of Castile and his wife lies beneath the openwork vault of this chapel of 1496.

Sacristy *(1765)*
The sacristy was rebuilt in Baroque style, with an exuberant plasterwork vault and Rococo altars.

Puerta de la Coronería
The tympanum of this portal of 1240 shows Christ flanked by the Evangelists. Statues of the apostles sit below.

Capilla de la Visitación

★ Crossing
The star-ribbed central dome, begun in 1539, is supported by four huge pillars. It is decorated with effigies of prophets and saints. Beneath it is the tomb of El Cid and his wife.

Capilla del Santísimo Cristo

Northern Spain

NORTHERN SPAIN ENCOMPASSES a variety of landscapes and cultures. In the far northwest of the peninsula, the Galicians are fiercely proud of their customs and language. Spain's greenest region, Galicia boasts some of the most attractive stretches of Atlantic coast, as well as the beautiful city of Santiago de Compostela. Popular with hikers and naturalists, the spectacular Picos de Europa massif sits astride the border between Asturias and Cantabria. The Basque Country is a unique part of Spain whose main attractions include superb cuisine, fashionable seaside resorts, and the cultural center of Bilbao, with its famous Guggenheim Museum.

Santiago de Compostela's grand cathedral towering over the city

Santiago de Compostela ❾

A Coruña. 🏃 100,000. ✈ 10 km (6 miles) N. 🚉 🚌 🅸 Calle Rúa do Villar 43 (981-58 40 81). 🎉 Fiesta (Jul 25).

IN THE MIDDLE AGES this fine city was Christendom's third most important place of pilgrimage after Jerusalem and Rome. In 813 the body of Christ's apostle James was supposedly discovered here, and in the following centuries pilgrims from all over Europe flocked to the city.

On the Praza do Obradoiro stands the city's **cathedral**, built in honor of St. James. The present structure dates from the 11th–13th centuries, but the Baroque west façade was added in the 18th century. The square's northern edge is flanked by the grand **Hostal de los Reyes Católicos**, built by the Catholic Monarchs (see p278) as a resting place for

sick pilgrims. It is now a hotel. Nearby are the 9th-century **Convento de San Paio de Antealtares**, one of the city's oldest monasteries, and the **Convento de San Martiño Pinario**, whose Baroque church has a wonderfully ornate Plateresque façade.

The **Convento de Santo Domingo de Bonaval**, east of the center, is also worth visiting. Part of the monastery now houses a Galician folk museum. There is also the

Centro Gallego de Arte Contemporáneo, with works by leading Galician artists.

🏛 **Centro Gallego de Arte Contemporáneo**
Calle Valle Inclán s/n. 🅲 981-54 66 29. 🕐 Tue–Sun. 🅿 by prior appointment (call 981-54 66 31). 🅱

Rías Baixas ❿

Pontevedra. 🚉 🚌 Pontevedra. 🅸 Calle General Mola 1, Pontevedra (986-85 08 14).

THE SOUTHERN part of Galicia's west coast consists of four large rías, or inlets, between pine-covered hills. Known as the Rías Baixas (Rías Bajas), they offer fine beaches, safe bathing, and lovely scenery.

The main town on the coast is lively **Pontevedra**, which has many historic monuments, such as the Gothic Convento de Santo Domingo, and an excellent provincial museum.

Many areas along the coast have become popular holiday resorts, such as **Sanxenxo**, west of Pontevedra. To the south, **Baiona** and **Panxón** both have good beaches, as well as sailing and a variety of water sports. In spite of tourism, much of the coastline, particularly the quieter northernmost part, remains unspoiled. Here you can visit many small fishing ports and watch the locals harvesting mussels and clams.

While in Rías Baixas look out for bórreos – traditional stone-built granaries raised on stilts. The waterfront of picturesque **Combarro** is lined with these buildings, typical of the whole of Galicia.

The tranquil fishing village of Combarro in the Rías Baixas

Santa María del Naranco, a Pre-Romanesque church in Oviedo

Oviedo ⓫

Asturias. 👥 201,000. ☐ ☐
ℹ️ Calle Uría 64 (985-21 33 85).

OVIEDO, THE CULTURAL and commercial capital of Asturias, is best known for its Pre-Romanesque buildings. This style flourished in the 8th–10th centuries and was confined to a small area of the kingdom of Asturias, one of the few areas of Spain that escaped invasion by the Moors.

With its huge barrel-vaulted hall and arcaded galleries, the church of **Santa María del Naranco**, in the north of the city, was originally built as a summer palace for Ramiro I in the 9th century. Equally impressive are the church of **San Miguel de Lillo** and the 9th-century church of **San Julián de los Prados**, noted for its glorious frescoes.

In the center of Oviedo, the Flamboyant Gothic **cathedral** and the 9th-century **Iglesia de San Tirso** are both worth taking some time to see.

The city has two museums of note: the **Museo Arqueológico**, which contains local prehistoric, Roman, and Romanesque treasures, and the **Museo de Bellas Artes** (Museum of Fine Arts).

🏛 **Museo Arqueológico**
Calle San Vicente 5. ☎ 985-21 54 05. ● for renovation until 2006.
🏛 **Museo de Bellas Artes**
Calle Santa Ana 1. ☎ 985-21 30 61. ☐ Tue–Sun.

Picos de Europa ⓬

Asturias, Cantabria, and Castilla y León. 🚌 Oviedo to Cangas de Onís.
ℹ️ Cangas de Onís (985-84 80 05).
Fuente Dé cable car ☎ 942-73 66 10. ☐ daily. ● Jan 7–early Mar.

THIS BEAUTIFUL mountain range – Europe's biggest national park – offers superb upland hiking and supports a diversity of wildlife.

The two main gateways to the Picos are **Cangas de Onís**, northwest of the park, and **Potes**, on the eastern side. About 8 km (5 miles) southeast of the former, **Covadonga** is where, in 722, the Visigoth Pelayo is said to have defeated a Moorish army, inspiring Christians in the north to reconquer the peninsula. The road south from Cangas de Onís follows the spectacular narrow gorge known as the Desfiladero de los Beyes.

The Fuente Dé cable car, in the heart of the park, climbs 900 m (2,950 ft) to a rocky plateau, offering magnificent panoramic views of the Picos's peaks and valleys.

Santander ⓭

Cantabria. 👥 181,000. ✈ ⛴ ☐ 🚌
ℹ️ Calle Hernán Cortés 4 (942-31 07 08). 🎭 International Festival (Jul–Aug).

CANTABRIA'S CAPITAL, Santander is a busy port that enjoys a splendid site on a deep bay on Spain's north Atlantic coast.

The early 20th-century Palacio de la Magdalena in Santander

The **cathedral** was rebuilt in Gothic style, following a fire in 1941 that destroyed the entire town. The 12th-century crypt has been preserved. Nearby, the **Museo de Bellas Artes** has works by Goya and Zurbarán, while the **Museo de Prehistoria y Arqueología** displays local finds, including Neolithic axe heads, Roman coins, pottery, and figurines.

On the Península de la Magdalena stands the **Palacio de la Magdalena**, built for Alfonso XIII in 1912. The upscale seaside resort of **El Sardinero**, to the north, has a long beach, chic cafés, and a majestic white casino.

🏛 **Museo de Bellas Artes**
Calle Rubio 6. ☎ 942-23 94 85.
☐ Mon–Sat.
🏛 **Museo de Prehistoria y Arqueología**
Calle Casimiro Saenz 4. ☎ 942-20 71 05. ☐ Tue–Sun.

19th-century Neo-Romanesque basilica in Covadonga, Picos de Europa

Frank Gehry's ultramodern Museo Guggenheim building in Bilbao

Bilbao ⓮

Vizcaya. 🏘 350,000. ✈ 🚢 🚇 🚌
🛈 Calle Rodriguez Arias 3 (944-79 57 60). 🎉 Fiesta (third week Aug).

BILBAO (BILBO) is the center of Basque industry and Spain's leading commercial port, yet it has many cultural attractions worth visiting. In the city's medieval quarter – the *Casco Viejo* – the **Museo Arqueológico, Etnográfico e Histórico Vasco** displays Basque art and folk artifacts, while in the newer town, the **Museo de Bellas Artes** is one of Spain's best art museums.

The jewel in Bilbao's cultural crown, however, is the **Museo Guggenheim Bilbao**, which has a superb collection of Modern and contemporary art. It is just one of the city's many pieces of modern architecture, which also include the striking **Palacio de la Música y Congresos Euskalduna**.

🏛 **Museo Guggenheim**
Avenida Abandoibarra. 📞 944-35 90 80. 🕐 10am–8pm. 🔴 Sep–Jun: Mon; public hols. 🎫 📷 📶 ♿
🌐 www.guggenheim-bilbao.es

San Sebastián ⓯

Guipúzcoa. 🏘 178,000. 🚇 🚌 🛈 Reina Regente 3 (943-48 11 66). 🎬 International Film Festival (late-Sep).

POPULAR WITH the aristocracy, San Sebastián (Donostia) became a fashionable seaside resort in the late 19th century.

At the heart of the old town are the handsome Plaza de la Constitución and the church of **Santa María del Coro**, with its Baroque portal. Behind the old town, Monte Urgull is worth climbing for the superb views from its summit. At the foot of the hill, the **Museo de San Telmo** holds exhibits ranging from Basque funerary columns to works by El Greco.

A short bus ride from the Calle Oquendo takes you to **Chillida-Leku**, a display of works by renowned Basque sculptor, Eduardo Chillida.

Between the city's two main beaches – the Playa de la Concha and the Playa de Ondarreta – is the **Palacio Miramar** (1889), built for Queen María Cristina.

🏛 **Museo de San Telmo**
Plaza Zuloaga. 📞 943-48 15 80.
🕐 Tue–Sun. ♿

Mural by Josep Maria Sert in the Museo de San Telmo, San Sebastián

Bulls scattering the runners during Sanfermines in Pamplona

Pamplona ⓰

Navarra. 🏘 183,000. ✈ 🚇 🚌
🛈 Calle Eslava 1 (948-20 65 40).
🎉 Sanfermines (Jul 6–14).

SUPPOSEDLY FOUNDED by the Roman general, Pompey, Pamplona is most famous for the fiesta of Los Sanfermines, with its daredevil bull running.

West of the city's mainly Gothic **cathedral** lies the old Jewish quarter. Here are the Baroque **Palacio de Navarra** and the medieval **Iglesia de San Saturnino**.

The **Museo de Navarra** is a museum of regional history, archaeology, and art.

Southeast of the center is Felipe II's massive **citadel**, erected in the 16th century.

🏛 **Museo de Navarra**
Calle Santo Domingo. 📞 948-42 64 92. 🕐 Tue–Sun. 🎫 free Sat pm & Sun am. ♿

BASQUE CULTURE

Possibly Europe's oldest race, the Basques are thought to be descended from Cro-Magnon people, who lived in the Pyrenees 40,000 years ago. Long isolated in their mountain villages, the Basques preserved their unique language (Euskera), myths, and art for millennia, almost untouched by other influences. Many families still live in the stone *caseríos*, or farmhouses, built by their forebears. The *fueros*, or ancient Basque laws, were suppressed under General Franco, but since 1975 the Basque region (Euskadi) has had its own parliament. Nevertheless, there is still a strong separatist movement seeking to sever links with the government in Madrid.

The Ikurriña, the flag of the Basque region

Catalonia

A NATION-WITHIN-A-NATION, Catalonia has its own semi-autonomous regional government, and its own language. Spoken by more than eight million people, Catalan has supplanted Castilian Spanish as the first language of the region, and is used on road signs and in place names everywhere. Barcelona is the region's capital, rivaling Madrid in economic and cultural importance. Catalonia offers a variety of attractions. The flower-filled valleys of the Pyrenees offer a paradise for naturalists and walkers, while inland are medieval towns, Roman ruins, and spectacular monasteries, such as Montserrat.

Parc Nacional d'Aigüestortes ⓱

Lleida. 🚃 La Pobla de Segur.
🚌 El Pont de Suert, La Pobla de Segur.
🏛 Barruera (973-69 61 89).

T HE PRISTINE mountain scenery of Catalonia's only national park is among the most spectacular in the Pyrenees. The main village in the area is the mountain settlement of Espot, on the park's eastern edge. Dotted around the park are waterfalls and more than a hundred lakes and tarns.

The most beautiful scenery is around Sant Maurici lake, from where several walks lead north to the towering peaks of Agulles d'Amitges. The park is home to a variety of wildlife: chamois, beavers, otters, and golden eagles have all found a habitat here.

Barcelona ⓲

See pp306–15.

Monestir de Montserrat ⓳

See pp316–7.

Poblet ⓴

Off N240, 10 km (6 miles) from Montblanc. 📞 977-87 02 54.
🚃 to L'Espluga de Francolí, then taxi.
🚌 ◯ 10am–12:30pm, 3–5:30pm daily. ◯ Jan 1, Dec 25 & 26. 🎫

S ANTA MARIA DE POBLET was the first and most important of three medieval monasteries, known as the "Cistercian triangle." In 1835, during the

The superb high altar reredos at Santa Maria de Poblet

Carlist upheavals, the abbey sustained serious damage. Restoration began in 1930, and monks returned a decade later.

Poblet is enclosed by fortified walls that have hardly changed since the Middle Ages. Its evocative, vaulted cloisters were built in the 12th and 13th centuries. Beautiful, carved scrollwork decorates the capitals. Behind the stone altar, an impressive alabaster reredos, carved by Damià Forment in 1527, fills the apse. Other highlights include the

Royal Tombs, where many Spanish monarchs are buried. Begun in 1359, they were reconstructed by Marès in 1950.

Tarragona ㉑

Tarragona. 🏛 125,000. ✈ 🚃 🚌
🏛 Carrer Fortuny 4 or Carrer Major 39 (977-24 50 64).

N OW A MAJOR industrial port, Tarragona preserves many remnants of its Roman past, when it was the capital of the Roman province, Tarraconensis.

Among the extensive ruins are the **Anfiteatro Romano** (Roman Amphitheater) and the Praetorium, a Roman tower that was later converted into a medieval palace. Also known as the Castell de Pilato (after Pontius Pilate), the tower houses the **Museu de la Romanitat**, which contains Roman and medieval finds and gives access to the cavernous passageways of the 1st-century AD Roman circus. In the adjacent building is the **Museu Nacional Arqueològic**, which holds the most important collection of Roman artifacts in Catalonia, including some beautiful frescoes. An archaeological walk follows part of the Roman city wall.

Tarragona's 12th-century **cathedral** was built on the site of a Roman temple and an Arab mosque, and exhibits a harmonious blend of styles.

🏛 Museu Nacional Arqueològic de Tarragona
Plaça del Rei 5. 📞 977-23 62 09.
◯ Jun–Sep: Tue–Sat, am Sun;
Oct–May: 10am–1:30pm, 4–7pm
Tue–Sat, am Sun. 🎫 🚻

View across the Roman amphitheater at Tarragona to the sea

Barcelona ⑱

BARCELONA, one of the Mediterranean's busiest ports, is more than the capital of Catalonia. In culture, commerce, and sport, it rivals not only Madrid, but also many of Europe's greatest cities. The success of the 1992 Olympic Games, staged in the Parc de Montjuïc, confirmed this to the world. Although there are many historical monuments in the Old Town, the city is best known for the scores of superb buildings left behind by the artistic explosion of Modernisme in the decades around 1900. Today, Barcelona still sizzles with creativity; its bars and public parks speak more of bold contemporary design than of tradition.

GREATER BARCELONA

SIGHTS AT A GLANCE

Barcelona Cathedral ①
Basílica de Santa
 Maria del Mar ④
Fundació Joan Miró ⑩
Montjuïc ⑨
Museu Nacional d'Art
 de Catalunya ⑪
Museu Picasso ⑤
Palau Reial Major ②
Quadrat d'Or ⑧
La Rambla ③
Sagrada Família
 pp312–3 ⑦
Vila Olímpica ⑥

Greater Barcelona
(see inset map)
Parc Güell ⑫
Tibidabo ⑬

KEY

Area of main map

KEY

■ Sight / Place of interest

✈ Airport

🚉 Train station

Ⓜ Metro station

🚌 Main bus stop

🚠 Cable car station

🚡 Funicular station

🅿 Parking

ℹ Tourist information

✝ Church

═ Pedestrian street

← One-way street

Pedestrian swing bridge in Port Vell, at the end of La Rambla

GETTING AROUND

The Old Town is well served by Metro lines 1, 3, and 4. Jaume I metro station is in the heart of the Barri Gòtic, and many buses pass through the Plaça de Catalunya on the edge of the district. Metro line 5 takes you to the Sagrada Família, a long walk from other sights. Set atop a steep hill, most of Montjuïc's attractions can be reached by buses 13, 50, and 100 from the Plaça d'Espanya, or by funicular and cable car from Metro Paral·lel.

Street-by-Street: Barri Gòtic

THE BARRI GOTIC (Gothic Quarter) is the true heart of Barcelona. This site was chosen by the Romans in the reign of Augustus (27 BC–AD 14) to found a new *colonia* (town), and has been the location of the city's administrative buildings ever since. The Roman forum was on the Plaça de Sant Jaume, where the medieval Palau de la Generalitat, Catalonia's parliament, and the Casa de la Ciutat, the town hall, now stand. Nearby are the Gothic cathedral and royal palace, where Columbus was received by the Catholic Monarchs on his return from the New World in 1492.

The Casa de l'Ardiaca (Archdeacon's House), a Gothic-Renaissance building on the Roman city wall, now houses Barcelona's historical archives.

Roman city wall

Plaça de Catalunya

SANT SEVER

CARRER DEL BISBE

CARRER DELS COMTES DE BARCELONA

SANT HONORAT

PLAÇA DE SANT JAUME

CARRER DE FARRAN

CARRER D

CARRER DE LA CIUTAT

La Rambla ←

★ Cathedral
The façade and spire are 19th-century additions to the original building. The cathedral's treasures include medieval Catalan paintings.

Palau de la Generalitat
The superb Gothic features of the Catalan Parliament include the chapel and a stone staircase rising to an arcaded gallery.

Casa de la Ciutat
Barcelona's town hall was built in the 14th and 15th centuries. The façade is a Neoclassical addition. In the entrance hall stands Three Gypsy Boys *by Joan Rebull (1899–1981), a 1976 copy of a sculpture he originally created in 1946.*

The Centre Excursionista de Catalunya, housed in a medieval mansion, displays Roman columns from the Temple of Augustus, whose site is marked by a millstone in the street outside.

Museu Frederic Marès
This medieval doorway is from an extensive display of Spanish sculpture – the mainstay of this museum's extraordinarily eclectic and high-quality collections.

★ **Palau Reial Major**
The 14th-century Capella Reial de Santa Àgata, with its 1466 altarpiece, is one of the best-preserved sections of the palace.

Capella Reial de Santa Àgata

Plaça del Rei

Palau del Lloctinent

Museu d'Història de la Ciutat
Housed in a 14th-century mansion, which was moved from the Carrer dels Mercaders in 1931, the museum focuses on Barcelona's rapid development in the 13th and 14th centuries, when commerce expanded dramatically.

KEY

– – – Suggested route

STAR SIGHTS

★ **Cathedral**

★ **Palau Reial Major**

0 meters 100
0 yards 100

Barcelona Cathedral ①

Plaça de la Seu. 93-315 15 54.
Jaume I. 17, 19, 45. 9am–1:30pm, 4–7:30pm daily.

BEGUN IN 1298 under Jaime II, on the foundations of a site dating back to Visigothic times, this compact Gothic cathedral was not finished until the late 19th century. The interior has beautiful Gothic cloisters and carved 15th-century choir stalls with painted coats of arms. Beneath the main altar, the crypt houses the sarcophagus of St. Eulalia, martyred in the 4th century AD. The nave has 28 side chapels, and a vaulted ceiling that rises to 26 m (85 ft).

The wide Catalan Gothic nave of Barcelona Cathedral

Palau Reial Major ②

Plaça del Rei. 93-315 11 11.
Jaume I. Jun–Oct: Tue–Sat, am Sun; Nov–May: pm Tue–Sat, am Sun. Jan 1, Good Fri, Jun 25, Dec 25–26. by appointment.

THE ROYAL PALACE was the residence of the count-kings of Barcelona from its foundation in the 13th century. The complex includes the 14th-century Gothic Saló del Tinell, with arches spanning 17 m (56 ft). On the right, built into the Roman city wall, is the Capella de Santa Àgata, with a painted wood ceiling by Jaume Huguet. Stairs to the right of the altar lead to the 16th-century tower of Martí the Humane (last of the count-kings), which offers splendid views over the royal complex.

La Rambla ③

M *Drassanes, Liceu, Catalunya.*

BUSY AROUND THE CLOCK, this is one of the most famous streets in Spain. A stroll down its tree-shaded, central walkway to the seafront, taking in the mansions, shops, and cafés, makes a perfect introduction to Barcelona life.

The name (Les Rambles in Catalan) comes from the Arabic *ramla*, meaning the dried-up bed of a seasonal river. Barcelona's 13th-century city wall followed the left bank of one such river. During the 16th century, convents, monasteries, and a university were built on the opposite bank. Later demolished, they have left their legacy in the names of the five sections of the street. Today La Rambla is thronged by street vendors, tarot readers, musicians, and mime artists.

Among its many famous buildings is the **Palau Güell**, a Neo-Gothic mansion that established the international reputation of Catalan architect Antoni Gaudí for outstanding,

The Gothic interior of the Basílica de Santa Maria del Mar

original architecture. Built in 1889, this fascinating work of art is located on a narrow street just off La Rambla. Nearby, the **Gran Teatre del Liceu**, the city's fine opera house, has been restored twice after fires in 1861 and 1994. Further along is the huge **Mercat de Sant Josep**, a colorful food market popularly known as "La Boqueria."

On the opposite side of La Rambla, midway between the Drassanes and Liceu metro stations, the **Plaça Reial** is Barcelona's liveliest square and dates from the 1850s. Also worth visiting, the **Museu de Cera** (wax-work museum) is housed in an atmospheric 19th-century building, and holds around 300 exhibits.

🏛 Palau Güell
Carrer Nou de la Rambla 3–5.
📞 *93-317 39 74.* **M** *Drassanes, Liceu.* **○** *Mar–Sep: 10am–8pm Mon–Sat; Oct–Feb: 10am–5pm Mon–Sat.* **●** *public hols.* 🎫 🔲

Basílica de Santa Maria del Mar ④

Plaza Sta Maria 1. **📞** *93-310 23 90.* **M** *Jaume I.* **○** *9am–1:30pm, 4:30–8pm Mon–Sat, 10am–8pm Sun.*

THIS BEAUTIFUL building, the city's favorite church, has superb acoustics for concerts. It is also the only surviving example of an entirely Catalan Gothic-style church.

The church took just 55 years to build. The speed of its construction – unrivaled in the Middle Ages – gave it a unity of style both inside and out. The west front has a 15th-century rose window of the Coronation of the Virgin. More stained glass, dating from the 15th to the 18th centuries, lights the wide nave and high aisles.

The choir and furnishings were destroyed during the Spanish Civil War (1936–9), which has enhanced the sense of space and simplicity.

Monument to Columbus at the southern end of the tree-lined Rambla

Museu Picasso ⑤

Carrer Montcada 15–23. 93-319
63 10. M Jaume I. 10am–7pm
Tue–Sat, 10am–2:30pm Sun. Jan
1, May 1, Jun 24, Dec 25–26.
W www.museupicasso.bcn.es

O NE OF BARCELONA'S most
popular attractions, the
Picasso Museum is housed
in five adjoining palaces on
the Carrer Montcada. It was
founded in 1963, displaying
works donated by Jaime
Sabartes, a great friend of
Picasso. Later, Picasso himself
donated paintings, including
some graphic works left in
his will. Several ceramic pieces
were given to the museum by
his widow, Jacqueline.

The strength of the 3,000-
piece collection is Picasso's
early drawings and paintings,
such as *The First Communion*
(1896), produced when he
was still an adolescent. The
most famous work on show
is the series *Las Meninas*,
based on Velázquez's 1656
masterpiece *(see p290)*.

**Yachts in the marina at the Port
Olímpic, overlooked by skyscrapers**

Vila Olímpica ⑥

M Ciutadella-Vila Olímpica.

T HE MOST DRAMATIC rebuilding
for the 1992 Olympics was
the demolition of the old
industrial waterfront and the
laying out of 4 km (2 miles) of
promenade and pristine sandy
beaches. Suddenly Barcelona
seemed like a seaside resort,
with a new estate of 2,000
apartments and parks called
Nova Icària. The area is still
popularly known as the Vila
Olímpica because the buildings
once housed Olympic athletes.

On the seafront there are
twin 44-floor towers – Spain's
tallest skyscrapers. They stand
beside the Port Olímpic, also
built for the Olympics. Two
levels of restaurants, shops,
and nightclubs around the
marina attract business people
at lunchtimes and pleasure
seekers at weekends.

Sagrada Família ⑦

See pp312–3.

Quadrat d'Or ⑧

M Diagonal, Passeig de Gracia.

C ALLED THE "Golden
Square" because it
contains so many of the
city's best Modernista
buildings, the Quadrat
d'Or is made up of
around a hundred city
blocks centering on the
Passeig de Gràcia. The
wealthy bourgeoisie,
who favored this area of
the Eixample, embraced
the new artistic and
architectural style, both

The rippled façade of Gaudí's Casa Milà "La Pedrera" in the Quadrat d'Or

for their homes and offices.
Many interiors are open to
the public, revealing a feast
of stained glass, ceramics,
and ironwork.

The most remarkable single
block is the **Illa de la
Discòrdia**, where four of
Barcelona's most famous
Modernista houses – all built
between 1900 and 1910 – vie
for attention. Nearby, the late
19th-century **Fundació Tàpies**,
by Domènech i Montaner,
houses paintings, sculptures,
and graphics, and is topped
by Tàpies' wire sculpture,
Cloud and Chair.

Gaudí's famous **Casa Milà
"La Pedrera"** has a wave-like
façade and a roofscape of
chimneys and vents resembling
abstract sculptures. The Palau
Baró de Quadras, designed
by Puig i Cadalfalch in 1904,
is now home to the Casa
Asia, which holds occasional
exhibitions dedicated to Asian
art and culture.

**Carving of a coiled beast on the doorway
of the Casa Asia, Quadrat d'Or**

Sagrada Família ⑦

EUROPE'S MOST unconventional church, the Temple Expiatori de la Sagrada Família is an emblem of a city that likes to think of itself as individualistic. Full of symbolism inspired by nature and striving for originality, it is the greatest work of Catalan architect Antoni Gaudí (1852–1926). In 1883, a year after work began on a Neo-Gothic church on the site, he was given the task of completing it. Gaudí changed everything, extemporizing as he went along. It became his life's work and he lived like a recluse on the site for 16 years. He is buried in the crypt. By the time of his death only one tower on the Nativity façade had been completed, but several more have since been finished to his original plans. After the Civil War, work resumed and continues today, financed by public subscription.

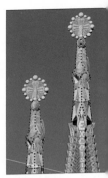

Bell Towers
Eight of the 12 spires, one for each apostle, have been built. Each is topped by Venetian mosaics.

THE FINISHED CHURCH

Gaudí's initial ambitions have been scaled down over the years, but the design for the building's completion remains impressive. Still to come is the central tower, which is to be encircled by four large towers representing the Evangelists. Four towers on the Glory (south) façade will match the existing four on the Passion (west) and Nativity (east) façades. An ambulatory – like an inside-out cloister – will run round the outside of the building.

Tower with elevator

The apse was the first part of the church Gaudí completed. Stairs lead down from here to the crypt below.

The altar canopy, designed by Gaudí, is still waiting for the altar.

★ Passion Façade
This bleak façade was completed in the late 1980s by artist Josep Maria Subirachs. A controversial work, its sculpted figures are angular and often sinister.

Entrance to Crypt Museum

Main entrance

Spiral Staircases
Steep stone steps allow access to the towers and upper galleries. Majestic views reward those who climb them or take the elevator.

Tower with elevator

VISITORS' CHECKLIST

Calle Mallorca 401. **(** 93-207 30 31. **M** Sagrada Familia. **🚌** 19, 33, 34, 43, 44, 50, 51, 54. **◻** Apr–Sep: 9am–8pm; Oct–Mar: 9am–6pm. **●** Jan 1 & 6, Dec 25 (pm) & 26. **✝** Apr–Sep: 9am, 10:30am, 11:45am, 1pm, 8:15pm. **🎦 ♿** ground floor. **W** www.sagradafamilia.org

★ **Nativity Façade**
The most complete part of Gaudí's church has doorways representing Faith, Hope, and Charity. Scenes of the Nativity and Christ's childhood contain imagery, such as doves, which symbolize the congregation.

★ **Crypt**
The crypt, where Gaudí is buried and services are currently held, was built by the original architect, Francesc de Paula Villar i Lozano, in 1882. A small museum traces the careers of both architects and the church's complicated history.

Nave
In the nave, which is still under construction, a forest of fluted pillars will support four galleries above the side aisles, while skylights let in natural light.

STAR FEATURES

★ **Passion Façade**

★ **Nativity Façade**

★ **Crypt**

Pretty whitewashed houses in Poble Espanyol, Montjuïc

Montjuïc ⑨

Ⓜ Espanya, Poble Sec, Paral·lel.
🚌 13, 50 from Plaça Espanya.

THE HILL OF MONTJUÏC, rising to 213 m (699 ft) above the commercial port on the south side of the city, is Barcelona's biggest recreation area. Its museums, art galleries, funfair, and nightclubs make it popular night and day. The hill is also a spectacular vantage point from which to view the city.

There was probably a Celt-iberian settlement here before the Romans built a temple to Jupiter on their Mons Jovis, which may have given Montjuïc its name. Another theory suggests that a Jewish cemetery on the hill inspired the name Mount of the Jews. Many buildings were erected in 1929, when an International Exhibition was held here, and later for the 1992 Olympics.

On Montjuïc's western edge is the popular **Poble Espanyol** – a "village" of cobbled streets and squares, created in 1929 to showcase different Spanish architectural styles. Also of interest, the **Museu Arqueològic** holds important finds from prehistoric cultures in Catalonia and the Balearic Islands. In the same complex, the **Museu Etnològic** houses artifacts from Oceania, Africa, Asia, and Latin America.

The summit of Montjuïc is occupied by the huge 18th-century **Castell de Montjuïc**, built for the Bourbon family. The castle is now a military museum with an extensive display of ancient weaponry.

♣ **Castell de Montjuïc**
Parc de Montjuïc. 🕻 93-329 86 13.
Ⓜ Paral·lel, then funicular & cable car (in winter Sat & public hols only).
Museum 🔾 Tue–Sun. ● Jan 1, Good Fri, May 1, Dec 25–26. 🗟
🏛 **Museu Arqueològic**
Passeig Santa Madrona 39. 🕻 93-424 65 77. Ⓜ Espanya, Poble Sec.
🔾 Tue–Sat, am Sun & public hols.
● Jan 1, Dec 25–26. 🗟 🕹

Fundació Joan Miró ⑩

Parc de Montjuïc. 🕻 93-329 19 08.
ⓦ www.bcn.fjmiró.es Ⓜ Espanya or Paral·lel, then bus 50. 🔾 Tue–Sat, am Sun & public hols. ● Jan 1, Dec 25 & 26. 🗟 🕹

HOUSED IN a boldly modern building designed in 1975 by Josep Lluís Sert, this collection of paintings, sculptures, and tapestries by Catalan artist Joan Miró (1893–1983) is lit by natural light.

An admirer of primitive Catalan art and Gaudí's Modernism, Miró developed a Surrealistic style, with vivid colors and fantastical forms that suggested dreamlike situations. Miró himself donated the works displayed here. Some of the best pieces at the museum include his *Barcelona Series* (1939–44), a set of 50 black-and-white lithographs. Temporary exhibitions of other artists' work are also held here.

The Palau Nacional, home of the Museu Nacional d'Art de Catalunya

Museu Nacional d'Art de Catalunya ⑪

Palau Nacional, Parc de Montjuïc.
🕻 93-622 03 60. Ⓜ Espanya.
🔾 Tue–Sat, am Sun & public hols.
● Jan 1, May 1, Dec 25–26. 🗟 call 93-622 03 75 in advance. 🕹

ORIGINALLY BUILT for the 1929 International Exhibition, since 1934 the austere Palau Nacional (National Palace) has been used to house the city's most important art collection.

The museum contains one of the greatest displays of Romanesque art in the world, its centerpiece being a series of magnificent 12th-century frescoes. These have been peeled from Catalan Pyrenean churches (to save them from the ravages of pollution and time) and pasted on to replicas of the original vaulted ceilings

A section of the 18th-century castle on the summit of Montjuïc

and apses they adorned. The most remarkable are the wall paintings from the churches of Santa Maria de Taüll and Sant Climent de Taüll in Vall de Boí.

The museum's superb Gothic collection covers the whole of Spain, but is particularly good on Catalonia. Several outstanding works by El Greco, Velázquez, and Zurbarán are on display in the Renaissance and Baroque section.

Parc Güell ⑫

Carrer d'Olot. █ 93-413 24 00. Ⓜ
Lesseps. ◯ daily. 🎟 ♿ Casa-Museu
Gaudí █ 93-219 38 11. ◯ daily.
● Dec 25 & 26 (am), Jan 1 & 6. 🎟

Designated a World Heritage Site by UNESCO, the Parc Güell is Gaudí's most colorful creation. He was commissioned in the 1890s by Count Eusebi Güell to design a garden city on 20 hectares (50 acres) of family estate. Little of Gaudí's grand plan for decorative buildings among landscaped gardens became reality. What we see today was completed between 1910 and 1914.

Most atmospheric is the Room of a Hundred Columns, a cavernous covered hall of 84 crooked pillars, which is brightened by glass and ceramic mosaics. Above it, reached by a flight of steps flanked by ceramic animals, is the Gran Plaça Circular, an

Mosaic-encrusted chimney by Gaudí at the entrance of the Parc Güell

open space with a snaking balcony of colored mosaics, said to have the longest bench in the world. It was executed by Josep Jujol, one of Gaudí's chief collaborators.

The two mosaic-decorated pavilions at the entrance are by Gaudí, but the **Casa-Museu Gaudí**, a gingerbread-style house where he lived from 1906–26, was built by Francesc Berenguer. The drawings and furniture inside are all by Gaudí.

Tibidabo ⑬

Plaça del Tibidabo 3–4. █ 93-211
79 42. Ⓜ Avda Tibidabo, then
Tramvia Blau & funicular. **Funfair**
◯ call to confirm opening times.
● Oct–Apr: Mon–Fri. ♿ **Temple
del Sagrat Cor** █ 93-417 56 86.
◯ daily.

The heights of Tibidabo are reached by Barcelona's last surviving tram, the Tramvia Blau, and a funicular

An ornate merry-go-round at the Parc d'Atraccions, Tibidabo

railway. The name, inspired by Tibidabo's views of the city, comes from the Latin *tibi dabo* (I shall give you) – a reference to the Temptation of Christ, who was taken up a mountain by Satan and offered the world spread at his feet.

The hugely popular funfair at **Parc d'Atraccions** first opened in 1908. The rides were completely renovated in the 1980s. While the old ones retain their charm, the newer ones provide the latest in vertiginous experiences. Their hilltop location at 517 m (1,696 ft) adds to the thrill. Also in the park is the **Museu d'Automates**, which displays automated toys, jukeboxes, and gaming machines.

Tibidabo is crowned by the **Temple Expiatori del Sagrat Cor** (Church of the Sacred Heart), built with religious zeal but little taste by Enric Sagnier between 1902 and 1911. Inside one of its towers, an elevator takes you up to an enormous statue of Christ.

Monestir de Montserrat ⓳

ITS HIGHEST PEAK rising to 1,236 m (4,055 ft), the "Serrated Mountain" (*mont serrat*) is a magnificent setting for Catalonia's holiest place, the Monastery of Montserrat, which is surrounded by chapels and hermits' caves. The earliest record of the monastery is from the 9th century. Enlarged in the 11th century, in 1409 it became independent of Rome. In 1811, when the French attacked Catalonia in the War of Independence, the monastery was destroyed and the monks killed. Rebuilt and repopulated in 1844, it was a beacon of Catalan culture during the Franco years. Today Benedictine monks live here. Visitors can hear the famous male choir, the Escolania, singing the *Salve Regina y Virolai* (the Montserrat hymn) at 11am and 7:10pm every day, except in July and from December 26 to January 8.

A Benedictine monk

Plaça de Santa Maria
The focal points of the square are two wings of the Gothic cloister built in 1477. The modern monastery façade is by Françesc Folguera.

Gothic cloister

Funicular to the holy site of Santa Cova

The Museum holds 19th- and 20th-century Catalan paintings and many archaeological exhibits from West Asia.

The Way of the Cross
This path passes 14 statues representing the Stations of the Cross. It begins near the Plaça de l'Abat Oliba.

View of Montserrat
The complex includes cafés and a hotel. A second funicular railway takes visitors to nature trails above the monastery.

STAR FEATURES

★ **Basilica Façade**

★ **Black Virgin**

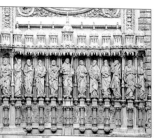

★ **Basilica Façade**
Agapit and Venanci Vallmitjana sculpted Christ and the apostles on the basilica's Neo-Renaissance façade. It was built in 1900 to replace the Plateresque façade of the original church, consecrated in 1592.

★ **Black Virgin**
La Moreneta looks down from behind the altar, protected behind glass. Her wooden orb protrudes for pilgrims to touch.

VISITORS' CHECKLIST

Montserrat (Barcelona province).
📞 93-877 77 77. 🚉 to Aeri de Montserrat (from Barcelona via Monistrol), then cable car.
🚌 from Barcelona. **Basilica**
🕐 Oct–Jun: 7:30am–7:30pm daily; Jul–Sep: 7:30am–8:30pm daily. ✝ from 9am Mon–Fri, from 7:30am Sat, from 8am Sun & religious hols. 📷 **Museum**
🕐 10am–6pm Mon–Fri, 9:30am–6:30pm Sat, Sun & public hols. 📷 ♿

Basilica Interior
The sanctuary in the domed basilica is adorned by a richly enameled altar and paintings by Catalan artists.

The rack railway, opened in 2003, follows the course of a historic rail line built in 1880.

Terminal for cable car from Aeri de Montserrat train station

THE VIRGIN OF MONTSERRAT

The small wooden statue of La Moreneta ("the dark one") is the soul of Montserrat. It is said to have been made by St. Luke and brought here by St. Peter in AD 50. Centuries later, the statue is believed to have been hidden from the Moors in the nearby Santa Cova (Holy Cave). Carbon dating suggests, however, that the statue was carved around the 12th century. In 1881 Montserrat's Black Virgin became patroness of Catalonia.

The Black Virgin of Montserrat

Inner Courtyard
On one side of the courtyard is the baptistry (1902), with sculptures by Charles Collet. Pilgrims may approach the Virgin through a door to the right.

Eastern Spain and the Balearic Islands

EASTERN SPAIN COVERS an extraordinary range of climates and landscapes, from the snowbound peaks of the Pyrenees in Aragón to the beaches of the Costa Blanca. The region has many historical sights, including the striking Mudéjar churches of Zaragoza and the great cathedral of Valencia. The coastal resorts of Eastern Spain are a popular destination, as are the Balearic Islands. Mallorca is the most culturally rich of the islands, while Menorca is dotted with prehistoric sites. Ibiza is chiefly known for its exuberant nightlife, but Formentera remains largely unspoiled. A dialect of the Catalan language, brought by 13th-century settlers, is still widely spoken on the islands.

Cupolas of the Basílica de Nuestra Señora del Pilar in Zaragoza

Zaragoza ㉒

Zaragoza. 700,000. Plaza del Pilar (976-20 12 00 or 902-20 12 12).

THE ROMAN SETTLEMENT of Caesaraugusta gave Zaragoza its name. Located on the fertile banks of the Río Ebro, it grew to become Spain's fifth largest city, and the capital of Aragón.

Badly damaged during the early 19th-century War of Independence, the old center nevertheless retains several fine monuments. Overlooking the vast Plaza del Pilar is the **Basílica de Nuestra Señora del Pilar**. With its 11 brightly tiled cupolas, it is one of the city's most impressive sights.

Also on the square are the Gothic-Plateresque **Lonja** (commodities exchange), the **Palacio Episcopal**, and Zaragoza's cathedral, **La Seo**, which displays a great mix of styles. Part of the exterior is faced with typical Mudéjar brick and ceramic decoration, while inside are a fine Gothic reredos and splendid Flemish tapestries. Nearby is the flamboyant Mudéjar bell tower of the **Iglesia de la Magdalena**, and remains of the Roman forum.

Parts of the Roman walls can be seen on the opposite side of the Plaza del Pilar near the **Mercado de Lanuza**, a market with sinuous ironwork in Art Nouveau style. The **Museo Camón Aznar** houses the eclectic collection of an art historian, whose special interest was the locally-born artist Goya.

The **Alfajería**, a beautiful 11th-century Moorish palace with gardens and a mosque, lies on the main road to Bilbao.

Ⅲ Museo Camón Aznar
Calle Espoz y Mina 23. 976-39 73 28. Tue–Sun.

Valencia ㉓

Valencia. 950,000. 8 km (5 miles) SW. Calle de la Paz 48 (96-398 64 22). Las Fallas (Mar 15–19).

VALENCIA, SPAIN'S third largest city, is famous for its ceramics, and for the spectacular fiesta of Las Fallas, marked by the erection and burning of elaborate papier-mâché monuments *(fallas)*.

Among the city's finest buildings are **La Lonja**, an exquisite Late Gothic hall built between 1482 and 1498, and the **cathedral** (1262) on Plaza de la Reina. Other monuments worth visiting include the Gothic **Palau de la Generalitat**, with its splendidly decorated first-floor chambers, and the 17th-century **Basílica de la Virgen de los Desamparados**.

Beyond the city center is the **Torres de Serranos** gateway, erected in 1238.

Valencia has a number of fine museums. The **Museo de Bellas Artes** holds 2,000 paintings and statues dating from antiquity to the 19th century, including six paintings by Goya, while the **Museo Domingo Fletcher** has a unique collection of local Stone Age engravings. Valencia's metro system takes tourists to the extensive beaches of El Cabañal and La Malvarrosa, east of the city.

La Lonja
Plaza del Mercado s/n.
96-352 54 78. Tue–Sun.

Effigy burning in Valencia during the annual fiesta of Las Fallas

The mountain village of Castell de Guadalest, Costa Blanca

🏛 **Palau de la Generalitat**
Plaza des Manises. 📞 *96-386 61 00 or 96-386 34 61.* ☐ *by prior appointment only.*

🏛 **Museo de Bellas Artes**
Museo San Pio V, Calle San Pio V 9.
📞 *96-360 57 93.* ☐ *Tue–Sun.* ●
Jan 1, Good Fri, Dec 25, 31. 📷 ♿

Costa Blanca ㉔

✈ 🚢 🚉 🚌 *Alicante.* 🛈 *Rambla Méndez Núñez 23, Alicante (96-514 34 52).* 🌐 *www.alicanteturismo.com*

THE COSTA BLANCA occupies a prime stretch of Spain's Mediterranean coastline. The main city, **Alicante** (Alacant), has an 18th-century Baroque town hall and a 16th-century castle, the Castillo de Santa Bárbara. The nearest beach to the city center is the popular Postiguet; slightly farther afield are the vast beaches of La Albufereta and Sant Joan.

The massive, rocky outcrop of the **Penyal d'Ifach** towers over Calp harbor, and is one of the Costa Blanca's most dramatic sights. Its summit offers spectacular views. A short drive inland, **Guadalest** is a pretty mountain village with castle ruins and a distinctive belfry perched precariously on top of a rock.

Also worth visiting are the whitewashed hilltop town of **Altea**, **Denia**, which has good snorkeling, and the cliffs and coves around **Xabia**. South of Alicante, **Guardamar del Segura** has a quiet beach bordered by aromatic pine woods, while **Torrevieja** is a highly-developed resort with sweeping, sandy shores.

Mallorca and the Balearic Islands ㉕

✈ 🚢 🚌 *Palma, Mallorca; Maó, Menorca.* 🛈 *Plaça Reina 2, Palma, Mallorca (971-71 22 16).*

THE LARGEST OF THE Balearic islands, Mallorca has a varied landscape and a rich cultural heritage. A massive Gothic cathedral is poised high on the sea wall of **Palma**, its capital. Completed in 1587 and known locally as Sa Seu, the cathedral is one of Spain's most breathtaking buildings. The interior was remodeled by Antoni Gaudí and a highlight is the Baldachino, his bizarre wrought-iron canopy above the altar.

Also worth visiting in Palma are the Basílica de Sant Francesc, the Moorish Palau de l'Almudaina, and the Fundació Pilar i Joan Miró – a stunning modern building housing Miró's studio and a collection of the artist's work.

Around the island, **Andratx** is a chic and affluent town with yachts moored along its harbor, while **Pollença** is a popular tourist resort which has remained relatively unspoiled. The 18th-century

family home, **La Granja**, and **Alfàbia**, which exudes a Moorish atmosphere, are aristocratic estates open to the public. The **Monasteri de Lluc**, in the remote mountain village of the same name, incorporates a guesthouse, a museum, and a church.

Menorca

Menorca's capital, **Maó**, has one of the finest harbors in the Mediterranean, an 18th-century Carmelite church, and a museum, the Collecció Hernández Mora, housing Menorcan art and antiques. The town of **Ciutadella** boasts an impressive main square and a delightful Art Nouveau market. Menorca's many Bronze Age villages – to which there is usually free access – are mostly the work of the "talaiotic" people, who lived from 2000–1000 BC.

Ibiza and Formentera

A popular package-tour destination, Ibiza has some of the wildest nightclubs in Europe. An hour's boat ride from Ibiza harbor are the tranquil shores of Formentera. The capital, **Sant Francesc**, has a pretty 18th-century church and a folk museum.

View across the marina at Palma, Mallorca to the spectacular cathedral

Southern Spain

ONE LARGE REGION – ANDALUSIA – extends across the south of Spain. It was here that the Moors lingered longest and left their greatest monuments in the cities of Granada, Córdoba, Málaga, and Seville. The eight southern provinces span a wide range of landscapes, with deserts in the east, sandy beaches along the Costa del Sol, and sherry-producing vineyards around Jerez. From flamingoes in the wetland Doñana National Park to flamenco – the uniquely Andalusian art form – the region has something to interest every visitor.

Antonio Palamino's cupola in the Monasterio de la Cartuja, Granada

Granada ㉖

Granada. 🏙 240,000. ✈ 12 km (7 miles) SW. 🚉 🚌 🛈 Corral del Carbón, Calle Mariana Pineda (958-24 71 28). 🎎 Corpus Christi (May – Jun).

THE ANCIENT CITY of Granada, founded by the Iberians, was for 250 years the capital of a Moorish kingdom. The Nasrid dynasty, who ruled from 1238 until 1492 when Granada fell to the Catholic Monarchs, left some out-standing examples of Moorish architecture here. The greatest legacy of their rule is the spectacular palace complex of the Alhambra (see pp322–3). Under the Nasrids the city enjoyed a golden age, acquiring an international reputation as a major cultural center. Later, under Christian rule, the city became a focus for the Renaissance.

Granada's 16th-century Gothic **cathedral** has a Renaissance façade and a Baroque west front. Nearby, the **Capilla Real** (Royal Chapel), built between 1505 and 1507, houses Carrara marble figures of the Catholic Monarchs, whose bodies lie in the crypt. Equally impressive are the **Casa de los Tiros**, a fortress-like palace built in Mudéjar style, and the **Monasterio de la Cartuja**, both dating from the 16th century. Founded by a Christian warrior, the latter has a dazzling cupola by Antonio Palomino.

Relics of the Moorish era in the old town include the **Corral del Carbón**, a former storehouse and inn for merchants, and the **Palacio de la Madraza**. Originally an Arab university, the palace has a Moorish hall with a finely decorated *mihrab* (prayer niche). It holds temporary art exhibitions.

Granada's Moorish ancestry is most evident in the hillside Albaicín district, which faces the Alhambra. Along its cobbled alleys stand *cármenes* – villas with Moorish decor and gardens – and **El Bañuelo**, the 11th-century brick-vaulted Arab baths. The churches here were mostly built on the sites of mosques. The most beautiful of these, the **Iglesia de Santa Ana**, has an elegant Plateresque portal. The **Real Chancillería**, or Royal Chancery (1530), boasts a beautiful Renaissance façade.

Also worth visiting in the Albaicín district is the **Museo Arqueológico**, with Iberian, Phoenician, and Roman finds.

From one end of the district, a road leads up to **Sacromonte**. Granada's gypsies once lived in the caves that line this hillside. Their legacy lives on in the flamenco shows performed here in the evenings.

From the northern side of the Alhambra, a footpath leads to the **Generalife** (see pp322–3), the country estate of the Nasrid kings. The gardens, begun in the 13th century, originally contained orchards and pastures. Today, their lush greenery, pools, and graceful water fountains provide a magical setting for the many events staged each year between mid-June and early July on the occasion of the city's international music and dance festival.

🏯 **Casa de los Tiros**
Calle Pavaneras. 🄲 958-22 10 72. ◯ Mon–Fri. ● main public hols.
🏯 **Palacio de la Madraza**
Calle Oficios 14. 🄲 958-24 34 84. ● for renovation.
🏛 **Museo Arqueológico**
Carrera del Darro 43. 🄲 958-22 56 40. ◯ Tue pm, 9am–8pm Wed–Sat, Sun am. ● main public hols.

Entrance to the Moorish *mihrab* in the Palacio de la Madraza, Granada

The main façade of Málaga's unusual cathedral, consecrated in 1588

Málaga ⓴

Málaga. 🏛 700,000. ✈ 🚢 🚉 🚌
🛈 Pasaje de Chinitas 4 (95-221 34 45).

MÁLAGA, the second largest city in Andalusia, was a thriving port under Phoenician, Roman, and Moorish rule. It also flourished during the 19th century, when sweet Málaga wine was one of Europe's most popular drinks.

At the heart of the old town is the **cathedral**, begun in 1528 by Diego de Siloé. The half-built second tower, abandoned in 1765 when funds ran out, gave the cathedral its nickname: La Manquita ("the one-armed one").

The **Casa Natal de Picasso**, where the painter spent his early years, is now the headquarters of the international Picasso Foundation. Málaga's old Museo de Bellas Artes has recently been renovated and transformed into a new museum dedicated to the painter.

The city's vast fortress – the **Alcazaba** – was built between the 8th and 11th centuries. Its major attractions are the display of Phoenician, Roman, and Moorish artifacts, as well as a recently restored Roman theater. The ruined **Castillo de Gibralfaro**, a 14th-century Moorish castle, lies behind the Alcazaba.

♠ Alcazaba
Calle Alcazabilla. 🎔 95-221 60 05.
🕐 9:30am–7:30pm Tue–Sun.

Costa del Sol ⓲

🏊 🏖 🅿 🚌 Málaga. 🛈 Pasaje de Chinitas 4, Málaga (95-221 34 45).

WITH ITS year-round sunshine and varied coastline, the Costa del Sol attracts crowds of vacationers every year and has half a million foreign residents.

Its most stylish resort is **Marbella**, frequented by royalty and film stars, who spend their summers here in the smart villas or luxury hotels overlooking the area's 28 beaches. Puerto Banús is its ostentatious marina. In winter the major attraction is golf: 30 of Europe's finest golf courses lie just inland.

Among the highlights of Marbella's old town is the Museo de Grabado Contemporáneo, which displays some of Picasso's least-known work, the peaceful Iglesia de Nuestra Señora de la Encarnación, and the town hall, with its exquisite, panelled Mudéjar ceiling.

Sotogrande, to the west of Marbella, is an exclusive resort of luxury villas. The marina is fronted by good seafood restaurants. In spite of tourism, **Estepona** preserves its Spanish character, with pretty tree-filled squares and inexpensive tapas bars.

To the east are the package-holiday resorts of **Fuengirola** and **Torremolinos**. Once the brash haunt of young northern European tourists, they are now more family-oriented.

Player on a green at one of Marbella's high-profile golf courses

MOORISH SPAIN

Typical Moorish *alcazaba*, dating from the 10th century

In the 8th century, the Iberian Peninsula came almost entirely under Moorish rule. The Muslim settlers called Spain "Al Andalus." A powerful caliphate was established in Córdoba, which became the center of one of the most brilliant civilizations of early medieval Europe. The Moors erected *alcazabas* (castles built into city ramparts) and palaces surrounded by patios, pools, and gardens, making lavish use of arches, stucco work, glazed wall tiles (*azulejos*), and ornamental calligraphy. They also introduced new crops to Spain, such as oranges and rice. By the 11th century the caliphate had collapsed into 30 *taifas* (splinter states) and the northern Christian kingdoms were reconquering parts of Moorish Spain. In 1492 the Catholic Monarchs took Granada, its last stronghold. Though many Muslims were expelled from Spain following the Reconquest, some were employed to build new churches and palaces for the Christian rulers. Known as Mudéjares (the name literally means "those permitted to stay"), these craftsmen developed a hybrid Christian-Islamic style that survived into the 18th century.

Granada: the Alhambra

A MAGICAL USE of space, light, water, and decoration characterizes this most sensual piece of architecture. It was built under Ismail I, Yusuf I, and Muhammad V, caliphs when the Nasrid dynasty (1238–1492) ruled Granada. Seeking to belie an image of waning power, they created their idea of paradise on earth. Modest materials were used (plaster, timber, and tiles), but they were superbly worked. Although the Alhambra suffered decay and pillage, including an attempt by Napoleon's troops to blow it up, it has recently been restored and its delicate craftsmanship still dazzles the eye.

Sala de la Barca

★ **Salón de Embajadores**
The ceiling of this sumptuous throne room, built between 1334 and 1354, represents the seven heavens of the Muslim cosmos.

★ **Patio de Arrayanes**
This pool, set amid myrtle hedges and graceful arcades, reflects light into the surrounding halls.

Patio de Machuca

Entrance

Patio del Mexuar
This council chamber, completed in 1365, was where the reigning sultan listened to the petitions of his subjects and held meetings with his ministers.

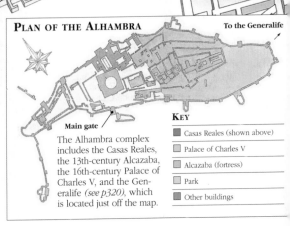

PLAN OF THE ALHAMBRA

To the Generalife

Main gate

The Alhambra complex includes the Casas Reales, the 13th-century Alcazaba, the 16th-century Palace of Charles V, and the Generalife *(see p320)*, which is located just off the map.

KEY

- Casas Reales (shown above)
- Palace of Charles V
- Alcazaba (fortress)
- Park
- Other buildings

Palacio del Partal

A pavilion with an arched portico and a tower is all that remains of this palace, the oldest building in the Alhambra.

VISITORS' CHECKLIST

For the Alhambra and
Generalife. 958-02 79 00.
Group reservations 958-22
09 12. 2. ☐ Mar–Oct:
8:30am–8pm daily; Nov–Feb:
8:30am–6pm daily.
Night visits: Mar–Oct:
10–11:30pm daily; Nov–Feb:
8–9:30pm Fri & Sat. ☐ ☐
W www.alhambra-patronato.es

Washington Irving's apartments

Baños Reales

Jardín de Lindaraja

The Sala de las Dos Hermanas, with its honeycomb dome, is regarded as a splendid example of Spanish-Islamic architecture.

Sala de los Reyes

This great banqueting hall was used to hold extravagant parties and feasts. Beautiful leather ceiling paintings, from the 14th century, depict tales of hunting and chivalry.

Puerta de la Rawda

★ Sala de los Abencerrajes

This hall takes its name from a noble family – rivals of the last Nasrid ruler, Boabdil. Legend claims he had the family massacred while they attended a banquet here. The geometrical ceiling was inspired by Pythagoras' theorem.

The Palace of Charles V (1526) houses a collection of Spanish-Islamic art, whose highlight is the Alhambra vase.

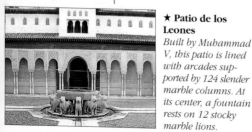

★ Patio de los Leones

Built by Muhammad V, this patio is lined with arcades supported by 124 slender marble columns. At its center, a fountain rests on 12 stocky marble lions.

STAR FEATURES

* ★ Salón de Embajadores

* ★ Patio de Arrayanes

* ★ Sala de los Abencerrajes

* ★ Patio de los Leones

The Puente Nuevo, spanning the deep Tajo gorge at Ronda

Ronda ㉙

Málaga. 🏠 35,000. 🚐 🚍
ℹ Plaza de España 9 (95-287 12 72).

RONDA SITS on a massive, rocky outcrop, straddling a precipitous limestone cleft. Because of its impregnable position, it was one of the last Moorish bastions, finally falling to the Christians in 1485.

On the south side perches a classic *pueblo blanco* – a white town – so-called because the houses are whitewashed in the Moorish tradition.

Among Ronda's historic buildings is the **Palacio Mondragón**, adorned with original Moorish mosaics. The façade of the 18th-century **Palacio del Marqués de Salvatierra** is decorated with images of South American Indians. From the **Casa del Rey Moro**, built on the site of a Moorish palace, 365 steps lead down to the river.

Across the **Puente Nuevo** or 'New Bridge,' which spans the deep Tajo gorge, is the modern town, and the site of one of Spain's oldest bullrings.

Inaugurated in 1785, the **Plaza de Toros** and its bull-fighting museum, the **Museo Taurino**, attract aficionados from all over the country.

🐂 Plaza de Toros & Museo Taurino
Calle Virgen de la Paz. ◯ daily.
🖼 ♿

Córdoba ㉚

Córdoba. 🏠 330,000. 🚐 🚍
ℹ Palacio de Congresos, Calle Torrijos 10 (957-47 12 35).

WITH ITS glorious mosque and pretty Moorish patios, Córdoba is northern Andalusia's star attraction. Its name may derive from Kartuba, Phoenician for "rich and precious city." In the 10th century the city enjoyed a golden age as the western capital of the Islamic empire.

Córdoba's most impressive Moorish monument is the mighty Mezquita *(see pp326–7)*. To the west of its towering walls, the **Alcázar de los Reyes Cristianos**, in the old Jewish quarter, is a stunning 14th-century palace-fortress built by Alfonso XI. The Catholic Monarchs stayed here during their campaign to wrest Granada from Moorish rule.

The small Mudéjar-style **synagogue** (c.1315) has decorative plasterwork with Hebrew script. Nearby, the **Museo Taurino**, a bullfighting museum, contains a replica of the tomb of Manolete, a famous matador, and the hide of the bull that killed him.

A Roman bridge, spanning the Río Guadalquivir, links the old town to the 14th-century **Torre de la Calahorra**. This defensive tower houses a small museum depicting life in 10th-century Córdoba.

In the newer part of the city, the **Museo Arqueológico** displays Roman and Moorish artifacts. The **Museo de Bellas Artes** contains sculptures by local artist Mateo Inurria (1867–1924) and paintings by Murillo and Zurbarán. Other notable buildings are the beautiful 17th-century **Palacio de Viana**, filled with works of art, and the handsome arcades of the **Plaza de la Corredera**.

♜ Alcázar de los Reyes Cristianos
Calle Caballerizas Reales s/n. 📞 957-42 01 51. ◯ 10am–3pm & 4:30–6:30pm Tue–Sat, 9:30am–2:30pm Sun & public hols. 🖼

Seville ㉛

See pp328–31.

Water gardens at the Alcázar de los Reyes Cristianos, Córdoba

Marshes and sand dunes of the Parque Nacional de Doñana

Parque Nacional de Doñana ㉜

Huelva & Sevilla. **ℹ** *La Rocina (959-44 23 40) or El Acebuche (959-44 87 11).* **Park interior** ◯ *summer: Mon–Sat; winter: Tue–Sun.* **☎** *959-43 04 32 for reservations.*

DOÑANA NATIONAL PARK is ranked among Europe's greatest wetlands, comprising more than 185,000 acres of marshes and sand dunes. The area, officially protected since 1969, was once a ducal hunting ground *(coto).*

A road suitable for drivers runs through part of the park and information points are located along it. There are also a number of self-guided walks on the park outskirts. The interior can be visited on official guided day tours only.

Doñana is home to wild cattle, fallow and red deer, and the lynx – one of Europe's rarest mammals. The greater flamingo and the rare imperial eagle can also be seen.

Jerez de la Frontera ㉝

Cádiz. **👥** *250,000.* **✈ 🚊 🚌**
ℹ *Plaza del Arenal sin Edificio Los Arcos (956-35 96 54).*

JEREZ IS THE CAPITAL of sherry production and many *bodegas* (cellars) can be visited. Among the well-known names are **González Byass** and **Pedro Domecq**.

The city is also famous for its **Real Escuela Andaluza de Arte Ecuestre**, a school

of equestrian skills. Public dressage displays are held on Thursdays. On the Plaza de San Juan, the 18th-century **Palacio de Penmartín** houses the Centro Andaluz de Flamenco, with exhibitions on this music and dance tradition. The 11th-century **Alcázar** encompasses a well-preserved mosque, now a church. Just to the north is the **cathedral**. Its most famous treasure, *The Sleeping Girl* by Zurbarán.

🍷 Sherry Bodegas
◯ *call for tour times.*
González Byass, Calle Manuel María González 12, Jerez.
☎ *956-35 70 00.*
Pedro Domecq, Calle San Ildefonso 3, Jerez.
☎ *956-15 15 00.*

Cádiz ㉞

Cádiz. **👥** *160,000.* **🚊 🚌 ℹ** *Plaza de San Juan de Dios 11 (956-24 10 01) or Calle Nueva 6 (956-25 86 46).*

SURROUNDED ALMOST entirely by water, Cádiz lays claim to being Europe's oldest city. After the Catholic reconquest, the city prospered on wealth brought from the New World.

Modern Cádiz is a busy port, with a pleasant waterfront, while the old town has narrow alleys and lively markets. The Baroque and Neoclassical **cathedral**, with its dome of golden yellow tiles, is one of Spain's largest.

At the **Museo de Cádiz** archaeological exhibits chart the history of the city, and you can also see one of the largest art collections in Andalusia.

The 18th-century **Oratorio de San Felipe Neri** has been a shrine to liberalism since 1812 when a provisional government assembled in the church to try to establish Spain's first constitutional monarchy. The **Torre Tavira**, an 18th-century watchtower, offers spectacular views of the city.

🏛 Museo de Cádiz
Plaza de Mina.
☎ *956-21 22 81.*
◯ *Tue–Sun.* ⬤ *main public hols.*

Golden chalice from the treasury of Cádiz cathedral

TAPAS

The light snacks known as tapas – and sometimes as *pinchos* – originated in Andalusia in the 19th century as an accompaniment to sherry. The name derives from a bartender's practice of covering a glass with a saucer or *tapa* (cover) to keep out flies. The custom progressed to a chunk of cheese, or a few olives, placed on a platter to serve with a drink. Today tapas range from cold snacks to elaborately prepared hot dishes, generally eaten standing at the bar rather than sitting at a table. Almost every village in Spain has a tapas bar. In the larger towns it is customary to move from bar to bar, sampling the specialties of each.

Olives

Jamón serrano (salt-cured ham)

Patatas bravas (potatoes in spicy tomato sauce)

Córdoba: the Mezquita

CÓRDOBA'S GREAT MOSQUE, dating back 12 centuries, embodied the power of Islam on the Iberian Peninsula. Abd al Rahman I built the original mosque between 785 and 787. The building evolved over the centuries, blending many architectural forms. In the 10th century al Hakam II made some of the most lavish additions, including the elaborate *mihrab* (prayer niche) and the *maqsura* (caliph's enclosure). During the 16th century a cathedral was built in the heart of the mosque, part of which was destroyed.

Patio de los Naranjos
Orange trees grow in the courtyard where the faithful washed before prayer.

Torre del Alminar
This bell tower, 93 m (305 ft) high, is built on the site of the original minaret. Steep steps lead to the top for a fine view of the city.

The Puerta del Perdón is a Mudéjar-style entrance gate, built during Christian rule in 1377. Penitents were pardoned here.

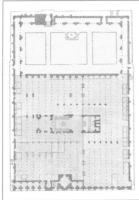

EXPANSION OF THE MEZQUITA

Abd al Rahman I built the original mosque. Extensions were added by Abd al Rahman II, al Hakam II, and al Mansur.

The Puerta de San Esteban is set in a section of wall from an earlier Visigothic church.

KEY TO ADDITIONS

☐ Original mosque (785–787)

☐ Added by Abd al Rahman II (848)

☐ Added by al Hakam II (c.961)

☐ Added by al Mansur (c.987)

☐ Patio de los Naranjos

STAR FEATURES

★ **Arches and Pillars**

★ **Mihrab**

★ **Capilla de Villaviciosa**

Cathedral
Part of the mosque was destroyed to accommodate the cathedral, begun in 1523. Featuring an Italianate dome, it was designed chiefly by members of the Hernán Ruiz family.

The cathedral choir
has Churrigueresque – excessive Baroque-style – stalls carved by Pedro Duque Cornejo in 1758.

Capilla Mayor

Capilla Real

★ Arches and Pillars
More than 850 columns of granite, jasper, and marble support the roof, creating a dazzling visual effect. Many were taken from Roman and Visigothic buildings.

★ Mihrab
This prayer niche, richly ornamented, held a gilded copy of the Koran. The worn flagstones indicate where pilgrims circled it seven times on their knees.

★ Capilla de Villaviciosa
The first Christian chapel was built in the mosque in 1371 by Mudéjar craftsmen (see p321). Its multi-lobed arches are stunning.

Street-by-Street: Seville ❸

THE MAZE of narrow streets that makes up the Barrio de Santa Cruz represents Seville at its most romantic and compact. This is a good place to begin an exploration of the city, since many of the best-known sights are located here. As well as the expected souvenir shops, tapas bars, and strolling guitarists, there are plenty of picturesque alleys, hidden plazas, and flower-decked patios to reward the casual wanderer. Once a Jewish ghetto, its restored buildings, with characteristic window grilles, are now a harmonious mix of upscale residences and tourist accommodations. Good restaurants and bars make the area well worth an evening visit.

Plaza Virgen de los Reyes
This delightful square, which is often lined with horse-drawn carriages, has an early 20th-century fountain by José Lafita.

Palacio Arzobispal, the 18th-century Archbishop's Palace, is still used by Seville's clergy.

Bus station

★ Cathedral and La Giralda
This huge Gothic cathedral and its Moorish bell tower are Seville's most popular sights (see p330).

Convento de la Encarnación (1591)

Archivo de Indias
Built in the 16th century as a merchants' exchange, the Archive of the Indies now houses documents and maps relating to the Spanish colonization of the Americas.

Plaza del Triunfo
The square was built to celebrate the city's survival of the great earthquake of 1755. I the center is a modern statue the Virgin Ma

Calle Mateos Gago
This street is filled with souvenir shops and tapas bars. Bar Giralda at No.2, whose vaults are the remains of a Moorish bath, is popular for its wide variety of tapas.

VISITORS' CHECKLIST

Sevilla. 🏙 700,000. ✈ 4 km (2.5 miles) NE. 🚆 Santa Justa, Avda de Kansas City. 🚌 Plaza de Armas, Calle de Arjona. 🛈 Avda de la Constitución 21 (95-422 14 04). **Archivo de Indias** ☎ 95-421 12 34. 🔒 for renovation until 2004.

Train station

The Plaza Santa Cruz is adorned by an ornate iron cross from 1692.

MESON DEL MORO

XIMENEZ ENCISO

SANTA TERESA

RODRIGO CARO

LA MERDANA

LOPE DE RUEDA

REINOSO

PLAZA

STA CRUZ

GLORIA

JUSTINO DE NEVE

PL DOÑA ELVIRA

SUSONA

PIMIENTA

VIDA

CALLEJON DEL AGUA

Hospital de los Venerables
The 17th-century home for elderly priests has a splendidly restored Baroque church (see p330).

Callejón del Agua
This whitewashed alleyway offers glimpses of enchanting plant-filled patios, such as the one pictured here.

★ Real Alcázar
Seville's Royal Palace is a rewarding combination of exquisite Mudéjar (see p321) craftsmanship, regal grandeur, and landscaped gardens (see p330).

| 0 meters | 50 |
| 0 yards | 50 |

KEY

– – – Suggested route

STAR SIGHTS

★ Cathedral and La Giralda

★ Real Alcázar

The mighty Giralda bell tower rising above the Gothic cathedral

🔒 Cathedral and La Giralda

Avenida de la Constitución. 📞 954-21 49 71. ◐ 11am–5pm daily (Sun: pm only). 🏷️ 🚻 except Giralda tower.

Seville's cathedral occupies the site of a great mosque, built by the Almohads in the late 12th century. La Giralda, its huge bell tower, and the beautiful Patio de los Naranjos, which is filled with orange trees, are a legacy of this Moorish structure. Work on the Christian cathedral began in 1401 and took just over a century to complete. The bronze spheres on the original Moorish minaret were replaced by Christian symbols, though the Giralda did not assume its present appearance until 1568. Today it is crowned by a bronze sculpture portraying Faith. This weathervane (giraldillo) has given the tower its name. Visitors can climb La Giralda for superb views of the city.

The cathedral houses many fine works of art, including the stunning high altar reredos with its 44 gilded reliefs, carved by Spanish and Flemish sculptors in 1482–1564.

🏛 Real Alcázar

Patio de Banderas. 📞 95-450 23 03. 🌐 www.patronato-alcazarsevilla.es ◐ Apr–Sep: Tue–Sun & public hols; Oct–Mar: Tue–Sat, am Sun & public hols. 🏷️

In 1364 Pedro I of Castile ordered the construction of a royal residence within the palaces that had been built in the 12th century by the Moors. Craftsmen from Granada and Toledo created a stunning complex of Mudéjar patios and halls, the Palacio Pedro I, now at the heart of Seville's Real Alcázar. Successive monarchs added their own distinguishing marks: Isabel I dispatched navigators to explore the New World from her Casa de Contratación, while Carlos I (the Holy Roman Emperor Charles V) had grandiose, richly decorated apartments built.

A star feature of the palace is the Salón de Embajadores (Ambassadors' Hall), with its dazzling dome of carved and gilded, interlaced wood. The hall overlooks the Patio de las Doncellas (Patio of the Maidens), which boasts some exquisite plasterwork.

Laid out with terraces, fountains, and pavilions, the tranquil gardens of the Real Alcázar provide a delightful refuge from the heat and bustle of the center of Seville.

🏛 Hospital de los Venerables

Plaza de los Venerables 8. 📞 95-456 26 96. ◐ 10am–2pm, 4–8pm daily. ● Jan 1, Good Friday, Dec 25. 🏷️ 🎦 🚻

This late 17th-century home for elderly priests has recently been restored as a cultural center, its upper floors, cellar, and infirmary serving as exhibition galleries. The Hospital church is a showcase of Baroque splendors, with frescoes by both Juan de Valdés Leal and his son Lucas Valdés. There are also fine sculptures by Pedro Roldán.

🏛 Torre del Oro

Paseo de Cristóbal Colón. 📞 95-422 24 19. ◐ 10am–2pm Tue–Fri, 11am–2pm Sat & Sun. ● Aug. 🎦 except Tue

The Moors built Seville's Torre del Oro (Tower of Gold) as a defensive lookout in 1220. Its turret was not added until 1760. The gold in the tower's name may refer to the gilded azulejos (ceramic tiles) that once clad its walls, or to treasures from

Fresco by Juan de Valdés Leal in the Hospital de los Venerables

Arcaded arena of the Plaza de Toros de la Maestranza, begun in 1761

the Americas unloaded here. It now houses the **Museo Marítimo**, which exhibits maritime maps and antiques.

▦ Plaza de Toros de la Maestranza

Paseo de Cristóbal Colón 12. **[** 95-422 45 77. ◯ *daily.* ● *for bullfights.*

Built between 1761 and 1881, Seville's famous bullring seats up to 14,000 spectators.

Visitors who take a guided tour of this enormous building are shown many interesting features, including a chapel where the matadors pray for success, and the stables where the horses of the *picadores* (lance-carrying horsemen) are kept. There is also a small museum.

Between Easter Sunday and October, *corridas* (bullfights) take place every Sunday evening. Tickets can be bought from the *taquilla* (ticket office) at the bullring.

▥ Museo de Bellas Artes

Plaza del Museo 9. **[** 95-422 07 90. ◯ *Wed–Sat, am Sun, pm Tue.* 🖼 &

The magnificently restored Convento de la Merced Calzada houses one of Spain's best art museums. Delightful tree-filled patios, colorful *azulejos*, and a church with a beautiful Baroque painted ceiling make this a wonderful setting for the fine works of art on display here.

The museum's collection of Spanish art and sculpture – which covers all periods from the medieval to the modern – focuses on the work of the Seville School artists. Among the star attractions are masterpieces by Murillo, Juan de Valdés Leal, and Zurbarán.

❦ Parque María Luisa

In 1893 Princess María Luisa donated part of the grounds of the Palacio San Telmo to the city for this park. Its most extravagant feature is the semicircular Plaza de España, designed by Aníbal González for the 1929 Ibero-American Exposition. At the center of the park, the Pabellón Mudéjar houses the **Museo de Artes y Costumbres Populares**, with displays of traditional Andalusian folk arts. Nearby, located in the grand Neo-Renaissance Pabellón de Bellas Artes, is the provincial **Museo Arqueológico** (Archaeological Museum).

☖ Monasterio de Santa María de las Cuevas

Calle Americo Vespucio 2, Isla de la Cartuja. **[** 95-503 70 70. ◯ *Tue–Sat, am Sun.* 🖼 🖻 *by prior appointment only.* &

This 15th-century Carthusian monastery was inhabited by monks until 1836. Columbus lay buried in the crypt of its church between 1507 and 1542.

The monastery stands at the heart of the Isla de Cartuja, the site of Expo '92. The area is also home to the **Museo de Arte Contemporáneo**, which has a collection of Spanish and international art, and the **Isla Mágica** theme park.

Seville's dazzling Plaza de España in the Parque María Luisa

Practical Information

SPAIN'S TOURIST INFORMATION service is efficient and extensive, with offices in most towns providing advice on lodgings, restaurants, and local events. In August, many businesses close and roads are busy. It is worth finding out whether local fiestas will coincide with your visit, as while these are enjoyable, they may also cause closures. Public telephones are widely available, but international call charges are high. When changing money, credit cards often offer the best exchange rate and can be used in cash dispensers. The Spanish lunch hour extends from 2pm to 5pm.

WHEN TO VISIT

AUGUST IS SPAIN'S busiest vacation month. Spanish holidaymakers and millions of foreign tourists flock to the coast. Easter is a good time to visit: temperatures are more bearable, especially in the south, the countryside is in full bloom, and the country's most important fiestas take place. In the Sierra Nevada and the Pyrenees the ski season is from mid-December until May.

TOURIST INFORMATION

ALL MAJOR CITIES and towns have a tourist information office (oficina de turismo), which will provide town plans, lists of hotels and restaurants, and details of local activities. There is a **Spanish National Tourist Office** in several large cities worldwide.

OPENING HOURS

MOST MONUMENTS and museums in Spain close on Mondays. On other days they are generally open from 10am to 2pm, and, in some cases, reopen from 5pm to 8pm. Most charge for entry. Some churches may only be opened for services.

In smaller towns, churches, castles, and other sights are often kept locked. The key, available on request, will be lodged in a neighboring house, in the town hall, or perhaps with the local bar owners.

VISA REQUIREMENTS AND CUSTOMS

CITIZENS OF THE EU do not require a visa for entry to Spain. A list of entry requirements – available from Spanish embassies – specifies other countries, including Canada and New Zealand, whose nationals do not need a visa for visits of less than 90 days. US and Australian citizens must have a valid visa to travel.

Non-EU residents can reclaim IVA (sales tax) on some single items. You pay the full price and ask the sales assistant for a formulario (tax exemption form). On leaving Spain, you must ask customs to stamp your formulario (this must be within six months of the purchase). You receive the refund by mail or on your credit card account.

PERSONAL SECURITY

VIOLENT CRIME is rare in Spain. Petty theft is the main problem in the cities, especially Barcelona, where visitors should be extra vigilant. Men may make complimentary remarks (piropos) to women in the street. This is customary and not intended to be intimidating.

POLICE

THERE ARE essentially three types of police force in Spain. The Guardia Civil (National Guard) mainly police rural areas and impose fines for traffic offenses. The Policía Nacional operate in larger towns. They are replaced by a regional force, the Ertzaintza, in the Basque country, and by the Mossos d'Esquadra in Catalonia. The Policía Local, also called Policía Municipal or Guardia Urbana, operate independently in each town and have a branch for city traffic control.

All three services will direct you to the relevant authority in the event of an incident requiring police help.

EMERGENCY SERVICES

ONLY THE Policía Nacional operates a nationwide emergency phone number (see Directory). Telephone

THE CLIMATE OF SPAIN

Spain's large landmass, with its mountain ranges and the influences of the Atlantic and Mediterranean, accounts for a varied climate. The eastern and southern coasts and islands have mild winters, but winter temperatures in the interior often fall below freezing. Summers everywhere are hot, except in upland areas. Northern Spain is wettest year round.

MADRID

°C/F	Apr	Jul	Oct	Jan
High	17/63	32/90	20/68	10/50
Low	5/41	16/61	8/46	0/32
Sun (hrs)	8	12	6.5	5
Rain (mm)	48	11	53	39

SEVILLE

°C/F	Apr	Jul	Oct	Jan
High	21/70	35/95	25/77	16/61
Low	10/50	18/64	13/55	5/41
Sun (hrs)	6	8	4.5	2
Rain (mm)	50	58	55	55

directories list local emergency numbers under *Servicios de Urgencia*. For emergency medical treatment call the Cruz Roja (Red Cross), look under *Ambulancias* in the phone book, or go to a hospital emergency room *(Urgencias)*.

HEALTH ISSUES

SPANISH PHARMACISTS have wide responsibilities. They can advise and, in certain cases, prescribe without consulting a doctor. In a non-emergency, a *farmacéutico* is a good person to see first. It is usually easy to find one who speaks English.

The pharmacy *(farmacia)* sign is a green or red illuminated cross. Those open at night are listed in the windows of all the local pharmacies.

FACILITIES FOR THE DISABLED

SPAIN'S NATIONAL association for the disabled, the Confederación Coordinadora Estatal de Minusválidos Físicos de España (**COCEMFE**), has a tour company, Servi-COCEMFE, which publishes

guides to facilities in Spain and will help plan a vacation to individual requirements. A Spanish travel agency, **Viajes 2000**, specializes in vacations for disabled people.

LANGUAGE AND ETIQUETTE

THE SPANISH commonly greet and say goodbye to strangers at bus stops and in stores and other public places. People shake hands when introduced and whenever they meet. In Catalonia and the Basque country, regional languages are as much in use as the national tongue, Castilian Spanish.

BANKING AND CURRENCY

THE SPANISH UNIT of currency was the peseta (pta). This has been replaced by the euro *(see p15)* which was introduced on January 1, 2002.

Generally, banks are open from 8am to 2pm Monday to Friday. Some branches, especially those in the larger towns and cities, open until 1pm on Saturdays, except in August. Most have a foreign exchange desk with the sign *Cambio* or *Extranjero*. Take

some form of ID when changing money. Bureaux de change charge higher rates of commission but are open longer hours and are commonly found in the main tourist destinations.

COMMUNICATIONS

AS WELL AS PUBLIC telephone booths *(cabinas)*, there are nearly always pay phones in bars. Most take coins, but some take tokens. Phonecards can be bought at newsstands and *estancos* (tobacconists). At public telephone offices, which are called *locutorios,* you can make a call and pay for it afterwards. Telefónica run the official ones, which are less expensive than private offices.

The Spanish postal service, Correos, is rather slow: a national or international delivery may take more than a week. Send important mail by *urgente* (express) or *certificado* (registered) mail. The main Correos offices open from 8am to 9pm from Monday to Friday and from 9am to 7pm on Saturday. Stamps for letters and postcards can also be bought from an *estanco*.

Travel Information

SPAIN HAS AN INCREASINGLY EFFICIENT transportation system. All the major cities and islands have airports, and flights from around the globe arrive at those of Madrid and Barcelona. Both the road and rail networks were greatly improved during the 1980s and in the run-up to the Barcelona Olympics in 1992. Intercity rail services are reliable, but buses are a faster and more frequent option between smaller towns. In much of rural Spain, however, public transportation is limited and a car is the most practical solution for getting around. Ferries connect mainland Spain with the Balearic Islands and ports in the UK.

FLYING TO SPAIN

OF THE SEVERAL US airlines serving Spain, **American Airlines** flies to Madrid, while **Delta Air Lines** flies to both Madrid and Barcelona. **Iberia**, the Spanish national airline, has direct flights to Madrid from New York, Miami, and Los Angeles, as well as flights to many destinations in Spain from Toronto and Montreal.

Iberia also offers scheduled flights daily to Madrid and Barcelona from all Western European capitals (except Dublin, which has four flights a week). **British Airways** has scheduled flights to Madrid and Barcelona and several other cities daily from London Heathrow or Gatwick; also Madrid from Manchester.

From Australasia the best connections are via Athens, Bangkok, and London.

CHARTERS AND PACKAGE DEALS

CHARTER FLIGHTS from the UK serve airports such as Alicante, Málaga, and Girona. These can be inexpensive, but are less reliable and often fly at unsociable hours. Make sure your agent is ABTA bonded before making a reservation. Special deals, particularly for weekend city breaks, are often offered in the winter and may include a number of nights at a hotel. Low-cost airline **easyJet** serves Madrid, Barcelona, Mallorca, and Málaga from London Luton and Liverpool, while rival **Go** flies from London Stansted to Alicante, Barcelona, Bilbao, Madrid, and Málaga.

DOMESTIC FLIGHTS

MOST OF Spain's domestic flights have traditionally been operated by **Iberia**. In recent years, however, this monopoly has been broken to encourage competition. The two main alternative Spanish carriers are **Air Europa** and **Spanair**.

The most frequent shuttle service is the Puente Aéreo, run between Barcelona and Madrid by Iberia. Flights leave every 15 minutes at peak business times. A ticket machine allows passengers to buy tickets up to 15 minutes before departure. The journey usually takes 50 minutes.

Air Europa and Spanair services between Madrid and the regional capitals are not as frequent as the Puente Aéreo, but their prices are usually slightly lower. Flights to provincial cities usually operate in the morning and evening. Air services to and within the Balearic Islands are run by **Binter**, which is affiliated to Iberia Airlines.

GETTING AROUND MADRID AND BARCELONA

THE METRO IS the quickest and least expensive way to travel around Madrid. It is open from 6am to 1:30am and consists of 11 color-coded lines, plus the Ópera-Príncipe Pío link and a service to the airport. Day buses run from 6am until midnight; night buses continue operating until 6am and leave from the Plaza de Cibeles. A *Metrobus* ticket, valid for ten trips on the buses and metro, can be bought at any metro station, as well as from newsstands and *estancos* (tobacconists). Sightseeing bus tours are run by **Madrid Vision** and **Juliá Tours**.

Barcelona's metro system generally runs from 5am to 11pm; on Fridays and Saturdays it stays open until 2am. There are various types of travelcard available, valid for bus, metro, and the FGC (*Ferrocarrils de la Generalitat de Catalunya*) suburban train network. The city buses in Barcelona are usually colored white and red. The *Nitbus* (night bus) runs from around 10pm to 5am; the *TombBus* covers the main shopping streets; and the *Aerobus* provides an excellent service between the Plaça de Catalunya and the airport.

Sightseeing tours in Barcelona are operated by Bus Turístic from April through to February on two routes from the Plaça de Catalunya.

RAIL TRAVEL

SPAIN OFFERS many options for users of the state railroad **RENFE**. The two high-speed services are the intercity TALGO trains and the AVE service between Madrid and Seville via Córdoba. Tickets for these are the most expensive and may be bought at train stations from the *taquilla* (ticket office) or obtained from travel agents. On certain days, so-called *días azules*, or blue days, there is a 10 percent discount on usual rail fares.

The *largo recorrido* (long-distance trains) and *regionales y cercanías* (regional and local) services are frequent, inexpensive, but slower. Tickets for local travel may be purchased from machines at the station.

In Madrid the major stations for long-distance trains are Atocha, Chamartín, and Norte. Barcelona's two principal train stations are Sants and Francia.

Regional rail companies operate in three areas of Spain. Catalonia and Valencia each has its own *Ferrocarrils de la Generalitat*, known respectively as the **FGC** and the **FGV**. The Basque country has the **ET** (*Eusko Trenbideale*).

Iberrail holidays offer rail-plus-hotel deals for traveling between Spanish cities. Two services similar to the Orient Express are also operated by Iberrail. The El Andalus Expres tours Andalusia, stopping at Seville, Córdoba, Granada, Jerez, and Ronda. The Transcantábrico, run by **FEVE** *(Ferrocarriles de Vía Estrecha)* leaves San Sebastián to travel the length of Spain's north coast, ending its journey in Santiago de Compostela. Passengers travel in style in 14 restored period carriages dating from between 1900–30.

LONG-DISTANCE BUSES

SPAIN HAS NO national long-distance bus company. The largest private company, **Autocares Juliá**, offers a variety of bus tours and sight-seeing trips nationwide.

Other companies operate in particular regions. Tickets and information for long-distance travel are available at main bus stations and from travel agents.

TRAVELING BY ROAD

SPAIN'S FASTEST roads are its *autopistas*. They are normally dual carriageways subject to *peajes* (tolls). *Autovías* are similar but have no tolls. Smaller roads are less well kept but are a more relaxed way to see rural Spain.

As well as the international car rental companies, a few Spanish companies, such as **Atesa**, operate nationwide. You can probably negotiate the best deal with an international company from home. There are also fly-drive package deals, which include car rental. *Gasolina* (gas) is priced by the liter.

Spanish law requires drivers to carry at all times valid insurance and registration documents, a driver's license, and ID, usually in the form of a passport.

FERRY SERVICES

TWO CAR FERRY routes link the Spanish mainland with the UK. **Brittany Ferries** sails between Plymouth in the UK and Santander in Cantabria; **P&O Portsmouth** sails from Portsmouth to Bilbao. The crossings take over 24 hours. Advance reservations are essential in the summer.

Trasmediterránea runs car ferry services from Barcelona and Valencia on the Spanish mainland to the Balearic Islands. The crossing takes about eight hours. The same company also operates frequent inter-island services.

DIRECTORY

IBERIA AND AFFILIATES

International and domestic flights
- 902-400 500 (Spain).
- 0845-601 2854 (UK).
- 800-772 4642 (US).
- w www.iberia.com

OTHER AIRLINES

Air Europa
- 902-401 501 (Spain).
- w www.air-europa.com

American Airlines
- 91-453 14 00 (Spain).
- 800-633 3711 (US).
- w www.aa.com

British Airways
- 902-111 333 (Spain).
- 0845-773 3377 (UK).
- 800-247 92 97 (US).
- w www.britishairways.com

Delta Air Lines
- 91-749 66 30 (Spain).
- 800-241 41 41 (US).
- w www.delta.com

easyJet
- w www.easyjet.com

Go
- w www.go-fly.com

Spanair
- 902-13 14 15 (Spain).
- w www.spanair.com

MADRID TOURS

Juliá Tours
Gran Vía 68, Madrid.
- 93-402 69 00.
- w www.juliatours.com

RAIL TRAVEL

ET
- 902-54 32 10.
- w www.euskotren.es

FEVE
- 902-100 818.
- w www.feve.es

FGC
- 93-205 15 15.
- w www.fgc.catalunya.net

FGV
- 96-526 27 31.
- w www.fgv.es

Iberrail
- 91-571 66 96.
- w www.iberrail.es

RENFE
- 902-24 02 02.
- w www.renfe.es

BUS COMPANIES

Autocares Juliá
- 902-40 00 80 (Spain).
- w www.julia.net

Eurolines
- 902-40 50 40 (Barcelona).
- 91-506 33 60 (Madrid).
- 01582-404 511 (UK).
- w www.eurolines.es
- w www.gobycoach.com

BUS STATIONS

Madrid
Estación Sur (for whole of Spain).
- 91-468 42 00.

Intercambiador des Autobuses (for northern Spain).
- 91-745 63 00.

Terminal Auto Res (for Valencia, Extremadura, Andalusia).
- 90-202 09 99.

Barcelona
Estació del Nord.
- 93-265 65 08.

Estació de Sants.
- 93-490 40 00.

CAR RENTAL

Atesa
- 902-10 01 01 (Spain).
- w www.atesa.com

Avis
- 902-18 08 54 (Spain).
- 0870-590 0500 (UK).
- w www.avis.com

Europcar
- 902-10 50 30 (Spain).
- 0845-722 2525 (UK).
- w www.europcar.com

Hertz
- 901-10 10 01 (toll-free in Spain).
- 0870-844 8844 (UK).
- w www.hertz.es

FERRY SERVICES

Brittany Ferries
- 942-36 06 11 (Spain).
- 0870-536 0360 (UK).
- w www.brittany-ferries.com

P&O Portsmouth
- 94-423 44 77 (Spain).
- 0870-600 3300 (UK).
- w www.poportsmouth.com

Trasmediterránea
- 93-295 91 39 (Barcelona).
- 971-70 73 77 (Palma de Mallorca).
- 96-367 65 12 (Valencia).
- 020-7491 4968 (UK).
- w www.trasmediterranea.es

Shopping

SHOPPING IN SPAIN is a pleasurable activity, particularly if you approach it in a leisurely way, punctuating it with frequent breaks for coffee. In small, family-run shops especially, people will go out of their way to fulfill your smallest request. Markets sell the freshest of produce and quality wines can be found at almost any grocer. Leatherwork is still highly regarded among Spain's many traditional crafts. Spanish design has come to the forefront in both fashion and decor.

OPENING HOURS

SHOPS USUALLY open at 10am, close at 2pm, and reopen from 5pm to 8pm. Bakeries generally open early, at around 8am. Supermarkets and department stores stay open over lunchtime.

Rural markets are held in the morning only. In some regions Sunday trading is just limited to the bakeries, *pastelerías* (pastry shops), and newspaper kiosks, but in many tourist resorts stores open on Sunday.

LARGER STORES

THE HIPERMERCADOS (super-stores) are sited outside towns and can often be found by following signs to the *centro comercial*. The best known are Carrefour, Alcampo, and Hipercor.

Spain's leading department store is **El Corte Inglés**. It has branches in all cities and in the larger regional towns.

Major seasonal sales are advertised by the word *Rebajas* displayed in store windows.

CLOTHING STORES

THE LARGER CITIES naturally offer the widest selection of clothing stores, but Spanish designer labels can be found even in the smaller towns.

The Calle de Serrano and Calle de José Ortega y Gasset are the main streets for fashionwear in Madrid, while the work of young designers is mostly located in the Chueca district. **Adolfo Domínguez** is the doyen of Madrid's minimalist look. The adventurous will appreciate the designs of **Agatha Ruiz de la Prada**.

In Barcelona, international fashion labels and clothes by young designers can be found in and around the Passeig de Gràcia, including **Armand Basi**, vendors of quality leisure and sportswear.

Victorio & Lucchino in Seville sells clothes with a distinctly Andalusian style.

LEATHER GOODS

LEATHER ACCESSORIES and shoes are a popular purchase and there is a wide range in terms of quality and price. It is the practice in mid-range stores for customers to choose from the selection in the window and give the sales assistant the code number indicated and the *talla* (size) required. If you want an all-leather shoe, look for *cuero*, the hide label mark. **Calzados E. Solé** in Barcelona is well known for its classic hand-made shoes and boots.

Leather clothes and bags of all kinds are usually of good quality and well designed. The prestigious **Loewe** hand-bags are sold in retail outlets in Madrid and other major Spanish cities. Madrid's **Piamonte** also offers stylish bags at affordable prices.

SPECIALTY STORES

SPECIALTY STORES are often run by generations of the same family. *Panaderías* (also called *hornos*) are bakeries selling bread and *bollos* (sweet buns). Cakes and pastries are sold in *pastelerías*.

Fresh meat can be bought in a *carnicería*, but a *char-cutería* will have the best selection of cold, cooked meats, and also sells a wide selection of cheeses.

Pescaderías sell fish and shell-fish, although the best fish is often to be found on the local market stands.

For fruit and vegetables, a *frutería* or *verdulería* will have better produce, because they stock only what is in season.

Hardware stores are called *ferreterías*. *Librerías* are in fact bookshops, not libraries, and *papelerías* are stationers. Anything you buy as a *regalo* (gift) will be gift-wrapped on request. When you buy flowers from a *floristería*, the assistant will expect to arrange them.

MARKETS

EVERY LARGE TOWN has a daily market *(mercado)*, open from 9am to 2pm, and from 5pm to 8pm. Small towns have one or more market days a week.

Markets usually have the best fresh produce, but they sell all types of food, including *frutos secos* (dried fruits) and seasonal produce, such as mushrooms, soft fruit, and game. There are also usually other types of goods on sale, such as flowers, hardware, and clothes.

Flea markets *(rastros)* are held everywhere in Spain, but the largest – known as **El Rastro** – is in Madrid, and is held on Sundays and public holidays. Prices on the clothes, records, antiques, and other items sold here can be bargained down. Madrid also has a coin, stamp, and postcard market held on Sundays in the Plaza Mayor.

The **Encants Vells**, the flea market in Barcelona, is held on Mondays, Wednesdays, Fridays, and Saturdays. The food market, **La Boquería**, is open daily on La Rambla.

FOOD AND DRINK

SPANISH REGIONAL specialties are often better value when bought where they are made. Each region produces its own type of sausage. In Burgos, for example, *morcilla* (blood sausage) is made, while a fiery red *chorizo* comes from Guijuelo, Extremadura. Andalusia is renowned for olives and olive oil, and Galicia for its cheeses.

Among the preserves and sweets of Spain, Seville marmalade is famous. The delicious almond-based nougat, called *turrón*, can be purchased from food stores around the country.

Wine can be bought by the liter at a *bodega* (local wine shop). It can also be purchased directly from vineyards (also called *bodegas*), but you may need an appointment to visit.

Spain's most famous vine-growing regions are La Rioja and Navarra, Penedés, home of *cava* (sparkling wine), Valdepeñas, Ribera del Duero, and Jerez, the sherry region.

TRADITIONAL CRAFTS

AUTHENTIC ITEMS such as guitars, fans, castanets, and flamenco shoes are sold in major cities. Madrid's **Almoraima** has a good selection of hand-painted

fans. **Guitarrería F. Manzanero** sells handmade guitars. Some traditional crafts originated with the Moors, such as Toledo's filigree metalwork and the *azulejos* (ceramic tiles) of Andalusia. **Cántaro**, near the Plaza de España in Madrid, **La Caixa de Fang** in Barcelona, and **Antonio Campos** in Seville all sell ceramics.

Catalan-style espadrilles are another popular buy. **La Manual Alpargatera** in Barcelona makes them by hand on the premises and sells them in a wide range of colors.

Lace from the villages of the Sierra de Gata in Extremadura and Galicia's Costa da Morte is prized. Spanish linen and silk shawls can be purchased from **Borca**, off the Puerta del Sol in Madrid. In Barcelona, **L'Arca de l'Avia** sells antique silk and lace. One of the most

celebrated traditional hat makers in Spain is the **Sombrerería Herederos de J. Russi** in Córdoba.

HOUSEHOLD AND KITCHEN GOODS

DEPARTMENT STORES have a good selection of household goods, but the *ferreterías* (small hardware shops) often have the more authentic selection. Traditional pottery, such as red clay *cazuelas* (dishes) that can be used in the oven and on the hob are inexpensive. Paella pans have always been made of iron or enamel, but now come in stainless steel or with non-stick finishes. Table linen is often a bargain on market stands. Spanish lighting design is widely admired and sold in *lampisterías*. Traditional wrought-iron goods, such as candlesticks and door hardware, are always popular.

DIRECTORY

DEPARTMENT STORES

El Corte Inglés
Calle de Preciados 1–3,
Madrid.
(91-309 05 35.
w www.elcorteingles.es

Plaça Catalunya 14,
Barcelona.
(93-306 38 00.

Plaza Duque de la Victoria 10, Seville.
(95-422 09 31.

CLOTHING STORES

Adolfo Domínguez
Calle de Serrano 18,
Madrid.
(91-577 82 80.

Passeig de Gràcia 89,
Barcelona.
(93-215 13 39.

Armand Basi
Passeig de Gràcia 49,
Barcelona.
(93-215 14 21.
w www.armandbasi.com

Agatha Ruiz de la Prada
Calle del Marqués de Riscal 8,
Madrid.
(91-310 44 83.

Victorio & Lucchino
Calle de las Sierpes 87,
Seville.
(95-422 79 51.

LEATHER GOODS

Calzados E. Solé
Carrer Ample 7,
Barcelona.
(93-301 69 84

Loewe
Calle de Serrano 26,
Madrid.
(91-577 60 56.

Plaza Nueva 12,
Seville.
(95-422 52 53.

Piamonte
Calle del Marqués de Monasterio 5,
Madrid.
(91-308 48 62.

MARKETS

La Boqueria
La Rambla 100,
Barcelona.

Encants Vells
Plaça de les Glòries Catalanes,
Barcelona.

El Rastro
Calle de la Ribera de Curtidores,
Madrid.

TRADITIONAL CRAFTS

Almoraima
Plaza Mayor 12,
Madrid.
(91-365 42 89.

Antonio Campos
Calle Alfarería 22,
Triana, Seville.
(95-434 33 04.

L'Arca de l'Avia
Carrer dels Banys Nous 20,
Barcelona.
(93-302 15 98.

Borca
Calle del Marqués Viudo de Pontejo 2,
Madrid.
(91-532 61 53.

La Caixa de Fang
Calle Freneria 1,
Barcelona.
(93-315 17 04.

Cántaro
Calle de la Flor Baja 8,
Madrid.
(91-547 95 14.

Guitarrería F. Manzanero
Calle de Santa Ana 12,
Madrid.
(91-366 00 47.

La Manual Alpargatera
Calle d'Avinyó 7,
Barcelona.
(93-301 01 72.

Sombrerería Herederos de J. Russi
Calle A. de Morales 1,
Córdoba.
(957-47 79 53.

Entertainment

THE SPANISH TAKE PARTICULAR pride in their cultural heritage. As well as the traditional art form of flamenco dance and the three-act drama of the bullfight *(corrida)*, the theaters and opera houses of Spanish cities provide one of the best ways of sharing the experience of Spain. Many activities begin well after midnight and taking full advantage of the afternoon siesta is a good way to prepare for the evening ahead. Spain's mountain ranges, woodlands, and extensive coast offer great potential for scenic tours and sports vacations as alternatives to lounging on the beach.

ENTERTAINMENT LISTINGS

FOR SPANISH SPEAKERS, the most complete guide to what's going on in Madrid and Barcelona can be found in the weekly *Guía del Ocio* (published on Fridays in Madrid, and Thursdays in Barcelona). Daily newspapers such as *El País, El Mundo,* and *ABC* have weekly entertainment supplements. The free monthly English-language publication, *In Madrid,* can be found in bookshops and Irish bars.

SEASONS AND TICKETS

THE MAIN CONCERT and theater season in Spain runs from September to June.

In Madrid, the easiest way to acquire tickets for the theater, concerts, and opera is by telephone. **Casa Madrid** and **Tel-Entrada** accept credit card payment and do not charge for the service. The **TEYCI** agency sells tickets for most events, but charges up to 20 percent commission. Another agency that holds tickets for a variety of events is **El Corte Inglés**.

In Barcelona, theater tickets can be bought from branches of the Caixa de Catalunya or La Caixa savings banks. Tickets for special events are sold at tourist offices.

In other parts of Spain, your hotel or local tourist office will provide details of events and where to purchase tickets.

Tickets for bullfights, generally held between mid-March and mid-October, are sold at the reservations office *(taquilla)* of the bullring.

OPERA AND ZARZUELA

A VISIT TO THE Spanish capital would not be complete without spending a night at the *zarzuela*, Madrid's own variety of comic opera. The best productions are those staged at the **Teatro de la Zarzuela**. Other venues include the **Teatro Albéniz** and the recently reopened **Teatro Príncipe – Palacio de las Variedades**. Several other theaters offer *zarzuela* productions in the summer.

The best place to see national and international opera, including Madrid's own opera company, is the **Teatro Real de Madrid**. The Teatro Calderón also hosts excellent classical and modern opera productions. Barcelona's opera house, the **Gran Teatre del Liceu**, is now fully operational following a fire in 1994.

THEATER

MADRID'S MOST prestigious theaters are the **Teatro de la Comedia** and the **Teatro María Guerrero**. The former stages classic works by Spanish playwrights, while the latter hosts foreign productions and modern Spanish drama. The **Teatro Muñoz Seca** and **Teatro Reina Victoria** put on comedy productions. Madrid's autumn festival of classical and modern drama (Festival de Otoño) takes place between mid-September and mid-November.

In Barcelona, the new **Teatre Nacional de Catalunya** is a fine show-case for Catalan drama.

CLASSICAL MUSIC

IN MADRID, the two concert halls of the **Auditorio Nacional de Música** host international classical music performances. The Orquesta Nacional de España plays here regularly. The newly-renovated **Teatro Real de Madrid** also hosts important classical music concerts.

Barcelona's Modernista **Palau de la Música Catalana** is one of the world's most beautiful concert halls, with world-renowned acoustics.

BULLFIGHTING

BULLFIGHTING continues to be a popular spectacle throughout the country, but it is not for the squeamish. The **Plaza de Toros de Las Ventas** in Madrid is the most famous bullring in the world. It holds *corridas* every Sunday during the bullfighting season. During the May Fiestas de San Isidro fights are held every day. Some of Spain's most important fights are held at the **Maestranza** bullring in Seville (a spring fair held during the fortnight after Easter). Most towns in Andalusia have their own bullrings: Ronda, Córdoba, and Granada are among the best-known venues.

FLAMENCO

A SPONTANEOUS musical art form, flamenco has its roots in the gypsy culture of Andalusia. However, many of the best exponents are now based in the capital.

In Madrid, **Casa Patas** is still the best place to catch the raw power of genuine flamenco guitar and *cante* singing. Both music and dance can be enjoyed at **Café de Chinitas**.

Flamenco is performed late at night with most venues offering dinner and a show. In Andalusia, visitors can enjoy top-quality performances in the *tablaos* (flamenco bars) of the Barrio de Santa Cruz, in Seville, and listen to soul-stirring songs in the bars of another of the city's districts,

Triana. One of the best-known flamenco venues in Granada is in the gypsy caves of Sacromonte (*see p320*).

SPECIAL INTEREST VACATIONS

ALL TOURIST OFFICES in Spain can provide details of special interest vacations. Cookery, wine, and painting courses, as well as history and archaeology tours, are popular. Nature lovers and hikers head for Spain's many national parks.

Information about Spanish language courses is provided by **Canning House** in London and the **Instituto Cervantes**.

OUTDOOR ACTIVITIES

FOR INFORMATION on horse riding and pony trekking in most regions, contact the **Federación Hípica Española**. Local Spanish tourist offices should also be able to help.

Picturesque minor roads in many parts of Spain are excellent for cycle-touring. Walking tours are also popular. The **Federación Española de Montañismo** can provide information about climbing and many other mountain sports.

Spain's most popular resorts for downhill skiing are the Vall d'Aran in Catalonia and the Sierra Nevada, near Granada.

As well as white-water rafting and canoeing, a wide variety of water sports is possible in Spain. Jet skis and windsurfing equipment are available to rent in many coastal resorts. Information about sailing can be obtained from the **Real Federación Española de Vela**.

Spain has an abundance of top-quality golf courses. The **Real Federación Española de Golf** will give locations and more detailed information. In most tourist areas there are tennis courts for rental by the hour. Travel agents arrange tennis holidays for enthusiasts. More information is available from the **Real Federación Española de Tenis**.

DIRECTORY

TICKETS

Casa Madrid
902-48 84 88
(Madrid).

El Corte Inglés
902-40 02 22
(Madrid).
www.
entradaselcorteingles.es

Tel-Entrada
902-10 12 12 (Madrid).
www.tel-entrada.com

TEYCI
Calle de Goya 7, Madrid.
91-576 45 32.
www.softguides.com

OPERA AND ZARZUELA

Gran Teatre del Liceu
Rambla de los Capuchinos 63, Barcelona.
93-485 99 00.

Teatro Albéniz
Calle de la Paz 11, Madrid.
91-521 99 98.

Teatro Príncipe – Palacio de las Variedades
Calle de las Tres Cruces 8, Madrid.
91-521 83 81.

Teatro Real de Madrid
Plaza de Oriente, Madrid.
91-516 06 06.

Teatro de la Zarzuela
Calle de Jovellanos 4, Madrid.
91-524 54 00.

THEATER

Teatre Nacional de Catalunya
Plaça de les Arts 1, Barcelona.
93-306 57 00.

Teatro de la Comedia
Calle del Príncipe 14, Madrid.
91-532 79 28.

Teatro María Guerrero
Calle de Tamayo y Baus 4, Madrid.
91-319 47 69.

Teatro Muñoz Seca
Plaza del Carmen 1, Madrid.
91-523 21 28.

Teatro Reina Victoria
Carrera de San Jerónimo 24, Madrid.
91-369 22 88.

CLASSICAL MUSIC

Auditorio Nacional de Música
Calle del Príncipe de Vergara 146, Madrid.
91-337 01 34.

Palau de la Música Catalana
Carrer de Sant Francesc de Paula 2, Barcelona.
93-295 72 00.

BULLFIGHTING

Plaza de Toros de la Maestranza
Paseo de Cristóbal Cólon 12, Seville.
95-422 45 77.

Plaza de Toros de las Ventas
Calle de Alcalá 237, Madrid.
91-356 22 00.

FLAMENCO

Café de Chinitas
Calle de Torija 7, Madrid.
91-547 15 02.

Casa Patas
Calle de Cañizares 10, Madrid.
91-369 04 96.

SPECIAL INTEREST VACATIONS

Canning House
2 Belgrave Square, London SW1X 8PJ.
020-7235 2303.

Instituto Cervantes (Spain)
Calle Libreros 23, 28801 Alcalá de Henares, Madrid.
91-885 61 00.

Instituto Cervantes (UK)
102 Eaton Square, London SW1W 9AN.
020-7235 0353.

OUTDOOR ACTIVITIES

Federación Española de Montañismo
Calle Floridablanca 84, 08015 Barcelona.
93-426 42 67.

Federación Hípica Española
Plaza del Marqués de Salamanca 2, 28006 Madrid.
91-577 78 92.

Real Federación Española de Golf
Calle Capitán Haya 5–9, 28002 Madrid.
91-555 26 82.

Real Federación Española de Tenis
Avinguda Diagonal 618 2°B, 08021 Barcelona.
93-200 53 55.

Real Federación Española de Vela
Calle Luis Salazar 9, 28002 Madrid.
91-519 50 08.

Where to Stay in Spain

Visitors to Spain have a wide variety of accommodations to choose from, at a range of prices. At the top of the scale are elegant suites in converted medieval castles or royal palaces – many of these are paradors, luxurious state-run hotels. Then there are stylish beach hotels and villas. For the budget traveler, family-run guesthouses offer simple but comfortable lodgings.

	NUMBER OF ROOMS	PRIVATE PARKING	AIR-CONDITIONING	GARDEN OR TERRACE
MADRID				
OLD MADRID: *Hostal Buenos Aires* €€ Gran Vía 61, 28013. **Map** B3. **(** *91-542 01 02.* **FAX** *91-542 28 69.* A simple, economical hotel, conveniently located on the busy Gran Vía. The public rooms are pleasantly decorated. Each of the bedrooms has its own balcony or small terrace. 🛏 📺 🍽	25		●	
OLD MADRID: *Carlos V* €€€€ Calle Maestro Vitoria 5, 28013. **Map** C4. **(** *91-531 41 00.* **FAX** *91-531 37 61.* Ⓦ www.hotelcarlosv.com A city-center, family-run hotel in a pedestrian street beside the Puerta del Sol. There are interconnecting bedrooms, family rooms, rooms with balconies, and top-floor rooms with sizeable sun terraces. 🛏 📺 🍽	67		●	
OLD MADRID: *Inglés* €€€€ Calle de Echegaray 8, 28014. **Map** C4. **(** *91-429 65 51.* **FAX** *91-420 24 23.* @ comercial@hotelingles.com A good-value, family-run hotel with its own garage. The rooms facing the street are sunny, but the back rooms are quieter. 🛏 📺 🍽	58	■		
OLD MADRID: *Arosa* €€€€€ Calle de la Salud 21, 28013. **Map** C3. **(** *91-532 16 00.* **FAX** *91-531 31 27.* Ⓦ www.bestwestern.com/es/arosa This centrally located hotel, off the Gran Vía and the Puerta del Sol, is popular with international and business visitors to Madrid. All the rooms are comfortable and well soundproofed. 🛏 📺 🍽	134	■	●	
OLD MADRID: *Gaudí* €€€€€ Gran Vía 9, 28013. **Map** C3. **(** *91-531 22 22.* **FAX** *91-531 54 69.* Ⓦ www.hoteles-catalonia.es A Modernista hotel, centrally located, decorated in the style of the famous Catalan architect, Gaudí. The suites at the top of the hotel have great views over the city, as well as a swimming pool and a jacuzzi. 🛏 📺 🏊 ♿ 🍽	185		●	
OLD MADRID: *Tryp Reina Victoria* €€€€€ Plaza Santa Ana 14, 28012. **Map** C4. **(** *91-531 45 00.* **FAX** *91-522 03 07.* Ⓦ www.solmelia.com Ernest Hemingway once lodged in this historic hotel, a graceful edifice and a traditional haunt of bullfighting aficionados. 🛏 📺 ♿ 🍽	201	■	●	
OLD MADRID: *Tryp Rex* €€€€€ Gran Vía 43, 28013. **Map** C3. **(** *91-547 48 00.* **FAX** *91-547 12 38.* Ⓦ www.solmelia.com A chain hotel in an old building between the Plaza del Callao and the Plaza de España, close to a large public car park. It has spacious public rooms and well-equipped bedrooms, each with its own safe. 🛏 📺 🍽	145		●	
BOURBON MADRID: *Mora* €€ Paseo del Prado 32, 28014. **Map** D4. **(** *91-420 15 69.* **FAX** *91-420 05 64.* A 1930s hotel with an attractive entrance. Its rooms and facilities are functional, but its prices are low and it is centrally located, near the Jardín Botánico and the Prado. 🛏 📺 🍽	75		●	
BOURBON MADRID: *Santander* €€ Calle de Echegaray 1, 28014. **Map** C4. **(** *91-429 46 44.* **FAX** *91-369 10 78.* This small, friendly family hotel, offering neat, comfortable, simple rooms, has been popular with travelers since it opened in the 1920s. 🛏 📺	35			
BOURBON MADRID: *Palace* €€€€€ Plaza de las Cortes 7, 28014. **Map** D4. **(** *91-360 80 00.* **FAX** *91-360 81 00.* Ⓦ www.luxurycollection.com/palacemadrid This gracious *belle époque* hotel has accommodated statesmen and the spy, Mata Hari. The bedrooms are elegant and the service welcoming and efficient. 🛏 📺 ♿ 🍽	465	■	●	

Map references refer to maps of Madrid and Barcelona on pp282–3 and pp306–7 respectively

Price categories are for a standard double room per night, with tax, breakfast, and service included:

€ under €50
€€ €50–75
€€€ €75–100
€€€€ €100–125
€€€€€ over €125

PRIVATE PARKING
Parking provided by the hotel in a private car park or private garage on the hotel site or nearby. Some hotels charge for use of private parking facilities.

SWIMMING POOL
Hotel pool outdoors unless otherwise stated.

CREDIT CARDS
Major credit cards are accepted in those hotels where the credit card symbol is shown.

	Price	NUMBER OF ROOMS	PRIVATE PARKING	AIR-CONDITIONING	GARDEN OR TERRACE
BOURBON MADRID: *Ritz* Plaza de la Lealtad 5, 28014. Map D4. 91-521 28 57. FAX 91-532 87 76. W www.ritz.es The Ritz is still one of Spain's most elegant hotels. It has an ornate, circular foyer and a terrace garden, and offers musical teas and brunches.	€€€€€	158	▪	●	▪
BOURBON MADRID: *Suecia* Calle Marqués de Casa Riera 4, 28014. Map D4. 91-531 69 00. FAX 91-521 71 41. W www.hotelsuecia.com Centrally located near the Puerta del Sol, the Suecia has a small, seventh-floor terrace for relaxing and sunbathing.	€€€€€	128	▪	●	▪
BOURBON MADRID: *Villa Real* Plaza de las Cortes 10, 28014. Map D4. 91-420 37 67. FAX 91-420 25 47. W www.derbyhotels.es Located close to the Prado, this stylish hotel is housed in an early 19th-century building.	€€€€€	115	▪	●	
FARTHER AFIELD: *NH Alcalá* Calle de Alcalá 66, 28009. Map E3. 91-435 10 60. FAX 91-435 11 05. W www.nh-hotels.com A hotel with a friendly atmosphere across the street from the Parque del Retiro. The back bedrooms overlook a pretty garden.	€€€€€	146	▪	●	
FARTHER AFIELD: *Wellington* Calle de Velázquez 8, 28001. Map E3. 91-575 44 00. FAX 91-576 41 64. W www.hotel-wellington.com A stylish hotel, built in the early 1950s, close to the Parque del Retiro. It is a meeting place for people interested in bullfighting.	€€€€€	260	▪	●	▪
BARCELONA					
OLD TOWN: *Hostal D'Avinyo* Avinyo 42, 08002. Map D3. 93-318 79 45. FAX 93-318 68 93. W www.hostalavinyo.com A centrally located youth hostel, close to the cathedral and the Museu Picasso. Some rooms have a balcony with a good view over the Old Town.	€	28			
OLD TOWN: *España* Carrer de Sant Pau 9–11, 08001. Map D3. 93-318 17 58. FAX 93-317 11 34. W www.hotelespana.com Domènech i Montaner, the outstanding Modernista architect, designed the lower floor of this hotel. The bedrooms are all modern.	€€€	84		●	
OLD TOWN: *Jardí* Plaça Sant Josep Oriol 1, 08002. Map D3. 93-301 59 00. FAX 93-342 57 33. @ hoteljardi@retemail.es A popular hotel overlooking a leafy square. Some rooms have been renovated and have good views; the others are less expensive.	€€€	40		●	
OLD TOWN: *Arts* Carrer de la Marina 19–21, 08005. Map F4. 93-221 10 00. FAX 93-221 10 70. W www.harts.es A modern, luxurious waterfront hotel in one of Spain's tallest towers. It has a huge swimming pool and a fitness center.	€€€€€	482	▪	●	▪
OLD TOWN: *Gaudí* Carrer Nou de la Rambla 12, 08001. Map D3. 93-317 90 32. FAX 93-412 26 36. W www.hotelgaudi.es A pleasant hotel in a street adjoining the Rambla de Catalunya, near Gaudí's Palau Güell. It has comfortable, well-equipped rooms.	€€€€€	73	▪	●	
OLD TOWN: *Le Meridien* La Rambla 111, 08002. Map D3. 93-318 62 00. FAX 93-301 77 76. W www.meridienbarcelona.com An exquisite hotel on La Rambla, popular with rock and film stars. It has an enormous presidential suite and a business center.	€€€€€	208	▪	●	

<table>
<tr><td>

Price categories are for a standard double room per night, with tax, breakfast, and service included:

€ under €50
€€ €50–75
€€€ €75–100
€€€€ €100–125
€€€€€ over €125

</td><td>

PRIVATE PARKING
Parking provided by the hotel in a private car park or private garage on the hotel site or nearby. Some hotels charge for use of private parking facilities.

SWIMMING POOL
Hotel pool outdoors unless otherwise stated.

CREDIT CARDS
Major credit cards are accepted in those hotels where the credit card symbol is shown.

</td></tr>
</table>

	NUMBER OF ROOMS	PRIVATE PARKING	AIR-CONDITIONING	GARDEN OR TERRACE
OLD TOWN: *Oriente* €€€€€ La Rambla 45–7, 08002. **Map** D3. 93-302 25 58. FAX 93-412 38 19. @ horiente@husa.es A former Franciscan friary makes a romantic setting for the Oriente. Some bedrooms have balconies overlooking La Rambla.	142		●	
OLD TOWN: *San Agustín* €€€€€ Plaça de Sant Agustí 3, 08001. **Map** D3. 93-318 16 58. FAX 93-317 29 28. @ hotelsa@hotelsa.com An attractive hotel with a pleasant first-floor lounge and bar looking out over a square. Some bedrooms have Catalan furniture.	75		●	
EIXAMPLE: *Gran Vía* €€€€ Gran Vía de les Corts Catalanes 642, 08007. **Map** D2. 93-318 19 00. FAX 93-318 99 97. @ hgranvia@nnhotels.es A hotel in a late 19th-century building with an aging grandeur, north of the Plaça de Catalunya adjoining the Passeig de Gràcia.	55		●	■
EIXAMPLE: *Condes de Barcelona* €€€€€ Passeig de Gràcia 73–5, 08008. **Map** D2. 93-467 47 80. FAX 93-467 47 85. W www.condesdebarcelona.com This Modernista hotel has an impressive pentagonal lobby. Advance reservations essential.	183	■	●	■
EIXAMPLE: *Gran Hotel Calderón* €€€€€ Rambla de Catalunya 26, 08007. **Map** D2. 93-301 00 00. FAX 93-412 41 93. W www.nh-hoteles.com A modern hotel near the Plaça de Catalunya, with spacious, comfortable rooms, indoor and rooftop pools, and a good restaurant.	253	■	●	■
EIXAMPLE: *Ritz* €€€€€ Gran Vía de les Corts Catalanes 668, 08010. **Map** E2. 93-318 52 00. FAX 93-318 01 48. W www.ritzbcn.com The most elegant of Barcelona's grand hotels, near the Plaça de Catalunya. The large, luxurious bedrooms are tastefully decorated.	125	■	●	
NORTHERN SPAIN				
BAIONA, RÍAS BAIXAS: *Parador de Baiona* €€€€€ Carretera de Baiona, 36300 (Pontevedra). 986-35 50 00. FAX 986-35 50 76. W www.parador.es This parador, built in the style of an old manor house or *pazo*, is located within the walls of Monterreal castle.	122	■		■
BILBAO (BILBO): *Gran Hotel Ercilla* €€€€€ Calle Ercilla 37–9, 48011 (Vizcaya). 94-470 57 00. FAX 94-443 93 35. W www.hotelercilla.es Bilbao's largest hotel is centrally located, comfortable, welcoming, and bustling with life. It has a very good restaurant.	345	■	●	
CANGAS DE ONÍS, LOS PICOS DE EUROPA: *Aultre Naray* €€€ Peruyes, 33547 (Asturias). 98-584 08 08. FAX 98-584 08 48. W www.aultrenaray.com There are mountain views from this country house hotel in one of Northern Spain's least-known corners. Every bedroom is different.	10	■		■
OVIEDO: *Hotel de la Reconquista* €€€€€ Calle Gil de Jaz 16, 33004 (Asturias). 98-524 11 00. FAX 98-524 11 66. W www.hoteldelareconquista.com This hotel occupies a magnificent 18th-century building. The public rooms are arranged around several arcaded courtyards.	142	■	●	
PAMPLONA (IRUÑA): *Tres Reyes* €€€€€ Jardines de la Taconera, 31001 (Navarra). 948-22 66 00. FAX 948-22 29 30. W www.hotel3reyes.com This large, modern hotel is located between the old and new towns. Services range from a gym and sauna to hairdressing and valeting.	160	■	●	■

Map references refer to map of Barcelona on pp306–7

PONTEVEDRA, RÍAS BAIXAS: *Parador de Pontevedra* €€€€€ | 47
Calle Barón 19, 36002. **C** 986-85 58 00. **FAX** 986-85 21 95. **W** www.parador.es
An elegant parador in a stately manor in the old town. The decor
incorporates antiques, gilt mirrors, chandeliers, and tapestries. 🛏 📺 🖥

SAN SEBASTIAN (DONOSTIA): *De Londres y de Inglaterra* €€€€€ | 148
Calle Zubieta 2, 20007 (Guipúzcoa). **C** 943-44 07 70. **FAX** 943-44 04 91. **W** www.hlondres.com
A 19th-century palace that was transformed into a hotel in 1902.
It enjoys a wonderful location on La Concha beach. 🛏 📺 🚹 🖥

SANTANDER: *Las Brisas* €€€€ | 13
Travesía de los Castros 14, 39005 (Cantabria). **C** 942-27 50 11. **FAX** 942-28 11 73.
W www.brisas.spain.info
A friendly hotel in a 19th-century white villa close to the popular Sardinero beach.
Breakfast is served on a terrace that looks out to sea. ● *Dec–Feb.* 🛏 📺 🖥

SANTIAGO DE COMPOSTELA: *Parador Reyes Católicos* €€€€€ | 136
Praza do Obradoiro 1, 15705 (A Coruña). **C** 981-58 22 00. **FAX** 981-56 30 94. **W** www.parador.es
Formerly a hospice for poor pilgrims, this 16th-century parador is one
of the world's grandest hotels. It is built around four arcaded patios
with fountains. 🛏 📺 🚹 🖥

CATALONIA & EASTERN SPAIN

ALICANTE (ALACANT), COSTA BLANCA: *Sidi San Juan* €€€€€ | 176
Playa San Juan, 03540. **C** 96-516 13 00. **FAX** 96-516 33 46. **W** www.hotelesside.es
A luxury hotel outside Alicante, with access to a beach through gardens.
The bedrooms have sea views and there is a health farm. 🛏 📺 ≋ 🚹 🖥

DÉNIA, COSTA BLANCA: *Rosa* €€€ | 39
Las Marinas, 03700 (Alicante). **C** 96-578 15 73. **FAX** 96-642 47 74.
A modern white villa close to the beach, run by a Parisian expatriate.
The comfortable rooms have Florentine-style balconies. 🛏 📺 ≋ 🚹 🖥

L'ESPLUGA DE FRANCOLI, NR POBLET: *Masía del Cadet* €€€ | 12
Les Masies de Poblet, 43449 (Tarragona). **C** & **FAX** 977-87 08 69.
An inexpensive hotel near the monastery of Poblet in a tastefully renovated,
15th-century house. The bedrooms are austere and quiet. Traditional
Catalan food is served in the restaurant. 🛏 📺 ≋ 🚹 🍴 🖥

TARRAGONA: *Lauria* €€€ | 72
Rambla Nova 20, 43004. **C** 977-23 67 12. **FAX** 977-23 67 00. **W** www.hlauria.com
A modern, functional hotel in the town center and close to the sea, with
an elegant entrance under balustraded stone stairs. 🛏 📺 ≋ 🖥

VALENCIA: *Inglés* €€€€€ | 65
Calle Marqués de Dos Aguas 6, 46002. **C** 96-351 64 26. **FAX** 96-394 02 51. **W** www.solmelia.com
This convenient city-center hotel is in the old palace of the Dukes of
Cardona. All the bedrooms look on to the street. The restaurant
serves Valencian cuisine. 🛏 📺 🚹 🖥

XÀBIA (JAVEA), COSTA BLANCA: *Parador de Jávea* €€€€€ | 70
Avda Mediterráneo 7, 03730 (Alicante). **C** 96-579 02 00. **FAX** 96-579 03 08. **W** www.parador.es
A parador on Arenales beach. The dining room looks across the terrace
to splendid gardens, and the bedroom balconies have sea views.
There are water sports facilities nearby. 🛏 📺 ≋ 🚹 🖥

ZARAGOZA: *Gran Hotel* €€€€ | 134
Calle Joaquín Costa 5, 50001. **C** 976-22 19 01. **FAX** 976-23 67 13. **W** www.nh-hoteles.com
Zaragoza's city-center hotel was opened in 1929 by Alfonso XIII.
It has colonnades and a magnificent domed salon. 🛏 📺 🍴 🖥

CENTRAL SPAIN

AVILA: *Palacio Valderrábanos* €€€€€ | 73
Plaza de la Catedral 9, 05001. **C** 920-21 10 23. **FAX** 920-25 16 91.
W www.palaciovalderrabanos.com
A spacious hotel in a stately 15th-century mansion beside the cathedral.
There is a suite in the watchtower. 🛏 📺 🖥

BURGOS: *Mesón del Cid* €€€€€ | 50
Plaza de Santa María 8, 09003. **C** 947-20 87 15. **FAX** 947-26 94 60. **W** www.mesondelcid.es
This stylish hotel, located near the cathedral, is dedicated to
the conquering medieval hero, El Cid *(see p299)*. 🛏 📺 🖥

For key to symbols see back flap

					Number of Rooms	Private Parking	Air-Conditioning	Garden or Terrace

Price categories are for a standard double room per night, with tax, breakfast, and service included:

€ under €50
€€ €50–75
€€€ €75–100
€€€€ €100–125
€€€€€ over €125

Private Parking
Parking provided by the hotel in a private car park or private garage on the hotel site or nearby. Some hotels charge for use of private parking facilities.

Swimming Pool
Hotel pool outdoors unless otherwise stated.

Credit Cards
Major credit cards are accepted in those hotels where the credit card symbol is shown.

Hotel	Rooms	Private Parking	Air-Conditioning	Garden or Terrace
León: *Parador de San Marcos* €€€€€ Plaza de San Marcos 7, 24001. ☎ 987-23 73 00. FAX 987-23 34 58. W www.parador.es This parador is in the Hostal San Marcos, a former convent and one of Spain's loveliest Renaissance buildings. It has a magnificent hall with a coffered ceiling and luxurious old and modern bedrooms. 🖥 TV 🛗 🌳	230	■		■
Salamanca: *Las Torres* €€€€ Plaza Mayor 26, 37002. ☎ 923-21 21 00. FAX 923-21 21 01. W www.mmteam.com/lastorres The restaurant of this hotel overlooks Salamanca's magnificent Plaza Mayor. Services include rapid clothes valeting. 🖥 TV 🛗 🌳	44		●	
San Lorenzo de El Escorial: *El Botánico* €€€€ Calle Timoteo Padros 16, 28200. ☎ 91-890 78 79. FAX 91-890 81 58. W www.valdesimonte.com Located in a quiet area of town, this former palace was converted into a hotel in 1997. A small and pleasant hotel with good views of the palace of El Escorial *(see p294)*. 🖥 TV 🍴 🌳	20	■	●	
Segovia: *Parador de Segovia* €€€€€ Carretera de Valladolid, 40003. ☎ 921-44 37 37. FAX 921-43 73 62. W www.parador.es This luxury parador has been strategically sited just outside Segovia so that guests can enjoy magnificent views of the city while sunbathing in the gardens. Facilities include a gym and an indoor pool. 🖥 TV 🏊 🌳	113	■		■
Toledo: *Pintor El Greco* €€€€ Calle Alamillos del Tránsito 13, 45002. ☎ 902-15 46 45. FAX 925-21 58 19. W www.hotelpintorelgreco.com Wrought iron and traditional ceramics add character to this hotel, which occupies a 17th-century house in Toledo's old Jewish quarter. 🖥 TV 🌳	33		●	
Toledo: *Parador de Toledo* €€€€€ Cerro del Emperador, 45002. ☎ 925-22 18 50. FAX 925-22 51 66. W www.parador.es There is a spectacular view of Toledo from the terrace of this parador, located on the brow of a hill overlooking the city. The hotel is popular with sightseers and photographers, so reserve in advance. 🖥 TV 🏊 🌳	76		●	■

SOUTHERN SPAIN

Hotel	Rooms	Private Parking	Air-Conditioning	Garden or Terrace
Córdoba: *Alfaros* €€€€ Calle Alfaros 18, 14001. ☎ 957-49 19 20. W www.maciahoteles.com In a busy street, but soundproofed against traffic noise, Alfaros has three attractive courtyards in Neo-Mudéjar style. 🖥 TV 🏊 🌳	133	■	●	■
Granada: *Hotel Navas* €€€ Calle Navas 22–4, 18009. ☎ 958-22 59 59. FAX 958-22 75 23. W www.hotelesporcel.com Located within a pedestrian area of Granada, close to several tapas bars, this modern hotel was constructed in 1993. 🖥 TV 🌳	40	■	●	
Granada: *Parador de Granada* €€€€€ Calle Real de la Alhambra s/n, 18009. ☎ 958-22 14 40. FAX 958-22 22 64. W www.parador.es This elegant parador in the gardens of the Alhambra was once a convent. For a room in such a spot you must reserve months ahead. 🖥 TV 🌳	36	■	●	■
Málaga: *Don Curro* €€€ Calle Sancha de Lara 7, 29015. ☎ 95-222 72 00. FAX 95-221 59 46. W www.hoteldoncurro.com The exterior may not be attractive, but inside, this hotel is charming and comfortable, with a friendly, welcoming atmosphere. 🖥 TV 🌳	118	■	●	
Marbella, Costa del Sol: *El Fuerte* €€€€€ Avenida El Fuerte s/n, 29600 (Málaga). ☎ 95-286 15 00. FAX 95-286 00 34. W www.fuertehoteles.com El Fuerte was the first hotel built in Marbella and it is still one of the best. Some rooms have mountain views, while others look out to sea. The hotel has a heated indoor pool and a health center. 🖥 TV 🏊 🌳	263	■	●	■

EL PUERTO DE STA MARÍA, NR CÁDIZ: *Monasterio San Miguel* €€€€€ | 150
Calle Larga 27, 11500. █ *956-54 04 40.* FAX *956-54 05 25.* W *www.jle.com/monasterio*
An elegant hotel in a Baroque building, well placed for visits
to Cádiz and Jerez de la Frontera. 🛏 📺 ♨ ⚿ 🌳

RONDA: *Parador de Ronda* €€€€€ | 78
Plaza España s/n, 29400 (Málaga). █ *95-287 75 00.* FAX *95-287 81 88.* W *www.parador.es*
A modern, purpose-built parador with stunning views of Ronda's famous
gorge, especially from the top-floor suites. 🛏 📺 ♨ ⚿ 🌳

SEVILLE: *Hostería del Laurel* €€ | 22
Plaza de los Venerables 5, 41004. █ *95-422 02 95.* FAX *95-421 04 50.* @ *laurel@sol.com*
A hotel in a small square near the Hospital de los Venerables. The reception
is in a covered courtyard and the rooms are spacious. 🛏 📺 ⚿ 🌳

SEVILLE: *Murillo* €€€ | 57
Calle Lope de Rueda 7 & 9, 41004. █ *95-421 60 95.* FAX *95-421 96 16.* W *www.hotelmurillo.com*
A pleasant, reasonably priced hotel in an old building, a short walk from
the cathedral. The management also have apartments to rent nearby. 🛏 🌳

SEVILLE: *Las Casas de la Judería* €€€€ | 95
Callejón de las Dos Hermanas 7, 41004. █ *95-441 51 50.* FAX *95-442 21 70.*
W *www.casasypalacios.com*
Less a hotel, more a labyrinth of suites, some with a private terrace.
It enjoys a peaceful location away from the bustle of the city. 🛏 📺 🌳

SEVILLE: *Alfonso XIII* €€€€€ | 146
Calle San Fernando 2, 41004. █ *95-491 70 00.* FAX *95-491 70 99.* W *www.westin.com*
Elegance and appropriately formal service are assured in Seville's grand hotel.
Inside there are chandeliers, outdoors palm tree-filled gardens. 🛏 📺 ♨ ⚿ 🌳

TORREMOLINOS, COSTA DEL SOL: *Hotel Miami* €€€ | 26
Calle Aladino 14, 29620 (Málaga). █ *95-238 52 55.* FAX *952-38 51 34.*
With its whitewashed walls and iron grilles and balconies, the Miami gives
welcome respite from the Costa del Sol's modern developments. 🛏 ♨ 🌳

THE BALEARIC ISLANDS

FORMENTERA, ES PUJOLS: *Sa Volta* €€€€€ | 18
Calle Miramar 94, 07871. █ *971-32 81 25.* FAX *971-32 82 28.*
A modern, family-run hotel within walking distance of the beach in one of
Formentera's main resorts. ● *Jan–Feb.* 🛏 📺 ♨ 🌳

IBIZA, IBIZA TOWN: *Hostal La Marina* €€€ | 24
Calle Barcelona 7, 07800. █ *971-31 01 72.* FAX *971-31 48 94.* W *www.hostal-lamarina.com*
An old hotel, modernized inside but retaining much of its 1862 decoration.
Airy front bedrooms overlook the harbor. 🛏 📺 🌳

MALLORCA, ANDRATX: *Villa Italia* €€€€€ | 16
Camino Sant Carles 13, Port d'Andratx, 07157. █ *971-67 40 11.* FAX *971-67 33 50.*
W *www.hotelvillaitalia.com*
A pink, Florentine-style villa, with stucco ceilings, marble floors, and
columns with Roman capitals. 🛏 📺 ♨ 🌳

MALLORCA, PALMA DE MALLORCA: *Born* €€€€ | 30
Calle Sant Jaume 3, 07012. █ *971-71 29 42.* FAX *971-71 86 18.* W *www.hotelborn.com*
The Marquis of Ferrandell's town mansion makes a splendid hotel. It has a
typical Mallorcan courtyard with palms and a grand staircase. 🛏 📺 🌳

MALLORCA, POLLENÇA: *Illa d'Or* €€€€€ | 120
Paseo de Colón 265, 07470. █ *971-86 51 00.* FAX *971-86 42 13.* @ *illador@fehm.es*
Built in the 1930s for elite northern Europeans who came to summer on the
island, the hotel retains its original furniture and atmosphere. 🛏 📺 ♨ 🌳

MENORCA, CIUTADELLA: *Patricia* €€€€€ | 44
Paseo San Nicolás 90–92, 07760. █ *971-38 55 11.* FAX *971-48 11 20.*
@ *hotel@hesperia-patricia.com*
A modern chain hotel on one of the town's main avenues, near to the
harbor. 🛏 📺 ♨ 🌳

MENORCA, MAÓ: *Port Mahón* €€€€€ | 82
Fort de L'Eau 13, 07702. █ *971-36 26 00.* FAX *971-35 10 50.* @ *portmahon@sethotels.com*
Housed in an attractive red and white colonial-style building, this hotel
overlooks Maó harbor. 🛏 📺 ♨ ⚿ 🌳

For key to symbols see back flap

Where to Eat in Spain

THE quickest and best-value places to eat in Spain are the bars and cafés that serve tapas, small appetizers traditionally eaten standing at the bar *(see p325)*. Family-run *ventas*, *posadas*, *fondas*, and *mesones* – all old words for an inn – serve reasonably priced, sit-down meals. Spain also has many top-quality restaurants, notably in the Basque Country, Galicia, Madrid, and Barcelona.

	TAPAS BAR	FIXED-PRICE MENU	GOOD WINE LIST	OUTDOOR TABLES
MADRID				
OLD MADRID: *La Bola Taberna* €€ **Calle de la Bola 5. Map** B3. 91-547 69 30. This restaurant, which dates back to 1870, is a true bastion of the *cocido madrileño*, a hearty stew made with *garbanzos* (chickpeas) and sausage, and served at lunch time only. ● *dinner Sun; Jul–Aug: dinner Sat.* &		■	●	
OLD MADRID: *Casa Ciriaco* €€ **Calle Mayor 84. Map** B4. 91-548 06 20. A traditional tavern near the Royal Palace, renowned for its *gallina en pepitoria* (a chicken stew with egg and saffron). ● *Wed, Aug.* &	●	■	●	
OLD MADRID: *Casa Patas* €€ **Calle Cañizares 10. Map** C4. 91-369 04 96. Known for its flamenco shows in the evening, Casa Patas also has a well-stocked tapas bar and an unbeatable fixed-price menu. ● *Sun.* &	●	■	●	
OLD MADRID: *Zacatín* €€ **Calle de Andrés Borrego 18. Map** C3. 91-532 1351. This popular restaurant offers a Spanish menu, changed monthly, in a charming rustic setting. The intimate atmosphere is complemented by friendly service. Worth booking ahead. ● *dinner Mon, lunch Sat, Sun.* &	●			
OLD MADRID: *Carmencita* €€€ **Calle de la Libertad 16. Map** C3. 91-531 66 12. What was once a neighborhood tavern (founded in 1850) patronized by impoverished intellectuals has become fashionable, serving refined home cooking. The menu of the day is excellent value. ● *Sun, lunch Sat.*		■		
OLD MADRID: *Botín* €€€€ **Calle de Cuchilleros 17. Map** B4. 91-366 42 17. Reputedly the oldest restaurant in the world, dating back to 1725. The original wood-burning oven is still used to cook the traditional Castilian roast lamb and suckling pig. Reasonable fixed-price menu.		■	●	
OLD MADRID: *Lhardy* €€€€ **Carrera de San Jerónimo 8. Map** C4. 91-521 33 85. Established in 1839 and conserving its traditional character with chandeliers, mirrors, and dark wood-paneled walls, this restaurant serves a classic *cocido madrileño* (sausage and vegetable stew). ● *dinner Sun & hols.*	●	■	●	
BOURBON MADRID: *Pimiento Verde* €€€ **Calle Lagasca 46. Map** E3. 91-576 41 35. A rustic tavern, lively and crowded, serves an assorted selection of tapas. The adjoining restaurant serves Basque specialties. ● *Sun.*	●		●	
BOURBON MADRID: *Teatriz* €€€ **Calle Hermosilla 15. Map** E3. 91-577 53 79. A restaurant in the stalls of an old theater, with a cocktail bar on the stage. The food is Italian-inspired. &	●	■	●	
BOURBON MADRID: *El Amparo* €€€€ **Callejón de Puigcerdá 8. Map** E3. 91-431 64 56. New Basque cuisine in what many consider to be Madrid's nicest setting, with a skylight that lets you gaze up at the stars. The tuna mousse with lobster and parsley oil is just one creation. ● *Sun, lunch Sat, public hols, Aug.*			●	
BOURBON MADRID: *Jockey* €€€€€ **Calle Amador de los Ríos 6. Map** E2. 91-319 10 03. Frequented by gourmets and celebrities, Jockey offers a seasonal menu. Excellent poultry and game dishes and a superb wine list. Smart dress only. ● *Sun, lunch Sat, public hols, Aug.* &			●	

Map references refer to maps of Madrid and Barcelona on pp282–3 and pp306–7 respectively

	TAPAS BAR	FIXED-PRICE MENU	GOOD WINE LIST	OUTDOOR TABLES

Price categories are for a three-course evening meal for one, including a half-bottle of house wine, tax, and service:

€ under €18
€€ €18–27
€€€ €27–36
€€€€ over €36

TAPAS BAR
In addition to the main dining room, there is a bar serving tapas.

FIXED-PRICE MENU
A good-value, fixed-price menu is offered at lunch or dinner, or both, usually with three courses.

GOOD WINE LIST
Denotes a wide range of good wines, or a more specialized selection of local wines.

BOURBON MADRID: *Al Mounia* €€€€ Calle de Recoletos 5. **Map** E3. **(** 91-435 08 28. Madrid's finest Moroccan restaurant, serving authentic couscous and *tajine* (lamb stew). Don't miss the rich house dessert. ● *Sun–Mon, Aug & Easter*			●	
BOURBON MADRID: *Paradis* €€€€ Calle Marqués de Cubas 14. **Map** D4. **(** 91-429 73 03. Part of a successful Catalan chain, offering top-quality Mediterranean cuisine. The grilled vegetables and the rice dishes make delicious first courses. They can be followed by any of the fresh fish items. ● *Sun, lunch Sat, public hols.*			●	
BOURBON MADRID: *Viridiana* €€€€ Calle Juan de Mena 14. **Map** E4. **(** 91-523 44 78. Innovative Spanish cuisine, complemented by an encyclopaedic wine list, is offered in this restaurant decorated with stills from Luis Buñuel's film *Viridiana*. The creative menu changes frequently. ● *Sun, Aug.*			●	

BARCELONA

OLD TOWN: *Can Culleretes* € Carrer d'En Quintana 5. **Map** D3. **(** 93-317 30 22. The city's oldest restaurant, established in 1786, serves traditional Catalan dishes like *pica pica de pescado* (a seafood medley). ● *Mon, dinner Sun, 3 weeks in Jul.*		■	●	
OLD TOWN: *Romesco* € Carrer de Sant Pau 28. **Map** D3. **(** 93-318 93 81. A popular spot just off La Rambla, with home-style cooking, a lively atmosphere, and unbeatable prices. The house specialty is *frijoles* (a Cuban dish of rice, black beans, fried banana, and egg). ● *Sun, Aug.*	●	■		
OLD TOWN: *Amaya* €€€ La Rambla 20–24. **Map** D3. **(** 93-302 10 37. This popular Basque-Catalan restaurant offers a good selection of tapas at the bar and half portions of many dishes that appear on the extensive menu. Fantastic wine list.	●	■	●	■
OLD TOWN: *Café de L'Academia* €€€ Lledó 1. **Map** D3. **(** 93-319 82 53. Situated in one of the prettiest squares in the old city, this restaurant is a mix of the old and new. Specialities include *lassanya freda* (Spanish lasagna with marinated anchovies) and risotto with *foie gras*. ● *Sat, Sun.*		■	●	■
OLD TOWN: *Los Caracoles* €€€ Carrer dels Escudellers 14. **Map** D3. **(** 93-302 31 85. Bustling restaurant in the Barri Xinès (Chinese Quarter), serving simple dishes such as paella, suckling lamb, and chicken roasted on a spit.	●		●	
OLD TOWN: *Set Portes* €€€ Passeig de Isabel II 14. **Map** E4. **(** 93-319 29 50. This lavishly decorated restaurant is reminiscent of an elegant Parisian café. Specialties include 11 different types of paella and delicious homemade cannelloni. Efficient service and a good wine list.		■	●	
OLD TOWN: *Cal Pep* €€€€ Plaça de les Olles 8. **Map** E4. **(** 93-310 79 61. Recommended dishes here include Pep's *pescado frito* (fried fish), clams with ham, and crayfish with onion. ● *Sun, lunch Mon, public hols.*	●		●	
OLD TOWN: *Talaia Mar* €€€€ Anexo Torre Mapfre, Carrer de la Marina 16. **Map** F4. **(** 93-221 90 90. This stunning, sleek restaurant, with views of the marina, offers extremely good food. The menu varies with the season. You can order half portions *(pica pica)* of most dishes.	●		●	

For key to symbols see back flap

<table>
<tr><td colspan="2">

Price categories are for a three-course evening meal for one, including a half-bottle of house wine, tax, and service:

€ under €18
€€ €18–27
€€€ €27–36
€€€€ over €36

</td><td colspan="5">

TAPAS BAR
In addition to the main dining room, there is a bar serving tapas.

FIXED-PRICE MENU
A good-value, fixed-price menu is offered at lunch or dinner, or both, usually with three courses.

GOOD WINE LIST
Denotes a wide range of good wines, or a more specialized selection of local wines.

</td></tr>
</table>

		TAPAS BAR	FIXED-PRICE MENU	GOOD WINE LIST	OUTDOOR TABLES
EIXAMPLE: *Roig Robí* Carrer de Sèneca 20. **Map** D1. (93-218 92 22. Small, intimate restaurant offering authentic Catalan cuisine, with a lovely interior courtyard for summer. ● *Sun, lunch Sat, public hols.* & ☕	€€€€		■	●	■
EIXAMPLE: *El Tragaluz* Passeig de la Concepció 5. **Map** D2. (93-487 06 21. Two different dining concepts are offered here: a sushi bar in front, and contemporary Mediterranean cuisine behind. & ☕	€€€€	●	■	●	

NORTHERN SPAIN

		TAPAS BAR	FIXED-PRICE MENU	GOOD WINE LIST	OUTDOOR TABLES
BAIONA, RIAS BAIXAS: *Moscón* Calle Alférez Barreiro 2 (Pontevedra). (986-35 50 08. Overlooking the harbor, Moscón offers Galician cuisine, including a tasty fish *caldeirada* (casserole) spiced with paprika. & ☕	€€€			●	
BILBAO (BILBO): *Zortziko* Calle Alameda Mazarredo 17 (Vizcaya). (94-423 97 43. Contemporary *haute cuisine* served in a beautiful building. The menu is seasonal and the creative Basque dishes are sublime. ● *Sun, dinner Mon.* ☕	€€€€	●	■	●	
CANGAS DE ONÍS, LOS PICOS DE EUROPA: *La Cabaña* Calle Susierra 34 (Asturias). (98-594 00 84. A popular grillroom with a wood fire, where suckling pig and baby lamb are roasted to perfection. ● *dinner Wed, Thu, mid-Dec–Feb.* & ☕	€€		■		■
OVIEDO: *El Raitán* Plaza de Trascorrales 6 (Asturias). (98-521 42 18. Discover the variety of Asturian cuisine with a nine-course, lunch-time *menú de degustación*, served by staff in regional dress. ● *dinner Sun.* ☕	€€	●	■	●	
PAMPLONA (IRUÑA): *Alhambra* Calle Bergamín 7 (Navarra). (948-24 50 07. Typical Navarrese cooking is served in this welcoming restaurant, together with a good selection of local wines. ● *Sun.* & ☕	€€€€		■	●	
PONTEVEDRA, RÍAS BAIXAS: *Doña Antonia* Calle Soportales, Plaza de la Herrería 4. (986-84 72 74. Contemporary European cuisine in a refined setting. The monkfish salad and the nougat ice cream with hazelnuts and pistachios are favorites. ● *Sun.* ☕	€€€			●	
SAN SEBASTIAN (DONOSTIA): *Arzak* Calle Alto de Miracruz 21 (Guipúzcoa). (943-27 84 65. According to many gourmets, this is Spain's best restaurant. Master chef Juan Mari Arzak's reputation for innovative Basque cuisine has been rewarded with three Michelin stars. ● *dinner Sun, Mon, Tue (in winter), late Jun & Nov.* & ☕	€€€€		■	●	
SANTANDER: *Zacarías* Calle Hernán Cortés 38 (Cantabria). (942-21 23 33. Featuring authentic Cantabrian dishes, this popular restaurant with a lively tapas bar offers a wide range of regional specialties. & ☕	€€€€	●	■	●	
SANTIAGO DE COMPOSTELA: *Moncho Vilas* Avenida de Vilagarcía 21 (A Coruña). (981-59 83 87. Exemplary Galician dishes are served at this restaurant. The fish and seafood, such as clams, scallops, and spiny lobster, are very fresh, and the meat is excellent. A separate bar serves tapas. ● *Mon.* ☕	€€€€	●	■	●	
VILAGARCÍA DE AROUSA, RÍAS BAIXAS: *Pazo Sobrán* Pazo Sobrán, Villajuan de Arosa (Pontevedra). (986-50 09 09. Housed in an old *pazo* (manor house), this popular establishment offers informal dining with good regional cooking. ● *dinner Sun & Mon.* & ☕	€€	●	■		

Map references refer to map of Barcelona on pp306–7

CATALONIA & EASTERN SPAIN

ALICANTE (ALACANT), COSTA BLANCA: *Dársena* €€€
Marina Deportiva, Muelle 6, Puerto. (96-520 75 89.
With 150 different rice dishes on the menu, you might be hard pressed
to choose. The generous portions are served in individual paella pans
that hold enough food for two persons. & 🥗

ALTEA, COSTA BLANCA: *Raco de Toni* €€€
Calle de la Mar 127 (Alicante). (96-584 17 63.
Regional food, including rice dishes and locally caught fish, is served in
this simple, cozy restaurant. The rice with salt cod and vegetables and the
anchovies stuffed with peppers are two of the specialties. ● *Nov.* & 🥗

TARRAGONA: *El Merlot* €€€
Carrer Caballers 6. (977-22 06 52.
Located in the old part of town, this restaurant serves Mediterranean
cuisine based on first-class local produce. Specialties include game dishes
(available in season) and homemade desserts. ● *Sun, lunch Mon.* 🥗

VALENCIA: *La Rosa* €€€
Paseo del Neptuno 70. (96-371 20 76.
Typical beachside restaurant with around 30 different rice dishes and a good
assortment of fresh fish and shellfish. ● *early Aug–early Sep.* & 🥗

VALENCIA: *Albacar* €€€€
Calle Sorní 35. (96-395 10 05.
Enjoy innovative cuisine in attractive surroundings. Try the lukewarm salad
of fish with tarragon vinaigrette, and finish with the ravioli of pina colada
with rum gelatin. ● *Sun, lunch Sat, public hols, Aug, Easter.* &

ZARAGOZA: *La Rinconada de Lorenzo* €€
Calle la Salle 3. (976-55 51 08.
Typical Aragonese cuisine is served at this restaurant, such as
migas con jamón (breadcrumbs with ham) and *ternasco al horno*
(roast lamb). Desserts include *higos con nueces* (figs with nuts).
● *dinner Sun, Easter, Jul–Aug: Mon.* & 🥗

CENTRAL SPAIN

AVILA: *Mesón del Rastro* €€€
Plaza del Rastro 1. (920-21 12 18.
Authentic regional dishes are offered in this truly Castilian restaurant
nestled in the city wall. The *Judías de El Barco de Avila* (dried white
beans served in a thick sauce with chorizo) is an all-time favorite. & 🥗

BURGOS: *Casa Ojeda* €€€
Calle Vitoria 5. (947-20 90 52.
A traditional restaurant serving classic dishes, such as roast suckling lamb
and *morcilla* (a black blood sausage) with red peppers. There is an
extensive choice of Ribera del Duero and La Rioja wines. ● *dinner Sun.* 🥗

LEÓN: *Mesón Leonés del Racimo de Oro* €€€
Calle Caño Vadillo 2. (987-25 75 75.
Enjoy traditional fare in a 17th-century inn. In winter there are game dishes
and stews, such as the *cocido leonés* (a hearty broth of *garbanzos* (chickpeas),
potatoes, bacon, blood sausage, and cabbage). ● *dinner Sun & Tue.* & 🥗

SALAMANCA: *Río de la Plata* €€€
Plaza del Peso 1. (923-21 90 05.
A tiny, popular restaurant next to the Plaza Mayor, serving a great variety
of fresh fish and Castilian dishes, all of superb quality. ● *Mon, Jul.* 🥗

SAN LORENZO DE EL ESCORIAL: *Taberna La Cueva* €€€
Calle San Antón 4. (91-890 15 16.
Juan de Villanueva, architect of the Prado, designed this 18th-century
inn, whose specialties include the *huevos a la cueva* (fried eggs and
ham served in a nest of straw potatoes). ● *Mon.* 🥗

SEGOVIA: *Mesón de Cándido* €€€
Plaza del Azoguejo 5. (921-42 81 03.
Don't leave town without visiting Mesón de Cándido, *the* place to eat
in Segovia. The restaurant has good views of the Roman aqueduct and
serves local specialties, such as roast lamb and suckling pig. & 🥗

					TAPAS BAR	FIXED-PRICE MENU	GOOD WINE LIST	OUTDOOR TABLES

Price categories are for a three-course evening meal for one, including a half-bottle of house wine, tax, and service:

€ under €18
€€ €18–27
€€€ €27–36
€€€€ over €36

TAPAS BAR
In addition to the main dining room, there is a bar serving tapas.

FIXED-PRICE MENU
A good-value, fixed-price menu is offered at lunch or dinner, or both, usually with three courses.

GOOD WINE LIST
Denotes a wide range of good wines, or a more specialized selection of local wines.

TOLEDO: *Hostal del Cardenal* €€
Paseo de Recaredo 24. (925-22 08 62.
Housed in an 18th-century palace, this restaurant serves garlic soup, suckling pig, and the famous Toledo *mazapán* (marzipan). 🗐
Fixed-Price Menu ■ *Good Wine List* ● *Outdoor Tables* ■

TOLEDO: *Adolfo* €€€€
Calle de Granada 6. (925-22 73 21.
Set in the heart of Toledo's Jewish quarter, the Adolfo, with its wonderful 15th-century Mudéjar coffered ceiling, serves game in winter and fresh trout from the Río Tajo. ● dinner Sun, late Jul. 🗐 🗐
Tapas Bar ● *Fixed-Price Menu* ■ *Good Wine List* ●

SOUTHERN SPAIN

CÁDIZ: *El Faro* €€€
Calle San Félix 15. (956-21 10 68. FAX 956-21 21 88.
@ elfaro_cadiz@raini-computer.net
El Faro's menu, which has a mix of modern and traditional dishes, changes daily, but always features local seafood. 🗐 🗐
Tapas Bar ● *Fixed-Price Menu* ■ *Good Wine List* ●

CÓRDOBA: *Caballo Rojo* €€€
Calle Cardenal Herrero 28. (957-47 53 75. FAX 957-47 47 42.
@ caballorojo@teleline.es
At this restaurant you can try dishes adapted from Moorish and Sephardic recipes. Enjoy lamb with honey or *Sefardi* salad of wild mushrooms, asparagus, roasted peppers, and salt cod. 🗐 🗐
Tapas Bar ● *Fixed-Price Menu* ■ *Good Wine List* ● *Outdoor Tables* ■

ESTEPONA, COSTA DEL SOL: *La Alborada* €€
Puerto Deportivo de Estepona (Málaga). (95-280 20 47.
This quayside eatery serves excellent paella and other rice dishes, such as *arroz a la banda* (fish risotto). ● Wed, weekdays in winter. 🗐 🗐
Good Wine List ● *Outdoor Tables* ■

FUENGIROLA, COSTA DEL SOL: *Portofino* €€
Edificio Perla 1, Paseo Marítimo 29 (Málaga). (952-47 06 43. FAX 952-66 56 15.
A seafood restaurant, popular for its friendly service and good Italian food. Try the fish and shellfish brochette. ● Mon, early Jul, mid-Jul–mid-Sep: lunch daily. 🗐
Outdoor Tables ■

GRANADA: *Don Giovanni.* €
Avenida de Cádiz Zaidin 65. (958-81 87 51.
It is hard to beat Don Giovanni's prices for oven-baked pizzas and the wide variety of pastas, meat dishes, and salads. ● Wed, 1 week in Aug. 🗐 🗐
Fixed-Price Menu ■ *Outdoor Tables* ■

GRANADA: *Mirador de Morayma* €€
Calle Pianista García Carillo 2. (958-22 82 90. FAX 958-22 81 25.
Situated in the Albaicín, with views of the Alhambra, this restaurant specializes in typical dishes of Granada, such as *remojón* (a salad of oranges and codfish) and *choto albaicinero* (kid fried with garlic). 🗐
Good Wine List ● *Outdoor Tables* ■

GRANADA: *Velázquez* €€
Calle Emilio Orozco 1. (958-28 01 09. FAX 958-28 79 66.
Modern interpretations of Moorish dishes, such as *bstella* (a meat pastry with pine nuts and almonds), are the specialty here. ● Sun, Aug. 🗐 🗐
Fixed-Price Menu ■ *Good Wine List* ●

JEREZ DE LA FRONTERA: *Gaitán* €€€
Calle Gaitán 3 (Cádiz). (956-34 58 59. @ jkl@arraquis.es
Gaitán's innovative chef combines Basque and Andalusian influences to create dishes such as hake confit with roasted vegetables and laurel, and breast of chicken with foie gras and pine nuts. 🗐
Fixed-Price Menu ■ *Good Wine List* ●

MÁLAGA: *Mesón Astorga* €€
Calle Gerona 11. (95-234 68 32. FAX 95-234 25 63.
Creative flair using Málaga's superb local produce makes this restaurant popular. Try the fried aubergine drizzled with molasses, or the salad of fresh tuna with sherry vinegar dressing. Lively tapas bar. ● Sun. 🗐 🗐
Tapas Bar ● *Good Wine List* ● *Outdoor Tables* ■

MARBELLA, COSTA DEL SOL: *Santiago* €€€
Paseo Marítimo 5 (Málaga). **[** 95-277 43 39. **FAX** 95-282 45 03.
One of the best places for seafood on the Costa del Sol. On any day,
there might be 40 to 50 fish and shellfish dishes, including paella, and
good meat dishes, such as pig and suckling lamb. ● *Nov.* **&** ●

RONDA: *Pedro Romero* €€
Calle Virgen de la Paz 18 (Málaga). **[** 95-287 11 10. **FAX** 95-287 10 61.
Facing Ronda's bullring, this restaurant serves well-prepared country
food. Try the rabbit with thyme or the braised bull's tail. **&** ●

SEVILLE: *Las Meninas* €
Calle Santo Tomás 3. **[** 95-422 62 26.
Hearty food and good prices make this a popular place. A variety
of local dishes include a tasty broth of *garbanzos* (chickpeas) and cod.

SEVILLE: *Bodegón Torre del Oro* €€
Calle Santander 15. **[** 95-422 08 80.
This combined bar and dining room specializes in *raciones* (appetizers).
Try the *garbanzos con espinacas* (chickpeas with spinach), *puntillitas*
(grilled cuttlefish), or the *punta de solomillo* (beef fillet tip). **&** ●

SEVILLE: *Enrique Becerra* €€€
Calle Gamazo 2. **[** 95-421 30 49.
A plush restaurant-bar. Besides a fine selection of fish and meat dishes,
the daily specials feature Andalusian home-style cooking. ● *Sun.* ●

SEVILLE: *La Isla* €€€
Calle Arfe 25. **[** 95-421 53 76. **FAX** 95-456 22 19.
An attractive, centrally located restaurant, featuring superb seafood: turbot,
bream, and delicacies such as *percebes* (barnacles). ● *Aug.* ●

SEVILLE: *Hostería del Laurel* €€€€
Plaza de los Venerables 5. **[** 95-422 02 95.
Rustic decoration, with wooden barrels and colorful wall tiles. Try local
specialties, *serrano* ham and *tortilla de patatas* (potato omelette). **&** ●

TORREMOLINOS, COSTA DEL SOL: *Frutos* €€€
Avda. Riviera 80, Los Alamos, Carretera a Cádiz km 228 (Málaga). **[** 95-238 14 50.
The *grande dame* of Costa del Sol restaurants, serving superb meat and
fish. Enjoy suckling pig, followed by *arroz con leche* (rice pudding). ●

THE BALEARIC ISLANDS

IBIZA, IBIZA TOWN: *Ca'n Alfredo* €€€
Paseo Vara de Rey 16. **[** 971-31 12 74.
Regional cuisine is served in this popular establishment, including *borrida
de ratjada* (ray stew). ● *Mon, May 1–15, Nov 15–30.* **&** ●

MALLORCA, ALGAIDA: *Es 4 Vents* €€€
Carretera Manacor. **[** 971-665 173.
A compulsory stop on the road to Manacor. Set in a traditional country
house, the menu specialises in typical Mallorcan dishes. ● *Jun 15–Jul 15.* **&** ●

MALLORCA, PALMA DE MALLORCA: *Porto Pí* €€€€
Calle Garita 25. **[** 971-40 00 87.
This elegant house, surrounded by gardens, is an ideal spot to savor
creative Mediterranean cuisine made with first-class ingredients. ● *Sat,
lunch Sun.* **&** ●

MALLORCA, PORT D'ANDRATX: *Miramar* €€
Avenida Mateo Bosch 22. **[** 971-67 16 17.
A family-run restaurant with views of the marina, offering good seafood and
great service. Specialties include shrimp in rock salt. ●

MENORCA, CIUTADELLA: *Club Nautico Ca's Quintu* €€
Cami Baex 8 (Puerto). **[** 971-38 10 02.
This restaurant serves traditional Menorcan food, with an emphasis on fresh
fish. The *caldera de langosta* (lobster casserole) is a house specialty. ●

MENORCA, MAÓ: *Jágaro* €€€
Moll de Levant 334. **[** 971-36 23 90.
Overlooking the harbor, this restaurant offers seafood dishes in the summer
and hearty stews in winter. ● *Feb: dinner Sun & Mon.* ● **&**

PORTUGAL

MOST VISITORS TO PORTUGAL *head for the sandy coves, pretty fishing villages, and manicured golf courses of the Algarve. But beyond the south coast resorts lies the least explored corner of Western Europe: a country of rugged landscapes, ancient cities with proud traditions, and quiet rural backwaters.*

Portugal appears to have no obvious geographical claim to nationhood, yet the country has existed within borders virtually unchanged for nearly 800 years, making it one of the oldest nation states in Europe. Its ten million people are proudly independent from, and distrustful of, neighboring Spain.

For a small country, the regions of Portugal are immensely varied. The rural Minho and Trás-os-Montes in the north are the most traditional – some might say backward. Over the last few decades many inhabitants of these neglected regions have been forced to emigrate in search of work. At the same time, the Algarve, with its beautiful sandy beaches and warm Mediterranean climate, has become a vacation playground for North Europeans as well as the Portuguese themselves. Lisbon, the capital, at the mouth of the Tagus, is a cosmopolitan metropolis with a rich cultural life. Oporto is a serious rival, especially in terms of commerce and industry, and is the center for the production and export of Portugal's most famous product – port wine, grown on steeply terraced vineyards hewn out of mountainsides in the wild upper reaches of the Douro valley.

HISTORY

The Romans, who arrived in 216 BC, called the whole peninsula Hispania, but the region between the Douro and Tagus rivers was named Lusitania after the Celtiberian tribe that lived there. After the collapse of the Roman Empire in the 5th century, Hispania was overrun first by Germanic tribes, then by Moors from North Africa in 711.

Reconquest by the Christian kingdoms of the north began in earnest in the 11th century. In the process Portucale, a small county of the kingdom of León and Castile, was declared an independent kingdom by its ruler, Afonso Henriques, in 1139. With the aid of English crusaders, he succeeded in recapturing Lisbon in 1147.

Fishing boats on the beach at the popular Algarve resort of Albufeira

◁ **Nave of the Manueline church of Santa Maria in the Jerónimos monastery, Belém, Lisbon**

The kingdom expanded south to the Algarve, and Portuguese sailors began to explore the African coast and the Atlantic. Portugal's golden age reached its zenith in the reign of Manuel I, with Vasco da Gama's voyage to India in 1498 and the discovery of Brazil in 1500. The era also produced the one uniquely Portuguese style of architecture: the Manueline. Trade with the East brought incredible wealth, but military defeat in Morocco meant that the prosperity was short-lived. Spain invaded in 1580 and ruled Portugal for the next 60 years.

After Portugal regained independence, its fortunes were restored by gold from Brazil. In the late 18th century, the chief minister, the Marquês de Pombal, began to modernize the country. However, Napoleon's invasion in 1807 and the

Manuel I (reigned 1495–1521), who made vast profits from Portugal's spice trade

loss of Brazil in 1825 left Portugal impoverished and divided. Absolutists and Constitutionalists struggled for power, until, in 1910, a republican revolution overthrew the monarchy.

The weakness of the economy led to a military coup in 1926 and a long period of dictatorship. António Salazar, who held power from 1928 to 1968, rid the country of its debts, but poverty was widespread and all opposition banned. The country was a virtual recluse in the world community, the prime concern of foreign policy being the defense of its African and Asian colonies. The bloodless Carnation Revolution ended the dictatorship in 1974, and full democracy was restored in 1976. Since its entry into the European Community in 1986, Portugal has enjoyed rapid economic growth and assumed the self-confident attitude of a modern Western European state.

LANGUAGE AND CULTURE

The family is the hub of Portuguese daily life and Catholicism remains a powerful force in rural communities. But the country has come a long way since the repression and self-censorship of the Salazar era. Urban Portugal, in particular, presents a secular, fairly emancipated and eagerly consumerist face to the world.

The national psyche encapsulates this dualism in its struggle between a forward-looking, realistic approach to life and the dreamy, inward-looking side that finds expression in the Portuguese notion of *saudade*, a melancholy yearning for something lost or unattainable.

The Portuguese language is a source of national pride, and visitors should take care not to assume that it is interchangeable with Spanish. Pride, too, is taken in *fado*, the native musical tradition that expresses *saudade*.

KEY DATES IN PORTUGUESE HISTORY

139 BC Romans subdue the Lusitani

415 AD Visigoths invade Iberian Peninsula

711 Muslim army of Arabs and Berbers from North Africa conquers Visigothic kingdom

1139 After defeating Moors at Ourique, Afonso Henriques declares himself king of Portugal

1147 Afonso Henriques takes Lisbon

1249 Conquest of Algarve complete

1385 João I defeats Castilians at Aljubarrota

1418 Prince Henry the Navigator made governor of Algarve; sponsors expeditions to Africa

1498 Vasco da Gama reaches India

1578 King Sebastião killed on ill-fated expedition to Morocco

1580 Philip II of Spain becomes king of Portugal

1640 Restoration; Duke of Bragança crowned João IV; start of war of independence

1668 Spain recognizes Portugal's independence

1755 Lisbon earthquake

1807 French invade; royal family flees to Brazil

1910 Revolution; Manuel II abdicates and flees to England; republic proclaimed

1932 António Salazar becomes prime minister

1974 Carnation Revolution

Exploring Portugal

Portugal IS A SMALL COUNTRY and there are fast road and train links between the country's three great cities, Lisbon, Coimbra, and Oporto. Many of the most famous sights, such as the royal palaces at Sintra and the monastery of Alcobaça, make a good day's outing from Lisbon. In the south, the great attractions are the sandy beaches of the Algarve. With the completion of the Lisbon-Algarve motorway, arriving from the north is quite easy, but most visitors fly direct to Faro airport and once there, traveling between the various resorts is no problem.

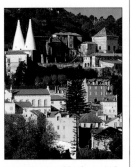

Sintra, dominated by the conical chimneys of the old royal palace

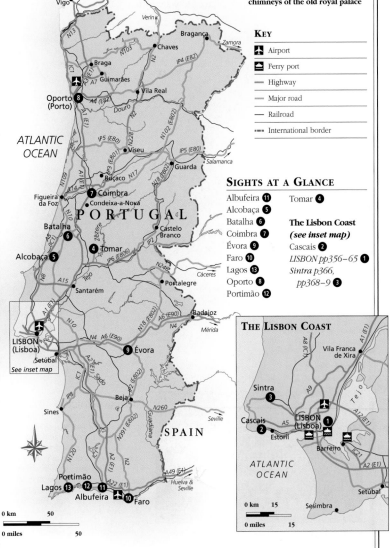

Key

- ✈ Airport
- ⛴ Ferry port
- — Highway
- — Major road
- — Railroad
- --- International border

SIGHTS AT A GLANCE

Albufeira ⑪
Alcobaça ⑤
Batalha ⑥
Coimbra ⑦
Évora ⑨
Faro ⑩
Lagos ⑬
Oporto ⑧
Portimão ⑫

Tomar ④

The Lisbon Coast
(see inset map)
Cascais ②
LISBON pp356–65 ①
Sintra p366,
* pp368–9* ③

THE LISBON COAST

Lisbon ❶

THE CAPITAL OF PORTUGAL occupies a hilly site on the estuary of the Tagus. Over the centuries, the city expanded along the coast to Belém, the starting point for the voyages of discovery in the 15th century, and even to the other side of the river, known as the Outra Banda. It has now spread far inland, making the population of Greater Lisbon nearly two million. The historic center (the Baixa) is a small, low-lying area, pinned between the heights of the Alfama to the east and the Bairro Alto to the west. The city underwent a great cleanup for the Expo '98 exhibition, especially in the old docks and industrial areas along the waterfront.

Portugal's coat of arms in the treasury of the Sé (cathedral)

SIGHTS AT A GLANCE

Alfama ④
Bairro Alto ⑨
Baixa ⑧
Castelo de São Jorge ⑤
Museu Nacional de Arte
 Antiga ⑪
Praça do Comércio ⑦
São Vicente de Fora ③
Sé ⑥

Greater Lisbon
(see inset map)
Museu Calouste
 Gulbenkian ⑩
Museu Nacional do
 Azulejo ②
Oceanário de
 Lisboa ①

Belém *(see inset map)*
Monument to the
 Discoveries ⑬
*Mosteiro dos Jerónimos
pp364–5* ⑭
Museu da Marinha ⑮
Museu Nacional dos
 Coches ⑫
Torre de Belém ⑯

Mosteiro dos Jerónimos overlooking Praça do Império

GETTING AROUND

Lisbon's limited metro system links the north of the city with sights in the center around Rossio square. Buses cover the whole city and are the most common form of public transportation. Take the Santa Justa lift to reach the Bairro Alto district and the 28 tram to climb the steep hill up to the Alfama. Belém is served by tram, train, and bus. Taxis are inexpensive, but a taxi ride can be alarming, as can any experience of driving in Lisbon.

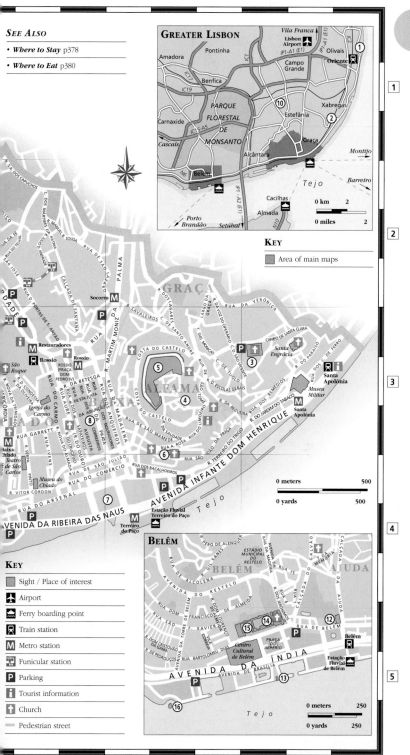

SEE ALSO

• **Where to Stay** p378
• **Where to Eat** p380

GREATER LISBON

Vila Franca
Lisbon
Airport
IP1-A1 (E1)
Olivais
IC1
Amadora
Pontinha
Campo
Grande
Oriente
Benfica
IC19
Xabregas
PARQUE
FLORESTAL
DE
MONSANTO
Estefânia
Carnaxide
Graça
Cascais
Alcântara
Montijo
N6
IP1-A2 (E1)
Belém
Barreiro
N10
Tejo
Cacilhas
0 km   2
Almada
0 miles   2
Porto
Brandão
Setúbal

KEY

Area of main maps

GRAÇA

RUA DA VERÓNICA

Socorro

Restauradores

São
Roque

Rossio
ROSSIO
(PRAÇA
DOM
PEDRO IV)

Rossio

Igreja do
Carmo

RUA GARRETT

Baixa
Chiado
Teatro
de São
Carlos

Museu do
Chiado

RUA DO ARSENAL

ALFAMA

COSTA DO CASTELO

CAMPO DE SANTA CLARA

Santa
Engrácia

Museu
Militar

Santa
Apolónia

Santa
Apolónia

RUA DE SÃO JULIÃO

RUA DO COMÉRCIO

RUA DOS BACALHOEIROS

AVENIDA INFANTE DOM HENRIQUE

Tejo

0 meters   500

0 yards   500

AVENIDA DA RIBEIRA DAS NAUS

Terreiro
do Paço

Estação Fluvial
Terreiro do Paço

BELÉM

ESTÁDIO
MUNICIPAL
DO
RESTELO

BELÉM

AJUDA

AVENIDA DO RESTELO

AVENIDA DE ALCOLENA

Centro
Cultural
de Belém

PRAÇA
DO
IMPÉRIO

RUA DE BELÉM

Belém

Estação
Fluvial
de Belém

AVENIDA DA ÍNDIA

AVENIDA DE BRASÍLIA

Tejo

0 meters   250

0 yards   250

KEY

■ Sight / Place of interest

✈ Airport

⛴ Ferry boarding point

🚉 Train station

Ⓜ Metro station

🚡 Funicular station

P Parking

ℹ Tourist information

✝ Church

Pedestrian street

D   E   F

Oceanário de Lisboa ①

Esplanada dom Carlos I, Parque das Nações. **(** 21-891 70 02. **M** Oriente. **🚌** 5, 10, 19, 21, 28, 44, 50, 68, 82, 208 (night). **🚃** Gare do Oriente. **◻** daily. **●** Dec 25. **🖼 ♿**

THIS HUGE oceanarium, on the banks of the Tagus, is the second largest in the world. It was designed for Expo '98 by the American architect, Peter Chermayeff, to illustrate the environmental theme of "The Oceans: A Heritage for the Future."

The central feature is a gigantic aquarium, the "Open Tank," with enough water to fill four Olympic swimming pools. Representing the open ocean, this contains fauna of the high seas, from sea bream to sharks. Around the main tank four smaller aquariums reconstruct the ecosystems of the Atlantic, Antarctic, Pacific, and Indian oceans.

Museu Nacional do Azulejo ②

Rua da Madre de Deus 4. **(** 21-814 77 47. **🚌** 18, 42, 104, 105. **◻** Tue pm–Sun. **●** Jan 1, Easter, May 1, Dec 25. **🖥 🎟 🖼**

THE IDEA OF DECORATIVE tiles was a legacy of the Moors. From the 16th century onward, Portugal started producing its own painted ceramic tiles *(azulejos)*. The blue-and-white tiles of the Baroque era are considered by many to be the finest.

The National Tile Museum is housed in the Convento da Madre de Deus, founded by Dona Leonor (widow of João II) in 1509. The interior of the church has striking Baroque decoration, added by João V.

An important surviving feature of the original convent is the Manueline cloister. Together with the larger Renaissance cloister, it provides a stunning setting for the museum. Decorative panels, individual tiles, and photographs trace tile-making from its introduction, through Spanish influence and the

Statue of woman praying beside tomb of Carlos I in São Vicente de Fora

development of Portugal's own styles, to today. Panels from churches, monasteries, and other sites around Portugal have been reassembled here. Highlights include a blue-and-white, 18th-century panorama showing Lisbon before the earthquake, and the colorful 17th-century carpet tiles (so-called because they imitated the patterns of Moorish rugs).

Detail from 16th-century altarpiece in the Museu Nacional do Azulejo

São Vicente de Fora ③

Largo de São Vicente. **(** 21-882 44 00. **🚃** 28. **🚌** 12. **◻** daily. **🖼** to cloisters.

ST. VINCENT was proclaimed Lisbon's patron saint in 1173, when his relics were brought to a church on this

site. The present church was completed in 1627. The Italianate façade has statues of Saints Vincent, Augustine, and Sebastian over the entrance. Inside, one's eye is immediately drawn to the striking Baroque altar canopy.

Behind the church is the old refectory, transformed into the Bragança Pantheon in 1885. The tombs of almost every Bragança king and queen are here, from João IV, who died in 1656, to Manuel II, last king of Portugal. Only Maria I and Pedro IV are not buried here. A stone mourner kneels at the tomb of Carlos I and his son Luís Felipe, assassinated in Praça do Comércio *(see p360)* in 1908.

Alfama ④

🚌 1, 12, 13, 37, 46, 91, 107. **🚃** 28.

A FASCINATING QUARTER at any time of day, the Alfama comes to life in the late afternoon and early evening, when the small restaurants and bars start to fill and music, often *fado*, can be heard in the alleyways. It is hard to believe that this, the oldest part of Lisbon, was once the most desirable quarter of the city. In the Middle Ages wealthy residents started to move away, fearing earthquakes, leaving the quarter to fishermen and paupers. Ironically, the Alfama was spared by the earthquake of 1755. Today, the area is a warren of narrow streets and small, picturesque houses clinging to the hillside below the Castelo de São Jorge.

The least strenuous way to see this area is to start at the castle at the top and work your way down. Attractions on the way include the **Museo de Artes Decorativas** (Museum of Decorative Arts), which has its own workshops, and the sweeping views from the terrace of the **Miradouro de Santa Luzia**. You could also visit, on a Tuesday or Saturday, the colorful **Feira da Ladra** (Thieves' Market) in Campo de Santa Clara to the east of the castle or the early morning fish market in Rua de São Pedro.

Castelo de São Jorge ⑤

Porta de S. Jorge, Rua do Chão da Feira. 🚪 *21-887 72 44.* 🚌 *37.* 🚋 *28.* ⬭ *daily (parts of castle grounds and Santa Cruz district currently closed for restoration).*

FOLLOWING THE RECAPTURE OF Lisbon from the Moors in 1147, King Afonso Henriques transformed their citadel – which crowned Lisbon's eastern hill – into the residence of the Portuguese kings. In 1511 Manuel I built a more lavish palace beside the river (*see p360*). In the centuries that followed the Castelo de São Jorge was used variously as a theater, a prison, and an

arms depot. After the 1755 earthquake, the ramparts lay in ruins until 1938 when the castle was completely rebuilt.

The castle gardens and narrow streets of the old Santa Cruz district, which lies within the walls, are a pleasant place for a stroll, and the views are the finest in Lisbon. Visitors can climb the towers, one of which has a camera obscura, walk along the reconstructed ramparts, or stand on the shaded observation terrace.

Sé ⑥

Largo da Sé. 🚪 *21-886 67 52.* 🚌 *37.* 🚋 *12, 28.* ⬭ *daily.* **Cloister & treasury** ⬭ *Mon–Sat.* 📷

IN 1150, AFONSO HENRIQUES built a cathedral for the first bishop of Lisbon (Gilbert of Hastings) on the site of the Moorish mosque. Sé denotes the seat of a bishop.

Though much renovated over the centuries, the Sé has kept its solid Romanesque façade. The Capela de Santo

The Sé, Lisbon's austere 12th-century cathedral

Ildefonso, one of nine Gothic chapels in the ambulatory behind the altar, contains two fine 14th-century tombs and in the Franciscan chapel by the entrance stands the font where St. Antony of Padua was baptized in 1195. In the Gothic cloister behind the Sé, excavations have unearthed Roman and other remains.

The treasury, located in one of the towers, has a splendid collection of exhibits, including the relics of St. Vincent. Legend has it that his remains were watched over by two ravens on their journey to Lisbon in 1173, hence the raven on the city's coat of arms.

View of the Castelo de São Jorge across the Baixa, Lisbon's lower town

Praça do Comércio, a grand entrance to the city of Lisbon

Praça do Comércio ⑦

🚌 2, 14, 40, 46, & many others.
🚋 15, 18.

MORE COMMONLY known as *Terreiro do Paço* (Palace Square), this was the site of the royal palace for 400 years. Manuel I transferred the royal residence here, from the Castelo de São Jorge, in 1511. The first palace, together with its library and 70,000 books, was destroyed in the 1755 earthquake. Its replacement was built around three sides of the square. After the 1910 revolution it became government administrative offices.

The south side looks across the Tagus and was once the finest gateway to Lisbon – used by royalty and ambassadors – with marble steps up from the river. In the center of the square is an equestrian statue of José I (1775) by Machado de Castro, leading Portuguese sculptor of the 18th century.

The impressive triumphal arch on the north side, decorated with statues of historical figures, leads into Rua Augusta and the Baixa.

On February 1, 1908, King Carlos and his son, Luís Felipe, were assassinated in the square. In 1974 it witnessed the first uprising of the Armed Forces Movement, which overthrew the Caetano regime in a bloodless coup that became known as the Carnation Revolution.

Baixa ⑧

🚌 2, 9, 14, 15, 36, 40, 44, 46, & many others. 🚋 15, 18. Ⓜ Rossio, Restauradores, Terreiro do Paço.

FOLLOWING THE 1755 earthquake, the Marquês de Pombal created an entirely new city center, one of Europe's first examples of town planning. Using a grid layout of streets, he linked the Praça do Comércio with the busy central square of Rossio. The streets were flanked by splendid Neoclassical buildings.

The Baixa (lower town) is still the commercial hub of the city, housing banks, offices, and stores. The streets are crowded by day, especially the central Rua Augusta, but less so after dark.

By the Restauradores metro station is the **Palácio Foz**, an 18th-century palace. Tourists are naturally drawn to Rossio, an elegant square and social focal point with cafés and *pastelarias*. The **National Theater** stands on the north side. Just to the east of Rossio is the less attractive Praça da Figueira, the city's main marketplace in Pombal's time. Rua das Portas de Santo Antão, north of the two squares, is a lively pedestrian street full of restaurants.

Bairro Alto ⑨

🚌 6, 9, 14, 20, 22, 27, 32, 38, & many others. 🚋 28 (also Elevador da Glória & Elevador da Santa Justa). Ⓜ Baixa-Chiado.

THE HILLTOP BAIRRO ALTO quarter, dating from the 16th century, is one of Lisbon's most picturesque districts. Its narrow, cobbled streets house a traditional, close-knit community, with small workshops and family-run *tascas* (cheap restaurants). This predominantly residential area has become fashionable at night for its bars, night clubs, and *fado* houses (see p377).

Rossio Square and the Neoclassical National Theater in the Baixa

THE EARTHQUAKE OF 1755

The first tremor of the devastating earthquake was felt at 9:30am on November 1. It was followed by a second, far more violent, shock a few minutes later, which reduced over half the city to rubble. A third shock was followed by fires which quickly spread. An hour later huge waves came rolling in from the Tagus, flooding the lower part of the city. Most of Portugal suffered damage, but Lisbon was the worst affected: an estimated 15,000 people died in

Marquês de Pombal

the city. Sebastião José de Carvalho e Melo, chief minister to King José I, later Marquês de Pombal, restored order and began a progressive town-planning scheme. His cool efficiency gained him almost total political control.

The Elevador de Santa Justa, which links the Baixa to the Carmo district

Very different in character is the neighboring, elegant, commercial district known as the Chiado, where affluent Lisboetas shop. On the main street, Rua Garrett, the Café Brasileira – once frequented by writers and intellectuals – remains popular. The Chiado was devastated by fire in 1988, but has been painstakingly renovated.

The best way to reach the Bairro Alto from the Baixa is via the Carmo district and the **Elevador de Santa Justa**, a Neo-Gothic elevator dating from 1901–2. Tourist attractions include the richly decorated **São Roque** church, the ruined **Igreja do Carmo**, once the largest church in Lisbon, and the **Museu do Chiado**, which houses art from 1850–1950.

Museu Calouste Gulbenkian ⑩

Avenida de Berna 45. 📞 *21-782 32 45.* 🅼 *Praça de Espanha, São Sebastião.* 🚌 *16, 18, 26, 31, 46, 56.* 🔲 *Tue–Sun (Tue: pm only).* ⬤ *Mon & public hols.* 🎫 🍴 🔲 ♿ 🆆 *www.gulbenkian.pt*

THANKS TO WEALTHY Armenian oil magnate, Calouste Gulbenkian, Portugal owns one of the finest personal art collections assembled during the 20th century. Gulbenkian moved to Portugal in World War II, because of the country's neutral status. This museum was inaugurated in 1969, as part of the charitable institution bequeathed to the nation. The building was devised to create the best layout for the founder's varied collection: the exhibits span over 4,000 years, from ancient Egypt and China, through an extensive collection of Islamic ceramics and carpets, to Art Nouveau. Gulbenkian was a friend of René Lalique, the great glassware and jewelry maker and one room is filled with his work.

Highlights of the European art collection include Van der Weyden's *St. Catherine* and Rembrandt's

Statue of the founder at Gulbenkian Museum

Portrait of an Old Man. Other major artists exhibited include Ghirlandaio, Rubens, Guardi, Gainsborough, Turner, Manet, and Renoir. The collection also includes sculpture, jewelry, textiles, manuscripts, porcelain, and a variety of decorative arts.

Museu Nacional de Arte Antiga ⑪

Rua das Janelas Verdes. 📞 *21-391 28 00.* 🚌 *27, 40, 49, 51, 60.* 🚊 *15, 18.* 🔲 *Tue–Sun (Tue: pm only).* ⬤ *public hols.* 🎫 ♿ 🔲 🍴

THE NATIONAL ART collection, housed in a 17th-century palace, was inaugurated in 1770. In 1940 a modern annex (including the main façade) was added. This was built on the site of a monastery, largely destroyed in the 1755 earthquake. Its only surviving feature, the chapel, has been integrated into the museum.

The ground floor houses 14th–19th-century European paintings, decorative arts, and furniture. Artists exhibited include Piero della Francesca, Hans Holbein the Elder, Raphael, Lucas Cranach the Elder, Hieronymus Bosch, and Albrecht Dürer. Oriental and African art, Chinese ceramics, and the gold, silver, and jewelry collection are on the second floor. The top floor houses Portuguese works.

The pride of the Portuguese collection is the *Adoration of St. Vincent* (c.1467–70), attributed to Nuno Gonçalves. It is an altarpiece painted on six panels, featuring portraits of a wide range of contemporary figures, from beggars and sailors to bishops and princes, including Henry the Navigator and the future João II, all paying homage to the saint. Another fascinating aspect of Portugal's great Age of Exploration is recorded in the 16th-century Japanese screens, which show Portuguese traders arriving in Japan.

Belém

At THE MOUTH of the Tagus, where the Portuguese mariners set sail on their voyages of discovery, Manuel I commissioned two grand monuments in the exuberant Manueline style of architecture: the Mosteiro dos Jerónimos and the Torre de Belém. Today Belém is a spacious, relatively green suburb with museums and gardens, including the vast Praça do Império, a formal square with a central fountain in front of the monastery. The area enjoys an attractive riverside setting with cafés and a promenade; on sunny days it has a distinct seaside feel. In Rua de Belém is the Antiga Confeitaria de Belém, a 19th-century café that sells the local specialty: *pastéis de Belém*, rich flaky-pastry custard tarts.

chaises used by young members of the royal family. There is also a 19th-century Lisbon cab, painted black and green, the colors of taxis right up to the 1990s. The 18th-century Eyeglass Chaise has a black leather hood pierced with sinister eyelike windows. It dates from the era of Pombal (*see p361*), when lavish decoration was discouraged.

Museu Nacional dos Coches ⑫

Praça Afonso de Albuquerque.
C 21-361 08 50. 14, 27, 28, 43, 49, 51. 15. Belém. ○ Tue–Sun.
● Jan 1, Easter, May 1, Dec 25.

THE NATIONAL COACH MUSEUM was established in 1905 by King Carlos's wife, Dona Amélia, whose pink riding cloak can be seen on display. It occupies the former riding school of the Palace of Belém. The rest of the elegant pink palace is now the residence of the president of Portugal.

Made in Portugal, Spain, Italy, France, and Austria, the coaches on display span three centuries and range from the practical to the preposterous. The main gallery, in Louis XVI style with a splendid painted ceiling, is the setting for two rows of coaches created for Portuguese royalty. The oldest is the comparatively plain 16th-century red leather and wood coach of Philip II of Spain. The coaches become increasingly sumptuous, interiors lined with red velvet and gold, exteriors carved with allegorical figures. The most extravagant of all are three Baroque coaches made in Rome for the Portuguese ambassador to the Vatican in the early 18th century.

The neighboring gallery has more royal carriages, including pony-drawn

Baroque coach in the Museu Nacional dos Coches

Monument to the Discoveries ⑬

Padrão dos Descobrimentos, Avenida de Brasília. **C** 21-303 19 50. 27, 28, 29, 43, 49, 51, 112. 15. ○ Tue–Sun. ● public hols. for elevator.

STANDING PROMINENTLY on the Belém waterfront, the Padrão dos Descobrimentos was built in 1960 to mark the 500th anniversary of the death of Henry the Navigator (*see p354*). The 52-m (170-ft) high monument was designed to resemble a caravel – the small, lateen-rigged ship that allowed Portuguese sailors to explore the coast of Africa –

EASTERN FACE OF THE MONUMENT TO THE DISCOVERIES

Afonso V (1432–81)

Henry the Navigator (1394–1460), patron of the first explorers

Pedro Álvares Cabral (1467–1520), discoverer of Brazil

Vasco da Gama (1460–1524)

Fernão Magalhães (Magellan), who crossed the Pacific in 1520–21

Padrão erected by Diogo Cão in the Congo in 1482

with Portugal's coat of arms on the sides. Henry the Navigator stands at the prow with a caravel in hand. In two sloping lines either side of the monument are heroes linked with the Discoveries.

In front of the monument is a huge mariner's compass cut into the paving. The central map, dotted with galleons and mermaids, shows the routes of the discoverers in the 15th and 16th centuries. Inside the monument, an elevator whisks you to the sixth floor where steps lead to the top for a splendid panorama.

Mosteiro dos Jerónimos ⑭

See pp364–5.

Museu de Marinha ⑮

Praça do Império. 🎫 21-362 00 19. 🚌 27, 28, 43, 49, 51, 112. 🚃 15. ⭕ Tue–Sun. ⬤ public hols. 📷 ♿

THE MARITIME MUSEUM was inaugurated in 1962 in the west wing of the Jerónimos monastery. A hall devoted to the Discoveries illustrates the rapid progress in ship design from the mid-15th century. Small replicas show the transition from the bark to the lateen-rigged caravel, through the faster square-rigged caravel, to the Portuguese *nau* or great ship. There is also a display of astrolabes and navigational instruments, and replicas of 16th-century maps. The pillars carved with the Cross of the Order of Christ are replicas of various kinds of *padrão*, a stone marker set up to denote Portuguese sovereignty over the new lands discovered.

Beyond the Hall of Discoveries are models of modern Portuguese ships and the Royal Quarters, housing the exquisitely furnished wood-paneled cabin of King Carlos and Queen Amélia from the royal yacht *Amélia*, built in Scotland in 1900.

The modern pavilion opposite houses original royal barges and the collection ends with a display of seaplanes.

The Torre de Belém, a landmark for sailors returning to Lisbon

Torre de Belém ⑯

Avenida da India. 🎫 *21-301 93 46.* 🚌 *27, 28, 43, 49, 51, 112.* 🚃 *15.* ⭕ *Belém* ⭕ *Tue–Sun.* ⬤ *Jan 1, Easter, May 1, Dec 25.* 📷 ♿ *ground floor only.*

COMMISSIONED BY Manuel I, the tower was built as a fortress in the middle of the Tagus in 1515–21. Before nearby land was reclaimed in the 19th century, the tower stood much further from the shore than it does today. As the starting point for the navigators who set out to discover the trade routes to the east, this Manueline gem became a symbol of Portugal's great era of expansion. On the terrace, facing the sea, stands a statue

Royal coat of arms on the Torre de Belém

of Our Lady of Safe Homecoming, watching over the lives of Portugal's sailors.

The beauty of the tower lies in the decoration of the exterior: Manueline ropework carved in stone, openwork balconies, and Moorish-style watchtowers. The distinctive battlements are in the shape of shields, decorated with the squared cross of the Order of Christ, the emblem that also adorned the sails of Portuguese ships. The space below the terrace, which served as a storeroom and a prison, is very austere, but the private quarters in the tower are worth visiting for the elegant arcaded Renaissance loggia and the wonderful panorama.

VASCO DA GAMA (c.1460–1524)

In 1498 Vasco da Gama sailed around the Cape of Good Hope and opened the sea route to India. Although the Hindu ruler of Calicut, who received him wearing diamond and ruby rings, was not impressed by his humble offerings of cloth and wash basins, da Gama returned to Portugal with a valuable cargo of spices. In 1502 he sailed again to India, establishing Portuguese trade routes in the Indian Ocean. João III nominated him Viceroy of India in 1524, but he died of a fever soon after.

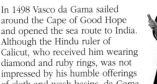

Portrait of Vasco da Gama, painted in India

Mosteiro dos Jerónimos ⑭

Armillary sphere in the cloister

A MONUMENT TO THE WEALTH of Portugal's Age of Discovery, the monastery is the culmination of the Manueline style of architecture. Commissioned by Manuel I around 1501, soon after Vasco da Gama's return from his historic voyage, it was funded largely by "pepper money," taxes on spices, precious stones, and gold. Various masterbuilders worked on the building, the most notable being Diogo Boitac, replaced by João de Castilho in 1517. The monastery was entrusted to the Order of St. Jerome (Hieronymites) until 1834, when all religious orders were disbanded.

Tomb of Vasco da Gama
The 19th-century tomb of the explorer (see p361) is carved with ropes, armillary spheres, and other seafaring symbols.

Refectory
The walls of the refectory are tiled with 18th-century azulejos. The panel at the northern end depicts the Feeding of the Five Thousand.

The fountain is in the shape of a lion, the heraldic animal of St. Jerome.

The modern wing, built in 1850 in Neo-Manueline style, houses the National Museum of Archaeology and part of the Maritime Museum *(see p361)*.

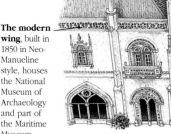

Entrance to church and cloister

View of the Monastery
The façade of the monastery church is dominated by the magnificent South Portal. This makes dramatic use of the Manueline style of architecture, essentially a Portuguese variant of Late Gothic.

Gallery

The West Portal was designed by the French sculptor Nicolau Chanterène. One of the niches holds a sculpture of the kneeling figure of King Manuel I.

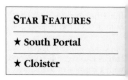

STAR FEATURES

★ **South Portal**

★ **Cloister**

★ Cloister
João de Castilho's pure Manueline creation was completed in 1544. Delicate tracery and richly carved images decorate the arches and balustrades.

VISITORS' CHECKLIST

Praça do Império. 21-362 00 34. 27, 28, 43, 49, 51, 112. 15. 10am–5pm (6pm May–Sep) Tue–Sun (last adm: 1 hr before closing). Jan 1, Easter, May 1, Dec 25. cloister.

Nave
The spectacular vaulting in the church of Santa Maria is held aloft by slender octagonal pillars. These rise like palm trees to the roof creating a feeling of space and harmony.

The chapter house holds the tomb of Alexandre Herculano (1810–77), historian and first mayor of Belém.

The chancel was commissioned in1572 by Dona Catarina, wife of João III.

The tombs of Manuel I, his wife Dona Maria, João III and Catarina are supported by elephants.

★ South Portal
The strict geometrical architecture of the portal is almost obscured by the exuberant decoration. João de Castilho unites religious themes, such as this image of St. Jerome, with the secular, exalting the kings of Portugal.

Tomb of King Sebastião
The tomb of the "longed for" Dom Sebastião stands empty. The young king never returned from battle in 1578 (see p354).

Beach at Estoril, east of Cascais

Cascais ②

🏠 30,000. 🚇 🚌 ℹ️ *Rua Visconde da Luz 14 (21-486 82 04).* 🛒 *first and third Sundays in month.*

A HARBOR since prehistoric times, Cascais became a fashionable resort in the 1870s, when Luís I's summer palace was sited here. Today it is a bustling cosmopolitan resort, with many upscale shops in the pedestrian streets of the old town and a new marina complex. Fishing is still an important activity, and the day's catch is auctioned near the harbor in the afternoon.

ENVIRONS: Along the coast, 3 km (2 miles) to the east, the resort of **Estoril** has been home to exiled European royalty. It has retained its sense of place with grand villas and hotels lining the coast.

Guincho, 10 km (6 miles) west of Cascais, has a magnificent sandy beach. Its Atlantic breakers make it popular with surfers. Further north is **Cabo da Roca**, the most westerly point of mainland Europe.

Sintra ③

🏠 23,000. 🚇 🚌 ℹ️ *Praça da República 23 (21-923 11 57).* 🛒 *2nd and 4th Sun of month in São Pedro.* 🎭 *Festival de Música (Jun–Jul).*

S INTRA'S SETTING among wooded ravines and fresh water springs made it a favorite summer retreat for the kings of Portugal, who built the fabulous **Palácio Nacional de Sintra** (*see pp368–9*) here.

Designated a UNESCO World Heritage Site in 1995, the town draws thousands of visitors, yet there are many tranquil walks in the surrounding hills.

Present-day Sintra is a maze of winding roads, and exploring the town on foot involves much walking and climbing; for a more leisurely tour, take a horse and carriage ride. The **Mira-douro da Vigia** in São Pedro offers impressive views, as does the cozy **Casa de Sapa** café, where you can sample *queijadas*, cheese tarts spiced with cinnamon.

Manueline window at Tomar's monastery

High above the town is the **Castelo dos Mouros**, an 8th-century Moorish castle. On a nearby hilltop stands the **Palácio da Pena**, built in the 19th century for Ferdinand, King Consort of Maria II, in a bizarre medley of architectural styles. A magnificent park surrounds the fairytale castle.

⛰️ Castelo dos Mouros

Estrada da Pena, 5 km (3 miles) S. 🚌 *(in summer) or taxi from Sintra.* ⭕ *daily.* ⬛ *Jan 1, Dec 25.*

🏛️ Palácio da Pena

Estrada da Pena, 5 km (3 miles) S. 📞 *21-910 53 40.* 🚌 *(in summer) or taxi from Sintra.* ⭕ *Tue–Sun.* ⬛ *Jan 1, Easter, May 1, Jun 29, Dec 25.* 🎫

Tomar ④

🏠 20,000. 🚇 🚌 ℹ️ *Avenida Dr. Cândido Madureira (24-932 24 27).* 🛒 *Fri.* 🎭 *Festa dos Tabuleiros (Jul, every 2 or 3 years).*

F OUNDED IN 1157 by Gualdim Pais, the first Grand Master of the Order of the Templars in Portugal, the town is dominated by the castle containing the **Convento de Cristo**. It was begun in 1162, built on land given to the Templars for services in battle, and preserves many traces of its founders and the inheritors of their mantle, the Order of Christ. The nucleus of the castle is the 12th-century Charola, the Templars' octagonal oratory. In 1356, Tomar became the headquarters of the Order of Christ.

Cloisters were built in the time of Henry the Navigator, but it was in the reigns of Manuel I (1495–1521) and his successor, João III (1521–57), that the greatest changes were made, with the addition of the Manueline church and Renaissance cloisters. The church window (c.1510), commissioned by Manuel I, is probably the best-known single example of the Manueline style of architecture.

Other fascinating features include the Terrace of Wax, where honeycombs were left to dry, and the "bread" cloister, where loaves were handed out to the poor.

The town of Tomar is the site of the curious Festa dos Tabuleiros, in which young girls carry towering structures made of 30 loaves of bread on their heads. They parade

Palácio da Pena in Sintra, the hilltop retreat of the last kings of Portugal

through the main square, Praça da República. The square's focal point is the 15th-century Gothic church of **São João Baptista**. Tomar is also home to one of Portugal's oldest synagogues, now the **Museu Luso-Hebraico de Abraham Zacuto**, a Jewish museum.

🛉 **Convento de Cristo**
📞 24-931 34 81. ⬜ daily.
⬛ Jan 1, Easter, May 1, Dec 25. 🖼

The Convento de Cristo, Tomar

Alcobaça ➎

Praça 25 de Abril, Alcobaça. 📞 262-50 51 20. 🚌 from Lisbon or Coimbra. ⬜ daily. ⬛ Easter, May 1, Dec 25. 🖼

THE MOSTEIRO de Santa Maria de Alcobaça is Portugal's largest church. Founded in 1153, the abbey is closely linked to the arrival of the Cistercian order in Portugal in 1138 as well as to the birth of the nation. In March 1147, Afonso Henriques conquered the Moorish stronghold of Santarém. To commemorate the victory, he gave land and

money to build a church to the Cistercians. Completed in 1223, the church is a beautiful building of austere simplicity. Portugal's rulers continued to endow the monastery, notably King Dinis (1279–1325), who added the main cloister, known as the Cloister of Silence. In the Sala dos Reis, 18th-century tiles depict the founding of the abbey, and statues of Portuguese kings adorn the walls.

Among those buried here are the tragic lovers King Pedro (1357–67) and his murdered mistress, Inês de Castro (d.1355), whose matching tombs face each other across the transept of the abbey church. Inês' death was ordered by Pedro's father, Afonso IV (1325–57). After Afonso's death, Pedro had two of Inês' murderers killed brutally. He then had her body exhumed and reburied.

One of Alcobaça's most popular features is the vast kitchen. Here whole oxen could be roasted on a spit inside the fireplace and a specially diverted stream provided a constant water supply.

Batalha ➏

Mosteiro de Santa Maria da Vitória, Batalha. 📞 244-76 54 97. 🚌 from Lisbon, Leiria, Porto de Mós, & Fátima. ⬜ daily. ⬛ Jan 1, Easter, May 1, Dec 25. 🖼

THE DOMINICAN ABBEY of Santa Maria da Vitória at Batalha is a masterpiece of Portuguese Gothic architecture. The pale limestone monastery

Manueline portal leading to the Unfinished Chapels at Batalha

was built to celebrate João I's victory at Aljubarrota (the battle which assured him the throne) in 1385. Today, the abbey still has military significance: two unknown soldiers from World War I lie in the chapter house. João I, his English wife, Philippa of Lancaster, and their son, Henry the Navigator, are also buried here, in the Founder's Chapel.

The abbey was begun in 1388 and work continued for the next two centuries. King Duarte, João's son, began an octagonal mausoleum for the royal house of Avis. The project was taken up again but then abandoned by Manuel I. It is now known as the Unfinished Chapels. Much of the decoration of the abbey is in the Manueline style.

The magnificent Gothic tomb of Pedro I in the transept of the monastery church at Alcobaça

Palácio Nacional de Sintra ❶

AT THE HEART of the old town of Sintra (Sintra Vila), a pair of strange conical chimneys rises high above the Royal Palace. The main part of the palace, including the central block with its plain Gothic façade and the large kitchens beneath

Swan panel, Sala dos Cisnes

the chimneys, was built by João I in the late 14th century, on a site once occupied by the Moorish rulers. The Paço Real, as it is also known, became the favorite summer retreat for the court and continued as a residence for Portuguese royalty until the 1880s. Additions to the building by the wealthy Manuel I, in the early 16th century, echo the Moorish style. Gradual rebuilding of the palace has resulted in a fascinating amalgamation of various different styles.

★ Sala das Pegas
It is said that King João I had the ceiling panels painted as a rebuke to the court women for indulging in idle gossip like chattering magpies (pegas).

The Torre da Meca has dovecotes below the cornice decorated with armillary spheres and nautical rope.

The Sala das Galés (galleons) houses temporary exhibitions.

★ Sala dos Brasões
The domed ceiling of this majestic room is decorated with stags holding the coats of arms (brasões) of 74 noble Portuguese families. The lower walls are lined with 18th-century Delft-like tiled panels.

Jardim da Preta, a walled garden

Sala de Dom Sebastião, the audience chamber

AZULEJOS – PAINTED CERAMIC TILES

Spanish-made, Moorish-style tiles from the palace chapel (1510)

The Palácio Nacional de Sintra contains *azulejos* from the 16th–18th centuries, many painted with Moorish-influenced designs. In the early 16th century, tiles were produced by compartmental techniques, using raised and depressed areas to prevent the tin-glaze colors from running. The maiolica technique appeared in the mid-16th century. This allowed artists to paint directly onto prepared flat tiles using several colors, as these did not run in the firing process. By the 18th century, no other European country was producing as many decorative tiles as Portugal, and there are many examples of 18th-century blue-and-white *azulejos* in the palace at Sintra, notably in the Sala dos Brasões.

★ Sala dos Cisnes
The magnificent ceiling of the former banqueting hall, painted in the 17th century, is divided into octagonal panels decorated with swans (cisnes).

The Sala dos Árabes
is decorated with fine *azulejos*.

Sala das Sereias
Intricate Arabesque designs on 16th-century tiles frame the door of the Room of the Sirens.

VISITORS' CHECKLIST

Largo Rainha Dona Amélia. 21-910 68 40. 10am–5:30pm Thu–Tue (last adm: 30 mins before closing). Jan 1, Easter, May 1, Jun 29, Dec 25. (free 10am–1pm Sun). w www.ippar.pt

The kitchens, beneath the huge conical chimneys, have spits and utensils once used for preparing royal banquets.

Entrance

Sala dos Archeiros, the entrance hall

Manuel I added the *ajimece* windows, a distinctive Moorish design with a slender column dividing two arches.

Chapel
Symmetrical Moorish patterns decorate the original 14th-century chestnut and oak ceiling and the mosaic floor of the private chapel.

STAR FEATURES

★ **Sala dos Brasões**

★ **Sala dos Cisnes**

★ **Sala das Pegas**

18th-century library of Coimbra University

Coimbra **7**

🏠 150,000. 🚉 🚌 🛈 *Praça da República (239-83 32 02); Largo Dom Dinis (239-83 25 91); Largo da Portagem (239-85 59 30).* 🛒 *Mon–Sat.* 🎭 *Queima das Fitas (early May).*

AFONSO HENRIQUES chose Coimbra as his capital in 1139, an honor it retained until 1256. Today, the city on the Mondego is famous as the home of Portugal's oldest university. Most sights are within walking distance of each other, so Coimbra is best explored on foot, despite the steep hill on which it is built.

Coimbra's two cathedrals, the **Sé Velha** ("old") and **Sé Nova** ("new"), lie in the shadow of the hilltop University. The Sé Velha, begun in 1064, is regarded as the finest Romanesque building in Portugal. The Sé Nova is only new in relative terms – it was founded in 1598, by the Jesuits.

The **University**, a short walk away, was founded in 1290 by King Dinis. Originally its location alternated between Lisbon and Coimbra, but it was finally installed in Coimbra's royal palace in 1537. Its oldest buildings are grouped around the Pátio das Escolas. The **belltower** (1733), symbol of the university, can be seen from all over the city. The **Library** was a gift of João V (1706–50). Its rooms,

of gilt and exotic wood, are lined with 300,000 books. Nearby is the similarly ornate **Capela de São Miguel**.

Each May, at the end of the academic year, the Queima das Fitas takes place, at which students hold a ceremonial burning of their faculty ribbons, a tradition that dates back 700 years.

Another fascinating site is the **Museu Nacional Machado de Castro**, which holds some of Portugal's finest sculpture set among the elegant 16th-century loggias and courtyards the former bishops' palace.

After visiting this area (the "upper town"), head to the "lower town." Largo da Portagem is a useful starting point, and river trips depart from nearby. In the Praça do Comércio, alongside coffee shops and bars, is the restored 12th-century church of **São Tiago**. North of this is **Santa Cruz**, founded in 1131, where Portugal's first two kings are buried.

In the southeast of the city is the **Jardim Botânico**. The gardens, Portugal's largest, were created in 1772 and house 1,200 plant species.

On the opposite bank of the Mondego are the two convents of **Santa Clara**; these have ties with Santa

Isabel, the widow of King Dinis (1279–1325), and Inês de Castro, stabbed to death here in 1355 *(see p367)*. Nearby is a fun place for those with children: the **Portugal dos Pequenitos** theme park.

🎪 **University**
Paço das Escolas. 📞 239-85 98 00. 🕐 *daily.* 🚫 *Dec 25.* 📷 ♿ *Library only.*

🏛 **Museu Nacional Machado de Castro**
Largo Dr. José Rodrigues. 📞 239-82 37 27. 🕐 *Tue–Sun.* 📷

🎡 **Portugal dos Pequenitos**
Santa Clara. 📞 239-80 11 70. 🕐 *daily.* 🚫 *Dec 25.* 📷 ♿

ENVIRONS: **Buçaco** National Forest lies 16 km (10 miles) north of Coimbra. Once the retreat of Carmelite monks, part ancient woodland and part arboretum, it is dotted with chapels and fountains. It also houses the Buçaco Palace Hotel, built in Neo-Manueline style as a royal hunting lodge in 1907. Buçaco was also the site of a crucial battle (1810) in the Peninsular War.

The Roman town of **Conímbriga** lay south of modern Coimbra. Portugal's largest Roman site, it has some opulent villas with fine floor mosaics, and there is an excellent museum.

Student in May celebrations

🏛 **Conímbriga**
2 km (1 mile) S of Condeixa-a-Nova. 🚌 *from Coimbra.* **Site** 🕐 *daily.* 🚫 *Dec 25.* **Museum** 📞 239-94 11 77. 🕐 *Tue–Sun.* 📷 ♿ *museum only.*

The Buçaco Palace Hotel *(see p381)* **in its enchanting woodland setting**

The old city of Oporto with the Ponte de Dom Luís I and the Douro in the foreground

Oporto ⓭

🏙 *300,000.* ✈ *10 km (6 miles) N.*
🚉 🚌 🛈 *Rua Clube dos Fenianos 25
(22-339 34 72); Rua Infante Dom
Henrique 63 (22-200 97 70); Praça
Dom João I 43 (22-205 75 14).*
🎉 *São João do Porto (Jun 23–24).*

EVER SINCE THE ROMANS built a fort here, at the mouth of the Douro, Oporto (Porto in Portuguese) has prospered from commerce. Today it is Portugal's second city and a thriving industrial center.

The commercial center of the city and the Baixa ("lower") district attract fashionable shoppers. Also in the Baixa is the colorful Bolhão market. Most of the tourist sights, however, are to be found in the older riverside quarters.

High above the river, on Penaventosa Hill, stands Oporto's cathedral, or **Sé**, originally a fortress church. A noteworthy 13th-century feature is the rose window, while the upper level of the beautiful 14th-century cloister affords splendid views.

Nearby are the Renaissance church of **Santa Clara**, and **São Bento Station**, completed in 1916, decorated with spectacular *azulejo* panels.

Below the Sé is the hillside **Barredo** quarter, seemingly unchanged since medieval days. This leads down to the riverside quarter, the **Ribeira**, its houses decorated with tiled or pastel-painted façades. The district is being restored, attracting restaurants and clubs.

Sights close to the river include the **Palácio da Bolsa**, the city's stock exchange,

built in 1842. Its highlight is the Arabian Room decorated in the style of the Alhambra. Close by is the 14th-century **São Francisco** church. Its interior is richly covered in carved and gilded wood.

In the Cordoaria district, west of the Sé, stands the 18th-century **Igreja dos Clérigos**. The church tower, at 75 m (246 ft), offers superb views.

Situated in the lovely Serralves park, the **Fundação de Serralves** is dedicated to contemporary art. It presents temporary exhibitions in the Art Deco Casa de Serralves, and its art collection, from the 1960s to the present, in the Modernist Museu de Arte Contemporânea, designed by Alvaro Siza Vieira.

The oldest of the five bridges spanning the Douro are the Dona Maria Pia rail bridge (1877), designed by Gustave Eiffel, and the two-tiered Ponte de Dom Luís I (1886), by one of Eiffel's assistants.

Across the river is the town of **Vila Nova de Gaia**, the center of port production, housing the lodges *(armazéns)* of over 50 companies. Many offer guided tours, which usually end with tastings.

🏛 **Fundação Serralves**
Rua Dom João de Castro 210. 📞 *80-820 05 43.* ⏰ *10am–7pm Tue–Wed Fri–Sun, 10am–10pm Thu.* ⭘ *Jan 1, Dec 25.* 🎟 *(free 10am–2pm Sun).* ♿ ▯ 🛈 ⓦ *www.serralves.pt*

THE STORY OF PORT

Port comes only from a demarcated region of the upper Douro valley. Its "discovery" dates from the 17th century, when British merchants added brandy to Douro wine to stop it turning sour in transit. Over the years, methods of maturing and blending were refined and continue today in the port lodges of Vila Nova de Gaia. Much of the trade is still in British control.

A classic after-dinner drink, port is rich and usually full-bodied. The tawnies are lighter in color than ruby or vintage, but can be more complex. All ports are blended from several wines, selected from scores of samples. White port,

Tiled panel of a *barco rabelo* on the Douro

unlike the other styles, is drunk chilled as an aperitif.

Traditionally the wine was shipped down the Douro from the wine-growing estates *(quintas)* to the port lodges on narrow sailing barges called *barcos rabelos*. Some of these can still be seen moored along the quay at Vila Nova de Gaia.

Southern Portugal

SOUTHERN PORTUGAL ENCOMPASSES the Alentejo and the Algarve, which are separated by ranges of hills. The Alentejo, nearly one-third of Portugal, stretches south from the Tagus. It is typified by vast rolling plains of olive trees, cork oaks, or wheat, as well as whitewashed villages, castles, and a sense of space and tranquility. The Algarve is very different from the rest of Portugal in climate, culture, and scenery. Its stunning coastline and year-round mild weather make it a popular vacation resort.

Renaissance fountain in Évora's main square, Praça do Giraldo

Carved figures of the Apostles on the portal of the Sé, Évora

Évora ❾

🏃 55,000. 🚪 🚌 🚹 Praça do Giraldo (266-73 00 30). 🔵 Sat & 2nd Tue of month. 🎭 Festa de São João (Jun).

RISING DRAMATICALLY out of the Alentejo plain, the enchanting city of Évora is set in Roman, medieval, and 17th-century walls. In 1986, UNESCO declared it a World Heritage Site.

The fortresslike cathedral, the **Sé**, on the Largo do Marquês de Marialva, was begun in 1186. The portal is flanked by a pair of unmatched towers. Inside, a glittering treasury houses sacred art. Beside it stands a 16th-century palace that houses the **Museu de Évora**, which has exhibits on the history of the city from Roman columns to modern sculpture. Opposite the museum is a **Roman temple** – erected in the 2nd or 3rd century AD – believed to have been dedicated to Diana.

Walk from the Sé past the craft shops of Rua 5 de Outubro to reach Praça do Giraldo, the main square, with its Moorish arcades and central fountain (1571). In 1573 the square was the site of an Inquisitional burning.

Just outside the city's Roman walls stands the **University**, founded by the Jesuits in 1559. It was closed in 1759 by the Marquês de Pombal *(see p361)*. The building, with its graceful cloister and notable *azulejos*, forms part of the present-day university and the 18th-century Baroque chapel is used for graduation ceremonies.

Évora has over 20 churches and monasteries, including the 15th-century **São Francisco**. The church's gruesome 17th-century **Capela dos Ossos** was created from the bones of 5,000 monks.

Northwest of the city stands the remaining 5 miles (9 km) of Évora's aqueduct, the **Aqueduto da Água de Prata**, (1531–37), which was damaged in the 17th century, during the Restoration War with Spain.

🏛 **Museu de Évora**
Largo do Conde de Vila Flor. 🕻 266-70 26 04. 🔵 Tue–Sun. 🌑 some public hols. 🖼

🏫 **University**
Largo dos Colegiais. 🕻 266-74 08 00. 🔵 daily. 🌑 public hols. 🖼 Sat pm, Sun.

Faro ❿

🏃 40,000. 🛬 🚉 🚌 🚹 Rua da Misericórdia 8–12 (289-80 36 04). 🔵 daily. 🎭 Dia da Cidade (Sep 7).

FARO HAS BEEN THE CAPITAL of the Algarve since 1756. It was damaged by the 1755 earthquake and, although some parts of the ancient city walls remain, most of the buildings date from the 18th or 19th centuries.

The old city is easy to explore on foot. At its heart is the Largo da Sé, lined with orange trees and flanked by the 18th-century bishops' palace, the **Paço Episcopal**, which is still in use today.

The **Sé** itself is a mixture of Baroque and Renaissance styles and has a fine 18th-century organ. Next to the Sé is the **Museu Arqueológico**, which contains local Roman, medieval, and Manueline archeological finds from the region. On the other side of the Old City wall is the impressive 18th-century church of **São Francisco**.

Orange trees in front of the Bishops' Palace in the old city of Faro

The lively center of modern Faro, along the Rua de Santo António, is stylish and pedestrianized, full of shops, bars, and restaurants.

A little to the north is Faro's parish church, the Baroque and Italianate **São Pedro**. In the nearby Largo do Carmo is the impressive **Igreja do Carmo**. Its magnificent façade and richly decorated interior are in sharp contrast to its somber **Capela dos Ossos** (Chapel of Bones), built in 1816.

At the far northeast corner of the town is the **Cemitério dos Judeus**. The Jewish cemetery served from 1838 until 1932; there is no Jewish community in Faro today.

🏛 **Museu Arqueológico**
Largo Dom Afonso III. ☎ 289-89 74 00. ◻ Mon–Fri. ● public hols. 🎟

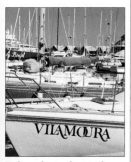

Yachts and power boats at the Vilamoura marina, near Albufeira

Albufeira ⓫

🏚 20,000. 🚉 🚌 🛈 Rua 5 de Outubro (289-58 52 79). 🍇 1st & 3rd Tue of month.

THIS CHARMING FISHING port has become the tourist capital of the Algarve. The Romans built a castle here and under the Arabs the town prospered from trade with North Africa. The oldest part of the town, around Rua da Igreja Velha, retains some original Moorish arches.

ENVIRONS: From **Praia de São Rafael**, 1 mile (2 km) west of Albufeira, to **Praia da Oura** due east, the area is punctuated by small sandy coves set between eroded ocher rocks.

East of Albufeira, **Vilamoura** is set to become Europe's largest leisure complex. It has a large marina with lively cafés, shops, and restaurants.

Portimão ⓬

🏚 40,000. 🚉 🚌 🛈 Avenida Zeca Afonso (282-47 07 17). 🍇 first Mon of month.

THE ROMANS were attracted to Portimão by its natural harbor. It is still a flourishing fishing port and one of the largest towns in the Algarve.

The town center, around the pedestrianized Rua Vasco da Gama, dates mainly from the 18th century, since it was rebuilt after the 1755 earthquake. The 14th-century origins of the church of Nossa Senhora da Conceição are revealed in its portico. The interior contains 17th- and 18th-century *azulejo* panels.

ENVIRONS: Just 3 km (2 miles) south of Portimão is **Praia da Rocha**, a series of fabulous sandy coves. At its east end is the 16th-century castle, Fortaleza de Santa Catarina, with a superb view of the beach and cliffs – and a swathe of high-rise hotels.

Inland from Portimão is the town of **Silves**, once the Moorish capital, Xelb. It has an impressive castle and picturesque groves of orange and lemon trees.

Ocher sandstone rocks sheltering the Praia de Dona Ana beach, Lagos

Lagos ⓭

🏚 20,000. 🚉 🚌 🛈 Sítio de São João (282-76 30 31). 🍇 first Sat of month.

LAGOS IS SET ON ONE of the Algarve's largest bays; it was the region's capital from 1576–1756. The town suffered badly in the 1755 earthquake, so as a result most of the buildings date from the late 18th and 19th centuries.

In the 15th century Lagos became an important naval center, unfortunately also becoming the site of the first slave market in Europe.

Lagos's parish church is the 16th-century **Santa Maria**. The 18th-century **Santo António** is worth a visit for its Baroque *azulejos* and carving. The statue of St. Antony, kept in the church, accompanied the local regiment during the Peninsular War (1807–11).

ENVIRONS: The promontory, **Ponta da Piedade**, shelters the bay of Lagos and should not be missed. **Praia de Dona Ana** beach is 25 minutes' walk from the town center, but **Praia do Camilo** may be less crowded. **Meia Praia**, east of Lagos, stretches for 4 km (2 miles).

If you are tired of beaches, 10 km (6 miles) north is the peaceful **Barragem de Bravura** reservoir. Another popular excursion is southwest to **Sagres** and the rocky headland of **Cabo de São Vicente**.

Practical & Travel Information

THE PORTUGUESE ARE a hospitable people and in Lisbon, Oporto and the Algarve the choice of hotels, restaurants and entertainment is vast, and English is widely spoken. Elsewhere, visitors will usually find help easily available, with locals keen to show off their region.

Travel and communication networks in Portugal have improved greatly in recent years. For national travel there are efficient rail and bus services. Cities have buses and trams, and Lisbon has a metro as well.

TOURIST INFORMATION

THE COUNTRY is divided into tourist regions, separate from its administrative districts. All cities and large towns have a *Posto de Turismo* (tourist office), where you can obtain information about the region, lists of hotels, and details of regional events. Visitors can also consult Portuguese tourist offices abroad.

Most state museums open from 10am to 5pm and are usually closed on Mondays. Many museums and sights also close for lunch for one, or even two hours.

In Lisbon, the convenient Lisboa Card entitles visitors to free public transportation and free or reduced entry to museums. It can be bought at the airport, the city's tourist offices, and some hotels, travel agents, and major sights. It is valid for up to three days.

VISA REQUIREMENTS

THERE ARE CURRENTLY no visa requirements for American, Canadian, Australian, and New Zealand nationals for stays up to 90 days. It is worth checking with the nearest Portuguese

embassy or consulate as this may change. Citizens of the EU need only a valid passport to enter Portugal.

PERSONAL SECURITY

VIOLENT CRIME is rare, but sensible precautions should be taken after dark, especially in Lisbon, Oporto, and the Algarve. To report a crime, contact the nearest police station. Ask for an interpreter if necessary. Theft of documents, such as a passport, should also be reported to your consulate or embassy. Remember that many travel insurance companies insist on policy holders reporting thefts within 24 hours to substantiate any subsequent claim.

EMERGENCY SERVICES

THE NUMBER TO CALL in an emergency is 112. Ask for either *polícia* (the police), *ambulância* (an ambulance), or *bombeiros* (the fire brigade). For emergency medical treatment you should go to the emergency room (*serviço de urgência*) of the nearest main hospital.

HEALTH ISSUES

FOR NON-EMERGENCY medical treatment, details of how to contact an English-speaking doctor can be found in English-language newspapers, such as the *Algarve Gazette*.

Pharmacies *(farmácias)* can dispense a range of drugs that would require a prescription in many other countries. They open from 9am to 1pm and 3 to 7pm and carry a sign with a green illuminated cross.

No vaccinations are needed for Portugal, although a typhoid shot and polio booster are recommended.

FACILITIES FOR THE DISABLED

THESE ARE LIMITED, although the situation is improving. Wheelchairs and adapted restrooms are available at airports and major stations, and ramps, reserved parking, and elevators are becoming more common. Lisbon has a special taxi service, but you have to book well in advance.

LANGUAGE AND ETIQUETTE

WRITTEN PORTUGUESE looks similar to Spanish, but its pronunciation is very different. The Portuguese do not take kindly to being spoken to in Spanish, so it is useful to learn a few basic phrases before you go. It is polite to address strangers as *senhor* or *senhora* and, when introduced to someone, to shake their hand.

Although dress is generally relaxed, especially in the more tourist-oriented areas, when visiting religious buildings arms and knees should be kept covered.

BANKING AND CURRENCY

THE EURO REPLACED the traditional Portuguese currency, the escudo, on January 1, 2002 *(see p15)*.

Money can be changed at most banks, hotels, and bureaux de change *(câmbio)*. Banks tend to offer a good rate of exchange. Traveler's checks can often be expensive to cash in Portugal

THE CLIMATE OF PORTUGAL

In the south, especially along the sheltered coast of the Algarve, winters are very mild, but July and August can be extremely hot. Between April and October, the north is pleasantly warm, though rain is not unusual. Winters in the north can be very cold, especially in the mountainous inland regions. The best times to visit are spring and fall.

LISBON

	Apr	Jul	Oct	Jan
High (°C/°F)	19/67	28/82	23/73	14/57
Low (°C/°F)	12/53	17/63	14/57	8/46
Sunshine (hrs)	9 hrs	12.5 hrs	7.5 hrs	5 hrs
Rainfall (mm)	47.5 mm	0 mm	65 mm	95 mm

although they are a safe way of carrying money. Most major credit cards can be used to make withdrawals from ATMs.

COMMUNICATIONS

THE POSTAL SERVICE is known as *Correios*. First-class mail *(correio azul)* and overseas letters are posted in blue mailboxes; second-class mail *(normal)* is posted in red mailboxes. Public payphones take either coins or cards (including credit cards). You can also make calls from post offices.

FLYING TO PORTUGAL

THE ONLY DIRECT flight from New York (Newark) to Lisbon is operated by **TAP Air Portugal**. Once in Lisbon, passengers can change for Faro or Oporto. Internal flights are operated by **Portugália** and **SATA**.

Many airlines operate flights from the US to European hubs, such as London, Paris, or Madrid, where passengers can change for Lisbon.

There are no direct flights to Portugal from Australia or New Zealand; visitors from these countries should fly via London or Madrid. Regular flights go from many European cities direct to Lisbon, Faro, and Oporto in Portugal.

RAIL TRAVEL

DIRECT TRAINS to Portugal go from Paris and Madrid. Once in Portugal, you can reach many places by rail, but services vary enormously. The high-speed Alfa service from Lisbon to Oporto via Coimbra is good, but local trains can be slow and infrequent. Fares are cheap compared to other parts of Europe and tourist tickets, valid for 7, 14, or 21 days, are available. It is always best to book in advance.

Lisbon can be confusing for visitors as there are five main stations. **Santa Apolónia** and **Oriente** (on the same line) serve international routes and the north; for the Algarve and the Alentejo, you must take a ferry to Barreiro on the south bank of the Tagus. Trains from Rossio go to Sintra and a few destinations on the coast; trains from Cais do Sodré serve Estoril and Cascais.

LONG-DISTANCE BUSES

SOME LONG-DISTANCE bus services – Lisbon to Évora for example – are quicker and more comfortable than going by train. There are no central bus stations because companies are private and operate separately, but tourist offices and travel agencies have information on routes.

TRAVELING BY CAR

PORTUGAL'S HIGHWAY network is expanding, but many older roads are in need of repair and minor roads can be treacherous. Driving can be a hair-raising experience – the country has one of the highest accident rates in Europe and traffic jams are a problem in and near cities. Beware of reckless drivers and do not drive in the rush hour if you can possibly avoid it.

If renting a car, check its condition and insurance very carefully. Always carry your passport, car insurance, license, and rental contract with you (or you may incur a fine).

Traffic drives on the right hand side and Continental European regulations apply. Seat belts must be worn. Speed limits are 60 kph (37 mph) in towns, 90 kph (55 mph) on other roads, and 120 kph (74 mph) on highways. Tolls are payable on highways and some bridges. Do not use the *Via Verde* (green lane) at tolls; this is for the use of drivers who have paid automatically. If you are involved in a car accident on a highway or a main road, use one of the orange SOS telephones to call for help.

Gas stations can be scarce in remote areas, so always fill up your car before leaving a town.

DIRECTORY

TOURIST OFFICES

Lisbon
Lisboa Welcome Center,
Rue do Arsenal 15.
(21-031 27 00.

Oporto
Rua Clube dos Fenianos 25.
(22-339 34 72.
w www.portoturismo.pt

UK
22–25a Sackville Street,
London W1.
(0906-364 0610.

US
590 Fifth Ave, 3rd floor,
New York, NY 10036.
(212-354 4403.
w www.portugal.org

EMBASSIES

Australia
Av. de Liberdade 196–200,
2° (Edifício Victoria),
1269-121 Lisbon.
(21-310 15 00.

Canada
Av. de Liberdade 196–200,
3° (Edifício Victoria),
1269-121 Lisbon.
(21-316 46 00.

Ireland
Rua da Imprensa à Estrela 1,
4°, 1250-684 Lisbon.
(21-392 94 40.

UK
Rua de São Bernardo 33,
1249-082 Lisbon.
(21-392 40 00.

US
Avenida das Forças
Armadas, 1600-081 Lisbon.
(21-727 33 00.

EMERGENCIES

**Ambulance, Police,
and Fire services**
(112.

AIRLINES

Portugália
(21-842 55 00.

SATA
(21-843 77 00.

TAP Air Portugal
(70-720 57 00 (Portugal).
(020-8762 7376 (UK).
(808-205 700 (US).
w www.tap-airportugal.us

TRAIN INFORMATION

(80-820 82 08.

CAR RENTAL

Auto Jardim, Faro
(289-81 84 91.

Budget, Oporto
(22-607 69 70.
w www.budgetrentacar.com

Sixt, Lisbon
(21-354 21 33.
w www.e-sixt.com

Europcar, Faro
(289-82 37 78.

Hertz, Lisbon
(21-381 24 30.
w www.hertz.com

Shopping & Entertainment

Traditional arts and crafts flourish in Portugal. A wide range of interesting pottery can be found in all parts of the country, while in the north embroidery, lace, and gold filigree jewelry from the Minho region make unusual presents. Many visitors come to Portugal for the sporting facilities, principally the golf courses of the Algarve. Water sports, both in the Algarve and on the wilder west coast, are another great attraction. Tourists are usually encouraged to sample *fado*, Lisbon's native folk music, and there are also classical cultural events to be enjoyed in the big cities and at annual festivals.

Where to Shop

Although it is not difficult to find shops that seem a little behind the times when compared with other European countries, modern shopping malls are now a common feature of most cities. In Lisbon, the **Amoreiras** shopping center led the way, with 370 shops, underground parking, cinemas, and restaurants. **Cascaishopping**, between Sintra and Estoril, is similar in style. Opening times for shopping centers are usually from 10am until 11pm daily (including Sunday). Ordinary stores open at 9 or 10am and close at 7pm, though smaller stores and those in quieter areas usually close for lunch between 1 and 3pm.

Reclaiming Tax

Value added tax (IVA) can be reclaimed by non-EU residents who stay for less than 180 days. Ask for an *Isenção de IVA* form or invoice in triplicate, describing the goods, quantity, value, and buyer's identity (best done where you see the "Tax Free for Tourists" signs). Present the forms at customs on departure.

What to Buy

Portugal is not expensive when compared with the rest of Europe, and prices are very reasonable for traditional crafts, especially away from the big cities and tourist centers. The Portuguese are well known for their delicate embroidery and fine lace. Some of the finest examples come from towns in the Minho such as Viana do Castelo, also famous for its brightly printed shawls. Embroidered bedspreads are made in Castelo Branco in the Beira Baixa, and colorful carpets are sold in the Alentejo.

Filigree jewelry *(filigrana)* from the Minho is typically worn at local festivals. Gold and silver threads are worked into intricate brooches, earrings, and pendants.

Woven baskets, produced throughout the country, make delightful souvenirs. Cork from the Alentejo is used to make articles such as mats and ice buckets.

Ceramics

In most cities you can buy as well as commission ceramic tiles and panels. Portugal has a long-standing tradition in ceramics, both for decorative purposes and for home use. Styles range from elegant Vista Alegre porcelain to simple glazed brown earthenware, plain or painted with simple patterns. Antique *azulejos* are highly sought after and very expensive, but you can buy reproductions of well-known historic designs at places such as Lisbon's Museu Nacional do Azulejo *(see p358)*.

Markets

A social and commercial occasion, the street market is integral to Portuguese life. It is usually held in the town's main square. Most markets sell a wide range of goods, from food to household items and clothes, but you will also see sites devoted to antiques, pottery, lace, rugs, clothes, and local crafts. Most markets are held in the morning only, but in tourist areas they may go on until late afternoon.

Food and Drink

Some visitors may want to buy regional produce such as Serra cheese from the Serra da Estrela mountains. However, more are likely to bring back a bottle as a souvenir – most probably of port. It is not especially cheap, but you will never have the opportunity to sample so many styles and vintages as you will on a tour of the port lodges of Vila Nova de Gaia *(see p371)*. Of table wines you might enjoy the young, slightly sparkling *vinho verde* from Dooro in the north, an aged red Dão, or one of the new southern wines from the Alentejo.

Entertainment Listings and Tickets

Tickets for almost all events in Lisbon can be reserved by visiting or phoning the Agência de Bilhetes para Espectáculos **(ABEP)**. Pay in cash when you collect them from the kiosk. Cinemas and theaters will not take phone or credit card reservations.

Previews of forthcoming events and listings of bars and clubs appear in several magazines in Lisbon. English-language publications include the monthly *Follow Me Lisbon* and the quarterly *Lisboa Step by Step*, both available free from tourist offices.

Classical Music, Opera, and Dance

Lisbon's top cultural centers are the **Fundação Calouste Gulbenkian** and the vast **Centro Cultural de Belém**. These host national and international events including ballet, opera, and concerts. The Portuguese national opera house is the **Teatro Nacional de São Carlos**.

Classical music festivals are held in many areas. One of the best is the annual summer festival in Sintra *(see p366)*.

THEATER AND CINEMA

IN LISBON theater-lovers can enjoy performances of Portuguese and foreign-language plays at the **Teatro Nacional Dona Maria II**.

Cult movies and international arthouse films can be seen at the **Cinemateca Portuguesa**, which has a comprehensive monthly film calendar.

In Portugal movies are almost always shown in the original language version with Portuguese subtitles.

FADO

FADO IS AN EXPRESSION of longing and sorrow. Literally meaning "fate," the term may be applied to an individual song as well as the genre itself. The dominant emotion is *saudade* – a longing for what has been lost or has never been attained. It is sung as often by women as men, accompanied by the *guitarra* (a flat-backed instrument shaped like a mandolin, with paired strings) and the *viola* (acoustic Spanish guitar).

The traditional way to enjoy *fado* is with a meal at a *fado* house. It can be an expensive night out, so make sure you like *fado* before you go. The best establishments are run by the *fadistas* themselves, for example the **Parreirinha de Alfama**, which is now run by the legendary performer, Argentina Santos.

OUTDOOR ACTIVITIES

ALTHOUGH A SMALL COUNTRY, Portugal offers a great variety of terrain, with sports and activities to match. Water sports are extremely popular along its 500 miles of coast. The best beach for surfing is the world-famous Guincho, near Cascais *(see p366)*. However, the ocean breakers there are only suitable for experienced surfers. In fact, all along the Atlantic coast conditions can be dangerous for swimming and water sports, hence the appeal of the sheltered bays of the Algarve. These are well-equipped for all kinds of activities. Windsurfing boards and small sailboats can be rented at most resorts and lessons are easily arranged. The marinas at Lagos and the giant vacation complex of Vilamoura are the most important yachting centers.

Many parts of Portugal's rugged interior are excellent for hiking, cycling, and horseback riding.

GOLF AND TENNIS

MOST OF PORTUGAL'S best golf courses are concentrated in the Algarve, which has gained a reputation as one of Europe's prime destinations for golfing vacations. The mild climate ensures that a game can be enjoyed all year round and many courses have been designed by top professionals. Some of the best courses insist that players show a reasonable degree of proficiency, while others welcome golfers of any ability and provide excellent coaching. Serious golfers might consider booking a specialist golf vacation. For information on golfing activities and vacations, contact the **Federação Portuguesa de Golfe** or, in the US, **Golf on Tour**.

Tennis courts are found virtually all over Portugal, especially alongside tourist facilities. Some of the larger Algarve resorts offer tennis coaching vacations. Based in London, **Jonathon Markson Tennis** organizes special vacation packages for tennis enthusiasts.

BULLFIGHTING

PORTUGUESE BULLFIGHTING differs from the Spanish version in many ways. The bull is not killed in the ring and the star of the show is the horseman *(cavaleiro)*. An added attraction is the *pega*, in which a team of men, the *forcados*, attempts to topple the bull and immobilize it with their bare hands.

The traditional center for bullfighting is the Ribatejo, but Lisbon has a splendid Neo-Moorish arena at Campo Pequeno, which is currently closed for renovation.

DIRECTORY

SHOPPING MALLS

Amoreiras
Avenida Eng. Duarte Pacheco.
21-381 02 40.

Cascaishopping
Estrada Nacional 9,
Alcabideche - Estoril.
21-467 90 78.

ENTERTAINMENT TICKETS

ABEP
Praça dos Restauradores,
Lisbon.
21-347 58 24.

CLASSICAL MUSIC, OPERA, & DANCE

Centro Cultural de Belém
Praça do Império, Belém,
Lisbon.
21-361 24 00.

Fundação Calouste Gulbenkian
Avenida de Berna 45,
Lisbon.
21-782 30 00 (tickets).

Teatro Nacional de São Carlos
Rua Serpa Pinto 9,
Lisbon.
21-325 30 00.

THEATER

Cinemateca Portuguesa
Rua Barata Salgueiro 39,
Lisbon.
21-359 62 62.

Teatro Nacional Dona Maria II
Praça Dom Pedro IV, Lisbon.
21-325 08 00.

FADO

Parreirinha de Alfama
Beco do Espírito Santo 1,
Lisbon.
21-886 82 09.

GOLF AND TENNIS

Federação Portuguesa de Golfe
Ave das Túlipas,
Edifício Miraflores, 17º,
1495-161 Algés.
21-412 37 80.

Golf on Tour
300 St. Andrews Trail,
Miamisburg,
OH 45342, US.
513-866 2523.

Jonathon Markson Tennis
Springside House,
84 North End Road,
London W14 9ES, UK.
020-7603 2422.

Where to Stay in Portugal

Hotels in Portugal vary enormously in quality, price, and facilities – from huge resort villages in the Algarve to the simple *pensão*, or guesthouse. In the main tourist areas, Lisbon and the Algarve, there are hotels to suit every budget. Many hotels have great character, especially the *pousadas*, inns run by the state, usually in converted historic buildings.

	Price	NUMBER OF ROOMS	RESTAURANT	GARDEN OR TERRACE	SWIMMING POOL
LISBON					
Avenida: *Lisboa Plaza* W www.heritage.pt Travessa do Salitre 7, 1250-205. **Map** C2. 21-321 82 18. FAX 21-347 16 30. Built in 1953, and situated off Praça da Alegria and Avenida da Liberade, with decor by the Portuguese interior designer, Graça Viterbo.	€€€€	112	●		
Avenida: *Tivoli Jardim* @ htjardim@mail.telepac.pt Rua J. César Machado 7–9, 1250-135. **Map** C2. 21-353 99 71. FAX 21-355 65 66. The stylish rooms are well appointed with spacious bathrooms. Extensive sports facilities include an unusual round pool in the garden.	€€€€	119	●	■	●
Baixa: *Internacional* @ reservas@hotel-internacional.com Rua da Betesga 3, 1100-090. **Map** D3. 21-324 09 90. FAX 21-347 86 35. Centrally located between Praça da Figueira and Rossio, this hotel has modern, spacious rooms, a large TV lounge, and a small bar.	€	52			
Baixa: *Mundial* @ mundial.hot@mail.telepac.pt Rua Dom Duarte 4, 1100-198. **Map** D3. 21-884 20 00. FAX 21-884 21 10. This hotel, located centrally off Praça da Figueira, has plain but comfortable rooms. The restaurant offers marvelous views.	€€	255	●		
Castelo: *Ninho das Águias* Costa do Castelo 74, 1100-199. **Map** E3. 21-885 40 70. The simple "Eagle's Nest" *pensão* sits below the castle walls. A stuffed eagle greets visitors on the terrace, which has amazing views. No breakfast.	€	16		■	
Chiado: *Lisboa Regency Chiado* W www.regency-hotels-resorts.com Rua Nova do Almada 114, 1200-290. **Map** D3. 21-325 61 00. FAX 21-325 61 61. Smallish, smart, and central, the Regency Chiado has a privileged location and fabulous views over the city. Parking can be a problem.	€€€€	40			
Lapa: *York House* @ yorkhouse@mail.telepac.pt Rua das Janelas Verdes 32, 1200-691. **Map** B4. 21-396 24 35. FAX 21-397 27 93. This enchanting *pensão* is housed in a 17th-century convent. Set around a plant-filled patio, the rooms are furnished with elegant antiques.	€€€€	34	●	■	
Marquês Pombal: *Jorge V* W www.hoteljorgev.com Rua Mouzinho da Silveira 3, 1250-165. **Map** C2. 21-356 25 25. FAX 21-315 03 19. This pleasant, comfortable hotel offers good value for the area. Roughly half the rooms have balconies, so request one when checking in.	€€	51			
Marquês Pombal: *Rex* @ sanaclassic.rex@sanahotels.com Rua Castilho 169, 1070-051. **Map** B1. 21-388 21 61. FAX 21-388 75 81. The Rex is located close to the Parque Eduardo VII. The rooftop conference room has good views.	€€€	68	●		
Marquês Pombal: *Ritz Four Seasons* W www.fourseasons.com Rua R. da Fonseca 88, 1099-039. **Map** C2. 21-381 14 00. FAX 21-383 17 83. The legendary Ritz is an elegant, comfortable hotel. Many of the rooms have balconies that overlook the Parque Eduardo VII.	€€€€	283	●	■	
Restauradores: *Avenida Palace* @ hotel.av.palace@mail.telepac.pt Rua 1° de Dezembro 123, 1200-359. **Map** D3. 21-321 81 00. FAX 21-342 28 84. This elegant hotel is conveniently central, with a grand Neoclassical façade and a luxurious interior retaining many original details.	€€€€	82			
REST OF PORTUGAL					
Albufeira: *Alfagar* W www.alfagar.com Semina, Santa Eulália, 8200. 289-54 02 20. FAX 289-54 19 79. On a clifftop overlooking the ocean, this attractive complex offers apartments with direct access to the Santa Eulália beach.	€€€	215	●	■	●

Map references refer to map of Lisbon on pp356–7

<table>
<tr><td colspan="2">

Price categories are for a standard double room per night, inclusive of breakfast and any other unavoidable charges, such as tax:

€ under €70
€€ €70–100
€€€ €100–150
€€€€ over €150

</td><td colspan="2">

RESTAURANT
The hotel has a restaurant open for lunch and dinner, sometimes closed to non-residents.

GARDEN OR TERRACE
Guests have use of garden, courtyard, or terrace.

SWIMMING POOL
The hotel has its own indoor or outdoor pool.

CREDIT CARDS
Major credit cards are accepted in those hotels where the credit card symbol is shown.

</td></tr>
</table>

	NUMBER OF ROOMS	RESTAURANT	GARDEN OR TERRACE	SWIMMING POOL
CASCAIS: *Cidadela* €€ Avenida 25 de Abril, 2750. **[** 21-482 76 00. **FAX** 21-486 72 26. A short walk from the town center, the Cidadela is surrounded by gardens. Most of the rooms have spectacular views of the bay. 🔆 TV ▤ **P** 🗩	113	●	■	●
CASCAIS: *Albatroz* €€€€ Rua Frederico Arouca, 100-102. **[** 21-483 28 21. **FAX** 21-484 73 80. Built as a retreat for the royal family, the Albatroz overlooks the ocean. It offers luxurious surroundings and excellent service. 🔆 TV ▤ **P** ♿ 🗩	46	●	■	●
COIMBRA: *Bragança* € Largo das Ameias 10, 3000-024. **[** 239-82 21 71. **FAX** 239-83 61 35. A slightly old-fashioned but very comfortable hotel located in the heart of Coimbra. The suites have marble bathrooms. 🔆 TV ▤ **P** 🗩	83	●		
COIMBRA: *Quinta das Lágrimas* €€€ Santa Clara, Aptdo. 5053, 3041-901. **[** 239-80 23 80. **FAX** 239-44 16 95. A handsome 18th-century country house. In the garden is the spring known as the "Fountain of Love," where Inês de Castro *(see p367)* was assassinated on the orders of Afonso IV. 🔆 TV ▤ **P** 🗩	39	●	■	●
ÉVORA: *Pousada dos Lóios* W www.pousadas.pt €€€€ Largo Conde Vila Flor, 7000-804. **[** 266-70 40 51. **FAX** 266-70 72 48. Originally a 15th-century monastery, the simple rooms in this elegant *pousada* were converted from the monks' cells and the dining room is in the cloister. Make reservations well in advance. 🔆 TV ▤ **P** 🗩	32	●	■	●
FARO: *Alnacir* @ hotel.alnacir@clix.pt € Estr. Senhora da Saúde 24, 8000-500. **[** 289-80 36 78. **FAX** 289- 80 35 48. A tidy, modern hotel, Alnacir is located on a quiet street close to the center of this busy town. Some rooms have a terrace. 🔆 TV ▤ **P** 🗩	53			
LAGOS: *Hotel Tivoli de Lagos* W www.tivolihotels.com €€€€ Rua C. dos Santos, 8600-678. **[** 282-79 00 79. **FAX** 282-79 03 45. This pleasant complex has five restaurants and a health club. Barbecues are prepared on the beach during the summer. 🔆 TV ▤ **P** ♿ 🗩	324	●	■	●
OPORTO: *Malaposta* € Rua da Conceição 80, 4050-214. **[** 22-200 62 78. **FAX** 22-200 62 95. Tucked away on a quiet side street and centrally located, the attractive and modern Malaposta is a friendly, bargain hotel. 🔆 TV ▤ 🗩	37			
OPORTO: *Pensão Paris* € Rua Fábrica 27, 4050-274. **[** 22-207 31 40. **FAX** 22-207 31 49. An old-world hotel in the Baixa area of the city whose atmosphere, location, and price more than compensate for the fairly basic facilities. 🔆 TV 🗩	38			
OPORTO: *Dom Henrique* W www.hotel-dom-henrique.pt €€€ Rua G. de Azevedo 179, 4049-009. **[** 22-340 16 16. **FAX** 22-340 16 00. Located right in the heart of the city, this hotel has 17 floors – two designated non-smoking – and a bar with a panoramic view. 🔆 TV ▤ 🗩	112	●		
PORTIMÃO: *Bela Vista* W www.hotelbelavista.net €€€ Avenida Tomas Cabreira, 8500. **[** 282-45 04 80. **FAX** 282-41 53 69. An attractive hotel above the popular Praia da Rocha beach, tastefully decorated with relaxing sofas and *azulejo* (painted ceramic tiling) panels. There is a terrace overlooking the sea. 🔆 TV **P** 🗩	14		■	
SINTRA: *Palácio de Seteais* W www.tivolihotels.com €€€€ Avenida B. du Bocage 8, 2710-517. **[** 21-923 32 00. **FAX** 21-923 42 77. Just outside town in a spectacular setting in the Sintra hills, this elegant hotel occupies a delightful 18th-century palace with beautifully decorated interiors and a topiary garden. 🔆 TV **P** 🗩	30	●	■	●

Where to Eat in Portugal

THERE ARE RESTAURANTS in Lisbon and the Algarve that serve standard international cuisine, but the Portuguese like to stick to their culinary traditions, so you will find many dishes using dried cod *(bacalhau)* and unusual combinations such as pork and clams. Marvelous fish dishes are available all along the coast, but vegetarians will find their choices rather limited.

	AIR-CONDITIONING	OPEN LATE	OUTDOOR TABLES	GOOD WINE LIST

LISBON				
AJUDA: *O Nobre* €€€€ Rua das Mercês 71a–b. **C** 21-363 38 27. Worth searching out on a trip to Belém, O Nobre serves crab soup, game stew, partridge, fish with olives, and roast pork with grapes. ● *Sun, lunch Sat.*		■		■
ALFAMA: *Faz Figura* €€€€ Rua do Paraíso 15b. **Map** F3. **C** 21-886 89 81. A chic restaurant with a panoramic view of the river. Specialties include *cataplana* (fish cooked in a covered pan like a wok). ● *Sun, lunch Sat.*	●		●	■
BAIRRO ALTO: *Adega da Tia Matilde* €€€ Rua da Beneficiência 77. **Map** C3. **C** 21-797 21 72. One of the reliable restaurants in Lisbon for good regional cooking. On offer are classic dishes with that home-cooked taste. ● *dinner Sat, Sun.*				
BAIRRO ALTO: *Casanostra* €€€ Travessa do Poço da Cidade 60. **Map** D3. **C** 21-342 59 31. Within the green, white, and black interior of this Italian restaurant you can choose from a six-page menu full of Italian delicacies. ● *Mon, lunch Sat.*	●			
BAIRRO ALTO: *Pap'Açorda* €€€€ Rua da Atalaia 57. **Map** C3. **C** 21-346 48 11. Both Lisboetas and tourists come here for the *açorda de mariscos* (bread and seafood stew). ● *Sun, lunch Mon, 2 weeks in Jul, 2 weeks in Oct.* &	●			■
BELÉM: *Já Sei* €€€€ Avenida Brasilia 202. **C** 21-301 59 69. This has a beautiful location, right on the river, so it is particularly good in the summer; the seafood-based menu is good all year round. ● *Mon, dinner Sun.*	●		●	■
CASTELO: *Restô do Chapitô* €€€ Costa do Castelo 7. **Map** E3. **C** 21-886 73 34. This cheerful restaurant with a bar and fine views of the harbor serves a wide range of international cuisine. ● *Mon.*		■	●	
CHIADO: *Tágide* €€€€€ Largo da Academia Nacional de Belas Artes 18–20. **Map** D4. **C** 21-342 07 20. An elegant restaurant with 18th-century tiles and a superb view over the Tagus. The luxurious dishes include partridge in port sauce. ● *Sun, lunch Sat.*	●			■
LAPA: *Sua Excelência* €€€€ Rua do Conde 34. **Map** A4. **C** 21-390 36 14. The owner here can recite the menu in five languages. Classic Portuguese dishes served in a relaxed atmosphere. ● *Wed, lunch Sat & Sun, Sep.* &	●		●	■
RESTAURADORES: *Lagosta Real* €€€€ Rua das Portas de Santo Antão 37. **Map** C2. **C** 21-342 39 95. Fish, and particularly shellfish, is the order of the day here. Shellfish casserole, lobster stew, and a grilled seafood platter are house specialties.	●	■	●	■
FARTHER AFIELD: *Espiral* €€ Praça da Ilha do Faial 14a. **C** 21-357 35 85. This vegetarian restaurant has a plain interior but a large menu, with fresh juice drinks and organic wine. ● *Jan 1, May 1.*	●			

REST OF PORTUGAL				
ALBUFEIRA: *Marisqueira Santa Eulália* €€€€ Praia de Santa Eulália. **C** 289-54 26 36. Overlooking the beach, this modern restaurant serves typical Portuguese seafood dishes *(mariscos)*, including grilled monkfish, salmon, shrimp in many styles, and clams. ● *Dec–Jan.* &		■	●	

Map references refer to map of Lisbon on pp356–7

Price categories are for a three-course meal for one with half a bottle of wine, including cover charge, service, and tax:

€ under €10
€€ €10–15
€€€ €15–22
€€€€ €22–30
€€€€€ over €30

OPEN LATE
The kitchen stays open after 10pm, and you can usually have a meal up until at least 11pm.

OUTDOOR TABLES
Tables for eating outdoors, in a garden or on a balcony, often with a pleasant view.

GOOD WINE LIST
The restaurant will have a good selection of quality wines.

CREDIT CARDS
Major credit cards are accepted in those restaurants where the credit card symbol is shown.

	Price	AIR-CONDITIONING	OPEN LATE	OUTDOOR TABLES	GOOD WINE LIST
ALCOBAÇA: *Trindade*	€€	●		●	
BATALHA: *Mestre Alfonso Domingues*	€€€€	●		●	■
BUÇACO: *Palace Hotel do Buçaco*	€€€€	●		●	■
CASCAIS: *Dom Manolo*	€€	●		●	
COIMBRA: *O Trovador*	€€	●			
ESTORIL: *Four Seasons*	€€€€€	●			■
ÉVORA: *O Grémio*	€€€€	●			
FARO: *Dois Irmãos*	€€€€		■	●	
OPORTO: *Portucale*	€€€€€	●	■		■
PORTIMÃO: *Vila Lisa*	€€€	●	■		
PORTIMÃO: *A Lanterna*	€€€€		■		■
SINTRA: *Tulhas*	€€€	●			■
TOMAR: *A Bela Vista*	€€			●	

ALCOBAÇA: *Trindade* €€
Praça Dom Afonso Henriques 22. (262-58 23 97.
Located in a beautiful square by the monastery. The specials include *açorda de mariscos* (bread and seafood stew). ● *2 weeks in May, 2 weeks in Oct.*

BATALHA: *Mestre Alfonso Domingues* €€€€
Largo Mestre Alfonso Domingues. (244-76 52 60.
This restaurant, found in the *pousada* named after the architect of the nearby monastery, serves such regional fare as fried pork with turnip tops.

BUÇACO: *Palace Hotel do Buçaco* €€€€
Mata do Buçaco. (231-93 79 70.
The dining room of this famous hotel is decorated in 15th-century style. The sumptuous dishes include roast suckling pig and cod *au gratin* with cream. Buçaco's fine house wines are bottled in the cellar.

CASCAIS: *Dom Manolo* €€
Avenida Marginal 11. (21-483 11 26.
A good-value mixed menu; the house specialty is *frango no churrasco* (spit-roast chicken). The *pastéis de bacalhau* (cod croquettes) are also good. ● *Jan.*

COIMBRA: *O Trovador* €€
Largo da Sé Velha 15–17. (239-82 54 75.
This rustic restaurant, set in the old town, offers excellent regional dishes such as *chanfana* (kid stew in wine sauce). ● *Sun.*

ESTORIL: *Four Seasons* €€€€€
Hotel Palácio Estoril, Rua do Parque. (21-464 80 00.
Exposed beams and leather seats furnish this luxurious restaurant. Try the flambéed shrimp with Pernod, cream, and hollandaise sauce.

ÉVORA: *O Grémio* €€€€
Rua Alcárcova de Cima 10. (266-74 29 31.
A wonderful restaurant built into the city's Roman wall. Try the tasty hare stewed with beans. ● *Wed.*

FARO: *Dois Irmãos* €€€€
Praça Ferreira de Almeida 13–14. (289-82 33 37.
One of the most popular restaurants in Faro, the Dois Irmãos offers fish or meat *cataplana* and a good variety of fresh fish dishes.

OPORTO: *Portucale* €€€€€
Rua da Alegria 598 (13th floor). (22-537 07 17.
This is one of the most famous restaurants in the country. It has a wide array of meat, fish, and game dishes, and spectacular views of the area.

PORTIMÃO: *Vila Lisa* €€€
Rua Francisco Bivar, Mexilhoeira Grande. (282-96 84 78.
Run by artist/chef José Vila, this characterful restaurant usually has a fixed menu with five dishes, dessert, wine, and coffee. ● *lunch; Oct–Jun: Sun–Thu.*

PORTIMÃO: *A Lanterna* €€€€
Rua Foz do Arade. (282-41 44 29.
An interesting menu of Portuguese dishes includes local clams, a selection of fish, and grilled duck with honey ● *Sun, Nov–Dec.*

SINTRA: *Tulhas* €€€
Rua Gil Vicente 4–6. (21-923 23 78.
This rustic restaurant, decorated with blue and yellow Sintra *azulejos*, serves superb traditional dishes such as veal steaks in Madeira sauce. ● *Wed.*

TOMAR: *A Bela Vista* €€
Fonte do Choupo 3–6. (249-31 28 70.
A Bela Vista offers beautiful views of the river and castle, and excellent regional specialties such as roast kid and *caldeirada* (fish stew). ● *dinner Mon, Tue; Nov.*

For key to symbols see back flap

ITALY AND GREECE

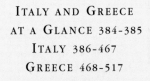

ΙΕΡΩΝΥΜΟΣ ΝΜ 53

Italy and Greece at a Glance

THE APPEAL OF ITALY AND GREECE is both cultural and hedonistic. As the cradles of Europe's two great Classical civilizations, both countries are famous for their ancient temples and monuments, concentrated principally in the cities of Rome and Athens. Located in the southern half of Europe, Italy and Greece share a sunny Mediterranean climate and a correspondingly laid-back way of life. Away from the main cultural sights, the peaceful countryside, beautiful beaches, and warm seas guarantee a relaxed vacation.

Milan

Verona

Venice

Turin

Genoa

Bologna

Florence

Siena

ROME

ITALY
(See pp386–4

Naples

Sardinia

Cagliari

Reggio di Cala

Palermo

Sicily

Venice (see pp432–41) *is a city quite unlike any other: a fabulous treasure house of art and architecture, built on a series of islands, where there are no cars and the streets are canals.*

Florence (see pp412–25) *embodies the Renaisssance of art and learning in the 15th century. Familiar masterpieces of the period, such as this copy of Michelangelo's David, adorn the streets.*

Rome (see pp392–405) *owes its grandest monuments to the era of papal rule. The vast colonnaded square in front of St. Peter's and the Vatican was created by Bernini in the 17th century.*

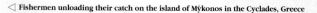

◁ Fishermen unloading their catch on the island of Mýkonos in the Cyclades, Greece

LOCATOR MAP

The Peloponnese (see pp490–93), *a large peninsula, connected to the rest of the Greek mainland by the Corinth isthmus, abounds in ancient and medieval ruins. The heavily fortified sea port of Monemvasía, in the southeastern corner, has many well-preserved Byzantine and Venetian buildings.*

Athens *(see pp474–81) is renowned for its unrivaled collection of Classical antiquities. The world-famous Acropolis is dominated by the 2,500-year-old Parthenon, built as an expression of the glory of ancient Greece.*

● Brindisi

● Thessaloníki

● Neápoli

Corfu

● Metéora

GREECE
(See pp468–517)

Ancient Olympia ●

● Náfplio

🏛 ATHENS

● Monemvasía

Rhodes Town ●

Rhodes

0 km	100
0 miles	100

● Irákleio

Crete

Crete *(see pp500–501), the largest and most southerly of the Greek islands, boasts clear blue seas and fine sandy beaches. Inland there are ancient Minoan palaces and dramatic mountainous landscapes.*

ITALY

ITALY HAS DRAWN PEOPLE *in search of culture and romance for centuries. Few countries can compete with its Classical origins, its art, architecture, musical, and literary traditions, its scenery, or its food and wine. Since World War II Italy has climbed into the top ten world economies, yet at its heart it retains many of the customs, traditions, and regional allegiances of its agricultural heritage.*

Italy has no single cultural identity. Between the snowy peaks of the Alps and the rugged shores of Sicily lies a whole series of regions, each with its own distinctive dialect, architecture, and cuisine. There is also a larger regional division. People speak of two Italies: the rich industrial north and the poorer agricultural south, known as *Il Mezzogiorno* (Land of the Midday Sun).

The north is directly responsible for Italy's place among the world's top industrial nations, a success achieved by names such as Fiat, Pirelli, Olivetti, Zanussi, Alessi, and Armani. The south, in contrast, has high unemployment, many areas in the grip of organized crime, and regions that rank among the most depressed in Europe.

History and geography have both contributed to the division. The north is closer both in location and spirit to Germany and France while the south has suffered a succession of invasions from foreign powers: Carthaginians and Greeks in ancient times, Saracens and Normans in the Middle Ages and until the middle of the last century, the Bourbons from Spain held sway.

HISTORY

Italy is a young country: it did not exist as a unified nation state until 1861. The idea of Italy as a geographic entity goes back to the time of the Etruscans, but prior to the 19th century, the only time the peninsula was united was under the Romans, who by the 2nd century BC had subdued the other Italian tribes and the Greek colonies around the coast. Rome became the capital of a huge empire, introducing its language, laws, and calendar to most of Europe before falling to Germanic invaders in the 5th century AD.

A timeless view and way of life: peaceful old age amid the hills of Tuscany

◁ **Piazza Navona, a Baroque fantasy created in papal Rome in the 17th century**

The ostentatious Victor Emmanuel Monument in Rome, built to commemorate the completion of the unification of Italy in 1870

Another important legacy of the Roman Empire was Christianity, with the pope as head of the Catholic church throughout western Europe. The medieval papacy summoned the Franks to drive out the Lombards from Italy and, in AD 800, crowned the Frankish king Charlemagne Holy Roman Emperor. Unfortunately, for five centuries popes and emperors fought to decide which of them should be in charge of their nebulous empire.

KEY DATES IN ITALIAN HISTORY

c.800 BC First Greek colonists reach Italy

c.700 BC Rise of the Etruscans

509 BC Foundation of Roman Republic after expulsion of Etruscan kings from Rome

202 BC Victory over Carthaginians makes Rome dominant power in the Mediterranean

27 BC Augustus establishes Roman Empire

AD 476 Collapse of Western Roman Empire

564 Lombards invade northern Italy

878 Saracens gain control of Sicily

1061 Start of Norman conquest of Sicily

11th–13th century Constant struggles between rival supporters of popes and emperors

1321 Dante writes *The Divine Comedy*

15th century Medici rule Florence; Renaissance

1527 Sack of Rome by Emperor's troops puts end to political ambitions of the papacy

1713 Much of the north passes to Austria

1735 Bourbon dynasty become rulers of Naples and Sicily (Kingdom of the Two Sicilies)

1860 Garibaldi and the Thousand capture Kingdom of the Two Sicilies

1861 Unification of most of Italy under House of Savoy, rulers of Piedmont and Sardinia

1870 Capture of Rome, which becomes capital of modern Italy

1922 Fascists come to power under Mussolini

1946 Foundation of modern Italian republic

Meanwhile, a succession of foreign invaders – Normans, Angevins, and Aragonese – conquered Sicily and the south. The north, in contrast, saw a growth of independent city states, the most powerful being Venice, fabulously wealthy from trade with the East. Northern Italy became the most prosperous and cultured region in western Europe and it was the artists and scholars of 15th-century Florence who inspired the Renaissance. Small, fragmented states, however, could not compete with great powers. In the 16th century Italy's petty kingdoms fell prey to a foreign invader, this time to Spain. The north subsequently came under the control of Austria, while the papacy ruled a small region in the center.

One small kingdom that remained independent was Piedmont and in the 19th century it was Piedmont that became the focus for a movement towards a united Italy, a goal that was achieved in 1870, thanks largely to the heroic military exploits of Garibaldi. In the 1920s, the Fascists seized power and, in 1946, the monarchy was abandoned for today's republic.

Governments in the postwar era have consistently been short-lived coalitions, dominated by the Christian Democrats. In 1993, however, Italy experienced a political crisis which blew its party system apart. Investigations in Milan in 1992 revealed an organized network of corruption which exposed a huge number of politicians and businessmen.

TRADITION AND PROGRESS

Variations between Italy's regions have much to do with the mountainous landscape and inaccessible valleys. Throughout the country, ancient techniques of husbandry endure and many livelihoods are linked to the land and the seasons. Main crops include wheat, olives, and grapes. Although some of the north's postwar economic prosperity can be attributed to industry (especially car production in Turin), much of it has grown from the expansion of family-owned artisan businesses exporting handmade goods abroad. The clothes chain, Benetton, is a typical example of Italian design flair capturing a large slice of the global market.

LANGUAGE AND CULTURE

A tradition of literary Italian was established back in the 14th century by the poets Dante and Petrarch, who wrote in a cultured Florentine dialect. Yet, even today, with national television and radio stations, Italy's regional dialects show an astonishing resilience and northerners have great difficulty understanding a Neapolitan or Sicilian.

The arts in Italy have enjoyed a long and glorious history and Italians are very proud of this. Given the fact that Italy has some 100,000 monuments of major historical significance, it is not surprising that there is a shortage of funds to keep them in good repair. However, with tourism accounting for 3 percent of Italy's GDP, efforts are being made to put as many great buildings and art collections on show as possible.

Alessi kettle, an icon of modern Italian design

The performing arts are also underfunded, yet there are spectacular cultural festivals. In the land of Verdi and Rossini, opera is naturally well supported, with almost every town of any size having its own opera house. Cinema is another art form that flourishes, keeping alive the tradition of great directors of the second half of the 20th century, such as Federico Fellini, Vittorio de Sica, and Luchino Visconti.

The Italian football team, losing finalists at the European Championships of 2000

Children on their way to take First Communion in the Basilica di Monte Berico in Vicenza

MODERN LIFE

The number of practising Catholics in Italy has been in decline for years. In spite of this, Italian society is still highly traditional, and Italians can be very formal. Italian chic decrees that whatever clothes you wear should give the impression of wealth. If people wear similar outfits, it is because Italians are conformists in fashion as in many other aspects of daily life.

The emphasis on conformity and a commitment to the family remain key factors in Italian society despite the country's low, and falling, birth rate. Grandparents, children and grandchildren still live in family units, although this is becoming less common. All children are pampered but the most cherished ones are, usually, male. Attitudes to women in the workplace have changed, particularly in the cities. However, the idea that men should help with housework is still a fairly foreign notion to the older generation.

Food and football are the great constants; Italians live for both. Much time is spent on preparing food and eating. The Italian diet, particularly in the south, is among the healthiest in the world. Football is a national passion and inspires massive public interest and media attention, not least as a way of expressing regional loyalties.

Despite the recession of the early 1990s and the political upheaval that followed the country's many corruption scandals, Italy appears little changed to foreign visitors, maintaining its regional identities and traditional values.

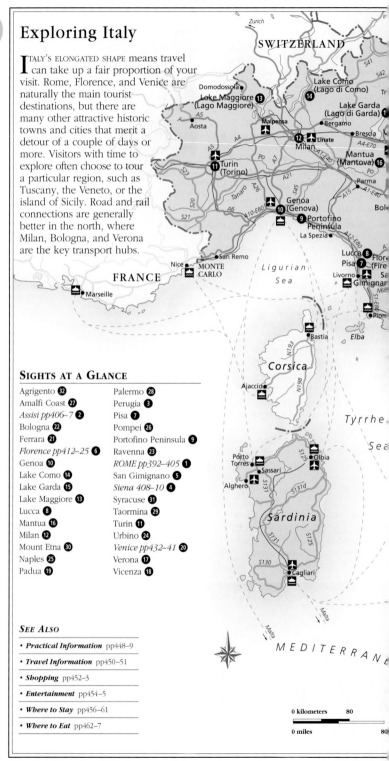

Exploring Italy

ITALY'S ELONGATED SHAPE means travel
can take up a fair proportion of your
visit. Rome, Florence, and Venice are
naturally the main tourist
destinations, but there are
many other attractive historic
towns and cities that merit a
detour of a couple of days or
more. Visitors with time to
explore often choose to tour
a particular region, such as
Tuscany, the Veneto, or the
island of Sicily. Road and rail
connections are generally
better in the north, where
Milan, Bologna, and Verona
are the key transport hubs.

SIGHTS AT A GLANCE

Agrigento ㉜
Amalfi Coast ㉗
Assisi pp406–7 ❷
Bologna ㉒
Ferrara ㉑
Florence pp412–25 ❻
Genoa ❿
Lake Como ⓮
Lake Garda ⓯
Lake Maggiore ⓭
Lucca ❽
Mantua ⓰
Milan ⓬
Mount Etna ㉚
Naples ㉕
Padua ⓳

Palermo ㉘
Perugia ❸
Pisa ❼
Pompei ㉖
Portofino Peninsula ❾
Ravenna ㉓
ROME pp392–405 ❶
San Gimignano ❺
Siena 408–10 ❹
Syracuse ㉛
Taormina ㉙
Turin ⓫
Urbino ㉔
Venice pp432–41 ⓴
Verona ⓱
Vicenza ⓲

SEE ALSO

0 kilometers   80

0 miles   80

Salzburg

AUSTRIA

Cortina d'Ampezzo

A23

SLOVENIA

Udine

S13

Ljubljana

Zagreb

Treviso

Trieste

Rijeka

20 Venice
dua (Venezia)
adova)

23 Ravenna

SAN
RINO Rimini

Pesaro

Urbino 24 Ancona

Gubbio S76

2 Perugia
3 Assisi

Todi

Ascoli
Piceno

Orvieto

Viterbo

Pescara

L'Aquila

tavecchia 1

Sulmona

ROME (Roma)

Anzio

S148

S 213

Naples
(Napoli)

Isola d'Ischia

Isola di Capri

Benevento

Pompei

25

26

27 Amalfi

Amalfi
Coast

Agri

Foggia

Bari

Taranto

Brindisi

Lecce

DISTANCE CHART

ROME								
383 238	*BOLOGNA*							
562 349	**783** 487	*BRINDISI*						
278 173	**106** 66	**832** 517	*FLORENCE*					
510 317	**291** 181	**1064** 661	**225** 140	*GENOA*				
575 357	**210** 130	**990** 615	**299** 186	**145** 90	*MILAN*			
219 136	**594** 369	**354** 220	**489** 304	**714** 444	**786** 488	*NAPLES*		
673 418	**332** 206	**1111** 691	**395** 245	**170** 106	**138** 86	**884** 549	*TURIN*	
530 329	**154** 96	**928** 577	**255** 158	**397** 247	**273** 170	**741** 460	**402** 250	*VENICE*

Distance in kilometers
Distance in miles

CROATIA

Split

**BOSNIA
AND
HERZEGOVINA**

Dubrovnik

Isole
Tremiti

A
D
R
I
A
T
I
C

S
E
A

Greece
Turkey
Egypt

Greece

Cosenza

Catanzaro

Ionian

Sea

Isole Eolie o Lipari

ole
adi

Trapani

Palermo

28

A29-E90 A19-E90

Agrigento 32

Sicily A19-E93

Messina

Reggio di
Calabria

A18-E45

Mount Etna 30 Taormina

29

Catania

Syracuse
(Siracusa)

31

S115-E45

*Isola di
Pantelleria*

Malta

KEY

✈	Airport
⚓	Ferry port
	Highway
	Major road
	Railroad
- - -	International border

Rome ❶

FROM ITS EARLY DAYS as a settlement of shepherds
on the Palatine hill, Rome grew to rule a vast
empire stretching beyond western Europe. Later,
after the fall of the Roman empire, Rome became the
center of the Christian world. The legacy of this
history can be seen all over the city. The Pope, head
of the Roman Catholic Church, still resides in the
Vatican City, an independent enclave at the heart of
Rome. In 1870 Rome became the capital of a newly
unified Italy, and now has over 2.6 million inhabitants.
In summer, many of the grand Baroque piazzas and
narrow medieval streets are crammed
with attractive sidewalk
bars and restaurants.

**View of the Roman Forum with
the Colosseum rising behind**

SIGHTS AT A GLANCE

GETTING AROUND

Rome has a subway system
known as *la metropolitana*
(metro for short). Line A crosses
the city from northwest to southeast, Line B from southwest to
northeast. The two lines meet
at Stazione Termini, the city's
central station, which is also the
starting point for many bus routes.
These cover most parts of the city.
Official taxis are white in color.
Driving is not advisable in Rome –
walking is the easiest way to
negotiate the city's narrow streets.

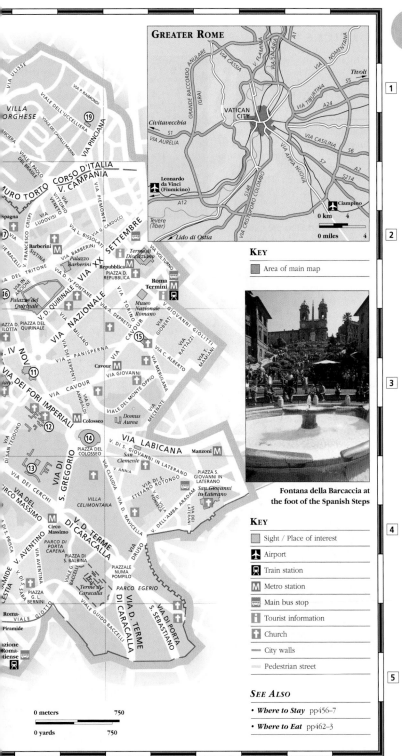

GREATER ROME

19

VILLA BORGHESE

Tivoli

VATICAN CITY

Civitavecchia

Leonardo da Vinci (Fiumicino)

Ciampino

Tevere (Tiber)

Lido di Ostia

0 km 4

0 miles 4

1

2

KEY

Area of main map

Fontana della Barcaccia at the foot of the Spanish Steps

3

KEY

| Sight / Place of interest |
| Airport |
| Train station |
| M Metro station |
| Main bus stop |
| Tourist information |
| Church |
| — City walls |
| Pedestrian street |

4

SEE ALSO

5

0 meters 750

0 yards 750

D E F

St. Peter's ①

CATHOLICISM'S most sacred shrine, the vast, marble-encrusted basilica draws pilgrims and tourists from all over the world. A shrine was erected on the site of St. Peter's tomb in the 2nd century and the first basilica, commissioned by Constantine, was completed around AD 349. By the 15th century it was falling down and in 1506 Pope Julius II laid the first stone of a new church. The present basilica, 187 m (615 ft) long, took more than a century to build and all the great architects of the Roman Renaissance and Baroque had a hand in its design. The dominant tone of the interior is set by Bernini, creator of the *baldacchino* below Michelangelo's magnificent dome.

★ Dome
The 137-m (448-ft) dome, designed by Michelangelo, was not completed until 1590, long after his death.

The apse is dominated by Bernini's spectacular bronze Throne of St. Peter in Glory.

Baldacchino
Commissioned by Urban VIII in 1624, Bernini's extravagant Baroque canopy stands above the Papal Altar, a plain slab of marble, at which only the pope may say mass. The altar is sited directly above the tomb of St. Peter in the Grottoes below.

Monument to Pope Alexander VII
Bernini's last work in St. Peter's was finished in 1678 and shows the pope surrounded by the allegorical figures of Truth, Justice, Charity, and Prudence.

The Treasury is reached through a door at the end of the left aisle. It houses ecclesiastical treasures, including reliquaries, tombs, and vestments.

STAR FEATURES

★ **Statue of St. Peter**

★ **Michelangelo's Pietà**

★ **Dome**

The Grottoes
A fragment of this 13th-century mosaic by Giotto, salvaged from the old basilica, is now in the Grottoes, where many popes are buried.

★ Statue of St. Peter
This 13th-century bronze is thought to be by Arnolfo di Cambio. The foot of the statue has worn thin from the kisses of millions of pilgrims over the centuries.

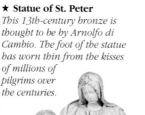

★ Michelangelo's Pietà
Protected by glass since an attack in 1972, the Pietà stands in the first side chapel on the right. It was created in 1499 when Michelangelo was only 25.

Two minor cupolas by Vignola (1507–73)

The façade (1614) is by Carlo Maderno, who lengthened the basilica to create its Latin-cross floorplan.

From this window, the pope blesses the faithful gathered in the piazza below.

Filarete Door
This bronze door, decorated with reliefs by Filarete (1439–45), was one of the doors of the old St. Peter's.

Entrance for stairs to dome

The nave floor has markings that show the lengths of other churches compared with St. Peter's.

Main entrance

Piazza San Pietro
The piazza in front of St. Peter's is enclosed by a vast pincer-shaped colonnade by Bernini. It is topped by statues of saints.

Vatican Museums ②

Four CENTURIES of papal patronage
and connoisseurship have resulted
in one of the world's great collections
of Classical and Renaissance art. The
Vatican houses many of the great
archaeological finds of central Italy,
including the *Laocoön* group and the
Apollo del Belvedere. The museums
are housed in palaces originally built
for wealthy Renaissance popes such as
Innocent VIII, Sixtus IV, and Julius II.
Parts of these were decorated with
wonderful frescoes by the finest
painters of the age – most notably the
Borgia Apartment, the Raphael Rooms
and the Sistine Chapel *(see p398)*.

**Gallery of the
Candelabra**
*Once an open
loggia, this gallery
of Greek and
Roman sculpture
has a fine view
of the Vatican
Gardens.*

**Room of the
Biga (a two-
horse chariot)**

**Gallery of
Tapestries**

Gallery of Maps
*The gallery is an important
record of 16th-century
cartography and history.
This painting shows
the Turkish siege of
Malta in 1565.*

**Etruscan
Museum**

The Raphael Loggia
contains Raphael
frescoes, but special
permission is needed
to visit it.

**Upper
floor**

**Sistine
Chapel**

**The Cortile
del Belvedere**
was laid out by
Bramante in 1503.

Raphael Rooms
This detail from the Expulsion
of Heliodorus from the Temple
*contains a portrait of Julius II.
It is one of a series of frescoes
painted by Raphael for the pope's
private apartments (see p398).*

The Borgia Apartment,
frescoed by Pinturicchio
in a highly decorative
style in the 1490s, also
houses a collection of
modern religious art.

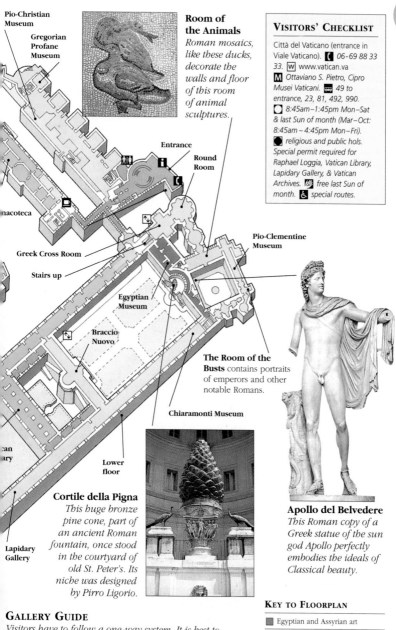

Pio-Christian Museum

Gregorian Profane Museum

Room of the Animals
Roman mosaics, like these ducks, decorate the walls and floor of this room of animal sculptures.

Entrance

Round Room

nacoteca

Greek Cross Room

Stairs up

Egyptian Museum

Braccio Nuovo

Pio-Clementine Museum

The Room of the Busts contains portraits of emperors and other notable Romans.

Chiaramonti Museum

can ary

Lower floor

Cortile della Pigna
This huge bronze pine cone, part of an ancient Roman fountain, once stood in the courtyard of old St. Peter's. Its niche was designed by Pirro Ligorio.

Lapidary Gallery

Apollo del Belvedere
This Roman copy of a Greek statue of the sun god Apollo perfectly embodies the ideals of Classical beauty.

VISITORS' CHECKLIST

Città del Vaticano (entrance in Viale Vaticano). 06-69 88 33 33. www.vatican.va Ottaviano S. Pietro, Cipro Musei Vaticani. 49 to entrance, 23, 81, 492, 990. 8:45am–1:45pm Mon–Sat & last Sun of month (Mar–Oct: 8:45am–4:45pm Mon–Fri). religious and public hols. Special permit required for Raphael Loggia, Vatican Library, Lapidary Gallery, & Vatican Archives. free last Sun of month. special routes.

GALLERY GUIDE

Visitors have to follow a one-way system. It is best to concentrate on a single collection or to choose one of the suggested itineraries. These are color-coded so that you can follow them throughout the museums. They vary in length from 90 minutes to five hours. If you are planning a long visit, make sure you allow plenty of time for resting. Conserve your stamina for the Sistine Chapel and the Raphael Rooms; they are 20–30 minutes' walk from the entrance, without allowing for any viewing time along the way.

KEY TO FLOORPLAN

	Egyptian and Assyrian art
	Greek and Roman art
	Etruscan and Italic art
	Early Christian and medieval art
	15th- to 19th-century art
	Modern religious art
	Non-exhibition space
	Open by special permit only

Exploring the Vatican's Collections

THE VATICAN'S GREATEST TREASURES are its Greek and Roman antiquities, which have been on display since the 18th century. The 19th century saw the addition of exciting discoveries from Etruscan tombs and excavations in Egypt. Then there are works by many of Italy's greatest Renaissance artists housed in the Pinacoteca (art gallery) and decorating the walls of chapels and papal apartments.

The *Laocoön*, a Roman copy of a Greek original, excavated in Rome in 1506

ANCIENT ART

THE EGYPTIAN COLLECTION contains finds from 19th- and 20th-century excavations, as well as items brought to Rome in Imperial times. There are also Roman imitations of Egyptian art. Genuine Egyptian works include the tomb of Iri, guardian of the Pyramid of Cheops (22nd century BC).

Prize Greek and Roman art in the Pio-Clementine Museum includes Roman copies of the 4th-century BC Greek statues *Apoxyomenos* and the *Apollo del Belvedere*, and a splendid *Laocoön* from the 1st century AD.

The Chiaramonti Museum is lined with ancient busts, and its extension, the Braccio Nuovo, has a 1st-century BC statue of Emperor Augustus.

The Etruscan Museum houses a superb collection, including the bronze throne, bed, and funeral cart, found in the 650 BC Regolini-Galassi tomb in Cerveteri.

In the Vatican Library is the *Aldobrandini Wedding*, a beautiful Roman fresco from the 1st century AD.

CHRISTIAN ART

THE PIO-CHRISTIAN Museum has Early Christian art, such as inscriptions and sculpture from catacombs and basilicas. The first two rooms of the Pinacoteca house medieval art, including Giotto's *Stefaneschi Triptych* (c.1300), which decorated the main altar of the old St. Peter's. Other rooms in the Pinacoteca contain Renaissance works. 15th-century highlights are a *Pietà* by Giovanni Bellini and Leonardo da Vinci's unfinished *St. Jerome*. Exceptional 16th-century pieces include an altarpiece by Titian, a *Deposition* by Caravaggio, *St. Helen* by Paolo Veronese, and a whole room devoted to Raphael.

THE SISTINE CHAPEL

THE SISTINE CHAPEL takes its name from Pope Sixtus IV: it was built in 1473 at his request. The walls were frescoed by some of the finest artists of the age, including Signorelli, Botticelli, Roselli, Ghirlandaio, and Perugino (who is credited with having overseen the project). There are 12 frescoes on the side walls, painted between 1481 and 1483. Their subjects are parallel episodes in the lives of Moses and Christ.

In 1508–12, at the request of Pope Julius II, Michelangelo created what has become his most famous work, the chapel ceiling. The main panels chart the *Creation of the World* and *Fall of Man.* They are surrounded by subjects from the Old and New Testaments.

In 1534–41 Michelangelo completed the chapel walls, painting *The Last Judgment* on the altar wall. It depicts the souls of the dead rising up to face the wrath of God and the damned being hurled down to hell. The artist's own tormented attitude to his faith is seen in his self-portrait, painted on the skin held by the martyr, St. Bartholomew.

RAPHAEL ROOMS

POPE JULIUS II chose Raphael (1483–1520) to redecorate four rooms *(stanze)* of his apartments. The frescoes in the Room of the Segnatura (1508–11) include the famous *School of Athens*, which centers on a debate between Plato and Aristotle. Raphael depicted Leonardo da Vinci and Michelangelo as philosophers. The decoration of the Room of Heliodorus (1512–4) incorporates a famous portrait of Julius II, whereas the Room of the Fire in the Borgo (1514–7) was painted during the reign of Pope Leo X, Julius II's successor. All the frescoes here exalt the new pope or his earlier namesakes.

The Hall of Constantine (1517–25) was largely the work of Raphael's pupils.

Original Sin, from Michelangelo's fresco on the Sistine Chapel ceiling

View across the Tiber to Castel Sant'Angelo, crowned by the figure of the angel that gave it its name

Castel Sant'Angelo ③

Lungotevere Castello. 📞 06-39 96 76 00. 🚌 23, 34, 280. 🕐 Tue–Sun. 🔴 public hols, 2nd & 4th Tue of month. 🎟️ ♿

THE MASSIVE FORTRESS of Castel Sant'Angelo takes its name from the vision of the Archangel Michael, experienced by Pope Gregory the Great in the 6th century, as he led a procession across the bridge, praying for the end of the plague.

The castle began life in AD 139 as the Emperor Hadrian's mausoleum. Since then it has been a bridgehead in the Emperor Aurelian's city wall, a medieval citadel and prison, and a place of safety for popes during times of war or political unrest.

Visitors are given a glimpse into all aspects of the castle's history – from its dank prison cells to the lavish apartments of Renaissance popes.

Villa Farnesina ④

Via della Lungara 230. 📞 06-68 02 72 68. 🚌 23, 280. 🕐 Mon–Sat. 🎟️

THE FABULOUSLY WEALTHY Sienese banker, Agostino Chigi, commissioned this villa in 1508 from his fellow Sienese, Baldassare Peruzzi. Chigi's main home was across the Tiber – the villa was just for extravagant banquets. Chigi also used it for sojourns

with the courtesan Imperia, who allegedly inspired one of the *Three Graces* painted by Raphael in the Loggia of Cupid and Psyche.

The simple, harmonious design of the Farnesina, with a central block and projecting wings, made it one of the first true villas of the Renaissance. Peruzzi decorated some of the interiors himself, such as the Sala della Prospettiva upstairs, in which illusionistic frescoes create the impression of looking out over Rome through a marble colonnade.

The painted vault of the main hall, the Sala di Galatea, shows the position of the stars at the time of Chigi's birth. After his death the banking business collapsed, and in 1577 the villa was sold off to the Farnese family.

Trompe l'oeil view in the Sala della Prospettiva, Villa Farnesina

Santa Maria in Trastevere ⑤

Piazza Santa Maria in Trastevere. 📞 06-581 48 02. 🚌 H, 23, 280. 🕐 daily. ♿

TRASTEVERE, THE AREA "across the Tiber," is one of the city's most attractive quarters: a maze of narrow, cobbled alleys. Once home to the city's poor, it has witnessed a proliferation of fashionable clubs, restaurants, and boutiques.

At the heart of Trastevere, overlooking an attractive traffic-free square stands the Basilica of Santa Maria – probably the first official place of Christian worship in Rome. It was founded by Pope Callixtus I in the 3rd century, when Christianity was still a minority cult. According to legend, it was built on the site where a fountain of oil had sprung up miraculously on the day that Christ was born.

The basilica became the focus of devotion to the Madonna. Mary and Christ are among the figures depicted in the façade mosaics (c.12th century). In the apse is a stylized 12th-century mosaic *Coronation of the Virgin*, and below it, a series of realistic mosaic scenes from the life of Mary by the 13th-century artist Pietro Cavallini. The oldest image of the Virgin is a 7th-century icon, which depicts her as a Byzantine empress flanked by a guard of angels.

Piazza Navona ⑥

🚌 *40, 46, 62, 64, 81, 87, 116, 492, 628.*

Rome's most spectacular Baroque piazza follows the shape of a 1st-century AD stadium, built by Domitian and used for athletic contests *(agones)*, chariot races, and other sports. The foundations of the surrounding buildings come from the ruined stadium, traces of which are visible below the church of Sant' Agnese in Agone. The church, created by the architects Girolamo and Carlo Rainaldi and Francesco Borromini, is dedicated to the virgin martyr, St. Agnes. When she was stripped naked to force her to renounce her faith, her hair grew miraculously long, concealing her body.

The piazza began to take on its present appearance in the 17th century, when Pope Innocent X commissioned a new church, palace, and fountain. The fountain, the Fontana dei Quattro Fiumi, is Bernini's most magnificent,

The Pantheon, a place of worship since the 2nd century AD

with statues of four gods personifying the world's greatest known rivers at the time – the Nile, the Plate, the Ganges, and the Danube – sitting on rocks below an obelisk. Bernini also sculpted the muscle-bound Moor in the Fontana del Moro, though the present statue is a copy.

Pantheon ⑦

Piazza della Rotonda. 📞 *06-68 30 02 30.* 🚌 *116 & many others.* 🕐 *daily.* ⬤ *Jan 1, May 1, Dec 25.* ♿

The Pantheon, the Roman "temple of all the gods," is the most extraordinary and best preserved ancient building in Rome. The first temple on the site is thought to have been a conventional rectangular affair erected by Agrippa between 27 and 25 BC; the present structure was built, and possibly designed, by Emperor Hadrian in AD 118.

The temple is fronted by a massive pedimented portico, screening what appears to be a cylinder fused to a shallow dome. Only from the inside can the true scale and beauty of the temple be appreciated: a vast hemispherical dome equal in radius to the height of the cylinder gives perfectly harmonious proportions to the building. A circular opening in the center of the coffered dome, the *oculus*, lets in the only light.

In the 7th century, Christians claimed that they were being plagued by demons as they passed by, and permission was given to turn the Pantheon into a church. Today it is lined with tombs, ranging from the restrained monument to Raphael to the huge marble and porphyry sarcophagi holding the bodies of Italian monarchs.

Palazzo Doria Pamphilj ⑧

Piazza del Collegio Romano 2. 📞 *06-679 73 23.* 🚌 *64, 70, 81, 85, 117, 119, 492.* 🕐 *Fri–Wed.* ⬤ *Jan 1, Easter Sun, May 1, Aug 15, Dec 25.* 🖼 by appt for private apartments. ♿

Palazzo Doria Pamphilj is a vast stone edifice, whose oldest parts date from 1435. It was owned by the della Rovere family and then by the Aldobrandini family, before the Pamphilj family took possession of it in 1647. The Pamphilj added a new wing, a splendid chapel, and a theater.

Personification of the Ganges, Fontana dei Quattro Fiumi, Piazza Navona

The family art collection has over 400 paintings dating from the 15th to the 18th century, including a portrait of Pope Innocent X by Velázquez and works by Caravaggio, Titian, Guercino, and Claude Lorrain. The opulent rooms of the private apartments retain many of their original furnishings, including Brussels and Gobelins tapestries, Murano chandeliers, and a gilded crib.

In the first half of the 18th century, Gabriele Valvassori created the gallery above the courtyard and a new façade along the Corso, using the highly decorative style of the period, known as the *barocchetto*, which now dominates the building.

Triumph of Faith over Heresy by Pierre Legros in the Gesù

Gesù ⑨

Piazza del Gesù. **C** 06-69 70 01. **H**, 46, 62, 64, 70, 81, 87, 186, 492, 628 & other routes. ○ daily.

THE GESÙ, built between 1568 and 1584, was Rome's first Jesuit church. The Jesuit order was founded in Rome in 1537 by a Basque soldier, Ignatius Loyola, who became a Christian after he was wounded in battle. The order was intellectual, austere, and heavily engaged in teaching and missionary activities.

The much-imitated design of the Gesù typifies Counter Reformation architecture: a large nave with side pulpits for preaching to crowds, and a main altar as the centerpiece for the mass. The illusionistic decoration that covers the nave ceiling and the dome was

added by Il Baciccia in the 17th century. The painting in the nave depicts the *Triumph of the Name of Jesus* and its message is clear: faithful, Catholic worshippers will be joyfully uplifted to heaven while Protestants and heretics are flung into the fires of hell. The message is reiterated in the Cappella di Sant'Ignazio, a rich display of lapis lazuli, serpentine, silver, and gold. The Baroque marble by Legros, *Triumph of Faith over Idolatry*, shows a female "Religion" trampling on the head of the serpent "Idolatry."

Capitoline Museums ⑩

Musei Capitolini, Piazza del Campidoglio. **C** 06-39 96 78 00. **▥** 40, 63, 64, 70, 75 & many others. ○ Tue–Sun. ● Jan 1, May 1, Dec 25. **▩** free last Sun of month. **☑ &**

WHEN EMPEROR Charles V announced he was to visit Rome in 1536, Pope Paul III asked Michelangelo to give the Capitol, formerly the citadel of Ancient Rome, a facelift. He redesigned the piazza, renovated the façades of its palaces and built a new staircase, the Cordonata. This gently rising ramp is now crowned with the massive Classical statues of Castor and Pollux.

The Capitoline Museums – the Palazzo Nuovo and the Palazzo dei Conservatori – stand on opposite sides of the impressive Piazza del Campidoglio. In the center of the piazza is an equestrian statue of Marcus Aurelius (it is a copy; the original bronze is in the Palazzo Nuovo).

The façade of the Palazzo Nuovo was designed by Michelangelo, but the work was finished in 1655 by the brothers Carlo and Girolamo Rainaldi.

The Palazzo dei Conservatori had been the seat of the city's magistrates during the late

Statue of Marcus Aurelius in the center of Piazza del Campidoglio

Middle Ages. Its frescoed halls are still used occasionally for political meetings and the ground floor houses the municipal registry office. The current building was begun in 1536, built by Giacomo della Porta, who also carried out Michelangelo's other designs for Piazza del Campidoglio.

A collection of Classical statues has been kept on the Capitoline Hill since the Renaissance. When the Palazzo Nuovo was completed, some of the statues were transferred there. In 1734 Pope Clement XII decreed that the building be turned into the world's first public museum.

The museum is still devoted chiefly to sculpture. Most of its finest works, such as *The Dying Galatian*, are Roman copies of Greek masterpieces. There are also two collections of busts, assembled in the 18th century, of the philosophers and poets of ancient Greece and the rulers of ancient Rome. Although much of the museum is given over to sculpture, it also houses a collection of porcelain, and its art galleries contain various works by Veronese, Titian, Caravaggio, Rubens, van Dyck, and Tintoretto.

Esquiline Venus, Capitoline Museums

The two museums have recently been restored, and a new subterranean passage now links them.

Ancient Rome

TRACES OF ANCIENT ROME are visible all over the city, occasionally a whole building, often just a column from a temple or an arch of an aqueduct recycled in a later construction. The major archaeological sites are to be found along Via dei Fori Imperiali, which runs from Piazza Venezia to the Colosseum. On the north side lie Trajan's Markets and the forums of various emperors; on the south side are the Roman Forum and the Palatine Hill. Many museums hold extensive collections of antiquities excavated in the city.

Romans fortifying a town in a detail from Trajan's Column

Trajan's Markets ⑪

Via IV Novembre. 📞 06-679 00 48. 🚌 64, 70, 170, 640 & many others. 🕐 Tue–Sun. ● public hols. 📷

ORIGINALLY CONSIDERED among the wonders of the Classical world, Trajan's Markets now show only a hint of their former splendor.

Emperor Trajan and his architect, Apollodorus of Damascus, built this visionary complex of 150 shops and offices in the early 2nd century AD. The Markets sold everything from Middle Eastern silks and spices to fresh fish, fruit, and flowers. It was also the place where the corn dole was administered: a free ration for Roman men.

Shops opened early and closed about noon. Almost all the shopping was done by men and the traders were almost exclusively male.

The **Forum of Trajan** (AD 107–13) was built in front of the market complex. It was a vast colonnaded open space with a huge basilica, and included two libraries.

Dominating the ruins today is **Trajan's Column**. Spiralling up its 30 m (98 ft) high stem are minutely detailed scenes from Trajan's successful campaigns in Dacia (present-day Romania).

Roman Forum ⑫

Entrances: Largo Romolo e Remo, Via del Foro Romano, and near the Arch of Titus on Via Sacra. 📞 06-39 96 77 00. Ⓜ Colosseo. 🚌 75, 81, 85, 87, 117, 175, 186, 810, 850. 🕐 daily. ● Jan 1, May 1, Dec 25. 📷

THE FORUM WAS the center of political, commercial, and judicial life in ancient Rome. As Rome's population grew, however, this ancient Forum became too small, so Julius Caesar built a new one (46 BC). This move was emulated by successive emperors. The newer forums are known as the "Imperial Fora."

The ruins of the Roman Forum date from many eras and the layout is confusing. It is a good idea to view them from the vantage point of the

Capitoline Hill, before walking around. From there you can make out the Via Sacra, the route of religious and triumphal processions.

The best preserved monuments are two triumphal arches. The **Arch of Titus** commemorates the crushing of the Jewish Revolt by Titus in AD 70. The later **Arch of Septimius Severus** (AD 203) records the emperor's victories over the Parthians.

Most of the other ruins are temples or basilicas. The latter were huge public buildings, which served as law courts and places of business. At the western end of the forum are the scant remains of the **Basilica Julia**, named after Julius Caesar, and the earlier **Basilica Aemilia**. Close to the latter stands the reconstructed **Curia**, where the Roman Senate once met.

The eastern end of the Forum is dominated by the shell of the **Basilica of Constantine and Maxentius** (4th century AD). The adjacent **Temple of Romulus** is now part of a church. Cross the Via Sacra from here to see the partly reconstructed **Temple of Vesta** and the **House of the Vestal Virgins**.

Further east past the Arch of Titus are the extensive ruins of the **Temple of Venus and Rome**, built in AD 121 by Hadrian. Attached to the ruined temple is the church of **Santa Francesca Romana** – patron saint of motorists. On March 9, drivers bring their cars here to have them blessed.

Central garden of the House of the Vestal Virgins in the Roman Forum

Ruins of oval fountain in the Domus Flavia on the Palatine

Palatine ⑬

Entrances: Via di San Gregorio and near the Arch of Titus on Via Sacra. 06-39 96 77 00. M *Colosseo.* 75, 85, 87, 117, 175 & many others. 3. daily. *public hols.*

THE PALATINE, the hill where the Roman aristocracy lived and emperors built their palaces, is the most pleasant and relaxing of the city's ancient sites. Shaded by pines and carpeted with wild flowers in the spring, it is dominated by the imposing ruins of the **Domus Augustana** and the **Domus Flavia**, two parts of Domitian's huge palace (1st century AD).

Other remains here include the **House of Augustus** and the **House of Livia**, where the Emperor Augustus lived with his wife Livia; and the **Cryptoporticus**, a long underground gallery built by Nero.

The **Huts of Romulus**, not far from the House of Augustus, are Iron Age huts (10th century BC), which provide archaeological support for the area's legendary links with the founding of Rome. According to legend Romulus and Remus grew up on this hill in the 8th century BC.

After admiring the ancient sights, visit the **Farnese Gardens**, created in the mid-16th century by Cardinal Alessandro Farnese, with tree-lined avenues, rose gardens, and glorious views.

Colosseum ⑭

Piazza del Colosseo. 06-3996 77 00. M *Colosseo.* 75, 81, 85, 87, 117, 175, 673, 810. 3. daily. Jan 1, May 1, Dec 25. *limited.*

ROME'S GREAT AMPHITHEATER, commissioned by the Emperor Vespasian in AD 72, was built on the marshy site of a lake in the grounds of Nero's palace.

It is likely that the arena took its name, not from its own size, but from that of an enormous statue, the Colossus of Nero, that stood nearby.

The Colosseum was the site of deadly gladiatorial combats and wild animal fights, staged free of charge by the emperor and wealthy citizens. It was built to a very practical design, its 80 entrances allowing easy access for 55,000 spectators. Excavations in the 19th century exposed a network of rooms under the arena, from which animals could be released.

The four tiers of the outside walls were built in differing styles. The lower three are arched: the bottom with Doric columns, the next with Ionic, and the third with Corinthian. The top level supported a huge awning, used to shade spectators from the sun.

Beside the Colosseum stands the **Arch of Constantine**, commemorating Constantine's victory in AD 312 over his co-emperor Maxentius. Most of the medallions, reliefs, and statues were scavenged from earlier monuments. Inside the arch are reliefs showing one of Trajan's victories.

ANCIENT ROMAN SITES AND MUSEUMS

Baths of Caracalla
Viale delle Terme di Caracalla 52. 06-575 86 26. M *Circo Massimo.* 160, 628. 3. *Tue–Sun & Mon am.* Extensive ruins of bath complex built in AD 217.

Domus Aurea
Viale della Domus Aurea. 06-39 96 77 00. M *Colosseo.* 85, 87, 117, 186, 810, 850. 3. *Wed–Mon (advance booking required).* Nero's Golden House – vast rooms of his palace, some with frescoes intact, buried beneath the Oppian Hill.

Museo Nazionale Romano
Palazzo Massimo, Largo di Villa Peretti 1. 06-399 67 700. M *Repubblica, Termini.* 36, 38, 64, 86, 110, 170, 175, H, and many others to Piazza dei Cinquecento. *Tue–Sun.* Sculpture, mosaics, wall-paintings and a Roman mummy. Another branch of the museum is at the Baths of Diocletian across the road.

Palazzo Altemps
Piazza Sant'Apollinare 46. 06-68 33 659. 70, 81, 115, 116, 280, 492, 628. *Tue–Sun.* Fine collection of Classical statuary in beautiful Renaissance palazzo.

Temples of the Forum Boarium
Piazza della Bocca della Verità. 44, 81, 95, 160, 170, 280, 628, 715, 716. Two miraculously preserved Republican-era temples.

The Colosseum, a majestic sight despite centuries of damage and neglect

Santa Maria Maggiore ⑮

Piazza di Santa Maria Maggiore.
📞 06-48 31 95. Ⓜ *Termini, Cavour.*
🚌 *16, 70, 71, 714.* 🚋 *14.*
🔲 *daily.* ✔

OF ALL THE GREAT Roman basilicas, Santa Maria has the most successful blend of different architectural styles. Its colonnaded triple nave is part of the original 5th-century building; the marble floor and Romanesque bell tower, with its blue ceramic roundels, are medieval; the Renaissance saw a new coffered ceiling; and the Baroque gave the church twin domes and its imposing front and rear façades.

Santa Maria is most famous for its mosaics. Those in the nave and on the triumphal arch date from the 5th century. Medieval mosaics include a 13th-century enthroned Christ in the loggia and Jacopo Torriti's *Coronation of the Virgin* (1295) in the apse.

The gilded ceiling was a gift of Alexander VI, the Borgia pope. The gold used is said to be the first brought back from America by Columbus.

Trevi Fountain ⑯

Piazza di Trevi. 🚌 *52, 53, 61, 62, 63, 71, 80, 95, 116, 119 & many others.*

MOST VISITORS gathering around the coin-filled fountain assume that it has always been there, but by the standards of the Eternal City, the Trevi is a fairly recent creation. Nicola Salvi's

The Spanish Steps, with the church of Trinità dei Monti above

theatrical design for Rome's largest and most famous fountain was completed only in 1762. The central figure is Neptune, flanked by two Tritons. One Triton struggles to master a very unruly "sea-horse," the other leads a far more docile animal. These symbolize the two contrasting moods of the sea.

The site was originally the terminal of the Aqua Virgo aqueduct (19 BC). A relief shows the legendary virgin, after whom the aqueduct was named, pointing to the spring from which the water flows.

Spanish Steps ⑰

Scalinata della Trinità dei Monti, Piazza di Spagna. Ⓜ *Spagna.*
🚌 *116, 117.*

THE STEPS, which link the church of Trinità dei Monti with Piazza di Spagna below, were completed in 1726. They combine straight sections, curves, and terraces to create one of the city's most dramatic and distinctive landmarks. To the right as you look at the steps from the square is the **Keats-Shelley Memorial House**, a small museum in the house where the poet John Keats died of consumption in 1821.

In the 19th century the steps were a meeting place for artists' models; today they are filled with people sitting, writing postcards, taking photos, flirting, busking, or just watching the passers-by. Eating here is not allowed.

The steps overlook Via Condotti and the surrounding streets. In the 18th century this area was full of hotels for foreigners doing the Grand Tour. It now contains the smartest shops in Rome.

The Trevi Fountain, the most famous of Rome's Baroque landmarks

Santa Maria del Popolo ⑱

Piazza del Popolo 12. ☏ 06-361 08 36. Ⓜ Flaminio. 🚌 95, 117, 119, 490, 495, 926. ⬭ daily.

Santa Maria del Popolo was commissioned by Sixtus IV in 1472. After his death in 1484, the pope's family chapel, the Della Rovere Chapel (first on the right), was frescoed by Pinturicchio.

In 1503 Sixtus IV's nephew Giuliano became Pope Julius II and had Bramante build a new apse. Pinturicchio was called in again to paint its vaults with Sibyls and Apostles framed by freakish beasts.

In 1513 Raphael created the Chigi Chapel (second on the left) – a Renaissance fusion of the sacred and profane – for the banker Agostino Chigi. Bernini later added the statues of Daniel and Habakkuk. In the Cerasi Chapel, left of the altar, are two Caravaggios: *The Crucifixion of St Peter* and *The Conversion of St Paul.*

The Chigi Chapel in Santa Maria del Popolo, designed by Raphael

Museo e Galleria Borghese ⑲

Piazzale Scipione Borghese 5.
☏ 06-328 10 (reservations). 🚌 52, 53, 116, 910. 🚊 3, 19. ⬭ Tue–Sun (reservations obligatory Sat & Sun).
⬤ public hols. 🚫

The Villa Borghese and its park were designed in 1605 for Cardinal Scipione Borghese, nephew of Pope

Detail from Bernini's *Rape of Proserpine* in the Museo Borghese

Paul V. The park was the first of its kind in Rome. It was laid out with 400 pine trees, sculpture by Bernini, and dramatic water features.

The villa was used for entertaining and displaying the cardinal's impressive collection of paintings and sculpture. Unfortunately, between 1801 and 1809 Prince Camillo Borghese, husband to Napoleon's sister Pauline, sold many of these to his brother-in-law, and swapped 200 of Scipione's Classical statues for an estate in Piedmont. The statues are still in the Louvre. However, some Classical treasures remain, including fragments of a 3rd-century AD mosaic of gladiators fighting wild animals.

The highlights of the remaining collection are the sculptures by the young Bernini. *Apollo and Daphne* (1624), shows the nymph Daphne being transformed into a laurel tree to escape being abducted by Apollo. Other striking works are *The Rape of Proserpine* and a *David*, whose face is said to be a self-portrait of Bernini.

The most notorious work is a sculpture by Canova of Pauline Borghese as *Venus Victrix* (1805), in which the semi-naked Pauline reclines on a chaise longue.

The Galleria Borghese, on the upper floor, houses some fine Renaissance and Baroque paintings. These include Raphael's *Deposition*, along with works by Pinturicchio, Correggio, Caravaggio, Rubens, and Titian.

Within the Villa Borghese park are other museums and galleries, foreign academies, a zoo, schools of archaeology, an artificial lake, and an array of fountains and follies.

Villa Giulia ⑳

Piazzale di Villa Giulia 9. ☏ 06-322 65 71. 🚌 52, 926, 88, 95, 490, 495. 🚊 3, 19. ⬭ Tue–Sun. ⬤ Jan 1, May 1, Dec 25. 🎫 🎧 audio. 🚫

Villa Giulia was built as a country retreat for Pope Julius III. Today it houses a world-famous collection of Etruscan and other pre-Roman remains. There are fascinating pieces of jewelry, bronzes, mirrors, and a marvelous terra-cotta sarcophagus of a husband and wife from Cerveteri.

The delightful villa was the work of architects Vasari and Vignola, and the sculptor Ammannati. Michelangelo also contributed. At the center of the garden is a *nympheum* – a sunken courtyard decorated with mosaics, statues, and fountains, built in imitation of ancient Roman models.

The cheerful figures of an Etruscan married couple on their sarcophagus, Villa Giulia

Assisi: Basilica di San Francesco

THE BURIAL PLACE of St. Francis, this basilica was begun in 1228, two years after the saint's death. Over the next century its Upper and Lower Churches were decorated by the foremost artists of their day, among them Cimabue, Simone Martini, Pietro Lorenzetti, and Giotto, whose frescoes of the *Life of St. Francis* are some of the most renowned in Italy. Many of the basilica's frescoes were badly damaged in the earthquake that hit Assisi in 1997, but all have been restored. The basilica, which dominates Assisi, is one of the great Christian shrines and receives vast numbers of pilgrims throughout the year.

★ Frescoes by Giotto
The Ecstasy of St. Francis is one of 28 panels that make up Giotto's cycle on the Life of St. Francis *(c.1290–95).*

St. Francis
Cimabue's simple painting (c.1280) captures the humility of the revered saint, who stood for poverty, chastity, and obedience.

Faded paintings by Roman artists line the walls above Giotto's *Life of St. Francis.*

The choir (1501) features a 13th-century stone papal throne.

The vaulting of the Lower Church is covered almost entirely in frescoes.

Steps to the Treasury

The crypt contains the tomb of St. Francis.

A Renaissance portico shelters the original Gothic portal of the Lower Church.

★ Frescoes by Lorenzetti
The bold composition of Pietro Lorenzetti's fresco, entitled The Deposition *(1323), is based around the truncated Cross, focusing attention on the twisted figure of Christ.*

★ Cappella di San Martino
The frescoes in this chapel on the life of St. Martin (1315) are by the Sienese painter Simone Martini. This panel shows the death of the Saint. Martini was also responsible for the fine stained glass in the chapel.

The Upper Church has soaring Gothic vaulting painted with a starry sky, symbolizing the heavenly glory of St. Francis. Its style influenced that of many later Franciscan churches.

The rose window is framed by the carved symbols of the four Evangelists

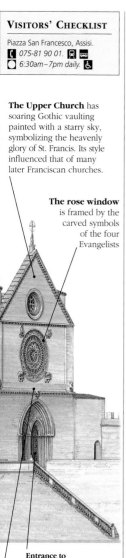

Entrance to Upper Church

The façade and its rose window are early examples of Italian Gothic.

STAR FEATURES

★ **Frescoes by Giotto**

★ **Frescoes by Lorenzetti**

★ **Cappella di San Martino**

The ancient Tempio di Minerva in the Piazza del Comune, Assisi

Assisi ❷

25,000. 🚉 🚍 ℹ Piazza del Comune (075-81 25 34). 🛒 Sat. 🌐 www.umbria2000.it

THIS BEAUTIFUL medieval town, with its geranium-hung streets, lovely views, and fountain-splashed piazzas, is heir to the legacy of St. Francis (c.1181–1226), who is buried in the **Basilica di San Francesco**.

Piazza del Comune, Assisi's main square, is dominated by the columns of the **Tempio di Minerva**, a Roman temple-front from the Augustan age. The Palazzo Comunale, opposite, houses an art gallery the **Pinacoteca Comunale**.

The town contains many other interesting churches. On Corso Mazzini is the **Basilica di Santa Chiara**. Here, St. Clare – Francis's companion and the founder of the Poor Clares (an order of nuns) – is buried. The **Duomo** has a superb Romanesque façade. **San Pietro** is a simple, well restored Romanesque church, while the nearby **Oratorio dei Pellegrini**, a 15th-century pilgrims' hospice, contains well-preserved frescoes by Matteo da Gualdo.

Perugia ❸

160,000. 🚉 🚍 ℹ Piazza IV Novembre 3 (075-572 33 27). 🛒 daily.

PERUGIA'S OLD CENTER hinges around Corso Vannucci, named after the local painter Pietro Vannucci (Perugino).

It is dominated by Umbria's finest building and former town hall, the monumental **Palazzo dei Priori**. Among its richly decorated rooms is the Sala dei Notari or Lawyers' Hall (c.1295), vividly frescoed with scenes from the Old Testament. Superlative frescoes (1498–1500) by Perugino cover the walls of the Collegio del Cambio, Perugia's medieval money exchange. The **Galleria Nazionale dell'Umbria** on the third floor displays a fine collection of paintings.

The Cappella del Santo Anello in Perugia's 15th-century **Duomo** houses the Virgin's agate "wedding ring," said to change color according to the character of its wearer. The Renaissance *Madonna delle Grazie* by Gian Nicola di Paolo hangs in the nave.

On Piazza San Francesco the **Oratorio di San Bernardino** (1457–61), has a colorful façade by Agostino di Duccio. Beyond the old city walls, the 10th-century **San Pietro** is Perugia's most extravagantly decorated church. **San Domenico** (1305–1632), on Piazza Giordano Bruno, is Umbria's largest church. It houses the tomb of Pope Benedict XI (c.1304) and the **Museo Archeologico Nazionale dell'Umbria**, a collection of prehistoric, Etruscan, and Roman artifacts.

🏛 Palazzo dei Priori

Corso Vannucci 19. 075-572 42 07. 🕐 daily. 🔴 Jan 1, May 1, Dec 25, 1st Mon of month. 🌀 ♿

Palazzo dei Priori, Perugia's imposing medieval town hall

Street-by-Street: Siena 4

SIENA'S PRINCIPAL SIGHTS cluster in the maze of narrow streets and alleys around the fan-shaped Piazza del Campo. One of Europe's greatest medieval squares, the piazza sits at the heart of the city's 17 *contrade*, the historic districts whose ancient rivalries are still acted out in the twice-yearly Palio *(see p410)*. Loyalty to the *contrada* of one's birth is fierce, and as you wander the streets you will see the parishes' animal symbols repeated on flags, plaques, and carvings.

Unicorn *contrada*

The Duomo dominating Siena's skyline

Via della Galluzza leads to the house of St. Catherine, Siena's patron saint *(see p410)*.

The Baptistry has fine frescoes and a font with reliefs by Donatello, Jacopo della Quercia, and Ghiberti.

★ **Duomo**
Striped black and white marble pillars, surmounted by a carved frieze of the popes, support the Duomo's vaulted ceiling, painted blue with gold stars to resemble the night sky (see p410).

Each tier of the Duomo's bell tower has one more window than the floor below.

Cafés and shops fill the streets around Piazza del Duomo.

Bus station

Train station

VIA D. GALLUZZA

PIAZZA INDIPENDENZA

VIA DI FONTEBRANDA

VIA DI DIACCETO

VIA DI CITTÀ

VIA FRANCIOSA

VIA DEI PELLEGRINI

PIAZZA SAN GIOVANNI

VIC. D. CAMPANE

VIA DEL FUSARI

PIAZZA DEL DUOMO

VIA DEL POGGIO

VIA DI CITTÀ

VIA DEL CAPITANO

Museo dell'Opera del Duomo
The museum (see p410) *houses weathered sculptures from the cathedral, including this battered she-wolf suckling Romulus and Remus.*

KEY

– – – Suggested route

| 0 meters | 300 |
| 0 yards | 300 |

VISITORS' CHECKLIST

👥 60,000. 🚂 Piazzale Rosselli. 🚌 Piazza San Domenico. ℹ️ Piazza del Campo 56 (0577-28 05 51). 🛒 Wed. 🎌 Palio (Jul 2, Aug 16); Settimana Musicale Chigiana – Classical music concerts (Jul). 🌐 www.siena.turismo.toscana.it

Loggia della Mercanzia
This graceful arcade (1417) was used by Siena's medieval merchants and money dealers.

Tourist information

Palazzo Piccolomini, built in 1460, now holds the Sienese state archives. Many of the original painted wooden bindings are on display.

A BANCHI DI SOTTO

VIA DI PANTANETO

VIA RINALDINA

VIA DEL PORRIONE

AZZA DEL AMPO

VIA DI SALICOTTO

PIAZZA DEL MERCATO

VIA DUPRE

★ **Palazzo Pubblico**
The graceful Gothic town hall was completed in 1342. At 102 m (330 ft), the bell tower, the Torre del Mangia, is the second highest medieval tower ever built in Italy.

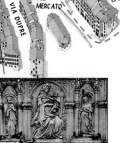

Fonte Gaia
The reliefs on the fountain are 19th-century copies of the 15th-century originals by Jacopo della Quercia.

STAR SIGHTS

★ **Duomo**

★ **Palazzo Pubblico**

🏛 **Palazzo Pubblico**
Piazza del Campo 1. 📞 0577-29 22 63. **Museo Civico & Torre del Mangia** ⏰ daily. 🎫
Although the Palazzo Pubblico (1297–1342) continues in its ancient role as Siena's town hall, the **Museo Civico** is also housed here. Many of the medieval rooms, some decorated with paintings of the Sienese School, are open to the public. They include the main council chamber, or Sala del Mappamondo, named after a map of the world painted here by Ambrogio Lorenzetti in the early 14th century. One wall is covered by Simone Martini's fresco *Maestà* (1315), which depicts the Virgin in Majesty. The Sala della Pace houses the famous *Allegory of Good and Bad Government*, a pair of frescoes by Lorenzetti finished in 1338.

In the palace courtyard is the magnificent **Torre del Mangia** bell tower, which offers superb views of the city.

🏛 **Piazza del Campo**
Italy's loveliest piazza occupies the site of the old Roman forum, and for much of Siena's early history was the city's principal market-place. The Council of Nine, Siena's ruling body, gave the order for work to start on the piazza in 1293. The red brick paving was finished in 1349. It is divided into nine sections, representing not only the authority of the council, but also the protective folds of the Madonna's cloak. The piazza has been the focus of city life ever since, a setting for executions, bullfights, and the drama of the Palio. Cafés, restaurants, and fine medieval palazzi now line the square, which is dominated by the Palazzo Pubblico and the Torre del Mangia.

Piazza del Campo, viewed from the top of the Torre del Mangia

Exploring Siena

O NCE A CAPITAL to rival Florence, Siena is still unspoiled and endowed with the grandeur of the age in which it was at its peak (1260–1348). The magnificent Duomo is one of Italy's greatest cathedrals. The best place to begin an exploration of the historic city center is Piazza del Campo and the surrounding maze of medieval streets. Siena's hilly position means that walks through the city are rewarded with countless sudden views of the surrounding countryside.

***Massacre of the Innocents*, a detail from the Duomo's marble floor**

Richly decorated façade of Siena's Duomo

🏠 Duomo

Piazza del Duomo. 📞 0577-28 30 48. ⭕ *daily.* ● *Nov–Mar: 1–2:30pm.*
Museo dell'Opera del Metropolitana
📞 0577-28 30 48. ⭕ *mid-Mar–Oct: 9am–7pm daily; Nov–mid-Mar: 9am–1:30pm daily.* ● *public hols.* 🎫
Siena's cathedral (1136–1382) is a spectacular example of Pisan-influenced Romanesque-Gothic architecture. Had the 14th-century plan to create a new nave come to fruition, it would have become the largest church in Christendom, but the idea was abandoned when the Black Death of 1348 virtually halved the city's population. Among the Duomo's treasures are sculptural masterpieces by Nicola Pisano, Donatello, and Michelangelo, a fine inlaid marble floor, and a magnificent fresco cycle by Pinturicchio.

In the side aisle of the unfinished nave, which has been roofed over, is the **Museo dell'Opera del Metropolitana**. The museum is devoted mainly to sculpture removed from the exterior of the Duomo, including a

tondo (circular relief) of a Madonna and Child, probably by Donatello. The highlight is Duccio's huge altarpiece, *Maestà* (1308–11), which depicts the *Madonna and Child* on one side, and *Scenes from the Life of Christ* on the other.

🏛 Pinacoteca Nazionale

Via San Pietro 29. 📞 0577-28 11 61. ● *Sun & Mon pm.* 🎫 ♿
Housed in the Palazzo Buonsignori, this gallery contains an unsurpassed collection of paintings by artists of the Sienese School. Highlights include Duccio's *Madonna dei Francescani* (1285) and Simone Martini's *The Blessed Agostino Novello and Four of his Miracles* (c.1330).

🏠 San Domenico

Piazza San Domenico. ⭕ *daily.*
The preserved head of the city's patroness, St. Catherine of Siena (1347–80), can be seen in a gilded tabernacle on the altar of a chapel dedicated to her in this huge, barn-like

Gothic church. The chapel itself was built in 1460 and is dominated by Sodoma's frescoes (1526), which show Catherine in states of religious fervor. The church has the only portrait of St. Catherine considered authentic, painted by her friend Andrea Vanni.

St. Catherine's house, the **Casa di Santa Caterina**, is also a popular shrine for visitors to Siena.

♣ Fortezza Medicea

Viale Maccari. **Fortezza** ⭕ *daily.*
Enoteca Italica 📞 0577-28 84 97. ⭕ *noon–8pm Mon, noon–1am Tue–Sat.* 🎫
This huge red-brick fortress was built by Cosimo I in 1560, following Siena's defeat by Florence in the 1554–5 war. After an 18-month siege, during which more than 8,000 Sienese died, the town's banking and wool industries were suppressed by the Florentines.

The fortress now houses the **Enoteca Italica**, where you can taste and buy Italian wines.

THE PALIO

The Palio is Tuscany's most celebrated festival and it occurs in the Campo each year on July 2 and August 16. This bareback horse race was first recorded in 1283, but it may have had its origins in Roman military training. The jockeys represent Siena's 17 *contrade* (districts) and the horses are chosen by the drawing of lots. Preceded by days of colorful pageantry and heavy betting, the races themselves last only 90 seconds each, the winner being rewarded with a silk *palio* (banner).

Drummer taking part in the Palio's noisy pre-race pageant

The skyline of San Gimignano, bristling with medieval towers

San Gimignano **5**

Siena. 🔼 7,000. 🚌 ℹ️ *Piazza del Duomo 1 (0577-94 00 08).* 🎭 *Thu.* 🎉 *San Gimignano (Jan 31).*

THE THIRTEEN TOWERS that dominate San Gimignano's skyline were built by rival noble families in the 12th and 13th centuries, when the town's position on the main pilgrim route to Rome brought it great prosperity. The plague of 1348, and later the diversion of the pilgrim route, led to its economic decline and its miraculous preservation.

Full of good restaurants and shops, the town is also home to many fine works of art. The **Museo Civico** holds works by Pinturicchio, Benozzo Gozzoli, and Filippino Lippi, while the church of **Sant'Agostino** has a Baroque interior by Vanvitelli (c.1740) and a fresco cycle on *The Life of St. Augustine* by Benozzo Gozzoli (1465).

Florence **6**

See pp412–25.

Pisa **7**

🔼 100,000. ✈️ *Galileo Galilei, 5 km (3 miles) S.* 🚉 🚌 ℹ️ *Via Carlo Cammeo 2 (050-56 04 64).* 🎭 *Wed & Sat.*

IN THE MIDDLE AGES, Pisa's navy dominated the western Mediterranean. Trade with Spain and North Africa brought vast wealth, reflected in the city's splendid buildings. The **Duomo**, begun in 1064, is a magnificent example of Pisan-Romanesque architecture, its four-tiered façade an intricate

medley of creamy colonnades and blind arcades. Inside, highlights include a pulpit (1302–11) by Giovanni Pisano and a mosaic of *Christ in Majesty* by Cimabue (1302).

Begun in 1173 on sandy silt subsoil, the famous **Leaning Tower** (Torre Pendente) was completed in 1350. The tower has attracted many visitors over the centuries, including Galileo, who came here to conduct experiments on falling objects. Recent engineering work has reduced the tower's tilt to approximately 4.12 m (13.5 ft).

The graceful **Baptistry** was begun in 1152 and finished a century later by Nicola and Giovanni Pisano.

The **Museo Nazionale di San Matteo** holds Pisan and Florentine art from the 12th to

the 17th centuries. Major 15th-century works include Masaccio's *St. Paul*, Gentile da Fabriano's radiant *Madonna of Humility*, and Donatello's reliquary bust of *San Rossore*.

🏛️ **Museo Nazionale di San Matteo**
Piazza San Matteo 1. 📞 *050-54 18 65.* 🕐 *Tue–Sun.* 🎫

Lucca **8**

🔼 100,000. 🚉 🚌 ℹ️ *Piazza Santa Maria 35 (0583-91 99 31).* 🎭 *Wed, Sat, 3rd Sun of month (antiques).*

THE CITY OF LUCCA is still enclosed within its 17th-century walls, and visitors can stroll along the ramparts, which were converted into a public park in the early 19th century. Within the walls, narrow lanes wind among dark medieval buildings, opening suddenly to reveal stunning churches and piazzas, including the vast Piazza del Anfiteatro, which traces the outline of the old Roman amphitheater. The finest of the churches are all Romanesque: **San Martino**, the 11th-century cathedral, **San Michele in Foro**, built on the sight of the old Roman forum, and **San Frediano**.

The Baptistry in front of Pisa's Duomo, with the Leaning Tower behind

Florence ⑥

FLORENCE IS A monument to the Renaissance, the artistic and cultural reawakening of the 15th century. The buildings of Brunelleschi and the paintings and sculptures of artists such as Botticelli and Michelangelo turned the city into one of the world's greatest artistic capitals. During this time Florence was at the cultural and intellectual heart of Europe, its cosmopolitan atmosphere and wealthy patrons, such as the Medici, providing the impetus for a period of unparalleled artistic growth. The legacy of the Renaissance draws many visitors to the city today, with its numerous museums, galleries, churches, and monuments the major attractions. Florence's best sights are encompassed within such a compact area that the city seems to reveal its treasures at every step.

SIGHTS AT A GLANCE

Bargello ⑥
Boboli Gardens ⑭
Duomo pp416–7 ①
Galleria dell'Accademia ④
Museo di Storia
  della Scienza ⑩
Palazzo Pitti ⑬
Palazzo Vecchio ⑨
Piazza della Signoria ⑧
Ponte Vecchio ⑫
San Lorenzo ②
San Marco ⑤
Santa Croce ⑦
Santa Maria Novella ③
Uffizi pp422–4 ⑪

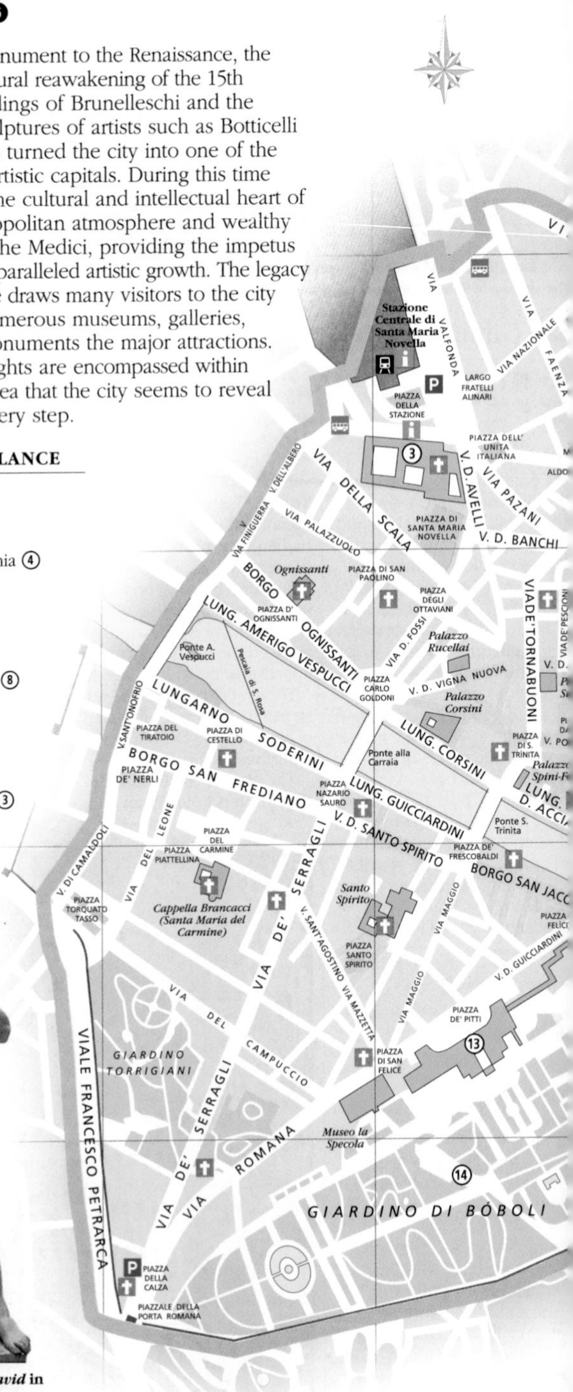

**Michelangelo's *David* in
the Galleria dell'Accademia**

The dome of the cathedral, or Duomo, Florence's greatest landmark

KEY

▢	Sight / Place of interest
🚆	Train station
🚌	Bus station
P	Parking
ℹ	Tourist information
✝	Church
—	Pedestrian street
—	City walls

SEE ALSO

• **Where to Stay** pp457–8

• **Where to Eat** pp463–4

0 meters   300

0 yards   300

GETTING AROUND

Buses in Florence are bright orange; most can be picked up at Santa Maria Novella station. Lines run until at least 9:30pm, the most popular until midnight or 1am. The most useful are Nos. 12 and 13, which make clockwise/counterclockwise circuits of the city. Official taxis are white, and are generally costly. What with one-way systems, erratic drivers, and limited traffic zones – where only authorized vehicles are permitted to go – driving is not recommended. Walking is easily the most enjoyable way to get around.

Duomo ①

See pp416–17.

San Lorenzo ②

Piazza di San Lorenzo. 🚌 *many routes.*
Basilica 📞 *055-21 66 34.* ⏰ *Mon–Sat.* ⚫ *religious hols.* 📚 **Biblioteca**
📞 *055-21 44 43.* ⏰ *am Mon–Sat.*
⚫ *public hols.* **Cappelle Medicee**
Piazza di Madonna degli Aldobrandini.
📞 *055-238 86 02.* ⏰ *daily (am only public hols).* ⚫ *1st, 3rd, & 5th Mon of month, Jan 1, May 1 & Dec 25.*

Sᴀɴ ʟᴏʀᴇɴᴢᴏ was the parish church of the Medici family, who lavished their wealth on its adornment. Rebuilt in Renaissance Classical style in 1419, the façade was never completed.

The inner façade of the Basilica was designed by Michelangelo. Cosimo il Vecchio, founder of the Medici dynasty, is buried under a stone slab before the High Altar. The bronze pulpits in the nave are Donatello's last works. Opposite is Bronzino's vast fresco of the human form in various poses (1659).

The **Biblioteca Mediceo-Laurenzia,** which housed the family's manuscripts, has an elaborate sandstone staircase, desks, and ceilings designed by Michelangelo in 1524.

The **Cappelle Medicee** incorporate three sacristies which epitomize different periods of art. Donatello's decoration of the Old Sacristy contrasts with the design of the New Sacristy

Detail from Donatello pulpit, San Lorenzo

by Michelangelo. The latter's funerary figures (1520–34) around its walls are among his greatest works. The Chapel of the Princes (1604), is opulently decorated with inlaid semiprecious stones and bright frescoes. Six Grand Dukes of the Medici family are buried here.

Santa Maria Novella ③

Piazza di Santa Maria Novella. 🚌 *A, 11, 12, 36, 37.* ♿ **Church** 📞 *055-215 98.* ⏰ *daily (pm only Fri–Sun & religious hols).* 📚 **Museum** 📞 *055-21 44 43.* ⏰ *am Sat–Thu.* ⚫ *Jan 1, Easter Sun, May 1, Dec 25.* 📷 ♿

Tʜᴇ ɢᴏᴛʜɪᴄ church of Santa Maria Novella, built by the Dominicans between 1279 and 1357, contains some of the most important works of art in Florence. The interior displays a number of superb frescoes, including Masaccio's *Trinity* (c.1428), which is renowned as a masterpiece of perspective and portraiture. The close spacing of the nave piers at the east end accentuates the illusion of length. The Tornabuoni Chapel contains Ghirlandaio's famous fresco cycle, *The Life of John the Baptist* (1485). In the Filippo Strozzi Chapel,

Façade of Santa Maria Novella, redesigned by Alberti in 1456–70

Lippi's dramatic frescoes show St. John raising Drusiana from the dead and St. Philip slaying a dragon. Boccaccio set the beginning of *The Decameron* in this chapel. The Strozzi Tomb (1493) is by Florentine sculptor Benedetto da Maiano.

The 14th-century frescoes in the Strozzi Chapel are by two brothers (Nardo di Cione and Andrea Orcagna) and were inspired by Dante's *Divine Comedy.*

Beside the church is a walled cemetery with grave niches. The cloisters on the other side of the church form a museum. The Green Cloister's name derives from the green tinge to Uccello's *Noah and the Flood* frescoes, damaged by the 1966 floods. The adjoining Spanish Chapel contains frescoes on the theme of salvation and damnation.

Galleria dell'Accademia ④

Via Ricasoli 60. 🚌 *many routes.*
📞 *055-238 86 09.* ⏰ *Tue–Sun (until midnight Jun–Sep).* ⚫ *Mon & public hols.* ♿

Tʜᴇ ᴀᴄᴀᴅᴇᴍʏ of Fine Arts in Florence, founded in 1563 was the first school in Europe set up to teach drawing, painting, and sculpture.

Since 1873, many of Michelangelo's most important works have been in the Accademia. Perhaps the most famous of all dominates the collection: Michelangelo's *David* (1504). This colossal nude depicts the biblical hero who killed the giant Goliath; it established Michelangelo, then aged 29, as the foremost sculptor of his time. The statue was moved here from the Palazzo Vecchio in 1873 to protect it from the elements.

Michelangelo's other masterpieces include a statue of St. Matthew finished in 1508, and the *Quattro Prigioni* (four prisoners), sculpted between 1521 and 1523. The muscular figures struggling to free themselves from the stone are among the most dramatic of his works.

The gallery contains an important collection of paintings by 15th- and 16th-century Florentine artists, and many major works including the *Madonna del Mare* attributed to Botticelli (1445–1510), Pacino di Bonaguida's *Tree of Life* (1310), and *Venus and Cupid* by Jacopo Pontormo (1494–1556). Also on display is an elaborately painted wooden chest, the *Cassone Adimari* (c.1440) by Lo Scheggia. It was originally used as part of a bride's trousseau, and is covered with details of Florentine daily life, clothing, and architecture.

The Salone della Toscana (Tuscany Room) exhibits more modest 19th-century sculpture and paintings by members of the Accademia.

Fra Angelico's *Annunciation*, in the monastery of San Marco

San Marco ⑤

Piazza di San Marco. 🚌 many routes. ♿ partial. **Church** 🕿 055-28 76 28. ◯ daily (pm only Sun and religious hols). **Museum** 🕿 055-238 86 08. ◯ daily (Mon–Fri: am only). ● Jan 1, May 1, Dec 25, 2nd & 4th Mon and 1st, 3rd, & 5th Sun each month. 🎫 ♿

THE CHURCH OF SAN MARCO, and the monastery built around it, date from the 13th century. Following the transfer of the site to the Dominicans of Fiesole by Pope Eugene IV in 1436, Cosimo il Vecchio paid a considerable sum for its reconstruction, overseen by his favorite architect, Michelozzo. The single-naved church holds valuable works of art, and the funerary chapel of St. Antony is considered Giambologna's main work of architecture.

To the right of the church, the oldest part of the monastery is now a museum. It contains a remarkable series of devotional frescoes by Fra Angelico. The former Pilgrims' Hospice houses *The Deposition* (1435–40), a poignant scene of the dead Christ; his *Crucifixion* (1441–2) can be seen in the Chapter House.

There are over 40 cells adorned with frescoes by Fra Angelico. *The Annunciation* (c.1445) demonstrates his mastery of perspective. Relics of the fiery orator Savonarola (1452–98), dragged from here and executed in Piazza della Signoria, are also on display.

The monastery houses Europe's first public library, designed by Michelozzo in a light and airy colonnaded hall. Valuable manuscripts and bibles are held here.

A scene from Lo Scheggia's *Cassone Adimari* in the Galleria dell'Accademia

Duomo ①

SET IN THE HEART of Florence, Santa Maria del Fiore – the Duomo, or cathedral, of Florence – dominates the city with its enormous dome. Its sheer size was typical of Florentine determination to lead in all things, and to this day, no other building stands taller in the city. The Baptistry, with its celebrated doors, is one of Florence's oldest buildings, dating perhaps from the 4th century. In his capacity as city architect, Giotto designed the Campanile in 1334; it was completed in 1359, 22 years after his death.

★ Campanile
At 85 m (276 ft), the Campanile is 6 m (20 ft) shorter than the dome. It is clad in white, green and pink Tuscan marble. The first-floor reliefs are by Andrea Pisano.

Gothic windows

The Neo-Gothic marble façade echoes the style of Giotto's campanile, but was only added in 1871–87.

★ Baptistry
Colorful 13th-century mosaics illustrating The Last Judgment *decorate the ceiling above the large octagonal font where many famous Florentines, including Dante, were baptized.*

The Baptistry doors demonstrate the artistic ideas that led to the Renaissance.

Main entrance

The east doors known as the "Gate of Paradise" (1424–52) were made by Ghiberti. The originals are in the Duomo museum.

STAR FEATURES
★ Dome
★ Baptistry
★ Campanile

South Door Panels
This scene from the south doors of the Baptistry, completed by the sculptor Andrea Pisano in 1336, depicts The Baptism of St. John the Baptist.

★ Dome
Brunelleschi's revolutionary
achievement was to build the
largest dome of its time without
scaffolding. As you climb the
463 steps to the top, you can
see how an inner shell provides a platform for the
timbers that support
the outer shell.

**The top of the
dome** offers
spectacular views
over the city.

VISITORS' CHECKLIST

Piazza del Duomo. 055-230
28 85. 1, 6, 14, 17, 23.
☐ Mon–Sat, Sun pm. ● Aug
15 & pm 1st Sat of month. &
Crypt ☐ Mon–Sat. **Dome**
☐ Mon–Sat. **Campanile**
☐ daily. **Baptistry** ☐ pm
Mon–Sat; Sun am. All buildings
● Jan 1 & religious hols.
W www.operaduomo.firenze.it

**Last Judgment
frescoes by**
Vasari

Bricks of varying size
were set in a self-
supporting herringbone
pattern – a technique
Brunelleschi copied
from the Pantheon
in Rome.

Chapels at the East End
The three apses each house
five chapels and are
crowned by a miniature
copy of the dome. The
15th-century stained glass
is by Lorenzo Ghiberti
and other artists.

**The octagonal marble
sanctuary** around the
High Altar was decorated
by Baccio Bandinelli.

**Entrance
to steps to
the dome**

Marble Pavememt
As you climb up to the dome,
you can see that the 16th-century
marble pavement, designed in part by
Baccio d'Agnelo, is laid out as a maze.

Steps to Santa Reparata
The crypt contains the remains of the church
of Santa Reparata, built in the 4th century,
and demolished in 1296 to make way for a
cathedral which would more fittingly represent
Florence and rival those of Siena and Pisa.

Bargello ⑥

Via del Proconsolo 4. 📞 *055-238 86 06.* 🚌 *A, 14.* 🕐 *8:30am–1:50pm daily.* ⬤ *1st & 3rd Sun and 2nd & 4th Mon of each month, Jan 1, May 1, Dec 25.* 📷 ♿

FLORENCE'S second-ranking museum after the Uffizi, the Bargello houses Italy's finest collection of Renaissance sculpture and some superb Mannerist bronzes. Begun in 1255, the fortress-like building was initially the town hall but later home to the chief of police (the *Bargello*). The renovated building opened as one of Italy's first national museums in 1865.

The key exhibits range over three floors, beginning with the Michelangelo Room. Here visitors can admire *Bacchus* (1497), the sculptor's first large free-standing work, a delicate circular relief depicting the *Madonna and Child* (1503–5), and *Brutus* (1539–40), his only known portrait bust. Among other sculptors' works in the same room is *Mercury* (1564), Giambologna's famous bronze. Across the courtyard, two more rooms contain exterior sculptures removed from sites around the city and an external staircase leads to a first-floor collection of bronze birds by Giambologna. To the right, the Salone del Consiglio Generale contains the cream of the museum's Early Renaissance sculpture, including Donatello's heroic *St George* (1416) and his androgynous *David* (c.1430), famous as the first free-standing nude by a Western artist since antiquity.

Donatello's statue of *David* in the Bargello

Beyond the Salone, the Bargello's emphasis shifts to the applied arts, with room after room devoted to rugs, ceramics, silverware, and

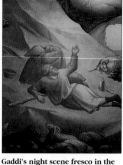
Gaddi's night scene fresco in the Baroncelli Chapel, Santa Croce

other *objets d'art*. The Salone del Camino on the second floor holds the finest collection of small bronzes in Italy. Benvenuto Cellini (1500–71) is among the artists featured.

Santa Croce ⑦

Piazza di Santa Croce. 📞 *055-24 46 19.* 🚌 *C, 23.* 🕐 *daily (Sun: pm only).* 📷 ♿

THE GOTHIC CHURCH of Santa Croce (1294) contains the tombs and monuments of many famous Florentines, among them Galileo, Michelangelo, and Machiavelli, as well as radiant early 14th-century frescoes by Giotto and his gifted pupil, Taddeo Gaddi. In 1842 the Neo-Gothic campanile of Santa Croce was added, and the façade in 1863.

In the Basilica, Rossellino's effigy (1447) of Leonardo Bruni, the great Humanist depicted in serene old age, is a triumph of realistic portraiture. Close by it is the 15th-century *Annunciation* by Donatello. The remainder of the monastic buildings scattered around the cloister form a museum of religious painting and sculpture.

The museum houses Cimabue's *Crucifixion*, a 13th-century masterpiece damaged in the flood of 1966, and Gaddi's magnificent *Last Supper* (c.1355–60).

Of the church's many chapels, the most famous is the Bardi Chapel, decorated by Giotto with frescoes of the life of St. Francis (1315–23). The Peruzzi Chapel houses further Giotto frescoes. Gaddi's 1338 fresco in the Baroncelli Chapel of an angel appearing to sleeping shepherds is notable as the first true night scene in Western art.

In the cloister alongside the church is Brunelleschi's Cappella de' Pazzi (Pazzi Chapel), a masterpiece of Renaissance architecture. The delicate gray stonework of the domed chapel is set off by white plaster, which is inset with terra-cotta roundels of the Evangelists by Luca della Robbia.

Piazza della Signoria ⑧

🚌 *A, B.*

PIAZZA DELLA SIGNORIA has been at the heart of Florence's political and social life for centuries. Citizens were once summoned to public meetings here, and the

Statue of Cosimo I in Piazza della Signoria

square's statues celebrate events in the city's history. That of Grand Duke Cosimo I (1595) by Giambologna commemorates the man who subjugated all Tuscany, while Ammannati's *Neptune Fountain* honors Tuscan naval victories. Michelangelo's original *David* stood here until 1873, when it was replaced by a copy. Donatello's original statue of the heraldic lion of Florence, known as the *Marzocco*, is now in the Bargello. Other notable statues include Cellini's bronze *Perseus*, and *The Rape of the Sabine Women* by Giambologna, carved from a single block of marble.

Painting of Penelope in Eleonora's rooms in the Palazzo Vecchio

The Putto fountain in Vasari's courtyard, at the Palazzo Vecchio

Palazzo Vecchio ⑨

Piazza della Signoria. 🕻 055-276 84 65. 🚌 A, B. ⬤ daily (Thu, am only). ⬤ Jan 1, Easter, May 1, Aug 15, Dec 25. 🎫 ♿

P ALAZZO VECCHIO, completed in 1322, has retained its external medieval appearance, and its imposing bell tower dominates the square. The "Old Palace" still fulfils its original role as Florence's town hall. Much of the interior was remodeled for Duke Cosimo I in the mid-16th century by Vasari, whose work includes several frescoes which laud the Duke's achievements.

The palazzo is entered via a courtyard, in which stands Verrochio's *Putto* fountain. A staircase leads to the Salone dei Cinquecento, which is graced by Michelangelo's *Victory* statue (1525), and to the tiny Studiolo decorated by 30 of Florence's leading Mannerist painters.

Eleonora of Toledo, wife of Cosimo I, had a suite of rooms in the palace, decorated with scenes of virtuous women. Highlights of the palace include the paintings by Il Bronzino in the Cappella di Eleonora and the loggia, which has wonderful views over the city. The Sala dei Gigli (Room of Lilies), contains frescoes of Roman heroes and Donatello's *Judith and Holofernes*.

A new Children's Museum is open at weekends to families, and several formerly secret passages and private rooms can now be visited.

Museo di Storia della Scienza ⑩

Piazza de' Giudici 1. 🕻 055-26 53 11. ⬤ 9:30am–5pm Wed–Mon. ⬤ Sat pm, public hols, Thu–Fri in winter. 🎫

T HIS LIVELY museum devotes numerous rooms on two floors to different scientific themes, illustrating each with fine displays and beautifully made early scientific instruments. It is also something of a shrine to the Pisa-born scientist, Galileo Galilei (1564–1642), and features two of his telescopes as well as large-scale reconstructions of his experiments into motion, weight, velocity, and acceleration. These are sometimes demonstrated by the attendants. Other exhibits come from the Accademia del Cimento (Academy for Experimentation), founded in memory of Galileo by Grand Duke Ferdinand II in 1657.

Some of the finest exhibits include early maps, antique microscopes, astrolabes, and barometers. Of equal interest are the huge 16th- and 17th-century Florentine globes illustrating the motion of the planets and stars. Be sure to see Lopo Homem's 16th-century map of the world, showing the newly charted coasts of the Americas, and the nautical instruments invented by Sir Robert Dudley, an Elizabethan marine engineer employed by the Medicis.

The second-floor rooms display fine old clocks, calculators, a horrifying collection of 19th-century surgical instruments, weights and measures, and graphic anatomical models.

Armillary sphere, Museo di Storia della Scienza

The Florentine Renaissance

FIFTEENTH-CENTURY ITALY saw a flowering of the arts and scholarship unmatched in Europe since Ancient Greek and Roman times. It was in wealthy Florence that this artistic and intellectual activity, later dubbed the Renaissance, was at its most intense. The patronage of the rich banking dynasty, the Medici, rulers of Florence from 1434, was lavished on the city, especially under Lorenzo the Magnificent (1469–92), and the city aspired to become the new Rome. Architects turned to Classical models for inspiration, while the art world, with a new understanding of perspective and anatomy, produced a series of painters and sculptors that included such giants as Donatello, Botticelli, Leonardo da Vinci, and Michelangelo.

ITALY IN 1492

▨ *Republic of Florence*

☐ *Papal States*

☐ *Aragonese possessions*

THE PROCESSION OF THE MAGI

Benozzo Gozzoli's fresco (1459) in the Palazzo Medici-Riccardi, Florence, depicts members of the Medici family and other contemporary notables. It contains references to the church council held in Florence in 1439, which, it was hoped, would effect a reconciliation between the Church of Rome and the Eastern Church.

Giuliano was the younger son of Piero de' Medici.

Piero de' Medici, Lorenzo's father, was given the nickname "the Gouty."

Self-portrait of the artist

Pope Leo X
There were two Medici popes: Giovanni, who reigned as Leo X (1513–21), and Giulio, who took his place as Clement VII (1521–34). Corruption in the church under Leo inspired Luther and the growth of Protestantism.

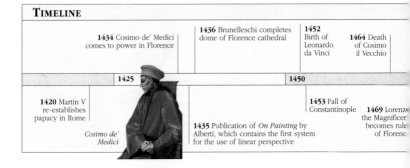

TIMELINE

1434 Cosimo de' Medici comes to power in Florence

1436 Brunelleschi completes dome of Florence cathedral

1452 Birth of Leonardo da Vinci

1464 Death of Cosimo il Vecchio

1425

1450

1420 Martin V re-establishes papacy in Rome

Cosimo de' Medici

1435 Publication of *On Painting* by Alberti, which contains the first system for the use of linear perspective

1453 Fall of Constantinople

1469 Lorenzo the Magnificent becomes ruler of Florence

Michelangelo's Sculpture

The Quattro Prigioni *(see p415), unfinished works intended for the tomb of Pope Julius II, illustrate Michelangelo's ideal of liberating "the figure imprisoned in the marble."*

RENAISSANCE ARCHITECTURE

In place of the spectacular Gothic style, Renaissance architects favored the rational, orderly, human scale of Greek and Roman buildings. The various stories of a palazzo were designed according to Classical proportions and there was a widespread revival in the use of Roman arches and the Doric, Ionic, and Corinthian orders of columns.

Filippo Brunelleschi

In order to realize his design for the dome of Florence's cathedral, Brunelleschi devised engineering techniques decades ahead of their time.

Palazzo Strozzi (1489–1536) is a typical Florentine building of the period. Rusticated stonework gives an impression of great strength. Decorative detail is largely on the upper stories above the fortress-like ground floor.

Lorenzo de' Medici (the Magnificent) is depicted as one of the three kings traveling to Bethlehem.

The Medici emblem of seven balls appears on the trappings of Lorenzo's horse.

The Spedale degli Innocenti*, an orphanage, was one of Brunelleschi's first buildings in Florence. Slender Corinthian columns support a delicate arcade.*

Humanism

Carpaccio's painting St. Augustine in his Study *(1502) is thought to show* **Cardinal Bessarion** *(c.1395–1472), one of the scholars who revived interest in Classical philosophy, especially Plato.*

		1498 Savonarola executed; Machiavelli secretary to ruling Council in Florence	**1513** Giovanni de' Medici crowned Pope Leo X	**1532** Machiavelli's book *The Prince* is published, five years after his death

1530 Medici restored as rulers of Florence

| **1500** | | **1525** |

Birth of elangelo

1483 Birth of Raphael

1494 Italy invaded by Charles VIII of France. Florence declared republic under leadership of the religious fanatic Savonarola

1512 Michelangelo completes Sistine Chapel ceiling

Niccolò Machiavelli

Uffizi ⑪

THE UFFIZI WAS BUILT in 1560–80 as a suite of offices (*uffici*) for Duke Cosimo I's new Tuscan administration. The architect, Vasari, used iron reinforcement to create an almost continuous wall of glass on the upper story. From 1581 Cosimo's heirs, beginning with Francesco I, used this well-lit space to display the Medici family art treasures, thus creating what is now the oldest art gallery in the world.

The café terrace merits a visit for its unusual views of Piazza della Signoria (*see pp418–19*).

Corridor ceilings are frescoed in the "grotesque" style of the 1580s, inspired by Roman grottoes.

The Vasari Corridor leads to the Palazzo Vecchio.

Main staircase

Entrance Hall

Entrance

Bar

GALLERY GUIDE

The Uffizi art collection is housed on the top floor. Ancient Greek and Roman sculptures are displayed in the corridor running round the inner side of the building. The paintings are hung in a series of rooms off the main corridor, in chronological order, to reveal the development of Florentine art from Gothic to High Renaissance and beyond. Most of the best-known paintings are grouped in rooms 7–18. To avoid the long queues, book your visiting time in advance.

The Ognissanti Madonna
Giotto's grasp of spatial depth in this altarpiece (1310) was a milestone in the mastery of perspective.

Buontalenti staircase

Entrance to the Vasari Corridor

STAR PAINTINGS

- ★ **The Duke and Duchess of Urbino** by Piero della Francesca

- ★ **The Birth of Venus** by Botticelli

- ★ **The Holy Family** by Michelangelo

- ★ **The Venus of Urbino** by Titian

★ **The Venus of Urbino** (*1538*)
Titian's sensuous nude was condemned for portraying the goddess in such an immodest pose.

★ **The Duke and Duchess of Urbino** *(1460)*
*Piero della Francesca's panels are among the first
true Renaissance portraits. He even recorded the
Duke's hooked nose – broken by a sword blow.*

VISITORS' CHECKLIST

Loggiato degli Uffizi 6.
[055-238 86 51
(to reserve time of visit call
055-29 48 83). B, 23.
8:15am–6:50pm Tue–Sun
(last adm: 45 mins before
closing); extended opening
hours in summer. Jan 1,
May 1, Dec 25.
Vasari Corridor 055-29
48 83 for guided tours.
W www.uffizi.firenze.it

The Tribune, decorated in red and gold, contains the works that the Medici valued most.

★ **The Birth of Venus** *(1485)*
*Botticelli's captivating image shows
the Roman goddess of love, born in a
storm in the Aegean sea. She is
blown ashore by the winds and
greeted by nymphs, ready to
wrap her in a cloak.*

**Boy Removing a
Thorn from his Foot**
*This ancient Roman statue is,
like many of the collection's
antique sculptures, based
on a Greek original.*

**Vasari's Classical
Arno façade**

KEY

☐ East Corridor
☐ West Corridor
☐ Arno Corridor
☐ Gallery Rooms 1–45
☐ Non-exhibition space

★ **The Holy Family** *(1507)*
*Michelangelo's painting, the
first to break with the
convention of showing
Christ on the Virgin's lap,
inspired subsequent Mannerist
artists through its expressive
handling of color and posture.*

Exploring the Uffizi's Collection

THE UFFIZI houses some of the greatest art of the
Renaissance. Accumulated over the centuries by
the Medici, the collection was first housed in the Uffizi
in 1581, and eventually bequeathed to the people of
Florence by Anna Maria Lodovica, the last of the Medici
(1667–1743). Roman statues collected by the Medici are
on display in the Arno Corridor, but the pride of the
gallery is its matchless collection of paintings.

Madonna of the Long Neck by
Parmigianino (c.1534)

GOTHIC ART

FOLLOWING THE collection of
statues and antiquities in
room 1, the gallery's next six
rooms are devoted to Tuscan
art from the 12th to the 14th
centuries, notably works by
Cimabue, Duccio, and Giotto,
the three greatest artists of this
period. Giotto (1266–1337)
introduced a degree of
naturalism new to Tuscan art.
This is apparent in the range
of emotions expressed by the
angels and saints in his
Ognissanti Madonna (1310).
There are also fine works
by Ambrogio and Pietro
Lorenzetti, and Simone
Martini of the Sienese School.

EARLY RENAISSANCE

A BETTER UNDERSTANDING of
geometry and perspective
allowed Renaissance artists
to create an illusion of space
and depth in their works. No
artist was more obsessed with
perspective than Paolo Uccello

(1397–1475), whose *Battle of
San Romano* is displayed in
room 7. Portraits include two
panels by Piero della Francesca
(1410–92), depicting the Duke
and Duchess of Urbino, while
Fra Filippo Lippi's *Madonna
and Child with Angels*
(1455–66) is a work of great
warmth and humanity.
For most visitors, however,
the famous Botticellis in rooms
10–14 are the highlight of the
gallery. In *The Birth of Venus*,
Botticelli replaces the Virgin
with the Classical goddess
of love, while in *Primavera*
(1480), he breaks with
Christian religious painting to
depict the pagan rite of spring.

HIGH RENAISSANCE
AND MANNERISM

ROOM 15 contains works
attributed to the young
Leonardo da Vinci. The
evolution of his masterly style
can be traced in *The
Annunciation* (1472–5) and
his unfinished *Adoration of
the Magi* (1481). The
octagonal Tribune
(room 18) displays
some of the best-loved
pieces of the Medici
collection, including
the 1st century BC
Medici Venus,
considered the most
erotic of ancient
statues. There are also
paintings of family
members, including
Bronzino's fine portrait
of Eleonora of Toledo,
Cosimo I's wife (1545).
Rooms 19 to 23
illustrate the spread of
Renaissance ideas and
techniques beyond
Florence to other parts
of Italy and beyond.
The Umbrian artist
Perugino (1446–1523)

and northern European
painters such as Dürer (1471–
1528) are well represented.
Michelangelo's *Holy Family*
(1507), in Room 25, is striking
for its vibrant colors and the
curious twisted pose of the
Virgin. This painting had
great influence on the next
generation of Tuscan painters,
notably Bronzino (1503–72),
Pontormo (1494–1556), and
Parmigianino (1503–40),
whose *Madonna of the Long
Neck* with its contorted
anatomy and unusual colors is
a classic example of what came
to be known as Mannerism.
Sublime examples of High
Renaissance art located
nearby include Raphael's
Madonna of the Goldfinch
and Titian's notorious *Venus
of Urbino* (1538), considered
by many to be the most
beautiful nude ever painted.

LATER PAINTINGS

ROOMS 41–45 of the Uffizi
hold paintings acquired
by the Medici in the 17th and
18th centuries. These include
works by Rubens (1577–1640)
and van Dyck (1599–1641)
and three paintings by
Caravaggio – *Bacchus*
(c.1589), *The Sacrifice of
Isaac* (c.1590), and *Medusa*
(1596–8). Room 44 is
dedicated to northern
European painting, and
features *Portrait of an Old
Man* (1665) by Rembrandt.

Madonna of the Golfinch (1506) by Raphael

Ponte Vecchio ⑫

🚌 *many routes.*

THE PONTE VECCHIO, the oldest surviving bridge in the city, was designed by Taddeo Gaddi, and built in 1345. The three-arched bridge rests on two stout piers with boat-shaped cutwaters. Its picturesque shops were originally occcupied by black-smiths, butchers, and tanners (who used the river as a convenient garbage dump). They were evicted in 1593 by Duke Ferdinando I and replaced by jewelers and goldsmiths who were able to pay higher rents. A bust of the most famous of Florence's goldsmiths, Benvenuto Cellini (1500–71), is located in the middle of the bridge.

The elevated Vasari Corridor runs along the eastern side of the bridge, above the shops. It was designed in 1565 to allow the Medici to move from the Palazzo Vecchio to Palazzo Pitti via the Uffizi, without having to mix with the public. The Mannelli family refused to demolish their tower to make way for the corridor, and it stands there defiantly to this day. The corridor passes around it, supported on brackets.

The "Old Bridge," at its most attractive when viewed at sunset, was the only one to escape destruction during World War II. Visitors today come to admire the views and to browse among the antiques and specialized jewelry shops.

The massive Renaissance Palazzo Pitti, home to several museums

Palazzo Pitti ⑬

Piazza Pitti. 🚌 *D, 11, 36, 37.* 📞 *055-238 86 14.* 🕐 *8:15am–6:50pm Tue–Sun.* ⬛ *public hols.* ♿ ⬛

PALAZZO PITTI was originally built for the banker Luca Pitti, but his attempt to outrival the Medici backfired when costs of the building, begun in 1457, bankrupted his heirs. The Medici moved in and subsequent rulers of the city lived here. Today the richly decorated rooms exhibit treasures from the Medici collections.

The Palatine Gallery contains numerous works of art and ceiling frescoes glorifying the Medici. Raphael's *Madonna dalla Seggiola* (c.1515) and Titian's *Portrait of a Gentleman* (1540) are among the exhibits. On the first floor of the south wing, the royal apartments – Appartamenti

Reali – are opulently decorated with ornate gold and white stuccoed ceilings. The rooms are hung with portraits of the Medici family and decorated with beautiful frescoes and Gobelins tapestries.

Other collections at the Palazzo include the Galleria d'Arte Moderna, with mainly 19th-century works of art, the Galleria del Costume, opened in 1983, which reflects changing taste in courtly fashions, and the Museo degli Argenti which displays the family's lavish tastes in silverware and furniture.

L'Isolotto with Giambologna's *Oceanus Fountain***, Boboli Gardens**

Boboli Gardens ⑭

Piazza de' Pitti. 🚌 *D, 11, 36, 37.* 🕐 *daily.* ⬛ *public hols.* ♿ ⬛

LAID OUT behind the Palazzo Pitti, the Boboli Gardens are an excellent example of highly stylized Renaissance gardening. Formal box hedges lead to peaceful groves of holly and cypress trees, all this gracefully interspersed with Classical statues.

Highlights include the stone amphitheater where early opera performances were staged and L'Isolotto (Little Island), with its statues of dancing peasants around a moated garden. The Grotta Grande is a Mannerist folly, which houses several statues including *Venus Bathing* (1565) by Giambologna and Vincenzo de' Rossi's *Paris with Helen of Troy* (1560).

View of the Ponte Vecchio and the Arno at sunset

Portofino Peninsula ❾

🏠 🚌 ℹ️ *Via Roma 35, Portofino (0185-26 90 24).*

PORTOFINO IS THE most exclusive harbor and resort town in Italy, crammed with the yachts of the wealthy. Cars are not allowed in the village but boats run regularly between here and the resort of **Santa Margherita Ligure**. Boats also run to the **Abbazia di San Fruttuoso**, an 11th-century abbey situated on the other side of the peninsula.

Further west along the coast is **Punta Chiappa**, a rocky promontory famous for the changing colors of the sea. Other attractive resorts along the Ligurian coast include the fishing village of **Camogli**, **Rapallo** and its patrician villas, and romantic **Portovenere**.

Genoa ❿

🏠 640,000. ✈️ *Cristoforo Colombo 6 km (4 miles) W.* 🚆 🚍 🚌 ℹ️ *Ponte Spinola, Area Porto Antico (010-24 87 11).* 🏠 *Mon, Wed, & Thu.* 🎭 *International Ballet Festival (Jul); Fiera Nautica (Oct).*

THE MOST IMPORTANT commercial port in Italy, Genoa (Genova in Italian) also possesses palaces, paintings, and sculptures

Gothic façade of San Lorenzo, Genoa

dotted around the city, which are among the finest in northwestern Italy.

The austere-looking **Palazzo Reale**, one-time residence of the Kings of Savoy, has a highly ornate Rococo interior, a collection of paintings including works by Parodi and van Dyck, and an attractive garden. Opposite the palace is the old **University** (1634), built on four levels and designed by the architect Bartolomeo Bianco.

Palazzo Bianco, on the **Via Garibaldi**, contains the city's prime collection of paintings, including works by Lippi, van Dyck, and Rubens. Across the

street, **Palazzo Rosso** houses works by Dürer and Caravaggio, and 17th-century frescoes by local artists.

Once the seat of the doges of Genoa and now an arts and cultural center, the **Palazzo Ducale** is located between **San Lorenzo** cathedral with its attached museum, and **Il Gesù**, a Baroque church.

All that remains of the Gothic church of **Sant' Agostino**, bombed in World War II, is the bell tower, which is decorated with colored tiles. Two surviving cloisters of its surrounding monastery have been turned into the **Museo di Sant' Agostino**, which contains the city's collection of sculptural and architectural fragments.

🏛️ **Palazzo Reale**
Via Balbi 10. 📞 010-271 02 72.
⏰ *daily (except pm Mon & Tue).*
⬤ *Jan 1, Apr 25, May 1, Dec 25.*
📷 ♿

🏛️ **Palazzo Bianco**
Via Garibaldi. 📞 010-557 22 03.
⏰ *Tue–Sun.* 📷 **Palazzo Rosso**
📞 010- 247 63 51. ⏰ *Tue–Sat.*
🏛️ **Museo di Sant' Agostino**
Piazza Sarzano 35. 📞 010-251 12 63. ⏰ *Tue–Sat & Sun am.*
⬤ *public hols.* 📷 ♿

Portofino's famous harbor, showing the large yachts moored here

The Dome of San Lorenzo in Turin

Turin ⑪

🏛 *1,000,000.* ✈ *Caselle 15 km (9 miles) N.* 🚉 🚌 🛈 *Stazione Porta Nuova (011-53 13 27).* 🛒 *Sat.* 🎉 *Festa di San Giovanni (Jun 24).*

HOME OF THE FIAT car company, the famous Shroud, and the Juventus football team, Turin (Torino to the Italians) is also a town of grace and charm, with superb Baroque architecture.

Many of Turin's monuments were erected by the House of Savoy (rulers of Piedmont and Sardinia) from their capital here, before Italian unification in 1861 made the head of the House of Savoy King of Italy.

The **Museo Egizio** – one of the world's great collections of Egyptian artifacts – was amassed by Bernardo Drovetti, Napoleon's Consul General in Egypt. Wall and tomb paintings, papyri, sculptures, and a reconstruction of the 15th-century BC **Rock Temple of Ellessya** are among its marvels.

The **Galleria Sabauda**, in the same building, was the House of Savoy's main painting collection, and houses a stunning array of works by Italian, French, Flemish, and Dutch masters.

Other notable buildings in the city include **San Lorenzo**, the former Royal Chapel designed by Guarino Guarini (1624–83), which boasts an extraordinary geometric dome. Inside the **Palazzo Reale**, seat of the Savoys, the **Armeria Reale** holds one of the largest arms collections in the world.

The **Duomo** (1497–8), Turin's cathedral dedicated to St. John the Baptist, is the only example of Renaissance architecture in the city. Inside, the **Cappella della Sacra Sindone**, also designed by Guarini, houses the famous Turin Shroud.

Inside the **Palazzo Madama**, the **Museo Civico d'Arte Antica**, which is closed for restoration until the end of 2004, contains a variety of Classical and antique treasures.

🏛 **Museo Egizio**
Via Accademia delle Scienze 6.
📞 011-561 77 76. 🕐 Tue–Sun.
⬤ Jan 1, Dec 25. 🎟 👜 🛈
🏛 **Palazzo Reale**
Piazzetta Reale. 📞 011-436 14 55.
🕐 Tue–Sun. ⬤ Jan 1, May 1, Dec 25. 🎟 👜 👜 🛈
🏛 **Armeria Reale**
Piazza Castello 191. 📞 011-54 38 89. 🕐 1:30–7:30pm Tue & Thu, 8:30am–2pm Wed & Fri, 10:30am–7:30pm Sat & Sun.
⬤ Jan 1, Dec 25. 🎟

The imposing façade of the Baroque Basilica di Superga

ENVIRONS: In the countryside around Turin, two superb monuments to the House of Savoy are worth visiting. About 9 km (5 miles) southwest of Turin, **Stupinigi** is a magnificent hunting lodge, sumptuously decorated with frescoes and paintings. It has a vast collection of 17th- and 18th-century furniture.

The Baroque **Basilica di Superga**, on a hill to the east of Turin, offers good views of the city. Its mausoleum commemorates kings of Sardinia and other members of the royal House of Savoy.

🏛 **Stupinigi**
Piazza Principe Amedeo 7. 📞 011-358 12 20. 🚌 63 to Piazza Caio Mario, then 41. 🕐 Tue–Sun. ⬤ Jan 1, Dec 25. 🎟 👜
🏛 **Basilica di Superga**
Strada Basilica di Superga 73.
📞 011-898 00 83. 🚂 Sassi, then 79 bus. 🕐 daily. **Tombs** 🕐 daily.

THE TURIN SHROUD

The most famous – and most dubious – holy relic of them all is kept in Turin's Duomo. The shroud, said to be the sheet in which the body of Christ was wrapped after the Crucifixion, bears the imprint of a man with a side wound, and bruises, possibly from a crown of thorns.

The shroud's early history is unclear, but the House of Savoy was in possession of it around 1450, and displayed it in Guarini's chapel in the Duomo from 1694. The "original" shroud sits in a silver casket inside an iron box within a marble coffer. This has been placed inside an urn on the chapel altar. A replica shroud is on view. In 1988 the myth of the shroud was exploded: a carbon-dating test showed it to be a 12th-century relic. The shroud remains an object of veneration nonetheless.

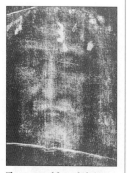

The supposed face of Christ imprinted on the Turin Shroud

The giant Gothic Duomo in central Milan, crowned with spires

Milan ⑫

🏃 1,465,000. ✈ Malpensa 55 km (34 miles) NW; Linate 8 km (5 miles) E. 🚉 🚌 🛈 Via Marconi 1 (02-72 52 43 01). 🚢 daily, major market Sat. 🎉 Sant'Ambrogio (Dec 7).

CENTER OF FASHION and business, Milan (Milano in Italian) also has a wealth of impressive sights reflecting its long and checkered history.

An important trading center since it was founded by the Romans in 222 BC, Milan's central position made it a favored location for the empire's rulers. It was here that Emperor Constantine declared that Christianity was officially recognized, following his own conversion (known as the Edict of Milan, AD 313).

By the Middle Ages Milan was one of many cities in Lombardy which opposed the power of the Holy Roman Emperor. A period of local dynastic rule followed the fall of the region to the Visconti family in 1277. They were succeeded by the Sforzas during the Renaissance. These dynasties became great patrons of the arts, with the result that Milan has acquired a host of artistic treasures. Today this chic, bustling, and prosperous metropolis offers opportunities for designer shopping and gastronomic pleasures along with plenty of cultural activities.

Situated at the very heart of Milan, the giant **Duomo** is one of the largest Gothic churches in the world. The roof is extraordinary with 135 spires and innumerable statues and gargoyles. Inside, there are remarkable stained-glass windows, bas-reliefs, and a medieval treasury. More religious artifacts can be seen in the **Museo del Duomo**, located in the Palazzo Reale.

An ornate shopping arcade completed in 1878, the **Galleria Vittorio Emanuele II** links the Piazza del Duomo with the Piazza della Scala. It boasts a superb metal and glass roof crowned with a central dome, has mosaic floors, and houses stylish shops and restaurants.

The Neo-Classical **Teatro alla Scala** opened in 1778 and is among the most prestigious opera houses in the world. Closed until 2005 for renovation, its stage is one of the largest in Europe. The adjoining **Museo Teatrale** displays past sets and costumes and offers a glimpse of the auditorium.

The **Castello Sforzesco**, a symbol of Milan, was initially the palace of the Visconti family. Francesco Sforza, who became lord of Milan in 1450, embellished it, turning it into a magnificent Renaissance residence. The building has a forbidding exterior, a delightful interior, and contains an impressive collection of furniture, antiquities, and paintings. Michelangelo's unfinished sculpture, known as the *Rondanini Pietà*, can also be seen here.

Milan's finest art collection is held in the imposing 17th-century Palazzo di Brera. Major works of Italian Renaissance and Baroque painters including *The Marriage of the Virgin* by Raphael, and Mantegna's

The glass dome of the Galleria Vittorio Emanuele II in Milan

Dead Christ, hang in the 38 rooms of the **Pinacoteca di Brera**. Works by some of Italy's 20th-century artists are also on display.

The beautiful 15th-century Renaissance convent of **Santa Maria delle Grazie,** in the southwest of the city, is a must-see because it contains one of the key images of western civilization: the *Last Supper* (or *Cenacolo*) of Leonardo da Vinci. The large wall painting has deteriorated badly but remains an iconic work of great subtlety.

Sant'Ambrogio is a mainly 10th-century Romanesque basilica dedicated to the patron saint of Milan whose tomb lies in the crypt. The 4th-century church of **San Lorenzo** holds an important collection of Roman and early Christian remains.

🏛 **Duomo**
Piazza del Duomo. 📷 *to roof.* ♿
Museo del Duomo 📞 *02-86 03 58.*
◻ *daily.* ● *public hols.* 📷
🏛 **Castello Sforzesco**
Piazza Castello. 📞 *02-88 46 37 01.*
◻ *Tue–Sun.* ● *public hols.* ♿
🏛 **Pinacoteca di Brera**
Via Brera 28. 📞 *02-72 26 31.*
◻ *Tue–Sun.* ● *Jan 1, May 1, Dec 25.* 📷 ♿ 🏛
🏛 **Santa Maria delle Grazie**
Piazza Santa Maria delle Grazie 2.
Cenacolo 📞 *02-89 42 11 46.*
◻ *Tue – Sun (booking compulsory).*
● *public hols.* 📷 ♿

Lake Maggiore ⓭

🚉 *to Stresa and Laveno.* 🚌
🚢 *Navigazione Lago Maggiore (800-55 18 01).* 🛈 *Piazza Marconi 16, Stresa (0323-301 50).*

LAKE MAGGIORE is a long expanse of water that nestles right against the mountains and stretches away into Alpine Switzerland. In the center lie the exquisite Borromean islands named after the chief patron of the lake, St. Carlo Borromeo, of whom there is a giant statue in **Arona.**

Further up the western coast of the lake is **Stresa,** the chief resort and main jumping-off point for visits to the islands. From here **Monte**

Statue of Carlo Borromeo, patron saint of Lake Maggiore, in Arona

Mottarone, a snow-capped peak offering spectacular panoramic views, can be reached by cable car.

Lake Como ⓮

🚉 *to Como and Lecco.* 🚌 🚢 *Navigazione Lago di Como (800-55 18 01).* 🛈 *Piazza Cavour 17, Como (031-330 01 11).*

SET IN AN IDYLLIC LANDSCAPE, Como has long attracted visitors who come to walk in the hills or to go boating. The long, narrow lake, also known as Lario, is shaped like an upside-down Y, and offers fine views of the Alps.

In the heart of the town of **Como** lies the elegant Piazza Cavour. The beautiful 14th-century **Duomo** nearby has 15th- and 16th-century reliefs and paintings, and fine tombs.

Bellagio, at the junction of the "Y," has spectacular views, and is one of the most popular spots on Lake Como.

In the lakeside town of **Tremezzo**, the 18th-century **Villa Carlotta** is adorned with sculptures and celebrated for its terraced gardens.

Lake Garda ⓯

🚉 *to Desenzano and Orta San Giulio.* 🚌🚢 *Navigazione Lago di Garda (800-55 18 01).* 🛈 *Via Repubblica 8, Gardone Riviera (0365-203 47).*

GARDA, THE LARGEST of the northern lakes, borders the three regions of Trentino, Lombardy, and Veneto.

Hydrofoils and catamarans ply the lake, offering stops at **Sirmione**, site of a medieval castle, **Gardone** with the curiosity-filled **Villa il Vittoriale**, and **Salò** where Mussolini established a short-lived Republic in 1943.

Lake Como, one of the most attractive summer resorts of northern Italy

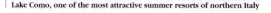

The Arena, Verona's Roman amphitheater – the setting for spectacular summer opera performances

Mantua ⑯

🚶 55,000. 🚉 🚌 🛈 *Piazza Andrea Mantegna 6 (0376-32 82 53).* 🗓 *Thu.*

A STRIKING if stern-looking city of fine squares and aristocratic architecture, Mantua (Mantova in Italian) is bordered on three sides by lakes. It was the birthplace of the poet Virgil and playground for three centuries of the Gonzaga dukes. Mantua was also the setting for Verdi's opera *Rigoletto*, and is mentioned in Shakespeare's *Romeo and Juliet*. These theatrical connections are celebrated in local street-names and monuments and are reinforced by the presence in the town of the 18th-century **Teatro Scientifico Bibiena**, a masterpiece of late Baroque theater architecture.

Mantua is focused on three attractive main squares. Piazza Sordello is the site of the **Palazzo Ducale**, the vast former home of the Gonzaga family which also incorporates

a 14th-century fortress and a basilica. The frescoes by Mantegna in the **Camera degli Sposi** (1465–74), are a highlight. They portray the Gonzaga family and court, and the room is completed by a light-hearted *trompe l'oeil* ceiling. The nearby **Duomo** has an 18th-century façade and fine interior stuccoes by Giulio Romano (c.1492–1546).

Piazza dell'Erbe is dominated by the Basilica di Sant' Andrea (15th century), designed largely by the early Renaissance architect and theorist, Alberti.

Across town is the vast 16th-century Palazzo del Tè, designed as the Gonzaga family's summer retreat. This extraordinary palace is decorated with frescoes by Giulio Romano and has rooms lavishly painted with horses and signs of the zodiac.

🏛 Palazzo Ducale
Piazza Sordello. 📞 0376-38 21 50. ⏰ Tue–Sun. 🚫 Jan 1, May 1, Dec 25. 📷 **Camera degli Sposi** ⏰ by appointment. 📞 in advance to book a viewing time.

The 13th-century façade of the Palazzo Ducale in Mantua

Verona ⑰

🚶 255,000. ✈ *Villafranca 14 km (9 miles) SW.* 🚉 🚌 🛈 *Via degli Alpini 9 (045-806 86 80).* 🗓 *daily.* 🎭 *Estate Teatrale Veronese (Jun–Aug); Opera Festival (Jun–Sep).*

V ERONA, A LARGE and prosperous city of the Veneto region, boasts magnificent Roman ruins, second only to those of Rome itself, as well as important medieval monuments.

The Arena, Verona's Roman amphitheater completed in AD 30, is the third largest in the world. Bullfights, fairs, and opera productions are staged here. Other Roman sites include the Roman Theater, and artifacts from Roman times can be seen in the Museo Archeologico.

The tragic story of Romeo and Juliet, first set here by Luigi da Porto in the 1520s and immortalized by Shakespeare, has inspired local monuments such as Romeo's House and the so-called Tomb of Juliet. Verona's focal point is Piazza Erbe, scene of colorful markets for 2,000 years.

The ornate tombs of members of the Scaglieri family, who ruled the city for 127 years from 1263, are situated beside the entrance to the church of Santa Maria Antica. Another legacy of the family is Castelvecchio, an impressive castle built by Cangrande II between 1355 and 1375. There is a fine art gallery in the castle, which has a collection of 15th-century late Renaissance Madonnas.

Built in 1125–35 to house the shrine of Verona's patron saint, **San Zeno Maggiore** is the most ornate Romanesque church in northern Italy, famous for its unusual medieval bronze door panels.

The **Duomo** also dates from the 12th century and displays Titian's *Assumption*. Other notable medieval churches in Verona are **San Fermo Maggiore** with many interior frescoes including the *Annunciation* by Pisanello (1377–1455), and **Sant' Anastasia,** which houses 15th-century frescoes and holy water stoups supported by figures of beggars known locally as *i gobbi*.

⌂ Arena
Piazza Brà. 🕻 045-800 32 04.
⬤ daily. ⬤ Jan 1, Dec 25–26. 🌠
♣ Castelvecchio
Corso Castelvecchio 2. 🕻 045-59 47 34. ⬤ daily. 🌠 🛅 🎧 (audio).

Vicenza ⑱

🏯 116,000. 🚉 🚌 🛈 Piazza
Matteotti 12 (0444-32 08 54).
🛒 Tue & Thu. 🎵 Concert season
(May–Jun); theater season (Sep–Oct).

V ICENZA IS CELEBRATED for
its splendid, varied
architecture. Known as the city
of Andrea Palladio (1508–80),
stonemason turned architect,
it offers a unique opportunity
to study the evolution of his
distinctive style.

Piazza dei Signori at the
heart of Vicenza is dominated
by the Palazzo della Ragione,
known also as the **Basilica.**

**The illusionistic stage set of the
Teatro Olimpico in Vicenza**

The Basilica di Sant'Antonio in Padua, with its Byzantine domes

Palladio's first public commission, it has a roof like an upturned boat, and a balustrade bristling with statues. Beside it stands the 12th-century **Torre di Piazza**.

The **Loggia del Capitaniato**, to the northwest, was built by Palladio in 1571. Its upper rooms contain the city's council chamber.

Europe's oldest surviving indoor theater, the **Teatro Olimpico** was begun by Palladio in 1579 and completed by his pupil, Vincenzo Scamozzi. It was Scamozzi who created the permanent stage, built largely of wood and plaster and painted to look like marble. It represents Thebes, a Greek city, and uses perspective to create an illusion of depth.

Palladio was also responsible for the **Palazzo Chiericati** which houses the **Museo Civico**, but the epitome of his work can be seen in the villa known as **La Rotonda**, located in the countryside to the south of Vicenza.

**Memorial to
Andrea Palladio
in Vicenza**

⛩ Piazza dei Signori
Basilica 🕻 0444-32 36 81.
⬤ for exhibitions. 🌠
⛩ Teatro Olimpico
Piazza Matteotti. 🕻 0444-22 28 00.
⬤ Tue–Sun. ⬤ 1 Jan, 25 Dec. 🌠 ♿
⛩ La Rotonda
Via Rotonda 25. 🕻 0444-3217 93.
Villa ⬤ Mar–Nov: Wed. 🌠
Garden ⬤ Tue–Sun. 🌠

Padua ⑲

🏯 220,000. 🚉 🚌 🛈 Piazzale
della Stazione (049-875 20 77).
🛒 Mon–Sat at Prato della Valle.
🎵 Concert season (Oct–Apr).

P ADUA IS AN OLD university
town with an illustrious
academic history. The city
(Padova in Italian) has two
major attractions – the
**Basilica di Sant'
Antonio**, one of the
most popular sites of
pilgrimage in Italy,
and the **Cappella
degli Scrovegni**, a
beautifully decorated
chapel. The exotic
Basilica was built from
1232 to house the
remains of the great
Franciscan preacher,
St. Antony of Padua.

The chapel (1303)
features a series of
frescoes depicting
the life of Christ,
painted by Giotto.
The **Museo Civico
Eremitani** on the same site
has a rich coin collection and
an art gallery.

Other attractions include
the **Duomo** and **Baptistry**,
which contains one of Italy's
most complete medieval fresco
cycles (painted by Giusto
de'Menabuoi in 1378), and the
Palazzo della Ragione, built
in 1218 to serve as Padua's
law court and council chamber.

⌂ Cappella degli Scrovegni
Piazza Eremitani. 🕻 049-201 00 20.
⬤ daily (advance booking necessary).
⬤ public hols. 🌠 ♿

Venice ⑳

CREATED ON A SERIES of mud banks in a lagoon, with canals in place of roads, Venice can truly claim to be unique. Originally a province of the Byzantine Empire, by the 12th century Venice was an independent city-state and, through its control of the spice and silk trade from the East, the richest trading nation in Europe. The banks of its canals are lined with magnificent palaces dating from this period up until the 18th century. By then Venice's power and influence were waning. It finally lost its independence in 1797, since when this astonishing city has remained more or less frozen in time.

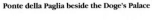

Ponte della Paglia beside the Doge's Palace

SIGHTS AT A GLANCE

Accademia ⑪
Doge's Palace pp436–7 ②
Grand Canal ⑥
Museo Correr ③
Peggy Guggenheim
 Collection ⑩
St. Mark's pp434–5 ①
Santa Maria Gloriosa
 dei Frari ⑤
Santa Maria della Salute ⑨
Santi Giovanni e Paolo ⑦
Scuola di San Giorgio
 degli Schiavoni ⑧
Scuola Grande di
 San Rocco ④

The Lagoon *(see inset map)*
Murano ⑫

GETTING AROUND

Venice's basic public transportation *(see p451)* is the *vaporetto*, a water bus that plies the canals of the city and links it to the various lagoon islands. There are some 15 routes. More exotic craft include gondolas, which are very expensive, and the more reasonable *traghetti* (gondola ferries) – useful for crossing the Grand Canal when exploring on foot. The speediest means of travel is water taxi.

SEE ALSO

• *Where to Stay* p458

• *Where to Eat* p464

A   B   C

VENICE: THE LAGOON

Treviso
S Dona
Marco Polo
Torcello
Burano

Mestre
Canale Oselino
Padua
Veneta
Laguna
VENICE
La Giudecca
Lido

0 km 4

0 miles 4

KEY

Area of main map

- - - Vaporetto route

Murano,
Burano
Fondamente Nuove

Ospedale
Civile

Madonna
dell'Orto

CAMPIELLO
PIAVE

Ca' Pésaro

Ca'd'Oro

Ca' d'Oro

Pescheria

Ponte
di Rialto

Fondaco dei
Tedeschi

Rialto

CAMPO
SAN
SILVESTRO

San
Silvestro

CORTE
TEATRO

CAMPO
SAN LUCA

CAMPO
SAN BENETO

CAMPO
MANIN

SAN MARCO

CAMPO
SAN
ANZOLO

CAMPIELLO
CALEGHERI

CAMPO
SAN
MAURIZIO

CAMPO
SAN MOISE

CAMPO DEL
TRAGHETTO

Santa Maria
del Giglio

Salute

CAMPO
SANT'ANTONIO

CAMPO
DEI GESUITI

CPLO D.
PIETA

CAMPO DEI
SANTI APOSTOLI

CPLO DEL
CASON

CAMPO S
MARIA NOVA

CPLO SANTA
MARIA NOVA

CAMPIELLO
WIDMAN

CAMPO
SAN
ZANIPOLO

CAMPO S
MARINA

CAMPO
SAN MARINA

CAMPO
SAN LIO

CAMPO
D. GUERRA

CAMPO S
MARIA
FORMOSA

CAMPO
SAN
LORENZO

CAMPO S
GIUSTINA

CAMPO DELLA
CONFRATERNITA

CASTELLO

PIAZZA
SAN
MARCO

San Marco

San
Zaccaria

CAMPO
SAN PROVOLO

CAMPO
SAN ZACCARIA

CAMPO
BANDIERA
E MORO

CPLO D.
PIOVAN

Canale di San Marco

Canale di San Marco

KEY

Sight / Place of interest

Airport

Train station

Vaporetto / ferry boarding point

Traghetto crossing

Gondola waiting point

Tourist information

Church

Synagogue

0 meters 300

0 yards 300

D E F

St. Mark's ①

THE BASILICA BLENDS architectural and decorative styles from East and West to create one of Europe's greatest buildings. Built on a Greek-cross plan and crowned with five huge domes, it is the third church to stand on this site. The first, built to enshrine the body of St. Mark in the 9th century, was destroyed by fire. The second was pulled down in the 11th century to make way for a truly spectacular edifice, reflecting the growing power of the Republic and its links with Byzantium. The dark interior is clad in wonderful mosaics, gleaming with gold. Many treasures – statues, icons, and the famous horses – were brought to St. Mark's after the 4th Crusade had plundered Constantinople in 1204.

★ Pentecost Mosaic
The interior of the dome above the nave is decorated with a 12th-century mosaic of the Holy Spirit descending on the Apostles in tongues of fire.

St. Mark flanked by Angels
The statues crowning the central arch were added in the early 15th century.

The atrium, or narthex, contains many fine mosaics, notably those of the Genesis Cupola showing the Creation.

The central arch features 13th-century carvings of the Labours of the Months.

★ Horses of St. Mark
The four horses are replicas of the gilded bronze originals, kept in the Museo Marciano, reached from the atrium.

Main entrance

★ Façade Mosaics
These are either heavily restored or replacements of the originals. This 17th-century work shows the body of St. Mark being smuggled out of Alexandria.

The Ascension Dome features a magnificent 13th-century mosaic of Christ surrounded by angels, the 12 Apostles, and the Virgin Mary.

★ Pala d'Oro
The greatest treasure of St. Mark's is kept behind the high altar. The magnificent altarpiece, created originally in the 10th century, is made up of 250 gold panels, adorned with enamels and precious stones.

VISITORS' CHECKLIST

Piazza San Marco. 041-522 52 05. San Marco. Apr–Sep: 9:30am–5pm Mon–Sat, 2–4pm Sun; Oct–Mar: 10am–4pm Mon–Sat, 2–4pm Sun. sightseeing limited during services. **Museo Marciano, Treasury, and Pala d'Oro** as above.

The altar canopy, or baldacchino, has alabaster columns carved with New Testament scenes.

St. Mark's body, thought to have been lost in the fire of 976, reappeared when the new church was consecrated in 1094. The remains are housed below the altar.

★ Treasury
This contains many treasures looted from Constantinople by the Venetians in 1204. This 11th-century silver-gilt reliquary is in the shape of a domed basilica.

Allegorical mosaics decorate the floor of the south transept.

Baptistry

The Tetrarchs
This porphyry sculptural group (4th-century Egyptian) may represent Diocletian, Maximian, Constantius, and Valerian – the four joint rulers of the Roman Empire c.AD 300, known as the tetrarchs.

STAR FEATURES

★ Mosaics

★ Horses of St. Mark

★ Treasury

★ Pala d'Oro

Doge's Palace ②

THE OFFICIAL RESIDENCE of the Venetian ruler (doge) was founded in the 9th century. The present palace owes its external appearance to the building work of the 14th and early 15th centuries. To create their airy Gothic masterpiece, the Venetians broke with tradition by perching the bulk of the palace (built of pink Veronese marble) on top of an apparent fretwork of loggias and arcades (built of white Istrian stone). A tour of the palace leads through a succession of richly decorated chambers and halls, ending with the Bridge of Sighs and the prisons.

Mars by Sansovino

In the Sala del Collegio the doge would receive ambassadors. The ceiling is decorated with 11 paintings by Veronese.

The Sala del Senato was the home of the senate, which had some 200 members.

Arco Foscari

Anticollegio

★ Porta della Carta
This 15th-century Gothic gate was the principal entrance to the palace. From it, a vaulted passageway leads to the Arco Foscari and the internal courtyard.

Exit

STAR FEATURES

★ **Giants' Staircase**

★ **Porta della Carta**

★ **Sala del Maggior Consiglio**

The balcony on the west façade was added in 1536 to mirror the early 15th-century balcony looking onto the quay.

★ Giants' Staircase
Statues by Sansovino of Neptune and Mars at the top of this late 15th-century staircase symbolize Venice's power at sea and on land. Doges were crowned with the glittering zogia or ducal cap on the landing.

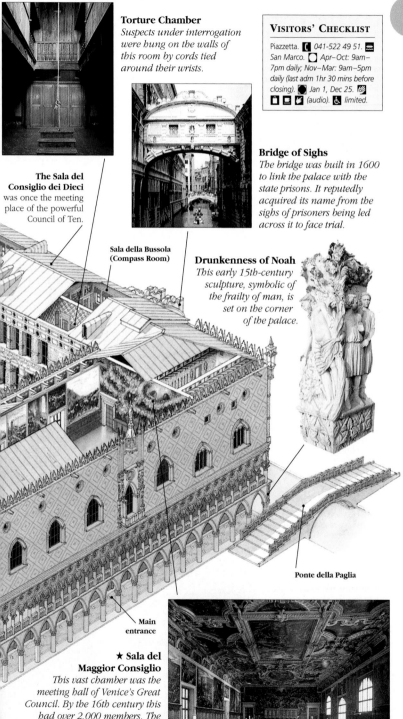

Torture Chamber
Suspects under interrogation were hung on the walls of this room by cords tied around their wrists.

VISITORS' CHECKLIST

Piazzetta. 041-522 49 51.
San Marco. Apr–Oct: 9am–7pm daily; Nov–Mar: 9am–5pm daily (last adm 1hr 30 mins before closing). Jan 1, Dec 25. (audio). limited.

The Sala del Consiglio dei Dieci was once the meeting place of the powerful Council of Ten.

Bridge of Sighs
The bridge was built in 1600 to link the palace with the state prisons. It reputedly acquired its name from the sighs of prisoners being led across it to face trial.

Sala della Bussola
(Compass Room)

Drunkenness of Noah
This early 15th-century sculpture, symbolic of the frailty of man, is set on the corner of the palace.

Ponte della Paglia

Main entrance

★ **Sala del Maggior Consiglio**
This vast chamber was the meeting hall of Venice's Great Council. By the 16th century this had over 2,000 members. The entire end wall is taken up by Tintoretto's Paradise *(1588–92).*

Carpaccio's *Portrait of a Young Man in a Red Hat*, Museo Correr

Museo Correr ③

Procuratie Nuove. Entrance in Ala Napoleonica. 041-522 56 25. San Marco. daily. Jan 1, Dec 25.

TEODORO CORRER bequeathed his extensive collection of works of art to Venice in 1830, thus forming the core of the city's fine civic museum.

Its first rooms form a suitably Neoclassical backdrop for early statues by Antonio Canova (1757–1822). The rest of the floor covers the history of the Venetian Republic, with maps, coins, armor, and a host of doge-related exhibits.

The second floor contains the picture gallery. Works are hung chronologically, enabling one to trace the evolution of Venetian painting. The most famous are by Carpaccio: *Portrait of a Young Man in a Red Hat* (c.1490), and *Two Venetian Ladies* (c.1507). The Museo del Risorgimento on the same floor looks at the history of Venice until unification with Italy in 1866.

Scuola Grande di San Rocco ④

Campo San Rocco. 041-523 48 64. San Tomà. daily. Jan 1, Easter, Dec 25. (audio).

FOUNDED IN HONOR of San Rocco (St. Roch), a saint who dedicated his life to helping the sick, the Scuola started out as a charitable

confraternity. Construction began in 1515. The work was financed by donations from Venetians keen to invoke San Rocco's protection, and the Scuola quickly became one of the wealthiest in Venice. In 1564 its members decided to commission Tintoretto to decorate its walls and ceilings. His earliest paintings, the first of over 50 works he eventually created for the Scuola, fill the small Sala dell'Albergo off the Upper Hall. His later paintings are in the Ground Floor Hall, just inside the entrance.

The ground floor cycle was executed in 1583–7, when Tintoretto was in his sixties, and consists of eight episodes from the life of Mary. They are remarkable for the tranquil serenity of paintings such as *The Flight into Egypt* and *St. Mary of Egypt*.

Scarpagnino's great staircase (1544–6), leads to the Upper Hall, which was decorated by Tintoretto in 1575–81. The ceiling is painted with scenes from the Old Testament. The three large square paintings in the center show episodes from the Book of Exodus, all alluding to the charitable aims of the Scuola in alleviating thirst, sickness, and hunger. The vast wall paintings feature episodes from the New Testament, linking with the ceiling paintings. Two of the most striking are *The Temptation of Christ*, which shows a handsome young Satan offering Christ two loaves of bread, and *The Adoration of the Shepherds*.

The carvings below the paintings were added in the 17th century by sculptor Francesco Pianta. They include (near the altar) a caricature of Tintoretto with his palette and brushes.

The Sala dell'Albergo contains perhaps the most breathtaking of all Tintoretto's masterpieces – the *Crucifixion* (1565). Henry James once remarked of this painting: "no single picture contains more of human life; there is everything in it, including the most exquisite beauty."

Santa Maria Gloriosa dei Frari ⑤

Campo dei Frari. 041-275 04 62. San Tomà. Mon–Sat & Sun pm. Jan 1, Dec 25. unless attending mass.

MORE COMMONLY known as the Frari (a corruption of Frati, meaning brothers), this vast Gothic church dwarfs the eastern area of San Polo. Its 83-m (272-ft) campanile is the tallest in the city after that of San Marco. The first church on the site was built by the Franciscans in 1250–1338, but was replaced by a larger building completed in the mid-15th century. The airy interior is striking for its sheer size and for the quality of its works of art, including master-pieces by Titian and Giovanni Bellini, and a statue by Donatello, and several grandiose tombs.

The sacristy altarpiece *The Madonna and Child* (1488)

Detail from Tintoretto's *Flight into Egypt*, Scuola Grande di San Rocco

by Bellini, with its sublime use of color, is one of Venice's most beautiful Renaissance paintings. The main altarpiece is *The Assumption of the Virgin*, a spectacular, glowing work by Titian (1518), which draws the eye through the Renaissance rood screen to the altar. Between the altar and the screen is the Monks' Choir (1468), its three-tiered stalls lavishly carved with saints and Venetian city scenes.

The Tomb of Canova, a marble, pyramid-shaped tomb, was built after Canova's death in 1822 by his pupils. It is similar to a design Canova himself had planned for a memorial for Titian. The Titian monument in the shape of a triumphal arch that stands opposite was built by two of Canova's pupils in 1853.

High altar of the Frari church with Titian's *Assumption of the Virgin*

Grand Canal ⑥

🚤 *1 from Ferrovia and many others.*

THE BEST WAY to view the Grand Canal as it winds through the heart of the city is from a *vaporetto*, or water bus. Several lines travel the length of the canal. The palaces lining the waterway were built over a span of five centuries and present a panoramic survey of the city's history, almost all bearing the name of some once-great Venetian family.

Nearly 4 km (2.5 miles) long, the canal varies in width from 30 to 70 m (100 to 230 ft) and is spanned by three

View across the Grand Canal to the Pescheria (fishmarket)

bridges, the Scalzi, the Rialto, and the Accademia. After passing the Rialto, the canal doubles back on itself along a stretch known as La Volta (the bend). It then widens out and the views become more spectacular approaching San Marco. Façades may have faded and foundations rotted, yet the canal remains, in the words of the French ambassador in 1495, "the most beautiful street in the world."

Santi Giovanni e Paolo ⑦

Campo Santi Giovanni e Paolo (also signposted San Zanipolo). 📞 041-523 75 10. 🚤 Fondamente Nuove or Ospedale Civile. 🕐 daily. 🌑 12:30–3:30pm. 🚻 🚫

KNOWN COLLOQUIALLY as San Zanipolo, Santi Giovanni e Paolo vies with the Frari as the city's greatest Gothic church. Built by the

Dominicans in the 14th century, it is striking for its vast scale and architectural austerity. Known as the Pantheon of Venice, it houses monuments to no fewer than 25 doges. Among these are several fine works of art, executed by the Lombardi family and other leading sculptors. Pietro Lombardo created the magnificent tombs of the doges Nicolò Marcello (died 1474) and Pietro Mocenigo (died 1476). His masterpiece, the Tomb of Andrea Vendramin (died 1478), takes the form of a Roman triumphal arch.

The main doorway, which is decorated with Byzantine reliefs and carvings, is one of Venice's earliest Renaissance architectural works. On the right as you enter the church is a polyptych by Giovanni Bellini (c.1465) showing St. Vincent Ferrer, a Spanish cleric, flanked by St. Sebastian and St. Christopher.

THE GONDOLAS OF VENICE

The gondola has been a part of Venice since the 11th century. With its slim hull and flat underside, the craft is perfectly adapted to negotiating narrow, shallow canals. There is a slight leftward curve to the prow, which counter-acts the force of the oar, preventing the gondola from going around in circles.

In 1562 it was decreed that all gondolas should be black to stop people making an ostentatious show of their wealth. For special occasions they were decorated with flowers. Today, gondola rides are expensive and usually taken by tourists.

Gondolas moored in a Venice canal

Scuola di San Giorgio degli Schiavoni ⑧

Calle Furlani. 🄲 *041-522 88 28.*
🚤 *San Zaccaria.* ○ *Tue–Sun (Sun: am only).* ● *Jan 1, May 1, Dec 25 and other religious hols.* 📷

WITHIN THIS small Scuola, established in 1451 and rebuilt in 1551, are some of the finest paintings of Vittore Carpaccio (c.1460–1525). Commissioned by the Schiavoni, or Dalmatian Slav trading community in Venice, Carpaccio's exquisite frieze (1502–08) shows scenes from the lives of three saints: St. George, St. Tryphon, and St. Jerome. Each episode of the narrative cycle is remarkable for its vivid coloring and minutely observed detail of Venetian life. *St. George Slaying the Dragon* and *The Vision of St. Jerome* are outstanding.

Santa Maria della Salute ⑨

Campo della Salute. 🄲 *041-520 85 65.*
🚤 *Salute.* ○ *daily.* 📷 *to sacristy.*

THE GREAT BAROQUE church of Santa Maria della Salute, standing at the entrance of the Grand Canal, is an imposing

The single-story palazzo housing the Peggy Guggenheim Collection

architectural landmark of Venice. Construction of the church, begun in 1630 by Baldassare Longhena, was not completed until 1687, five years after his death.

The comparatively sober interior of Santa Maria della Salute consists of a large octagonal space below the cupola and six chapels radiating from the ambulatory. The sculptural group around the grandiose high altar is by Giusto Le Corte and represents the Virgin and Child protecting the city of Venice from the plague.

In the sacristy to the left of the altar, Titian's early altarpiece *St. Mark Enthroned with St. Cosmas, St. Damian, St. Roch and St. Sebastian* (1511–12) and his dramatic ceiling paintings of *David and Goliath*, *Cain and Abel*, and *The Sacrifice of Isaac* (1540–9) are considered the finest paintings in the church. *The Wedding at Cana* (1551) on the wall opposite the entrance, is a major work by Jacopo Tintoretto.

The church was named *Salute*, which means both "health" and "salvation," in thanksgiving for the deliverance of the city from the plague epidemic of 1630. Each November, in a moving ceremony of remembrance, worshipers light candles and approach the church across a bridge of boats which spans the mouth of the Grand Canal.

The Baroque church of Santa Maria della Salute, viewed from the other side of the Grand Canal

Peggy Guggenheim Collection ⑩

Palazzo Venier dei Leoni. 🄲 *041-240 54 11.* 🚤 *Accademia.* ○ *Wed–Mon* ● *Dec 25.* 📷 📷 *(audio).* 🄿 🛒

INTENDED AS A four-story palace, the 18th-century Palazzo Venier dei Leoni in fact never rose beyond the ground floor – hence its nickname "The Unfinished Palace." In 1949 the building was bought by Peggy Guggenheim (1898–1979), an American collector, dealer, and patron of the arts. One of the most visited sights of Venice, the palace is the best place in the city to see modern art. The light-filled rooms and modern canvases are in striking contrast to the majority of the art on display in Venice.

Her collection consists of 200 fine paintings and sculptures, representing the 20th century's most influential modern art movements. The dining room has notable Cubist works of art, including *The Poet* by Pablo Picasso, and an entire room is devoted to Jackson Pollock, who was "discovered" by Guggenheim. There are also works by Braque, Chagall, Dalí, Klee, Mondrian, and Magritte, whose Surreal *Empire of Light* (1953–4) shows a night scene of a darkened house with bright daylight above.

The sculpture collection, which includes Constantin Brancusi's elegant *Bird in Space* (c.1923), is laid out in the house and the garden.

Perhaps the most provocative piece, on the terrace overlooking the Grand Canal, is Marino Marini's *Angelo della Città* (1948). It shows a man sitting on a horse, erect in all respects.

Accademia ⑪

Campo della Carità. 📞 041-522 22
47. 🚤 Accademia. 🕐 daily (Mon:
am only). ⬤ Jan 1, May 1, Dec 25.
📷 🎫 (audio). 🚻

SPANNING FIVE CENTURIES, the matchless collection of paintings in the Accademia provides a complete spectrum of the Venetian school, from the Byzantine period through the Renaissance to the Baroque and later.

Housed in three former religious buildings, the basis of the collection was the Accademia di Belle Arti, founded in 1750 by the painter Giovanni Battista Piazzetta. In 1807 Napoleon moved the academy to its present premises, greatly enlarging the collection with artworks from churches and monasteries he suppressed.

The paintings are housed on one floor divided into 24 rooms, more or less in date order. A highlight of the Byzantine and Gothic section is Paolo Veneziano's *Coronation of the Virgin* (1325), which contrasts with the delicate naturalism of Giambono's painting of the same name (1448).

The Bellini family played a dominant role in the early Venetian Renaissance, and outstanding examples of their work include Giovanni Bellini's *Madonna and Child between St. John the Baptist and a Saint* (c.1504), and other paintings of his Madonna collection in rooms 4 and 5. One of Bellini's students, Giorgione, painted the famous,

The colonnaded apse of Murano's Basilica dei Santi Maria e Donato

atmospheric *Tempest* (c.1507). Among Renaissance works on display are Veronese's Feast in the *House of Levi* (1573), and *The Miracle of the Slave* (1548) which made the reputation of Jacopo Tintoretto.

The long gallery of Baroque, genre, and landscape paintings alongside Palladio's inner courtyard (1561) features works by Giambattista Tiepolo, the greatest Venetian painter of the 18th century, and a view of Venice (1763) by Canaletto.

Rooms 20 and 21 contain two cycles of 16th-century paintings: *The Stories of the Cross*, and *Scenes from the Legend of St. Ursula*, painted by Carpaccio in the 1490s and portraying Venetian settings.

Murano ⑫

🚤 41 and 42 from San Zaccaria; "Dir"
from Ferrovia and Piazzale Roma.

LIKE THE CITY of Venice, Murano consists of a cluster of small islands, connected by bridges. In the 15th and 16th

centuries Murano was the principal glass-producing center in Europe and today most tourists visit to tour the furnaces and buy traditionally designed glass from the manufacturers' showrooms.

The **Museo Vetrario** in the Palazzo Giustinian houses a fine collection of antique pieces. The prize exhibit is the dark blue wedding cup (1470–80) with enamel work by Angelo Barovier.

The architectural highlight of the island is the 12th-century **Basilica dei Santi Maria e Donato** with its lovely colonnaded apse. Of particular note are the Gothic ship's-keel roof, the mosaic Madonna in the apse, and the beautiful medieval mosaic floor, which dates from 1140.

🏛 **Museo Vetrario**
Palazzo Giustinian. 📞 041-73 95 86.
🕐 Thu–Tue. ⬤ Jan 1, May 1,
Dec 25. 📷 🚻
⛪ **Basilica dei Santi Maria e Donato**
Fondamenta Giustinian. 📞 041-73
90 56. 🕐 daily.

Veronese's painting of Christ's Last Supper, retitled *The Feast in the House of Levi* (1573), in the Accademia

Ferrara ㉑

🏛 140,000. 🚉 🚌 ℹ *Castello Estense, Largo Castello (0532-20 93 70).* 🛒 *Mon & Fri.*

THE D'ESTE DYNASTY has left an indelible mark on Ferrara, one of the Emilia-Romagna region's greatest walled towns. The noble family took control of the town under Nicolò II in the late 13th century, holding power until 1598. **Castello Estense**, the family's dynastic seat, with its moats, towers, and battlements, looms over the town center.

Bronze statues of Nicolò III and Borso d'Este, one of Nicolò's reputed 27 children, adorn the medieval **Palazzo del Comune**. The d'Este summer retreat was the **Palazzo Schifanoia**. Begun in 1385, it is famous for its Salone dei Mesi, whose walls are covered with murals by Cosmè Tura and other Ferrarese painters.

Ferrara's **cathedral** has an excellent museum, which contains marble reliefs of the *Labours of the Months* (late 12th century), two painted organ shutters (1469) of *St. George* and the *Annunciation* by Tura, and the *Madonna of the Pomegranate* (1408) by Sienese sculptor Jacopo della Quercia (c.1374–1438).

♠ **Castello Estense**
Largo Castello. 📞 *0532-29 92 33.*
◯ *daily.* ● *public hols.* 📷
🎪 **Palazzo Schifanoia**
Via Scandiana 23. 📞 *0532-641 78.*
◯ *Tue–Sun.* ● *public hols.* 📷

The medieval Castello Estense and surrounding moat in Ferrara

Flagged medieval street with shady, arcaded buildings, typical of central Bologna

Bologna ㉒

🏛 400,000. ✈ *Marconi 9 km (5 miles) NW.* 🚉 🚌 ℹ *Piazza Maggiore I, 1 (051-24 65 41).* 🛒 *Fri & Sat.* 🎭 *Bologna Music Festival (Mar–Jun).*

CAPITAL OF Emilia-Romagna and one of Italy's most prosperous cities, Bologna has a rich cultural heritage, ranging from medieval palaces and churches to leaning towers.

Celebrated in the Middle Ages for its university – believed to be the oldest in Europe – Bologna came under papal rule in 1506 and a large part of the city was given over to monasteries and convents. Following the arrival of Napoleon's occupying force in 1797, the university was moved from its Catholic cradle in the **Archiginnasio** to a science building where Marconi later studied. After unification the old city walls were demolished and an era of prosperity was ushered in.

The two central squares of the city, the Piazza Maggiore and the Piazza del Nettuno, are bordered to the south by the churches of **San Petronio** and **San Domenico**. The former ranks among the greatest of Italy's brick-built medieval buildings. Founded in 1390, its construction was halted halfway due to financial constraints, and the planned central row of columns became the eastern flank. Twenty-two chapels open off the nave of the Gothic interior, many with fine works of art.

San Domenico is the most important of Italy's many Dominican churches, housing, as it does, the tomb of St. Dominic himself. A magnificent composite work, the tomb features statues and reliefs by Nicola Pisano, while the figures of angels and saints are early works by Michelangelo.

The **Torri degli Asinelli e Garisenda** are among the few surviving towers of the 200 that once formed the sky-line of Bologna. Both were begun in the 12th century. The Garisenda tower leans some 3 m (10 ft), while the Asinelli tower has a 500-step ascent and offers fine views of Bologna and the hills beyond.

The Romanesque-Gothic church of **San Giacomo Maggiore**, begun in 1267 but altered substantially since, is visited mainly for the superb Bentivoglio family chapel, decorated with frescoes by Lorenzo Costa (1460–1535). The Bentivoglio tomb is among the last works of Jacopo della Quercia.

Bologna's principal art gallery, the **Pinacoteca Nazionale**, stands on the edge of the city's university district. The two highlights are Perugino's *Madonna in Glory* (c.1491) and Raphael's famous *Ecstasy of St. Cecilia*, painted around 1515.

The cuisine of Bologna is reputed to be Italy's finest. To try the famous Bolognese meat sauce you should order *spaghetti al ragù.*

🎪 **Torri degli Asinelli e Garisenda**
Piazza di Porta Ravegnana. ◯ *daily.* 📷
🏛 **Pinacoteca Nazionale**
Via delle Belle Arti 56. 📞 *051-421 19 84.* ◯ *Tue–Sun.* ● *Jan 1, May 1, Aug 15, Dec 25.* 📷 ♿

Ravenna ㉓

🏛 90,000. 🚉 🚌 🛈 *Via Salara 8–12 (0544-354 04).* 🛒 *Wed & Sat.*

RAVENNA ROSE to power in the 1st century BC when Emperor Augustus built a port and naval base nearby, but gained in prominence after becoming the administrative capital of the Byzantine Empire in AD 402.

Most people visit the city for its superb early Christian mosaics. Spanning the years of Roman and Byzantine rule, they can be seen in many of Ravenna's 5th- and 6th-century buildings. In the church of **San Vitale**, apse mosaics (526–547) show the saint being handed a martyr's crown. Another mosaic depicts Emperor Justinian, who ruled from 527 to 565, and members of his court. Next door, the tiny **Mausoleo di Galla Placidia** is adorned with a mosaic of *The Good*

Apse of San Vitale, Ravenna, showing 6th-century mosaics

Shepherd. Galla Placidia ran the Western Empire for 20 years after the death of her husband, the Visigothic King Altauf. The 6th-century church of **Sant'Apollinare Nuovo** is dominated by two rows of mosaics which depict processions of martyrs and virgins bearing gifts.

Travelers in Ravenna can also visit **Dante's Tomb** – the great writer died here in 1321 – and the **Museo Nazionale**, which houses icons, paintings, and archaeological displays. The best place to relax and take a break from sightseeing is among the lovely ensemble of medieval buildings in the Piazza del Popolo.

🔓 **San Vitale & Mausoleo di Galla Placidia**
Via Fiandrini. ☎ *0544-21 99 38.*
🕐 *daily.* ⬤ *Jan 1, Dec 25.* 📷 ♿
🔓 **Sant'Apollinare Nuovo**
Via di Roma. ☎ *0544-390 81.*
🕐 *daily.* ⬤ *Jan 1, Dec 25.* 📷 ♿

BYZANTINE ITALY

By the 5th century AD the Roman Empire was split into two. Rome and the Western Empire could not stem the tide of Germanic invaders as they migrated southwards and Italy fell to the Goths. In the years after 535 AD, however, the Eastern Empire reconquered most of Italy. Its stronghold, Ravenna, became the richest, most **Byzantine Emperor Justinian** powerful Italian city. Most of the peninsula was subsequently lost to the Lombards who invaded in 564, but Ravenna, protected by marshes and lagoons, was able to hold out until 752 when the Lombard King Aistulf finally recaptured the city.

Urbino ㉔

🏛 16,000. 🚌 🛈 *Piazza Rinascimento 1 (0722-26 13).* 🛒 *Sat.*

URBINO TRACES its origins to the Umbrians, centuries before Christ, and became a Roman municipality in the 3rd century BC. The city's zenith, however, came in the 15th century under the rule of the philosopher-warrior Federico da Montefeltro, who commissioned the building of the **Palazzo Ducale** in 1444. This beautiful Renaissance palace has an extensive library, hanging gardens, and numerous fine paintings. Two great 15th-century works, *The Flagellation* by Piero della Francesca, and *Ideal City* attributed to Luciano Laurana, are notable for their use of perspective.

Of special interest in the Neoclassical **Duomo**, built in 1789, is the painting of the *Last Supper* by Federico Barocci (c.1535–1612). The **Museo Diocesano** contains a collection of ceramics, glass, and religious artifacts.

The **Casa Natale di Raffaello**, home of Urbino's famous son, the painter Raphael (1483–1520), is also open to visitors.

🏛 **Palazzo Ducale**
Piazza Duca Federico 13. ☎ *0722-27 60.* 🕐 *8:30am–7:15pm Tue–Sun, 9am–2pm Mon.* ⬤ *Jan 1, Dec 25.*
📷 ♿
🏛 **Casa Natale di Raffaello**
Via di Raffaello 57. ☎ *0722-32 01 05.*
🕐 *Mon–Sat, Sun am.* ⬤ *Jan 1, Dec 25.* 📷

The Palazzo Ducale, rising above the rooftops of Urbino

View across the Bay of Naples to the slopes of Mount Vesuvius

Naples ㉕

🏛 1,000,000. ✈ Capodichino 4 km (2.5 miles) NW. 🚉 🚌 ⛴ 🛈 Piazza del Gesù Nuovo (081-551 27 01). 🖐 daily. 🎭 Maggio dei Monumenti (May), San Gennaro (Sep 19).

THE CHAOTIC yet spectacular city of Naples (Napoli) sprawls around the edge of a beautiful bay in the shadow of Mount Vesuvius.

Originally a Greek city named Neapolis, founded in 600 BC, Naples became an "allied city" of Rome two centuries later. It has since had many foreign rulers. The French House of Anjou controled Naples between 1266 and 1421, when power passed to Alfonso V of Aragón. A colony of Spain by 1503, in 1707 Naples was ceded to Austria, and in 1734 Charles III of Bourbon took over. In 1860, Naples became part of the

Tomb of King Ladislas of Naples in San Giovanni a Carbonara

new kingdom of Italy. The centuries of occupation have left Naples with a rich store of ancient ruins, churches, and palaces, many of which can be seen in the compact center of the old city. The **Museo Archeologico Nazionale** holds treasures from Pompeii and Herculaneum, including a bust of Seneca, fine glassware, frescoes, mosaics, and the fabulous Farnese Classical sculptures. Nearby, the church of **San Giovanni a Carbonara** houses some glorious medieval works of art, such as the tomb of King Ladislas of Naples (1386–1414). The French Gothic **Duomo** holds the relics of San Gennaro, martyred in 305 AD. Next to it is one of Italy's finest Renaissance gateways, the **Porta Capuana**, completed in 1490.

Also worth visiting, the **Monte della Misericordia**, a 17th-century octagonal church, houses Caravaggio's huge *Seven Acts of Mercy* (1607).

Central Naples is particularly rich in 14th- and 15th-century churches. **San Domenico Maggiore** contains some fine Renaissance sculpture while **Santa Chiara** houses the tombs of the Angevin monarchs and a museum whose exhibits include the

Farnese Hercules, Museo Archeologico Nazionale

ruins of a Roman bathhouse. Southeast Naples is home to the city's castles and the royal palace of **Castel Nuovo**, built for Charles of Anjou in 1279–82. Another star sight, the **Palazzo Reale** was designed for the viceroy Ruiz de Castro, and has a superb library, richly adorned royal apartments, and a court theater. Begun in 1600, the palace was not completed until 1843.

The Palazzo Reale di Capodimonte, once a hunting lodge, now houses the **Museo di Capodimonte**, with its magnificent collection of Italian paintings, including works by Titian, Botticelli, and Raphael. This part of Naples is also known for its "Spanish Quarter," or **Quartieri Spagnoli**, a neighborhood of narrow, cobbled alleys often used to represent the archetypal Neapolitan street scene.

ENVIRONS: A trip by funicular railway up **Vomero** hill brings you to the **Certosa di San Martino**. This 14th-century charterhouse has been lavishly redecorated over the centuries. The Church and the Prior's Residence are particularly impressive. Just behind the Certosa lies the **Castel Sant Elmo**, which offers fine views of the city center and the Bay of Naples.

Boat excursions can be taken along the Posillipo coast, and to the islands of **Capri**, **Ischia**, and **Procida**. Inland, **Caserta** has its own **Palazzo Reale**, which boasts over 1,000 sumptuously decorated rooms. The town of **Santa Maria Capua Vetere** has a Roman amphitheater and a Mithraeum.

🏛 **Museo Archeologico Nazionale**
Piazza Museo Nazionale 19. 📞 081-564 89 41. Ⓜ Piazza Cavour. ⏰ Wed–Mon. 🔴 Jan 1, Dec 25. 🎟

🏛 **Museo di Capodimonte**
Parco di Capodimonte. 📞 081-741 14 76. ⏰ Tue–Sun. 🎟 ♿

A breathtaking view of the steep village of Positano on the **Amalfi Coast**

Pompeii 26

Piazza Esedra 5. (081-537 03 28.
🚌 🚋 ◯ daily. ◯ Jan 1, Easter Mon,
May 1, Aug 15, Dec 25. 🕮 ♿ 🎥

A NCIENT POMPEII, destroyed
in AD 79 by an eruption
of Vesuvius, lay buried under
rock and ash until the 18th
century. When excavations
began in 1748, a city frozen
in time was revealed. Many
buildings survived, some
complete with paintings and
sculptures. The villa of the
wealthy patrician Casii is
known as House of the Faun
after its bronze statuette. The
House of the Vettii, named
after its owners, contains rich
wall decorations.

The original layout of the
city can be clearly seen. The
Forum was the center of
public life, with administrative
and religious institutions
grouped around it. Theaters,
the marketplace, temples,
stores, and even brothels can
be visited. Around 2,000
people died at Pompeii and
casts of numerous recumbent
figures have been made.

Much of our knowledge of
the daily lives of the ancient
Romans has been derived
from the excavations at
Pompeii and nearby
Herculaneum. The baths were
divided into separate sections
for men and women, but the
citizens of Pompeii were not
prudish – graphic frescoes
reveal the services offered by
male and female prostitutes in
the *lupanares*, or brothels.

Many works of art, domestic
items, and other artifacts were
preserved by the mud and
ash are on permanent display
in the Museo Archeologico
Nazionale in Naples.

Amalfi Coast 27

⛴ 🚌 *Amalfi*. 🛈 *Corso Roma 19,
Amalfi (089-87 11 07).*

T HE MOST ENCHANTING and
most visited route in
Campania is that skirting the
southern flank of Sorrento's
peninsula: the Amalfi Coast
(Costiera Amalfitana). Among
the popular pleasures here
are dining on locally caught
grilled fish and sipping icy
Lacrima Christi from Vesuvian
vineyards, interspersed with
beach-hopping.

From **Sorrento**, a well-
developed holiday resort, the
road winds down to **Positano**,
a village clambering down a
vertiginous slope to the sea.
Further on, **Praiano** is
another fashionable resort.

Amalfi – the coast's largest
town – was a maritime power
before it was subdued in 1131
by King Roger of Naples. Its
most illustrious citizens were
buried in the 13th-century
Chiostro del Paradiso, flanking
the 9th-century Duomo.
Above Amalfi, **Ravello** offers
peace and quiet and superb
views of the coast.

Sacrarium of the Lares, shrine of Pompeii's guardian deities

Sicily

LOCATED AT A CROSSROADS in the Mediterranean, Sicily was a magnet for colonists and invaders from half the ancient civilized world. As Greek, Arab, and Norman conquerors came and went, they left behind a rich and varied cultural heritage. This has evolved into a colorful mixture of language, customs, and cuisine, and is reflected in the diverse art and architecture of the island. Sicily has magnificent beaches, remote hilltowns, flower-covered mountain ranges, and an active volcano whose lava flows over the centuries have created a fertile land of walnut trees, citrus groves, and vineyards.

Front façade of the Norman Duomo (cathedral) in Palermo

Palermo 🄰

🄰 800,000. ✈ Punta Raisi 32 km (20 miles) W. ⛴ 🚉 🚌 🛈 Piazza Castelnuovo 35 (091-605 83 51) and railway station. ▨ Mon–Sat. 🎭 U Festinu for Santa Rosalia (Jul 10–15).

CAPITAL OF SICILY and situated along the bay at the foot of Monte Pellegrino, Palermo was originally called Panormos, or "port" by the Phoenicians. A prosperous Roman town, Palermo's golden age came later, while under Arab domination. The Baroque period (17th–18th centuries) has also left a lasting mark on the city's civic and religious buildings.

Palermo suffered heavy bombardment by the Allies in World War II, but, despite chaotic rebuilding, the city remains an exotic mix of the oriental and the European, and an exciting place to explore.

The old Arab quarter can be found in North Palermo, typified by the medieval, casbah-style market of **Vucciria**. On Piazza Marina, the focal point of North Palermo, the 15th-century

Palazzo Abatellis houses the **Galleria Regionale di Sicilia**, which has a fine collection of sculptures, medieval crucifixes, frescoes, and paintings.

On the Piazza della Vittoria in South Palermo, the **Palazzo Reale** – a focus of power since Byzantine rule – is now home to Sicily's regional government. Its splendid **Cappella Palatina** is adorned with mosaics. The **Duomo**, founded in 1184, has a Catalan Gothic portico (1430), a cupola in Baroque style, and slender turrets with lancet windows.

🏛 Galleria Regionale di Sicilia

Via Alloro 4. 📞 091-623 00 11. 🕒 am daily, pm Tue–Thu. 📷

🏯 Palazzo Reale

Piazza Indipendenza. 📞 091-705 43 17. 🕒 am Mon, Fri, & Sat. **Cappella Palatina** 🕒 daily. ● Easter, Apr 25, May 1, Dec 26. 📷

ENVIRONS: A few miles inland from Palermo, the cathedral at **Monreale**, founded in 1172, is one of the great sights of Norman Sicily. The interior of the building glitters with mosaics and the cloisters, with their Saracenic-style arches, represent Norman artistry at its peak.

🔒 Monreale

Piazza Vittorio Emanuele. 🚌 ✔ **Cloister** 📞 091-640 44 13. 🕒 daily (am only Sun & hols). 📷 for treasury.

Taormina 🄲

Messina. 🄰 10,000. 🚉 🚌 🛈 Palazzo Corvaja, Piazza Santa Caterina (0942 232 43). ▨ Wed.

SICILY'S MOST POPULAR tourist resort, Taormina is a delight to visit, with sandy beaches and numerous restaurants.

The most illustrious relic of the past is the 3rd-century BC **Theater**, begun by the Greeks, and rebuilt by the Romans. Among other Classical ruins are the **Odeon** (a musical theater) and the **Naumachia** (a man-made lake for mock battles).

The 14th-century **Palazzo Corvaia** and the 13th-century **Duomo**, renovated in 1636, are also worth visiting.

Taormina's Greek theater with Mount Etna in the background

Fishing boats moored in the picturesque harbor of Syracuse

Mount Etna ⑳

Catania. 🚆 *to Linguaglossa or Randazzo; Circumetnea (095-374 842).* 🚌 *to Nicolosi.* ℹ️ *Via G Garibaldi 63, Nicolosi (095-91 15 05).*

ONE OF THE WORLD'S largest active volcanoes, Mount Etna was thought by the Romans to have been the forge of Vulcan, the god of fire. To view it in comfort, take the Circumetnea railway, which runs around the base from Catania to Riposto.

Now a protected area, about 58 sq km (22 sq miles) in size, Etna offers numerous opportunities for excursions. One of the most popular is from Zafferana to the Valle del Bove. Hikes can also be taken up to the large craters at the summit.

Syracuse ㉛

🏛️ *120,000.* ✈️ 🚆 🚌 ℹ️ *Via San Sebastiano 45 (0931-677 10).* 🍴 *Wed.*

THE MOST IMPORTANT and powerful Greek city from 400 to 211 BC when it fell to the Romans, Syracuse (Siracusa in Italian) was also regarded as the most beautiful.

The peninsula of Ortigia is the hub of the old city. A highlight is the 18th-century **Duomo**. Its Baroque façade masks the **Temple of Athena** (5th century BC), which has been absorbed into it. Nearby is the **Palazzo Beneventano del Bosco** (1778–88) where

Admiral Nelson once stayed. At Ortigia's farthest point is the **Castello Maniace**, built by Frederick II around 1239, and the **Galleria Regionale di Palazzo Bellomo**, where Caravaggio's *Burial of St. Lucy* (1608) may be seen.

One of the world's most important examples of ancient theater architecture, the 5th-century BC **Greek Theater** has a 67-tier auditorium or *cavea*. The great Greek playwrights, including Aeschylus, staged their works here.

At Tyche, north of Syracuse, the **Museo Archeologico Regionale Paolo Orsi** houses an important collection of artifacts excavated from local digs, which date from the Paleolithic to the Byzantine era.

🏛️ **Galleria Regionale di Palazzo Bellomo**
Palazzo Bellomo, Via Capodieci 16. ☎️ *0931-696 17.* 🕐 *Tue–Sat, Sun am.*
🏛️ **Museo Archeologico Regionale Paolo Orsi**
Viale Teocrito 66. ☎️ *0931-46 40 22.* 🕐 *Tue–Sat, Sun am.*

Agrigento ㉜

🏛️ *57,000.* ✈️ 🚆 🚌 ℹ️ *Via Empedocle 73 (0922-203 91).* 🍴 *Fri.*

MODERN AGRIGENTO occupies the site of Akragas, an important city of the ancient Greeks. Following the Roman conquest of 210 BC, Agrigento was renamed and successively occupied by Byzantines, Arabs, and Normans.

The historic medieval core of the city focuses on the Via Atenea. The 13th-century abbey complex of **Santo Spirito** houses stuccoes by Giacomo Serpotta (1695).

ENVIRONS: South of Agrigento, the **Valley of Temples** is the principal sacred site of ancient Akragas. The mainly 5th- and 6th-century ruins rank among the most impressive complexes of ancient Greek buildings outside Greece. The **Museo Regionale Archeologico** houses outstanding artifacts from the temples and the city.

🏛️ **Museo Regionale Archeologico**
Contrada San Nicola, Viale Panoramica. ☎️ *0922-40 15 65.* 🕐 *Tue–Sat, Sun–Mon am only.*

The Temple of Concord (c.430 BC) in the Valley of Temples, Agrigento

Practical Information

ITALY'S CHARM AND ALLURE help to mask an idiosyncratic public sector in which delays and long lines are common. Be prepared to wait in offices and banks, and to persevere when seeking information. However, communications – other than the post office – are good, and banking and exchange facilities are widely available. Italy is generally safe for visitors and there is a visible police presence should a crisis arise. Personal belongings should nevertheless be watched at all times. Many shops and offices close at lunch for the siesta, reopening in the late afternoon. Pharmacies are a useful first stop for health advice.

WHEN TO VISIT

ITALY'S TOWNS and historic sites are extremely popular attractions and it is worth considering this when planning your trip. Rome, Florence, and Venice are all crowded from spring to October and it is advisable to reserve a hotel well in advance. In August the cities are generally slightly less busy, and the seaside resorts fill up. June and September can be as hot as midsummer, but the beaches are less crowded. The skiing season runs from December to March.

TOURIST INFORMATION

THE NATIONAL tourist board, ENIT, has branches in capital cities worldwide and offers general information on Italy. Locally, there are two types of tourist office: an EPT (*Ente Provinciale di Turismo*) has information on its town and surrounding province, whereas an **APT** (*Azienda di Promozione Turistica*) deals exclusively with an individual town. Both can help with practical issues such as hotel reservations and local tour guides. They also provide free maps and guidebooks in several languages.

OPENING HOURS

ITALIAN MUSEUMS are gradually conforming to new regulations, particularly in the north, opening daily from 9am to 7pm, except for two or more Mondays each month. In summer, many museums stay open longer at weekends. In winter, opening times are more limited. It is advisable to check beforehand. Archaeological sites usually open from 9am to an hour before sunset, Tuesday to Sunday. Churches are open from about 7am to 12:30pm and 4 to 7pm, but they often prefer not to admit tourists during services.

Visits to some of the more popular tourist sights, such as Leonardo da Vinci's painting of *The Last Supper* in Milan, must be organized in advance.

VISA REQUIREMENTS

CITIZENS OF the European Union (EU), US, Canada, Australia, and New Zealand do not require a visa for stays of up to three months. Most European Union visitors need only a valid identity document to enter Italy, but visitors from the UK, Ireland, Sweden, and Denmark need a passport.

PERSONAL SECURITY

ALTHOUGH PETTY CRIME in the cities is frequent, violent crime in Italy is rare. However, it is common for people to raise their voices aggressively during an argument. Usually, remaining calm and being polite will help to defuse the situation. Unofficial tour guides, taxi drivers, or strangers who try to advise you on accommodations may expect money in return.

Women traveling alone in Italy are likely to meet with a lot of attention, although this is often more of an irritation than a danger. Staff at hotels and restaurants generally treat their single female customers with extra care and attention.

POLICE

THERE ARE SEVERAL different police forces in Italy and each one fulfills a particular role. The state police, *la polizia*, deals with most crimes. The *carabinieri* deal with a variety of offences, and also conduct random security checks. The *vigili urbani*, the municipal traffic police, issue fines for traffic and parking

THE CLIMATE OF ITALY

The Italian peninsula has a varied climate falling into three distinct geographical regions. Cold Alpine winters and warm, wet summers characterize the northern regions. In the extensive Po Valley, arid summers contrast with freezing, damp winters. The rest of Italy has a pleasant climate with long, hot summers and mild, sunny winters.

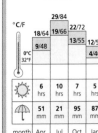

ROME			
°C/F	29/84		
18/64	19/66	22/72	
9/48		13/55	12/54
0°C 32°F			4/40
6 hrs	10 hrs	7 hrs	5 hrs
51 mm	21 mm	95 mm	87 mm
month Apr	Jul	Oct	Jan

VENICE			
°C/F	28/82		
17/63	18/64	18/64	
7/44		9/48	7/44
0°C 32°F			0/32
7 hrs	9 hrs	4 hrs	2 hrs
112 mm	108 mm	134 mm	90 mm
month Apr	Jul	Oct	Jan

offences. If you have anything stolen, you should go to the nearest police station and file a report *(denuncia)*.

EMERGENCY SERVICES

IN CASE OF EMERGENCIES while on vacation the appropriate numbers to call are listed in the directory below.

HEALTH ISSUES

NO INOCULATIONS are needed for Italy, but it is advisable to carry mosquito repellent in the summer months. If emergency medical treatment becomes necessary, go to the *Pronto Soccorso* (emergency room) of the nearest hospital.

Various medical products, including homeopathic medicines, are available in any pharmacy *(farmacia)*, but a prescription is often required. Thanks to a night rota *(servizio notturno)* – listed in the local pages of daily newspapers and on pharmacy doors – there is always a pharmacy open in all cities and most towns.

LANGUAGE AND ETIQUETTE

PEOPLE IN ITALY are very dress-conscious and unusual or risqué clothes get noticed. Strict dress codes are enforced in many places of worship, where your torso, knees, and upper arms should be covered.

Forms of address are still governed by traditional social formalities. *Ciao* should only be used as a greeting for familiar friends, otherwise *piacere* (pleased to meet you), *buon giorno* (good day), or *buona sera* (good evening) are polite greetings. Say *arrivederci* on parting. Kissing on the cheeks is common among friends, but shake hands with strangers.

Tipping in restaurants is expected when the service charge (usually 15 percent) is not included. However, as much as 10 percent would be considered generous and a tip is often not expected at all in family-run restaurants. Taxi drivers and hotel porters expect a reasonable tip if they have been helpful.

FACILITIES FOR THE DISABLED

PUBLIC AWARENESS of the needs of the disabled is low, but improving. **CO.IN** (Consorzio Cooperative Integrale) provides information on facilities for the disabled.

BANKING AND CURRENCY

ITALY'S CURRENCY was the lira (plural lire). However, on January 1, 2002 it was replaced by the euro *(see p15)*.

Banks open between 8:30am and 1:30pm Monday to Friday. Most also open from 2:15 to 3pm or 2:30 to 3:30pm. Electronic exchange machines, with multilingual

instructions, are located at all major airports, train stations, and banks. Bureaux de change can be found in main towns, and are usually open all day, and into the evening in resorts. However, they quite often tend to have less favorable exchange rates and charge a higher commission than banks.

COMMUNICATIONS

POST OFFICES OPEN from 8:25am to 1:50pm weekdays, and from 8:25am to noon on Saturday. Main post offices are open from 8:25am to 7pm non-stop. The red mailboxes (blue in the Vatican City) usually have two slots labeled *per la città* (for the city only) and *tutte le altre destinazioni* (for all other destinations). Italian post is renowned for its unreliability, and letters can take from four days to two weeks to arrive. For a faster service, send mail *prioritaria*.

Public telephones are increasingly card-operated. A telephone card *(carta or scheda telefonica)* can be purchased from bars, newspaper kiosks, post offices, and tobacconists *(tabacchi)*. Remember to break off the corner of the card before attempting to make a call. Alternatively, main towns have telephone offices *(Telefoni)* where you are assigned a booth and pay after calls are completed. No premium is charged.

Travel Information

ITALY HAS TRANSPORTATION SYSTEMS of varying efficiency, from the modern road, bus, and rail networks of the north to the slower and more antiquated systems of the south. Numerous airlines operate flights to the country's major airports. Highways are good, but busy at weekends and peak periods, and delays are common at Alpine passes. Train travel is inexpensive and services generally frequent, although they can be overcrowded during local holidays. The major Italian cities have a number of transportation options and that most suited to the tourist varies from place to place: the bus is more practical in Rome and the metro in Milan.

FLYING TO ITALY

IF YOU ARE FLYING from the United States, **Delta** and **United Airlines** operate direct scheduled flights to Rome and Milan from New York, Washington, Los Angeles, Boston, and Chicago. **Air Canada** flies from Montreal and Toronto, and **Qantas** flies from Sydney and Melbourne.

The Italian state airline, **Alitalia**, has regular services between Rome and Milan and New York, San Francisco, Philadelphia, Boston, Chicago, Detroit, Washington, Montreal, Toronto, and Sydney. It may, however, be more convenient and less expensive for long-haul passengers to take a budget flight to London, Frankfurt, Paris, or Amsterdam before continuing their journey to Italy from there.

Low-cost airlines **easyJet** and **Ryanair** offer flights from London Stansted to as many as 15 Italian airports according to season.

Rome's Leonardo da Vinci (Fiumicino) and Milan's Malpensa are the key airports for long-haul flights into Italy. Milan's Linate airport handles European flights.

CHARTERS AND PACKAGE DEALS

PACKAGE HOLIDAYS to Italy are usually less costly than traveling independently, unless you are on a tight budget and are prepared to make use of youth hostels and campsites. Rome, Florence, and Venice are often offered as separate or linked package deals, and many operators have packages to Tuscany and Umbria, the Lakes, the Riviera, Naples, Sicily, and the Amalfi Coast. Several firms organize fly-drive packages. In winter, ski packages to many Alpine resorts are available. Specialty walking, gastronomy, and art tours are increasingly common.

DOMESTIC FLIGHTS

ALITALIA RUNS regular services between many Italian cities. Long-haul passengers can transfer to domestic flights in Rome and Milan.

As internal flights are expensive, and busy at peak periods, it is worth trying the train as an alternative to domestic flights. Flights to airports in the north can be disrupted by fog in the winter.

TRAVELING IN CITIES

MILAN AND ROME both have a metro system known as *la metropolitana* (*metro* for short). Rome's network amounts to just two lines – A and B – which converge at Stazione Termini, the city's central train station. Several stations are useful for key sights but the system is designed for commuters and carriages are usually stiflingly hot in summer.

Milan has three principal lines – MM1 (the red line), MM2 (green), and MM3 (yellow) – that give easy access to the city's main sights.

Cars are a liability in all city centers and some, such as Florence, have a large limited-traffic zone. Walking is in many cases the easiest way to negotiate the narrow streets of historic town centers. Trams still run in some cities such as Milan and Rome. Taxis must be met at official taxi stands or reserved by telephone; in theory, you cannot hail a taxi in the street.

Most Italian cities and towns have a bus system which is inexpensive, comprehensive, and as efficient as traffic will allow. Bus stops are known as *fermate*, and buses (*autobus*) usually run from about 6am to midnight. Train stations are invariably linked to the city centers by shuttle buses. Tickets (*biglietti*) must usually be bought before boarding the bus, and are available from kiosks, bars, and *tabacchi* (tobacconists). Buses are boarded via the front and rear doors and exited via the central doors. Tickets are validated by being punched in machines on board.

GETTING AROUND VENICE

THE WATER BUSES (*vaporetti*) are an entertaining form of public transportation in Venice, although most journeys within the city can easily be covered on foot. The main route for the water buses is the Grand Canal. They also link the city to the islands in the lagoon. Tickets can be purchased from kiosks at each stop, and the main routes run every 10 to 20 minutes until early evening. For general inquiries, contact the **Hello Venice Information Office**.

Gondolas are a luxury form of transportation. Before boarding, agree on a price with the gondolier. *Traghetti* (gondola ferries), on the other hand, are an inexpensive, convenient way of crossing the Grand Canal.

For those with sufficient funds, the most practical means of traveling around Venice is by water taxi. These motorboats run from 16 water taxi ranks and can reach the airport in 20 minutes. Extra charges are made for luggage, waiting, night service, and calling out a taxi.

RAIL TRAVEL

THE BULK OF ITALY'S rail network is an integrated state-run system operated by the **Ferrovie dello Stato** (FS). Train journeys into Italy from other parts of Europe wind through the Alps and are an exciting way to travel to the country. High-speed trains, which operate on main lines to the coast or between cities, almost always require pre-booking of seats. Intercity (IC) trains and Eurocity (EC) trains only stop at main stations and require the payment of a first- or second-class supplement (*supplemento*). *Espresso* and *Diretto* trains make more stops and require no supplement.

There are three types of rail pass: the Biglietto Chilometrico gives a limited mileage allowance or 20 journeys for up to 5 people traveling together; the Italy Railcard is for non-residents and allows unlimited travel for a defined period; the Italy Flexi-Railcard gives unlimited travel for 4, 8, or 12 days in a month.

Before traveling, tickets need to be validated in one of the machines on the platform.

TRAVELING BY BUS

LONG-DISTANCE buses (*pullman* or *corriere*) operate between towns and can be less expensive and more frequent than the trains. Tickets can be purchased on board, and services usually depart from a town's train station or main square. Buses in some areas may be run by several companies (*see Directory below*).

TRAVELING BY ROAD

A CAR IS INVALUABLE for touring the Italian countryside. Drivers should take into account high gas (*benzina*) prices, the difficulty of parking in towns, and the Italians' often erratic approach to driving. Italy has a good network of highways, but most have tollbooths, often leading to congestion. Care should be taken at night when many traffic lights switch to flashing amber. Car theft is rife in Italy and valuables should not be left unattended.

Car rental (*autonoleggio*) is expensive in Italy, and should be organized beforehand through fly-drive deals or prebooked with firms that have branches in Italy. Local firms may be less expensive than the international firms. Most airports have rental offices on site (*see Directory below*). Visitors from outside the EU need an international license, but in practice not all rental firms insist on this.

FERRY SERVICES

ITALY'S LARGE NUMBER of off-shore islands means that it has a well-developed network of ferries. Boats of various kinds also operate on the Italian Lakes.

Ferries depart for Sicily from Naples and Reggio di Calabria. They also run from the mainland and from Sicily to surrounding islands and archipelagoes, for example from Naples to Capri and Ischia. Boats for Sardinia leave from Civitavecchia near Rome, Livorno, and Genoa. There are car ferry services from Brindisi to Corfu and Patras in Greece. In summer, these ferries can get very crowded, so make sure you reserve well in advance.

DIRECTORY

AIRLINES

Air Canada
(06-659 1300 (Italy).
(888-247 2262 (Canada).
W www.aircanada.com

Alitalia (Italy)
(06-656 43 (information).
(06-656 41 (domestic flights).
(06-656 42 (international flights).
W www.alitalia.it

Alitalia (UK)
(0870-544 8259.
W www.alitalia.co.uk

Alitalia (US)
(800-223 5730.
W www.alitaliausa.com

British Airways
(199-71 22 66 (Italy).
(0845-773 3377 (UK).
W www.britishairways.com

Delta
(800-241 4141 (US).
W www.delta.com

easyJet
W www.easyjet.com

Qantas
(06-5248 2725 (Italy).
(612-13 13 13 (Australia).
W www.qantas.com

Ryanair
W www.ryanair.com

United Airlines
(02-482 9000 (Italy).
(800-622 1015 (US).
W www.ual.com

GETTING AROUND VENICE

Hello Venice Information Office
Piazzale Roma, Venice.
(041-528 24 24.

Consorzio Motoscafi Rialto (Water Taxis)
(041-522 23 03.

RAIL TRAVEL

Ferrovie dello Stato
Toll-free number; information and inquiries.
(89-20 21.
W www.trenitalia.it

BUS COMPANIES

Cotral
Rome: (06-575 31.

Lazzi
Rome: (06-884 0840.
Florence and national:
(055-215 155.

Sita
Florence:
(800-373 760.
National & international:
(055-294 955.

CAR RENTAL

Avis
(99-10 01 33 (Rome).
W www.avis.com

Europcar
(800-01 44 10 (Rome).
W www.europcar.co.it

Hertz
(06-650 11553 (Rome airport).
W www.hertz.it

Maggiore
(06-488 00 49 (Rome).
W www.maggiore.it

Sixt
(06-659 651 (Rome).

Shopping

ITALY IS KNOWN FOR ITS QUALITY designer goods, ranging from chic clothing and sleek cars to stylish household items. There is a strong tradition of craftsmanship, often from family-run businesses, and there are numerous markets selling regional specialties. Apart from the town markets, it is not a country for bargains, but the joys of window-shopping will offer plenty of compensation.

OPENING HOURS

OPENING TIMES for shops are usually 9:30am–1pm and around 3:30–8pm. Stores are traditionally closed on Monday mornings, but shopkeepers are increasingly working more flexible hours.

DEPARTMENT STORES

DEPARTMENT STORES are often open without a lunchbreak (orario continuato) from 9am to 8pm Monday to Saturday. **La Rinascente** stores are good for ready-to-wear clothes, haberdashery, and perfumes.

DESIGNER FASHION

ITALY IS FAMOUS worldwide for its fashion industry. Milan, its designer capital, is stormed each year by Italians and foreigners alike in search of the latest catwalk novelty. **Giò Moretti**, in Via della Spiga, features articles by the top names, as well as pieces by up-and-coming designers.

Retail outlets of famous designers can be found in most Italian city centers. In Venice, **Armani** and others have stylish shops just off the Piazza San Marco. Rome's most famous designer is **Valentino**. His and other top fashion names dominate Rome's Via Condotti, Via de' Tornabuoni in Florence, and the Chiaia district of Naples.

CLOTHING STORES

LESS EXPENSIVE CLOTHES are available in high-street stores, where the styles tend to be more conventional and classical. Sales, called saldi, are held during summer and winter. Secondhand shops may seem expensive, but the quality of the clothes is good.

JEWELRY

GLITZY GOLD JEWELRY is very popular in Italy and every gioielleria (jewelry shop) will offer a wide selection of items. Elegant, classic jewelry can be purchased at **Cusi** in Milan, while Venice's smartest jewelers are **Missiaglia** and **Nardi** in the arcades of the Piazza San Marco. **Bulgari**, known for its beautiful jewelry and watches, has a number of retail outlets, as does **Buccellati**, famous for its delicately engraved designs inspired by the Italian Renaissance. For made-to-order jewelry try the **Gioie d'Arte** store in Rome. Naples has several jewelers' and goldsmiths' shops where traditional engraving and cameo work can still be seen. Unusual and original items can often be found in artisan shops (oreficeria).

ACCESSORIES

STYLISH ITALIAN LEATHER shoes and handbags have an international market, and are a popular purchase of visitors to all parts of the country. **Ferragamo**, the well-known Italian designer, has stores in most Italian cities, offering elegant, classic shoes. The **Mandarina Duck** shops stock casual bags and luggage and **Borsalino** is the place to go for top-quality classic hats.

One-off pieces by local designers can also be found by the intrepid shopper. In Naples, **Marinella** has a store selling her famous ties worn by many celebrities.

HOUSEHOLD ITEMS

HOUSEHOLD STORES in cities and towns throughout the country sell the well-designed utensils for which Italy is famous. Stainless steel and copper kitchenware is a favorite buy with visitors.

REGIONAL CRAFTS

TRADITIONAL CRAFTS are still practised in Italy and range from delicate lacework and glassware in the Veneto to leatherwork, jewelry, and marbled paper in Florence. Elaborate Tuscan pottery, hand-painted dishes from around Amalfi, and De Simone's stylized designer plates from Sicily are among many ceramic styles available.

Among the best craft workshops in Rome is **Arte e Mestieri**, which specializes in original, hand-made wood and terra-cotta items. Naples' **Il Cantuccio della Ceramica** is the place to go for ceramics.

In Venice, the best place to buy local blue- and claret-colored glass is the island of Murano. Here, **Barovier e Toso** produce original designs. Some of the most expensive glass in Venice can be bought from **Venini**. Carnival masks, available from **Tragicomica**, and traditional Burano lace are also popular buys.

The Etruscan art of working alabaster is best seen in Volterra. Hand-made perfumes and toiletries, and hand-painted majolica are favorite purchases in Tuscany. Sicily is well known for its ceramics, and for traditional rod puppets. The latter, now rare, can still be found in antique shops.

GOURMET FOODS

MANY OF ITALY'S regional food specialties are world-famous: Parma ham, Chianti wine, olive oil, and grappa. Regional sweets, including the Sienese panforte and Sicilian marzipan, are also well-known, as are cheeses such as Gorgonzola from Lombardy and Parmesan from Emilia-Romagna. Tuscan delicacies include bottled antipasti and sunflower honey. The Veneto region produces the famous panettone cake and amaretto biscuits. Vesuvio chocolate with rum from Naples is delicious.

To make the most of Italian food, try to buy what is in season. Mushrooms and grapes are best in the fall, whereas spring is the season for asparagus, strawberries, and artichokes. In winter, cauliflower and broccoli are at their best, as are lemons from Amalfi and Sicilian blood oranges. Summer is the time for plums, pears, and cherries, as well as zucchini, eggplant, tomatoes, and melon.

FOOD STORES

SPECIALTY STORES are the most interesting way to shop for food in Italy. A *fornaio* has the best bread and a *macellaio* has the finest meat (go to a *norceria* for pork products). Vegetables are freshest from market stands or the *frutti-* *vendolo*. You can buy cakes at the *pasticceria*, milk at the *latteria*, and pasta, ham, and cheese at the well-stocked *alimentari* and delicatessens.

To buy wine, head for the *enoteca*, *vineria*, or *vinaio*, where you can sometimes taste the products first. Italy is a major wine producer and stores stock a wide range of labels, from the prized Barolo and Barbaresco vintages to the inexpensive but palatable local *vino da tavola*.

MARKETS

ALL ITALIAN TOWNS have at least one market a week. Large towns have small, daily markets in addition to a weekly flea market, usually held on a Sunday. Traders set up at 5am and start to clear away at about 1:30pm. Bargaining is not usual when buying food, but it is worth asking for a discount *(sconto)* for clothes and other items.

Larger markets have stands piled high with secondhand clothes, and many markets sell fake Rayban sunglasses, Lacoste T-shirts, and Levi's jeans. Popular gifts from Italy include the characteristic brown espresso and cappuccino cups sold in all markets.

Specialty markets can be found in many cities. Milan's antique market, the Mercatone dell'Antiquariato, is held on the last Sunday of the month, and the Via Sannio and Porta Portese markets of Rome are a mecca for secondhand clothes. The fish market by the Grand Canal in Venice is an interesting place to visit.

DIRECTORY

DEPARTMENT STORES

La Rinascente
Via del Corso 189, Rome.
☎ 06-679 76 91.

Piazza Fiume, Rome.
☎ 06-884 12 31.

Piazza della Repubblica 1, Florence.
☎ 055-21 91 13.

Piazza Duomo, Milan.
☎ 02-885 21.

DESIGNER FASHION

Armani
Via Condotti 77, Rome.
☎ 06-699 14 61.

Via de Tournabuoni 48r, Florence.
☎ 055-21 90 41.

Via Manzoni 31, Milan.
☎ 02-62 31 26 00.

Piazza dei Martiri 61, Naples.
☎ 081-42 58 16.

Calle dei Fabbri, Venice.
☎ 041-523 78 08.

Giò Moretti
Via della Spiga 4, Milan.
☎ 02-76 00 31 86.

Valentino
Via Bocca di Leone 16, Rome.
☎ 06-678 36 56.

Via della Vigna Nuova 47r, Florence.
☎ 055-29 31 42.

Salizzada San Moisè, San Marco 1473, Venice.
☎ 041-520 57 33.

JEWELRY

Buccellati
Via Condotti 31, Rome.
☎ 06-679 03 29.

Via della Vigna Nuova 71/73r, Florence.
☎ 055-239 65 79.

Via Montenapoleone 23, Milan.
☎ 02-76 00 21 53.

Bulgari
Via Condotti 10, Rome.
☎ 06-679 38 76.

Via della Spiga 6, Milan.
☎ 02-77 70 01.

Cusi
Via Montenapoleone 21a, Milan.
☎ 02-76 02 19 77.

Missiaglia
Procuratie Vecchie, San Marco 125, Venice.
☎ 041-522 44 64.

Nardi
Procuratie Nuove, Piazza San Marco 69, Venice.
☎ 041-522 57 33.

Gioie d'Arte
Via de'Gigli d'Oro 10, Rome.
☎ 06-687 75 24.

ACCESSORIES

Borsalino
Piazza del Popolo 20, Rome.
☎ 06-32 65 08 38.

Galleria Corso V Emanuele 92, Milan.
☎ 02-89 01 54 36.

Ferragamo
Via Condotti 73–74, Rome.
☎ 06-679 15 65.

Via de' Tornabuoni 14r, Florence.
☎ 055-29 21 23.

Via Montenapoleone 3, Milan.
☎ 02-76 00 00 54.

Mandarina Duck
Via di Propaganda 1, Rome.
☎ 06-69 94 03 20.

Corso Europa/corner of Galleria San Carlo, Milan.
☎ 02-78 22 10.

Marinella
Riviera di Chiaia 287, Naples.
☎ 081-764 42 14.

REGIONAL CRAFTS

Studio Arti e Mestieri
Via dei Baullari 146, Rome.
☎ 06-687 24 67.

Barovier e Toso
Fondamenta Vetrai 28, Murano.
☎ 041-73 90 49.

Il Cantuccio della Ceramica
Via B. Croce 38, Naples.
☎ 081-552 58 57.

Tragicomica
Calle dei Nomboli, San Polo 2800, Venice.
☎ 041-72 11 02.

Venini
Piazzetta dei Leoncini San Marco 314, Venice.
☎ 041-522 40 45.

Entertainment

WITH WORLD-CLASS SPORTING and a host of cultural events, Italy has something to offer everyone. The cities boast a varied and lively nightlife, while its Riviera resorts, hill villages, and classical sites are ideal for the avid sightseer or walker. Skiing in the Alps, water sports of all kinds on the coast, and pony trekking in the countryside, are tourist favorites. The open-air theater and music performances in summer are world-famous. Or simply join the Italians in their traditional evening stroll, the *passeggiata*, followed by a drink at a bar or café in a picturesque piazza.

ENTERTAINMENT LISTINGS

INFORMATION ABOUT what's on in Rome can be found in *Trovaroma*, the weekly Thursday supplement to the *La Repubblica* newspaper. There is also a weekly listings publication, *Roma C'È*, which has a section in English.

In Florence, the monthly magazines *Firenze Spettacolo* and *Florence Today* have restaurant and café guides, as well as details of concerts, exhibitions, and sporting events. *Milano Mese* is a free brochure listing concerts and other cultural events held in and around the city.

Un Ospite di Venezia (A Guest in Venice), produced by the Hotels' Association, comes out fortnightly in summer and monthly in winter and is free.

If you can read Italian, regional newspapers are also a good source of information about current events. Local tourist offices display posters advertising forthcoming events.

TICKETS

MAKING ADVANCE reservations for concerts is not the custom in Italy, where decisions are often made on the spur of the moment. To guarantee a seat you will have to visit the box office in person, as reservations are not usually taken over the telephone. You may also have to pay an advance booking supplement, or *prevendita,* which is generally about 10 percent of the price of the seat.

Tickets for popular music concerts are normally sold through record and music shops, whose names are displayed on the publicity material distributed.

Whereas tickets for classical concerts are sold on the spot for same-day performances, opera tickets are purchased months in advance. Prices vary significantly according to the artists scheduled to perform and the type of venue.

ENTERTAINMENT VENUES

ROME'S CITY CHURCHES and the new **Parco della Musica** are favorite venues for classical music lovers. Venice also makes good use of its most magnificent churches as concert halls. **La Pietà** was Vivaldi's own church and is still used for classical music performances. In Milan, by contrast, the **San Siro** football stadium is often used as a concert venue along with the 5,000-capacity Palalido and the even larger **Mazdapalace**.

OPEN-AIR VENUES

DURING THE SUMMER months, Italy's historic buildings and classical ruins become dramatic settings for open-air events. Concerts are held in the grounds of Rome's 16th-century Villa Giulia *(see p405)* while Greek and Roman plays are staged in the restored theater of **Ostia Antica**, southwest of Rome.

In Venice the gardens of the Baroque palace, **Ca'Rezzonico**, and the ornate, enclosed courtyard of the Doge's Palace *(see pp436–7)* are used as outdoor concert venues. The 1st-century Teatro Romano *(see pp430–31)* in Verona also stages open-air concerts.

OPERA

OPERA IS ONE OF the great cultural delights of Italy, whether experienced in the magnificent opera houses of **La Scala** in Milan or Venice's **La Fenice Viva!**, or in a spectacular open-air venue like Verona's superb **Arena**. The opera house of Naples, **San Carlo**, also boasts world-class performers. The **Teatro dell'Opera** in Rome has a late winter season and an open-air summer festival.

The opera season at the Verona Arena runs from the first week in July until the beginning of September, and every year features a lavish production of Verdi's *Aida*.

CLUBS AND DISCOS

CITIES AND RESORTS in Italy are packed with trendy discos, and upscale night-clubs. **Gilda**, with its two elegant restaurants and large dancefloor, is a favorite with Rome's jet set. A younger crowd frequents **Alien**. In the summer months the nightlife shifts to the Roman seaside resort of Fregene.

Currently drawing in the fashion crowd of Milan is the **Hollywood** club. Also popular with celebrities is the **Grand Café**. The **Martini Scala** is a well-known late-night club in Venice and there are a number of discos at Mestre on the mainland.

ITALIAN FESTIVALS

THE DISTINCTIVE regionalism which has survived in modern Italy is marked by the diverse local festivals celebrated each year. For example, on April 25 Venetians commemorate St. Mark with a gondola race and on June 24 Florence relives its past with a procession of people in 16th-century costumes. The Sienese celebrate the Palio – a bareback horse race dating from 1283 – on July 2 and August 16 each year. Traditional dress is worn in the processions and pre-race pageants. Other *festas* celebrate the harvesting of local produce: the wine festivals held in September and October in Chianti, Tuscany, and the Castelli Romani south of Rome, are popular with visitors.

Many events have an international flavor, such as the film festivals held in Venice (Aug–Sep) and in Taormina, Sicily (Jul–Aug). From May to June Florence hosts an arts festival and Syracuse celebrates Greek drama. Ravello, near Naples, hosts an international festival of music each May.

Masked Venetians spill onto the streets during Carnival in February, and on summer evenings throughout Italy tourists can join in street dancing at local *festas*.

SPECIAL INTEREST VACATIONS

IN RECENT YEARS, culinary holidays run by English-speaking experts in Italian cooking have become very popular. **Tasting Places**, for example, organizes wine tours and week-long courses in Italian cuisine. The course locations include the Veneto, Sicily, Tuscany, and Umbria.

The **Società Dante Alighieri** provides courses in the Italian language, literature, history of art, and culture. There are both full- and part-time courses available, for every level of ability.

The **Gruppo Archeologico Romano** runs two-week digs in various regions. There are summer and winter trips for both adults and children.

For those with an interest in more energetic activities, the **Federazione Arrampicata Sportiva Italiana** has a list of mountain-climbing schools that organize climbs for people of all abilities. Ski holidays are best arranged with agents offering package deals. Trekking excursions can be organized with **Club Alpino Italiano (CAI)**. Nature walks

and bird-watching trips are run by the **Italian Birds Protection League (LIPU)**. Cyclists will find miles of flat and scenic cycling routes in the Po Delta.

WATER SPORTS

MOST LAKESIDE TOWNS and many seaside resorts in Italy rent out sailboats, canoes, and windsurfing equipment. Lessons and courses in a variety of water sports are organized by clubs, which usually require membership.

The **Federazione Italiana di Attività Subacquee** runs underwater diving courses. Most travel agents have a selection of sailing vacations.

Swimming pools are expensive in Italy and you often have to pay a membership fee and a monthly tariff. Water parks are popular and provide pools, slides, wave machines, and games.

DIRECTORY

ENTERTAINMENT VENUES

Ca'Rezzonico
Fondamenta Rezzonico 3136, Venice.
☎ 041-241 01 00.

La Pietà
Riva degli Schiavoni, Venice.
☎ 041-523 73 95.

Mazdapalace
Via San Elia 33, Milan.
☎ 02-33 40 05 51.

Ostia Antica
Viale dei Romagnoli 717, Rome.
☎ 06-56 35 80 99.

Parco della Musica
Viale de Coubertin, Rome.
☎ 06-80 24 13 50.

San Siro
Via Piccolomini 5, Milan.
☎ 02-48 71 37 13.

OPERA

La Fenice Viva!
Cassa di Risparmio,
Campo San Luca, Venice.
☎ 041-78 65 11.

Teatro alla Scala
Piazza alla Scala, Milan.
☎ 02-720 03 744.

Teatro dell'Opera
Piazza Beniamino Gigli 1, Rome.
☎ 06-48 16 02 87.

Teatro San Carlo
Via San Carlo 93/f, Naples.
☎ 081-797 23 31.

Verona Arena
Box Office
ENTE Arena, Piazza Brà 28, 37121 Verona.
☎ 045-800 51 51.

Ticket Agent
Virtours,
Galleria Pelliciai 13, 37121 Verona.
☎ 045-800 51 12.

CLUBS AND DISCOS

Alien
Via Velletri 13, Rome.
☎ 06-841 22 12.

Gilda
Via Mario de' Fiori 97, Rome.
☎ 06-678 48 38.

Grand Café
Via Vetere 6, Milan.
☎ 02-89 40 29 97.

Hollywood
Corso Como 15, Milan.
☎ 02-659 89 96.

Martini Scala
Campo San Fantin,
San Marco 2007, Venice.
☎ 041-522 41 21.

SPECIAL INTEREST VACATIONS

Club Alpino Italiano
Corso Vittorio Emanuele II 305, 00186 Rome.
☎ 06-68 61 01 11.

Federazione Arrampicata Sportiva Italiana
Via del Pilastro 8, Bologna.
☎ 051-633 3357.
ⓦ www.federclimb.it

Gruppo Archeologico Romano
Via degli Scipioni 30a, 00192 Rome.
☎ 06-39 73 36 37.

Italian Birds Protection League
Via Trento 49, 43100 Parma.
☎ 0521-27 30 43.
ⓦ www.lipu.it

Società Dante Alighieri
Piazza Firenze 27, 00186 Rome.
☎ 06-687 36 94.
ⓦ www.soc-dante-alighieri.it

Tasting Places
Bus Space, Unit 108, Conlan St, London W10 5AP, England.
☎ 020-7460 0077.
ⓦ www.tastingplaces.com

WATER SPORTS

Federazione Italiana di Attività Subacquee
Via Vittoria Colonna 27, 00193 Rome.
☎ 06-322 56 87.

Where to Stay in Italy

ACCOMMODATIONS IN ITALY range from the family-run *pensione* to the Renaissance palazzo, and prices vary accordingly. The top hotels in Venice and Florence are very expensive. Italian lodgings tend to have fewer facilities than in other countries, but you can find excellent value in all price ranges. Book as early as you can, especially if you want a room with a particular view.

	NUMBER OF ROOMS	RESTAURANT	SWIMMING POOL	GARDEN OR TERRACE
ROME				
AVENTINE: *Sant'Anselmo* W www.aventinohotels.com €€ Piazza Sant'Anselmo 2, 00153. **Map** D4. 06-574 35 47. **FAX** 06-578 36 04. A charming hotel in a pretty villa on the peaceful Aventine Hill within walking distance of the Colosseum. It has a secluded garden. 🚪 TV P 🌿	45			■
CAMPO DE' FIORI: *Teatro di Pompeo* @ hotel.teatrodipompeo@tiscali.it €€ Largo del Pallaro 8, 00186. **Map** C3. 06-68 30 01 70. **FAX** 06-68 80 55 31. A small hotel run by courteous staff. The highlight is the basement breakfast room, which is in located in the ruins of Pompey the Great's theater. All the bedrooms have beamed ceilings. 🚪 TV P 🌿	13			
FORUM: *Lancelot* W www.lancelothotel.com €€ Via Capo d'Africa 47. **Map** E4. 06-70 45 06 15. **FAX** 06-70 45 06 40. Close to the Colosseum, this welcoming family-run hotel offers tastefully furnished rooms, some with terraces and views. 🚪 TV 🍽 P 🌿	60	■		■
FORUM: *Forum* W www.hotelforumrome.com €€€€ Via Tor de' Conti 25, 00184. **Map** D3. 06-679 24 46. **FAX** 06-678 64 79. An old-fashioned hotel with wood-paneled public rooms and a sunny roof-terrace restaurant with views over the ancient Forum. 🚪 TV 🍽 P 🌿	76	■		■
PANTHEON: *Nazionale* W www.nazionaleroma.it €€€€€ Piazza di Montecitorio 131, 00186. **Map** C2. 06-69 50 01. **FAX** 06-678 66 77. Opposite the Chamber of Deputies, the Nazionale's comfortable and sometimes huge rooms are furnished with British and Italian antiques. The hotel is popular with business travelers and well-heeled tourists. 🚪 TV 🌿	87	■		
PANTHEON: *Sole al Pantheon* W www.hotelsoleal.pantheon.com €€€€€€ Piazza della Rotonda 63, 00186. **Map** C3. 06-678 04 41. **FAX** 06-69 94 06 89. A historic hotel dating from 1467. Some of its beautiful modernized rooms have painted paneled ceilings and magical views of the Pantheon. 🚪 TV 🍽 🌿	25			
PIAZZA NAVONA: *Due Torri* W www.hotelduetorriroma.com €€€ Vicolo del Leonetto 23–25, 00186. **Map** C2. 06-687 69 83. **FAX** 06-686 54 42. An amiable hotel tucked into an alleyway in the artisans' district. Rooms vary in size and style. Public rooms have a country house feel. 🚪 TV 🍽 🌿	25			■
PIAZZA NAVONA: *Raphael* W www.raphaelhotel.com €€€€€ Largo Febo 2, 00186. **Map** C2. 06-68 28 31. **FAX** 06-687 89 93. An ivy-clad luxury hotel whose reception is full of antique statues and modern sculpture. It has a restaurant and elegantly furnished bedrooms. 🚪 TV 🍽 🌿	59	■		
PIAZZA DI SPAGNA: *Margutta* €€ Via Laurina 34, 00187. **Map** C2. 06-322 36 74. **FAX** 06-320 03 95. The Margutta offers pretty rooms on a quiet street. The three attic rooms share a roof terrace, but booking well in advance for these is advisable. 🚪 🌿	24			
PIAZZA DI SPAGNA: *Hassler* W www.hotelhasslerroma.com €€€€€€ Piazza Trinità dei Monti 6, 00187. **Map** D2. 06-69 93 40. **FAX** 06-678 99 91. Venetian glass chandeliers and wood-paneled bathrooms retain the air of a more extravagant era. There are magnificent views from the roof terrace. 🚪 TV 🍽 P 🌿	102	■		■
TERMINI: *Diana* W www.hoteldianaroma.it €€ Via Principe Amedeo 4. **Map** E3. 06-482 75 41. **FAX** 06-48 69 98. This pleasant hotel has tastefully furnished rooms. The restaurant offers traditional Italian cuisine, served on the roof terrace in summer. 🚪 TV 🍽 🌿	171	■		■
TRASTEVERE: *San Francesco* W www.hotelsanfrancesco.net €€€ Via Jacopa de Settesoli 7. **Map** C4. 06-583 00 051. **FAX** 06-583 33 413. The rooms in this new hotel are elegantly furnished. A rooftop terrace and breakfast overlooking a small cloister add a nice touch. 🚪 🍽 🍽 TV 🌿	24			

Map references refer to maps of Rome and Florence on pp392–3 and pp412–13 respectively

	NUMBER OF ROOMS	RESTAURANT	SWIMMING POOL	GARDEN OR TERRACE
Price categories are for a standard double room for one night, including tax and service charges but not including breakfast: € under €75 €€ €75–150 €€€ €150–230 €€€€ €230–310 €€€€€ over €310 **SWIMMING POOL** Hotel swimming pools are usually quite small and are normally outdoors. **GARDEN OR TERRACE** Hotels with a garden, courtyard, or terrace. **CREDIT CARDS** Major credit cards are accepted in those hotels where the credit card symbol is shown.				

VATICAN: *Columbus* W www.hotelcolumbus.net €€€
Via della Conciliazione 33, 00193. **Map** B2. (06-686 54 35. **FAX** 06-686 48 74.
A hotel occupying a former monastery near St. Peter's Square. The function
room in the old refectory has retained its original frescoes. ⊞ TV ▤ P ✿

	100	■		■

VATICAN: *Visconti Palace* W www.viscontipalace.com €€€
Via Federico Cesi 37, 00193. **Map** C2. (06-36 84. **FAX** 06-32 00 551.
This modern and efficient hotel is in an ideal location and provides large common
spaces and well-decorated rooms. There is a piano bar nightly. ⊞ TV ▤ P ✿

	247			

VIA VENETO: *Ambasciatori Palace* W www.hotelambasciatoripalace.com €€€€€
Via Vittorio Veneto 62, 00187. **Map** D2. (06-474 93. **FAX** 06-474 36 01.
This hotel offers hospitality in the grand tradition. Set within a historical
building, the plush furnishings add to the air of luxury. ⊞ TV ▤ ✿

	148	■		

VILLA BORGHESE: *Villa Borghese* @ hotel.villaborghese@tiscali.it €€€
Via Pinciana 31, 00198. **Map** D1. (06-854 96 48. **FAX** 06-841 41 00.
This pleasant hotel has the atmosphere of a private home rather than a hotel.
Rooms are small but comfortable, and are tastefully decorated. ⊞ TV P ✿

	32			■

FLORENCE

CITY CENTER: *Hotel Porta Rossa* €€€
Via Porta Rossa 19, 50123. **Map** C3. (055-28 75 51. **FAX** 055-28 21 79.
Italy's second-oldest hotel, the Porta Rossa dates from 1386 and has
a warm and welcoming atmosphere. The huge bedrooms are airy
and pleasantly decorated with antique furnishings. ⊞ TV ▤ ✿

	78			

CITY CENTER: *Hotel Tornabuoni Beacci* @ info@bthotel.it €€€
Via de' Tornabuoni 3, 50123. **Map** C3. (055-21 26 45. **FAX** 055-28 35 94.
This former palazzo is situated on a busy central street. Wide, carpeted hallways
lead to lounge areas furnished with antiques and tapestries. ⊞ TV ▤ P ✿

	40	■		■

CITY CENTER: *Hotel Hermitage* W www.hermitagehotel.com €€€€
Vicolo Marzio 1, 50122. **Map** D3. (055-28 72 16. **FAX** 055-21 22 08.
There are spectacular views from the more expensive upper-story rooms of
this medieval building a few yards from the Ponte Vecchio. ⊞ ▤ ✿

	28			■

CITY CENTER: *Londra* W www.hotellondra.com €€€€
Via Jacopo da Diacceto, 16-18, 50123. **Map** B1. (055-238 27 91. **FAX** 055-21 06 82.
Conveniently located near the train station, this hotel is equipped
for the business or leisure traveler. There is a gym and sauna; bikes
can be rented; and there are special services for children. ⊞ TV P ✿

	158	■		■

CITY CENTER: *Hotel Brunelleschi* W www.brunelleschi.it €€€€€
Piazza Santa Elisabetta 3, 50122. **Map** D3. (055-273 70. **FAX** 055-21 96 53.
This unique hotel was built inside a Byzantine tower. It is therefore wonderfully
atmospheric with stunning views over Florence from the roof terrace. ⊞ TV P ✿

	88	■		

CITY CENTER: *Hotel Excelsior* @ info@hotelexcelsior.it €€€€€
Piazza d'Ognissanti 3, 50123. **Map** B3. (055-27 151. **FAX** 055-21 02 78.
Occupying two houses rebuilt in 1815, the hotel is decorated with gracious
marble floors and stained glass, with lovely views over the Arno. ⊞ TV ▤ P ✿

	168	■		■

CITY CENTER: *Hotel Montebello Splendid* @ info@montebellosplendid.it €€€€€
Via Montebello 60. **Map** B3. (055-239 80 51. **FAX** 055-21 18 67.
A 19th-century villa elegantly transformed into an intimate hotel near the city center.
There is a lovely garden and a restaurant with outdoor seating. ⊞ TV ▤ P ✿

	48	■		■

CITY CENTER: *Hotel Regency* @ info@regency-hotel.com €€€€€
Piazza Massimo d'Azeglio 3, 50121. **Map** F2. (055-24 52 47. **FAX** 055-234 67 35.
Behind the modest exterior of a Florentine town house lies a grand, Classical-
style reception area and bar, decorated with wood paneling. ⊞ TV P ✿

	34	■		■

	NUMBER OF ROOMS	RESTAURANT	SWIMMING POOL	GARDEN OR TERRACE
Price categories are for a standard double room for one night, including tax and service charges but not including breakfast: € under €75 €€ €75–150 €€€ €150–230 €€€€ €230–310 €€€€€ over €310 **SWIMMING POOL** Hotel swimming pools are usually quite small and are normally outdoors. **GARDEN OR TERRACE** Hotels with a garden, courtyard, or terrace. **CREDIT CARDS** Major credit cards are accepted in those hotels where the credit card symbol is shown.				

SOUTH OF THE ARNO: *Hotel Silla* W www.hotelsilla.it   €€€ | 36 | | | ■

Via dei Renai 5, 50125. **Map** D4. (055-234 28 88. FAX 055-234 14 37.
This 16th-century hotel is approached through an elegant courtyard with a grand staircase. There is a pretty terrace giving views of the Arno.

VENICE

CANNAREGIO: *Continental* @ continental@ve.nettuno.it   €€€ | 93 | ■ | | ■

Lista di Spagna 166. **Map** C2. (041-71 51 22. FAX 041-524 24 32.
A large, well-equipped, modern hotel. Some rooms overlook the Grand Canal, while others are quieter with views of a tree-shaded square.

CASTELLO: *Paganelli* @ hotelpag@tin.it   €€€ | 22 | | | ■

Riva degli Schiavoni 4686. **Map** F4. (041-522 43 24. FAX 041-523 92 67.
The Paganelli affords excellent views of St. Mark's Basin from cozy old-fashioned bedrooms. The *dipendenza* (annexe) is less attractive but quieter.

CASTELLO: *Danieli* @ reso72danieli@starwoodhotels.com   €€€€€ | 253 | ■ | | ■

Riva degli Schiavoni, 4196. **Map** E4. (041-522 64 80. FAX 041-520 02 08.
This luxurious hotel was the palace of the Dandolo family and has strong literary and musical connections. Service is impeccable.

DORSODURO: *American* @ reception@hotelamerican.com   €€€ | 30 | | | ■

Fondamenta Bragadin San Vio 628. **Map** C5. (041-520 47 33. FAX 041-520 40 48.
A comfortable hotel tucked away beside a small canal near the Accademia. The rooms are well-appointed and the management is friendly.

LIDO DI VENEZIA: *Villa Mabapa* @ info@villamabapa.com   €€€€ | 70 | ■ | | ■

Riviera San Nicolo 16. (041-526 05 90. FAX 041-526 94 41.
Originally built as a private residence in the 1930s, this lovely villa on the promenade by the lagoon retains its original style and atmosphere.

LIDO DI VENEZIA: *Excelsior Palace* W www.westin.com   €€€€€ | 197 | ■ | ● | ■

Lungomare Marconi 41. (041-526 02 01. FAX 041-526 72 76.
The hotel presents a flamboyantly Moorish exterior (even the beach huts are like Arabian tents). Service and comfort are equally splendid.

RIALTO: *Rialto*   €€€ | 89 | ■ | | ■

San Marco 5149. **Map** E3. (041-520 91 66. FAX 041-523 89 58. @ info@rialtohotel.com
From its spectacular position by the Rialto bridge, the hotel looks out onto the bustle of the city center and graceful gondolas.

SAN MARCO: *Flora* @ info@hotelflora.it   €€€ | 44 | | | ■

Calle Larga XXII Marzo 2283a. **Map** D4. (041-520 58 44. FAX 041-522 82 17.
A charming and quiet hotel on a secluded alley near Piazza San Marco. During the summer breakfast is served in the flower-filled garden.

SAN MARCO: *Europa & Regina* @ europaregina@westin.com   €€€€€ | 185 | ■ | | ■

San Marco 2159. **Map** D4. (041-520 04 77. FAX 041-523 15 33.
Once the residence of the 18th-century Italian painter Tiepolo, this splendid property has been completely restyled. The terrace overlooking the Grand Canal houses a flamboyant bar and restaurant.

SAN MARCO: *Gritti Palace* W www.luxurycollection.com   €€€€€ | 91 | ■ | | ■

Santa Maria del Giglio 2467. **Map** D4. (041-79 46 11. FAX 041-520 09 42.
An elegant, sumptuous hotel housed in the 15th-century palazzo that once belonged to the Gritti family. Rooms are superb and it is charmingly old-fashioned. Ernest Hemingway stayed here while in Venice.

SANTA CROCE: *Al Sole* @ info@albergoalsolevenice.com   €€€€ | 80 | | | ■

Fondamenta Minotta 136. **Map** C3. (041-71 08 44. FAX 041-72 22 87.
This 14th-century building is conveniently situated in a quiet corner near the station. It has pleasant rooms and a marble-floored reception area.

Map references refer to maps of Florence and Venice on pp412–13 and pp432–3 respectively

NORTHERN ITALY

GENOA: *Nuovo Astoria*
Piazza Brignole 4, 16122. **(** *010-87 33 16.* **FAX** *010-831 73 26.* **@** *astorige@tin.it*
A simple, no frills, modern hotel in the center of Genoa, very close to the
station and a short walk from the city's main sights. 🛏 📺 🅿 ▤ ☙
€€ — 69

LAKE COMO: *Florence* **@** *hotflore@tin.it*
Piazza Mazzini 46, Bellagio 22021. **(** *031-95 03 42.* **FAX** *031-95 17 22.*
This friendly hotel has a bar, and its rooms overlook the lively port of Lake
Como. The hotel has plenty of charm, with tastefully furnished rooms. 🛏 📺 ☙
€€€ — 30

LAKE COMO: *Hotel du Lac* **W** *www.albergodulac.com*
Via del Prestino 4, Varenna 23829. **(** *0341-83 02 38.* **FAX** *0341-83 10 81.*
There are wonderful views from this delightfully peaceful hotel in a
romantic setting overlooking the lake. All the rooms are different; the
furnishings are simple but comfortable and modern. 🛏 📺 ▤ 🅿 ☙
€€€ — 17

LAKE GARDA: *Bisesti* **@** *bisesti@infogarda.com*
Corso Italia 34, Garda 37016. **(** *045-725 57 66.* **FAX** *045-725 59 27.*
Well placed near the town center and the lake, this modern holiday hotel has
a private beach. Many of the rooms have their own balcony. 🛏 ▤ 📺 🅿 ☙
€ — 90

LAKE MAGGIORE: *Giardino* **W** *www.giardinoarona.com*
Corso Repubblica 1, Arona 28041. **(** *0322-459 94.* **FAX** *0322-24 94 01.*
A friendly, comfortable lakeside hotel. A large terrace offers spectacular views
over Lake Maggiore and bedrooms are tastefully furnished. 🛏 📺 ▤ ☙
€€ — 56

LAKE MAGGIORE: *Verbano* **W** *www.hotelverbano.it*
Via Ugo Ara 1, Isola dei Pescatori 28049. **(** *0323-304 08.* **FAX** *0323-331 29.*
A rambling island villa is the setting for this friendly hotel with views
over the lake to Isola Bella and Palazzo Borromeo. All of the prettily
decorated bedrooms have their own balcony. 🛏 ☙
€€ — 12

MANTUA: *Rechigi* **W** *www.rechigi.com*
Via Calvi 30, 46100. **(** *0376-32 07 81.* **FAX** *0376-22 02 91.*
Although located in the historic city center, the Rechigi is innovatively modern.
The hotel regularly houses contemporary art exhibitions. 🛏 📺 ▤ 🅿 ♿ ☙
€€€ — 60

MILAN: *Cavour* **W** *www.hotelcavour.it*
Via Fatebenefratelli 21, 20121. **(** *02-657 20 51.* **FAX** *02-659 22 63.*
Very well placed for Milan's main sights, this modern city hotel has
good-sized, comfortable rooms and a pleasant bar. 🛏 📺 ▤ 🅿 ☙
€€€ — 113

MILAN: *Capitol Millennium* **@** *info@capitolmillennium.com*
Via Cimarosa 6. **(** *02-48 00 30 50.* **FAX** *02-469 47 24.*
After major refurbishment this hotel now boasts excellent facilities. The
rooms are wood-paneled with marble bathrooms. The public spaces are
tastefully decorated and there is a gym, restaurant, and bar. 📺 ▤ ☙ ♿
€€€€ — 66

MILAN: *Pierre Milano* **W** *www.hotelpierremilano.it*
Via de Amicis 32, 20123. **(** *02-72 00 05 81.* **FAX** *02-805 21 57.*
A luxurious hotel that blends traditional and modern styles in its interior design
and furnishings. The restaurant is one of the best in Milan. 🛏 📺 ▤ ♿ ☙
€€€€ — 51

PADUA: *Plaza* **@** *plaza@plazapadova.it*
Corso Milano 40, 35139. **(** *049-65 68 22.* **FAX** *049-66 11 17.*
An established and efficiently-run hotel with a high reputation that is richly
deserved. It provides a full range of services and a warm welcome. 🛏 📺 ▤ 🅿 ☙
€€€ — 142

PORTOFINO: *Eden* **@** *eden@ifree.it*
Via Dritto 18, 16034. **(** *0185-26 90 91.* **FAX** *0185-26 90 47.*
Just behind the piazza of the pretty harbor, the Eden is, as its name suggests, set
in an attractive garden. Bedrooms are simple but well equipped. 🛏 📺 ▤ ☙
€€€ — 9

TURIN: *Victoria* **W** *www.hotelvictoria-torino.com*
Via Nino Costa 4, 10123. **(** *011-561 19 09.* **FAX** *011-561 18 06.*
The comfortable, pretty rooms in this modern hotel combine function with
innovative decor; choose from Egyptian or New Orleans rooms. 🛏 📺 ▤ ☙
€€€ — 106

TURIN: *Turin Palace* **@** *palace@thi.it*
Via Sacchi 8, 10128. **(** *011-562 55 11.* **FAX** *011-561 21 87.*
Dating from 1872, Turin's smartest hotel has an impressive array of modern
facilities. The sumptuous rooms are furnished with antiques. 🛏 📺 ▤ 🅿 ♿ ☙
€€€€ — 121

<table>
<tr><td colspan="2">

Price categories are for a standard double room for one night, including tax and service charges but not including breakfast:

€ under €75
€€ €75–150
€€€ €150–230
€€€€ €230–310
€€€€€ over €310

</td></tr>
</table>

SWIMMING POOL
Hotel swimming pools are usually quite small and are normally outdoors.

GARDEN OR TERRACE
Hotels with a garden, courtyard, or terrace.

CREDIT CARDS
Major credit cards are accepted in those hotels where the credit card symbol is shown.

	NUMBER OF ROOMS	RESTAURANT	SWIMMING POOL	GARDEN OR TERRACE
VERONA: *Giulietta e Romeo* @ info@giuliettaeromeo.com €€€ Vicolo Tre Marchetti 3, 37121. (045-800 35 54. FAX 045-801 08 62. Situated in a quiet street just behind the Arena, the bedrooms are spacious and comfortable with modern furnishings. Breakfast is served in the bar. 🔲 TV 🔲 ✉	31			
VERONA: *Due Torri Hotel Baglioni* W www.baglionihotels.com €€€€€ Piazza Sant'Anastasia 4, 37121. (045-59 50 44. FAX 045-800 41 30. Right in the heart of medieval Verona, this is one of Italy's most eccentric hotels. Each of the huge bedrooms is decorated and furnished in the style of a different era. Many of the walls and ceilings are frescoed. 🔲 TV 🔲 P ✉	91	▦		
VICENZA: *Campo Marzio* @ info@hotelcampomarzio.com €€€ Via Roma 21, 36100. (0444-54 57 00. FAX 0444-32 04 95. A stylish hotel with good facilities near the city center. Bedrooms are large, light, and well furnished, and the location is peaceful. 🔲 TV 🔲 ✉ P	35	▦		

CENTRAL ITALY

	NUMBER OF ROOMS	RESTAURANT	SWIMMING POOL	GARDEN OR TERRACE
ASSISI: *Dei Priori* €€ Corso Mazzini 15, 06081. (075-81 22 37. FAX 075-81 68 04. @ hpriori@edisons.it Set in a 17th-century building in the historic center, the bedrooms are pretty and fresh and there is a lovely vaulted dining room. 🔲 TV 🔲 P ✉	34	▦		
BOLOGNA: *Corona d'Oro 1890* €€€ Via Oberdan 12, 40126. (051-23 64 56. FAX 051-26 26 79. @ hotcoro@tin.it Parts of this building date back to the 14th century and there has been a hotel here for more than 100 years. Today it has a late 19th-century elegance, with Art Nouveau friezes combined with modern facilities. 🔲 TV 🔲 P ✉	35			
FERRARA: *Duchessa Isabella* €€€€ Via Palestro 70, 44100. (0532-20 21 21. FAX 0532-20 26 38. @ isabellad@tin.it A splendid hotel set in a 15th-century palazzo in the center of Ferrara, named after Isabella d'Este. Impeccable service and luxurious bedrooms. 🔲 TV 🔲 P ✉	27	▦		▦
LUCCA: *Piccolo Hotel Puccini* €€ Via di Poggio 9, 55100. (0583-554 21. FAX 0583-534 87. @ info@hotelpuccini.com Housed in a lovely old stone building, this smart, small hotel has an attractive bar that overlooks the pretty narrow street outside. 🔲 TV ✉	14			
PERUGIA: *Brufani* €€€€ Piazza Italia 12, 06100. (075-573 25 41. FAX 075-572 02 10. @ brufani@tin.it Opened in 1884, the public rooms of this exclusive hotel were painted by Lillis, the German interior designer. The views are spectacular. 🔲 TV 🔲 P ✉	82	▦		▦
PISA: *Royal Victoria Hotel* €€ Lungarno Pacinotti 12, 56126. (050-94 01 11. FAX 050-94 01 80. @ rvh@csinfo.it A dignified hotel originally built in the 19th century. It retains several original features, including exquisite *trompe l'oeil* drapery. 🔲 TV P ✉	40			
RAVENNA: *Bisanzio* @ info@bisanziohotel.com €€ Via Salara 30, 48100. (0544-21 71 11. FAX 0544-325 39. A faded façade hides a welcoming, modern interior overlooking a pretty garden, conveniently located in the center of Ravenna. 🔲 TV 🔲 ✉	38			▦
SAN GIMIGNANO: *Villa San Paolo* @ sanpaolo@iol.it €€€ Strada per Certaldo, 53037. (0577-95 51 00. FAX 0577-95 51 13. The San Paolo is an attractive hillside villa set in terraced gardens. Inside there are pretty bedrooms and intimate lounges. ● Jan–Mar. 🔲 TV 🔲 P ✉	18		●	▦
SIENA: *Santa Caterina* @ hsc@sienanet.it €€ Via Enea Silvio Piccolomini 7, 53100. (0577-22 11 05. FAX 0577-27 10 87. The comfortable rooms overlook the marvelous flower garden which has charming views of the red roofs of Siena. 🔲 TV 🔲 P ✉	19			▦

SIENA: *Villa Scacciapensieri* €€€€ | 28
Via di Scacciapensieri 10, 53100. [0577-414 41. FAX 0577-27 08 54. @ villasca@tin.it
Set in attractive grounds, this villa features an old-fashioned lounge with a huge
stone fireplace. The spacious bedrooms have views of Siena. 🔒 TV 目 P 🌅

URBINO: *Bonconte* W www.viphotels.it €€ | 23
Via delle Mura 28, 61029. [0722-24 63. FAX 0722-47 82.
A recently refurbished old villa, whose furnishings include some antiques among
the more modern suites. The bright rooms are well equipped. 🔒 TV 目 🌅

NAPLES AND THE SOUTH

AMALFI: *Santa Caterina* W www.hotelsantacaterina.it €€€€€€ | 62
Via S.S. Amalfitana 9, 84011. [089-87 10 12. FAX 089-87 13 51.
This is a luxurious property set amid lemon groves. Two elevators can
whisk you from the spectacular suites to the private beach in seconds. Enjoy
the sea view from the hotel's terraces or the high-tech gym. 🔒 TV 目 P 🌅

CAPRI: *Villa Sarah* W www.villasarah.it €€€ | 20
Via Tiberio 3a, 80073. [081-837 78 17. FAX 081-837 72 15.
A peaceful family-run villa hotel set among the island's vineyards. Rooms
are clean and pretty, and home produce is served for breakfast. 🔒 TV 🌅

NAPLES: *Britannique* W www.hotelbritannique.it €€€ | 86
Corso Vittorio Emanuele 133, 80121. [081-761 41 45. FAX 081-66 04 57.
A smart, modern hotel in the city center with spectacular views from its garden.
Suites with cooking facilities are available for longer stays. 🔒 TV 目 P 🌅

NAPLES: *Grande Albergo Vesuvio* W www.vesuvio.it €€€€ | 163
Via Partenope 45, 80121. [081-764 00 44. FAX 081-764 44 83.
Founded in 1882, the Grande Hotel overlooks the marina in central Naples.
It is furnished with marble bathrooms and antiques. 🔒 TV 目 P 🔒 🌅

NAPLES: *Hotel San Francesco al Monte* W www.hotelsanfrancesco.it €€€€ | 50
Corso Vittorio Emanuele 328, 80135. [081-423 91 11. FAX 081-251 24 85.
Originally a monastery, the San Francesco offers modern comforts in an historic
setting, with views over Naples, and a pool in its own gardens. 🔒 TV 目 P 🌅

POSITANO: *L'Ancora* €€€ | 18
Via Colombo 36, 84017. [089-87 53 18. FAX 089-81 17 84.
Excellent value in expensive Positano is available from this modern, central hotel
with sea views. The good-sized bedrooms are comfortable. 🔒 TV 目 P 🌅

SICILY

AGRIGENTO: *Villa Athena* W www.hotelvillaathena.com €€€€ | 40
Via Panoramica dei Templi 53, 92100. [0922-59 62 88. FAX 0922-40 21 80.
Set in an 18th-century villa just outside Agrigento, the decor of the Athena is
modern. There are great views of the Temple of Concord. 🔒 TV 目 P 🌅

CATANIA: *Nettuno* W www.hotel-nettuno.it €€€ | 101
Viale Ruggero di Lauria 121, 95126. [095-712 52 52. FAX 095-49 80 66.
A well-equipped, modern hotel in a quiet location. It overlooks the sea and
has a breakfast terrace above the outdoor swimming pool. 🔒 TV 目 P 🌅

PALERMO: *Grand Hotel Villa Igiea* W www.thi.it €€€ | 114
Salita Belmonte 43, 90142. [091-63 12 111. FAX 091-54 76 54.
An exquisite hotel dating from the early 20th century with Art Nouveau stained
glass and wall paintings. It is set by the sea in gardens with their own ancient
ruins. An elegant cocktail bar opens onto the terrace. 🔒 TV 目 P 🌅

PALERMO: *Splendid Hotel La Torre* W www.latorre.com €€€ | 168
Via Piano Gallo 11, Mondello 90151. [091-45 02 22. FAX 091-45 00 33.
A large, traditional seaside hotel, set on a promontory with its own private
beach. Some bedrooms have their own balcony with sea views. 🔒 TV 目 P 🌅

TAORMINA: *Villa Belvedere* W www.villabelvedere.it €€€ | 46
Via Bagnoli Croci 79, 98039. [0942-237 91. FAX 0942-62 58 30.
A very comfortable, family hotel in the center of Taormina. Some rooms have
sea views and balconies. Lunch is served by the pool. 🔒 TV 目 P 🌅

TAORMINA: *San Domenico Palace* W www.thi.it €€€€€€ | 108
Piazza San Domenico 5, 98039. [0942-61 31 11. FAX 0942-62 55 06.
A peaceful, 15th-century monastery restored and furnished with
genuine antiques, with a beautiful formal garden. 🔒 TV 目 P 🌅

Where to Eat in Italy

EACH REGION has its own distinctive cuisine, making use of locally-grown seasonal ingredients, although national favorites, such as classic pasta dishes, pizzas, and desserts, are produced all over the country. Risotto and polenta often replace pasta in the north. Among the countless delights of Italian food, look out for Sicilian fish, game and steaks in Tuscany, and the rich cuisine of Emilia-Romagna.

	FIXED-PRICE MENU	GOOD WINE LIST	AIR-CONDITIONING	OUTDOOR TABLES
ROME				
CAMPO DE' FIORI: *Dal Pompiere* €€€ Via Santa Maria dei Calderari 38. **Map** C3. **(** 06-686 83 77. In the heart of the Jewish ghetto, Al Pompiere is located in the Palazzo Cenci Bolognetti. The food is classical Roman, including fried zucchini flowers and *rigatoni con la pajata* (rigatoni with sweetbreads). ● *Sun; Aug.* ●		■	●	
CAMPO DE' FIORI: *Il Drappo* €€€ Vicolo del Malpasso 9. **Map** C3. **(** 06-687 73 65. An intimate restaurant, serving Sardinian cuisine, including *seadas* (sweet cheese-filled ravioli) and *mirto* liqueur. ● *Sun; 3 weeks Aug.* ● ●	●		●	■
CAMPO DE' FIORI: *Camponeschi* €€€€€ Piazza Farnese 50. **Map** C3. **(** 06-687 49 27. Modern and regional Italian cooking, and French specialties, served in a restaurant on one of the most beautiful piazzas in Rome. ● *Sun, lunch daily; 3 weeks Aug.* ● ●		■	●	■
ISOLA TIBERINA: *Sora Lella* €€€€€ Via di Ponte Quattro Capi 16. **Map** C3. **(** 06-686 16 01. Situated on the picturesque Tiber Island, this restaurant is popular with the locals. Traditional Roman dishes are served in elegant surroundings. ● *Sun; Aug.* ●		■	●	
PANTHEON: *Da Gino* €€ Vicolo Rosini 4. **Map** C2. **(** 06-687 34 34. An ancient, traditional Roman trattoria full of journalists, politicians, and the initiated. Daily dishes include gnocchi and *baccalà* (dried, salted cod) as well as some classic sturdy soups. ● *Sun; Aug.*				
PANTHEON: *El Toulà* €€€€€ Via della Lupa 29b. **Map** C2. **(** 06-687 34 98. One of Rome's most exclusive and traditional restaurants. The cuisine is mainly Venetian; the service and the wines are superb. ● *Sun, lunch Sat, lunch Mon; Aug.* ●	●	■	●	
PIAZZA NAVONA: *La Taverna da Giovanni* €€ Via della Lupa 29b. **Map** C2. **(** 06-686 41 16. A crowded trattoria with a family atmosphere. The *rigatoni all'amatriciana* (pasta with spicy bacon and tomato) is a specialty. ● *Mon.* ●	●	■	●	■
PIAZZA DI SPAGNA: *Birreria Viennese* €€ Via della Croce 21. **Map** C2. **(** 06-679 55 69. Traditional Austrian beers, sausages, and other specialties have been served in this long and crowded room for more than 60 years. ●	●		●	■
PIAZZA DI SPAGNA: *Porto di Ripetta* €€€€ Via di Ripetta 250. **Map** C2. **(** 06-361 23 76. A friendly restaurant serving wonderful dishes with fish and seafood brought in daily. Try the swordfish or the fish soup. ● *Sun lunch, Mon; Aug.* ● ●	●	■	●	
QUIRINAL: *Colline Emiliane* €€€ Via degli Avignonesi 22. **Map** D2. **(** 06-481 75 38. A small, family trattoria serving specialties from Emilia-Romagna, including home-made pasta, salami, and boiled meats with *salsa verde*. ● *Fri; Aug.* ● ●		■	●	
QUIRINAL: *Il Posto Accanto* €€€ Via del Boschetto 36a. **Map** D3. **(** 06-474 30 02. This elegant family-run restaurant owes its success to a carefully chosen menu based on home-made pasta, fish, and meat. ● *Sun, lunch Sat; Aug.* ● ●		■	●	
TRASTEVERE: *La Cornucopia* €€€ Piazza in Piscinula 18. **Map** C4. **(** 06-580 03 80. Come here for excellent antipasti and simply cooked fish dishes such as *spigola al vapore* (steamed sea bass). Candlelight adds to the ambience. ● *Tue.* ●	●		●	■

Map references refer to maps of Rome and Florence on pp392–3 and pp412–13 respectively

Price categories are for a three-course meal for one, including a half-bottle of house wine, tax, and service: € under €18 €€ €18–30 €€€ €30–40 €€€€ €40–50 €€€€€ over €50	**FIXED-PRICE MENU** A fixed-price menu is on offer, usually with three courses. **GOOD WINE LIST** Denotes a wide range of good quality wines. **CREDIT CARDS** Credit cards are accepted at those restaurants where the credit card symbol is shown.	FIXED-PRICE MENU	GOOD WINE LIST	AIR-CONDITIONING	OUTDOOR TABLES

TRASTEVERE: *Alberto Ciarla* €€€€€ Piazza San Cosimato 40. **Map** C4. 📞 06-581 86 68. This is the place to enjoy fish and seafood. From oysters to scampi, the menu is based on the day's fish from the market. The decor is dramatic. ● *lunch, Sun.* 🔲 🗐		●	■	●	■
VATICAN: *San Luigi* €€ Via Mocenigo 10. **Map** A2. 📞 06-39 72 07 04. After a long walk round the nearby Vatican Museums, this is just the place to rest and relax. The San Luigi offers traditional Roman cuisine – the pastas and desserts are particularly good. ● *Sun; Aug.* 🗐		●			
VIA VENETO: *Tullio* €€€€ Via San Nicola da Tolentino 26. **Map** D2. 📞 06-474 55 60. A genuine Tuscan restaurant frequented by an enthusiastic crowd. Dishes include *porcini* mushrooms prepared in numerous ways. ● *Sun; Aug.* 🗐 🗐			■	●	
VILLA BORGHESE: *Al Ceppo* €€€€€ Via Panama 2. 📞 06-841 96 96. Run by two sisters who serve a strictly seasonal menu of traditional dishes with flashes of inspiration in a hospitable atmosphere. ● *Mon; 2 weeks Aug.* 🗐 🗐			■	●	■

FLORENCE

CITY CENTER: *San Zanobi* € Via San Zanobi 33r. **Map** D1. 📞 055-47 52 86. Delicate, inventive food served in a sedate, refined dining room. The dishes, based on a Florentine theme, are light and well presented. ● *Sun.* 🗐					
CITY CENTER: *Da Pennello* €€ Via Dante Alighieri 4r. **Map** D3. 📞 055-29 48 48. This popular restaurant is famous for its extensive antipasti, a meal in themselves. Book well ahead or risk a long wait for a table. ● *Mon; dinner Sun; Aug, 1 week Dec.*		●	■		
CITY CENTER: *Paoli* €€ Via dei Tavolini 12r. **Map** D3. 📞 055-21 62 15. A spectacular setting: the dining room is a vaulted hall smothered in medieval frescoes. The restaurant specializes in Tuscan dishes. ● *Tue; Aug.* 🗐		●	■		
CITY CENTER: *Buca dell'Orafo* €€€ Volta de' Girolami 28r. **Map** D4. 📞 055-21 36 19. The cooking is based on home-made pasta, and daily specials include Tuscan *ribollita* (vegetable soup) and *pasta e fagioli* (beans). ● *Sun, lunch Mon; Aug.*				●	
CITY CENTER: *Cafaggi* €€€ Via Guelfa 35r. **Map** C1. 📞 055-29 49 89. This Tuscan trattoria uses oil and wines from the family farm. The *crostini* (toasts) and *involtini* (roulade) are particularly good. ● *Sun; 2 weeks Jul, 2 weeks Aug.* 🗐		●	■		
CITY CENTER: *Dino* €€€ Via Ghibellina 51r. **Map** D3. 📞 055-24 14 52. A well-regarded restaurant in a beautiful 14th-century palazzo, with one of the best wine lists in Florence. Regional dishes are served. ● *Mon; dinner Sun.* 🗐			■		
CITY CENTER: *Il Santo Bevitore* €€€ Via di Santo Spirito 64r. **Map** C4. 📞 055-21 12 64. The relaxed restaurant, housed in a former stable, features delicately flavored, innovative, seasonal dishes. ● *Sun.* 🗐 🗐			■	●	
CITY CENTER: *Alle Murate* €€€€ Via Ghibellina 52r. **Map** E3. 📞 055-24 06 18. The Tuscan food here combines Italian staples with more far-flung Mediterranean dishes, and there are light and interesting desserts. ● *Mon, lunch daily; 2 weeks Dec.* 🗐		●	■		

Price categories are for a three-course meal for one, including a half-bottle of house wine, tax, and service:

€ under €18
€€ €18–30
€€€ €30–40
€€€€ €40–50
€€€€€ over €50

FIXED-PRICE MENU
A fixed-price menu is on offer, usually with three courses.

GOOD WINE LIST
Denotes a wide range of good quality wines.

CREDIT CARDS
Credit cards are accepted at those restaurants where the credit card symbol is shown.

	FIXED-PRICE MENU	GOOD WINE LIST	AIR-CONDITIONING	OUTDOOR TABLES
CITY CENTER: *Lobs* €€€€ Via Faenza 75r. **Map** C2. 055-21 24 78. A small and informal fish restaurant, decorated with warm beach colours, offering pasta lunches and assorted fish 'platters' in the evening.		■	●	
CITY CENTER: *Enoteca Pinchiorri* €€€€€ Via Ghibellina 87. **Map** E3. 055-24 27 77. Often described as Italy's best restaurant with the finest wine cellar in Europe, the Pinchiorri is situated in a 15th-century palazzo. The Tuscan- and French-inspired cuisine includes a wonderful mix of dishes. ● *Sun, Mon, lunch Wed; Aug.*	●	■	●	■

VENICE

	FIXED-PRICE MENU	GOOD WINE LIST	AIR-CONDITIONING	OUTDOOR TABLES
BURANO: *Antica Trattoria alla Maddalena* €€ Mazzorbo 7/b. 041-73 01 51. This modest restaurant acts as a local bar as well as an eating house. The wild duck served with polenta is famous throughout the area. ● *Thu.*		■		■
CANNAREGIO: *Vini Da Gigio* €€€ Fondamenta San Felice 3628a. **Map** D2. 041-528 51 40. A cozy restaurant serving traditional Venetian cuisine with a difference. The risotto of shrimp and grilled cuttlefish is particularly good. ● *Mon; mid-Jan–Feb, late Aug.*		■	●	
CASTELLO: *La Corte Sconta* €€€€ Calle del Pestrin 3886. **Map** F4. 041-522 70 24. La Corte Sconta ("the hidden courtyard") is a simple eating house which has become one of the city's top restaurants. The fish and the home-made pasta are both superb. ● *Sun, Mon; Jan 7–Feb 7, Jul 21–Aug 16.*		■	●	■
DORSODURO: *Da Silvio* €€€ Calle San Pantalon 3748. **Map** C4. 041-520 58 33. A genuine local restaurant with a lovely garden for summer eating. The menu has no surprises but the food is fresh and home-made. ● *Sun, lunch Sat.*		■		■
DORSODURO: *Ai Gondolieri* €€€€ San Vio 366. **Map** D5. 041-528 63 96. A sympathetically restored old inn, where friendly hosts offer good regional specialties, including *sformati* (soufflés) with wild herbs, hand-carved prosciutto, or mushroom soup. ● *Tue.*		■	●	
GIUDECCA: *Cipriani* €€€€€ Giudecca 10. 041-520 77 44. One of Venice's most exclusive restaurants, the Cipriani offers impeccable food and service in elegant surroundings. Panoramic terrace. ● *Nov–Mar.*	●	■	●	■
SAN MARCO: *Al Conte Pescaor* €€€€ Piscina San Zulian 544b. **Map** E3. 041-522 14 83. A small restaurant with a superb fish menu. The customers are mainly locals, which guarantees the high quality of the food. ● *Sun; Jan 7–Feb 7.*	●		●	■
SAN MARCO: *Da Raffaele* €€€€ Ponte delle Ostreghe 2347. **Map** D4. 041-523 23 17. A romantic setting in which to eat regional dishes. Try the *granseola* (spider crab), risotto with scampi, and *rombo alla Raffaele* (turbot). ● *Thu; Dec–early Feb.*		■	●	■
SAN MARCO: *Da Arturo* €€€€€ Calle degli Assassini 3656. **Map** D4. 041-528 69 74. This restaurant must be the only place in Venice that does not serve fish, but the menu does include a variety of meat dishes and vegetarian salads. ● *Sun; Aug.*		■	●	
SAN POLO: *Da Fiore* €€€€ Calle del Scaleter 2202a. **Map** C3. 041-72 13 08. Fish specialties include a wonderful seafood antipasto, grilled fish, and *fritto misto* (mixed fried fish). ● *Sun, Mon; 3 weeks Aug, 2 weeks Dec.*		■	●	

Map references refer to maps of Florence and Venice on pp412–13 and pp432–3 respectively

NORTHERN ITALY

GENOA: *Da Genio* €€
Salita San Leonardo 61r. ☎ 010-58 84 63.
Popular with locals, the Da Genio has an animated atmosphere. The delicious food includes grilled swordfish and anchovies stuffed with capers. ● *Sun; Aug.*

LAKE COMO: *Silvio* €€
Via Carcano 12, Bellagio. ☎ 031-95 03 22.
Silvio and his son Cristian catch much of the lake fish which is used for patés, pasta sauces, ravioli, and risottos. There is a relaxed atmosphere in this lovely restaurant and hotel with beautiful lakeside views. ● *Jan, Feb.*

LAKE GARDA: *Locanda San Vigilio* €€€
Località San Vigilio, Garda. ☎ 045-725 66 88.
This excellent restaurant overlooking the lake has an antipasto buffet and an astounding range of freshwater fish and seafood dishes. ● *Nov–Mar.*

MANTUA: *Il Cigno Trattoria dei Martini* €€€
Piazza Carlo d'Arco 1. ☎ 0376-32 71 01.
Fine Mantuan cuisine is accompanied by excellent wines. Try the *tortelli di zucca* (pumpkin). ● *Mon, Tue; Aug, 1st week Jan.*

MILAN: *Geppo* €
Via Morgagni 37. ☎ 02-29 51 48 62.
A fun atmosphere and a wide range of pizzas are on offer here. Try the *valdostana* (spinach, tomato, mozzarella, and taleggio cheese). ● *Sun.*

MILAN: *La Capanna* €€
Via Donatello 9. ☎ 02-29 40 08 84.
Don't be put off by the plain appearance; the food, based on Tuscan cuisine, is exceptional. Fresh pasta and home-made desserts. ● *Wed, lunch Sat.*

MILAN: *Lucca* €€€
Via Castaldi 33. ☎ 02-29 52 66 68.
A great place for business lunches and popular for dinner, the cuisine at the Lucca is Tuscan and Mediterranean in style. ● *Mon; Easter, Dec 23–Jan 7.*

MILAN: *Il Luogo di Aimo e Nadiá* €€€€€
Via Montecuccoli 6. ☎ 02-41 68 86.
A small, chic restaurant which is famed for its delicious, imaginative dishes, prepared with select, seasonal ingredients. ● *Sun, lunch Sat; Aug, 10 days Jan.*

PADUA: *San Pietro* €€€
Via San Pietro 95. ☎ 049-876 03 30.
The place to try regional specialties, cooked with fresh ingredients. The service is friendly and the atmosphere informal. ● *Sat in summer, Sun; Jul, 2 weeks Dec.*

PORTOFINO: *Puny* €€€€€
Piazza Martiri Olivetta 5. ☎ 0185-26 90 37.
A spectacular view of the bay of Portofino accompanies the well-prepared regional dishes and crisp Ligurian wines. ● *Thu; Jan, Feb, 2 weeks Dec.*

TURIN: *Porto di Savona* €€
Piazza Vittorio Veneto 2. ☎ 011-817 35 00.
A friendly restaurant set in an 18th-century building in central Turin. The regional cuisine includes such dishes as gnocchi with gorgonzola and meats braised in Barolo wine. ● *Mon, lunch Tue; 2 weeks Jan, 2 weeks Aug.*

TURIN: *Neuv Caval 'd Brôns* €€€€
Piazza San Carlo 151. ☎ 011-562 74 83.
An elegant, spacious restaurant offering excellent food from a range of cuisine, including vegetarian dishes. Specialties include the renowned mint and chocolate dessert *Santa Vittoria*. ● *Sun, lunch Sat; 2 weeks Aug.*

VERONA: *Al Bersagliere* €€
Via dietro Pallone 1. ☎ 045-800 48 24.
Traditional Veronese food in a friendly atmosphere. Dishes include mixed grilled meats and polenta with wild mushrooms. ● *Sun.*

VERONA: *Il Desco* €€€€€
Via dietro San Sebastiano 5–7. ☎ 045-59 53 58.
One of Italy's best restaurants, set in a 16th-century palazzo. Imaginative dishes include veal with ginger and lobster risotto. ● *Sun, Mon; 2 weeks Jan, 2 weeks Jun.*

Price categories are for a three-course meal for one, including a half-bottle of house wine, tax, and service:

€ under 18
€€ 18–30
€€€ 30–40
€€€€ 40–50
€€€€€ over 50

FIXED-PRICE MENU
A fixed-price menu is on offer, usually with three courses.

GOOD WINE LIST
Denotes a wide range of good quality wines.

CREDIT CARDS
Credit cards are accepted at those restaurants where the credit card symbol is shown.

Restaurant	Price	Fixed-Price Menu	Good Wine List	Air-Conditioning	Outdoor Tables
VICENZA: *Taverna Aeolia* — Piazza Conte da Schio 1, Costozza di Longare. 0444-55 50 36. This restaurant is housed in an elegant villa with a beautiful frescoed ceiling. The menu specializes in creative meat dishes. *Tue; Nov 1–15.*	€	●	■	●	

CENTRAL ITALY

Restaurant	Price	Fixed-Price Menu	Good Wine List	Air-Conditioning	Outdoor Tables
ASSISI: *Medioevo* — Via Arco dei Priori 4b. 075-81 30 68. An elegant restaurant in old Assisi, serving home-made pastas (try them with black truffles in season). Meats are cooked to traditional recipes. *Wed, dinner Sun; Jan.*	€€		■	●	
BOLOGNA: *Antica Trattoria Spiga* — Via Broccaindosso 21a. 051-23 00 63. An authentic trattoria, with immaculately prepared traditional cuisine. Specialties include lasagna, tortellini, and gnocchi. *Sun, dinner Mon; Aug.*	€€	●			
BOLOGNA: *Pappagallo* — Piazza Mercanzia 3c. 051-23 28 07. Housed in a 14th-century palazzo in the historic center, this elegant restaurant serves Bolognese dishes – tortellini and lasagna. *Sun; Aug.*	€€€€		■		
FERRARA: *La Sgarbata* — Via Sgarbata 84. 0532-71 21 10. A country trattoria on the outskirts of Ferrara which serves fish dishes as well as rich and tasty pizzas. *Mon, Tue.*	€€	●			■
LUCCA: *Buca di Sant'Antonio* — Via della Cervia 3. 0583-558 81. Lucca's most famous restaurant of traditional rustic cooking. Local dishes, such as *fettuccine sul piccione* (pasta and pigeon), are served. *Mon, dinner Sun; Jul.*	€€€				
PERUGIA: *Giò Arte e Vini* — Via Ruggero d'Andreotto 19. 075-573 11 00. A restaurant famous for its spectacular selection of wines and well-chosen regional dishes with special touches. The pumpkin ravioli and the *trecciola di agnello* (lamb) are particularly good. *dinner Sun, lunch Mon.*	€€	●	■	●	■
PISA: *Al Ristoro dei Vecchi Macelli* — Via Volturno 49. 050-204 24. Innovative dishes in a pleasant, intimate restaurant that serves light Tuscan food with an adventurous twist. The desserts are a delight. *Wed; 2 weeks Aug.*	€€€€	●	■	●	
RAVENNA: *Trattoria Capannetti* — Vicolo Capannetti 21. 0544-666 81. A peaceful restaurant in the historic center, the Capannetti serves creative, regional home-made cuisine that changes with the season. *dinner Sun, Mon.*	€€€	●	■		■
SAN GIMIGNANO: *Le Terrazze* — Albergo la Cisterna, Piazza della Cisterna 24. 0577-94 03 28. One of the dining rooms at Le Terrazze is part of a 13th-century palazzo. Regional specialties with some novelties are served. *Tue, lunch Wed; Jan–Mar.*	€€€€		■	●	
SIENA: *Al Marsili* — Via del Castoro 3. 0577-471 54. Set in an 11th-century building, Al Marsili – long regarded as one of the best restaurants in Siena – offers good regional specialties. *Mon.*	€€€		■	●	
SIENA: *Osteria le Logge* — Via del Porrione 33. 0577-480 13. This is Siena's prettiest restaurant, with a dark wood and marble interior. Home-produced oils and Montalcino wines accompany dishes that include guinea fowl, duck and fennel, and rabbit with capers. *Sun; Nov.*	€€€€		■		■

URBINO: *Vecchia Urbino* €€
Via del Vasari 3–5. [0722-44 47.
A restaurant with views over the historic center. Local rustic dishes include *vincisgrassi* (the local lasagna), rabbit, and polenta with mushrooms. ● Tue. & 🖅

NAPLES AND THE SOUTH

AMALFI: *La Marinella* €€€
Via Lungomare dei Cavalieri di San Giovanni di Gerusalemme 1. [089-87 10 43.
A lively, friendly restaurant overlooking the the Amalfi coast. Much fish is served along with traditional local specialties. ● Fri in winter; Jan–Feb. & 🖅

CAPRI: *La Savardina da Eduardo* €€
Via Lo Capo 8. [081-837 63 00.
One of the most traditional restaurants in Capri, with orange trees, sea views, and tasty regional specialties, such as ravioli. ● Tue (in winter); Nov–Feb/Mar. 🖅

NAPLES: *Da Ettore* €€
Via Santa Lucia 56. [081-764 04 98.
Excellent antipasta, pasta, and pizza are served in this popular pizzeria. Friendly, efficient service and outside tables, ideal for people-watching. ● Sun. & limited. 🖅

NAPLES: *Amici Miei* €€€
Via Monte di Dio 78. [081-764 60 63.
Intimate, old-fashioned restaurant specialising in home-made pasta and meat dishes. Prestigious wine list and excellent value. ● Sun dinner, Mon; Aug. 🖅

NAPLES: *La Cantinella* €€€€€
Via Cuma 42. [081-764 86 84.
One of Naples' most famous restaurants, with a richly-deserved reputation for its carefully prepared regional cuisine. Need to book. ● Sun; 3 weeks Aug. 🖅 🖅

POMPEII: *Il Principe* €€€€€
Piazza B. Longo 8. [081-850 55 66.
This acclaimed restaurant is close to the Pompeii excavations. Its cuisine is based on fish. ● dinner Sun, Mon; 3 weeks Aug. 🖅 & 🗎 🖅

POSITANO: *La Sponda* €€€€
Via Colombo 30. [089-87 50 66.
A sumptuous restaurant, where guests are treated like family friends and offered a tempting range of modern and traditional dishes based on fresh fish. ● Dec–Feb. 🖅

SICILY

AGRIGENTO: *Trattoria del Pescatore* €€
Lungomare Falcone e Borsellino 20, Località Lido di San Leone. [0922-41 43 42.
The chef at the Pescatore chooses the fish daily for simple but delicious dishes with oil and lemon juice, sometimes served raw. The pasta specialty is spaghetti with swordfish, eggplant, and basil. ● Wed (in winter); Nov. 🖅

PALERMO: *Simpaty* €€€
Via Piano Gallo 18, Località Mondello. [091-45 44 70.
The dining room of the Simpaty looks out over the bay of Mondello. The menu is almost exclusively fish – try *ricci* (little sea urchins) as an antipasto. ● Mon; Nov. 🖅

PALERMO: *La Scuderia* €€€€
Viale del Fante 9. [091-52 03 23.
Set in the Parco della Favorita, this elegant restaurant sticks to traditional Sicilian cuisine, carefully and deliciously prepared. ● Sun; 2 weeks Aug. & 🖅

SYRACUSE: *Jonico 'a Rutta 'e Ciauli* €€
Riviera Dionisio il Grande 194. [0931-655 40.
The attractive, bright dining room here has walls covered with Sicilian ceramics and agricultural artifacts. The cuisine is regional and traditional. ● Tue; Christmas week, Easter week. & 🖅

TAORMINA: *Pizzeria Vecchia Taormina* €
Vico Ebrei 3. [0942-62 55 89.
A traditional pizzeria in the old Jewish quarter of Taormina. There is a massive range of Sicilian-style pizzas and delicious antipasti. ● Wed; 2 weeks Jul. 🖅 🖅

TAORMINA: *La Giara* €€€€
Vicolo La Floresta 1. [0942-233 60.
A pretty restaurant with beautiful views over the bay of Taormina. Try ravioli with eggplant and wild fennel *involtini* (parcels). ● Mon; Nov–Mar: Sun–Thu. 🖅

GREECE

GREECE IS ONE *of the most visited countries in Europe, yet remains one of the least known. Although most visitors will be familiar with the images of Ancient Greece, the modern Greek state dates only from 1830. Situated at a geographical crossroads, Greece combines cultural elements of the Balkans, the Middle East, and the Mediterranean.*

For a small country, Greece possesses marked regional differences. Nearly three-quarters of the land is mountainous, uninhabited, or uncultivated. On the mainland, fertile agricultural land supports tobacco farming in the northeast, with orchard fruits and vegetables grown farther south. A third of the population lives in the capital, Athens, the cultural, financial, and political center, where ancient and modern stand side by side. Of the myriad islands, only about a hundred are today inhabited.

For centuries a large number of Greeks have lived abroad. Currently there are over half as many Greeks outside the country as in, although recent years have seen reverse immigration, with expatriates returning home, especially to the islands.

Rural and urban life in contemporary Greece has been transformed since the start of the 20th century, despite foreign occupation and civil war. Until the 1960s, the country remained underdeveloped, with many rural areas lacking basic amenities. Since then, a number of improvements, including the growth of tourism, the country's largest hard-currency earner, have helped Greece develop into a relatively wealthy, modern state.

HISTORY

Early Greek history is marked by a series of internal struggles, from the Mycenaean and Minoan cultures of the Bronze Age to the competing city-states of the 1st millennium BC. In spite of warfare, the 4th and 5th centuries BC were the high point of ancient Greek civilization, a golden age of exceptional creativity in philosophy and the arts.

In 338 BC the Greeks were conquered by Philip II of Macedonia at Chaironeia, and Greece soon became absorbed into Alexander the Great's vast empire. With the defeat of

Whitewashed stone windmills, a common feature of the Cyclades and the Dodecanese islands

◁ The awe-inspiring rock "towers" of Metéora in central Greece, first settled by hermits in the 10th century

the Macedonians by the Romans in 168 BC, Greece was made a province of Rome. As part of the Eastern Empire, it was ruled from Constantinople and became a powerful element within the Orthodox Christian, Byzantine world.

Following the Ottomans' momentous capture of Constantinople in 1453, the Greek mainland was ruled by the Turks for the next 350 years. Crete and the Ionian islands were seized for long periods by the Venetians. Eventually the Greeks rebelled and, in 1821, the Greek War of Independence began. In 1832 the Great Powers that dominated Europe established a protectorate over Greece, marking the end of Ottoman rule. During the 19th century the Greeks expanded their national territory, reasserting Greek sovereignty over many of the islands.

Almost a century of significant territorial gains came to a disastrous end in 1922, when millions of Greeks were expelled from Smyrna in Turkish Anatolia, bringing to a close thousands of years of Greek presence in Asia

19th-century lithograph celebrating the Greek War of Independence

Minor. The ensuing years were a time of hardship and instability. The Metaxás dictatorship was followed by Italian, German, and Bulgarian occupation during World War II, and then a bitter civil war. The present boundaries of the Greek state date from 1948, when the Dodecanese were finally returned by the Italians. Today, Greece is a stable democracy and has been a member of the European Union since 1981.

KEY DATES IN GREEK HISTORY

3000–1200 BC Bronze Age; Cycladic, Minoan, and Mycenaean cultures flourish

800 Emergence of city-states

5th century Classical period; high point of Athenian culture under Perikles

431–404 Peloponnesian Wars; defeat of the Athenians by the city-state of Sparta

338 Greek army conquered by Philip II of Macedonia

333 Alexander the Great declares himself king of Asia; Greece absorbed into his vast empire

168 Romans defeat Macedonians; Greece becomes province of Rome

AD 49–54 St. Paul preaches Christianity in Greece

395 Greece becomes part of the new Eastern Roman Empire, ruled from Constantinople

1453 Constantinople falls to the Ottoman Turks

1821 Start of the Greek War of Independence

1832 Great Powers establish protectorate over Greece, and appoint Otto of Bavaria king

1922 Greeks fail to capture Smyrna from Turks

1940 Greece enters World War II

1946–9 Civil war leaves thousands dead or homeless

1981 Admission to the European Union

RELIGION, LANGUAGE, AND CULTURE

During Venetian and Ottoman domination, the Greek Orthodox church succeeded in preserving the Greek language and identity. Today, the Orthodox church is still a powerful force. Great importance is placed on baptisms and church weddings, although civil marriages are valid in law. Sunday mass is very popular with women, for whom church is a meeting place for socializing, just as the *kafeneía* (cafés) are for men.

The Greek language was for a long time a field of conflict between *katharévousa*, an artificial form devised around the time of independence, and the slowly evolved everyday speech, or *dimotikí*. Today's prevalence of *dimotikí* was perhaps a foregone conclusion in an oral culture. The art of storytelling is as prized now as it was in Homer's time, with conversation pursued for its own sake in *kafeneía* and at dinner tables. Singers, writers, and poet-lyricists have all kept *dimotikí* alive until the present day.

DEVELOPMENT AND DIPLOMACY

Compared to its Balkan neighbors, Greece is a wealthy country, but it remains one of the poorer members of the European Union. It still bears the hallmarks of a developing economy, with agriculture and the service sector accounting for two-thirds of the GNP. Nevertheless, with a nominally capitalist orientation, it has overcome its resemblance to pre-1989 Eastern Europe. Loss-making state enterprises have been sold off, and inflation and interest rates have fallen. However, unemployment remains high. Tourism has compensated for the decline in other industries, such as world shipping.

The fact that the Greek state is less than 200 years old, combined with recent periods of political instability, means that there is little faith in government institutions. Life operates on networks of personal friendships and official contacts. In the political sphere, the years following World War II were largely shaped by the influence of two men: Andréas Papandréou of the Pan-hellenic Socialist Movement (PASOK) and Conservative Konstantínos Karamanlís, who between them held office for the most part of the 1980s and 90s.

Typical scene at a Greek taverna, a popular place for friends and family to socialize

With the Cold War over and improvements in relations with its Balkan neighbors, Greece now seems poised to become a significant regional power.

HOME LIFE

The family is still the basic Greek social unit. Traditionally, one family would farm its own land independently, and today family-run businesses are common in urban settings. Family life and social life are usually one and the same, and tend to revolve around eating out. Arranged marriages and dowries, though officially banned, persist. Most single young adults live with their parents and outside the largest cities, few unmarried couples dare to cohabit. Despite the renowned Greek love of children, Greece has one of the lowest birth rates in Europe. Recently, the status of urban Greek women has greatly improved. They are now better represented in medicine and law, and many women run their own firms. However, in the country macho attitudes still exist, women often sacrificing a career to look after the house and children. New imported attitudes have crept in, especially in the cities, but generally the Greek traditional way of life remains resolutely strong.

The late Andréas Papandréou, three times Greek premier

Fishermen mending their nets on one of the Greek islands

Exploring Greece

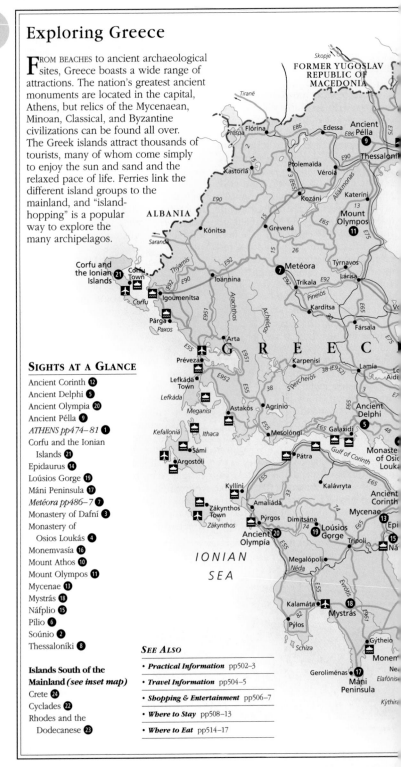

FROM BEACHES to ancient archaeological sites, Greece boasts a wide range of attractions. The nation's greatest ancient monuments are located in the capital, Athens, but relics of the Mycenaean, Minoan, Classical, and Byzantine civilizations can be found all over. The Greek islands attract thousands of tourists, many of whom come simply to enjoy the sun and sand and the relaxed pace of life. Ferries link the different island groups to the mainland, and "island-hopping" is a popular way to explore the many archipelagos.

SIGHTS AT A GLANCE

Ancient Corinth **12**
Ancient Delphi **5**
Ancient Olympia **20**
Ancient Pélla **9**
ATHENS pp474–81 **1**
Corfu and the Ionian
  Islands **21**
Epidaurus **14**
Loúsios Gorge **19**
Máni Peninsula **17**
Metéora pp486–7 **7**
Monastery of Dafní **3**
Monastery of
  Osios Loukás **4**
Monemvasía **16**
Mount Athos **10**
Mount Olympos **11**
Mycenae **13**
Mystrás **18**
Náfplio **15**
Pílio **6**
Soúnio **2**
Thessaloníki **8**

**Islands South of the
Mainland (see inset map)**
Crete **24**
Cyclades **22**
Rhodes and the
  Dodecanese **23**

SEE ALSO

• *Practical Information* pp502–3

• *Travel Information* pp504–5

• *Shopping & Entertainment* pp506–7

• *Where to Stay* pp508–13

• *Where to Eat* pp514–17

BULGARIA

Kastaniés
Orestiáda
Istanbul

dirókastro
Dráma
14
Sérres
Néa
Zíchni
Amfípoli
Kavála
Keramotí
Alexandroúpoli
Istanbul
Soufli
Komotiní
Xánthi
E90
E90
E85

Néstos
Angítis
E90

Moudaniá
Ouranoúpoli
10 Mount Athos

Thásos

THRACIAN   SEA

Samothráki

Ímvros

Ténedos

TURKEY

Límnos

Agios
Efstrátios

áthos
Alónnisos
Gioúra
Kyrá Panagiá
Peristéra
Skópelos

AEGEAN

Lésvos

Skýros

Kými
Chalkída
44

SEA

Psará
Chíos
Oinoússes

tery
afní
3
Marathónas
1 ATHENS
eus
1

Kárystos

Andros

Sámos

Aígina
thana
Póros
ra
Makrónisos
Soúnio
2
Kéa

Gyáros

Kýthnos
Sýros
Tínos

Sérifos
Antíparos
Sifnos
Páros

Mílos
Kímolos
Polýaigos
Sikínos
Folégandros

KEY

✈ Airport
⛴ Ferry port
— Highway
— Major road
— Railroad
-·-·- International boundary

ISLANDS SOUTH OF THE MAINLAND

ATHENS
Andros
Chíos
TURKEY

Kéa
Tínos
Sámos
Ikaría

Kýthnos
Sýros
Délos
Mýkonos
Pátmos

Sérifos
Sifnos
Páros
Náxos
Kálymnos
Kos

Mílos
22 The Cyclades
Íos
Amorgós
Astypálaia

Santoríni
Anáfi
23 Rhodes and
the Dodecanese
Rhodes Town
Líndos

MEDITERRANEAN
SEA
Rhodes

Kárpathos
Kásos

Chaniá
Sea of Crete
Irákleio
Ágios
Nikólaos
24 Crete

0 km   50
0 miles   50

0 kilometers   50
0 miles   50

Athens ●

ATHENS HAS BEEN INHABITED for 7,000 years. The city's greatest glory was during the Classical period (4th and 5th centuries BC) of ancient Greece, from which so many buildings and artifacts survive. The city is dominated by the world-famous Acropolis and its theaters and temples, including the Parthenon, erected by Perikles as part of his grand building plan in the mid-5th century BC. Within the Byzantine Empire and under Ottoman rule, Athens played only a minor role. It returned to prominence in 1834, when King Otto made it capital of Greece. When the king's architects planned the new, European-style city, they included many splendid Neoclassical public buildings, which today provide elegant homes for some of Athens' best museums and galleries.

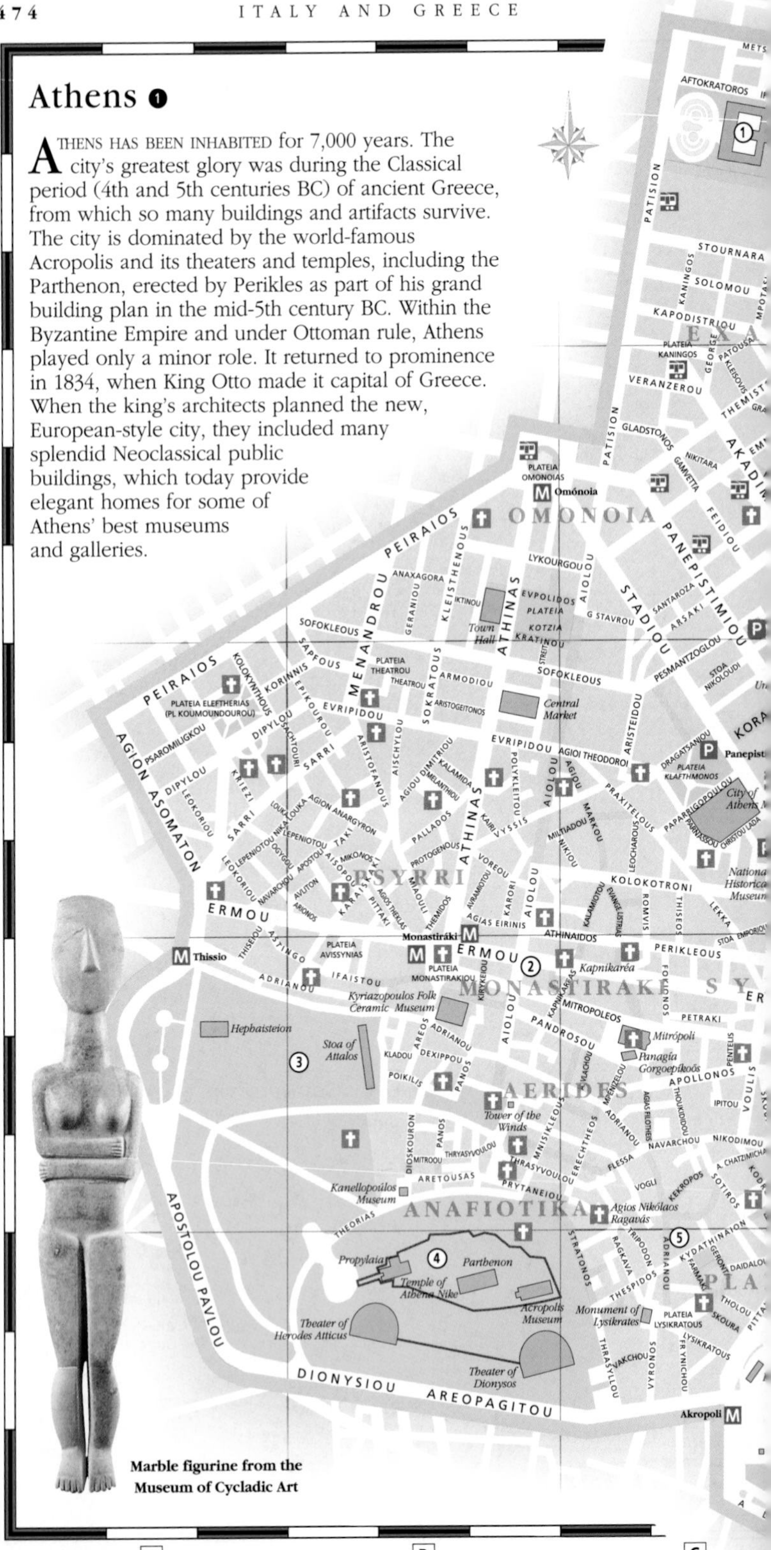

Marble figurine from the Museum of Cycladic Art

1

2

3

4

5

AFTOKRATOROS
METS

STOURNARA

PLATEIA
OMONOIAS
M Omónoia

OMONOIA

PANEPISTIMIOU

PEIRAIOS

LYKOURGOU

ANAXAGORA

KLEISTHENOUS

EVPOLIDOS
PLATEIA

Town
Hall
KOTZIA
KRATINOU

SOFOKLEOUS

PEIRAIOS

PLATEIA ELEFTHERIAS
(PL KOUMOUNDOUROU)

MENANDROU

PLATEIA
THEATROU

Central
Market

AGION ASOMATON

SARRI

DIPYLOU

EVRIPIDOU

EVRIPIDOU AGIOI THEODOROI

Panepist

City of
Athens

PSYRRI

ERMOU

KOLOKOTRONI

Nationa
Historica
Museum

M Thissio

M Monastiráki

PLATEIA
AVISSYNIAS

ERMOU ②

Kapnikaréa

MONASTIRAKI

SYR

ADRIANOU

PLATEIA
MONASTIRAKIOU

IFAISTOU

Kyriazopoulos Folk
Ceramic Museum

MITROPOLEOS

PETRAKI

Hephaisteion

PANDROSOU

Mitrópoli

Stoa of
Attalos ③

ADRIANOU

Panagía
Gorgoepíkoos

APOLLONOS

AERIDES

Tower of the
Winds

NAVARCHOU

NIKODIMOU

Kanellopoilos
Museum

ANAFIOTIKA

Agios Nikólaos
Ragavás

Propylaia ④ Parthenon

Temple of
Athena Nike

Acropolis
Museum

Monument of
Lysikrates ⑤

PLA

Theater of
Herodes Atticus

Theater of
Dionysos

PLATEIA
LYSIKRATOUS

DIONYSIOU AREOPAGITOU

APOSTOLOU PAVLOU

Akropoli **M**

| A | B | C |

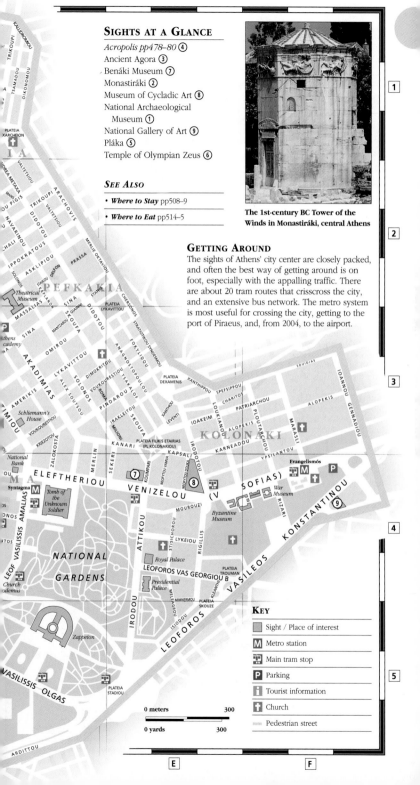

SIGHTS AT A GLANCE

Acropolis pp478–80 ④
Ancient Agora ③
Benáki Museum ⑦
Monastiráki ②
Museum of Cycladic Art ⑧
National Archaeological
  Museum ①
National Gallery of Art ⑨
Pláka ⑤
Temple of Olympian Zeus ⑥

SEE ALSO

- **Where to Stay** pp508–9
- **Where to Eat** pp514–5

The 1st-century BC Tower of the Winds in Monastiráki, central Athens

GETTING AROUND

The sights of Athens' city center are closely packed, and often the best way of getting around is on foot, especially with the appalling traffic. There are about 20 tram routes that crisscross the city, and an extensive bus network. The metro system is most useful for crossing the city, getting to the port of Piraeus, and, from 2004, to the airport.

KEY

▨	Sight / Place of interest
Ⓜ	Metro station
🚋	Main tram stop
🅿	Parking
ⓘ	Tourist information
✝	Church
---	Pedestrian street

0 meters   300

0 yards   300

Neoclassical entrance to the National Archaeological Museum

National Archaeological Museum ①

Patission 44, Exárcheia. 210-821 7717. www.culture.gr Omónoia. for renovation work until Apr 2004.

WHEN IT WAS OPENED in 1891, this museum brought together antiquities that had previously been stored in different places all over the city. New wings were added in 1939, but during World War II the museum's priceless exhibits were dispersed and buried underground to protect them from possible damage. The museum reopened in 1946, but it has taken another 50 or so years of renovation and reorganization to finally do justice to its formidable collection. With the combination of such unique exhibits as the Mycenaean gold, and an unrivaled assembly of sculpture, pottery, and jewelry, it can definitely be claimed as one of the finest museums in the world. It is a good idea to plan ahead and be selective when visiting the museum and not attempt to cover everything in one visit.

The museum's exhibits can be divided into seven main collections: Neolithic and Cycladic, Mycenaean, Geometric and Archaic sculpture, Classical sculpture, Roman and Hellenistic sculpture, the pottery collections, and the Thíra frescoes. There are also other smaller collections that are well worth seeing. These include the stunning Eléni Stathátou jewelry collection and the recently opened Egyptian rooms.

High points of the museum include the unique finds from the grave circle at Mycenae *(see p490)*, in particular the gold Mask of Agamemnon. Also not to be missed are the Archaic *kouroi* statues and the unrivaled collection of Classical and Hellenistic statues. Two of the most important and finest of the bronzes are the *Horse with the Little Jockey* and *Poseidon*. One of the world's largest collections of ancient ceramics can also be found here, comprising a vast array of elegant red- and black-figure vases from the 6th and 5th centuries BC and some Geometric funerary vases that date back as far as 1000 BC.

Monastiráki ②

Monastiráki. **Market** daily.

THIS LIVELY and atmospheric area, which is named after the little monastery in Plateía Monastirakíou, is synonymous with Athens' famous flea market. Located next to the ancient Agora, it is bounded by Sari in the west and Aiólou in the east. The streets of Pandrósou, Ifaístou, and Areos leading off Plateía Monastirakíou are full of shops, selling a range of goods from expensive antiques, leather, and silver to tourist trinkets.

The heart of the flea market is in Plateía Avyssinías, west of Plateía Monastirakíou, where every morning junk dealers arrive with pieces of furniture and various odds and ends. During the week the shops and stalls are filled with antiques, second-hand books, rugs, leatherware, taverna chairs, army surplus gear, and tools.

On Sunday mornings, when the shops are closed, the market itself still flourishes along Adrianoú and in Plateía Agíou Filíppou. There are always numerous bargains to be had. Items particularly worth investing in include some of the brightly colored woven and embroidered cloths and an abundance of good silver jewelry.

Shoppers browsing in Athens' lively Monastiráki market

View across the Agora, showing the reconstructed Stoa of Attalos on the right

Ancient Agora ③

Main entrance at Adrianoú, Monastiráki. ☎ 210-321 0185. Ⓜ Thiseío, Monastiráki. **Museum and site** ◐ Tue–Sun. ◐ main public hols. 📷 ♿ limited.

THE AMERICAN SCHOOL of Archaeology commenced excavations of the Ancient Agora in the 1930s, and since then a complex array of public buildings and temples has been revealed. The democratically governed Agora was the political and religious heart of ancient Athens. Also the center of commercial and daily life, it abounded with schools and elegant stoas, or roofed arcades, filled with shops. The state prison was here, as was the city's mint. Even the remains of an olive oil mill have been found.

The main building standing today is the impressive two-story Stoa of Attalos. This was rebuilt in the 1950s on the original foundations and using ancient building materials. Founded by King Attalos of Pergamon (ruled 159–138 BC), it dominated the eastern quarter of the Agora until it was destroyed in AD 267. It is used today as a museum, exhibiting the finds from the Agora. These include a *klepsydra* (a water clock that was used for timing plaintiffs' speeches), bronze ballots, and items from everyday life such as some terra-cotta toys and leather sandals. The best-preserved ruins on the site are the

Odeion of Agrippa, a covered theater, and the Hephaisteion, a temple to Hephaistos, also known as the Theseion.

Acropolis ④

See pp478–80.

Pláka ⑤

Ⓜ Monastiráki. 🚌 1, 2, 4, 5, and many others.

THE AREA OF PLAKA is the historic heart of Athens. Even though only a few buildings date back farther than the Ottoman period, it remains the oldest continually inhabited area in the city. One probable explanation of its name comes from the word used by Albanian soldiers in the service of the Turks who settled here in the 16th century – *pliaka* (old) was how they used to describe the area. Despite the

constant swarm of tourists and Athenians, who come to eat in old-fashioned tavernas or browse in the antique and icon shops, Pláka still retains the atmosphere of a traditional neighborhood. The **Lysikrates Monument** in Plateía Lysikrátous is one of a number of monuments that were built to commemorate the victors at the annual choral and dramatic festival at the Theater of Dionysos. Taking its name from the sponsor of the winning team, it is the only such monument still intact in Athens.

Many churches are worth a visit: the 11th-century **Agios Nikólaos Ragavás** has ancient columns built into the walls.

The **Tower of the Winds**, in the far west of Pláka, lies in the grounds of the Roman Agora. It was built by a Syrian astronomer in the 2nd century BC as a weather vane and water clock. The name comes from external friezes depicting the eight mythological winds.

The Byzantine church of Agios Nikólaos Ragavás in Pláka

Acropolis ④

I N THE MID-5TH CENTURY BC, Perikles persuaded
the Athenians to begin a grand program of
new building work. The resulting transformation
has come to embody the political and cultural
achievements of ancient Greece. Three
contrasting temples were built on the Acropolis,
together with a monumental gateway. The
Theater of Dionysos and the Theater of Herodes
Atticus were added later, in the 4th century BC
and the 2nd century AD respectively.

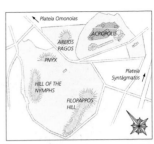

LOCATOR MAP

★ Porch of the Caryatids
*These statues of
women were used
in place of columns
on the south porch
of the Erechtheion.
The originals, four
of which can be
seen in the Acropolis
Museum, have been
replaced by casts.*

An olive tree now
grows where Athena
first planted her tree
in a competition
against Poseidon.

The Propylaia was built
in 437–432 BC to form a
new entrance to the
Acropolis.

★ Temple of Athena Nike
*This temple to Athena of
Victory is on the west side
of the Propylaia. It was
built in 426–421 BC.*

The Beulé Gate
was the first
entrance to
the Acropolis.

**Pathway to
Acropolis
from ticket
office**

STAR SIGHTS

- **★ Parthenon**
- **★ Porch of the Caryatids**
- **★ Temple of Athena Nike**

Theater of Herodes Atticus
*Also known as the Odeion of
Herodes Atticus, this superb
theater was originally built
in AD 161. It was restored in
1955 and is used today
for outdoor concerts.*

★ Parthenon
Although few sculptures are left on this famous temple to Athena, some can still be admired, such as this one from the east pediment (see p480).

Acropolis Museum
(see p480)

VISITORS' CHECKLIST

Dionysíou Areopagítou (main entrance), Pláka. 210-321 0219. Acropolis. 230, 231. **Site** Apr–Oct: 8am–6:30pm daily; Nov–Mar: 8am–2:30pm daily. Jan 1, Mar 25, Easter Sun, May 1, 25 & 26 Dec.
Museum 210-323 6665. Apr–Oct: 8am–6:30pm daily; Nov–Mar: 8am– 2:30pm daily. Jan 1, Mar 25, Easter Sun, May 1, 25 & 26 Dec.
www.culture.gr

Two Corinthian columns are the remains of choregic monuments erected by sponsors of successful dramatic performances.

Panagía Spiliótissa is a chapel set up in a cave in the Acropolis rock.

Theater of Dionysos
This figure of the comic satyr, Silenus, can be seen here. The theater visible today was built by Lykourgos in 342–326 BC.

Shrine of Asklepios

Stoa of Eumenes

The Acropolis rock was an easily defended site. It has been in use for nearly 5,000 years.

THE ELGIN MARBLES

These famous sculptures, also called the Parthenon Marbles, are held in the British Museum in London. They were acquired from the occupying Turkish authorities by Lord Elgin in 1801–3. He sold them to the British nation for £35,000 in 1816. There is great controversy surrounding the Marbles. While some argue that they are more carefully preserved in the British Museum, the Greek government does not accept the legality of the sale and believes they belong in Athens.

The newly arrived Elgin Marbles at the British Museum, in a painting by A. Archer

Exploring the Acropolis

ONCE YOU ARE THROUGH THE PROPYLAIA, the grand entrance to the site, the Parthenon exerts an overwhelming fascination. The other fine temples on "the Rock" include the Erechtheion and the Temple of Athena Nike. Since 1975, access to all the temple precincts has been banned. However, it is a miracle that anything remains at all. The ravages of war, the removal of treasures, and pollution have all taken their irrevocable toll on the Acropolis.

View of the Parthenon from the southwest at sunrise

♪ The Parthenon

One of the world's most famous monuments, the Parthenon was commissioned by Perikles as part of his rebuilding plan. Work began in 447 BC, when the sculptor Pheidias was entrusted with supervising the building of a new Doric temple to Athena, the patron goddess of the city. Built on the site of earlier Archaic temples, it was designed primarily to house the *Parthenos,* Pheidias's impressive cult statue of Athena.

Taking just nine years to complete, the temple was dedicated to the goddess in the course of the Great Panathenaia festival of 438 BC. Designed and constructed in Pentelic marble by the architects Kallikrates and Iktinos, the Parthenon replaces straight lines with slight curves. It is thought that this complex architectural style was used to create an illusion of perfection *(see pp482–3).*

For the pediments and the friezes that ran all the way around the temple, an army of sculptors and painters

was employed. Agorakritos and Alkamenes, both pupils of Pheidias, are two of the sculptors who worked on the frieze, which depicted the people and horses in the Panathenaic procession.

Despite much damage and alterations made to adapt it to various uses, which have included a church, a mosque, and even an arsenal, the Parthenon remains a majestic sight today.

🏛 Acropolis Museum

Opened in 1878, this museum houses a collection devoted solely to finds from the Acropolis. Among the treasures are some beautiful statues dating from the 5th century BC and segments of the Parthenon frieze.

The collection begins chronologically with the 6th-century BC works in Rooms I, II, and III. The *Moschophoros* or Calf-bearer (c.570 BC) is displayed in this section of the museum, along with fragments of pedimental statues of mythological scenes. Room V contains a pediment from the old Temple of Athena, while Rooms IV and VI hold a

collection of *kórai* (550–500 BC), votive statues of maidens offered to the goddess Athena.

Exhibits in Rooms VII and VIII include fragments from the Erechtheion frieze and a well-preserved *metope* from the south side of the Parthenon. The collection ends in Room IX with the four remaining caryatids from the Erechtheion, carefully kept behind glass in a temperature-controlled environment.

Around the Acropolis

The area around the Acropolis was the center of public life in Athens. In addition to the Agora in the north *(see p477),* there were two theaters on the southern slope, the Theater of Herodes Atticus and the Theater of Dionysos. Political life was largely centered on the Areopagos and the Pynx Hills to the west of the Acropolis: the *Ekklesia* (citizens' assembly) met on the latter, while the former was the seat of the Supreme Judicial Court. Filopáppos Hill, the highest summit in the south of Athens, has always played an important defensive role in the city's history – an important fort was built here overlooking the strategic Piraeus road in 294 BC. On the tree-clad Hill of the Nymphs, the 19th-century Danish-built Asteroskopeíon (Observatory) occupies the site of an old sanctuary dedicated to nymphs associated with childbirth.

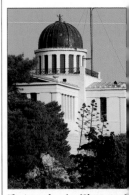

The Asteroskopeíon (Observatory) on the Hill of the Nymphs

Temple of Olympian Zeus ⑥

Corner of Amalías & Vasilíssis Olgas, Pláka. (210-922 6330. 🚌 2, 4, 11. ◯ daily. ● main public hols. 📷 & limited.

THIS VAST TEMPLE is the largest in Greece, exceeding even the Parthenon in size. The tyrant Peisistratos allegedly initiated the building of the temple in the 6th century BC to gain public favor. It was not completed until 650 years later.

In AD 132 the Roman Emperor Hadrian dedicated the temple to Zeus Olympios and set up a statue of the god inside, a copy of the original by Pheidias at Olympia (see p493). Next to it he placed a huge statue of himself. Both statues have since been lost.

Only 15 of the original 104 columns remain, but enough to give a sense of the once enormous size of this temple – approximately 96 m (315 ft) long and 40 m (130 ft) wide. Roman-style Corinthian capitals were added to the original, simple Doric columns in 174 BC.

The temple lies next to Hadrian's Arch, which was built in AD 131 and marked the boundary between the ancient city and the new Athens of Hadrian.

Benáki Museum ⑦

Corner of Koumpári & Vasilíssis Sofías, Kolonáki. (210-367 1000. 🚌 3, 7, 8, 13. ◯ Mon & Wed–Sun. ● public hols. 📷 except Thu. & limited.

THIS MUSEUM contains a superb collection of Greek art and crafts, jewelry, regional costumes, and political memorabilia from the Neolithic era to the 20th century. It was founded by Antónios Benákis (1873–1954), who was interested in Greek, Persian, Egyptian, and Ottoman art from an early age and started collecting while living in Alexandria. On moving to Athens in 1926, he donated his collection to the Greek state. The family home, an elegant 19th-century

The remains of the Temple of Olympian Zeus

Neoclassical mansion, was used as a museum and opened to the public in 1931.

A major part of the Benáki collection consists of gold jewelry dating from as far back as 3000 BC. Also on display are icons, liturgical silverware, Egyptian artifacts, and Greek embroideries.

Museum of Cycladic Art ⑧

Neofýtou Doúka 4 (new wing at Irodótou 1), Kolonáki. (210-722 8321. 🚌 3, 7, 8, 13. ◯ Mon & Wed–Sat. ● main public hols. 📷 &.

A MAGNIFICENT selection of ancient Greek art, including the world's most important collection of Cycladic figurines, is on view at this modern museum.

Clearly laid out over five floors, the displays start on the first floor, with the Cycladic

collection. Dating back to the 3rd millennium BC, the Cycladic figurines were found mostly in graves, although their exact usage remains a mystery. Ancient Greek art is exhibited on the second floor and the Charles Polítis collection of Classical and Prehistoric art on the fourth floor. The third floor is currently used for temporary exhibitions.

A new wing, which opened in the adjoining Stathátos Mansion in 1992, contains the Greek Art Collection of the Athens Academy.

National Gallery of Art ⑨

Vasiléos Konstantínou 50, Ilísia. (210-723 5937. 🚌 3, 13. ◯ 9am–3pm Thu–Sun, 9am–3pm 6–9pm Mon & Wed. ● main public hols. 📷 &

THIS MODERN building holds a permanent collection of European and Greek art. European exhibits include various works by van Dyck, Cézanne, Dürer, Rembrandt, Picasso, and Caravaggio. The majority of the collection, however, is made up of Greek art from the 18th to 20th centuries, and includes paintings of the Greek War of Independence, seascapes, and some excellent portraits.

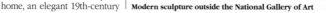

Modern sculpture outside the National Gallery of Art

Temple Architecture

TEMPLES WERE THE most important public buildings in ancient Greece, largely because religion was a central part of everyday life. Often placed in prominent positions, temples were also statements about political and divine power. The earliest temples, in the 8th century BC, were built of wood and sun-dried bricks. Many of their features were copied in marble buildings from the 6th century BC onward.

The Parthenon on the Acropolis in Athens

TEMPLE CONSTRUCTION
This drawing is of an idealized Doric temple, showing how it was both built and used.

The pediment, triangular in shape, often held sculpture.

The cella, or inner sanctum, housed the cult statue.

The cult statue was of the god or goddess to whom the temple was dedicated.

Fluting on columns was carved *in situ*, guided by that on top and bottom drums.

A ramp led up to the temple entrance.

The stepped platform was built on a stone foundation.

The column drums were initially carved with bosses for lifting them into place.

THE ILLUSION OF PERFECTION

Every aspect of the Parthenon was built on a 9:4 ratio to make the temple completely symmetrical. The sculptors also used visual trickery to counteract the laws of perspective. The illustration *(right)* is exaggerated to show the techniques they employed.

The base of the temple is higher in the middle than at the edges.

Entasis (a bulge in the middle) makes each column look straight.

Each column leans slightly inward.

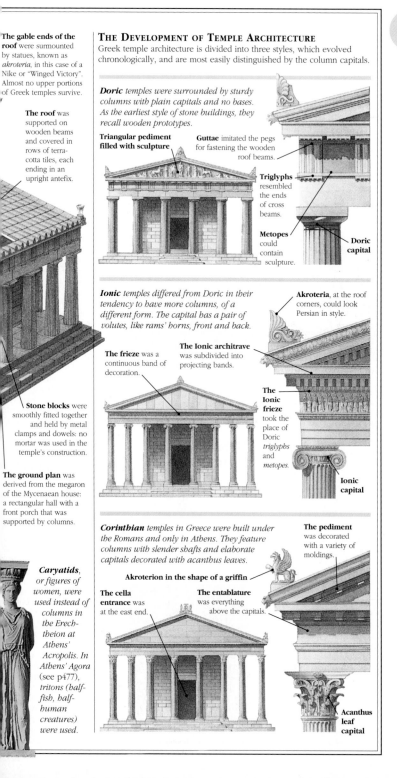

The gable ends of the roof were surmounted by statues, known as *akroteria*, in this case of a Nike or "Winged Victory". Almost no upper portions of Greek temples survive.

The roof was supported on wooden beams and covered in rows of terra-cotta tiles, each ending in an upright antefix.

Stone blocks were smoothly fitted together and held by metal clamps and dowels: no mortar was used in the temple's construction.

The ground plan was derived from the megaron of the Mycenaean house: a rectangular hall with a front porch that was supported by columns.

Caryatids, *or figures of women, were used instead of columns in the Erechtheion at Athens' Acropolis. In Athens' Agora (see p477), tritons (half-fish, half-human creatures) were used.*

THE DEVELOPMENT OF TEMPLE ARCHITECTURE

Greek temple architecture is divided into three styles, which evolved chronologically, and are most easily distinguished by the column capitals.

Doric *temples were surrounded by sturdy columns with plain capitals and no bases. As the earliest style of stone buildings, they recall wooden prototypes.*

Triangular pediment filled with sculpture

Guttae imitated the pegs for fastening the wooden roof beams.

Triglyphs resembled the ends of cross beams.

Metopes could contain sculpture.

Doric capital

Ionic *temples differed from Doric in their tendency to have more columns, of a different form. The capital has a pair of volutes, like rams' horns, front and back.*

Akroteria, at the roof corners, could look Persian in style.

The frieze was a continuous band of decoration.

The Ionic architrave was subdivided into projecting bands.

The Ionic frieze took the place of Doric *triglyphs* and *metopes*.

Ionic capital

Corinthian *temples in Greece were built under the Romans and only in Athens. They feature columns with slender shafts and elaborate capitals decorated with acanthus leaves.*

Akroterion in the shape of a griffin

The pediment was decorated with a variety of moldings.

The cella entrance was at the east end.

The entablature was everything above the capitals.

Acanthus leaf capital

Central Greece

BEYOND THE ENDLESS urban sprawl of Athens, the vast expanse of central Greece has a little of everything for the visitor, from sandy beaches and fishing ports, to one of the country's most important archaeological sites, Ancient Delphi. Not to be missed is the Byzantine splendor of the monasteries of Dafní and Osios Loúkas, while the extraordinary mountain-top monasteries of Metéora are another of the region's principal attractions. The beautiful wooded mountain slopes of the Pílio offer some of the best scenery on the mainland.

The Temple of Poseidon on the cape at Soúnio

Soúnio ❷

9 km (5.5 miles) S of Lávrio, Attica.
C 22920-39363. 🚌 to Lávrio.
◯ daily. 🌐

THE TEMPLE OF POSEIDON, situated at the top of sheer cliffs tumbling into the Aegean Sea at Soúnio (Cape Sounion), was ideally located as a place to worship the powerful god of the sea. Its brilliant white marble columns have been a landmark for ancient and modern mariners alike.

The present temple, built in 444 BC, stands on the site of older ruins. An Ionic frieze, made from 13 slabs of Parian marble, is located on the east side of the temple's main approach path. It is very eroded, but is known to have depicted scenes from mythological battles, as well as the adventures of the hero Theseus, said in some legends to be the son of Poseidon.

Local marble from the quarries at Agriléza was used for the temple's 34 slender Doric columns, of which 15 survive today. In 1810 the British Romantic poet, Lord

Byron, carved his name on one of the columns, setting an unfortunate precedent for vandalism at the temple.

Monastery of Dafní ❸

10 km (6 miles) NW of Athens, Attica.
C 210-581 1558. 🚌 ◯ until 2004 for restoration. 🌐 ♿ limited.

FOUNDED IN THE 5TH century AD, the Monastery of Dafní is named after the laurels (*dáfnes*) that once grew here. It was built with

The 5th-century Byzantine Monastery of Dafní near Athens

the remains of an ancient sanctuary of Apollo, which had occupied the site until it was destroyed in AD 395. In the early 13th century, Otto de la Roche, the first Frankish Duke of Athens, bequeathed it to Cistercian monks in Burgundy. Greek Orthodox monks took the site in the 16th century, erecting the elegant cloisters just south of the church. The monastery is presently closed for restoration, due to an earthquake which hit in the year 2000.

Among the monastery's principal attractions are the beautiful gold-leaf Byzantine mosaics in the *katholikón* (main church). Byzantine church architecture was concerned almost exclusively with decoration. Mosaics and frescoes portraying the whole body of the Church, from Christ downward, had a dual purpose: they gave inspiration to worshipers and represented windows to the spiritual world. The most impressive mosaics at Dafní are the Esonarthex Mosaics, which include the *Last Supper*, the *Washing of the Feet*, and the *Betrayal of Judas*. Equally magnificent, the *Christ Pantokrátor* is a mosaic of Christ in judgement that fills the church's huge dome.

Monastery of Osios Loúkas ❹

8 km (5 miles) E of Dístomo, Stereá Elláda. **C** 22670-22228. 🚌
◯ daily. 🌐

DEDICATED to a local hermit and healer, Osios Loúkas ("Holy Luke"), who lived in the 10th century, this splendid monastery was one of medieval Greece's most important buildings architecturally. It was built around AD 1011 by the Emperor Romanós, who extended an earlier church dating from 944. The octagonal style of the main church, the *katholikón*, became a hallmark of late Byzantine church design, while the mosaics inside lifted Byzantine art into its final great period.

Among the most impressive features of the monastery are the 10th-century crypt, which

Detail from an 11th-century mosaic in the Monastery of Osios Loúkas

is from the original church and contains the sarcophagus of Holy Luke, and a mosaic entitled *Washing of the Apostles' Feet*. This 11th-century work, based on a style dating back to the 6th century, is the finest of a number of mosaics found in the narthex, the western entrance hall. The monastery's main dome is decorated with an imposing mural of Christ, painted in the 16th century to replace fallen mosaics.

Ancient Delphi ❺

Mount Parnassus, Stereá Elláda.
☎ *22650-82312*. **🚌** **○** *daily*.
● *main public hols.* **♿**

I N ANCIENT TIMES Delphi was believed to be the center of the earth. The site was renowned as a dwelling place of Apollo, and from the late 8th century BC people came here to worship and seek advice from the god. With the political rise of Delphi in the 6th century BC, and the establishment of the Pythian Games – a cultural, religious, and athletic festival – the site entered a golden age that lasted until the arrival of the Romans in 191 BC. The Delphic Oracle was abolished in AD 393 after Christianity was introduced as the state religion.

The Sanctuary of Apollo, also known as the Sacred Precinct, forms the heart of the complex, and one of its most impressive sights is the **Temple of Apollo**. A temple has stood on this spot since the 6th century BC, but the

remains visible today date from the 4th century BC. Leading from the sanctuary entrance to the Temple of Apollo is the **Sacred Way**, once lined with some 3,000 statues and treasuries. Also worth seeing is the well-preserved **Stadium**. The present structure dates from Roman times, and most of the seating is still intact.

The Marmaria Precinct, or marble quarry, is where the **Sanctuary of Athena Pronaia** is found. Here, the most remarkable monument is the *tholos*, which dates from the 4th century BC. The purpose of this circular structure, originally surrounded by 20 columns, remains a mystery.

The museum at Ancient Delphi houses an impressive collection of sculptures and architectural remains.

Pílio ❻

Thessaly. **🚌** *Vólos.* **🚗** **ℹ** *Plateía Riga Feraíou, Vólos (24210-23500).*

T HE PILIO PENINSULA is one of the most beautiful areas of the mainland. The mountain air is sweet with the scent of herbs, which in ancient times were renowned for their healing properties. The area became populated in the 13th century by Greeks retreating

Traditional-style guesthouses in the Pílio village of Vyzítsa

from the Ottomans. After centuries of protecting its culture, the Pílio is known for its strong local cuisine.

The main town on the peninsula is **Vólos**, which has an excellent Archaeological Museum. From here you can make a tour of the many traditional hillside villages and fishing ports. Worth visiting are **Miliés**, with its Folk Museum and fresco-adorned church, and picturesque **Vyzítsa**. **Argalastí** has a busy market, though its tavernas and cafés retain a peaceful atmosphere. For fine sandy beaches and excellent seafood, visit the popular coastal resorts of **Plataniá** or **Agios Ioánnis**.

The *tholos* beside the Sanctuary of Athena Pronaia at Ancient Delphi

Metéora **❼**

THE EXTRAORDINARY sandstone towers of Metéora (or "suspended rocks") were formed by the action of the sea that covered the plain of Thessaly around 30 million years ago. The huge columns of rock were first used as a religious retreat in AD 985, when a hermit named Barnabas occupied a cave here. In the mid-14th century Neílos, the Prior of Stagai convent, built a small church. A few years later, in 1382, the monk Athanásios, from Mount Athos, founded the huge monastery of Megálo Metéoro on one of the many pinnacles. A further 23 monasteries were built, though most had fallen into ruin by the 19th century. In the 1920s stairs were cut in the rock faces to make the remaining six monasteries more accessible, and today a religious revival has seen the return of many monks and nuns.

Monastic cells

Outer walls

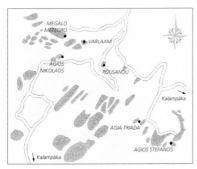

LOCATION OF MONASTERIES OF METEORA

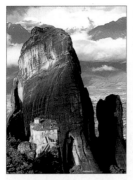

Rousánou
Moní Rousánou, perched precariously on the very tip of a narrow spire of rock, is the most spectacularly located of all the monasteries. Its church of the Metamórfosis (1545) is renowned for its harrowing frescoes, painted in 1560 by the iconographers of the Cretan school.

VARLAÁM
Founded in 1518, the monastery of Varlaám is named after the first hermit to live on this rock in 1350. The *katholikón* (main church) was built in 1542 and contains frescoes by the Theban iconographer Frágkos Katelános.

Megálo Metéoro
Also known as the Great Meteoron, this was the first and, at 623 m (2,045 ft), highest monastery to be founded. By the entrance is a cave in which Athanásios first lived. His body is buried in the main church.

Katholikón
*Dedicated to Agioi Pántes
(All Saints), the church is
adorned with frescoes,
including one of
Theofánis (right)
and Nektários,
its founders.*

The refectory
contains a
small icon
museum.

VISITORS' CHECKLIST

Thessaly. 🚌 ℹ️ Chatzipétrou
10, Kalampáka (24320-76100).
Megálo Metéoro 📞 24320-
22278. ◯ Mon, Wed–Sun.
Varlaám 📞 24320-22277.
◯ Sat–Thu. **Agíou Nikoláou**
📞 24320-22649. ◯ daily. **Rousánou**
📞 24320-22649. ◯ daily.
Agías Triádas 📞 24320-22220.
◯ daily. **Agiou Stefánou**
📞 24320-22279. ◯ Tue–Sun.
All Metéora monasteries
● 1–3pm. 📷 🚻 Agías Triádas
& Agiou Stefánou.

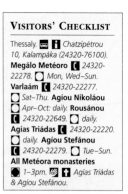

Ascent Tower
*Goods and people were
brought to the top of the rock
in a net that was pulled up
by a winch mechanism,
made in 1536.*

**Net descending
from tower**

Entrance

THE BUILDING OF
THE MONASTERIES

Though it is unknown how the
first hermits at Metéora reached
the tops of these often vertical
rock faces, it is likely that they
hammered pegs into tiny gaps
in the rock and hauled building
materials to the summits.
Another theory is that kites
were flown over the tops,
carrying strings attached to
thicker ropes, which were made
into the first rope ladders. How
the ladders were anchored to
the rock is uncertain.

Northern Greece

NORTHERN GREECE offers an appealing combination of comparatively unexplored natural beauty and a rich cultural heritage. The stunning scenery of places like Mount Olympos holds special appeal to walking enthusiasts, while of historical interest in the region are several ancient archaeological sites, including Pélla, the birthplace of Alexander the Great. Many of northern Greece's finest examples of Byzantine architecture and art are to be found on the Athos Peninsula and in the bustling city of Thessaloníki.

The 15th-century White Tower on the waterfront in Thessaloníki

Thessaloníki ❽

🏙 1,000,000. ✈ 25 km (15 miles) SE. 🚉 🚌 🚢 ℹ Ferry terminal (2310-271888).

THESSALONIKI, also known as Salonica, is Greece's second city, and was founded by King Kassandros in 315 BC. The capital of the Roman province of Macedonia Prima from 146 BC, it later became part of the Byzantine Empire. In 1430 it was captured by the Turks, who held it until 1912. Today Thessaloníki is a bustling cosmopolitan city and a major religious center.

On the *paralía*, the city's attractive waterfront, stands one of Thessaloníki's most famous sights, the **White Tower**. Built in 1430, this is one of three towers that were added to the city walls by the Turks. Today it is used to house a collection of Byzantine icons and historical displays.

The **Arch of Galerius** was built in AD 303 by the Emperor Galerius to celebrate victory over the Persians, and is the principal architectural legacy of Roman rule. Standing north of the arch is the **Rotónda**, believed to have been constructed as a mausoleum for Galerius. Now closed, it has been used in the past as both a church and a mosque.

Thessaloníki has a number of museums, including the **Museum of Byzantine Culture** and the **Museum of the Macedonian Struggle**, whose exhibits recount the story of centuries of Turkish domination. The star attractions at the city's **Archaeological Museum** are the Roman floor mosaics, and the splendid Dervéni Krater, a 4th-century BC bronze wine-mixing bowl. The gold burial caskets from the Royal Tombs at Vergína form the centerpiece of the museum's stunning collection of Macedonian gold.

Visitors should not miss the city's rich array of Byzantine churches, which include the 5th-century **Agios Dimítrios** – the largest church in Greece. Dating from the mid-8th century, **Agía Sofía** is an important building, both for its mosaics and for its role in influencing future architectural development, while the 14th-century **Agios Nikólaos Orfanós** contains the best-preserved collection of late Byzantine frescoes in the city.

🏛 **Archaeological Museum**
Manóli Andrónikou & Leof Stratoú. 📞 031-830538. 🚌 3. 🕐 daily (Mon: pm only). 🔴 main public hols. 🖼 ♿

Ancient Pélla ❾

38 km (24 miles) NW of Thessaloníki. 📞 23820-31160. 🚌 🕐 Tue–Sun. 🔴 main public hols. 🖼 ♿

THIS SMALL site was once the flourishing capital of Macedonia. The court was moved here from Aigai (near modern Vergína) in 410 BC

THE MACEDONIAN ROYAL FAMILY

The gold burial casket found at Vergína is emblazoned with the Macedonian Sun, the symbol of the king. Philip II was from a long line of Macedonian kings that began in about 640 BC with Perdiccas I. Philip was the first ruler to unite the whole of Greece as it existed at that time. Much of Greece's pride in the symbol lies in the fact that Alexander the Great used it throughout his empire. He was just 20 when his father was assassinated in 336 BC. He inherited his father's already large empire and also his ambition to conquer the Persians. In 334 BC Alexander crossed the Dardanelles with 40,000 men and defeated the Persians in three different battles, advancing as far as the Indus Valley before he died at the age of 33. With his death the Macedonian empire divided.

Gold burial casket from the Royal Tombs at Vergína

Russian Orthodox monastery, Agíou Panteleímonos, on Mount Athos

by King Archelaos, who ruled from 413 to 399 BC. It is here that Alexander the Great was born in 356 BC, and was later tutored by the philosopher Aristotle. Some sense of the existence of a city can be gained from a plan of the site, which shows where the main street and stores were located. The palace, believed to have been north of the main site, is still being excavated.

At the site, and in the museum, are some of the best-preserved pebble mosaics in Greece. Dating from about 300 BC, the mosaics depict vivid hunting scenes. One of the most famous is of Dionysos riding a panther; it is housed in the now-covered, 4th-century BC House of the Lion Hunt. Originally comprising 12 rooms around three open courtyards, this building was constructed at the end of the 4th century BC.

Mount Athos ⓾

Athos Peninsula. 🚢 *Dáfni (boat trips from Ouranoúpoli & Thessaloníki for the west coast, or from Ierissós for the east coast).* 🚌 *to Karyés.* 💰 *donation.*

ALSO KNOWN as the Holy Mountain, Mount Athos is the highest point on the Athos Peninsula – an autonomous republic, ruled by the 1,700 monks who live in its 20 monasteries. Only adult males may visit the peninsula, but it is possible to see many of the monasteries from a boat trip along the coast. They include some fine examples of Byzantine architecture and provide a fascinating insight into Orthodox monastic life.

For the monks who live here, the day begins at 3 or 4am with morning services and prayers. They eat two meals a day, which consist mainly of food they grow themselves. There are 159 fasting days in the year. Between meals the monks spend their time working, resting, and praying.

Ouranoúpoli is the main town on Athos and where the boat trips for the peninsula's west coast start. Among the monasteries that can be viewed are the 10th-century **Docheiaríou**, **Agíou Panteleímonos**, an 11th-century Russian Orthodox monastery, and **Moní Agíou Pávlou**. On the east coast, **Megístis Lávras** was the first monastery to be founded on Athos, while 10th-century **Moní Vatopedíou**, farther north, is one of the largest and best-preserved buildings.

Adult males wishing to visit any of the monasteries must obtain a letter of recommendation from the Greek consul in their country. The Ministry of Foreign Affairs in Athens, or Ministry of Macedonia and Thrace in Thessaloníki, will then issue a permit allowing a stay of up to four nights. Accommodations are free, though donations are expected.

Mount Olympos ⓫

17 km (10 miles) W of Litóchoro. 🚏 *Litóchoro.* 🛈 *EOS: Evángelou Karavákou 20, Litóchoro (23520-82444).*

THE NAME Mount Olympos refers to a whole range of mountains, 20 km (12 miles) across. The highest peak in the range is Mýtikas, at 2,917 m (9,570 ft). The entire area constitutes the Olympos National Park, an area of outstanding natural beauty that attracts naturalists and walkers alike. The park's rich flora and fauna include 1,700 plant species, in addition to chamois, boars, and roe deer. From **Litóchoro**, which has several hotels and tavernas, walkers can follow a series of trails.

A short distance from Litóchoro is **Ancient Díon**, considered a holy city by the ancient Macedonians. The flat plains were used as a military camp by King Philip II of Macedon in the 4th century BC. The ruins visible today – which include mosaics, baths, and a theater – date mainly from the Roman era. A museum shows finds from the site.

The peaks of the Mount Olympos range rising above Litóchoro

The Peloponnese

O NE OF THE PRIMARY strongholds and battlefields of the 1821–31 Revolution, the Peloponnese is the kernel from which the modern Greek state grew. The region boasts a wealth of ancient and medieval ruins, from Bronze Age Mycenae to the Byzantine town of Mystrás. As popular as its vast array of historical sites is the Peloponnese's spectacularly varied landscape. The breathtaking scenery of places like the Loúsios Gorge attracts walkers and naturalists in their thousands.

The ruins of Acrocorinth, south of Ancient Corinth

Ancient Corinth ⑫

7 km (4 miles) SW of modern Corinth.
☎ 27410-31207. 🚍 ⬜ daily.
⬤ main public hols. 📷 ♿ limited.

A SETTLEMENT since Neolithic times, Ancient Corinth was razed in 146 BC by the Romans, who rebuilt it a century later. Attaining a population of 750,000 under the patronage of the Roman emperors, the town gained a reputation for licentious living, which St. Paul attacked when he came here in AD 52. Excavations have revealed the vast extent of the ancient city, which was destroyed by earthquakes in Byzantine times. The ruins constitute the largest Roman township in Greece.

Among the most impressive remains are the **Lechaion Way**, the marble-paved road that linked the nearby port of Lechaion with the city, and the **Temple of Apollo**, with its striking Doric columns. The temple was one of the few buildings preserved by the Romans when they rebuilt the city in 44 BC. Of the **Temple of Octavia**, once dedicated to the sister of Emperor Augustus, three ornate Corinthian columns, overarched by a restored architrave, are all that remain. The **Odeion** is one of several buildings endowed to the city by Herodes Atticus, the wealthy Athenian and friend of the Emperor Hadrian.

Close to the Odeion, the **Museum** houses a collection of exhibits representing all periods of the town's history. The Roman gallery is particularly rich, containing some spectacular 2nd-century AD mosaics lifted from the floors of nearby villas.

Just 4 km (2 miles) south of Ancient Corinth is the bastion of **Acrocorinth**, to which there is access between 8:30am and 3pm each day. Held and refortified by every occupying power in Greece from Roman times onward, it was one of the country's most important fortresses in medieval times. The ruins show evidence of Byzantine, Turkish, Frankish, and Venetian occupation. The summit of Acrocorinth affords one of the most sweeping views in the whole of Greece.

RECONSTRUCTION OF ANCIENT CORINTH (C.AD 100)

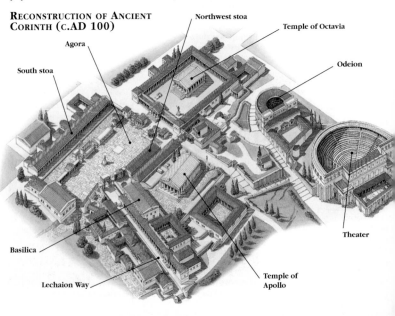

Northwest stoa

Temple of Octavia

Agora

Odeion

South stoa

Basilica

Lechaion Way

Temple of Apollo

Theater

Interior of the tomb known as the Treasury of Atreus, at Mycenae

Mycenae ⑬

2 km (1 mile) N of Mykínes.
📞 27510-76585. 🚌 to Mykínes.
◯ daily. ● main public hols. 📷
🚹 Treasury of Atreus only.

DISCOVERED in 1874, the fortified palace complex of Mycenae is an early example of sophisticated citadel architecture. The Mycenaeans were a Bronze Age culture that existed between 1700 and 1100 BC. Only the ruling class inhabited the palace, with artisans and merchants living outside the city walls. The citadel was abandoned in 1100 BC after much disruption in the region.

The tombs at Mycenae are one of the most famous attractions of the site. The city's nobles were entombed in shaft graves, such as those at **Grave Circle A**, or, later, in *tholos* ("beehive") tombs, so-called because of their shape. The *tholos* tombs, found outside the palace walls, were buried under an earth mound, the only entrance being via a *dromos*, or open-air corridor. The 14th-century BC **Treasury of Atreus** is the most outstanding of the *tholos* tombs. Here a Mycenaean king was buried with his weapons and enough food and drink for his journey to the underworld. The so-called **Tomb of Klytemnestra** is equally well preserved.

Also of interest at the site are the remains of the **Royal Palace**, the **Secret Stairway**, which leads down to a cistern deep beneath the citadel, and the 13th-century BC **Lion Gate**, the grand entrance to Mycenae.

Epidaurus ⑭

30 km (19 miles) E of Náfplio.
📞 27530-22009. 🚌 ◯ daily
● main public hols. 📷
🚹 limited. 📷

ACTIVE FROM the 6th century BC until at least the 2nd century AD, the Sanctuary of Epidaurus was an extensive therapeutic and religious center, dedicated to the healing god Asklepios.

The site is most renowned for its magnificent **Theater**, whose *cavea* (cavity) is 114 m (374 ft) across and surrounds a 20-m (66-ft) diameter *orchestra* (stage). Designed in the late 4th century BC, the theater is well known for near-perfect acoustics, and has the only circular *orchestra* to have survived from antiquity. Today, it is the venue for an annual summer festival of ancient drama.

Most of the **Asklepieion**, or Sanctuary of Asklepios, is currently being re-excavated. Accessible remains include the *propylaia*, or monumental gateway, a late Classical stadium, and the *tholos* – a circular building, thought to have been used either as a pit for sacred serpents, or as the setting for religious rites. Of Asklepios's temple, to the east of the *tholos*, only the foundations have survived.

Náfplio ⑮

🏠 12,000. 🚉 🚌 🚹 Ikosispémptis Martíou 24 (27520-24444).

ONE OF THE MOST elegant towns in mainland Greece, Náfplio emerged in the 13th century and later endured many sieges during the struggles between the Turks and the Venetians for the ports of the Peloponnese. From 1829 to 1834, it was the first capital of liberated Greece.

A number of fortifications today testify to the town's checkered history. The island fortress of **Boúrtzi** is a legacy of the second Venetian occupation (1686–1715). **Akronafplía**, also known as Its Kale ("Inner Castle" in Turkish), was the site of the Byzantine and early medieval town, while the huge Venetian citadel of **Palamídi** was built between 1711 and 1714.

The Plateía Syntágmatos, the hub of public life, looks much as it did three centuries ago, when two mosques were built by the victorious Ottomans. These are now the cathedral, **Agios Geórgios**, and the **Catholic church**.

The town has two museums of note: the award-winning **Folk Art Museum**, and the **Archaeological Museum**, which houses mainly local pre-Mycenaean artifacts.

Located 4 km (2 miles) outside Náfplio, the 12th-century convent of **Agía Moní** is worth visiting.

🏛 **Archaeological Museum**
Plateía Syntágmatos. 📞 27520-27502.
◯ 8:30am–3pm Tue–Sun. ● main public hols.

The fortified isle of Boúrtzi, north of Náfplio harbor

The cliff-top church of Agía Sofía, Monemvasía upper town

Monemvasía **16**

🏛 800. 🚤 🚌 ℹ️ 27320-61210.

THIS FORTIFIED town is built on two levels on a rock rising 350 m (1,150 ft) above the sea. A town of 50,000 in its 15th-century halcyon days, Monemvasía was for centuries a semi-autonomous city-state, which prospered thanks to its strategic position astride the sea lanes from Italy to the Black Sea. After a long and protracted siege, the town was finally surrendered by the Turks in 1821 during the War of Independence.

In the restored lower town, enclosed by the formidable 16th-century walls, are a number of mosques and churches. They include the 18th-century **Panagía Myrtidióssa** and the 13th-century cathedral, **Christós Elkómenos**, with its Venetian belfry. Also found in the lower town is **Giánnis Rítsos's House**, where this prominent 20th-century Greek poet and communist was born.

The upper town, which lies largely in ruins, has been uninhabited since 1911. It was first fortified in the 6th century, and is the oldest part of Monemvasía. Here, the most impressive sight is the still-intact, cliff-top church of **Agía Sofía**, founded by Emperor Andronikos II (1282–1328) and modeled on the Monastery of Dafní (*see p484*). Visitors can also see the remains of a 13th-century fortress.

Máni Peninsula **17**

🛳 Gýtheio. 🚌 Kalamáta (Outer Máni), Areópoli (Inner Máni). ℹ️ Vasiléos Georgiou 20, Gýtheio (27330-24484).

THE HARSH and remote Máni Peninsula is divided into two areas, Outer Máni and Inner Máni, separated by a ravine at Oítylo. The area is most famous for its history of internal feuding, which led to the building of many fine tower houses. From the 15th century, rival clansmen, fighting over the inadequate land, used the towers to shoot at their opponents. After years of bloodshed, the clans finally united, instigating the Greek Independence uprising in 1821.

The main places of interest in more fertile Outer Máni are **Oítylo**, with its elegant 19th-century mansions, and **Kardamýli**, the lair of the Troupákis family, one of the most important Maniot clans. In the environs of Kardamýli are the stunning **Vyrós Gorge**, and **Stoúpa**, popular for its two sandy bays. **Mount Taÿgetos** is one of the area's beauty spots, and can offer several days of wilderness trekking to experienced, well-equipped mountaineers.

In Inner Máni, bustling **Gýtheio** is one of the most attractive coastal towns in the southern Peloponnese. Its 18th-century fortress houses the Museum of the Máni. **Areópoli**, "the city of Ares" (god of war), was where the Maniot uprising against the Turks was proclaimed by Pétros Mavromichális. Nearby

Fishing boats moored in Gýtheio harbor in Inner Máni

is the 17th-century Ottoman **Kelefá Castle**. Visitors to Inner Máni should also see the **Pýrgos Diroú** cave system, and the many Byzantine churches scattered along the west coast. Built between the 10th and 14th centuries, the finest churches include **Taxiarchón**, at Charoúda, **Agios Theódoros**, at Vámvaka, and, near Ano Mpoulárioi village, **Agios Panteleímon** contains 10th-century frescoes. Overlooking the sea and Cape Taínaro, **Vátheia** is one of the most dramatically located of the villages in the Máni. It is worth visiting just to see its collection of tower houses.

Ruins of the Despots' Palace in the Byzantine town of Mystrás

Mystrás **18**

5 km (3 miles) W of Spárti. ☎ 27310-83377. 🚌 to Néos Mystrás. ◷ daily. ● main public hols. 🎫

MAJESTIC MYSTRAS occupies a panoramic site on a spur of the severe Taÿgetos range. Founded by the Franks in 1249, the town soon passed to the Byzantines, under whom it attained a population of 20,000 and, after 1348, became the seat of the Despots of Morea. The despotate acted semi-independently and, by the 15th century, Mystrás had become the last major Byzantine cultural center, attracting scholars and artists from Italy, Constantinople, and Serbia. One result was the uniquely cosmopolitan decoration of Mystrás's churches, whose pastel-colored frescoes, crowded with detail, reflect Italian Renaissance influence.

Now in ruins, Mystrás consists of an upper and lower town, with a wealth of churches, monasteries, palaces, and houses lining its narrow, winding streets. Among the churches and monasteries worth visiting are **Mitrópoli** – the oldest church in Mystrás, dating from 1291 – **Moní Perivléptou**, and **Moní Pantánassas**. The **Vrontóchion**, a 13th-century monastic complex, was the cultural heart of medieval Mystrás. Visitors can also explore the ruins of the **Despots' Palace**, and the **Kástro**, an impressive fortification that crowns the summit of the upper town, and affords magnificent views of the entire site.

Loúsios Gorge ⑲

Dimitsána. **All monasteries** dawn to dusk daily. **Moní Aimyalón** 2–5pm.

A**LTHOUGH MERELY** a tributary of the Alfeiós River, the Loúsios stream boasts one of the most impressive canyons in Greece. Scarcely 5 km (3 miles) long, the Loúsios Gorge is nearly 300 m (985 ft) deep at its narrowest section.

Moní Agíou Ioánnou Prodrómou in the Loúsios Gorge

Remains of the Palaestra, or training center, at Ancient Olympia

A number of hiking trails connect the area's highlights, which include several churches and monasteries clinging to the steep cliffs of the gorge. Of these, the most impressive are **Moní Aimyalón**, founded in 1605 and containing some magnificent frescoes, the 17th-century **Néa Moní Filosófou**, and the 10th-century **Moní Agíou Ioánnou Prodrómou**, wedged into the canyon's east flank. Occupying a sunken excavation on the stream's west bank is the Asklepieíon, or therapeutic center, of **Ancient Gortys**. On this site lie the foundations of a 4th-century BC temple to Asklepios, the god of healing.

Overlooking the gorge, the beautiful hillside towns of **Dimitsána** and **Stemnítsa** make a good base from which to explore the area.

🏛 Ancient Gortys
daily. main public hols.

Ancient Olympia ⑳

26240-22517. 🚌 daily. main public hols, May–mid-Oct: Mon am.

T**HE SANCTUARY** of Olympia enjoyed over 1,000 years of renown as a religious and athletics center. Though it flourished in Mycenaean times, its historic importance dates to the coming of the Dorians, at the beginning of

the first millennium BC. They brought the worship of Zeus, after whose abode on Mount Olympos the site was named. Olympia reached its zenith in the 5th century BC, but by the end of the reign of Roman Emperor Hadrian (AD 117–38), it had begun to have less religious and political significance. The first Olympian Games, the forerunner of the Olympic Games, took place here in 776 BC, but were banned in AD 393 by Emperor Theodosius I, who took a dim view of the pagan festival.

The most important ruins include the 5th-century BC Doric **Temple of Zeus**, of which only column bases and tumbled sections remain, and the partly reconstructed **Palaestra**, which was a training center for athletes. In **Pheidias's Workshop**, a huge statue of Zeus was sculpted in the 5th century BC.

Also not to be missed is the **Archaeological Museum**, one of the richest museums in Greece, with exhibits from prehistory, through the Classical period, to the Roman era. The central hall houses the pediment and metope sculpture from the Temple of Zeus, and another room is dedicated entirely to the Olympian Games.

🏛 Archaeological Museum
26240-22742. daily. main public hols, May–mid-Oct.

Corfu and the Ionian Islands ㉑

THE IONIAN ISLANDS are the greenest and most fertile of all the island groups. Lying off the west coast of mainland Greece, they have been greatly influenced by Western Europe. Periods of rule by the Venetians, French, and British have left their mark on many of the islands, especially in the mixed architecture of places like Corfu town. The Ionians first became a holiday destination during the Roman era, and today their beaches remain one of their most popular attractions.

The elegant parade of cafés known as the Liston in Corfu town

Corfu

🏛 100,000. ✈ 3 km (1.5 miles) S of Corfu town. 🚢 Xenofóntos Stratigoú, Corfu town. 🚌 ℹ Corfu town (26610-43420).

CORFU OFFERS the diverse attractions of secluded coves, bustling resorts, and traditional hill villages. Between 229 BC and AD 337 it was part of the Roman empire. It remained under Byzantine rule until the 14th century, when the Venetians took control. French and British occupation followed, before unification with Greece in 1864. Though the island is most popular for its beaches, inland there are many places where you can still observe the traditional lifestyle of the Corfiot people.

Corfu Town

The checkered history of the island is reflected in Corfu town's varied architecture. With its grand French-style colonnades, elegant Italianate buildings, and famous cricket pitch, the town is a delightful blend of European influences.

The **Palace of St. Michael and St. George** was built by the British between 1819 and 1824 to serve as the residence of a high commissioner. Used for a short time by the Greek royal family after the British left the island, the palace is now home to the **Museum of Asiatic Art**.

The palace overlooks the Esplanade, or Spianáda, a mixture of park and town square, and the site of the cricket ground. Once a Venetian firing range, the cricket pitch was developed by the British, and local teams play here regularly. Nearby, the Enosis Monument commemorates the 1864 union of the Ionian Islands with the rest of Greece. The **Liston**, a parade of cafés that was built in 1807 as a copy of the Rue de Rivoli in Paris, lines one side of the square.

Another of the town's most famous sights, the distinctive red-domed belfry of **Agios Spyrídon** is the tallest belfry on Corfu. The church was built in 1589 and dedicated to the island's patron saint.

Also worth seeing are the **Town Hall** – a grand Venetian building located in the Plateía Dimarcheíou – the **Byzantine Museum**, and the fascinating **Archaeological Museum**. The latter's centerpiece is a stunning Gorgon frieze.

On the town's eastern side stands the 16th-century Venetian-built **Old Fortress**, which affords magnificent views of the town and along the island's east coast. The **New Fortress** was built shortly after the old one to strengthen the town's defenses.

✠ Palace of St. Michael and St. George
Plateía Spianáda. ℂ 26610-30443. ◯ Tue–Sun. ● main public hols.

Northern Corfu
Northern Corfu, in particular the northeast coast, is a busy vacation destination, which boasts a whole host of popular resorts and beaches.

The multiple picturesque bays of Palaiokastrítsa in northern Corfu

Vacation apartments at Fiskárdo on the island of Kefalloniá

Set around a fishing harbor, **Kassiópi** has retained its character in spite of the influx of tourists. Nearby are the ruins of a 13th-century castle, and the church of Kassiopítissa, which occupies the site of a former temple of Jupiter.

The bustling vacation center of **Sidári** is famous for its sandy beaches and unusual rock formations, while picturesque **Palaiokastrítsa** has safe swimming and water sports, as well as boat trips to nearby grottoes. Vacationers wanting a diversion from the busy resort atmosphere can visit the 17th-century monastery, **Moní Theotókou**.

Mount Pantokrátor, a short drive north of Corfu town, is popular with walkers and naturalists. The highest point on Corfu, it offers fine views of the whole island.

Southern Corfu

More varied than the north, southern Corfu offers other attractions apart from beaches. Tranquil hillside villages, such as **Vátos** and **Pélekas**, contrast with noisy resorts like **Benítses**, offering a more traditional image of Greece.

Among the more peaceful spots in the south is the **Korisíon Lagoon**, a 5-km (3-mile) stretch of water, separated from the sea by some of the most beautiful dunes and beaches on Corfu. The area provides a habitat for many species of birds and wild flowers.

A popular day trip from any of Corfu's resorts is to the **Achílleion Palace**, built between 1890 and 1891 as a personal retreat for the Empress Elizabeth of Austria (1837–98). After a tour of the palace and its gardens, visit the Vasilákis Tastery opposite, and sample this local distiller's products.

🏛 Achílleion Palace
19 km (12 miles) SW of Corfu town.
📞 26610-56210. ◯ daily.

Kefalloniá

🏠 31,000. ✈ 9 km (6 miles) S of Argostóli. ⛴ Argostóli, Fiskárdo. 🚌 Ioánnou Metaxá, Argostóli. 🛈 Waterfront, Argostóli (26710-28835).

THE LARGEST island in the Ionians, Kefalloniá has a range of attractions, from busy beach resorts to areas of outstanding natural beauty.

The capital, **Argostóli**, is a busy town located by a bay. Of interest are the Historical and Folk Museum and the Archaeological Museum.

Around the island the liveliest places are **Lássi** and the south-coast resorts, but elsewhere there are quiet villages and stunning scenery.

Mount Aínos and the **Mount Aínos National Park**, in the south, and the haunting, subterranean **Melissaní Cave-Lake** are sights not to be missed. **Fiskárdo**, with its 18th-century Venetian houses clustered by the harbor, is Kefalloniá's prettiest village. From here ferry services are available to the islands of **Ithaca** and **Lefkáda**.

Zákynthos

🏠 30,000. ✈ 4 km (2.5 miles) S of Zákynthos town. ⛴ 4 km (2.5 miles) S of Zákynthos town. ⛴ Zákynthos town, Agios Nikólaos. 🚌 Zákynthos town. 🛈 Tzoulátí 2, Zákynthos town (26950-42064).

ZÁKYNTHOS IS an attractive and green island, with good beaches and beautiful scenery to be enjoyed.

Zákynthos town is the point of arrival on the island. Here, the impressive church of Agios Dionýsios, and the Byzantine Museum, which houses a breathtaking array of frescoes, both deserve a visit.

The growth of tourism on Zákynthos has been heavily concentrated in **Laganás** and its 14-km (9-mile) sweep of soft sand. The town's hectic nightlife continues until dawn. Alternatively, visitors can head to the island's north coast for the beach resorts of **Tsiliví** and **Alykés**, the latter being especially good for windsurfing. At the northernmost tip of the island are the unusual and spectacular **Blue Caves**. The caves can be visited by boat from the resort of **Agios Nikólaos**.

The Blue Caves of Zákynthos at the northern tip of the island

Cyclades ⑳

LOCATOR MAP

THE MOST VISITED island group, the Cyclades are everyone's Greek island ideal, with their whitewashed, cliff-top villages, blue-domed churches, and stunning beaches. The islands vary greatly, from the quiet and traditional to the more nightlife-oriented. The cradle of the Cycladic civilization (3000–1000 BC), they also offer a rich ancient history. Important archaeological sites, such as those on Delos and Santoríni, provide a fascinating insight into the past.

Working 16th-century windmill, part of the Folk Museum in Mýkonos town

Mýkonos

🏛 4,500. ✈ 3 km (1.5 miles) SE of Mýkonos town. ⛴ Mýkonos town. 🚌 Polykandrióti, Mýkonos town (for north of island); on road to Ornós, Mýkonos town (for south of island). 🛈 Harborfront, Mýkonos town (22890-22201).

SANDY BEACHES and dynamic nightlife combine to make Mýkonos one of the most popular islands in the Cyclades. Visited by intellectuals in the early days of tourism, today it thrives on its reputation as the glitziest island in Greece. In addition to offering sun, sea, and sand, the island is a good base from which to visit the ancient archaeological site on Delos.

Mýkonos Town
The supreme example of a Cycladic town, Mýkonos town (or Chóra) is a tangle of dazzling white alleys and cube-shaped houses. It has a bustling port, from where taxi boats for the island of **Delos** leave. To the south, the **Archaeological Museum** has a fine collection of exhibits, including finds from the excavations of the ruins on Delos.

In the Kástro, the oldest part of town, is the excellent **Folk Museum**. The 16th-century Vonís Windmill, still in working order, is part of the museum. Nearby, the most famous church on the island is **Panagía Para-portianí**, which dates back to 1425. From Kástro, the lanes run down into picturesque Venetía, or Little Venice, the artists' quarter. Also worth visiting are the **Maritime Museum of the Aegean** and the **Municipal Art Gallery**.

🏛 **Archaeological Museum**
Harborfront. 【 22890-22325. ◯ Tue–Sun. ◉ main public hols. 🈂

Around the Island
Mýkonos is popular primarily for its beaches and one of the best is stylish **Platýs Gialós**, 3.5 km (2 miles) south of Mýkonos town. There are also several nudist beaches, including quiet **Parága** and the more lively **Paradise**, **Super Paradise**, and **Eliá**.

Inland, the traditional village of **Ano Merá** remains largely unspoiled by tourism. The main attraction here is the 16th-century monastery **Panagía i Tourlianí**.

🏴 **Delos**
2.5 km (1 mile) SW of Mýkonos town.
【 22890-22259. ⛴ 8–10am daily from Mýkonos town returning 12–2pm. ◯ Tue–Sun. ◉ main public hols. 🈂 🈂

The tiny, uninhabited island of Delos is one of the most important archaeological sites in Greece. The legendary birthplace of Artemis and Apollo, from 1000 BC it was home to the annual Delian Festival, held in honor of the god Apollo. By 700 BC it had become a major religious center and place of pilgrimage. In addition to some impressive 2nd-century BC mosaics and temple ruins, the most important remains on Delos are the magnificent 7th-century BC **Lion Terrace**, the **Theater**, built in 300 BC to hold 5,500 people, and the **Theater Quarter**.

Lions carved from Naxian marble along the Lion Terrace on Delos

Whitewashed buildings lining the cliff top in Firá, Santoríni

Santoríni

🏠 12,500. ✈ 5 km (3 miles) SE of Firá. ⛴ Skála Firón. 🚌 50 m (160 ft) S of main square, Firá. ℹ Firá (22860-22649).

COLONIZED BY the Minoans in 3000 BC, this volcanic island erupted in 1450 BC, forming Santoríni's distinct crescent shape. A popular tourist destination, it is a stunning island, as famous for its ancient archaeological sites as for its white-washed villages, volcanic cliffs, and black sand beaches.

Firá

Founded in the late 18th century, Firá was destroyed by an earthquake in 1956 and rebuilt along terraces in the volcanic cliffs. Packed with hotels, bars, and restaurants, its streets enjoy magnificent views out to sea. The tiny port of Skála Firón, 270 m (890 ft) below, is connected to the town by cable car or by mule up 580 steps.

Among Firá's most interesting sights are the **Archaeological Museum**, with finds from Ancient Thíra and Minoan Akrotíri, and the 18th-century church of **Agios Minás**. The pretty ocher chapel of **Agios Stylianós** is also worth a visit on the way to the Frangika, or Frankish quarter, with its maze of arcaded streets.

🏛 **Archaeological Museum**
Opposite cable car station.
📞 22860-22217. ◯ Tue–Sun. ⬤ main public hols.

Around the Island

Within easy reach of Firá, on the headland of Mésa Vounó, the ruins of the Dorian town of **Ancient Thíra** are not to be missed. Most of the ruins date from the Ptolemies, who built temples to the Egyptian gods in the 4th and 3rd centuries BC. There are also Hellenistic and Roman remains. Below the site are the popular beaches of **Períssa** and **Kamári**. Another of the Cyclades' most inspiring archaeological sites, the Minoan settlement of **Akrotíri** was unearthed in 1967, still wonderfully preserved after some 3,500 years of burial under volcanic ash. Some of the frescoes discovered here are now on display in the National Archaeological Museum in Athens (see p476).

A donkey ride in Firá, Santoríni

🏛 **Ancient Thíra**
11 km (7 miles) SW of Firá.
🚌 to Kamári. ◯ Tue–Sun.
⬤ main public hols.

Náxos

🏠 20,000. ✈ 2 km (1 mile) S of Náxos town. ⛴ 🚌 Harborfront, Náxos town. ℹ Harborfront, Náxos town (22850-25201).

THE LARGEST of the Cyclades, Náxos was a major center of the Cycladic civilization. The Venetians, who arrived in the 13th century, built many fortifications that still stand on the island today. History and superb beaches make Náxos an ideal vacation destination.

Náxos Town

Overlooking Náxos town's bustling harbor is the huge, marble, 6th-century BC Portára gateway, built as the entrance to the unfinished Temple of Apollo. To the south, **Agios Geórgios** is the main tourist center, with a wealth of hotels, apartments, and restaurants. The old town divides into the Kástro – the 13th-century Venetian fortifications – and the medieval Bourg. The fine 18th-century Orthodox cathedral, the **Mitrópoli Zoödóchou Pigís**, stands in the Bourg, which also has a busy market area. In the Kástro, the **Archaeological Museum**, in the Palace of Sanoúdo, has one of the best collections of Cycladic marble figurines in the Greek islands.

🏛 **Archaeological Museum**
Palace of Sanoúdo. 📞 22850-22725. ◯ Tue–Sun. ⬤ main public hols. 📷

Around the Island

South of Náxos town are many fine beaches, including **Agía Anna** and **Kastráki** – both good for water sports – and tranquil **Pláka**.

Inland the Tragaía Valley is a walkers' paradise. It is dotted with picturesque villages, such as **Chalkí**, with its Byzantine and Venetian architecture, and **Filóti**, which sits on the slopes of 1,000-m (3,300-ft) Mount Zas.

The Portára gateway that overlooks Náxos town's harbor

Rhodes and the Dodecanese ㉓

THE DODECANESE OFFER a wide range of landscapes and activities. Their hot climate and fine beaches attract many visitors, but the islands also boast lush, fertile valleys and wooded mountains. The Dodecanese have been subject to several invasions, with periods of occupation by the medieval Knights of St. John, the Ottomans, and the Italians. This checkered history is still apparent in the islands' impressively varied architecture and wealth of historical sites.

LOCATOR MAP

The Palace of the Grand Masters in Rhodes town

Rhodes

🚶 100,000. ✈ 25 km (15 miles) SW of Rhodes town. ⚓ Commercial harbor, Rhodes town. 🚤 Mandráki, Rhodes town. 🛈 Plateía Rímini, Rhodes town (22410-22661).

AN IMPORTANT center from the 5th to 3rd centuries BC, Rhodes was later part of both the Roman and Byzantine empires before being conquered by the Knights of St. John, the order founded in the 11th century to tend Christian pilgrims in Jerusalem. They occupied the island from 1306 to 1522, and their medieval walled city still dominates Rhodes town. Ottoman and Italian rulers followed, leaving their own traces of occupation. Rhodes' rich and varied history, sandy beaches, and lively nightlife attract tens of thousands of tourists each year.

Rhodes Old Town
The town of Rhodes has been inhabited for over 2,400 years. A city was first built here in 408 BC, and when the Knights of St. John arrived in 1306 they built their citadel over these ancient remains. Surrounded by moats and 3 km (2 miles) of walls, the Knights' medieval citadel forms the center of the Old Town, which is divided into the Collachium and the Bourg. The Collachium was the Knights' quarter, while the Bourg was home to the rest of the population.

Dominating the Old Town is the 14th-century **Palace of the Grand Masters**, the seat of 19 Grand Masters of the Knights during two centuries of occupation. The palace houses several priceless mosaics from sites in Kos, as well as two permanent exhibitions about ancient and medieval Rhodes.

The medieval **Street of the Knights** is lined by the Inns of the Tongues of the Order of St. John. The Inns – there was one for each of the seven Tongues, or nationalities, into which the Order was divided – were used as meeting places for the Knights. Begun in the 14th century in Gothic style, they were restored by the Italians in the early 20th century.

The **Archaeological Museum** and the **Byzantine Museum**, both located in the Collachium, contain many fine exhibits from different periods in Rhodes' history.

In the Bourg area, the **Mosque of Suleiman the Magnificent** was built to commemorate the Sultan's victory over the Knights in 1522. The **Library of Ahmet Havuz**, which houses the chronicle of the Turks' siege of Rhodes, and the **Hammam**, the public baths, provide further reminders of the town's Turkish past.

🏛 Palace of the Grand Masters
Ippotón. 🎧 22410-23359. ☐ Tue–Sun. ● main public hols. 🈲 👢 limited.

Rhodes New Town
Beyond the original citadel walls, the new town of Rhodes is made up of a number of areas. These include **Néa Agora**, with its Moorish domes and lively market, and **Mandráki harbor** in the eastern half of town. Close to the harbor are the mock Venetian Gothic **Government House** – a legacy of the Italian occupation of the 1920s – and the **Mosque of Murad Reis**, with its graceful minaret. The west side of town is a busy tourist center, with lively streets and a packed beach.

The minaret of the Mosque of Murad Reis

The acropolis overlooking Líndos town on Rhodes

Western Rhodes

A short distance southwest of Rhodes town, set on the beautiful green and wooded hillsides of Filérimos, is **Moní Filerímou**. A place of worship for 2,000 years, this monastery has layers of history and tradition, from Phoenician to Byzantine, Orthodox, and Catholic.

A few kilometers farther southwest, **Ancient Kámeiros** is one of the best-preserved Classical Greek cities. Its remains include a 3rd-century BC Doric temple.

Also worth visiting are the wine-making village of **Emponas**, and **Petaloúdes**, or Butterfly Valley. Popular with walkers, this valley teems with Jersey tiger moths from June to September.

⋔ Ancient Kámeiros
36 km (22 miles) SW of Rhodes town.
◯ *Tue–Sun.* ◉ *main public hols.* 📷
♿ *to lower sections only.*

Eastern Rhodes

Halfway along Rhodes' sheltered east coast, **Líndos** is one of the island's most popular resorts. A magnet for tourists seeking sun, sea, and sand, it is also famous for its cliff-top acropolis overlooking the bay. This temple site, crowned by the 4th-century BC Temple of Lindian Athena, was one of the most sacred spots in the ancient world.

Located in the Valley of Aíthona, between Líndos and Rhodes town, **Archángelos** is famous for its pottery, hand-woven rugs and leather boots. Above the town are the ruins of the Crusader Castle, built in 1467 by the Knights of St. John as a defense against the Turks.

⋔ Acropolis at Líndos
1 km (0.5 miles) E of Líndos village.
📞 *22440-31258.* ◯ *Jul–Sep: daily (Mon: pm only); Oct–Jun: Tue–Sun.* ◉ *main public hols.* 📷

Kos

🚹 *27,000.* ✈ *27 km (16 miles) W of Kos town.* ⛴ 🚌 *Aktí Koudouriótou, Kos town.* 🛈 *Vasiléos Georgíou, Kos town (22420-28724).*

Mᴀɪɴʟʏ ꜰʟᴀᴛ and fertile, Kos is known as the "Floating Garden." It has a wealth of archaeological sites, Hellenistic and Roman ruins, and Byzantine and Venetian castles, many of which can be found in **Kos town**. Here, the 16th-century Castle of the Knights, the Ancient Agora, and the Roman remains should not be missed.

Most visitors to Kos come for the sandy beaches. The best of these are easily reached from the resort of **Kamári** on the island's southwest coast. **Kardámaina** is Kos's biggest and noisiest resort, while the northwest bays, such as **Tigkáki**, are ideal for water sports. In spite of tourist development, inland you can still see remnants of Kos's traditional lifestyle.

Kos is a good base from which to explore the more northerly islands of the Dodecanese, including **Pátmos**, home to the 11th-century Monastery of St. John.

Kárpathos

🚹 *5,000.* ✈ *17 km (11 miles) S of Kárpathos town.* 🚌 *corner of 28 Oktovríou & Dimokratías, Kárpathos town.* ⛴ *Kárpathos town, Diáfani.* 🛈 *Kárpathos town (22450-22222).*

Dᴇsᴘɪᴛᴇ ᴀ ʀᴇᴄᴇɴᴛ increase in tourism, wild and rugged Kárpathos remains largely unspoiled. Its capital, **Kárpathos town**, is a busy center, with hotels, cafés, and restaurants around its bay. Nearby is the main resort of **Amoopí**, with its sweep of sandy shore. In addition to some magnificent beaches on the west coast, including **Lefkós** and **Apélla**, the island has places of archaeological and historical interest. **Vroukoúnda** is the site of a 6th-century BC city, while in the village of **Olympos** traditional Greek life and customs can still be observed.

Windmills in the traditional village of Olympos on Kárpathos

Crete

R UGGED MOUNTAINS, sparkling seas, and ancient history combine with the Cretans' relaxed nature to make this island an idyllic vacation destination. The center of the Minoan civilization over 3,000 years ago, Crete has also been occupied by Romans, Byzantines, Venetians, and Turks. Historic towns such as Irákleio, Chaniá, and Réthymno, and the famous Minoan palaces at Knossos and Phaestos, give a fascinating insight into some of the most important periods in Cretan history.

LOCATOR MAP

Irákleio's boat-lined harbor, dominated by the vast Venetian fortress

Irákleio

116,000. 5 km (3 miles) E. Xanthoudídou 1 (2810-228225).

A BUSY, SPRAWLING town of concrete buildings, Irákleio nevertheless has much of interest to the visitor. Four centuries of Venetian rule have left a rich architectural legacy, evident in the imposing 16th-century **fortress** overlooking the harbor, and the elegantly-restored 17th-century **Loggia**, a former meeting place for the island's nobility. Among Irákleio's many churches, **Agios Márkos**, built by the Venetians in 1239, and 16th-century **Agios Títos** deserve a visit. Also not to be missed are the Archaeological Museum *(see below)* and the **Historical Museum**, which traces the history of Crete from early Christian times. The heart of the town is the Plateía Eleftheríou Venizélou, a bustling pedestrianized zone of cafés and shops.

Those interested in the beaches should head to the package-tour resorts of **Mália** and **Chersónisos**, just a short drive east of the town.

🏛 Irákleio Archaeological Museum

Corner of Xanthoudídou & Mpofór, Plateía Eleftherías. 2810-226092. daily (Mon: pm only). main public hols; some areas due to ongoing renovation work. ground floor only.

This impressive museum displays Minoan artifacts from all over Crete. Its most magnificent exhibits include the famous Minoan frescoes from Knossos, and the Phaestos Disk, discovered at the site of the palace of Phaestos in 1903. Inscribed with pictorial symbols, the disk's meaning and origin remain a mystery. Among the museum's many other treasures are the Snake Goddesses, two figurines dating from around 1600 BC.

🏛 Palace of Knossos

5 km (3 miles) S of Irákleio. 2810-231 940. daily. main public hols.

The capital of Minoan Crete, Knossos was the largest and most sophisticated of the Minoan palaces on the island. Built around 1900 BC, the first palace of Knossos was destroyed by an earthquake in about 1700 BC and was soon completely rebuilt. The ruins visible today are almost entirely from this second palace. They were restored by Sir Arthur Evans in the early 20th century; although the subject of academic controversy, his reconstructions give one of the best impressions of life in Minoan Crete to be found anywhere on the island.

Highlights of a tour of the site – the focal point of which is the vast Central Court – include the replica of the Priest-King Fresco, the Giant Pithoi, one of over 100 *pithoi* (storage jars) unearthed at Knossos, the Throne Room, believed to have served as a shrine, and the Royal Apartments. The original frescoes from the palace are now housed in Irákleio's Archaeological Museum.

The South Propylon (entrance) of the Palace of Knossos

Phaestos

65 km (40 miles) SW of Irákleio.
📞 28920-42315. 🚌 🅿️ daily.
⬤ main public hols. 🎫

PHAESTOS WAS ONE OF THE most important Minoan palaces on Crete. In 1900 Italian-led excavations unearthed two palaces. Remains of the first palace, constructed around 1900 BC and destroyed by an earthquake in 1700 BC, are still visible. Most of the present ruins, however, are of the second palace. Phaestos was finally destroyed in the 2nd century BC by the ancient city-state of Górtys.

The most impressive remains are the Grand Staircase, which was the main entrance to the palace, and the Central Court.

A few kilometers northeast of Phaestos, the archaeological remains of ancient **Górtys** date from about 1000 BC to the late 7th century AD.

Agios Nikólaos

🏘️ 10,000. 🚌 🚌 ℹ️ Koundoúrou 21 (28410-22357). ⬤ Wed.

THE MAIN transport hub for the east of the island, delightful Agios Nikólaos is a thriving vacation center with an attractive harbor and fine beaches, as well as an interesting **Folk Museum** and an **Archaeological Museum**.

A few kilometers north is the well-established resort of **Eloúnta**, boasting attractive sandy coves and a good range of accommodations.

Chaniá

🏘️ 50,000. ✈️ 16 km (10 miles) E.
🚌 🚌 ℹ️ Kriári 40 (28210-92943).

ONE OF CRETE'S most appealing cities, Chánia was ruled by the Venetians from 1204 to 1669, and is dotted with elegant houses, churches, and fortifications dating from this period. Many of these can be found in the Venetian quarter around the harbor, and in the picturesque Splántzia district. The **Mosque of the Janissaries**, on one side of the harbor, dates back to the arrival of the Turks in 1645, and is the oldest Ottoman building on Crete. The lively covered market, with its many shops and fresh produce stalls, is an area worth exploring. Nearby the **Archaeological Museum** is housed in the Venetian church of San Francesco.

A short walk west of Chaniá is the relatively undisturbed beach of **Agioi Apóstoloi**.

Samariá Gorge

44 km (27 miles) S of Chaniá. 🚌 to Xylóskalo. 🚤 Agía Rouméli to Sfakía or Palaiochóra (via Soúgia); last boat back leaves at 5pm. ⬤ May–mid-Oct: 6am–4pm daily; Apr 10–30 & Oct 16–31: if weather permits.

CRETE'S MOST spectacular scenery lies along the Samariá Gorge, the longest ravine in Europe. When it became a national park, the inhabitants of the village of Samariá moved elsewhere, leaving behind the ruined buildings and chapels seen here today. Starting from the Xylóskalo (Wooden Stairs), an 18-km (11-mile) trail leads to the seaside village of Agía Rouméli. A truly impressive sight along the route is the Sideróportes, or Iron Gates, where the path squeezes between two towering walls of rock, only 3 m (9 ft) apart. Upon reaching Agía Rouméli walkers can take a boat to Sfakía, Soúgia, or Palaiochóra to join the road and buses back to Chaniá.

The narrow defile known as the Iron Gates in the Samariá Gorge

Réthymno

🏘️ 24,000. 🚌 🚌 ℹ️ Eleftheriou Venizélou (28310-29148). 🍷 Wine Festival (mid-Jul).

DESPITE TOURISM and modern development, Réthymno has retained much of its charm. The old quarter is rich in well-preserved Venetian and Ottoman architecture, including the elegant 16th-century Venetian **Lótzia** (Loggia) and the **Nerantzés Mosque**, converted from a church by the Turks in 1675. The huge **Fortétsa** was built by the Venetians in the 16th century to defend the port against both pirates and the Turks. Below it is a pretty harbor, lined with cafés and restaurants. Also worth visiting in the town is the **Archaeological Museum**.

East of Réthymno there are several resorts, while to the west lies a 20-km (12-mile) stretch of uncrowded beach.

Tavernas and bars along Réthymno's waterfront

Practical Information

TOURISM IS ONE OF GREECE'S most important industries, and as a consequence, visitors to the country are well catered for: transportation networks are relatively efficient, there are banks and exchange facilities in all the major resorts, and telecommunications have improved dramatically in recent years. The country's hot climate, together with the easy-going outlook of its people, are conducive to a relaxed vacation, and it is usually best to adopt the philosophy *sigá, sigá* (slowly, slowly). In summer, almost everything closes for a few hours after lunch, reopening later in the day when the air cools and Greece comes to life again.

WHEN TO VISIT

TOURIST SEASON in Greece – May to October – is the hottest and most expensive time to visit, as well as being very crowded. December to March are the coldest and wettest months, with reduced public transportation facilities, and many restaurants and hotels closed for the winter. Spring is a good time to visit; there are fewer tourists, and the weather and the countryside are at their best.

TOURIST INFORMATION

TOURIST INFORMATION is available in many towns and villages throughout Greece, from government-run **EOT** offices (Ellinikós Organismós Tourismoú), municipally run tourist offices, the local tourist police, or privately owned travel agencies. However, visitors should be aware that not all of the information published by the EOT is reliable or up-to-date.

OPENING HOURS

OPENING HOURS tend to be vague in Greece, varying from day to day, season to season, and place to place. To avoid disappointment, visitors are advised to confirm the opening times of sites covered in this chapter once they arrive in the country.

All post offices and banks, and most stores, offices, state-run museums, and archaeological sites close on public holidays. Some facilities may also be closed on local festival days.

The main public holidays in Greece are as follows: January 1, March 25, Good Friday, Easter Sunday, May 1, December 25 and 26.

VISA REQUIREMENTS AND CUSTOMS

VISITORS FROM EU countries, the US, Canada, Australia, and New Zealand need only a valid passport for entry to Greece (no visa is required), and can stay for up to 90 days.

The unauthorized export of antiquities and archaeological artifacts from Greece is treated as a serious offence, incurring hefty fines or even a prison sentence.

Prescription drugs brought into the country should be accompanied by a prescription note for the purposes of the customs authorities.

PERSONAL SECURITY

THE CRIME RATE in Greece is very low compared with other European countries, but it is worth taking a few sensible precautions, such as keeping all personal possessions secure. If you have anything stolen, you should contact either the police or the tourist police.

Foreign women traveling alone in Greece are usually treated with respect, especially if they are dressed modestly. However, hitchhiking alone is not advisable.

POLICE

GREECE'S POLICE are split into three forces: the regular police, the port police, and the tourist police. The tourist police provide advice to vacationers in addition to carrying out normal police duties. Should you suffer a theft, lose your passport, or have cause to complain about shops, restaurants, tour guides, or taxi drivers, you should contact them first. Every tourist police office claims to have at least one English speaker. Their offices also offer maps, brochures, and useful advice on finding accommodations in Greece.

EMERGENCY SERVICES

IN THE UNLIKELY event of an emergency while on vacation, the appropriate numbers to call are listed in the Directory opposite.

HEALTH ISSUES

NO INOCULATIONS are required for visitors to Greece, though tetanus and typhoid boosters may be recommended by your doctor.

THE CLIMATE OF GREECE

On the mainland, summers are very hot, while spring and autumn generally bring milder but wetter weather. In winter, rainfall is at its greatest everywhere. Mountainous regions usually get heavy snow, but around Athens, temperatures rarely drop below freezing. Throughout the islands, the tendency is for long, dry summers and mild but rainy winters.

ATHENS

°C/F	Apr	Jul	Oct	Jan
high	18/64	31/88	22/72	12/54
low	11/52	22/72	15/59	6/43
sun	8 hrs	12 hrs	7 hrs	4 hrs
rain	23 mm	6 mm	51 mm	62 mm
month	Apr	Jul	Oct	Jan

Tap water in Greece is generally safe to drink, but in remote communities it is a good precaution to check with the locals.

Jellyfish, sea urchins, and weaver fish are potential hazards on beach holidays.

PHARMACIES

GREEK PHARMACIES, *farmakeía*, are open from 8:30am to 2pm Monday to Friday, but are usually closed in the afternoon and all day on Saturdays. In larger towns there is often a rota system to maintain a service from 7:30am to 2pm and from 5:30 to 10pm. Details are posted in pharmacy windows, in both Greek and English.

FACILITIES FOR THE DISABLED

THERE ARE FEW facilities in Greece for assisting the disabled, so careful, advance planning is essential.

ETIQUETTE

THOUGH FORMAL attire is rarely needed, modest clothing (trousers for men and skirts for women) should be worn when visiting churches and monasteries.

In restaurants, the service charge is always included in the check, but tips are still appreciated – the custom is to leave between 10 and 15 percent. Public restroom attendants should also be tipped. Taxi drivers, hotel porters, and chambermaids do not expect a tip, but are not averse to them either.

PHOTOGRAPHY

TAKING PHOTOGRAPHS inside churches and monasteries is officially forbidden in Greece. Inside museums, photography is usually permitted, although flashes and tripods are often not. Wherever you go, it is best to gain permission before using a camera, as rules vary.

BANKING AND CURRENCY

THE GREEK UNIT of currency was the drachma, but since January 2002 it has been replaced by the euro (*see p15*).

Greek banks open from 8am to 2pm Monday to Thursday, and 8am to 1:30pm on Friday. In major cities and resorts, at least one bank usually opens its exchange desk for a few hours on weekday evenings and on Saturday mornings in summer.

Exchange facilities are also available at post offices, travel agents, hotels, tourist offices, and car rental agencies. Take your passport with you when cashing traveler's checks. Cash point machines (ATMs) operate 24 hours a day.

COMMUNICATIONS

PUBLIC TELEPHONES can be found in many locales, including hotel lobbies, street kiosks, or local offices of the **OTE** (Organismós Tilepikoinonión Elládos – the Greek national telephone company). OTE offices are open daily from 7am to 10pm or midnight in larger towns, or until around 3pm in smaller communities. Long-distance calls are very expensive in Greece. They are best made in a telephone booth using a phonecard – available at any street kiosk.

Greek post offices (*tachydromeía*) are generally open from 7:30am to 2pm Monday to Friday; some main branches close as late as 8pm and occasionally open for a few hours at weekends. All post offices are closed on public holidays. Those displaying an "Exchange" sign will change money in addition to offering the usual services.

DIRECTORY

TOURIST INFORMATION

Greek National Tourist Board
W www.gnto.gr

EOT in Greece:
Amerikis 2,
10564 Athens.
210-331 0692 or 331 0561.
FAX 210-325 2895.

In Australia:
51–57 Pitt St,
Sydney, NSW 2000.
2-9241 1663.

In Canada:
91 Scollard St,
2nd Floor, Toronto,
Ontario M5R 1G4.
416-968-2220.

In the UK:
4 Conduit St,
London W15 2DJ.
020-7495 9300.

In the US:
Olympic Tower, 645 Fifth Ave, New York, NY 10022.
212-421-5777.

EMBASSIES

Australia
Dimitríou Soútsou 37,
11521 Athens.
210-645 0404.

Canada
Gennadíou 4,
11521 Athens.
210-727 3400.

New Zealand
Kifissías 268,
11528 Athens.
210-687 4700.

Ireland
Vassiléos Konstantínou 7,
10674 Athens.
210-723 2405.

UK
Ploutárchou 1,
10675 Athens.
210-727 2600.

US
Vasilíssis Sofías 91,
10160 Athens.
210-721 2951.

EMERGENCY NUMBERS (NATIONWIDE)

Police
100.

Ambulance
166.

Fire
199.

Road assistance
104.

Coastguard patrol
108.

EMERGENCY NUMBERS (ATHENS)

Tourist police
171.

Doctors
1016 (2pm–7am).

Pharmacies
For information on 24-hour pharmacies:
107 (central Athens).
102 (suburbs).

Travel Information

DURING THE TOURIST SEASON (May to October), there are countless international flights bringing millions of vacationers to the shores of Greece, especially from the colder parts of northern Europe and North America. Traveling within Greece is easy enough. While many of the larger islands can be reached from the mainland by plane, there are ferry routes to even the remotest destinations. Greece's extensive bus network serves virtually everywhere, from the largest city to the tiniest community. Renting a car or motorcycle is another popular way of exploring the country.

FLYING TO GREECE

THERE ARE around 20 international airports in Greece that can be reached directly from Europe. Only Crete, Rhodes, and Corfu among the islands, and Athens and Thessaloníki on the mainland, handle both charter and scheduled flights. The other international airports can only be reached directly by charter flights.

Direct scheduled flights from London to Athens and Thessaloníki are operated by **Olympic Airways** (the Greek national airline), British Airways, and easyJet (Athens only). From outside Europe, all scheduled flights to Greece arrive in Athens, and only a few airlines offer direct flights. Olympic and Delta Air Lines operate direct flights daily from New York.

Flights from Australasia to Athens are run by Qantas, Singapore Airlines, Thai Airways, and KLM.

Athens' new international airport, Eléfthérios Venizélos, opened in March 2001 and is located 27 km (17 miles) northeast of the center. There are two 24-hour bus services from the city to the airport: the E95 from the Plateía Syntágmatos takes approximately 1 hour; the E96 departs from Piraeus and takes 1 hour and 20 minutes. Rail and metro links are due to open in 2004.

CHARTERS AND PACKAGE DEALS

CHARTER FLIGHTS to Greece are nearly all from within Europe, and mostly operate between May and October.

Tickets are sold by travel agencies either as part of an all-inclusive package tour or as a flight-only deal.

DOMESTIC FLIGHTS

MOST INTERNAL flights in Greece are operated by **Olympic Airways** and its affiliate, **Olympic Aviation**. Olympic Airways operates direct flights from Athens and Thessaloníki to many of the islands. In addition, there are a number of inter-island services available throughout the year. Private companies, such as **Aegean Airlines**, also provide services between Athens and some of the major mainland and island destinations. Fares for domestic flights are at least double the equivalent bus journey or deck-class ferry trip.

GETTING AROUND ATHENS

ATHENS HAS A NETWORK of buses and trams, in addition to a metro system. Buses are inexpensive, but can be very slow, as well as crowded. Tickets for buses and trams must be purchased in advance from a *periptero* (street kiosk), a transport booth, or certain other designated places. A brown, red, and white logo, with the words *eisitíria edó*, indicates where you can buy them. Each ticket is valid for one journey only, regardless of the distance traveled.

Since most of the major sights in the city center are within walking distance of one another, you can avoid using public transportation.

RAIL TRAVEL

GREECE'S RAIL network is operated by the state-owned **OSE** (Organismós Sidirodrómon Elládos). Limited to the mainland, it is fairly skeletal by European standards. First- and second-class tickets are less expensive than the equivalent bus journey, but services tend to be slower. Though more costly, tickets for intercity express trains are worth it for the time they save. A Greek Rail Pass allows the user 10, 20, or 30 days of unlimited rail travel on first- and second-class services, anywhere in Greece.

TRAVELING BY BUS

INTERNATIONAL BUSES connect Greece with the rest of Europe, though during the tourist season fares are more expensive than charter flights.

Within Greece, the long-distance bus network is extensive, with buses stopping at least once a day at even the remotest destinations, and frequent express services on all the major routes.

From Athens there are regular departures to all the larger mainland towns, apart from those in Thrace, which are served by buses from Thessaloníki. Athens' Terminal A serves Epirus, Macedonia, the Peloponnese, and the Ionian islands of Corfu, Kefalloniá, Lefkáda, and Zákynthos. Terminal B serves most destinations in central Greece, including Delphi.

TRAVELING BY CAR

ON THE MAINLAND there are express highways between Athens, Thessaloníki Vólos, and Pátra. These roads are very fast, but tolls are charged for their use. There has been much upgrading of the roads on the islands, but they are still often poorly surfaced, particularly in more remote areas.

Car rental agencies are found in every tourist resort and major town. International companies such as **Budget**, **Avis**, **Hertz**, and **Europcar** tend to be more expensive than their local counterparts. The car rental agency should have an agreement with an emergency recovery company, such as Express, Hellas, or the InterAmerican Towing Company, in the event of a vehicle breakdown. Mopeds and motorcycles are also available for rent in many tourist resorts.

Greece has one of the highest road traffic accident rates in Europe; visitors are advised to take extra care when driving around.

FERRY SERVICES

THERE ARE REGULAR, year-round ferry crossings from Italy, Israel, and Turkey to the Greek mainland and islands.

Piraeus, the port of Athens, is Greece's busiest port, with ferry routes to international destinations, as well as to scores of locations on the mainland and islands. A number of companies run the ferry services, each with their own ticket agency on the dockside. All fares except first class are set by the Ministry of Transport, so a journey should cost you the same, regardless of which shipping company you choose.

Ferry tickets can be purchased from the shipping line office on the dockside, or any authorized travel agency. Advance reservations are essential in peak season, which runs from June to August. In off season, services may be reduced or suspended altogether. Check local sources – such as the Greek tourist office or a travel agency – for the latest information before you travel. The port police, who have an office at Piraeus, are also a good source of reliable, up-to-date information.

In addition to the large ferries, there are smaller vessels that make inter-island crossings in summer.

HYDROFOILS AND CATAMARANS

THE MAIN OPERATORS of hydrofoil and catamaran services between the mainland and the islands are **Dodecanese Hydrofoils** and **Flying Dolphin** (run by Minoan Lines). However, all hydrofoils, regardless of which company they are operated by, are known locally as "Flying Dolphins." They are twice as fast as ferries, but twice as expensive. Most vessels function only in the summer months and are often cancelled in bad weather.

DIRECTORY

OLYMPIC AIRWAYS

w www.olympic-airways.gr

Athens
Syngroú 96,
11741 Athens.
(210-966 6666.

Thessaloníki
Kountouriótou 3,
Thessaloníki.
(2310-368 666.

UK
11 Conduit Street,
London W1R OLP.
(020-7399 1500 or
0870-606 0460.

US
645 Fifth Avenue,
New York,
NY 10022.
(212-838 3600.

DOMESTIC AIRLINES

Aegean Airlines
Leof. Vouliagménis 572,
16451 Athens.
(80-11 12 00 00.

TRAVEL AGENCIES IN GREECE

National Travel Information.
(1440 (boat, train,
coach times).

American Express Travel Services
Ermoú 2,
10225 Athens.
(210-324 4975.

Ginis Vacances
3rd floor, Ermoú 23–25,
10563 Athens.
(210-325 0401.

Oxygen Travel
Eslin 4, Athens.
(210-641 0881.

RAIL TRAVEL

OSE (Information & Reservations)
Sína 6, Athens.
(210-362 4402.

Rail Europe
(08705-848 848 (UK).
w www.raileurope.co.uk

Train Stations in Athens
Laríssis station (for
northern Greece)
(210-823 1514.

Peloponnísou station
(for Peloponnese)
(210-513 1601.

BUSES

Bus Terminals in Athens
Terminal A:
Kifisoú 100
(210-513 2834.

Terminal B:
Liosíon 260
(210-832 9585.

Eurolines
52 Grosvenor Gardens,
Victoria, London
SW1, England.
(020-7730 8235.
w www.eurolines.co.uk
w www.gobycoach.com

CAR RENTAL AGENCIES

Avis
Leofóros Amalías 48,
10558 Athens.
(210-322 4951.
w www.avis.com

Budget
Syngroú 8, 11742 Athens.
(210-921 4771.
w www.budgetrentacar.com

Europcar
Syngroú 4,
11742 Athens.
(210-924 8810.
w www.europcar.com

Hertz
Leofóros Vouliagménis
576A, 16451 Argyroúpoli.
(801-11 100100.
w www.hertz.gr

PIRAEUS PORT

(01-422 6000
(port police).
(1440
(ferry timetable).

HYDROFOIL AND CATAMARAN SERVICES

Dodecanese Hydrofoils
Mandráki Harbor,
Rhodes.
(224-107 8052.

Flying Dolphin
Goúnari 2,
Piraeus.
(210-422 4775.

Shopping & Entertainment

THE CHOICE OF PLACES TO SHOP in Greece ranges from colorful, bustling street markets, found in almost every town and village, through traditional arts and crafts shops, to the designer fashion boutiques of Athens. Entertainment is as varied; visitors can try an open-air concert in the atmospheric setting of an ancient theater, or enjoy some late-night dining in a local taverna before heading for a bar or disco. With its dry, sunny climate and clear, warm seas, Greece offers countless opportunities for outdoor activities, from snorkeling to windsurfing, sailing, and hiking.

WHAT TO BUY

TRADITIONAL HANDICRAFTS, though often expensive, are the most genuinely Greek souvenirs. In Athens, Monastiráki and Pláka are the best places to purchase such items. There are also many unusual shops offering unique services, such as that of self-styled poet, **Stávros Melissinós**, who makes a wide variety of sturdy sandals and leather items. An excellent selection of goods, including tapestries and rugs, is available at the **National Welfare Organization**, while at the fascinating **Center of Hellenic Tradition** you can buy, among other things, finely crafted ceramics.

Some of the country's best ceramics can be found in the markets and shops of Athens' northern suburb Maroúsi, and on the island of Crete.

Brightly colored embroidery and wall-hangings are produced in many Greek villages. Colorful *flokáti* rugs, which are handwoven from sheep or goat's wool, are made mainly in the Píndos mountains, but can also be found in other parts of the mainland and on the islands.

Sold throughout Greece, leather goods are particularly noted on Crete, where the town of Chaniá hosts a huge leather market.

Well-crafted copies of ancient and Byzantine Greek art can be found in museum shops in many of the major cities. In Pláka in Athens, **Orféas** offers good quality marble and pottery copies of Classical Greek works, in addition to glittering Byzantine icons.

For jewelry, Athens is the best place to shop. Exclusive names include **Vourákis** and **Anagnostópoulos**, on Voukourestíou. The **Ilías Lalaoúnis Jewelry Museum** has over 3,000 designs, inspired by Classical and other archaeological sources.

MARKETS

MOST TOWNS IN GREECE have a weekly street market (*laïkí agorá*), where fresh produce is sold alongside shoes, fabrics, and sundry household items. In Athens, the one on Xenokrátous in centrally located Kolonáki takes place every Friday. The busy Central Market is excellent for food, while the famous Sunday-morning flea market in Monastiráki should not be missed.

FOOD AND DRINK

CULINARY DELIGHTS to look for in Greece include honey, olives, olive oil, pistachios, and cheeses, such as the salty feta. Also worth trying are ouzo (an anise-flavored liquor), retsina (wine flavored with pine resin), and the firewater *tsípouro*.

ENTERTAINMENT LISTINGS AND TICKETS

FOR DETAILED INFORMATION on entertainment in Athens, try *Athenscope* or *Downtown*, both published on Fridays, or the weekly *Athens News*.

Most theaters and music clubs in the capital sell tickets at the door on the day of the performance. However, tickets for the summer Athens Festival and for concerts at the Mousikís Mégaron Concert Hall should be purchased in advance; there is a central ticket office, open daily from 10am to 4pm, located near the Plateía Syntágmatos.

Elsewhere, your nearest tourist office should be able to provide information on what is happening locally.

ENTERTAINMENT VENUES

THE MAIN ENTERTAINMENT venues in Athens host a wide variety of events. As well as excellent productions of 19th-century Greek and European plays, the **National Theater** puts on opera, ballet, and contemporary dance. The **Mousikís Mégaron Concert Hall** is a first-class classical concert venue, while the Olympia Theater is home to the **Lyrikí Skiní** (National Opera). At the **Dóra Strátou Dance Theater** there is traditional regional Greek dancing nightly between May and September.

OPEN-AIR CINEMAS AND THEATERS

FOUND IN TOWNS and cities all over Greece, the outdoor cinema is extremely popular with Greeks and an experience not to be missed by anyone visiting the country in summer. Most movies are in English with Greek subtitles.

Open-air performances of Classical and modern drama, held at famous ancient archaeological sites, are an equally popular form of entertainment. The **Herodes Atticus Theater** hosts plays, as well as opera, ballet, and classical music concerts, during the annual Athens Festival (mid-June to mid-September). The theater at **Epidaurus** in the Peloponnese is another well-known venue.

TRADITIONAL GREEK MUSIC

TO HEAR TRADITIONAL Greek music in Athens head for **Diogénis Studio** or **Rex**. At **Taksími** and **Rempétiki Istoría** you can hear genuine *bouzouki* (Greek mandolin) music. In smaller towns and resorts around the country, the local taverna is often a good place to watch traditional musicians perform while you dine.

SPECIAL INTEREST VACATIONS

COMPANIES OFFERING special interest vacations include **Filoxenía** and **Ramblers Holidays**, which organize archaeological tours, and **Pharos Travel & Tourism**. Filoxenía also runs courses on creative writing, drawing, and painting in Greece. For specialist wildlife tours contact **Peregrine Holidays**, **Sunbird**, or **Ornitholidays**.

OUTDOOR ACTIVITIES

WITH MILES of coastline, and crystal clear seas, Greece is the perfect place to pursue water sports. Windsurfing, water-skiing, jet-skiing, and parasailing are all available in the larger resorts. Snorkeling and scuba diving are also popular, although the latter is restricted. A list of places where it is permissible to dive with oxygen equipment can be obtained from the **Department of Underwater Archaeology** in Athens, or from the EOT *(see p502).*

For information on sailing vacations and chartering yachts, contact the **Hellenic Yachting Federation**.

Cruises on luxury liners can be booked through **Swan Hellenic Cruises**, while inexpensive mini-cruises and boat trips are best arranged at a local travel agent on the spot.

Those wishing to simply relax on the beach should look for one with a Blue Flag; this indicates that the water is regularly tested for purity, and that the beach meets over a dozen other environmental criteria for both cleanliness and safety.

Inland the range of leisure opportunities is very varied, ranging from kayaking, white-water rafting, and canoeing, to hiking. **Trekking Hellas** organizes vacations based on these and other activities.

DIRECTORY

ART AND CRAFTS

Center of Hellenic Tradition
Mitropóleos 59 (Arcade) – Pandrósou 36,
Monastiráki, Athens.
(210-321 3023.

National Welfare Organization
Ypatías 6 and Apóllonos,
Monastiráki, Athens.
(210-321 8272.

Stávros Melissinós
Pandrósou 89,
Monastiráki, Athens.
(210-321 9247.

MUSEUM COPIES

Orféas
Pandrósou 28, Pláka,
Athens.
(210-324 5034.

JEWELRY

Anagnostópoulos
Voukourestíou 21,
Kolonáki, Athens.
(210-360 4426.

Ilías Lalaoúnis Jewelry Museum
Karyatidon 4a, Pláka,
Athens.
(210-922 1044.

Vourákis
Voukourestíou 8, Kolonáki,
Athens.
(210-331 1089.

THEATERS

Dóra Strátou Dance Theater
Filopáppou Hill,
Filopáppou, Athens.
(210-921 4650.

National Theater
Agíou Konstantínou 22,
Omónoia, Athens.
(210-322 3242.

CLASSICAL MUSIC AND OPERA

Lyrikí Skiní, Olympia Theater
Akadimías 59,
Omónoia, Athens.
(210-361 2461.

Mousikís Mégaron Concert Hall
V Sofías & Kókkali,
Stégi Patrídos, Athens.
(210-728 2333.

OPEN-AIR THEATERS

Herodes Atticus Theater
Dionysíou Areopagítou,
Acropolis, Athens.
(210-323 9132.

TRADITIONAL GREEK MUSIC

Diogénis Studio
Leof A Syngroú 259,
N. Smyrni, Athens.
(210-942 5754.

Rempétiki Istoría
Ippokrátous 181,
Neápoli, Athens.
(210-642 4937.507

Rex
Panepistimíou 48,
Omonoia, Athens.
(210-381 4591.

Taksími
C Trikoúpi & Isávron 29,
Neápoli, Athens.
(210-363 9919.

SPECIAL INTEREST VACATIONS

Filoxenía
Sourdock Hill,
Barkisland, Halifax,
West Yorkshire,
HX4 0AG, England.
(01422-371 796.

Ornitholidays
29 Straight Mile, Romsey,
Hants SO51 9BB, England.
(01794 519445.

Peregrine Holidays
29a Main Street,
Lyddington, Oakham,
Rutland LE15 9LR.
(01572-821 330.

Pharos Travel & Tourism
230 W. 31st Street,
New York,
NY 10001 USA.
(212-736 6070.
FAX 212-736 3921.

Ramblers Holidays
Box 43, Welwyn Garden
City, Herts AL8 6PQ,
England.
(01707-331 133.

Sunbird
PO Box 76, Sandy,
Bedfordshire SG19 1DF,
England.
(01767-682 969.

OUTDOOR ACTIVITIES

Department of Underwater Archaeology
Kallispéri 30,
11742 Athens, Greece.
(210-924 7249.

Hellenic Yachting Federation
Akti Possidónas 51,
Moschato, Athens, Greece.
(210-940 3111.

Swan Hellenic Cruises
Richmond Hse, Perminus
Terrace, Southampton,
SO14 3PN, England.
(0845-355 5111.
W www.swanhellenic.com

Trekking Hellas
Filellinou 7,
10557 Athens,
Greece.
(210-331 0323.
W www.trekking.gr

Where to Stay in Greece

I N A COUNTRY so heavily dependent on tourism, accommodations are always easily found, and are very inexpensive compared with those in most other European destinations. Visitors to Greece can choose to stay in an extensive range of surroundings, from modern luxury chain hotels, through restored historic buildings, to inexpensive and informal *domátia* (rooms) in a family home.

	NUMBER OF ROOMS	RESTAURANT	GARDEN OR TERRACE	SWIMMING POOL	AIR-CONDITIONING
ATHENS					
EXÁRCHEIA: *Exarcheíon* €€€ Themistokléous 55, 10683. **Map** D1. (210-380 0731. FAX 210-360 3296. This hotel is close to the late-night action of Plateía Exarcheíon. Rooms are basic, but there is a roof garden and a good sidewalk café. ▣ 占 ⌷	50				
EXÁRCHEIA: *Museum* €€€ Mpoumpoulínas 16, 10682. **Map** C1. (210-380 3296. FAX 210-728 1111. Located opposite the National Archaeological Museum, this hotel is frequented by academics. The rooms are clean and quiet. ▣ P 占 ⌷	58				▪
ILISIA: *Hilton* w www.hilton.com €€€€€ Leofóros Vasilíssis Sofías 46, 11528. **Map** F3. (210-728 1000. FAX 210-728 1111. Athens' best-known modern hotel. All the rooms have large balconies, providing stunning views across the city. ▣ P 占 ⌷	517	●	▪	●	▪
KOLONÁKI: *St. George Lycabettus* w www.sglycabettus.gr €€€€€ Kleoménous 2, 10675. **Map** E3. (210-729 0711. FAX 210-729 0439. Located beneath Lykavittós Hill, this small, luxury hotel offers large rooms with good views. The rooftop restaurant is excellent. ▣ P 占 ⌷	167	●		●	▪
MAKRYGIANNI: *Divani Palace Acropolis* €€€€€ Parthenónos 19–25, 11742. **Map** B5. (210-928 0100. FAX 210-921 4993. Beautifully upgraded to deluxe standard, this hotel is just a short stroll from the Acropolis. ▣ P ⌷	251	●	▪	●	▪
MONASTIRÁKI: *Attalos* @ atthot@aol.gr €€€ Athinás 29, 19554. **Map** B3. (210-321 2801. FAX 210-324 3124. Ideally located for shopping, near Monastiráki and Athinás, the Attalos offers adequate rooms, some with balconies. The hotel also has a roof garden with good views of the Acropolis. ▣ 占 ⌷	80		▪		▪
MONASTIRÁKI: *Témpi* @ tempihotel@travelling.gr €€€€ Aiólou 29, 10551. **Map** B3. (210-321 3175. FAX 210-325 4179. Overlooking the flower market and Agía Eiríni church, this hotel is ideal for those who want to explore Athinás market's food and stalls. ⌷	24		▪		
OMÓNOIA: *La Mirage* €€€€ Maríkas Kotopoúli 3, 10431. **Map** B2. (210-523 4071. FAX 210-523 3992. A favorite for those who want to be close to the 24-hour hustle and bustle of Plateía Omonoías. All rooms are double glazed. ▣ P 占 ⌷	208	●			
OMÓNOIA: *Dorian Inn* @ dorianho@otenet.gr €€€€€ Peiraiós 15–17, 10552. **Map** B2. (210-523 9782. FAX 210-522 6196. Located in the heart of the city center, the roof garden of this smart hotel offers spectacular views of Athens and the Acropolis. ▣ P 占 ⌷	146	●	▪	●	▪
OMÓNOIA: *Titania* @ titania@netplan.gr €€€€€€ Panepistimíou 52, 10678. **Map** C2. (210-330 0111. FAX 210-330 0700. The entrance to the Titania is through a shopping mall, close to Plateía Omonoías. Rooms are well-equipped. ▣ P 占 ⌷	396	●	▪		▪
PLÁKA: *John's Place* €€€€ Patróou 5, 10557. **Map** C4. (210-322 9719. One of the better bargain backpacking hotels. The rooms are small but very clean, and bathrooms are shared.	15				
PLÁKA: *Koúros* €€€€ Kódrou 11, 10557. **Map** C4. (210-322 7431. Located in the heart of Pláka, this inexpensive small *pension* is housed in a converted Neo-Classical mansion house. Rooms are basic but clean and have balconies – some with a view of the Acropolis.	10				

Map references refer to map of Athens on pp474–5

Price categories are for a standard double room for one night in peak season, including tax, service charges, and breakfast:

€ under €25
€€ €25–35
€€€ €35–45
€€€€ €45–60
€€€€€ over €60

RESTAURANT
Restaurant within the hotel, sometimes reserved for residents only.

SWIMMING POOL
Hotel swimming pools are usually outdoors unless otherwise stated.

AIR-CONDITIONING
Hotel with air-conditioning in all rooms.

CREDIT CARDS
Major credit cards are accepted in those hotels where the credit card symbol is shown.

Hotel	Price	Number of Rooms	Restaurant	Garden or Terrace	Swimming Pool	Air-Conditioning
PLÁKA: *Acropolis House Pension* €€€€€ Kóudrou 6–8, 10557. **Map** C4. 210-322 2344. **FAX** 210-324 4143. Housed in a converted 19th-century building, the rooms in this *pension* are large and airy. All rooms have private balconies.		19				■
PLÁKA: *Adónis* €€€€€ Kódrou 3, 10557. 210-324 9737. **FAX** 210-323 1602. A modern, reasonably priced hotel, offering decent rooms with balconies and views across Athens from its roof garden.		26		■		■
PLÁKA: *Aphrodite* €€€€€ Apóllonos 21, 10557. **Map** C4. 210-323 4357. **FAX** 210-322 5244. This hotel is well located and offers clean, good-value rooms, some of which enjoy wonderful views of the Acropolis.		84	●	■		■
PLÁKA: *Myrtó* €€€€€ Níkis 40, 10558. **Map** C4. 210-322 7237. **FAX** 210-323 4560. Close to the central areas of Plateía Syntágmatos and Pláka, this small hotel is ideal for short stays and is popular with young couples.		12				■
PLÁKA: *Neféli* €€€€€ Angelikís Chatzimicháli 2, 10558. **Map** C4. 210-322 8044. **FAX** 210-322 5800. A modern hotel, hidden away in a peaceful backwater in Pláka. The rooms are clean and of a good, basic standard.		18		■		
PLÁKA: *Pláka* €€€€€ Kapnikareas & Mitropoleos 7, 10556. **Map** C4. 210-322 2096. **FAX** 210-322 2412. Set in the heart of Pláka, with a superb view of the Acropolis, this is a comfortable hotel with a friendly atmosphere.		67	●	■		■
STATHMÓS LARISSÍS: *Novotel Athens* @ novotel@hol.gr €€€€€ Michaíl Vóda 4–6, 10439. 210-820 0700. **FAX** 210-820 0777. Run by the French group, Novotel, this smart, centrally located hotel has modern, well-equipped rooms and a stunning rooftop garden and swimming pool.		195	●	■	●	■
SÝNTAGMA: *Metropolis* €€€€ Mitropóleos 46, 10563. **Map** C4. 210-321 7469. **FAX** 210-321 7469. Friendly staff greet you at this five-story hotel enjoying views over Athens' Mitrópoli (cathedral). Rooms are large and clean.		25		■		
SÝNTAGMA: *Aretoúsa* w www.arethusahotel.gr €€€€€ Mitropóleos 6–8 & Níkis 12, 10563. **Map** C4. 210-322 9431. **FAX** 210-322 9439. Good value characterizes this centrally located hotel. The rooms are modern and there is a roof garden, as well as a lively bar.		87	●	■		
SÝNTAGMA: *Astor* €€€€€ Karageórgi Servías 16, 10562. **Map** D4. 210-335 1000. **FAX** 210-325 5115. The popular all-year-round rooftop restaurant of this hotel boasts stunning views over Athens. The double rooms from the sixth floor and above share the impressive view of the city.		130	●	■		
SÝNTAGMA: *Esperia Palace* @ esper@otenet.gr €€€€€ Stadíou 22, 10564. **Map** C3. 210-323 8001. **FAX** 210-323 8100. A smart city hotel with marble lobbies and tastefully decorated rooms. Its restaurant and bar are popular with Athenians.		184	●			■
SÝNTAGMA: *Grande Bretagne* @ info@hotelgrandebretagne-ath.gr €€€€€ Plateía Syntágmatos, 10563. **Map** D4. 210-333 0000. **FAX** 210-322 8034. This luxurious hotel was built in 1852 and is the landmark of Plateía Syntágmatos, the most desirable hotel location in Athens. The lobby and rooms are beautiful and the service is excellent.		450	●	■		■

For key to symbols see back flap

Price categories are for a standard double room for one night in peak season, including tax, service charges, and breakfast:

€ under €25
€€ €25–35
€€€ €35–45
€€€€ €45–60
€€€€€ over €60

RESTAURANT
Restaurant within the hotel, sometimes reserved for residents only.

SWIMMING POOL
Hotel swimming pools are usually outdoors unless otherwise stated.

AIR-CONDITIONING
Hotel with air-conditioning in all rooms.

CREDIT CARDS
Major credit cards are accepted in those hotels where the credit card symbol is shown.

	NUMBER OF ROOMS	RESTAURANT	GARDEN OR TERRACE	SWIMMING POOL	AIR-CONDITIONING
REST OF MAINLAND GREECE					
AGIOS IÓANNIS, PÍLIO: *Eftychía* €€€€	17	●	■		
ANCIENT CORINTH: *Shadow* €€€€	12	■			■
AREÓPOLI, MÁNI PENINSULA: *Pyrgos Kapetanákou* €€€€€	7		■		
DELFOÍ: *Olympic* €€€€€	20				■
DIMITSÁNA, LOÚSIOS GORGE: *Dimitsána* €€€€	27		■		
GÝTHEIO, MÁNI PENINSULA: *Aktaíon* €€€€€	22	●			
KALAMPÁKA, NEAR METÉORA: *Antoniádi* €€€€	70	●	■	●	■
KARDAMÝLI, MÁNI PENINSULA: *Kardamýli Beach* €€€€€	30		■	●	
LITÓCHORO, MOUNT OLYMPOS: *Myrtó* €€€	32		■		
MONEMVÁSIA: *Malvásia* €€€€	28				
MYCENAE: *Belle Hélène* €€€	8	●	■		

AGIOS IÓANNIS, PÍLIO: *Eftychía*
Main road into village, 37012. 24260-31150.
Located in Agios Ioánnis, 25 km (16 miles) north of Miliés, the Eftychía is a typical Pílio-style hotel, with stone roof tiles and a whitewashed exterior. There are sea views but no rooms with balconies. Sep–May.

ANCIENT CORINTH: *Shadow*
On access road to village, 20007. 27410-31481. FAX 27410-31481.
The rear rooms of this simple family hotel overlook Acrocorinth and the lush Kórinthos plain. The affiliated restaurant has live music.

AREÓPOLI, MÁNI PENINSULA: *Pyrgos Kapetanákou*
Off Plateía Areopóleos, 23062. 27330-51233. FAX 27330-51401.
This hotel is housed in a three-story tower dating from 1865. The rooms vary sharply in price and range from a lone single to a family quintuple loft. There are mature gardens and a lovely breakfast salon.

DELFOÍ: *Olympic*
Freideríkis 53B, 33054. 22650-82793. FAX 22650-82639.
Located in Delfoí, just east of Ancient Delphi, this luxurious hotel has rooms with private bathrooms and views over an olive-filled valley.

DIMITSÁNA, LOÚSIOS GORGE: *Dimitsána*
Off Dimitsána–Stemnítsa road, 22100. 27950-31518. FAX 27950-31040.
A recently modernized hotel located in a lush and leafy setting overlooking the Loúsios Gorge. Most of the rooms have balconies.

GÝTHEIO, MÁNI PENINSULA: *Aktaíon*
Vasiléos Pávlou 39, 23200. 27330-23500. FAX 27330-22294.
Housed in a restored Neo-Classical building on the dockside, the Aktaíon offers clean rooms and balconies with sea views.

KALAMPÁKA, NEAR METÉORA: *Antoniádi*
Trikálon 148, 42200. 24320-24387. FAX 24320-24319.
A new, but homely, small hotel which lacks views of Metéora but has a very friendly atmosphere and a first-class restaurant.

KARDAMÝLI, MÁNI PENINSULA: *Kardamýli Beach*
Kardamýli beach, 24022. 27210-73180. FAX 27210-73184.
Located in Kardamýli, 34 km (21 miles) south of Kalamáta, this modern, friendly hotel sits at the foot of the Taÿgettos range and has excellent views of the sea and the mountains.

LITÓCHORO, MOUNT OLYMPOS: *Myrtó*
Agíou Nikoláou 5, 60200. 23520-81398. FAX 23520-82298.
Situated in Litóchoro, 21 km (13 miles) south of Kateríni, this hotel offers large rooms with private bathrooms and a friendly atmosphere.

MONEMVÁSIA: *Malvásia*
Kástro, 23070. 27320-61323. FAX 27320-61722.
This restoration complex is scattered about the old town on three different sites that vary in price. Each room, furnished in wood, marble, and bright textiles, has its own individual charm.

MYCENAE: *Belle Hélène*
Chrístou Ioúda, 21200. 27510-76225. FAX 27510-76179.
Dating from 1862, this simple but atmospheric building housed the archaeologist Schliemann during his excavations here. The ground floor restaurant features an impressive guest register. Jan–Feb.

NÁFPLIO: *Byron* @ byronhotel@otenet.gr €€€€ 18
Plátonos 2, 21100. (27520-22351. FAX 27520-26338.
A beautifully restored hotel located near the top of the old town.
Some of the upper floor rooms have views of the sea. 🟢

NÁFPLIO: *Epídavros* €€€€ 35
Kokkínou 2, 21100. (27520-27541. FAX 27520-27541.
Every room of this tastefully renovated hotel is different, though all
have pine floors and coffered ceilings. Some have balconies. 🔲 P

NÁFPLIO: *King Othon* €€€€€ 12
Farmakopoúlou 3, 21100. (27520-27585. FAX 27520-27595.
Housed in a Neo-Classical building, the King Othon has high ceilings
and windows, which contribute to its atmosphere.

NÉOS MYSTRÁS: *Byzántion* €€€€ 22
Main square, 23100. (27310-83309. FAX 27310-20019.
Located in Néos Mystrás, 1 km (0.5 miles) east of Byzantine Mystrás, this
recently restored hotel has individually decorated rooms with vaulted ceilings
and wooden furniture. Prices vary depending on the view. 🟢 *Nov–Mar.* 🔲 P

OLYMPIA: *Pelops* €€ 25
Varelá 2, 27065. (26240-22543. FAX 26240-22213.
Situated in Olympia, this hotel is run by an Australian-Greek team. The family
atmosphere and ivy-covered bar area make for a pleasant stay. 🟢 *mid-
Nov–mid-Feb.* 🔲 🟢

OLYMPIA: *Europa* @ hoteleuropa@hellasnet.gr €€€€ 80
Droúva 1, 27065. (26240-22650. FAX 26240-23166.
This welcoming, family-run hotel (a member of the Best Western chain)
enjoys a superb hillside site in Olympía, 500 m (1,600 ft) east of Ancient
Olympia. Facilities include a tennis court and riding stable. 🔲 P 🟢

OURANOÚPOLI, ATHOS: *Skítes* €€€€€ 29
Road to Mount Athos, 63075. (23770-71140. FAX 23770-71322.
A family-run hotel set in a peaceful spot, surrounded by pine woods, with
whitewashed bungalows that are decorated in a rustic style. The veranda
restaurant has spectacular views of the sea. 🟢 *Nov–Apr.* 🔲 P 🔵 🟢

STEMNÍTSA, LOÚSIOS GORGE: *Trikolóneio* €€€€ 20
Off main square, 22024. (27950-81297. FAX 27950-81483.
The traditional-style Trikolóneio is housed in two 19th-century mansions
with an annex. There is an excellent restaurant attached. 🔲 P

THESSALONÍKI: *Anatolia* €€€€ 70
Langadá 13, 54629. (2310-522421. FAX 2310-512892.
A Neoclassical-style hotel within walking distance of the central square
and port, and close to the bazaar. All rooms have balconies. 🔲 P 🟢

THESSALONÍKI: *Electra Palace* €€€€€ 138
Plateía Aristotélous 9, 54624. (2310-232221. FAX 2310-235947.
An upscale central hotel, situated just off the waterfront. All rooms
are fully equipped with a telephone, television, and minibar. 🔲 🔵 🟢

THESSALONÍKI: *Olympía* €€€€ 111
Olýmpou 65, 54631. (2310-235421. FAX 2310-276133.
This is a well-kept hotel with good facilities. It is located in the quieter
back streets, but is just a short stroll from the city center. 🔲 P 🟢

THESSALONÍKI: *Panórama* €€€€€ 50
Analípseos 26, Panórama, 55236. (2310-344871. FAX 2310-344871.
Located in the eastern hilltop suburb of Panórama, this comfortable
hotel has a wonderful view of the city. Cars or taxis are needed to
reach the city center, but the superior rooms compensate for this. 🔲

VÓLOS, PÍLIO: *Park* €€€€€ 119
Deligiórgi 2, 38221. (24210-36511. FAX 24210-28645.
This is one of the best hotels in Vólos. The rooms are modern, stylishly
decorated, and have balconies that overlook the sea or park. 🔲 P 🔵 🟢

VYZÍTSA, PÍLIO: *Karagiannopoulos Mansion* €€€€ 6
Off main road, 37010. (24230-86717. FAX 24230-86878.
This hotel is housed in a traditional mansion, with woodcut ceilings
and a garden terrace. 🔲

For key to symbols see back flap

<table>
<tr><td colspan="2">

Price categories are for a standard double room for one night in peak season, including tax, service charges, and breakfast:

€ under €25
€€ €25–35
€€€ €35–45
€€€€ €45–60
€€€€€ over €60

</td><td colspan="5">

RESTAURANT
Restaurant within the hotel, sometimes reserved for residents only.
SWIMMING POOL
Hotel swimming pools are usually outdoors unless otherwise stated.
AIR-CONDITIONING
Hotel with air-conditioning in all rooms.
CREDIT CARDS
Major credit cards are accepted in those hotels where the credit card symbol is shown.

</td></tr>
</table>

	NUMBER OF ROOMS	RESTAURANT	CLOSE TO BEACH	SWIMMING POOL	AIR-CONDITIONING
CORFU AND THE IONIAN ISLANDS					
CORFU: *Akrotíri Beach* €€€€€ T Desýlla 155, Palaiokastrítsa, 49083. 📞 26630-41237. 🖷 26630-41277. One of the best hotels in this popular resort, the Akrotíri Beach enjoys a lovely setting on a headland. ● Nov–Apr. 🛏 ♿ 🗐	127	●	▨	●	
CORFU: *Bella Venezia* @ belvenht@hol.gr €€€€€ N Zampéli 4, Corfu town, 49100. 📞 26610-46500. 🖷 26610-20708. Close to the town center, this Neoclassical mansion has comfortable and tasteful rooms. The staff are hospitable and courteous. 🛏 🗐	32		▨		▨
CORFU: *Corfu Palace* €€€€€ Leofóros Dimokratías 2, Corfu town, 49100. 📞 26610-39485-7. 🖷 26610-31749. This luxury hotel is set in beautiful tropical gardens, with a peaceful, waterfront location and views of the Greek mainland. 🛏 ♿ 🗐	106	●	▨	▨	▨
CORFU: *San Stéfano* @ sanstefano@hol.gr €€€€€ Waterfront, Benítses, 49081. 📞 26610-71118. 🖷 26610-71124. This smart hotel was once used to accommodate European politicians at conferences, so facilities are excellent. ● Nov–Mar. 🛏 🗐	259	●	▨	●	▨
KEFALLONIÁ: *Kefalloniá Star* €€€€€ Ioánnou Metaxá 60, Argostóli, 28100. 📞 26710-23181. 🖷 26710-23180. A long-established hotel on the main harbor road, it has some balconied front rooms and fine sea views. A comfortable place to stay. 🛏 ♿ 🗐	42		▨		▨
KEFALLONIÁ: *Rosa's Studio* €€€€€ Lourdata Beach, 28083. 📞 26710-31105. 🖷 26710-23469. These well-equiped studios have balconies overlooking the sea with steps leading down to the pretty beach below. ● Oct–Apr. 🛏 🗐	15		▨		
ZÁKYNTHOS: *Montreal* €€€€€ Alykés, 29090. 📞 26950-83241. 🖷 26950-83342. Right on the busy beach of this popular holiday resort, all of the rooms have sea views and are modern and well kept. ● Nov–Mar. 🛏 ♿ 🗐	35	●	▨		
THE CYCLADES					
MÝKONOS: *Cavo Tagoo* €€€€€ 500 m (1,650 ft) N of port, Mýkonos town, 84100. 📞 22890-23692. 🖷 22890-24923. This stylish yet friendly hotel features a range of beautifully furnished Cycladic maisonettes, overlooking the bay at Tagoo. ● Nov–Mar. 🛏 🗐	72	●	▨	●	▨
MÝKONOS: *The Princess of Mýkonos* €€€€€ Agios Stéfanos beach, 84600. 📞 22890-23806. 🖷 22890-23031. A Cycladic-style hotel that has all the luxury facilities, from gym to conference rooms and satellite TV. ● Nov–Mar. 🛏 ♿ 🗐	38	●	▨	●	▨
NÁXOS: *Nissaki Beach Hotel* @ nissaki@naxos_island.com €€€€€ Agios Geórgios, Náxos town, 84300. 📞 22850-25710. 🖷 22850-23876. Recently renovated in traditional Cycladic décor, this hotel is located next to the beach. Some rooms have views of the sea, others the pool. 🛏 🗐	40	●	▨	●	▨
SANTORÍNI: *Ermís* €€€€€ Kamári beach, 84700. 📞 22860-31664. 🖷 22860-33240. Set among beautiful gardens, this friendly, family-run hotel offers well-appointed rooms, not far from the town center. ● Nov–Apr. 🛏 ♿ 🗐	36		▨	●	
SANTORÍNI: *Kavalári* @ info@kavalari.com €€€€€ Near bus station, Firá, 84700. 📞 22860-22455. 🖷 22860-22603. Formerly a sea captain's home, this unusual hotel is terraced into the rock face. It offers spectacular views. ● Nov–Mar. 🛏 🗐	18	●	▨		▨

RHODES AND THE DODECANESE

KÁRPATHOS: *Amoopí Bay* €€€€ | 65
Amoopí beach, 85700. ☎ 22450-81184. FAX 22450-81105.
Located right on the beach, the rooms of this small hotel are
basic but all have balconies and are good value for money.

Kos: *Afentoúlis* €€€€ | 17
Evripídou 1, Kos town, 85300. ☎ 22420-25321. FAX 22420-25797.
A small family-run hotel with very friendly management, in a quiet spot
close to the sea. There is a lovely jasmine-filled garden. ● Oct–Mar.

Kos: *Porto Bello Beach* €€€€€ | 350
Waterfront, W of Kardámaina, 85300. ☎ 22420-91217. FAX 22420-91168.
Located on the beach, this resort hotel consists of whitewashed
bungalows, sea views, and a children's playground. ● Nov–Apr.

RHODES: *Nikolís* @ nikoliss@hol.gr €€€€€ | 10
Ippodámou 61, Rhodes town, 85100. ☎ 22410-34561. FAX 22410-32034.
Housed in an atmospheric medieval building in the heart of the old town,
this hotel has rear rooms with terraces overlooking a garden.

RHODES: *Rhodos Palace* €€€€€ | 785
Ialyssós bay, Ixiá, 85101. ☎ 22410-25222. FAX 22410-25350.
A luxury hotel with apartments and bungalows in extensive grounds.
Facilities include indoor and outdoor pools. ● Dec–Feb.

RHODES: *Spartális* €€€€€ | 79
N Plastíra 2, Rhodes town, 85100. ☎ 22410-24371. FAX 22410-20406.
A basic but friendly hotel, handily placed close to the harbor for ferries
and boat trips. There is a lovely breakfast terrace.

CRETE

AGIOS NIKÓLAOS: *Istron Beach* €€€€€ | 117
13 km (8 miles) E of Agios Nikólaos. ☎ 28410-61303. FAX 28410-61383.
This delightfully secluded resort hotel overlooks a spectacular cove and
has the luxury of its own sandy beach. The atmosphere is friendly.

CHANIÁ: *Terésa* €€€ | 8
Angélou 8, 73100. ☎ 28210-92798. FAX 28210-92798.
Renovated Venetian house with fabulous views of the harbor from
its roof terrace and some of the rooms. Excellent value for money.

CHANIÁ: *Vílla Androméda* €€€€€ | 8
Eleftheríou Venizélou 150, 73133. ☎ 28210-28300. FAX 28210-28303.
This elegantly restored Neoclassical mansion was built in 1870
and was once home to the German consulate. The hotel comprises
eight luxuriously decorated suites. ● Nov 20–Dec 20, Jan 25–Feb 25.

ELOÚNTA: *Eloúnta Beach Hotel* €€€€€ | 280
2 km (1 mile) N of Eloúnta, 72053. ☎ 28410-41412. FAX 28410-41373.
The Eloúnta offers every amenity imaginable from jacuzzis, Turkish baths,
and saunas, to scuba diving and parasailing. ● Nov–Feb.

IRÁKLEIO: *Galaxy* €€€€€ | 140
Dimokratías 67, 71306. ☎ 2810-238812. FAX 2810-211211. @ galaxyer@otenet.gr
This attractive, modern hotel is set around a central court and
swimming pool. The rooms are tastefully decorated.

IRÁKLEIO: *Lató* €€€€€ | 50
Epimenídou 15, 71202. ☎ 2810-228103. FAX 2810-240350. @ lato@her.forthnet.gr
A pleasant hotel with superb views over the Venetian harbor and in
a good central location below the Archaeological Museum.

RÉTHYMNO: *Fortétsa* €€€€€ | 54
Melisinoú 16, 74100. ☎ 28310-55551. FAX 28310-54073. @ milodak@ret.forthnet.gr
One of the nicest hotels in Réthymno, on a quiet backstreet just behind
the Fortétsa, and a short walk from the waterfront. ● Dec–Feb.

RÉTHYMNO: *Grecotel Creta Palace* €€€€€ | 355
Misiría, 74100. ☎ 28310-55181. FAX 28310-54085.
A resort hotel with its own beach in Misiría, 4 km (2 miles) east of Réthymno.
The full range of facilities includes a fitness club. ● Nov–Mar.

For key to symbols see back flap

Where to Eat in Greece

EATING OUT IS AN IMPORTANT PART of Greek social life, enjoyed by rich and poor, old and young alike. As a result, the country boasts a vast array of eating places. With a host of stylish restaurants serving international fare, friendly tavernas offering traditional, local cooking, and lively cafés and bars, Greece caters for almost every taste.

	AIR-CONDITIONING	OUTDOOR TABLES	LIVE ENTERTAINMENT	LOCAL WINES

ATHENS

ACROPOLIS: *Strofí* €€ Rovértou Gkálli 25, 11742. **Map** B5. 210-921 4130. The rooftop views of the Acropolis attract a constant stream of diners. The menu features all the mainstays of a Greek taverna. ● *Sun, lunch daily.* 🍽		●	■		■
EXÁRCHEIA: *Ama Lachei* €€ Kallidromíou 69, 10681. **Map** A3. 210-382 4138. This well-known *mezedopoteío* is about as authentic as they get. It is situated in the heart of Exárcheia, well off the usual tourist route. ● *lunch, Sun.*			■		
KOLONÁKI: *The Food Company* € Corner of Anagnostopoúlou & Dimokrítou, 10673. **Map** E3. 210-363 0373. This American-owned café offers wholesome, tasty food at excellent prices, including salads, great pasta, and delicious cakes. ● *Aug 1–15.*			■		
KOLONÁKI: *Dekaoktó* €€€€ Souidías 51, 10676. **Map** F3. 210-723 5561. A dozen candlelit tables, seductive *mezédes* (appetizers), perfectly grilled fish, and a good wine list make for a romantic place to dine. 🍽		●			■
KOLONÁKI: *Kíku* €€€€€ Dimokrítou 12, 10673. **Map** D3. 210-364 7033. The city's finest Japanese restaurant has all the ingredients you would expect: understated decor, perfect *sushi* and *sashimi*. ● *Sun, lunch daily; mid-Jul–mid-Aug.* 🍽		●			■
MONASTIRÁKI: *Thánasis* € Mitropóleos 69, 10555. **Map** B4. 210-324 4705. Thánasis has some of the best and least expensive grilled food in the city. Try the kebabs of spiced meat, onion, tomato, and parsley. ● *Jan 1, Easter Sun, Dec 25.*		●			
MONASTIRÁKI: *Cafe Avissynía* €€€€ Plateía Avissynías, 10555. **Map** B4. 210-321 7047. Tables are always packed for the accordionist and singer who perform here every weekend. During the week, when the café is quieter, is a better time to sample the unusual Macedonian dishes. ● *dinner daily; Aug.* 🍽		●	■	●	■
OMÓNOIA: *Néon* €€ Plateía Omónoias, 10431. **Map** B2. 210-523 6409. All-day eating at this self-service chain restaurant includes a salad bar, fresh pasta, grills, and typical oven baked dishes.		●			
OMÓNOIA: *Ideal* €€€ Panepistimíou 46, 10678. **Map** C2. 210-330 3000. Since 1922 this much-loved institution has been serving excellent Greek and international cuisine. Specials include milk-fed veal with eggplant, stuffed zucchini, and *agkináres a la políta* (artichokes in lemon juice). ● *Sun.* 🍽		●			■
PLÁKA: *Byzantinó* €€ Kydathinaíon 18, 10558. **Map** C5. 210-322 7368. Excellent daily specials such as the *chtapódi krasáto* (octopus in wine) and baked vegetable dishes entice the locals to this old-fashioned taverna. 🍽		●	■		
PLÁKA: *Eden* €€ Lysíou 12, off Mnisikléous,10556. **Map** B4. 210-324 8858. Housed in a Neoclassical building with a modern interior, this is Athens' oldest vegetarian restaurant. Food is made with organically-grown produce. ● *Tue.* 🍽		●			
PLÁKA: *Symposion* €€ Mnisikléous 24, 10556. **Map** B4. 210-325 4940. This lively *ouzerí* serves traditional Greek food. Retsina is served from the barrel and live *rempétika* music is played every day. 🍽		●	■	●	■

Map references refer to the map of Athens on pp474–5

Price categories are for a three-course meal for one, including a half-bottle of house wine, and any extra charges, such as tax or service: € under €10 €€ €10–18 €€€ €18–25 €€€€ €25–33 €€€€€ over €33	**OUTDOOR TABLES** Tables for eating outdoors, often with a good view. **LIVE ENTERTAINMENT** Dancing or live music performances on various days of the week. **LOCAL WINES** The restaurant offers an interesting selection of local Greek wines.	AIR-CONDITIONING	OUTDOOR TABLES	LIVE ENTERTAINMENT	LOCAL WINES
SÝNTAGMA: *GB Corner* €€€€€ Hotel Grande Bretagne, Plateía Syntágmatos, 10563. **Map** D4. ☎ 210-333 0000. This is a long-established restaurant serving good quality Greek and international food. The service is impeccable. ⊟		●	▦		▦
THISEÍO: *Pil Poul* €€€€€ Corner of Apostólou Pávlou & Poulopoúlou, 11851. **Map** A4. ☎ 210-342 3665. Mediterranean cooking and views of the Acropolis draw the crowds to this busy and expensive restaurant, located west of the Hephaisteion. ● *lunch, Sun.* ⊟		●	▦	●	▦

REST OF MAINLAND GREECE

AGIOS IOÁNNIS, PÍLIO: *Ostriá* €€ On shore road, 37012. ☎ 24260-32132. This restaurant serves typical Pílio dishes such as rabbit stew *(kounéli kokkinistó)* and wild greens pie *(chortópita).* ● *lunch Mon–Fri; Oct–Apr.*		●	▦		▦
ANCIENT CORINTH: *Archontikó* €€ On shore road, 20100. ☎ 27410-27968. A family-run concern where fair-sized portions are accompanied by the excellent house rosé. ● *lunch daily; Easter.*		●	▦		▦
GÝTHEIO, MÁNI PENINSULA: *Saga Fish Tavern* € Tzanni Tazznetaki, 23200. ☎ 27330-23220. This tavern is in a wonderful location on the beach – enjoy a dish of shrimp or grilled fish seated on the wooden veranda looking out to sea.			▦		
KALAMPÁKA, NEAR METÉORA: *Metéora* € Plateía Dimarcheíou, 42200. ☎ 24320-22316. Wholesome Greek food, prepared by the owner's wife, and the usual menu of salads, moussakas, and grills can be enjoyed here. ● *mid-Nov–mid-Mar.*			▦		
LITÓCHORO, MOUNT OLYMPOS: *Damaskiniá* € Vasiléos Konstantínou 4, 60200. ☎ 23520-81247. Located in Litóchoro, 21 km (13 miles) south of Katerína, this lively taverna offers good home-cooked Greek fare. Meals include grilled fish and stews.			▦		
MONEMVASÍA: *I Matoúla* €€ Main through road, 23070. ☎ 27320-61660. For many decades this was the only taverna in Monemvasía. All traditional dishes can be enjoyed under a giant fig tree in the garden.			▦		
NÁFPLIO: *O Vasílis* € Staïkopoúlou 22, 21100. ☎ 27520-25334. Of all the competing restaurants along Staïkopoúlou, this is one of the oldest and the best for hearty Greek food. ● *Oct–Mar: Tue; Nov 15–30.*		●	▦		
NÁFPLIO: *Zorbás* € Staïkopoúlou 30, 21100. ☎ 27520-25319. This family-run taverna prepares all the standard Greek dishes. Try the delicious homemade fish soup or the octopus. ⊟		●	▦		
NÉOS MYSTRÁS: *O Mystrás* € Main square, 23100. This traditional taverna, 1 km (0.5 miles) east of Byzantine Mystrás, serves large portions of the tastiest vegetable stews in the Peloponnese, as well as olives and various grilled meats.			▦		▦
OLYMPIA: *Praxitelous* € Spiliopoúlou 7, 27065. ☎ 26240-23570. The emphasis here is on traditional, local food, served in a very Greek atmosphere. Located very near the site of Ancient Olympia, you can enjoy your meal outside in the garden. ● *mid-Nov.* ⊟			▦		▦

For key to symbols see back flap

	AIR-CONDITIONING	OUTDOOR TABLES	LIVE ENTERTAINMENT	LOCAL WINES

Price Categories are for a three-course meal for one, including a half-bottle of house wine, and any extra charges, such as tax or service:
€ under €10
€€ €10–18
€€€ €18–25
€€€€ €25–33
€€€€€ over €33

OUTDOOR TABLES
Tables for eating outdoors, often with a good view.

LIVE ENTERTAINMENT
Dancing or live music performances on various days of the week.

LOCAL WINES
The restaurant offers an interesting selection of local Greek wines.

THESSALONÍKI: *Tiffany's*   €€
Iktínou 3, 54622. 📞 2310-274022.
This modern-style restaurant serves a wide selection of both Greek and international food. 🍽

| | ● | ▦ | | ▦ |

THESSALONÍKI: *Ta Nisiá*   €€€€
Proxénou Koromilá 13, 54623. 📞 2310-285991.
A popular spot, this taverna specializes in fresh fish and game dishes. Imaginative combinations, such as shrimp and bacon, and a good dessert menu are on offer. The walnut pie is a regular feature. ● dinner Sun. 🍽

| | ● | | | |

CORFU AND THE IONIAN ISLANDS

CORFU: *Rex*   €€
Kapodistríou 66, Corfu town. 📞 26610-39649.
Housed in a 19th-century town house, the Rex is a truly traditional Greek restaurant serving genuine Greek and Corfiot food. Specialties include swordfish *mpourdétto* – a spicy fish stew with peppers and potatoes. 🍽

| | ● | ▦ | | ▦ |

CORFU: *Tría Adélfia*   €€
Harborfront, Kassiópi. 📞 26630-81211.
Despite the increasing tourist trade, this restaurant retains its Greek atmosphere. The menu includes standard Greek fare such as moussaka and salads, while its fish is caught daily by the owner. ● Nov–Mar. 🍽

| | | ▦ | ● | ▦ |

CORFU: *Vráchos*   €€
Palaiokastrítsa beach. 📞 26630-41233.
This well-located taverna offers good, reliable food. The restaurant specializes in seafood, from lobster and swordfish to mullet. ● Nov–Mar. 🍽

| | | ▦ | | ▦ |

KEFALLONIÁ: *Dásos*   €€
Harborfront, Fiskárdo. 📞 26740-41276.
This restaurant serves fresh fish as well as a good example of the island specialty, Kefalloniá meat pie *(kreatópita)*. ● Oct–Mar. 🍽

| | | ▦ | | ▦ |

KEFALLONIÁ: *Patsoúras*   €€
Ioánnou Metaxá 40, Argostóli. 📞 26710-22779.
This small, family-run restaurant, also known as Perivoláki, has a pleasant garden and serves authentic island dishes such as *krasáto* (pork in wine) and the ubiquitous Kefalloniá meat pie. ● Nov, Easter Sun, Dec 25. 🍽

| | ● | ▦ | | ▦ |

ZÁKYNTHOS: *I Mantaléna*   €
Waterfront, 1 km (0.5 miles) E of Alykés. 📞 26950-83487.
A superb family-run restaurant that serves wine from the family vines and wonderful home-cooked dishes. ● main public hols; Oct–Apr: Mon–Fri.

| | | ▦ | | ▦ |

THE CYCLADES

MÝKONOS: *Antoníni's*   €€
Plateía Mantó, Mýkonos town. 📞 22890-22319.
For many this is the island's best eating place serving authentic Greek dishes at palatable prices. ● Nov–Mar.

| | | ▦ | | |

MÝKONOS: *Chez Katrin*   €€€€
Nikíou, Mýkonos town. 📞 22890-22169.
Commonly known as Bobby's and beloved by the locals, this is one of the island's oldest international restaurants, known for its French cuisine and delicious chocolate mousse. Reservations advisable. ● Nov–Apr. 🍽

| | ● | ▦ | | |

NÁXOS: *Oneiro*   €€€
Parapórti area, Náxos town. 📞 22850-23846.
Fine views from the roof garden, romantic candlelit tables, and an international menu make the Oneiro a good choice. ● lunch daily; Nov–Apr. 🍽

| | | ▦ | ● | ▦ |

SANTORÍNI: *Camille Stefaní* €€€
Kamári beach. 22860-31716.
This elegant restaurant is located by the beach and offers French-influenced
cuisine. The restaurant also has its own wine label. ● *Nov–Mar.*

SANTORÍNI: *Nikólas* €€€
Above central square, Firá. 22860-24550.
Long-established, traditional taverna in the heart of Firá, with
an authentic Greek menu, fresh fish, and wines from the barrel.

THE DODECANESE

KÁRPATHOS: *Kalí Kardiá* €
On road to Vróntis beach, Kárpathos town. 22450-22256.
This friendly Greek/American, family-run taverna is situated at the water's edge
and offers a good selection of oven dishes as well as fresh fish. ● *Oct–Mar.*

KOS: *Frangolis* €€
Plateía Arístonis, Kakó Prinári, Kos town. 22420-28761.
Considered one of the island's best traditional tavernas, the Frangolis
has an authentic Greek menu – rare in Kos town. Barbecued meat
and oven dishes can be sampled in the tree-shaded garden.

KOS: *O Plátanos* €€€
Plateía Plátanou, Kos town. 22420-28991.
Named after Hippocrates' plane tree, this café overlooks the ancient agora.
Classical music and cakes can be enjoyed under a shady canopy. ● *Nov–Apr.*

RHODES: *Bombay* €€
Agiou Fanouriou, Rhodes town. 22410-70527.
This restaurant is situated off a quiet cobbled street in the heart of the
old town. Authentic Indian dishes created by the Bangladeshi chef are
served in atmospheric surroundings. ● *lunch; Dec–Mar.*

RHODES: *Paliá Istoría* €€€
Mitropóleos 108, Ammos district, Rhodes town. 22410-32421.
This award-winning eatery offers Greek and Mediterranean dishes with a twist.
The imaginative and healthy creations range from beets with walnuts to lobster
spaghetti. Dine beneath the shady pergola. Reservations advisable. ● *lunch daily.*

CRETE

AGIOS NIKÓLAOS: *I Tráta* €€
Akti Pangálou 17. 28410-22028.
A fish taverna and grill house, the I Tráta offers fresh fish and meat grills,
as well as most traditional Greek dishes and Italian food, such as pizza.

CHANIÁ: *The Well of the Turk* €€
Kaliníkou Zarpáki 1–3. 28210-54547.
This cozy restaurant, with candlelit tables and eastern music, is set in a stone-
built cellar. Spicy, original-tasting food is on offer, including eggplant meatballs
and stuffed *kalamári* (squid). ● *Tue, lunch Sun; mid-Nov–mid-Dec: lunch daily.*

IRÁKLEIO: *O Kyriákos* €€
Leofóros Dimokratías 53. 2810-222464.
Traditional Cretan food can be enjoyed at this old restaurant
with a wooden interior. Customers select their dishes in the
kitchen and see how they are prepared. ● *dinner Wed; Jun–Sep.*

IRAKLEIO: *Loukoulos* €€€
Odos Korai 5. 2810-224435.
Fine architecture and luxurious décor make this an elegant restaurant. Listen
to classical music on the terrace while sampling the Mediterranean cuisine.

RÉTHYMNO: *O Goúnos* €
Koronaíou 6. 28310-28816.
Traditional Greek dishes such as rabbit *stifádo* (casserole) and goat soup are on
offer at this taverna, a 150-year old building. There is traditional dance in summer.

RÉTHYMNO: *Tavérna tou Kómpou* €
On Réthymno–Chaniá road. 28310-29725.
Cretan specialties such as *apátzia* (smoked pork sausages) and *glykádia*
(goat's meat) are served at this taverna with cozy alcoves and a fireplace. Meats
are charcoal-grilled and there is a tree-filled garden. *lunch daily; Nov–Apr: Mon.*

For key to symbols see back flap

GERMANY, AUSTRIA, AND SWITZERLAND

Germany, Austria, and Switzerland at a Glance

EUROPE'S THREE MAIN German-speaking countries occupy a broad swathe of Europe stretching from the Alps to the North Sea and the Baltic. Germany has many great cities, the former capitals of the small states that made up Germany under the Holy Roman Empire. It also has beautiful countryside, rivers, and forests. Austria's main attractions are the former imperial capital Vienna, the river Danube, and its mountains. More than half of Switzerland, which also has important French- and Italian-speaking regions, is mountainous, dominated by its permanently snow-capped Alpine peaks.

Lüb

Hamburg •

• Bremen

Hanover •

• Münster

GERMANY
(See pp520–58

• Düsseldorf
  Cologne   • Kasse

• Bonn
      Frankfurt
      am Main
Trier   Würzbur
      Mainz

• Stuttgar

The Rhine Valley (see pp558–9) *attracts hordes of visitors in summer, drawn by the beautiful scenery, medieval and mock-medieval castles, and Germany's finest white wines. You can either tour by car or take a river cruise from cities such as Mainz and Koblenz.*

• Freiburg
  am Breisgau
Basel •
      • Zürich
• BERN

SWITZERLAND
(See pp612–633)

• Geneva

The Swiss Alps (see pp619–24) *are a popular destination all year round: in winter for the skiing and other winter sports, in summer for the excellent walking or simply for the crisp, clean air and unrivaled scenery.*

Salzburg (see pp602–3) *trades on the legacy of Mozart, its most famous son, and stages one of the world's great music festivals. It also boasts a rich architectural heritage from the prince-archbishops who ruled the city from 1278 to 1816.*

◁ **Swiss lakeland scene, Interlaken**

Rostock

BERLIN

Magdeburg

Leipzig

Dresden

LOCATOR MAP

Berlin (see pp528–41), since 1990 once more the capital of a united Germany, combines relics of its imperial past, such as the Berliner Dom, with modern landmarks such as the towering Fernsehturm.

Munich (see pp546–54) is the cultural capital of southern Germany. It owes many of its great buildings and art collections to the kings of Bavaria. The city is also remarkable for its 18th-century churches, such as the astonishingly ornate Asamkirche.

mberg

Munich

Linz

VIENNA

Salzburg

AUSTRIA
(See pp586–611)

Innsbruck

Graz

0 kilometers   100

0 miles   100

Vienna (see pp590–99) was largely the the creation of the 18th- and 19th- century Habsburg emperors. More modern land-marks include the ferris wheel in the Prater funfair, immortalized in The Third Man, the 1949 film starring Orson Welles.

GERMANY

BY REPUTATION THE GERMANS *are a hard-working, efficient, competitive people and this is borne out by their recent economic success. However, Germany's turbulent, divided past and the centuries when it was a patchwork of many tiny states mean that there are profound regional differences, apparent in a wealth of fascinating historical sights and colorful local traditions.*

Thanks initially to American aid, industry and commerce boomed in West Germany following World War II. This so-called *Wirtschaftswunder* (economic miracle) made West Germany a dominant member of the European Economic Community (now the European Union). Demand for labor led to reliance on migrant workers or *Gastarbeiter* (guest workers). As a result, over 7 million immigrants now live in Germany, the largest number coming from Turkey, but many too from Italy, Greece, and increasingly the former Yugoslavia. In the manufacturing city of Stuttgart one inhabitant in three is an immigrant.

Despite its many industrial cities and a population of over 80 million, Germany is large enough to also possess a great variety of attractive rural landscapes. For many the Rhine epitomizes Germany, especially the romantic stretch between Mainz and Cologne. However, the country has much more to offer in the way of scenery, especially its forests, heaths, and mountains. In the far south the Alps are the major attraction, especially around Lake Constance (the Bodensee), the large lake that borders Austria and Switzerland.

History

Germanic tribes became established in the region sometime during the 1st millennium BC. They clashed with the Romans, defeating them in AD 9 at the Teutoburger forest. Thereafter the Romans fixed their frontier along the Rhine and the Danube. Although relations were often hostile, the Goths and other Germanic tribes traded and made alliances with Rome, and as the Roman Empire collapsed, these peoples carved out kingdoms of their own.

The dome of Berlin's Reichstag – home to the Bundestag (Federal Parliament)

◁ Neuschwanstein, King Ludwig II's theatrical castle in the Bavarian Alps

The people who eventually inherited the largest kingdom were the Franks, who conquered France and in the early 9th century, under Charlemagne, subdued most of the German tribes, including the Saxons, Swabians, and Bavarians. The pope gave his blessing to Charlemagne's overlordship, thus creating the Holy Roman Empire.

After Charlemagne, the German kingdom became separated from the rest of the empire. The next strong German ruler was the Saxon Otto I, who earned the title of emperor through his defeat of the Magyars in 955.

Frederick II (the Great), King of Prussia (1740–86)

The Middle Ages saw the development of a complicated feudal system with hundreds of dukedoms, counties, and ecclesiastical estates owing allegiance to the German emperor, as well as free "imperial cities." In the 11th and 12th centuries popes and emperors joined in a fierce struggle over who should grant lands,

appoint bishops, and collect revenues. Each would try to bribe the Electors *(Kurfürsten)* – princes and bishops who chose the emperor. The role of the Electors was clarified in the Golden Bull issued by Emperor Charles IV in 1356, but by the 16th century the position had become the more or less hereditary right of the Austrian Habsburgs.

The power of the church created many problems and it was no surprise that the Reformation began in Germany in 1517 with Martin Luther's *95 Theses* pointing out the abuses of the clergy. In the ensuing wars of religion, princes saw a chance to increase their lands at the expense of the Church. The Peace of Augsburg in 1555 established the principle *cuius regio eius religio* – each state followed the religion of its ruler. In the 17th century religious differences were again a major factor in the Thirty Years' War. Other countries, such as France and Sweden, joined the conflict, which laid waste most of Germany.

In the 17th and 18th centuries Germany remained a patchwork of small states, theoretically still part of the Habsburg Empire. However, Prussia gradually became a power to rival the Habsburgs. During the Enlightenment and Romantic periods German literature found its voice, especially in the dramas of Goethe and Schiller, and Napoleon's invasion of Germany sparked ideas of nationalism. In the mid-19th century it was Prussia that assumed the leadership of Germany through the skilful politics of Otto von Bismarck, the Prussian chancellor. After the Prussians had defeated the Austrians in 1866 and the French in 1870, the Second German Reich was declared with the Prussian King as Kaiser Wilhelm I.

Wilhelm's grandson Wilhelm II had great ambitions for the new empire and rivalry with Britain, France, and Russia plunged Europe into World War I. The humiliation of defeat and the terms of the Treaty of Versailles (1919) left

---

KEY DATES IN GERMAN HISTORY

5th century AD Germanic peoples overrun large parts of Roman Empire

c.750 Mission of St. Boniface to Germany

843 Charlemagne's empire divided; Louis the German rules lands east of the Rhine

962 Otto I crowned emperor

1074 Pope Gregory VII and Emperor Heinrich IV clash over investiture of bishops

1155 Frederick Barbarossa crowned Emperor

13th century North German Hanseatic League starts to dominate trade in Baltic region

1356 Golden Bull establishes role of Electors

1517 Martin Luther attaches his *95 Theses* to the door of a church in Wittenberg

1555 Peace of Augsburg ends religious wars

1618–48 Germany ravaged by Thirty Years' War

1740–86 Reign of Frederick the Great

1806 Napoleon abolishes Holy Roman Empire

1871 German Empire proclaimed

1914–18 World War I

1933 End of Weimar Republic; Hitler comes to power

1939–45 World War II: after Germany's defeat country divided into West and East

1990 Reunification of Germany

Germany in economic chaos. The Weimar Republic struggled on until 1933 when Hitler seized power. His nationalist policies appealed to a demoralized people, but his territorial ambitions led the country into World War II and a second defeat.

Despite the atrocities committed by the Nazis, the Germans were soon forgiven by both America and Russia as they divided the country in such a way that it became the theater for the Cold War between East and West. The Berlin Wall erected in 1961 to stop East Germans fleeing to the West became the symbol of an era. Its fall in 1989 was the start of the process of reunification.

Modern Germany, the Bundesrepublik, is a federal country, with each *Land* (state) electing its own parliament. Regional differences due to Germany's checkered history are still much in evidence, the Catholic south being much more conservative than the north. Differences between the former West Germany and the old DDR (East Germany) are also very visible. The East suffers from high unemployment and its people tend to be suspicious of the motives of the West Germans, despite all the money poured into the region to equalize living standards.

Celebrating the fall of the Berlin Wall in 1989

Of all the arts it is to classical music that Germany has made the greatest contribution, Johann Sebastian Bach from the Baroque period and Ludwig van Beethoven from the Romantic period being perhaps the two most influential figures. In the 19th century poems by Goethe, Schiller, and others were set to music by composers Robert Schumann, Johannes Brahms, and Hugo Wolf.

Germany has also produced many of the world's most influential philosophers: from Immanuel Kant (1724–1804), father of modern philosophy, to Karl Marx (1818–83), founder of the 20th century's most potent political ideology.

CULTURE AND THE ARTS

Germany is rich in legends and sagas, such as the tale of Siegfried told in the epic poem the *Nibelungenlied*, written down around 1200. It has been reworked many times, notably in Richard Wagner's great *Ring* opera cycle.

MODERN LIFE

The German economy tends to be dominated by long-established giants such as Siemens in the electrical and electronic sectors, Volkswagen and BMW in cars, and Hoechst in chemicals. Despite the continuing success of German industry and banking, and the people's reputation for hard work, the Germans actually enjoy longer annual holidays and spend more money on foreign travel than any other European nation. When at home they are enthusiastic participants in many sports, and have enjoyed great success in recent years at football, motor racing, and tennis. They also enjoy gregarious public merrymaking, for example at *Fasching* (carnival) and the Oktoberfest, Munich's annual beer festival.

Munich's Olympic Stadium, created for the 1972 Olympic Games

Exploring Germany

Visitors in search of classical German landscapes flock
to the Black Forest, the Rhine Valley, and the Bavarian
Alps. The attractive German countryside is easily accessed
thanks to the best road network in Europe. Of the cities,
the most popular destinations are the capital Berlin, a
vibrant metropolis in a state of transition since
reunification in 1990, and Munich, the historic
former capital of the Kingdom of Bavaria. East
Germany, now open for tourism, has many
attractions to draw visitors – particularly the
city of Dresden, rebuilt after World War II.

SIGHTS AT A GLANCE

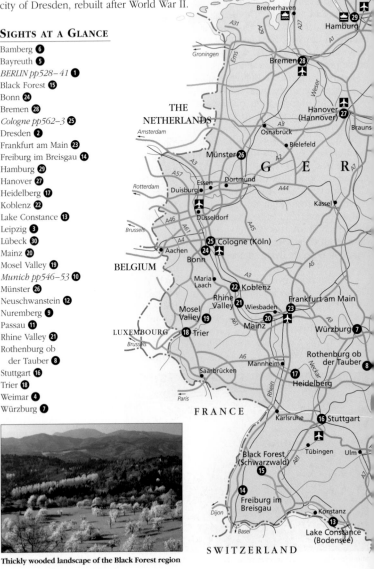

Thickly wooded landscape of the Black Forest region

DISTANCE CHART

Distance in kilometers
Distance in miles

BERLIN								
574 356	COLOGNE							
198 123	**629** 390	DRESDEN						
540 335	**189** 117	**511** 317	FRANKFURT					
285 177	**431** 268	**483** 300	**495** 307	HAMBURG				
288 179	**294** 183	**376** 233	**354** 220	**156** 97	HANOVER			
585 363	**590** 366	**474** 294	**400** 248	**781** 485	**616** 382	MUNICH		
415 258	**415** 258	**304** 189	**231** 143	**585** 363	**441** 274	**170** 105	NUREMBERG	
629 397	**374** 232	**522** 324	**208** 129	**652** 405	**508** 315	**231** 143	**218** 135	STUTTGART

SEE ALSO

• **Practical Information** pp566–7

• **Travel Information** pp568–9

• **Shopping** pp570–71

• **Entertainment** pp572–3

• **Where to Stay** pp574–9

• **Where to Eat** pp580–85

Kaiser-Wilhelm-Gedächtniskirche with its octagonal extension and bell tower, Berlin

KEY

✈ Airport

⛴ Ferry port

— Highway

— Major road

— Railroad

--- International border

Berlin ①

Since becoming the capital of the Federal Republic of Germany following reunification in 1990, Berlin has become an ever popular destination for visitors. The historic heart of the city is located around the wide avenue Unter den Linden, with its grand Baroque and Neoclassical monuments, and on Museum Island, which takes its name from the fine museums built there in the 19th and early 20th centuries. South of Unter den Linden is Checkpoint Charlie, a legacy of Berlin's status as a divided city during the Cold War. To the west are the green open spaces of Tiergarten and Kurfürstendamm, the center of the former West Berlin. Farther afield, the splendid palaces of Potsdam, now almost a suburb of Berlin, are not to be missed.

The grand approach to the 18th-century Rococo Schloss Sanssouci in Potsdam

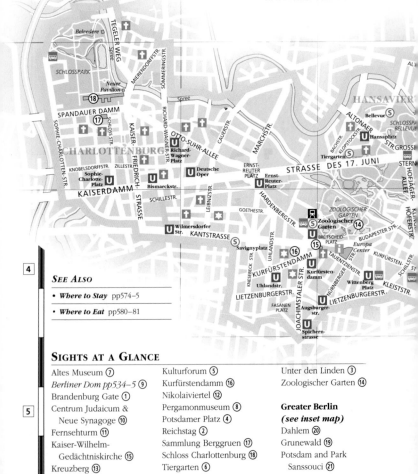

See Also

- **Where to Stay** pp574–5
- **Where to Eat** pp580–81

Sights at a Glance

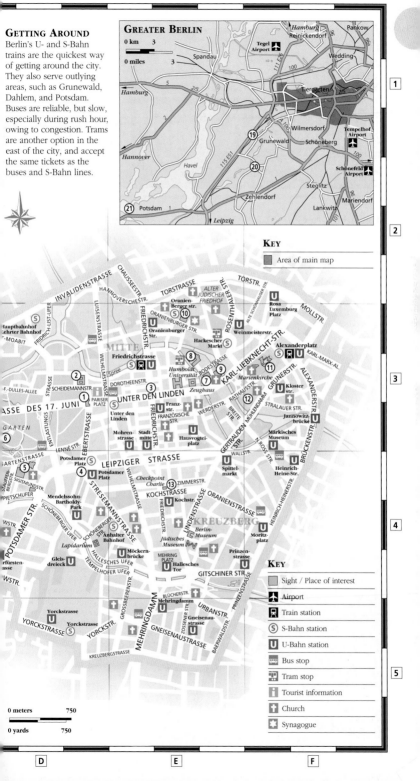

GETTING AROUND

Berlin's U- and S-Bahn trains are the quickest way of getting around the city. They also serve outlying areas, such as Grunewald, Dahlem, and Potsdam. Buses are reliable, but slow, especially during rush hour, owing to congestion. Trams are another option in the east of the city, and accept the same tickets as the buses and S-Bahn lines.

GREATER BERLIN

0 km 3

0 miles 3

KEY

Area of main map

KEY

Sight / Place of interest

✈ Airport

🚉 Train station

Ⓢ S-Bahn station

Ⓤ U-Bahn station

🚌 Bus stop

🚊 Tram stop

ℹ Tourist information

✝ Church

✡ Synagogue

0 meters 750

0 yards 750

The imposing Brandenburg Gate in Pariser Platz, at the western end of Unter den Linden

Brandenburg Gate ①

Pariser Platz. **Ⓢ** *Unter den Linden.* 🚌 *100.*

THE BRANDENBURG GATE is the quintessential symbol of Berlin. This magnificent Neo-classical structure was designed by Carl Gotthard Langhans and modeled on the Propylaia of the Acropolis in Athens *(see p478)*. It was erected between 1788 and 1791, although the sculptural decorations were not completed until 1795. Pavilions frame its simple Doric colonnade, and bas-reliefs on the entablature above the columns depict scenes from Greek myth. The structure is crowned by the famous sculpture of a *quadriga* – a chariot drawn by four horses – designed by Johann Gottfried Schadow.

The Brandenburg Gate has witnessed many important historical events. Military parades and demonstrating workers have marched under its arches, and it was the site of celebrations marking the birth of the Second Reich in 1871. It was here, too, that the Soviet flag was raised in 1945.

Restored between 1956 and 1958, for the next 30 years the gate stood watch over the divided city, until the fall of the Berlin Wall in 1989. It was renovated once again in 2002.

Reichstag ②

Platz der Republik. **Ⓢ** *Unter den Linden.* 🚌 *100, 200, 248, 257.* 📞 *030-2273 5908.* **Dome & Assembly Hall** ☐ *daily.* ● *Jan 1, Dec 24, 26 & 31.* ▱

BUILT TO HOUSE the German Parliament, the Reichstag was intended as a symbol of national unity and to showcase the aspirations of the new German Empire, declared in 1871. Constructed between 1884 and 1894, the Neo-Renaissance building by Paul Wallot captured the prevailing spirit of German optimism. On the night of February 28, 1933, a fire destroyed the main hall. Rebuilding work undertaken between 1957 and 1972 removed the dome and most of the ornamentation on the façades. On December 2, 1990, the Reichstag was the first meeting place of a newly-elected Bundestag following German reunification.

The latest rebuilding project, completed in 1999 to a design by Sir Norman Foster, transformed the Reichstag into a modern meeting hall crowned by an elliptical glass dome.

Unter den Linden ③

Ⓢ *Unter den Linden.* 🚌 *100, 157, 200, 348.*

ONE OF THE MOST famous streets in Berlin, Unter den Linden was once the route to the royal hunting grounds that were transformed into the Tiergarten. In the 17th century it was planted with lime trees, to which it owes its name.

In the 18th century, Unter den Linden became the main street of the westward-growing city. It gradually filled with prestigious buildings, such as the Baroque **Zeughaus**, home of the Deutsches Historisches Museum, and the **Humboldt Universität** (1753). Next door, the **Neue Wache** (1816–1818) commemorates the victims of war and dictatorship.

Since reunification, Unter den Linden has acquired several cafés and restaurants, as well as many smart new shops. The street is also the venue for many outdoor events.

The Reichstag, crowned by a dome designed by Sir Norman Foster

Potsdamer Platz ④

U **S** *Potsdamer Platz.*

BEFORE THE ONSET of World War II, Potsdamer Platz was one of the busiest and most densely built-up areas of Berlin. Most of the area's landmarks ceased to exist after the bombing of 1945, and the destruction was completed when the burned-out ruins were finally pulled down to build the Berlin Wall.

Since the mid-1990s a new financial and business district has sprung up on this empty wasteland, which once divided East and West Berlin. The huge new complex comprises not only office buildings, but also a concert hall, a multi-screen cinema, and the Arkaden shopping mall. The first finished structure was the Daimler-Benz-Areal office block, designed by Renzo Piano and Christoph Kohlbecker. To the north lies the impressive Sony-Center complex, by Helmut Jahn.

Silver and ivory tankard from the Kunstgewerbemuseum

Kulturforum ⑤

U **S** *Potsdamer Platz.* **C** *030-2090 5555.* **Kunstgewerbemuseum** ▢ *Tue–Sun.* ● *first Tue after Easter, Whitsun, Oct 1, Dec 24, 25 & 31.* **Gemäldegalerie** ▢ *Tue–Sun.* ● *first Tue after Easter, Whitsun, May 1, Dec 24, 25 & 31.* **Neue Nationalgalerie** ▢ *Tue–Sun.*

THE IDEA OF creating a new cultural center in West Berlin was first mooted in 1956. The first building to go up was the

Philharmonie (Berlin Philharmonic concert hall), built to an innovative design by Hans Scharoun in 1961. Most of the other plans for the Kulturforum were realized between 1961 and 1987. With many museums and galleries, the area attracts millions of visitors every year.

The **Kunstgewerbe-museum** (Museum of Arts and Crafts) holds a rich collection of decorative art and crafts dating from the early Middle Ages to the modern day. Goldwork is very well represented, and the museum takes great pride in its late Gothic and Renaissance silver.

The **Gemälde-galerie** fine art collection is in a modern building designed by Heinz Hilmer and Christopher Sattler. Works by German Renaissance artists, including Albrecht Dürer and Hans Holbein, dominate the exhibition space, but there are also pieces by van Dyck, Rembrandt, Raphael, Velázquez, and Caravaggio.

Housed in a striking building with a flat steel roof over a glass hall, the **Neue National-galerie** contains mainly 20th-century art, but begins with artists of the late 19th century, such as Edvard Munch and Ferdinand Hodler. Paintings from the *Die Brücke* movement include pieces by Ernst Ludwig Kirchner and Karl Schmidt-Rottluff. Also on display are works by Picasso, Léger, Dalí, Magritte, and Max Ernst.

A tranquil stretch of water in Berlin's 19th-century Tiergarten

Tiergarten ⑥

S *Tiergarten, Bellevue.* ▦ *100, 187, 341.*

THE TIERGARTEN is the largest park in Berlin. Situated at the geographical center of the city, it occupies a 200-ha (495-acre) area. Once the Elector's hunting reserve, the forest was transformed into a landscaped park by Peter Joseph Lenné in the 1830s. A triumphal avenue was built at the end of the 19th century, lined with statues of the nation's rulers and statesmen.

World War II inflicted huge damage on the Tiergarten, including the destruction of the triumphal avenue, many of whose surviving monuments can now be seen in the Lapidarium in Kreuzberg (*see p536*). Replanting has restored the Tiergarten, and many of its avenues are now lined with statues of national celebrities, including Goethe and Wagner.

The Philharmonie, with the later addition of the Kammermusiksaal (1984–7) in front, at Kulturforum

Mosaic from Hadrian's Villa (2nd century AD), at the Altes Museum

Altes Museum ⑦

Am Lustgarten. 📞 030-2090 5555.
Ⓢ Hackescher Markt. 🚌 100, 157,
348. 🕐 Tue–Sun. 📷

THE ALTES MUSEUM, designed
by Karl Friedrich Schinkel,
is undoubtedly one of the
world's most beautiful Neoclassical structures, with an
impressive 87-m (285-ft) high
portico supported by Ionic
columns. The stately rotunda
is decorated with sculptures
and ringed by a colonnade.

Officially opened in 1830,
this was one of the first
purpose-built museums in
Europe, designed to house
the royal collection of
paintings and antiquities.
Following World War II, the
building was used to display
temporary exhibitions. Since
1998 the Altes Museum has
housed a portion of the
Antikensammlung, a magnificent collection of Greek and
Roman antiquities. Among the

highlights of the collection are
a colorful floor mosaic from
Hadrian's Villa near Tivoli, and
Perikles' Head, a Roman copy
of the sculpture by Kresilas
that stood at the entrance to
the Acropolis in Athens.

Pergamonmuseum ⑧

Bodestrasse 1–3 (entrance from Am
Kupfergraben). 📞 030-2090 5555.
Ⓢ Hackescher Markt, Friedrich-
strasse. 🚌 100, 147, 257, 348.
🕐 Tue–Sun. ● Jan 1, first Tue after
Easter and Pentecost, Dec 24, 25 &
31. 📷 ♿

BUILT BETWEEN 1912 and 1930
to a design by Alfred
Messel and Ludwig Hoffmann,
the Pergamonmuseum is one
of Berlin's major attractions.
The museum's three large
independent collections, the
result of extensive archaeological excavations, form one
of the most famous collections
of antiquities in Europe.

The highlight of Berlin's
collection of Greek and Roman
antiquities (Antikensammlung)
is the huge Pergamon Altar
from the acropolis of ancient
Pergamon in Asia Minor. This
magnificently restored altar,
which gives the museum its
name, is thought to have
been commissioned by King
Eumenes in 160 BC. Roman
architecture is represented by
the market gate from the
Roman city of Miletus, which
dates from the 2nd century BC.

Major excavations begun in
the 1820s form the basis of a
royal collection at the Museum
of Near Eastern Antiquities
(Vorderasiatisches Museum).
One striking exhibit is the
splendid Ishtar Gate, built
during the reign of
Nebuchadnezzar II
(604–562 BC) in
ancient Babylon.
Also on display
are pieces from
the neighboring
regions of Persia,
Syria, and Pales-
tine, including a
basalt sculpture of
a bird from Tel
Halaf and a glazed
wall relief of a
spear-bearer from
Artaxerxes II's
palace in Susa,
capital of the   **Persian relief,**
Persian Empire.   **Pergamon-**
  The history of   **museum**
the Museum of
Islamic Art (Museum für
Islamische Kunst) begins in
1904 when Wilhelm von Bode
donated his extensive
collection of carpets. He also
brought to Berlin a 45-m
(150-ft) long section of the
façade of a Jordanian desert
palace, dating from the Oma-
yyad period (AD 661–750).
Another fascinating exhibit is
a beautiful 13th-century
mihrab (Islamic prayer
niche). Made in the Iranian
town of Kashan, the *mihrab*
is covered in lustrous metallic
glazed tiles. The collection's
many carpets come from as
far afield as Iran, Asia Minor,
Egypt, and the Caucasus.

Berliner Dom ⑨

Relief carving of Athena from the Pergamon Altar, Pergamonmuseum

See pp534–5.

The splendidly reconstructed gilded domes of the Neue Synagoge

Centrum Judaicum & Neue Synagoge ⑩

Oranienburger Strasse 29 & 30. 🇨 *030-2840 1316 (Centrum Judaicum)*. Ⓢ *Oranienburger Strasse.* 🚋 *1, 13.* 🚌 *157.* ⬚ *Sun–Thu, am Fri.* ⬤ *Jewish festivals.* 🔲

OCCUPYING THE former premises of the Jewish community council, the Centrum Judaicum contains an extensive library, archives, and a research center all devoted to the history and cultural heritage of Berlin's Jews. Next door, the restored rooms of the Neue Synagoge are used as a museum, exhibiting material relating to the local Jewish community.

The building of the New Synagogue was started in 1859 and completed in 1866. The narrow façade is flanked by a pair of towers and crowned with a dome containing a round vestibule. Now in use again for services, the synagogue's main hall has space for 3,000 worshipers.

This fascinating structure was Berlin's largest synagogue. However, on November 9, 1938, it was partially destroyed during the infamous "*Kristallnacht*" ("Night of the Broken Glass"), when thousands of synagogues, cemeteries, and Jewish homes and shops all over Germany were looted and burned. The building was damaged further by Allied bombing in 1943, and was finally demolished in 1958. Reconstruction began in 1988 and was completed in 1995.

Fernsehturm ⑪

Panoramastrasse. 🇺 Ⓢ *Alexanderplatz.* 🚌 *100, 157.* ⬚ *daily.*

KNOWN AS the *Telespargel*, or toothpick, by the locals, this 365-m (1,197-ft) high television mast soars above the massive Alexanderplatz. It is the second tallest structure in Europe – only the Palace of Culture in Warsaw (*see p752*) is taller.

The concrete shaft contains elevators that carry passengers to the viewing platform. Situated inside a steel-clad giant sphere, this platform is 203 m (666 ft) above the ground. Visitors can also enjoy the revolving café, from where it is possible to get a bird's-eye view of the whole city while sipping a cup of coffee. Visibility can reach up to 40 km (25 miles).

Nikolaiviertel ⑫

🇺 *Alexanderplatz, Klosterstrasse.* Ⓢ *Alexanderplatz.* 🚌 *100, 142, 157, 257, 348.*

THIS SMALL AREA on the bank of the Spree, known as the Nikolaiviertel (St. Nicholas Quarter), is a favorite strolling ground for both Berliners and tourists. Some of Berlin's oldest houses stood here until they were destroyed in World War II. The redevelopment of the area, carried out between

Berlin's massive Fernsehturm, towering over the city

1979 and 1987, proved to be an interesting, if somewhat controversial, attempt at recreating a medieval village.

Today the area consists mostly of newly built replicas of historic buildings. The narrow streets are filled with small shops, cafés, bars, and restaurants, among them the popular Zum Nussbaum, a historical inn that was once located on Fischer Island. Dating from 1507, the original building was destroyed, and subsequently reconstructed at the junction of Am Nussbaum and Propststrasse.

Riverside buildings of the Nikolaiviertel

Berliner Dom ⑨

Royal crest of Friedrich III

THIS PROTESTANT CATHEDRAL was built by Johann Bormann between 1747 and 1750 on the site of a Dominican church. It incorporated the crypt of the Hohenzollern dynasty, which ruled the city for nearly 500 years, and is one of the largest of its kind in Europe. The present Neo-Baroque structure is the work of Julius Raschdorff and dates from 1894–1905. The central copper dome reaches 98 m (322 ft), with an inner cupola which is 70 m (230 ft) high. Following severe damage sustained in World War II, the building has been restored in a simplified form, including the dismantling of the Hohenzollern memorial chapel, which originally adjoined the northern wall.

Philipp der Grossmütige
At the base of the arcade stand statues of church reformers and princes who supported the Reformation. The statue of Philip the Magnanimous, Landgrave of Hesse (1509–67) is the work of Walter Schott.

Figures of the Apostles

★ Church Interior
The impressive, richly-decorated interior was designed by Julius Raschdorff at the turn of the 20th century.

Sauer's Organ
The organ, the work of Wilhelm Sauer, is set against an exquisitely carved backdrop.

Main entrance

★ Elector's Tomb
This tomb is the oldest in the cathedral, dating from c.1530. It was commissioned from the Vischer studio in Nuremberg by Joachim II for his grandfather, Elector Johann Cicero.

The Four Evangelists
Mosaics depicting the Four Evangelists decorate the ceilings of the smaller niches in the cathedral. They were designed by Woldemar Friedrich.

VISITORS' CHECKLIST

Am Lustgarten. 📞 030-20 26 91
19. Ⓢ Hackescher Markt.
🚌 100, 157, 200, 348. ⏰
9am–8pm Mon–Sat, noon–8pm
Sun. 🎫 ✝ 10am & 6pm Sun.

The Ascension
The stained glass in the windows of the apses, designed by Anton von Werner, shows scenes from the life of Jesus.

The main altar, saved from the previous cathedral, is the work of Friedrich August Stüler and dates from 1850.

Pulpit
This elaborate Neo-Baroque pulpit is part of the cathedral's ornate decor dating from the early 20th century.

★ Sarcophagi of Friedrich I and his Wife
Both of these were designed by Andreas Schlüter. The sculpture on Sophie Charlotte's sarcophagus depicts death.

STAR FEATURES

★ Elector's Tomb

★ Church Interior

★ Sarcophagi of Friedrich I and his Wife

Kreuzberg ⑬

Checkpoint Charlie Friedrichstrasse 43–45. **C** 030-253 7250.
U Kochstrasse. 129. **O** 9am–10pm daily. **Jüdisches Museum** Lindenstrasse 14. **U** Hallesches Tor, Kochstrasse. 240. **C** 030-259 933. **O** 10am–10pm Mon, 10am–8pm Tue–Sun.

KREUZBERG IS an area of contrasts, with luxury apartments next to dilapidated buildings. The district's attractions are its wealth of restaurants and Turkish bazaars, as well as a wide selection of theaters, cinemas, and galleries.

Checkpoint Charlie was once the notorious border crossing between the Soviet and American sectors, and witness to a number of dramatic events during the Cold War. The museum close by, Haus am Checkpoint Charlie, houses exhibits connected with the ingenious attempts by East Germans to escape to the West.

The imaginative architecture of the **Jüdisches Museum**, dedicated to Jewish history and art, conveys something of the tragic history of the millions of Jews who lost their lives in the Holocaust. The zigzag layout recalls a torn Star of David, while the interior arrangement is dominated by a long empty area, which symbolizes the void left in Europe by the exile and murder of countless thousands of Jews.

Berlin Wall sculpture at entrance to Haus am Checkpoint Charlie

Zoologischer Garten, home to over 1,400 animal species

Zoologischer Garten ⑭

Hardenbergplatz 8 or Budapester Strasse 34. **C** 030-254 010.
U S Zoologischer Garten. 100, 109, 145, 146 & many others. **O** daily.

THE ZOOLOGICAL GARDEN forms part of the Tiergarten and dates from 1844, making it the oldest zoo in Germany. It offers a number of attractions, including the monkey house, which contains a family of gorillas, and a specially darkened pavilion for observing nocturnal animals. The hippopotamus pool has a glazed wall that enables visitors to watch these enormous creatures moving through the water. The aquarium, one of the largest in Europe, contains sharks, piranhas, and unusual animals from coral reefs. There is also a huge terrarium with an overgrown jungle that is home to a group of crocodiles.

Kaiser-Wilhelm-Gedächtniskirche ⑮

Breitscheidplatz. **C** 030-218 5023.
U Zoologischer Garten, Kurfürstenstrasse. **S** Zoologischer Garten. 100, 119, 129, 146, X-9.
Gedenkhalle O Mon–Sat.

THE DAMAGED ROOF of this former church has become one of the best-known symbols of postwar Berlin. The vast Neo-Romanesque building was consecrated in 1895, but was destroyed by bombs in 1943. After World War II the ruins were removed, leaving only the massive front tower, at the base of which the Gedenkhalle (Memorial Hall) is situated. This hall documents the history of the church and contains some of the original ceiling mosaics, marble reliefs, and liturgical objects. The latter include the Coventry Crucifix, a modest cross fashioned from nails found in the ashes of Coventry Cathedral, England, which was destroyed in the bombing raids of the 1940s.

In 1963, Egon Eiermann designed a new octagonal church in blue glass. His hexagonal bell tower stands on the site of the former nave of the destroyed church.

New and old bell towers of the Kaiser-Wilhelm-Gedächtniskirche

**A bustling outdoor café
on the Kurfürstendamm**

Kurfürstendamm ⑯

🇺 *Kurfürstendamm.* 🚌 *109, 119,
129, 219.*

Tʜɪs ᴡɪᴅᴇ ᴀᴠᴇɴᴜᴇ was
established in the 1880s on
the site of a former track that
led to the Grunewald forest
(*see p538*). It quickly acquired
many imposing buildings and
grand hotels. In the 20 years
between World Wars I and II,
the Ku'damm, as it is popularly
called, was renowned for its
cafés, visited by famous film
directors, writers, and painters.

After World War II, the
damaged houses were replaced
with modern buildings, but
this did not change the
character of the finest street
in West Berlin. Elegant shops
and cafés with pretty summer
gardens attract a chic crowd.

Sammlung
Berggruen ⑰

Schlossstrasse 1. 📞 *030-3269 5815.*
🇺 *Richard-Wagner-Platz, Sophie-
Charlotte-Platz.* Ⓢ *Westend.* 🚌 *109,
110, 145, X-21, X-26.* 🔲
10am–6pm Tue–Sun. 📷 🚻 ♿

Hᴇɪɴᴢ ʙᴇʀɢɢʀᴜᴇɴ assembled
this tasteful collection of
art dating from the late 19th
and first half of the 20th
centuries. Opened in 1996,
the museum is particularly
well-known for its impressive
array of paintings, drawings,
and gouaches by Pablo
Picasso. There is also a display
of more than 20 works by
Paul Klee and paintings by Van
Gogh, Braque, and Cézanne.
The exhibition is supplemented
by some excellent sculptures.

Schloss
Charlottenburg ⑱

Spandauer Damm. 📞 *030-3209
1275.* 🇺 *Richard-Wagner-Platz,
Sophie-Charlotte-Platz.* Ⓢ *Westend.*
🚌 *109, 110, 145, X-26.* 🔲 *Tue–Sun.*
📷 *compulsory on ground floor.* 📷

Tʜᴇ ᴘᴀʟᴀᴄᴇ in Charlottenburg
was intended as a summer
residence for Sophie Charlotte,
Elector Friedrich III's wife.
Construction began in 1695 to
a design by Johann Arnold
Nering. Between 1701 and
1713 the palace was enlarged,
and a Baroque cupola and
an orangery were added.
Subsequent extensions were
undertaken by Frederick the
Great (King Friedrich II), who
added the Neuer Flügel (New
Wing) between 1740 and 1746.

Restored to its former
elegance after World War II,
the palace's richly decorated
interior is unequalled in Berlin.
In the central section of the
palace, the mirrored gallery of
the Porzellankabinett has
walls lined with fine Japanese
and Chinese porcelain.

The Neuer Flügel, the new
wing of the palace, used to
house the popular Galerie der
Romantik. It is currently being
renovated, and will reopen in
2005 as the Hohenzollern-
Museum. This will present a
wide variety of precious items
from Germany's imperial
family, the Hohenzollern.

The Neoclassical pavilion
that houses the **Museum für
Vor- und Frühgeschichte**,
a museum of pre- and early
history, was added to the
orangery wing in 1787–91.

The park surrounding the
palace is one of the most
picturesque places in Berlin.
Among the many fine
monuments dotted around
the grounds are the charming
Neoclassical **Neuer Pavilion**
(New Pavilion), whose
interior is furnished in period
style, and the **Belvedere**
(1788), housing a large
collection of porcelain.

Central tower and 18th-century cupola of Schloss Charlottenburg

Restaurant in the Forsthaus Paulsborn in the Grunewald

Grunewald ⑲

Ⓢ *Grunewald.* 🚌 *115.* **Jagdschloss Grunewald.** 📞 *030-813 3597.* 🕐 *May 15–Oct 15: Tue–Sun.*

JUST A SHORT S-Bahn ride from central Berlin lie the vast forests of the Grunewald, bordering some of the city's most elegant suburbs. Once the haunt of politicians, wealthy industrialists, and renowned artists, some of the villas here now serve as the headquarters of Berlin's academic institutes.

On the shore of the picturesque Grunewaldsee stands the **Jagdschloss Grunewald**, one of the oldest civic buildings in Berlin. Built by Elector Joachim II in 1542, it was rebuilt in the Baroque style around 1700. Inside the small palace is Berlin's only surviving Renaissance hall, which houses canvases by Rubens and van Dyck among others. In the east wing is the small Waldmuseum, with various illustrations depicting forest life. It is currently being restored after nearly burning down in 2003.

Opposite the Jagdschloss, the **Jagdmuseum** (Hunting Museum) holds displays of historic hunting equipment.

To the southwest of the Grunewaldsee is **Forsthaus Paulsborn**. This picturesque hunting lodge, which now houses a very good restaurant, was constructed in 1905.

Dahlem ⑳

Ⓤ *Dahlem Dorf.* 🚌 *110, 183, X-11, X-83.* **Museumszentrum** 📞 *030-20 90 55 55.* 🕐 *Tue–Sun.*

FIRST MENTIONED in 1275, by the 19th century Dahlem had grown from a small village into an affluent, tranquil city suburb. At the beginning of the 20th century, a number of museums, designed by Bruno Paul, were built. They were extended considerably in the 1960s, when the **Museumszentrum** was created to rival East Berlin's Museum Island (*see pp532–4*).

Highlights from this cluster of museums include bronzes from Benin in West Africa and gold Inca jewelry from South America at the Ethnologisches Museum (Museum of Ethnography). The other collections range from the Museum für Indische Kunst (Museum of Indian Art) and the Museum für Ostasiatische Kunst (Museum of Far Eastern Art), to the Nordamerica Ausstellung (Exhibition of Native North American Cultures).

Not far from the Museumszentrum, the **Museum Europäischer Kulturen** specializes in European folk art and culture. Among the exhibits you can expect to see are earthenware items, costumes, jewelry, toys, and tools.

Domäne Dahlem is a rare oasis of country life in the Berlin suburbs. Part of the Stadtmuseum Berlin (Museum of the City of Berlin), the Baroque manor house (c.1680) boasts splendid period interiors, while the 19th-century farm buildings hold a collection of agricultural tools.

The elegant Functionalist building occupied by the **Brücke-Museum** was built by Werner Düttmann in 1966–7. The museum houses a collection of German Expressionist paintings by members of the artistic group known as *Die Brücke*.

The combined museum and working farm of Domäne Dahlem

Potsdam and Park Sanssouci ㉑

A N INDEPENDENT CITY close to Berlin, Potsdam has almost 150,000 inhabitants and is the capital of Brandenburg. The first documented reference to the town dates from AD 993; it was later granted municipal rights in 1317. The town blossomed in the 1600s, during the era of the Great Elector, and then again in the 18th century, when the splendid summer palace, Schloss Sanssouci, was built for Frederick the Great. Potsdam suffered badly in World War II, particularly on April 14 and 15, 1945, when the Allies bombed the town's center.

VISITORS' CHECKLIST

Brandenburg. 🚇 150,000.
🚉 from Bahnhof Zoo, Berlin
to Potsdam-Stadt. Ⓢ 🚊 🚍
ℹ Friedrich-Ebertstrasse 5
(0331-27 55 80) or Am Neuen
Markt 1.

A Russian-style wooden house in the charming Alexandrowka district

Exploring Potsdam

Despite its wartime losses, today Potsdam is one of Germany's most attractive towns. Tourists flock to see the magnificent royal estate, Park Sanssouci (*see pp540–41*), to stroll in the Neuer Garten, which boasts its own grand palaces, and to see the pretty Alexandrowka district and the historic Dutch quarter.

🏛 Marmorpalais

Am Ufer des Heiligen Sees (Neuer Garten). 📞 0331-969 4246.
🚍 695. ◯ May 15– Oct 31:
Tue–Sun; Nov 1–May 14: Sat & Sun.
The Marmorpalais (Marble Palace) is located on the edge of the lake in the Neuer Garten, a park northeast of Potsdam's center. Completed in 1791, the grand Neoclassical building owes its name to the Silesian marble that decorates its façade. The rooms in the main part of the palace contain Neoclassical furnishings from the late 18th century, including Wedgwood porcelain and furniture from the workshops of Roentgen. The concert hall in the right wing, whose interior dates from the 1840s, is particularly impressive.

🏛 Schloss Cecilienhof

Am Neuen Garten. 📞 0331-969
4244. 🚍 695. ◯ Apr–Oct:
Tue–Sun; Nov–Mar: Tue–Sun.
Schloss Cecilienhof was built for the Hohenzollern family between 1914 and 1917. In July 1945 the palace played an important role in history, when it served as the venue for the Potsdam Conference – an event that played a major part in establishing the political balance of power in Europe following the end of World War II.

🏛 Alexandrowka

Russische Kolonie Allee/ Puschkinallee.
🚍 138, 604, 609, 650, 692, 697.
🚊 92, 95.
A trip to Alexandrowka, in the northeast of the city, takes the visitor into the world of Pushkin's fairy tales. Wooden log cabins, set in their own gardens, form a charming residential estate. The houses were built in 1826 for singers in a Russian choir established to entertain military troops. Peter Joseph Lenné was responsible for the overall appearance of the estate, named after the Tsarina, the Prussian Princess Charlotte.

🏛 Holländisches Viertel

Friedrich-Ebertstrasse/ Kurfürsten-strasse/ Hebbelstrasse/ Gutenberg-strasse. 🚍 138, 601, 602, 603, 604 & many others.
The Dutch Quarter attracts crowds of tourists, with numerous stores, galleries, cafés, and beer cellars, especially along Mittelstrasse. The area was built up in the first half of the 18th century, when Dutch workers, invited by Friedrich Wilhelm I, began to settle in Potsdam. Today, you can still see the pretty red-brick, gabled houses that were built for them.

🏛 Filmpark Babelsberg

Grossbeerenstrasse. 📞 0331-721
2750. ◯ Mar 16–Nov 2: daily. 🎬
This amazing film park was laid out on the site of the film studios where Germany's first movies were made in 1912. From 1917, the studios belonged to Universum-Film-AG, which produced some of the most renowned movies of the silent era, such as Fritz Lang's futuristic *Metropolis* (1927) and films starring Marlene Dietrich and Greta Garbo. Later, Nazi propaganda films were also made here. The studio is still in operation today, but part of the complex is open to the public. Visitors can see old film sets, exciting special effects demonstrations, and stuntmen in action.

Original film prop on display at the Filmpark Babelsberg

Park Sanssouci

T HE ENORMOUS PARK SANSSOUCI, occupying an area of 287 hectares (709 acres), is among the most beautiful palace complexes in Europe. The first building to be constructed, Frederick the Great's Schloss Sanssouci, was built on the site of an orchard in 1745–7. Its name – *sans souci* is French for "without a care" – gives an indication of the building's flamboyant character. Over the years, the park has been enriched by other palaces and pavilions. Today, the park is made up of small gardens dating from different eras, all maintained in their original style.

Communs (1766–9)
This house for the palace staff has an unusually elegant character, and is situated next to a pretty courtyard.

★ Neues Palais
The monumental New Palace, constructed in 1763–1769, is crowned by a massive dome. Bas-reliefs on the triangular tympanum depict figures from Greek mythology.

0 meters	200
0 yards	200

Schloss Charlottenhof
The most interesting interior of this Neoclassical palace is the Humboldt Room, also called the Tent Room due to its resemblance to a marquee.

The Lustgarten
(pleasure garden) has a symmetrical layout lined with rose beds.

STAR SIGHTS

★ Schloss Sanssouci

★ Neues Palais

The Römische Bäder
(Roman Baths) date from 1829 and include a mock-Renaissance villa and a suite of Roman-style rooms.

The Chinesisches Teehaus
(Chinese Teahouse) features an exhibition of exquisite Oriental porcelain.

VISITORS' CHECKLIST

Schopenhauerstrasse/Zur
Historischen Mühle. 🚌 612, 614,
695. **Chinesisches Teehaus**
Ökonomieweg (Rehgarten).
🚃 0331-969 4202. 🚌 606.
🚊 94, 96. ◯ mid-May–mid-
Oct: Tue–Sun. **Communs** Am
Neuen Palais. 🚌 606, 612.
Römische Bäder Lenné-Strasse
(Park Charlotten-hof). 🚃 0331-
969 4202. 🚌 606. 🚊 91, 94,
96, 98. ◯ mid-May–mid-Oct:
Tue–Sun.

Orangerie

*This Neo-Renaissance palace,
the largest in the park, was
built in the mid-19th
century to house
foreign royalty
and guests.*

**Neue
Kammern**

**Bildergalerie
(art gallery)**

🛕 Neues Palais

Am Neuen Palais. 🚃 0331-969 4255.
🚌 606, 695. ◯ Sat–Thu. 🎫 🅿

This imposing Baroque palace
was begun at the request of
Frederick the Great in 1763.
Decorated with hundreds of
sculptures, the vast two-story
building contains more than
200 richly adorned rooms.
Especially unusual is the
Grottensaal (Grotto Salon),
where man-made stalactites
hang from the ceiling.

🛕 Schloss Sanssouci

Zur Historischen Mühle. 🚃 0331-
969 4202. 🚌 695. 🚊 94, 96.
◯ Tue–Sun. 🎫

Schloss Sanssouci is an enchanting Rococo palace, built in
1745–7. The original sketches
for the building were made
by Frederick the Great.
Inside, the walls of the
Konzertzimmer (Concert Hall)
are lined with paintings by
Antoine Pesne. The greatest
treasures are the paintings
of *fêtes galantes* by Antoine
Watteau (1684–1721), a favorite
artist of Frederick the Great.

🛕 Orangerie

Maulbeerallee (Nordischer Garten).
🚃 0331-969 4281. 🚌 695.
◯ mid-May–mid-Oct: Tue–Sun.

The highlight of this guest
house is the Raphael Hall,
which is decorated with copies
of works by the great Italian
Renaissance artist. The view
from the observation terrace
extends over Potsdam.

🛕 Schloss Charlottenhof

Geschwister-Scholl-Strasse. 🚃 0331-
969 4202. 🚌 606. 🚊 94, 96.
◯ mid-May–mid-Oct: Tue–Sun.

This small Neoclassical palace
was designed by Friedrich
Schinkel and Ludwig

**The elegant Baroque exterior
of the Neue Kammern**

Persius in 1829, in the style of
a Roman villa. The rear of the
palace has a portico that
opens out onto the garden
terrace. Some of the wall
paintings, produced by
Schinkel, are still in place.

🛕 Neue Kammern

Zur Historischen Mühle (Lustgarten).
🚃 0331-969 4202. 🚌 X-15, 695.
◯ Apr–mid-May: Sat–Sun; mid-
May–mid-Oct: Tue–Sun. 🎫 🅿

Originally built as an orangery
for Schloss Sanssouci in 1747,
the Neue Kammern (New
Chambers) was remodeled
as guest accommodations in
1777. The most impressive of
the building's four elegant
Rococo halls is the Ovidsaal,
with its rich reliefs and
marble floors.

🏛 Bildergalerie

Zur Historischen Mühle. 🚃 0331-
969 4202. 🚌 X15, 695. ◯ mid-
May–mid-Oct: Tue–Sun. 🎫

Constructed between 1755
and 1764 to a design by
J.G. Buring, the Bildergalerie
holds an exhibition of paintings
once owned by Frederick the
Great. Highlights include
Caravaggio's *Doubting
Thomas* (1597), and Guido
Reni's *Cleopatra's Death* (1626),
as well as a number of works
by Rubens and van Dyck.

★ **Schloss Sanssouci**

*The oldest building in
the complex, this palace
contains the imposing
Marmorsaal (Marble
Hall), decorated with
pairs of columns made
from Carrara marble.
Frederick the Great
wanted the room to be
based on the Pantheon
in Rome (see p400).*

Eastern Germany

Closed to the west for over 40 years of Communist rule, Eastern Germany is now fast rebuilding its reputation as an attractive tourist destination. The powerful duchy of Saxony, whose rulers were also Electors and, in the early 18th century, kings of Poland, has left behind a rich cultural heritage for visitors to explore. After Berlin, the area's main attractions are Dresden, the ancient capital of Saxony, the old university town of Leipzig, and the important cultural center of Weimar in Thuringia.

Dresden ❷

Saxony. 480,000. 15 km (9 miles) N. Prager Strasse 2A (0351- 49 19 20). W www.dresden.de

One of Germany's most beautiful cities, Dresden blossomed during the 18th century, when it became a cultural center and acquired many magnificent buildings. Almost all of these, however, were completely destroyed during World War II, when Allied air forces mounted vast carpet-bombing raids on the city.

Today, meticulous restoration work is in progress to return the city to its former glory, now with renewed effort after the city was flooded in 2002.

The most famous monument in Dresden is the **Zwinger**, an imposing Baroque building constructed in 1709–32. Its spacious courtyard is surrounded on all sides by galleries that house several museums, including the **Gemäldegalerie Alte Meister**. This contains one of Europe's finest art collections, with canvases by Antoine Watteau, Rembrandt, van Eyck, Velázquez,

Vermeer's *Girl Reading a Letter*, Gemäldegalerie Alte Meister

Vermeer, Raphael, Titian, and Albrecht Dürer.

The imposing 19th-century **Sächsische Staatsoper** (Saxon State Opera) has been the venue for many world premieres, including *The Flying Dutchman* and *Tannhäuser* by Wagner, as well as works by Richard Strauss.

The **Hofkirche**, a monumental Baroque cathedral, was rebuilt after damage in World War II. The interior features a magnificent Rococo pulpit and a huge organ – the last work of Gottfried Silbermann.

Dresden's **Residenzschloss** was built in stages from the late 15th to the 17th centuries. Parts of the palace have been restored and are used for temporary exhibitions. Housed in the 16th-century royal stables, the Verkehrsmuseum has been a museum of transportation since 1956. The Residenzschloss also houses the famous **Grünes Gewölbe**, a vast royal treasury full of precious jewelry.

Once part of the town's fortifications, the **Brühlsche Terrasse** was subsequently transformed into magnificent

The Baroque Wallpavilion, part of the Zwinger building in Dresden

REBUILT FROM THE ASHES

Once known as the "Florence of the north," Dresden was one of the most beautiful cities in Europe. Then, on the night of February 13, 1945, 800 British aircraft launched the first of five massive firebomb raids on the city made by Allied air forces. The raids completely destroyed the greater part of the city, killing over 35,000 people, many of whom were refugees. The rebuilding of Dresden began soon after the war, when it was decided to restore the Zwinger and other historic buildings, and create a new city of modern developments on the levelled land around the old city center. Much of Dresden has now been reconstructed, though some reminders of the city's destruction remain.

The center of Dresden after Allied carpet-bombing

gardens by Heinrich von Brühl. Offering splendid views over the Elbe river, it is known as "the balcony of Europe." The **Albertinum** houses several magnificent collections, including the **Gemälde-galerie Neue Meister**, which holds paintings from the 19th and 20th centuries. These include landscapes by Caspar David Friedrich, canvases by the Nazarene group of painters, and works by Degas, van Gogh, Manet, and Monet.

On the banks of the Elbe stands **Schloss Pillnitz**, the charming summer residence of Augustus the Strong. The main attraction is the park, laid out in English and Chinese styles.

🏛 Gemäldegalerie Alte Meister

Theaterplatz 1. 📞 0351-491 46 78. ⭕ Tue–Sun. 📷

ENVIRONS: Meissen, 19 km (12 miles) northwest of Dresden, is famous for its porcelain manufacture. The **Albrechtsburg** is a vast fortified hilltop complex with a cathedral and a palace once used by the Electors. Europe's first porcelain factory was set up in the palace in 1710 and moved to its present premises in Talstrasse in 1865. Documents relating to the history of the factory and examples of its products are on display in the palace rooms.

♣ Albrechtsburg

Domplatz 1. 📞 03521-470 70. ⭕ daily. ● Jan 10–31. 📷

Leipzig ❸

Saxony. 🏙 475,000. ✈ 🚉 🚌 ℹ Richard-Wagner-Strasse 1 (0341-710 42 60).

LEIPZIG IS NOT ONLY one of Germany's leading commercial towns, but also a center of culture and learning. Most of the interesting sights can be found in the old town, including Europe's biggest train station, the **Hauptbahnhof**.

Lovers of Johann Sebastian Bach's music can visit the **Thomaskirche** (1482–96), where he was choirmaster from 1723. It now contains his tomb.

The lofty Neoclassical interior of the Nikolaikirche, Leipzig

The **Bacharchive und Bachmuseum** houses items relating to the composer.

The 16th-century **Nikolaikirche** (Church of St. Nicholas) was redecorated in Neoclassical style in 1784–97. The grand Renaissance **Altes Rathaus** (Old Town Hall), built in only nine months in 1556, is now the municipal museum. The **Museum der Bildenden Künste** has an excellent collection of German masters, including works by Caspar David Friedrich and Lucas Cranach the Elder, as well as van Eyck, Rubens, and Rodin.

Currently under renovation, the **Grassimuseum** complex houses three collections: a museum of ethnography, a museum of decorative arts, and a large collection of musical instruments.

🏛 Museum der Bildenden Künste

Grimmaische Strasse 1–7 (until 2004, then Katharinenstr 10). 📞 0341-216 990. ⭕ Tue–Sun (Wed: 1–8pm).

Weimar ❹

Thuringia. 🏙 62,000. 🚉 🚌 ℹ Markt 10 (03643-240 00). 🅦 www.weimar.de

WEIMAR ROSE to prominence due to the enlightened sponsorship of its rulers, particularly Duke Carl Augustus and his wife Anna Amalia in the 18th century. Former residents include Goethe, Schiller, and Nietzsche, as well as the artists, designers, and architects of the Bauhaus School, founded here in 1919.

Weimar is relatively small, and most of its museums are in the town center. To the north stands the **Neues Museum**, which holds a large collection of modern art. The nearby **Stadtmuseum** is devoted to Weimar's history, while the **Goethe-Museum** displays items associated with the famous writer.

The Neoclassical **Deutsches Nationaltheater**, built in 1906–7, was the venue for the world premiere of Wagner's *Lohengrin*. In 1919 the National Congress sat here to pass the new constitution for the Weimar Republic.

The vast ducal castle, **Weimar Schloss**, has original interiors and fine paintings by Peter Paul Rubens. Also known as the Grünes Schloss (Green Castle), the **Herzogin-Anna-Amalia Bibliothek** was converted into the duchess' library in 1761–6. It has a splendid Rococo interior.

Set in attractive Belvedere Park, the ducal summer residence of **Schloss Belvedere** (1761–6) has fine collections of Rococo decorative art and vintage vehicles.

♣ Weimar Schloss

Burgplatz 4. 📞 03643-54 61 30. ⭕ Tue–Sun. 📷

Weimar Schloss in Burgplatz, with its tall Renaissance tower

Bavaria

BAVARIA IS THE LARGEST STATE in the Federal Republic of Germany. Ruled by the Wittelsbach dynasty from 1180, the duchy of Bavaria was elevated to the status of a kingdom in 1806. In addition to historic cities, fairy-tale castles, and exquisite Baroque and Renaissance palaces, the region has more than its fair share of glorious Alpine scenery, beer halls, and colorful festivals.

The auditorium of Bayreuth's Markgräfliches Opernhaus

Bayreuth ❺

🏛 75,000. 🚉 🛈 Luitpoldplatz 9 (0921-885 88). 🎭 Richard-Wagner-Festspiele (Jul–Aug).

MUSIC LOVERS associate this city with the German composer Richard Wagner (1813–83), who took up residence here in 1872. The **Villa Wahnfried** was built for Wagner by Carl Wölfel and today houses a museum dedicated to the famous musician. Nearby, the **Franz-Liszt-Museum** occupies the house where the Hungarian composer died in 1886.

Other sights of interest in Bayreuth include the **Mark-gräfliches Opernhaus**, the lavish Baroque opera house, which dates from the mid-18th century, and the **Neues Schloss**. Built for Margravine Wilhelmine in the 18th century, the palace retains its splendid Baroque and Rococo interiors, and its English-style gardens.

Bamberg ❻

🏛 70,000. 🚉 🛈 Geyerswörth-strasse 3 (0951-297 62 00).

BAMBERG'S MOST interesting historical monuments are clustered around Domplatz, including the magnificent **Cathedral of St. Peter and St. George**. Begun around 1211, the cathedral combines the late Romanesque and early French-Gothic styles. The eastern choir contains the famous equestrian statue of the "Bamberg Rider" (1225–30), whose identity remains a mystery to this day.

The west side of Domplatz is flanked by the **Alte Hofhaltung**, the former bishop's residence. Built in the 15th and 16th centuries, it houses a museum of local history. The more recent Baroque **Bishop's Palace** (1763) stands behind the cathedral.

Also on Dom-platz is the **Neue Residenz** (1695–1704), with its richly decorated apartments. Inside, the Staatsgalerie has a collection of old German masters.

On the east side of the town, the **Altes Rathaus** was originally Gothic in style, but was remodeled in 1744–56 by Jakob Michael Küchel.

🏛 Neue Residenz
Domplatz 8. 📞 0951-519 390. ◯ daily. 📷

Bamberger Reiter (Bamberg Rider) in the city's cathedral

Würzburg ❼

🏛 130,000. 🚉 🛈 Am Congress Centrum (0931-37 23 35).

LOCATED ON the bank of the Main river, Würzburg is an important cultural and commercial center, and home of the excellent Franconian wine.

The city's most impressive landmark is the **Residenz**, where Würzburg's prince-bishops lived from 1744. A highlight of this lavish Baroque palace is the huge Treppenhaus (staircase), by Balthasar Neumann (1687–1753). Above it is a glorious ceiling fresco by the Venetian artist, Giovanni Battista Tiepolo. Before the Residenz was built, the city's prince-bishops resided in the fortress known as the **Festung Marienberg**, which has stood on a hill overlooking the river since 1210. The Mainfränkisches Museum, housed inside the fortress, illustrates the history of the town and holds a number of works by the renowned German sculptor Tilman Riemen-schneider (1460–1531).

Würzburg's cathedral, the **Dom St. Kilian**, dates from 1045 and is one of Germany's largest Romanesque churches. North of it is the 11th-century basilica **Neumünster**. Its imposing Baroque dome and sandstone façade are 18th-century additions. Dating from the 13th century, the picturesque **Rathaus** (Town Hall) has a late-Renaissance tower, added in 1660.

🏛 Residenz
Residenzplatz 2. 📞 0931-35 51 70. ◯ daily. 📷
🏰 Festung Marienberg
📷 Apr–Oct: 11am, 2pm, 3pm Tue–Fri; 10am, 11am, 1pm, 2pm, 3pm, 4pm Sat–Sun. 📷 **Mainfränkisches Museum** 📞 0931-205 940. ◯ Tue–Sun. 📷

Neumann's stunning Treppenhaus (staircase) at Würzburg's Residenz

Rothenburg ob der Tauber ❽

🏛 12,000. 🚉 ℹ️ Marktplatz 2 (09861-404 92).

ENCIRCLED BY ramparts, Rothenburg is a perfectly preserved medieval town in a picturesque setting on the banks of the Tauber river.

At the heart of the town is Marktplatz, whose focal point is the **Rathaus** (Town Hall), combining Renaissance and Gothic styles. Off the main square, **St. Jakobs Kirche** (1373–1464) and the **Franziskanerkirche** both contain many historical treasures.

Two museums of note are the **Reichsstadtmuseum**, devoted to the town's history, and the **Mittelalterliches Museum**, which contains a large collection of medieval instruments of torture.

Through the Burgtor, a gateway in the city walls, you arrive at the **Burggarten** – pretty gardens giving views over the town and river.

Rothenburg's Rathaus (Town Hall), begun in the 14th century

massive 15th and 16th-century ramparts. A short walk away is the **Germanisches Nationalmuseum**. Founded in 1853, the museum houses a superb collection of antiquities from the German-speaking world, including masterworks by Tilman Riemenschneider, Lucas Cranach the Elder (1472–1553), and Albrecht Dürer (1471–1528).

Overlooking the bustling Lorenzer Platz, the Gothic **St. Lorenz-Kirche** is one of the city's most important churches. Begun in 1270, it boasts some glorious stained-glass windows.

As you cross over the Pegnitz to the north side of town, look out for the **Heilig-Geist-Spital** (Hospital of the Holy Spirit), which dates from 1332 and spans the river.

A major landmark north of the river is the **Frauenkirche**, commissioned by the Holy Roman Emperor Charles IV in the mid-14th century. Also of importance is the **Albrecht-Dürer-Haus**, where the

celebrated Renaissance painter lived in 1509–28. Copies of a wide selection of his works are on display here.

A climb up Burgstrasse brings you to the **Kaiserburg**, the imperial castle complex. The oldest surviving part is a pentagonal tower, the **Fünfeckturm**, which dates from 1040. At its foot is the Kaiserstallung (Imperial Stables), now a youth hostel.

At the Christkindlmarkt, the lively Christmas fair held during Advent in the Hauptmarkt, you can warm yourself with a glass of hot red wine spiced with cloves and buy locally made crafts.

🏛 **Germanisches Nationalmuseum**
Kornmarkt. 📞 0911-13 310.
🕐 Tue–Sun. 🚫
🏛 **Albrecht-Dürer-Haus**
Albrecht-Dürer-Strasse 39. 📞 0911-231 25 68. 🕐 Tue–Sun. 🚫 📷

Nuremberg ❾

🏛 490,000. ✈️ 🚉 ℹ️ König Strasse 93 (0911-233 60).

THE LARGEST TOWN in Bavaria after Munich, Nuremberg (Nürnberg) flourished in the 15th and 16th centuries, when many prominent artists, craftsmen, and intellectuals worked here, making it a leading European cultural center. The city is divided in two by the Pegnitz river. In the southern half, the mighty **Frauentor** is one of several gateways in the

The half-timbered buildings of Nuremberg's Kaiserburg at the top of Burgstrasse

Munich ⓾

FOUNDED IN 1158, Munich became the capital of Bavaria in the 16th century. The town rapidly overshadowed once powerful neighbors, such as Augsburg and Nuremberg, to become southern Germany's main metropolis. The period of greatest growth was in the 19th century, when the city was developed along Neoclassical lines. Many of the grand buildings around Königsplatz and along Ludwigstrasse date from this time. As well as historic monuments, Munich has first-class museums and excellent shopping. It also hosts the world-famous annual beer festival, the Oktoberfest.

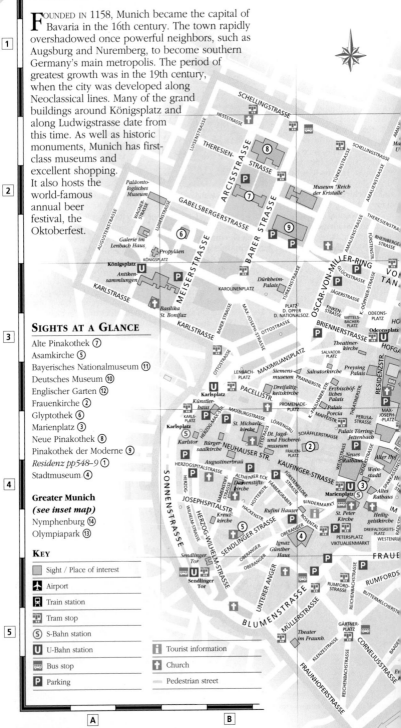

SIGHTS AT A GLANCE

Alte Pinakothek ⑦
Asamkirche ⑤
Bayerisches Nationalmuseum ⑪
Deutsches Museum ⑩
Englischer Garten ⑫
Frauenkirche ②
Glyptothek ⑥
Marienplatz ③
Neue Pinakothek ⑧
Pinakothek der Moderne ⑨
Residenz pp548–9 ①
Stadtmuseum ④

Greater Munich
(see inset map)
Nymphenburg ⑭
Olympiapark ⑬

KEY

▢	Sight / Place of interest
✈	Airport
🚉	Train station
🚊	Tram stop
Ⓢ	S-Bahn station
Ⓤ	U-Bahn station
🚌	Bus stop
P	Parking

ℹ	Tourist information
✝	Church
—	Pedestrian street

GETTING AROUND

Most of the main sights of interest can be reached by Munich's efficient U- and S-Bahn train networks, including sights located farther afield, such as Olympia-park and Nymphenburg. Buses and trams also serve many of the main tourist spots. There is a large pedestrianized zone at the heart of the city making walking a pleasant alternative to public transportation.

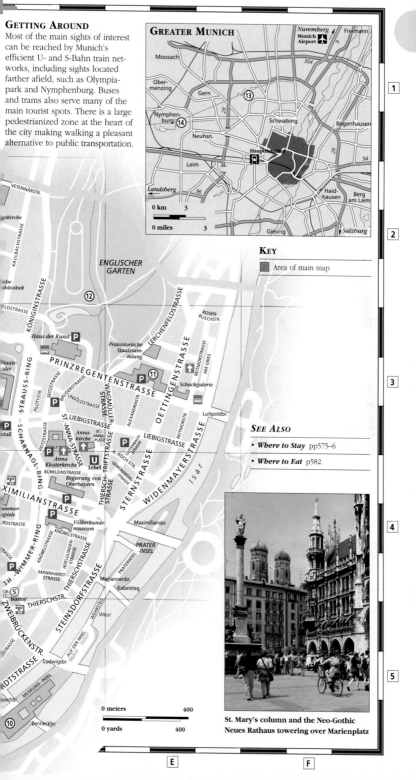

GREATER MUNICH

Nuremberg
Munich Airport
Freimann

Moosach

Ober-menzing
Gern
⑬
304

Nymphen-burg
⑭
Schwabing

Neuhsn.
Bogenhausen

Hauptbahnhof
2R
94

Laim

Landsberg 96
Haid-hausen
Berg am Laim

0 km 3

0 miles 3
Giesing
Salzburg

KEY

Area of main map

VETERINÄRSTR.

gskirche

KAULBACHSTRASSE

che bliotbek

ENGLISCHER GARTEN

KÖNIGINSTRASSE

ELDSTRASSE

⑫

Haus der Kunst P

Prähistorische Staatssamm-lung

LERCHENFELDSTRASSE

ROSEN-BUSCHSTR.

OETTINGENSTRASSE

REITMORSTRASSE

AM GRIES

staats-zlei

STRAUSS-RING

PRINZREGENTENSTRASSE

P

WAGMÜLLER-STRASSE

P ⑪

Schackgalerie

SEITZSTRASSE

PILOTYSTR.

BRUDERSTRASSE

UNSÖLDSTRASSE

ALEXANDRASTR.

Luitpoldbr.

Isar

SCHARNAGL-RING

ST. LIEBIGSTRASSE

SEITZSTRASSE

Anna-kirche

ST.-ANNA-PLATZ

ANNASTRASSE

LIEBIGSTRASSE

R.-KOCH-STR.

SEE ALSO

• *Where to Stay* pp575–6

• *Where to Eat* p582

stall

Anna Klosterkirche

BÜRKLEINSTRASSE

U Lehel

TRIFTSTRASSE

THIERSCH-STRASSE

GEWÜRZMÜHL-STR.

STERNSTRASSE

WIDENMAYERSTRASSE

Regierung von Oberbayern

XIMILIANSTRASSE

ammer-spiele

RDSTRASSE

Völkerkunde-museum

Maximiliansbr.

KNOBELSTRASSE

KNÖBELSTRASSE

ADELGUNDEN-STRASSE

TH.-WIMMER-RING

P

RASSE

MANNHARDT-STRASSE

PRATER-INSEL

Pratermr.

④

THIERSCHSTRASSE

Mariannenbr.

ORT-Z S Isartor

THIERSCHSTR.

Kabelsteg

ZWEIBRÜCKENSTR.

STEINSDORFSTRASSE

WEIDSTEG

Weur

DTSTRASSE

Ludwigsbr.

AUF DER INSEL

RDSTRASSE

oschbr. MUSEUMS-INSEL

⑩

Zenneckbr.

0 meters 400

0 yards 400

St. Mary's column and the Neo-Gothic Neues Rathaus towering over Marienplatz

E

F

Residenz ①

THE ORIGINS OF Munich's grand Residenz – the former residence of Bavarian kings – go back to the 14th century, when a castle was built here for the Wittelsbach dynasty. In the following centuries the fortress was replaced by a palace complex, which in turn was gradually modified and extended. Major work in the 17th century included the construction of two chapels, the Reiche Kapelle and the Hofkapelle. The Königsbau, containing the superb Nibelungensäle, was added by Leo von Klenze in the first half of the 19th century. Since 1920 the palace has been open to the public as a museum, displaying a wealth of magnificent treasures. In addition to the collections of the Residenzmuseum and the Schatzkammer (Treasury), there is an interesting museum of Egyptian art, the Staatliches Museum Ägyptischer Kunst.

Hofkapelle
This imposing chapel, which dates from the early 17th century, was modelled on nearby St. Michael's Church.

The Staatliches Museum Ägyptischer Kunst
(Museum of Egyptian Art) is housed in this wing of the Residenz.

Main entrance

Patrona Boiariae
The Renaissance façade features two magnificent portals, and a statue of the Holy Virgin as Patroness of Bavaria (Patrona Boiariae).

The Reiche Kapelle, built for Maximilian I, contains lavish furnishings.

Grottenhof (Grotto Court)

★ Nibelungensäle
The Nibelungensäle (Halls of the Nibelungs), a series of five rooms in the Königsbau, take their name from the wall paintings depicting scenes from the great German epic, the Nibelungenlied.

STAR FEATURES

★ **Nibelungensäle**

★ **Schatzkammer**

★ **Antiquarium**

★ Antiquarium
This magnificent vaulted chamber, with its stunning frescoes, was begun in the second half of the 16th century to house the royal collection of antiquities.

Cuvilliés-Theater
*Designed in 1751–3 by
François de Cuvilliés,
this is Europe's finest
surviving Rococo theater
and is still in use today.*

Entrance

★ Schatzkammer
*The rooms of the treasury
hold many priceless arti-
facts, including liturgical
objects, jewelry, and items
of gold. The highlight of Room V
is the Bavarian crown jewels.*

The Brunnenhof has
as its centerpiece an
elaborately decorated
fountain dedicated to
the Wittelsbachs.

Frauenkirche ②

Frauenplatz 1. **U** or **S** *Karlsplatz, Marienplatz.* 🚋 *19.* **Tower**
🔲 *Apr–Oct: Mon–Sat.* 📷

THE SITE of the Frauenkirche was originally occupied by a small chapel dedicated to the Virgin Mary, built in the 13th century. Some 200 years later, a new much larger church was built here by the architects Jörg von Halspach and Lukas Rottaler. The new Frauenkirche (or Dom) was completed in 1488, although the distinctive copper onion domes were not added to its towers until 1525. The church is one of southern Germany's largest Gothic structures. Over 100 m (330 ft) long and 40 m (130 ft) wide, it can accommodate a congregation of about 2,000 people. The vast triple-naved hall has no transept. There are long rows of side chapels and a gallery surrounding the choir. For a good view of central Munich, you can take an elevator to the top of one of the towers.

Partly demolished in 1944–5, the church was rebuilt after World War II. Church treasures that escaped destruction include a painting of the Virgin by Jan Polack (c.1500), the altar of St. Andrew in the Chapel of St. Sebastian, and the huge monumental tomb of Ludwig IV the Bavarian, the first member of the house of Wittelsbach to be elected Holy Roman Emperor (c.1283–1347). The monument was the work of Hans Krumpper (1619–22).

Altes Rathaus and the Talbruktor on Marienplatz

Marienplatz ③

U or **S** *Marienplatz.*
Spielzeugmuseum 📞 *089-29 40 01.*
🔲 *daily.* 📷

IN MEDIEVAL TIMES Marienplatz was Munich's salt- and cornmarket. In the center stands a column with a statue of the Virgin Mary dating from 1623. The square is dominated by the Neo-Gothic **Neues Rathaus** (New Town Hall), built in 1867–1909. Its walls are adorned with statues of Bavarian rulers, mythological figures, saints, and monstrous gargoyles. At 11am and 5pm the center of attention is the clocktower. The bells ring out a carillon, while figures of knights fight a tournament and a crowd dances. The dance is the "Coopers' Dance," first performed in 1517 to raise citizens' morale during a plague epidemic.

At the eastern end of the square stands the **Altes Rathaus** (Old Town Hall). Originally built in the late 15th century, it has been rebuilt many times since. The high tower, above the old city gate beside the town hall, was rebuilt in 1975 to a design based on pictures dating from 1493. Since 1983 the tower has been the home of the city's **Spiel-zeugmuseum** (toy museum).

Stadtmuseum ④

St. Jakobsplatz 1. 📞 *089-23 32 23 70.*
U or **S** *Marienplatz.* **U** *Sendlinger Tor.* 🔲 *Tue–Sun.* 📷

THE COLLECTION of the city museum has been housed since 1880 in the former arsenal, built in 1491–3 by Lukas Rottaler. It is filled with exhibits illustrating daily life in Munich throughout the ages. One of the museum's greatest treasures is the "Dancing Moors" by Erasmus Grasser (1480), which used to decorate the ballroom of the Altes Rathaus. Originally there were 18 highly expressive limewood carvings of dancing figures surrounding the figure of a woman, but only ten survive.

The Waffenhalle on the ground floor has a fine collection of arms and armor. There are also fascinating displays of furniture, paintings, prints, posters, photographs, brewing equipment, dolls, and musical instruments. The vast doll collection includes paper dolls from India and China, as well as automata and puppets. The museum stages regular temporary exhibitions and there is also a film museum and a cinema with nightly screenings.

Asamkirche ⑤

Sendlinger Strasse 32. **U** *Sendlinger Tor.* 🚋 *18, 20, 21, 27.* 🚌 *31, 56.*
🔲 *daily.*

THIS EXTRAORDINARY Rococo church is dedicated to St. John Nepomuk, but is known as the Asamkirche after the brothers Cosmas Damian and

The distinctive onion domes of the Frauenkirche rising above the city

Egid Quirin Asam, who built it as a private family church. Completed in 1746, the tiny church is a riot of decoration with a dynamically shaped single nave, where no surface is left unembellished. The eye is drawn to the altar, and its sculptural group of the Holy Trinity. The house next door to the church was the residence of Egid Quirin Asam, who was a stuccoist and sculptor. From one of the windows of his house he could see the altar.

The richly decorated altar of the Rococo Asamkirche

Glyptothek ⑥

Königsplatz 3. 🄲 089-28 61 00.
🅄 Königsplatz. 🄾 Tue–Sun. 📷
Staatliche Antikensammlung
Königsplatz 1. 🄲 089-59 83 59.
🄾 Tue–Sun. 📷

O N THE NORTHERN SIDE of Königsplatz stands the Glyptothek, a collection of Greek and Roman sculpture, notably statues from the

Temple of Aphaia on the Greek island of Aegina. The museum's imposing façade, with the portico of an Ionic temple at the center, is part of a kind of Neoclassical forum created in the first half of the 19th century to house the archaeological finds acquired by King Ludwig I of Bavaria. On the opposite side of the square, the **Staatliche Antikensammlung** houses smaller treasures, in particular a vast array of Greek vases.

Alte Pinakothek ⑦

Barer Strasse 27. 🄲 089-23 80 52 16.
🅄 Königsplatz. 🚋 27. 🚌 53.
🄾 Tue–Sun. 📷 ♿

T HIS MAGNIFICENT gallery is filled with masterpieces of European art from the Middle Ages to the mid-18th century. Many of the Wittelsbach rulers of Bavaria were great collectors, the first being Wilhelm IV the Steadfast, who ruled from 1508 to 1550. The Alte Pinakothek (Old Picture Gallery) was built for Ludwig I by Leo von Klenze in 1826–36 in the form of a Florentine Renaissance palazzo. The ground floor is devoted to the works of German and Flemish Old Masters from the 16th and 17th centuries. On the first floor are works by Dutch, Flemish, French, German, Italian, and Spanish artists.

Of the German works, pride of place goes to Albrecht Dürer's famous *Self-Portrait* (1500) and two panels of an altarpiece showing *Four Apostles*. Among the other German artists represented are Lucas Cranach the Elder and Grünewald. Early Flemish

Four Apostles **(1526) by Albrecht Dürer, in the Alte Pinakothek**

masterpieces include *St. Luke Painting the Madonna* by Roger van der Weyden, and works by Hans Memling and Pieter Brueghel the Elder.

Of later artists, the one with most works on display is the prolific Rubens. There are also interesting works by El Greco, Rembrandt, Raphael, Titian, and Tintoretto.

Neue Pinakothek ⑧

Barer Strasse 29. 🄲 089-23 80 51 95.
🅄 Theresienstrasse. 🚋 18. 🚌 53.
🄾 Wed–Mon. 📷

B AVARIA'S COLLECTION of late 18th- and 19th-century European painting and sculpture occupies a purpose-built gallery completed in 1981. German painting of every artistic movement of the 19th century, including Romanticism, the "Nazarenes", German and Austrian Bieder-meier, and Impressionism is well represented. There are also works by French Realists, Impressionists, and Symbolists purchased when the gallery's director was the art historian Hugo von Tschudi.

The open space between the Neue and Alte Pinakothek has been turned into a sculpture park.

Neoclassical façade of the Glyptothek, which houses a collection of Greek and Roman sculpture

Pinakothek der Moderne ⑨

Barer Straße 40. 📞 089-23 80 53 60.
Ⓤ Königsplatz. 🚋 27. 🚌 53. ◐
10am–5pm Tue–Wed Sat–Sun, 10am–
8pm Thu–Fri. 🎫 except Sun. ♿ ▯
W www.pinakothek-der-moderne.de

DESIGNED BY THE German
architect Stephan
Braunfels, this new museum
brings together the worlds of
art, design, graphics, and
architecture under one roof.
The collections of four
previously separate museums,
including the Staatlich
Graphische Sammlung, the
design collection of Die Neue
Sammlung, and the models,
drawings, and objects of the
Architekturmuseum, are now
housed here. As well as the
individual permanent displays,
there are also temporary and
mixed exhibitions.

Deutsches Museum ⑩

Museuminsel 1. 📞 089-217 91.
Ⓢ Isartor. 🚋 18. 🚌 52, 56.
◐ daily. 🎫 W www.deutsches-
museum.de

REPUTED TO BE the largest
science and technology
museum in the world, the
Deutsches Museum is also
the most popular museum in
Germany. Founded in 1904,
the vast collection features
more than 18,000 exhibits
across a wide range of subject
areas, from agriculture to
telecommunications.

In the basement and on the
ground floor are some of the
museum's largest exhibits.
The aeronautics
section holds an
aeroplane that
belonged to
the

**Benz's tricycle, the first petrol-driven
car, on display at the Deutsches Museum**

Neapolitan crib in the Bayerisches Nationalmuseum

Wright brothers and a 1936
Messerschmitt ME 109. A hall
charting the history of seafaring houses a 14th-century
cog, a trading ship used by
the Hanseatic League, and a
19th-century fishing vessel.

The museums's superb
collection of automobiles and
other exhibits related to land
travel are now in the
Deutsches Museum Verkehrs-
zentrum at Theresienhöhe
14a, in the west of the city.

Temporary exhibitions are
regularly held at the museum,
which also has an excellent
library archive and a range
of multimedia facilities.

Bayerisches Nationalmuseum ⑪

Prinzregentenstrasse 3. 📞 089-211
24 01. 🚋 20. 🚌 53, 55. ◐ Tue–Sun.

FOUNDED IN 1855 by King
Maximilian II, the Bavarian
National Museum holds a
superb collection of fine and
applied arts and historical
artifacts. Since 1900 the
museum has occupied an
impressive building on
Prinzregentenstrasse.
designed

by Gabriel von Seidel. The
ground floor contains works
from the Romanesque,
Gothic, Renaissance, Baroque,
and Neoclassical periods. Star
exhibits are German sculptor
Conrad Meit's *Judith* (1515)
and a beautiful sculpture of
the Madonna by Tilman
Riemenschneider (c.1460-
–1531). The first-floor
collections include German
porcelain, clocks, glassware,
ivory carvings, textiles, and
items of gold.

In the basement rooms, the
Christmas nativity scenes by
Bavarian and Italian artists
are especially worth seeing.

Englischer Garten ⑫

Ⓤ Giselastrasse. 🚌 54.

THE IDEA OF creating a park
in the heart of the city
open to all Munich's citizens
came from the American-born
Count von Rumford, who
lived in Bavaria from 1784.
In 1789, taking advantage of
his position as Bavaria's
Minister of War, he persuaded
Elector Karl Theodor to put
his plans into action. Opened
in 1808, the Karl-Theodor-
Park is today simply known
as the Englischer Garten
(English Garden). The park
covers an area of 5 sq km
(1,235 acres), and has become
a popular place for walking,
jogging, or simply relaxing.

Several interesting buildings
dotted about the gardens
include the Monopteros, a
Neoclassical temple (1837)
by Leo von Klenze, and the
Chinese Tower (1789–90),
similar to the pagoda in

London's Kew Gardens *(see p63)*. In the delightful Japanese Teahouse, demonstrations on the art of tea brewing are held. Within the Englischer Garten are three beer gardens, where locals and tourists alike come to drink and listen to live music. Visitors can also take out rowing boats on the park's lake, the Kleinhesseloher See.

The late 18th-century Chinese Tower in the Englischer Garten

Olympiapark ⑬

C 089-30 67 24 14. **U** Olympia-zentrum. **⊞** 20, 25, 27. **Pavilion** ◯ daily.

BUILT FOR the 1972 Olympic Games, the Olympiapark is visible from almost anywhere in Munich, identifiable by the 290-m (950-ft) high television tower, the Olympiaturm. The site has three main facilities: the Olympic stadium, which seats over 60,000 spectators, the Olympic Hall, and the Swimming Hall. All three are covered by a vast transparent canopy, stretched between several tall masts to form an irregular-shaped pavilion. Also within the complex are an indoor skating rink, a cycle racing track, and tennis courts.

As well as sporting occasions, the Olympiapark hosts many popular cultural events, such as fireworks displays and open-air rock and pop concerts during the summer months.

Schloss Nymphenburg ⑭

C 089-17 90 80. **U** Rotkreuzplatz. ◯ daily. **⚑ Botanischer Garten** ◯ daily. **⚑**

LOCATED NORTHWEST of the city center, the stunning Schloss Nymphenburg grew up around an Italianate villa, built in 1663–4 for Electress Henrietta-Adelaide. The Electress dedicated the palace, which became the summer residence of the Wittelsbachs, to the pastoral pleasures of the goddess Flora and her nymphs, hence the name. Several additions were made in the following century, including the construction of four pavilions, connected to the original villa by arcaded passageways.

The palace's interior boasts some magnificent examples of the Rococo style. One of the most impressive rooms is the **Festsaal** – a sumptuous ballroom, designed by father and son, Johann Baptiste and Franz Zimmermann. Equally impressive is the **Schön-heitengalerie** (Gallery of Beauties). Hanging here are 38 portraits of beautiful women – favorites of King Ludwig I. The palace also houses a small natural history and science museum. The old stables are now home to the **Marstallmuseum**, a collection of wonderfully ornate carriages that once belonged to Bavarian rulers.

Interior of the Amalienburg, in the grounds of Schloss Nymphenburg

The approach to the palace is dominated by a broad canal, bordered by immac-ulately presented gardens. On the edge of the gardens is the Porcelain Factory, established in 1741, and one of the oldest factories of its type in Europe.

Behind the palace stretches the **Schlosspark**, an English-style country park dotted with lakes and various royal lodges. The most notable of these is François de Cuvilliés's **Amalienburg**, a hunting lodge with a lavish Rococo interior. Its highlight is the splendid Spiegelsaal (Hall of Mirrors). Joseph Effner, the principal architect of the palace's extensions, was also responsible for designing the **Pagodenburg**, used for entertaining, and the Baroque bathing house, the **Badenburg**. Also in the park is the **Magdalenenklause**, built as a hermitage for Maximilian Emmanuel, but not completed until after the Elector's death in 1725.

North of the palace, the **Botanischer Garten** (Botanical Garden) holds many rare and exotic species.

Façade of the splendid Schloss Nymphenburg, begun in the 17th century

The Beers of Germany

ALTHOUGH GERMANY produces many fine wines, it is for its beer that the country has won worldwide renown. Nowhere is the business of brewing and beer drinking taken so seriously as in Munich. Bavarians are probably the world's greatest consumers of beer, with an annual intake of 240 liters per head. However, this figure is possibly inflated by the

Logo of the Paulaner brewery in Munich

vast quantities downed at the annual Oktoberfest, when some 7 million lovers of beer converge on Munich for 16 days of revelry lasting from late September to early October. When traveling in Germany, make a point of trying the specialties of the local brewery, in a *Bierkeller* (beer cellar) or *Bierstube* (pub) in winter, and in summer in a *Biergarten* (beer garden).

The tankard known as a Mass *(measure) holds one liter, although German beer is always served with a considerable head on it. Waitresses at the Oktoberfest have no difficulty carrying eight or nine of these at once.*

PILSENER

The most widely drunk beer in Germany is Pils (short for Pilsener), a light lager-style beer produced by bottom-fermentation. This method was perfected in Pilsen (Plzeň in the Czech Republic) in the 19th century. Fermentation occurs at low temperatures, so takes longer than with other beers. The essential ingredients are barley, hops, and crystal-clear water. Two of the main breweries producing this kind of beer in Munich are Löwenbräu and Paulaner.

Paulaner Pilsener   **Löwenbräu Pilsener**

Munich's Oktoberfest attracts so many visitors, a great tented village, with stalls, a funfair, and loud music, is set up on Theresienwiese, just to the west of the city center. This open space was where the marriage of King Ludwig was celebrated in 1810.

OTHER GERMAN BEERS

Germany produces many varieties of beer, some of which are brewed only at certain times of year. Of these seasonal beers, it is worth trying spring beers such as the strong *Maibock*. Other interesting beers include dark styles – known as *Dunkelbier* or *Schwarzbier* – and *Weizenbier*, a beer made from wheat rather than barley. The Berlin version of the latter, *Berliner Weisse* (white beer), is served with fruit juice. Many local breweries have their own specialties. Bamberg is famous for its *Rauchbier*, which has a light smokiness. In the lower Rhine valley, *Altbier* is still produced; this is a top-fermented beer, prepared by traditional methods.

Berliner Weisse (wheat beer)   **Dunkel-bier**   **Oktoberfest beer**

St. Stephans Dom, Passau's imposing Baroque cathedral

Passau **⓫**

🏛 50,000. 🚇 🚍 🛈 *Rathaus-platz 3 (0851-95 59 80).*

Passau LIES on a peninsula between the Danube and the Inn, near the Austrian border. In 739 the Irish monk St. Boniface founded a major bishopric here. After two destructive fires in 1662 and 1680, the town was rebuilt by Italian architects, who left many fine Baroque buildings, including the cathedral, **St. Stephans Dom**. However, the town retains a medieval feel in its narrow alleys and archways. The Gothic town hall dates from the 14th and 15th centuries. Opposite it is the **Passauer Glasmuseum**, which has a fine collection of Bohemian, Austrian, and Bavarian glass. High above the Inn stands a pretty Baroque pilgrimage church, the **Wallfahrtskirche Mariahilf**.

Neuschwanstein **⓬**

🚍 *to Schwangau.* 📞 *08362-93 98 86.* 🕐 *Oct–Mar: 10am–4pm daily; Apr–Sep: 9am–6pm (8pm Thu) daily.* 🎟 📷 ♿ *(limited access).*

SET AMID magnificent mountain scenery on the shores of the Alpsee, this fairy-tale castle was built in

1869–86 for the eccentric Bavarian King Ludwig II, to a design by the theater designer Christian Jank. Its pinnacled turrets have provided the inspiration for countless models, book illustrations, and film sets.

The walls of the vestibule and other rooms in the castle are lavishly covered with paint-

Gilded apse of the throne room, Neuschwanstein

ings depicting scenes from German myths and legends. The gilded interior of the throne room is reminiscent of a Byzantine basilica, while the dining room has intricately carved panels and fabulous pictures and furniture. The pale grey granite castle, which draws on a variety of historical styles, is a 20-minute walk from the village of Schwangau.

In the village itself is another 19th-century castle, **Hohenschwangau**, built over the ruins of a medieval castle in 1832 by Maximilian, heir to the throne of Bavaria. A tour of the Neo-Gothic castle gives a fascinating insight into the history of the Wittelsbach family, rulers of Bavaria from 1180 to 1918. There are also some fine 19th-century furnishings and the castle's terraced gardens afford magnificent views.

⚜ **Hohenschwangau**
📞 *08362-811 27.* 🕐 *daily.* 🌑 *Dec 24.* 🎟 📷

Lake Constance **⓭**

🚉 *Konstanz.* 🚍 🛈 *Bahnhofplatz 13, Konstanz (07531-13 30 30).*

LAKE CONSTANCE (in German, the Bodensee) lies on the borders of Germany, Austria, and Switzerland. The area surrounding the lake is one of the most attractive in Germany, in terms of both natural beauty and cultural heritage. The best time to visit is summer, when local fishermen stage colorful festivals and there are plenty of opportunities for water sports and cruises on the lake.

Konstanz (Constance) is the largest town in the region, and its main attraction is the magnificent 11th-century Romanesque cathedral. The town is in two parts: the old town (Altstadt) is a German enclave in Switzerland on the southern shore, while the newer part stands on a peninsula between the two main arms of the lake.

The many romantic old towns and beautiful islands of Lake Constance attract hordes of visitors every summer. The exquisite little town of **Meersburg** opposite Konstanz is a very popular destination. So too is **Mainau**, the "Island of Flowers." The most beautiful gardens on the island are in the park of the Baroque palace, built in 1739–46. At the northeastern (Bavarian) end of the lake, the medieval island town of **Lindau** is the major draw.

Lake Constance, with the Swiss Alps rising above the southern shore

Baden-Württemberg

BADEN-WÜRTTEMBERG, which includes territories of the former Grand Duchy of Baden, is one of Germany's most popular tourist destinations. Its magnificent castles, luxurious resorts, and the beautiful recreation areas of the Black Forest guarantee a memorable vacation, while the region's long and turbulent history has given it a rich cultural and religious diversity. Germany's oldest university, Heidelberg, is also located in the region.

The Kaufhaus, Freiburg's historic merchants' meeting hall

Freiburg im Breisgau ⓮

🏛 197,000. 🚉 🚌 ℹ️ Rotteckring 14 (0761-388 18 80). 🎭 Fasnet (end of carnival), Weintage (Jun).

FREIBURG IS a natural gateway to the Black Forest. The counts von Zähringen first established the town in 1120, and since 1805 it has been part of Baden. From the Middle Ages, fast-flowing canals, or *bächle*, have run through the town, providing water to help extinguish the once frequent fires.

The **cathedral** was built in the 13th century in Gothic style. Münsterplatz, the picturesque cathedral square, is lined with houses from various architectural periods.

Completed in 1520, with ground-floor arcades and richly adorned gables, the **Kaufhaus** was used by merchants for meetings and conferences.

Black Forest ⓯

🚉 to Freiburg. 🚌 to all towns. ℹ️ Wehratalstrasse 19, Todtmoos (07674-906 00).

DENSELY PLANTED with tall firs and spruces, the Black Forest (Schwarzwald) is one of Germany's most picturesque regions. The area is famous for *Schwarzwälder Kirschtorte* (Black Forest gateau) and *Kirschwasser* (schnaps), as well as for its therapeutic spring waters.

Todtnau is a popular sports center and a base for hikers. Nearby, Hangloch-Wasserfall is one of the most magnificent waterfalls in the region.

The heart of the resort of **Todtmoos** is the Baroque pilgrimage church, which dates from the 17th–18th centuries. Popular dog-sled races are held annually in the town.

In the health resort of **St. Blasien** stands a Benedictine Abbey, founded in the 9th century. Its church (1783) is an excellent example of early Neoclassical style.

The main attraction of **Furtwangen** is its clock museum (Uhrenmuseum), which houses a collection of more than 4,000 chronometers.

In the open-air museum near the small town of **Gutach** visitors can see the Black Forest's oldest house – the 16th-century Vogtsbauernhof.

Rembrandt's *St. Paul in Prison* **(1627), Staatsgalerie, Stuttgart**

Stuttgart ⓰

🏛 586,000. 🚆 🚉 🚌
ℹ️ Königstrasse 1A (0711-222 820).

STUTTGART GREW from humble beginnings as a stud farm to become the ducal and royal capital of Württemberg. It is now one of the largest and most important towns of the Federal Republic. Beautifully situated among picturesque hills, the town is a major industrial and cultural center, with a world-famous ballet company, chamber orchestra, and splendid art collections.

When Württemberg castle burned down in 1311, the family seat was moved to Stuttgart. The ducal residence, the **Altes Schloss**, was given its present square layout in 1553–78. The palace now houses the Württembergisches Landesmuseum, which holds vast collections of decorative art and jewelry.

The Vogtsbauernhof in Gutach, the oldest house in the Black Forest

On the east side of Stuttgart's main square is a huge palace complex, the **Neues Schloss**, built in 1746–1807. The palace gardens have maintained much of their original charm, with neat avenues and impressive sculptures.

The **Staatsgalerie** grew from a fine art museum containing King Wilhelm I of Württemberg's private collection. Among the Old Masters on display are Rembrandt and Bellini, while modern artists include Monet, Picasso, and Modigliani.

A building exhibition held in 1927 left behind a complete housing estate, the **Weissenhofsiedlung**, which contains houses by Mies van der Rohe, Le Corbusier, Peter Behrens, and Hans Scharoun. Another must for all lovers of modern architecture, the **Liederhalle** congress center is a successful synthesis of tradition and modernism.

The **Linden Museum** is one of Germany's finest ethnology museums, containing exhibits from all over the world. Figures from the Indonesian theater of shadows and a 6th–8th-century mask from Peru are among the eclectic items on display.

To the east of the center is the famous **Mercedes-Benz-Museum**. Its splendid collection illustrates the development of the automobile with over 70 historic vehicles, all in immaculate condition. Stuttgart's other famous car manufacturer has created the **Porsche-Museum**, which includes around 50 examples of these high-speed, expensive vehicles.

Once an independent health resort, **Bad Cannstatt** is now a district of Stuttgart. Set in a beautiful park, it has a late-Gothic church, a Neoclassical town hall, and a *kursaal* (spa-house). One of its main attractions is the Neoclassical Schloss Rosenstein (1824–9).

🏛 **Staatsgalerie**
Konrad-Adenauer-Strasse 30–32.
📞 0711-470 400. ⏰ Tue–Sun.
(free Wed).
🏛 **Mercedes-Benz-Museum**
Mercedesstrasse 137. 📞 0711-172 25 78. ⏰ Tue–Sun.

Classic cars on display in the Mercedes-Benz-Museum, Stuttgart

Heidelberg ⑰

🏠 139,000. 🚗 🚆 ℹ *Hauptbahnhof (06221-194 33).*

SITUATED ON THE BANKS of the Neckar river, Heidelberg is one of Germany's most beautiful towns. For centuries it was a center of political power, with a lively and influential cultural life. In 1386, Germany's first university was established here by the Elector Ruprecht I. The construction of the town's palace began during his reign, continuing until the mid-17th century. However,

French incursions in the late 17th century totally destroyed medieval Heidelberg. The town was subsequently rebuilt in the 18th-century in Baroque style.

Towering over the town, the **Heidelberger Schloss** is a vast residential complex that was built and repeatedly extended between the 13th and 17th centuries. Originally a supremely well-fortified Gothic castle, it is now mostly in ruins.

The **Universitätsbibliothek** (University Library), erected in 1901–5, has one of the largest book collections in Germany, with over two million volumes.

The French Count Charles de Graimberg built up an extensive collection of fine drawings, paintings, arms, and other curios. His collection forms the core of the **Kurpfälzisches Museum**, which also has a fascinating archaeology section.

The Baroque domes of the **Heiliggeistkirche** are city landmarks. Former canons of the college were university scholars, and the church aisle features special galleries for extensive collections of books.

🏛 **Kurpfälzisches Museum**
Hauptstrasse 97. 📞 06221-58 34 02.
⏰ Tue–Sun (Wed: 10am–9pm). 🎫

Heidelberger Schloss rising above Heidelberg's Alte Brücke (Old Bridge)

The Rhine and Mosel Valleys

THE RHINE AND MOSEL VALLEYS offer a series of fairy-tale landscapes – spectacular gorges, rocky crags topped by romantic castles, and picturesque villages surrounded by vineyards producing excellent white wines. After flowing into Germany from France, the Mosel meanders between steep-sided banks to join the Rhine at Koblenz. South of Koblenz lies one of the most stunning stretches of the Rhine, which is also the birthplace of German myths such as the Lorelei and the *Nibelunglied*, the great medieval epic poem of vengeance and honor.

The colorful portal of Trier's Kurfürstliches Schloss

Trier 18

Rhineland-Palatinate. 99,000.
Simeonstrasse 60 (0651-97 80 80).

ONE OF GERMANY's oldest towns, Trier was founded by the Emperor Augustus in 16 BC. Its monumental Roman gateway, the **Porta Nigra**, was built in the 3rd century AD. Among the city's other Roman relics are the **Aula Palatina** (AD 310), a vast, austere building that served as the throne hall of Roman emperors and is now a church, and the 4th-century **Kaisertherman** (Imperial Baths). A superb collection of Roman artifacts is held in the **Rheinisches Landesmuseum**.

Close by the museum is the **Basilika und Kurfürstliches Schloss**. The basilica was built for Emperor Constantine around AD 305. In the 16th century part of it was incorporated into a Renaissance castle, later transformed into a Baroque palace for the archbishop-electors of Trier.

Rheinisches Landesmuseum
Weimarer Allee 1. 0651-977 40.
Tue–Sun.

Mosel Valley 19

Am Gestade 6, Bernkastel-Kues (06531-4023). Firtia Michels (06531-8222); Gebrüder Kolb, Briedern (02673-1515).

ON THE STRETCH of the Mosel between Trier and Koblenz, romantic castles tower above extensive vineyards. Between May and October river trips are available all along the river – either short daytrips or longer cruises. However, progress can be slow because of the number of locks. A tour by car or bus is an attractive alternative. Two of the most popular excursions are from Trier to Bernkastel-Kues and from Koblenz to Cochem. Wine-tasting and eating play a big part in visitors' enjoyment of the region. Of the many castles that line the river be sure to visit **Burg Eltz** – the core of which has survived more or less intact since it was built in the 12th century – a short walk from the town of Wierschem.

Burg Eltz
to Wierschem. Apr–Oct: daily.

Mainz 20

Rhineland-Palatinate. 190,000.
Im Brückenturm am Rathaus (06131-28 62 10).

MAINZ ENJOYED power and influence under the Holy Roman Empire, as the city's Archbishop was one of the Electors. The **Kaiserdom**, the Romanesque cathedral, dates back to the 11th century. Like others from this period it has a choir at each end – one for the emperor and one for the clergy. The nave is

Burg Eltz, the most authentic and evocative castle in the Mosel Valley

The apse and towers at the east end of the Kaiserdom, Mainz

filled with the splendid tombs of the archbishops, ranging in date from the 13th to the 19th century. The **St. Gotthard-Kapelle** beside the cathedral was the private chapel of the archbishops. It has a fine 12th-century arcaded loggia.

Other attractions include the well-preserved old half-timbered houses of the **Kirschgarten** area and the Baroque **Kurfürstliches Schloss**, now a museum of Roman and other relics.

Mainz is also famous for the development in the 1440s by Johannes Gutenberg of printing with movable metal type. The **Gutenberg Museum** has a recreation of his studio and a copy of his famous 42-line Bible.

🏛 **Gutenberg Museum**
Liebfrauenplatz 5. 📞 06131-12 26 40. 🕐 Tue – Sun. ● public hols.

Rhine Valley ㉑

🛈 Bahnhofplatz 17, Koblenz (0261-313 04). 🚢 K-D Linie, Rheinwerft, Koblenz (0261-310 30).

CRUISES on the Rhine are available along much of its length, but the most scenic and popular stretch is the Rhine Gorge between Mainz and Bonn. The gorge starts at Bingen, where the Nahe joins the Rhine on its 1,320-km (825-mile) journey from Switzerland to the North Sea. Popular sights along the route include **Bacharach**, a pretty

town on the left bank, and the striking white-walled island castle of **Pfalzgrafenstein**, which levied tolls on passing ships until the mid-19th century. Past the town of Kaub on the right bank is the rock of the **Lorelei**, a legendary siren who lured sailors to their deaths with her song and her beauty. A modern statue marks the spot. Across the river is the town of **St. Goar**, dominated by the ruined Burg Rheinfels, blown up by French troops in 1797. **Burg Katz** offers one of the best-known views of the Rhine valley. At **Boppard** the attractions include the 13th-century Church of St. Severus and more spectacular views of the Rhine. Just south of Koblenz stands **Schloss Stolzenfels**, created in the early 19th century for King Friedrich Wilhelm IV. There are no bridges on this stretch of the river, but if you are exploring by car, there are ferries at various points along the route. However, the best way to enjoy the Rhine's magnificent scenery is by boat.

Koblenz ㉒

Rhineland-Palatinate. 🏠 109,000.
🚉 🚌 🛈 Bahnhofplatz 17 (0261-313 04), Jesuitenplatz (0261-129 16 10).

KOBLENZ STANDS at the confluence of the Mosel and Rhine rivers. On the **Deutsches Eck**, the spur of land between the two rivers, stands a huge equestrian statue of Emperor Wilhelm I.

Florinsmarkt takes its name from the Romanesque-Gothic **Church of St. Florin**, which dates from the 12th century. Nestling among the square's historic buildings is the **Mittelrheinisches Museum**, with medieval art and archaeological collections.

The present appearance of the **Alte Burg**, with its fine Renaissance façade, dates from the 17th century, but a fortress has stood on this site since the early Middle Ages.

Other sights of interest are the **Liebfrauenkirche**, which has a beautiful Gothic choir, the **Kurfürstliches Schloss** (the Electors' palace), and **Festung Ehrenbreitstein**, where the archbishops of Trier resided from 1648 to 1786.

Detail on tomb of Heinrich II, Maria Laach

ENVIRONS: Northwest of Koblenz in the Eifel range, the Benedictine abbey of **Maria Laach** is a masterpiece of Romanesque architecture. It was begun in 1093 on the orders of Count Palatine Heinrich II, who lies buried here. The Paradise courtyard, meant to symbolize the Garden of Eden, resembles the Alhambra in Granada (see pp322–3).

🛈 **Maria Laach**
Off A61, 25 km (16 miles) NW of Koblenz. 📞 02652-590. 🚌 from Andernach or Niedermendig. 🕐 daily.

Burg Katz above the town of St. Goarhausen in the Rhine Gorge

Frankfurt's skyscraper district, nicknamed "Mainhattan"

Frankfurt am Main ㉓

Hesse. 🏠 660,000. ✈ 🚆 🚌 🚇
ℹ *Hauptbahnhof (069-21 23 88 00).*

FRANKFURT AM MAIN is one of the main economic and cultural centers of Europe. The headquarters of many major banks and newspaper publishers are based here, and the city's International Book Fair is the world's largest event of its kind.

Since 1878, the **Städelsches Kunstinstitut** has occupied a Neo-Renaissance building on Schaumainkai, the picturesque "museum embankment." The ground floor houses a collection of Dutch and German prints and drawings, the first floor is devoted to 19th- and 20th-century art, and the second floor displays works by Old Masters such as Botticelli, van Eyck, Vermeer, and Rembrandt.

Another interesting museum in the Schaumainkai complex is the **Deutsches Architektur-museum**, which concentrates mainly on developments in 20th-century architecture.

Nearby is the **Deutsches Filmmuseum**, which holds documents and objects relating to the art of filmmaking and the development of film technology. The museum has its own cinema, which shows old and often long-forgotten films.

The great German poet, novelist, and dramatist Johann Wolfgang von Goethe was born at the **Goethehaus** in 1749. The house was totally destroyed in World War II, but later lovingly restored, its interior reconstructed in typical 18th-century style. The desk at which Goethe wrote his early works, such as *The Sorrows of Young Werther* (1774), remains.

Located in the center of the old town, the **Römer** is a collection of 15th- to 18th-century houses, including the Altes Rathaus (Old Town Hall), rebuilt after World War II. Opposite is a group of half-timbered houses, known as the **Ostzeile**.

On the banks of the Main stands **St. Leonhardkirche**, a fine example of Gothic and Romanesque architecture.

Portrait of a Woman (c.1480) by Botticelli, Städelsches Kunstinstitut

Built in stages in the 13th and 15th centuries, the church contains many treasures, including a copy of Leonardo da Vinci's *Last Supper* by Hans Holbein the Elder, from 1501.

The **Historisches Museum** has an interesting display of items relating to Frankfurt's history, including a fascinating model of the medieval town, a collection of local prehistoric finds, and several decorative fragments from buildings destroyed during World War II.

The twin-naved **Alte Nikolaikirche**, or Church of St. Nicholas, is popular with visitors for its fine statues of St. Nicholas and the 40-bell carillon, which plays German folk songs twice a day.

The **Kaiserdom**, an imperial cathedral, was built between the 13th and 15th centuries. It has several priceless masterpieces of Gothic artwork, including the 15th-century Maria-Schlaf-Altar.

The collection at the **Museum für Moderne Kunst** (Museum of Modern Art) represents all the major artistic trends from the 1960s until the present day, with works by Roy Lichtenstein and Andy Warhol.

The **Liebieghaus**, a museum of sculpture, has works ranging from antiquity through to Mannerism and Rococo. There are some superb examples of ancient Egyptian and Far Eastern art, as well as splendid works from the Middle Ages and the Renaissance.

🏛 **Städelsches Kunstinstitut**
Schaumainkai 63. 📞 069-605 09 80.
🕐 Tue–Sun. 🎟 (free Tue). 🔲
🏛 **Museum für Moderne Kunst**
Domstrasse 10. 📞 069-21 23 04 47.
🕐 Tue–Sun. 🎟

ENVIRONS: Hanau, 30 km (19 miles) east of Frankfurt, is the birthplace of the brothers Wilhelm and Jakob Grimm. There is an exhibition devoted to their lives and work at the local historical museum.

The Ostzeile on the Römerberg, one of the symbols of Frankfurt

The Baroque Elector's palace, housing Bonn University

Bonn ㉔

North Rhine-Westphalia. 🏛 *310,000.*
🚇 🚊 🚌 🛈 *Windeckstrasse 1
(0228-77 50 00).*

THERE HAS BEEN a crossing over the Rhine at Bonn since pre-Roman times, but the settlement first rose to prominence under the Archbishops of Cologne in the 13th century. Bonn was the capital of the Federal Republic of Germany between 1949 and 1991.

The central market square is surrounded by a mixture of modern and Baroque architecture, including the late-Baroque **Rathaus** (Town Hall), built in 1737–8. Just north of the market square stands the 18th-century Baroque house where Beethoven was born. The **Beethovenhaus** is now a museum housing an impressive collection of memorabilia.

Bonn has many fine museums. The **Rheinisches Landesmuseum** has a vast collection of archaeological exhibits dating back to Roman times, as well as medieval and modern art. A Neanderthal skull is also exhibited here. The **Kunstmuseum Bonn**, a museum of modern art, has a superb display of Expressionist paintings.

Cologne ㉕

North Rhine-Westphalia.
🏛 *1,000,000.* 🚇 🚊 🚌 🛈 *Unter
Fettenhennen 19 (0221-22 13 04 00).*

ORIGINALLY FOUNDED by the Romans, Cologne (Köln) is one of the oldest settlements in Germany. Present-day Cologne is an important ecclesiastical and cultural center, boasting 12 Romanesque churches and the famous cathedral (see pp562–3), as well as several excellent museums, historic buildings, and superb galleries.

The **Wallraf-Richartz-Museum** contains 14th- to 19th-century paintings organized by the schools of art they represent. Featured artists include Rubens, Dürer, Munch, and Max Liebermann.

Housing archaeological finds from Cologne and the Rhine Valley, the modern **Römisch-Germanisches Museum** displays Roman weapons, tools, and decorative objects, as well as the superb Dionysus mosaic from around 250 BC.

The **Museum Ludwig** boasts one of Europe's best collections of modern art. German Expressionists, Surrealists, and American Pop Artists are all represented.

The Romans built a sports arena on the site now occupied by the 12th-century **Groß St. Martin**. Remains of the baths have been uncovered underneath the crypt.

Cologne's **Rathaus** (Town Hall) is an irregular-shaped building, the result of successive modifications after 1330. Under a glass pyramid at the front are the remains of 12th-century Jewish baths.

Highlights of the late-Gothic **Church of St. Peter**, built in 1515–39, are its stained-glass windows and the magnificent *Crucifixion of St. Peter* (c.1637) by Peter Paul Rubens.

The southern chamber of the **Church of St. Ursula** is lined with many shrines. According to legend, they hold the remains of St. Ursula and 11,000 virgins, reputedly killed by the Huns.

🏛 **Wallraf-Richartz-Museum**
Martinstrasse 39. 📞 *0221-22 12
11 19.* ⭘ *Tue–Sun.* 🚫

Skyline of Cologne, dominated by the spires of the Rathaus, Gross St. Martin, and the cathedral

Cologne Cathedral

The north tower, at 157.38 m (516 ft), is slightly higher than the south tower.

THE HISTORY of Germany's greatest Gothic cathedral is long and complicated. The foundation stone was laid on August 15, 1248, the chancel was consecrated in 1322, and building work continued until about 1520. The cathedral then stood unfinished until the 19th century, when the original Gothic designs were rediscovered. It was finally completed in 1842–80. Precious works of art include the fabulous Shrine of the Three Kings, the Altar of the Magi, and an early-Gothic carving of the Virgin Mary (c.1290) known as the Mailänder (Milanese) Madonna.

Mailänder Madonna

Elaborately decorated pinnacles top the supporting pillars.

Cathedral Interior
The chancel, the ambulatory, and the chapels retain a large number of Gothic, mainly early 14th-century, stained-glass windows.

Main entrance

The Petrusportal is the only entrance built in the Middle Ages. Of the figures flanking the doorway, five were original Gothic statues, but these have been replaced by copies.

Buttresses support the entire bulk of the cathedral.

Englebert Reliquary (c.1630)
The treasury in the cloister on the north side of the cathedral is famous for its large collection of gold objects, vestments, and the beautifully decorated liturgical books.

★ Choir
The massive oak stalls were built in 1308–11. They are backed by beautiful painted wooden panels.

★ Shrine of the Three Kings
This huge Romanesque reliquary was made by Nikolaus von Verdun in 1181–1220, to hold the relics of the Three Kings. These were brought to Cologne from Italy in 1164 by Emperor Friedrich I Barbarossa.

High Altar
The Gothic altar dates back to the consecration of the chancel. The frieze depicts the Coronation of the Virgin Mary, flanked by the twelve Apostles.

★ Altar of the Magi
This magnificent altarpiece (c.1442) by Stephan Lochner depicts The Adoration of the Magi. When the panels are closed, it shows The Annunciation.

STAR FEATURES

★ Choir

★ Shrine of the Three Kings

★ Altar of the Magi

Northern Germany

THREE FEDERAL STATES – Lower Saxony and the city-states of Hamburg and Bremen – occupy a huge swathe of northern Germany. Lower Saxony's capital, Hanover, has splendid architecture and fine museums. Hamburg and Bremen were wealthy Hanseatic trading towns, and today their ports still play an important role in city life. The region's other main attractions are the well-preserved medieval towns of Münster, in North Rhine-Westphalia, and Lübeck in Schleswig-Holstein.

The beautifully restored façade of Münster's Gothic Rathaus

Münster ㉖

🏛 280,000. ✈ 🚊 🚻 *Klemens-strasse 9 (0251-492 27 10).*

MÜNSTER'S MAIN sights of interest are located in the Altstadt, the historic heart of the city. The imposing Gothic **Rathaus** (Town Hall), carefully restored following damage during World War II, dates from the late 12th century. In 1648 the Treaty of Westphalia was signed here, ending the Thirty Years' War.

Münster's great cathedral, the **Dom St. Paulus**, on Dom-platz, was built in 1225–65. Its best-known treasure is the astronomical clock (1540). Also on the square is the **Westfälisches Landes-museum**, which specializes in Gothic art. Nearby, the **Lambertikirche** (1375–1450) is a fine example of the hall-churches typical of Westphalia.

West of the center stands the **Residenzschloss**. Built in 1767–87, the splendid Baroque palace, now the headquarters of Münster's university, over-looks pleasant gardens.

Hanover ㉗

🏛 520,000. 🚉 🚻 *Ernst-August-Platz 2 (0511-16 84 97 00).*
🎪 *Schützenfest (Jun–Jul).*

HANOVER (Hannover) is the capital of Lower Saxony, and for more than a century, from 1714 to 1837, shared a succession of rulers with Britain. Heavily bombed during World War II, the city has been largely rebuilt.

Among the city's finest landmarks are the grand **Opernhaus** (Opera House), built in Neoclassical style in 1845–57, and, on Tramm-platz, the **Neues Rathaus** (Town Hall), which dates from 1901–13 and combines Neo-Gothic and Secessionist detail. The latter's massive central dome offers fine views of the city.

On Marktplatz, in the old town, are many restored, 15th-century, half-timbered houses, as well as the **Markt-kirche St. Georg und St. Jacobus** with its 14th-century nave and fine Gothic altar.

One of Europe's best museums of modern art, the **Sprengel-Museum** holds works by Munch, Chagall, Picasso, and Christo. Also worth visiting is the **Niedersächsisches Landesmuseum**, whose picture gallery has German medieval and Renaissance paintings, Dutch and Flemish works by Rubens, Rembrandt, and van Dyck, and 19th- and 20th-century German art.

West of the city center, the **Herrenhauser Gärten** are among the most beautiful Baroque gardens in Germany.

🏛 **Sprengel-Museum**
Kurt-Schwitters-Platz. 📞 *0511-168 438 75.* 🕐 *Tue–Sun.* 🎨
🏛 **Niedersächsisches Landesmuseum**
Willy-Brandt-Allee 5. 📞 *0511-98 075.* 🕐 *Tue–Sun.*

Bremen ㉘

🏛 560,000. ✈ 🚊 🚻 *Am Bahnhofplatz (0421-30 800 51).*

A MEMBER OF THE Hanseatic League from 1358, in the Middle Ages Bremen was a thriving seaport, trading in grain, wine, and salt. Today, the independent city-state still prospers from its port, Germany's second-largest.

Bremen's **Rathaus** (Town Hall), on Marktplatz, was built in 1405–10 and boasts a fine Renaissance façade, added to the original Gothic structure 200 years later. Opposite is the 11th-century Romanesque

Hanover's medieval quarter, with the Church of St. George and St. Jacobus

Attractive gabled houses and the statue of Roland in Bremen's Marktplatz

Dom, which contains some fine bas-reliefs. In Marktplatz itself stand a tall statue of Charlemagne's knight Roland (1404) and a sculpture of the *Musicians of Bremen* (1953), recalling the Grimm fairy tale.

Two museums of note are the **Kunsthalle**, with European art dating from the Middle Ages to the 20th century, and the **Focke-Museum**, a museum of local history and decorative arts.

Musicians of Bremen sculpture

🏛 Rathaus
Marktplatz. ◯ for guided tours only (11am, noon, 3pm, 4pm daily) book at
🏛 Kunsthalle
Am Wall 207. 📞 0421-32 90 80.
◯ Tue–Sun.

Hamburg ㉙

🏠 1,700,000. ✈ 🚆 🚌 ℹ Hauptbahnhof, Kirchenallee (040-30 05 12 00).

F OR MANY YEARS Hamburg, Germany's second largest city, was a leading member of the Hanseatic League and an independent trading town. In 1945 it became a city-state of the Federal Republic.

Hamburg sustained considerable damage during World War II, and little of the old town remains. The ruined tower of the Neo-Gothic **Nikolai-kirche** serves as a

monument to the tragic consequences of war. Nearby, the **Jakobikirche** (1340) has been rebuilt in its original style. Inside is a massive 17th-century Baroque organ by Arp Schnitger. Another fine church is the Baroque **Michaeliskirche**, whose 132-m (433-ft) tower gives splendid views of the city.

Hamburg's Neo-Renaissance town hall, on the Rathausmarkt, is the fifth in the city's history. Just north of it is a large recreational lake, the Binnenalster. Also nearby, the prestigious **Kunst-halle** traces the history of European art from medieval times to the 20th century. The section devoted to the 19th-century German Romantics is especially good.

The best-known example of the city's collection of Expressionist buildings is Fritz Höger's **Chilehaus** (1922–4) in Kontorhausviertel.

Hamburg is the second largest port in Europe after Rotterdam, and a tour is highly recommended. There

Triptych adorning the main altar in Hamburg's Jakobikirche

are two museum ships moored here: the freighter *Cap San Diego* and the sailing boat *Rickmer Rickmers* (1896).

🏛 Kunsthalle
Glockengiesserwall. 📞 040-428 13 12 00. ◯ Tue–Sun.
🚢 Port
Ⓤ Baumwall or St-Pauli-Landungs-brücken. **Cap San Diego** 📞 040-36 42 09. ◯ daily. **Rickmer Rickmers** 📞 040-319 59 59. ◯ daily.

Lübeck's 15th-century Holstentor, on the western edge of the town

Lübeck ㉚

🏠 215,000. 🚆 ℹ Breitestrasse 62 (0451-12 25 420).

T HE MOST IMPORTANT town in the Baltic basin at the end of the Middle Ages, Lübeck is known for its wealth of superb medieval architecture.

The city's 13th-century **Marienkirche** (St. Mary's Church), boasts the highest vaulted brick nave in the world. A short walk away, the turreted **Rathaus** (Town Hall) dates from 1226 and is a fine example of Lübeck's distinctive Gothic brick architecture. The Gothic **Dom** (Cathedral) was begun in 1173. Nearby, the **St-Annen-Museum** has historical artifacts dating from the 13th to the 18th centuries. Another famous monument is the **Holstentor** (1466–78), the western gateway to the city.

The **Buddenbrook-Haus** is a museum devoted to the great writers Thomas and Heinrich Mann, whose family lived here in 1841–91.

🏛 Buddenbrook-Haus
Heinrich-und-Thomas-Mann-Zentrum, Mengstrasse 4. 📞 0451-122 4192. ◯ daily. ⬤ Dec 24, 25 & 31.

Practical Information

Gᴇʀᴍᴀɴʏ ɪꜱ ʀᴇɴᴏᴡɴᴇᴅ as a safe, clean, and efficient country to visit. Travelers will find that every town has a helpful tourist information center offering advice on restaurants, attractions, and activities. Larger cities also have Internet web sites which give up-to-the-minute information. Hotels are plentiful but may be busy during the festivals and fairs which occur throughout the year in different parts of the country.

Wʜᴇɴ ᴛᴏ Vɪꜱɪᴛ

Tʜᴇ ᴄʟɪᴍᴀᴛᴇ in Germany is pleasantly temperate. Cities and historic monuments are best visited in spring or early fall, particularly in the south of the country where it can be very warm. July and August are ideal months for a restful holiday by the sea, in the lake districts or in the mountains. In Bavaria during the second half of September and early October the Oktoberfest takes place. This is an annual beer-drinking event which is open to all visitors. In December everybody is preoccupied with Christmas shopping, while during winter, skiing is a popular pursuit in the Black Forest, the Alps, and the Harz Mountains. The roads are busiest during the school holidays, dates of which vary from state to state, and during the "long weekends" at Easter, Whitsun, and other national public holidays.

Vɪꜱᴀ Rᴇǫᴜɪʀᴇᴍᴇɴᴛꜱ ᴀɴᴅ Cᴜꜱᴛᴏᴍꜱ

Cɪᴛɪᴢᴇɴꜱ ᴏꜰ countries that are members of the EU, as well as citizens from the US, Canada, Australia, and New Zealand, do not need a visa to visit Germany, so long as their stay does not exceed three months. Visitors from South Africa must have a visa. Visitors from EU countries do not require a passport to enter Germany, as long as they have a national ID card.

Drugs, animals, animal products, such as cured meats, and exotic plants under special protection are totally prohibited from importation into Germany. Regulations also restrict the importation of cigarettes and wine.

Pᴇʀꜱᴏɴᴀʟ Sᴇᴄᴜʀɪᴛʏ

Aꜱ ɪɴ ᴏᴛʜᴇʀ countries, visitors are far safer in small towns and villages than in big cities, where extra care must be taken against street theft – particularly when traveling on public transport during the rush hour. Pickpockets tend to frequent popular tourist sights and any events where large groups of people gather. It is worth using a money belt to conceal your money and documents. Also keep cameras and audio equipment out of sight. Better still, leave valuable items in the hotel safe.

Pᴏʟɪᴄᴇ

Gᴇʀᴍᴀɴ ᴘᴏʟɪᴄᴇ uniforms and signs are mostly green. Look out for motorized police units, the *Verkehrspolizei*, which are concerned with safety on the streets, roads, and highways, and are distinguished by their white caps. Uniformed police officers patroling city streets have a green cap. Certain town police have navy-blue uniforms and their job is to catch motorists for parking offences for which they can impose an on-the-spot fine. Remember that you should carry ID such as a passport, driving license or student card with you at all times.

Pʜᴀʀᴍᴀᴄɪᴇꜱ

Lᴏᴏᴋ ᴏᴜᴛ ꜰᴏʀ the stylized letter "A" *(Apotheke)* which indicates a pharmacy. They are usually open from 8am to 6pm; in small towns they close between 1 and 3pm. In larger towns there is always a rota and this is displayed in the window of each pharmacy with a note of addresses. Information on rota pharmacies may also be obtained from tourist offices.

Aᴄᴄɪᴅᴇɴᴛꜱ ᴀɴᴅ Eᴍᴇʀɢᴇɴᴄɪᴇꜱ

Iꜰ ʏᴏᴜ ʜᴀᴠᴇ an accident or a serious breakdown on the motorway, it is best to use one of the special telephones that are situated at regular intervals along the hard shoulder. Throughout the country a special emergency

Tʜᴇ Cʟɪᴍᴀᴛᴇ ᴏꜰ Gᴇʀᴍᴀɴʏ

Germany lies in a temperate climatic zone. In the north, with marine influences predominating, summers tend to be quite cool and winters mild, with relatively high rainfall. In the eastern part of the country, however, the climate is more continental and this produces harsher winters and hotter summers. Germany's highest rainfall and lowest temperatures are recorded in the Alps.

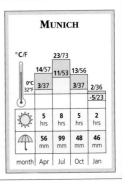

BERLIN			
°C/F	23/73		
	13/56 12/54	14/57	
0°C 32°F 3/37		3/37	1/34
			-5/23
6 hrs	8 hrs	4 hrs	2 hrs
24 mm	60 mm	41 mm	31 mm
month Apr	Jul	Oct	Jan

MUNICH			
°C/F	23/73		
	14/57 11/53	13/56	
0°C 32°F 3/37		3/37	2/36
			-5/23
5 hrs	8 hrs	5 hrs	2 hrs
56 mm	99 mm	48 mm	46 mm
month Apr	Jul	Oct	Jan

number, 110, is answered by an operator who will inform the appropriate emergency services. This number is free on all telephones, including mobiles. If you lose your passport, you should go to your consulate.

TOURIST INFORMATION

A WELL-DEVELOPED network of tourist information centers exists in Germany. These are usually run by the city or regional tourist authorities, *Verkehrsamt.* They provide advice on accommodations, addresses, and opening hours of monuments, museums, tours, and excursions, as well as brochures covering the most important tourist attractions. They may also be able to find and book you a hotel room.

OPENING HOURS

T HE OPENING HOURS of stores, offices, and most other businesses depend to a great extent on the size of the town. In larger cities, office hours are usually from 9am until 6pm, and larger shops are open

from 9am to 8pm weekdays, and until 6pm on Saturday. Banks operate shorter hours: 9am–3:30pm Monday–Friday, with a lunchbreak between noon and 1pm. They usually stay open later one evening a week until 6pm. Some new shopping malls are open on Sundays. In smaller towns, not much tends to open before 10am, and many businesses close from 1–2pm for lunch, on Saturday afternoons, Sundays and public holidays

DISABLED TRAVELERS

T HERE ARE RAMPS or lifts for people confined to wheelchairs at large museums and major historical sites. Banks are also accessible by wheelchair and there are lifts at railroad stations and larger underground stations. Some public transport is adapted to take wheelchairs. Most higher grade hotels have suitably equipped bedrooms. Public restroom facilities in parking lots, train stations, and airports usually have suitable cubicles. For information contact **Bundesverband Selbsthilfe Körperbehinderter (BSK)**.

COMMUNICATIONS

M AIL AND TELEPHONE services in Germany are very efficient. Mailboxes are bright yellow and call booths can be found everywhere. The oldest types are coin-operated, but others take telephone cards which can be bought at mail offices. Many public phone booths have a number so they can receive incoming calls. Call booths with the word "*National*" can only be used to ring numbers with German dialling codes, but overseas calls can be made from other phones. You can book a call at mail offices at the window marked "*Ferngespräche.*" Calls are cheaper in the evening from 6–9pm and at weekends.

BANKING AND CURRENCY

T HE DEUTSCHMARK was the German currency until 2002 when the euro, common currency of the European Union, was introduced into general circulation. Foreign currency can be changed at banks, most hotels, or bureau de change *(Wechselstube).*

DIRECTORY

TOURIST INFORMATION

German National Tourist Office
☏ 069-97 46 40.
🅆 www.germantourism.de

Berlin
Am Karlsbad 11,
10785 Berlin.
☏ 030-25 00 25.
🅆 www.btm.de

Frankfurt am Main
Kaiserstrasse 56,
60329 Frankfurt am Main.
☏ 069-21 23 88 00.
🅆 www.frankfurttourismus.de

Munich
Sendlinger Strasse 1,
80331 Munich.
☏ 089-233 03 00.
🅆 www.munichtourist.de

Stuttgart
Lautenschlagerstr. 3,
70173 Stuttgart.
☏ 0711-22 28 252.
🅆 www.stuttgarttourist.de

EMBASSIES

Australia
Wallstrasse 76–79,
10179 Berlin.
☏ 030-880 08 80.
℻ 030-22 48 92 91.
🅆 www.australianembassy.de

Canada
Friedrichstrasse 95,
10117 Berlin.
☏ 030-20 31 20.
℻ 030-20 31 21 34.
🅆 www.kanada-info.de

New Zealand
Friedrichstrasse 60,
10117 Berlin.
☏ 030-20 62 10.
℻ 030-20 62 11 14.
@ nzemb@t-online.de

South Africa
Tiergartenstrasse 17–18,
12683 Berlin.
☏ 030-22 07 30.
℻ 030-22 07 31 90.
🅆 www.suedafrika.org

United Kingdom Embassy
Wilhelmstrasse 70,
10117 Berlin.
☏ 030-20 45 70.
℻ 030-20 45 75 78.
🅆 www.britischebotschaft.de

Consulate
Harvestehuder Weg 8a,
20148 Hamburg.
☏ 040-448 03 20.
℻ 040-410 72 59.

United States Embassy
Neustädtische Kirchstrasse 4–5, 10117 Berlin.
☏ 030-238 51 74.
℻ 030-238 62 90.
🅆 www.usembassy.de

Consulate
Königinstrasse 5,
80539 Munich.
☏ 089-288 80.
℻ 089-280 99 98.

EMERGENCY NUMBERS

Police and Fire services
☏ 110.

Ambulance
☏ 19222.

DISABLED TRAVELERS

Mobility International
North America
☏ 541-343 1284.

Bundesverband Selbsthilfe Körperbehinderter (BSK)
Postfach 20,
74238 Krautheim.
☏ 06294-42810.
🅆 www.bsk-ev.de

Travel Information

TRAVELING TO AND AROUND Germany is fast and easy. In every large city there is an airport, and most of these offer international connections. The whole of Germany is linked by a dense network of highways, while the main roads are of a high standard and well signposted. Train travel throughout the country is comfortable and reliable; for longer journeys it is worth taking advantage of the fast connections offered by InterCityExpress (ICE). Buses are also comfortable and efficient and can be essential in rural areas that cannot be reached by train. Large cities have tram, bus, and sometimes subway services.

ARRIVING BY AIR

GERMANY'S MOST important airports are Berlin, Frankfurt am Main, Munich and Düsseldorf. You can get connecting flights from these to other cities such as Hamburg and Stuttgart. The country's national airline is **Lufthansa**, which operates regular, scheduled flights between Germany and most of the world's major destinations.

There are frequent flights from the US to Germany, mainly to Berlin and Frankfurt, which is Germany's largest airport and one of the busiest in Europe. Direct flights are available from many major US cities, including New York (JFK), Newark, Washington DC, Boston, Chicago, Miami, San Francisco, and Los Angeles.

Although Canada does not have many direct flights to Germany, **Air Canada** operates a regular flight from Toronto to Frankfurt and its subsidiary Canadian Airlines flies from Vancouver to Frankfurt.

DOMESTIC FLIGHTS

IN ADDITION to Lufthansa, there are a number of smaller airlines in Germany including the British **Deutsche BA**, which may offer cheaper fares than Lufthansa on internal routes, as well as providing air links with small airports, such as Augsburg, Dortmund, and Erfurt.

BORDER CROSSINGS

THERE ARE MANY crossings into Germany and provided that you carry the necessary documents and your car does not look disreputable, you should experience a minimum of delay and formalities at the border. There are limits on the amount of duty-free items that can be brought in by non-EU citizens *(see p13)*.

TRAVELING BY CAR

THE FASTEST and most comfortable way to travel around the country is by road. Germany's excellent network of toll-free highway routes guarantees fast journeys over long distances, while a well-maintained system of good smaller roads means that many interesting places throughout the country are within easy reach. On smaller roads and in remote areas, filling stations may be few and far between.

The German *Autobahn* (highway) network is extensive. An *Autobahn* is indicated by the letter "A" followed by a number – some also have a letter "E" and a number, denoting that the road crosses the German border. They are all toll-free and have regularly spaced filling stations, as well as parking lots with restrooms, restaurants, and motels. A *Bundesstrasse* (main road) has the letter "B" and a number.

In the event of an accident on an *Autobahn*, or if sudden traffic congestion means you have to brake hard, drivers should turn on their flashing emergency lights to warn drivers behind of the danger. Along the hard shoulder there are yellow poles with emergency buttons, which can be used to call for help if you have a breakdown or an accident. The two automobile associations **Allgemeiner Deutscher Automobil Club (ADAC)** and **Automobilclub von Deutschland (AvD)** offer roadside assistance.

RULES OF THE ROAD

IN GERMANY, the same road traffic regulations apply as in most European countries. The car must carry a plate indicating country of origin, and be equipped with a red warning triangle for use in case of breakdown.

The wearing of seatbelts is compulsory and children under 12 must sit in the back, with babies and toddlers secured in child-seats.

Driving after drinking a small amount of alcohol is allowed, but if you have an accident, the consequences will be more severe if a breathalyzer shows alcohol in your blood.

In built-up areas the speed limit is 50 km/h (31 mph); beyond this it is 100 km/h (62 mph), and on highways there is no limit, of which many drivers take full advantage. When traveling with a caravan or camping trailer outside built-up areas, drivers should not exceed 70 km/h (44 mph), and on highways 100 km/h (62 mph). Road traffic police are strict about imposing fines for speeding. Drivers can also be fined for driving too close to the vehicle in front and for parking in prohibited areas.

PARKING IN TOWNS

FINDING A PLACE to park is not easy: it is often best to use a multi-level parking lot, which is indicated by *"Parkhaus"*; a sign with the word *"Frei"* indicates that spaces are available. It is never worth leaving your car in a prohibited area. If you do risk it, a traffic warden may find your car, immediately impose a fine and arrange for the car to be towed away. Retrieving your car is then expensive and difficult.

Cars left in a parking zone must either display a parking ticket or be at a meter.

TRAVELING BY TRAIN

TRAVELING AROUND Germany by train is not the cheapest form of transport, but it is undoubtedly one of the most efficient. Trains operated by **Deutsche Bahn**, the German rail company, are renowned for their punctuality, safety, and cleanliness. The fastest are InterCityExpress (ICE) trains; these are aero-dynamically designed, painted white, with air-conditioning in the coaches and airline-style seats. Unfortunately, there is not much room for luggage. These trains can travel at more than 200 km/h (125 mph), which means that a journey from Hamburg to Munich takes just under six hours. ICE trains operate on just a few routes linking the largest cities. The InterCity (IC) trains, which stop only at certain stations, are cheaper but still offer an express service. For short distances, it is best to take the Regional Express (RE) trains. The *S-Bahn* (short for *Schnellbahn*) is a fast commuter rail network which operates in some of the major German cities.

TRAIN FARES

TRAIN FARES in Germany are quite expensive and there is a compulsory surcharge *(Zuschlag)* for express train travel. It is not usually necessary to reserve seats, but in the high season this is a good idea and it does not cost a lot. If you are staying for some time and want to use trains frequently, one way to travel more cheaply is to buy a *BahnCard*. After an initial hefty outlay, this gives you a 50 percent discount on rail tickets for a whole year.

CITY TRANSPORT

SEVERAL MAJOR CITIES in Germany, including Berlin, Hamburg, Munich, and Nuremberg, have a network of fast connections by subway *(U-Bahn)*. *U-Bahn* stations are indicated by square signs with a white "U" on a dark blue background, while *S-Bahn* stations have round signs with a white "S" on a green background. The *U-Bahn* offers very frequent services – at peak hours trains normally run every 3–5 minutes – and stations are only a short distance from each other. The *S-Bahn* trains are less frequent and the stations are farther apart.

In some cities (especially in eastern Germany) trams are the most common method of travel; in some cities they also have underground sections. Trams are ideal urban transport because they do not get stuck in traffic jams. You can use the same tickets as on buses and the *S-Bahn*. When they are above ground, remember that trams have right of way.

Various types of ticket can be bought from machines located by the entrance to stations. Children under six travel free while those under 14 get a reduced rate.

TRAVELING BY BUS

THERE IS A GOOD network of inter-city bus services in Germany, though journeys are generally no cheaper than traveling by train. Most towns have a *Zentraler Omnibus Bahnhof* (ZOB) close to the train station. Most bus services originate here and you can also get timetables and buy your tickets here.

CYCLING TOURS

CYCLING is a slow but environmentally friendly means of getting around. It also enables you to combine sightseeing with physical exercise. It is easy to rent bikes in some tourist areas, particularly at main train stations from April to October. Bikes can be taken on trains, on the *U-Bahn*, and the *S-Bahn*. For cycling routes, you will find that many newsstands, book-stores, and tourist offices have excellent maps.

DIRECTORY

AIRLINES

Air Canada
Canada: 1888-247 2262. Frankfurt: 069-27 11 51 11. www.aircanada.ca

American Airlines
US: 800-433 7300.
Frankfurt: 01803-242324. www.AA.com

British Airways
UK: 0845-773 3377.
Frankfurt: 01805-26 65 22. www.britishairways.com

Delta Air Lines
US: 1800-221 12 12.
Berlin: 0180-333 78 80. www.delta.com

Deutsche BA
01805-35 93 22. www.deutsche-ba.de

Lufthansa
UK: 0844-5544.
US: 800-645 3880.
Berlin: 01805-83 84 26. www.lufthansa.com

Qantas
Australia: 612-131313.
Frankfurt: 01805-25 06 30. www.qantas.com

United Airlines
US: 800-241 6522.
Frankfurt: 069-50 07 03 87. www.unitedairlines.de

AIRPORT INFORMATION

Berlin Schönefeld
0180-500 01 86.

Berlin Tegel
0180-500 01 86.

Berlin Tempelhof
0180-500 01 86.

Frankfurt am Main
0180-53 72 46 36.

Munich
089-97 52 13 13.

CAR RENTAL

Avis
06171-68 18 00. www.avis.com

Hertz
0180-533 35 35. www.hertz.com

Sixt Rent-a-Car
0180-525 25 25. www.e-sixt.com

EMERGENCY SERVICES

ADAC
0180-510 11 12.

AvD
069-660 60.

TRAIN TRAVEL

Deutsche Bahn
National Rail Inquiries:
0800-150 70 90. www.deutsche-bahn.de

Shopping

STORES IN GERMANY are generally of high quality but many products are not cheap. In Berlin almost anything can be bought, so long as you know where to look; outside Berlin, you'll discover that in many areas of the country the tradition of producing handicrafts and various types of folk art continues. A visit to a local market could give you the chance to buy a regional specialty to take home as a souvenir. The vast shopping malls that are springing up in every large city offer a wide choice of stores and top-quality brands.

MARKETS

A WEEKLY MARKET, known as a *Wochenmarkt*, is held in many towns throughout Germany. In smaller towns, stalls are set up in the market square, while in larger towns and cities markets may be held in specially designated squares in different neighborhoods. At these markets, you can buy fresh fruit and vegetables, cheeses, and many everyday items. Specialist fairs are often held at weekends – for example *Blumenmärkte*, where flowers are sold, or *Kunstmärkte*, where artists and craftsmen display their work for sale.

Every large town also has its *Flohmarkt* (fleamarket) where, among the masses of junk, pieces of amusing kitsch and genuine antiques can sometimes be found. In Berlin the **Antik und Trödelmarkt** is worth a visit.

In Munich there is a famous market specializing in crafts, antiques, and hardware called **Auer Dult**. This is held during the last weeks of April, July, and October.

REGIONAL SPECIALTIES

A LMOST EVERY state in Germany produces its own regional specialty and although you might not be able to take certain fresh foods back home, you could try them while you are visiting. For example, Lübeck is known for marzipan, while Nuremberg is synonymous with gingerbread. The Spreewald region is known for its pickled cucumbers, while you'll find the cherry jam produced in the Black Forest region is excellent. In Friesland

and Schleswig in the north, marinated herrings and excellent cheeses are worth trying. The hams of Westphalia have a well-deserved reputation, as do sausages from Braunschweig (Brunswick).

GIFTS AND SOUVENIRS

J UST ABOUT EVERY region of Germany has something special to offer. You could buy a beer stein from a beer hall, or a cuckoo clock from the Black Forest, for instance. If you are keen on dressing up, traditional clothes such as lederhosen and dirndl skirts can be found in Bavaria. For children, handmade puppets and marionettes are good gifts, while in Nuremberg there is a wide selection of toys. Don't forget that German optical items such as cameras, binoculars, and lenses are top quality and may be cheaper than at home.

ALCOHOLIC DRINKS

R ENOWNED German beers are best drunk straight from the barrel, but it is also worth looking out for the bottled beers that are rarely seen outside Germany.

There are a number of fine German wines, especially those from vineyards in the Mosel and Rhine valleys. Excellent wines are also produced in Bavaria and Baden-Württemberg.

Various types of spirits, as well as herbal and root-flavored liqueurs and bitters, are produced on a large scale. If you visit a monastery you may be able to buy a bottle of a herbal infusion or a liqueur that is made to a centuries-old recipe.

SHOPPING IN BERLIN

A LTHOUGH GERMAN CITIES all boast shopping malls and every town has a shopping district popular with local residents, Berlin stands out with its choice and quality of shops. If it is luxury you want, you must head for the large stores on the Kurfürstendamm, Friedrichstrasse, and Potsdamer Platz, where all the major fashion houses and perfume makers have their stores. Alternatively, if you want to explore the smaller boutiques of lesser-known designers, make your way to Berlin's Hackescher Markt in the Mitte district, or to Prenzlauer Berg.

Kaufhaus des Westens, better known as **KaDeWe** in Wittenbergplatz, is the biggest and the best department store in Berlin. Only products of the highest quality are sold in these luxurious halls, where virtually everything you need is on sale – from unusual perfumes and elegant underwear to *haute couture*, all sold in a system of stores-within-stores. The food hall on the sixth floor is legendary for its restaurant overlooking Tauentzienstrasse.

Galeries Lafayette on Friedrichstrasse is nothing less than a slice of Paris placed in the heart of Berlin. Its perfumes, household items, and clothing attract an enormous clientele, many of whom also visit the food counter, which offers a wide range of French specialties. An extraordinary glass cone rises through the middle of the store, reflecting the interiors of the stores.

Another very popular store is **Wertheim** on the Kurfürstendamm. Although its range of goods is not as broad as that at Galeries Lafayette, there is still an enormous choice and its top-floor restaurant offers excellent views over the city.

New shopping malls are being opened all the time, usually situated conveniently close to S-Bahn stations. *Passagen* (arcades) are massive three-level structures, resembling huge arcaded passageways, which contain an enormous number of stores, ranging from supermarkets and pharmacies to bars, fashion outlets, and bookstores. Like most of the stores in Berlin, they stay open until 8pm during the week and are open on Sundays.

One of the newest shopping malls is the **Potsdamer Platz Arkaden**. Built in October 1998 this is now very popular both as a shopping mall and a meeting place for Berliners and visitors.

The **Gesundbrunnencenter** is the biggest shopping arcade in Berlin, and has countless stalls and tables offering every kind of bargain. A large number of bars also makes this a popular place to meet friends for a beer or a coffee.

SHOPPING IN OTHER CITIES

MOST SHOPPERS in Munich make a beeline for the pedestrian precinct in the old town center between Karlsplatz and Marienplatz. Here you will find many big department stores such as **Ludwig Beck am Rathauseck** and chain stores where you can buy fashion and shoes as well as jewelry, souvenirs, and music.

For haute couture in Munich, the big-name stores are concentrated in these streets: Maximilianstrasse, Theatinerstrasse, Residenzstrasse, and Briennerstrasse.

The place to shop for food in Munich is the colorful **Viktualienmarkt** near Marienplatz. This has been the city's main food market for over 200 years.

The largest and most interesting shopping area in Frankfurt is the Zeil, while in Hamburg it is the Alsterhaus. Hamburg also prides itself on its many fine shopping arcades, several of which are covered and heated, making them ideal for window shopping.

CERAMICS AND GLASS

PORCELAIN MADE by Meissen is among the most sought-after in the world but it is expensive. Meissen porcelain can be found in the town itself at the **Staatliche Porzellan-Manufaktur** (see p543) or in several shops situated along the popular Kurfürstendamm in Berlin. Munich's **Porzellan Manufaktur Nymphenburg**, which has a factory and a shop in the grounds of Schloss Nymphenburg (see

p553), produces china of similarly exquisite quality. Berlin's **KPM** (Königliche Porzellan-Manufaktur), which has been in operation for over 250 years, also makes excellent porcelain.

German glassware is renowned. Old glassworks in Saxony and Bavaria still make glassware by traditional techniques: for example, beautifully cut and polished crystal tableware and ruby-colored glassware.

Some porcelain and glass-ware factories operate retail outlets with showrooms. Visitors can arrange to have purchases sent to their home.

BOOKSTORES

WHEN YOU NEED a book in English or an American newspaper, **Buchexpress** is the place to go in Berlin. In Munich, look for the **Words' Worth** and **Geobuch** for good maps and guides. In Frankfurt try the **British Bookshop**.

The **Bücherbogen** chain offers a huge choice of books and has several outlets in Berlin and elsewhere; the one under the S-Bahn bridge near Savignyplatz in Berlin has the largest stock.

DIRECTORY

MARKETS

Antik und Trödelmarkt
Erich-Steinfurth-Strasse, Berlin.
🕐 10am–5pm Sat–Sun.

Auer Dult
Mariahilfplatz, Munich.
🕐 last weeks of Apr, Jul & Oct.

SHOPPING IN BERLIN

Galeries Lafayette
Friedrichstrasse 76–78, Berlin.
📞 030-20 94 80.

Gesundbrunnen-center
Gesundbrunnen S-Bahn, Berlin.

KaDeWe
Tauentzienstrasse 21–24, Berlin.
📞 030-212 10.

Potsdamer Platz Arkaden
Debis Gelände, Berlin.

Wertheim
Kurfürstendamm 231, Berlin.
📞 030-880 030.

SHOPPING IN OTHER CITIES

Ludwig Beck am Rathauseck
Am Marienplatz 11, Munich.
📞 089-236 91 00.

Viktualienmarkt
Peterplatz–Frauenstrasse, Munich.
🕐 Mon–Sat.

CERAMICS AND GLASS

KPM
Berlin Pavillon, Berlin.
📞 030-39 00 92 15.

Porzellan Manufaktur Nymphenburg
Schloss Nymphenburg, Nördliches Schlossrondell 8, Munich.
📞 089-179 19 70.
Odeonsplatz 1, Munich.
📞 089-28 24 28.
Fünf Höfe, Salvatorpassage, Theatinerstrasse 5, Munich.
📞 089-15 90 37 18.

Staatlich Porzellan-Manufaktur
Talstrasse 9, Meissen.
Showroom
🕐 May–Oct: 9am–6pm; Nov–Apr: 9am–5pm.
📞 03521-4680.

BOOKSTORES

British Bookshop
Börsenstrasse 17, Frankfurt am Main.
📞 069-28 04 92.

Bücherbogen
Savignyplatz, Berlin.
📞 030-31 86 95 11.

Buchexpress
Unter den Eichen 97, Berlin.
📞 030-831 40 04.

Geobuch
Rosental 6, Munich.
📞 089-26 50 30.

Words' Worth
Schellingstrasse 3 & 21, Munich.
📞 089-280 9141.

Entertainment

WITH SO MUCH ON OFFER in Germany, it is possible to indulge just about any taste, whether you are looking for avant-garde theater and performance art, atmospheric clubs, or prestigious music festivals. Outside Berlin the larger cosmopolitan cities, such as Munich and Frankfurt, also offer a wide range of entertainment, from classical drama to eclectic nightclubs, from grand opera to discos.

ENTERTAINMENT LISTINGS

TOURIST INFORMATION centers offer basic information in every city and town, but the most comprehensive guides are in the local press and listings magazines. In Berlin there are *Tip* and *Zitty*, which are published every other Wednesday. The daily *Berliner Morgenpost* publishes its supplement *bm Live* on Fridays, while *Ticket* comes out on Wednesdays, together with *Tagesspiegel*.

Useful listing magazines in Munich are *In München* and *Münchener Stadtmagazin*. There is also a monthly review in English called *Munich Found*, available from the Tourist Office. You can get a monthly jazz magazine called *Münchener Jazz-Zeitung* in music shops and at jazz cafés and clubs.

In Frankfurt a magazine detailing events called *Prinz* is on sale from news kiosks. There are also free publications such as *Fritz*, while the *Frankfurter Woche* is available from the tourist office for a small sum.

BOOKING TICKETS

THEATER AND CONCERT tickets can usually be booked up to two weeks in advance, and you can buy directly at the box office or by telephone. Reserved tickets must be picked up and paid for at least half an hour before the performance. In Berlin you can also pre-book tickets at special outlets: the best one in the city center is the **Fullhouse Service**.

One Berlin agency that specializes in last-minute ticket purchase is **Hekticket Theaterkassen** on

Hardenbergerstrasse, where you can get tickets on the day, even an hour before a show. These tickets are usually sold at a 50 percent discount.

Students, senior citizens, and the disabled are entitled to a 50 percent discount on tickets, for which they must present proof of their status.

THEATER

AS YOU WOULD EXPECT in the land of Goethe and Schiller, theatrical traditions are very strong in Germany. Almost every large town has a good local theater. Berlin's most famous theater is the magnificent **Berliner Ensemble**, which was once managed by Bertold Brecht. The **Deutsches Theater** offers an ambitious program, while the **Volksbühne** stages works by young playwrights.

Munich has many theaters, with most of the productions in German. A venerable venue is the **Cuvilliéstheater** in the Residenz (*see pp548–9*), while the **Deutsches Theater** offers some foreign plays. The **Kammerspiele** is dedicated to contemporary works.

Frankfurt has a theater that offers productions in English, aptly called the **English Theater**. You will find a range of old and new plays put on at the city's main theater, the **Schauspielhaus**.

CLASSICAL MUSIC AND DANCE

BERLIN HAS one of the finest orchestras in the world — the Berlin Philharmonic Orchestra, whose home, the **Philharmonie**, is also one of the world's most beautiful concert halls. The city boasts three opera houses: the **Staatsoper Unter den**

Linden and the **Komische Oper** are in the eastern part of city, while the **Deutsche Oper Berlin** is in the west. The three opera houses have ballet programs built into their repertoires and these are performed largely by resident dance companies.

Munich has two opera houses and several distinguished resident orchestras. A visit to the **Bayerische Staatsoper** is a must if you appreciate grand opera and ballet. The **Gasteig** is a modern complex offering a range of classical concerts, large and small. Munich's **Prinzregententheater** is the main venue for ballet and other musical performances.

Frankfurt has a wide choice of musical events. At the **Alte Oper**, there are three halls for orchestral and vocal performances, while the **Jahrhunderthalle** also offers classical recitals and concerts.

JAZZ, ROCK, AND POP

BERLIN IS ALWAYS a popular destination for world-famous musicians, whose concerts are often held in the **Waldbühne**. Numerous music clubs offer daily opportunities to hear good music. Favorite venues are **Quasimodo** in the western part of the city center, **Schlot** in Prenzlauer Berg and **Junction Bar** in Kreuzberg. Good traditional jazz can be heard at Berlin's annual Jazzfest in the first week of November. At the same time experimental modern works are performed at the Total Music Meeting.

In Munich in the late evening you could drop into a small, hip club like **Atomic Café** or go to hear blues, rock, or jazz at **Feierwerk**. Dixieland jazz is played at the **Alabamahalle** and traditional jazz at **Jam**. There are often free rock concerts in Munich in summer at the Theatron in Olympiapark.

Frankfurt has an enthusiastic jazz scene which is centered around *Jazzgasse* (Jazz Alley) or Kleine Bockenheimer Strasse. Apart from many bars here, you will find the city's top jazz venue, **Jazzkeller**, in a cellar. If you like to listen to different kinds of live music such as African, Asian, and salsa, try **Brotfabrik**, which also has a café.

Discos in Munich and Frankfurt mainly cater, naturally enough, for a young crowd and play music of all kinds: from chart hits, funk, and techno to heavy metal. Some have a dress policy.

FESTIVALS AND FAIRS

GERMANS LOVE festivals and fairs and this country probably has more than most other European countries. The most famous is the *Oktoberfest* in Munich *(see p554)*, which is a huge event that celebrates beer with two weeks of drinking, from the last week in September. Not to be outdone, wine-drinkers can enjoy a wine festival *(Weinfest)* in August in the Rhine-Mosel area and in October in the Rhineland.

Germany has produced many of the world's foremost musicians, so classical music festivals are popular and take place in many German towns. To give a few examples, there is a Bach Festival in May in Leipzig *(see p543)*, while Bonn *(see p561)* is the venue for the International Beethoven Festival from late September. Beginning in late July, Bayreuth *(see p540)* hosts the annual *Opernfest* of Richard Wagner's *Ring Cycle*. However, be aware that you cannot just turn up for a performance here – you will have to book tickets at least a year in advance or else get them with a package holiday.

December brings a rush of fairs. Many towns and cities, including Berlin and Munich, stage a Christmas market *(Christkindlmarkt)*, but the one in Nuremberg is considered to be the most impressive.

OUTDOOR ACTIVITIES

GERMANY IS the ideal destination for a range of outdoor activities, including hiking, cycling, fishing, and sailing. It also has a number of winter-sports resorts with first-class ski slopes, the best being in the Bavarian Alps, which lie only an hour's drive from Munich.

There is a tradition of great horsemanship in Germany. Keen riders will find excellent facilities in many areas, as well as the chance to attend international competitions.

Tennis is the second most popular sport (after soccer) and there are several annual professional tournaments. You can play on the many public courts, or find a hotel with its own facilities. Golfers with the appropriate handicap can play on most golf courses simply by paying a green fee.

DIRECTORY

BOOKING TICKETS

Fullhouse Service
Unter den Linden 36–38, Berlin.
030-3087 85685.

Hekticket Theaterkassen
Hardenbergstrasse 29d, Berlin.
030-230 99 30.

THEATER

Berliner Ensemble
Bertold-Brecht-Platz 1, Berlin.
030-28 40 81 55.

Cuvilliéstheater
Residenzstrasse 1, Munich.
089-21 85 19 40.

Deutsches Theater
Schumannstrasse 13a, Berlin.
030-28 44 12 25.

Deutsches Theater
Schwanthalerstrasse 13, Munich.
089-55 23 44 44.

English Theater
Kaiserstrasse 52, Frankfurt.
069-24 23 16 20.

Kammerspiele
Maximillianstrasse 28, Munich.
089-233 966 00.

Schauspielhaus
Willy-Brandt-Platz, Frankfurt.
069-13 40 400.

Volksbühne
Rosa-Luxemburg-Platz, Berlin.
030-247 67 72.

CLASSICAL MUSIC AND DANCE

Alter Oper
Opernplatz, Frankfurt.
069-134 04 00

Bayerische Staatsoper
Max-Joseph-Platz 1, Munich.
089-21 85 19 20.

Deutsche Oper
Bismarckstrasse. 34–37, Berlin.
030-341 02 49.

Gasteig
Rosenheimer Strasse 5, Munich.
089-54 81 81 81.

Jahrhunderthalle
Pffafenwiese, Höchst, Frankfurt.
069-360 12 40.

Komische Oper
Behrenstrasse. 55–57, Berlin.
030-47 99 74 00.

Philharmonie
Herbert-von-Karajan-Strasse 1, Berlin.
030-25 48 81 32.

Prinzregenten-theater
Prinzregentenplatz 12, Munich.
089-21 85 19 20.

Staatsoper
Unter den Linden 7, Berlin.
030-20 35 45 55.

JAZZ, ROCK, AND POP

Alabamahalle
Domagkstrasse 33, Munich.
089-324 42 53.

Atomic Café
Neuturmstrasse 5, Munich.
089-30 77 72 32.

Brotfabrik
Bachmannstrasse 2–4, Frankfurt.
069-97 84 55 13.

Feierwerk
Hansastrasse 39, Munich.
089-72 48 80.

Jam
Rosenheimer Strasse 4, Haidhausen, Munich.
089-48 44 09.

Jazzkeller
Kleine Bockenheimer Strasse 18a, Frankfurt.
069-28 85 37.

Junction Bar
Gneisenaustrasse 18, Berlin.
030-694 66 02.

Quasimodo
Kantstrasse 12a, Berlin.
030-312 80 86.

Schlot
Chausseestrasse 18, Berlin.
030-448 21 60.

Waldbühne
Glockenturmstrasse 1, Berlin.
030-23 08 82 30.

Where to Stay in Germany

M OST GERMAN CITIES have several deluxe and international chain hotels offering a high level of comfort. Finding less expensive accommodations can be difficult, unless you stay outside the center. Away from the cities, high prices generally apply to hotels in historic buildings or peaceful locations; a room in a pension or private home is usually more reasonable.

	NUMBER OF ROOMS	RESTAURANT	PRIVATE PARKING	AIR-CONDITIONING

BERLIN

EAST OF CENTER: *Märkischer Hof* €€ · 20 · · ■ ·
Linienstrasse 133, 10 115. **Map** E3. (*030-282 71 55.* FAX *030-282 43 31.*
Housed in a historic 19th-century building, not far from Oranienburger Strasse, this small hotel has a family atmosphere. The standard is astonishingly high in relation to the prices. 🔒 TV 📶

| | 20 | | ■ | |

EAST OF CENTER: *Hackescher Markt* €€€ · 31 · ● · ■ ·
Grosse Präsidentenstrasse 8, 10 178. **Map** E3. (*030-28 00 30.*
FAX *030-28 00 31 11.* W www.hackescher-markt.com
A charming small hotel, the Hackescher Markt boasts an excellent restaurant and elegantly furnished rooms. 🔒 TV 📶

| | 31 | ● | ■ | |

EAST OF CENTER: *Berlin Hilton* €€€€ · 589 · ● · ■ · ●
Mohrenstrasse 30, 10 117. **Map** E3. (*030-202 30.* FAX *030-20 23 42 69.*
W www.hilton.com
The Berlin Hilton enjoys superb views of the Deutscher Dom. All the rooms are spacious and comfortable, and there are three very good restaurants, a gym, and a swimming pool. 🔒 TV 🏊 📶

| | 589 | ● | ■ | ● |

EAST OF CENTER: *DeragHotel Grosser Kurfürst* €€€€ · 144 · ●
Neue Ross Strasse 11–12, 10 179. **Map** F3. (*030-24 60 00.* FAX *030-24 60 03 00.*
W www.deraghotels.de
This mid-range chain hotel is located near a U-Bahn station. It overlooks the Spree river and is a pleasant mix of modern style and minimalist Berlin architecture. 🔒 TV 📶

| | 144 | ● | | |

EAST OF CENTER: *Four Seasons Hotel* €€€€€ · 204 · ● · ■ · ●
Charlottenstrasse 49, 10 117. **Map** E3. (*030-203 38.* FAX *030-20 33 61 19.*
W www.fourseasons.com
Regarded as one of Berlin's most exclusive hotels, the Four Seasons has exquisite Neo-Baroque style interiors. Guests can make use of a wide range of facilities, such as a gym and a business center. 🔒 TV 📶

| | 204 | ● | ■ | ● |

WEST OF CENTER: *Hotel Palace Berlin* €€€€ · 282 · ● · ■ · ●
Budapester Strasse 45, 10 787. **Map** C4. (*030-250 20.* FAX *030-25 02 11 09.*
W www.palace.de
This elegant hotel, frequented by politicians and film stars, is valued for its intimate atmosphere, impeccable service, and famous gourmet restaurant, First Floor *(see p581)*. There are also business facilities and a fitness center. 🔒 TV 📶

| | 282 | ● | ■ | ● |

WEST OF CENTER: *Grand Hyatt Berlin* €€€€€€ · 342 · ● · ■ · ●
Marlene Dietrich Platz 2, 10 785. **Map** D4. (*030-25 53 12 34.* FAX *030-25 53 12 35.*
Reservations (*0180-523 12 34.* W www.hyatt.com
One of the most luxurious hotels in Berlin, the Grand Hyatt offers all the modern conveniences one expects of a first-class hotel, including a good restaurant (the Vox), a discreet café (the Tizian), a sushi bar, a gym, and a conference center. 🔒 TV 🏊 📶

| | 342 | ● | ■ | ● |

WEST OF CENTER: *Hotel Brandenburger Hof* €€€€€ · 82 · ● · ■
Eislebener Strasse 14, 10 789. **Map** B4. (*030-21 40 50.* FAX *030-21 40 51 00.*
W www.brandenburger-hof.com
A tranquil location, perfect service, and luxury rooms, furnished in the Bauhaus style and decorated with works of art, ensure this hotel's reputation as one of the city's best. The restaurant, Die Quadriga *(see p581)* is also well-known. 🔒 TV 📶

| | 82 | ● | ■ | |

WEST OF CENTER: *Kempinski Hotel Bristol Berlin* €€€€€ · 301 · ● · ■ · ●
Kurfürstendamm 27, 10 719. **Map** B4. (*030-88 43 40.* FAX *030-883 60 75.*
W www.kempinskiberlin.de
Occupying a distinctive semicircular building, this renowned hotel offers spacious, luxurious accommodations and an unrivaled range of amenities. In addition there is an excellent restaurant and bistro-café. 🔒 TV 🏊 📶

| | 301 | ● | ■ | ● |

Map references refer to map of Berlin on pp528–9

<table>
<tr><td colspan="2"></td><td>NUMBER OF ROOMS</td><td>RESTAURANT</td><td>PRIVATE PARKING</td><td>AIR-CONDITIONING</td></tr>
</table>

Price categories for a double room with private bathroom or shower, and including breakfast, service, and tax:

€ under €80
€€ €80–130
€€€ €130–180
€€€€ €180–230
€€€€€ over €230

RESTAURANT
Hotel restaurant or dining room usually open to non-residents as well as to hotel guests.

PRIVATE PARKING
Parking provided by the hotel in a private car park or private garage on the hotel site or nearby. Some hotels charge for use of private parking facilities.

CREDIT CARDS
The credit card symbol indicates that the hotel accepts the major credit cards.

		Number of Rooms	Restaurant	Private Parking	Air-Conditioning
FARTHER AFIELD: *Best Western Hotel City-Consul* Rathausstrasse 2–3, 10367. 📞 030-55 75 70. FAX 030-55 75 72 72. w www.consul-hotels.com This modern hotel is just a 10-minute walk from Alexanderplatz. It is furnished to a high standard, and offers fax and modem facilities for guests' use. An excellent buffet breakfast is served. 🛏 TV 🗂	€€	98	●	■	●
FARTHER AFIELD: *Villa Kastania* Kastanienallee 20, 14 052 Berlin-Charlottenburg. 📞 030-300 00 20. FAX 030-30 00 02 10. w www.villakastania.com Situated in a quiet street, with good connections by U-Bahn to the city center, the intimate Villa Kastania maintains high standards. Some rooms are fitted with small kitchens. 🛏 TV 🏊 🗂	€€€	48	●	■	●
EASTERN GERMANY					
DRESDEN: *art'otel Dresden* Ostra-Allee 33, 01 067. 📞 0351-492 20. FAX 0351-492 27 77. w www.artotel.de An interestingly designed hotel, located near the Zwinger building. Its comfortable rooms feature paintings by well-known artists, while there is also an art gallery with regular exhibitions. The excellent recreational facilities include a sauna. 🛏 TV 🗂	€€	174	●	■	
DRESDEN: *Romantik Hotel Pattis* Merbitzer Strasse 53, 01 157 Dresden-Briesnitz. 📞 0351-425 50. FAX 0351-425 52 55. w www.pattis.net Occupying a former 16th-century mill, this hotel enjoys an unrivaled setting in a beautiful park. The restaurant's renowned chef prepares dishes based on recipes from the Saxon royal court. 🛏 TV 🏊 🗂	€€€€	47	●	■	
LEIPZIG: *Balance Hotel Leipzig Alte Messe* Breslauerstrasse 33, 04 299 Leipzig-Stötteritz. 📞 0341-867 90. FAX 0341-867 94 44. w www.balancehotel-leipzig.com This chain hotel is housed in an Art Nouveau building and has tastefully decorated rooms. The restaurant serves international cuisine. 🛏 TV 🗂	€€	126	●		●
LEIPZIG: *Hotel Fürstenhof* Tröndlinring 8, 04 105. 📞 0341-14 00. FAX 0341-140 37 00. w www.arabellasheraton.com The attentive staff and grand surroundings, including marble floors and beautifully decorated ceilings, add to the pleasure of a stay here. 🛏 TV 🏊 🗂	€€€	92	●	■	●
WEIMAR: *Hotel Elephant* Markt 19, 99 423. 📞 03643-80 20. FAX 03643-80 26 10. w www.arabellasheraton.com Guests, including many celebrities, have been received here since the 16th century. The rooms are comfortable, and the hotel has two restaurants that include Thuringian dishes in their repertoire. 🛏 TV 🗂	€€€€	99	●	■	
MUNICH					
CENTRAL MUNICH: *Cosmopolitan Hotel* Hohenzollernstrasse 5, 80 801. 📞 089-38 38 10. FAX 089-38 38 11 11. w www.cosmopolitan-hotel.de Located in the Schwabing district, this hotel has comfortable, modern rooms. The hotel bar is a popular meeting place in the evenings. 🛏 TV 🗂	€€	71		■	
CENTRAL MUNICH: *Romantik Hotel Insel Mühle* Von-Kahr-Strasse 87, 80 999 München-Untermenzing. 📞 089-810 10. FAX 089-812 05 71. w www.weber-gastronomie.de One of the most beautiful hotels in Munich. Most of its stylish rooms have balconies and the restaurant is highly recommended. 🛏 TV 🗂	€€€	38	●	■	

	NUMBER OF ROOMS	RESTAURANT	PRIVATE PARKING	AIR-CONDITIONING
Price categories for a double room with private bathroom or shower, and including breakfast, service, and tax: € under €80 €€ €80–130 €€€ €130–180 €€€€ €180–230 €€€€€ over €230 **RESTAURANT** Hotel restaurant or dining room usually open to non-residents as well as to hotel guests. **PRIVATE PARKING** Parking provided by the hotel in a private car park or private garage on the hotel site or nearby. Some hotels charge for use of private parking facilities. **CREDIT CARDS** The credit card symbol indicates that the hotel accepts the major credit cards.				
CENTRAL MUNICH: *Bayerischer Hof* €€€€€ Promenadeplatz 2–6, 80 333. **Map** C4. (089-212 00. FAX 089-212 09 06. W www.bayerischerhof.de The internationally renowned Bayerischer Hof has a central location, and lavishly furnished rooms. There is a good choice of restaurants, as well as swimming pool, designer boutiques, and a business center.	399	●	■	●
CENTRAL MUNICH: *Kempinski Hotel Vier Jahreszeiten München* €€€€€ Maximilianstrasse 17, 80 539. **Map** D3. (089-212 50. FAX 089-21 25 20 00. W www.kempinski-vierjahreszeiten.de Known for its excellent service and elegant restaurant, this luxurious hotel will not fail to impress. All the rooms are well-equipped.	316	●	■	●
SOUTHERN GERMANY				
BAMBERG: *Romantik Hotel Weinhaus Messerschmitt* €€ Lange Strasse 47, 96 047. (0951-297 800. FAX 0951-297 8029. W www.hotel-messerschmitt.de This hotel has been owned by the same family for many years. The cozy atmosphere and classic regional cuisine are key attractions.	19	●		
BAMBERG: *Residenzschloss* €€€ Untere Sandstrasse 32, 96 049. (0951-609 10. FAX 0951-609 17 01. W www.residenzschloss.com The Residenzschloss has a wonderful riverside setting. You can expect a high standard of accommodation and ample facilities.	185	●	■	
BAYREUTH: *Treff Hotel Rheingold* €€ Austrasse 2/Unteres Tor, 95 445. (0921-756 50. FAX 0921-756 58 01. W www.ramada-treff.de Guests are well-catered for at this hotel, which has a magnificent swimming pool, gym, sauna, solarium, and golf course.	146	●	■	
FREIBURG IM BREISGAU: *Colombi-Hotel* €€€€ Rotteckring 16, 79 098. (0761-210 60. FAX 0761-314 10. A quiet, centrally located hotel, offering impeccable service, luxurious accommodations, and a superb range of facilities.	120	●	■	●
HEIDELBERG: *Heidelberg Marriott Hotel garni* €€€ Vangerowstrasse 16, 69 115. (06221-90 80. FAX 06221-90 86 60. W www.marriott.com Heidelberg's Marriott hotel, on the bank of the Neckar river, has a private jetty as well as a well-equipped conference hall, and atmospheric wine bar. From the café there is a beautiful view along the river.	247	●	■	
HEIDELBERG: *Holländer Hof garni* €€€ Neckarstaden 66, 69 117. (06221-605 00. FAX 06221-60 50 60. W www.hollaender-hof.de Close to all the main sights of interest and with views of Heidelberg's famous castle, this hotel has a long tradition of warm hospitality.	39	●		
NUREMBERG: *Burghotel-Grosses Haus* €€ Lammsgasse 3, 90 403. (0911-23 88 90. FAX 0911-23 88 91 00. W www.altstadthotels-nuernberg.de The Burghotel-Grosses Haus boasts stunning views of the old town. Amenities include a swimming pool, sauna, and rustic bar.	57		■	
NUREMBERG: *Romantik Hotel Am Josephsplatz* €€ Josephsplatz 30/32, 90 403. (0911-21 44 70. FAX 0911-21 44 72 00. W www.romantikhotels.com This splendid hotel lies in the heart of the old town. Parts of the building date back to the 17th century. Some of the elegant rooms open onto a flower-filled courtyard.	36			

Map references refer to map of Munich on pp546–7

NUREMBERG: *Maritim* €€€€ 316
Frauentorgraben 11, 90 443. [0911-236 30. FAX 0911-236 38 23.
W www.maritim.de
A hotel of international standard, close to the train station. The rooms are
lovingly decorated and there are several dining options. 🛏 TV ⛱ 🖎

PASSAU: *Passauer Wolf* €€ 40
Rindermarkt 6–8, 94 032. [0851-931 51 10. FAX 0851-931 51 50.
W www.passauerwolf.de
Modern rooms and excellent cuisine make for a pleasant stay in this
attractive historic building between the old town and the Danube. 🛏 TV 🖎

ROTHENBURG OB DER TAUBER: *Markusturm Romantik Hotel* €€€ 25
Rödergasse 1, 91 541. [09861-942 80. FAX 09861-942 8113.
W www.markusturm.de
Housed in an old building dating from 1264, this hotel has rooms
furnished with beautiful antique furniture. 🛏 TV 🖎

STUTTGART: *Kronen-Hotel* €€€ 84
Kronenstrasse 48, 70 174. [0711-225 10. FAX 0711-225 14 04.
W www.vch.de
The Kronen is located in a tranquil part of the city, close to the train station.
Breakfast is very good and there is a garden with a terrace. 🛏 TV 🖎

STUTTGART: *Inter-Continental* €€€€ 276
Willy-Brandt-Strasse 30, 70 173. [0711-202 00. FAX 0711-20 20 20 20.
W www.stuttgart.interconti.com
This modern chain hotel offers high standards of accommodations and a wide
range of facilities, including a business center and golf course. 🛏 TV ⛱ 🖎

WÜRZBURG: *Alter Kranen* € 14
Kärrmergasse 11, 97 070. [0931-351 80. FAX 0931-500 10.
W www.hotel-alter-kranen.de
The Alter Kranen is a mid-range hotel located on the bank of the Main
river. A generous buffet breakfast is served in the morning. 🛏 TV 🖎

WESTERN GERMANY

BONN: *Schlosshotel Kommende Ramersdorf* €€ 18
Oberkasslerstrasse 10, 53 227 Bonn-Beuel. [0228-44 07 34. FAX 0228-44 44 00.
This hotel is housed in the imposing castle of the Teutonic Knights.
Former meeting halls have been converted into a restaurant and
function rooms. 🛏 TV 🖎

BONN: *Kaiser Karl* €€€ 42
Vorgebirgsstrasse 56, 53 119. [0228-98 55 70. FAX 0228-985 57 77.
W www.kaiser-karl-hotel-bonn.de
Comfort and good service are guaranteed at this exclusive hotel. Breakfast
is served in the lounge or garden, and there is also a bar. 🛏 TV 🖎

BONN: *Best Western Domicil* €€€€ 44
Thomas-Mann-Strasse 24–26, 53 111. [0228-72 90 90. FAX 0228-69 12 07.
W www.bestwestern.de
In addition to modern, well-furnished rooms, the hotel has a pleasant bar,
a winter garden, and a restaurant serving international cuisine. 🛏 TV 🖎

COLOGNE: *Coellner Hof* €€ 79
Hansaring 100, 50 670. [0221-166 60. FAX 0221-166 61 66. W www.coellnerhof.de
Staff at this well-known, beautifully furnished hotel always give guests top-
quality service. The restaurant is recommended. 🛏 TV 🖎

COLOGNE: *Rheinblick garni* €€ 27
Uferstrasse 20, 50 996 Köln-Rodenkirchen. [0221-340 91 40. FAX 0221-39 21 39.
A major attraction of this inexpensive hotel is its location on the banks
of the Rhine. Enjoy the views of the river while you take breakfast in
the garden. 🛏 TV 🖎

COLOGNE: *Im Wasserturm* €€€€ 88
Kaygasse 2, 50 676. [0221-200 80. FAX 0221-200 88 88.
W www.hotel-im-wasserturm.de
Housed in a 19th-century water tower, this hotel is set in a park near the
old town. The wonderful interiors were designed by a Parisian architect.
Sophisticated service and a panoramic restaurant on the 11th floor add to
guests' enjoyment of their stay here. 🛏 TV ⛱ 🖎

<table>
<tr><td colspan="2">

Price categories for a double room with private bathroom or shower, and including breakfast, service, and tax:

€ under €80
€€ €80–130
€€€ €130–180
€€€€ €180–230
€€€€€ over €230

</td><td colspan="4">

RESTAURANT
Hotel restaurant or dining room usually open to non-residents as well as to hotel guests.

PRIVATE PARKING
Parking provided by the hotel in a private car park or private garage on the hotel site or nearby. Some hotels charge for use of private parking facilities.

CREDIT CARDS
The credit card symbol indicates that the hotel accepts the major credit cards.

</td></tr>
</table>

		NUMBER OF ROOMS	RESTAURANT	PRIVATE PARKING	AIR-CONDITIONING
COLOGNE: *Hyatt Regency* Kennedy-Ufer 2a, 50 679. **(** 0221-828 12 34. **FAX** 0221-828 13 70. **W** www.cologne.regency.hyatt.de Lush greenery and fountains grace the entrance hall of the Hyatt Regency, giving it the feel of a botanical garden. High levels of comfort and a great range of facilities put it among the city's best hotels.	€€€€€	305	●	■	●
FRANKFURT AM MAIN: *Borger garni* Triebstrasse 51, 60 388 Frankfurt-Bergen-Enkheim. **(** 06109-309 00. **FAX** 06109-30 90 30. A long-established, family-run hotel. The rooms are comfortable and the area has good transport connections to the city center.	€€	34	●	■	
FRANKFURT AM MAIN: *Best Western Alexander am Zoo garni* Waldschmidtstrasse 59–61, 60 316. **(** 069-94 96 00. **FAX** 069-94 96 07 20. **W** www.alexanderamzoo.de The Best Western features modern Italian-style decor. There is a pleasant bar and a varied breakfast buffet. Ideal venue for business travelers.	€€€	59		■	
FRANKFURT AM MAIN: *Frankfurt Hotel Savoy* Wiesenhüttenstrasse 42, 60 329. **(** 069-27 39 60. **FAX** 069-27 39 67 95. **W** www.savoyhotel.de This superior hotel has spacious rooms decorated in Swedish style and a roof-top fitness center and swimming pool.	€€€	144	●		●
FRANKFURT AM MAIN: *Steigenberger Frankfurter Hof* Kaiserplatz, 60 311. **(** 069-215 02. **FAX** 069-21 59 00. **W** www.frankfurter-hof.steigenberger.de From the vast presidential suite to the standard rooms, accommodations at the Steigenberger chain's flagship hotel are truly luxurious. Guests can choose between a number of excellent restaurants.	€€€€€€	332	●		●
KOBLENZ: *Top Hotel Krämer garni* Kardinal-Krementz-Strasse 12, 56 073. **(** 0261-40 62 00. **FAX** 0261-413 40. **W** www.tophotel-k.de A warm and friendly welcome is extended to all at this family-owned hotel in a quiet area of the city center.	€€	22		■	
KOBLENZ: *Mercure* Julius-Wegeler-Strasse 6, 56 068. **(** 0261-13 60. **FAX** 0261-136 11 99. **W** www.mercure.com The Mercure has a vast, mirrored façade and a stylish restaurant. Rooms are comfortable and tastefully furnished.	€€€	169	●	■	
MAINZ: *Dorint Hotel Mainz* Augustusstrasse 6, 55 131. **(** 06131-95 40. **FAX** 06131-95 41 00. **W** www.dorint.de Baroque cellars dating from the 17th century have been integrated into this unique hotel building, which offers superior accommodations. Guests have the use of a number of business and recreational facilities. The Bajazzo restaurant serves international and regional cuisine.	€€€	217	●		●
MAINZ: *Günnewig Bristol Hotel* Friedrich-Ebert-Strasse 20, 55 130 Mainz-Weisenau. **(** 06131-80 60. **FAX** 06131-80 61 00. **W** www.guennewig.de Popular with business travelers, this conveniently located hotel has air-conditioned rooms and a good restaurant.	€€€	75	●	■	●
TRIER: *Dorint Hotel Porta Nigra* Porta-Nigra-Platz 1, 54 292. **(** 0651-270 10. **FAX** 0651-270 11 70. **W** www.dorint.de One of the finest hotels in Trier, with rooms providing a high degree of comfort and a restaurant to satisfy gourmets.	€€€	106	●	■	

NORTHERN GERMANY

BREMEN: *Lichtsinn garni* €€ 30
Rembertistrasse 11, 28 203. **[** *0421-36 80 70.* **FAX** *0421-32 72 87.*
W www.hotel-lichtsinn.de
Ten suites equipped with small kitchens, as well as individual rooms, are
available in this family-run hotel in the city center. ☐ TV 🛒

BREMEN: *Park Hotel* €€€€€ 149
Im Bürgerpark, 28 209. **[** *0421-340 80.* **FAX** *0421-340 86 02.*
W www.park-hotel-bremen.de
A luxurious hotel, renowned for its family atmosphere, excellent service,
and well-equipped conference rooms. Try the restaurant for some
delicious fish, poultry, and game dishes. ☐ TV 🏊 🛒

HAMBURG: *Europäischer Hof* €€€ 320
Kirchenallee 45, 20 099. **[** *040-24 82 48.* **FAX** *040-24 82 47 99.*
W www.europaeischer-hof.de
The Europäischer Hof offers modern, luxurious interiors and
faultless service. The hotel also issues guests with a card entitling them
to three days' free travel on Hamburg's public transportation system.
☐ TV 🏊 🛒

HAMBURG: *Hafen Hamburg* €€€ 355
Seewartenstrasse 9, 20 459. **[** *040-31 11 30.* **FAX** *040-31 11 37 55.*
W www.hotel-hamburg.de
Formerly a sailor's house, this building has been extended and
refurbished as a hotel with large comfortable rooms. Enjoy the panoramic
views of the port from the restaurant. ☐ TV 🛒

HAMBURG: *Vier Jahreszeiten* €€€€€ 154
Neuer Jungfernstieg 9–14, 20 354. **[** *040-349 40.* **FAX** *040-34 94 26 00.*
W www.raffles-hvj.de
The interior of this lavish establishment features precious woods,
expensive rugs, and antiques. The restaurant, well-stocked wine bar, and
excellent patisserie are very popular. ☐ TV 🛒

HANOVER: *Best Western Premier Parkhotel Kronsberg* €€€ 200
Gut Kronsberg 1. 18, 30 539. **[** *0511-874 00.* **FAX** *0511-86 71 12.*
W www.kronsberg.bestwestern.de
Opposite the Hanover trade fair area, this modern hotel, which offers a wide
range of amenities, is surrounded by beautiful greenery. ☐ TV 🏊 🛒

HANOVER: *Grand Hotel Mussmann garni* €€€ 140
Ernst-August-Platz 7, 30 159. **[** *0511-365 60.* **FAX** *0511-365 61 45.*
W www.grandhotel.de
A well-maintained hotel in the city center, across the road from
the train station. The rooms are well-equipped and the service
commendable. ☐ TV 🛒

HANOVER: *Hotel Georgenhof* €€€ 14
Herrenhäuser Kirchweg 20, 30 167. **[** *0511-70 22 44.* **FAX** *0511-70 85 59.*
Famous for having one of the best restaurants in the country, with an
extensive wine list, the Georgenhof is close to Hanover's center. ☐ TV 🛒

LÜBECK: *Alter Speicher garni* €€ 45
Beckergrube 91–93, 23 552. **[** *0451-710 45.* **FAX** *0451-70 48 04.*
W www.hotel-alter-speicher.de
Built in the style of a traditional granary, this hotel has comfortably
furnished rooms and its own sauna and solarium. ☐ TV 🛒

LÜBECK: *Kaiserhof garni* €€ 60
Kronsforder Allee 11–13, 23 560. **[** *0451-70 33 01.* **FAX** *0451-79 50 83.*
W www.kaiserhof-luebeck.de
A modern hotel has been created within two restored bourgeois
houses. All the rooms are beautifully decorated and the hotel
has a terrace and a communal lounge area. ☐ TV 🏊 🛒

MÜNSTER: *Schloss Wilkinghege* €€€ 36
Steinfurter Strasse 374, 48 159 Münster-Ausserhalb. **[** *0251-21 30 45.*
FAX *0251-21 28 98.* **W** www.schloss-wilkinghege.de
Guests return here again and again for the modern, elegantly furnished
rooms and the highly recommended restaurant specializing in regional
dishes. There is also a golf course. ☐ TV 🛒

For key to symbols see back flap

Where to Eat in Germany

GERMAN CUISINE does not enjoy the same reputation as that of some European countries, but nevertheless you can eat very well here. Many establishments specialize in regional dishes, which, although somewhat heavy, are always very appetizing. In the past few years, some fine restaurants have opened. Run by renowned master chefs, they serve excellent international cuisine of the very highest standard.

	VEGETARIAN DISHES	OUTDOOR TABLES	GERMAN WINE LIST

BERLIN

EAST OF CENTER: *Oren* — €
Oranienburger Strasse 28, 10 117. **Map** E3. 030-282 82 28.
This restaurant specializes in Jewish and Arabic vegetarian dishes for groups of 10 people or more. The menu includes such delicacies as falafels, tofu-stuffed peppers, and excellent eggplant dishes. Wines from Israel.
Vegetarian Dishes ●, Outdoor Tables ■, German Wine List ●

EAST OF CENTER: *Zum Nussbaum* — €
Am Nussbaum 3, 10 178. **Map** E3. 030-242 30 95.
This inn, located in one of the lanes of the Nikolaiviertel, is one of the most popular places in town. The cuisine is traditional Berlin style – both pork knuckle and herrings feature on the menu.
Outdoor Tables ■, German Wine List ●

EAST OF CENTER: *art'otel Berlin Mitte* — €€€
Wallstrasse 70–73, 10 179. **Map** F3. 030-24 06 20.
Good regional cuisine, with a light, modern touch, and an excellent selection of imported wines. The function room is located in an 18th-century palace and has an ornamental Rococo ceiling. ● *Sun, Mon.*
Vegetarian Dishes ●, Outdoor Tables ■, German Wine List ●

EAST OF CENTER: *Mare Bê* — €€€
Rosenthaler Strasse 46–48, 10 178. **Map** E3. 030-283 65 45.
An excellent establishment for lovers of southern French, Italian, and Spanish cooking, with a hint of the Middle East. It is worth eating here on a Tuesday, when the house specialty – oysters – is served. The restaurant has a peaceful garden.
Vegetarian Dishes ●, Outdoor Tables ■

EAST OF CENTER: *Reinhard's* — €€€
Poststrasse 28, 10 178. **Map** F3. 030-242 52 95.
A captivating restaurant with a stylish interior reminiscent of the 1920s. The specialty is *Das Geheimnis aus dem Kaiserhof* ("The Secret from the Emperor's Court") – a succulent steak served in a special sauce, apparently created for Max Liebermann.
Vegetarian Dishes ●, Outdoor Tables ■, German Wine List ●

EAST OF CENTER: *Borchardt* — €€€€
Französische Strasse 47, 10 117. **Map** E3. 030-20 38 71 10.
One of a small number of restaurants that have retained their original early 20th-century interiors, with marble columns, mosaics, and parquet floors. Prices are reasonable, and the Italian food is very good.
Vegetarian Dishes ●, Outdoor Tables ■, German Wine List ●

EAST OF CENTER: *Lorenz Adlon* — €€€€€
Unter den Linden 77, 10 117. **Map** E3. 030-226 10.
Thanks to the culinary art of its chef, Karlheinz Hauser, L'Etoile is easily one of the best restaurants in town, serving French gourmet cuisine.
Vegetarian Dishes ●, German Wine List ●

EAST OF CENTER: *Margaux* — €€€€€
Unter den Linden 78, 10 117. **Map** E3. 030-226 520 11.
The Michelin-starred Margaux represents the new Berlin better than any other gourmet restaurant. It is stylish and urbane, in the classic yet creative French dishes, the sophisticated interior, the service and the patrons. ● *Sun lunch.*
Vegetarian Dishes ●, German Wine List ●

WEST OF CENTER: *Ottenthal* — €€€
Kantstrasse 153, 10 623. **Map** B4. 030-313 31 62.
Almost opposite the Theater des Westens, the modest interior of this restaurant is decorated in rural Austrian style. The owner/chef serves good Austrian food and an excellent selection of Austrian wines, accompanied by music from Mozart. Try the delicious Wiener Schnitzel.
Vegetarian Dishes ●

WEST OF CENTER: *First Floor* — €€€€
Budapester Strasse 45, 10 787. **Map** C4. 030-25 02 10 20.
A restaurant of the highest caliber, situated in the Hotel Palace Berlin *(see p574)*. The menu includes traditional German fare, as well as more sophisticated creations with fish, crab, and aromatic truffles. A reservation is necessary. ● *lunch Sat.*
Vegetarian Dishes ●, German Wine List ●

Map references refer to map of Berlin on pp528–9

	Vegetarian Dishes	Outdoor Tables	German Wine List

Price categories for a three course meal without drinks, including cover charge, tax, and service:

€ under €20
€€ €20–30
€€€ €30–40
€€€€ €40–50
€€€€€ over €50

VEGETARIAN DISHES
Available as a starter, a main course, or both.

OUTDOOR TABLES
Restaurants with a garden, courtyard, or terrace.

GERMAN WINE LIST
A good selection of German wines is available.

CREDIT CARDS
Major credit cards are accepted in restaurants where the credit card symbol is shown.

WEST OF CENTER: *Ana e Bruno* €€€€€
Sophie-Charlotten Strasse 101, 14 059. **Map** A3. ☎ 030-325 71 10.
The elegant pastel interior and soft Italian melodies at the Ana e Bruno create an ideal setting for the delicious specialties created by the chef. This is quite definitely the finest Italian restaurant in town. ● *Sun, Mon.* ▣

Vegetarian Dishes ● Outdoor Tables ■

WEST OF CENTER: *Die Quadriga* €€€€€
Eislebener Strasse 14, 10 789. **Map** B4. ☎ 030-21 40 50.
This gourmet restaurant is based in the Brandenburger Hof Hotel *(see p574)*. The small dining room has elegant furniture designed by Frank Lloyd Wright. Impeccable service complements the sophisticated French cuisine. ● *Sat, Sun.* ♿ ▣

German Wine List ●

WEST OF CENTER: *Harlekin* €€€€€
Lützowufer 15, 10 785. **Map** C4. ☎ 030-25 47 88 58.
Diners can observe the chefs at work in the open kitchen of this hotel restaurant. The exceptional menu lists European and Asian dishes. ● *Sun, Mon.* ♿ ▣

Vegetarian Dishes ● Outdoor Tables ■ German Wine List ●

FARTHER AFIELD: *Speckers Gaststätte zur Ratswaage* €€€
Am neuen Markt 10, 14 467 Potsdam. ☎ 0331-280 43 11.
An unpretentious, modern, family-run restaurant. The exquisite and original creations, mainly French-influenced, are prepared from locally grown produce. Excellent service. ● *Sun & Mon.* ♿ ▣

Vegetarian Dishes ● Outdoor Tables ■ German Wine List ●

EASTERN GERMANY

DRESDEN: *Fischgalerie* €€
Maxstrasse 2, 01 067. ☎ 0351-490 35 06.
Decorated in avant-garde style, this restaurant specializes in fish and seafood dishes. Guests can watch the dishes being prepared. ● *Sun, dinner Mon, dinner Sat.* ▣

Vegetarian Dishes ● Outdoor Tables ■

DRESDEN: *Intermezzo* €€€€
Am Taschenberg 3, 01 067. ☎ 0351-491 2712.
This elegant restaurant in the Kempinski Taschenberg Palais, the former "guesthouse of the kings", serves fresh and unconventional food with a mediterranean touch. Try the Vierländerente or "four-country duck". ♿ ▤ ▣

Vegetarian Dishes ● Outdoor Tables ■ German Wine List ●

DRESDEN: *Das Caroussel* €€€€€
Rähnitzgasse 19, Dresden-Neustadt. ☎ 0351-800 30.
The hotel and restaurant are housed in a recently restored 18th-century Baroque palace in the historic city center. In culinary terms, this is one of the most famous addresses in Saxony. French cuisine. ♿ ▣

Vegetarian Dishes ● Outdoor Tables ■ German Wine List ●

LEIPZIG: *Yamato* €€
Gerberstrasse 15, 04 105. ☎ 0341-988 10 88.
Yamato is a very popular Japanese restaurant, and it is best to reserve a table. The majority of dishes are prepared in front of diners. The service is extremely courteous, and guests are given small aprons and hot towels. ♿ ▣

Vegetarian Dishes ●

LEIPZIG: *Kaiser Maximilian* €€€
Neumarkt 9–19, 04 109. ☎ 0341-998 69 00.
A bright restaurant, pleasantly decorated, with small recesses for the tables. It offers a large selection of Italian dishes, and the menu changes every other week. ♿ ▣

Vegetarian Dishes ● Outdoor Tables ■ German Wine List ●

MEISSEN: *Mercure Park Hotel Meissen* €
Hafenstrasse 27–31, 01 662. ☎ 03521-722 50.
This classy hotel-restaurant is based in a large Art Nouveau villa. It serves regional and international food, including a variety of fish dishes. Guests can also dine in the café, which has a terrace, or in the intimate hotel bar. ▣

Vegetarian Dishes ● Outdoor Tables ■

WEIMAR: *Wolff's Art Hotel & Restaurant* €
Freiherr-vom-Stein-Allee 3a/b, 99 425. ☎ 03643-540 60.
Both the Art Hotel and its restaurant are furnished in the style created by the Bauhaus School. The menu includes international as well as German dishes. ● *Sun.* ♿ ▣

Vegetarian Dishes ● Outdoor Tables ■

	VEGETARIAN DISHES	OUTDOOR TABLES	GERMAN WINE LIST

Price categories for a three course meal without drinks, including cover charge, tax, and service:

€ under €20
€€ €20–30
€€€ €30–40
€€€€ €40–50
€€€€€ over €50

VEGETARIAN DISHES
Available as a starter, a main course, or both.

OUTDOOR TABLES
Restaurants with a garden, courtyard, or terrace.

GERMAN WINE LIST
A good selection of German wines is available.

CREDIT CARDS
Major credit cards are accepted in restaurants where the credit card symbol is shown.

WEIMAR: *Alt Weimar* Prellerstrasse 2, 99 423. **(** 03643-861 90. For over a century this restaurant has been a popular meeting place for actors from the nearby theater. Its cooking, consisting mainly of Italian dishes, is renowned throughout the region. 🥗	€€		■	●
WEIMAR: *Anna Amalia* Markt 19, 99 423. **(** 03643-80 26 50. Anna Amalia has a venerable tradition – Richard Wagner and Thomas Mann dined here – and it has remained popular to this day. The finest Italian cooking in Thuringia is served here, with a new menu to choose from every day. The interior is decorated in Art-Deco style. 🔵 🥗	€€€	●	■	●

MUNICH

CENTRAL MUNICH: *Dallmayr* Dienerstrasse 14, 80 331. **Map** C4. **(** 089-213 51 00. This exceptionally elegant restaurant is popular with locals and visitors alike, just like the famous coffee of the same name. Traditional German and international dishes are served. ● *Sun, lunch Sat.* 🔵 🥗	€€€	●		●
CENTRAL MUNICH: *Königshof* Karlsplatz 25, 80 335. **Map** B4. **(** 089-55 13 60. A beautifully furnished restaurant in the center of the old town, which is very highly esteemed by gourmets. Wine lovers will be astonished by the vast selection: 1,000 different labels are on offer. 🥗	€€€€€			●
EASTERN MUNICH: *Käferschänke* Prinzregentenstrasse 73, 81 675. **Map** F3. **(** 089-416 82 47. Serving French and Italian food, this restaurant is one of the finest in Munich. The owners have a delicatessen next door, selling regional delicacies. ● *Sun.* 🥗	€€€€€	●	■	●
NORTHERN MUNICH: *Bistro Terrine* Amalienstrasse 89, 80 799 München-Schwabing. **Map** C2. **(** 089-28 17 80. The former chef of the Tantris now cooks here, preparing delicious, low-calorie dishes, particularly with lamb and fish. Try the ray with artichokes or the exquisite *crème brûlée*. The restaurant has a romantic ambience. ● *lunch Mon, lunch Sat, Sun.*	€€€	●	■	●
NORTHERN MUNICH: *Tantris* Johann-Fichte-Strasse 7, 80 805 München-Schwabing. **(** 089-361 95 90. One of the very best restaurants in Germany, the Tantris will satisfy even the jaded palate of a seasoned gourmet. It is luxuriously furnished, and the service is of a very high standard. Advance reservations are recommended. ● *Sun, Mon.* 🥗	€€€€€	●	■	●

SOUTHERN GERMANY

BAMBERG: *St. Nepomuk* Obere Mühlebrücke 9, 96 049. **(** 0951-984 20. A good restaurant located on an island in the Regnitz river, offering beautiful views over the surrounding area. St. Nepomuk is an old, cozy restaurant which specializes in fish and game dishes. 🥗	€€	●		●
BAYREUTH: *Schloss Thiergarten* Oberthiergärtner Strasse 36, 95 448. **(** 09209-9840. There are two restaurants in the castle, the elegantly furnished Schloss-Restaurant, and the less expensive Jagdstübchen. The latter occupies a former hunting lodge and specializes in game dishes. 🔵 🥗	€€	●	■	●
BAYREUTH: *Eremitage-Cuvée* Eremitage 6, 95 448. **(** 0921-79 99 70. Cosima Wagner, the composer's wife, used to dine in this beautifully furnished restaurant, one of the finest gastronomic establishments in town. The excellent cooking is much revered by diners. 🥗	€€€		■	

Map references refer to map of Munich on pp546–7

FREIBURG IM BREISGAU: *Enoteca* €€
Gerberau 21, 79 098. ▮ 0761-389 91 30.
Enoteca is a modern, elegant, and stylishly furnished restaurant located
in Freiburg's old town, beautifully set amid period buildings. The restaurant
specializes in light Italian cuisine. ▮

HEIDELBERG: *Simplicissimus* €€
Ingrimstrasse 16, 69 117. ▮ 06221-18 33 36.
This restaurant, situated in the old town, is as popular with tourists as with the
locals, especially since the service is excellent. French cuisine predominates; even
the simplest dishes are very tasty. Advance reservations essential. ▮ *Tue.*

HEIDELBERG: *Schlossweinstube Schönmehls* €€€
Im Schlosshof, 69 117. ▮ 06221-979 70.
A modern and elegantly furnished restaurant, housed in a castle. When the weather
permits, tables are set out on the terrace. Among the many dishes on the menu,
the roast duck with all the trimmings is outstanding. ▮ *Wed; Dec 20–Jan 15.* ▮

NUREMBERG: *Seewald* €€€
Weinmarkt 14, 90 403. ▮ 0911-38 13 03.
With a traditional tiled stove and walls hung with many pictures, the Seewald has a
cozy atmosphere. Courteous staff serve appetizing Italian and German dishes. ▮ ▮

NUREMBERG: *Essigbrätlein* €€€€€
Weinmarkt 3, 90 403. ▮ 0911-22 51 31.
The Essigbrätlein is a small and intimate restaurant, with excellent cooking
and elegant table settings. Reservations are recommended. The lunch menu
is considerably less expensive. ▮

PASSAU: *Heilig-Geist-Stift Schenke/Stiftskeller* €
Heiliggeistgasse 4, 94 032. ▮ 0851-26 07.
A rustic restaurant and wine bar specializing in Bavarian food, including
fish dishes and delicious Austrian cakes. Open until late. ▮ *Wed.* ▮

PASSAU: *Wilder Mann* €€
Am Rathausplatz, 94 032. ▮ 0851-350 71.
Enjoying a prime location right in the city center, this restaurant draws diners
with its good cooking and stylish surroundings. ▮ ▮

ROTHENBURG OB DER TAUBER: *Eisenhut* €€
Herrngasse 3–7, 91 541. ▮ 09861-70 50.
The Eisenhut, in the hotel of the same name, offers a pleasingly stylish interior,
sophisticated dishes, and friendly service. There is also a garden restaurant,
a café with a terrace, and a hotel bar. ▮ *Jan 3–Feb 28.* ▮

STUTTGART: *Ecco* €
Plieninger Strasse 100, 70 567. ▮ 0711-900 72 72.
The specialty of this modern bistro is international cuisine. Try the liver
with spinach, which is highly rated by regulars. ▮ ▮

STUTTGART: *Weber's Gourmet im Turm* €€€
Jahnstrasse 120, 70 597 Stuttgart-Degerloch. ▮ 0711-24 89 96 10.
This restaurant has a fantastic position high up inside a television tower, with stunning
views over the town. All the dishes, mainly Italian and French influenced, are
carefully prepared, and the service is highly professional. ▮ *Sun, Mon.* ▮ ▮

STUTTGART: *Schloss Solitude* €€€€€
Kavaliersbau Haus 2, 70 197 Stuttgart. ▮ 0711-69 20 25.
The breathtakingly beautiful castle chambers and regal cuisine ensure a first-class
culinary as well as an aesthetic experience. Receptions are held in the castle
banqueting halls. ▮ *Mon, dinner Sun.* ▮

WÜRZBURG: *Schloss Steinburg* €€€
Auf dem Steinberg, 97 080 Würzburg-Unterdürrbach. ▮ 0931-970 20.
The Schloss Steinburg, a hotel-restaurant housed in a castle, boasts attractive
furnishings. German cuisine is its specialty, and it is open late at night. ▮ *Dec 20–26.* ▮

WESTERN GERMANY

BONN: *Zur Lindenwirtin Aennchen* €€€
Aennchenplatz 2, 53 173 Bonn-Bad Godesberg. ▮ 0228-31 20 51.
A romantic restaurant, known throughout Rhineland for its fantastic selection of
wines. The chef often uses wine in the preparation of his elaborate dishes, based on
both traditional German and international recipes. ▮ *Sat lunch, Sun.* ▮

<table>
<tr><td colspan="2">

Price categories for a three course meal without drinks, including cover charge, tax, and service:

€ under €20
€€ €20–30
€€€ €30–40
€€€€ €40–50
€€€€€ over €50

</td><td colspan="2">

VEGETARIAN DISHES
Available as a starter, a main course, or both.

OUTDOOR TABLES
Restaurants with a garden, courtyard, or terrace.

GERMAN WINE LIST
A good selection of German wines is available.

CREDIT CARDS
Major credit cards are accepted in restaurants where the credit card symbol is shown.

</td></tr>
</table>

	VEGETARIAN DISHES	OUTDOOR TABLES	GERMAN WINE LIST
BONN: *Halbedel's Gasthaus* €€€€€ Rheinallee 47, 53 173 Bonn-Bad Godesberg. ☎ 0228-35 42 53. A favorite haunt of politicians, this restaurant is housed in a beautiful Art Nouveau villa. Specialties include rabbit in French pastry. Courteous service. ● Mon. ✉	●	■	●
COLOGNE: *Fischers* €€€ Hohenstaufenring 53, 50 674. ☎ 0221-310 84 70. Fischers doubles as a wine bar, and the landlady is a great authority on the subject. Accordingly, there is a large selection of wines on offer, which is matched by the choice of food. The menu features specialties from around the world. ✉		■	●
COLOGNE: *Landhaus Kuckuck* €€€ Olympiaweg 2, 50 933. ☎ 0221-485 360. The Kuckuck is a refined and elegant establishment, specializing in poultry dishes. Try the delicious liver or the succulent roast goose. ✉	●	■	●
COLOGNE: *Börsen-Restaurant Maître* €€€€ Unter Sachsenhausen 10–26, 50 667. ☎ 0221-13 30 21. This stylish and elegant restaurant has a wonderful menu, consisting of the most ingenious French dishes. It is characterized by a pleasant atmosphere and courteous service. ● lunch Sat, Sun; 2 weeks at Easter, 4 weeks in summer. ✉	●	■	●
FRANKFURT AM MAIN: *L'Artichoc* €€€ Bockenheimer Landstrasse 89–91, 60 325. ☎ 069-90 74 87 71. Located in the basement of the Palmenhof Hotel, close to the botanical gardens, this popular establishment serves traditional German and Asian cuisine. ● Sat, Sun. ✉	●		●
FRANKFURT AM MAIN: *Zum Schwarzen Stern* €€€ Römerberg 6, 60 311. ☎ 069-29 19 79. This modern, elegant restaurant is in the heart of the old town, conveniently situated right next to the cathedral. It serves good regional cuisine. ♿ ✉	●	■	●
FRANKFURT AM MAIN: *Tigerpalast* €€€€€ Heiligenkreuzgasse 20, 60 313. ☎ 069-92 00 22 25. It is easy to spend a pleasant evening at this restaurant watching the excellent variety show, which includes circus artistes and other performers. A large selection of wines and many interesting Italian dishes are served. Excellent service. ● Sun, Mon. ✉	●		●
KOBLENZ: *Loup de Mer* €€ Neustadt 12, 56 068. ☎ 0261-161 38. One of the best restaurants in town, serving mainly seafood and fish dishes. Diners can also enjoy the gallery of modern art which is situated on the premises. ● Sun. ✉	●	■	●
MAINZ: *Der Halbe Mond* €€€ In der Witz 12, 55 252 Mainz-Kastel. ☎ 06134-239 13. Diners here can try local specialties from the Rhineland-Palatinate region. The venue is tastefully furnished, and the service is good. ● Sun & Mon. ✉		■	●
MARIA LAACH (KOBLENZ): *Seehotel Maria Laach* €€€ Ortsteil Maria Laach, 56 653 Glees-Maria Laach. ☎ 02652-58 40. This well-known restaurant, situated in quiet and tranquil surroundings next to the famous Benedictine monastery, specializes in fish dishes. Its delicious eel and salmon are highly recommended. There is also a café. ♿	●	■	●
TRIER: *Pfeffermühle* €€ Zurlaubener Ufer 76, 54 292 Trier-Zurlauben. ☎ 0651-261 33. The Pfeffermühle occupies an 18th-century fishermen's house on the banks of the Mosel River. It serves classic and regional cuisine. Among the specialties are game, lamb, and goose dishes. Reservations are recommended. ● Sun, lunch Mon. ✉		■	●
TRIER: *Römischer Kaiser-Taverne* €€ Porta-Nigra-Platz 6, 54 292. ☎ 0651-977 00. A split-level restaurant in Trier's main square. The romantic setting, stylish decor, and tasty German and international cuisine make it a popular spot. ♿ ✉		■	●

NORTHERN GERMANY

BREMEN: *Meierei* €€€
Im Bürgerpark, 28 209. 📞 0421-340 86 19.
A smart restaurant with rustic furniture, the Meierei is beautifully situated
in the middle of a park. The restaurant's stone oven, used for baking bread
and other dishes, is a particularly interesting feature. ● *Mon.* 🍴

BREMEN: *L'Orchidée* €€€€
Am Markt, 28 195. 📞 0421-305 98 88.
The interior of this modern restaurant, located in the center of the city near the
main train station, is elegant and luxurious. Diners come here for the excellent
French and regional cuisine. There is also a bar. ● *Sun, Mon; early Jan, Apr.* ♿ 🍴

HAMBURG: *Fischereihafen-Restaurant* €€€
Grosse Elbstrasse 143, 22 767 Hamburg-Altona. 📞 040-38 18 16.
From the restaurant there are fantastic views of the harbor. The restaurant and bar
have received many celebrities, whose autographs now adorn the walls. The menu
features international fare, with a large selection of fish dishes. ♿ 🍴

HAMBURG: *Jacobs Restaurant* €€€€
Elbchaussee 401–403, 22 609 Hamburg-Nienstedten. 📞 040-82 25 50.
The master chef here is amazingly imaginative and very skilled at his craft,
serving light French cuisine with Italian accents as well as German dishes.
The wine list has 900 different wines. ♿ 🍴

HAMBURG: *Tafelhaus* €€€€
Holstenkamp 71, 22 525 Hamburg-Bahrenfeld. 📞 040-89 27 60.
The Tafelhaus is a bistro-style restaurant offering international cuisine.
The service is very good. ● *Sun, Mon.* ♿ 🍴

HANOVER: *Gallo Nero* €€
Gross-Bucholzer Kirchweb 72b, 30 655 Hanover. 📞 0511-546 34 34.
The furnishings in the "Black Cockerel" are elegant and the service excellent. The
menu includes Italian dishes and there is a large wine list. ● *Sun; 4 weeks in summer.* 🍴

HANOVER: *Die Insel* €€€
Rudolf-von-Bennigsen-Ufer 81, 30 519. 📞 0511-83 12 14.
A modern restaurant, bar, and café are combined in one gastronomic complex that
attracts many guests. The restaurant affords superb views of the Masch lake. The
menu includes interesting Asian specialties and game dishes. ♿ 🍴

HANOVER: *Le Chalet* €€€
Isernhagener Strasse 21, 30 161 Hannover-List. 📞 0511-31 95 88.
"Klein aber fein" ("small but good") is an appropriate epithet for Le Chalet. The chef
is very experienced, and the restaurant specializes in French cuisine. ● *Mon.* 🍴

LÜBECK: *Haus der Schiffergesellschaft* €€
Breite Strasse 2, 23 552. 📞 0451-767 76.
Dating from the 16th century, this well-known historic restaurant is adorned
with mementos of Lübeck's yachtsmen. The menu features many fish dishes
and excellent lamb. Reservations are advisable as the venue is very popular. ♿

LÜBECK: *Das kleine Restaurant* €€€
An der Untertrave 39, 23 552. 📞 0451-70 59 59.
This unique little restaurant offers ten-course meals that are highly affordable.
The many portions are small enough to manage. ● *Sun.* 🍴

LÜBECK: *Wullenwever* €€€
Beckergrube 71, 23 552. 📞 0451-70 43 33.
A restaurant for connoisseurs housed in a 16th-century building. It boasts
captivating decor, excellent service, and a large selection of wines. ● *Sun, Mon.* 🍴

MÜNSTER: *Landhaus Eggert* €€
Zur Haskenau 81, 48 157 Münster-Handorf. 📞 0251-32 80 40.
The Landhaus Eggert comprises a hotel, restaurant, and beer garden and is set
on a former gentleman's estate, amid charming meadows and forests. The large
selection of dishes includes specialties from around the world. ♿ 🍴

MÜNSTER: *Villa Medici* €€€
Ostmarkstrasse 15, 48 145. 📞 0251-342 18.
Diners flock to this attractively furnished restaurant for the excellent
Italian food. The chef is very attentive to his customers' needs, and he
also offers wine tours of Italy. ● *Sun, Mon; 3 weeks in summer, 1 week in winter.* 🍴

AUSTRIA

A USTRIA HAS EXISTED *as a country for less than 100 years but, despite inauspicious beginnings, has thrived thanks to its position at the heart of Europe. Visitors are attracted by the glories of its Imperial Habsburg past, especially in the capital, Vienna. Austria also has a strong musical tradition and great natural beauty, especially in the Alps and the valley of the Danube.*

Present-day Austria emerged in 1919, when the lands of its former empire were granted independence, as a curiously shaped, landlocked country. It is bordered by Switzerland and Germany to the west and north. Along the rest of its border lie the former lands of the old Habsburg Empire, the Czech Republic, Slovakia, Hungary, Slovenia, and the South Tyrol. The regions of the west, the Vorarlberg and the Tyrol, are mountainous, dominated by the eastern Alps. This is where you will find the most familiar images of Austria: well-appointed skiing resorts, snow-capped peaks, and beautiful valleys cloaked in forest.

The Alps are not the traditional heart of Austria – this lies in the regions of Upper and Lower Austria in the northeast, where the Danube (Donau) flows eastwards across the country for 360 km (225 miles). Vienna stands at a

point just beyond where the great river emerges from the mountains to flow into the Hungarian plain. The east of the country is more populous, with more agriculture and industry.

HISTORY

In the 1st millennium BC, settlements in the region of present-day Austria prospered from mining iron and salt. One settlement, Hallstatt, has given its name to an important Iron Age culture that spread across Europe. It was iron that first drew the Romans to occupy the region, where they established the provinces of Rhaetia, Noricum, and Pannonia, making the Danube the frontier of their empire. When the Romans withdrew, the region was settled by Germanic tribes, such as the Alemanni and the Bavarians, and Slavs, but it was the German-speaking peoples who prevailed.

Ruined castle of Aggstein overlooking the Danube in the Wachau region

◁ **The magnificent staircase at the entrance to the Vienna State Opera House**

The geographical kernel of Austria (Österreich) was the Ostmark (eastern march or border county) established by Charlemagne in the 9th century to protect the frontier of his empire. In the 10th century, the Babenbergs acquired the county, which was elevated to a dukedom in 1156. Their dynasty died out in the 13th century and their lands were fought over until they came under the control of Rudolf of Habsburg, who was elected Holy Roman Emperor in 1273.

The Central, one of the grandest of Vienna's coffee houses

Over the next three centuries the Habsburg domains grew, occasionally by conquest, but usually by means of marriages and inheritances. In time it became a matter of course that they were elected as Holy Roman Emperors.

From the 15th century, Turkish invasions threatened the Habsburg lands. In 1683 the Turks laid siege to Vienna, but they were dispersed by a relieving army. This marked the start of many successful campaigns in the Balkans. In the 18th century Austria was a major power, although the rise of Prussia and Napoleon's occupation of Vienna in 1809 dented Habsburg pride.

The Austrian empire was considerably weakened in the 19th century by the growth of nationalist movements, but Vienna enjoyed its heyday as a great cosmopolitan European capital.

After World War I, the defeated Austrian Empire was dismembered and countries such as Czechoslovakia and Hungary gained their independence. There followed bitter struggles between Right and Left for control of the new Austrian republic. The country was annexed by Germany in 1938 and then, following Hitler's defeat in 1945, came under Allied control until 1955, when it

Exploring Austria

A USTRIA'S MAIN ATTRACTIONS are the alpine resorts in the west of the country around Innsbruck and the capital, Vienna, in the east. In between there are many other sights worth seeking out: ancient monasteries and castles, well-preserved medieval cities, such as Salzburg and Graz, the picturesque lakes of the Salzkammergut region, and the scenic stretch of the Danube known as the Wachau. Road and rail communications along the main axis of the country between Vienna, Linz, Salzburg, and Innsbruck are very good.

Skiing at the fashionable resort of Kitzbühel in the Austrian Alps

0 kilometers   50

0 miles   50

became a sovereign state once more. As a keen member of the European Union, Austria has flourished economically, but the old political divisions have arisen in a new form. When the ultra-conservative nationalist party, the FPÖ, led by Jörg Haider, joined the government coalition in 2000, the EU briefly imposed diplomatic sanctions on Austria.

LANGUAGE AND CULTURE

Austria is linguistically homogenous, with 98 percent of the population speaking German. There are, however, considerable differences in dialect between the various regions.

Culturally, Austria is synonymous with music, the long list of great Austrian composers containing names such as Mozart, Haydn, Schubert, and Mahler, not forgetting the Strausses, father and son, and their famous waltzes. Vienna's intellectual and artistic life enjoyed an extraordinary flowering in the late 19th and early 20th century with the Secession movement in painting, architecture, and design. It was also the period of Sigmund Freud's investigations, which laid the foundations of modern

KEY DATES IN AUSTRIAN HISTORY
c.800 BC Rise of Hallstatt culture
15 BC Noricum occupied by Romans
AD 976–1246 Babenberg dynasty rules Eastern March of the Holy Roman Empire
1276 Rudolf of Habsburg ruler of Austria
1519 Charles V, after inheriting Spain and Burgundy, is elected Holy Roman Emperor
1618–48 Thirty Years' War
1683 Siege of Vienna
1740–80 Reign of Maria Theresa
1805 Napoleon defeats Austrians at Austerlitz
1815 Congress of Vienna
1848 Revolutions throughout Habsburg Empire
1918 Defeat in World War I brings Habsburg rule to an end – Austria declared republic
1938 Anschluss – Austria absorbed by Germany
1945–55 Vienna occupied by Allies
1994 Austria joins EU

psychology. However, alongside the intellectual excitement of this period, older, more conservative Austrian values survived. One still cherished today is the idea of *Gemütlichkeit*, coziness, embodied in family life, coffee and cakes, and old-fashioned courtesy.

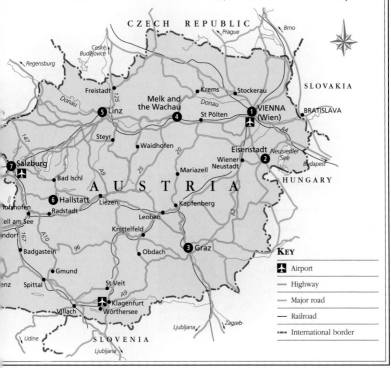

KEY	
✈	Airport
—	Highway
—	Major road
—	Railroad
•••	International border

Vienna ●

GREATER VIENNA has a population of 1.5 million, but the Austrian capital is a compact city with many of the important sights, especially those that date from the Habsburg era, clustered around the Hofburg, the former imperial court. In the mid-19th century the city's old defenses were pulled down and a wide circular boulevard, the Ringstrasse, was built linking new political and cultural institutions, such as Vienna's great art gallery, the Kunsthistorisches Museum. Completed in the 1880s, the Ringstrasse still defines the Innere Stadt or heart of the city. The Danube (Donau) river flows through the east of the city, where it has been canalized to prevent flooding.

SIGHTS AT A GLANCE

Albertina ⑫
Applied Arts Museum ⑨
Burgtheater ②
Freud Museum ⑧
Hofburg pp592–4 ①
Karlskirche ⑪
Kunsthistorisches Museum ⑥
MuseumsQuartier Wien ⑦
Naturhistorisches Museum ⑤
Secession Building ⑩
Staatsoper ④
Stephansdom ③

Greater Vienna *(see inset map)*

Belvedere ⑭
Prater ⑬
Schönbrunn Palace
  and Gardens ⑮

GETTING AROUND

The center of the city is easily explored on foot. Trams 1 and 2 take you round the Ringstrasse past many of the important sights. To see these in old-world style, but at great expense, hire a horse-drawn *Fiaker*. The suburbs are served by the U-bahn (subway) and S-bahn services, although the latter is of more use to locals.

Lipizzaner stallion at the Winter Riding School in the Hofburg

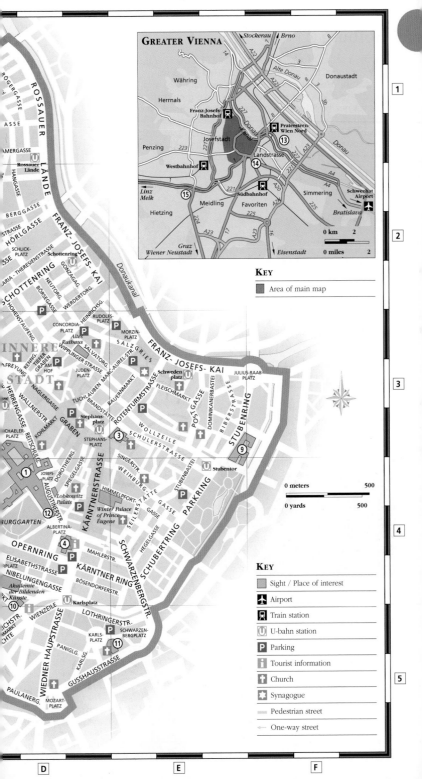

GREATER VIENNA

Stockerau Brno

Währing

Herrnals

Franz-Josefs-Bahnhof

Josefstadt

Penzing

Westbahnhof

Landstrasse ⑬ ⑭

Meidling Südbahnhof ⑮

Hietzing Favoriten

Simmering

Schwechat Airport

Donaustadt

Alte Donau

Praterstern-Wien Nord

Bratislava

Linz Melk

Graz Wiener Neustadt Eisenstadt

0 km 2

0 miles 2

KEY

Area of main map

ROSSAUER

FRANZ- JOSEFS- KAI

INNERE STADT

Schottenring

Alles Rathaus

Morzin-Platz

Schwedenplatz

Julius-Raab-Platz

Stephansplatz

Stephans-Platz ③

Schulerstrasse

Wollzeile

Stubentor ⑨

Winter Palace of Prince Eugene

Lobkowitz Palais

Albertina-Platz ④

Opernring

Karlsplatz

Karls-Platz ⑪

Burggarten ⑫

① ⑩

Akademie der Bildenden Künste

Schwarzenberg-Platz

0 meters 500

0 yards 500

KEY

	Sight / Place of interest
✈	Airport
🚉	Train station
Ⓤ	U-bahn station
P	Parking
i	Tourist information
✝	Church
✡	Synagogue
	Pedestrian street
←	One-way street

D   E   F

1 2 3 4 5

Hofburg ①

WHAT BEGAN AS A SMALL FORTRESS in 1275 grew over the centuries into a vast palace, the Hofburg. It was the seat of Austrian power for over six centuries, and successive rulers were all anxious to leave their mark. The various buildings range in style from Gothic to late 19th-century Neo-Renaissance. The complex was still expanding up until a few years before the Habsburgs fell from power in 1918. The presence of the imperial court had a profound effect on the surrounding area, with noble families competing to site their palaces as close as possible to the Hofburg.

Burggarten

The Albertina, recently renovated, houses a collection of Old Master drawings and prints.

Statue of Joseph II (1806) in Josefsplatz

★ **Augustinerkirche**
The former parish church of the Habsburgs houses the spectacular late 18th-century tomb of Maria Christina, Maria Theresa's favorite daughter, by Antonio Canova.

Prunksaal
The showpiece of the Austrian National Library (1722–35) is the grand, wood-paneled Prunksaal, or Hall of Honor.

Stallburg

The Schatzkammer (treasuries) are housed in the Alte Burg, the core of the old palace.

The Michaelertor is the gate through which visitors reach the older parts of the palace.

STAR FEATURES

★ **State Apartments**

★ **Winter Riding School**

★ **Augustinerkirche**

★ **Winter Riding School**
The white Lipizzaner horses are stabled in the Stallburg opposite the Riding School itself, where they are trained and give performances.

Mozart Memorial (1896)
*Viktor Tilgner's statue of
the composer stands just
inside the Ringstrasse
entrance.*

VISITORS' CHECKLIST

Michaelerplatz 1, A-1010.
U Stephansplatz, Herrengasse,
Volkstheater. 2A, 3A. D,
J, 1. For details of individual
museums, see p594.

The Burgtor or outer
gate was built to a
design by Peter Nobile
in 1821–4.

Neue Burg
*A monument to
the great general,
Eugene of Savoy
(1663–1736), stands
in front of the newest
wing of the palace,
completed in 1913.*

Volksgarten

Heldenplatz

Schweizertor
*This 16th-century
gateway leads to the
Schweizerhof, the oldest part
of the Hofburg, originally a
stronghold with four towers.*

The Burgkapelle,
the Hofburg's
chapel, is where the
famous Vienna
Boys' Choir sings.

★ **State Apartments**
*The table in the state
banqueting hall is laid
as it used to be in the latter
part of the reign of Franz
Joseph I (1848–1916).*

Exploring the Hofburg Complex

THE VAST HOFBURG COMPLEX contains the former imperial apartments and treasuries (Schatzkammer) of the Habsburgs, several museums, a chapel, a church, the Austrian National Library, the Winter Riding School, and the President of Austria's offices. The entrance to the imperial apartments and the treasuries is through the Michaelertor on Michaelerplatz.

10th-century crown of the Holy Roman Empire, Schatzkammer

Portrait of the Empress Elisabeth by Winterhalter (1865)

Neue Burg
Burgring. [01-5252 4484.
○ Wed–Mon. 🖾
The massive curved Neue Burg on Heldenplatz was added to the Hofburg in 1881–1913. Today, it is home to a number of museums. Archaeological finds from Ephesus are on display in the **Ephesos Museum**, while pianos that belonged to Beethoven, Schubert, and Haydn are among countless items housed in the musical instrument museum – the **Sammlung alter Musikinstrumente**. The weapons collection in the **Hofjagd und Rüstkammer** is one of the finest in Europe. There is also an excellent ethnological collection – the **Völkerkundemuseum**.

Augustinerkirche
Augustinerstrasse 3. [01-533 7099. ○ daily.
The church has one of the best-preserved 14th-century Gothic interiors in Vienna. In the Loreto Chapel are a series of silver urns that contain the hearts of the Habsburg family. The church is also celebrated for its music, with masses by Schubert or Haydn performed here on Sundays.

State Apartments
Michaelerkuppel-Feststiege. [01-533 7570. ○ 9am–4:30pm daily. 🖾 🖾 Sat & Sun.
The State Apartments (Kaiserappartements) in the Reichskanzleitrakt (1723–30) and the Amalienburg (1575) include the rooms occupied by Franz Joseph from 1857 to 1916, Empress Elisabeth's apartments from 1854 to 1898, and the rooms where Czar Alexander I lived during the Congress of Vienna in 1815.

Winter Riding School
[01-533 9032. ○ for performances. ● public hols. 🖾 🖾 some areas.
The Spanish Riding School is believed to have been founded in 1572 to cultivate the classic skills of *haute école* horsemanship. By breeding and training horses from Spain, the Habsburgs formed the Spanische Reitschule. Today, 80-minute shows take place in the building known as the Winter Riding School, built in 1729–35 to a design by Josef Emanuel Fischer von Erlach.

Schatzkammer
Schweizerhof. [01-525 240. ○ 10am–6pm Wed–Mon. ● Jan 1, May 1, Nov 1, Dec 25. 🖾 🖾
Sacred and secular treasures amassed during centuries of Habsburg rule are displayed in 21 rooms, known as the Schatzkammer or Treasury. They include relics of the Holy Roman Empire, the crown jewels, and liturgical objects of the imperial court. Visitors can also admire the dazzling gold, silver, and porcelain once used at state banquets.

Burgkapelle
Schweizerhof. [01-533 9927. ○ 11am–3pm Mon–Thu, 11am–1pm Fri. ● Nov 1, Dec 8, Jan 1. 🖾
Vienna Boys' Choir Jan–Jun & Sep–Dec: 9:15am Sun (book by phone). 🖾
From the Schweizerhof, steps lead up to the Burgkapelle, originally constructed in 1296. The interior has Gothic statues in canopied niches. On Sundays, visitors can hear the Wiener Sängerknaben, the Vienna Boys' Choir (see p607).

Burggarten and Volksgarten
Burgring/Opernring/Dr-Karl-Renner-Ring. ○ daily.
Some of the space left around the Hofburg after Napoleon had razed part of the city walls was transformed by the Habsburgs into gardens. The Volksgarten opened to the public in 1820, but the Burggarten remained the palace's private garden until 1918.

Ornamental pond in the Volksgarten, with Burgtheater in the background

Burgtheater ②

Dr Karl-Lueger-Ring, A-1014.
📞 01-5144 44440. Ⓤ Schottentor.
🚋 1, 2, D. ◯ for performances.
● Good Fri, Dec 24; Jul & Aug
(except for guided tours). 🎞 ♿
📷 afternoons (call 01-5144 44140).

THE BURGTHEATER is the most
prestigious stage in the
German-speaking world. The
original theater, built in Maria
Theresa's reign, was replaced
in 1888 by today's Italian
Renaissance-style building by
Karl von Hasenauer and
Gottfried Semper. It closed for
refurbishment in 1897 after the
discovery that several seats had
no view of the stage. At the
end of World War II a bomb
devastated the building, leaving
only the side wings containing
the Grand Staircases intact. The
restoration was so successful
that today it is hard to tell the
new parts from the old.

**Detail from the Wiener Neustädter
Altar in the Stephansdom**

Stephansdom ③

Stephansplatz 3, A-1010. 📞 01-5155
2530. Ⓤ Stephansplatz.
🚋 1A. ◯ daily. ♿

THE STEPHANSDOM, with its
magnificent glazed-tile
roof, is the heart and soul of
Vienna. It is no mere
coincidence that the urns
containing the entrails of
some of the Habsburgs lie in
a vault beneath its main altar.
    A church has stood on the
site for over 800 years, but
all that remains of the original
13th-century Romanesque
church are the Giants'
Doorway and Heathen

Auditorium of the Staatsoper, the Vienna State Opera House

Towers. The Gothic nave, the
choir, and the side chapels are
the result of rebuilding in the
14th and 15th centuries, while
some of the outbuildings,
such as the Lower Vestry, are
Baroque additions.
    The lofty vaulted interior
contains an impressive
collection of works of art.
Masterpieces of Gothic sculpture include the fabulously
intricate pulpit, several of the
figures of saints adorning
the piers, and the canopies
over many of the side altars.
To the left of the High Altar
is the 15th-century winged
Wiener Neustädter Altar
bearing the painted images
of 72 saints. The altar panels
open out to reveal delicate
sculpture groups. The most
spectacular Renaissance work
is the tomb of Friedrich III,
while the High Altar adds a
flamboyant Baroque note.

Staatsoper ④

Opernring 2, A-1010. 📞 01-5144
7880. Ⓤ Karlsplatz. 🚋 1, 2, D, J.
◯ for performances. 🎞 ♿ 📷 by
arrangement (call 5144 42613).

VIENNA'S OPERA HOUSE,
the Staatsoper, was
the first of the grand
Ringstrasse buildings
to be completed; it
opened on May 25,
1869 to the strains
of Mozart's Don
Giovanni. Built in
Neo-Renaissance style,
it initially failed to
impress the Viennese.
Yet when it was
hit by a bomb in
1945 and largely

destroyed, the event was seen
as a symbolic blow to the
city. With a brand new
auditorium and stage
incorporating the latest
technology, the Opera House
reopened in November 1955
with a performance of
Beethoven's Fidelio.

Naturhistorisches Museum ⑤

Maria-Theresien-Platz, A-1014.
📞 01-521 77. Ⓤ Volkstheater.
🚌 2A, 48A. 🚋 1, 2, D, J, 46, 49,
52, 58. ◯ 9am–6pm Wed–Mon. ●
Jan 1, May 1, Nov 1, Dec 25. 🎞 ♿

ALMOST THE MIRROR image of
the Kunsthistorisches
Museum, the Natural History
Museum was designed by the
same architects, and opened
in 1889. Its interior decoration
reflects the nature of the
collections. These include
archaeological, anthropological,
mineralogical, zoological, and
geological displays. There are
casts of dinosaur skeletons,
the world's largest display of
skulls illustrating the history
of man, one of Europe's
most comprehensive
collections of gems,
prehistoric sculpture,
Bronze Age items,
and extinct birds
and mammals. In
the archaeological
section look out for
the celebrated
Venus of Willendorf,
a 24,000-year-old
Palaeolithic fertility
figurine, and finds from
the early Iron Age
settlement at
Hallstatt (see p602).

**Venus of Willendorf,
Naturhistorisches Museum**

Hunters in the Snow by Peter Brueghel the Elder (1565)

Kunsthistorisches Museum ⑥

Maria-Theresien-Platz. 📞 01-525 24. 🚇 Babenberger Strasse, Volkstheater. 🚊 2A, 57A. ◯ 10am–6pm Tue–Sun; picture gallery also 6–9pm Thu. ● Jan 1, May 1, Nov 1, Dec 25. 📷 ♿ 🎁 ✏ ⧠ www.khm.at

THE MUSEUM of the History of Art attracts more than one and a half million visitors each year. Its collections are based largely on those built up over a number of centuries by the Habsburgs.

The picture gallery occupies the whole of the first floor. The collection focuses on Old Masters from the 15th to the 18th centuries. Because of the links between the Habsburgs and the Netherlands, Flemish painting is especially well represented. About half the surviving works of Peter Brueghel the Elder (c.1525–69) are held by the museum, including *The Tower of Babel* and most of the cycle of *The Seasons*.

The Dutch paintings range from genre scenes of great domestic charm to magnificent landscapes. All the Rembrandts on show are portraits, including the famous *Large Self-Portrait* of the artist in a plain smock (1652). The only Vermeer is the enigmatic allegorical painting, *The Artist's Studio* (1665). The

Blue ceramic hippopotamus from Egypt (around 2000 BC)

Italian galleries have a strong collection of 16th-century Venetian paintings, with a comprehensive range of Titians and great works by Giovanni Bellini and Tintoretto. Also on show are the bizarre vegetable portrait heads, representing the four seasons, made for Emperor Rudolf II by Giuseppe Arcimboldo (1527–93).

The German section is rich in 16th-century paintings. There are several works by Dürer, including his *Madonna with the Pear* (1512). The most interesting of the Spanish works are the portraits of the Spanish royal family made by Diego Velázquez (1599–1660).

On the ground floor are the Greek, Roman, Egyptian, and Near Eastern collections, as well as collections of European sculpture and the decorative arts. Among the Egyptian and Near Eastern antiquities is an entire 5th-Dynasty tomb chapel from Giza (c.2400 BC) and a splendid bust of King Tuthmosis III (c.1460 BC).

The sculpture and decorative arts collection contains some fine, late Gothic religious statues by artists such as Tilman Riemenschneider (c.1460–1531). There is also a collection of curiosities bought or commissioned by various Habsburg monarchs, such as automata and scientific instruments.

MuseumsQuartier Wien ⑦

Museumsplatz 1. 📞 523-5881/1730. 🚇 MuseumsQuartier, Volkstheater. 🚌 2a to the MuseumsQuartier, 48a to Volkstheater. 🚋 49 to Volkstheater. **Visitor Centre** ◯ 10am–7pm daily. 📷 🎁 ♿ 🍴 ⧠ ⧠ www.mqw.at

THIS MUSEUM COMPLEX is one of the largest cultural centers in the world, housed in what was once the imperial stables and carriage houses. Here you will find art museums, venues for film, theater, architecture, dance, new media, and a children's creativity center. The visitor center is a good starting point.

Among the attractions is the **Leopold Museum** which focuses on Austrian art, including many works by Egon Schiele and Gustav Klimt. The **Museum of Modern Art Ludwig Foundation Vienna** shows contemporary and modern art from around the world. **ZOOM Kindermuseum** offers a lively introduction to the world of the museum for children. **Architekturzentrum** is dedicated to 20th- and 21st-century architecture.

Freud Museum ⑧

Berggasse 19. 📞 01-319 1596. 🚇 Schottentor. ◯ 9am–5pm daily. 📷

NO. 19 BERGGASSE is very like any other 19th-century apartment in Vienna, yet it is now one of the city's most famous addresses. The father of psychoanalysis, Sigmund Freud, received patients here from 1891 to 1938. The flat housed Freud's

Beautifully restored patients' waiting room in the Freud Museum

family as well as his practice. Memorabilia on display include letters and books, furnishings, photographs, and various antiquities. Even his hat and cane are on show. Although it was abandoned when the Nazis forced Freud to leave, the apartment still preserves an intimate domestic atmosphere.

Applied Arts Museum ⑨

Stubenring 5. 📞 01-711 360.
Stubentor. 🚊 1A, 74A. 🚋 1, 2.
Landstrasse. ◯ 10am–midnight Tue, 10am–6pm Wed–Sun. ● Jan 1, May 1, Nov 1, Dec 25.

T HE MAK (Museum für angewandte Kunst) was founded in 1864 as a museum for art and industry. Over the years, it also acquired objects representing new artistic movements. The museum has a fine collection of furniture, including some classical works of the German cabinet-maker David Roentgen, textiles, glass, Islamic and East Asian art, and fine Renaissance jewelry. There is also a whole room full of Biedermeier furniture. The most important Austrian artistic movement was the Secession, formed by artists who seceded from the Vienna academy in 1897. Their style, also known as Jugendstil, is represented through the many and varied productions of the Wiener Werkstätte (Viennese Workshops), a cooperative arts and crafts studio, founded in 1903.

Brass vase (1903) by Kolo Moser

Secession Building ⑩

Friedrichstrasse 12. 📞 01-587 5307.
Karlsplatz. ◯ 10am–6pm Tue–Sun.

J OSEPH MARIA OLBRICH designed the unusual Secession Building in Jugendstil style as a showcase for the Secession

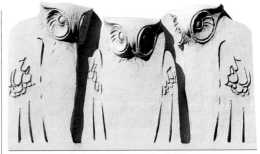
Group of stone owls decorating the Secession Building

movement's artists in 1898. The almost windowless building is a squat cube with four towers. The filigree globe of entwined laurel leaves on the roof gave rise to the building's nickname: "The Golden Cabbage."

Inside, Gustav Klimt's *Beethoven Frieze* is the building's best-known work of art. Designed in 1902, it covers three walls and stretches 34 m (110 ft) from end to end.

Karlskirche ⑪

Karlsplatz. 📞 01-504 6187.
Karlsplatz. 🚊 4A. ◯ daily.

D URING VIENNA'S plague epidemic of 1713, Karl VI vowed that, as soon as the city was delivered, he would build a church dedicated to St. Charles Borromeo (1538–84), a patron saint of the plague.

Karlskirche, with column showing scenes from the life of St. Charles Borromeo

Johann Bernhard Fischer von Erlach's design produced a richly eclectic Baroque masterpiece, borrowing from the architecture of ancient Greece and Rome.

The interior was embellished with carvings and altarpieces by leading artists of the day. Johann Michael Rottmayr's huge fresco in the cupola (1725–30) depicts St. Charles in heaven interceding for deliverance from the plague.

Albertina ⑫

Augustinestrasse 1. 📞 01-534 830.
Karlsplatz, Stephansplatz. ◯ 10am–6pm daily (to 9pm Wed).
🔲 www.albertina.at

H IDDEN AWAY IN a corner of the Hofburg is the Albertina, a palace named after Duke Albert of Sachsen-Teschen, Maria Theresa's son-in-law. Its collection includes one million prints, 65,000 watercolors and drawings, and over 70,000 photographs. The gems of the collection are by Durer, with Michelangelo and Rubens also well represented. Picasso heads a fine 20th-century section. These are displayed through a series of temporary exhibitions in three halls.

The palace was recently restored to its former glory and now, for the first time in over 200 years, it is possible to visit the Hapsburg State Rooms, a fine example of Neoclassical architecture and interior decoration.

Vienna: Farther Afield

For a city of over two million inhabitants, Vienna is surprisingly compact. Nonetheless, some of the most interesting sights are away from the city center. At Belvedere, the palace and gardens of Prince Eugene impress with their scale and grandeur. Farther away at Schönbrunn sprawls the immense palace and gardens so loved by Empress Maria Theresa. There are also many parks and gardens around the city, the largest and most interesting of which is the Prater. A former hunting ground of the Habsburgs, it is now open to the public for numerous leisure activities.

The colorful Volksprater Funfair, Prater

Prater ⑬

Prater. **U** **S** *Praterstern.* 🚌 *74A.* **Park** ⬜ *daily.* **Ferris Wheel** ⬜ *daily.* 📷

Originally an imperial hunting ground, this huge area of woods and meadows between the Danube and the Danube Canal was opened to the public by Joseph II in 1766. The central avenue, or Hauptallee, stretches for 5 km (3 miles) through the center of the Prater, and was for a long time the preserve of the nobility and their footmen. During the 19th century the northern end of the Prater became a massive funfair,

dominated by a giant ferris wheel, one of Vienna's most famous landmarks. There is also a planetarium, an exhibition center, and a trotting stadium nearby.

The southern side of the Prater contains extensive woodland – interlaced with cycle paths, a municipal golf course, and the Freudenau Racetrack, where flat racing meetings are held from April to November.

Belvedere ⑭

Upper Belvedere Prinz-Eugen-Strasse 27. **[** 01-795 57. 🚌 *13A.* **S** *Süd-bahnhof.* 🚊 *0, 18, D, 71.* ⬜ *10am–6pm Tue–Sun (Good Fri, Dec 24 & 31: 10am–3pm).* ● *Jan 1, May 1, Nov 1, Dec 25.* 📷 ♿ 🏛 **Lower Belvedere** Rennweg 6a. **[** 01-795 57. 🚊 *71, D.* ⬜ *as above.* ● *as above.* 📷 ♿ 🏛 **Gardens** ⬜ *daily.* ♿

The Belvedere was built by Johann Lukas von Hildebrandt as the summer residence of Prince Eugene of Savoy, the brilliant military commander whose strategies helped vanquish the Turks in 1683. Situated on a gently sloping hill, the Belvedere consists of two palaces linked by a formal garden laid out in the French style by Dominique Girard. The huge garden is sited on three levels, linked by two elaborate cascading waterfalls. Different areas of the garden are meant to convey a complicated series of Classical allusions: the lower part of the garden represents the domain of the Four Elements, the center is Parnassus, and the upper section is Olympus.

Standing at the highest point of the garden, the Upper Belvedere has a more elaborate façade than the Lower Belvedere, with lavish stone ornamentation, statues, and balustrades. The domed copper roofs of the end pavilions were designed to resemble Turkish tents – an allusion to Prince Eugene's many victories over the Turks. In fact, the whole palace was intended to be a symbolic reflection of the prince's power and glory, and was appropriate to the grand festive occasions for which it was originally used. The many impressive interiors include the Sala Terrena, with four Herculean figures supporting the ceiling, and a grand, sweeping staircase, the ornately decorated chapel, and the opulent Marble Hall.

Sphinx from U
Belvedere gar

Imposing Baroque façade of Prince Eugene's Upper Belvedere palace

The Sala Terrena, the grand entrance hall of the Upper Belvedere

The building also houses the collections of 19th- and 20th-century paintings belonging to the Austrian Gallery. Many of the works are by Austrian painters, including an excellent collection by Gustav Klimt. There are also works by Ferdinand Georg Waldmüller and Van Gogh.

The Lower Belvedere was used by Prince Eugene for day-to-day living, and the building itself is less elaborate than the Upper Belvedere. Many of the rooms are just as grand, however, for example the ornate, golden Hall of Mirrors. Part of the palace now houses the Museum of Austrian Baroque Art, which displays works of art by the artists and sculptors who shaped the city during Vienna's Golden Age (c.1683–1780). There are paintings by J. M. Rottmayr, Martino Altomonte, Daniel Gran, and Paul Troger among others, and sculptures by Franz Xavier Messerschmidt and Georg Raphael Donner.

Next door to the Lower Belvedere is the handsome Orangery, originally used to shelter tender garden plants in winter. The Museum of Austrian Medieval Art is housed here, and the gallery contains masterpieces of Gothic and early Renaissance painting and sculpture. Notable among the sculptures is the 12th-century Romanesque Stammerberg Crucifix, one of the oldest surviving examples of Tyrolean woodcarving. The seven painted panels by Rueland Frueauf the Elder (1490–94) show the Passion taking place in an Austrian setting.

Schönbrunn Palace and Gardens ⑮

Schönbrunner Schloss Strasse 47, Schönbrunn. 【 01-811 13239. ⓤ Schönbrunn. 🚌 10A. 🚋 10, 58. ◯ daily. 🌃 (gardens free). ♿ ▯ ▯ ▯

THIS MAGNIFICENT former summer residence of the imperial family takes its name from a "beautiful spring" that was found nearby. An earlier hunting lodge was destroyed by the Turks, so Leopold I asked Johann Bernhard Fischer von Erlach to design a grand Baroque residence here in 1695. The project was finally completed by Nikolaus Pacassi in the mid-18th century, under Empress Maria Theresa.

The strict symmetry of the architecture is complemented by the extensive formal gardens, with their neat lawns and careful planting. An array of fountains and statues is framed by trees and alleyways. The gardens also contain a huge tropical Palm House with an interesting collection of exotic plants, a small zoo, a butterfly house, an orangery, and the Gloriette – a large Neoclassical arcade which crowns the hill behind the palace. Inside the palace, the Rococo decorative schemes were devised by Nikolaus Pacassi. In the state rooms, the dominant features are white paneling, often adorned with gilded ornamental framework. The rooms vary from the extremely sumptuous – such as the Millionen-Zimmer, paneled with fig-wood inlaid with Persian miniatures – to the quite plain apartments of Franz Joseph and Empress Elisabeth. The Memorial Room contains the portrait and effigy of the Duke of Reichstadt, the son of Napoleon and Princess Maria Louisa, daughter of Austrian Emperor Franz I. A virtual prisoner in the palace after Napoleon's fall from power, the duke died here in 1832 aged 21. Alongside the palace is a museum of imperial coaches and sleighs.

The beautiful Schönbrunn Palace, as seen from the gardens

The historic center of Graz, overlooked by the thickly-wooded Schlossberg

Eisenstadt ❷

🏠 13,000. 🚉 🚌 🛈 Schloss Esterházy (02682-719 3000).

THE PRINCIPAL attraction of Eisenstadt is the grand residence of the Esterházy princes, the Hungarian aristocrats who claimed to be descendants of Attila. **Schloss Esterházy** was built for Prince Paul Esterházy in 1663–73. In the Haydnsaal, a huge hall of state decorated with 18th-century frescoes, the famous composer Joseph Haydn (1732–1809) conducted the family orchestra. Haydn lived on Haydngasse, and his house is now a museum. He is buried in the **Bergkirche**, west of the palace.

Until World War II, Eisenstadt had a large Jewish community, and there is a **Jewish Museum** near the palace.

Schloss Esterházy, a mix of Baroque and Neoclassical styles

🏛 **Schloss Esterházy**
Esterházyplatz. 📞 02682-719 3000.
🕐 Easter–Oct: daily. 🈯

Graz ❸

🏠 250,000. ✈ 9 km (6 miles) S. 🚉 🚌 🛈 Herrengasse 16 (0316-807 50).

ALMOST ENTIRELY surrounded by mountains, Graz is Austria's second largest city. During the Middle Ages its importance rivaled that of Vienna. In the late 14th century, the Habsburg Duke Leopold III chose Graz as his base, and in the following century the town played a vital strategic role in the war against the invading Turks.

The city is dominated by the Schlossberg, the huge hill on which the town's medieval defenses were built. During the Napoleonic Wars Graz was occupied by French troops, who blew up most of the fortifications in 1809. Among the ruins that can be seen today are a 28-m (92-ft) high clock tower, the **Uhrturm**, dating from 1561, and the **Glockenturm** (bell tower), erected in 1588. The former houses the **Schlossmuseum**, with exhibits illustrating the history of Graz. From the summit of the hill there are splendid views over the city and the Mur valley.

At the foot of the Schlossberg lies the Old Town. The medieval **Burg** (fortress) was built in several stages and completed in 1500. To the south are the late-Gothic **Cathedral of St. Ägydius**, with its striking Baroque interior, and the **Mausoleum of Ferdinand II**, designed by the Italian Pietro de Pomis in the late 17th century.

Graz's **Landesmuseum Joanneum** consists of two sections, the Alte Galerie (Old Gallery) which has a rich collection of paintings, including works by Lucas Cranach the Elder (1472–1553) and Peter Brueghel the Younger (1564–1638), and a natural history department. Also of interest are the **Landeszeughaus**, with its impressive array of over 30,000 weapons and pieces of armor, and the **Neue Galerie**.

🏛 **Landesmuseum Joanneum**
Neutorgasse 45 (Alte Galerie);
Raubergasse 10 (Natural History).
📞 0316-8017 9700. 🕐 Tue–Sun. 🈯
🏛 **Neue Galerie**
Herberstein Palace, Sackstrasse 16.
0316-829 155. 🕐 Tue–Sun. 🈯

ENVIRONS: A few kilometers west of the city, **Schloss Eggenberg** was built by Johann Ulrich von Eggenberg in 1625–35. Open daily, the Baroque palace houses a collection of 19th- and 20th-century art, as well as a collection of local prehistoric finds, coins, antiquities, and gemstones. There are displays of stuffed animals in the Jagdmuseum (Hunting Museum).

Melk and the Wachau ❹

🚉 🚌 *Melk*. 🛈 *Babenbergerstr., Melk (02752-555 232)*. **Benedictine abbey** ⭘ *Palm Sunday–early Nov: daily; early-Nov–Palm Sunday: guided tours only (11am and 2pm daily).* 🖼

MELK LIES at the western end of one of the loveliest stretches of the River Danube, the Wachau, which extends 40 km (25 miles) downstream to Krems.

Dotted with Renaissance houses and old towers, **Melk** itself is most famous for its Baroque Benedictine abbey, a treasure trove of paintings, sculptures, and decorative art. One of its most impressive rooms is the Marble Hall, with beautiful ceiling paintings depicting mythological scenes.

A boat trip is the best way to enjoy the Wachau, though for the energetic there are cycle paths along the banks of the river. Landmarks to look for traveling downstream include the picturesque castle of **Schönbühel** and the ruined medieval fortress at **Aggstein**. Though not visible from the river, nearby **Willendorf** is the site of famous prehistoric finds.

At the eastern end of the Wachau are the well-preserved medieval towns of **Dürnstein** and **Krems**. The latter's tiny hillside streets offer fine views across the Danube to the Baroque **Göttweig Abbey**.

The opulent interior of the 17th-century Church of St. Ignatius in Linz

Linz ❺

🏙 *210,000*. ✈ *10 km (6 miles) SW.* 🚉 🚌 🛈 *Hauptplatz 1 (0732-7070 1777)*.

AUSTRIA'S THIRD CITY, Linz has been inhabited since Roman times, when it was a port called Lentia. In the early 16th century it developed into an important trading center. Although, today, Linz is a busy industrial city, the Old Town contains many historic buildings and monuments.

The Hauptplatz, one of the largest medieval squares in Europe, is bordered by splendid Baroque façades. Among the finest buildings is the **Town Hall**, home to the Museum Linz-Genesis, which tells the history of the city. The 20-m (66-ft) high marble Dreifaltigkeitssäule (Trinity Column) was completed in 1723.

In the southeast corner of the square is the **Church of St. Ignatius**. Also known as the Alter Dom, it was built in the 17th century in Baroque style and boasts a wonderfully ornate pulpit and altarpiece. Nearby, the **Landhaus** is well worth seeing for its three beautiful Renaissance courtyards and loggia.

The streets west of the Hauptplatz lead up to Linz's hilltop **castle**, built for Friedrich V (Holy Roman Emperor Friedrich III) in the 15th century. The castle houses the Schlossmuseum, with paintings, sculptures, and historical artifacts.

On the other side of the river, the **Ars Electronica Center** is a superb new museum that allows visitors to experiment with the latest technological innovations. Hidden away in the Lentia 2000 shopping mall is the **Neue Galerie**, containing a fine collection of 19th- and 20th-century Austrian art, including works by Egon Schiele (1890–1918) and Gustav Klimt (1862–1918).

For splendid panoramic views of Linz, take a ride on the Pöstlingbergbahn, a train that climbs to the summit of the hill known as Pöstlingberg.

River cruises along the Danube west to Passau, in Germany, and east to Vienna depart from the quay at the Nibelungenbrücke. On-board entertainment includes themed events, such as a "Bavarian afternoon" or an "Italian night".

🏛 **Ars Electronica Center**
Hauptstrasse 2. 📞 *0732-727 20.* ⭘ *Wed–Sun.* 🖼
🏛 **Neue Galerie**
Lentia 2000, Blütenstrasse. 📞 *0732-7070 3600.* ⭘ *Wed–Mon.* 🖼

Melk's massive Benedictine abbey on the banks of the Danube

Hallstatt, an attractive lakeside village in the Salzkammergut

Hallstatt ⑥

🏛 1,200. 🚇 🚌 ☒ 🛈 Seestrasse 169 (06134-8208).

THIS PRETTY VILLAGE on the bank of the Hallstätter See lies in the Salzkammergut, a stunning region of lakes and mountains. The area takes its name from the rich deposits of salt (salz) that have been mined here since the 1st millennium BC. From Hallstatt, it is possible to visit a working mine, the **Salzbergwerk**, by taking the cable car from the southern end of the village up to the mine entrance on the Salzberg mountain. The **Rudolfsturm**, the tower that stands close to the station at the top, was completed in 1284 to defend the mine workings.

Hallstatt's **Prähistorisches Museum** contains Celtic Iron Age artifacts discovered near the mines, such as tools, weapons, and jewelry. Today, the name Hallstatt is used to refer to the Celtic culture that flourished from the 9th to the 5th centuries BC.

Behind the **Pfarrkirche**, the town's late-Gothic parish church, the **Beinhaus** (Charnel House) has been used to store human remains since 1600.

🏛 **Salzbergwerk Hallstatt**
📞 06132-200 2990. ☐ Apr–Oct: daily. 📷
🏛 **Prähistorisches Museum**
📞 06245-807 83. ☐ Mar–Oct. 📷

ENVIRONS: The mountains and the crystal clear waters of the Hallstätter See offer many opportunities for swimming, water sports, scuba diving, hiking, and cycling. There are also boat trips on the lake.

At the southern end of the Hallstätter See, about 2 km (1 mile) from Hallstatt, are the **Dachstein limestone caves**, open daily from May to mid-October. A cable car, which leaves from a station south of Obertraun village, climbs to the entrance of the caves, giving superb views of the lake and surrounding mountains.

Salzburg ⑦

🏛 144,000. ✈ 3 km (2 miles) W.
🚉 🚌 🛈 Mozartplatz 5 (0662-88987). ⬥ Salzburger Festspiele (late Jul–Aug).

SALZBURG FIRST rose to prominence in about AD 700, when a church and a monastery were established here. Until 1816, when it became part of the Habsburg empire, the independent city-state of Salzburg was ruled by a succession of prince-archbishops. Best known as the birthplace of Wolfgang Amadeus Mozart, today the city has a thriving musical tradition. Each summer large numbers of tourists arrive for the Salzburger Festspiele, a festival of opera, classical music concerts, and theater.

Salzburg's medieval fortress, the **Festung Hohensalzburg**, looms over the city from its hilltop position. The castle dates from the 11th century, but the state apartments are an early 16th-century addition.

The **Residenz**, where Salzburg's prince-archbishops lived and held court, owes its early Baroque appearance to Archbishop Wolf Dietrich von Raiteneau, who resided here from 1587. The palace contains the Residenzgalerie, a collection of European art of the 16th to 19th centuries.

WOLFGANG AMADEUS MOZART

Wolfgang Amadeus Mozart (1756–91)

Salzburg's most famous son, Wolfgang Amadeus Mozart, was born in 1756, the son of Leopold, a member of the Prince-Archbishop's chamber orchestra. He learnt to play the harpsichord at the age of 3, and by the age of 5 had already written his first compositions. From 1763 Mozart traveled widely, performing for the aristocracy across Europe. His mastery of all the musical genres of the day swiftly earned him renown at home and abroad. During his short life, his prodigious output included 56 symphonies, over 20 concertos, and 15 operas, among them *The Marriage of Figaro* and *Don Giovanni*. Mozart's aspirations to lead the kind of lifestyle enjoyed by his patrons, however, led him into financial difficulties. In his final years, the musician was continually debt-ridden and prone to depression. He died in 1791 and was buried in a mass grave.

Among the city's fine religious buildings are **St. Peter's Abbey** and **Benedictine monastery**, dating from c.AD 700, and the **Cathedral** (Dom), begun in 1614 to a design by Santino Solari. The **Franziskanerkirche** boasts a magnificent Baroque altarpiece (1709) by Johann Bernhard Fischer von Erlach.

Notable museums include the **Museum Carolino-Augusteum**, with its historical and fine arts collections, and the **Haus der Natur**, a museum of natural history. The **Mozarts Geburtshaus** is Mozart's birthplace, while the **Mozart Wohnhaus** features audio-visual displays telling the story of the composer's life.

On the right bank of the Salzach, **Schloss Mirabell** was built by Archbishop Wolf Dietrich for his Jewish mistress, Salome Alt. The palace gardens house the **Barock-museum** (Baroque Museum), with its collection of 17th- and 18th-century works of art.

🏔 **Festung Hohensalzburg**
Mönchsberg 34. 📞 0662-8424 3011. ⬜ daily. 🈸 📷
🏛 **Residenz**
Residenzplatz 1. 📞 0662-8042 2690. ⬜ daily. (Residenzgalerie ● Oct–Mar: Wed.) 🈸 📷
🏛 **Museum Carolino-Augusteum**
Museumplatz 1. 📞 0662-620 808 200. ⬜ daily. 🈸
🏛 **Barock-museum**
📞 0662-877 432. ⬜ Tue–Sun. 🈸

Innsbruck's Annasäule, crowned by a statue of the Virgin Mary

Innsbruck ⓼

🏠 127,000. ✈ 4 km (2.5 miles) W.
🚉 🚌 ℹ Burggraben 3 (0512-5356 recorded information).

CAPITAL OF the Tyrol region, Innsbruck grew up at the crossroads of the old trade routes between Germany and Italy, Vienna, and Switzerland.

One of the city's finest pieces of architecture is the **Goldenes Dachl** (Golden Roof), commissioned by Emperor Maximilian I, who chose Innsbruck as his imperial capital at the end of the 15th century. Made of gilded copper tiles, the roof was constructed in the 1490s to cover a balcony used by members of the court to observe events in the square below. Beneath the balcony is the **Museum Maximilianeum**, which focuses on the life of the Habsburg emperor, who ruled from 1493 to 1519.

Innsbruck's **Hofburg** (Imperial Palace) dates from the 15th century, but was rebuilt in Rococo style in the 18th century by Empress Maria Theresa (ruled 1740–80).

Built in 1555–65, the **Hofkirche** contains the impressive mausoleum of Maximilian I, which features 28 bronze statues. The high-light of the **Domkirche St. Jakob** (1717–22) is Lucas Cranach the Elder's painting of the *Madonna and Child*, which adorns the high altar.

Innsbruck's many museums include the **Tiroler Landes-museum Ferdinandeum**, which has European art from the 15th to the 20th centuries, and the **Tiroler Volkskunst-museum**, with exhibitions of local folk art and crafts.

🏛 **Museum Maximilianeum**
Herzog-Friedrichstrasse 15. 📞 0512-581 1111. ⬜ daily. ● Oct–Apr: Mon. 🈸
🏛 **Hofburg**
Rennweg 1. 📞 0512-587 186.
⬜ daily. ● Aug 15. 🈸
🏛 **Tiroler Landesmuseum Ferdinandeum**
Museumstrasse 15. 📞 0512-59489.
⬜ daily. ● Oct–May: Mon. 🈸
🏛 **Tiroler Volkskunst-museum**
Universitätsstrasse 2. 📞 0512-584 302. ⬜ daily. 🈸

Salzburg's magnificent Baroque cathedral, dominating the skyline of the Old Town

Practical & Travel Information

AUSTRIA IS WELL-EQUIPPED for tourism in both winter and summer. The extensive winter-sports facilities mean that even in the mountainous west of the country, communications are good and most roads are kept open all year. Public transport, especially the train services between the main cities, is reliable, and banking and exchange facilities are widely available. The country is generally safe for visitors except for a few unsavory bits of Vienna. Hospitals are of a high standard and, for lesser ailments, pharmacists are highly respected.

TOURIST INFORMATION

AUSTRIA HAS a wide network of local and regional tourist offices and the **Austrian National Tourist Office** has branches in many countries abroad. In the busier skiing resorts in winter, local offices often stay open as late as 9pm. In Vienna, **Wiener Tourismusverband** is a very helpful organization, especially with regard to forthcoming events and booking accommodations.

VISA REQUIREMENTS

CITIZENS of the US, Canada, Australia, and New Zealand need just a passport to visit Austria. No visa is required for stays of up to three months. Most European Union (EU) visitors need only a valid identity card to enter the country.

PERSONAL SECURITY

ALTHOUGH CRIME in the cities is rare, there are a few parts of Vienna that are best avoided at night, especially around the Karlsplatz station. Fights and pickpocketing are quite common at the Prater funfair at night.

In case of emergencies while on vacation, the appropriate services to call are listed in the Directory opposite.

HEALTH ISSUES

IT IS BEST to take out full health insurance which also covers flights home for medical reasons. This is true even for visitors from EU countries such as Great Britain. There is a reciprocal arrangement with Austria whereby emergency hospital treatment is free upon presentation of a British passport, but obtaining free treatment can involve rather a lot of bureaucracy.

In the case of a medical emergency, call an ambulance *(Rettungsdienst)* or the local **Doctor on Call**. For minor ailments or injuries, visit an *Apotheke* (pharmacy). All pharmacies display a distinctive red "A" sign. When closed, they give the address of the nearest open pharmacy.

FACILITIES FOR THE DISABLED

PUBLIC AWARENESS of the needs of the disabled is growing in Austria. Wiener Tourismusverband has a good online information service with details of the ease of wheelchair access at tourist sights, hotels, and public restrooms.

ETIQUETTE

AUSTRIANS on the whole are a conservative people and formal in their modes of address. Waiters are summoned with a deferential "Herr Ober," and greetings in the street are accompanied by the use of titles, such as "Herr Doktor," and much handshaking.

BANKING AND CURRENCY

THE UNIT OF CURRENCY in Austria was, until 2002, the Austrian Schilling. On January 1, 2002, it was replaced by the euro *(see p15)*.

Banks are usually the best places to change money. Most are open Monday to Friday from 8am to 12:30pm and from 1:30pm to 3pm (5:30pm on Thursdays). Some banks, generally those at main train stations and at airports, stay open longer and do not close for lunch. Though major credit cards are accepted at most large stores, hotels, and restaurants, they are not used as frequently as, for instance, in the UK or France, so it is a good idea to carry some cash with you.

COMMUNICATIONS

THE AUSTRIAN telecommunications network is run by Telekom Austria. Calls are among the most expensive in Europe. Public phones are coin- or card-operated, and you can buy phonecards from post offices and newsagents. Lower-rate calling times from Vienna are from 6pm to 8am Monday to Friday, and all day on Saturday and Sunday. Numbers starting in 05- can be dialled from anywhere in Austria at a local call rate. The postal service is reliable, verging on the pedantic, and

---

THE CLIMATE OF AUSTRIA

Altitude obviously plays an important role in the climate of Austria, the Alpine part of the country experiencing lower temperatures and receiving more rain and snow than Vienna and the east. Snow cover in the Alps lasts from November to May. Daytime temperatures in summer can be high, but the evenings are cool. There is a risk of thunderstorms from June to August.

VIENNA			
°C/F	25/77		
	13/55	15/59	13/55
0°C 5/41		6/43	
32°F			2/36
			-2/28
☀ 5.5 hrs	8 hrs	4.5 hrs	1.5 hrs
☂ 51 mm	74 mm	40 mm	38 mm
month	Apr	Jul	Oct	Jan

posting a letter can take some time. Each letter is carefully weighed and every size and shape coded separately.

Most post offices are open between 8am and noon and 2pm and 6pm from Monday to Friday. You can also buy stamps at newsagents.

FLYING TO AUSTRIA

IF YOU FLY from the United States, there are direct flights with **Delta Air Lines** from New York and Orlando to Vienna's Schwechat airport. **Austrian Airlines** flies from New York, Washington, and Chicago and **Lauda Air** has flights from Miami. The only direct flights from Australia are run by Lauda Air, which operates services from Sydney and Melbourne.

Connections to all of the major European cities are good. There are several flights a day from London's Gatwick and Heathrow airports. British Airways is the main British airline with regular flights to Vienna, and the main Austrian carrier is Austrian Airlines.

You can get APEX tickets if you make a booking two weeks in advance and charters are available at very competitive prices. Weekend package deals, including the price of two nights at a good Viennese hotel, can be

excellent value, sometimes costing less than the economy-class ticket price.

RAIL TRAVEL

AUSTRIA'S RAIL NETWORK is run by the state-owned Österreichische Bundesbahnen (ÖBB). Like London and Paris, Vienna has several mainline stations, three of which serve international connections. Generally, the Westbahnhof handles trains from the west, with good, frequent services to Innsbruck and Salzburg. Southern and eastern areas are served by the Südbahnhof, and trains from the north arrive at Franz-Josefs-Bahnhof.

The city of Vienna has two local train services: the U-Bahn (subway) and the Schnellbahn (a fast commuter service). The Westbahnhof has interchanges with the U3 and U6 subway lines, the Schnellbahn, and several tram and bus routes. The Südbahnhof is linked to the Schnellbahn and tram and bus lines, while Franz-Josefs-Bahnhof is served by the Schnellbahn and the cross-city D tram, which goes directly to the Ringstrasse.

The travel agency (*Reisebüro*) at Westbahnhof, open from 8am to 7pm Monday to Friday, and 8am to 1pm on Saturday, provides

rail information and also helps with hotel bookings. The travel agency at the Südbahnhof, which offers a similar service, operates the same hours in the high season, but shorter hours from November to April.

TRAVELING BY BUS

AUSTRIA'S LONG-DISTANCE buses serve those parts of the country that are not reached by train. Bus and train timetables are well integrated. In most towns, buses leave from the train station or the post office.

TRAVELING BY CAR

EVEN IN WINTER, Austrian road conditions are good and autobahns (highways) link all the major cities. There are also convenient routes into Austria from neighboring countries, such as those from Munich to Salzburg and Innsbruck. Highways are subject to a toll, which is paid by buying a windshield sticker valid for a certain period of time, ranging from a week to two months or a year. Stickers can be bought at the border or at post offices, gas stations, and tobacconists throughout the country. Tolls are also payable on certain mountain roads and tunnels.

DIRECTORY

TOURIST OFFICES

Austrian National Tourist Office
W www.austria-tourism.at

In Australia:
36 Carrington Street, 1st floor, Sydney, NSW 2000.
C 02-9299 3621.

In Canada:
2 Bloor Street East, Suite 3330, Toronto, Ontario M4W 1A8.
C 416-967 4867.

In the UK:
14 Cork St, London W1S 3NS.
C 020-7629 0461.

In the US:
500 Fifth Avenue, Suite 2009-2022, New York NY 10110.
C 212-944 6880.

Wiener Tourismusverband
Corner of Albertinaplatz/ Tegethoffstrasse/ Meysedergasse, Vienna.
C 01-24555.
W www.info.wien.at

EMBASSIES

Australia
Mattiellistrasse 2–4, A-1010 Vienna.
C 01-506 740.

Canada
Laurenzerberg 2, A-1010 Vienna.
C 01-5313 83000.

UK
Jaurèsgasse 12, A-1030 Vienna.
C 01-716130.

US
Boltzmanngasse 16, A-1090 Vienna.
C 01-31339.

EMERGENCY NUMBERS

Ambulance
C 144.

Doctor on Call
C 141.

Fire
C 122.

Police
C 133.

AIRLINES

Austrian Airlines
C 05-1789 (Austria).
C 020-7434 7350 (UK).
C 800-843 0002 (US).
W www.aua.com

Delta Air Lines
C 01-79567 023 (Vienna).
C 800-241 4141 (US).
W www.delta.com

Lauda Air
C 01-7000 (Vienna).
C 0845-601 0934 (UK).
C 800-588 8399 (US).
W www.laudaair.com

RAIL INFORMATION

C 05-1717.
W www.oebb.at

Shopping and Entertainment

S HOPPING IN AUSTRIA can be expensive, but it is a good place to buy certain high-quality traditional goods, such as Loden coats, porcelain, and glass. Famous for its coffee shops, Christmas markets, world-class opera, and orchestras, Vienna is the center of entertainment in Austria, although some important music festivals are held across the country. Outside the city, such rural pleasures as skiing and hiking are available in the west of the country, in the Tyrol, Salzburger Land, and Salzkammergut regions.

OPENING HOURS

S TORES USUALLY OPEN at 8:30 or 9am and close at 6 or 7pm. Smaller ones may close for an hour at lunch. In the past all stores closed at noon on Saturday, a routine that some still follow, though most now stay open until 5pm. Shops are still closed on Sundays and public holidays, but you can buy items such as groceries, flowers, books, camera film, and newspapers at major train stations.

FOOD AND DRINK

A USTRIA IS JUSTLY famous for its cakes and pastries, and in Vienna and large towns a good *Café-Konditorei* (cake shop and café) will mail cakes back home for you. Buy a prettily-packaged *Sachertorte*, the world-famous Viennese chocolate cake. In November and December try the buttery Advent *Stollen*, stuffed with fruit and nuts and dusted with icing sugar, available from the **Julius Meinl** delicatessen or any good baker. Specialist chocolate shops, such as **Altmann & Kühne**, are also worth a visit, both for the unusual packaging and the chocolates themselves.

Sweet *Eiswein* (so-called because the grapes are left on the vines until the first frosts) is an unusual and delicious white dessert wine. **Zum Schwarzen Kameel** in Vienna also sells the rarer red variety.

LUXURY GOODS

D ESIRABLE AUSTRIAN goods include clothes made of *Loden*, a felt-like woollen fabric, custom-made sheets, and high-quality down pillows and duvets. Petit point embroidery, which adorns handbags, powder compacts, and similar articles, is a Viennese specialty. A wide range is available at **Petit Point** and **Maria Stransky**.

Trachten (Austrian costume) shops are fun, selling a wide selection of hats, children's dresses, jackets, and blouses.

Glassware – including superb chandeliers – and Augarten porcelain come in highly original designs, but are very expensive. **Rasper & Söhne** is a good glass and porcelain shop for such items. The **Schloss Augarten** porcelain factory is open to visitors.

BOOKING TICKETS

Y OU CAN BUY tickets direct from the appropriate box office or reserve them by phone. Agencies are reliable; try the **Reisebüro Mondial**. Vienna's four state theaters, the Burgtheater, Akademietheater, Opera House, and Volksoper have a central booking office, the **Bundestheaterkassen**. In most cases tickets go on sale one month before the performance. Written applications for tickets must reach the Österreichische Bundestheater Verband (address as Bundestheaterkassen) at least three weeks in advance for opera tickets, and 10 days ahead for the theaters. Standing-room tickets (over 500 at the Opera House) are sold at the evening box office one hour before the start of the performance.

THEATER

V IENNESE THEATER enjoys a high reputation and the Burgtheater (*see p594*) is the most prestigious venue.

Classic and modern plays are performed here and at the associated Akademietheater.

The **Volkstheater** offers more modern plays as well as the occasional classic and some operetta performances.

The historic **Theater an der Wien** and the large **Raimund Theater** are part of the Vereinigte Bühnen Wien, the city's own theaters. Both specialize in lavish musicals. The Wiener Festwochen is held in May and June, and includes productions by guest companies, which are staged at these two theaters as part of the festival programme.

Vienna has a wide range of fringe theater from one-man shows to *Kabarett* – satirical shows not cabarets – but fairly fluent German is needed to appreciate them.

OPERA AND OPERETTA

T HE OPERA SEASON runs from September to June. At the Staatsoper in Vienna, operas are normally performed in the original language. At the **Wiener Volksoper**, where the repertoire includes light opera by Mozart and Puccini and operettas by Strauss and Lehár, they are sung in German. The same singers often appear at the two venues. The New Year's Eve performance at the Opera House is always Johan Strauss the Younger's *Die Fledermaus*, and famous guests sometimes make surprise appearances during the second act.

A wonderful smaller opera house is the **Wiener Kammeroper**. Here you can expect anything from Rossini and classic operetta to rock versions of familiar operas and opera parodies. From mid-July until mid-August the Wiener Kammeroper also plays at the **Soirée bei Prinz Orlofsky** festival at the Schönbrunner Schlosstheater.

CLASSICAL MUSIC

T HE PRINCIPAL VENUES for classical music concerts are the **Musikverein** (including the restored Brahms-Saal) and the concert halls of the **Konzerthaus**. Performances are also held in many other halls and historic palaces around Vienna.

The New Year's Concert is televised live from the Grosser Musikvereinsaal in the Musikverein every year. You can apply for tickets by writing direct to the **Wiener Philharmoniker**. Applications must be received on January 2 (not before, not after) for the next year's concert. You can order from abroad by telegram.

The city supports two great orchestras, the Wiener Philharmoniker and the Wiener Symphoniker. There are also a number of chamber music ensembles and church music is often of concert quality. The world-famous Vienna Boys' Choir can be heard during mass at the Burgkapelle in the Hofburg complex (see p594) every Sunday and religious holiday at 9:15am except from July to about mid-September (the box office is open the Friday before). You can also hear them at the Konzerthaus every Friday at 3:30pm in May, June, September, and October. Tickets are available from hotel porters and from Reisebüro Mondial.

MUSIC FESTIVALS

SEASONAL EVENTS in Vienna include the Vienna Festival in May and June, and the Klangbogen Wien in July and August, which includes opera performances held at the Theater an der Wien.

Inaugurated in 1920, the **Salzburg Festival** of opera, drama, and music claims to be the largest of its kind in the world. It is held annually in late July and August, attracting the world's finest conductors, soloists, and opera and theater companies. The spectacular venues include the Felsenreitschule, the riding school of the prince-archbishops of Salzburg. There is always a strong emphasis on Mozart, the city's most famous son, but the festival has also won acclaim for its contemporary music and innovative productions of classic and modern drama.

Another smaller festival is the **Haydn Festspiele**, held at the magnificent Schloss Esterházy in Eisenstadt (see p600). The festival itself is in September, but Haydn concerts are given in the palace throughout the summer.

COFFEE HOUSES AND HEURIGE

THE VIENNESE coffee house is a throwback to a more leisured age, serving coffee in a bewildering range of styles and allowing patrons to sit and read newspapers at their leisure. The Heuriger is a uniquely Austrian establishment. Its literal meaning is "this year's," and it refers both to the youngest available local wine and to venues that sell it. The most famous are in villages to the north and west of Vienna, such as Heiligenstadt and Grinzing. A sign reading Eigenbau means that the wine is from the owner's vineyards.

WINTER SPORTS

AUSTRIA'S facilities for winter sports are second only to Switzerland's. Ski resorts vary from fashionable Kitzbühel and St. Anton to small family resorts with less demanding slopes. Package tours are available from many countries around the world. Information on 800 resorts can be found on the **Austria Tourism** website, along with snow reports and other useful information.

DIRECTORY

FOOD AND DRINK

Altmann & Kühne
Graben 30, Vienna.
(01-533 0927.

Julius Meinl
Graben 19, Vienna.
(01-532 3334.

Zum Schwarzen Kameel
Bognergasse 5, Vienna.
(01-533 8125.

LUXURY GOODS

Maria Stransky
Hofburg Passage 2,
Vienna.
(01-533 6098.

Petit Point
Kärntner Strasse 16,
Vienna.
(01-512 4886.

Rasper & Söhne
Graben 15, Vienna.
(01-534 330.

Schloss Augarten
Obere Augartenstrasse 1,
Vienna.
(01-211 240.

BOOKING TICKETS

Bundestheater-kassen
Hanuschgasse 3, Vienna.
(01-514 440.

Reisebüro Mondial
Faulmanngasse 4, Vienna.
(01-5880 4141.

THEATER

Raimund Theater
Wallgasse 18, Vienna.
(01-599 770.

Theater an der Wien
Linke Wienzeile 6, Vienna.
(01-588 300.

Volkstheater
Neustiftgasse 1, Vienna.
(01-524 7263.

OPERA AND OPERETTA

Soirée bei Prinz Orlofsky
Schönbrunner Schloss-theater, Schönbrunn.
(01-512 0100.

Wiener Kammeroper
Fleischmarkt 24, Vienna.
(01-512 010077.

Wiener Volksoper
Währinger Strasse 78,
Vienna.
(01-514 443 318.

CLASSICAL MUSIC

Konzerthaus
Lothringerstrasse 20,
Vienna.
(01-242 002.

Musikverein
Bösendorferstrasse 12,
Vienna.
(01-505 8190.

Wiener Philharmoniker
Bösendorferstrasse 12,
Vienna.
(01-5056 5250.

MUSIC FESTIVALS

Haydn Festspiele
Schloss Esterházy,
A-7000 Eisenstadt.
(02682-618 66.

Salzburg Festival
Hofstallgasse 1, Postfach
140, A-5100 Salzburg.
(0662-804 5579.

WINTER SPORTS

Austria Tourism
w www.austria-tourism.at

Where to Stay in Austria

ACCOMMODATIONS IN AUSTRIA range from large, well-equipped, five-star hotels to simple pensions, and generally you can expect a high standard of comfort and cleanliness everywhere. Room rates in Vienna are disproportionately high compared to other costs. However, you can save money by staying in a hotel outside the Ringstrasse or by looking out for any special deals.

	NUMBER OF ROOMS	PRIVATE PARKING	RESTAURANT	AIR-CONDITIONING
VIENNA				
CENTRAL VIENNA: *Christina* €€ Hafnersteig 7, A-1010. Map E3. 01-533 2961. FAX 01-533 29611. W www.pertschy.com The Christina is a quiet, unassuming pension, where you are guaranteed a warm welcome. It has been renovated in Art Deco style.	33			
CENTRAL VIENNA: *Nossek* €€ Graben 17, A-1010. Map D3. 01-533 70410. FAX 01-535 3646. You will need to book well in advance for a room with a balcony over-looking the Graben at this family-run pension. Most bedrooms, though short on facilities and with rudimentary bathrooms, are elegantly furnished.	28			
CENTRAL VIENNA: *Pension City* €€ Bauernmarkt 10, A-1010. Map E3. 01-533 9521. FAX 01-535 5216. Housed in a late 19th-century building, this small, friendly hotel is close to shops, bars, and restaurants. Some of the rooms have good views.	19	■		
CENTRAL VIENNA: *Kärntnerhof* €€€ Grashofgasse 4, A-1011. Map E3. 01-512 1923. FAX 01-513 222833. W www.karntnerhof.com The interior of this well-run establishment has splendid Art Deco features. Breakfast is served in rustic, beamed surroundings.	43	●		
CENTRAL VIENNA: *Wandl* €€€ Petersplatz 9, A-1010. Map E3. 01-534 550. FAX 01-534 5577. W www.hotel-wandl.com The centrally located Wandl is a characterful, old-fashioned hotel that has been in the same family for generations. All but four of the rooms have a private bathroom, and some have views of the Stephansdom.	138			
CENTRAL VIENNA: *Am Schubertring* €€€€ Schubertring 11, A-1010. Map E4. 01-717 020. FAX 01-713 9966. Art Deco prints, murals, and lamps decorate the smart bar, breakfast and sitting rooms of this fine hotel. The same level of detail has gone into the design of the luxurious rooms. Professional, attentive staff.	39	●		●
CENTRAL VIENNA: *Astoria* €€€€€ Führichgasse 1, A-1015. Map D4. 01-515 770. FAX 01-515 7782. W www.austria-trend.at It is worth paying a little more for the extra space, fine stucco work, and splendid period furnishings at this turn-of-the-century hotel, where opera stars often pop in for drinks.	108	●	■	
CENTRAL VIENNA: *König von Ungarn* €€€€ Schulerstrasse 10, A-1010. Map E3. 01-515 840. FAX 01-515 848. W www.kvu.at A highly recommended hotel, offering great value for money. The large, comfortable rooms have appealing, rustic furniture. Visit the vaulted dining rooms for well-prepared, traditional specialties.	33	●	■	●
CENTRAL VIENNA: *Sacher* €€€€€ Philarmonikerstrasse 4, A-1010. Map D4. 01-514 56. FAX 01-514 56810. W www.sacher.com Vienna's most famous hotel boasts opulent interiors and an excellent range of amenities. The service is outstanding.	119	●	■	●
FARTHER AFIELD: *Wild* € Lange Gasse 10, A-1080. Map B3. 01-406 5174. FAX 01-402 2168. W www.pension-wild.com Located in the heart of the Josefstadt area, a short distance west of the city center, this friendly pension has spotlessly clean bedrooms. A toilet and shower are shared between every two or three rooms.	22			
FARTHER AFIELD: *Im Palais Schwarzenberg* €€€€€ Schwarzenbergplatz 9, A-1030. Map 5E. 01-798 4515. FAX 01-798 4714. This intimate hotel occupies part of the huge Baroque Schwarzenberg Palace and is set in a beautiful landscaped park. Here guests can escape the hurly-burly of Vienna's busier luxury hotels.	44	●	■	●

Map references refer to map of Vienna on pp590–1

Price categories are for a double room with bathroom per night, including tax, and service:

€ under €70
€€ €70–110
€€€ €110–145
€€€€ €145–195
€€€€€ over €195

CREDIT CARDS
Hotels that accept major credit cards are indicated in the text.

PRIVATE PARKING
Parking provided by the hotel in a private car park or private garage on the hotel site or nearby. Some hotels charge for use of private parking facilities.

REST OF AUSTRIA

	NUMBER OF ROOMS	PRIVATE PARKING	RESTAURANT	AIR-CONDITIONING
GRAZ: *Erzherzog Johann* €€€€ Sackstrasse 3–5, A-8010 Graz. 0316-81 16 16. FAX 0316-81 15 15. www.erzherzog-johann.com This luxurious former Baroque palace has been functioning as a hotel for 140 years. The 60 rooms and 2 suites are furnished with antique furniture and rugs. Amenities include a cocktail bar, sauna, and conference facilities.	62		■	
GRAZ: *Schlossberghotel* €€€€€ Kaiser-Franz-Josef-Kai 30, A-8010 Graz. 0316-80 70 0. FAX 0316-80 70 70. www.schlossberg-hotel.at Guests at this attractive, upscale hotel can enjoy many facilities, including a sauna, steam room, gym, and a roof-top swimming pool.	54	●	■	
HALLSTATT: *Gasthof Hirlatz* € Malerweg 125, A-4830 Hallstatt. 06134-84 43 0. FAX 06134-8443 33. www.interactive.com.hotel/HIRLATZ A homey chalet-style guesthouse with splendid mountain views and traditional home cooking. There is an outdoor swimming pool in the gardens.	12	●	■	
INNSBRUCK: *Best Western Parkhotel Leipzigerhof* €€ Defreggerstrasse 13, A-6020 Innsbruck. 0512-34 35 25. FAX 0512-39 43 57. www.parkhotel-leipzigerhof.at A pleasant hotel, conveniently located for the main shopping district and the Altstadt. Rooms are tastefully appointed and well-equipped.	120	●	■	●
INNSBRUCK: *Tautermann* €€ Stamser Feld 5, A-6020 Innsbruck. 0512-28 15 72. FAX 0512-28 15 72 10. www.tautermann-hotel.at The town center is only a 5-minute walk from this quiet, chalet-style bed-and-breakfast hotel. The spacious rooms have light wooden furnishings.	32	●		
LINZ: *Mühlviertlerhof* € Graben 24, A-4020 Linz. 0732-77 22 68. FAX 0732-77 22 68 34. www.hotel-muehlviertlerhof.at The Mühlviertlerhof is centrally located. It is a modest but well-kept hotel, with clean, comfortable rooms, and friendly and attentive staff.	22			
LINZ: *Austria Classic Hotel Drei Mohren* €€€ Promenade 17, A-4020 Linz. 0732-77 26 26 0. FAX 0732-77 26 26 6. www.drei-mohren.at Occupying an old town house in the city center, this family-run hotel has tastefully decorated, well-equipped rooms.	20	●		
SALZBURG: *Blaue Gans* €€ Getreidegasse 41–43, A-5020 Salzburg. 0662-84 24 91 0. FAX 0662-84 24 91 9. www.blauegans.at A charming, friendly hotel located in the heart of the old town. There are family rooms, as well as a babysitting service.	44	●	■	
SALZBURG: *Weisse Taube* €€€ Kaigasse 9, A-5020 Salzburg. 0662-84 24 04. FAX 0662-84 17 83. www.weissetaube.at Housed in a historic building, the Weisse Taube is a traditional-style hotel with comfortable rooms. The hotel staff are both helpful and informative.	31	●		
SALZBURG: *Sacher Salzburg Osterreichischer Hof* €€€€€ Schwarzstrasse 5–7, A-5020 Salzburg. 0662-88 97 73 51. FAX 0662-88 97 75 51. salzburg@sacher.com Owned by the same family as the Sacher in Vienna, this long-established hotel is one of Salzburg's finest, and enjoys a wonderful location overlooking the river. Choose from a range of luxury rooms and suites.	120	●	■	●

For key to symbols see back flap

Where to Eat in Austria

AUSTRIA HAS A RANGE OF RESTAURANTS to suit most tastes and budgets. In the capital, the most luxurious establishments are found in or near the Stephansdom Quarter. Some, including those in the big hotels, offer international menus. There are also many ethnic restaurants serving Chinese, Greek, Indian, or Turkish cuisine. In smaller towns and cities, most venues prepare local specialties.

	FIXED-PRICE MENU	OUTDOOR TABLES	VEGETARIAN DISHES	GOOD WINE LIST
VIENNA				
CENTRAL VIENNA: *Bei Max* €€ Landhausgasse 2. **Map** D3. ☎ 01-533 7359. Specialties here are the *Fleischnudel* or *Kasnudel* – pastry parcels stuffed with meat or cheese. There are also some interesting Austrian wines on offer. ● *Sat, Sun; 2 weeks at Christmas.* ▯	●			
CENTRAL VIENNA: *Hedrich* €€ Stubenring 2. **Map** E3. ☎ 01-512 9588. Most popular at lunchtime, this small, thriving restaurant serves modern cuisine. The veal dishes are particularly good, as are the desserts. ● *Sat, Sun.*		▮		
CENTRAL VIENNA: *Zu den Drei Hacken* €€ Singerstraße 28. **Map** E4. ☎ 01-512 58 95. Crammed into a couple of small, plain rooms, this intimate, somewhat old-fashioned restaurant offers excellent traditional Viennese and regional Austrian cooking, with laid-back service. ● *Sun and hols.* ♿ ▯	●	▮		▮
CENTRAL VIENNA: *Schnattl* €€€ Lange Gasse 40. **Map** B3. ☎ 01-405 3400. Wilhelm Schnattl's fresh and innovative interpretation of standard Viennese dishes, together with the pleasant setting and affordable prices, more than compensates for the rather slow service here. ● *Sat, Sun, last 2 weeks Aug.* ▯	●	▮	●	▮
CENTRAL VIENNA: *Do & Co* €€€€ Haas-Haus, 7th Floor, Stephansplatz 12. **Map** D3. ☎ 01-535 39 69. Do & Co is something of a Viennese institution with Vienna's most sought-after view of the Stephansdom. International seafood specialties jostle for attention with perfect *schnitzels.* ♿ ▯				▮
CENTRAL VIENNA: *Grotta Azzurra* €€€€ Babenbergerstrasse 5. **Map** C3. ☎ 01-5861 0440. This light and spacious restaurant offers a range of classic Italian cooking, elegantly presented. The lengthy wine list is exclusively Italian. ▯			●	▮
CENTRAL VIENNA: *Drei Husaren* €€€€€ Weihburggasse 4. **Map** E4. ☎ 01-5121 0920. A sedate and very comfortable restaurant, serving excellent traditional Viennese dishes. Drei Husaren is famous for its carefully composed hors d'oeuvres, such as calves' brains on spinach and miniature steak tartare. ♿ ▯			●	▮
CENTRAL VIENNA: *Korso* €€€€€ Hotel Bristol, Mahlerstrasse 2. **Map** D4. ☎ 01-5151 6546. Modern Viennese haute cuisine is accompanied by a magnificent wine list. Efficient service, though a little unfriendly. ● *lunch Sat; mid-Jul–mid-Aug.* ♿ ▯	●		●	▮
CENTRAL VIENNA: *Palais Schwarzenberg* €€€€€ Hotel im Palais Schwarzenberg, Schwarzenbergplatz 9. **Map** E5. ☎ 01-798 4515. The cooking here is unashamedly luxurious, with ample use of ingredients such as truffles, caviar, and champagne. There is a mix of Viennese and international dishes. Very good Austrian wines are available by the glass. ♿ ▯		▮		▮
FARTHER AFIELD: *Hunger-Künstler* € Gumpendorfer Strasse 48. ☎ 01-587 9210. This quiet, unpretentious establishment has a varied menu of traditional Austrian and Italian dishes. Open until 1am every day. ● *lunch daily.* ♿ ▯			●	
FARTHER AFIELD: *Vikerls Lokal* €€€ Würffelgasse 4. ☎ 01-894 3430. First-rate ingredients and generous portions are guaranteed at this friendly, family-run restaurant. Try the *Schmankerl von Kalb* – veal fillet, kidneys, and sweet-breads in a thyme and rosemary sauce. ● *Mon, dinner Sun.* ♿	●	▮		▮

Map references refer to the map of Vienna on pp590–91

Price categories are for a three-course meal for one, including a ¼ liter of house wine, tax, and service:

€ under €20
€€ €20–30
€€€ €30–40
€€€€ €40–50
€€€€€ over €50

FIXED-PRICE MENU
A good-value fixed-price menu on offer at lunch, dinner, or both, usually with three courses.

VEGETARIAN DISHES
Restaurant serves a selection of dishes suitable for vegetarian diners.

CREDIT CARDS
Major credit cards are accepted in those hotels where the credit card symbol is shown.

	FIXED-PRICE MENU	OUTDOOR TABLES	VEGETARIAN DISHES	GOOD WINE LIST

REST OF AUSTRIA

INNSBRUCK: *Altstadt Stüberl* — €
Reisengasse 13, Innsbruck. 0512-58 23 47.
Housed in a 500-year-old building, this snug restaurant is a favorite with locals. It specialises in Tyrolean dishes, such as *Tiroler gröstl* and *schlutz-krapfen*, but the menu also extends throughout Austria. ● Sun & hols. &

| | ● | | | |

GRAZ: *Stainzerbauer* — €€
Bürgergasse 4, Graz. 0316-82 11 06.
This restaurant serves a good selection of hearty Styrian dishes. In summer, diners can sit out in the garden. All wines are Austrian. ● Sun & hols. &

| | ● | ■ | ● | |

GRAZ: *Johan* — €€€
Landhausgasse 1, Graz. 0316-82 13 120.
Housed in a medieval hall, this restaurant has been praised in architecture reviews for its modern design. The cuisine (modern international) is equally impressive. There is a stylish cocktail bar on site. ● Sun, Mon, & hols. &

| | ● | ■ | ● | ■ |

INNSBRUCK: *Theresien Bräu* — €
Maria-Theresien-Strasse 51–53, Innsbruck. 0512-58 75 80.
This one-time cinema is now decked out with fishing nets and other nautical paraphenalia and offers an Austrian-International menu. Specialties include noodles with ham, cheese, and herb-flavored cream sauce. ● Dec 24. &

| | ● | ■ | ● | |

LINZ: *Stieglbräu im Klosterhof* — €€
Landstrasse 30, Linz. 0732-77 33 73.
One of the most popular places to eat in Linz, the Stieglbräu serves traditional Austrian cuisine with a Bavarian touch. There is a huge garden seating over 1,000 people, and the beer is great. Open until midnight.

| | | ■ | | |

LINZ: *Restaurant Verdi* — €€€
Pachmayrstrasse 137, Linz. 0732-73 30 05.
With views over Linz and a relaxed setting and leather-covered chairs, the Verdi serves up a seasonal menu with an experimental touch. Worth trying is the roasted lamb served with *gnocchi*, thyme, and peppers. ● Sun.

| | ● | | ● | ■ |

MELK: *Hotel Restaurant zur Post* — €
Linzer Strasse 1, Melk. 0275-25 23 45.
A charming place with a courtyard, situated just below Melk's famous monastery. Good Austrian food is on offer, including Wiener Schnitzel, strudel, and traditional soups and fish dishes. ● Mon, Oct–Feb. &

| | ● | ■ | ● | |

SALZBURG: *Augustiner Bräu* — €
Kloster Mülln, Augustinergasse 4, Salzburg. 0662-43 12 46.
This huge hall in the well-known brewery can seat over 1,000 diners. Cheap Austrian food is available buffet-style on a self-serve basis. Or you can bring your own food and just go for the beer. There is a pleasant garden. Opens at 3pm.

| | | ■ | ● | |

SALZBURG: *Gasthof Krimpelstätter* — €€
Müllner Hauptstrasse 31, Salzburg. 0662-43 22 74.
Serves good local dishes such as dumplings, and wonderful house beer or Augustiner beer from the nearby brewery. The old building has an interesting interior and a beautiful garden. It is popular with local actors. ● Sun, Mon.

| | | ■ | ● | |

SALZBURG: *Schlossrestaurant Paris Lodron* — €€€€€
Mönchsberg Park 26, Salzburg. 0662-84 85 55-0.
Situated in the first-class Hotel Schloss Mönchstein, this restaurant has a similar high standard, with prize-winning cuisine. &

| | ● | ■ | ● | ■ |

SCHÜTZEN IM GEBIRGE: *Taubenkogel* — €€€€€
Hauptstrasse 33, Schützen im Gebirge. 0268-42 29 7.
Situated 5 km (3 miles) from Eisenstadt, this small but excellent restaurant has received much critical acclaim. ● Mon, Tue. &

| | ● | ■ | ● | ■ |

For key to symbols see back flap

SWITZERLAND

T HE STEREOTYPICAL IMAGES OF SWITZERLAND – *brightly-painted wooden chalets, alpine meadows, and chic skiing resorts – are easy to find. But there are many other sides to this small, diverse country that are equally accessible, from picturesque medieval towns to world-class art and fine gastronomy. Switzerland's rural retreats offer wonderful opportunities for relaxing and recharging.*

Switzerland lies at the very heart of Europe, landlocked between the Alps and the Jura mountains. It is bordered to the west by France, to the north by Germany, to the east by Austria and Liechtenstein, and to the south by Italy.

Mountains make up 70 percent of Switzerland's 41,285 sq km (15,949 sq miles). The St. Gotthard Massif in the center of Switzerland is the source of many lakes and two of Europe's major rivers, the Rhine and the Rhône. The central Mittelland has the highest concentration of picturesque Alpine peaks and mountain villages, although the loftiest Alps are those of the Valais in the southwest. The isolated valleys of Graubünden in the east provide the setting for many quality winter resorts. In the west, the cities lining the northern shore of Lake Geneva make up the bulk of French Switzerland, while a series of high passes in southern Ticino provides overland access to Italy.

With almost a quarter of its area comprising high Alps, lakes, and barren rock, and with no seaboard and few natural resources other than water power, the country has managed to preserve a proud and united spirit of independence.

HISTORY

Switzerland's unique geography has presented both opportunities and disadvantages. Its story has been of a gradual coming together, not without bloodshed, of a population of diverse races, religions, and languages, making what is today viewed as a haven of peace and reason.

The Jura mountains provide the earliest evidence of Switzerland's habitation, which dates to over 50,000 years ago. By the start of the Christian era, Celtic peoples were living in western Switzerland and Germanic tribes in the north and east. Many of

The snow-capped Jungfrau, one of the Alps' most famous peaks

◁ The colorful façade of a typical Swiss chalet, Interlaken

these communities were under the control of the expanding Roman Empire, whose influence spread after 58 BC.

The Germanic tribes to the north eventually broke through Roman defenses; by the 5th century AD the era of Roman rule had ended. During the so-called "Dark Ages," the Burgundian tribe controlled the west, the Alemanni the center and east. In the 5th century, both tribes came under the control of the Franks, and later the Holy Roman Empire. The 13th century saw the rise of powerful local families such as the Habsburgs and the Zähringen, who established feudal rule over the area.

Huldrych Zwingli (1484–1531), leader of the Swiss Reformation

In 1291 three forest cantons around Lake Lucerne – Uri, Schwyz, and Unterwalden – came together to swear an Oath of Allegiance, thus forming an independent Swiss state. Over the coming centuries, more cantons came to join the Confederation. These included lands south of the Alps known as the Ticino, and those to the west, where Charles of Burgundy was defeated by the Swiss in 1477. Switzerland was famous at this period for producing skilled mercenaries, who were paid handsomely to fight battles well beyond Swiss frontiers.

Protestantism took root in Switzerland in the 16th century, spread by the teachings of Zwingli and Calvin. Swiss cities embraced the new doctrines, whereas rural cantons remained mostly Catholic. Tensions between the two communities erupted into violence from time to time, and apart from a brief period at the turn of the 19th century when Napoleon established the Helvetic Republic, these issues were not resolved until the adoption of a federal constitution in 1848.

With stability came development – railways were built, agriculture diversified, resorts developed. A tradition

Exploring Switzerland

SWITZERLAND IS A SMALL COUNTRY – only 300 km (190 miles) by 180 km (110 miles) at its greatest extent. The Alps run across the southern part of the country, and in the northwest, the Jura mountains stretch along the French border. Mediterranean influences can be felt and seen in mild winters and palm-lined esplanades south of the Alps. Traveling by car is the most flexible mode of transportation, but the reliable rail network makes sightseeing by train easy and surprisingly affordable.

SIGHTS AT A GLANCE

Basel ❹
Bern ❺
Chur ❿
Geneva ❶
Interlaken and
  the Jungfrau ❻
Lake Geneva ❷
Lucerne ❽
Neuchâtel ❸
Swiss National Park ⓫
Ticino ⓬
Zermatt ❼
Zürich ❾

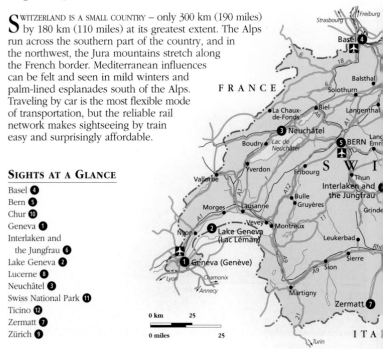

0 km   25

0 miles   25

of humanitarianism began in the mid-19th century with the founding of the International Red Cross. In the 20th century Switzerland remained neutral during the two world wars, and concentrated on furthering its economic development, notably in the sectors of finance and pharmaceuticals.

LANGUAGE AND CULTURE

Switzerland is a quadrilingual nation. German, French, Italian, and Romansch (the language of a few valleys in the canton of Graubünden) are spoken in different parts of the country, though German is the language of the majority.

For many centuries Swiss culture had a predominantly rural tradition, and wine festivals are still a feature of village life. Great pride is taken in traditional crafts and regional specialties, such as the famous Emmental cheese. Swiss chocolate is also renowned for its high quality. Switzerland is now an outward-looking country, keen to export its expertise in finance and watchmaking worldwide.

KEY DATES IN SWISS HISTORY

58 BC–AD 400 Roman occupation

AD 400–1100 Germanic peoples – the Allemani and Burgundians – inhabit the area

12th century Holy Roman Empire extends feudal law over much of present-day Switzerland

1220 Gotthard Pass opened

1291 Oath of Allegiance marks beginning of the Swiss Confederation

1351 Zürich joins the Confederation

1477 Charles the Bold of Burgundy defeated by Swiss troops at Battle of Nancy

16th century Reformation; Protestantism takes firm hold in Swiss cities

1798 Napoleon creates the Helvetic Republic

1815 Power of cantons re-established

1830–48 Federal constitution drawn up

1864 International Red Cross set up

1914–18 & 1939–45 Switzerland remains neutral during two world wars

1946 UN offices established in Geneva

1998 Global settlement sum agreed by Swiss banks by way of reparations for Holocaust claims

2002 Switzerland declared member of the UN

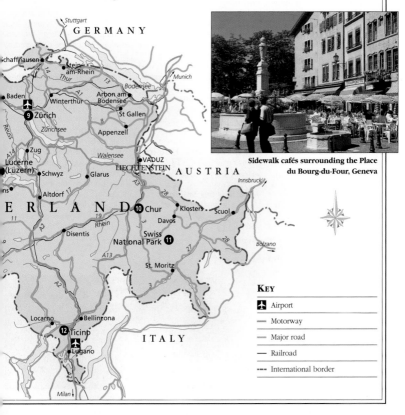

Sidewalk cafés surrounding the Place du Bourg-du-Four, Geneva

KEY

✈ Airport

— Motorway

— Major road

— Railroad

▪▪▪ International border

Narrow, winding street in Geneva's historic old town

Geneva ❶

Geneva. 🚶 *416,000*. ✈ 🚆 🚌
ℹ *Rue du Mont-Blanc 18 (022-909 7000)*. 📅 *Fêtes de Genève (early Aug)*.

G ENEVA IS an ancient settlement with origins that go back to Roman times. The **old town**, situated on a craggy hill up above the western end of Lake Geneva, is the most attractive part of the city, with narrow, cobbled lanes and streets, stately stone townhouses, fountain-filled squares, and a tempting array of galleries, shops, and cafés.

In the heart of the old town stands the **Cathédrale St-Pierre**. Although the building dates from the 12th century it was much altered in the 16th century – the plain façade and interiors are in keeping with its Reformist heritage. A splendid 14th-century town-house close by, the **Maison Tavel**, gives a good insight into life in the developing city of Geneva through the centuries. In Rue Jean-Calvin the **Barbier-Müller Museum** displays artifacts and objects from traditional societies in Africa and the Asia-Pacific region. There is a mesmer-izing array of beautiful carvings, jewelry, and textiles.

Geneva's grandest museum, however, is the **Musée d'Art et Histoire**, at the eastern end of the old town. The stately early 19th-century edifice houses a diverse array of Swiss and European art

and artifacts, from prehistory to the modern age. It also has a sizeable collection of Egyptian antiquities.

At the foot of the old town Geneva's main shopping street – the Rue de Rive – runs parallel to the lake shore. The quays either side of the lake are pleasant places to stroll, with the Jardin Anglais and the **Jet d'Eau** (one of the world's largest fountains) on the Left Bank, and the Quai du Mont-Blanc on the right. It is from the latter that the ferries and paddlesteamers operate pleasure cruises and regular services to towns along the lake. Farther along the Right Bank are the city's **botanic gardens**, and if you take the road bordering them you will come to the international quarter of the city. Here the **Palais des Nations** – European head-quarters of the UN – runs frequent guided tours through the day. Opposite, the **International Museum of the Red Cross and Red Crescent** offers a moving testimony to the world's need for such an organization.

Jet d'Eau fountain, Geneva harbor

🏛 **Musée d'Art et Histoire**
Rue Charles-Galland 2. ☎ *022-418 2600*. ⏰ *Tue–Sun*. ⚙ 🎟 *for temporary exhibitions*.

🏛 **Palais des Nations**
Avenue de la Paix 14. ☎ *022-914 4896*. ⏰ *daily*. ● *Nov–Mar: Sat & Sun*. 🎟 ♿

Lake Geneva ❷

Vaud. 🚆 🚌 ⛴ ℹ *Avenue d' Ouchy 60, Lausanne (021- 613 2626)*. 📅 *Nyon Paléo Music Festival (Jul)*.

T HE REGION skirting Lake Geneva offers a string of interesting settlements in a landscape replete with rolling hills, pretty stone-built villages, vine-clad slopes, and palm-fringed esplanades.

Coppet, 15 km (10 miles) north along the lake, is a quaint medieval village. The 17th-century Château de Coppet was the home of Madame de Staël, whose literary soirées and opposition to Napoleon enhanced the popularity of the château in the 18th century.

Another 15 km (10 miles) farther along the lake, **Nyon** is a charming lakeside town dating from Roman times, a heritage displayed at the excellent Roman Museum. With its fortress-like château and network of lanes, Nyon commands a fine hilltop view over the lake. Pretty gardens cover the western slopes down to the lake shore.

Lausanne, 60 km (38 miles) east of Geneva, is a bustling city with a fine old town, a beautiful Gothic cathedral, and excellent shopping. The city is also home to the international Olympic movement – at the lakeside district of Ouchy, the Musée Olympique is a must for all sports enthusiasts.

Wine château and vineyards near the hilltop town of Nyon

The resort of **Montreux** at the eastern end of the lake has a palm-lined promenade and a busy marina. There are Belle Epoque hotels and health resorts in abundance, and the town boasts one of Switzerland's top attractions – the **Château de Chillon**. This former bastion of the dukes of Savoy has all the accoutrements of a medieval castle – damp dungeons, weaponry, and huge banqueting halls.

About 25 km (15 miles) north of Montreux, the wonderfully preserved medieval hilltop town of **Gruyères** is also a major tourist attraction. The walled town is divided by a cobbled main street flanked by tempting restaurants. You can see the famous cheese being made in the traditional way in Moléson-sur-Gruyères.

Pit Stop (1984), sculpture in the Museum Jean Tinguely, Basel

♣ Château de Chillon
1820 Veytaux, Montreux. 【 021-966 8910. ◯ daily. 🈂 🅂 limited.

Neuchâtel ❸

Neuchâtel. 🏠 32,000. 🚉 🚌
ℹ Hôtel des Postes (032- 889 6890).
🍷 Wine Festival (late Sep).

NEUCHÂTEL, an old religious center and university town, lies at the eastern end of Lake Neuchâtel at the base of the Jura mountains. It is a little off the beaten track as far as tourism is concerned, but has an extensive and attractive old town overlooked by the partly Romanesque **Collegiate Church**. Just below the church, the **Tour des Prisons** offers a stunning view of the lake and city. The market square – Place des Halles – is bounded by elegant 17th-century buildings, including the turreted **Maison des Halles**, now a restaurant. The area around Neuchâtel is known for its wines, including Perdrix Blanche.

ENVIRONS: 20 km (12 miles) northwest of Neuchâtel lies **La Chaux-de-Fonds**, the largest of Switzerland's watchmaking towns. Located 992 m (3,255 ft) above sea level, it does not have the feel of a typical Swiss town. Its rigid grid pattern was adopted when the town was rebuilt after a devastating fire in the 18th century. Le Corbusier and Louis Chevrolet are famous sons, though there is little evidence of the former in the town's architecture. The **Musée International d'Horlogerie** has a wonderful collection devoted to the watch industry, and is well worth a visit.

🏛 Musée International d'Horlogerie
Rue des Musées 29. 【 032-967 6861.
◯ Tue–Sun. ● public hols. 🈂

Enameled watch (c.1665) in the Musée International d'Horlogerie

Basel ❹

Basel. 🏠 188,000. ✈ 🚉 🚌
ℹ Basel Tourismus, Steinenberg 14 (061-268 6868). 🍷 Fair (Oct–Nov).

BASEL SITS in the northernmost corner of Switzerland and shares borders with both Germany and France. The city straddles the Rhine at the farthest point that the river is navigable to sea-going vessels. It is a large commercial city, and a world center for the chemical and pharmaceutical industries. This specialization is a legacy of its liberal past, when the city offered a home to Huguenots fleeing persecution. Their traditional silk-weaving skills eventually led to the development of synthetic dyes, and then on to other chemical and pharmaceutical processes.

The **old town** remains the heart of the city and is a maze of fine streets and squares, including Marktplatz with its daily fruit and vegetable market. The striking red painted **rathaus** (town hall) stands here, on the southern bank of the Rhine.

The twin sandstone towers of the Gothic **cathedral** are major landmarks. This imposing 12th-century building stands in a grand square – site of the famous autumn fair which has been an annual event since the 15th century.

Basel has a modern side too, with a vibrant cultural scene and a number of interesting museums, most notably the **Kunstmuseum**, a collection which includes an impressive range of 20th-century artists including Picasso.

Switzerland's most famous artist, Jean Tinguely (1925–91), has a museum devoted to his outlandish mechanical sculptures – **Museum Jean Tinguely**.

🏛 Kunstmuseum
St. Alban-Graben 16. 【 061-206 6262. ◯ Tue–Sun. 🈂 🅂
🏛 Museum Jean Tinguely
Grenzacherstrasse. 【 061-681 9320. ◯ Wed–Sun. 🈂 🅂

The tall spire of Bern Cathedral rising above the city skyline

Bern ❺

Bern. 🏛 300,000. ✈ 🚉 🚌
ℹ️ *Bahnhof (031-328 1212).*
🎭 *Mattenfest (Sep).*
🌐 *www.bernetourism.ch*

BERN IS THE CAPITAL of Switzerland and its most attractive city – it has the best-preserved medieval town center in the country. It is located on raised land in a bend of the Aare River. From the city's terraces there are spectacular views over the river and across to the peaks of the distant Alps.

The city was founded at the end of the 12th century by the Duke of Zähringen and allegedly named after the first animal – a bear – killed in the forests which previously covered the area. The bear has been the city's emblem ever since. Most of the center of Bern, with its many fine stone Renaissance houses and covered arcades, dates from the 16th and 17th centuries.

Since 1848 Bern has been the capital of the Confederation. The massive **Bundeshaus** (Capitol) is the home of the Swiss Parliament, and the building is open to visitors when parliament is not in session. It is situated at the end of the city's main market squares – Bärenplatz and Bundesplatz. These linked squares are also the site of the annual onion market which takes place on the fourth Monday in November, when the local onion harvest is traditionally celebrated.

The grotesque Kindlifresser or Ogre Fountain

The attractive **old town** at the heart of Bern is a UNESCO World Heritage Site, famous for its arcaded streets. The old town is lovely to wander around in both fair weather and foul – the continuous arcading offers comprehensive protection from the elements. The main streets – Kramgasse, Münstergasse, Marktgasse, and Gerechtigkeitsgasse – are all lined with tempting shops, galleries, and cafés.

The city's famous **clocktower** stands where Kramgasse meets Marktplatz. The clock dates from 1530, and on the hour a series of figures – including bears, a jester, and a rooster – plays out its performance. The old town is filled with magnificent fountains, each of which depicts a famous historical or legendary figure. A wander around the city center will reveal the likenesses of Moses, the Duke of Zähringen, and the gruesome child-eating ogre, the Kindlifresser.

The **cathedral** on Münstergasse was built in the 15th century and is a beautiful example of late Gothic

architecture. The building's most magnificent element is the main portal – a masterpiece of carved and painted stone, which depicts the Last Judgment. The tall spire was only added in the late 19th century. To the right of the cathedral is a delightful small park overlooking the Aare flowing far below. This makes a good picnic spot in summer.

The **Bärengraben**, or bear pits, are to be found at the eastern end of the old town, over the Nydeggbrücke bridge. These date from the mid-1800s and today only a handful of bears are kept here. The city's **Historical Museum** – located just south of the old town over the river across Kirchenfeldbrücke – provides a great introduction to the city's history. Among the notable exhibits are wonderful Flemish tapestries, which were recently restored, and details of Niklaus Manuel's *Dance of Death* paintings, which once adorned the city walls in the 16th century.

🏛 **Historical Museum**
Helvetiaplatz 5. 【 *031-350 7711.*
🕐 *Tue–Sun.* 🖼 ♿ ✔

ENVIRONS: To the southeast of Bern is the **Emmental Valley**. This verdant agricultural region, with its lush grazing, is famous for the cheese of the same name. A drive around the region can make an ideal half-day countryside tour. Take in some of the delightful towns and villages – Burgdorf, Affoltern, or Langnau im Emmental – and the gentle rolling hills dotted with covered wooden bridges and distinctive gabled wooden farmhouses of the area.

The Last Judgment, in the tympanum of Bern Cathedral's main portal

Interlaken cruise ship moored by the banks of the Thunersee

Interlaken and the Jungfrau ❻

Bern. 🏔 *15,000.* 🚉 🚌 ℹ
Höheweg 37 (033-826 5300).
Ⓦ *www.interlaken.ch*

INTERLAKEN, as its name suggests, lies between two lakes – the Thunersee and the Brienzersee – in the foothills of the Alps. To the south is the classic landscape of the Jungfrau mountains – one of the first regions of Switzerland to be opened up to tourism in the middle of the 19th century. Tourism is virtually the only industry in town, which caters for skiers in winter and sightseers by the busload in summer. The oldest and quaintest part of Interlaken is Unterseen, at its northwestern edge, but there is little of real interest to visitors in the town. However, hotels and restaurants are good and plentiful, and with its lakeside setting and fantastic views of the Jungfrau, it makes a good base for exploring the region.

ENVIRONS: One of the Alps' most famous peaks, the 4,158-m (13,642-ft) **Jungfrau** lies 20 km (12 miles) to the south of Interlaken. The almost equally high **Mönch** and **Eiger** mountains are neighbors and the stretch between Interlaken and the mountains is full of pretty alpine valleys and villages. From **Wengen** and **Grindelwald** you can take a train up to Kleine Scheidegg, and another to Jungfraujoch, a viewpoint high on the Jungfrau. Another popular viewpoint is the **Schilthorn** peak at the head of the Lauterbrunnen valley. This can be reached via **Mürren** and **Gimmelwald**, by cable car on the last stretch. The region is perfect skiing and hiking territory, with walking trails to suit all ability levels.

A few kilometers east of Brienz, the main town on Brienzersee, lies the Swiss Open Air Museum (known as the **Ballenberg**). Original buildings from all over the country have been brought to this living museum. There are demonstrations of traditional crafts and you also get the chance to join in activities and to buy regional produce. A special bus runs from Brienz train station to the museum.

🏛 Ballenberg
☎ *033-952 1030.* ☐ *May–Oct: daily.* 📷 ♿ 📹

Zermatt ❼

Valais. 🏔 *6,000.* 🚉
ℹ *Bahnhofplatz (027-966 8100).*
Ⓦ *www.zermatt.ch*

THE CHALET-FILLED resort of Zermatt sits directly below the **Matterhorn**, a peak of 4,478 m (14,688 ft), which has been a mountain-climbers' mecca for the best part of two centuries. In addition to mountaineering, Zermatt offers top-quality skiing and hiking. Skiing is possible all year round at this, the highest of Swiss resorts, and there are miles of well-marked trails accessible to all walkers.

The most scenic way to arrive in Zermatt is via the Glacier Express from St. Moritz, but you can also take the less expensive train from Täsch 5 km (3 miles) down the valley. The only other alternative is a minibus service, as Zermatt is car free. If you are driving to Zermatt, you can leave your car in Täsch.

Hinterdorf is the most historic part of town. The parish church and cemetery contain some poignant reminders of the dangers of the high mountains. The displays at the **Alpine Museum** reflect the importance of the region's mountaineering tradition.

Gornergrat is probably the best viewing point for the Matterhorn, and can be reached by taking a cog-wheel railroad. You can carry on by cable car to the **Stockhorn** peak for more mountain views.

Cog-wheel mountain railroad, with the Matterhorn peak rising behind

The Alps

THE ALPS ARE ONE of the oldest mountain ranges in the world, formed 65 million years ago when the Eurasian and African tectonic plates collided. They dominate Switzerland's landscape, covering more than half its surface area, and have shaped its history and economy. Switzerland is home to many well-known, distinctive peaks – such as the Matterhorn, Jungfrau, and Eiger – which were early tourist attractions in the 18th and 19th centuries. Trade and pilgrimage routes have crossed the Alps since Roman times but it is only in the last century that this wild and beautiful landscape has become truly accessible, with the development of long road and rail tunnels, mountain railroads, and cable cars.

Peak of the Matterhorn and the Gornergrat mountain railroad

Lake Lucerne surrounded by peaks and alpine meadows

ALPINE FLORA

Deciduous trees are common on the lower slopes of the Alps, but these gradually give way to coniferous spruce and pine. Between the tree line and the snow line lie lush alpine meadows famous for their wildflowers.

The Alpine aster is one of many beautiful, brief-flowering, alpine plants found throughout the higher slopes and pastures. It blooms from July to August.

Androsace alpina, or rock jasmine, grows in mats which cling to alpine rockfaces. The shoots produce pinky-white flowers between July and August.

Edelweiss is the country's most famous flower, a symbol of purity and everlasting love. Increasingly rare, it is now a protected species.

ALPINE WILDLIFE

Several national parks amid the Alps ensure the preservation of the unique native fauna. Although some animals have disappeared, a few species have adapted well to the higher altitudes, such as the marmot, chamois, ibex, mountain hare, and alpine chough.

Marmots are difficult to spot but quite easy to hear, and live in burrows high on the valley slopes. Found throughout the Alps, these mammals are particularly abundant in Graubünden and Ticino.

Chamois are goat-like antelopes which can be seen adeptly scaling the highest mountain ridges. In the past they were hunted for their hide, which makes a very soft leather, but strict hunting controls are now imposed.

The alpine chough, a crow-like bird with a yellow bill, glossy blue-black plumage, and gregarious disposition, spends the summer above the tree line. They descend to the valleys and villages in winter, where they accept food from tourists.

THE ALPS IN SUMMER

Long before skiing became popular, foreign visitors were coming to Switzerland's alpine areas for quiet, relaxing holidays full of fabulous vistas and fresh air. In general, alpine resorts are quieter in summer than during the ski season, but there are good outdoor activities provided in most areas. Some resorts, such as Verbier and Gstaad, host summer music festivals of some note. Most cable cars and mountain railroads operate throughout the summer, transporting hikers and sightseers.

Hikers and mountain bikers are very well-catered for in summer, as Switzerland has thousands of kilometers of designated footpaths. Trails are well-marked and maintained, with regular refreshment stops en route.

Désalpe, a traditional Swiss festival, celebrates the return of herds of cows from the high mountain pastures at the end of summer. In alpine valleys and the Jura, lines of groomed and festooned cattle are herded down the country roads, stopping off at village cattle troughs and fountains for refreshment, on their way back to the lowland farms.

THE ALPS IN WINTER

Switzerland has ski resorts to suit most tastes and budgets, from the chic, five-star hotels of St. Moritz, where celebrity spotting is almost as popular as skiing, to family-oriented resorts with facilities and slopes for all abilities such as Grindelwald. Some are predominantly modern – Verbier has grown from the unvisited hamlet of 50 years ago into one of the biggest ski resorts in Switzerland. Others, such as Zermatt – with its historic town center, alpine museum, and slow pace of life – are more traditional.

Davos is the largest resort in Switzerland, attracting visitors from all over the world. The twin towns of Davos Dorf and Davos Platz offer a wide choice of activities off piste, with an indoor sports center and many bars, nightclubs, and restaurants.

EDWARD WHYMPER

An illustrator by profession, the mountaineeer Edward Whymper (1840–1911) was one of a long line of British climbers who came to the Swiss Alps in the 19th century to scale hitherto unconquered peaks. In 1865, he reached the peak of the Matterhorn at 4,478 m (14,688 ft), together with two Swiss guides. Today, the Matterhorn remains one of the key challenges on the international mountaineering list.

Winter snow is what draws most visitors to the Alps, whether for traditional skiing or trendy snowboarding. More bizarre sports include horseboarding (like water-skiing with a horse) and "zorbing" (tumbling down the slopes strapped to the inside of a balloon).

Breathtaking Lake Lucerne and its surrounding mountain peaks

Lucerne ⑧

Lucerne. 🚶 60,000. 🚉 🚌
ℹ️ Zentralstrasse 5 (041-227 1717).
📅 Lucerne Festival Sommer (mid-
Aug–mid-Sep). 🌐 www.luzern.org

THE CITY of Lucerne makes
a good base for touring
most of central Switzerland.
The surrounding countryside
is possibly the most stereo-
typically Swiss – crystal-clear
lakes ringed with snow-capped
mountains, hemmed with lush
pastures in summer, and criss-
crossed with cog-wheel railroads. This is also the heartland
of the Swiss Confederation –
the three forest cantons of
Uri, Schwyz, and Unterwalden,
which swore the original Oath
of Allegiance in 1291 (see
p613), border the shores of
Lake Lucerne. Today the region
remains the most conservative
part of Switzerland.
   The town's historic center
stands on the north bank of
the Reuss river, which flows
out of Lake Lucerne at its
westernmost corner. Stretches
of the ancient city wall and its
watchtowers can be clearly
seen bounding a ridge that
marks the northern edge of
the old town. The cobbled
streets and shady squares are
bustling both day and night.
   The **Kapellbrücke** is the
city's most famous symbol.
Spanning the river at the lake
end, this covered wooden

bridge was built in 1333,
and formed part of the city's
original boundary. Much of the
bridge, including its decorative
paintings, had to be renovated
following a destructive fire in
1993. Farther downstream, a
second, shorter covered
bridge, the **Spreuerbrücke**,
dates from 1408 and is
decorated with paintings by
Kaspar Meglinger from 1635.
   Next to the town hall on
Furrengasse lies the **Picasso
Museum**, which focuses on
the later works of the artist.
Photographs of Picasso, taken
during the last 20 years of his
life by British photographer
David Douglas Duncan, further
illuminate the artist's character.

🏛 Picasso Museum
Furrengasse 21. 📞 041-410 3533.
🕐 daily. 🈵 🚫

ENVIRONS: Less than 2 km
(1 mile) southeast of the town
center stands the **Richard
Wagner Museum**, where the
composer lived and worked
from 1866 to 1872. There are
letters, manuscripts, and
photographs relating to
Wagner's life, and a fine
collection of 17th-, 18th-,
and 19th-century instruments.
   About 28 km (17 miles) east
of Lucerne, **Schwyz** is the
capital of one of the original
three forest cantons, and has
given the country its name.
The charter detailing the 1291
Oath of Allegiance which
marks the beginning of the
Swiss Confederation is
housed in the town's
Bundesbriefmuseum. More
interesting is the **Ital Reding
Hofstatt**, a fine 17th-century
mansion on the northwest side
of town, built on the proceeds
of one of Switzerland's first
exports – mercenaries. The
fighting skills of the men of
Schwyz were highly prized by
warring European rulers until
well into the 18th century.
   Pilatus and **Rigi** mountains
tower over the area and both
are easily accessible. Mount
Rigi has the distinction of being
the first mountain in Europe
to have a rail line constructed
to the summit. This starts at
Vitznau on the lake shore.
Mount Pilatus to the south is
higher and gives unrivaled
views of the Alps. Its peak
can be reached either by cable
car from Kriens or cog-wheel
railroad from Alpnachstad.

🏛 Richard Wagner Museum
Wagnerweg 27. 📞 041-360 2370.
🕐 mid-Mar–Nov: Tue–Sun. 🈵 🚫

The 17th-century mansion of Ital Reding Hofstatt in Schwyz

Zürich ⑨

Zürich. 🏙 340,000. ✈ 10 km
(6 miles) N. 🚉 🚌 🛈 Haupt-
bahnhof (01-215 4000).
Ⓦ www.zuerich.com

THE DOMINANT position of
Zürich in the nation's
economy has long been felt –
in medieval times the guilds
ruled the city and, boosted by
the Reformation, Zürich and
its inhabitants developed a
talent for hard work and
accumulating wealth. The
stock exchange, which is the
world's fourth largest, opened
in 1877, and today Swiss
bankers control the purse
strings of many international
companies and organizations.

Despite this tradition, the
city also knows how to enjoy
itself, and the medieval town
center, which stretches either
side of the Limmat river, is a

Grossmünster and Fraumünster in Zürich, separated by the Limmat river

**Lively flea market at a lakeside
park in Zürich's old town**

hive of cafés, bars, and hip
boutiques. On the east bank
the warren of streets and alleys
lies close to the university,
adding to the café culture of
this district. Also on the east
bank, the extremely austere
Grossmünster dominates the
city. This was the church from
which Ulrich Zwingli launched
the Reformation on the
receptive burghers of Zürich
in 1520. Along Limmat Quai
you can see the town hall
(rathaus) built out on supports
over the river, opposite one
of Zürich's grand guildhalls.

On the other side of the
river there are a number of
interesting sights. **Lindenhof**,

a small hill, overlooks the city
and was the site chosen by
the Romans to build a customs
post and thus found the city.
Fraumünster and **St. Peter's**
churches are nearby; the
latter, with its Romanesque
cloisters and stained-glass
windows created by Marc
Chagall, is well worth a visit.

Augustinergasse, which
leads down from St. Peter's, is
a delightful street with traces
of medieval storefronts. It is a
world away from Zürich's main
shopping street, which it
meets; Bahnhofstrasse is one
of the world's most famous
shopping areas – a wide, tree-
lined avenue with trams
running along its length. There
are plenty of high-priced
emporia, especially towards the
southern lake end, but interesting and reasonably priced
shops and department stores
can be found here or in the
streets nearby. At No.
70, **Orell Füssli** is
Switzerland's largest
English-language
bookshop, and
nearby on Löwen-
platz you will find
hard-to-resist outlets
of the celebrated
Lindt & Sprüngli
confectioner.

Just behind the
main train station at
the top of Bahnhof-
strasse, housed in a
suitably schloss-like
building, the **Swiss
National Museum**
contains a compre-
hensive collection of
art and artifacts
detailing the history
and cultural diversity
of the country.

🏛 **Swiss National Museum**
Museumstrasse 2. 📞 01-218 6511.
🕐 Tue–Sun. 🛗 Ⓦ www.musee-
suisse.ch

ENVIRONS: **Winterthur**, 25 km
(15 miles) northwest of
Zürich, is an interesting and
little visited Swiss town. Its
history as an industrial center
in the 19th century has left a
legacy of old factory and mill
architecture. It also boasts
excellent museums; the best
of these are the eclectic Oskar
Reinhart Collection am Römer-
holz and the Fotomuseum.

The nucleus of medieval
Stein-am-Rhein, 40 km
(25 miles) northeast of Zürich,
has stood unchanged since
the 16th century. Rathausplatz
and Understadt, at the heart of
town, are lined with buildings
covered in colorful frescoes,
ornate oriel windows, and
overflowing window boxes.

**Oriel window and frescoed façade of the
Gasthaus zur Sonne, Stein-am-Rhein**

Chur ⓾

Graubünden. 🏘 *35,000*. 🚉
🛈 *Grabenstrasse 5 (081-252 1818).*
🎭 *Spring Festival (Mar).*
🅆 www.churtourismus.ch

CHUR, THE CAPITAL of Switzerland's largest canton Graubünden, is a quiet, ancient town with origins that go back 2,000 years. It is located on the upper reaches of the Rhine, on an ancient route between northern Europe and Italy. It has long been a religious center – the bishop of Chur controls dioceses as far away as Zürich – as well as a commercial center, and is famous throughout the country for the Passugger mineral water which is bottled just outside the town.

The pedestrianized historic town center is a maze of cobbled streets and small squares, including Arcas Square with its sunny, café-filled corners in summer. At the southern tip of the old town the late-Romanesque **cathedral**, set in a square, overlooks the rest of town. The highlight of the cathedral is its intricately carved and gilded 15th-century altarpiece, depicting Christ stumbling under the weight of the cross and scenes from the life of St. Catherine. Unfortunately, lighting levels are so low inside the building that its full

Elaborate 15th-century gilded altarpiece in Chur Cathedral

glory is hard to discern. Next to the cathedral stands the **Bishop's Palace** (not open to the public) and at the bottom of the small flight of steps leading up to the cathedral square is the **Rätisches Museum**, which focuses on the history and culture of the canton of Graubünden.

🏛 **Rätisches Museum**
Hofstrasse 1. 📞 *081-257 2889.*
🕐 *Tue–Sun.* ⓰

ENVIRONS: To the east of Chur there are a number of world-class ski resorts. The two best-known, with very different characters, are **Klosters** and **Davos**. The former, famous as the favorite ski destination of British royalty, is a small traditional resort filled with charming chalets. Davos, on the other hand, is a big, brash town with plenty in the way of diversions away from the slopes. It has grown from a mountain health resort in the 19th century to a major winter-sports venue – apart from skiing, there are opportunities for snowboarding, tobogganing, and paragliding.

Swiss National Park ⓫

Graubünden. 🚉 *Zernez, Scuol, Schanf.* 🛈 *National Park House, Zernez (081-856 1378).* 🕐 *May–Oct: daily.* ⓰ 🅆 www.nationalpark.ch

SWITZERLAND HAS many small nature reserves but only one national park. By international standards it is small, covering only 172 sq km (66 sq miles), but it is an area where conservation measures have been strictly enforced for the best part of a century, and people always take second place to the natural environment.

The Ofenpass road, linking Switzerland with Austria, cuts through the center of the park and affords good views of one of the park's valleys. Otherwise the best way to see the park is to take some of the 80 km (50 miles) of marked trails – walkers are not allowed to deviate off the paths.

The landscape is one of wooded lower slopes and jagged scree-covered ridges, including the park's highest peak at 3,173 m (10,407 ft) – Piz Pisoc. Among the abundant wildlife you may see are chamois, ibex, marmots, and the glorious bearded vultures, which are very rare in Europe and were reintroduced into the park in 1991. From June to August, with the retreat of the snows at higher altitudes, a carpet of beautiful alpine flowers, including edelweiss and Swiss androsace, appears. Plans to enlarge the park, since its small size is compromising the range of creatures that can be conserved and reintroduced, have recently been shelved.

The lively winter-sports resort of Davos, in the mountains east of Chur

Hilltop sanctuary of Madonna del Sasso, Ticino, with its lakeside views

Ticino ⑫

🛬 Agno. 🚉 Bellinzona, Locarno, Lugano. ℹ️ Viala della Statzione, Bellinzona (091-825 2131); Riva Albertolli 5, Lugano (091-921 4664). 🎬 Locarno International Film Festival (early Aug).

THE TICINO, Switzerland's most southerly canton, feels much more Italian than Swiss with its mild climate and Italian cuisine and language. It lies south of the Alps, bordering the Italian lakes (see p429), and is traversed by routes up the Alpine passes of St. Gotthard and San Bernadino. The three main towns of Bellinzona, Locarno, and Lugano all make attractive bases for exploring the region, with plenty of attractions and tempting cafés and restaurants. Beyond, the valleys of the Ticino offer great sightseeing opportunities.

Bellinzona is the capital of the canton. Lying on the main north–south route between the Alps and Italy, it provides the first hint of Italian life with elegant piazzas, hilltop fortresses, and fine Renaissance churches. In the heart of town, the 13th-century **Castelgrande**, with its imposing battlements, was the stronghold of the Visconti family during medieval times. At the base of the castle the piazzas Collegiata and Nosetto form the commercial heart of town – lively with pavement cafés.

Locarno is located at the northern end of Lake Maggiore. The suitably named Piazza Grande is the heart of town, which for two weeks in August becomes a giant open-air cinema during the International Film Festival.

Winding lanes filled with restaurants and boutiques radiate off the piazza. Above the town, easily accessible by a funicular railroad, the sanctuary of **Sasso del Madonna** is a major tourist and pilgrimage site. There has been a church here since 1480 when a vision of the Virgin Mary appeared to a local monk. The Baroque church is filled with marvelous frescoes and commands a fantastic view over the lake.

Probably the most charming of the three main centers of the region is **Lugano**, with its palm-lined lakeside location and attractive historic center of elegant piazzas. The arcaded streets are full of interesting old shops selling local produce. Not far from town, set in classical lakeside gardens, is the Villa Favorita. This is home to the **Fondazione Thyssen-Bornemisza**, a fine collection of art covering the 18th century to the present day.

Away from the main centers there are plenty of quaint villages along the Maggiore and Lugano lakes, such as **Ascona** and **Gandria**. These are now filled with waterside restaurants and arts and crafts shops. The valleys to the north offer great hiking and beautiful, peaceful scenery. Val Verzasca, north of Locarno, is one such valley, with the photogenic stone hamlet of **Corippo** clinging to the steep sides, and the pretty villages of **Brione** and **Sonogno** towards the head of the valley.

⛪ **Castelgrande**
Monte San Michele, Bellinzona.
📞 091-825 8145. 🕐 daily. 🅿️ ♿
⛪ **Madonna del Sasso**
Locarno. 📞 091-743 6265. 🕐 daily.
🏛️ **Fondazione Thyssen-Bornemisza**
Villa Favorita, Lugano. 📞 091-972 1741. 🕐 Apr–Oct: Fri–Sun. 🅿️

Crowd gathered for Locarno's annual International Film Festival

Practical & Travel Information

THANKS TO THE FAMOUS Swiss efficiency, traveling around Switzerland is generally a pleasant and hassle-free experience. The country prides itself on its excellent transportation systems, with an extensive national rail network and frequent tram and bus services in the big cities. There are abundant tourist information offices and banking and communication facilities are of a high standard. Switzerland has four national languages – German, French, Italian, and Romansh – but the use of English is widespread, especially in tourist destinations.

TOURIST INFORMATION

UP-TO-DATE information on many of Switzerland's towns and cities can be obtained from brochures and internet sites. Most large cities have at least one centrally located tourist information office (*Verkehrsverein, Tourismus,* or *Office du Tourisme*), offering a wide range of information and facilities. Even the smallest towns and resorts have tourist offices, but the opening hours of those in ski resorts may be limited in summer. Most embassies are located in Bern, but many countries also have a consulate in Geneva.

OPENING HOURS

THE 24-HOUR society has yet to reach Switzerland and while large stores in cities may have late-night opening (usually on a Thursday), most shops, museums, and offices close at 5 or 6pm. Many museums are closed on Mondays and village restaurants often close on one or two days a week.

VISA REQUIREMENTS

VISITORS TO Switzerland must have a valid passport to enter the country. A visa is not required for visitors from the UK, Ireland, the United States, Canada, Australia, and New Zealand for stays of up to 90 days. EU citizens should remember that Switzerland is not a member of the European Union, so there is no "express" blue channel at customs.

SAFETY AND EMERGENCIES

SWITZERLAND IS one of the world's safest countries but you should still take all the usual precautions. Since Switzerland has no public health system, travel and health insurance are essential, especially considering the medical costs associated with skiing accidents. Hospitals have 24-hour emergency cover and in cities and towns there is always a pharmacy open. All pharmacies should post details of a 24-hour roster in their window.

Emergency services, including **helicopter rescue**, are very efficient, and there is also an **avalanche bulletin** hotline. If skiing or hiking at altitude, remember that dehydration or sunburn can cause problems.

BANKING AND CURRENCY

THE UNIT OF CURRENCY in Switzerland is the Swiss franc (CHF). Banking hours are generally 8:30am–4:30pm Monday to Friday, with some branches in tourist resorts also opening on Saturdays. Outside the big cities some banks may close for lunch between noon and 2pm. Money can be changed at banks or at bureaux de change. The latter can be found in hundreds of locations across the country, including at major train stations. Credit cards are widely accepted in Switzerland.

COMMUNICATIONS

EVEN THE SMALLEST villages in Switzerland have a post office, and the bright yellow mail boxes are easy to spot. Post offices usually open from 7:30am to noon and 1:30 to 6:30pm Monday to Friday, and from 8 to 11am on Saturday. However, times can vary from region to region, and smaller post offices often have more restricted hours. Public telephones are plentiful, and take both phonecards – available from post offices and newsagents – and credit cards. Internet facilities are found at airports and train stations, among other places.

The principal newspapers with nationwide circulation are the *Neue Zürcher Zeitung* from Zürich and *Le Temps* from Geneva. Most British newspapers are available in major centers from lunchtime.

FLYING TO SWITZERLAND

SWITZERLAND HAS international airports at Zürich, Geneva, Basel, Bern, and Lugano. Among the major airlines that fly to Switzerland are Qantas, American Airlines, **Swissair** and British Airways. Low-cost airline easyJet (*see p17*) flies

---

THE CLIMATE OF SWITZERLAND

Generally summers are sunny with temperatures frequently reaching 25° C (77° F), though thunderstorms can be a feature of summer evenings. Winters are cold with plenty of snow, but many places get a lot of winter sunshine, especially the ski resorts of the Valais. South of the Alps, in the Ticino, the climate is milder and much more Mediterranean in character.

BERN

°C/F	Apr	Jul	Oct	Jan
		23/73		
	12/54	13/55	13/55	
0°C / 32°F	3/37		6/43	2/36
				-2/38
sun (hrs)	6 hrs	8 hrs	4 hrs	2 hrs
rain (mm)	70 mm	85 mm	65 mm	75 mm
month	Apr	Jul	Oct	Jan

from London Gatwick and from London Luton to Zürich and Geneva.

Because of the large numbers of business travelers who fly to Switzerland on a weekly basis, Monday and Friday flights can be hard to obtain, especially during the skiing season.

TRAVELING BY TRAIN

SWITZERLAND IS at the heart of Europe and rail links to major European cities are fast and efficient. The journey time from Zürich to Paris is six hours; from Geneva to Paris it is four hours.

Switzerland's rail network is operated by the state-owned **Swiss Federal Railways** and private companies. The network reaches all major cities and towns and even the smallest villages in hills and mountains. There is an integrated ticketing and fare system. When traveling to a major city, ask for a ticket that covers your destination's transportation network too – this usually costs only a small amount more. Swiss Passes allow unlimited travel on trains, lake ferries, and many mountain railroads. They are available for 4-, 8-, 15- or 22-day periods, or for a month.

Switzerland has a number of spectacular train routes. The best-known are those that pass through the Alps, such as the Glacier Express between St. Moritz and Zermatt. These services are expensive, but often include meals and offer a thrilling day out. Local tourist offices and Swiss Federal Railways can provide details.

TRAVELING BY CAR

THE MOST direct route by car from Great Britain to Switzerland is via the Channel Tunnel and French freeways to western Switzerland. Drivers must carry a driver's license and a valid vehicle registration document. If you want to make use of Switzerland's excellent freeway network you will need to purchase a freeway sticker (*vignette*), available at border crossings, tourist offices, and gas stations.

Renting a car in Switzerland is expensive. Most of the international rental firms have offices at airports and in the major towns. Many allow you to leave the car at a destination in France, Germany, or Italy.

As in the rest of continental Europe, the Swiss drive on the right. Since most freight is moved by rail in Switzerland, the majority of country routes,

main roads, and freeways are free of congestion. Driving around major cities, however, can be more difficult. Road signs are generally clear, with main roads in blue and freeways in green. Historic sights are usually signposted in brown. Speed limits are strictly enforced – 120 km/h (75 mph) on freeways, 80 km/h (50 mph) on main roads, and 50 km/h (30 mph) in built-up areas. Many mountain passes are closed from November to April. A sign at the foot of the pass will indicate whether the road is open or closed.

GETTING AROUND CITIES AND TOWNS

BUSES AND TRAMS are found in the major cities and they provide frequent and reliable services. Tickets can be purchased from machines at bus and tram stops. Taxis are generally very expensive. Some cities such as Bern offer bicycle rental facilities, as do most of the major train stations. Many small villages that are not served by trains are on a "post bus" route, which usually originates at the train station of the nearest main town. Buses are timed to coincide with the arrival and departure of trains.

DIRECTORY

TOURIST INFORMATION

Australia
Swissair Building, Level 8, 33 Pitt Street, Sydney.
[02-9231 3744.

UK
10th Floor, Swiss Centre, 10 Wardour Street, London W1D 6QF.
[0800-100 200 30.

US
Swiss Center, 608 Fifth Ave, New York, NY 10020.
[1-877-794-8037.

Geneva
Case Postale 1602, 1211 Geneva.
[022-909 7072.

Zürich
P.O. Box 695, 8027 Zürich.
[01-288 1111.
[w] www.myswitzerland .com

EMBASSIES

Australia
Chemin des Fins 2, Case Postale 172, Geneva 1211.
[02-2799 9100.

Canada
Kirchenfeldstrasse 88, 3005 Bern.
[031-357 3200.

Ireland
Kirchenfeldstrasse 68, 3005 Bern.
[031-352 1442.

UK
Thunstrasse 50, 3000 Bern.
[031-359 7700.

US
Jubiläumstrasse 93, 3001 Bern.
[031-357 7011.

EMERGENCY NUMBERS

Ambulance
[144.

Avalanche Bulletin
[187.

Fire
[140.

Helicopter Rescue
[1414 / 1415.

Police
[117.

SWISSAIR

Australia
[1-800 883 199.

Ireland
[01-890 200 515.

New Zealand
[09-977 2238.

Switzerland
[01-258 3355.

UK
[0845-601 0956.
[w] www.swiss.com

US & Canada
[1-877 359 7947.

TRAVELING BY TRAIN

Swiss Federal Railways
Hochschulstrasse 6, 3000 Bern.
[0512-201 111.
[w] www.sbb.ch

Shopping & Entertainment

THERE ARE PLENTY of high-quality Swiss-made products to take away from your trip, including, of course, watches and chocolate. Porcelain, lace, wine, and cheese are also popular purchases. Apart from major events, such as the Montreux Jazz Festival, there is entertainment on a smaller scale throughout the country. Classical and jazz concerts abound in the large cities, which also have cinemas, theater, opera halls, and dance venues. Most regions hold a number of seasonal local events, from wine festivals to antiques and bric-à-brac fairs. Switzerland's greatest attractions, however, are its landscape and outdoor sports. The mountains welcome skiers in winter and climbers, hikers, and cyclists in summer, with all levels of ability catered for.

WHERE TO SHOP

IN THE LARGE CITIES the old town areas usually have the most rewarding shopping – narrow streets crammed with interesting, if often expensive, specialist stores and galleries. Bern's old town, with its arcaded streets, offers varied and sheltered shopping whatever the weather. The major department stores such as Jelmoli and Globus offer a fairly standard international shopping experience, but in nationwide chains such as Manor and Migros (both supermarkets) you can pick up some interesting and reasonably priced items, especially when it comes to food and wine.

WHAT TO BUY

AFTER YOU HAVE stocked up with Swiss chocolate, other items you might consider taking away with you as souvenirs and gifts are linen and lace. Switzerland has a long tradition of textile-working in the northeast of the country and the quality is generally very good.

Swiss army knives are popular and incredibly useful. Victorinox is the make to look out for. Swiss porcelain and pottery can also be a good buy. Many of the designs favor strong colors and rural motifs.

Basketry and carved wooden items (such as toys) make ideal gifts, and these can sometimes be found on market stalls. A wide range of

watches and jewelry is available, particularly at the top end of the market. Watches are one of Switzerland's most important exports, so the quality of Swiss watchmaking is very high.

Other places where you might find suitable gifts include any branch of **Schweizer Heimatwerk**, which is a national chain of Swiss handicraft stores. They have outlets in many large towns and cities, as well as at the airports if you leave your present-buying late.

Major museums, cheese showrooms and similar locations will often have a small store. In the major tourist destinations, such as Gruyères, there is no shortage of shops selling cheap tourist souvenirs, but you will also find knowledgeable retailers offering high-quality genuine Swiss-made items.

MARKETS

OUTDOOR PRODUCE and craft markets are common in Switzerland. Most towns and cities have a market on one or two mornings a week, and almost always on a Saturday morning. These are great places to try out local wines and cheeses, as well as simply to savor the lively atmosphere.

FOOD AND DRINK

VERY LITTLE SWISS WINE is exported, so it makes an unusual gift. Some of the Valais wines, such as *Fendant* (white) and *Dôle* (red), are the best.

Among more transportable food items are dried meats from the German parts of Switzerland, such as *bündner-fleisch*, alpine cheeses such as Gruyère, and spicy *leckerli* biscuits from Lucerne. Even packets of ready-made *rösti* mixture from supermarkets can make a fun gift.

ENTERTAINMENT LISTINGS AND TICKETS

A GREAT VARIETY of small town- and village-based concerts, festivals, and events takes place in Switzerland throughout the year. Local tourist offices can supply details of what's happening during your visit, while the Swiss Tourist Board offices abroad can provide comprehensive listings of all major sporting and cultural events taking place in Switzerland over the coming year.

Most major cities have a variety of venues dedicated to the arts, whether it be classical music, theater, cabaret, or jazz. In Zürich, the listings magazines *Züritip* and *Zürich Next* provide information on all concerts, venues, and shows around town. Tickets for most events in the city are available from **Billetzentrale**, while the music shop **Musik Hug** sells theater, concert, and opera tickets.

ENTERTAINMENT VENUES

MANY VENUES in Switzerland are not dedicated to a specific type of entertainment. The **Reitschule** in Bern is used for live music, theater, film, and dance, while the **Théâtre de l'Usine** in Geneva hosts concerts, theater, film, and cabaret.

The Zürich Tonhalle Orchestra is based at the **Opernhaus**, a popular venue for opera and ballet. Zürich's nightlife is centered on the Neiderdorfstrasse, where the **Casa Bar** and the **Widder Bar** are popular venues to hear live jazz performances.

Cinemas in Switzerland usually show films in their original language, often with subtitles in French, German, Italian, or English. Zürich has more than 40 cinemas, almost all of which have regular showings of English-language films.

FESTIVALS AND PUBLIC HOLIDAYS

ACROSS SWITZERLAND, public holidays and religious events are celebrated in different ways. Lent and Easter are marked by masked parades, lantern processions, music concerts, and tree- and fountain-dressing in many parts of the country. Swiss National Day (August 1) commemorates the swearing of the Oath of Allegiance between the original forest cantons. Bonfires are lit and huge firework displays put on all over the country. Even the smallest village has a party with wine, food, and music.

Switzerland has many other annual festivals and themed events. Geneva's famous International Motor Show is held every year in the spring. The **Montreux International Jazz Festival** takes place in July, as does the **Paléo Music Festival**, a week-long open-air concert of world music at the town of Nyon on Lake Geneva. August brings the **Locarno International Film Festival** and Lucerne's International Music Festival.

Other annual festivals include the huge autumn fair in Basel, harvest festivals in the country's wine-growing regions, and the summer-long Combats de Reines, a form of cow fighting popular in the Valais. The animals are pitted against each other to determine which cow will lead the herds to the summer pastures – the animals themselves are rarely hurt.

WINTER SPORTS

SKIING AND snowboarding are just a couple of the many activities that Switzerland has to offer. Despite the country's reputation for high costs, it is possible to ski inexpensively. There is a wide range of options, from small, traditional villages to large modern resorts packed with lots of additional facilities such as swimming pools and ice-skating rinks. Advice on the range and suitability of different resorts can be sought from the Switzerland Travel Centre or the **Ski Club of Great Britain**, which provides information, advice, and holiday and tuition packages. Cross-country skiing is very popular – some of the best places to try this are the villages of the Jura and the Lower Engadine Valley.

SUMMER SPORTS

IN THE SUMMER, mountaineering and hiking take over from skiing as the most popular draw, though skiing all year round is an option at one or two high-altitude resorts, such as Zermatt. There are thousands of kilometers of marked hiking trails all over the country, including some long-distance ancient trade and pilgrimage routes, such as the Grand St-Bernard trail. Yellow markers indicate standard hiking trails. Higher, rougher trails have red and white markers and the very high-altitude trails are marked in blue. These should only be attempted with an experienced guide. Mountain biking is also catered for, with trails clearly indicated. Maps and information are available from the **Swiss Alpine Club** or the **Swiss Hiking Federation**.

OTHER OUTDOOR ACTIVITIES

SAILING AND swimming are possible during summer at the country's clean lakes. River rafting is also a popular activity, especially along the Rhine. If slightly gentler sports – such as hot-air ballooning or horseback riding – are more your thing, tourist offices will be able to provide suggestions.

DIRECTORY

HANDICRAFTS

Schweizer Heimatwerk
W www.heimatwerk.ch
Schneidergasse 2, Basel.
C 061-261 9178.
Airport, Geneva.
C 022-788 3300.
Bahnhofstrasse 2, Zürich.
C 01-221 0837.
Rudolf-Brun-Brücke, Zürich.
C 01-217 8317.

ENTERTAINMENT TICKETS

Billetzentrale
Bahnhofstrasse 9,
Zürich.
C 01-221 2283.

Musik Hug
Limmatquai 28-30, Zürich.
C 01-269 4141.
FAX 01-269 4101.
W www.musikhug.ch

ENTERTAINMENT VENUES

Casa Bar
Münstergasse 30, Zürich.
C 01-261 2002.

Opernhaus
Falkenstrasse 1, Zürich.
C 01-268 6666.
FAX 01-268 6555.

Reitschule
Neubrückstrasse 8, Bern.
C 031-306 6969.
FAX 031-306 6967.

Théâtre de l'Usine
4 Place des Volontaires,
Geneva.
C 022-328 0818.
FAX 022-781 4138.

Widder Bar
Widdergasse 6,
Zürich.
C 01-224 2526.

FESTIVALS

Locarno International Film Festival
W www.pardo.ch

Montreux International Jazz Festival
W www.montreuxjazz.com

Paléo Music Festival
W www.paleo.ch

OUTDOOR ACTIVITIES

Ski Club of Great Britain
57–63 Church Road,
London SW19.
C 0845-458 0780.
W www.skiclub.co.uk

Swiss Alpine Club
Monbijoustrasse 61, Bern.
C 031-370 1818.
W www.sac-cas.ch

Swiss Hiking Federation
Im Hirshalm 49, Reihen.
C 061-606 9340.
W www.swisshiking.ch

Where to Stay in Switzerland

SWITZERLAND HAS ALWAYS BEEN a highly popular European tourist destination and, not surprisingly, its hoteliers are famous for their courteous enthusiasm and attention to detail. It is all too easy to think of Switzerland only as mountains and wooden ski chalets, but there are many smart town hotels, too, as well as spectacular lakeside accommodations.

	NUMBER OF ROOMS	RESTAURANT	GARDEN OR TERRACE	PRIVATE PARKING
LAKE GENEVA				
GENEVA: *Hotel le Montbrilliant* @ contact@montbrilliant.ch ⓕⓕⓕ Rue de Montbrilliant 2, 1201 Geneva. (022-733 7784. FAX 022-733 2511. Centrally located opposite the main train station, this hotel has recently been renovated. Rooms are furnished in a cozy, rustic style. There are two restaurants and an attractive sun terrace for those long summer evenings. 🖫 TV 🗐	52	●		●
GENEVA: *Mon-Repos* W www.hmrge.ch ⓕⓕⓕ Rue de Lausanne 131–133, 1202 Geneva. (022-909 3909. FAX 022-909 3993. This hotel overlooks a beautiful park on the shores of Lake Geneva. Rooms are elegant and tranquil, and there are also self-catering apartments available. The restaurant serves classic French cuisine. 🖫 TV 🗐	108	●	■	●
GENEVA: *Hotel Bristol* W www.bristol.ch ⓕⓕⓕⓕ Rue du Mont-Blanc 10, 1201 Geneva. (022-716 5700. FAX 022-738 9039. Close to Lake Geneva, at the heart of the financial, business, and shopping district, the Hotel Bristol has an elegant *à la carte* restaurant, as well as a gym, sauna, jacuzzi, and steam bath. 🖫 TV 🗐	95	●	■	
GRUYÈRES: *Hostellerie des Chevaliers* W www.gruyeres-hotels.ch ⓕⓕ 1663 Gruyères, Fribourg. (026-921 1933. FAX 026-921 2552. A family-run mountain inn. The kitchen provides a gourmet menu as well as more traditional food. Bedrooms have magnificent views of the meadows and mountains around this medieval town. ● *Jan–mid-Feb.* 🖫 TV 🗐	34	●	■	●
LAUSANNE: *Hotel au Lac* W www.aulac.ch ⓕⓕⓕ Place de la Navigation 4, Lausanne, Vaud. (021-613 1500. FAX 021-613 1515. The ornamental rooftop of this hotel is surmounted by a pretty clock tower. While traditional on the outside, the interior is furnished in a modern style. A restaurant serves Swiss and international cuisine. 🖫 TV 🗐	84	●	■	
LAUSANNE: *Royal Savoy* W www.royal-savoy.ch ⓕⓕⓕⓕ Avenue d'Ouchy 40, Lausanne, Vaud. (021-614 8888. FAX 021-614 8878. The Savoy is set in its own magnificent park, a popular spot for jogging. The late 19th-century building itself has three restaurants, a bar, a gym, a sauna, and 10 function rooms for business travelers. 🖫 TV ▦ 🗐	108	●	■	●
WESTERN SWITZERLAND				
BASEL: *Teufelhof* W www.teufelhof.com ⓕⓕⓕ Leonhardsgraben 49, 4051 Basel. (061-261 1010. FAX 061-261 1004. Each room of this hotel, which is run by theater people, has been designed by a different artist. A small theater on the premises hosts cabaret, satire, and concerts. 🖫 🗐	33	●	■	
GRINDELWALD: *Fiescherblick* W www.fiescherblick.ch ⓕⓕ 3818 Grindelwald, Bern. (033-854 5353. FAX 033-854 5350. The Fiescherblick is always busy, since Grindelwald is one of the few resorts in the area accessible by car. Staff can provide packed lunches and advice on mountain trails. ● *Oct–Dec.* 🖫 TV 🗐	25	●	■	●
INTERLAKEN: *Goldey* W www.goldey.ch ⓕⓕⓕ Obere Goldey 85, 3800 Interlaken, Bern. (033-826 4445. FAX 033-826 4440. This family-run hotel commands spectacular views of the Jungfrau peaks. Rooms which are not north-facing have balconies, and a spacious apartment is available for families. There is also a sauna. ● *Dec–mid-Jan.* 🖫 TV 🗐	40	●	■	●
SCHANGAU IM EMMENTAL: *Kemmeriboden-Bad* W www.kemmeriboden.ch ⓕⓕ Schangau im Emmental, 6197 Bern. (034-493 7777. FAX 034-493 7770. Set in a beautiful valley, the hotel was originally built for visitors to the nearby sulfur springs. Now tourists come for the fishing, walking, skiing, and climbing. ● *2 weeks before Christmas.* 🖫 TV 🗐	30	●	■	●

		Price categories description						

Price categories are for a standard double room per night, inclusive of breakfast, service charges, and any additional taxes:

Ⓕ under 100 CHF
ⒻⒻ 100–200 CHF
ⒻⒻⒻ 200–300 CHF
ⒻⒻⒻⒻ over 300 CHF

RESTAURANT
Hotel restaurant or dining room, usually open to non-residents.

PRIVATE PARKING
Parking is available in a private car park or garage on the hotel site, or in a public car park nearby. Some hotels charge for use of private parking facilities.

CREDIT CARDS
Major credit cards are accepted in those hotels where the credit card symbol is shown.

		Number of Rooms	Restaurant	Garden or Terrace	Private Parking
ZERMATT: *Julen* �W www.zermatt.ch/julen 3920 Zermatt, Valais. ⓒ 027-966 7600. ℻ 027-966 7676. A family hotel with a working sheepdog. The bedrooms are lavish, and each is decorated in its own style. Don't miss the *Schaeferstube* (sheep room). The garden is large, and there are marvelous views of the Matterhorn.	ⒻⒻⒻ	32	●	■	

ZÜRICH AND LUCERNE

		Number of Rooms	Restaurant	Garden or Terrace	Private Parking
LUCERNE: *Spatz* �W www.hotelspatz.ch Obergrundstrasse 103, 6005 Lucerne. ⓒ 041-310 6384. ℻ 041-310 1084. Located south of the town center, this small hotel-restaurant is popular with families, and some rooms have three or four beds. Two banquet rooms are also available for family occasions or business travelers.	ⒻⒻ	14	●	■	●
LUCERNE: *Baslertor* �W www.baslertor.ch Pfistergasse 17, 6003 Lucerne. ⓒ 041-249 2222. ℻ 041-249 2233. The Baslertor stands in the center of town, close to the Spreuerbrücke. There is a welcoming atmosphere, and guests can relax on the terrace overlooking the outdoor swimming pool.	ⒻⒻⒻ	30		■	
ZÜRICH: *Montana* �W www.hotelmontana.ch Konradstrasse 39, 8005 Zürich. ⓒ 01-271 6900. ℻ 01-272 3070. A glass elevator in the atrium links the five floors of this hotel. Most rooms are spacious and furnished in a modern style. The bistro *Le Lyonnais* specializes in classic French cuisine and is very popular with local residents.	ⒻⒻⒻ	74	●		●
ZÜRICH: *Seidenhof* �W www.seidenhof.ch Sihlstrasse 9, 8021 Zürich. ⓒ 01-228 7500. ℻ 01-228 7575. This centrally located hotel has modern decor and furnishings. The restaurant has an international flavor, with an alternative menu – "Leong's Nouvelle Chinese Cuisine" – available in the evening.	ⒻⒻⒻⒻ	84	●	■	
ZÜRICH: *Steigenberger Bellerive du Lac* �W www.zuerich.steigenberger.ch Utoquai 47, 8008 Zürich. ⓒ 01-254 4000. ℻ 01-254 4001. The hospitality is always warm at this hotel, situated along Zürich's lakeside promenade. The winter garden terrace has superb views over the lake, and the restaurants offer a choice of seafood or Mediterranean dishes.	ⒻⒻⒻⒻ	51	●	■	

GRAUBÜNDEN AND TICINO

		Number of Rooms	Restaurant	Garden or Terrace	Private Parking
DAVOS: *Hotel Sunstar* �W www.sunstar.ch Parkstrasse 1, 7270 Davos-Platz, Graubünden. ⓒ 081-413 1414. ℻ 081-413 1579. A free hotel bus runs to the ski-lifts and the train station. There is a comfortable lounge and bar, and a spacious dining room where a buffet breakfast and a four-couse dinner are served. The hotel has a sauna and solarium.	ⒻⒻ	69	●	■	●
KLOSTERS: *Hotel Sport* �W www.hotel-sport.ch Landstrasse, 7250 Klosters, Graubünden. ⓒ 081-422 2921. ℻ 081-422 4953. As the name suggests, this hotel offers many leisure facilities, with a gym, sauna, solarium, billiard room, and even a bowling alley. Guests can relax in the cozy lounge, which has a large open fireplace.	ⒻⒻ	45	●	■	●
KLOSTERS: *Silvretta Parkhotel* �W www.silvretta.ch Landstrasse 190, 7250 Klosters, Graubünden. ⓒ 081-423 3435. ℻ 081-423 3450. Just a short walk from the main lift to the Parsenn ski area, this hotel has a gym, jacuzzi, sauna, piano bar, and nightclub for guests' use. All rooms have either a balcony or terrace.	ⒻⒻⒻ	110	●	■	●
LUGANO: *Villa Principe Leopoldo* �W www.leopoldohotel.com Via Montalbano 5, 6900 Lugano, Ticino. ⓒ 091-985 8855. ℻ 091-985 8825. Enjoy the stunning views of Lugano, the mountains, and the lake from the flower-filled terrace. The bedrooms are luxurious and the restaurant serves good-quality imaginative cuisine.	ⒻⒻⒻⒻ	37	●	■	●

For key to symbols see back flap

Where to Eat in Switzerland

THERE IS NO "NATIONAL DISH" in Switzerland, since menus vary from region to region. In French Switzerland, fondue is a local specialty, while in German Swiss restaurants *rösti* (hash brown potatoes) is a favorite. Pizzerias are popular throughout Switzerland but, naturally, they are most numerous in the Italian-speaking Ticino region. For a landlocked country, seafood is surprisingly popular.

	VEGETARIAN DISHES	FIXED-PRICE MENU	OUTDOOR TABLES	GOOD WINE LIST
LAKE GENEVA				
GENEVA: *Au Pied-de-Cochon* ⒻⒻⒻ Place du Bourg-de-Four 4. ☎ 022-310 4797. A crowded bistro offering simple Lyonnais dishes, including the *pieds-de-cochon* (pig's feet) that give this restaurant its name. They are served grilled, with mushrooms or lentils, or *désossés* (boned). 🍴 ⚒ 🍷			■	
GENEVA: *Café de la Paix* ⒻⒻⒻ Hotel de la Paix, Quai du Mont-Blanc 11. ☎ 022-732 6150. The Café de la Paix, situated opposite the lake, offers the best of local and international cuisine. Sample the Viennese and Mediterranean specialties; the *entrecôte de la Paix* is a must. 🍷	■	●		●
GENEVA: *La Perle du Lac* ⒻⒻⒻⒻ Rue de Lausanne 126. ☎ 022-909 1020. The grand wooden chalet of La Perle du Lac features an open-air terrace and a beautiful garden with an idyllic view of the lake, the city, and Mont-Blanc. French cuisine, with fish specialties. ● Mon; Dec 22–Jan 25. ⚒ 🍷	■	●	■	●
GENEVA: *Le Neptune* ⒻⒻⒻⒻ Hotel du Rhône, Quai Turrettini 1. ☎ 022-731 9831. A fresco of Neptune's watery kingdom hints at the specialty of this eatery. Dishes such as lobster cannelloni and sweek seabass with almonds, make it a haven for lovers of seafood. ● Sat–Sun & public hols. ⚒ 🍷	■	●	■	●
LAUSANNE: *Olympia* ⒻⒻⒻ Continental Hotel, Place de la Gare 2. ☎ 021-321 8800. Opposite the main train station, this restaurant offers Mediterranean specialties as well as local cuisine. The contemporary decor attracts a mix of tourists and businessmen. ⚒ 🍷	■	●	■	●
MONTREUX: *Du Pont* ⒻⒻⒻ Rue du Pont 12. ☎ 021-963 2249. Diners can either eat informally in the smoky café, or enjoy full service in the lovely dining room upstairs. The menu and prices are exactly the same, including a cheap daily special. Generous portions of veal *piccata*, steaks, and game. ● Mon dinner. 🍷	■	●	■	●
WESTERN SWITZERLAND				
BASEL: *Le Jardin Euler* ⒻⒻⒻ Hotel Euler, Centralbahnplatz 14. ☎ 061-272 4500. Professional and friendly service at this French restaurant make it popular for business lunches. In summer, specialties from the grill are served on the terrace, while seafood is a favorite in winter. ● Sat–Sun in winter. ⚒ 🍷	■	●	■	●
BERN: *Zimmermania* ⒻⒻⒻⒻ Brunngasse 19. ☎ 031-311 1542. This bistro has been in business for more than 150 years and is a local favorite for authentic French cooking. Try their cheese soufflé, veal kidneys in mustard sauce, or any of their fish specialties. ● Sun–Mon; Jul. ⚒ 🍷	■	●	■	●
GRINDELWALD: *Onkel Tom's Hütte* ⒻⒻ Grindelwald, Bern. ☎ 033-853 5239. This tiny pizza-parlor is extremely cozy. Wooden floors accommodate ski boots, and tables share space with a huge iron stove, which produces fresh pizzas. There are generous salads and homemade desserts. ● Jun, Nov. 🍴 ⚒ 🍷	■		■	
INTERLAKEN: *Im Gade* Ⓕ Hotel du Nord, Höheweg 70. ☎ 033-822 2631. This welcoming restaurant fills up with appreciative locals. Seasonal specialties (game, mushrooms) stand out. The restaurant's forte is its selection of hearty veal dishes, lake fish, and generous daily specials. ● Mon; Dec–Apr. ⚒ 🍷	■	●	■	●

		Price categories include a three-course meal for one, half a bottle of house wine, and all extra charges, such as cover, service, and tax:

Price categories include a three-course meal for one, half a bottle of house wine, and all extra charges, such as cover, service, and tax:

ⓕ under 40 CHF
ⓕⓕ 40–60 CHF
ⓕⓕⓕ 60–100 CHF
ⓕⓕⓕⓕ over 100 CHF

VEGETARIAN DISHES
Vegetarian dishes, sometimes as both starters and main courses.

FIXED-PRICE MENU
Fixed-price menu available for lunch, dinner, or both.

GOOD WINE LIST
Denotes a wide range of good wines, or a more specialized selection of local wines.

CREDIT CARDS
Major credit cards are accepted in those restaurants where the credit card symbol is shown.

	Price	Vegetarian Dishes	Fixed-Price Menu	Outdoor Tables	Good Wine List
ZÜRICH AND LUCERNE					
LUCERNE: *Rotes Gatter* Hotel des Balances, Weinmarkt. ☎ 041-418 2828. Rotes Gatter lies just a few steps from many of Lucerne's major sights, on the banks of the Reuss river. An incredible view of the river and opposite bank complements very fresh, high-quality Swiss cuisine. ♿ ☕	ⓕⓕⓕ	■	●	■	●
LUCERNE: *Wirtshaus Galliker* Schützenstrasse 1. ☎ 041-240 1002. The menu at this historic, family-run restaurant features recipes that are special family secrets. One of the most popular specialty dishes is *Kalbskopf* (calf's head). Booking advisable. ● Sun–Mon; mid-Jul–mid-Aug. ♿ ☕	ⓕⓕⓕ	■	●		●
ZÜRICH: *Hummerbar* Hotel St-Gotthard, Bahnhofstrasse 87. ☎ 01-227 7621. This lobster and oyster bar is the only restaurant in Zürich where a full range of seafood is available all year round. The menu is rounded off with smoked salmon and caviar as well as seasonal produce such as truffles and asparagus. ♿ ☕	ⓕⓕⓕⓕ	■			
ZÜRICH: *La Rotonde* Dolder Grand Hotel, Kurhausstrasse 65. ☎ 01-269 3870. This elegant restaurant is well known for its traditional cuisine. Everything is perfect – the quality and presentation of the meals, the attentive service, even the extraordinary view of the Alps. Book in advance. ♿ ☕	ⓕⓕⓕⓕ	■	●	■	
ZÜRICH: *Rive Gauche* Hotel Baur au Lac, Talstrasse 1. ☎ 01-220 5060. Furnished in a contemporary style, this restaurant exudes a serene atmosphere, complementing the light and refreshing dishes. The inner bar is more traditional in style, with more than 100 varieties of whisky on offer. ● Sun; mid-Jul–mid-Aug. ♿ ☕	ⓕⓕⓕⓕ	■			●
GRAUBÜNDEN AND TICINO					
BELLINZONA: *Castelgrande* Monte San Michele. ☎ 091-826 2353. This restaurant, situated in the oldest castle in Bellinzona, is chic, modern, and sophisticated. The cuisine is Mediterranean with regional variations, based on local produce. On the terrace, meals are served throughout the day. ● Mon. ♿ ☕	ⓕⓕⓕ	■	●	■	●
CHUR: *Controversa* Steinbruchstrasse 2. ☎ 081-252 9944. A modern restaurant attracting a lively, young clientele. The immense salad bar is the main draw, although many of the daring main courses – such as tagliatelle with chicken, mango, and hot curry sauce – are delicious too. ● Sun lunch. ♿ ☕	ⓕⓕ	■			
KLOSTERS: *Walserhof* Landstrasse 141. ☎ 081-410 2929. This restaurant, with its two Michelin stars, specializes in international and regional fare. Popular specialties from the Davos-Klosters region include poultry with duck liver, and trout with potatoes on lentils. ● Apr–Jun: Tue–Wed; Oct–Dec. ♿ ☕	ⓕⓕⓕⓕ	■	●	■	●
LOCARNO: *Dell'Angelo* Piazza Grande. ☎ 091-751 8175. A lively pizzeria at the end of the Piazza Grande, the Dell'Angelo uses an old-style wood-burning oven to prepare its pizzas. The same menu is available in the restaurant upstairs, where diners can eat in a more formal atmosphere. ♿ ☕	ⓕⓕ	■		■	
LUGANO: *Le Relais* Grand Hotel, Viale Castagnola 31. ☎ 091-971 2213. A relaxed and inviting restaurant, serving light Mediterranean cuisine. Highlights include the seafood and fresh market produce. In summer, the terrace offers wonderful views of Lake Lugano and the peak of San Salvatore. ♿ ☕	ⓕⓕⓕ	■	●	■	●

SCANDINAVIA

Scandinavia at a Glance

THE SCANDINAVIAN COUNTRIES – Denmark, Norway, Sweden, and Finland – are, arguably, among the least known countries in Europe. In Norway, Sweden, and Finland the majority of the population lives in the south, in affluent, modern cities, which are also rich in history and tradition. Away from the main towns and cities lie vast expanses of unspoiled, often wild terrain, from the breathtaking Norwegian fjords to the dense pine forests and clear lakes of Finland. Smaller and largely flat and rural, Denmark shares characteristics with both mainland Europe and Scandinavia proper.

Oslo (see pp660–64), *Norway's capital, is an attractive city of grand Neoclassical buildings, wide boulevards, and green open spaces. In Frogner Park, one of the largest parks, is a collection of works by the eccentric Norwegian sculptor Gustav Vigeland (1869–1943).*

Bergen (see p666) *was the largest town and most important port in medieval Norway. Its streets are lined with fine historic monuments, including the 12th-century Mariakirken, the oldest building in the city.*

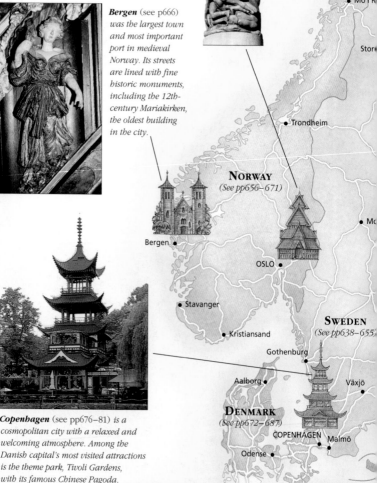

Mo i R

Stor

Trondheim

NORWAY
(See pp656–671)

Bergen

OSLO

Mc

Stavanger

Kristiansand

SWEDEN
(See pp638–655)

Gothenburg

Aalborg

Växjö

DENMARK
(See pp672–687)

COPENHAGEN   Malmö

Odense

Copenhagen (see pp676–81) *is a cosmopolitan city with a relaxed and welcoming atmosphere. Among the Danish capital's most visited attractions is the theme park, Tivoli Gardens, with its famous Chinese Pagoda.*

◁ **Pulpit Rock, giving spectacular views of the Lysefjord near Stavanger in Norway**

LOCATOR MAP

omsø

Kemijärvi

Luleå

FINLAND
(See pp688–701)

Vaasa

Turku

HELSINKI

STOCKHOLM

sby

Helsinki (see pp692–6), the capital of Finland, boasts an impressive mix of Neoclassical and modern 20th-century architecture. The city's hub of activity is Market Square on the waterfront, which in summer fills with crowds browsing the craft and food stalls.

Stockholm (see pp642–7) enjoys an unrivaled setting surrounded by water and unspoiled countryside that stretches right into the center. Overlooking the Riddarfjärden channel is the Stadshuset (City Hall), a symbol of the city.

Visby (see p649), on the island of Gotland, was a major Viking trading post, and later a wealthy Hanseatic port. Clustered within the old city walls are ruined churches, timber merchants' houses, and many wonderfully preserved medieval warehouses.

SWEDEN

THE SWEDES ARE JUSTLY PROUD *of the natural beauty of their country. From the snow-capped mountains of the north, through rolling countryside dotted with forests and lakes, to the tiny islands of the Baltic archipelagos around Stockholm, the country is a mecca for outdoor enthusiasts. Like its people, Sweden's cities are modern and dynamic, but also rich in tradition.*

Sweden is Europe's fifth-largest country, with an area about the size of California. Roughly 1,600 km (1,000 miles) lie between its southernmost and northernmost points. About 15 percent of its area lies north of the Arctic Circle, where, for a few days each summer, the sun never sets, and never rises for a similar period in winter. The Swedish climate is not severe, thanks to the warming influence of the Gulf Stream.

Only 7 percent of Sweden's area is cultivated farmland; more than half the country is covered by timberlands, consisting mainly of coniferous forests. Mountains, fells, and wetlands occupy nearly a quarter of the country. Sweden has about 100,000 lakes, which include Vänern, the third-largest body of fresh water in Europe. Norrland, the northern three-fifths of the country, is rich in natural resources, including timber, ore deposits, and rivers, whose waterfalls contribute to the national energy supply. It is here that the Sami (formerly known as the Lapps) earn their traditional livelihood herding reindeer.

HISTORY

Although the Swedish Vikings were seafaring warriors like their Danish and Norwegian cousins, they were primarily known as Sweden's first traders, opening up routes along the Russian rivers to the east as far as the Black Sea. Ruthlessly exploiting the Slav population of the area, they dealt mainly in slaves and furs. The Viking reign ended with the successful Christianization of Sweden at the end of the 11th century.

The German traders of the Hanseatic League arrived in Sweden some time during the 13th century, and dominated Swedish life for the next hundred years. In 1397, the Germans were forced out by the Union of Kalmar, which brought

Dancers in traditional folk costume in the village of Sundborn, Dalarna province

◁ **View across the Strömmen in Stockholm to the dome of Katarina Kyrka on Södermalm**

Scandinavia under Danish rule. This state of affairs continued until Gustav Vasa, resenting Denmark's influence, succeeded in ousting the Danes in 1523, becoming king of an independent Sweden.

The 17th and early 18th centuries were dominated by two military giants, Gustav II Adolf and Karl XII, whose conquests made Sweden for the first time more powerful than Denmark. In the 18th century, the Swedes contributed to Europe's Age of Enlightenment with advances in science and major developments in the arts, especially under the patronage of Gustav III. He opened the magnificent Royal Opera House in 1782, and was responsible for the construction of the Royal Dramatic Theater in 1788.

Karl XII of Sweden (1697–1718), the "warrior king"

By 1809, Sweden's military power had waned to such an extent that the country was forced to surrender Finland to Russia. A new constitution transferred power from the king to Parliament, marking the beginning of Sweden's democratic monarchy. In the early 19th century, Sweden was also a poor country, suffering from stagnation in the spheres of agriculture and trade. In the course of the century nearly one million Swedes migrated, mostly to America. Their departure was a sobering lesson to those that remained, inspiring the philosophy of cradle-to-grave care that was put into practice in 20th-century Sweden's welfare state.

In a single century, Sweden was transformed from a poor rural economy to a leading industrial nation. The 1990s saw many significant changes take place. Engineering expanded rapidly, particularly in the field of telecommunications, led by the Ericsson company. Sweden joined the EU, and the church severed its role with the state after more than 400 years. In the year 2000, Malmö in Sweden and the Danish capital of Copenhagen were connected by the completion of the Öresund Bridge, symbolic of the long-standing friendship that has replaced the animosity between these once warring nations.

KEY DATES IN SWEDISH HISTORY

AD 800–1060 Era of the Swedish Vikings

13th century Hanseatic League of German merchants at height of its power in Sweden

1397 Kalmar Union links the Nordic countries

1523 Gustav Vasa becomes king of an independent Sweden

1611–32 Reign of Gustav II Adolf, "the Lion of the North," whose campaigns turn Sweden into a great European power

1718 Death of Karl XII, Sweden's last great military king, at siege of Fredriksten in Norway

1721 Sweden cedes Baltic provinces to Russia in the Peace of Nystad

1772 Gustav III crowned and mounts coup d'état giving the monarchy absolute power

1809 Sweden loses Finland to Russia

1814 Sweden gains Norway from Denmark

1869 Emigration to North America increases due to crop failure

1905 Parliament dissolves union with Norway

1939 Sweden declares neutrality in World War II

1995 Sweden joins European Union

2000 Öresund Bridge opens, finally connecting Sweden and Denmark

LANGUAGE AND CULTURE

Swedish belongs to the northern group of Germanic languages, along with Norwegian, Danish, Icelandic, and Faeroese. Various dialects are spoken, most notably in Skåne, southern Sweden, where the accent is almost Danish.

A nation of nature lovers, the Swedes are apt to retreat to their country cottages in all seasons. Deeply traditional, they love their rituals, from maypole dances at midsummer to the St. Lucia procession in December. Beneath their reserve the Swedes are a friendly people, their warmth readily unleashed with a *skål* (toast) and a round of schnapps.

Swedes are open-minded, trend-hungry, and tech-friendly. Stockholm offers the latest in design and architecture, and Sweden has become increasingly multicultural. While this new Sweden doesn't always blend easily with the old, most Swedes recognize that the country is richer for its diversity.

Exploring Sweden

THE NATURAL STARTING POINT for exploring Sweden is the capital Stockholm, built on a cluster of Baltic Sea islands. From here, visitors can explore the castles of Lake Mälaren or head north to Uppsala, a thriving university town. On the way south to Malmö or west to Gothenburg lies the Glass Kingdom, where some of the world's best-known glassmakers ply their trade. Travel throughout Sweden can be conducted quite easily by high-speed trains or by car, though the long distances involved make travel quite expensive.

SIGHTS AT A GLANCE

Dalarna **4**
Gothenburg **6**
Gotland and Visby **5**
Lake Mälaren **2**
Malmö **8**
STOCKHOLM pp642–7 **1**
Uppsala **3**
Växjö **7**

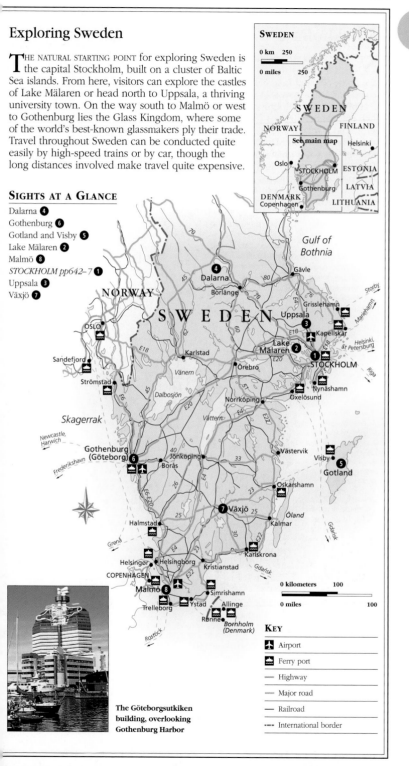

SWEDEN

0 km   250

0 miles   250

SWEDEN

NORWAY   FINLAND

See main map   Helsinki

Oslo   STOCKHOLM   ESTONIA

DENMARK   Gothenburg   LATVIA

Copenhagen   LITHUANIA

Gulf of Bothnia

Dalarna **4**   Gävle

Borlänge   Grisslehamn

S W E D E N   Uppsala **3**

NORWAY   Kapellskär

OSLO   Lake Mälaren **2**   Helsinki, St Petersburg

Karlstad   STOCKHOLM **1**

Sandefjord   Örebro   Riga

Strömstad   Nynäshamn

Vänern   Oxelösund

Skagerrak   Norrköping

Dalbosjön   *Vättern*

Newcastle, Harwich

Frederikshavn   Gothenburg (Göteborg) **6**   Jönköping   Västervik   Visby **5**

Borås   Gotland

Oskarshamn

Växjö **7**   Öland

Halmstad   Kalmar

Grenå

Karlskrona

Helsingør   Helsingborg   Kristianstad

COPENHAGEN

0 kilometers   100

Malmö **8**   Simrishamn

0 miles   100

Trelleborg   Ystad   Allinge

Rønne   Bornholm (Denmark)

Rostock

KEY

✈ Airport

⛴ Ferry port

— Highway

— Major road

— Railroad

- - - International border

The Göteborgsutkiken building, overlooking Gothenburg Harbor

Stockholm ❶

STOCKHOLM WAS FOUNDED around 1250 on a small island in the narrow Strömmen channel between the Baltic Sea and Lake Mälaren. Today, the Swedish capital stretches across 14 islands. As well as a stunning waterside location, Stockholm boasts a rich cultural heritage. Its 750-year history has produced a wealth of beautiful buildings, such as the Royal Palace and Drottningholm – symbols of Sweden's era as a great power in the 17th and early 18th centuries. Many other impressive treasures from the past can be discovered in the city's fine museums.

The Stadshuset, Stockholm's City Hall, on the island of Kungsholmen

GETTING AROUND

Most of the main sights are served by Tunnel-bana (underground train), and there are also numerous bus routes. Bus 47 goes to the Vasamuseet, the Nordiska Museet, and Skansen, which you cannot reach by Tunnelbana. Small ferries travel between the city center and Djurgården, while archipelago boats take visitors on day trips to some of the thousands of islands in the Stockholm archipelago.

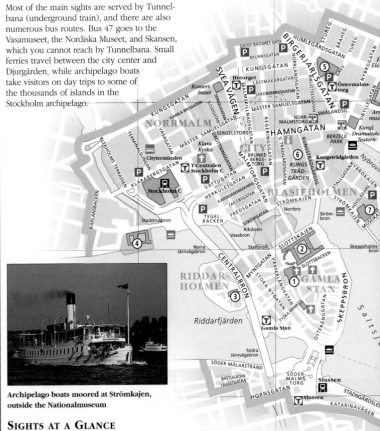

Archipelago boats moored at Strömkajen, outside the Nationalmuseum

SIGHTS AT A GLANCE

Historiska Museet ⑫
Kungsträdgården ⑥
Moderna Museet ⑧
Nationalmuseum ⑦
Nordiska Museet ⑪
Riddarholmskyrkan ③
Royal Palace ②
Skansen ⑩

Stadshuset ④
Storkyrkan ①
Stureplan & Sturegallerian ⑤
Vasamuseet ⑨

**Greater Stockholm
(see inset map)**
Drottningholm ⑬

SEE ALSO

- *Where to Stay* p654
- *Where to Eat* p655

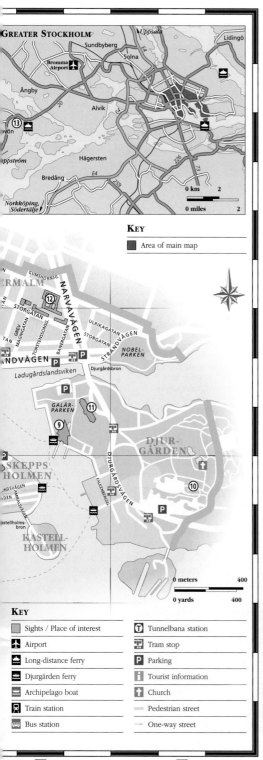

GREATER STOCKHOLM

Uppsala

Lidingö

Sundbyberg

Solna

Bromma Airport

Ångby

⑬

Alvik

ppström

Hägersten

Bredäng

Norrköping, Södertälje

0 km 2

0 miles 2

KEY

Area of main map

RMALM

GUMSHORNSG.

⑫

NARVAVÄGEN

STORGATAN

GREV MAGNIGATAN

TORSTENSSONG.

BANÉRGATAN

ULRIKAGATAN

STORGATAN

STRANDVÄGEN

NOBEL-PARKEN

NDVÄGEN

Ladugårdslandsviken

Djurgårdsbron

GALÄR-PARKEN

⑪

⑨

DJUR-GÅRDEN

DJURGÅRDSVÄGEN

SKEPPS HOLMEN

NDSVÄGEN

FALKENBERGSG.

⑩

stellholms-bron

KASTELL-HOLMEN

0 meters 400

0 yards 400

KEY

◼ Sights / Place of interest	🚇 Tunnelbana station
✈ Airport	🚊 Tram stop
⛴ Long-distance ferry	🅿 Parking
⛴ Djurgården ferry	ℹ Tourist information
⛴ Archipelago boat	✝ Church
🚉 Train station	— Pedestrian street
🚌 Bus station	→ One-way street

D   E

Storkyrkan ①

Trångsund 1. 📞 08-723 30 16.
🚇 Gamla Stan. 🚌 43, 46, 55, 59,
76. ◯ daily. 🎫 May–Aug. 🖼 in
English: Jul–mid-Aug: 1pm. ♿

STOCKHOLM'S 700-year-old
cathedral, known as the
Storkyrkan, or, literally, "big
church," is of great national
religious importance. From
here the Swedish reformer
Olaus Petri (1493–1552) spread
his Lutheran message around
the kingdom. The cathedral is
also used for royal ceremonies.

A small church was built on
this site in the 13th century,
probably by the city's founder
Birger Jarl. In 1306 it was
replaced by a much bigger
basilica, St. Nicholas.

The 15th-century Gothic
interior was revealed in 1908
during restoration work. The
late Baroque period provided
the cathedral's so-called
"royal chairs," the pews
nearest the chancel, which
were designed by Nicodemus
Tessin the Younger (1654–
1728) to be used by royal
guests on special occasions.
The 66-m (216-ft) high tower
was added in 1743.

The cathedral houses some
priceless artifacts, such as
Bernt Notke's late-Gothic
sculpture of *St. George and
the Dragon* (1489), celebrating
Sten Sture the Elder's 1471
victory over the Danes. Other
prized treasures are the silver
altar (1650s) and the *Parhelion
Painting*, which depicts a
light phenomenon observed
over Stockholm in 1535. Recent
research has proved the
painting is not the original,
but a copy from the 1630s.

**The Italian Baroque-style façade
of Stockholm's Storkyrkan**

The grand façade of Stockholm's Kungliga Slottet (Royal Palace)

Royal Palace ②

Kungliga Slottet. **☎** 08-402 61 30.
Ⓣ Gamla Stan. **🚌** 43, 46, 55, 59,
76. **🕐** mid-May–Aug: daily;
Sep–mid-May: noon–3pm Tue–Sun
(except Royal Chapel & Museum of
Antiquities). **●** during official
functions of the Court. **🎫 ✆** for
tours in English call 402 61 30. **♿**
W www.royalcourt.se

COMPLETED IN the mid-13th century, the Tre Kronor (Three Crowns) fortress was turned into a royal residence by the Vasa kings during the following century. In 1697 it was destroyed by fire. In its place the architect Nicodemus Tessin the Younger (1654–1728) created a new palace with an Italianate exterior and a French interior that also shows Swedish influences.

Though the palace is no longer the king's residence, the **State Apartments** are still used for official functions. Banquets for visiting heads of state are often held in the magnificent Karl XI's Gallery, which is modeled on the Hall of Mirrors at Versailles outside Paris *(see pp168–9)*, and is a fine example of Swedish Late Baroque. Look out for the exquisite ivory and silver saltcellar, designed by Flemish painter Rubens. The two-story Hall of State, designed by Tessin and Carl Hårleman, combines Rococo and Classical elements, and contains

one of the palace's most valuable treasures, the splendid silver coronation throne of Queen Kristina (reigned 1633–54).

Below the Hall of State is the **Treasury**, where the State regalia are kept, including King Erik XIV's crown, scepter, and orb. Other priceless artifacts, such as two crystal crowns belonging to the present monarchs, King Carl XVI Gustaf and Queen Silvia, are on view in the **Royal Chapel**.

Within the palace are two museums. **Gustav III's Museum of Antiquities** opened in 1794 in memory of the murdered king, and contains artifacts collected during his journey to Italy in 1783–4. The **Tre Kronor Museum** illustrates the palace's 1,000-year history, and has relics rescued from the

Tre Kronor (Three Crowns) symbol atop the 106-m (348-ft) tower of the Stadshuset

burning palace in 1697. A very popular tourist event, the daily changing of the guard, takes place at midday in the palace's Outer Courtyard.

Riddarholms-kyrkan ③

Birger Jarls Torg. **☎** 08-402 61 30.
Ⓣ Gamla Stan. **🚌** 3, 53. **🕐** mid-
May–Aug: daily; Sep: noon–3pm Sat
& Sun. **🎫 ✆** in English: 1pm daily. **♿**

BUILT ON THE SITE of the late 13th-century Greyfriars abbey, founded by Magnus Ladulås, this majestic brick church is best known for its ornate burial vaults. Dating back to the 16th century, the vaults hold the remains of all the Swedish monarchs, from Gustav II Adolf in the 17th century, with two exceptions: Queen Kristina, buried at St. Peter's in Rome in 1689, and Gustav VI Adolf, who was interred at Haga, on the city outskirts, in 1973. Especially moving are the graves of royal children who met an early death, including the many small tin coffins that surround the tombs of Gustav II Adolf and his queen, Maria Eleonora.

Stadshuset ④

Hantverkargatan 1. **☎** 08-508 290
58. **Ⓣ** Centralen. **🚌** 3, 62. **🕐** for
guided tours. **●** Jan 1, Easter,
Dec 24–26 & 31, and during special
activities. **🎫 ✆** obligatory. **♿**
W www.stockholm.se/cityhall

PROBABLY Sweden's biggest architectural project of the 20th century, the Stadshuset (City Hall) was completed in

1923 and has become a symbol of Stockholm. It was designed by Ragnar Östberg (1866–1945) and displays influences of both the Nordic Gothic and Northern Italian schools. Many leading Swedish artists contributed to the rich interior design, including Einar Forseth (1892–1988), who created the stunning Byzantine-inspired gold-leaf wall mosaics in the Golden Room.

The building contains the Council Chamber and 250 offices for administrative staff. As well as a work place for the city's councillors, the Stadshuset also provides a venue for special events, such as the annual Nobel Prize ceremony, which takes place in the lavish Blue Hall.

Kungsträdgården, known as Stockholm's "open-air living room"

Stureplan, a popular meeting place for Stockholmers

Stureplan and Sturegallerian ⑤

ⓣ *Östermalmstorg.* 🚌 *1, 46, 55, 56, 91.* **Sturegallerian** *Stureplan 4.* 📞 *08-611 46 06.* ◯ *daily (Sun: pm only).* **Sturebadet** 📞 *08-545 015 00.* ◯ *Mon–Sat.*

Aᶠᵗᵉʳ ᴬ ꜰɪʀᴇ at the Sturebadet swimming pool in 1985, the Stureplan district was revamped and restored to its late 19th-century glory.

Part of the renovation of the area included building a stylish shopping mall, the Sturegallerian, which boasts some 50 retail outlets. The Sturebadet public baths, within the mall, have been rebuilt according to their original late 19th-century Art Nouveau design.

Kungsträdgården ⑥

ⓣ *Kungsträdgården.* 🚌 *46, 47, 55, 59, 62, 65, 76.* **Kungliga Operan** 📞 *08-791 43 00.* 🎫 *by arrangement.* ♿

Tʜᴇ ᴄɪᴛʏ's oldest park, the Kungsträdgården (King's Garden) takes its name from when it was a royal kitchen garden in the 15th century. During the summer open-air theater, dancing, concerts, and food festivals take place here. In winter the skating rink is a popular attraction. At the center of the park is a bronze fountain (1866) by J.P. Molin, who also designed the statue of Karl XII (1868) at the park's southern end. Overlooking this part of the park is the city's royal opera house, the **Kungliga Operan** (1898), whose ornate interior includes the Gold Foyer, with ceiling paintings by Carl Larsson.

In the 16th century, the kitchen garden was transformed into a Renaissance garden, and later a summer house was built for Queen Kristina. The 17th-century building still stands on the park's western flank.

Nationalmuseum ⑦

Södra Blasieholmshamnen. 📞 *08-519 543 00.* ⓣ *Kungsträdgården.* 🚌 *65, 46, 55, 59, 62, 76.* ◯ *Tue–Sun.* ● *some public hols.* 🎫 📷 ♿ 🅦 *www.nationalmuseum.se*

Tʜᴇ ʟᴏᴄᴀᴛɪᴏɴ of the Nationalmuseum, on the Strömmen channel, inspired the 19th-century German architect August Stüler to design a building in the Venetian and Florentine Renaissance styles. Completed in 1866, the museum houses some 500,000 paintings, sculptures, prints, and drawings from the 15th to the early 20th centuries. The focus of the painting and sculpture section is Swedish 18th- to early 20th-century art, but the 17th-century Dutch and Flemish, and 18th-century French schools are also well represented. Highlights include Rembrandt's *The Conspiracy of the Batavians under Claudius Civilis* (1661–62) and *The Lady with the Veil* (1769) by Swedish portrait painter Alexander Roslin. There is also a decorative arts department, which contains 30,000 works spanning the last five centuries. Among the wide range of exhibits on show is Scandinavia's largest display of porcelain, glass, silver-ware, and furniture. Another exhibit, Design 19002000, tracks the history of design to the present day.

The opulent interior of Stockholm's Nationalmuseum

The Moderna Museet's airy interior, designed by Catalan Rafael Moneo

Moderna Museet ⑧

c/o Klarabergsviadukten 61 (until Aug 2003). █ 08-519 552 00. ⑪ Centralen. █ 52. ○ Tue–Sun. ● Jan 1, Apr 30, May 1, Jun 25, Dec 24, 25 & 31. ☐ W www.modernamuseet.se

T HE LIGHT and spacious building that the Moderna Museet has occupied since 1998 provides a perfect setting for the museum's world-class collection of modern art, photography, and film.

Following a recent period of renovation, during which the museum moved to another location and put on a variety of exhibitions and events, it is now back in its own building.

All the works on display date from between 1900 and the present day. Two of the star exhibits are *The Child's Brain* (1914) by Italian artist Giorgio de Chirico, widely considered a precursor to the Surrealists, and *Monogram* (1955–59) by the American Robert Rauschenberg. Among the collection of Swedish works is Nils Dardel's Expressionistic painting, *The Dying Dandy* (1918).

Vasamuseet ⑨

Galärvarvet, Djurgården. █ 08-519 548 00. █ 44, 47. █ 7. ▣ Djurgårdsfärja. ○ daily. ● Jan 1, May 1, Dec 23–25 & 31. ▨ ᴔ ☞
Museifartygen █ 519 548 91. ○ Jun 10–Aug: pm daily. ▨ ☞ W www.vasamuseet.se

T HE CENTERPIECE of the city's most popular museum is the massive royal warship, *Vasa*, which capsized in Stockholm harbor on its maiden voyage in 1628. Rediscovered in 1956, the vessel has been painstakingly restored to 95 percent of its original appearance.

The warship is decorated with around 700 sculpted figures and carved ornaments, designed as a type of war propaganda. King Gustav II Adolf, who commissioned *Vasa*, was known as the Lion of the North, so a springing lion was the obvious choice for the figurehead on the ship's prow. It is 4 m (13 ft) long and weighs 450 kg (990 lb).

Although visitors cannot board the ship, full-scale models of *Vasa*'s upper gun deck and the Admiral's cabin provide a glimpse of what life on board was like. There is also a fascinating display of items retrieved in the salvage operation, including medical equipment, an officer's back-gammon set, and a chest still neatly packed with clothing and other personal belongings.

Moored in the dock alongside the museum are two other historic vessels, collectively referred to as the **Museifartygen**. The lightship *Finngrundet* was built in 1903 and worked for 60 years before becoming a museum. *Sankt Erik* was commissioned in 1915 and was Sweden's first sea-going icebreaker.

Midsummer celebrations at the open-air museum, Skansen

Skansen ⑩

Djurgårdsslätten 49–51. █ 08-442 80 00. █ 44, 47. █ 7. ▣ Djurgårdsfärja. ○ daily. ● Dec 24. ▨ ☞ Jun–Aug (call in advance).

T HE WORLD'S first open-air museum opened in 1891 to show an increasingly industrialized society how people once lived. Around 150 buildings were assembled from all over Scandinavia, to portray the life of peasants and landed gentry, as well as Lapp *(Same)* culture.

In the Town Quarter are 19th-century town-houses, where glassblowers, shoe-makers, and other crafts-men demonstrate their skills. Two of Skansen's oldest "exhibits" are a 650-year-old wooden farmhouse from Dalarna, and a 14th-century storehouse from eastern Norway.

Nordic flora and fauna can be seen, with elks, bears, and wolves in natural habitat enclosures and marine animals in an aquarium. Traditional festivals and concerts are held here throughout the year.

The restored 17th-century royal warship, *Vasa*, at the Vasamuseet

Nordiska Museet ⑪

Djurgårdsvägen 6–16. 08-45 70
660. 44, 47. 7. *Djurgårdsfärja.* *late Jun–Aug: daily; Sep–
mid-Jun: Tue–Sun.* *midsummer
hol, Dec 24, 25, 31; Jan 1.*
www.nordiskamuseet.se

HOUSED IN a Renaissance-
style building, the
Nordiska Museet's collection
was started by Artur Hazelius
(1833–1901), founder of the
Skansen open-air museum.
Hazelius' intention was to
assemble a variety of objects
that would remind future
generations of the old Nordic
farming culture. Today, the
museum has over 1.5 million
exhibits portraying everyday
life in Sweden from the 1520s
to the present day. Items on
display range from priceless
jewelry, to furniture, dolls'
houses, and replicas of period
rooms, such as the splendid
17th-century state bedchamber
from Ulvsunda Castle. Highlights include the monumental
gilded oak statue of King
Gustav Vasa (1924), and 16
paintings by the Swedish
author and dramatist August
Strindberg (1849–1912).

**Carl Milles' huge statue of King
Gustav Vasa in the Nordiska Museet**

Historiska Museet ⑫

Narvavägen 13–17. 08-519 556 00.
Karlaplan. 44, 56. *mid-
May–mid-Sep: daily; mid-Sep–mid-May:
Tue–Sun.* *some public hols.*
www.historiska.se

SWEDEN'S Museum of National
Antiquities was opened in
1943. It originally made its
name with relics from the
Viking era, as well as its
outstanding collections from
the Middle Ages. The latter
include one of the museum's
star exhibits – a richly gilded
wooden Madonna figure,
from Sweden's early medieval
period. In the prehistoric
collection is the Alunda
Elk, a ceremonial stone
axe, discovered in 1920
at Alunda and thought
to have been made
around 2000 BC.
    Since the early
1990s the museum's
priceless collection
of gold and silver,
dating from the
Bronze Age to the
Middle Ages, has
been on show in
the Guld-rummet
(Gold Room). Look out
for the stunning Elisabeth
Reliquary, an 11th-century
goblet, with a silver cover
made in 1230 to enclose the
skull of St. Elisabeth.

**Madonna figure in
the Historiska Museet**

Drottningholm ⑬

10 km (6 miles) W of Stockholm.
08-402 62 80. *Brommaplan,*
then bus 177, 300–323.
May–Sep from Stadshusbron.
*May–Sep: daily; Oct–Apr: Sat &
Sun. (Chinese Pavilion: May–Sep only;
Theater Museum: May–Sep only.)*
Dec 22–Jan 5.
www.royalcourt.se

WITH ITS SUMPTUOUS
palace, theater, park,
and Chinese pavilion, the
whole of the Drottningholm
estate has been included in
UNESCO's World Heritage list.

The magnificent Drottningholm palace, on the island of Lovön

Contemporary Italian and
French architecture inspired
Nicodemus Tessin the Elder
(1615–81) in his design of the
royal palace. Begun in the
1660s on the orders of King
Karl X Gustav's widow, Queen
Hedvig Eleonora, the building
was completed by Tessin the
Younger. Today, the present
royal family still uses parts
of the palace as a private
residence. The most lavish
rooms open to the public
include Queen Lovisa
Ulrika's library,
designed by Jean
Eric Rehn (1717–93),
and Queen Hedvig
Eleonora's state
bedroom, decorated
in Baroque style.
    The Baroque and
Rococo gardens and
lush parkland surrounding
the palace are dotted with
monuments and splendid
buildings. The blue and gold
Chinese Pavilion (Kina Slott)
was built for Queen Lovisa
Ulrika in the latter half of the
18th century, and contains
many interesting artifacts from
China and Japan. The designer
of the Chinese Pavilion,
Carl Fredrik Adelcrantz,
was also responsible for the
Drottningholm Court Theater
(Slottsteatern), which dates
from 1766. This simple
wooden building is the world's
oldest theater still preserved
in its original form. The
scenery, with its wooden
hand driven machinery, is still
in working order. In summer
the theater hosts opera and
ballet. There is also a
museum, which focuses on
18th-century theater.

The Renaissance Gripsholms Slott, on the shore of Lake Mälaren

🏛 **Birkamuseet**
📞 08-560 514 45. ⏱ May 1–
Sep 26: daily. 🖼 🎫
♟ **Gripsholms Slott**
📞 0159-101 94. ⏱ mid-May–
mid-Sep: daily; mid-Sep–mid-May:
noon–3pm Sat & Sun. 🎫 🖼

Uppsala ❸

👥 190,000. 🚂 🚌 ℹ Fyris
Torg 8 (018-727 48 00).

O NE OF SWEDEN'S oldest settlements, Uppsala, on the banks of the Fyrisån river, is also a lively university town. On the last day of April, crowds of students wearing white caps parade through the town for the traditional spring season celebrations.

Dominating the town's attractive medieval center is the **Domkyrkan**, Scandinavia's largest Gothic cathedral. Its vaults, which date from 1435, contain the relics of Sweden's patron saint, Saint Erik. The onion-domed **Gustavianum**, opposite the cathedral, dates from the 1620s and houses the Uppsala University Museum. Among the museum's many exhibits are a 17th-century anatomical theater and Egyptian, Classical, and Nordic antiquities. Just a short walk away stands the **Carolina Rediviva**, the impressive university library.

Uppsala Slott, the town's hilltop fortress, was built in the 16th century by King Gustav Vasa, although it was later destroyed by fire. Now restored, it also houses the Uppsala Art Museum.

Lake Mälaren ❷

Birka 🚢 May–Sep daily from Stadshusbron, Stockholm. **Mariefred** 🚢 in summer from Stadshusbron, Stockholm. 🚂 from Centralstationen, Stockholm to Läggesta, then bus or steam train.

T O THE WEST of Stockholm lies Lake Mälaren, a vast stretch of water, whose pretty shores and islands offer several day excursions from the city.

Sweden's first town, **Birka**, was founded on the island of Björkö in the 8th century, although archaeological finds indicate that trading activity took place here at least 1,500 years ago. In the 9th and 10th centuries Birka grew into a busy Viking center. The **Birkamuseet** has displays of local archaeological finds and provides a fascinating insight into the daily lives of the town's early inhabitants. There are also guided tours of ongoing excavations.

The most striking feature of the pretty town of **Mariefred** is the majestic **Gripsholms Slott**, built for King Gustav Vasa in 1537, and later modified under Gustav III in the 18th century. The palace is known for its well-preserved interiors, and also houses the National Portrait Gallery, with over 4,000 paintings spanning some 500 years.

Mariefred itself has a lovely 17th-century church and an 18th-century timber Rådhus (law courts' building), as well as several specialist stores, galleries, and antique shops. In summer, one of the most enjoyable ways to travel there from Stockholm is aboard the *Mariefred*, a historic, coal-fired steamboat. The trip takes around three and a half hours and allows passengers to enjoy the spectacular scenery along the route.

Aerial view of Uppsala, with its massive Gothic cathedral, the Domkyrkan

A short bus ride north of the town center, Gamla Uppsala is the site of the Kungshögarna, royal burial mounds believed to date from the 6th century. The **Historiskt Centrum** acquaints visitors with the history, legends, and lore surrounding the burial mounds and contains displays of local archaeological finds.

🏛 **Gustavianum**
Akademigatan 3. 📞 018-471 75 71.
🕐 Tue–Sun. 🚫 ♿
[w] www.gustavianum.uu.se

⚓ **Uppsala Slott**
Slottet, entrance E. 📞 018-727 24 82.
🕐 Wed–Sun. 🚫 ♿ Jun–Aug.

🏛 **Historiskt Centrum**
Disavägen. 📞 018-23 93 00.
🕐 May–Aug: daily; at other times: call for information. 🚫 ♿

Dalarna ❹

🚃 Falun, Mora. 🚌 Falun, Mora.
ℹ Trotzgatan 10–12 (023-640 04);
Stationsväg 3, Mora (0250-59 20 20).

WITH ITS PROUD tradition of music, dance, and handicrafts, Dalarna is Sweden's folklore district. The charming rural landscape, dotted with red, wooden cottages, attracts many tourists seeking a quiet country retreat in the summer. In winter, the area's mountain resorts, Sälen and Idre, are packed with skiers.

The main sights of interest are located around Lake Siljan. **Mora**, the largest of the lakeside towns, was home to one of Sweden's best-known artists, Anders Zorn (1860–1920). Open daily, the Zorn Museum, at No. 36 Vasagatan, holds paintings by the artist, and you can also visit his former home and studio.

Dalarna is famous for its midsummer festivals. In **Leksand** and **Rättvik** you may see traditionally dressed locals dancing and playing musical instruments or rowing on the lake in wooden longboats during the towns' colorful celebrations.

Around 15 km (9 miles) from the provincial capital and largely industrial town of

Female musician at a midsummer festival in Dalarna

Falun is **Sundborn**, where Swedish painter Carl Larsson (1853–1919) and his wife, Karin, a textile artist, lived in the early 20th century. Their work still has a big influence on contemporary Swedish design. The couple's lakeside house is open to the public.

Gotland and Visby ❺

🏛 60,000. ✈ 🚢 to Visby.
ℹ Hamngatan 4, Visby (0498-20 17 00).

THE ISLAND of Gotland, Sweden's most popular holiday destination, boasts a stunning coastline, a rich cultural heritage, and a superb climate, enjoying more hours of sunshine than anywhere else in the country.

In the Viking Age, Gotland, the largest island in the Baltic Sea, was a major trading post and later its capital, Visby, became a prosperous Hanseatic port. Surrounded by one of the best-preserved city walls in the world, Visby is like a living museum, with pretty step-gabled houses and a web of narrow cobbled streets and small squares. The original Hanseatic harbor is now a park, but the **Burmeisterska Huset** (Burmeister's House), dating

The Norderport, one of the gateways in Visby's medieval city walls

from 1645, is a fine surviving example of the architecture of the Post-Hanseatic period. Strandgatan contains some of Visby's most attractive historic buildings, the former homes of wealthy merchants. In the same street is the excellent historical museum, **Gotlands Fornsal**, which holds a collection of artifacts spanning 8,000 years. The **Domkyrkan** (Cathedral of St. Maria) below Kyrkberget is the only medieval church still intact and in use in Visby.

Away from Visby, the rest of Gotland is dotted with many unspoilt farmhouses, old medieval churches, and secluded beaches. Among the most impressive sights are the subterranean limestone caves of **Lummelundagrottorna**, 13 km (8 miles) north of the city, and, off the northeastern tip of the island, **Fårö**. This island, known for its severe beauty, can be reached by a daily, half-hourly ferry from Fårösund. Besides old fishing hamlets such as Helgumannen, visitors can enjoy the long stretch of white sandy beach and the swimming at Sudersands. Look out for Fårö's spectacular *raukar*. These are huge limestone rock formations, rising out of the sea on the west side of the island.

🏛 **Gotlands Fornsal**
Strandgatan 14. 📞 0498-29 27 00.
🕐 May–mid-Sep: daily; mid-Sep–Apr: pm Tue–Sun. 🚫 📷 in summer. ♿

Poseidon fountain, at the end of Kungsportsavenyn in Gothenburg

Gothenburg ❻

🏛 *463,000.* ✈ *25 km (16 miles) E.*
🚉 🚌 ⛴ ℹ *Kungsportsplatsen 2
(031-612 500).*

GOTHENBURG (Göteborg), Sweden's second largest city, has a distinctive character, with beautiful architecture, pleasant café-lined boulevards, a bustling harbor, and a dynamic cultural life.

Scandinavia's largest seaport is dominated by the **Göteborgsutkiken**, a huge lookout tower providing stunning panoramic views of the city and its surroundings. A short walk west along the quayside are the daring, industrial-style **Göteborgsoperan** (Opera House), built in 1994, and the **Maritima Centrum**, reputedly the world's largest floating ship museum. Moored in the dock are a dozen different types of vessel, all open to the public. They include a light ship, a destroyer, and a submarine.

The pulse of the city is Kungsportsavenyn, simply known as Avenyn, or "The Avenue." This 900-m (2952-ft) long boulevard is lined with restaurants, pubs, and cafés,

and is a favorite haunt of street musicians and hawkers. On a side street off Avenyn, **Röhsska Museet** is Sweden's only museum devoted to arts, crafts, and industrial design. At the southern end of the avenue is Götaplatsen, whose focal point is the famous Poseidon fountain by the Swedish sculptor Carl Milles. The square is flanked by the fine **Konst-museet** (Art Museum), which specializes in 19th- and 20th-century Scandinavian art.

Southeast of Götaplatsen is **Lisebergs Nöjespark**, the largest amusement park in Sweden.

🏛 **Maritima Centrum**
Packhuskajen 8. 📞 031-10 59 50.
⭕ *Mar–Nov: daily; Dec–Feb: advance bookings only.* ♿
🏛 **Röhsska Museet**
Vasagatan 37–39. 📞 031-61 38 50.
⭕ *pm Tue–Sun.* ♿
🖥 www.designmuseum.se
🏛 **Konstmuseet**
Götaplatsen. 📞 031-61 29 80. ⭕
May–Aug: daily; Sep–Apr: Tue–Sun. ♿

Växjö ❼

🏛 *77,000.* 🚉 🚌 ℹ *Stationen,
Norra Järnsvägsgatan (0470-414 10).*

LOCATED RIGHT at the heart of Småland, Växjö is an ideal base from which to begin an exploration of the Glasriket, or "Kingdom of Glass," Sweden's world-famous region of glassworks. The town's main attraction is the **Smålands Museum**, which tells the story of 400 years of glassmaking, and provides a good introduction to a visit to any one of the numerous glassworks scattered throughout the surrounding forests.

The best-known glassworks are at **Orrefors** and **Kosta**, within 90 km (56 miles) of Växjö, but other factories worth visiting include **Åfors** and **Strömbergshyttan**. Most of the factories have excellent glassblowing demonstrations, and all have a shop where you can choose from a wide selection of products. In the past, Småland's glassworks were more than just a place of work. Locals used to meet here in the evenings to bake herrings and potatoes in the furnace, while music was provided by a fiddler. Today the Orrefors and Kosta glassworks arrange similar forms of entertainment, known as *hyttsill* evenings.

Visitors to Växjö should not miss the **Utvandrarnas Hus** (House of Emigrants). This interesting museum recounts the story of the one million Swedes who, in the face of famine in the late 19th and early 20th centuries, left their homes in Småland for a better life in America.

Swedish glassware from Småland

🏛 **Smålands Museum**
Södra Järnvägsgatan 2. 📞 0470-7042 00. ⭕ *Jun–Aug: daily; Sep–May: Tue–Sun.* ♿ ♿
🏛 **Kosta Glassworks**
Kosta, on route 28. 📞 0478-34529.
⭕ *daily.* ⬤ *some public hols.*
🛍 *daily.*
🏛 **Utvandrarnas Hus**
Vilhelm Mobergsgatan 4. 📞 0470-201 20. ⭕ *daily.* ⬤ *public hols.*

Malmö  **8**

🏛 260,000. 🚶 🚢 🚉 🚌 ℹ️
Central Station (040-34 1200).

Mälmo's main square, overlooked by the Renaissance Rådhuset

MALMÖ IS the capital of the province of Skåne in southwestern Sweden. In the 16th century, it was a major fishing port, competing with Copenhagen as Scandinavia's most influential city. Today the city is well-known for its busy harbor, as well as for its rich architectural heritage.

The imposing 16th-century Malmöhus was built by the Danish king Christian III, when Skåne formed part of Denmark. It contains the **Malmömuseer** (Malmö Museums), which include the Art Museum, the Museum of Natural History, the City Museum, the Science & Technology and Maritime Museum, and the Kommendants Hus (Commander's House).

The Dutch Renaissance style is evident in Malmö's impressive **Rådhuset** (Town Hall), which dates from 1546 and dominates the city's main square, Stortorget. Northeast of here is the 14th-century **St. Petri's Kyrka**, built in the Baltic Gothic style. The church's most beautiful features include the altarpiece (1611), Scandinavia's largest,

and a wonderfully ornate pulpit. Amid the city's maze of pedestrianized streets, lined with shops and cafés, is Lilla Torg (Little Square), with its cobblestones and charmingly restored houses. The square has a lively atmosphere and draws crowds of tourists and locals alike, especially in fine weather. At the northwest corner of the square, the bustling Saluhallen is a covered market, with many restaurants, cafés, and specialist food stores.

Heading east from Lilla Torg brings you to the **Rooseum**. This excellent museum of modern art was founded in 1988 by the Swedish art collector and financier Fredrik Roos. Retrospectives of a number of leading international contemporary artists are held here regularly.

🏛 **Malmömuseer**
Malmöhus, Malmöhusvägen.
📞 040-34 44 37. ⭕ pm daily. 📷

🏛 **Rooseum**
Gasverksgatan 22. 📞 040-12 17 16.
⭕ pm Wed–Sun. 📷 ♿

THE ÖRESUND LINK

Despite a legacy of mutual warfare and rivalry, in May 2000 the close ties between Denmark and Sweden were strengthened with the inauguration of the Öresund Link. A 16-km (10-mile) long combined suspension bridge and tunnel now connects the Danish capital, Copenhagen, with the Swedish provincial capital Malmö on either side of the channel of water known as the Öresund. The bridge is the strongest cable stay bridge in the world, designed to carry the combined weight of a motorway and a dual-track railway, while the tunnel is the world's largest immersed tunnel in terms of volume. The project has been hailed as a renaissance for southern Sweden, which now seems poised to become a prospering center of trade, science, industry, and culture at the heart of the cross-border Danish-Swedish Öresund region.

The newly constructed Öresund Link, spanning the Öresund channel

Practical & Travel Information

WITH SWEDEN GROWING RAPIDLY as an important tourist destination, standards in the travel industry have improved greatly. Foreign visitors will enjoy a comfortable stay in Sweden, not least because most people speak English. Sweden's infrastructure is constantly being improved – there are many new highways and the rail system has recently been upgraded for high-speed trains. There is also a direct link to Denmark via the new Öresund Bridge. In Stockholm, public transportation on buses, subway trains, ferries, and local trains is efficient, and covers the entire city and surrounding region.

TOURIST INFORMATION

TOURIST INFORMATION offices are located throughout Sweden, and are run by the **Swedish Travel & Tourism Council**. Stockholm's official tourist information organization is the **Stockholm Visitors Board**. Most hotels in the capital, as well as many department stores and museums, stock the free monthly listings brochure *What's On Stockholm*.

Most museums and other sights in Sweden are open between 10 or 11am and 5 or 6pm all year round, and often have longer opening hours in the summer. They are usually closed on Monday.

VISA REQUIREMENTS

PASSPORTS ARE not required for visitors from most EU countries, but visitors from the US, Canada, the UK, Ireland, Australia, and New Zealand still need a valid passport. Citizens of almost all countries can enter Sweden without a visa.

PERSONAL SECURITY

VIOLENT CRIME against tourists is rare in Sweden, although pickpockets are known to frequent the busier pedestrian shopping streets in the main cities. Sweden has a well-developed network of emergency services, which are efficient and reliable. Swedish police are extremely helpful and most speak good English.

HEALTH ISSUES

NO SPECIAL vaccinations are necessary to visit Sweden. Hygiene standards are among the highest in the world, and the tap water is safe to drink. For prescription and non-prescription medicines visit a pharmacy *(apotek)*, open during normal store hours. A 24-hour *apotek* service is also available in major cities.

CURRENCY AND BANKING

THE SWEDISH UNIT of currency is the krona, abbreviated to SEK or kr. Banking hours are generally

10am–3pm Monday to Friday, though some banks stay open until 6pm at least one day a week. Traveler's checks can be changed at all banks. Bureaux de change are located throughout the main cities and airports, and normally provide a better exchange rate than banks.

All the well-known credit cards are widely accepted in Sweden. Withdrawals can be made from cash machines using all internationally accepted credit cards.

COMMUNICATIONS

PUBLIC TELEPHONE kiosks are owned by the state-run Telia company, and are usually operated by card only. Phonecards can be bought at tobacconists and newspaper kiosks, though normal credit cards or international telephone cards work just as well.

Post offices are open from 10am to 6pm on weekdays and from 10am to 1pm on Saturdays. Many of the post offices have recently been closed and postal services moved to gas stations and stores instead. Stamps can be purchased at these locations as well as at post offices, Pressbyrån kiosks, and tourist information offices.

FLYING TO SWEDEN

MOST MAJOR European cities have direct flights to Stockholm. Many of the world's leading airlines serve Arlanda Airport, located about 40 km (25 miles) north of the city center. International flights also serve Gothenburg and Malmö. Services from the UK are operated by **Finnair**, **SAS** (Scandinavian Airlines), British Airways, and low-cost airline **Ryanair**. Direct flights from North America are available from SAS and Finnair, and from the US airline American.

TRAVELING BY FERRY

FERRIES TO GOTHENBURG from Fredrikshavn in Denmark (2–3 hours), and from Kiel in Germany (20–22 hours), are operated by **Stena Line**.

THE CLIMATE OF SWEDEN

Sweden's summers are usually fairly cool, although sometimes there can be heatwaves for several weeks at a time. Winter temperatures often fall below freezing, but it is rarely severely cold, except in the far north. The snow may lie until well after March in the north, but in the rest of the country some recent winters have been virtually free of snow.

STOCKHOLM			
°C/F	23/73		
	14/57	12/54	
10/50		7/44	
0°C	2/36		0/32
32°F			-4/25
☀ 6 hrs	8 hrs	3.5 hrs	1.5 hrs
☂ 21 mm	65 mm	48 mm	27 mm
month	Apr	Jul	Oct	Jan

Large passenger and car ferries sail to Stockholm from Finland; both **Viking Line** and **Silja Line** operate daily services from Helsinki (with a crossing time of about 15 hours) and Turku (with a crossing time of about 11 hours).

DFDS Seaways has a year-round service twice a week from Newcastle in Great Britain to Gothenburg via Kristiansand (with a crossing time of about 24 hours).

Within Sweden, ferries to Visby in Gotland leave from Nynäshamn, about 75 km (47 miles) south of Stockholm. There are two crossings daily by catamaran (2 hours 50 mins) and one or two crossings daily by regular ferry (5 hours). Both services are run by **Destination Gotland**.

RAIL TRAVEL

R^AIL TRAVEL to Sweden from mainland Europe is fast and comfortable. Journey times have been cut considerably with the opening of the Öresund Bridge; traveling from Copenhagen to Malmö now takes only 40 minutes.

Within Sweden, the state-owned rail company Statens Järnvägar (SJ) operates many of the long-distance trains. Some routes are run by private companies – Tågkompaniet runs trains from Stockholm to Narvik, Umeå, and Luleå in the far north of Sweden.

In recent years domestic air travel in Sweden has faced strong competition from the new X 2000 high-speed trains. The journey time by train from Malmö to Stockholm is about 5 hours, and from Gothenburg to the capital takes about 3 hours.

TRAVELING BY CAR

V^ISITORS DRIVING from Denmark can use the spectacular new Öresund toll bridge between Copenhagen and Malmö. On the Swedish side, the bridge connects with the E4, a 550-km (340-mile) highway to Stockholm.

Fines for speeding are high, and even if the limit is only slightly exceeded, you can lose your license. The maximum permitted blood alcohol level is so low that drinking is effectively banned for drivers. When driving in the Swedish countryside, be particularly cautious, as elk and deer may appear unexpectedly in the middle of the road.

TRAVELING IN STOCKHOLM

V^IRTUALLY ALL of Stockholm's sights and attractions can be reached by subway train or bus. Tunnelbana, the underground rail system, has 100 stations on three main routes. Travelcards are available for one-day, three-day, and monthly periods, and are also valid on bus and ferry services.

Traveling by bus is a pleasant and economical way to see the city. The best routes for sightseeing are 3, 4, 46, 47, 62, and 69, which cover the central area and stop near many sights.

Stockholm's waterways play an important role in urban life, and boats and ferries provide a delightful way of getting to know the city and its environs. **Strömma Kanalbolaget** runs various hour-long excursions during the summer months, and also organizes longer tours of the archipelago and Lake Mälaren throughout the year.

A worthwhile purchase for any visitor to the capital is the Stockholm Card, which allow free travel on Tunnelbana trains, local buses, and local trains, free parking at official city parking areas, and free admission to more than 70 museums and attractions.

DIRECTORY	**EMBASSIES**	**EMERGENCY NUMBERS**	**FERRY SERVICES**
TOURIST OFFICES	**Australia**		**Destination Gotland**
	11th floor, Sergels Torg 12, Stockholm.	**Ambulance, Police and Fire**	☎ 08-20 10 20.
Stockholm Visitors Board	☎ 08-613 29 00.	☎ 112.	**DFDS Seaways**
Sweden House, Hamngatan 27, Stockholm.	☎ www.austemb.se		☎ 031-65 06 50.
☎ 08-789 24 90.	**Canada**	**AIRLINES**	☎ www.dfdsseaways.com
☎ www.stockholmtown.com	Tegelbacken 4, Stockholm.	**Finnair**	**Silja Line**
	☎ 08-453 3000.	☎ 020-78 11 00 (toll-free in Sweden).	☎ 08-22 21 40.
Swedish Travel & Tourism Council	☎ www.canadaemb.se	☎ 0870-241 4411 (UK).	☎ www.silja.se
Kungsgatan 36, Stockholm.	**Ireland**	☎ 800-950 5000 (US).	**Stena Line**
☎ 08-725 55 00.	Östermalmsgatan 97, Stockholm.	☎ www.finnair.com	☎ 031-704 00 00.
☎ www.visit-sweden.com	☎ 08-661 80 05.	**Malmö Aviation**	☎ www7.stenaline.co.uk
In the UK:	**UK**	☎ 020-55 00 10.	**Viking Line**
5 Upper Montague Street, London W1H 2AG.	Skarpögatan 6-8, Stockholm.	☎ www.malmoaviation.se	☎ 08-452 40 00.
☎ 0800-3080 3080.	☎ 08-671 30 00.	**Ryanair**	☎ www.vikingline.se
In the US:	☎ www.britishembassy.com	☎ www.ryanair.com	
P.O. Box 4649, Grand Central Station, New York, NY 10163-4649.	**US**	**SAS**	**TRAVELING IN STOCKHOLM**
☎ 212-885 9710.	Dag Hammarskjölds Väg 31, Stockholm.	☎ 0770-727 727 (toll-free in Sweden).	**Strömma Kanalbolaget**
🖷 212-885 9765.	☎ 081-783 53 00.	☎ 0845-6072 7727 (UK).	☎ 08-587 140 00.
	☎ www.usemb.se	☎ 800-221 2350 (US).	☎ www.strommakanal-bolaget.com
		☎ www.scandinavian.net	

Where to Stay in Sweden

Sweden's hotels are not usually built on the same grandiose scale as their counterparts in southern Europe, but they offer a high level of comfort and service and often have magnificent views or locations. Major hotels in the larger cities can be fairly expensive, but rooms are available at reduced rates during the summer and for weekend breaks all year round.

	NUMBER OF ROOMS	RESTAURANT	PRIVATE PARKING	SWIMMING POOL
STOCKHOLM				
CENTRAL STOCKHOLM: *Lydmar Hotel* Ⓚ Ⓚ Ⓚ Ⓚ Sturegatan 10. **Map** C2. 〖 08-566 113 00. 🅕🅐🅧 08-556 113 01. Ⓦ www.lydmar.se A new hotel with the accent on quality, both in the rooms – adorned with antiques and modern art – and in the two restaurants. The hotel plays host to regular jazz evenings and art exhibitions. 🔲 📺 🖼	62	●		
CENTRAL STOCKHOLM: *Scandic Hotel Sergel Plaza* Ⓚ Ⓚ Ⓚ Ⓚ Brunkebergstorg 9. **Map** B3. 〖 08-517 263 00. 🅕🅐🅧 08-517 263 11. The Plaza has been voted "Hotel of the Year" four times since its opening in 1984. It offers a full range of services for both tourists and business travelers. 🔲 📺 🖼 🖼	403	●	■	
CENTRAL STOCKHOLM: *Victory Hotel* Ⓚ Ⓚ Ⓚ Ⓚ Lilla Nygatan 5. **Map** B4. 〖 08-506 400 00. 🅕🅐🅧 08-506 400 10. Ⓦ www. victory-hotel.se A hotel with a Lord Nelson theme. An original letter written by him to Lady Hamilton is one of the many unique treasures displayed here. ⬤ *Christmas.* 🔲 📺 🖼	45	●	■	
SOUTHERN STOCKHOLM: *Tre Små Rum Hotel* Ⓚ Högbergsgatan 81. 〖 08-641 23 71. 🅕🅐🅧 08-642 88 08. Ⓦ www.tresmarum.se Guests can prepare their own breakfast in this modern small hotel. Rooms have the air of a home away from home. Shared bathrooms. 🔲 *hotel.* 🖼	7			
SOUTHERN STOCKHOLM: *Ersta Konferens & Hotell* Ⓚ Ⓚ Erstagatan 1K. **Map** D5. 〖 08-714 63 41. 🅕🅐🅧 08-714 63 51. Ⓦ www.ersta.se/konferens Complex in a historic setting with a hotel, conference facilities, restaurant, bookshop, museum, and church, with a fantastic view of Stockholm. Each floor has a mini-kitchen with microwave oven. 🔲 📺 🖼 🔲 *hotel.* 🖼	22	●		
WESTERN STOCKHOLM: *Långholmen Hotell & Vandrarhem* Ⓚ Ⓚ Kronohäktet, Långholmen. 〖 08-668 05 00. 🅕🅐🅧 08-720 85 75. Ⓦ www.langholmen.com This former prison offers converted cells on a leafy island near the city center. There is an excellent restaurant and a large wine cellar. Also runs a youth hostel with 26 rooms (more in summer). ⬤ *Dec 21–Jan 1.* 🔲 📺 🖼 🔲 *hotel.* 🖼	102	●	■	
REST OF SWEDEN				
DALARNA: *Hotell Siljan* Ⓚ Ⓚ Moragatan 6, Mora. 〖 0250-130 00. 🅕🅐🅧 0250 -130 98. Ⓦ www. hotellsiljan.se This small, modern hotel affords views over the lake that shares its name. Comfortable and clean rooms (all renovated in 2000). 🔲 📺 🖼	40	●	■	
GOTHENBURG: *Hotel Eggers* Ⓚ Ⓚ Ⓚ Drottningtorget. 〖 031-806 070. 🅕🅐🅧 031-154 243. Ⓦ www. hoteleggers.se Close to many of Gothenburg's major attractions, the Eggers is the third oldest hotel in Sweden, with plenty of classic charm and character. Each room has an individual style, and most are large with high ceilings. ⬤ *Dec 23–26.* 🔲 📺 🖼	67	●	■	
MALMÖ: *Mäster Johan Hotel* Ⓚ Ⓚ Ⓚ Mäster Johansgatan 13. 〖 040-664 6400. 🅕🅐🅧 040-664 6401. Ⓦ www.masterjohan.se A completely modern hotel with generously sized rooms. The highlight of the Mäster Johan is the attention to detail, with recessed lighting, oak floors, Oriental carpets, and French cherrywood furnishings. ⬤ *Dec 21–Jan 6.* 🔲 📺 🖼 🖼	69		■	

<table>
<tr><td>

Price categories are for a standard double room per night, with additional tax, breakfast, and service charges included:

Ⓚ under 700 SEK
Ⓚ Ⓚ 700–1,400 SEK
Ⓚ Ⓚ Ⓚ 1,400–2,100 SEK
Ⓚ Ⓚ Ⓚ Ⓚ over 2,100 SEK

</td><td>

RESTAURANT
Hotel restaurant or dining-room usually open to non-residents.

PRIVATE PARKING
Parking provided by the hotel in either a private car park or a private garage close by.

CREDIT CARDS
Major credit cards are accepted in those hotels where the credit card symbol is shown.

</td></tr>
</table>

Map references refer to map of Stockholm on pp642–3

Where to Eat in Sweden

GOOD SWEDISH RESTAURANTS tend to be small and informal. Food can be very expensive, with lunch often the best value. Some restaurants serve a *smörgåsbord*, where you can eat as much as you like at a fixed price. Many menus feature *husmanskost* – traditional dishes of Swedish "home-cooking" – such as Swedish meatballs (also popular in a *smörgåsbord*) or boiled salted brisket of beef.

		OPEN LATE	VEGETARIAN DISHES	FIXED-PRICE MENU	GOOD WINE LIST
STOCKHOLM					
CENTRAL STOCKHOLM: *Bakfickan* Operahuset. **Map** C3. 08-676 58 09. www.operakallaren.se A little pearl with many regular customers, including artists from the Opera House. Swedish *husmanskost* is served over the bar counter, and other meals come from the legendary kitchens of the Opera House. ● *Sun.*	ⓚⓚ	■	●		●
CENTRAL STOCKHOLM: *Fem Små Hus* Nygränd 10. **Map** C4. 08-108 775. www.femmahus.se Restaurant set in a cozy cellar location with many nooks and crannies and larger dining rooms. Elegant modern Swedish cuisine and professional service.	ⓚⓚⓚ		●	■	●
CENTRAL STOCKHOLM: *Sturehof* Stureplan 2. **Map** C2. 08-440 57 30. www.sturehof.com This classic 19th-century seafood restaurant has four bars, and elegant dining room, as well as the outdoor restaurant. Food includes fish and shellfish, delicious snacks, and the very best *husmanskost*.	ⓚⓚⓚ	■	●	■	●
CENTRAL STOCKHOLM: *Gondolen* Stadsgården 6, top of Katarinahissen. **Map** C4. 08-641 70 90. www.eriks.se As well as the top-class cuisine, this restaurant has a great location, with the city's most fantastic view. The Gondolen's adjoining Köket restaurant also serves superb food in a rustic setting at significantly lower prices. ● *Sun.*	ⓚⓚⓚⓚ	■	●	■	●
CENTRAL STOCKHOLM: *Leijontornet* Lilla Nygatan 5. **Map** B4. 08-506 400 80. www.leijontornet.se Stylish but austerely decorated restaurant in a medieval cellar, with courtyard bar. The cuisine includes many Swedish ingredients, with excellent desserts. ● *lunch, Sun; Jul, Dec 22–Jan 7.*	ⓚⓚⓚⓚ		●	■	●
WESTERN STOCKHOLM: *Mälarstrandskrogen* Norr Mälarstrand 30. **Map** A3. 08-653 47 77. www.lunchinfo.se This small but highly popular local restaurant offers high-quality classic French and Swedish specialties at surprisingly low prices. ● *public hols.*	ⓚ		●		
REST OF SWEDEN					
GOTHENBURG: *Räkan* Lorensbergsgatan 16. 031-169 839. www.rakan.se Diners at this gimmicky shellfish restaurant sit on tables around a large tank of water, and their orders arrive on radio-controlled miniature boats. ● *Dec 22–Jan 6.*	ⓚⓚ	■		■	
MALMÖ: *Årstiderna I Kockska Huset* Stortorget. 040 -230 910. www.arstiderna.se The atmosphere at this restaurant is intimate. The menu offers generous portions of fish, reindeer, cheese, and other Swedish specialties. ● *public hols.*	ⓚⓚⓚ	■	●	■	●
UPPSALA: *Domtrappkällaren* St. Eriksgränd 15. 018-130 955. www.domtrappkallaren.se Popular with the locals, this restaurant is in a 14th-century cellar close to Uppsala Cathedral. The cuisine is a mixture of Swedish and French fare, with game dishes being the specialty. The salmon is also popular. ● *Sun in summer.*	ⓚⓚⓚ		●	■	●

Price categories are for a three-course meal for one, half a bottle of house wine, and all unavoidable extra charges such as cover and service:

ⓚ under 300 SEK
ⓚⓚ 300–400 SEK
ⓚⓚⓚ 400–500 SEK
ⓚⓚⓚⓚ over 500 SEK

OPEN LATE
Restaurants that remain open with their full menu available after 10pm.

VEGETARIAN DISHES
Available as a starter, a main course, or both.

FIXED-PRICE MENU
Available at lunch, dinner, or both.

CREDIT CARDS
Major credit cards are accepted in restaurants where the credit card symbol is shown.

NORWAY

ORWAY'S GREAT ATTRACTION *is the grandeur of its scenery. The landscape is one of dramatic contrasts: great mountain ranges, sheer river valleys, mighty glaciers, deep green forests, and the spectacular fjords that indent the western coast. In the far north, above the Arctic Circle, visitors can marvel at the Northern Lights and the long summer nights of the Land of the Midnight Sun.*

The fjords that make the coastline of Norway one of the most jagged in the world were carved by glaciers during the last Ice Age. As the glaciers began to recede about 12,000 years ago, the sea level rose and seawater flooded back to fill the deep, eroded valleys. Norway's extraordinary geography has had a great influence on its people and development. In the past, scarcity of agricultural land led to economic dependence on the sea. In contrast, Norway today has abundant hydro-electric power as well as rich oil and gas deposits on its continental shelf.

The first settlers arrived 10,000 years ago as the Scandinavian icesheets retreated. They were hunters of reindeer, deer, bears, and fish. By the Bronze Age (1500–500 BC) rock carvings show that these early Norwegians had learnt to ski. Other inhabitants of the region were the Sami (formerly known as the Lapps),

with origins in the northern regions of Russia, Finland, Sweden, and Norway, where they haved lived for thousands of years by fishing and herding reindeer. Some still follow the nomadic life of their forefathers but the majority now live and work in much the same way as Norwegians.

HISTORY

It is for the Viking Age (c.800–1050) that Norway is best known. As a result of overpopulation and clan warfare, the Norwegian Vikings traveled to find new lands. They mostly sailed west, their longships reaching the British Isles, Iceland, Greenland, and even America. The raiders soon became settlers and those who remained at home benefited both from the spoils of war and the fact that farmland was no longer in such short supply. The country was united by Harald the Fairhaired in the 9th century. This

The harbor at Bergen, the main center for tours of Norway's fjords

◁ Borgund stave church, one of the best-preserved of Norway's distinctive medieval churches

The Norwegian explorer, Roald Amundsen, checking his position after reaching the South Pole in 1911

great age of expansion, however, effectively ended in 1066, when King Harald Hardråde was defeated at the battle of Stamford Bridge in England.

The 11th and 12th centuries were marked by dynastic conflicts and the rising influence of the church. In 1217 Haakon IV came to power, ushering in a "Golden Age," when Norway flourished under strong centralized government. In 1262 both Iceland and Greenland came under Norwegian rule. However, in the following century, after suffering terrible losses in the Black Death, Norway was reduced to being the least important of the Scandinavian countries. From 1380 to 1905 it was under the rule first of Denmark and then of Sweden.

The 19th century saw the growth of a national identity and a blossoming of Norwegian culture. Most of Norway's most famous individuals were born in this century, among them the composer Edvard Grieg, dramatist Henrik Ibsen, Expressionist painter Edvard Munch, and polar explorer Roald Amundsen.

Following independence from Sweden in 1905, the government set about industrializing the country, expanding the merchant fleet, and establishing healthcare and education as the cornerstones of a welfare state.

Norway pursued a policy of neutrality in World War I and World War II. The price was high in World War I, since German submarines attacked shipping indiscriminately and Norway lost half its chartered tonnage. In World War II Germany occupied the country, but encountered a massive resistance movement. Norway's part in the war helped it gain in status and it became one of the founding members of the UN in 1945 and entered NATO in 1949.

The biggest issue of the postwar years has been whether or not to join the EU. Twice Norway has refused, but the economy thrives regardless, thanks in large part to revenues from North Sea oil.

KEY DATES IN NORWEGIAN HISTORY

AD 800–1050 Viking Age

866 Vikings control most of England

900 Norway united under hereditary rule

1030 Christianity established

1217–63 Reign of Haakon IV

1380–1814 Norway in union with Denmark

1397 Kalmar Union unites crowns of Denmark, Sweden, and Norway

1660 Modern boundaries of Norway established, through peace of Copenhagen

1814 Union with Sweden, but Norwegian parliament, the Storting, has extensive powers

1887 Norwegian Labour party is founded

1905 Norway established as a separate kingdom

1940–45 German occupation of Norway during World War II

1969 Discovery of oil and gas in North Sea

1972 Following a referendum Norway declines membership of the EU

1994 Second referendum on membership of the EU; majority again votes "no"

LANGUAGE AND CULTURE

There are two official Norwegian languages: *Bokmål* (book language), a modernization of old Dano-Norwegian used in the days of Danish rule, and *Nynorsk*, based on rural dialects, which was codified in the 19th century as part of the resurgence of nationalism. Despite the government's efforts to preserve the use of *Nynorsk*, it is in decline. As in other parts of Scandinavia, you don't need to speak Norwegian to get by, since most people speak English.

Perhaps because independence was so long in coming, most Norwegians are great patriots. National Independence Day (May 17) is celebrated the length and breadth of the country, with festive gatherings even at remote farms. Norwegians also have a great attachment to outdoor pursuits – fishing, hiking, walking, and skiing – and many families have a *hytte* (cottage or cabin) in the mountains or on the coast.

Exploring Norway

Norway is so long and narrow that, if Oslo remained fixed and the rest were turned upside down, it would stretch all the way to Rome. There are two main areas of attraction: Oslo, a lively, open city, particularly in summer, and Bergen and the fjords in the west. Elsewhere, up to 95 percent of the country is forested or uncultivated. Transportation (which comprises trains, buses, and coastal ferries) is reliable, though services can be cut back severely in the winter months, especially in the north.

Cruise ships moored in the Geiranger Fjord between Bergen and Trondheim

SIGHTS AT A GLANCE

Bergen and the Fjords ❸
OSLO pp660–64 ❶
Stavanger ❷
Trondheim ❹

See inset map
Tromsø ❺

KEY

- ✈ Airport
- ⛴ Ferry port
- — Highway
- — Major road
- — Railroad
- --- International border

0 kilometers 100

0 miles 100

Oslo ❶

Founded around 1048 by Harald Hardråde; Oslo is the oldest of the Scandinavian capital cities and occupies an enormous area, although it has only 500,000 inhabitants. The heart of the city is largely made up of late 19th- and early 20th-century Neoclassical buildings, wide avenues, and landscaped parks. Once the poor cousin to Stockholm and Copenhagen in terms of nightlife and cultural activities, in recent years Oslo has undergone a rebirth, and there are now more restaurants and entertainment venues than ever before. Most of the city's sights are within walking distance of each other. The Nordmarka area of forests to the north of the center gives a glimpse of the beautiful Norwegian countryside.

Sights at a Glance

Aker Brygge ③
Akershus Slott and
   Hjemmefrontmuseet ①
Frammuseet ⑨
Kongelige Slottet ④
Kon-Tiki Museum ⑩
Munch-museet ⑦
Nasjonalgalleriet ⑥
Nationaltheatret ⑤
Norsk Folkemuseum ⑫
Rådhus ②
Vigelandsparken ⑧
Vikingsskipshuset ⑪

See Also

• *Where to Stay* p670

• *Where to Eat* p671

Boats moored along the quayside, in front of the Akershus Slott

Getting Around

Oslo has around 60 bus and tram routes. Buses are faster than trams, and most set out from the terminal a few hundred meters northwest of Oslo Sentralstasjon, the main train station. Route 30 goes to the museums on the Bygdøy Peninsula. From late April to September you can also reach the peninsula by ferry from the boarding point by the Rådhus. The Tunnelbanen is most useful for reaching the city suburbs, including Nordmarka.

Busy shopping street in Oslo's city center

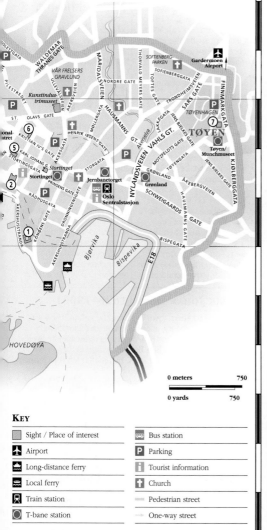

KEY

▢ Sight / Place of interest	🚌 Bus station
✈ Airport	🅿 Parking
⚓ Long-distance ferry	ℹ Tourist information
⚓ Local ferry	✝ Church
🚆 Train station	Pedestrian street
Ⓣ T-bane station	One-way street

D   E

Akershus Slott and Hjemmefront-museet ①

Festningsplassen. 🚆 10, 12. **Akershus Slott** ☎ 22 41 25 21 or 23 09 39 17. ◯ May 2–Sep 15: daily (Sun pm only). ● May 17. 📷 ✦
Hjemmefrontmuseet
☎ 23 09 31 38. ◯ daily. 📷
● Dec 24–26 & 31, Jan 1 & Easter.

Located on a knoll over-looking the Oslofjorden, the Akershus Slott (Akershus Castle) is the city's most notable memorial to medieval times. Built around 1300, the castle was besieged several times before King Christian IV of Denmark transformed it into a lavish Renaissance residence in the 1620s. He also built a new fortress around the castle. Known as the Akershus Festning, it is still in use today. Little remains of the castle's former glory, most of the rooms being relatively bare, although the tapestries in the Romerike Hall are impressive. You can also visit the royal chapel and the royal mausoleum, where members of the present Norwegian dynasty lie buried.

The most somber period in the Akershus Slott's history was during World War II, when the occupying Nazis tortured and shot members of the Norwegian resistance here. Pictorial displays at the Hjemmefrontmuseet (Resistance Museum), located by the gates of the castle, provide a moving account of the war in Norway, from occupation through resistance to liberation.

Akershus Slott, Oslo's finest surviving medieval monument

Rådhus ②

Rådhuset i Oslo. 【 *23 46 16 00.*
Ⓣ *Nationaltheatret.* 🚌 *30, 31, 32,*
45, 81. 🚋 *10, 12, 13, 19.* ⭘ *daily*
(Sun: pm only). ◐ *public hols.* ♿

INAUGURATED IN 1950 to
commemorate Oslo's 900th
year, the brown brick Rådhus
(City Hall) is the city's most
conspicuous landmark. The
building was a subject of
contention when it opened,
with many commenting
that it seemed particularly
un-Norwegian, but in time
the Rådhus has become a
popular symbol of civic pride.
Providing a complete contrast
to the exterior, the colorful
murals, sculptures, and frescoes
inside the building celebrate
Norwegian artistic and
intellectual achieve-
ments, as well as
those in exploration.
  The Rådhus is
famous as the place
where the Nobel
Peace Prize is
presented. This award
owes its inception,
ironically enough, to a
Swedish chemist, Alfred
Nobel, who invented
dynamite in 1867
and a smokeless
gunpowder in 1889.
He left his fortune in
trust for the endow-
ment of five Nobel
prizes – for physics,
chemistry, medicine, literature,
and peace, choosing the
Norwegian government to
make the peace award. All
the other prizes are awarded
at the Stadshuset in Stockholm
(see p644). Past recipients of
the prize have included the
Red Cross, Martin Luther
King, and Mother Teresa.

**Viking warrior
detail from Rådhus
main doors**

Aker Brygge ③

Aker Brygge. 🚌 *21.* 🚋 *10, 12.*

THE OLD Aker shipyard is
now a glass-and-chrome
leisure complex, centered
around an open sculpture
court, which includes shops,
restaurants, bars, cinemas,
and a theater. It is one of the
most popular places in the
city to go for a beer and a
meal, especially during the
long Scandinavian summer
evenings, when you can sit
outside and enjoy the lovely
scenery of the Oslo Fjord.

Kongelige Slottet ④

Drammensveien 1. 【 *22 04 87 00.*
Ⓣ *Nationaltheatret.* 🚌 *30, 31, 32.*
🚋 *13, 19.* ⭘ *Jun 22–Aug 17.* 🎫 *in
English, 2pm & 5:20pm.* **Changing of
the guard:** *1:30pm daily.*

THE NEOCLASSICAL Royal
Palace is a monument to
openness, standing as it does
in the freely accessible Palace
gardens (Slottsparken). Without gates or walls, the gardens
symbolize Norway's "open"
monarchy. The palace itself
was built in 1825–48 at
the request of King
Karl Johan. An
equestrian statue of
the king stands in
front of the building.
Every day at 1.30pm
the ceremony of the
changing of the
guard takes place.
Once a year during
Norway's National
Day on May 17, the
palace becomes the
focal point of cele-
brations when the
royal family stands
on the balcony to
greet the processions
of school children.

**Oslo's Nationaltheatret, overlooking
its attractive, busy piazza**

Nationaltheatret ⑤

Johanne Dybwads plass 1. 【 *22 00
14 00.* Ⓣ *Nationaltheatret.* 🚌 *30,
31, 32.* 🚋 *13, 19.* ⭘ *Aug–mid-Jun:
daily.* 🎫 *(call in advance).*

BUILT IN 1899, Norway's
National Theater is Neo-
classical in style, and flanked
by imposing statues of the
nation's two greatest 19th-
century playwrights – the
internationally famous Henrik
Johan Ibsen and Bjørnstjerne
Bjørnson, who is little known
outside Scandinavia these
days, but was a prolific writer
of plays and poetry during the
19th century. The theater has
four stages, and a varied
program, with all perfor-
mances given in Norwegian.
Visitors can make special
arrangements to have a
guided tour of the interior.

HENRIK JOHAN IBSEN (1828–1906)

Born in the southern town of Skien, the young Ibsen was
brought up in poverty, after his timber merchant father
suffered bankruptcy in 1836. Managing to escape, he lived
first in Kristiania and then Bergen, where he began writing
and producing his first dramas. In 1864 he left for Germany
and Italy, where he spent the next 27
years. His most famous plays include
Peer Gynt (1867), *A Doll's House*
(1879), and *Hedda Gabler* (1890).
Regarded as one of the founders
of modern drama, Ibsen's legacy
to the European stage was his
introduction of themes such as
the alienation of the individual
from a morally bankrupt society,
loss of religious faith, and women's
desire to free themselves of their
roles as wives and mothers – a clear
departure from the unchallenging
theater of the time. After returning
to Norway, he died in 1906.

**Playwright Henrik
Johan Ibsen**

Simple, red brick façade of the Nasjonalgalleriet

Nasjonalgalleriet ⑥

Universitetsgaten 13. 📞 22 20 04 04.
🚇 Nationaltheatret. 🚌 30, 31, 32.
🚋 10, 11, 13, 17, 18, 19. 🕐 Wed–
Mon. 🌐 www.nasjonalgalleriet.no

NORWAY'S BIGGEST collection of art is housed in this grand 19th-century building. It includes an impressive collection of works by the country's most famous painter, Edvard Munch, from the 1880s to 1916. Although rather rambling in its layout, the main part of the collection is housed on the second floor. There is a strong international collection including Impressionist paintings by Manet, Monet, and Degas, Post-Impressionist works by Gauguin and Cézanne, and early 20th-century paintings by Picasso and Braque. The museum also holds an important collection of Norwegian art. Among the paintings on display are some spectacular fjord and country scenes from the 19th-century National Romantic period by leading Norwegian landscape painters, notably Johan Christian Dahl. There are also works by Realist artists such as Harriet Becker, Christian Krohg, and Erik Werenskiold, as well as sculptures by Gustav Vigeland. The Munch room contains such important works as *The Sick Child* (1885) and *The Scream* (1893), the swirling forms and colours of which were to greatly inspire the growing Expressionist movement.

Munch-museet ⑦

Tøyengaten 53. 📞 23 24 14 00.
🚇 Tøyen. 🚌 20, 60. 🕐 Jun–mid-
Sep: daily; mid-Sep–May: Tue–Sun.
♿ ♻ 🌐 www.munch.museum.no

ONE OF SCANDINAVIA'S leading artists, Edvard Munch (1863–1944) left an amazing 1,100 paintings, 4,500 drawings, and 18,000 graphic works to the city of Oslo when he died. Most of these are housed at the Munch-museet, which opened in 1963.

Munch led a troubled life, plagued by melancholy and depression due, in part, to the untimely deaths of his favorite sister and younger brother. He nevertheless remained a highly prolific artist whose intensely psychological work remains one of the great cornerstones of early Expressionist art. Since the Munch-museet is a fairly small museum, only a fraction of his work can be shown at any one time, which prevents it from being overwhelming and means that displays are frequently changed. The core of the collection is the series of outstanding paintings from the 1890s, although other periods of his life are well represented. As well as being a painter, Munch was also a prolific graphic artist, and the print room reveals his talents using etching, lithographic, and woodcut techniques. The museum's basement houses a permanent display of Munch's life and times, and there is also a comprehensive library.

Young Woman on the Shore (1896) by Edvard Munch, at the Munch-museet

View back towards the city across Vigelandsparken sculpture park

Vigelandsparken ⑧

Kirkeveien. 📞 22 54 25 30.
🚇 Majorstua. 🚌 20. 🚋 12.

VIGELANDSPARKEN lies within the larger green expanse of Frognerparken. The park takes its name from the larger-than-life sculptures of Gustav Vigeland (1869–1943), which form extraordinary tableaux of fighting, play, and love. Work on display includes a series of 58 bronzes of men, women, and infants, flanking the footbridge over the river and leading up to his most famous creation, a 17-m (55-ft) granite obelisk of no fewer than 121 intertwined figures depicting the cycle of life. One of Oslo's most visited attractions, the park is a monumental artistic creation that took Vigeland some 40 years of his life to complete. Some other examples of his work can be seen at Vigelandsmuseet near the park or at the Nasjonalgalleriet.

The Bygdøy Peninsula

No TRIP TO OSLO is complete without a visit to the Bygdøy Peninsula, which lies off the western edge of the city. The area offers beaches, walking, numerous historic sites, and fascinating museums. These include a folk museum showing traditional ways of life, the Vikingsskipshuset, which traces Norway's maritime history, and others celebrating the famous Norwegian explorers Roald Amundsen and Thor Heyerdahl.

Frammuseet ⑨

Bygdøynes. 〖 23 28 29 50. 🚌 30.
�︎ 🔾 daily. 🌑 public hols. 📷
🅆 www.fram.museum.no

DESIGNED IN 1892 by Scottish-Norwegian shipbuilder Colin Archer, the *Fram* is best known as the ship that carried Norwegian explorer Roald Amundsen on his epic journey to the South Pole in 1912. The *Fram* was an ideal vessel for this undertaking. Its sides are perfectly smooth, making it impossible for ice to get a grip on the hull. Visitors can ease themselves between the remarkable array of beams in the ship's hull and marvel at the assortment of equipment – ranging from a piano to surgical instruments – that the crew managed to take with them. A series of fascinating displays around the ship relate the history of Arctic exploration.

Kon-Tiki Museum ⑩

Bygdøynesveien 36. 〖 23 08 67 67.
🚌 30. �︎ 🔾 daily. 🌑 public hols.
📷 📷 🅆 www.kon-tiki.no

ON DISPLAY at the superb Kon-Tiki Museum are the unbelievably fragile-looking vessels used by Thor Heyerdahl to make his legendary journeys across the Pacific and Atlantic Oceans. The aim of his voyages was to prove that transoceanic contact was possible between ancient civilisations. The balsawood *Kon-Tiki* raft carried Heyerdahl and a crew from Peru to Polynesia in 1947, confirming his theory that the first Poly-nesian settlers could have sailed from pre-Inca Peru. In 1970 he sailed a papyrus boat, *Ra II*, from Morocco to the Caribbean to prove that the

Thor Heyerdahl's vessel, *Ra II*, at the Kon-Tiki Museum

ancient peoples of Africa or Europe might have had contact with South America. These, and other eventful sagas, are outlined in the exhibition.

Vikingskipshuset ⑪

Huk Aveny 35. 〖 22 13 52 80. 🚌 30.
🚫 🔾 daily. 🌑 public hols. 📷 📷
🅆 www.ukm.uio.no/vikingskipshuset

NORWAY IS best known for its Viking explorers, and this museum contains three beautifully preserved 9th-

century longships. All three were unearthed from burial mounds in Norway, and funeral goods from each of the vessels are on display, including ceremonial sleighs, chests, and tapestries. Viewing platforms allow visitors to study the magnificent 22 m by 5 m (72 ft by 16 ft) Oseberg ship and the slightly larger Gokstad boat, both of which were discovered on the western side of the Oslofjord. Fragmented sections of a smaller boat, the Tune, remain much as they were when they were found on the eastern side of the fjord in 1867.

Norsk Folkemuseum ⑫

Museumsveien 10. 〖 22 12 37 00.
🚌 30. 🚫 🔾 daily. 🌑 Dec 31, Jan 1.
📷 ♿ 🅆 www.norskfolke.museum.no

ESTABLISHED IN 1894, this excellent attraction is devoted largely to Norwegian rural life, and visitors should set aside half a day to view the many (over 150) restored buildings. These include various dwellings, barns, storehouses, and a splendid stave church (c.1200) with typical steep, shingle-covered roofs and dramatic dragon finials. The indoor collections consist of displays of folk art, toys, folk dress, the playwright Ibsen's study, and a pharmacy museum. On Sundays in the summer there are displays of folk dancing, and guides demonstrate skills such as weaving tapestries or baking traditional flatbread.

A reassembled grass-roofed house at the Norsk Folkemuseum

The Vikings

FROM THE 8TH TO the 11th century the Vikings, or Northmen, sailed from their overpopulated fjords in Scandinavia and made their way across Europe, plundering, looking for trade, and offering mercenary service. The Swedes (or Varangians) established themselves throughout the Baltic and controlled the overland route to the Black Sea, while the Danes invaded parts of England, Portugal, and France. The Norwegians, however, were unparalleled in their success, and their adventures became the stuff of Viking legend. After overrunning the Orkneys,

Gold and silver box brooch

the Shetlands, the Hebrides, and parts of Ireland, the Norwegians established colonies in the Faroes, Iceland, and Greenland. They even sailed to the coast of North America.

The Vikings were undoubtedly the most feared Europeans of their day, and their impact on history was immense. Fear of the Viking raid unified many otherwise disparate tribes and kingdoms, and many new political states were created by the Vikings themselves. Despite profiting from the spoils of war, it was their success as settlers and traders that was the Vikings' greatest achievement.

Burial "ships" made of stone for warriors from poorer families, near Aalborg in Denmark

Viking religion *was dominated by the supreme gods Odin (god of war), Thor (thunder), and Frey (fertility). Valhalla was their equivalent of heaven. Warriors were buried with whatever it was thought the afterlife required, and the rich were entombed in ships, often with their servants. Most had converted to Christianity by the late 10th century, but Sweden remained pagan well into the 11th century.*

Frey, god of fertility

The longship *was the main vessel of the Viking raid. Longer, slimmer, and faster than the usual Viking ship, it had a large rectangular sail and between 24 and 50 oars. The sail was used in open sea and navigation was achieved by taking bearings from the stars.*

The prow, curled into a "shepherd's crook," formed a high defensive barrier.

The keel was characteristically shallow to allow for flat beach landings.

The beautifully restored Oseberg ship, unearthed in 1904, on display at the Vikingskipshuset in Oslo

Weapons and armor *were the backbone of Viking culture, so the blacksmith's art was always in demand. Bronze and iron swords were endlessly produced, many of which followed their bearers to the grave. Arrows, axes, shields, helmets, and coats of mail were standard military gear, examples of which survive in pristine condition today.*

Viking helmet with noseguard

Gold armlet

Jewelry design *often showed Arab and eastern European influence, which illustrates the extent of the Viking trading network. Gold and silver were a sign of wealth and prestige, although many ornaments were made of bronze, pewter, colored glass, jet, and amber.*

Picture stones *were memorial blocks that celebrated the glory of dead relatives. They were carved with pictures and runic writing.*

Picture stone from Gotland

View of the waterfront at
Stavanger's attractive marina

Stavanger ❷

🏠 110,000. ✈ 🚢 🚌 🚃
ℹ Rosenkildetorget 1 (51 85 92 00).
🎭 Maijazz (May); Glad Mat food
festival (Jul).

STAVANGER IS best known
today as Norway's major
oil town, with North Sea oil
having provided its prosperity
since the 1970s. Earlier in
its history, in the mid-19th
century, the town grew rich
on herring exports.

Small enough to be seen
on foot, much of the center
of Stavanger is modern. One
exception is the cathedral,
the **Stavanger Domkirke**,
which dates back to the
12th century but has been
restored several times since.
Later 17th-century additions
include a flamboyant pulpit
and a number of huge, richly
carved memorial tablets
hanging in the aisles.

Stavanger's main attraction
is Gamle Stavanger (Old
Stavanger), west of the
harbor. Visitors can wander
down the narrow cobble-
stone streets of this old city
quarter, amid the white-
painted wooden houses,
and imagine life here in the
19th century. An interesting
museum in the town is the
Hermetikkmuseet (Canning
Museum) at No. 88 Øvre
Strandgate, which tells the
story of Stavanger's fisheries.
Overlooking the harbor,
the **Norsk Oljemuseum**
(Norwegian Petroleum
Museum) gives an insight into
North Sea oil exploration.

Bergen and
the Fjords ❸

🏠 233,000. ✈ 🚢 🚌 🚃
ℹ Vågsalmenningen 1 (55 55 20 00).
🎭 Bergen International Festival (May).

SURROUNDED BY no fewer
than seven mountains,
Norway's most westerly port
offers the visitor plenty to do
and see, although it rains
relentlessly here. Founded in
the 12th century, Bergen is one
of Norway's prettiest cities,
with a medieval quarter dating
back to the days when the port
was an important center of
European trade for the all-
powerful German Hanseatic
League. Many of the surviving
Hanseatic buildings are found
on the **Bryggen** (quay), where
brightly-painted old wooden
warehouses – now museums,
shops, and restaurants – make
up an attractive harborside.

Close by the harbor is the
busy Fisketorvet (Fish Market)
where fresh fish, produce, and
local crafts can be found. Also
nearby are the 12th-century
Mariakirken (St. Mary's
Church) and the **Hanseatisk
Museum** – an excellently
preserved late Hansa house
from the 18th century.
Around Lille Lungegårds-
vann, the city's central lake,
are a number of interesting
art galleries. Finally, no
visitor to Bergen should miss
the chance to take a trip up
Mount Ulriken for a panoramic
view of the area. A cable car
takes you from the edge of
the city to the summit.

Elaborate Baroque pulpit in the
Mariakirken, Bergen

ENVIRONS: Sights to see just
outside the city include
Troldhaugen, an enchanting
villa filled with paintings,
prints, and other memorabilia,
where Norway's most famous
composer Edvard Grieg
(1843–1907) spent the later
years of his life and composed
much of his work. A short
way beyond is **Fantoft
Stavkirke**, a traditional,
ancient wooden church,
originally built in Sognefjord,
but later moved here.
Bergen also makes a good
base for viewing the western
fjord scenery, which extends
from south of Bergen to
distant Kristiansund in the
north. Boat trips leave from
Bergen throughout the
summer (a few run year-
round), visiting local fjords.
One of the closest is
Osterfjord, but **Hardanger-
fjord**, with its majestic
waterfalls, is perhaps the most

The stunning scenery of the Sognefjord, north of Bergen

spectacular. To the north, **Sognefjord**, at 200 km (120 miles) long and 1,300 m (4,260 ft) deep, is the deepest and longest fjord in the world.

♨ Troldhaugen
Troldhaugveien 65, Paradis. 📞 55 92 29 92. ⬜ Apr–Nov: daily; mid-Jan–Mar: Mon–Fri. 🎫 ♿ 📷

Trondheim ❹

🏠 150,000. 🚆 ✈ 🚌 🚐
ℹ Munkegaten 19 (73 80 76 60).
🎭 St. Olav Festival (Jul).

CALLED NIDAROS (which means the mouth of the River Nid) until the 16th century, Trondheim has benefited from having a good harbor and being situated in a wide and fertile valley. Founded in AD 997, the city was for many centuries the political and religious capital of Norway, with the earliest Parliament (or *Ting*) being held here. This period saw the construction of Trondheim's most beautiful building – and one of Norway's architectural highlights – the **Nidaros Cathedral**, begun around 1077. Until the Reformation in the 16th century, the cathedral attracted pilgrims from all over Scandinavia. Notable features of this colossal building include the Gothic-style great arched nave and a magnificent stained-glass rose window above the entrance – the work of Gabriel Kjelland in 1930. Since 1988,

Detail from the façade of Nidaros Cathedral, Trondheim

the cathedral has been home to the Norwegian Crown jewels and the modest but beautiful regalia of the King, Queen, and Crown Prince, which are on display in a side chapel.

Another reminder of Trondheim's medieval past is provided by the wharves running alongside the harbor and the narrow streets that wind between brightly-painted warehouses. Although the buildings you see today only date back to the 18th century, the layout of the area is much as it was in earlier times when fishing and timber were the main source of the town's wealth.

Other attractions of the city include Scandinavia's largest wooden building, the **Stiftsgården**, built between 1774 and 1778 as a private home. Today it serves as the king's official residence in Trondheim. The **Nordenfjeldske Kunstindustrimuseum** (Decorative Arts Museum) houses an extensive collection of furniture, tapestries, ceramics, silver, and glassware from the 16th to the 20th century, including a particularly fine collection of Art Nouveau pieces. It also stages exhibitions of contemporary arts, crafts, and design.

🏛 Nordenfjeldske Kunstindustrimuseum
Munkegaten 5. 📞 73 80 89 50. ⬜ Jun–mid-Aug: daily; mid-Aug–May: Tue–Sun. 🎫 ♿

Tromsø ❺

🏔 60,000. 🚆 ✈ 🚌
ℹ Storgaten 61–63 (77 61 00 00).
🎭 Northern Lights Festival (Jan).

SITUATED ABOVE the Arctic circle, Tromsø, the so-called capital of North Norway, is a lively university town. There are not many specific sights and attractions in the town itself, but its fine mountain and fjord setting makes it well worth a visit. The most spectacular time to stay is in

Tromsø's modern concrete and glass Arctic Cathedral

the summer, during the period of the "midnight sun." Due to the high latitude, the sun remains above the horizon from May 21 to July 21, and the sky often glows red throughout the night. Tromsø is also a good place to view the Northern Lights.

Since Tromsø is a compact town, it is possible to stroll through the center, which sits upon a small hilly island reached by a bridge, in around 15 minutes. The major sight here is the striking white **Ishavskatedralen** (Arctic Cathedral). The cathedral is intended to represent the type of tent used by the Sami, the region's indigenous semi-nomadic people. Tromsø's **Polarmuseet** (Polar Museum) documents the history of the local economy – seal trapping played a big part until the 1950s – and polar expeditions, in particular the voyages undertaken by Norwegian explorer Roald Amundsen. Tromsø is a famous starting point for Arctic expeditions, and Amundsen made his last expedition from here to the Arctic ice cap, where he died in 1928. Visitors should not miss the opportunity to take the cable car (Fjellheisen) up the mountain behind the city to get a real sense of the setting of this polar town.

🏛 Polarmuseet
Søndre Tollbugate 11. 📞 77 68 43 73. ⬜ daily. ⬤ public hols. 🎫

Practical & Travel Information

NORWAY HAS A REPUTATION as an expensive destination, but the cost of traveling around the country is fairly reasonable. Norway's public transportation system is comprehensive and reliable, although visitors should expect a reduced service during winter. Once within the Arctic Circle, there is a period around midsummer during which the sun never sets (the "midnight sun"). Conversely, there is a "polar night" around midwinter, during which the sun never rises at all. These effects occur for longer periods the farther north you travel.

TOURIST INFORMATION

NORWAY HAS around 350 local tourist offices, as well as almost 20 regional offices. Visitors to the capital, Oslo, can use the **Norwegian Information Center** in the center of town. For brochures and more general information on all parts of the country, contact the **Norwegian Tourist Board** before you leave home.

As well as providing information on hiking routes and guided mountain tours, **Den Norske Turistforening** (Norwegian Mountain Touring Association) sells maps and hiking gear, and maintains more than 300 mountain huts throughout the country.

OPENING HOURS

MANY ATTRACTIONS are open all year round, although a few have seasonal opening hours. Stores are generally open from 9am to 5pm Monday to Friday, and from 9am to 1 or 3pm on Saturday. Many stores stay open until 7 or 8pm on Thursdays.

VISA REQUIREMENTS

CITIZENS OF THE EU, the US, Canada, Australia, and New Zealand do not require a visa for stays of less than three months. Citizens of most EU countries can use a national identity card instead of a passport for entry to Norway.

SAFETY AND EMERGENCIES

NORWAY IS a safe country, and crime against tourists is relatively rare. Standards of healthcare are excellent. Hotels and tourist offices have lists of local doctors, or you can look in the telephone directory under doctors *(leger)*. You will have to pay a fee for a doctor's appointment and for prescriptions, but EU citizens with an E111 form will be reimbursed for part of the cost of any treatment.

BANKING AND CURRENCY

THE NORWEGIAN UNIT of currency is the Norwegian krone, abbreviated to NOK. Cash and traveler's checks

can be changed at banks and post offices for a small commission. Outside banking hours, you can change money at hotels, some campsites, and (in Oslo) exchange booths, although exchange rates are less favorable. Major credit and charge cards are accepted in most places.

Banks are open from 8:15am to 3pm Monday to Wednesday and Friday, and 8:15am to 5pm on Thursday. Between June and August, they close 30 minutes earlier.

COMMUNICATIONS

TELECOMMUNICATIONS and postal services in Norway are very efficient and reliable. Coin-operated phone booths are gradually being phased out in favor of those that will only take phonecards (Telekort). These cards can be purchased in news kiosks.

E-mail can be collected at the country's growing number of Internet cafés (all major cities have at least a couple) or at most public libraries.

Thanks to state subsidies and loans there is a large number of newspapers in Norway. Most British and some American newspapers are sold in large towns from Narvesen newsstands.

TAX-FREE SHOPPING

VISITORS TO NORWAY can benefit from the nation's decision not to join the EU by taking advantage of the tax-free shopping scheme. This means that if you purchase goods over a certain value from any one of the 3,000 outlets that participate in the scheme you can have the VAT refunded. You will receive a tax-free voucher, which you must present upon your departure from the country. The goods must be unused for you to receive the refund.

ARRIVING BY AIR

MOST INTERNATIONAL flights arrive at Oslo's new airport, **Gardermoen**, 60 km (37 miles) north of the city, although some carriers also

THE CLIMATE OF NORWAY

The climate of Norway experiences intense seasonal changes. The short summer (roughly mid-June to mid-August) can be quite hot, though rain is regular and temperatures in the far north can plunge during the summer nights. Winter is long and dark, and the north is subject to sub-zero temperatures which can persist for months at a time.

OSLO

	Apr	Jul	Oct	Jan
High °C/F	9/48	21/70	9/48	0/32
Low °C/F	1/34	12/54	3/37	-6/21
Sunshine (hrs)	5 hrs	7 hrs	3 hrs	2 hrs
Rainfall (mm)	48 mm	79 mm	99 mm	58 mm

fly to Stavanger, Bergen, Tromsø, and Kristiansand. From Britain, daily direct flights are operated by British Airways, **SAS** (Scandinavian Airline System), and Ryanair. SAS offers direct flights from other major European cities, such as Stockholm, Berlin, and Amsterdam.

Flying to Norway from North America may involve changing planes, although SAS offers a direct service from New York to Oslo.

Domestic flights can be useful if you are short on time – especially if you wish to visit the far north – and are operated by a variety of carriers, including SAS.

TRAVELING BY SEA

FERRIES FROM Germany, Denmark, and Sweden make daily crossings to Norway. It is also possible to travel directly from Newcastle in the UK, but the journey can take as long as 27 hours. Routes are operated by **Fjord Line** and **DFDS Seaways**.

Once in Norway, you are never very far from the sea and local ferries are an invaluable means of transportation across the fjords.

Hurtigruten, the Norwegian Coastal Express service, sails from Bergen to Kirkenes, far above the Arctic Circle, putting in at 35 ports en route. It is a superb way to see Norway's dramatic coastline. Call ferry companies **OVDS** or **TFDS** to make a reservation.

RAIL TRAVEL

MANY RAIL SERVICES link Norway with the rest of Scandinavia and mainland Europe. The major point of entry to Scandinavia from mainland Europe is Copenhagen, where trains cross the new Øresund Bridge before heading to Oslo. Within Norway, the **Norges Statsbaner** (Norwegian State Railroad) operates a more extensive network in the south than in the north, but there are routes to all the major towns.

A Norway rail pass allows unlimited travel on all trains in Norway for a specified number of days in a given period. The pass is available from rail ticket agents in Norway and abroad.

Oslo's Tunnelbanen (T-bane) consists of eight metro lines, which converge in the city center. The system runs from around 6am to 12:30am.

BUSES AND TAXIS

BUSES COVER the length and breadth of Norway, and are useful for getting to places the train network does not reach. Bus journeys are also reasonably priced. Most long-distance buses are operated by the national company, **Nor-Way Bussekspress**.

Taxis are extremely expensive in the cities and towns, but in Oslo the excellent public transportation network generally means that you can avoid having to use taxis at all.

TRAVELING BY CAR

CAR RENTAL is fairly costly, although Norway's main roads are fast and extremely well maintained. All of the major international car rental companies are represented. EU driver's licenses are honored in Norway, but visitors from other countries will need an international driver's license. Road regulations are strictly enforced, particularly those relating to drunken driving.

Due to poor visibility and bad weather, many minor roads in Norway close during the dark winter months.

DIRECTORY

TOURIST INFORMATION

Den Norske Turistforening
📞 22 82 28 00.
🌐 www. turistforeningen.no

Oslo Promotion Tourist Information
Vestbanen, Brynjulf Bullsplass 1, N-0250 Oslo.
📞 23 11 78 80.
🌐 www.visitoslo.com

Norwegian Tourist Board
🌐 www.visitnorway.com

In Norway:
Norges Turistråd,
PO Box 722 Centrum,
N-0105 Oslo.
📞 24 14 46 00.

In the UK:
5th Floor, Charles House,
5 Regent Street,
London SW1Y 4LR.
📞 020-7839 2650.

In the US:
655 Third Avenue,
Suite 1810,
New York 1.
📞 212-885 9700.

EMBASSIES

Australia
Jernbanetorget 2, Oslo.
📞 22 47 91 70.

Canada
Wergelandsveien 7, Oslo.
📞 22 99 53 00.

UK
Thomas Heftyes Gate 8,
Oslo.
📞 23 13 27 00.

US
Drammensveien 18, Oslo.
📞 22 44 85 50.

EMERGENCY NUMBERS

Ambulance
📞 113.

Fire
📞 110.

Police
📞 112.

AIR TRAVEL

Gardermoen Airport
📞 815-502 50.

SAS
📞 815-20 400 (Norway).
📞 0845-60 727 727 (UK).
📞 800-221 2350 (US).
🌐 www.scandinavian.net

FERRY SERVICES

DFDS Seaways
📞 22 41 90 90 (Norway).
📞 0191-293 6215 (UK).
🌐 www.dfds.com

Fjord Line
📞 55 54 88 00 (Norway).
📞 0191-296 1313 (UK).
🌐 www.fjordline.com

OVDS/TFDS
📞 76 96 76 93 (OVDS).
📞 77 64 82 00 (TFDS).

RAIL TRAVEL

Norges Statsbaner
📞 81 50 08 88.

BUSES

Nor-Way Bussekspress
Schweigaardsgata 8–10
(Visitor Centre), Oslo.
📞 815-444 44.

Where to Stay in Norway

Accommodations in norway are not as expensive as might be expected for Scandinavia; almost all hotels offer weekend and summer discounts, which can reduce the cost considerably. Hotel breakfasts are huge, all-you-can-eat buffet affairs, and are normally included in the price. Guests can expect attentive service and neat, spotlessly clean rooms.

		Number of Rooms	Restaurant	Private Parking	Garden or Terrace
Oslo					
Central Oslo: *Norrøna* (K)(K)(K)		93	■		
Grensen 19. **Map** D3. (23 31 80 00. FAX 23 31 80 01. W www.norrona.no This hotel in downtown Oslo has been completely renovated. A café serves Norwegian specialties. There is also a library, gym, and sauna.					
Central Oslo: *Grand Hotel* (K)(K)(K)(K)		289	■	●	
Karl Johans Gate 31. **Map** D3. (23 21 20 00. FAX 23 21 21 00. W www.grand.no The Grand offers tradition, comfort, and style from a prime position on Oslo's main street. Each year, the winner of the Nobel Peace Prize stays here for the ceremony. Comfortable rooms and excellent breakfasts.					
Northwest Oslo: *Holmenkollen Park Hotel Rica* (K)(K)(K)(K)		220	■	●	
Kongeveien 26. **Map** A1. (22 92 20 00. FAX 22 14 61 92. W www.holmenkollenparkhotel.no This grand old-style wooden building offers a breathtaking view over Oslo, and also overlooks Norway's most famous ski jump. Forest trails pass right by the entrance, suitable for hikers in summer and skiers in winter.					
West Oslo: *Gabelshus* (K)(K)(K)(K)		43		●	■
Gabels Gate 16. **Map** C3. (23 27 65 00. FAX 23 27 65 60. W www.gabelshus.no Situated at the heart of a residential area in the embassy district, this is an intimate hotel, recently renovated, with excellent service.					
West Oslo: *Frogner House Hotel* (K)(K)(K)(K)(K)		60		●	
Skovveien 8. **Map** C3. (22 56 00 56. FAX 22 56 05 00. W www.frognerhouse.com An elegant hotel in what was once a handsome 19th-century townhouse. Each of the bedrooms is individually decorated.					
Rest of Norway					
Bergen: *Clarion Hotel Admiral* (K)(K)(K)(K)		211	■		
C. Sundts Gate 3–9. (55 23 64 00. FAX 55 23 64 64. W www.admiral.no Set in a renovated maritime warehouse, the Admiral is one of Bergen's finest hotels, with superb harbor views and a seafood restaurant. Rooms are small but comfortable, with Art Nouveau styling.					
Stavanger: *Skagen Brygge* (K)(K)(K)(K)		110			
Skagenkaien 30. (51 85 00 00. FAX 51 85 00 01. W www.skagenbryggehotell.no Built in the style of an old maritime warehouse – but with more glass – this quayside hotel is well-known for its friendly service.					
Tromsø: *Comfort Hotel Saga* (K)(K)(K)(K)		67		●	
Richard Withs Plass 2. (77 60 70 00. FAX 77 68 23 80. W www.choicehotels.no On Tromsø's beachfront, this hotel lies close to the town harbor and main shopping district. The rooms are basic but comfortable, and are decorated in a contemporary style. ● *Easter & Christmas.*					
Trondheim: *Radisson SAS Royal Garden Hotel* (K)(K)(K)(K)(K)		298	■	●	■
Kjøpmannsgaten 73. (73 80 30 00. FAX 73 80 30 50. W www.radissonsas.com Trondheim's largest hotel is situated close to the town's docks and marina. The many sports and fitness facilities include a gym, sauna, solarium, and whirlpool. Guests can unwind at the jazz club some evenings.					

Price categories are for a standard double room per night, inclusive of breakfast, service charges, and any unavoidable taxes:

(K) under 700 NOK
(K)(K) 700–1,000 NOK
(K)(K)(K) 1,000–1,200 NOK
(K)(K)(K)(K) 1,200–1,500 NOK
(K)(K)(K)(K)(K) over 1,500 NOK

Restaurant
Hotel restaurant or dining-room, usually open to non-residents.

Private Parking
Parking provided by the hotel in either a private car park or a private garage close by.

Credit Cards
Major credit cards are accepted in those hotels where the credit card symbol is shown.

Map references refer to map of Oslo on pp660–61

Where to Eat in Norway

Eating out, and food in general, is often expensive in Norway, especially when the price of alcohol is added to the bill. Lunchtimes are usually simple affairs, consisting of *smørbrød* (open sandwiches) and light pastries. A three-course evening meal at many traditional Norwegian restaurants will often involve soup as a starter and fruits or berries for dessert.

Restaurant	Open Late	Vegetarian Dishes	Fixed-Price Menu	Good Wine List
OSLO				
CENTRAL OSLO: *Kaffistova* (Kr)(Kr) **Rosenkrantz Gate 8. Map D3.** *23 21 42 10.* www.bondeheimen.com Decorated in a modern style, this unpretentious restaurant is part of the Bondesheimen hotel. Traditional Norwegian specialties, homemade bread and cakes, are served from breakfast to early evening. No alcohol.		■		
CENTRAL OSLO: *Kafé Celsius* (Kr)(Kr)(Kr) **Rådhusgata 19. Map D3.** *22 42 45 39.* www.kafecelsius.no A laid-back café-bar in one of Oslo's oldest buildings, offering light snacks such as sandwiches, pasta, and Mediterranean-inspired food. Closed: *Mon in winter.*		■		
CENTRAL OSLO: *Grand Café* (Kr)(Kr)(Kr)(Kr) **Karl Johansgate 31. Map D3.** *24 14 53 00.* www.grand.no/en/rest_grand.asp The old-fashioned formality of this atmospheric restaurant has made it the place to be seen by the fashionable elite. Ibsen spent many hours here during his final sojourn in Oslo. Good for coffee and cakes, as well as main courses.	●	■	●	■
CENTRAL OSLO: *Brasserie A Touch of France* (Kr)(Kr)(Kr)(Kr) **Øvre Slottsgate 16. Map D3.** *23 10 01 65.* This brasserie offers French cuisine in a lively atmosphere. Fixed-price menu available for groups booked in advance. Closed: *Sun; Oct–Apr: lunch; Dec 22–Jan 3.*	●	■		■
CENTRAL OSLO: *Engebret Café* (Kr)(Kr)(Kr)(Kr) **Bankplassen 1. Map D3.** *22 82 25 25.* www.engebretcafe.no Since it opened in 1857, not much has changed in this historic building. The Norwegian and French menu is popular all year round. Closed: *Sun.*	●	■		■
CENTRAL OSLO: *Theatercaféen* (Kr)(Kr)(Kr)(Kr) **Stortings Gate 24–26. Map D3.** *22 82 40 50.* www.hotel-continental.no This famous Viennese-style café is popular with Oslo's intelligentsia and entertainers, with live music and early 20th-century decor. The desserts here are particularly good.	●	■		■
REST OF NORWAY				
BERGEN: *Enhjørningen* (Kr)(Kr)(Kr)(Kr) **Bryggen 29.** *55 32 79 19.* www.enhjorningen.no Enhjørningen (The Unicorn) offers a mouth-watering range of seafood and local Norwegian specialties, all served on the second floor of a superbly restored 18th-century merchant's house. Closed: *Sep–May: Sun; Easter & Christmas.*	●	■		■
STAVANGER: *Sjøhuset Skagen* (Kr)(Kr)(Kr)(Kr) **Skagenkaien 16.** *51 89 51 80.* www.sjohusetskagen.no Monkfish is a specialty at this fine seafood restaurant. The delicious Norwegian-style marinated salmon is also highly recommended. Closed: *Easter & Christmas.*	●	■	●	■
TRONDHEIM: *Bryggen Restaurant* (Kr)(Kr)(Kr)(Kr) **Øvre Bakklandet 66.** *73 87 42 42.* www.bryggen-restaurant.no This traditional Norwegian restaurant has an intimate atmosphere. Seafood is the specialty here, though dishes such as reindeer fillet salad can also be found on the menu. Closed: *Sun, Easter week, Dec 22–Jan 2.*	●	■	●	■

Price categories are for a three-course meal for one, half a bottle of house wine, and all unavoidable extra charges, such as cover, service charge, and tax:

(Kr) under 150 NOK
(Kr)(Kr) 150–300 NOK
(Kr)(Kr)(Kr) 300–450 NOK
(Kr)(Kr)(Kr)(Kr) over 450 NOK

OPEN LATE
Restaurants which remain open with their full menu available after 10pm.

VEGETARIAN DISHES
Available as a starter, a main course, or both.

FIXED-PRICE MENU
Available at lunch, dinner, or both.

CREDIT CARDS
Major credit cards are accepted in restaurants where the credit card symbol is shown.

For key to symbols see back flap

DENMARK

ENMARK IS A PEACEFUL AND PLEASANT PLACE. *Its landscape is largely green, flat, and rural – with a host of half-timbered villages reminiscent of a Hans Christian Andersen fairy tale. It is an easy country to visit – not only do the majority of Danes speak English, but they are friendly and extremely hospitable. Above all, the pace of life is not as frenetic as in some European mainland countries.*

Denmark consists of no fewer than 405 islands and the Jutland peninsula, which extends north from Germany. Located as it is between Scandinavia proper and mainland Europe, Denmark not surprisingly shares characteristics with both. It has the least dramatic countryside of the Scandinavian countries, yet there are also a number of important Viking sites dotted throughout the land. Zealand, the largest island, is the focal point for Denmark's 5.3 million inhabitants, a quarter of whom live in Copenhagen. Funen is a much more tranquil island, its sandy beaches popular with Danish youth. The Jutland peninsula has Denmark's most varied scenery, with marshland and desolate moors alternating with agricultural land.

HISTORY

Although nomadic hunters inhabited Jutland some 25,000 years ago, the first mention of the Danes as a distinct people is in the chronicles of Bishop Gregor of Tours from 590. Their strategic position in the north made them a central power in the Viking expansion that followed. Constant struggles for control of the North Sea with England and western Europe, for the Skagerrak – the straits between Denmark and Norway – with Norway and Sweden, and for the Baltic Sea with Germany, Poland, and Russia, ensued. But thanks to their fast ships and fearless warriors, by 1033 the Danes controlled much of England and Normandy, as well as most trading routes in the Baltic.

The next three hundred years were characterized by Denmark's attempts to maintain its power in the Baltic with the help of the German Hanseatic League. During the reign of Valdemar IV (1340–1375), Sweden, Norway, Iceland, Greenland, and the Faroe Isles came under Danish rule.

Ice skating in the Tivoli Gardens, Copenhagen

◁ **Frederiksborg Slot, a grand Renaissance palace northwest of Copenhagen**

Valdemar's daughter Margrethe presided over this first Scandinavian federation, known as the Kalmar Union.

The next period of Danish prosperity occurred in the 16th century, when Denmark profited from the Sound dues, a levy charged to ships traversing the Øresund, the narrow channel between Denmark and Sweden. Christian IV (reigned 1588–1648), the "builder king," instigated a huge program of construction that provided Denmark with a number of architectural masterpieces, such as the Rosenborg Palace in Copenhagen (see p681).

Christian IV of Denmark (1588–1648)

By the 18th century, Denmark had discovered lucrative trading opportunities in the Far East, and consolidated its position in the Baltic. However, an alliance with the French in the Napoleonic Wars (1803–15) led to the bombardment of Copenhagen by Britain's Admiral Nelson, and King Frederik VI was forced to hand over Norway to Sweden in 1814.

The remainder of the 19th century witnessed the rise of the social democrats and the trade unions. The year 1901 saw the beginnings of parliamentary democracy and a number of social reforms, including income tax on a sliding scale and free schooling.

Denmark declared itself neutral during both world wars, but during World War II the country was occupied by the Nazis, a move that heralded the development of a huge underground resistance movement. Social reforms continued after the war, and in the 1960s laws were passed allowing abortion on demand and the abolition of all forms of censorship. In 1972, Denmark became the first Scandinavian country to join the European Community, and has developed a reputation for addressing environmental issues and supporting the economies of developing nations.

As the 21st century begins, Danish citizens have a high standard of living and state-funded education and health systems, although this has been achieved through high tax bills. Nevertheless, Denmark remains less expensive than either Norway or Sweden.

LANGUAGE AND CULTURE

A North Germanic language, Danish is similar to Norwegian and Swedish, but there are some significant differences in word meaning ("frokost" for example, means "lunch" in Danish, but "breakfast" in Norwegian) and pronunciation. English and German are widely spoken, so visitors should have few problems in making themselves understood.

For such a small country Denmark has produced a number of world-famous writers and philosophers, including Hans Christian Andersen (see p683) and the 19th-century philosopher Søren Kierkegaard, who is claimed to have laid the foundations of modern existentialism. However, it is best known for its 20th-century design and craftsmanship, which have given the country an international reputation. The works of companies such as Georg Jensen silversmiths and Royal Copenhagen porcelain, and the furniture of architect Arne Jacobsen, enjoy a worldwide reputation.

KEY DATES IN DANISH HISTORY

AD 590 First written account of the Danes in the chronicle of Bishop Gregor of Tours

960 Denmark becomes officially Christian with the baptism of King Harald "Bluetooth"

1033 Danes control much of England and Normandy and dominate trade in the Baltic

1282 Erik V forced to grant nobles a charter limiting his powers – first Danish constitution

1397 Queen Margrethe I unites Scandinavia under the Danish throne in the Kalmar Union

1814 Norway transferred from the Danish to the Swedish crown

1849 Under Frederik VII, Denmark becomes a constitutional monarchy

1890s Social reforms lay the foundations of the present welfare state

1914–18 Denmark neutral in World War I

1940–45 Despite declaring its neutrality, Denmark invaded and occupied by the Nazis

1945 Becomes a charter member of the United Nations and signs the North Atlantic Treaty

1972 Denmark becomes the first Scandinavian country to join the EC (now the EU)

Exploring Denmark

COPENHAGEN IS DENMARK'S main attraction, a
small yet lively capital with a considerable
number of sights concentrated in the center.
Outside the capital, the pace of life is slow, and
the flat countryside is punctuated by half-timbered
villages and the occasional manor house. Roads
are of a high standard, and the trains and buses
extremely punctual and efficient. Denmark's lack
of hills makes it an excellent place for cycling.

Tranquil park at Odense, the principal
town of the fertile island of Funen

SIGHTS AT A GLANCE

Aalborg **7**
Århus **6**
COPENHAGEN pp676–81 **1**
Frederiksborg Slot **3**
Helsingør **2**
Legoland **8**
Odense **5**
Roskilde **4**

KEY

✈	Airport
⛴	Ferry port
—	Highway
—	Major road
—	Railroad
---	International border

0 km   40

0 miles   40

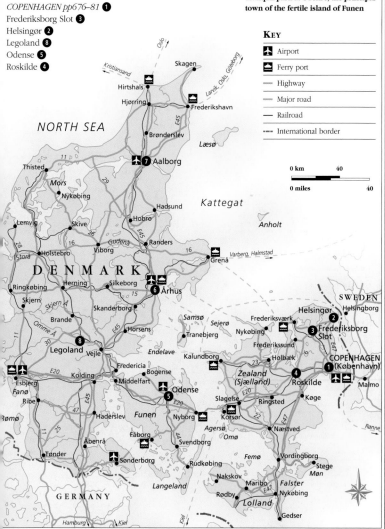

Copenhagen ❶

COPENHAGEN IS Denmark's largest city, with a
population of around 1.4 million. Founded in
1167 by Bishop Absalon, who built a fortress on
the island of Slotsholmen, the town grew quickly,
prospering from trade in the Baltic. In 1461 it was
declared the capital of Denmark. During the reign
of Christian IV (1588–1648), the city was endowed
with many fine Renaissance buildings, some of
which still stand today, including the splendid
Rosenborg Slot and the Børsen. As a change from
sightseeing, visitors can head for the lively,
cosmopolitan shopping area of Strøget, Europe's
longest pedestrian street, or simply relax in one of
the many restaurants and cafés of bustling Nyhavn,
with its charming, gabled townhouses.

**Cannon in the grounds of the city's
16th-century fortress, the Kastellet**

SIGHTS AT A GLANCE

Amalienborg ⑨
Børsen ⑥
Christiania ⑭
Christiansborg Palace ⑤
Kastellet and
  Frihedsmuseet ⑪
Little Mermaid ⑩
National Museum ④
Ny Carlsberg Glyptotek ②
Nyhavn ⑧
Rådhuset ③
Rosenborg Slot ⑬
Statens Museum for Kunst ⑫
Strøget ⑦
Tivoli Gardens ①

SEE ALSO

KEY

▢	Sight / Place of interest
🛳	Ferry boarding point
🚆	Train station
🚌	Bus station
Ⓜ	Metro station
🅿	Parking
🛈	Tourist information
✝	Church
✡	Synagogue
▬	Pedestrian street
→	One-way street

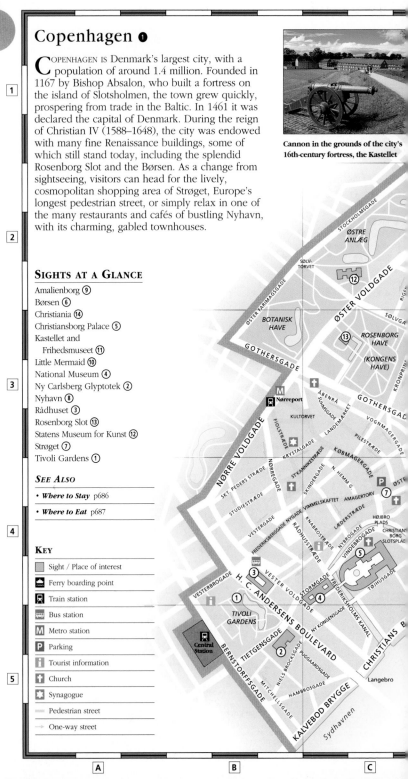

A   B   C

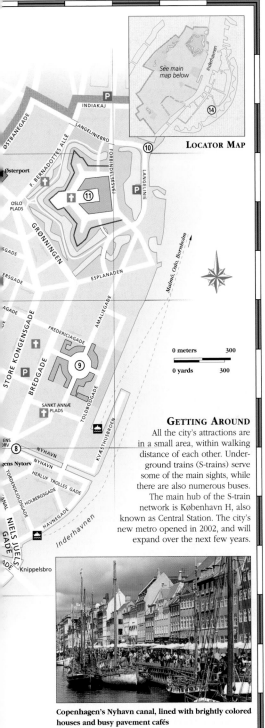

See main map below

LOCATOR MAP

The Nimb building, with its domes and minarets, at Tivoli Gardens

Tivoli Gardens ①

Vesterbrogade 3. **[** 33 15 10 01.
⊠ København H. **🚌** 8, 14, 16, 34.
◯ mid-Apr–Sep: daily; late Nov–late Dec: daily (for Christmas Fair).

Ｏ NE OF COPENHAGEN'S most famous tourist attractions, the Tivoli Gardens opened in 1843. This highly popular entertainment park combines all the fun of fairground rides with fountains and fireworks, concerts and ballets, top-quality restaurants and fast-food outlets. Based on the 18th-century ornamental gardens popular in Europe at the time, Tivoli features Chinese-style pagodas and Moorish pavilions, as well as modern additions, such as the Hanging Gardens and the Bubble Fountain.

Among the many fairground rides are a traditional roller coaster, a ferris wheel, and a "freefall" tower, as well as rides designed especially for children. You can also have fun in the amusement arcades and shooting galleries.

The gardens are at their most enthralling after dusk, when thousands of tiny lights illuminate the park. At night, open-air theaters host all forms of entertainment, from jugglers to jazz bands and performances of Italian *Commedia dell'Arte*. On Wednesdays and Saturdays there is a spectacular fireworks display just before midnight.

A good time to visit Tivoli is between late November and Christmas. At this time, the gardens are transformed into a bustling Christmas fair, where you can sample traditional Danish seasonal fare, buy many specialty Christmas gifts, and ice-skate on Tivoli Lake.

GETTING AROUND

All the city's attractions are in a small area, within walking distance of each other. Underground trains (S-trains) serve some of the main sights, while there are also numerous buses. The main hub of the S-train network is København H, also known as Central Station. The city's new metro opened in 2002, and will expand over the next few years.

0 meters 300
0 yards 300

Copenhagen's Nyhavn canal, lined with brightly colored houses and busy pavement cafés

The richly decorated Neoclassical façade of Ny Carlsberg Glyptotek art gallery

Ny Carlsberg Glyptotek ②

Dantes Plads 7. **(** *33 41 81 41.* 🚉 *København H.* 🚌 *1, 2, 5, 6, 8, 10, 28, 29, 30, 32, 34.* 🕐 *Tue–Sun.* 🔵 *Jan1, Jun 5, Dec 24, 25.* 🖼 *except Wed & Sun.* 🔵 🌐 *www.glyptoteket.dk*

COPENHAGEN'S MOST elegant art gallery was opened in 1897 by Carl Jacobsen, son of the founder of the Carlsberg Brewery, to give more people the chance to see classical art. Housed in a magnificent Neoclassical building, the Glyptotek is best-known for its exquisite antiquities, in particular a collection of Etruscan art and what is claimed to be Europe's finest collection of Roman portraits.

The main building's collections are completed with Egyptian, Greek, Roman, and French sculpture and works from the "Golden Age" of Danish painting (1800–1850). A modern wing, designed by acclaimed Danish architect Henning Larsen, contains Impressionist paintings by Monet, Sisley, Pissarro, and works by David and Bonnard.

Rådhuset ③

Rådhuspladsen. **(** *33 66 70 32.* 🚉 *København H.* 🚌 *8, 14, 16, 34.* 🔵 *Sun, public hols.* 🎫 *in English with* 🖼 *3pm Mon–Sat.*

AT THE EDGE of the Indre By (city center), in the middle of a wide open square, stands the Baroque-style Rådhuset or City Hall, built at the start of the 20th century. A statue of Copenhagen's 11th-century founder, Bishop Absalon, sits

above the entrance. A 300-step staircase leads to the top of the bell tower for a view of the city. The tower also houses the first World Clock. This super-accurate, multi-dialed timepiece, with a 570,000-year calendar, was designed by Jens Olsen and took 27 years to complete. The clock was started in 1955.

The modern, central atrium of Denmark's National Museum

National Museum ④

Ny Vestergade 10. **(** *33 13 44 11.* 🚉 *København H.* 🚌 *1, 2, 5, 6, 8, 10, 28, 29, 30, 32, 34.* 🕐 *10am–5pm Tue–Sun.* 🔵 *Dec 24–25 & 31.* 🖼 *(free on Wed).* 🔵 🎫 *audio.* 🌐 *www.natmus.dk*

LIKE SO MANY of Denmark's museums, the National Museum contains beautifully presented exhibits. The extensive ethnographic and antiquities collections detail Danish history from prehistoric to modern times, and include fascinating exhibits of Viking life. Many of the items on display come from the Danish isles, such as items of jewelry, bones, and even several bodies found preserved in peat bogs,

as well as imposing rune stones with inscriptions dating from around AD 1000. There is also a children's museum and a host of educational activities, all housed in the restored 18th-century royal residence. Close by, and part of the museum, is a Danish home with authentic interiors from the 1890s, complete with decorated panels and carvings, a profusion of paintings, and elaborately carved furniture.

Christiansborg Palace ⑤

Slotsholmen. **(** *33 92 64 92.* 🚌 *1, 2, 6, 8, 9, 10, 28, 29, 31, 37.* 🕐 *May–Sep: daily; Oct–Apr: Tue, Thu, Sat, Sun.* 🖼 🎫 🌐 *www.slotte.dk* **Teatermuseet:** *Christiansborg Ridebane 18.* **(** *33 11 51 76.* 🕐 *Wed, Sat, Sun.* 🔵 *Dec 23–Jan 1.* 🖼 **Thorvaldsens's Museum:** *Porthusgade 2.* **(** *33 32 15 32.* 🕐 *Tue–Sun.* 🖼

SITUATED ON the island of Slotsholmen, the **Christiansborg Palace** has been the seat of the Danish Parliament since 1918, and also houses the Royal Reception Rooms, the Queen's Library, the Supreme Court, and the Prime Minister's Office. Built on the site of a fortress constructed in 1167 by Copenhagen's founder, Bishop Absalon, the palace has twice burnt down and been rebuilt, then altered and extended. Much of this work was carried out during the 18th century under Christian VI, whose elaborate visions were realized both in the architecture and in the lavish interiors. The current palace dates mostly from the early 20th century, and it is possible to visit the Royal

Reception Rooms, the Harness Room, the Stables and Coach House, and some ruins from the original fortress.

Above the riding stables is the Royal Court Theater, built by Christian VI in 1767. Now a museum, much of it has been restored to its original 18th-century appearance. Exhibits illustrate the history of Danish theater up to the present day. The auditorium, with its plush, red furnishings and small, gold side boxes, houses a wealth of memorabilia – including costumes, old theater programs, wigs, and even old make-up boxes and a reconstructed dressing room. The whole theater is dominated, however, by the grand royal box, built for King Frederik VII in 1852. Situated at the back of the auditorium, it seems almost to upstage the stage itself. Unusually, the king's wife, the former ballet dancer Louise Rasmussen, had a private box to the right of the royal box, where she sat if she was alone.

Along the north side of the palace, the **Thorvaldsen's Museum** houses the work of the country's most celebrated sculptor, Bertel Thorvaldsen (1770–1844). After completing his education in Denmark, Thorvaldsen lived for nearly 40 years in Rome, where he gained a worldwide reputation. As well as his own impressive Neoclassical sculptures, the museum houses his collection of antiquities and 19th-century Danish art. There is also a detailed account of his life.

The Børsen, Copenhagen's beautiful old stock exchange

Børsen ⑥

Børsgade. 🚌 1, 2, 5, 6, 8, 9, 10, 28, 29, 31, 37, 43. ⬤ to public.

Built in 1619–40 by King Christian IV, Denmark's old stock exchange is an architectural masterpiece. The building combines tiny windows, steep roofs, and decorative gables, and is topped by a spire representing four intertwined dragon's tails. Originally a marketplace, it became a commodities and stock exchange in the 19th century. Today the building is used only for special occasions, since the modern stock exchange has long since moved to the Strøget. It is not open to the public.

Strøget ⑦

Frederiksberggade to Østergade.
🚉 København H, Nørreport. 🚌 5, 14, 16, 29, 31, 42, 43.

Running between Rådhuspladsen (town hall square) and Kongens Nytorv (marketplace), Strøget (pronounced "Stroyet") is the world's longest pedestrian street. Located at the center of a large traffic-free zone in the heart of the city, Strøget consists of five streets – Frederiksberggade, Nygade, Vimmelskaftet, Amagertorv, and Østergade. The area is home to several exclusive stores, including top international designers Hermes, Gucci, and Chanel. Other stores sell the best in Danish porcelain, modern design, glass, and furnishings – all areas in which Denmark has a world-class reputation.

The best selection can be found in the Royal Copenhagen shopping mall, facing Amagertorv, which includes Royal Copenhagen, Georg Jensen, and Illums Bolighus. There are also many bustling cafés and restaurants, street performers, and musicians, making it a lively place for walking or for relaxing with a coffee. The area is extremely popular with locals and visitors, particularly on a Saturday, but it is still possible to enjoy the atmosphere and admire the many surviving 18th-century buildings.

The impressive Christiansborg Palace, once a seat of royalty and now home to the Danish Parliament

Nyhavn ⑧

Kongens Nytorv. 🚌 *1, 6, 9, 10, 28, 29, 31, 41.*

A NARROW CANAL flanked by a wide promenade, Nyhavn (New Harbor) was originally built 300 years ago to attract trade. It leads up to the Kongens Nytorv (New Royal Market). For much of its history the district was far from inviting, being mainly frequented by sailors, but after the 1970s the area was transformed. The harbor is lined either side with brightly painted town houses, a number of which date from the 18th century. Author Hans Christian Andersen lived in three of them (numbers 18, 20, and 67). Shops, restaurants, and bars have replaced all but one or two of the tattoo parlors that used to be here.

The attractive buildings, as well as the dozens of old wooden sailing ships moored on the water, make Nyhavn a lively and picturesque place to spend an hour or two enjoying a meal or a beer. It is also a good starting point for seeing the city, as some pleasure-boat tours of Copenhagen's canals leave from here.

Changing of Queen Margrethe's guard, Amalienborg

Amalienborg ⑨

Amaliegade. 📞 *33 12 21 86.* 🚊 Østerport. 🚌 *1, 6, 9, 10, 29.* ⭕ May–Oct: daily. 📷 for museum. 📸 call in advance. ♿ **Changing of the guard:** noon daily. 🌐 www. slotte.dk

THE AMALIENBORG (Amalia's Castle) consists of four identical Rococo buildings

Nyhavn, Copenhagen's picturesque and popular harborside promenade

arranged symmetrically around a large cobbled square with an imposing equestrian statue of Frederik V in the middle. The buildings have housed the Danish royal family since 1784, and two of them still serve as royal residences. Changing of the guard takes place every day at noon outside the palace of the present queen, Margrethe II. The palace directly opposite is now a museum and is home to part of the Royal Collection, the bulk of which is housed at the Rosenborg Slot. Some of the official and private rooms have been opened to the public, the latest of which to be shown is the study of Frederik IX. However the highlights are undoubtedly the study of King Christian IX (1818–1906) and the drawing room of his wife, Queen Louise, which are filled with family presents, photographs, and the occasional Fabergé treasure.

There are two attractive, but completely contrasting views from the square. On the harborside is Amaliehaven (Amalia's Garden), with lush greenery and a fountain; in the opposite direction lies the Marmorkirken, a white marble church officially known as Frederikskirken, which has one of Europe's

largest domes, inspired by St. Peter's in Rome. Its construction was begun in 1749 with expensive Norwegian marble, but was not completed until 150 years later (with less expensive Danish limestone) owing to the huge costs incurred. Inside, the church is decorated with many frescoes and statues.

Little Mermaid ⑩

Langelinie. 🚊 Østerport. 🚌 *29.* 🚢 *901, 902.*

THE SUBJECT OF many Danish postcards, the Little Mermaid (Den Lille Havfrue) has become the emblem of Copenhagen and is much visited by tourists. Sitting on a stone by the promenade at Langelinie, and looking out over the Øresund, she is difficult to spot from the road and smaller than her pictures would have you believe. Sculpted by Edvard Erichsen and first unveiled in 1913, this bronze statue was inspired by the Hans Christian Andersen character, who left the sea after falling in love with a prince. The mermaid has suffered over the years at the hands of mischievous pranksters, even losing her head and an arm. Happily, she is currently in possession of all her "parts."

Copenhagen's famous Little Mermaid

Kastellet and Frihedsmuseet ⑪

Churchillparken. 📞 33 13 77 14.
🚇 Østerport. 🚌 1, 6, 9, 29.
Kastellet ⭕ daily. **Frihedsmuseet**
⭕ Tue–Sun. 🎫 May–mid-Sep. ♿

THE GRASSY GROUNDS of this fortress, built by Christian IV in the 16th century (and added to by his successors), are good for strolling around or sitting quietly by the moat. Currently occupied by the Danish army, its buildings are closed to the public, but near the south entrance is the museum of the Danish Resistance Movement (Frihedsmuseet). This charts the German occupation of Denmark in World War II and the growth of the organization that saved more than 7,000 Jews from the Nazis by hiding them in "safe houses" and then helping them escape to neutral Sweden.

Statens Museum for Kunst ⑫

Sølvgade 48–50. 📞 33 74 84 94.
🚇 Nørreport, Østerport. 🚌 10, 14, 42, 43. ⭕ Tue–Sun. 🎫 ♿

THE EXTENSIVE Statens Museum for Kunst (State Art Museum) holds Danish and European art from the 14th century to the present day. Among its many paintings and sculptures are works by Titian, Rubens, Rembrandt, El Greco, Picasso, and Matisse. Danish artists are particularly well represented in the new modern art wing. There is also a vast collection of prints and drawings.

The enchanting Rosenborg Slot, set within magnificent parkland

Rosenborg Slot ⑬

Østervoldgade 4A. 📞 33 15 32 86.
🚇 Nørreport. 🚌 5, 10, 14, 16, 31, 42, 43. ⭕ May–Oct: daily; Nov–Apr: Tue–Sun. ⬤ end Dec, Jan 1. 🎫 🎫

ORIGINALLY BUILT by Christian IV as a summer residence in 1606–7, the Rosenborg Slot was inspired by the Renaissance architecture of the Netherlands. The "builder king" continued to add to it over the next 30 years until the castle looked much as it does today – a playful version of a fortress. The interiors are particularly well preserved and its sumptuous chambers, halls, and ballrooms are full of objects including amber chandeliers, life-size silver lions, tapestries, thrones, portraits, and gilded chairs, making the castle a veritable treasure trove.

Two of the 24 rooms open to the public are stacked from floor to ceiling with porcelain and glass. The Porcelain Cabinet includes examples from the famous *Flora Danica* dinner service made for 100 guests, created by the Royal Copenhagen Porcelain factory between 1790 and 1803. The colorful Glass Cabinet houses nearly 1,000 examples of old Venetian glass as well as glass from the Netherlands, Bohemia, England, and most of the German glassworks.

Christiania ⑭

Bådsmandsstræde 43. 📞 32 95 65 07. 🚇 Christianshavn. 🚌 48. ⭕ daily. 🎫 for prebooked groups only.
Ⓦ www.christiania.org

ORIGINALLY SET UP in 1971, this "free town" is an enclave of an alternative lifestyle: colorful, anarchic, community-based, self-governing, and with an active drug scene. With around 1,000 permanent inhabitants, it has also become Denmark's third largest tourist attraction. Shops, galleries, workshops, cafes, bakeries, and music venues cater for the 500,000 visitors a year.

Modern art wing of the Statens Museum for Kunst

Helsingør ❷

Zealand. 🏃 *60,000.* ⛴ 🚉 🚌
ℹ *Havnepladsen 3 (49 21 13 33).*

H ELSINGØR, OR ELSINORE, lies
at the narrowest point of
the Øresund, the waterway
dividing Denmark and Sweden.
Its attractive medieval quarter
has many well-preserved merchants' and ferrymen's houses.

The town is dominated by
the **Kronborg Slot** (Kronborg
Castle), which stands on a
spit of land overlooking the
sea. It is famous as the setting
of Shakespeare's *Hamlet*,
although the present fortress
dates from the 16th century,
much later than the legendary
Hamlet would have lived.
Highlights include the 62-m
(210-ft) banqueting hall and the
ornate royal chapel. A statue of
the Viking chief Holger Danske
slumbers in the castle cellars –
according to legend he will
awaken to defend Denmark
should the need ever arise.

⚓ **Kronborg Slot**
Kronborg. ☎ *42 21 30 78.*
◯ *May–Sep: daily; Oct–Apr:*
Tue–Sun. 🎫 ☑

Frederiksborg Slot ❸

Hillerød, Zealand. ☎ *42 26 04 39.*
🚉 *to Hillerød, then bus 701 or 702.*
◯ *daily.* 🎫 ⛓

O NE OF SCANDINAVIA'S most
magnificent royal castles,
the Frederiksborg Slot is built
across three small islands

The spires and turrets of the Kronborg Slot, Helsingør

surrounded by an artificial
lake. Created as a residence
for Frederik II (1559–88), the
castle was rebuilt in the Dutch
Renaissance style by his son,
Christian IV (1588–1648).

The vaulted black marble
chapel, where monarchs were
once crowned, sits directly
below the Great Hall, with its
fine tapestries, paintings, and
reliefs. The castle also houses
the National History Museum.

Roskilde ❹

Zealand. 🏃 *52,000.* 🚉 🚌
ℹ *Gullandstræde 15 (46 35 27 00).*

T HE SETTLEMENT of Roskilde
has existed since pre-
historic times. It first came to
prominence in AD 980, when a
Viking king, Harald Bluetooth,
built Zealand's first Christian
church here. Once the center
of Danish Catholicism, the
town declined after the
Reformation. Today Roskilde
is a quiet town, although it
also hosts northern Europe's
largest annual music festival.

The **Roskilde Domkirke**
stands on the site of Harald
Bluetooth's original church.
Begun by Bishop Absalon in
1170, the building is now a
mix of architectural styles.
The cathedral also functions
as Denmark's royal mausoleum
– some 39 Danish kings and
queens are buried here.

Overlooking Roskilde Fjord
is the **Vikingeskibsmuseet**.
This Viking ship museum
contains five reconstructed
Viking ships, first built around
AD 1000, excavated from the
bottom of the fjord in 1962. In
the waterside workshops
Viking ship replicas are built
using authentic period tools
and traditional techniques.

🏛 **Vikingeskibsmuseet**
Strandengen. ☎ *46 30 02 53.*
◯ *daily.* ◉ *Dec 24–25 & 31.* 🎫
📷 *in summer.* ⛓ *call in advance.*

Odense ❺

Funen. 🏃 *185,000.* 🚉 🚌
ℹ *Rådhus, Vestergade (66 12 75 20).*

L OOKING LIKE a storybook
village, Odense is never-
theless Denmark's third-largest
urban center. It lies at the
heart of an area dubbed the
"Garden of Denmark" for the
variety of fruits and vegetables
produced here. The town is
most famous as the birthplace
of Hans Christian Andersen.

Thanks to its compact size,
Odense is easily explored on
foot. The old town contains
some fine museums, including
three art museums, one of
which is dedicated to photography. Odense's showpiece is
the **Hans Christian Andersen
Hus,** where the storyteller's life
is detailed through drawings,

View from the outer courtyard of the Frederiksborg Slot

photographs, letters, and personal belongings. A library contains his works in more than 90 languages. The **H.C. Andersens Barndomshjem** (H.C. Andersen's Childhood Home) shows where Andersen lived with his parents in a room measuring barely 2 m (6 ft) by 1.5 m (5 ft).

⬚ Hans Christian Andersen Hus

Munkemollestræde 3–5. **☎** 65 51 46 01. **◯** mid-Jun–Aug: daily; Sep–mid-Jun: Tue–Sun. **◲ ◪** by prior arrangement only.

Half-timbered buildings at Den Gamle By outdoor museum, Århus

Århus ❻

Jutland. **⬚** 300,000. **✈** 44 km (27 miles) NE. **⬚ ⬚ ⬚ ⬚** Rådhus, Park Allé (89 40 67 00).

DENMARK'S SECOND city and Jutland's main urban center, Århus is small enough to see within a few hours. The city is well worth a visit, however, as it is something of a showcase for innovative 20th-century architecture.

The city divides clearly into two parts. The old town is a cluster of medieval streets with several fine churches. **Den Gamle By**, the city's open-air museum, consists of 60 or so half-timbered houses and a watermill, transported from locations all over Jutland and carefully reconstructed.

In the modern part of the city, the controversial **Rådhus** (City Hall) was built by Arne Jakobsen and Erik Møller in 1941. Its coating of pale Norwegian marble still provokes differing opinions to this day.

⬚ Den Gamle By

Viborgvej. **☎** 86 12 31 88. **◯** daily. **◯** Dec 24–25 & 31, Jan 1. **◲**

Aalborg ❼

Jutland. **⬚** 160,000. **⬚ ⬚ ⬚ ⬚** **ℹ** Østerågade 8 (98 12 60 22).

THE PORT OF AALBORG spreads across both sides of the Limfjord, which slices through the tip of the Jutland peninsula. Aalborg is the leading producer of the spirit aquavit, the fiery Danish national drink.

The well-preserved old town has several sights of interest, including the suitably dark and atmospheric dungeons of the town castle, the **Aalborghus Slot** (1539). The **Budolfi Domkirke**, a 16th-century Gothic cathedral, houses a collection of portraits depicting Aalborg merchants from the town's prosperous past.

Aalborg's best museum is the **Nordjyllands Kunstmuseum** (North Jutland Art Museum). It houses a fine collection of Danish modern art, as well as works by foreign artists such as Max Ernst and Chagall.

On the edge of Aalborg is the important historical site of **Lindholm Høje**. Set on a hilltop overlooking the city, it contains more than 650 marked graves from the Iron Age and Viking Age *(see p665)*. A museum depicting the history of the site stands nearby.

⬚ Lindholm Høje

Vendilavej. **☎** 96 31 04 10. **◯** daily. **Museum ◯** Easter–mid-Oct: daily; in winter: Tue & Sun. **◲ ◪**

Legoland transportation – the colorful Lego train and monorail

Legoland ❽

Billund, Jutland. **☎** 75 33 13 33. **⬚** **⬚** to Vejle, then bus. **◯** Apr–Oct: daily. **◲ ◪**

THE LEGOLAND BILLUND theme park celebrates the tiny plastic blocks that have become a household name worldwide. The park opened in 1968, and more than 45 million Lego bricks were used in its construction.

Aimed primarily at 3–13 year olds, Legoland is divided into different zones. As well as Lego sculptures of animals, buildings, and landscapes, there are many rides and stage shows. Highlights include Miniland, a collection of miniature Lego towns that represent places around the world, and a driving track where children can take a safety test in a Lego car.

HANS CHRISTIAN ANDERSEN

Denmark's most internationally famous writer, Hans Christian Andersen (1805–75) was born in Odense, the son of a poor cobbler. Andersen was admitted to the University of Copenhagen in 1832, and the following year made his debut as an author with his first novel. Several plays and other novels followed but he remains best known for his children's fairy tales, published between 1835 and 1872. Andersen used everyday language, thus breaking with the literary tradition of the time. Some of his tales, such as "The Little Mermaid" *(see p680)*, are deeply pessimistic and unhappy. A strong autobiographical element runs through these sadder tales; throughout his life Andersen saw himself as an outsider and he also suffered deeply in his closest relationships.

Statue of Hans Christian Andersen, Copenhagen

Practical & Travel Information

VISITORS ARE ALWAYS TREATED with courtesy and hospitality in Denmark; the Danes are one of the most tolerant nations in the world, and the Danish concept of *hygge* (coziness) makes the country a very comfortable place to stay. Denmark's travel facilities are plentiful, reliable, and easy to use. There is an extensive rail network and city public transportation services function efficiently. The capital, Copenhagen, is a compact city, which makes getting around by public transport quite straightforward. Since most Danes speak fluent English, you should have no problems with communication.

TOURIST INFORMATION

GENERAL AND location-specific information on all parts of Denmark can be obtained from the **Danish Tourist Board**, which has offices in many countries worldwide, including the US and the UK. Visitors to the capital can obtain brochures, maps, and other useful information at the **Wonderful Copenhagen** office.

OPENING HOURS

MANY TOURIST attractions close on Mondays, and a few have seasonal opening hours. Stores are open 10am to 5:30pm Monday to Thursday, 10am to 7 or 8pm on Friday, and 9am to 2pm on Saturday. Office hours are generally 9am to 4pm Monday to Friday.

VISA REQUIREMENTS

VISITORS WHO are not citizens of a Scandinavian country require a valid passport to enter Denmark. Citizens of the EU may use a national identity card in lieu of their passport. No visa is required for visitors from the US, Canada, the UK, Ireland, Australia, or New Zealand.

SAFETY AND EMERGENCIES

DENMARK IS a peaceful country and street crime is rare, although travelers are advised to take out comprehensive travel insurance. Danish tourist offices and health offices have lists of doctors and local hospitals. For prescriptions (obtainable at a pharmacy or *apotek*) or a doctor's consultation, you will have to pay the full cost on the spot, but EU citizens can obtain a refund by taking their passport and form E111 to a local health office.

BANKING AND CURRENCY

THE DANISH UNIT of currency is the krone (DKr), which is divided into 100 øre.

Danish banks usually open from 9:30am to 4pm Monday to Wednesday and Friday, and from 9:30am to 6pm on Thursday. For the most favorable exchange rates, change money and traveler's checks at a bank. Outside bank opening hours there are exchange booths at post offices, and most airports, main train stations, and ferry terminals. Major credit and charge cards are accepted in most places, and local currency can be obtained with credit or debit cards from cashpoint machines (ATMs).

COMMUNICATIONS

PUBLIC PHONE BOOTHS are plentiful and generally very reliable. Phone cards are becoming common in the larger cities and can be purchased from all post offices and kiosks.

Most post offices open from 10am to 6pm Monday to Friday, and 10am to 1pm on Saturday, although smaller branches may have restricted opening times. Visitors can have letters sent *poste restante* to anywhere in Denmark (some places will even hold mail ahead of your arrival). Cyber cafés are springing up in many of the larger cities.

English-language newspapers are usually available the day after publication at train stations and many of the larger newsagents.

FLYING TO DENMARK

MOST INTERNATIONAL flights arrive at Copenhagen's **Kastrup Airport**, 8 km (5 miles) from the city center. British Airways, British Midland, Go, Ryanair, and **SAS** (Scandinavian Airline System) operate direct flights from Britain. SAS also offers direct flights from New York; most flights from North America, however, require a stopover. **Maersk Air** is the largest Danish domestic airline.

TRAVELING BY SEA

IF YOU ARE considering traveling to Denmark by sea, **DFDS Seaways** operates a ferry service between Harwich in England and Esbjerg, on Denmark's west

THE CLIMATE OF DENMARK

The climate of Denmark is the least extreme of the Scandinavian countries, but the country's close proximity to the sea means that the weather can change very quickly. The summer months are generally sunny; temperatures in July can top 26° C (78° F). Winters are cold and rainy, although not severe, and there may be snow from December to February.

COPENHAGEN

°C/F	Apr	Jul	Oct	Jan
	9/48	20/68	11/52	
	2/36	12/54	6/43	2/36
				-1/30
sun (hrs)	5 hrs	8 hrs	3 hrs	1 hrs
rain (mm)	45 mm	70 mm	60 mm	55 mm
month	Apr	Jul	Oct	Jan

coast, three or four times a week. The crossing takes around 20 hours. Special midweek offers are often available, which can cut the cost of travel considerably.

Norway and Sweden are also well connected to Denmark by sea. Ferries from Oslo call at Copenhagen, Hirtshals, and Frederikshavn, and journeys to Helsingør from Helsingborg in Sweden take just 15 minutes.

Ferries also link all the Danish islands and range in size from the car- and bus-carrying catamarans and ferries of **Mols-Linien**, which travel between Zealand and Jutland, to tiny vessels serving small settlements off the mainland and major islands.

RAIL TRAVEL

L IKE THE REST of the public transportation system in Denmark, the trains are clean and reliable, and are by far the best way to get around. **Danish State Railways** – Danske Statsbaner (DSB) – operates an efficient network that covers most parts of the country, with the exception of Funen and northeast Jutland.

In Copenhagen a local train service, the **S-tog**, provides transportation between the city center and the surrounding areas, including Helsingør.

TRAVELING BY CAR

C AR RENTAL in Denmark is expensive. To rent a vehicle you must be at least 20 years of age, and hold an international driver's license.

Driving in central Copenhagen is not advisable due to the traffic and lack of parking.

The Danish authorities conduct random breath tests on those suspected of driving under the influence of alcohol, and penalties are severe. Denmark's motoring organization, the **Forenede Danske Motorejere (FDM)**, offers a breakdown service.

BUSES, TAXIS, AND BICYCLES

B USES ARE CHEAPER than trains, but on the whole not as comfortable. However, they are useful for traveling to remote areas not covered by the train network. Copenhagen's **HT Kunde-center** has a bus information hotline.

Most taxi drivers speak English, but cabs are often expensive, especially at night and all day at weekends.

Cycling is an excellent way to enjoy Denmark's mostly flat landscape, since traffic is light on the country roads and most towns have cycle tracks. Bikes can be rented at most youth hostels, tourist offices, and bike stores, and at some train stations. In Copenhagen, **Kobenhavns Cykelbørs** is a reliable bike rental store. Contact the **Dansk Cyklist Forbund** (Danish Cycling Association) for more information.

SIGHTSEEING IN COPENHAGEN

I F YOU PLAN to do a lot of sightseeing in Copenhagen, it is worth investing in a Copenhagen Card (valid for one, two, or three days). The card gives unlimited use of public transportation in the metropolitan area (including North Zealand), free or discounted admission to many museums, as well as price reductions with certain car rental companies and on ferry crossings to Sweden.

DIRECTORY

TOURIST OFFICES

Danish Tourist Board
W www.visitdenmark.com

In Denmark:
Bernstorffsgade 1,
Copenhagen V.
C 70 22 24 42.
FAX 70 22 24 52.

In the UK:
55 Sloane Street,
London SW1X 9SY.
C 020-7259 5959.
FAX 020-7259 5955.

In the US:
655 Third Avenue,
Suite 1810, New York.
C 212-885 9700.
FAX 212-885 9726.

Wonderful Copenhagen
Gammel Kongevej 1,
Copenhagen V.
C 70 22 24 42.

EMBASSIES

Australia
Dampførgevej 26,
Copenhagen Ø.
C 70 26 36 76.

Canada
Kristen Bernikows Gade 1,
Copenhagen K.
C 33 48 32 00.

Ireland
Østbanegade 21,
Copenhagen Ø.
C 35 42 32 33.

UK
Kastelsvej 36–40,
Copenhagen Ø.
C 35 44 52 00.

US
Dag Hammarskjölds
Allè 24,
Copenhagen Ø.
C 35 55 31 44.

EMERGENCY NUMBERS

Ambulance, Fire and Police
C 112.

AIR TRAVEL

Kastrup Airport
C 32 31 32 31.
W www.cph.dk

Maersk Air
C 32 31 44 44.
W www.maersk-air.com

SAS
C 70 10 20 00 (Denmark).
C 0845-60 727 727 (UK).
C 800-221 2350 (US).
W www.sas.dk

FERRY SERVICES

DFDS Seaways
C 33 42 33 42 (Denmark).
C 08705-333 000 (UK).

Mols-Linien
C 70 10 14 18 (Denmark).

RAIL TRAVEL

Danish State Railways
C 70 13 14 18.

S-tog Information
C 33 14 17 01.

ROAD TRAVEL

HT Kunde-center (bus information)
C 36 13 14 15.

Dansk Cyklist Forbund
C 33 32 31 21.
FAX 33 32 76 83.

Forenede Danske Motorejere (FDM)
C 45 27 07 07.
FAX 45 27 09 93.

Kobenhavns Cykelbørs
Gothersgade 157,
Copenhagen K.
C 33 14 07 17.

Where to Stay in Denmark

ALTHOUGH DENMARK is a less expensive country to visit than either Sweden or Norway, a large chunk of a traveler's budget will still be spent on accommodations. However, most hotels offer discount rates for summer or weekend stays, and an all-you-can-eat breakfast is included in the price. As many Danish hotels are found in very old buildings, rooms can vary enormously, but are always clean.

	NUMBER OF ROOMS	RESTAURANT	PRIVATE PARKING	GARDEN OR TERRACE
COPENHAGEN				
CENTRAL COPENHAGEN: *Ascot* ⓚⓚⓚ Studiestræde 61. **Map** B4. 📞 33 12 60 00. **FAX** 33 14 60 40. **W** www.dkhotellist.dk A charming hotel with a striking wrought-iron staircase as its centerpiece. Comfortable rooms are equipped with modern furniture and decorated in bright colors. The hotel has a fitness center and a solarium. 🔲 📺 🔲 🔲	165	●		
CENTRAL COPENHAGEN: *Copenhagen Admiral* ⓚⓚⓚⓚ Toldbodgade 24–28. **Map** D3. 📞 33 74 14 14. **FAX** 33 74 14 16. **W** www.admiralhotel.dk A short stroll from Nyhavn, the Admiral was once a grain warehouse, but now offers visitors comfortable accommodations overlooking old Copenhagen. The hotel is equipped with a sauna, solarium, snack bar, and nightclub. 🔲 📺 🔲 🔲	366	■	●	■
CENTRAL COPENHAGEN: *Copenhagen Strand Hotel* ⓚⓚⓚⓚ Havnegade 37. **Map** D4. 📞 33 48 99 00. **FAX** 33 48 99 01. **W** www.copenhagenstrand.dk A modern hotel down by the waterfront with small but extremely comfortable rooms and marble bathrooms. The decor is rustic in style. 🔲 📺 🔲	174	■		
CENTRAL COPENHAGEN: *Phoenix Copenhagen* ⓚⓚⓚⓚ Bredgade 37. **Map** D3. 📞 33 95 95 00. **FAX** 33 33 98 33. **W** www.phoenixcopenhagen.dk The favored lodgings of the Danish aristocracy, this elegant 17th-century hotel lies at the center of Copenhagen's business district. 🔲 📺 🔲 🔲	213	■		■
CENTRAL COPENHAGEN: *D'Angleterre* ⓚⓚⓚⓚ Kongens Nytorv 34. **Map** D3. 📞 33 12 00 95. **FAX** 33 12 11 18. **W** www.remmen.dk A deluxe hotel that was once a palace, this is one of Denmark's finest hotels. Its gourmet restaurant, specializing in Danish and French cuisine, is decorated with glassware masterpieces by the Rosenthal artist Bjørn Wiinblad. 🔲 📺 🔲 🔲 🔲 🔲	123	■	●	
WEST COPENHAGEN: *Ibsens* ⓚⓚ Vendersgade 23. **Map** B3. 📞 33 13 19 13. **FAX** 33 13 19 16. **W** www.ibsenshotel.dk Centrally located in a residential area, Ibsens has been completely renovated, with new furnishings, bathrooms, bar, and breakfast restaurant. 🔲 📺 🔲 🔲	118	■		
REST OF DENMARK				
AALBORG: *Helnan Phønix* ⓚⓚⓚ Vesterbro 77. 📞 98 12 00 11. **FAX** 98 10 10 20. **W** www.helnan.dk The Phønix is the largest and oldest hotel in Aalborg. Rooms are elegantly furnished, and the restaurant serves Danish and international cuisine. 🔲 📺 🔲 🔲	219	■	●	■
ÅRHUS: *Plaza* ⓚⓚⓚ Banegårdspladsen 14. 📞 87 32 01 00. **FAX** 87 32 01 99. **W** www.scandic-hotels.com A few minutes' walk from the harbor, this hotel is encircled by the City Hall park. The in-house Restaurant Brazil serves Latin American barbecues. There is also a bar, as well as fitness facilities with a jacuzzi. 🔲 📺 🔲 🔲 🔲	162	■	●	■
ODENSE: *City Hotel Odense* ⓚ Hans Mules Gade 5. 📞 66 12 12 58. **FAX** 66 12 93 64. **W** www.city-hotel-odense.dk A modern and cozy hotel close to Odense town center. It has no restaurant of its own, but the Old Inn, which serves traditional and French cuisine, has the same owners and is located just around the corner. ● *Dec 20–Jan 6.* 🔲 📺 🔲 🔲	43		●	■

Price categories are for a standard double room per night, inclusive of breakfast, service charges, and any unavoidable taxes:

ⓚ under 1,000 DKK
ⓚⓚ 1,000–1,200 DKK
ⓚⓚⓚ 1,200–1,500 DKK
ⓚⓚⓚⓚ 1,500–2000 DKK
ⓚⓚⓚⓚⓚ over 2,000 DKK

RESTAURANT
Hotel restaurant or dining-room, usually open to non-residents.

PRIVATE PARKING
Parking provided by the hotel in either a private car park or a private garage close by.

CREDIT CARDS
Major credit cards are accepted in those hotels where the credit card symbol is shown.

Map references refer to map of Copenhagen on pp676–7

Where to Eat in Denmark

AN EVENING MEAL can be an expensive proposition in Denmark, especially in the capital. Visitors are advised to have a hearty meal at lunchtime, when a few helpings of *smørrebrød* (Danish open sandwiches piled with meat, fish, cheese, and vegetables) at one of the numerous Danish cafés will reduce the need for a large dinner – without reducing the size of your wallet.

	OPEN LATE	VEGETARIAN DISHES	FIXED-PRICE MENU	GOOD WINE LIST
COPENHAGEN				
CENTRAL COPENHAGEN: *Café Sorgenfri* ⓚ Brolæggerstræde 8. **Map** C4. 〖 33 11 58 80. A 150-year-old basement restaurant in central Copenhagen serving classic *smørrebrød*, pickled herring, and tasty roast pork. Very popular, so be sure to book in advance. ● *Dec 24 & 31.* 🐟				
CENTRAL COPENHAGEN: *Ida Davidsen* ⓚ Store Kongensgade 70. **Map** D3. 〖 33 91 36 55. 〚w〛 www.idadavidsen.dk With the finest *smørrebrød* in Copenhagen, Ida's restaurant serves over 250 varieties of sandwich. ● *Sat, Sun, dinner daily, Jul, Dec 23–Jan 2, public hols.* ♿ 🐟		▧		
CENTRAL COPENHAGEN: *Riz Raz* ⓚ Kompagnistræde 20. **Map** C4. 〖 33 15 05 75. 〚w〛 www.rizraz.dk The specialty of this North African restaurant is the all-you-can-eat Mediterranean buffet, which includes feta cheese, eggplants, olives, hummus, and falafel. ♿ 🐟	●	▧		▧
CENTRAL COPENHAGEN: *Skt. Gertruds Kloster* ⓚⓚⓚ Hauser Plads 32. **Map** C3. 〖 33 14 66 30. 〚w〛 www.sgk.as Entering this restaurant is like stepping back into the Middle Ages. Situated in roomy vaults under the streets of Copenhagen, the Kloster has a selection of "banquet halls" for varying numbers of guests. ● *lunch daily, Dec 24–26, Jan 1.* 🐟		▧	●	▧
CENTRAL COPENHAGEN: *Café Victor* ⓚⓚⓚⓚ Ny Østergade 8. **Map** C4. 〖 33 13 36 13. This exclusive restaurant combines Danish and French cuisines, complemented by an extensive wine cellar. ● *Easter, Dec 24.* 🐟		▧		▧
CENTRAL COPENHAGEN: *Kong Hans Kælder* ⓚⓚⓚⓚ Vingårdsstræde 6. **Map** C4. 〖 33 11 68 68. 〚w〛 www.konghans.dk This Gothic vaulted cellar was at one time the basement of Hans Christian Andersen's house. The present restaurant serves up fantastic French gourmet cuisine. ● *Sun, lunch daily, two weeks Jul, public hols.* 🐟		▧	●	▧
CENTRAL COPENHAGEN: *Krogs Fiskrestaurant* ⓚⓚⓚⓚ Gammel Strand 38. **Map** C4. 〖 33 15 89 15. 〚w〛 www.krogs.com A top seafood restaurant housed in an imposing late 18th-century townhouse. The *bouillabaisse* (fish soup) is recommended. In summer, guests can dine alfresco, enjoying views of Christianborg Palace. ● *Sep–Apr: Sun; Dec 22–26, Jan 1, Easter.* 🐟			●	▧
REST OF DENMARK				
AALBORG: *Duus Vinkælder* ⓚ Østerå 9. 〖 98 12 50 56. This basement bar is a popular place for a drink before or after dinner. *Smørrebrød* and good lunches are always available, and in winter the menu includes *frikadeller* (Danish meatballs) and *biksemad* (potato, meat, and onion hash). ● *Sun.*	●	▧		▧
ODENSE: *Le Provence* ⓚⓚ Pogestræde 31. 〖 66 12 12 96. A restaurant giving a Danish twist to traditional Provençal cuisine. Has specialities such as venison in blackberry sauce. ● *lunch daily, Sun, Dec 24–25.* ♿ 🐟			●	▧

Price categories are for a three-course meal for one, half a bottle of house wine, and all unavoidable extra charges, such as cover, service, and tax:

ⓚ under 200 DKK
ⓚⓚ 200–400 DKK
ⓚⓚⓚ 400–600 DKK
ⓚⓚⓚⓚ over 600 DKK

OPEN LATE
Restaurants which remain open with their full menu available after 10pm.

VEGETARIAN DISHES
Available as a starter, a main course, or both.

FIXED-PRICE MENU
Available at lunch, dinner, or both.

CREDIT CARDS
Major credit cards are accepted in those restaurants where the credit card symbol is shown.

For key to symbols see back flap

1st millennium BC the arrival of more groups, including the ancestors of the present-day Finns, forced the Sami to withdraw northwards to Lapland.

Even before the beginning of the Viking age (8th–11th century AD), Swedes had settled on the southwest coast of Finland, and in 1216 Finland became part of Sweden. Under Swedish sovereignty, the Finnish tribes gradually developed a sense of unity, which would later form the basis for a proud national identity.

From the 13th to the 18th centuries, Finland was a battleground for power struggles between Sweden and Russia. Eventually, Sweden ceded Finland to Russia in 1809, and the territory became an autonomous Grand Duchy of Russia. Helsinki was decreed the Finnish capital in 1812, and by the 1830s the transformation of this rocky fishing harbor into a major Baltic trading city was well underway.

When Czar Nicholas II unwisely removed Finland's autonomous status, a determination to achieve independence took root. This independence was finally won in 1917, aided by the maneuverings of General Carl Gustaf Emil Mannerheim (1867–1951). Mannerheim ousted the Russian soldiers still garrisoned in Finland and thus averted the immediate danger

Statue of General Mannerheim, architect of independence

that the fledging USSR might extend its Communist regime into the country. Finland's declaration of independence was finally recognized by the Soviet government on December 31, 1917.

Between the two world wars, Finland was dominated by a controversy over language. The Finns fought for the supremacy of their native tongue, and the use of Swedish suffered a sharp decline.

Despite its independent status, tensions between Finland and the Soviet Union remained strained throughout the early 20th century. Years of fear culminated in the 1939–40 Winter War against an invading Soviet army, swiftly followed by the "War of Continuation" (1941–44), in which Finland aided German troops against the Soviet Union. Deep suspicion of the Soviet Union continued for decades, but following the demise of the USSR in 1991, Finland reached a new agreement with Russia which pledged to end disputes between them peacefully.

In recent years, Finland has carved for itself a peace-brokering reputation, and has expanded economically through membership of the European Union and the efforts of its entrepreneurs.

LANGUAGE AND CULTURE

What began as a tentative linguistic and cultural exploration of Finnishness in the 19th century has evolved into a confident, outward-looking sense of nationhood. At the heart of Finnishness lies the notion of *sisu*, a kind of courage against the odds, but it also embraces everything in which the Finns take pride, such as the freedom to harvest berries and mushrooms in the forests.

Outdoor pursuits have an important place in the national psyche, especially cross-country skiing, swimming, boating, and cycling. Finland is also successful in some competitive sports, such as long-distance running and rally driving.

In the arts, the music of composer Jean Sibelius *(see p696)* remains Finland's best known cultural export. Finnish architects and designers, in particular Alvar Aalto (1898–1976), are renowned worldwide.

KEY DATES IN FINNISH HISTORY

1155 First Swedish crusade to Finland

1216 Finland becomes a duchy of Sweden

1550 New market town of Helsinki established

1714 & 1721 Russia and Finland are at war

1748 Island fortress of Suomenlinna under construction to defend Finland against Russians

1809 Finland is separated from Sweden and becomes an autonomous Grand Duchy of Russia

1812 Helsinki becomes capital of Grand Duchy

1917 Declaration of independence

1939–44 Russia and Finland at war

1995 Finland joins the European Union

1999 EU Presidency held by Finland

2000 Helsinki is European City of Culture and celebrates its 450th anniversary

Exploring Finland

AFTER MANY YEARS in the tourism wilderness, Finns are working hard to put their country on the map of world travel destinations. Wonderful natural amenities, a manageable and attractive capital city, and excellent public transportation make Finland an easy country to promote. Trains are the most convenient way to get around the country, although long-distance buses are often faster on east–west journeys. Destinations in the populous south are all easy to reach, but in the far north traveling takes more time and planning.

SIGHTS AT A GLANCE

HELSINKI pp692–6 ❶
Savonlinna ❸
Turku ❷

Lake Saimaa sightseeing cruise leaving Savonlinna

KEY

✈ International airport

⛴ Ferry port

— Highway

— Major road

— Railroad

▪▪▪ International border

Helsinki ❶

Finland's capital since 1812, Helsinki is called the "White City of the North," a reference to the gleaming white Neoclassical buildings commissioned by its Russian rulers in the 19th century. It also boasts impressive modern architecture, from the copper, glass, and rock Temppeliaukio Church to the futuristic Kiasma center. The city is at its best in summer, when long days and clear light lift the mood of Finns, and the parks and waterfront cafés fill with lively crowds.

Eila Hiltunen's eye-catching Sibelius Monument in the leafy Sibelius Park

Sights at a Glance

Finlandia Hall ⑦
Helsinki Cathedral ④
Helsinki Central Station ⑤
Kiasma, Museum of
  Contemporary Art ⑥
Market Square ①
National Museum ⑧
Senate Square ③
Sibelius Monument ⑩
Temppeliaukio Church ⑨
Uspenski Cathedral ②

Greater Helsinki
(see inset map)
Suomenlinna Island Fortress ⑪

Helsinki skyline, viewed from the Gulf of Finland

Key

▢	Sight / Place of interest
✈	Airport
⛴	Long-distance ferry
⛴	Local ferry
🚉	Train station
Ⓜ	Metro station
🚌	Bus station
🅿	Parking
ℹ	Tourist information
✝	Church
✡	Synagogue
—	Pedestrian street
→	One-way street

See Also

• *Where to Stay* p700
• *Where to Eat* p701

Getting Around

The center of Helsinki is easily explored on foot. The city's efficient transportation network consists of buses, trams, and a metro system, although the latter is of limited use to tourists. Virtually all bus and tram routes converge on the streets around Helsinki Central Station. Suomenlinna Island Fortress can be reached by ferry only, from Market Square.

KEY

Area of main map

Market Square ①

Head of South Harbor. 🚊 *1, 3.* 🚢
*6.30am–6pm Mon–Fri, 6:30am–4pm
Sat, 10am–4pm Sun.* ⬤ *Sun in winter.*

IN SUMMER, a short season
that must sustain a nation
through a long winter, the
people of Helsinki sun themselves in the cobbled Market
Square (Kauppatori). Looking
out over the harbor, the Finns
while away the hours, eating
sugar peas, strawberries, and
ice cream or drinking coffee.

Finnish craftsmen sell
handmade wares alongside
colorful fish, fruit, and
vegetable stalls. On a good
day, farmers will travel from
many miles away by small
wooden boat to sell fresh
produce, such as berries, new
potatoes, and dill, grown on
their smallholdings, just as
their forefathers did.

Among the fine buildings
surrounding the square are
the blue-painted **City Hall**,
by Neoclassical architect Carl
Ludwig Engel (1778–1840),
and, nearby, the 19th-century
red- and yellow-brick **Old
Market Hall**, which houses
a number of gourmet and
specialist food shops.

Leading westward from the
Market Square area is the
Esplanadi park, a favorite
gathering place for Finns, who
can be seen strolling down
its wide boulevards on long
summer evenings. At the
eastern end of the park is a
bronze statue of a nude,
Havis Amanda (1905) by
Ville Vallgren. Although it is
not known who the woman
was, this famous statue has
become a symbol of the city.

**Stall holder moored alongside the
quay at Helsinki's Market Square**

The red-brick exterior and "onion" domes of Uspenski Cathedral

Uspenski Cathedral ②

Kanavakatu 1. **C** 09-634 267.
P 2, 4. ○ daily. **&** ask the information desk for assistance.

WITH ITS DARK-RED brick exterior, this Russian Orthodox cathedral is a colorful landmark in the ubiquitous white of the historic city center. Its green copper roof and gold "onion" domes make it highly visible on Helsinki's skyline.

Designed in the Byzantine-Russian architectural tradition by A.M. Gornostayev of St. Petersburg, the cathedral was built in 1868. Uspenski is the biggest Russian Orthodox church in Scandinavia, and its spacious interior is resplendent in gold, silver, red, and blue. From the surrounding terrace there is a splendid view over the heart of Helsinki, and the immediate area has been improved by converting old warehouses into restaurants and shops.

The sheer exuberance of the building forms a sharp contrast to the Lutheran austerity of Helsinki Cathedral.

Senate Square ③

P 1, 2, 3, 4, 7.

SENATE SQUARE – *Senaatintori* in Finnish – is the masterpiece of Carl Ludwig Engel (1778–1840). It was built by Finland's Russian rulers in the early 19th century, and a

The steep south-facing steps leading to the Neoclassical Helsinki Cathedral

statue of Czar Alexander II of Russia stands in the center. The entire square is paved with red and grey granite cobblestones. There are reputed to be more than 400,000 of them in total.

The pleasing proportions of the square are best viewed from the top of the flight of steps to Helsinki Cathedral. From here, the **Senate Building** lies to the left. This houses the Council of State, seat of the Finnish government. Forming a symmetrical pair with the Senate Building, the **University of Helsinki** lies to the right. This building was designed by Engel to accommodate the relocated university after the great fire of Turku in 1827. The **University Library** occupies the north-eastern corner of the square.

Adjacent to the square is **Sederholm House** (1757), the oldest stone building in Helsinki. Restored to preserve its original appearance, it is now home to an exhibition which relates the history of the house and of Helsinki.

Helsinki Cathedral ④

Senaatintori. **C** 09-709 2455.
P 1, 2, 3, 4 & 7. ○ daily (Sun: pm only). **&** call in advance.
Crypt ○ Jun–Aug: daily.

THE FIVE GREEN cupolas of the gleaming white Lutheran Cathedral – formally named St. Nicholas' Cathedral – are a much-loved landmark on Helsinki's skyline. Designed by C.L. Engel and built between 1830 and 1840, the Neoclassical building sits at the top of a steep flight of steps. In summer, Finns use the south-facing steps for sunbathing and picnicking.

White Corinthian columns decorate the splendid exterior, which dominates Senate Square. Inside, the cathedral is surprisingly spartan, with little ornamentation to ruffle its austere atmosphere. There are, however, statues of the 16th-century Protestant reformers Martin Luther, Philipp Melanchthon, the great humanist scholar, and Mikael Agricola, translator of the Bible into Finnish. Beneath the cathedral is a crypt, which is now used for concerts and exhibitions, and houses a small café in summer. The entrance to the crypt is at the rear of the cathedral.

Helsinki Central Station ⑤

Kaivokatu. ☎ 0307-20901. ♿

A BUSTLING HUB which connects Helsinki with the rest of Finland, the railroad station is a remarkable building in its own right. Architect Eliel Saarinen won the competition for the design of the building in 1905, but it was not completed until 1919. Clad in pink granite, it features a 48-m (160-ft) clock tower. Imposing, muscular statues by sculptor Emil Wikström guard the station's exterior. The interior is spacious. Carved wooden fittings are noteworthy features, as is the painting by Eero Järnefelt that decorates the Eliel Restaurant.

Lantern-holding statues at Helsinki Central Station

Kiasma, Museum of Contemporary Art ⑥

Mannerheiminaukio 2. ☎ 09-173 36501. 🚌 🚊 3T & many routes. ◯ 10am–8:30pm Wed–Sun, 9am–5pm Tue. ● public hols. 📷 🎫 ♿ Ⓦ www.kiasma.fi

T HIS STRIKING GLASS and metal-paneled building, designed by American architect Steven Holl, was completed in 1998 at a cost of over 227 million Finnish markka. Holl took Arctic light as his inspiration, and the museum is built in a curve to maximize natural light in the exhibition spaces. Kiasma's

The glass entrance to Kiasma, Museum of Contemporary Art

fluid lines and white interior appeal to modernists, and the changing light of the passing day creates a variety of lighting effects. Intended as an exhibition space for post-1960 art, Kiasma also hosts mixed media shows, art installations, and contemporary drama. This modern museum also has an educational role, offering art workshops and a center for children that makes use of the latest technology. Kiasma's inter-disciplinary and inter-national function is reflected in its name – *chiasma* means "crossing point" in Greek.

Finlandia Hall ⑦

Mannerheimintie 13E. ☎ 09-40241. 🚊 3T, 4. 📷 🎫 by arrangement. ♿

C LOSE TO the edge of Töölönlahti Bay is one of architect Alvar Aalto's best-known works. Located at the heart of Helsinki, Finlandia Hall stands in the tranquil setting of Hesperia Park, a popular spot for joggers and walkers.

Aalto designed both the exterior and the interior, and building began in 1967. The concert hall was completed in 1971 and the congress hall was finished four years later. The external cladding of white Carrara marble had to be renovated during the 1990s, as years of exposure to the harsh weather had taken its toll.

The hall is a leading concert venue. In addition to perform-ances by international artists, there are regular concerts by the Helsinki Philharmonic and the Radio Symphony Orchestra. Unfortunately, the concert hall's acoustics are considered poor and efforts are continually being made to remedy this. Visually, however, Finlandia Hall remains striking.

National Museum ⑧

Mannerheimintie 34. ☎ 09-405 09 544. 🚌 🚊 4, 10 & many routes. ◯ 11am–8pm Tue–Wed, 11am–6pm Thu–Sun. ● public hols. 📷 ♿ Ⓦ www.nba.fi

D ATING FROM the start of the 20th century, the National Museum is one of Helsinki's most notable examples of Finnish National-Romantic architecture. The museum illustrates the history of Finland, from prehistoric times to the present day, through a variety of artifacts, media, and displays. Many exhibits are enlivened by film, costumes, and touch screens.

Among the historical artifacts are furniture, jewelry, fabrics, and glassware. One of the highlights is the throne of Czar Alexander I from 1809.

The striking and much-reproduced wall painting by Akseli Gallen-Kallela (1865–1931) in the entrance hall depicts scenes from Finland's national epic, a poem known as the *Kalevala*.

The National Museum of Finland, with its landmark tower

Interior of Temppeliaukio Church, with its copper and glass dome

Temppeliaukio Church ⑨

Lutherinkatu 3. 📞 09-494 698.
🚌 3T. 🔲 daily. ♿

BUILT INTO a granite outcrop with walls of stone, this circular "Church in the Rock" is an astonishing piece of modern architecture. Consecrated in 1969, it is the work of architects Timo and Tuomo Suomalainen. The ceiling is an enormous, domed, copper disk, separated from the rough-surfaced rock walls by a ribbed ring of glass, which allows light to filter in from outside. The austere interior is relatively free of iconography and religious symbolism.

As well as being a major visitor attraction – some half a million people come to admire the church each year – this popular Lutheran place of worship is also used for organ concerts and choral music.

Sibelius Monument ⑩

Sibelius Park. 🚌 24, 18, 14, 14B.
🔲 daily.

THIS STAINLESS STEEL sculpture by Eila Hiltunen (born in 1922) stands on a rocky outcrop in Sibelius Park in Töölö, an affluent area of Helsinki. It was the winning design in a competition held to find a suitable monument to Jean Sibelius, the composer who played such an important role in the development

---

JEAN SIBELIUS (1865–1957)

Composer Jean Sibelius first came into contact with Finnish literature during his student days at the Finnish Normal School in Helsinki. He was particularly affected by the *Kalevala*, the mythological epic of Finland, which remained a constant source of inspiration throughout his lifetime. He soon abandoned his law studies, devoting himself entirely to composing music. By drawing on many aspects of Finnishness in his music, especially landscape and folklore, Sibelius came to represent the emergent nationalism of the late 19th century, epitomized in his tone poem, *Finlandia* (1899). Other major works include seven symphonies and his violin concerto.

Bust of Jean Sibelius on the rock base of the Sibelius Monument

---

of Finnish national identity. Perversely, the monument imitates the one instrument, the organ, that Sibelius is reputed to have disliked intensely. It attracted much publicity, as tastes were then much divided between abstract and figurative art. As a compromise, a small bust of the composer was installed on the sculpture's rock base.

Suomenlinna Island Fortress ⑪

🚢 from Market Square to residential area of island. 📞 09-684 1880.
🔲 by appointment. ♿ limited.

THE SWEDES constructed this island fortress between 1748 and 1772. It is the biggest sea fortress in Scandinavia, and is now a UNESCO World Heritage Site. Designed to defend the Finnish coast, Suomenlinna offered security

to Helsinki's burghers and merchants and enabled the city to flourish. The fortress spans a cluster of six islands and contains about 200 buildings, most of which date from the 18th century. Until the early 19th century, the fortress had more residents than Helsinki.

Today, 900 people still live on the Suomenlinna islands, just 15 minutes away from Market Square. As Helsinki's main tourist attraction, the Island Fortress receives around 700,000 visitors a year. People come to enjoy its cobbled castle courtyards, marinas, and outdoor picnic, walking, and swimming areas. There is a visitors' center at the fortress, as well as many cafés, restaurants, galleries, and museums, including a popular doll and toy museum. Suomenlinna offers that rare experience – a magnificent historical monument which is still very much alive.

Suomenlinna Island Fortress, the largest sea fortress in Scandinavia

Turku ②

🏛 *174,000.* ✈ 🚉 🚌 🚤 🛈
Aurakatu 4 (02-262 7444). 🎷 *Music Festival (Aug).*

A BUSTLING PORT with a modern city center a short distance inland, Turku is the western gateway to Finland. Turku (or Åbo in Swedish) was Finland's principal city during the sovereignty of Sweden, and remains the center of Finland's second language, Swedish. Finland's first university was established here in the 17th century.

Completed in 1300, **Turku Cathedral** is the principal place of worship for the Evangelical-Lutheran Church of Finland. The museum holds many ecclesiastical treasures.

Work began on **Turku Castle** in the late 13th century, but it was in the mid-16th century that the castle reached its prime, during the reign of Duke Johan and Katarina Jagellonica. Around this period the Renaissance Floor, the King's Hall, and the Queen's Hall were added. The history of the castle, and of Turku itself, is presented in the **Historical Museum of Turku**, located in the castle bailey.

Aboa Vetus and **Ars Nova** ("Old Turku" and "New Art") form a double museum. Aboa Vetus is a fascinating exhibition about life in medieval Turku, while Ars Nova is a collection of 20th-century art by Finnish and international artists.

Other attractions include the west bank of the River Aura – largely designed by C.L. Engel, the German architect of much of Neoclassical Helsinki – and the indoor market, where you can try a local specialty – "raisin" or "saltwater" sausage. Archipelago steamship cruises are also available.

♣ Turku Castle
Linnankatu 80. 📞 *02-262 0300.*
🕐 *mid-Apr–mid-Sep: daily.* ● *mid-Sep–mid-Apr: Mon, public hols.* 🎫 *in summer* 📷

🏛 Aboa Vetus and Ars Nova
Itäinen Rantakatu 4–7. 📞 *02-250 0552.* 🕐 *May–mid-Sep: daily; mid-Sep–Apr: Thu–Sun (Sat–Sun only in Dec).* ● *public hols.* 📷 🎫 *in summer.* ♿

The medieval fortifications of Olavinlinna (St. Olav's Castle) in Savonlinna

ENVIRONS: Approximately 16 km (10 miles) west of Turku lies **Naantali**, one of Finland's most popular seaside resorts. The old town is very pleasant to stroll around, and cruises are available from the harbor. Naantali's other attraction is **Moominworld**, a popular children's theme park based on Tove Jansson's creations.

🏛 Moominworld
Naantali. 🚌 *11, 110, 111 from Turku.* 📞 *02-511 1111.* 🕐 *Jun 7–Aug 10: daily; weekends for rest of Aug.* 📷
🖥 *www.muumimaailma.fi*

Exploring the courtyard of the late 13th-century Turku Castle

Savonlinna ③

🏛 *29,000.* 🚉 🚌 🚤 *in summer.* 🛈 *Puistokatu 1 (015-517 510).* 🎷 *International Opera Festival (Jul).* 🖥 *www.savonlinnatravel.com*

A GOOD BASE from which to make excursions into Finland's Saimaa Lakelands, Savonlinna also has charms of its own. Spread over several islands, the town boasts the celebrated medieval castle of **Olavinlinna** (St. Olav's Castle), the venue for the world-renowned Savonlinna International Opera Festival. Lasting a month, the summer festival is a magnet for visitors, who flock to the area to combine culture with nature. Olavinlinna itself is one of the best-preserved medieval castles in Scandinavia.

Founded in 1475, the castle consists of three towers and a bailey with an encircling wall reinforced by more towers. There are two museums: the **Castle Museum** illustrates the history of the castle through various artifacts and exhibits, while the **Orthodox Museum** displays items of Russian Orthodox iconography from both Finland and Russia. The castle has been the main tourist attraction in Finland since the late 19th century.

♣ Olavinlinna
📞 *015-531 164.* 🕐 *daily.* ● *some public hols.* 📷 📷 *(free for children under 7).*

ENVIRONS: The Lakeland area (also known as Savo) is widely considered to have Finland's most beautiful scenery. From Savonlinna harbor, steamships make excursions on lakes Haapavesi and Pihlajavesi.

A half-hour boat trip from Savonlinna lies the village of Lehtiniemi, home of the **Rauhalinna Villa**. This wooden manor house was built in 1900 by a lieutenant general of Czar Nicholas II as a wedding gift for his wife. It is open as a hotel and restaurant in the summer.

Practical & Travel Information

The Finnish are a practical people, and tourists can expect the local information services to be both accurate and helpful. Finland's main cities are all served by an efficient railroad system and regular, inexpensive internal flights. Finns take pride in their public transportation systems and promote environmentally-friendly modes of travel. Cycling and walking in summer and cross-country skiing in winter are an in-built part of the national psyche. The capital, Helsinki, is easy to navigate on foot, by bicycle, or using public transportation.

Tourist Information

For general and location-specific information, get in touch with the **Finnish Tourist Board**, which has offices in major cities all over the world. The Finnish Tourist Board office in Helsinki has information about different parts of Finland in several languages. Helsinki, Turku, and Savonlinna all have a local tourist office.

The best time to visit Finland is between May and September, but winter in northern Finland has its own special, snow-laden charm. Many tourist attractions in Finland close on Mondays, and some have seasonal opening hours.

Visa Requirements

Visitors who are not citizens of Norway, Denmark, Sweden, or Iceland must have a passport to enter Finland. Members of most EU countries may use an official EU identity card in lieu of their passport. Visas are not required for visitors from the UK, Ireland, the United States, Canada, Australia, or New Zealand. At Finnish customs, there is a blue channel for citizens of EU countries.

Safety and Emergencies

Finland has very low crime statistics, although drunks (largely harmless) have been a common sight in Finnish towns and cities for years. Mosquitoes are very active during the summer months near water (which is just about everywhere), but their bites do not carry disease. Tap water is safe to drink.

In case of emergencies the appropriate number to call is listed in the Directory opposite.

Language

Finland has two official languages – Finnish, which is spoken by 94 percent of the population, and Swedish, which is spoken by 6 percent. Road signs and maps are often in both languages and there are different national newspapers for each language, too. Younger Finns invariably speak some English, and are very eager to practise it.

Banking and Currency

The Finnish currency unit was the markka until 2002, when it was replaced by the euro, the common currency of the European Union (*see p15*).

Banks usually open from 9:15am to 4:15pm Monday to Friday. Most international credit cards are accepted in many places all over Finland.

Communications

Post offices in Finland usually open from 9am to 6pm Monday to Friday, although the main post office in Helsinki operates longer hours. You can buy stamps from kiosks and bookstores, as well as at post offices.

Public telephones are found in thousands of locations, and are usually always well maintained. Many take phonecards, available at kiosks and post offices.

Saunas

Many hotels have a sauna, but they are usually electric ones. For a memorable sauna experience, seek out a wood-fired sauna – preferably close to a lake or the sea – or a traditional "smoke sauna" (*savusauna*). The sauna is a popular and family-friendly place in which to relax and unwind – there are over a million in Finland. Helsinki boasts the superb Kotiharjan wood-fired sauna (call 09-753 1535). The Finnish Sauna Society has two wood-fired saunas and three smoke saunas set beside the sea (call 09-686 0560 for more information).

Flying to Finland

Most international flights arrive at Helsinki's **Vantaa Airport**, which is 19 km (12 miles) north of Helsinki. **Finnair** and British Airways both operate daily scheduled services from London Heathrow to Helsinki. Some special "visit Father

The Climate of Finland

In northern Finland (beyond the Arctic Circle), the sun remains above the horizon for a month in summer. This gives Finland its sobriquet "Land of the Midnight Sun." Even in Helsinki, there are almost 20 hours of daylight in summer. In winter, the average temperature falls well below 0º C (32º F), but low humidity makes the extreme cold less raw.

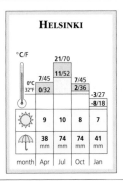

HELSINKI

°C/F	Apr	Jul	Oct	Jan
	7/45	21/70 11/52	7/45	
0°C 32°F	0/32		2/36	-3/27 -8/18
☀	9	10	8	7
☂	38 mm	74 mm	74 mm	41 mm
month	Apr	Jul	Oct	Jan

Christmas" winter flights fly direct from the UK to Rovaniemi on the Arctic Circle. KLM and SAS operate regular flights from Amsterdam and Copenhagen respectively to Helsinki. Travel from North America to Helsinki usually involves connecting flights (changing in Greenland or in Europe) but Finnair flies direct from New York to Helsinki.

ARRIVING BY SEA

THE LUXURY FERRIES that ply the waters between Stockholm in Sweden and the Finnish ports of Helsinki and Turku have a reputation for offering a state-of-the-art cruising experience. The superliners – operated by **Silja Line** and **Viking Line** – take about 13 hours to make the crossing, which allows plenty of time to enjoy shopping, entertainment, and the celebrated *smörgåsbord* buffets.

RAIL TRAVEL

FINLAND'S NATIONAL rail network is run by the State Railroads of Finland (Valtion Rautatiet or VR). Finnish trains are reliable and clean. Advance reservations are recommended for long-distance, intercity (IC), and some express (EP) trains. In

Helsinki, tickets can be bought either at **Helsinki Central Station** or from **TourShop**, which is located at the Helsinki City Tourist Office.

TRAVELING BY BUS

BUSES IN RURAL AREAS are infrequent (but reliable), while intercity buses are fast and efficient. Long-distance journeys are very time-consuming, so it is worth considering the relatively inexpensive domestic flights.

TRAVELING BY CAR

CAR RENTAL has come down in cost since Finland joined the EU. Even so, car hire using the main international agencies is still pricey. **Europcar** offers some of the more reasonable rates.

Laws about driving under the influence of alcohol are strict and rigidly enforced, as are speed restrictions. Elk and reindeer are a serious road danger, so do pay attention to animal hazard signs.

GETTING AROUND HELSINKI

HELSINKI IS manageable on foot or by bicycle, but buses, trams, and the metro provide easy alternatives. The

3T tram circles central Helsinki, stopping at several important sights. Cycle tours, city walks, and cruises are all available from the TourExpert office. Taxis are an expensive way of getting around; ask the driver for an idea of the cost before you embark on your journey.

Finland's island-hopping passenger motorcruisers are a fun form of transportation, giving a real taste of relaxed Finnish summer living.

If you plan to visit several attractions, it is worth investing in a Helsinki Card (available from the Helsinki City Tourist Office and from most hotels). Valid for one, two, or three days, the Card gives unlimited travel on public transportation and on some ferries, reductions on some theater, dance, and opera tickets, and free admission to all major Helsinki sights and nearly 50 museums. Other benefits include reductions on sightseeing tours and on goods in some shops.

Another option is the Helsinki City Transport tourist ticket, which entitles you to unlimited travel on all buses, trams, the metro, and local trains in Helsinki. The ticket is valid for one, three, or five days and is available at all Helsinki City Transport (HKL) points and tourist offices.

DIRECTORY

TOURIST INFORMATION

Finnish Tourist Board
W www.mek.fi
W www.finland-tourism.com

In Finland:
Eteläesplanadi 4,
FIN-00131 Helsinki.
C 09-4176 9300.

In the UK:
PO Box 33213,
London W6 8JX.
C 020-7365 2512.

In the US:
655 Third Avenue,
New York NY10017.
C 212-885 9700.

Helsinki City Tourist Office
Pohjoisesplanadi 19,
FIN-00100 Helsinki.
C 09-169 3757.
W www.hel.fi/tourism

EMBASSIES

Canada
Pohjoisesplanadi 25b,
Helsinki.
C 09-228 530.

UK
Itäinen Puistotie 17,
Helsinki.
C 09-2286 5100.

US
Itäinen Puistotie 14b,
Helsinki.
C 09-616 250.

EMERGENCIES

Ambulance and Fire
C 112.

Police
C 10022.

AIR TRAVEL

Finnair
C 09-818 8383 (Finland).
C 0870-241 4411 (UK).
C 800-950 5000 (US).
W www.finnair.com

Vantaa Airport
C 0200-14636.

FERRY SERVICES

Silja Line
C 09-18041.
W www.silja.fi

Viking Line
C 09-12 351.
W www.vikingline.fi

RAIL TRAVEL

Helsinki Central Station
C 0307-20901.

TourShop
C 09-2288 1500 (Finland).

CAR RENTAL

Avis
C 09-859 8356 (Finland).

Budget
C 09-686 6500 (Finland).

Europcar
C 09-7515 5700 (Finland).

Hertz
C 020-555 2300 (Finland).

Where to Stay in Finland

Finns ARE VERY KEEN on sleek, modern hotels. As a result, Helsinki offers plenty of middle-range and upscale hotels. A general lack of character in city-center accommodations is mitigated by convenience, cleanliness, and efficiency. Most global hotel chains are represented in Helsinki, and the Finnish chain Sokos has several hotels in the capital. Prices often include a morning sauna and swim.

	NUMBER OF ROOMS	RESTAURANT	PRIVATE PARKING	SAUNA
HELSINKI				
CENTRAL HELSINKI: *Hotel Anna* €€€ Annankatu 1. **Map** C4. 09-616 621. FAX 09-602 664. W www.hotelanna.com This small central establishment enjoys a reputation with its regular clientele for being quiet, low-key, and unpretentious.	64		■	●
CENTRAL HELSINKI: *Lord Hotel* €€€ Lönnrotinkatu 29. **Map** D4. 09-615 815. FAX 09-680 1315. W www.lordhotel.fi Formerly a castle called Vanha Poli – constructed in Finnish National Romantic style in 1903 – this granite building has since been given a modern extension, and opened as a characterful hotel in 1990.	48	●		●
CENTRAL HELSINKI: *Sokos Hotel Helsinki* €€€ Kluuvikatu 8. **Map** D4. 09-43 320. FAX 09-176 014. W www.sokoshotels.fi This relaxed hotel, which has stood near Senate Square for many years, was refurbished in 1997. Some rooms have their own private sauna.	202	●		
CENTRAL HELSINKI: *Scandic Hotel Marski* €€€€ Mannerheimintie 10. **Map** C3. 09-68061. FAX 09-642 377. W www.scandic-hotels.com Situated opposite Stockmans department store, this modern hotel is convenient for all city center attractions – shopping, sightseeing, and dining. There is a new Brazilian-style coffee bar in the lounge.	289	●	■	●
CENTRAL HELSINKI: *Sokos Hotel Vaakuna* €€€€ Asema-aukio 2. **Map** D4. 09-43 370. FAX 09-433 77100. W www.sokoshotels.fi Built for the Helsinki Olympics in 1952, this hotel is undergoing discreet renovation work. Located opposite Central Station, the Vaakuna is best known for its 10th floor, which offers a range of dining options and a nightclub.	164	●		●
CENTRAL HELSINKI: *Hotel Kämp* @ hotelkamp@luxurycollection.com €€€€€ Pohjoisesplanadi 29. **Map** D4. 09-576 111. FAX 09-576 1122. Originally a haven for artists and now Helsinki's most exclusive hotel, the Kämp has a health club. Afternoon tea is served in the library.	179	●	■	●
EAST HELSINKI: *Eurohostel* € Linnankatu 9. 09-622 0470. FAX 09-655 044. W www.eurohostel.fi Offering budget accommodations in single, double, triple, and family rooms, the Eurohostel has self-catering facilities and shared bathrooms on each floor. A morning sauna is included in the room rate.	135	●		●
REST OF FINLAND				
SAVONLINNA: *Hotel Seurahuone* €€ Kauppatori 4-6. 015-5731. FAX 015-273 918. W www.savonhotillit.fi Built in 1956, the Seurahuone enjoys lake and market views. The hotel's restaurants and nightclub are a fixture on the local scene too.	84	●		●
TURKU: *Sokos Hotel Hamburger Börs* €€€ Kauppiaskatu 6. 02-337 381. FAX 02-2311 010. W www.sokoshotels.com Recently renovated, the Hamburger Börs enjoys a reputation locally for its seven restaurants and its nightclub. New conference facilities have broadened the appeal of this very well-established hotel.	346	●		●

Price categories are for a standard double room per night, with tax, breakfast, and service included:

€ under €65
€€ €65–135
€€€ €135–200
€€€€ €200–270
€€€€€ over €270

RESTAURANT
Hotel restaurant or dining-room, usually open to non-residents.

PRIVATE PARKING
Parking provided by the hotel in either a private car park or a private garage close by.

CREDIT CARDS
Major credit cards are accepted in those hotels where the credit card symbol is shown.

Map references refer to map of Helsinki on pp692–3

Where to Eat in Finland

HELSINKI RESTAURANTS HAVE all the diversity, quality, and originality that you would expect to find in an energetic capital city. Eating out used to be a prohibitively expensive experience for tourists in Finland, but a wider range of restaurants means that even city-center dining now caters for all budgets. Lunchtime is a good time of day to find bargain set menus throughout Finland.

	OPEN LATE	VEGETARIAN DISHES	FIXED-PRICE MENU	OUTDOOR TABLES
HELSINKI				
CENTRAL HELSINKI: *Omenapuu* € Keskuskatu 6. **Map** D4. 📞 09-6844 0331. 🖳 www.center-inn.fi This restaurant offers a large variety of staple dishes such as meatballs, chicken, and salmon. There is a lunchtime buffet and children's play area. ♿ 🖊	▦	●	▦	
CENTRAL HELSINKI: *Zetor* €€€ Mannerheimintie 3–5. **Map** C3. 📞 09-666 966. 🖳 www.zetor.net Decorated like an old Finnish farmhouse (complete with tractors, cartwheels, log piles, and swings), this restaurant offers food that is similarly hearty and traditional. Meatballs and sausages with mashed potatoes come in giant portions. ♿ 🖊	▦	●		
CENTRAL HELSINKI: *Kappeli* €€€€ Eteläesplanadi 1. **Map** D4. 📞 09-681 2440. 🖳 www.ravintolakappeli.com Several culinary choices exist under one long-established roof – dining room, bar, café, and beer cellar. A confirmed favorite from a menu of Scandinavian classics is sautéed reindeer with mashed potatoes. ♿ 🖊	▦	●	▦	●
CENTRAL HELSINKI: *Lappi* €€€€ Annankatu 22. **Map** C4. 📞 09-645 550. 🖳 www.lappires.com Lappish specialties are reindeer in every shape and form (fillet, tongue, liver, and stew), white fish and salmon, and Lappish coffee served in a wooden cup. A favorite dessert is farmcheese with cloudberries. Book in advance. ♿ 🗏 🖊	▦	●	▦	
CENTRAL HELSINKI: *Ravintola Savoy* €€€€ Eteläesplanadi 14. **Map** D4. 📞 09-684 4020. 🖳 www.royalravintolat.com Architect Alvar Aalto designed the dining room's burnished wood interior in 1937. Modern cooking styles revitalize traditional Finnish dishes. ● *Sat, Sun.* ♿ 🗏 🖊	▦	●	▦	
NORTHWEST HELSINKI: *Elite* €€€€ Eteläinen Hesperiankatu 22. **Map** B3. 📞 09-434 2200. 🖳 www.royalravintolat.com/elite Just on the edge of the city center, Elite is popular with business people at lunchtime and a more relaxed crowd in the evening. Favorite Finnish dishes – such as onionsteak – are embellished with international flavors. ♿ 🖊	▦	●	▦	●
SOUTH HELSINKI: *Saslik* €€€€ Neitsytpolku 12. **Map** E5. 📞 09-7425 5500. 🖳 www.saslik.com The taste and ambience of old Russia are recreated in Saslik's two dining rooms. Live music is played every evening. ♿ 🗏 🖊	▦	●	▦	
REST OF FINLAND				
SAVONLINNA: *Majakka* €€ Satamakatu 11. 📞 015-531 456. This popular restaurant is near the market and the harbor, and overlooks the lake. It serves traditional Finnish food as well as fried local fish. ♿ 🖊		●	▦	●
TURKU: *Teini* €€€ Uudenmaankatu 1. 📞 02-233 0203. In the heart of historical Turku, this relaxed restaurant offers an *à la carte* menu with meat, fish, and poultry served in lovely surroundings. Baltic herring is a traditional favorite. ♿ 🖊	▦	●		

Price categories are for a three-course meal for one, half a bottle of house wine, and all unavoidable extra charges such as cover, service, and tax:

€ under €15
€€ €15–25
€€€ €25–35
€€€€ over €35

OPEN LATE
Restaurants which remain open with their full menu available after 10pm.

VEGETARIAN DISHES
Available as a starter, a main course, or both.

FIXED-PRICE MENU
Available at lunch, dinner, or both.

CREDIT CARDS
Major credit cards are accepted in restaurants where the credit card symbol is shown.

For key to symbols see back flap

CENTRAL AND EASTERN EUROPE

Central and Eastern Europe at a Glance

AT THE GEOGRAPHICAL HEART of mainland Europe, Hungary, Poland, and the Czech Republic have witnessed a huge surge in visitor numbers since the end of Communism in the late 1980s and early 1990s. Despite the widespread destruction caused by two world wars, their towns and cities retain a wealth of historic monuments, many of which have been painstakingly restored to their former glory. Fortunately, tourism has not destroyed the unique cultural identity of these once little-known countries.

Prague (see pp710–21), *the capital of the Czech Republic, is a vibrant city with a rich architectural and cultural heritage. The hilltop castle complex is dominated by the magnificent St. Vitus's Cathedral, whose treasures include many royal tombs.*

Słupsk

Szczecin

Poznań

Wrocław

Karlsbad

PRAGUE ● Kutná Hora

Plzeň

CZECH REPUBLIC
(See pp706–727)

Olomouc

Český Krumlov

Bohemia *(see pp722–3) holds the greatest appeal for most foreign visitors to the Czech Republic. The region boasts elegant spas, fairy-tale castles perched high on thickly wooded hillsides, and many perfectly preserved medieval towns, such as Český Krumlov in the far south.*

Gy

Balatonf

Pé

Lake Balaton *(see p738), a huge freshwater lake in western Hungary, is the country's most popular summer vacation destination. Bordered by dozens of resorts, it offers beaches, safe bathing, and water sports, and also provides a habitat for a wide variety of flora and fauna.*

◁ **Charles Bridge and buildings of the Old Town in Prague, Czech Republic**

dańsk

Augustów •

LOCATOR MAP

•WARSAW

POLAND
(See pp744 – 761)

•Cracow

Warsaw (see pp748–53) *was largely rebuilt during the Communist era following complete destruction in World War II. Many of its grandest buildings date from the Baroque period, including the splendid Royal Castle.*

•Eger

•BUDAPEST

HUNGARY
(See pp728 – 743)

Cracow (see pp754–7), *in southern Poland, has historic monuments spanning hundreds of years, and has been declared a UNESCO World Heritage Site. Its skyline is dominated by dozens of churches, the most important being the Gothic St. Mary's Church in Market Square.*

0 km	75
0 miles	75

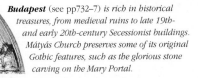

Budapest (see pp732–7) *is rich in historical treasures, from medieval ruins to late 19th- and early 20th-century Secessionist buildings. Mátyás Church preserves some of its original Gothic features, such as the glorious stone carving on the Mary Portal.*

CZECH REPUBLIC

THE CZECH REPUBLIC *is one of Europe's youngest states. In the years after World War II, foreign visitors to what was then Czechoslovakia rarely ventured farther than the capital, Prague. Today the country's beautifully preserved medieval towns and castles are attracting an ever-increasing number of tourists.*

The Czech Republic is divided into two regions, Bohemia and Moravia. Rolling plains and lush, pine-clad mountains, dotted with medieval chateaux and 19th-century spa resorts, characterize the landscape of southern and western Bohemia. In spite of the recent influx of tourists, life here still proceeds at a gentle, relaxed pace. In contrast, much of northern Bohemia has been given over to mining and other heavy industry, with devastating effects on the local environment. Moravia has orchards and vineyards in the south, and a broad industrial belt in the north of the region.

Bohemia's largest city and the capital of the Czech Republic, Prague is a thriving cultural and commercial center that bears little relation to most people's expectations of an "Eastern" European city. Its wealth of magnificent architecture, spanning over a thousand years, has withstood two world wars in the last century.

Since the early 1990s the Czech Republic has emerged as a relatively healthy democratic state. Its economy has been boosted by tourism, and the country, already a member of NATO, has signed up for entry to the EU.

HISTORY

From 500 BC the area now known as the Czech Republic was settled by Celtic tribes, who were later joined by Germanic peoples. The first Slavs, the forefathers of the Czechs, came to the region around 500 AD. Struggles for supremacy led to the emergence of a ruling dynasty, the Přemyslids, at the start of the 9th century. The Přemyslids were involved in many bloody family feuds. In 935 Prince Wenceslas was murdered by his brother, Boleslav. Later canonized, Wenceslas became Bohemia's best-known patron saint.

The reign of Holy Roman Emperor Charles IV in the 14th century heralded a Golden Age for Bohemia.

Rooftops of Prague's Malá Strana (Little Quarter), covered in snow

◁ **The medieval Karlstein Castle, rising above picturesque wooded valleys in Bohemia**

Charles chose Prague as his imperial residence and founded many prestigious institutions there, including central Europe's first university.

In the early 15th century, central Europe shook in fear of an incredible fighting force – the Hussites, followers of the reformer Jan Hus, who preached in Prague and attacked the corrupt practices of the Catholic Church. His execution for heresy in 1415 led to the Hussite wars. The radical wing of the Hussites, the Taborites, were finally defeated at the Battle of Lipany in 1434.

At the start of the 16th century the Austrian Habsburgs took over, beginning a period of rule that would last for almost 400 years. Religious turmoil led, in 1618, to the Protestant revolt and the 30 Years' War. The end of the war ushered in a period of persecution of all non-Catholics and a systematic Germanization of the country's institutions.

Engraving showing the radical cleric Jan Hus being burnt at the stake

The 19th century saw a period of Czech national revival and the burgeoning of civic pride. But, a foreign power still ruled, and it was not until 1918 and the collapse of the Habsburg Empire that the independent republic of Czechoslovakia was declared. World War II brought German occupation, followed by four decades of Communism. In 1968, a program of liberal reforms was introduced, known as the "Prague Spring"; the reforms were swiftly quashed by Soviet leaders, who sent in troops to occupy the country. The overthrow of Communism did not come until 20 years later: in November 1989 a protest rally in Prague against police brutality led to the "Velvet Revolution" – a series of mass demonstrations and strikes that resulted in the resignation of the existing regime. The most recent chapter in Czech history was closed in 1993 with the peaceful division of Czechoslovakia into two independent states – Slovakia and the Czech Republic.

LANGUAGE AND CULTURE

Under the Habsburgs, Czech identity was largely suppressed and the Czech language became little more than a dialect, mainly spoken among the peasant population. In the 19th century, however, Austrian rule relaxed, and the Czechs began rediscovering their own culture. The first history of the Czech nation was written by the Moravian František Palacký, and Czech was re-established as an official language.

Since the Golden Age of the 14th century Prague has prided itself on its reputation as a flourishing cultural center. In the early 20th century the city had a Cubist movement to rival that of Paris. The Czech Republic has produced writers, artists, and musicians of world renown including Franz Kafka, Alfons Mucha, and Antonín Dvořák.

KEY DATES IN CZECH HISTORY

500 BC Celts in Bohemia and Moravia. Joined by Germanic tribes in 1st century AD

AD 500–600 Slavs settle in the region

800 Dynasty of Přemyslids founded

870 Přemyslids build Prague Castle

1333 Charles IV makes Prague his home, marking the start of the city's Golden Age

1415 Jan Hus burnt at the stake for heresy; start of the Hussite Wars

1526 Habsburg rule begins with Ferdinand I

1583 Accession of Habsburg Emperor Rudolf II; Rudolf encourages the arts and sciences

1618 Protestant revolt leads to the 30 Years' War

1627 Beginning of Counter-Reformation committee in Prague

19th century Czech National Revival

1918 Foundation of Czechoslovakia

1948 Communist Party assumes power

1989 Year of the "Velvet Revolution"; Communist regime finally overthrown

1993 Czechoslovakia ceases to exist; creation of the new Czech Republic

Exploring the Czech Republic

ONE OF EUROPE'S most beautiful capital cities, Prague is undoubtedly the highlight of a visit to the Czech Republic. Away from this bustling, cosmopolitan city, however, the tranquil Bohemian countryside is home to dozens of castles and historic towns, whose appearance has remained virtually unchanged for hundreds of years. Most of the main sights of interest can be visited on a day trip from Prague, and are easily reached from the capital by good public transportation and road networks. Slightly farther afield, Český Krumlov merits at least a couple of days' exploration.

Prague's Charles Bridge and the buildings of the Old Town

CZECH REPUBLIC

0 km   100

0 miles   100

GERMANY

Dresden • Liberec

POLAND

PRAGUE (Praha) • CZECH REPUBLIC

Katowice

BOHEMIA

MORAVIA • Olomouc

Ostrava

Brno

AUSTRIA

SLOVAKIA

Vienna (Wien) • Bratislava

---

0 km   45

0 miles   45

Berlin Leipzig

Děčín

GERMANY

Teplice

Liberec

Chomutov

Terezín

Turnov

Žatec

Elbe

Mladá Boleslav

Karlsbad (Karlovy Vary)

Kladno

PRAGUE (Praha)

Poděbrady

Hradec Králové

Marienbad (Mariánské Lázně)

Karlstein (Karlštejn)

Kutná Hora

Pilsen (Plzeň)

CZECH REPUBLIC

MORAVIA

Nuremberg

Vltava

BOHEMIA

Humpolec

Klatovy

Tabor

Jihlava

Strákonice

Písek

Brno

Jindřichův Hradec

Budweis (České Budějovice)

Znojmo

KEY

✈ Airport

— Highway

— Major road

— Railroad

▪▪▪ International border

Munich

Český Krumlov

Vienna

AUSTRIA

Vienna

Linz

Prague ❶

PRAGUE, CAPITAL OF the Czech Republic, has a population of just over one million. In the late Middle Ages, during the reign of Charles IV, Prague's position as the crossroads of Europe aided its growth into a magnificent city, larger than Paris or London. In the 16th century the Austrian Habsburgs took over and many of the Baroque palaces and gardens that delight visitors today were built. Some of these palaces now house important museums and galleries. Prague's Jewish Quarter has a handful of synagogues and a cemetery, which remarkably survived the Nazi occupation. Despite neglect under Communist rule, the historic center of the city has been preserved.

The Three Fiddles, an old house sign in Nerudova Street

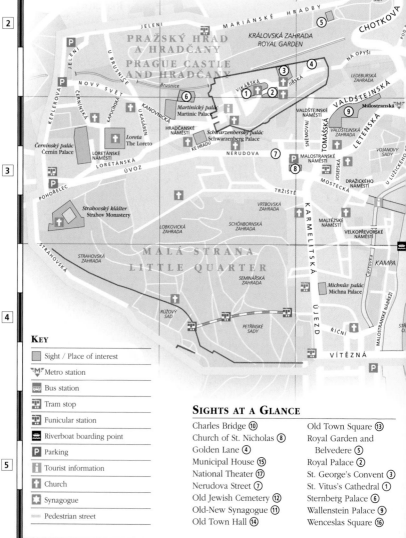

KEY

▨	Sight / Place of interest
Ⓜ	Metro station
🚌	Bus station
🚋	Tram stop
🚋	Funicular station
🚢	Riverboat boarding point
🅿	Parking
ℹ	Tourist information
✝	Church
✡	Synagogue
━━	Pedestrian street

SIGHTS AT A GLANCE

Charles Bridge ⑩
Church of St. Nicholas ⑧
Golden Lane ④
Municipal House ⑮
National Theater ⑰
Nerudova Street ⑦
Old Jewish Cemetery ⑫
Old-New Synagogue ⑪
Old Town Hall ⑭

Old Town Square ⑬
Royal Garden and Belvedere ⑤
Royal Palace ②
St. George's Convent ③
St. Vitus's Cathedral ①
Sternberg Palace ⑥
Wallenstein Palace ⑨
Wenceslas Square ⑯

GETTING AROUND

Prague's subway, known as the
metro, is the fastest way of getting
around the city. It has three lines,
A, B, and C, and 53 stations. Line A
covers all the main areas of the city
center. Trams are the city's oldest
method of public transport. There are
also a number of night trams. Routes
14, 17, 22, and 23 pass many major
sights on both banks of the Vltava.

SEE ALSO

• *Where to Stay* p726

• *Where to Eat* p727

Corner of Old Town Square, with the Church of St. Nicholas

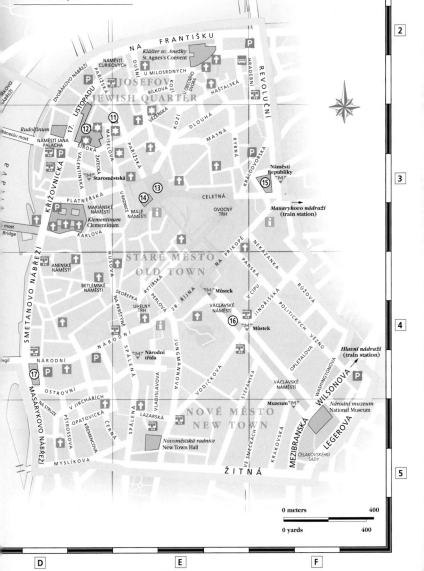

Street-by-Street: Prague Castle

THE HISTORY OF PRAGUE begins with the castle, founded by Prince Bořivoj in the 9th century. Despite periodic fires and invasions, it has retained churches, chapels, halls, and towers from every period of its history, from the Gothic splendor of St. Vitus's Cathedral to the Renaissance additions of Rudolph II, the last Habsburg to use the castle as his principal residence. The courtyards date from 1753–75, when the whole area was rebuilt in Late Baroque and Neoclassical styles. The castle became the seat of the Czechoslovak president in 1918, and the current president of the Czech Republic has an office here.

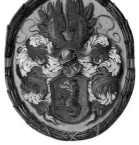

★ Royal Palace
The uniform exterior of the palace (see p714) conceals many fine Gothic and Renaissance halls. Coats of arms cover the walls and ceiling of the Room of the New Land Rolls.

The Powder Tower was used in the past for storing gunpowder and as a bell foundry. It is now a museum.

To Royal Garden

★ St. Vitus's Cathedral
This stained-glass window by Alfons Mucha is one of many 20th-century works of art added to the cathedral.

The Picture Gallery of Prague Castle, in the restored stables of the castle, has a good collection of Renaissance and Baroque paintings.

President's office

To Hradčanské náměstí (Castle Square)

Matthias Gate (1614)

Church of the Holy Rood

Steps down to Little Quarter

KEY

– – – Suggested route

0 meters   60
0 yards   60

STAR SIGHTS

★ St. Vitus's Cathedral

★ St. George's Basilica

★ Royal Palace

South Gardens
Various gardens have been laid out along the old ramparts over-looking the Little Quarter. These statues date from the 18th century.

Dalibor Tower
This grim 15th-century tower takes its name from the first man imprisoned in it, a young knight sentenced to death for harboring outlawed serfs.

Golden Lane (see p714) is lined with picturesque artisans' cottages, built in the late 16th century for the Castle's guards and gunners.

White Tower

Steps down to Malostranská metro

The Lobkowicz Palace houses the historical collection of the National Museum.

St. George's Convent (see p714) houses Mannerist and Baroque art from Bohemia.

★ **St. George's Basilica**
The vaulted chapel of the royal Bohemian martyr St. Ludmilla is decorated with 16th-century paintings.

THE DEFENESTRATION OF 1618

On May 23, 1618, more than 100 Protestant nobles stormed the Royal Palace to protest against the succession of the Habsburg Archduke Ferdinand. The two Catholic Governors, Jaroslav Martinic and Vilém Slavata, were confronted and thrown out of the eastern window along with their secretary, Philipp Fabricius. Falling some 15 m (50 ft), they landed in a dung heap. This event signaled the beginning of the Thirty Years' War. The Catholics attributed the survival of the Governors to the intervention of angels.

St. Vitus's Cathedral ①

Prague Castle, third courtyard.
M *Hradčanská, Malostranská.*
22, 23 to Prague Castle (Pražský hrad) or U Prašného mostu. ⬜ *daily (except during services).* ♿ **Steeple** ⬜ *daily.* ⬤ *in bad weather.* 📷

WORK BEGAN on the city's most distinctive landmark in 1344 on the orders of John of Luxemburg. The Gothic cathedral replaced an earlier Romanesque basilica that stood on the site of a small rotunda dating back to the time of St. Wenceslas (c.925). The first architect of the new Gothic structure was the Frenchman Matthew of Arras. After his death, the Swabian Peter Parler took over. The eastern end of the cathedral dates from this period. The original entrance was the Golden Portal on the south side of the building. The present entrance, the western end of the nave, and the façade with its twin spires were added in 1872–1929.

The chapels house many saintly relics, the Bohemian crown jewels, and a number of royal tombs. The tomb of "Good King" Wenceslas stands in the St. Wenceslas Chapel, which is decorated with Gothic frescoes. Another spectacular memorial is the huge silver tomb (1736) of St. John Nepomuk, whose cult was encouraged during the Counter-Reformation.

Spectacularly vaulted chancel of St. Vitus's Cathedral

Royal Palace ②

Prague Castle, third courtyard. **℡** 22-
43 73 368. **W** www.hrad.cz
M Hradčanská, Malostranská.
☰ 22, 23. **○** daily. 🎫 🚻

FROM THE TIME Prague Castle
was first fortified in stone
in the 11th century, the Royal
Palace was the seat of a long
line of Bohemian kings.

The building consists of
three different architectural
layers. A Romanesque palace,
built around 1135, forms the
basement of the present
structure. In the course of the
next 200 years, two further
palaces were built above this –
the first by Přemysl Otakar II
in 1253, and the second by
Charles IV in 1340. On the
top floor, and dominating the
entire palace structure, is the
massive Gothic Vladislav Hall,
with its splendid rib vaulting.
Designed by Benedikt Ried for
King Vladislav Jagiello, the
hall was completed in 1502.
The Riders' Staircase, just off
one side of the hall, is a flight
of wide sloping steps with a
magnificent Gothic rib-vaulted
ceiling. It was used by knights
on horseback to get to the
hall for jousting contests.

Under Habsburg rule, the
palace housed government
offices, courts, and the old
Bohemian Diet (seat of the
parliament). The Bohemian
Chancellery, the former royal
offices of the Habsburgs, is
the site of the famous 1618
defenestration (see p713). In
1619 the Bohemian nobles
deposed Emperor Ferdinand II

**The Riders' Staircase leading to
the Vladislav Hall, Royal Palace**

**Simeon and the Infant Jesus (1725) by the
Baroque painter Petr Brandl**

as King of Bohemia, electing
in his place Frederick of the
Palatinate. This led to the
Battle of the White Mountain
(1620), the first major battle of
the Thirty Years' War, fought
just outside Prague. The defeat
of the Bohemians ushered in
a period of persecution of all
non-Catholics and the
systematic Germanization of
the country's institutions.

Also worth seeing at the
Royal Palace are the New
Land Rolls, a set of rooms
decorated with the crests of
clerks who worked here from
1561 to 1774, and the All
Saints' Chapel, built by Peter
Parler for Charles IV.

St. George's Convent ③

Prague Castle, Jiřské náměstí. **℡** 25-75
31 644. **M** Hradčanská, Malostranská.
☰ 22, 23. **○** Tue–Sun. 🎫

BOHEMIA'S FIRST convent was
founded here in 973 by
Prince Boleslav II. Rebuilt
over the centuries, it was
finally abolished in 1782 when
it was converted into barracks.
Today, the convent holds a
fine collection of Bohemian
art dating from the era of the
Habsburg Emperor Rudolph II
to the end of the Baroque.

With his passion for the
unusual and the artificial,
Rudolph loved Mannerist
artists and invited many to

work at his court
in Prague. The
emperor's great
collection was
dispersed when
Prague Castle was
looted in 1648, but
the few works on
show here give an
idea of his tastes.
Among the best are
the paintings of the
German-born Hans
von Aachen and
the sculptures of
the Dutch-born
Adriaen de Vries.

The gallery of the
Baroque period
contains some
excellent religious
canvases by Petr
Brandl, including the
particularly moving
painting Simeon and the
Infant Jesus, as well as several
masterly portraits by Karel
Škréta and Jan Kupecký.

Adjoining the convent,
St. George's Basilica was
founded by Prince Vratislav
in 920 and is the best-
preserved Romanesque
church in Prague. The huge
twin towers and austere
interior have been restored to
give an idea of the church's
original appearance. The rusty
red façade was a 17th-century
Baroque addition.

Golden Lane ④

M Hradčanská, Malostranská.
☰ 22, 23. 🎫

NAMED AFTER the goldsmiths
who lived here in the
17th century, this is one of
the most picturesque streets
in Prague. The tiny, brightly
painted houses that line one
side of it were built in the late
1500s for Rudolph II's castle
guards. A century later the
goldsmiths moved in. By the
19th century the area had
degenerated into a slum,
populated by Prague's poor
and the criminal community.
In the 1950s the area was
restored to something like its
original state, and most of the
houses were converted into
shops selling books, Bohemian
glass, and other souvenirs for
the tourists who flock here.

Golden Lane has been home to a number of well-known writers, including Franz Kafka (1883–1924), who stayed at No. 22 for a few months between 1916 and 1917.

Royal Garden and Belvedere ⑤

Prague Castle, U Prašného mostu. Ⓜ *Hradčanská, Malostranská.* 🚋 *22, 23.* **Garden** ⏲ *May–Oct: daily.* 🎫 ♿ **Belvedere** ⏲ *only for exhibitions.* 🎫 ♿ Ⓦ *www.hrad.cz*

P RAGUE'S WELL-KEPT Royal Garden was created in 1535 for Ferdinand I. The garden contains some fine examples of 16th-century architecture, including the Belvedere, a beautiful arcaded summerhouse with slender Ionic columns and a blue-green copper roof. Also known as the Royal Summer Palace (Královský letohrádek), the Italian Renaissance building was commissioned in the mid-16th century for Ferdinand's wife. It is now used as an art gallery. In front of it is the Singing Fountain, which owes its name to the musical sound the water makes as it hits the bronze bowl.

Also in the garden is the Ball Game Hall (Míčovna), built in 1569, and used primarily for playing a form of real tennis.

At the entrance to the garden, the Lion Court was where Rudolph II had his zoo (now a restaurant).

Artisans' cottages on Golden Lane, Prague Castle

Sternberg Palace ⑥

Hradčanské náměstí 15. 📞 *22-05 14 598.* Ⓜ *Hradčanská, Malostranská.* 🚋 *22, 23 to Pohořelec or Prague Castle.* ⏲ *Tue–Sun.* 🎫 🗲 Ⓦ *www.ngprague.cz*

F RANZ JOSEF STERNBERG founded the Society of Patriotic Friends of the Arts in Bohemia in 1796. Fellow noblemen would lend their finest pictures and sculpture to the society, which had its headquarters in the early 18th-century Sternberg Palace. Since 1949 the fine Baroque building has been used to house the National Gallery's collection of European art.

The palace has an impressive array of exhibits, including some particularly fine examples of Italian medieval art, Neapolitan works of the 17th and 18th centuries, Dutch and Flemish masterpieces, and German art of the 15th to 17th centuries. The 19th- and 20th-century exhibits, including works by Klimt, Picasso, and Miró, were moved to the Veletržní Palace, northeast of the city center, in 1996.

Among the highlights at the palace are Albrecht Dürer's *The Feast of the Rosary* (1506), *Head of Christ*, painted by El Greco in the 1590s, and Rembrandt's *Scholar in his Study* (1634).

Visitors can also see a collection of Renaissance bronzes, as well as the fascinating Chinese Cabinet. This richly decorated chamber, which combines the Baroque style with Far Eastern motifs, is now on display again after several years of restoration work.

The Belvedere, Emperor Ferdinand I's summer palace in the Royal Garden beside Prague Castle

Malá Strana

MALÁ STRANA (THE LITTLE QUARTER) is the part of Prague that has been least affected by recent history. Hardly any new building has taken place here since the 18th century, and the quarter is rich in splendid Baroque palaces and churches, and old houses with attractive signs. Founded in 1257, it is built on the slopes below the castle, enjoying magnificent views across the river to the Old Town. The center of Malá Strana is Little Quarter Square, dominated by the impressive Church of St. Nicholas.

Cupola and bell tower of the Church of St. Nicholas

Sign of Jan Neruda's house, At the Two Suns, 47 Nerudova Street

Nerudova Street ⑦

M *Malostranská.* 🚋 *12, 22, 23.*

THIS NARROW picturesque street is named after the 19th-century writer Jan Neruda, who wrote many short stories set in this part of Prague. He lived in the house known as At the Two Suns (No. 47) between 1845 and 1857.

Before the introduction of house numbers in 1770, the city's houses were distinguished by signs. Nerudova's houses have a splendid selection of heraldic beasts and emblems. Ones to look for in particular

are the Red Eagle (No. 6), the Three Fiddles (No. 12), the Golden Horseshoe (No. 34), the Green Lobster (No. 43), and the White Swan (No. 49).

Nerudova Street also has a number of grand Baroque buildings, including the Thun-Hohenstein Palace (No. 20) – now the Italian embassy – and the Morzin Palace (No. 5) – home of the Romanian embassy. The latter has an interesting façade featuring two massive statues of Moors.

Church of St. Nicholas ⑧

Malostranské náměstí. **C** 25-75 34 215. **M** *Malostranská.* 🚋 *12, 22, 23.* 🕐 *daily.* 📷 ✔

DOMINATING Little Quarter Square, at the heart of Malá Strana, is the Church of St. Nicholas. Begun in 1703, it is the acknowledged master-

piece of architects Christoph and Kilian Ignaz Dientzenhofer, who were responsible for the greatest examples of Jesuit-influenced Baroque architecture in Prague. Neither father nor son lived to see the completion of the church – their work was finished in 1761 by Kilian's son-in-law, Anselmo Lurago.

Among the many works of art inside the church is Franz Palko's magnificent fresco, *The Celebration of the Holy Trinity*, which fills the 70-m (230-ft) high dome. A fresco of St. Cecilia, patron saint of music, watches over the church's splendid Baroque organ. Built in 1746, it was played by Mozart in 1787. Another star feature is the ornate 18th-century pulpit, lavishly adorned with golden cherubs. The impressive statues of the Church Fathers, which stand at the four corners of the crossing, are the work of Ignaz Platzer, as is the statue of St. Nicholas that graces the high altar.

Wallenstein Palace ⑨

Valdštejnský Palác, Valdštejnské náměstí 4. **C** 25-70 71 111. **W** www.senat.cz **M** *Malostranská.* 🚋 *12, 18, 22, 23.* 🕐 *Sat–Sun.* **Riding school** 🕐 *Tue–Sun.* 🔊 **Garden** 🕐 *Apr–Oct: daily.* 🔊

THE FIRST LARGE secular building of the Baroque era in Prague, this palace was commissioned by imperial military commander Albrecht

The superbly ornamented Baroque organ in the Church of St. Nicholas

von Wallenstein (1581–1634). His victories in the 30 Years' War made him vital to Emperor Ferdinand II. Already showered with titles, Wallenstein started to covet the crown of Bohemia. He began to negotiate independently with the enemy, and in 1634 was killed on the Emperor's orders by mercenaries.

Wallenstein's intention was to overshadow even Prague Castle with his vast palace, built between 1624 and 1630. The magnificent main hall has a ceiling fresco of the commander portrayed as Mars, riding in a triumphal chariot. Now used by the Czech Senate, the palace is currently closed to the public.

Dotted with bronze statues and fountains, the gardens are laid out as they were when Wallenstein resided here. The Grotesquery is an unusual feature – an imitation of the walls of a cave, covered in stalactites. There is also a fine frescoed pavilion. The old Riding School is today used to house exhibitions by the National Gallery.

Charles Bridge and the Little Quarter Bridge Tower

Charles Bridge ⑩

🚋 *12, 22, 23 to Malostranské náměstí (for Little Quarter side); 17, 18 to Křižovnické náměstí (for Old Town side).* **Little Quarter Bridge Tower** ◻ *Apr – Oct: daily.* 🖼 **Old Town Bridge Tower** ◻ *daily.* 🖼

O NE OF THE MOST familiar sights in Prague, the Charles Bridge (Karlův Most) connects the Old Town with the Little Quarter. Although it is now pedestrianized, at one time it took four carriages abreast. The bridge was commissioned by Charles IV in 1357 after the Judith Bridge was destroyed by floods.

The bridge's original decoration consisted of a simple wooden cross. In 1683 a statue of St. John Nepomuk – the first of the many Baroque statues that today line each side of the bridge – was added. The vicar general Jan Nepomucký was arrested in 1393 by Wenceslas IV for having displeased the king. He died under torture and his body was later thrown from the bridge. A number of finely worked reliefs depict the martyrdom of this saint, who was revered by the Jesuits as a rival to Jan Hus.

Between 1683 and the latter half of the 19th century several more statues were erected. Sculpted by Matthias Braun at the age of 26, the statue of St. Luitgard is regarded as one of the most artistically remarkable.

Another splendid piece of decoration, the 17th-century Crucifixion bears the Hebrew inscription "Holy, Holy, Holy Lord," paid for by a Jew as punishment for blasphemy.

At the Little Quarter end of the bridge stand two bridge towers. The shorter of these is the remains of the Judith Bridge and dates from 1188. The taller pinnacled tower was built in 1464. It offers a magnificent view of the city, as does the late 14th-century Gothic tower at the Old Town end of the bridge.

The vast 17th-century Wallenstein Palace and its gardens

Old-New Synagogue ⑪

BUILT AROUND 1270, this is the oldest synagogue in Europe, and one of the earliest Gothic buildings in Prague. The synagogue has survived fires, the slum clearances of the 19th century, and many Jewish pogroms. Residents of the Jewish Quarter have often had to seek refuge within its walls, and today it is still the religious center for Prague's Jews. It was originally called the New Synagogue, until another synagogue was built nearby – this was later destroyed.

Right-hand Nave
The glow from the bronze chandeliers provides light for worshippers using the seats lining the walls.

14th-century stepped brick gable

★ Jewish Standard
The historic banner of Prague's Jews is decorated with a Star of David, within which is depicted the hat that had to be worn by Jews in the 14th century.

These windows
formed part of the 18th-century extension, built to allow women a view of the service.

Candlestick holder

★ Five-rib Vaulting
Two massive octagonal pillars inside the main hall support the five-rib vaults.

The cantor's platform and its lectern are surrounded by a wrought-iron Gothic grille.

Entrance to the synagogue from Červená Street

Entrance Portal
The tympanum above the door in the south vestibule is carved with a vine, which bears 12 bunches of grapes, symbolizing the tribes of Israel.

STAR FEATURES

- ★ **Rabbi Löw's Chair**
- ★ **Five-rib Vaulting**
- ★ **Jewish Standard**

The Ark is the holiest place
in the synagogue and holds
the sacred scrolls of the
Torah. The tympanum
above it is decorated
with 13th-century
leaf carvings.

View across the Old Jewish Cemetery towards the Klausen Synagogue

Old Jewish Cemetery ⑫

Široká 3 (main entrance). 22-23
17 191 (reservations); 22-48 19 456
(Jewish museum). M Staroměstská.
17, 18. ◯ Sun–Fri. includes
entry to all Jewish sites except Old-
New Synagogue.

FOUNDED IN 1478, for over
300 years this was the
only burial ground permitted
to Jews. Because of the lack
of space, people had to be
buried on top of each other,
up to 12 layers deep. Today
you can see over 12,000
gravestones, but around
100,000 people are thought
to have been buried here –
the last person, Moses Beck,
in 1787. The most visited
grave in the cemetery is that
of Rabbi Löw (1520–1609).
Visitors place hundreds of
pebbles and wishes on his
grave as a mark of respect.

On the northern edge of the
cemetery, the **Klausen
Synagogue** (1694) stands on
the site of a number of small
Jewish schools and prayer
houses, known as *klausen*.
Today it is home to the **Jewish
Museum**, whose exhibits
trace the history of the Jews
in Central Europe back to the
Middle Ages. Next to the
synagogue is the former
ceremonial hall of the Jewish
Burial Society, built in 1906.
It now houses a permanent
exhibition of childrens'
drawings from the Terezín
concentration camp.

Also bordering the cemetery,
the **Pinkas Synagogue** was
founded in 1479, and now
serves as a memorial to all the
Jewish Czechoslovak citizens
who were imprisoned at
Terezín. Excavations at the
synagogue have turned up
fascinating relics of life in the
medieval ghetto, including a
mikva, or ritual bath.

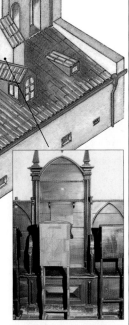

★ **Rabbi Löw's Chair**
*A Star of David marks
the chair of the Chief
Rabbi, placed where the
16th-century scholar,
Rabbi Löw, used to sit.*

PRAGUE'S JEWISH QUARTER

In the Middle Ages Prague's Jewish community was
confined in an enclosed ghetto. For
centuries the Jews suffered from
oppressive laws – in the 16th
century they had to wear a yellow
circle as a mark of shame.
Discrimination was partially
relaxed in 1784 by Joseph II,
and the Jewish Quarter was
named Josefov after him. In
1850 the area was officially
incorporated as part of Prague. A
few years later the city authorities
razed the ghetto slums, but many
synagogues, the Town Hall, and the
Old Jewish Cemetery were saved.

**Ten Commandments motif
on the Spanish Synagogue**

The Old and New Towns

THE HEART OF THE CITY is the Old Town (Staré Město) and its central square. In the 11th century the settlements around the castle spread to the right bank of the Vltava. A marketplace in what is now Old Town Square was first mentioned in 1091, and houses and churches quickly sprang up around it. Founded in 1348 by Charles IV, the New Town (Nové Město) was mainly inhabited by tradesmen and craftsmen. In the late 19th century, much of it was demolished and completely redeveloped, giving it the appearance it has today.

Church of Our Lady before Týn in the Old Town Square

Old Town Square ⑬

Ⓜ *Staroměstská.*

FREE OF TRAFFIC, except for a handful of horse-drawn carriages, and ringed with historic buildings, Prague's enormous Old Town Square (Staroměstské náměstí) ranks among the finest public spaces of any European city.

Dominating the east side of the square is the **Church of Our Lady before Týn**, with its magnificent Gothic steeples. Begun in 1365, from the early 15th century until 1620 it was the main Hussite church in Prague.

Also on the east side of the square, the **House at the Stone Bell** has been restored to its former appearance as a Gothic town palace. The splendid 18th-century Rococo **Kinský Palace**, with its pretty pink and white stucco façade,

was designed by Kilian Ignaz Dientzenhofer. Today, it houses art exhibitions by the National Gallery.

At the northern end of the square, the **Church of St. Nicholas** stands on the site of a former church dating from the 12th century. The present building, completed by Kilian Ignaz Dientzenhofer in 1735, has a dramatic white façade, studded with statues by Antonín Braun. In summer, evening concerts are held here.

A colorful array of arcaded buildings of Romanesque or Gothic origin, with fascinating house signs, graces the south side of the square. Among the most attractive are the house called **At the Stone Ram** and the Neo-Renaissance **Štorch House**, also known as At the Stone Madonna.

At one end of the square stands the huge monument dedicated to the reformist Jan Hus, who was burnt at the stake for heresy in 1415.

In addition to historic buildings, there are also many shops, as well as restaurants and cafés, whose tables and chairs spill out onto the pavements of the square in summer.

Old Town Hall ⑭

Staroměstské náměstí 1. Ⓒ 22-42 28 456. Ⓜ *Staroměstská, Můstek.* ⊞ 17. ◯ *daily.* 🎨 ♿ ✔

STANDING AT the southwest corner of the Old Town Square, the Old Town Hall is one of the most striking buildings in Prague.

Established in 1338 after King John of Luxemburg agreed to set up a town

council, the Town Hall grew in the course of the next few centuries and today consists of a row of colorful Gothic and Renaissance buildings.

The Old Town Hall Tower is one of the building's star features and dates from 1364. The gallery at the top provides a magnificent view of the city. Located on the first floor is the 14th-century Oriel Chapel, with its ornate, recently restored ceiling.

Another famous sight is the Astronomical Clock, built by the clockmaker Hanuš in 1490. The mechanism of the clock we see today was perfected by Jan Táborský between 1552 and 1572. The clock records three different kinds of time, Old Bohemian time, time as we know it, and so-called Babylonian time. It also shows the movement of the sun and moon through the 12 signs of the zodiac. Every time the clock strikes the hour, mechanical figures perform above the zodiac signs, drawing crowds of spectators. The lower section of the clock consists of the

Astronomical Clock and Calendar on the Old Town Hall Tower

Calendar. This beautifully decorated revolving dial, designed by celebrated artist Josef Mánes, dates from 1866.

Municipal House ⑮

Náměstí Republiky 5. ☎ 22-20 02 111. Ⓦ www. obecni-dum.cz
Ⓜ Náměstí Republiky. 🚋 5, 14, 26. **Gallery** ⬜ daily. 🖼 by prior arrangement.

PRAGUE'S MOST prominent Art Nouveau building occupies the site of the former Royal Court palace, the king's residence between 1383 and 1485. The attractive exterior is embellished with allegorical statuary, and above the main entrance there is a mosaic entitled *Homage to Prague* by Karel Špillar. Inside is Prague's principal concert venue, the Smetana Hall, also used as a ballroom. The interior is decorated with works by leading Czech artists of the early 20th century, including Alfons Mucha, one of the most successful exponents of the Art Nouveau style.

On October 28, 1918, Prague's Municipal House was the scene of the momentous proclamation of the new independent state of Czechoslovakia.

Wenceslas Square ⑯

Ⓜ Můstek, Muzeum. 🚋 3, 9, 14, 24.

ORIGINALLY A medieval horse market, today Wenceslas Square remains an important commercial center, with shops, hotels, restaurants, and clubs.

At one end of the square is the **National Museum**. This grand building, with its monumental staircase and rich marbled interior, was completed in 1890 as a symbol of national prestige. The museum's collections are devoted mainly to mineralogy, archaeology, anthropology, and natural history.

View across the Vltava River to the National Theater

The huge equestrian statue of St. Wenceslas that stands in front of the National Museum was erected in 1912, the work of the 19th-century sculptor Josef Myslbek. At the foot of the pedestal there are smaller statues of Czech patron saints. Also worth seeing are the Art Nouveau-style **Hotel Europa** (1906) and the **Church of Our Lady of the Snows**. This towering Gothic building is only part of a vast church planned in the 14th century but never completed.

Wenceslas Square has witnessed many important events in recent Czech history. In November 1989, a protest rally against police brutality took place here, leading to the Velvet Revolution and the overthrow of Communism.

Statue of St. Wenceslas flanked by Czech patron saints in St. Wenceslas Square

National Theater ⑰

Národní divadlo, Národní 2. ☎ 22-49 12 673. Ⓜ Národní třída. 🚋 17, 18, 22, 23 to Národní třída. ⬜ for performances only. ♿

THE NATIONAL THEATER has always been an important symbol of the Czech cultural revival. Work began on the building in 1868. The original Neo-Renaissance design was by the Czech architect Josef Zítek. After it was completely destroyed by fire – just days before the official opening – Josef Schulz was given the job of rebuilding the theater, and all the best Czech artists of the period contributed toward its lavish decoration. During the late 1970s and early 80s the theater underwent restoration work and the New Stage was built.

The theater's auditorium is a splendid sight, its elaborately painted ceiling adorned with allegorical figures representing the arts. Equally impressive are the sumptuous gold and red stage curtain, which shows the origin of the theater, and the ceiling fresco in the theater's lobby. The fresco is the final part of a triptych, painted by Františeck Ženíšek in 1878, depicting the *Golden Age of Czech Art*.

The theater's vivid sky-blue roof, covered with stars, is said to symbolize the summit all artists should aim for.

Excursions in Bohemia

THE SIGHTS THAT ATTRACT most visitors away from the capital are Bohemia's picturesque towns and castles, and its famous spa resorts. The castle at Karlstein, for example, stands in splendid isolation above wooded valleys that have changed little since Charles IV hunted here in the 14th century. Further south, the historic town of Český Krumlov retains a medieval atmosphere. Still popular as a therapeutic retreat, the spa town of Karlsbad is located in the leafy Teplá valley and offers a welcome respite from Prague's crowds.

Karlstein Castle, built by Emperor Charles IV in the 14th century

Karlstein ❷

Karlštejn, 25 km (16 miles) SW of Prague. [311-68 16 95.
[W] www.hradkarlstejn.cz ⬚ to Karlštejn (1.5 km/1 mile from castle). ⬚ to Karlštejn (1 km/0.6 miles from castle). ◯ Apr–Nov: Tue–Sun. 🎫 obligatory. **Chapel of the Holy Rood** ◯ Aug–Nov: Tue–Sun. 🎫 obligatory and by advance reservation only.

KARLSTEIN CASTLE was founded by Charles IV as a country retreat and a treasury for the imperial crown jewels. The present structure is largely a 19th-century reconstruction by Josef Mocker. The original building work took place between 1348 and 1367, supervised by the French master mason Matthew of Arras, and after him by Peter Parler. You can still see the audience hall and the bed-chamber of Charles IV in the Royal Palace.

The central tower houses the Church of Our Lady, with its faded 14th-century wall paintings. A passage leads to the Chapel of St. Catherine, whose walls are adorned with semiprecious stones. The Chapel of the Holy Rood in the Great Tower, where the crown jewels were once kept, has gilded vaulting studded with glass stars. At one time the chapel held 127 panels painted by Master Theodoric (1357–65), one of the greatest painters of Charles IV's reign. Some panels have been restored and can now be seen in Prague's St. Agnes's Convent.

Kutná Hora ❸

70 km (45 miles) east of Prague.
🏛 20,000 ⬚ ⬚ 🛈 Palackého náměstí 377 (327-51 23 78).

AFTER DEPOSITS of silver were found here in the 13th century, Kutná Hora evolved from a small mining community into the second most important town in Bohemia after Prague. The Prague *groschen*, a silver coin that was in circulation all over Europe, was minted at the **Italian Court** (Vlašský dvůr), so-called because Florentine experts were employed to set up the mint. Strongly fortified, the Italian Court was also the ruler's seat in the town. In the late 14th century a palace was built, containing reception halls and the Chapel of St. Wenceslas and St. Ladislav. They can be visited by guided tour.

Kutná Hora's **Mining Museum**, housed in a former fort called the Hrádek, and the splendid Gothic **Cathedral of St. Barbara**, which dates from the late 14th century, are also worth visiting.

Karlsbad ❹

Karlovy Vary, 140 km (85 miles) west of Prague. 🏛 60,000 ⬚ ⬚
🛈 Lázeňská 1 (353-23 63 77).

LEGEND HAS it that Charles IV discovered one of the sources of mineral water that would make Karlsbad's fortune when one of his staghounds fell into a hot

The three steeples of Kutná Hora's great Cathedral of St. Barbara

The spa town of Karlsbad with its 19th-century Mill Colonnade

spring. By the end of the 16th century more than 200 spa buildings had been built in the town. Today there are 12 hot mineral springs. The best-known is the Vřídlo (Sprudel), which, at 72˚C (162˚F), is also the hottest.

Among the town's historic monuments are a number of churches, including the 18th-century Baroque parish **church of Mary Magdalene**. The elegant 19th-century **Mill Colonnade** (Mlýnská kolonáda) is by Josef Zítek, architect of the National Theater *(see p721)* in Prague.

Karlsbad is also known for its Karlovy Vary china and Moser glass, and for summer concerts and cultural events.

ENVIRONS: Around 60 km (38 miles) southwest of Karlsbad is another of Bohemia's spa towns, **Marienbad** (Mariánské Lázně). Here the cast-iron colonnade, with frescoes by Josef Vyletěl, is an impressive sight. There are also many pleasant walks in the local countryside, especially in the protected Slavkov Forest.

Český Krumlov ⑤

170 km (106 miles) south of Prague.
🚶 15,000 🚉 🚌 🛈 *náměstí Svornosti 2 (337-70 44 21-3).*

OF ALL THE Czech Republic's medieval towns, Český Krumlov must rank as the finest. Almost entirely enclosed by a bend in the River Vltava, the beautifully preserved Old Town (Staré Město) appears to have changed very little in the last few hundred years, although some buildings are being repaired after suffering flood damage in 2002. A maze of narrow cobbled streets radiates out from the main square (náměstí Svornosti), which is lined with elegant arcaded Renaissance buildings and the Gothic former town hall. On one of these streets – Horní – is the magnificent 16th-century sgraffitoed **Jesuit College** (now a hotel). Opposite it is the **museum**, with temporary exhibitions explaining the town's history. **Schiele Centrum** is housed in a 15th-century former brewery. The museum has an excellent collection of works by the Austrian painter Egon Schiele.

Český Krumlov's most famous sight is its 13th-century castle – the **Krumlovský Zámek** – in the Latrán quarter. In the older, lower part of the castle complex, the splendidly restored castle tower can be climbed for superb views of the whole town. Other highlights of the castle include a Rococo chapel, a lavishly decorated ballroom – the Maškarní sál – and the ornate 18th-century Rococo theater. The castle gardens provide a tranquil spot to sit and relax, while performances of opera and ballet take place in the gardens' open-air theater in July and August.

In summer, renting a canoe from one of a number of outlets in the town is a good way to enjoy the fine views of Český Krumlov from the river.

♣ **Krumlovský Zámek**
Latrán. ⏰ *Apr–Oct: Tue–Sun.* 📷 ✔

CZECH BEERS

Czech beer-bottle cap

The best-known Czech beer is Pilsner, which is made by the lager method: top fermented and matured at low temperatures. The word "Pilsner" (now used as a generic name for similar lagers brewed all over the world) derives from Plzeň, a town 88 km (55 miles) southwest of Prague, where this type of beer was first brewed in 1842.

The brewery that developed the beer still makes Plzeňský pivo, as well as Plzeňský prazdroj (original source), better known by its German export name Pilsner Urquell. Guided tours of the brewery include a tasting. České Budějovice is Bohemia's other famous brewing town – home to the Czech Republic's biggest selling export beer, Budweiser Budvar.

Selection of Czech beers

Český Krumlov's castle tower rising above the medieval Old Town

Practical & Travel Information

SINCE 1989 the Czech Republic has become far more open to visitors. The country has responded well to the huge influx of tourists, and facilities such as communications, banks, and information centers have improved considerably. The best way to explore Prague is on foot; if you are traveling to places of interest outside the capital, buses and trains are reliable and inexpensive.

WHEN TO VISIT

THE BUSIEST MONTHS are August and September, although Prague can be very crowded in June and at Easter also. The main sights are always packed at these times, but the crowds lend a carnival atmosphere, which can make a visit all the more enjoyable. Many sights are closed between the end of October and the beginning of April.

TOURIST INFORMATION

TOURIST INFORMATION offices in the Czech Republic range from private agencies to the state-owned **Čedok**. Many employ English speakers and offer a variety of English-language publications, maps, and guides. The efficient **Prague Information Service (PIS)** is the best source of tourist information for visitors to the capital. It has three offices in the city center, providing information in English, German, and Czech.

VISA REQUIREMENTS

CITIZENS OF THE EU and US need a valid passport to enter the Czech Republic, and can stay for up to 30 days (US citizens) or 90 days (EU citizens). At present, New Zealand, Canadian, and Australian nationals require a visa, valid for one month.

SAFETY AND EMERGENCIES

VIOLENT CRIME against tourists is rare in the Czech Republic. The main problem, especially in Prague, is petty theft from cars, hotel rooms, and pockets. At night, lone women are advised to avoid Prague's Wenceslas Square, which used to be a hangout for prostitutes.

It is an unwritten law that you should have your passport with you at all times in the Czech Republic. Although you are unlikely to be asked to produce it, having it could save a lot of problems.

In case of an emergency, the numbers to call are listed in the directory opposite.

HEALTH ISSUES

NO INOCULATIONS are required for the Czech Republic. Visitors should take note that in winter sulphur dioxide levels in Prague often exceed the World Health Organization's safety levels.

For prescription and non-prescription medicines, visit a pharmacy *(lékárna)*.

FACILITIES FOR THE DISABLED

DISABLED TRAVELERS seeking advice on transportation, accommodations, and sight-seeing tours should contact the **Czech Association of Persons with Disabilities** or, alternatively, the **Prague Wheelchair Association**.

BANKING AND CURRENCY

THE CZECH unit of currency is the Czech crown (Kč). Banking hours are generally 8am to 5pm Monday to Friday, with some branches closing at lunch. Bureaux de change in tourist spots are open every day, and some offer a 24-hour service. Although they give much better exchange rates than the banks, their commission charges are huge, often as high as 12 percent. Traveler's checks can only be changed in banks. Credit cards are becoming more widely accepted in the Czech Republic, but never assume that you can pay with them.

COMMUNICATIONS

COIN- AND card-operated public phone booths are found all over the Czech Republic. You can buy phone-cards *(telefonní karta)* from most tobacconists and news-stands. International calls can be made from a public phone, a post office or a hotel, although the latter option is usually highly expensive.

Most post offices are open from 8am until 6pm, Monday to Friday, and on Saturday mornings. Stamps *(známky)* can be purchased at most tobacconists and newsstands, as well as from post offices.

FLYING TO THE CZECH REPUBLIC

IF YOU ARE traveling from the United States, **Czech Airlines (ČSA)** is the only airline that offers direct flights to Prague. A number of other carriers, including **Delta Air**

THE CLIMATE OF THE CZECH REPUBLIC

The Czech Republic enjoys long, warm days in summer, the hottest months being June, July, and August. The winter months can get bitterly cold; temperatures often drop below freezing and heavy snowfall is not uncommon. The wettest months are October and November but frequent light showers can occur in the summer months as well.

PRAGUE			
°C/F	24/75		
	13/55 14/57	16/61	
0°C 3/37		5/41	
32°F			0/32
			-5/23
5.5 hrs	8.5 hrs	4 hrs	1.5 hrs
73 mm	19 mm	95 mm	60 mm
month	Apr	Jul	Oct	Jan

Lines, **Air Canada**, **KLM**, and **Lufthansa** operate flights from the US and Canada to the Czech Republic, via another European city.

Carriers operating direct scheduled flights daily from the UK to Prague include **British Airways** and Czech Airlines (ČSA). The low-cost airline **easyJet** has flights to Prague from London Stansted.

Among a number of airlines flying from Australia and New Zealand to Prague are Lufthansa and KLM. Flights from Australasia require a stopover in Europe or Asia.

Čedaz runs an inexpensive and efficient minibus service from Prague's Ruzyně airport to the city center.

RAIL TRAVEL

PRAGUE IS connected by rail to all the major capitals of Europe, although it can be a rather slow way of getting to the Czech Republic. For example, the journey time from London to Prague is 19 hours. Nearly all international trains arrive at and depart from Hlavní nádraží, the city's biggest and busiest station.

The Czech Republic's state-run rail company, České Dráhy (ČD), operates two types of domestic routes. Express trains *(rychlík)* stop only at the major towns and cities and you pay a premium to travel on them. The slow trains, or *osobní*, stop at every station on the line.

For help with timetables and advice on fares in Prague, visit the local PIS or Information at Hlavní nádraží station.

TRAVELING BY BUS

TRAVELING BY BUS between Prague and other major European cities can be slow and tiring, but it is significantly less expensive than rail or air travel. Seats get booked up very quickly, especially in summer, so reserve well in advance. **Eurolines** is one of the main operators of inter-national bus routes to Prague.

Within the Czech Republic, long-distance buses are run by Československá státní automobilová doprava (ČSAD). There is an extensive route network, and buses are often a less expensive way of traveling between towns than the trains. For popular routes you should buy your ticket in advance from the bus station.

The main bus terminal in Prague is Florenc, which serves all international and long-distance domestic routes.

TRAVELING BY CAR

THERE ARE FEW highways in the Czech Republic, which can make car travel slower than in other European countries. To travel on them you must purchase a tax disc *(dálniční známka)*, valid for either 10 days or a month and available at the border or from post offices and gas stations.

Most of the major car rental firms have offices in Prague and at Ruzyně airport, but renting is relatively expensive.

DIRECTORY

CZECH TOURIST OFFICES ABROAD

UK
95 Great Portland Street, London W1N 5RA.
☎ 207-291 9920.
ⓦ www.czechcentre.org.uk

US
1109 Madison Avenue, New York, NY 10028.
☎ 212-288 0830.
ⓦ www.czechcenter.com

TOURIST OFFICES IN PRAGUE

Čedok
Na příkopě 18, Prague.
☎ 22-41 97 616.
FAX 22-22 44 421.

Prague Information Service
Na příkopě 20, Prague.
☎ 22-17 141 38.
☎ 22-44 825 62 (for walking tours).
ⓦ www.pis.cz

EMBASSIES AND CONSULATES

Australian Consulate
Klimentská 10, Prague.
☎ 25-10 18 350.

Canadian Embassy
Mickiewiczova 6, Prague.
☎ 27-21 01 800.

UK Embassy
Thunovská 14, Prague.
☎ 25-74 02 111.

US Embassy
Tržiště 15, Prague.
☎ 25-75 30 663.

EMERGENCY NUMBERS

Ambulance
Rychlá lékařská pomoc
☎ 155.
☎ 112 (English).

Fire
Tísňové volání hasičů
☎ 150.

Police
Tísňové volání policie
☎ 158.

FACILITIES FOR THE DISABLED

Czech Association of Persons with Disabilities
Karlínské náměstí 12, Prague.
☎ 22-48 15 915 or 22-48 16 976.

Prague Wheelchair Association
Benediktská 6, Prague.
☎ 22-48 26 078.

AIRLINES

Air Canada
☎ 888-247 2262 (Canada).
☎ 22-48 10 181 (Czech Republic).
ⓦ www.aircanada.ca

British Airways
☎ 0845-773 3377 (UK).
☎ 800-955 2748 (US).
☎ 22-21 14 444 (Czech Republic).
ⓦ www.britishairways.com

Czech Airlines
☎ 020-7255 1898 (UK).
☎ 800-223 2365 (US).
☎ 22-20 10 41 11 (Czech Republic).
ⓦ www.csa.cz

Delta Air Lines
☎ 800-241 4141 (US).
☎ 22-49 46 733 (Czech Republic).
ⓦ www.delta.com

easyJet
☎ 0845-605 4321 (UK).
ⓦ www.easyjet.com

KLM
☎ 800-447 4747 (US).
☎ 22-33 09 09 33 (Czech Republic).
ⓦ www.klm.cz

Lufthansa
☎ 800-645 3880 (US).
☎ 22-01 14 456 (Czech Republic).
ⓦ www.lufthansa.cz

BUS COMPANIES

Eurolines
☎ 08705-143 219 (UK).
ⓦ www.gobycoach.com

Where to Stay in the Czech Republic

Since the "Velvet Revolution" of 1989, the Czech Republic has received an ever-increasing number of tourists. To meet the demand for accommodations, old hotels have been revamped and many new establishments have sprung up. The top-range hotels are as good as any in Europe – but often just as expensive. In Prague, budget accommodations are unfortunately scarce.

	Number of Rooms	Private Parking	Recommended Restaurant
Prague			
Malá Strana (Little Quarter): *U Páva* @ hotelupava@iol.cz (Kč)(Kč)(Kč)(Kč) U lužického semináře 32, 110 00 Prague 1. **Map C3.** *25-75 33 573.* FAX *25-75 30 919.* A few minutes' walk from the Charles Bridge, this stylish hotel is decorated with dark, wooden furniture and chandeliers. Spacious, comfortable rooms. TV	11	■	
Malá Strana (Little Quarter): *U Pštrosů* @ info@upstrosu.cz (Kč)(Kč)(Kč)(Kč)(Kč) Dražického náměstí 12, 118 00 Prague 1. **Map C3.** *25-75 32 410.* FAX *25-75 33 217.* This family-run hotel, with an intimate atmosphere, has an excellent reputation, so reserve in advance. The large bedrooms have recently been refurbished. TV	18	■	●
New Town: *Hotel Anna* @ reception@hotelanna.cz (Kč) Budecska 17, Prague 2. *22-25 13 111.* FAX *22-25 15 158.* Located within a 10-minute walk of Wenceslas Square, the Hotel Anna is an elegant establishment, with an Art Nouveau interior, set in a quiet street. TV	24	■	
New Town: *Pension Páv* @ pav@vol.cz (Kč) Křemencova 13, 110 00 Prague 1. **Map D5.** *22- 49 33 760.* FAX *22-49 33 080.* The rooms and apartments of the Pension Páv, located in a fairly quiet street, are simple, but of a good size. There is a cozy bar and a reasonable restaurant. TV	8		
New Town: *City Hotel Morá§* @ bw-moran@login.cz (Kč)(Kč)(Kč)(Kč) Na Moráni 15, 120 00 Prague 2. **Map D5.** *22-49 15 208.* FAX *22-49 20 625.* Although the size of the rooms varies, the standard of comfort is high at the Morá§, with all the conveniences you would expect of a modern hotel. TV	57	■	
Old Town: *Harmony* (Kč) Na poříčí 31, 110 00 Prague 1. **Map F3.** *22-23 20 720.* FAX *22-23 10 009.* An immaculate hotel, run by young, friendly staff. Two small restaurants give a choice of Czech or international cuisine.	60		
Old Town: *Praha Renaissance* @ renaissance.prague@renaissance.cz (Kč)(Kč)(Kč)(Kč) V celnici, PO Box 726, 110 00 Prague 1. **Map F3.** *22-18 22 100.* FAX *22-18 22 333.* The rooms here come with soft furnishings, plump bedcovers, and fluffy bath-robes. There is a choice of restaurants and a swimming pool. TV	309	■	
Further Afield: *Corinthia Towers* W www.corinthia.cz (Kč)(Kč)(Kč)(Kč)(Kč) Kongresová 1, 140 69 Prague 4. *26-11 91 111.* FAX *26-12 25 011.* Two stops south of the Muzeum metro station on Line C, this hotel boasts first-class accommodations, a superb sports center, and stunning views. TV	551	■	●
Rest of the Czech Republicublic			
Český Krumlov: *Růže* W www.hotelruze.cz (Kč)(Kč)(Kč)(Kč) Horní 154, 381 01 Český Krumlov. *38-07 72 100.* FAX *38-07 13 346.* A luxurious hotel, housed in a former Jesuit monastery and furnished in the Renaissance style. It offers a superb range of facilities. TV	71	■	●
Karlsbad (Karlovy Vary): *Embassy* (Kč) Nová Louka 21, 360 01 Karlovy Vary. *35-32 21 161.* FAX *35-32 23 146.* The Embassy is a family-run, elegantly decorated hotel. The good-sized rooms are tastefully furnished and some have views of the river. TV	18	■	

Price categories for a double room per night in high season, with breakfast, tax, and service:

(Kč) up to 4,000 Kč
(Kč)(Kč) 4,000–5,000 Kč
(Kč)(Kč)(Kč) 5,000–6,000 Kč
(Kč)(Kč)(Kč)(Kč) 6,000–7,000 Kč
(Kč)(Kč)(Kč)(Kč)(Kč) over 7,000 Kč

Recommended Restaurant
The hotel has a restaurant that is especially recommended.

Private Parking
Parking provided by the hotel in either a private car park or a private garage nearby. Some hotels charge for the use of private parking facilities.

Map references refer to map of Prague on pp710–11

Where to Eat in the Czech Republic

FUELLED BY THE BOOMING TOURIST INDUSTRY, new restaurants are opening constantly in the Czech Republic. Many of them, above all in Prague, are foreign-owned, offering the discerning diner an ever-increasing choice. There are also plenty of traditional eateries for those who wish to sample local cuisine. Compared to western European prices, eating out in the Czech Republic is inexpensive.

	FIXED-PRICE MENU	OUTDOOR TABLES	VEGETARIAN DISHES

PRAGUE

JEWISH QUARTER: *U Maxima* Ⓚ Ⓚ Ⓚ
Bílkova 4. **Map** E2. 22-23 19 996. www.umaxima.cz
The specialty at this elegant restaurant is the "Czech plate" – pork, duck, smoked meat, cabbage, and dumplings. Live piano music adds to the restaurant's charm.
— | ▪ | ● | ▪

MALÁ STRANA (LITTLE QUARTER): *Square* Ⓚ Ⓚ Ⓚ Ⓚ
Malostranské náměstí 5. **Map** C3. 25-75 32 109.
This stylish eatery has an international menu with an innovative touch. On offer are excellent tapas, and main dishes such as fried quail eggs with parsley.
— | ▪ | ● | ▪

NEW TOWN: *Kmotra* Ⓚ
V jirchářích 12. **Map** D4. 22-49 34 100.
Large, tasty pizzas at reasonable prices are the order of the day here. Students, travelers, and business people all rub elbows in the whitewashed vaulted rooms.

NEW TOWN: *La Perle de Prague* Ⓚ Ⓚ Ⓚ Ⓚ
Rašín Building, Rašínovo nábřeží 18. **Map** D5. 22-19 84 160.
Occupying the top two floors of Frank Gehry's famous "Ginger and Fred" building, this much talked-about restaurant offers Parisian-style haute cuisine in a striking, postmodern setting. There is a separate cocktail bar. ● Sun, Mon lunch.
— | ▪ | | ▪

OLD TOWN: *Klub Architektů* Ⓚ Ⓚ
Betlémské nam 5a. **Map** D4. 22-44 01 214.
Eager diners try to keep this eatery something of a secret. It has plentiful servings of hearty cuisine, with a good choice for vegetarians as well as carnivores.
— | | | ▪

OLD TOWN: *Pivnice Skořepka* Ⓚ Ⓚ
Skořepka 1. **Map** E4. 22-42 14 715.
Most people visit this Czech establishment to eat the medieval banquet-style pork knee joints. Alternatively try the chicken cutlets stuffed with ham or blue cheese.

OLD TOWN: *Kogo Slovanský dům* Ⓚ Ⓚ Ⓚ
Na Příkopě 22. **Map** F3. 22-14 51 259.
Located in the Slovanský dům, this Italian restaurant is especially popular with the fashionable crowd.
— | | ● | ▪

PRAGUE CASTLE AND HRADČANY: *Palffy Palace* Ⓚ Ⓚ Ⓚ Ⓚ
Valdštejnská 14. **Map** C3. 25-75 31 420.
The innovative, continental cuisine served here includes dishes such as beef tenderloin with gorgonzola butter, and scallops with red onion and fennel sauce.
— | | ● | ▪

REST OF THE CZECH REPUBLICBLIC

ČESKÝ KRUMLOV: *Restaurant Na Ostrově* Ⓚ
Na Ostrově 171. 38-07 11 326.
This relaxed establishment serves hearty Czech meals, with a wide variety of chicken and fish dishes. Although the service can be slow, the setting is lovely.
— | | ● | ▪

KARLSBAD (KARLOVY VARY): *Promenáda* Ⓚ Ⓚ Ⓚ
Tržiště 31. 35-32 25 648.
A highly popular establishment offering well-prepared Czech and international cuisine, including wild game and mixed grills. Reserve in advance.
— | | | ▪

Price categories for a three-course meal for one, half a bottle of house wine, and all unavoidable extra charges, such as cover, service, and tax:

Ⓚ under 250 Kč
Ⓚ Ⓚ 250–450 Kč
Ⓚ Ⓚ Ⓚ 450–650 Kč
Ⓚ Ⓚ Ⓚ Ⓚ over 650 Kč

VEGETARIAN DISHES
In general, vegetarians are not well catered for in the Czech Republic, where meat forms the basis of most meals. We have included a selection of restaurants that serve dishes suitable for vegetarian diners.

FIXED-PRICE MENU
Available at lunch, dinner, or both.

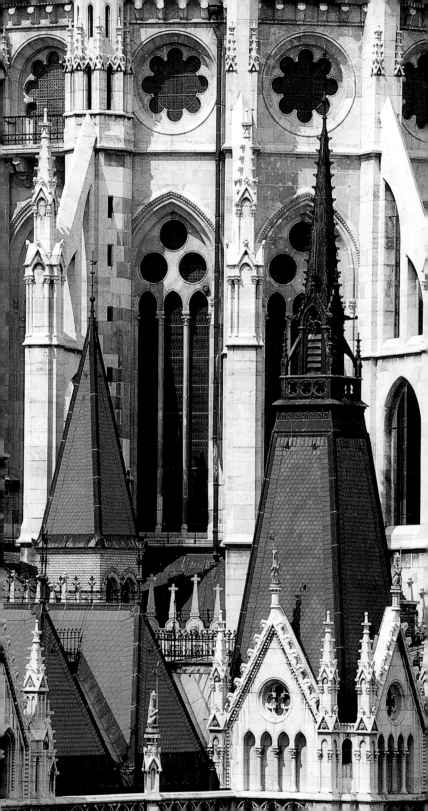

HUNGARY

*U*NIQUELY IN CENTRAL EUROPE, *Hungary is peopled by descendants of the Magyars, a race from central Asia who settled here at the end of the 9th century. In recent times the country has fought against Turkish, German, Austrian, and Russian occupiers, yet its rich indigenous culture remains intact. In 1989 Hungary became the first Soviet Bloc country to embrace Western-style democracy.*

Hungary has an extremely varied landscape, with forests and mountains dominating the north and a vast plain covering the rest of the country. The Tisza river and its tributaries shape the eastern regions, while the west has Lake Balaton, one of the largest lakes in Europe. The Danube flows through the heart of the country, bisecting the capital, Budapest, where one-fifth of the population lives. Ethnically the country is 92 percent Magyar, 4 percent Romany, 2 percent German, and one percent Slovak, the final one percent being of Jewish origin.

HISTORY

In AD 100 the Romans established the town of Aquincum near modern-day Budapest, and ruled the area corresponding roughly to Hungary (then called Pannonia) for three centuries. The arrival of the Huns in the early 5th century led to the complete withdrawal of the Romans. After the death of Attila the Hun in 453, the area was ruled by the Goths, the Longobards, and the Avars. The ancestors of the modern Hungarians, the Magyars, migrated from the Urals in 896, under the leadership of Prince Árpád, whose dynasty ruled until 1301, when King András III died without leaving an heir.

The throne then passed to a series of foreign kings, including the French Angevins and the Lithuanian Jagiellos, but the country flourished, and during the reign of Mátyás Corvinus (1458–90) it became the greatest monarchy in Middle Europe. Mátyás's marriage to Beatrice, a Neapolitan princess, saw the Renaissance blossom throughout Hungary, but all was soon eclipsed by a series of Turkish invasions. The Turks won a major victory at the Battle of Mohács in 1526, then they returned in 1541 to take Buda, which

The Gellért monument in Budapest, dedicated to a martyred 11th-century bishop

◁ Neo-Gothic spires, flying buttresses, and stained-glass windows on Hungary's Parliament building

became the capital of Ottoman Hungary. To quell the Turkish advance, the Austrians, under Ferdinand of Habsburg, occupied western (or "Royal") Hungary, while the central plains stayed under Ottoman control; the eastern region, including Transylvania (now in Romania), became a semi-autonomous land, feudally tied to the Turks.

Christian armies led by the Habsburgs fought to recapture Buda, and finally defeated the Turks in 1686. Economic prosperity came with Austrian rule, but nationalism was cruelly suppressed, culminating in a major uprising in 1848. After crushing the rebellion, Emperor Franz Joseph I sought to unite the two nations, and so created the Dual Monarchy of Austro-Hungary in 1867.

Mátyás Corvinus, King of Hungary (1458–90)

Following World War I, the Habsburg Empire was dismantled, and Hungary lost two-thirds of its territory to the "successor states" of Yugoslavia, Czechoslovakia, and Romania. It was to regain these territories that Hungary backed Germany in World War II, but in 1945 Budapest was taken by the Russians. The subsequent Communist rule was ruthlessly upheld, most visibly in 1956 when demonstrations were crushed by Soviet tanks. Nevertheless, free elections finally took place in 1989, resulting in victory for the democratic opposition. Since then, the country has invested heavily in tourism, which is now a major source of income.

LANGUAGE AND CULTURE

Modern Hungarian, like Finnish, derives from a language originally spoken by the Finno-Ugric tribes of the Urals. It differs greatly from most other European languages, although Slavic, German, Caucasian, Latin, and Turkic words have been incorporated.

Traditional peasant culture was all but destroyed in the 20th century, but folk songs and dances still survive; Christmas and Easter are the best times to witness these, particularly in the countryside, where holy days are celebrated in style.

Exploring Hungary

BUDAPEST has a pivotal location at the heart of central Europe, and it is also the perfect base for exploring Hungary itself. Szentendre, with its Serbian religious art, and Esztergom, where Hungary's first Christian king was crowned, are both only a short drive north, while Lake Balaton lies only a little further west. Pécs, a treasure trove of European history, lies to the south, while Eger and Tokaj stand in the wine-producing area to the east; the former, with its castle and Turkish minaret, is one of Hungary's most popular towns.

SIGHTS AT A GLANCE

Chess-players in a bathhouse in Budapest

Musically, the country has always had much to be proud of, including composers Franz Liszt and Béla Bartók, while in literature the Communist years produced some very powerful voices, among them Tibor Déry and István Örkény. Otherwise the country is best known for its cuisine, which incorporates a wide range of beers and meat-based dishes (such as goulash), the latter invariably spiced with paprika, the country's most famous export.

KEY DATES IN HUNGARIAN HISTORY

c.AD 100 Romans establish Aquincum

c.410 Huns overrun the region

896 Magyar tribes arrive

1001 Coronation of István I, Hungary's first king

1300s Angevin rule begins

1458–90 Reign of Mátyás Corvinus

1526 Turks win the Battle of Mohács

1526–41 Turks conquer Buda on three occasions

1541 The start of Ottoman rule

1686 Christian troops enter Buda, ending Turkish rule in Hungary

1848 Hungarian Nationalist uprising

1867 Compromise with Austria gives Hungary independence in internal affairs

1873 Buda and Pest become Budapest

1918 With the break-up of the Austro-Hungarian Empire, Hungary gains independence after nearly 400 years of foreign rule

1941 Hungary enters World War II

1945 Russian army takes Budapest

1956 Russia suppresses a nationalist uprising

1989 Hungary proclaimed a democratic republic

KEY

🛪 Airport

— Highway

— Major road

— Railroad

▪▪▪ International border

Budapest ❶

B UDAPEST WAS FOUNDED IN 1873 after the unification of three separate towns, Buda and Óbuda on the west bank of the Danube and Pest on the east. The city dates largely from the late 19th and early 20th centuries and is very much the creation of the nationalist enthusiasm of that era. All three towns had originally grown up in the second half of the twelfth century and Buda was the seat of Hungary's rulers from 1247. Turkish rule from 1541 to 1686, when it was recaptured by the Habsburgs, left little mark, except for the city's wonderful bathhouses.

SIGHTS AT A GLANCE

Gellért Hill Hotel and Baths ③
Hungarian National Museum ⑤
Inner City Parish Church ④
Mátyás Church ②
Museum of Fine Arts ⑨
Parliament ⑧
Royal Palace ①
St. Stephen's Basilica ⑦
State Opera House ⑥
Vajdahunyad Castle ⑩

Barrel-organist playing in the Castle district of Buda

0 meters   600
0 yards   600

GETTING AROUND

Trams are possibly the most convenient means of transportation for tourists, in particular the 18, 19, and 61 on the Buda side and the 2, 4, and 6 in Pest. There are also some 200 bus routes. The three metro lines, which converge at Deák tér station, and the HÉV rail lines link the center with the suburbs.

Chain Bridge (Széchenyi lánchid), the first permanent bridge over the Danube, completed in 1849

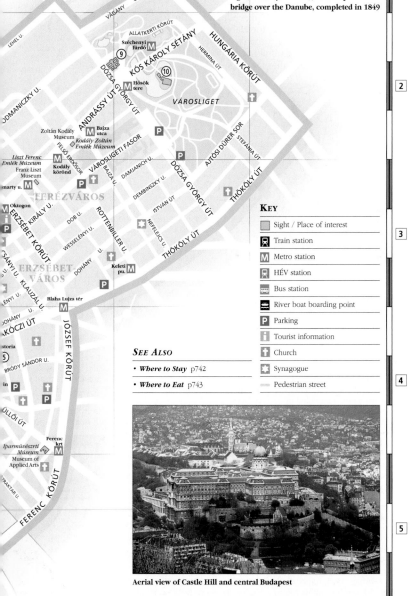

KEY

▢	Sight / Place of interest
🚊	Train station
Ⓜ	Metro station
🚉	HÉV station
🚌	Bus station
🚢	River boat boarding point
🅿	Parking
🛈	Tourist information
✝	Church
✡	Synagogue
—	Pedestrian street

SEE ALSO

• **Where to Stay** p742

• **Where to Eat** p743

Aerial view of Castle Hill and central Budapest

Buda

IN 1247, BÉLA IV CHOSE Buda, on the Danube's west bank, as his capital city. Its position, at 60 m (197 ft) above the river, made it a strategic choice. Buda expanded during Angevin rule, reaching a zenith under Mátyás Corvinus (1458–90), although further development was hindered by the Turkish occupation of 1541–1686. The Habsburgs' attempts to recover the city were devastating and by the time of its liberation, the city had been largely destroyed. In the 18th and 19th centuries, the Habsburgs set about rebuilding the palace and the old town, adding some magnificent buildings, but most had to be rebuilt again after the siege of 1945.

The rebuilt Royal Palace with the heroic statue of Eugene of Savoy

Royal Palace ①

Szinház utca. 🚌 5, 16, 78, Várbusz.

KING BÉLA IV (1235–70) built a royal castle in Buda, but its exact location is unknown. Around 1400 it was replaced by a Gothic palace, subsequently remodeled in Renaissance style by King Mátyás in 1458. Under Turkish rule, the palace was used to stable horses and store gunpowder, leading to its destruction in 1686 during the reconquest. A new palace, begun in 1719 by the Habsburgs, grew in size and grandeur under Maria Teresa, but this too was destroyed in the uprising of 1849 and had to be rebuilt in the second half of the 19th century.

When the Habsburg palace was again razed to the ground in February 1945, remains of the 15th-century Gothic palace were uncovered. These were incorporated into the restored palace that visitors see today.

Various statues, gateways, and fountains have survived from the 19th-century palace. In the northwest courtyard stands the Mátyás Fountain (1904), depicting Mátyás Corvinus (1458–90) and his legendary love, the peasant girl, Ilonka. In front of the palace's rebuilt dome stands an equestrian statue (1900) of Prince Eugene of Savoy, victor of the Battle of Zenta against the Turks in 1697.

Today the palace houses a series of important national collections, including the Széchenyi National Library, with over five million books and manuscripts, the National Gallery, the Budapest History Museum, and the Museum of Contemporary History and Ludwig Collection.

🏛 Hungarian National Gallery

Királyi Palota, Szent György te'r 6.
📞 1-375 7533. ◯ Tue–Sun. 🎟 🚻

Established in 1957, the National Gallery has a superb collection of Hungarian art stretching from medieval times to the 20th century. The permanent exhibitions include a section of sculpture and stonework – the Lapidarium. There are also regular temporary exhibitions.

Highlights include a carved stone head of King Béla III, from c.1200, religious artifacts spanning several centuries, including many fine Gothic altarpieces, some Renaissance and Baroque art, and a

St. Anne Altarpiece, National Gallery

wonderful selection of 19th- and 20th-century Hungarian works.

Notable early works include *The Madonna of Ba'rtfa* (1465–70), and the folding St. Anne Altarpiece (1510–20).

Among the 19th-century works, look out for the historical scenes by Bertalan Székely and the landscapes of Mihály Munkácsy, (1844–1900), widely held to be Hungary's greatest artist. The early 20th-century paintings of Tivadar Kosztka Csontváry display a unique, idiosyncratic vision of the world.

🏛 Budapest History Museum

Szent György te'r 2. 📞 1-255 7809.
🚌 5, 16, 78, Várbusz.
◯ Tue–Sun. 🎟

The city's history museum (*Budapesti Történeti Múzeum*), also known as the Castle Museum, is housed in the Royal Palace. It illustrates the city's evolution from its origins under the Romans.

Damage to the palace in World War II led to chambers dating from the Middle Ages being uncovered in the south wing. These were recreated in the basement.

The ground floor exhibits cover the period from Roman times to the 15th century and include some Gothic statues, unearthed here in 1974. The first floor traces the history of the city from 1686 (the end of Turkish rule) to the present.

15th-century majolica floor in the Budapest History Museum

West front of the Mátyás Church, with tiled Béla Tower on the left

Mátyás Church ②

Szenthdromság te'r 2. 【 1-355 56 57. 🚌 Várbusz. ⏺ daily. ⏺ Sat pm, Sun pm. 🎫 🚻

THIS CHURCH IS mainly a Neo-Gothic reconstruction dating from 1874–96. Most of the original church (13th–15th centuries) was lost when the Turks turned it into their Great Mosque in 1541. The building had to be restored again after damage in World War II. The great rose window has been faithfully reproduced in its original Gothic style.

The tombs of King Béla III (13th century) and his wife, Anne de Châtillon, can be seen in the Trinity Chapel, while the Mary Portal (near the main altar) is considered the finest example of Gothic stone carving in Hungary. Also fascinating is a Baroque statue of the Madonna: according to legend, the original was set into a wall during the Turkish occupation. When the church was virtually destroyed in 1686, the Madonna made a miraculous reappearance, which the Turks took as an omen of defeat.

Mátyás church stands in the heart of Buda's old town, which developed to the north of the Royal Palace from the 13th century onward.

In front of the church is Holy Trinity Square, with a memorial column to those who died in the devastating plague of 1691. On the square stands the Old Town Hall, an elegant Baroque building with an onion-domed clock tower.

Baroque Madonna, Mátyás Church

Gellért Hill Hotel and Baths ③

Szent Gellért tér. 【 1-466 61 66. 🚌 7, 7A, 86. 🚃 18, 19, 47, 49. 🚻 **Baths** Entrance on Kelenhegyi út. ⏺ daily. 🎫 🚻

THE EARLIEST REFERENCE to the existence of healing waters at this site is found in the 13th century. In the later Middle Ages a hospital stood here and then, during the Turkish occupation, baths were built. The area takes its name from Bishop Gellért, whose monument on the hill is visible from many parts of the city. He was supposedly martyred here in 1046 by a group opposed to the introduction of Christianity. From the top of the hill one can admire a beautiful view of the whole of Budapest.

The Gellért Hotel, with its famous spa, was built between 1912 and 1918 in the Secession style, at the foot of the hill. It boasts elaborate mosaics, stained-glass windows, statues, and fanciful balconies fronting the rooms. Its eastern-style towers and turrets offer superb views.

The complex houses an institute of water therapy. The baths are separated into different areas for men and women. Each has plunge pools, a sauna, and a steam bath. The facilities have been modernized, but the glorious Secession interiors remain.

There is also an outdoor swimming pool with a wave machine, installed in 1927 and still in operation. The baths and health spa, with their sun terraces, restaurants, and cafés, are open to the public as well as to hotel guests.

The men's section at the Gellért Baths

OTHER MUSEUMS IN BUDAPEST

Franz Liszt Museum
Vörösmarty út 35. 【 1-322 98 04. Ⓜ Vörösmarty utca. ⏺ Mon–Sat. 🎫 🎫 by arrangement. Museum in a house built for Liszt (1811–86) in 1877, where he composed his later works.

Museum of Applied Arts
Üllői út 33–37. 【 1-218 58 21. Ⓜ Ferenc körút. ⏺ Tue–Sun. 🎫 Fine collection of decorative arts, especially Art Nouveau artifacts, housed in beautiful Secession building.

Museum of Contemporary Art and Ludwig Museum
Disz tér 17. 【 1-375 91 75. 🚌 5, 16, 78, Várbusz. ⏺ Tue–Sun. 🎫 🚻 A contemporary art museum, in the Royal Palace, with works by Warhol (1930–87) and Hockney (b.1937).

Zoltán Kodály Museum
Kodály Körönd 1. 【 1-342 84 48. Ⓜ Kodály Körönd. ⏺ Wed–Sun. 🎫 The house in which the composer Kodály (1882–1967) lived and worked.

Pest

AT THE END OF THE 17TH CENTURY, much of the walled city of Pest, on the east bank of the Danube, was in ruins and few residents remained. Gradually new residential districts began to be developed, extending beyond the medieval walls, and people started to return.

After a flood in 1838, which destroyed most of the rural dwellings in the areas around Pest, redevelopment schemes introduced grand houses and apartment blocks. The area of Városliget (City Park), once an expanse of marshland, was also developed in the 19th century.

The first bridge linking Pest and Buda was built in 1766. The two cities were united as Budapest in 1873.

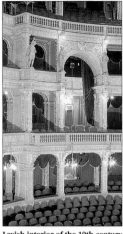

Lavish interior of the 19th-century State Opera House

The predominantly Baroque nave of the Inner City Parish Church

Inner City Parish Church ④

Március 15 tér 2. 🔲 *1-318 3108.* Ⓜ *Ferenciek tere.* ⃝ *for services.*

DURING THE REIGN of István I (AD 1001–38), a small church stood on this site. St. Gellért was buried here after his martyrdom in 1046.

Work began on the Inner City Parish Church (*Belvárosi Plébánia templom*), adding to the existing building, in the 12th century. It is the oldest building in Pest. In the 14th century it was remodeled in Gothic style, and later used as a mosque by the Turks. After the fire of 1723, it was partly rebuilt in the Baroque style.

On the south side of the church is a Renaissance tabernacle bearing the Crest of Pest, created in the 16th century. Close to the main altar is a reminder of Turkish occupation: a *mihrab*, or prayer niche, indicating the direction of Mecca.

Hungarian National Museum ⑤

Múzeum körút 14–16. 🔲 *1-338 21 22.* ⃝ *Tue–Sun.* Ⓜ *Kálvin tér, Astoria.* 🚌 *9, 15.* 🚊 *47, 49.* 📷 ✓

THE HUNGARIAN NATIONAL Museum was founded in 1802, when Count Ferenc Széchényi gave his personal collection to the nation. It is housed in an impressive Neoclassical edifice (1837–47).

In 1848, on the steps of the museum, poet Sándor Petőfi first read his *National Song*, which sparked the uprising against Habsburg rule. A reenactment is staged each year on March 15.

The museum's eclectic exhibits span the 11th century to the present day. Items on display include an 18th-century campaign chest from the time of Ferenc Rákóczi II, decorative weapons of Transylvanian princes, and a printing press used to print nationalist propaganda in 1848.

The museum is home to the Coronation Mantle donated by St. Stephen in 1031. It is made of Byzantine silks and is one of the oldest and best-preserved textile masterpieces in Europe.

Baroque campaign chest in the National Museum

State Opera House ⑥

Andrássy út 22. 🔲 *1-331 25 50.* Ⓜ *Opera.* ⃝ *daily.* 📷 ✓ *obligatory.* ♿ 🎧

THE STATE OPERA House (*Magyar Állami Operaház*), opened in 1884, was the life's work of architect Miklós Ybl. The façade expresses musical themes, with statues of two of Hungary's most prominent composers, Ferenc Erkel and Franz Liszt. The opulence of the foyer, with its chandeliers, murals, and vaulted ceiling, is echoed in the grandeur of the sweeping main staircase and of the three-story auditorium.

St. Stephen's Basilica ⑦

Szent István tér. 🔲 *1-311 28 59.* Ⓜ *Deák Ferenc tér.* **Treasury** ⃝ *daily.* 📷 🔒 *daily.*

THIS NEOCLASSICAL church, dedicated to St. Stephen, or István, Hungary's first Christian king (1001–38), was built in 1851–1905 on a Greek cross floor plan. The church received the title Basilica Minor in 1938, the 900th anniversary of the king's death.

On the main altar is a marble statue of the saint; scenes from his life are depicted behind the altar. A painting to the right of the main entrance shows István dedicating Hungary to the Virgin Mary. His mummified forearm is kept in the Chapel of the Holy Right Hand.

The main entrance to the basilica is a massive door, decorated with carved heads of the 12 apostles. The dome reaches 96 m (315 ft) and is visible all over Budapest. Its interior is decorated with mosaics by Károly Lotz.

The basilica also has two distinctive towers. The one to the left of the main door houses a bell weighing 9 tons. This was funded by German Catholics to compensate for the loss of the original bell, which was looted by the Nazis in 1944.

Parliament ⑧

Kossuth Lajos tér 1–3. **C** *1-441 49 04.* **M** *Kossuth tér.* 🚋 *70, 78.* 🚃 *2, 2A.* ⭕ *for guided tours only.* 🎦 🚻 *call 1-441 49 04 to arrange.* ♿ ▯

THE PARLIAMENT (*Országház*) is Hungary's largest building – 268 m (880 ft) long, 96 m (315 ft) high, with 691 rooms. Built between 1884 and 1902, it was based on London's Houses of Parliament *(see p45)*. Although the façade is Neo-Gothic, the ground plan follows Baroque conventions, with a magnificent dome at the center. Beneath it is the Domed Hall, off which is the Gobelin Hall, with a Gobelin tapestry of Árpád *(see p729)* and fellow Magyar chiefs taking a blood oath.

Tapestry of Árpád and Magyar chiefs in the Parliament building

The greatest artists of the day were invited to decorate the interior of the building, and there are some spectacular ceiling frescoes by Károly Lotz and György Kiss.

Between the Domed Hall and the south wing is the National Assembly Hall. On the opposite side is the Congress Hall, a virtual mirror image of the National Assembly Hall. Both have public galleries.

Since 2000, the royal insignia have been displayed here.

Museum of Fine Arts ⑨

Hősök tere. **C** *1-469 71 00.* **M** *Hősök tere.* 🚌 *4, 20, 30, 105.* 🚋 *75, 79.* ⭕ *Tue–Sun.* 🎦 🚻 ♿

IN 1870 the state bought a magnificent collection of paintings from the Esterházy family. Enriched by donations and acquisitions, the collection moved to its present location in 1906. As well as great European paintings from every era from the Middle Ages to

the 20th century, there are Egyptian, Greek, and Roman antiquities. Renaissance pieces include a wonderful unfinished Raphael known as the *Esterházy Madonna* and a small bronze by Leonardo da Vinci of François I of France on horseback. There are also paintings by Holbein and Dürer, no less than seven works by El Greco, and a fabulous collection of old master drawings.

Of more recent art, 19th-century French painting is very well represented, with works by Manet, Gauguin, and Toulouse-Lautrec.

Vajdahunyad Castle ⑩

Városliget. **C** *1-363 19 73.* **M** *Széchenyi Fürdő.* ⭕ *daily.* 🎦 🚻 ♿

THIS FANTASTICAL castle stands among trees at the edge of the lake in Városliget. It is in fact a complex of pavilions illustrating the evolution of Hungarian architecture. Created for the 1896 Millennium Celebrations as a temporary exhibit, it proved so popular that it was rebuilt permanently, in brick.

The pavilions are grouped in chronological order of style: Romanesque is followed by Gothic, Renaissance, Baroque, and so on, but the elements are linked to suggest a single, cohesive design. Details from more than 20 of Hungary's best-loved buildings are reproduced. The greatest emphasis is given to the medieval period, considered the most glorious in the country's history, while the controversial Habsburg era is pushed into the background.

View across the lake of the Gothic *(left)* and Renaissance *(right)* sections of the Vajdahunyad Castle

Szentendre ❷

🏛 20,000. 🚉 🚌 🚢 from Budapest. 🛈 Dumtsa Jenő utca 22 (26-317 965).

SZENTENDRE WAS SETTLED by Serbian refugees, who first came here in the 14th century. After the Turkish occupation of Belgrade in 1690, more Serbs arrived, ushering in a period of great prosperity.

The Slavic interiors of the town's many churches are filled with incense, icons, and candlelight. **Blagovestenska Church** on Fő tér, the main square, has a magnificent iconostasis, while other sites worth visiting are **Belgrade Cathedral**, for Sunday Mass, and the bishop's palace. Next door, the **Museum of Serbian Art** contains displays of icons and other religious artifacts.

Many artists have made their home in Szentendre, including the Hungarian ceramic artist, Margit Kovács (1902–77). Her work can be seen at the **Margit Kovács Museum**.

🏛 **Margit Kovács Museum**
Vastaggyörgy utca 1. 📞 26-310 244. ◷ Tue–Sun. 🌐 🎫

Esztergom ❸

🏛 30,000. 🚉 🚌 🚢 from Budapest.

ST. ISTVÁN, Hungary's first Christian king, was baptized in Esztergom and later crowned here on Christmas Day in AD 1000.

Dominating the city's skyline is the huge **Catholic Cathedral**, built in the early 19th century on the site of a 12th-century church. In the

The Tihany Peninsula, jutting out into Lake Balaton

treasury are religious artifacts from the original church. The 16th-century marble Bakócz burial chapel, next to the southern entrance, was built by Florentine craftsmen. South of the cathedral, the remains of Esztergom's **Castle** date from the 10th century.

In the picturesque old town, Esztergom's central square is bordered by many lively pavement cafés.

⛨ **Castle**
Szent István tér 1. 📞 33-415 986. ◷ Tue–Sun.

Lake Balaton ❹

Siófok 🚉 🚌 🚢 to/from Balatonfüred. 🛈 Viztorony, Pf: 75 (84-315 355). **Balatonfüred** 🚉 🚌 🚢 to/from Siófok and Tihany. 🛈 Petőfi U, 68 (87-581 227).

EVERY SUMMER Lake Balaton, Europe's largest fresh-water lake, attracts thousands of vacationers. The southern

shore is the more developed, with sandy beaches and a wide choice of tourist accommodations. The largest resort is **Siófok**, characterized by high-rise buildings, lively bars, and noisy nightlife. By day, windsurfing, sailing, and pleasure cruises are available.

Those in search of a more peaceful atmosphere should head for **Balatonvilágos**, set atop attractive wooded cliffs, or **Balatonberény**, which has a nudist beach. Southwest of Balatonberény, the tiny lake known as **Kis-Balaton** (Little Balaton) is a protected nature reserve, home to over 80 species of birds.

One of the most popular destinations on Balaton's northern shore is the spa town of **Balatonfüred**, whose mineral springs have been used for curative purposes since Roman times. From here you can visit the **Tihany Peninsula**, which became Hungary's first national park in 1957, and boasts some of the most beautiful scenery in the area.

At the far northwestern tip of the lake, the university town of **Keszthely** has three beaches, as well as a number of other attractions, including the Balaton Museum, which covers the history and natural history of the region, and the imposing Festetics Palace. A 15-minute drive from Keszthely brings you to **Hévíz**, an old 19th-century spa resort, where you can bathe in the world's second largest thermal lake.

Esztergom's vast cathedral, on the banks of the Danube River

Pécs ❺

👤 180,000. 🚉 🚌 ℹ️ Széchenyi tér 9 (72-213 315).

FIRST A CELTIC, then a Roman settlement, Pécs was later ruled by the Turks from 1543 until 1686. Several monuments testify to these different periods of Pécs' history.

The city's main square, Széchenyi tér, is overlooked by the **Catholic Church**, formerly the Mosque of Gazi Kassim Pasha, built under Turkish occupation. Inside, a delicately decorated *mihrab* (prayer niche) serves as a reminder of the building's origins. Behind the church is the **Archaeological Museum**, whose exhibits date from prehistoric times to the Magyar conquest.

On Dom tér are Pécs' four-towered, Neo-Romanesque **Cathedral**, which stands on the foundations of an 11th-century basilica, and the Neo-Renaissance **Bishop's Palace** (1770). South of here, on Szent István tér, a stairway leads to the ruins of a 4th-century underground **chapel**, which contains a wonderful collection of frescoes. On nearby Apáca utca, recent excavations have unearthed a collection of **Roman tombs**. Remains of the city's **medieval walls**, erected after an invasion by the Mongols in the 13th century, include a 15th-century barbican.

Candlelit interior of Pécs' Neo-Romanesque cathedral

Pécs' museums include the **Csontváry Museum**, showing works by the artist Kosztka Tivadar Csontváry (1853–1919), and the **Vasarely Museum**, dedicated to Hungarian Op artist Victor Vasarely (1908–97).

🏛️ **Archaeological Museum**
Széchenyi tér 12. 📞 72-312 719.
⭕ Tue–Sat. 🔒

🏛️ **Vasarely Museum**
Káptalan utca 3. 📞 72-324 822.
⭕ Tue–Sun. 🔒

Eger ❻

👤 60,000. 🚉 🚌 ℹ️ Dobó István tér 2 (36-517 715).

ONE OF THE most popular tourist destinations in Hungary, Eger is also famous for its world-class wines.

At the heart of the town, on Eszterházy tér, are the Neoclassical **Cathedral** (1830s) and the **Lyceum**. A highlight of the latter is the observatory, which affords stunning views of the town and surrounding vineyards.

Eger's 40-m (130-ft) **minaret** is a relic of 16th-century Turkish occupation, while the splendid Baroque **Minorite Church** on Dobó István tér dates from the 1770s.

Eger Castle was built in the 13th century following the Mongol invasion. The castle complex includes the Bishop's Palace (1470), which houses a museum of historical artifacts, and underground casemates.

♟️ **Eger Castle**
Mekcsey utca. 📞 36-312 744.
⭕ daily. 🔒

ENVIRONS: A short distance west of the town, in the **Szépasszony Valley**, you can sample the region's wines, including the famous dry red, Egri Bikavér, or Bull's Blood.

Tokaj ❼

👤 20,000. 🚉 🚌 ℹ️ Serház utca 1 (47-352 259).

TOKAJ IS located at the center of one of Hungary's most important wine-growing areas. Tokaji dessert wines range from sweet to dry and owe their distinctive full-bodied flavor to the volcanic soil in which the vines grow, and a type of mold peculiar to the region. The best cellars to visit for a tasting are the

Hungarian dessert wine Tokaji Aszú

Rákóczi Cellar, run by a foreign company, and the privately-owned **Hímesudvar** at No. 2 Bem utca.

Tokaj has a **synagogue** and a **Jewish cemetery**, relics of the period before World War I, when the town had a large Jewish population. The **Tokaj Museum** gives an interesting insight into the history of the town and its environs.

🍷 **Rákóczi Cellar**
Kossuth tér 15. 📞 47-352 408. ⭕ Apr–Oct daily (call in advance). 🔒

Eger's Baroque Minorite church, towering over Dobó István tér

Practical & Travel Information

IN RECENT YEARS, tourism has become an important part of the Hungarian national economy, and as a result, there have been vast improvements in communications, banking facilities, and public transportation. The biggest problem tourists face is the formidable language barrier. However, staff at many tourist offices, hotels, and other attractions, usually speak English or German.

WHEN TO VISIT

THE MOST POPULAR times to visit Hungary are between April and the end of June, and from the middle of August until October. July is usually extremely hot, and it is almost unbearable to stay in Budapest, although away from the capital the heat is less severe. From November until March, many museums have shorter opening hours or may close altogether.

TOURIST INFORMATION

BEFORE LEAVING for Hungary, you can obtain various information leaflets and maps from the Hungarian National Tourist Office, which has branches worldwide.

Within Hungary, there are tourist information offices in most large towns, many of them run by Tourinform. In Budapest, advice on sight-seeing, accommodations, and cultural events is given in several languages by **Tourinform Budapest**. The **Vista Visitor Center** also offers these services, as well as a reduced-rate telephone center, left-luggage lockers, a bureau de change, and an internet café. Visitors to the capital may wish to invest in the Budapest Card, which entitles card-holders, together with one child under 14 years of age, to unlimited use of the city's public transport system, free entry to 60 museums, the zoo and funfair, 50 per cent discount on guided tours by Tourinform, and 10 to 20 per cent discount on selected cultural events, swimming centers, and restaurants.

VISA REQUIREMENTS

CITIZENS OF THE US, Canada, New Zealand, and the European Union need only a valid passport to visit Hungary for up to 90 days. Visitors from Australia require a visa, which can be obtained from any Hungarian embassy or at the airport. A tourist visa allows you to stay for up to 30 days.

PERSONAL SECURITY

HUNGARY IS on the whole a safe country to travel in. As in most cities that attract large numbers of tourists, pickpockets operate in Budapest, targeting crowded metro stations, buses, and shopping malls. Rákóczi tér and Mátyás tér, in district VIII, are traditional hangouts for prostitutes; lone women should avoid these areas at night.

In the case of an emergency while on vacation, the relevant numbers to call are listed in the directory opposite.

HEALTH ISSUES

NO SPECIAL vaccinations are required for Hungary. Allergy sufferers and people with breathing difficulties who intend to visit Budapest should take account of the summer smog conditions, which are particulary acute in Pest. Those susceptible might consider staying in the castle district, where cars are banned, or retreating to the wooded Buda hills.

For treatments for minor ailments, visit a pharmacy *(Gyógyszertár* or *Patika)*. If your nearest store is closed, it should display a list of 24-hour emergency pharmacies.

People with heart conditions who wish to use Hungary's thermal baths should seek a physician's advice beforehand.

FACILITIES FOR THE DISABLED

HUNGARY'S public transport-ation systems, museums, and other attractions are gradually being renovated to make them wheelchair-friendly, but people with disabilities may still encounter problems. For more detailed information contact the **Hungarian Disabled Association**.

BANKING AND CURRENCY

THE HUNGARIAN currency is the forint (HUF or Ft). If you need to change money, the best rates of exchange are offered by banks and bureaux de change. Branches of the National Bank of Hungary and Budapest Bank are open from 10:30am until 2pm, Monday to Friday. Other banks open from 8am to 5pm, Monday to Friday. While all banks are closed at the weekends, bureaux de change and ATMs remain open. Credit cards are more widely accepted now than before, but don't expect to be able to use them everywhere.

THE CLIMATE OF HUNGARY

Hungary enjoys some of the sunniest weather in Europe, with an average of eight hours of sunshine a day in summer. June, July, and August are the hottest months. In winter, temperatures can fall well below freezing and there may also be snowfall. Hungary has comparatively low rainfall. June usually gets the most rain, while the fall is the driest season.

BUDAPEST

°C/F		26/79		
	15/59	15/59	15/59	
0°C 32°F	5/41		6/43	2/36
				-3/27
☀	6 hrs	10 hrs	5 hrs	2 hrs
☔	42 mm	56 mm	40 mm	40 mm
month	Apr	Jul	Oct	Jan

COMMUNICATIONS

THE HUNGARIAN telephone system used to be notoriously bad, but improvements are now slowly being made. Phonecards – available from tobacconists, post offices, and some newspaper kiosks – are the best option when using public phones, although some booths still accept coins.

Post offices open from 8am to 6pm, Monday to Friday, and on Saturday mornings. Service can be slow and there are often long lines, so be prepared to wait. If you need only stamps (*bélyeg*), you can buy them at a *trafik* (a newspaper kiosk or tobacconist).

FLYING TO HUNGARY

DIRECT SCHEDULED flights between New York's JFK airport and Budapest's international airport at Ferihegy are operated by **Malév**, the Hungarian national airline. Other major airlines flying from the US and Canada to Hungary include **Air France, British Airways, KLM, Lufthansa**, and **Northwest Airlines**, although services

entail a transfer or touchdown at another European city. British Airways and Malév each operate two daily scheduled flights between London's Heathrow airport and Budapest.

Ferihegy airport is located 16 km (10 miles) from the center of Budapest. The efficient **Airport Minibus Shuttle** will take passengers from the airport to any address in the capital. Taxis are a quick and comfortable way of getting into the city.

RAIL TRAVEL

THE HUNGARIAN national rail network is very efficient, with trains invariably departing and arriving on time. Budapest has direct international rail links with 25 other capital cities, Keleti pu station handling the majority of the international traffic. High-speed trains to Vienna, the main communications hub for western Europe, depart approximately every three hours and take around 2 hours 25 minutes. There are also car-train services from Keleti pu to Thessaloníki in Greece.

Within Hungary, local trains are categorized according to speed: "slow" (*személy*), "speedy" (*sebes*), or "fast" (*gyors*). There are also modern intercity services between Budapest and the larger cities. A number of concessionary fares are available for those planning on doing a lot of rail travel in Hungary.

TRAVELING BY BUS

INTERNATIONAL BUSES to all European destinations, depart from Népliget station. Nationally, buses are run by Volánbusz, which operates routes to most cities and towns in Hungary.

TRAVELING BY CAR

TO RENT A CAR in Hungary you must be aged 21 years or over, and have held a full driver's license for at least a year. An international drivers' license helps also. Most of the big, international firms have offices at the airport in Budapest, or you can arrange rental at hotels and travel agencies throughout the country.

DIRECTORY

HUNGARIAN NATIONAL TOURIST OFFICES

W www. hungarytourism.hu

In the UK:
46 Eaton Place,
London SW1X 8AL.
C 020-7823 1032.
FAX 020-7823 1459.

In the US:
150 East 58th Street,
33rd Floor, New York,
NY 10155-3398.
C 212-355 0240.
FAX 212-207 4103.
W www.gotohungary.com

TOURIST INFORMATION

Tourinform Hotline
C 06-80 66 00 44
(within Hungary).
C 60 55 00 44 (abroad).

Tourinform Budapest
Sütő utca 2, Budapest V.
C 1-438 80 80.

Vista Visitor Center
Paulay Ede utca 7–9,
Budapest.
C 1-268 08 88.
W www.vista.hu

EMBASSIES

Australia
Királyhágó tér 8–9,
Budapest.
C 1-201 88 99.
FAX 1-201 97 92.

Canada
Budakeszi út 32,
Budapest.
C 1-392 33 60.
FAX 1-392 33 90.

UK
Harmincad utca 6,
Budapest.
C 1-266 28 88.
FAX 1-266 09 07.

US
Szabadság tér 12,
Budapest.
C 1-475 44 00.
FAX 1-374 00 34.

EMERGENCY NUMBERS

Ambulance
C 104
(also 1-311 16 66).

Fire
C 105
(also 1-321 62 16).

Police
C 107.

FACILITIES FOR THE DISABLED

Hungarian Disabled Association
San Marco utca 76,
Budapest.
C & FAX 1-388 23 88.

AIR TRAVEL

Ferihegy Airport General Information
C 1-296 96 96.

Air France
C 1-318 04 11 (Hungary).
C 800-237 2747 (US).

British Airways
C 1-411 5555 (Hungary).
C 0845-773 3377 (UK).
C 877 428 2228 (US).

KLM
C 1-373 77 37 (Hungary).
C 800-374 7747 (US).

Lufthansa
C 1-266 45 11 (Hungary).
C 800-645 3880 (US).

Malév
C 1-235 35 35 (Hungary).
C 800-223 6884 (US).

Northwest Airlines
W www.nwa.com

Where to Stay in Hungary

VISITORS TO HUNGARY can choose from a range of accommodations, from top-class chain hotels to family-run pensions and hostels. In Budapest, bargain hunters can take advantage of the substantial weekend reductions offered by many luxury hotels in the low season. When choosing where to stay in the capital, take account of the often uncomfortable smog conditions in Pest at the height of summer.

	NUMBER OF ROOMS	RESTAURANT	PRIVATE PARKING
BUDAPEST			
BUDA: *Citadella* (HUF)	15	■	●
1118, Citadella sétány. **Map** C4. **[** 1-466 57 94. **FAX** 1-386 05 05. **W** www.citadella.hu			
An inexpensive, hostel-style hotel, occupying part of the old Citadel. The double and multi-occupancy rooms are all kept neat and clean.			
BUDA: *Budapest Hilton* (HUF)(HUF)(HUF)(HUF)(HUF)	295	■	●
1014, Hess András tér 1-3. Map B3. **[** 1-488 66 00. **FAX** 1-488 66 44. **W** www.budapest.hilton.com			
This modern hotel offers a full range of facilities, with excellent service, and commanding views across the Danube.			
BUDA: *Gellért* (HUF)(HUF)(HUF)(HUF)(HUF)	234	■	●
1111, Szent Gellért tér 1. **Map** C4. **[** 1-385 22 00. **FAX** 1-466 66 31. **W** www.danubiusgroup.com			
This first-class hotel has been made famous by its attractive indoor and outdoor pools and luxurious spa treatments.			
PEST: *Benczúr* (HUF)(HUF)(HUF)	93	■	●
1068, Benczúr utca 35. **Map** E2. **[** 1-342 79 70. **FAX** 1-342 15 58. **W** www.hotelbenczur.hu			
Situated in a quiet spot, the Benczúr has small but comfortable rooms and a pretty garden. Rates are sometimes considerably reduced out of the high season.			
PEST: *Astoria* **W** www.danubiusgroup.com (HUF)(HUF)(HUF)(HUF)	131	■	●
1053, Kossuth Lajos utca 19–21. **Map** C3. **[** 1-484 32 00. **FAX** 1-318 67 98.			
This old hotel boasts beautiful, refurbished interiors. Its café-bar is especially recommended. Rooms at the front can be noisy. Book limited parking.			
PEST: *Sofitel Atrium Budapest* (HUF)(HUF)(HUF)(HUF)(HUF)	351	■	●
1051, Roosevelt tér 2. **Map** C3. **[** 1-266 12 34. **FAX** 1-266 91 01. **W** www.sofitel.hu			
With fine views of the city, the modern Hyatt Regency has excellent facilities including a casino, a gym, and a choice of stylish restaurants.			
FARTHER AFIELD: *Danubius Grand Hotel Margitsziget* (HUF)(HUF)(HUF)(HUF)(HUF)	164	■	●
1138, Margitsziget. **[** 1-452 62 00. **FAX** 1-452 62 72. **W** www.danubiusgroup.com			
The Danubius Grand enjoys a tranquil setting on Margaret Island, north of the city center. Guests can make use of the superb spa facilities.			
REST OF HUNGARY			
BALATONFÜRED (LAKE BALATON): *Annabella Hotel* **W** www.danubiusgroup.com (HUF)(HUF)(HUF)	388	■	●
H-8230 Balatonfüred, Deák Ferenc utca 25. **[** 87-342 222. **FAX** 87-343 084.			
The amenities at this modern, high-rise hotel on the shore of Lake Balaton include a sauna and massage parlor, as well as water-sports equipment rental.			
EGER: *Senator House Hotel* (HUF)(HUF)	11	■	●
H-3300 Eger, Dobó tér 11. **[** 36-320 466. **FAX** 36-411 711 **@** senator@enternet.hu			
This centrally-located hotel occupies a charming 18th-century patrician's house. All the rooms are well-equipped. Early reservations are essential.			
PÉCS: *Hotel Platinus* (HUF)(HUF)	88	■	
H-7621 Pécs, Király u.5. **[** 72-514 260. **FAX** 72-514 738. **W** www.danubiusgroup.com			
This sumptuous Art Deco hotel couldn't be better located, situated as it is on the main shopping street. The facilities and service are to a high standard.			

Price categories are for a double room with ensuite bathroom per night, including breakfast and service:

(HUF) up to 10,000 HUF
(HUF)(HUF) 10,000–20,000 HUF
(HUF)(HUF)(HUF) 20,000–30,000 HUF
(HUF)(HUF)(HUF)(HUF) 30,000–40,000 HUF
(HUF)(HUF)(HUF)(HUF)(HUF) over 40,000 HUF

CREDIT CARDS
Major credit cards are accepted in those hotels where the credit card symbol is shown.

PRIVATE PARKING
Parking provided by the hotel in either a private car park or a private garage nearby. Some hotels charge for the use of private parking facilities.

Map references refer to the map of Budapest on pp732–3

Where to Eat in Hungary

HUNGARY OFFERS A VARIETY of places to eat at prices to suit most budgets. Two of the most common types of establishment are the *étterem*, a restaurant that offers a selection of Hungarian and international dishes, and the *csárda*, a folky taverna typically serving local specialties. In recent years, many ethnic venues have sprung up in Budapest, where you can sample cuisine from all over the world.

Columns (right): FIXED-PRICE MENU · VEGETARIAN DISHES · OUTDOOR TABLES

BUDAPEST

BUDA: *Aranyszarvas* (HUF)(HUF)(HUF) · ● · ■
Szarvas tér 1. **Map** B4. 1-375 64 51.
This charming inn in the Castle District serves tasty Hungarian fare. Game dishes, such as the roast venison, are the house specialty.

BUDA: *Rivalda* (HUF)(HUF)(HUF)(HUF) · ● · ■
Színház u.5–9. **Map** B4. 1-489 0236.
This is one of the better seafood and vegetarian restaurants in the city, with theatrical decor and a charming courtyard.

PEST: *Stex Hauz* (HUF) · ●
József Kut 55-57. **Map** D4. 1-318 5716.
A vast gymnasium-sized restaurant serving traditional Hungarian dishes at very reasonable prices. Try the gourmet's platter.

PEST: *Apostolok Étterem* (HUF)(HUF)(HUF)(HUF) · ●
Kígyó utca 4–6. **Map** C4. 1-267 02 90.
An intimate restaurant with woodcarvings of the Apostles hanging above alcoves. The menu is good, offering *foie gras*, tasty soups, and desserts. Booking advisable.

PEST: *Belcanto* (HUF)(HUF)(HUF)(HUF)(HUF) · ■ · ●
Dalszínhaz utca 8. 1-269 31 01.
Next to the Opera House, music is on the menu nightly from classical musicians. The fare, mainly steaks, fish, and game, is almost secondary. Booking essential.

PEST: *Gundel Étterem* (HUF)(HUF)(HUF)(HUF)(HUF) · ■ · ● · ■
Állatkerti út 2. **Map** D2. 1-468 40 40.
Top-quality French/Hungarian cuisine is served in this magnificent historic building. The restaurant has one of the most extensive selections of wines in Hungary.

PEST: *Lou Lou* (HUF)(HUF)(HUF)(HUF)(HUF) · ■ · ●
Vigyázó Ferenc utca 4. **Map** C3. 1-312 45 05.
This small, intimate French restaurant is ideal for a romantic meal. Dishes include salmon with lemongrass and parmesan-encrusted rack of lamb. ● Sun.

REST OF HUNGARY

BALATONFÜRED (LAKE BALATON): *Tölgyfa Csárda* (HUF) · ■ · ■
H-8230 Balatonfüred, Meleghegy. 87-343 036.
Set atop a hill, this restaurant enjoys stunning views of the Tihany peninsula. Typical Hungarian fare with live gypsy music in the evenings for group bookings. ● Nov–Apr.

EGER: *Talizman-Tulipankert* (HUF) · ■ · ● · ■
H-3300 Eger, Szépasszonyvölgy utca 45. 36-412 533.
A selection of traditional Hungarian and international meals is served in an old-fashioned, homey interior. The service is friendly and attentive.

ESZTERGOM: *Prímás Pince* (HUF)(HUF)(HUF) · ■ · ● · ■
H-2500 Esztergom, Szent István tér 4. 33-313 495.
Dark wooden tables and exposed brick vaults create an attractive setting in which to try a variety of refined Hungarian dishes. ● Jan–Mar: dinner.

Price categories are for a three-course meal with half a bottle of wine, including service:

(HUF) up to 2,000 HUF
(HUF)(HUF) 2,000–3,000 HUF
(HUF)(HUF)(HUF) 3,000–4,000 HUF
(HUF)(HUF)(HUF)(HUF) 4,000–5,000 HUF
(HUF)(HUF)(HUF)(HUF)(HUF) over 5,000 HUF

FIXED-PRICE MENU
Restaurants offering a good-value, fixed-price meal at lunch or dinner.

VEGETARIAN DISHES
In general, vegetarians are not well catered for in Hungary, where meat forms the basis of most meals. Restaurants serving dishes suitable for vegetarian diners are indicated.

For key to symbols see back flap

POLAND

LOCATED BETWEEN RUSSIA AND GERMANY, *Poland has always been a fiercely contested land. Released from the eastern bloc in 1989, the country is now developing rapidly, especially in the cities of Warsaw, Cracow, Gdańsk, and Katovice. Monuments attest to a stormy history, but Poland is famed for its virtues, especially the generosity of its people and the excellence of its vodka.*

Although situated on the plains of central Europe, Poland has an extremely varied landscape. Alpine scenery predominates in the Tatra Mountains to the south, while the north is dominated by lakes. Mountain lovers can make use of the well-developed infrastructure of hostels and shelters, such as those found in the Tatras. The countless lakes of Warmia and Mazuria, collectively known as the Land of a Thousand Lakes, are a haven for water-sports enthusiasts.

Poland's inhabitants, who number almost 39 million, all but constitute a single ethnic group, with minorities accounting for less than 4 percent of the population. The largest minorities are Belorussians and Ukrainians, who inhabit the east of the country, and Germans, who are concentrated mainly around the city of Opole in Silesia. The majority of Poles are Catholic, but large regions of the country, such as Cieszyn Silesia, have a substantial Protestant population. In the east there are also many Orthodox Christians. Religious denomination does not necessarily coincide with ethnic identity, although Belorussians tend to be Orthodox, while Ukrainians belong to the Greek Catholic (Uniate) Church.

HISTORY

Poland's borders have changed continually with the course of history. The origins of the Polish nation go back to the 10th century, when Slav tribes living in the area of Gniezno united under the Piast dynasty, which ruled Poland until 1370. Mieszko I converted to Christianity in 966, thus bringing his kingdom into Christian Europe, and made Poznań the seat of Poland's first bishop. The Piast dynasty ruled Poland with variable fortune and

Statue of the great 19th-century poet and patriot Adam Mickiewicz in Market Square, Cracow

◁ **Altarpiece depicting the Assumption in St. Mary's Church, Cracow, carved by Veit Stoss (1447–1533)**

Solidarity demonstrators staging a mass rally during a papal visit to Poland in 1987

embroiled the nation in domestic quarrels for 150 years. After this dynasty died out, the great Lithuanian prince Jagiello took the Polish throne and founded a new dynasty. The treaty with Lithuania signed in 1385 initiated the long process of consolidation between these nations, culminating in 1569 with the signing of the Union of Lublin. Nevertheless, the so-called Republic of Two Nations (*Rzeczpospolita Obojga Narodow*) lasted only until 1572, when the Jagiellonian dynasty died out, after which the Polish authorities introduced elective kings, with the nobility having the right to vote.

KEY DATES IN POLISH HISTORY

966 Adoption of Christianity under Mieszko I

1025 Coronation of Bolesław the Brave, first king of Poland

1320 The unification of the Polish state

1385 Poland and Lithuania unite under the Treaty of Krewa

1569 The Union of Lublin creates the Polish-Lithuanian Republic of Two Nations

1596 The capital moves from Cracow to Warsaw

1655 Beginning of the "Deluge" (the Swedish occupation), ending in 1660

1772–1918 Poland divided three times between Russia, Prussia, and Austria. The final partition (1795) is made after a Polish uprising led by Tadeusz Kościuszko

1918 Poland regains independence

1939 Soviet and German forces invade

1940 Auschwitz-Birkenau established. Two million Poles are gassed during the war

1945 Communist government takes control

1980 Solidarity formed, led by Lech Wałęsa

1989 First free post-war elections are held. Lech Wałęsa wins the Presidency by a landslide

1999 Poland joins NATO

The 17th century was dominated by wars with Sweden, Russia, and the Ottoman Empire, and although the country survived, it was considerably weakened, and its time of dominance was over. In 1795 it was partitioned by Russia, Prussia, and Austria, and was wiped off the map for more than 100 years. Attempts to wrest independence by insurrection were unsuccessful, and Poland did not regain its sovereignty until 1918. The arduous process of rebuilding and uniting the nation was still incomplete when, at the outbreak of World War II, a six-year period of German and Soviet occupation began. The price that Poland paid was very high: millions were murdered, including virtually its entire Jewish population. The country suffered devastation and there were huge territorial losses, which were only partly compensated by the Allies' decision to move the border westwards. After the war, Poland was subjugated by the Soviet Union, but the socialist economy proved ineffective. The formation of Solidarity (*Solidarność*) in 1980 accelerated the pace of change, which was completed when Poland regained its freedom after the June 1989 elections.

In 1999 Poland became a member of NATO, and it is currently preparing to join the European Union.

LANGUAGE AND CULTURE

The legacy of more than 100 years of partition rule is still visible in Poland's cultural landscape. Russian, Prussian, and Austrian administrations left their mark not only on rural and urban architecture, but also on the customs and mentality of the people.

The Poles have a deep reverence for religious symbols and rituals, and the presence of the church can be seen everywhere, either in the form of lavish Baroque buildings or images of the Black Madonna. Wayside shrines are also a regular feature.

Polish is a West Slavic language closely related to Slovak and Czech. Many of its words (such as *Solidarność*) are borrowed from Latin, although German, Italian, and English words are also common.

Exploring Poland

BORDERING THE BALTIC SEA, Poland is one of the largest countries of Central Europe, with a population of around 39 million. Warsaw, the capital, is located at the center of Poland, on the banks of the River Vistula (Wisła). Its location makes it an ideal base for visiting other cities, such as Cracow, the ancient royal capital; Gdańsk, the Hanseatic city whose shipyards gave birth to Solidarity; and Poznań, one of the oldest Polish cities. Cracow is one of the country's greatest treasures, offering excursions to the Polish mountains and the Cracow-Częstochowa Valley.

Children in traditional dress on a Polish public holiday, Cracow

SIGHTS AT A GLANCE

Cracow pp754–7 **2**
WARSAW pp748–53 **1**

The Neoclassical entrance to Warsaw's Wilanów Palace and Park

KEY

✈	Airport
⛴	Ferry port
—	Highway
—	Major road
—	Railroad
▪▪▪	International border

0 kilometers 100

0 miles 100

Warsaw ❶

THE CITY OF WARSAW is unique among European capitals. By the end of World War II, some 80 percent of the buildings had been reduced to rubble. What you see today is the product of meticulous reconstruction undertaken during the Communist era. Despite the devastation, Warsaw is rich in museums and sights and the Varsovians are immensely proud of their history of resistance to oppression. The center has been declared a UNESCO World Heritage Site. Warsaw is believed to have been founded in the late 13th century, when Duke Bolesław built a castle here overlooking the Vistula. It became capital of Poland in 1596, and the present castle and other grand buildings of the Old Town date largely from the Renaissance and Baroque periods.

Wilanów Palace, a 17th-century royal retreat, which stands in a magnificent park on the outskirts of the city

SIGHTS AT A GLANCE

Grand Theater ⑥
Monument to the Ghetto Heroes ⑦
Monument to those Fallen and
   Murdered in the East ⑧
National Museum ⑩
Old Town Market Square ①
Palace of Culture and
   Science ⑨
Royal Castle ③
Royal Route ⑤
St. Anna's Church ④
St. John's Cathedral ②

Greater Warsaw
(see inset map)
Łazienki Park ⑪
Wilanów Palace and Park ⑫

SEE ALSO

0 metres		350
0 yards		350

GETTING AROUND

The sights in the Old and New Town areas are easily visited on foot, since most of the streets are pedestrianized. Trams are best for short trips across the center. There is also an extensive bus service, but Warsaw's single metro line only serves suburbs to the south and is of little use to tourists. Taxis are reasonably priced, but use a reputable firm. Driving is getting more problematic, but the streets are still less crowded than in most European cities.

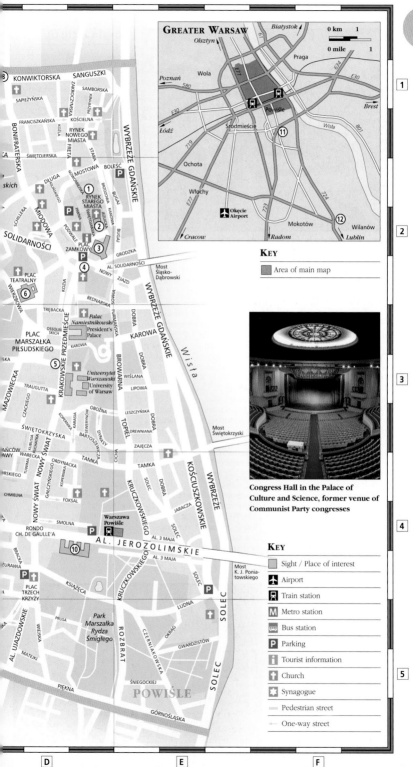

GREATER WARSAW

0 km   1
0 mile   1

Białystok
Olsztyn
Poznań
Wola
Praga
Brest
Śródmieście
Wisła
Łódź
Ochota
Włochy
Okęcie Airport
Mokotów
Wilanów
Cracow   Radom   Lublin

KEY

Area of main map

KONWIKTORSKA   SANGUSZKI
SAPIEŻYŃSKA
SAMBORSKA
ZAKROCZYMSKA
PRZYRYNEK
FRANCISZKAŃSKA   KOŚCIELNA
BONIFRATERSKA
KOZŁA
ŚWIĘTOJERSKA
RYNEK NOWEGO MIASTA
STARA
DŁUGA
MIODOWA
BOLEŚĆ
MOSTOWA
skich
SCHILLERA
SOLIDARNOŚCI
RYNEK STAREGO MIASTA
PODWALE
PLAC ZAMKOWY
GRODZKA
AL. SOLIDARNOŚCI
Most Śląsko-Dąbrowski
NOWY   ZJAZD
PLAC TEATRALNY
WIERZBOWA
BEDNARSKA
WYBRZEŻE GDAŃSKIE
TRĘBACKA
DOBRA
Pałac Namiestnikowski
President's Palace
KAROWA
PLAC MARSZAŁKA PIŁSUDSKIEGO
OSSOLIŃSKICH
KRAKOWSKIE PRZEDMIEŚCIE
BROWARNA
WIŚLANA
Wisła
MAZOWIECKA
TRAUGUTTA
CZACKIEGO
KOPERNIKA
Uniwersytet Warszawski
University of Warsaw
OBOŻNA
LESZCZYŃSKA
DOBRA
LIPOWA
ŚWIĘTOKRZYSKA
DYNASY
TOPIEL
BARTOSZEWICZA
Most Świętokrzyski
NOWY ŚWIAT
WARECKA
TAMKA
TAMKA
CICHA
ZAJĘCZA
KOŚCIUSZKOWSKIE
WYBRZEŻE
ORDYNACKA
KOPERNIKA
GAŁCZYŃSKIEGO
CHMIELNA
DOBRA
FOKSAL
JARACZA
SMOLNA
Warszawa Powiśle
NOWY ŚWIAT
RONDO CH. DE GAULLE'A
AL. 3 MAJA
AL. JEROZOLIMSKIE
AL. 3 MAJA
Most K. J. Poniatowskiego
BRACKA
SOLEC
ŻURAWIA
PLAC TRZECH KRZYŻY
KSIĄŻĘCA
KRUCZKOWSKIEGO
LUDNA
AL. UJAZDOWSKIE
PRUSA
WIEJSKA
Park Marszałka Rydza Śmigłego
ROZBRAT
CZERNIAKOWSKA
OKRĄG
GWARDZISTÓW
SOLEC
MATEJKI
ŚNIEGOCKIEJ
PIĘKNA
POWIŚLE
GÓRNOŚLĄSKA

Congress Hall in the Palace of Culture and Science, former venue of Communist Party congresses

KEY

▪ Sight / Place of interest
✈ Airport
🚆 Train station
M Metro station
🚌 Bus station
P Parking
i Tourist information
✝ Church
✡ Synagogue
— Pedestrian street
← One-way street

Horse-drawn carriages in the colorful Old Town Market Square

Old Town Market Square ①

Rynek Starego Miasta. 🚇 *E-1, 116, 122, 174, 175, 179, 195, 495, 503.* **History Museum** 📞 *022-635 16 25.* ⭕ *Tue–Sun.* 🎟 *(free Sun).*

Painstakingly restored after World War II, the Old Town Market Square was the center of Warsaw public life until the 19th century, when the focus of the growing, modern city moved. The tall, ornate, and colorful houses, which lend the square its unique character, were built or restyled by wealthy merchant families in the 17th century.

The houses on one side form the **Warsaw History Museum** (Muzeum Historyczne m st Warszawy). This displays the city's history through paintings, photographs, sculpture, and archaeological finds. There is also a film show, with footage of the Nazis' systematic destruction of Warsaw in 1944. Today, café tables and stalls line the square, and horse-drawn carriages offer tours the of the Old Town.

St. John's Cathedral ②

Świętojańska 8. 📞 *022-831 02 89.* 🚇 *E-1, 116, 122, 175, 179, 195, 495, 503.* ⭕ *daily (Sun: pm only).*

Completed in the early 15th century, St. John's Cathedral (katedra św Jana) was originally a parish church. Gaining collegiate status in 1406, it was not until 1798 that St. John's became a cathedral. Important events that took place here include the coronation of Poland's last king, Stanisław August Poniatowski, in 1764, and the swearing of an oath by the deputies of the *Sejm* (Parliament) to uphold the 1791 Constitution.

After World War II, various elaborate 19th-century additions were removed from the façade, and the cathedral was restored to its original Mazovian Gothic style. The interior features religious art, richly carved wooden stalls, and ornate tombs, including those of Gabriel Narutowicz (1865–1922), Poland's first president, assassinated two days after taking office, and Nobel prize-winning novelist Henryk Sienkiewicz (1846–1916). In a chapel founded by the Baryczka family hangs a 16th-century crucifix, which is credited with several miracles.

Royal Castle ③

Plac Zamkowy 4. 📞 *022-657 21 70.* 🚇 *E-1, 116, 122, 174, 175, 179, 195, 495, 503.* ⭕ *daily (separate tickets for Royal Apartments and Parliament).* ⬤ *Oct–Apr 14: Mon; public hols.* 🎟 *(free Sun).*

Warsaw's royal castle (Zamek Królewski) stands on the site of an original castle built here by the Mazovian dukes in the 14th century. It was transformed between 1598 and 1619 by King Zygmunt III Waza, who asked Italian architects to restyle the castle into a polygon. The king chose this castle as his royal residence in 1596, after the *Sejm* (Parliament) had moved here from Cracow in 1569. In the 18th century, King Augustus III remodeled the east wing in Baroque style and King Stanisław August Poniatowski added a library.

In 1939, the castle was burned, and then blown up by the Nazis in 1944. Reconstruction, which was funded by public donations, took from 1971 to 1988, and the castle is now a museum.

The castle's fascinating interiors are the result of its dual role: being a royal residence as well as the seat of parliament. Meticulously reconstructed, the castle has royal apartments, as well as the Chamber of Deputies and the Senate. Some of the woodwork and stucco is original, as are many of the furnishings and much of the art. Among the paintings are 18th-century works by Bellotto and Bacciarelli.

The opulent interior of the Marble Room in the Royal Castle

The magnificent Rococo organ loft of St. Anna's Church

St. Anna's Church ④

Krakowskie Przedmieście 68.
116, 122, 195, 503. daily.

THIS IMPOSING CHURCH on the Royal Route was founded by Anna, the widow of Duke Bolesław III, and built in the late 15th century, along with a Bernardine monastery. Extended between 1518 and 1533, the church was destroyed during the Swedish invasion of 1655, but later rebuilt in Baroque style. The Neoclassical façade was a subsequent addition, as was the freestanding bell tower, which dates from the 1820s.

The church has a magnificent interior, with several Rococo altars, a splendid organ, and frescoes by Walenty Żebrowski. A side chapel contains the relics of St. Ładysław of Gielniów, Warsaw's patron saint. St. Anna's is a popular choice for weddings, partly due to the superstition that any marriage celebrated here will be a happy one.

Next to the church are the remains of the 16th-century Bernardine monastery, which was closed in 1864. The old cloisters in the monastery's east wing, however, have retained their original vaulted ceilings. Behind St. Anna's there is an attractive Neoclassical colonnade, known as Odwach. This is the city's best location for second-hand booksellers, and is an interesting place to browse.

Royal Route ⑤

Krakowskie Przedmieście and Nowy Świat. 116, 122, 195, 503.

THE ROYAL ROUTE (Trakt Królewski) is one of Warsaw's most historic and beautiful streets. Starting by Castle Square (Plac Zamkowy), and continuing all the way to the royal palace at Wilanów, the most interesting part of the route is along Krakowskie Przedmieście and Nowy Świat. These thoroughfares developed in the late Middle Ages, with their rural setting, by the banks of the Vistula river, attracting Warsaw's aristocracy and wealthy merchant class.

This social elite built grand summer residences and town houses here, while religious orders established lavish churches and monasteries. Krakowskie Przedmieście features many buildings from the 17th and 18th centuries, with several imposing palaces standing back from the road behind tree-lined squares and courtyards. Alongside, there are impressive town houses and some of the city's most interesting churches, including **St. Anna's**, **St. Joseph's**, and the **Church of the Assumption**. **Warsaw University** and the **Fine Arts Academy** are also located here, while various monuments pay tribute to eminent Poles.

Nowy Świat is lined with long rows of 18th- and 19th-century town

Statue of Poland's most famous astronomer, Nicholas Copernicus (1473–1543), on the Royal Route

houses. It is also one of the busiest shopping streets in the world, and full of large stores, fashionable boutiques, colorful sidewalk cafés, and a wide choice of restaurants.

Imposing Neoclassical façade of the Grand Theater

Grand Theater ⑥

Plac Teatralny. 022-826 50 19.
107, 111. Ticket office daily.

ONE OF THE city's largest buildings that stand before World War II, the Grand Theater was built in 1825–33, to a design by Antonio Corazzi and Ludwik Kozubowski. Many renowned craftsmen also contributed to the sublime, palatial interiors. Initially the building was to be named the National Theater, but the defeat of the 1830 November Uprising forced a change of name. The two statues that stand in front of the building are of the 19th-century composer Stanisław Moniuszko, known as the father of Polish opera, and of Wojciech Bogusławski, the man who instigated the construction of the theater.

The theater currently houses the National Opera and Ballet and a small theater museum. Severely damaged during World War II, the theater retained only its impressive Neoclassical façade and a few of its rooms. Greatly enlarged in the course of reconstruction, it acquired many modern interiors and far more extensive backstage facilities.

Monument to the Ghetto Heroes ⑦

Pomnik Bohaterów Getta, Zamenhofa. 🚋 *111, 180, 516.*

THE NAZIS CREATED the Jewish ghetto in 1940 by driving the Jewish inhabitants of Warsaw and nearby villages into an area in the northwest of the city. The ghetto initially housed around 450,000 people, but by 1942 over 300,000 had been transported to death camps, and 100,000 others had died or been killed in the ghetto. The Ghetto Uprising of 1943 was an action of heroic defiance against the Nazis, planned not as a bid for liberty, but as an honorable way to die. Built to commemorate this action, the Monument to the Ghetto Heroes stands in the center of the former ghetto. It depicts men, women, and children struggling to flee the burning ghetto, together with a procession of Jews being driven to Nazi death camps.

A **Path of Remembrance**, lined with a series of granite blocks dedicated to events or heroes of the ghetto, links the ghetto memorial to the nearby Bunker Monument – on the site from where the uprising was co-ordinated – and the Umschlagplatz Monument. Engraved with hundreds of names, it marks the place from where many Jews were deported to the death camps, and represents the cattle trucks used for transportation.

Detail from the Monument to the Ghetto Heroes

Monument to Those Fallen and Murdered in the East ⑧

ul. Muranowska. 🚋 *116, 122, 127, 157, 174, 175, 195, 303, 503, 518.* 🚊 *2, 4, 15, 18, 35, 36.*

THIS EMOTIONALLY stirring monument, designed by Mirosław Biskupski, has the form of a typical railway wagon in which Poles were deported into the depths of the Soviet Union. It is filled with a pile of crosses symbolising the hundreds of thousands of Poles carted off to the East in cattle vans and subsequently murdered in Soviet prison camps.

Palace of Culture and Science ⑨

Plac Defilad 1. 📞 *022-656 62 01.* **Viewing Terrace** ◯ *daily.* 📷

THIS MONOLITHIC BUILDING was a "gift" from Soviet Russia to the people of Warsaw, and intended as a monument to "the inventive spirit and social progress." Built in 1952–5 by the Russian architect, Lev Rudniev, it resembles Moscow's Socialist Realist tower blocks.

The palace still inspires extreme emotions among Varsovians, ranging from admiration to demands for its demolition. Since the end of Soviet domination, the building's role has changed. The tower itself now provides office space, and the Congress Hall, which once held Communist Party congresses, is now a venue for concerts and festivals. The palace remains a cultural center in other ways, with the Theater of Dramatic Art, a cinema, puppet theater, technology museum, and a sports complex.

The imposing Socialist Realist Palace of Culture and Science

National Museum ⑩

Aleje Jerozolimskie 3. 📞 *022-622 57 81.* 🚋 *101, 102, 111, 117, 158.* 🚊 *7, 22, 24, 25.* ◯ *10am–4pm Tue–Wed & Fri–Sun, 10am–6pm Thu.* ◯ *public hols.* 📷 *(free Sat).* **Military Museum** 📞 *022-629 52 71.* ◯ *Tue–Sun.* ◯ *some public hols.* 📷 *(free Sat).* 📷

ORIGINALLY ESTABLISHED in 1862 as the Fine Art Museum, the National Museum (Muzeum Narodowe) was created in 1916. Its vast collection was started in 1862 with the purchase of 36 paintings. Subsequent acquisitions have turned the museum into one of the city's finest. Collections include ancient Greek, Roman, and Egyptian art, archaeological finds from Faras in present-day Sudan, and medieval Polish religious paintings, altarpieces, and sculptures.

The foreign art collection features Italian, French, Dutch, and Flemish works. There is a fine *Madonna and Child* by Sandro Botticelli. In the vast Polish art collection are works by Bernardo Bellotto (1720–80), nephew of Canaletto, who settled in Warsaw and painted fine views of the city. Of native Polish artists, Jan Matejko (1838–93) is one of the finest on display. He painted historical subjects such as *The Battle of Grunwald*. In an east wing of the museum, the **Military Museum** illustrates the history of Polish firearms and armor.

The impressive Neoclassical façade of Wilanów Palace, designed for King Jan III Sobieski

Łazienki Park ⑪

Łazienki Królewskie, Agrykola 1.
📞 022-621 62 41. 🚌 108, 116, 118, 119, 195. **Park** ⬜ daily until dusk.
Palace on the Water ⬜ Tue–Sun until dusk. ⬛ days after public hols.
🎫 (free Sat).

THIS HUGE PARK, studded with palaces, temples, and monuments, originally dates from the Middle Ages, when it belonged to the Mazovian dukes. By the early 17th century, it was owned by the Polish crown, and housed a royal menagerie. In 1674 the Grand Crown Marshal Stanisław Herakliusz Lubomirski acquired the park, and Tylman of Gameren designed its hermitage and bathing pavilion. The pavilion gave the park its name, as *łazienki* means "baths."

In the 18th century, the park was owned by King Stanisław August Poniatowski, and he commissioned Karol Agrykola, Karol Schultz, and Jan Schuch to lay it out as a formal garden. A number of new buildings were also completed during this time, and the pavilion was redesigned, by Dominik Merlini, as a royal summer residence. This became known as the **Palace on the Water**, and is one of the finest examples of Neoclassical architecture in Poland. It now houses an architecture museum. Unfortunately the king was only able to enjoy the palace for a few years, as after the Third Partition of Poland he was forced to abdicate, and left Warsaw on January 7, 1795. The Nazis planned to blow it up but, lacking time on their withdrawal, set fire to it instead. It was rebuilt by 1965.

Solomon's Hall, reception room of Palace on the Water, Łazienki Park

Wilanów Palace and Park ⑫

S.K. Potockiego 10–16. 📞 022-842 07 95. 🚌 130, 180, 410, 414, 522.
Palace ⬜ Wed–Mon (until 2:30pm). ⬛ Jan. 🎫 🡇 **Park** ⬜ daily until dusk. 🎫 (free Thu). 🡇

ALTHOUGH IT WAS a royal residence, Wilanów Palace, which is set within parkland and beautiful formal gardens, was actually designed as a private retreat for King Jan III Sobieski, who valued family life above material splendor. The original property, known as Villa Nova, was purchased in 1677 and within two years had been rebuilt as a mansion, designed by royal architect Augustyn Locci. The elaborate façades were adorned with sculptures and murals, while the interiors were decorated by Europe's finest craftsmen.

Enlarged over subsequent years by its many different owners, the palace gained two large wings, a pair of towers, and a first-floor banqueting hall. The north wing comprises 19th-century rooms, formerly used as living quarters and as a gallery. The largest room, the Great Crimson Room, is used as a venue for entertaining VIPs. The south wing includes the late Baroque Great Dining Room, designed for King August II Mocny, as well as Princess Izabela Lubomirska's apartments, which feature a bathroom dating from 1775.

The most interesting rooms in the main part of the palace are the Neoclassical Great Hall, with marble detailing and allegorical friezes, and the ornate King's Bedchamber, with its 17th-century Turkish bed canopy. There are also apartments once occupied by King Jan III Sobieski and his wife Marysieńka, which retain many of their original 17th-century features, as well as an old nursery, governesses' rooms, and a fascinating portrait gallery. Outside the palace, in the old riding school building, there is an interesting poster museum.

The enchanting Palace on the Water, Łazienki Park

Cracow ❷

FOR NEARLY SIX CENTURIES Cracow was the capital of Poland and the country's largest city. Polish rulers resided at Wawel Castle until the court and parliament moved to Warsaw in 1609. Even then Cracow continued to be regarded as the official capital and rulers were still crowned and buried in the cathedral on Wawel Hill. The city still plays an important role in preserving the national identity. The prestigious Jagiellonian University is the oldest in the country and the city is full of memorials to illustrious Poles. Perhaps Cracow's greatest attraction lies in the fact that, unlike so many Polish cities, it was scarcely damaged in World War II. In recent years many buildings and monuments have been restored to their former glory.

Head in Deputies' Hall, Royal Castle

Royal Castle
The Birds Hall, with its gilded coffered ceiling and marble fireplace, is one of the later 17th-century rooms in the castle's Royal Apartments.

WAWEL HILL

In about 1038 Kazimierz the Restorer made the citadel on Wawel Hill the seat of Polish political power. In the 16th century the Jagiellonian rulers transformed the Gothic castle into a magnificent Renaissance palace and endowed the cathedral with new chapels and works of art.

Lost Wawel Exhibition

Statue of Tadeusz Kościuszko

Cathedral Museum

Fortified walls

Dragon's Lair

Cracow Cathedral
The Zygmunt Chapel with its striking gilded dome was one of many additions to the cathedral made in the early 16th century.

The foundations of medieval houses that stood within the castle walls have been excavated here. The houses were razed by the Austrians in 1805–6 to create a parade ground.

♠ Royal Castle

Wawel 5. 012-422 16 97. 103, 124, 444, 502. 6, 8, 10, 18. *daily.* Royal Appartments, "Orient in the Wawel" & Nov 1–Mar 31: Mon; public hols. *(free Sun in winter, Mon in summer).*

The present Renaissance castle was built in the first half of the 16th century. After the royal court moved from Cracow to Warsaw in the early 17th century, the castle fell gradually into decay. At the start of the 20th century it was given to the city of Cracow and work began to restore it to its former grandeur.

The richly decorated Royal Apartments are the main reason for visiting the castle. Most of the rooms reflect the tastes of the last Jagiellonian kings. They contain Italian paintings and furniture, painted friezes around the walls, and a fine collection of Flemish tapestries. The Hall of Deputies was where the lower house of the Polish parliament, the *Sejm*, met for debates. It is also known as the Hall of Heads because the ceiling is decorated with carved heads. On the top floor there is a suite of rooms from the 17th century, with portraits of the Waza kings, including one of Prince Władysław (later Władysław IV) by Rubens. The Crown Treasury and Armory are situated on the ground floor. The treasury's collection of royal jewels and regalia includes the coronation sword of the Polish kings.

The "Orient in the Wawel" collection on the first and second floors features Turkish tents and banners seized by the victorious Christian troops at the Siege of Vienna in 1683.

Royal Castle with the so-called Hen's Claw Wing on the right

🏛 Lost Wawel Exhibition

Wawel Hill. 012-422 16 97. *Wed–Mon.* *(free Sun in winter, Mon in summer).*

An exhibition in the castle basement includes the remains of an early church, thought to date from the 11th century. Computer models illustrate the development of Wawel Hill through the Middle Ages.

Baroque silver reliquary of St. Stanisław by Peter von der Rennen (1669–71), Cracow Cathedral

⛪ Cracow Cathedral

Wawel 3. 012-422 26 43. 103, 124, 502. 6, 8, 10, 18. *daily (Sun: pm only).* **Cathedral Museum** 012-422 09 04. *Tue–Sun.*

Originally founded in 1020, the present cathedral is the third to stand on this site. It was completed in 1364 in the reign of Kazimierz the Great. The resting place of many Polish kings, the cathedral has always had great symbolic significance for the nation. It is dedicated to St. Stanisław, whose relics are housed in an ornate reliquary in the shape of a coffin beneath an eye-catching Baroque altar canopy in the center of the nave.

The original Gothic cathedral has seen many subsequent additions, notably the Baroque spire built in the early 18th century and the side chapels, which have been remodeled many times. There are many fine tombs of Polish rulers. The Renaissance Zygmunt Chapel was built in 1519–33 by the Italian Bartolomeo Berrecci. It contains an impressive double monument in red marble to Zygmunt the Old (reigned 1506–48) and his son Zygmunt August (reigned 1548–72). Look out too for the late Gothic canopied sarcophagus of Kazimierz Jagiellończyk carved by Veit Stoss (1492) in the Chapel of the Holy Cross. The marble tomb of Stefan Batory (reigned 1576–86), created by Santi Gucci in 1595, stands behind the altar.

The crypt is divided into sections containing the tombs and sarcophagi of other Polish rulers, leading poets, and national heroes, including Tadeusz Kościuszko, leader of the failed insurrection of 1794.

The Cathedral Museum houses a collection of sacred art and a selection of Polish royal regalia, including the coronation robe of the last Polish king, Stanisław August Poniatowski (reigned 1764–95).

🏛 Dragon's Lair

Wawel Hill. *May–Oct: daily.* Beneath Wawel Hill is a series of caves associated with the legend of a dragon. In summer part of the cave system can be reached by a set of spiral steps. Children take delight in the bronze, fire-breathing statue of a dragon at the entrance.

Turkish tent in the "Orient in the Wawel" exhibition in the castle

Cracow: the Old Quarter

IN 1257 CRACOW WAS GRANTED a charter by Duke Bolesław the Chaste. This was of key importance to the city, ensuring local government and trade privileges and stimulating the city's future development. The charter stipulated certain conditions: a large centrally located square, surrounded by a regular grid of streets, was to become the city center. The size of each plot determined the size of the houses. Although the architecture became ever more opulent over the centuries, this urban scheme has survived almost intact. To this day the Old Quarter remains the heart of modern Cracow. Many of the streets are pedestrianized, allowing visitors to enjoy the great concentration of historic sights.

The Slacker Crucifix (1496) by Veit Stoss in St. Mary's Church

The City Hall Tower in the western corner of Market Square

🏛 Market Square

Rynek Główny.

The Market Square is said to be the largest town square in Europe. In summer nearly 30 street cafés remain open here until the early hours. Flower stalls, street musicians, and artists selling their works all contribute to the lively atmosphere. The ornate Cloth Hall virtually divides the square in two. Two other buildings stand in the square: the small green-domed Church of St. Adalbert, below which is a museum of the history of the square, and the City Hall Tower, a relic of the original Gothic town hall. There is also a monumental statue of the great Polish poet Adam Mickiewitz (1798–1855).

Buildings around the square retain elements from every era in the history of the city. Many are decorated with an emblem that gives the house its name, for example the Palace of the Rams on the west side of the square, home of a famous cabaret since 1956. Christopher Palace takes its name from a 14th-century statue of St. Christopher. The house was remodeled in 1682–5 around a beautiful arcaded courtyard. It is home to the Museum of Cracow, where paintings, gold artifacts from local workshops, documents, and memorabilia are displayed in a series of grand stuccoed rooms.

🏛 Cloth Hall

Market Square 1/3. 📞 012-422 11 66. ◯ Tue–Sun. 🖼 🎫

The Cloth Hall (Sukiennice) in the middle of Market Square originated in medieval times as a covered market. It was rebuilt after a fire in 1555 and then remodeled entirely in 1875 with arcades along the exterior that give it a Venetian look. Most of the stalls today sell souvenirs of various kinds and there is a gallery of 19th-century Polish painting on the upper floor. The Cloth Hall also contains a number of cafés – the Noworolski Café is one of the best in Cracow.

⛪ St. Mary's Church

Mariacki Square 5. 📞 012-422 05 21. ◯ Mon–Fri & during services. 🖼 🎫

St. Mary's façade with its two impressive Gothic towers is set at an angle on the east side of Market Square. The left-hand tower is topped by a spire added in 1478. It served as the city's watch tower and still today a bugle call is played every hour. It is even broadcast on Polish radio at noon. The projecting porch between the towers was added in the Baroque period.

The church's greatest treasure is the huge altarpiece, 12 m (39 ft) high, by Veit Stoss, who lived in Cracow from 1477 to 1496. The outer panels show scenes from the lives of Christ and the Virgin. The middle shutters are opened each day at noon to reveal the huge carved centerpiece, *The Assumption of the Virgin* (see p742). There is also a fine crucifix by Veit Stoss, known as the Slacker Crucifix.

Horse-drawn cabs lined up in front of the Cloth Hall in Market Square

🏛 Czartoryski Museum

Św. Jana 19. 📞 012-422 55 66.
🚌 124, 152, 192, 194. 🚊 3, 4, 5,
7, 12, 15, 19. 🕐 Tue–Sun. 🔴 Mon,
one Sun a month. 🎫 💳 (free Sun).

The core of the museum is
the art collection assembled by
Princess Isabella Czartoryska
in the late 18th century. It
contains some magnificent
paintings, notably Leonardo
da Vinci's *Lady with an Ermine*
and Rembrandt's *Landscape
with the Good Samaritan*. The
museum also has decorative
arts from all over Europe and
a section on Polish history.

**Leonardo's *Lady with an Ermine*
in the Czartoryski Museum**

🏫 Collegium Maius

Jagiellonska 15. 📞 012-422 05 49.
🚌 124, 144, 152, 192. 🚊 14, 15,
18. 🕐 Mon–Fri. 🎫 💳 obligatory
(call to book visit).

This is the oldest building of
the Jagiellonian University. In
the 15th century a number of
houses were amalgamated to
create lecture rooms and
housing for professors. It was
extensively remodeled in the
mid-19th century. At the heart
of the building is an attractive
Gothic cloister. The University
Museum moved here after
World War II. Visitors can see
the 16th-century Libraria and
Great Hall, rooms still used
by the Senate of the university,
and the Treasury. There is also
a Copernicus Room dedicated
to the great astronomer, who
studied here in 1491–95.

🌿 Planty

🕐 daily.

The Planty green belt follows
the outline of Cracow's
medieval walls, which were
demolished in the early 19th

century. A circuit through the
park of about 5 km (3 miles)
starting from Wawel leads
along tree-lined paths and
avenues, past fountains and
statues. Only a small stretch of
the city walls survives beside
St. Florian's Gate at the north
end of the Old Town. Nearby
stands a well-preserved round
bárbican built in 1498–9,
when Turkish incursions were
a serious threat to the city.

✡ Old Synagogue

Szeroka 24. 📞 012-422 09 62. 🚌
184, 198. 🚊 3, 6, 9, 13. 🕐 daily.
🔴 Oct 16–Apr 15: Tue.

In the late 15th century
Cracow's Jewish quarter was
established in the Kazimierz
district, east of Wawel Hill. At
the outbreak of World War II
there was a community of
some 70,000 Jews. The Nazis
moved them all to a ghetto
across the river, from where
they were eventually deported
to concentration camps.

Amazingly, a number of
Jewish sites have survived.
The Old Synagogue, carefully
restored after the war, is not
used for worship, but houses
the Jewish Museum. The
Remu'h Synagogue (c.1553),
also on Szeroka Street, still
functions. It is named after
Rabbi Moses Remu'h, a 16th-
century philosopher, whose
tomb in the **Remu'h
Cemetery** attracts pilgrims
from all over the world. Most
of the graves were destroyed
by the Nazis, but fragments
from them have been piled
up to form a "wailing wall."

Hall of Prayers in Cracow's Old Synagogue

**Entrance gate to the Auschwitz
extermination camp**

ENVIRONS: Although the
name Oświęcim means little
to most foreigners, its German
form **Auschwitz** evokes fear
and horror in people all
round the world. It was here
near the little town of
Oświęcim, about 55 km (35
miles) west of Cracow, that
the Nazis established their
largest complex of con-
centration and extermination
camps. The Auschwitz camp
opened in June 1940, and in
March 1941 a much larger
camp was set up at nearby
Birkenau (Brzezinka in Polish).
In all, over 1,500,000 Jews and
others were murdered here.
The gas chambers, capable of
killing thousands daily, were
in use from 1942 to January
1945, when the camps were
liberated by Soviet troops.

The area has been declared
a UNESCO World Heritage
Site and the two camps are
preserved as the **Muzeum
Oświęcim-Brzezinka** – a grim
warning to future generations
of mankind's capacity for
inhumanity. Many
structures were
destroyed as the
Nazis left, but the
gate, with the
chilling words
"Arbeit macht frei"
("Work makes
free") written above
it, still stands.

🏛 Muzeum Oświęcim-Brzezinka

ul. Więzniów Oświęcimia
20. 🚉 🚌
📞 033-843 2022.
🕐 daily (closing time
varies between 3pm
in winter and 6pm in
summer). 💳

Practical & Travel Information

SINCE THE FALL OF COMMUNISM in 1989, tourism has greatly increased in Poland. New shops and hotels have sprung up, and the quality of service has improved, especially in banks and post offices. Nevertheless, much of Poland's economy has yet to adjust to the post-Communist era; the health service has been reformed, but it lags behind the country's many developing sectors. In general, goods in Poland are much cheaper than in Western Europe.

VISAS AND CUSTOMS INFORMATION

A VALID PASSPORT is required for admittance to Poland, but you may not need a visa; contact the Polish embassy in your country for details. Personal items may be brought into the country, but limits are imposed on the import and export of alcohol, tobacco, and cigarettes. Antiques exported from the country require a special permit. Gifts worth up to 170 Euros may be imported duty free.

PERSONAL SECURITY

POLISH CITIES suffer from the same crime and security problems as most European capitals, so vigilance and care are needed. Security is provided by the state police, the highway police, and a number of private security organizations. The latter are often hired to protect public buildings and private houses, and to keep order at various events. In the city of Warsaw, it is advisable for tourists to avoid the Praga district, and in particular Ulica Brzeska.

MEDICAL EMERGENCIES

CITIZENS of the following countries are entitled to free medical treatment in Poland: Belarus, the Czech Republic, Denmark, Finland, Sweden, Tunisia, the UK, Ukraine, Mongolia, China, and the countries of the former Yugoslavia. For visitors from other countries, first aid is provided free of charge at hospitals, but other types of treatment may incur a charge. Nevertheless, all visitors are advised to take out full medical insurance before arriving in Poland. Keep your policy documents with you at all times, as well as a passport for identifying yourself to hospital staff. An ambulance service is available 24 hours a day.

TOURIST INFORMATION

INFORMATION CENTERS are generally found at train stations; these provide general regional information. For specific enquiries about accommodations, tickets, and trains, **Orbis** agencies are preferable. Hotel employees are also a good source of information.

CURRENCY AND BANKING

THE OFFICIAL POLISH currency is the złoty, each of which is divided into 100 grosze. In January 1997, four zeros were knocked off the złoty, so that 10,000 złoty became one Polish New Złoty (PLN). The old złoty banknotes were withdrawn and replaced with new notes, but they can still be exchanged in banks. Money can also be changed at bureaux de change, many of which offer better rates than banks. The majority of banks are open from 8am to 6pm.

DISABLED TRAVELERS

POLAND HAS a poor record for providing for disabled people, but things are rapidly changing. All renovated or new public buildings have ramps or lifts built into them, and there are also special taxis available. Nevertheless, many traditional sites of interest may prove difficult to enter. For general advice or for information about specific sites, contact the **Disabled People's National Council**.

COMMUNICATIONS

IN RECENT YEARS phonecard-operated telephones have been installed throughout Poland, replacing the older token-operated models. Phonecards can be bought at post offices and newsagents. Charges for long-distance national calls vary according to the time of day. The highest charges are made between 8am and 6pm. Local calls are cheaper from 10pm to 6am. The charges for international calls do not vary with time of day. Poland has three mobile telephone networks, which operate on two wavelengths, 900 MHz and 1,800 MHz, and cover almost all of the country.

Poczta Polska, the Polish postal service, provides a wide range of services, and its offices are open from 8am to 8pm on weekdays; the main post office in Warsaw is open 24 hours a day, seven days a week. Letters to destinations within Poland usually arrive

THE CLIMATE OF POLAND

Poland's climate is influenced by cold polar air from Scandinavia, and sub-tropical air from the south. Polar-continental fronts dominate in winter, bringing crisp, frosty weather, while late summer and autumn (the most popular times to visit) enjoy plenty of warm sunny days. Winters, which always bring snow, can be very cold in the north.

WARSAW			
°C/F	21/70		
	11/52		
0°C 7/45		7/45	
32°F 0/32		2/36	
			-3/27
			-8/18
5 hrs	7.5 hrs	3 hrs	1.5 hrs
42 mm	56 mm	40 mm	40 mm
month	Apr	Jul	Oct	Jan

within 2 or 3 days of posting, while international mail may take up to a week; intercontinental mail can take up to three weeks to reach its destination. Local correspondence (within a town) should be posted in the green post boxes, and all other mail should be posted in the red boxes. For urgent mail, Poczta Polska provides both an express service and a courier service. The international DHL and UPS courier agencies also operate in Poland.

TRAVELING BY PLANE

POLAND IS well connected with the rest of the world. International flights from some 50 cities in 30 countries arrive in Warsaw. The airports at Gdańsk, Katowice, Szczecin, Poznań, Wrocław and Cracow also have international flights, linking Poland with much of Western Europe, as well as Prague, Budapest, Sofia, Bucharest, and the capitals of the former Soviet Union. Some 25 airlines, including British Airways, Air France, SAS (Scandinavia), and Lufthansa (Germany), operate from **Warsaw Okęcie** airport, which has direct connections with Canada, the US, Israel, and Thailand. **Cracow Balice**,

the second largest airport in Poland, offers a substantial number of domestic and international flights.

TRAVELING BY BUS

MOST LONG-DISTANCE routes within Poland are served by Polish Motor Transport, Polska Komunikaja Samochodowa (PKS). A competitor is Polski Express, which offers cheaper fares, air-conditioned coaches, and pleasant staff, but the journeys tend to be longer, for the routes are rarely direct.

Local buses are sometimes the only means of getting to minor towns and villages. The services are generally punctual, although before 8am and in the afternoon they may be crowded. Tickets for these are always bought from the driver.

TRAVELING BY TRAIN

INTERNATIONAL TRAIN services run between all major European and Polish cities. The journeys by fast train from Warsaw to Prague and Berlin take just six and nine hours respectively. The main rail route runs across Poland from east to west, connecting Russia with western Europe.

Express lines connect almost all the big cities, and the trains

are fast and usually arrive on time. The most comfortable, and most expensive, are the InterCity trains, which also give passengers a free meal. Euro and InterCity trains both provide compartments for mothers with children and for disabled people. Fares for ordinary and fast trains are very reasonable; express trains and sleeping cars are expensive, although not by the standards of the rest of Europe.

Suburban routes are served by electric trains, which sometimes consist of open-plan, double-decker cars.

TRAVELING BY CAR

POLAND HAS FEW highways, and those that exist are generally in poor condition. An exception is the Cracow–Katowice highway, the first stretch of what promises to be a network of highways spanning the entire country.

Wherever you drive in Poland, always carry your passport, car insurance, license, green card, and rental contract with you, and if you are driving a foreign car, display the international symbol of its country of origin.

All the major international car rental companies operate in Warsaw and Cracow.

Where to Stay in Poland

ONLY A FEW YEARS AGO the standard of Polish hotels was much lower than that of their Western counterparts. Since 1989, however, many new luxury hotels have been built, the majority of them part of international hotel chains. In Warsaw there is a shortage of good, moderately priced hotels. In central Cracow, however, a number of historic 19th-century hotels have been modernized.

		NUMBER OF ROOMS	RESTAURANT	PRIVATE PARKING	SWIMMING POOL

WARSAW

CITY CENTER: *Harenda* Krakowskie Przedmieście 4–6. **Map** D3. 022-826 00 71. **FAX** 022-826 00 71. Located in one of the most picturesque streets in Warsaw's historic center, close to many of the main sights, this hotel offers modest accommodations at reasonable rates. 📶 TV 🖥	ZŁ	45	●	▣	
CITY CENTER: *Grand* Krucza 28. **Map** D4. 022-583 21 00. **FAX** 022-621 97 24. @ wagrand@orbis.pl W www.orbis.pl The Grand lives up to its name: it is a large hotel built at the end of the 1950s for visiting heads of state and other officials. 📶 TV 🖥	ZŁZŁ	385	●	▣	
CITY CENTER: *Le Royal Meridien–Bristol* Krakowskie Przedmieście 42–44. **Map** D3. 022-625 25 25. **FAX** 022-625 25 77. @ bristol@it.com.pl W www.lemeridien-bristol.com This most elegant and exclusive hotel opened in 1900. Its Secessionist interior, designed by Otto Wagner of Vienna, has been renovated. The Paderewski Suite is especially fine. 📶 TV 🔧 🖥	ZŁZŁZŁ	206	●	▣	●
FARTHER AFIELD: *Maria* Aleja Jana Pawła II 71. 022-838 40 62. **FAX** 022-838 38 40. W www.hotelmaria.pl This small hotel, set at the northern edge of the town center, has a friendly, intimate atmosphere. The rooms are large and tastefully furnished, as well as being spotlessly clean. 📶 TV 🖥	ZŁ	24	●	▣	

CRACOW

NOWY ŚWIAT: *Logos* Szujskiego 5. 012-632 33 33. **FAX** 012-632 42 10. @ logos-kr@hotel-logos.pl W www.hotel-logos.pl This modern building blends perfectly with its historic surroundings. Located just off Market Square, the hotel offers comfortable, attractively furnished rooms at reasonable prices. 📶 TV 🔧 🖥	ZŁ	49	●	▣	
OLD QUARTER: *Pod Różą* Floriańska 14. 012-422 12 44. **FAX** 012-421 75 13. @ pod-roza@hotel.com.pl W www.hotel.com.pl Dating from the mid-19th century, this hotel has luxurious, finely furnished rooms and an excellent location. 📶 TV 🖥	ZŁZŁ	54	●		
OLD QUARTER: *Polski "Pod Bialym Orlem"* Pijarska 17. 012-422 11 44. W www.podorlem.com.pl This hotel was much neglected during the Communist regime but it has recently been revived. It has a prime location opposite the remnants of the city wall. It now offers excellent service at moderate prices. 📶 TV 🖥	ZŁZŁ	54			
STRADOM QUARTER: *Royal* św Gertrudy 26–29. 012-421 49 79 or 421 35 00. **FAX** 012-421 58 57. W www.royal.com.pl The Royal is recommended for those who are on a budget but appreciate an interesting location. The renovated building, at the foot of Wawel Hill, dates back to the times of Austro-Hungarian rule. 📶 TV 🖥	ZŁ	115	●	▣	

Price categories are for a standard double room per night, with tax, breakfast, and service included:

ZŁ under 300–450 złoty
ZŁZŁ 450–600 złoty
ZŁZŁZŁ over 600 złoty

RESTAURANT
Hotel restaurant or dining room usually open to non-residents.

PRIVATE PARKING
Parking provided by the hotel in either a private car park or a private garage close by.

CREDIT CARDS
Major credit cards are accepted in those hotels where the credit card symbol is shown.

Map references refer to map of Warsaw on pp748–9

Where to Eat in Poland

POLISH FOOD suffers from a poor international image, but this is changing with the opening of a new generation of restaurants all over Poland. Many take pride in reviving and updating traditional Polish specialties, such as *pierogi* (ravioli), pancakes, soups, and dumplings. It is not difficult to find a good restaurant in Warsaw or Cracow, but prices are often inflated in the popular tourist areas.

	Price	Open Late	Vegetarian Dishes	Good Wine List	Outdoor Tables
WARSAW					
CITY CENTER: *La Boheme* Pl. Teatralny (inside the National Theater). **Map** D2. 022-692 06 81. La Boheme is a restaurant that specializes in sophisticated French cuisine and traditional Polish dishes. Some of the restaurant's dishes are also available at a nearby bar, which serves snacks and takeouts.	ZL ZL	●	■	●	
CITY CENTER: *Fukier* Rynek Starego Miasta (Old Market Square) 27. **Map** D2. 022-831 10 13. Cozy, antique interiors and Magda Gessler's masterly cooking skills guarantee an excellent, though by no means cheap, dinner. Polish national dishes predominate, but there are also delicacies from other parts of Europe. The delicious wild mushroom soup is highly recommended.	ZL ZL ZL	●	■	●	
ROYAL ROUTE (TRAKT KRÓLEWSKI): *Restauracja Polska* ul. Nowy Świat 21. **Map** D3. 022-826 38 77. Located on one of Warsaw's most beautiful streets, a lively atmosphere and good Polish food make this a popular place to eat.	ZL ZL	●	■	●	
ROYAL ROUTE (TRAKT KRÓLEWSKI): *Studio Buffo* Konopnickiej 6. **Map** D5. 022-626 89 07. This restaurant specializes in traditional Polish cuisine. It is prepared by Maciej Kuroń, a well-known local chef.	ZL ZL	●	■	●	■
CRACOW					
KAZIMIERZ QUARTER: *Alef* Szeroka 17. 012-421 38 70. This excellent restaurant specializes in Jewish cuisine. Diners may sample such delicacies as stuffed carp, stuffed vine leaves, and goose livers fried with almonds and raisins, while listening to live music, including gypsy and Russian love songs.	ZL ZL			●	■
OLD QUARTER: *Hawełka* Rynek Główny 34. 012-422 47 53. Hawełka consists of two restaurants: the one on the ground floor specializes in Cracovian cuisine, including Cracovian-style duck (stewed with wild mushrooms), while the second, on the first floor, is more expensive and serves sophisticated international dishes.	ZL ZL	●		●	
OLD QUARTER: *Cyrano de Bergerac* Sławkowska 26. 012-411 72 88. This French restaurant is fairly expensive, but its quality fully justifies the price. The menu includes quail with *ceps* and *foie gras*, frog legs with cream of candied garlic, and the fish dishes are particularly good.	ZL ZL ZL	●	■	●	■
STRADOM QUARTER: *Chłopskie Jadło* św Agnieszki 1. 012-421 85 20. This fine restaurant, with interiors designed to resemble a peasant's cottage, serves traditional Polish dishes, including wild mushroom soup, stuffed cabbage, black pudding, and *pierogi* (ravioli). Fish dishes are served in the part of the restaurant called *Baba Ryba*.	ZL	●			

Price categories are for a three-course meal for one, half a bottle of house wine, and all unavoidable extra charges such as cover, service, and tax:

ZL under 70 złoty
ZL ZL 70–100 złoty
ZL ZL ZL over 100 złoty

OPEN LATE
Restaurants that remain open with their full menu available after 10pm.

VEGETARIAN DISHES
Available as a starter, a main course, or both. (Traditional Polish cuisine tends to be heavily meat and fish oriented).

CREDIT CARDS
Major credit cards are accepted in restaurants where the credit card symbol is shown.

For key to symbols see back flap

Acknowledgments

DORLING KINDERSLEY would like to thank the following people whose contributions and assistance have made the preparation of this book possible.

MAIN CONTRIBUTORS
Amy Brown, Nina Hathway, Vivien Stone, Kristina Woolnough.

ADDITIONAL CONTRIBUTORS
John Ardagh, Rosemary Bailey, David Baird, Josie Barnard, Rosemary Barron, Gretel Beer, Ros Belford, Susie Boulton, Gerhard Bruschke, Caroline Bugler, Christopher Catling, Juliet Clough, Deidre Coffey, Marc Dubin, Paul Duncan, Joanna Egert-Romanowska, Olivia Ercoli, Judith Fayard, Stephanie Ferguson, Lisa Gerard-Sharp, Mike Gerrard, Andrew Gumbel, Andy Harris, Vicky Hayward, Zöe Hewetson, Adam Hopkins, Lindsay Hunt, Nick Inman, Tim Jepson, Colin Jones, Marion Kaplan, Alister Kershaw, Michael Leapman, Philip Lee, Alec Lobrano, Sarah McAlister, Jerzy S. Majewski, Fred Mawer, Lynette Mitchell, Colin Nicholson, Tadeusz Olsański, Małgorzata Omilanowska, Robin Osborne, Robin Pascoe, Alice Peebles, Tim Perry, Polly Phillimore, Paul Richardson, Anthony Roberts, Barnaby Rogerson, Zöe Ross, Kaj Sandell, Jane Shaw, Vladimír Soukup, Robert Strauss, Martin Symington, Allan Tillier, Nigel Tisdall, Roger Thomas, Tanya Tsikas, Roger Williams, Timothy Wright.

ILLUSTRATORS
Acanto Arquitectura y Urbanismo S.L., Stephen Conlin, Gary Cross, Richard Draper, Nick Gibbard, Paul Guest, Stephen Gyapay, Studio Illibill, Kevin Jones Associates, Paweł Marczak, Maltings Partnership, Chris Orr and Associates, Otakar Pok, Robbie Polley, Jaroslav Staněk, Paul Weston, Andrzej Wielgosz, Ann Winterbotham, John Woodcock, Martin Woodward, Piotr Zubrzycki.

DESIGN AND EDITORIAL ASSISTANCE
Douglas Amrine, Marina Carter, Lucinda Hawksley, Matthew Ibbotson, Jacky Jackson, Michelle de Larrabeiti, Helen Partington, Dave Pugh, Marisa Renzullo, Simon Ryder, Hugh Thompson, Conrad van Dyk, Karen Villabona, Simon Wilder.

FACTCHECKER
Jessica Hughes.

PROOFREADER
Stewart J. Wild.

INDEX
Hilary Bird.

ADDITIONAL PICTURE RESEARCH
Nicole Kaczynski.

PRODUCTION
Joanna Bull, Sarah Dodd, Marie Ingledew.

PUBLISHING MANAGER
Helen Townsend.

MANAGING ART EDITOR
Jane Ewart.

DIRECTOR OF PUBLISHING
Gilllian Allan.

ADDITIONAL PHOTOGRAPHY
Max Alexander, Peter Anderson, Gabor Barka, Steve Bere, Clive Bournsnell, Maciej Bronarski, Demetrio Carrasco, Andrzej Chec, Krzysztof Chojnacki, Stephen Conlin, Joe Cornish, Andy Crawford, Michael Crocket, Wojciech Czerniewicz, Tim Daly, Jiří Doležal, Philip Dowell, Mike Dunning, Philip Enticknap, Jane Ewart, Foto Carfagna + Associati, Philip Gatward, Steve Gorton, A. Hayder, Heidi Grassley, John Heseltine, Gabriel Hilderbrandt, Roger Hilton, Rupert Horrox, Ed Ironside, Dorota Jarymowicz, Mariusz Jarymowicz, Piotr Jamski, Colin Keates, Paul Kenward, Alan Keohand, Dave King, Jiří Kopřiva, Mariusz Kowalewski, Vladimír Kozlík, Adrian Lascom, Cyril Laubscher, Neil Lukas, Eric Meacher, Wojciech Mędrzak, Neil Mersh, John Miller, John Moss, Roger Moss, David Murray, Hanna Musiał, Maciej Musiał, Tomasz Myśluk, Stephen Oliver, John Parker, Agencja "Piękna," Milan Posselt, František Přeučil, Rob Reichenfeld, Tim Ridley, Kim Sayer, Jules Selmes, Anthony Souter, Clive Streeter, Stanislav Tereba, Matthew Ward, Alan Williams, Peter Wilson, Jeremy Whitaker, Linda Whitwam, Stephen Whitehorn, Paweł Wójcik, Stephen Wooster, Francesca Yorke, Jan Zych.

ADDITIONAL ASSISTANCE

DORLING KINDERSLEY would like to give special thanks to Britt Lightbody of the Danish Tourist Board, Henrik Thierlein, International Press Officer for Wonderful Copenhagen, Petter Ree of the Norwegian Embassy in London, Riitta Balza at the Finnish Tourist Board, London, and journalist Tone Sendberg.

PHOTOGRAPHY PERMISSIONS

DORLING KINDERSLEY would like to thank all the churches, museums, galleries, and other sights that kindly gave their permission for us to photograph their establishments and works of art.

PICTURE CREDITS

t = top; tl = top left; tlc = top left center; tc = top center; tr = top right; cla = center left above; ca = center above; cra = center right above; cl = center left; c = center; cr = center right; clb = center left below; cb = center below; crb = center right below; bl = bottom left; b = bottom; bc = bottom center; bcl = bottom center left; br = bottom right; d = detail.

Every effort has been made to trace the copyright holders and we apologize in advance for any unintentional omissions. We would be pleased to insert the appropriate acknowledgments in any subsequent edition of this publication.

Works of art have been reproduced with the permission of the following copyright holders:
© Munch Museum/Munch-Ellingsen Group BONO, Oslo, DACS, London 2001, 663bl; © Succession Picasso/DACS 2001, 31bc.

The publisher would like to thank the following individuals, companies, and picture libraries for permission to reproduce their photographs:

AKG LONDON: *Cosimo de Medici* 420b, *St. Augustine* by Carpaccio 421crb, *Niccolò Machiavelli* 421br; Museo Archeologico Nazionale, *Farnese Hercules* 444c; Collection Archiv für Kunst und Geschichte, Berlin 718cla, 470t; Staatliche Kunstsammlungen, Kassel, *William I of Orange* by Anthonis Mor (1556) 246t; Museum Boijmans-van Beuningen, Rotterdam, *The Tower of Babel* (c.1525) by Peter Brueghel the Elder 263br; Naturhistorisches Museum/Eric Lessing 595brc; Niedersächsisches Landesmuseum, Hanover, *Friedrich II* by Antoine Pesne 524t; Rijksmuseum, *Winter Landscape with Skaters* (1618) by Hendrick Avercamp 256tc; San Francesco, Assisi/ Stefan Diller, *St. Francis Appears to the Monks at Arles* by Giotto (c.1295) 28br; Staatliche Kunstsammlungen, Dresden/ Gemäldegalerie Alte Meister, *Girl Reading a Letter* by Vermeer 542tr; Vatican Museums, Rome 27tl; ALVEY AND TOWERS: 147br; MUSEUM AMSTELKRING: 250tr; AMSTERDAMS HISTORISCH MUSEUM: 252br, 253cl; ANCIENT EGYPT PICTURE LIBRARY: The Trustees of the British Museum 24cla; APEX PHOTO AGENCY: 39t; ARENAS FOTOGRAFIA ARTISTICA: 325cr; ARQUIVO ICONOGRAFICO S.A., BARCELONA: Museo del Prado, *The Triumph of Bacchus* by Velázquez 288tl; THE ART ARCHIVE: The Imperial War Museum 231bl; The British Library 125bl; ART DIRECTORS & TRIP: C. Rennie 639bc, 641b, 649b; ARTOTHEK SPECIALARCHIV FÜR GEMÄLDEFOTOGRAFIE, PEISSENBERG: *Four Apostles* (1526) by Albrecht Dürer 551tr; JAMES AUSTIN: 152b; AUSTRIAN NATIONAL TOURIST BOARD: 592bc.

JAUME BALAYNA: 313crb; C.H. BASTIN & J. EVRARD: 232bc; BAYERISCHES NATIONAL-MUSEUM, MUNICH: 552t; LA BELLE AURORE: 193b; BETHNAL GREEN MUSEUM OF CHILDHOOD/VICTORIA & ALBERT MUSEUM, LONDON: 57b; BILDARCHIV PREUSSISCHER KULTURBESITZ: 532t; Kunstgewerbe-museum, Berlin 531c; Pergamon Museum, Berlin 25t; GÉRARD BOULLAY: 155c, 155bl; THE BRIDGEMAN ART LIBRARY: Basilica di San Francesco, Assisi, *The Ecstasy of St. Francis* by Giotto 406tr; The British Museum 52c, 53tl, *The Festival of Sekhtet* 52br, *The Young Prince with his Parents* 53c; Lauros-Giraudon/Chateau de Versailles, France, *Equestrian Portrait of Louis XIV* (c.1692) by Pierre Mignard 29tr; Crown Institute/Institute of Directors, London, UK, *Field Marshal King Leopold I of Belgium* by Nicholas Pieneman 220t; Galleria degli Uffizi, Firenze, *The Venus of Urbino* (1538) by Titian 422b, *The Duke of Urbino* (1460) by Piero della Francesca 423tr, *The Duchess of Urbino* (1460) by Piero della Francesca 423tl, *Madonna of the*

Goldfinch (1506) by Raphael 424b; Kunsthistorisches Museum, Vienna, *Matthias I, Hunyadi* (1440–90) 730t; Louvre, Paris, *Virgin of the Rocks* (c.1478) by Leonardo da Vinci 29bl, *The Oath of the Horatii* (1784) by Jacques-Louis David 30clb; Munch-Museet, Oslo, *Young Woman on the Shore* (1896) by Edvard Munch 663bl; Musée Carnavalet, Paris 30cla; Museo del Prado, Madrid, *The Three Graces* (1635) by Rubens 288cr, *The Clothed Maja* (c.1800) by Goya 289tr, *The Naked Maja* (c.1800) by Goya 289cra, *The Martyrdom of St. Philip* (c.1639) by José de Ribera 289cr, *The Annunciation* by Fra Angelico (c.1387–1455) 290cr, *The Santo Domingo el Antiguo Altarpiece*, depicting *The Adoration of the Shepherds*, by El Greco (1541–1614) 290bl; Museo Nacional Centro de Arte Reina Sofia, Madrid, *Guernica* (1937) by Pablo Picasso 31bc; Private Collection, *Queen Elizabeth I* by Marcus Gheeraerts the Younger 38t; Royal Holloway & Bedford New College, *Princes Edward and Richard in the Tower* by Sir John Everett Millais 61b; St. Peter's, Vatican, *Pietà* by Michelangelo 2r; THE BRITISH MUSEUM: 26br, 53br, 479r; BRITSTOCK-IFA: F. Aberham 619br; Erich Bach 623bl; S. Bohnacker 600t; Bernd Ducke 600bl; Torsten Fleer 235br; P. Graf 650t; G. Grafenhain 235cla, 601bl, 620cla, 651tr, 683br; S. Gräfenwhain 622tl; B. Moller 648b; 624bl; AP&F/Thomas Ulrich 621bc; BUDAPESTI TORTENETI MUZEUM: 734br; BUDAPESTI TURISZTIKAI HIVATAL: 735bl; INTERNATIONAL BULBFLOWER CENTRE: 261tc; MICHAEL BUSSELLE: 140–141.

CAMERA PRESS: Cecil Beaton 46cb; GIUSEPPE CARFAGNA & ASSOCIATI: 427bc; BIÈRES DE CHIMAY S.A: 220b; CHUR TOURISMUS: 624tc; COLLECTIONS DU MUSÉE INTERNATIONAL D'HORLOGERIE, LA CHAUX-DE-FONDS, SUISSE: Photo Institut l'homme et le Temps 617c; COLOGNE CATHEDRAL DOMBAUARCHIV: 562tl, 562cl, 562bl, 563tl, 563cra, 563crb, 563bl; ALAN COPSON PHOTOGRAPHY: 228cl; CORBIS: Archivo Iconografico, S.A., *An Old Woman Cooking Eggs* by Velázquez 85b; Arte & Immagini srl, *The Annunciation* by Fra Angelico 415tr; Yann Arthus-Betrand 304tl; Bettman Archive 525bl, 658t; Ric Ergenbright 522; Macduff Everton 650c; Historical Picture Archive 31bl; Hulton-Deutsch Collection 331cr;

Bob Krist 588t; Dennis Marsico 407tc; NATIONAL GALLERY, LONDON: *Bathers at Asnières* by Seurat 49br; Richard T. Nowitz 623tr; José F. Poblete 625tl; Michael St. Maur Sheil 757tr; Gregor Schmid 523c; Ted Spiegel 665cl; Adam Woolfitt 143crb; JOE CORNISH: 77b, 78br, 79bl, 80b, 84t, 85t, 86b, 86t, 108c, 109b, 111tr, 124tr, 124bl, 126cl, 126cr, 126bl, 127tl, 127cr, 127br, 128cl, 128cr, 128bl, 128bl, 128br, 157t, 280t, 300tr, 319br, 366c, 367tr, 367cl, 367b, 471tr, 490t, 491br, 492b, 492t, 493b, 493t, 157t, 157t, 700–701; COVER ARCHIVO: Ilenas Quim 304br; CZARTORYSKI MUSEUM, CRACOW: *Lady with an Ermine* by Leonardo da Vinci 757cl.

IL DAGHERROTIPO: Riccardo D'Errico 443t; DEAN AND CHAPTER OF WESTMINSTER: 47bl; DEUTSCHES MUSEUM, MUNICH: 552b; C.M. DIXON: Vatican Museums, Rome 25br; JURGEN DRENTH: 244c; DUCHAS, THE HERITAGE SERVICE: 122b; DEUTSCHE PRESSE-AGENTUR GMBH: 542br, 554cla.

EMPICS LTD: Tony Marshall 389bl; ENGLISH HERITAGE: by kind permission of the Provost and Fellows of King's College, Cambridge 73tr; MARY EVANS PICTURE LIBRARY: 8r, 9c, 21c, 28tr, 30tr, 33c, 75bl, 81b, 110tl, 141c, *Napoleon Bonaparte* (c.1804) by Jacques-Louis David 146t, 273c, 278cr, 383c, 579c, 602bc, 635c, 640t, 674t, 701c; EYE UBIQUITOUS: James Davis 316br.

SIGMUND FREUD MUSEUM, VIENNA: 596br.

GETTY IMAGES/STONE: Hideo Kuihara 2; Hugh Sitton 65t; James Strachan 704clb; GODO-FOTO: 318br; NICHOLAS P. GOULANDRIS FOUNDATION MUSEUM OF CYCLADIC AND ANCIENT GREEK ART: 474bl; MICHAEL GRYCHOWSKI: 754tr; ©FMBG GUGGENHEIM BILBAO MUSEOA: London 2001. Erica Barahona Ede (All rights reserved. Total or partial reproduction is prohibited) 31bra; GUINNESS IRELAND ARCHIVES, DUBLIN: 121c.

SONIA HALLIDAY PHOTOGRAPHS: 35ca; ROBERT HARDING PICTURE LIBRARY: 23c, 23t, 27br, 159br, 171t, 279tr, 395b, 603tc, 620tr, 621tr, 621bla, 623cl, 637b, 649t, 682tl, 689bc, 697tr; G. Hellier 603b, 739bl; K. Gillam 691b; Simon Harris 602t; John

Rainford 520br; Chris Rennie 279tr; Adina Tovy 38b; Adam Woolfitt 637cla, 675t, 683cl; GORDON HENDERSON 81t; HISTORIC ROYAL PALACES 1999 (CROWN COPYRIGHT): 63t; ANGELO HORNAK LIBRARY: 78cla; HULTON ARCHIVE: 29tc, 30b, 146b, 228br, 253cr, 471c, 662bl, 708t; Imperial War Museum 31tl; HUNGARIAN NATIONAL GALLERY: 734tr; HUNGARIAN TOURIST BOARD: 739tr.

IDEAL PHOTO S.A.: T. Passios 489t; IMAGES COLOUR LIBRARY: 293ca, 293cb; IMPACT PHOTOS: Brian Harris 387b; INDEX FOTOTECA: 323c; INSTITUTO PORTUGUÊS DE MUSEUS: Museu Grão Vasco 362tr; ISTITUTO E MUSEO DI STORIA DELLA SCIENZA, FLORENCE: 419br.

STANISŁAWA JABŁOŃSKA: 744, 755bl; PAUL JACKSON 49tl; JARROLD PUBLISHING: ©2001 His Grace Duke of Marlborough 75c; MICHAEL JENNER PHOTOGRAPHY: 124bc; JOODS HISTORISCH MUSEUM, AMSTERDAM: 251tr; JORVIK, YORK: 79tl.

OLDRICK KARASEK: 706, 722b, 722t, 723tl, 723b; KONINKLIJK MUSEUM VOOR SCHONE KUNSTEN, ANTWERP: As the Old Sang, The Young Play Pipes (1638) by Jacob Jordaen 230bl; KUNSTHISTORISCHES MUSEUM, VIENNA: 594tr, 596c, Empress Elisabeth (1865) by Winterhalter 594tl, Hunters in the Snow (1565) by Peter Brueghel the Elder 596t.

LOCARNO FILM FESTIVAL: 625bl; LUXEMBOURG TOURIST OFFICE: pictures by kind permission of the Luxembourg Tourist Office, London 221b.

TOM MACKIE: 32–33; MADAME TUSSAUD'S, LONDON: 54bla; MAGYAR NEMZETI MUZEUM: 736bc; MARIA LAACH KUNSTVERLAG: 559c; MAK – ÖSTERREICHISCHE MUSEUM FÜR ANGEWANDTE KUNST: 597cl; MARKGRÄFLICHES OPERNHAUS, BAYREUTH: 557t; MERCEDES-BENZ MUSEUM, STUTTGART: 557t; MUSEI CAPITOLINI, ROME: 27bl; MUSEI VATICANI E CAPELLA SISTINA, ROME: 394c, 394bl, 394t, 395tl, 395cr, 395ca, 396c, 396cl, 397tc, 397cr, 397cb, 398t; MUSEU DA CIDADE, LISBON: Portrait of Marquês de Pombal 361t; MUSEUM HUIS LAMBERT VAN MEERTEN, RBK: 263cl; MUSEUM JEAN TINGUELY BASEL: 617tr; MUSEUM OF LONDON: 58b; MUSEU DA MARINHA, LISBON: Manuel I by Alberto

Cutileiro 354t, Vasco da Gama 363br; MUSÉE NATIONAL DU CHÂTEAU DE VERSAILLES: 168tr, 168cl, 168bl, 169tr, 169tlb, 169bc; MUSÉES ROYAUX DES BEAUX-ARTS DE BELGIQUE: 226bc; MUSEO NACIONAL DEL PRADO, MADRID: The Garden of Delights (1505) by Hieronymus Bosch 288crb; MUSEO THYSSEN-BORNEMISZA, MADRID: Our Lady of the Dry Tree (c.1450) by Petrus Christus 286bl.

NÁRODNÍ GALERIE V PRAZE, PRAGUE: Simeon and the Infant Jesus by Petr Brandl 714t; NATIONAL GALLERY OF IRELAND, DUBLIN: The Taking of Christ (1602) by Caravaggio (Reproduction courtesy of the National Gallery of Ireland, Dublin) 117b; NATIONAL TRUST PHOTOGRAPHIC LIBRARY: 130b; Nick Meers 77c; TRUSTEES OF THE NATIONAL MUSEUMS OF SCOTLAND: 28tr; NIPPON TELEVISION NETWORK CORPORATION: Original Sin by Michelangelo, detail from the Sistine Chapel ceiling, Vatican, Rome 398br.

ORONOZ ARCHIVO FOTOGRÁFICO: 293cla, 299c, 326c; J.A Fernandez 304tr.

PA PHOTOS: DPA 31tr; EPA 525tr; PALACE OF CULTURE AND SCIENCE, WARSAW: 749cr; PALAIS HET LOOS: E. Boeijinga 261bl; PICTURES COLOUR LIBRARY: 682b, 738tr; ROBBIE POLLEY: 232bla; POWERSTOCK/ZEFA LTD: 750tl; Mauritius Gallery 598bc; PRISMA ARCHIVO FOTOGRÁFICO, BARCELONA: Palacio del Senado, The Fall of Granada by Francisco Pradilla 278tl.

REX FEATURES: 66c, 67br, 71c; Denis Cameron 325tr; Pertti Jenytin 688c; Sipa Press 196tr; RIJKSMUSEUM AMSTERDAM: 257c; The Wedding Portrait (c.1622) by Frans Hals 24tr; The Kitchen Maid (1658) by Jan Vermeer 256cl; St. Elizabeth's Day Flood (1500) 256bc; The Night Watch (1642) by Rembrandt 257tl; Woman at her Toilet (1660) by Jan Steen 257br; The Jewish Bride by Rembrandt 258br; RÉUNION DES MUSÉES NATIONAUX AGENCE PHOTOGRAPHIQUE: Louvre/Lewandowski/LeMage Mona Lisa (La Joconde) by Leonardo da Vinci 160t; Louvre/Herve Lewandowski 160c; Gilles or Pierrot (c.1717) by Watteau 24clb; THE ROYAL COLLECTION: ©2001 Her Majesty Queen Elizabeth II: 60br, 60b, 61tl, 66tr, 67tl, 67tr, 67bl.

SCALA GROUP S.P.A: 394br, 394bla, 396b; Basilica di San Francesco, *St. Francis* (1280) by Cimabue 406cl, *The Deposition* (1323) by Lorenzetti 406bl, *The Life of St. Martin* (1315) by Simone Martini 406br; *Pope Leo X* 420clb; Palazzo Medici Riccardi, Firenze, *The Procession of the Magi* by Gozzoli 420–421; 421tl, 421ca, 443bla; Accademia, Venice, *The Feast in the House of Levi* by Veronese 441b; Bargello, Firenze, *David* by Donatello 418cl; Galleria degli Uffizi, Firenze 423cb; *The Ognissanti Madonna* (1310) by Giotto 422c, *The Birth of Venus* (1485) by Botticelli 423c, *The Holy Family* (1507) by Michelangelo, *Madonna of the Long Neck* (c.1534) by Parmigianino 424t; *The Annunciation* by Leonardo da Vinci 25crb; Galleria dell'Accademia: *Cassone Adimari* by Lo Scheggia 415b; SCHLOSSVERWALTUNG, MUNICH: 544b, 549t, 555c; HERMAN SCHOLTEN: 245b; SCIENCE MUSEUM, LONDON: 56tl, 56bl; SCIENCE PHOTO LIBRARY: M-SAT Ltd 10c; SCOPE: 186tr, 187c, 187br; SPECTRUM COLOUR LIBRARY: 8; STAATSGALERIE, STUTTGART: *St. Paul in Prison* (1627) by Rembrandt 556tr; STAD BRUGGE STEDLIJKE MUSEA: 234tc; STÄDELSCHES KUNSTINSTITUT UND STÄDTISCHE GALERIE, FRANKFURT AM MAIN: *Portrait of a Woman* (1480) by Sandro Botticelli 560c; STATENS HISTORISKA MUSEUM: 647c, 665tc, 665cr; STIFTUNG PREUSSISCHE SCHLÖSSER UND GÄRTEN BERLIN-BRANDENBURG: 541br; STOCKPHOTOS: David Hornback 277b; SWISS NATIONAL MUSEUM, ZÜRICH: 614c; SWISS NATIONAL PARK: 620clb, 620cb, 620bl; SWISS TOURIST OFFICE: 622b.

TATE, LONDON 2001: Marcus Lee, *Maman* (1999) by Louise Bourgeois 59t; TOPHAM PICTUREPOINT: 621cr; TOROS MAGAZINE: 293cr; THE TRAVEL LIBRARY: Galleria dell'Accademia 412bl; TRINITY COLLEGE, DUBLIN: Courtesy of the Board of Trinity College, Dublin 115t, 116tl, *Portrait of St. Matthew* from *The Book of Kells* 116c, 125t.

VAN GOGH MUSEUM, AMSTERDAM: Courtesy of the Vincent van Gogh Foundation 259c; *The Bedroom at Arles* by Vincent van Gogh 259t; VASA MUSEUM, STOCKHOLM: Hans Hammarskiold 646bl.

JEREMY WHITAKER: 75bl; CHRISTOPHER WILSON: 78bl; PETER WILSON: 468; JEPPE WIKSTRÖM: 20–21, 638c, 642b, 644b, 645t; WONDERFUL COPENHAGEN: 672c, 673bc, 679tr, 681bl, 683tr; WORLD PICTURES: 588b.

YORK CASTLE MUSEUM: 79c.

ZEFA, WARSAW: 520cla, 555b, 556br, 561b.

Jacket:
Front - DK Picture Library: cr; John Heseltine cl; Stephen Oliver bc; Getty Images: Veronica Jones main image.
Back - DK Picture Library: Rob Reichenfeld tl; Peter Wilson br.
Spine - Getty Images: Veronica Jones..

All other images © Dorling Kindersley. For further information see: www.dkimages.com

Europe's Rail Network

IT WAS IN BRITAIN that railroads were first developed in the second quarter of the 19th century, and Europe is still criss-crossed by tens of thousands of kilometers of track. Only the main routes are shown on this map. Although many lines are badly in need of modernization, the main intercity routes use high-speed, comfortable trains, making rail a quick and convenient form of transportation for many journeys both within and between countries (*see p18*). London to Paris, for example, takes just three hours, and you can travel from Paris to Marseille in the same time. Prices vary considerably from country to country. In Great Britain, for example, standard tickets are almost three times the price for equivalent journeys in Italy. Details on the rail services of individual countries are given in the *Travel Information* sections of the appropriate chapters.

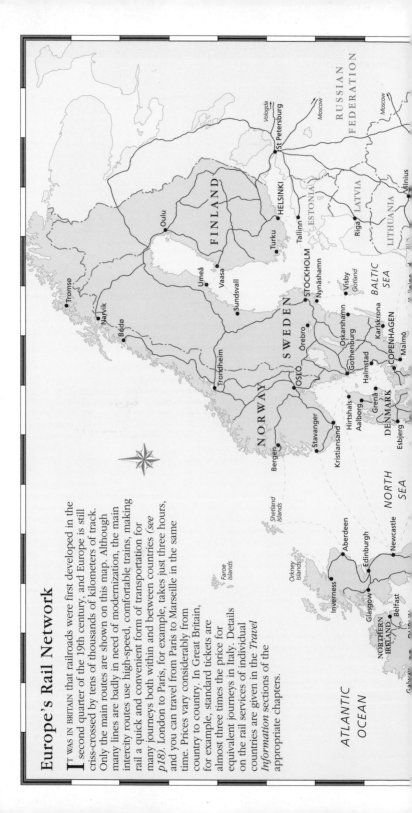